P9-CCO-121

International Law

Ethics Spotlight

BUSINESS LAW

SEVENTH EDITION

Legal Environment, Online Commerce, Business Ethics, and International Issues

Henry R. Cheeseman

Clinical Professor of Business Law
Director of the Legal Studies Program, Marshall School of Business
University of Southern California

Pearson Prentice Hall
UPPER SADDLE RIVER, NEW JERSEY 07458

Library of Congress Cataloging-in-Publication Data

Cheeseman, Henry R.
    Business law : legal environment, online commerce, business ethics, and international issues/Henry R. Cheeseman. —7th ed.
        p. cm.
    Includes bibliographical references and index.
    ISBN-13: 978-0-13-608554-6
    ISBN-10: 0-13-608554-7
    1. Business law—United States.   I. Title.

KF889.C433 2009
346.7307—dc22

2008052772

Editorial Director: Sally Yagan
AVP/Editor-in-Chief: Eric Svendsen
Product Development Manager:
    Ashley Santora
Editorial Project Manager: Kierra Kashickey
Editorial Assistant: Christina Rumbaugh
Associate Director, Production Editorial:
    Judy Leale
Production Project Manager: Kerri Tomasso
Permissions Coordinator: Charles Morris
Senior Operations Specialist: Arnold Vila
Operations Specialist: Benjamin Smith
Art Director: Kristine Carney

Interior Designer: Jonanthan Boylan
Cover Designer: Jonanthan Boylan
Director, Image Resource Center: Melinda Patelli
Manager, Rights and Permissions: Zina Arabia
Manager, Visual Research: Beth Brenzel
Image Permission Coordinator: Ang'John Ferreri
Manager, Cover Visual Research & Permissions:
    Karen Sanatar
Composition/Full-Service Project Management:
    Heidi Allgair, GGS Higher Education Resources,
    a Division of PreMedia Global, Inc.
Printer/Binder: Courier/Kendallville
Typeface: 10/12 ACaslon Regular

Credits and acknowledgments borrowed from other sources and reproduced, with permission, in this textbook appear on appropriate page within text.

Photo Credits: Cover: PictureNet/Corbis RF; page 1: Douglas Toombs/Shutterstock; page 6: The Granger Collection, New York; page 24: istockphoto.com; page 34: istockphoto.com; page 51: Getty Images; page 73: Stephen Fin/Shutterstock; page 89: Peter Wilson © Dorling Kindersley; page 105: Matthew Ward © Dorling Kindersley; page 108: © Dorling Kindersley; page 151: Valery Potapova/Shutterstock; page 152: Chas Howson © The Trustees of the British Museum; page 166: Irene Springer/Pearson Education/PH College; page 180: Philip Entricknap © Dorling Kindersley; page 207: FOTOG/Getty Images, Inc. Tetra Images; page 218: Roger Dixon © Dorling Kindersley; page 227: Geoff Brightling © Dorling Kindersley; page 231: Photodisc/Getty Images; page 279: Martin Trebbin/Shutterstock; page 280: Jochen Sand/Getty Images/Digital Vision; page 295: Dorling Kindersley © Daid Peart; page 305: Chas Howson © The British Museum; page 309: Vincent P. Walter/Pearson Education/PH College; page 325: istockphoto.com; page 336: Chris Stowers © Dorling Kindersley; page 339: Eyalos/Shutterstock; page 340: Getty Images, Inc.—Stockbyte Royalty; page 355: Photodisc/Getty Images; page 370: Chas Howson © The Trustees of the British Museum; page 405: zimmytws/Shutterstock; page 406: Irene Springer/Pearson Education/PH College; page 419: Anthony Johnson © Dorling Kindersley; page 434: Ed Bohon/Corbis/ Stock Market; page 457: Alex Saberi/Shutterstock; page 458: Stewart Cohen/Getty Images/Digital Vision; page 499: Laima Druskis/Pearson Education/PH College; page 527: Getty Images; page 544: Photolibary.com; page 556: istockphoto.com; page 577: Stephen Jaffe/AFP/Getty Images; page 597: Punit Paranjpe/Corbis/Reuters America LLC; page 612: istockphoto.com; page 677: Yegor Korzh/Shutterstock; page 691: Getty Images, Inc.—Purestock Royalty Free; page 702: John Foxx/Getty Images, Inc.—Stockbyte Royalty Free; page 737: Photodisc/Getty Images; page 783: unopix/Shutterstock; page 815: istockphoto.com; page 847: serg64/Shuttestock.

Copyright © 2010, 2007, 2004, 2001, 1998 by Pearson Education, Inc., Upper Saddle River, New Jersey, 07458.
Pearson Prentice Hall. All rights reserved. Printed in the United States of America. This publication is protected by Copyright and permission should be obtained from the publisher prior to any prohibited reproduction, storage in a retrieval system, or transmission in any form or by any means, electronic, mechanical, photocopying, recording, or likewise. For information regarding permission(s), write to: Rights and Permissions Department.

Pearson Prentice Hall™ is a trademark of Pearson Education, Inc.
Pearson® is a registered trademark of Pearson plc
Prentice Hall® is a registered trademark of Pearson Education, Inc.

Pearson Education LTD., London
Pearson Education Singapore, Pte. Ltd
Pearson Education, Canada, Ltd
Pearson Education–Japan

Pearson Education Australia PTY, Limited
Pearson Education North Asia Ltd
Pearson Educación de Mexico, S.A. de C.V.
Pearson Education Malaysia, Pte. Ltd.

Prentice Hall
is an imprint of

10 9 8 7 6 5 4 3
ISBN-13: 978-0-13-608554-6
ISBN-10: 0-13-608554-7

Dedication

Jin Du

ABOUT THE AUTHOR

Henry R. Cheeseman is clinical professor of Business Law, director of the Legal Studies Program, and co-director of the Minor in Business Law Program at the Marshall School of Business of the University of Southern California (USC), Los Angeles, California.

Professor Cheeseman earned a bachelor's degree in finance from Marquette University, both a master's in business administration (MBA) and a master's in business taxation (MBT) from the University of Southern California, a juris doctor (J.D.) degree from the University of California at Los Angeles School of Law, a master's of business administration with emphasis on law and economics from the University of Chicago, and a master's in law (L.L.M.) degree in financial institutions law from Boston University.

Professor Cheeseman has earned the "Golden Apple" Teaching Award on many occasions by having been voted by the students as the best professor at the Marshall School of Business of the University of Southern California. He was named a fellow of the Center for Excellence in Teaching at the University of Southern California by the dean of the Marshall School of Business. The USC's Torch and Tassel Chapter of the Mortar Board has named Professor Cheeseman Faculty of the Month of USC.

Professor Cheeseman writes leading business law and legal environment textbooks that are published by Prentice Hall. These include *Business Law: Legal Environment, Online Commerce, Business Ethics, and International Issues, Contemporary Business and Online Commerce Law, The Legal Environment of Business and Online Commerce, Essentials of Contemporary Business Law,* and *Introduction to Law: Its Dynamic Nature.*

Professor Cheeseman is an avid traveler and amateur photographer. Many of the interior photographs for this book were taken by Professor Cheeseman.

BRIEF CONTENTS

CONTENTS

To the Students

Each semester, as I stand up in front of a new group of students in my business law and legal environment classes, I am struck by the thought that, cases and statutes aside, I know two very important things that the students have yet to learn. The first is that I draw as much from them as they do from me. Their youth, enthusiasm, and questions—and even the doubts a few of them hold about the relevance of law to their futures—fuel my teaching. They don't know that every time they open their minds to look at an issue from a new perspective or critically question something, I have gotten a wonderful reward for the work I do.

The other thing I know is that both teaching and learning the legal environment are all about stories. These stories come from the legal cases in this book, as well as the important cases and stories that each professor personally brings to the classroom. These stories provide the framework on which students will hang everything they learn about the law in class. It is my hope that long after the specific language of cases or statutes have faded, they will retain that framework. Several years from now, "unintentional torts" may draw only a glimmer of recognition with business managers who learn about them as students in my class this year. However, they will likely recall the story of the woman who sued McDonald's for damages for serving her coffee that was too hot and caused her injuries. The story sticks and gives students the hook on which to hang the concepts.

I remind myself of these two facts every time I sit down to work on writing and revising *Business Law*, as well. My goal is to present business law, ethics, and the legal environment in a way that will spur students to ask questions, to go beyond rote memorization.

Business law is an evolving outgrowth of its environment, and the legal environment keeps changing. This new seventh edition of *Business Law* emphasizes

coverage of online law and e-commerce as key parts of the legal environment. In addition, this book covers social, ethical, and international issues that are important to the study of business law.

It is my wish that my commitment to these goals shines through in this labor of love, and I hope you have as much pleasure in using it as I have had in creating it for you.

Henry Cheeseman

SUPPLEMENTS THAT ACCOMPANY *BUSINESS LAW*, SEVENTH EDITION

For Instructors

We offer a variety of both print and electronic supplements to meet the unique teaching needs of each instructor. Electronic versions of the supplements that accompany this text are available for download by instructors only at our Instructor Resource Center, at **www.pearsonhighered.com/irc**.

NEW! Video Cases   Taken from the ABC News Video Library, includes a selection of brief video cases for use in class. Each case contains a real news clip as well as an optional introductory and conclusion section designed to stimulate classroom discussion. Cases are available on the Instructor's DVD.

Instructor's Manual   A comprehensive outline of each text chapter. Also included are "teacher to teacher dialogues" that offer teaching suggestions for each chapter as well as key chapter objectives.

Test Item File   Now featuring 500 new questions written specifically for this edition. Each question includes a corresponding difficulty level, allowing for the creation of tailor-made testing material.

TestGen   Test management software containing all the material from the Test Item File. This software is completely user friendly and allows instructors to view, edit, and add test questions with just a few mouse clicks.

PowerPoint Presentation   A ready-to-use PowerPoint slideshow designed for classroom presentation. Use it as-is or edit content to fit your individual classroom needs.

Instructor's Resource Center on DVD   A compilation of instructor's tools, including videos, the Instructor's Manual, the PowerPoint presentation, the Test Item File, and TestGen.

Web Exercises Moved Online   To offer you the most current web experience, all web exercises have been completely revised and moved online to **www.pearsonhighered.com/cheeseman**. For each chapter, we provide at least one new web exercise to assign to your students to help them use the web for legal research. Further, notes for using and assigning these exercises are available at the Instructor Resource Center for this text.

For Students

Study Guide   A student aid designed to facilitate learning by enforcing key concepts. Each chapter contains a chapter overview, a list of objectives, and an explanation of the practical applications of the chapter. Also included are a "helpful hints" section and a practice quiz in addition to several exercises.

Companion Website   Access at **www.pearsonhighered.com/cheeseman**. This website contains an online study guide, including true/false and multiple-choice questions, PowerPoint presentations for each chapter, and the completely revised web exercises.

Customizing This Text

You can easily customize this text via Prentice Hall Custom Business Resources (PHCBR), which offers you the flexibility to select specific chapters from the text to create a customized book to exactly fit your course needs. When you customize a book with PHCBR, your book will have the chapters in the order that matches your syllabus, with sequential pagination. All cross-references to other chapters will be removed. You even have the option to add your own material or third-party content!

To receive your free evaluation copy, build your book online (**www.prenhall.com/custombusiness**), contact your Pearson representative, or contact us directly, at dbase.pub@pearsoncustom.com or 800-777-6872. You can expect your evaluation copy to arrive within 7 to 10 business days.

ACKNOWLEDGMENTS

When I first began writing this book, I was a solitary figure, researching cases in the law library and writing text at my desk. As time passed, others entered upon the scene—copy editors, a developmental editor, research assistants, reviewers, and production personnel—and touched the project and made it better. Although my name appears on the cover of this book, it is no longer mine alone. I humbly thank the following persons for their contributions to this project.

THE EXCEPTIONAL PRENTICE HALL PROFESSIONALS AND SUPPLEMENTS TEAM

Many thanks to Kerri Tomasso, production project manager, for shepherding this seventh edition of *Business Law* through the many phases of editing and production at Prentice Hall. I'd also like to thank Heidi Allgair and Kitty Wilson of GGS Higher Education Resources, as the editors who skillfully and cheerfully navigated this complex project to publication. Kerri, Heidi, and Kitty have worked on several of my previous books, and I hope that they will each work on my future books.

The supplements package has been authored by a remarkable team, with exceptional contributions from Linda Fried at The University of Colorado–Denver, Robert McDonald at Franciscan University, Melinda Hickman at Fort Hayes State University, Jeffrey Penley at Catawba Valley Community College, and Tonia Hap Murphy at Notre Dame University.

I also appreciate the ideas, encouragement, effort, and decisions of the management team at Prentice Hall, including Eric Svendsen, editor-in-chief, Kierra Kashickey, editorial project manager, and Benjamin Paris, developmental editor, for their support in the publication of this book.

I would especially like to thank the professionals of the sales staff of Prentice Hall, particularly all the knowledgeable sales representatives, without whom the success of this textbook would be impossible.

PERSONAL ACKNOWLEDGMENTS

My family

Family counts the most, no matter how far away they are geographically. Thanks to my parents—Henry B. and Florence, deceased—who had a profound effect on me and my ability to be a professor and writer; my brother Gregory and the special bond that exists between us as twins; and the rest of my family, Gregory's wife Lana, my sister Marcia, my nephew Gregory and niece Nikki, and my great-nieces Lauren, Addison, and Shelby. My entire family lives in St. Ignace, Michigan, which I will always call home.

Students

I'd like to acknowledge the students at the University of Southern California (USC) and the students at other colleges and universities in the United States and around the world. Their spirit, energy, and joy are contagious. I love teaching my students (and, as importantly, their teaching me). At the end of each semester, I am sad that the students I have come to know are moving on. But each new semester brings another group of students who will be a joy to teach. And the cycle continues.

Research Assistant

Ashley Anderson has been my research assistant for the past three years. Ashley has done an absolutely excellent job in researching new cases to be used in this seventh edition of

Business Law and working on the editing and production of the book. Ashley has now moved on to law school, and I will miss her.

Colleagues

Certain people and colleagues are enjoyable to work with and have made my life easier as I have endeavored to write this new edition of *Business Law*. I would like to thank Kerry Fields, my colleague in teaching business law courses at USC, who is an excellent professor and a wonderful friend. I would also like to thank Helen Pitts, Terry Lichvar, Marilyn Johnson, and Debra Jacobs, at the Marshall School of Business, who are always a joy to work with. I would also like to thank the professors who teach business law and legal environment courses for their dedication to the discipline and to their students.

Reviewers

The author and publisher would like to acknowledge the following reviewers for their time and valuable feedback:

Denise Bartles, Western State College
Eli Bortman, Babson College
Chester Brough, Utah State University
Nigel J. Cohen, University of Texas, Pan American
Thomas Eppink, University of South Carolina
Deborah Frey, Southern Illinois University
Wendy Gelman, Florida International University
Howard Hammer, Ball State University
Richard Kohn, Southeast Community College
Linda Moran, Sonoma State University
Tonia Hap Murphy, Notre Dame University
Mark Patzkowski, North West Oklahoma State University
Frank Primiani, Green River Community College
Donald Sanders, Southwest Texas State University
Charles Soos, Livingston College, Rutgers University
Robert Young, University of Nebraska, Kearney
Eric Yordy, Northern Arizona University

AUTHOR'S PERSONAL STATEMENT

While writing this Preface and Acknowledgment, I have thought about the thousands of hours I have spent researching, writing, and preparing this manuscript. I've loved every minute, and the knowledge gained has been sufficient reward for the endeavor.

I hope this book and its supplementary materials will serve you as well as they have served me.

With joy and sadness,
emptiness and fullness,
honor and humility,
I surrender the fruits of this labor

Henry R. Cheeseman

Part I
LEGAL ENVIRONMENT
OF BUSINESS
AND E-COMMERCE

1

1 | LEGAL HERITAGE AND THE INFORMATION AGE

▲ **Statue of Liberty, New York Harbor.** *The Statue of Liberty stands majestically in New York harbor. During the American Revolution, France gave the colonial patriots substantial support in the form of money for equipment and supplies, officers and soldiers who fought in the war, and ships and sailors who fought on the seas. Without the assistance of France, it is unlikely that the American colonists would have won their independence from Britain. In 1886, the people of France gave the Statue of Liberty to the people of the United States in recognition of their friendship that was established during the American Revolution. Since then, the Statue of Liberty has become a symbol of liberty and democracy throughout the world.*

CHAPTER OBJECTIVES

After studying this chapter, you should be able to:

1. Define *law*.
2. Describe the functions of law.
3. List and describe the sources of law in the United States.
4. Explain the development of the U.S. legal system.

CHAPTER CONTENTS

▶ **INTRODUCTION TO LEGAL HERITAGE AND THE INFORMATION AGE**

▶ **WHAT IS LAW?**
Landmark U.S. Supreme Court Case · *Brown v. Board of Education*

▶ **SCHOOLS OF JURISPRUDENTIAL THOUGHT**
International Law · *Immigration to the United States of America*

▶ **HISTORY OF AMERICAN LAW**
International Law · *Adoption of English Common Law in America*
International Law · *The Civil Law System*

▶ **SOURCES OF LAW IN THE UNITED STATES**

separate trial. In writing the opinion of the Court, Chief Justice Warren Burger stated, "This case does no more than manifest the simple, if discomforting, reality that different juries may reach different results under any criminal statute. That is one of the consequences we accept under our jury system."

Flexibility of the Law

U.S. law evolves and changes along with the norms of society, technology, and the growth and expansion of commerce in the United States and the world. The following quote by Judge Jerome Frank discusses the value of the adaptability of law:

> *Law must be stable and yet it cannot stand still.*
>
> Roscoe Pound
> *Interpretations of Legal History (1923)*

The law always has been, is now, and will ever continue to be, largely vague and variable. And how could this be otherwise? The law deals with human relations in their most complicated aspects. The whole confused, shifting helter-skelter of life parades before it— more confused than ever, in our kaleidoscopic age.

Men have never been able to construct a comprehensive, eternalized set of rules anticipating all possible legal disputes and formulating in advance the rules which would apply to them. Situations are bound to occur which were never contemplated when the original rules were made. How much less is such a frozen legal system possible in modern times?

The constant development of unprecedented problems requires a legal system capable of fluidity and pliancy. Our society would be straightjacketed were not the courts, with the able assistance of the lawyers, constantly overhauling the law and adapting it to the realities of ever-changing social, industrial, and political conditions; although changes cannot be made lightly, yet rules of law must be more or less impermanent, experimental and therefore not nicely calculable.

Much of the uncertainty of law is not an unfortunate accident; it is of immense social value.[5]

LANDMARK U.S. SUPREME COURT CASE

Brown v. Board of Education

"We conclude that in the field of public education the doctrine of 'separate but equal' has no place."

—Justice Warren

When the original 13 states ratified the Constitution of the United States of America in 1788, it created a democratic form of government and granted certain rights to its people. But all persons were not treated equally, as many people, including drafters of the Constitution such as Thomas Jefferson, owned African American slaves. It was more than 75 years before the Civil War was fought between the northern states and the southern Confederate states over the preservation of the Union and slavery. Slavery was abolished by the Thirteenth Amendment to the Constitution in 1865. The Fourteenth Amendment, added to the Constitution in 1868, contains the Equal Protection Clause, which provides that no state shall "deny to any person within its jurisdiction the equal protection of the laws." The original intent of this amendment was to guarantee equality to freed African Americans.

But equality was denied to African Americans for years to come. This included discrimination in housing, transportation, education, jobs, service at restaurants, and other activities. In 1896, the U.S. Supreme Court decided the case Plessy v. Ferguson.[6] *In that case, the state of Louisiana had a law that provided for separate but equal accommodations for African American and white railway passengers. An African American passenger challenged the state law. The Supreme Court held that the "separate but equal" state law did not violate the Equal Protection Clause of the Fourteenth Amendment. The "separate but equal" doctrine was then applied to all areas of life, including public education. Thus, African American and white children attended separate schools, often with unequal facilities.*

It was not until 1954 that the U.S. Supreme Court decided a case that challenged the separate but equal doctrine as it applied to public elementary and high schools. In Brown v. Board of Education,[7] *a consolidated case that challenged the separate school systems of four states—Kansas, South Carolina,*

(case continues)

Virginia, and Delaware—the Supreme Court decided to revisit the separate but equal doctrine announced by its forbearers in another century. This time, a unanimous Supreme Court, in an opinion written by Chief Justice Earl Warren, reversed prior precedent and held that the separate but equal doctrine violated the Equal Protection Clause of the Fourteenth Amendment to the Constitution. In its opinion, the Court stated:

> We cannot turn the clock back to 1868 when the Amendment was adopted, or even to 1896 when Plessy v. Ferguson was written. Today, education is perhaps the most important function of state and local governments.
>
> We conclude that in the field of public education the doctrine of "separate but equal" has no place. Separate educational facilities are inherently unequal. Therefore,

we hold that the plaintiffs and others similarly situated for whom actions have been brought are, by reason of the segregation complained of, deprived of the equal protection of the laws guaranteed by the Fourteenth Amendment.

After Brown v. Board of Education was decided, it took court orders as well as U.S. Army enforcement to integrate many of the public schools in this country. The Brown v. Board of Education case demonstrates that one Supreme Court case can overrule prior Supreme Court cases to promote justice. The U.S. Supreme Court's Brown v. Board of Education opinion is set forth in Exhibit 1.1. Brown v. Board of Education, 347 U.S. 483, 74 S.Ct. 686, 98 L.Ed. 873, **Web** 1954 U.S. Lexis 2094 (Supreme Court of the United States, 1954)

Case Questions

Critical Legal Thinking What does the Equal Protection Clause of the Fourteenth Amendment to the U.S. Constitution provide?

Business Ethics Was the Equal Protection Clause properly applied in the early U.S. Supreme Court decision *Plessy v. Ferguson*? Explain.

Contemporary Business It has been said that the U.S. Constitution is a "living document"—that is, one that can adapt to changing times. Do you think this is a good policy? Or should the U.S. Constitution be interpreted narrowly and literally, as originally written?

Supreme Court of the United States

No. 1 ——— , October Term, 19 54

Oliver Brown, Mrs. Richard Lawton, Mrs. Sadie Emmanuel et al.,

Appellants,

vs.

Board of Education of Topeka, Shawnee County, Kansas, et al.

Appeal from the United States District Court for the ——————————— District of Kansas.

This cause came on to be heard on the transcript of the record from the United States District Court for the ——————— District of Kansas, ——————— and was argued by counsel.

On consideration whereof, It is ordered and adjudged by this Court that the judgment of the said District ——————— Court in this cause be, and the same is hereby, reversed with costs; and that this cause be, and the same is hereby, remanded to the said District Court to take such proceedings and enter such orders and decrees consistent with the opinions of this Court as are necessary and proper to admit to public schools on a racially nondiscriminatory basis with all deliberate speed the parties to this case.

Per Mr. Chief Justice Warren,

May 31, 1955.

1469

▶ **Exhibit 1.1 OPINION OF THE U.S. SUPREME COURT:** *BROWN V. BOARD OF EDUCATION*

▶ SCHOOLS OF JURISPRUDENTIAL THOUGHT

jurisprudence
The philosophy or science of law.

The philosophy or science of the law is referred to as **jurisprudence**. There are several different philosophies about how the law developed, ranging from the classical natural theory to modern theories of law and economics and critical legal studies. Classical legal philosophies are discussed in the following paragraphs.

Natural Law School

The **Natural Law School** of jurisprudence postulates that the law is based on what is "correct." Natural law philosophers emphasize a **moral theory of law**—that is, law should be based on morality and ethics. Natural law is "discovered" by humans through the use of reason and choosing between good and evil.

Examples Documents such as the U.S. Constitution, the Magna Carta, and the United Nations Charter reflect this theory.

The law is not a series of calculating machines where definitions and answers come tumbling out when the right levers are pushed.

William O. Douglas
The Dissent, A Safeguard of Democracy (1948)

Historical School

The **Historical School** of jurisprudence believes that the law is an aggregate of social traditions and customs that have developed over the centuries. It believes that changes in the norms of society will gradually be reflected in the law. To these legal philosophers, the law is an evolutionary process.

Example Historical legal scholars look to past legal decisions (precedent) to solve contemporary problems.

Analytical School

The **Analytical School** of jurisprudence maintains that the law is shaped by logic. Analytical philosophers believe that results are reached by applying principles of logic to the specific facts of the case. The emphasis is on the logic of the result rather than on how the result is reached.

Sociological School

The **Sociological School** of jurisprudence asserts that the law is a means of achieving and advancing certain sociological goals. The followers of this philosophy, known as *realists*, believe that the purpose of law is to shape social behavior. Sociological philosophers are unlikely to adhere to past law as precedent.

Command School

The philosophers of the **Command School** of jurisprudence believe that the law is a set of rules developed, communicated, and enforced by the ruling party rather than a reflection of the society's morality, history, logic, or sociology. This school maintains that the law changes when the ruling class changes.

Critical Legal Studies School

The **Critical Legal Studies School** proposes that legal rules are unnecessary and are used as an obstacle by the powerful to maintain the status quo. Critical legal theorists (the *Crits*) argue that legal disputes should be solved by applying arbitrary rules that are based on broad notions of what is "fair" in each circumstance. Under this theory, subjective decision making by judges would be permitted.

Pyongyang, North Korea.
This is the Kim Il Sung statue and Mount Paekto–Mansudae Grand Monument in Pyongyang, North Korea. North Korea—the Democratic People's Republic of Korea (or DPRK)—is a communist dictatorship, first commanded by the late Kim Il Sung. North Koreans pay homage to the Dear Leader's statue in Pyongyang, the capital of North Korea.

Law and Economics School

The **Law and Economics School** (or the "**Chicago School**," named after the University of Chicago, where it was first developed) believes that promoting market efficiency should be the central goal of legal decision making.

Example Proponents of law and economics theory suggest that the practice of appointing counsel, free of charge, to prisoners who bring civil rights cases should be abolished. They believe that if a prisoner cannot find a lawyer who will take the case on a contingency-fee basis or *pro bono* (free of charge), the case is probably not worth bringing.

CONCEPT SUMMARY
SCHOOLS OF JURISPRUDENTIAL THOUGHT

School	Philosophy
Natural Law	Postulates that law is based on what is "correct." It emphasizes a moral theory of law—that is, law should be based on morality and ethics.
Historical	Believes that law is an aggregate of social traditions and customs.
Analytical	Maintains that law is shaped by logic.
Sociological	Asserts that the law is a means of achieving and advancing certain sociological goals.
Command	Believes that the law is a set of rules developed, communicated, and enforced by the ruling party.
Critical Legal Studies	Maintains that legal rules are unnecessary and that legal disputes should be solved by applying arbitrary rules based on fairness.
Law and Economics	Believes that promoting market efficiency should be the central concern of legal decision making.

INTERNATIONAL LAW

Immigration to the United States of America

"That I will support and defend the Constitution and laws of the United States of America against all enemies, . . ."

—Oath of Citizenship
United States of America

The United States of America was originally founded by immigrants, primarily those from western Europe. Many sought wealth and prosperity; some sought religious freedom, and others were running from their debts. But no matter the reason, during the sixteenth, seventeenth, and eighteenth centuries, the immigrants kept coming, and they moved increasingly further inland from the Atlantic Ocean. Many immigrants also came from the continent of Africa, most forcibly to become slaves.

After winning a bloody revolution and gaining freedom from Great Britain, immigrants continued to pour into the country during the nineteenth and twentieth centuries, and they continue to do so in the twenty-first century. Immigrants to the United States come from all over the world.

In 1921, the United States enacted its first immigration quota law, setting a limit on the number of immigrants that could be admitted to the United States from each foreign country each year. During different times, the quotas for each foreign country have been raised or lowered, depending on the world situation. For example, after World War II, the United States increased the quotas dramatically to accept many persons who had been displaced by the war. This quota system is still in effect today.

Currently, the immigration laws of this country are administered by the **United States Citizenship and Immigration Services (USCIS)**, which is part of the U.S. Department of Homeland Security.

Foreign nationals who qualify, and have met the requirements to do so, may become citizens of the United States. During their swearing-in ceremony, they must swear the following Oath of Citizenship:

The Oath of Citizenship

I hereby declare, on oath, that I absolutely and entirely renounce and adjure all allegiance and fidelity to any foreign prince, potentate, state, or sovereignty of whom or which I have heretofore been a subject or citizen; that I will support and defend the Constitution and laws of the United States of America against all enemies, foreign and domestic; that I will bear true faith and allegiance to the same; that I will bear arms on behalf of the United States when required by law; that I will perform noncombatant service in the Armed Forces of the United States when required by the law; that I will perform work of national importance under civilian direction when required by the law; and that I take this obligation freely without any mental reservation or purpose of evasion; so help me God. In acknowledgement whereof I have hereunto affixed my signature.

Ellis Island, New York.
Ellis Island, New York, was the primary entry point for immigrants entering the United States from the late 1800s until 1954.

▶ HISTORY OF AMERICAN LAW

When the American colonies were first settled, the English system of law was generally adopted as the system of jurisprudence. This was the foundation from which American judges developed a common law in America.

English Common Law

English common law was law developed by judges who issued their opinions when deciding cases. The principles announced in these cases became *precedent* for later judges deciding similar cases. The English common law can be divided into cases decided by the *law courts*, *equity courts*, and *merchant courts*.

Law Courts   Prior to the Norman Conquest of England in 1066, each locality in England was subject to local laws, as established by the lord or chieftain in control of the local area. There was no countrywide system of law. After 1066, William the Conqueror and his successors to the throne of England began to replace the various local laws with one uniform system of law. To accomplish this, the king or queen appointed loyal followers as judges in all local areas. These judges were charged with administering the law in a uniform manner, in courts that were called **law courts**. Law at that time tended to emphasize the form (legal procedure) over the substance (merit) of a case. The only relief available at law courts was a monetary award for damages.

Chancery (Equity) Courts   Because of the unfair results and the limited remedy available in the law courts, a second set of courts—the **Court of Chancery** (or **equity court**)—was established. These courts were under the authority of the lord chancellor. Persons who believed that the decision of the law court was unfair or believed that the law court could not grant an appropriate remedy could seek relief in the Court of Chancery. Rather than emphasize legal procedure, the chancery court inquired into the merits of the case. The chancellor's remedies were called *equitable remedies* because they were shaped to fit each situation. Equitable orders and remedies of the Court of Chancery took precedence over the legal decisions and remedies of the law courts.

Merchant Courts   As trade developed in the Middle Ages, the merchants who traveled about England and Europe developed certain rules to solve their commercial disputes. These rules, known as the "law of merchants," or the **Law Merchant**, were based on common trade practices and usage. Eventually, a separate set of courts was established to administer these rules. This court was called the **Merchant Court**. In the early 1900s, the Merchant Court was absorbed into the regular law court system of England.

common law
Law developed by judges who issued their opinions when deciding a case. The principles announced in these cases became precedent for later judges deciding similar cases.

Two things most people should never see made: sausages and laws.

An old saying

 INTERNATIONAL LAW

Adoption of English Common Law in America

All the states of the United States of America (except Louisiana) base their legal systems primarily on the English common law. In the United States, the law, equity, and merchant courts have been merged. Thus, most U.S. courts permit the aggrieved party to seek both law and equitable orders and remedies.

The importance of common law to the American legal system is described in the following excerpt from

Justice Douglas's opinion in the 1841 case *Penny v. Little*:

The common law is a beautiful system, containing the wisdom and experiences of ages. Like the people it ruled and protected, it was simple and crude in its infancy and became enlarged, improved, and polished as the nation advanced in civilization, virtue, and intelligence. Adapting itself to the conditions and circumstances of the people and relying upon them for its administration, it necessarily improved as the condition of the people was elevated. The inhabitants of this country always claimed the common law as their birthright, and at an early period established it as the basis of their jurisprudence.[8]

INTERNATIONAL LAW

The Civil Law System

One of the major legal systems that has developed in the world in addition to the Anglo-American common law system is the **Romano-Germanic civil law system**. This legal system, which is commonly called the **civil law**, dates to 450 B.C., when Rome adopted the Twelve Tables, a code of laws applicable to the Romans. A compilation of Roman law, called the *Corpus Juris Civilis*

("Body of Civil Law"), was completed in A.D. 534. Later, two national codes—the French Civil Code of 1804 (the Napoleonic Code) and the German Civil Code of 1896—became models for countries that adopted civil codes.

In contrast to the Anglo-American common law, in which laws are created by the judicial system as well as by congressional legislation, the Civil Code and parliamentary statutes that expand and interpret it are the sole sources of the law in most civil law countries. Thus, the adjudication of a case is simply the application of the code or the statutes to a particular set of facts. In some civil law countries, court decisions do not have the force of law.

Many countries in Europe still follow the civil law system.

▶ SOURCES OF LAW IN THE UNITED STATES

In the more than 200 years since the founding of the United States and adoption of the English common law, the lawmakers of this country have developed a substantial body of law. The *sources of modern law* in the United States are discussed in the paragraphs that follow.

Constitutions

constitution of the United States of America
The supreme law of the United States.

The **Constitution of the United States of America** is the *supreme law of the land*. This means that any law—whether federal, state, or local—that conflicts with the U.S. Constitution is unconstitutional and, therefore, unenforceable.

The principles enumerated in the Constitution are extremely broad because the founding fathers intended them to be applied to evolving social, technological, and economic conditions. The U.S. Constitution is often referred to as a "living document" because it is so adaptable.

The U.S. Constitution established the structure of the federal government. It created the following three branches of government and gave them the following powers:

The Constitution of the United States is not a mere lawyers' document: it is a vehicle of life, and its spirit is always the spirit of age.

Woodrow Wilson
Constitutional Government in the United States (1927)

- The **legislative branch (Congress)** has the power to make (enact) the law.
- The **executive branch (president)** has the power to enforce the law.
- The **judicial branch (courts)** has the power to interpret and determine the validity of the law.

Powers not given to the federal government by the Constitution are reserved for the states. States also have their own **constitutions**. These are often patterned after the U.S. Constitution, although many are more detailed. State constitutions establish the legislative, executive, and judicial branches of state government and establish the powers of each branch. Provisions of state constitutions are valid unless they conflict with the U.S. Constitution or any valid federal law.

Treaties

treaty
A compact made between two or more nations.

The U.S. Constitution provides that the president, with the advice and consent of two-thirds of the Senate, may enter into **treaties** with foreign governments. Treaties become part of the supreme law of the land. With increasing international economic relations among nations, treaties will become an even more important source of law that will affect business in the future.

Codified Law

Statutes are written laws that establish certain courses of conduct that must be adhered to by covered parties. The U.S. Congress is empowered by the Commerce Clause and other provisions of the U.S. Constitution to enact **federal statutes** to regulate foreign and interstate commerce. State legislatures enact **state statutes**. The statutes enacted by the legislative branches of the federal and state governments are organized by topic into code books. This is often called **codified law**.

State legislatures often delegate lawmaking authority to local government bodies, including cities and municipalities, counties, school districts, water districts, and such. These governmental units are empowered to adopt **ordinances**. Ordinances are also codified.

statute
Written law enacted by the legislative branch of the federal and state governments that establishes certain courses of conduct that must be adhered to by covered parties.

ordinance
Law enacted by local government bodies, such as cities and municipalities, counties, school districts, and water districts.

U.S. Congress, Washington, DC. *The U.S. Congress, which is a bicameral system made up of the U.S. Senate and the U.S. House of Representatives, creates federal law by enacting statutes. Each state has two senators and is allocated a certain number of representatives, based on population.*

Executive Orders

The executive branch of government, which includes the president of the United States and state governors, is empowered to issue **executive orders**. This power is derived from express delegation from the legislative branch and is implied from the U.S. Constitution and state constitutions.

executive order
An order issued by a member of the executive branch of the government.

Example When the United States is at war with another country, the president of the United States usually issues executive orders prohibiting U.S. companies from selling goods or services to that country.

Regulations and Orders of Administrative Agencies

administrative agencies
Agencies (such as the Securities and Exchange Commission and the Federal Trade Commission) that the legislative and executive branches of federal and state governments are empowered to establish.

The legislative and executive branches of federal and state governments are empowered to establish **administrative agencies** to enforce and interpret statutes enacted by Congress and state legislatures. Many of these agencies regulate business.

Examples Congress has created the Securities and Exchange Commission (SEC) to enforce federal securities laws and the Federal Trade Commission (FTC) to enforce consumer protection statutes.

Congress or the state legislatures usually empower these agencies to adopt **administrative rules and regulations** to interpret the statutes that the agency is authorized to enforce. These rules and regulations have the force of law. Administrative agencies usually have the power to hear and decide disputes. Their decisions are called **orders**. Because of their power, administrative agencies are often informally referred to as the "fourth branch of government."

Judicial Decisions

judicial decision
A decision about an individual lawsuit issued by a federal or state court.

When deciding individual lawsuits, federal and state courts issue **judicial decisions**. In these written opinions, a judge or justice usually explains the legal reasoning used to decide the case. These opinions often include interpretations of statutes, ordinances, and administrative regulations and the announcement of legal principles used to decide the case. Many court decisions are printed (reported) in books that are available in law libraries.

precedent
A rule of law established in a court decision. Lower courts must follow the precedent established by higher courts.

***Doctrine of* Stare Decisis**   Based on the common law tradition, past court decisions become **precedent** for deciding future cases. Lower courts must follow the precedent established by higher courts. That is why all federal and state courts in the United States must follow the precedents established by U.S. Supreme Court decisions.

The courts of one jurisdiction are not bound by the precedent established by the courts of another jurisdiction, although they may look to each other for guidance.

Example State courts of one state are not required to follow the legal precedent established by the courts of another state.

stare decisis
Latin: "to stand by the decision." Adherence to precedent.

Adherence to precedent is called the **doctrine of *stare decisis*** ("to stand by the decision"). The doctrine of *stare decisis* promotes uniformity of law within a jurisdiction, makes the court system more efficient, and makes the law more predictable for individuals and businesses. A court may later change or reverse its legal reasoning if a new case is presented to it and change is warranted. The doctrine of *stare decisis* is discussed in the following excerpt from Justice Musmanno's decision in *Flagiello v. Pennsylvania*:

> *Without* stare decisis, *there would be no stability in our system of jurisprudence.* Stare decisis *channels the law. It erects lighthouses and flies the signal of safety. The ships of jurisprudence must follow that well-defined channel which, over the years, has been proved to be secure and worthy.*[9]

CONCEPT SUMMARY

SOURCES OF LAW IN THE UNITED STATES

Source of Law	Description
Constitutions	The U.S. Constitution establishes the federal government and enumerates its powers. Powers not given to the federal government are reserved to the states. State constitutions establish state governments and enumerate their powers.
Treaties	The president, with the advice and consent of two-thirds of the Senate, may enter into treaties with foreign countries.
Codified law: statutes and ordinances	Statutes are enacted by Congress and state legislatures. Ordinances are enacted by municipalities and local government bodies. They establish courses of conduct that covered parties must follow.

Executive orders	Issued by the president and governors of states. Executive orders regulate the conduct of covered parties.
Regulations and orders of administrative agencies	Administrative agencies are created by the legislative and executive branches of government. They may adopt rules and regulations that regulate the conduct of covered parties as well as issue orders.
Judicial decisions	Courts decide controversies. In doing so, a court issues an opinion that states the decision of the court and the rationale used in reaching that decision.

Priority of Law in the United States

As mentioned previously, the U.S. Constitution and treaties take precedence over all other laws in the United States. Federal statutes take precedence over federal regulations. Valid federal law takes precedence over any conflicting state or local law. State constitutions rank as the highest state law. State statutes take precedence over state regulations. Valid state law takes precedence over local laws.

Where law ends, there tyranny begins.

William Pitt, First Earl of Chatham

TEST REVIEW TERMS AND CONCEPTS

Administrative agency
Administrative rules and regulations
Analytical School
Civil law
Codified law
Command School
Constitution
Constitution of the United States of America
Court of Chancery (equity courts)

Critical Legal Studies School
Doctrine of *stare decisis*
English common law
Executive branch (president)
Executive order
Federal statutes
Historical School
Judicial branch (courts)
Judicial decision

Jurisprudence
Law
Law courts
Law and Economics School ("Chicago School")
Law Merchant
Legislative branch (Congress)
Merchant Court
Moral theory of law
Natural Law School

Order
Ordinance
Precedent
Romano-Germanic civil law system
Sociological School
State statute
Statute
Treaty
United States Citizenship and Immigration Services (USCIS)

CASE PROBLEM

1.1 Fairness of the Law   In 1909, the state legislature of Illinois enacted a statute called the "Woman's 10-Hour Law." The law prohibited women who were employed in factories and other manufacturing facilities from working more than 10 hours per day. The law did not apply to men. W. C. Ritchie & Co., an employer, brought a lawsuit that challenged the statute as being unconstitutional, in violation of the Equal Protection Clause of the Illinois constitution. In upholding the statute, the Illinois supreme court stated:

It is known to all men (and what we know as men we cannot profess to be ignorant of as judges) that woman's physical structure and the performance of maternal functions place her at a great disadvantage in the battle of life; that while a man can work for more than 10 hours a day without injury to himself, a woman, especially when the burdens of motherhood are upon her, cannot; that while a man can work standing upon his feet for more than 10 hours a day, day after day, without injury to himself, a woman cannot; and that to require a woman to stand upon her feet for more than 10 hours in any one day and perform severe manual labor

while thus standing, day after day, has the effect to impair her health, and that as weakly and sickly women cannot be mothers of vigorous children.

We think the general consensus of opinion, not only in this country but in the civilized countries of Europe, is, that a working day of not more than 10 hours for women is justified for the following reasons: (1) the physical organization of women, (2) her maternal function, (3) the rearing and education of children, (4) the maintenance of the home; and these conditions are, so far, matters of general knowledge that the courts will take judicial cognizance of their existence.

Surrounded as women are by changing conditions of society, and the evolution of employment which environs them, we agree fully with what is said by the Supreme Court of Washington in the Buchanan case; "law is, or ought to be, a progressive science."

Is the statute fair? Would the statute be lawful today? Should the law be a "progressive science"? *W. C. Ritchie & Co. v. Wayman, Attorney for Cook County, Illinois*, 244 Ill. 509, 91 N.E. 695, **Web** 1910 Ill. Lexis 1958 (Supreme Court of Illinois)

BUSINESS ETHICS CASE

1.2 Business Ethics   In 1975, after the war in Vietnam, the U.S. Government discontinued draft registration for men in this country. In 1980, after the Soviet Union invaded Afghanistan, President Jimmy Carter asked Congress for funds to reactivate draft registration. President Carter suggested that both males and females be required to register. Congress allocated funds only for the registration of males. Several men who were subject to draft registration brought a lawsuit that challenged the law as being unconstitutional, in violation of the Equal Protection Clause of the U.S. Constitution. The U.S. Supreme Court upheld the constitutionality of the draft registration law, reasoning as follows:

The question of registering women for the draft not only received considerable national attention and was the subject of wide-ranging public debate, but also was extensively considered by Congress in hearings, floor debate, and in committee. The foregoing clearly establishes that the decision to exempt women from registration was not the "accidental by-product of a traditional way of thinking about women."

This is not a case of Congress arbitrarily choosing to burden one of two similarly situated groups, such as would be the case with an all-black or all-white, or an all-Catholic or all-Lutheran, or an all-Republican or all-Democratic registration. Men and women are simply not similarly situated for purposes of a draft or registration for a draft.

Justice Marshall dissented, stating:

The Court today places its imprimatur on one of the most potent remaining public expressions of "ancient canards about the proper role of women." It upholds a statute that requires males but not females to register for the draft, and which thereby categorically excludes women from a fundamental civil obligation. I dissent.

Is the decision fair? Is the law a "progressive science" in this case? Is it ethical for males but not females to have to register for the draft? *Rostker, Director of Selective Service v. Goldberg*, 453 U.S. 57, 101 S.Ct. 2646, 69 L.Ed. 2d 478, **Web** 1981 U.S. Lexis 126 (Supreme Court of the United States)

ENDNOTES

1. *The Spirit of Liberty*, 3rd ed. (New York: Alfred A. Knopf, 1960).
2. "Introduction," *The Nature of Law: Readings in Legal Philosophy*, ed. M. P. Golding (New York: Random House, 1966).
3. *Black's Law Dictionary*, 5th ed. (St. Paul, MN: West).
4. 447 U.S. 10, 100 S.Ct. 1999, 64 L.Ed.2d 689, **Web** 1980 U.S. Lexis 127 (Supreme Court of the United States).
5. *Law and the Modern Mind* (New York: Brentano's, 1930).
6. 163 U.S. 537, 16 S.C. 1138, 141 L.Ed 256, **Web** 1896 U.S. Lexis 3390 (Supreme Court of the United States, 1896).
7. 347 U.S. 483, 74 S.Ct. 686, 98 L.Ed. 873, **Web** 1954 U.S. Lexis 2094 (Supreme Court of the United States, 1954).
8. 4 Ill. 301, 1841 Ill. Lexis 98 (Ill.).
9. 417 Pa. 486, 208 A.2d 193, **Web** 1965 Pa. Lexis 442 (Supreme Court of Pennsylvania).

▲ **Las Vegas, Nevada** *This is a federal government courthouse—the Lloyd D. George United States District Court for the District of Nevada—located in Las Vegas, Nevada. This is a federal trial court. Federal courts hear and decide cases over which the court has jurisdiction.*

CHAPTER OBJECTIVES

After studying this chapter, you should be able to:

1. Describe state court systems.
2. Describe the federal court system.
3. List and describe the types of decisions that are issued by the U.S. Supreme Court.

4. Compare the jurisdiction of state courts with that of federal courts.
5. Define *standing to sue* and *venue*.

CHAPTER CONTENTS

"I was never ruined but twice; once when I lost a lawsuit, and once when I won one."

Voltaire

▶ INTRODUCTION TO COURT SYSTEMS AND JURISDICTION

There are two major court systems in the United States: (1) the federal court system and (2) the court systems of the 50 states, the District of Columbia, and territories of the United States. Each of these systems has jurisdiction to hear different types of lawsuits. This chapter discusses the various court systems and the jurisdiction of different courts to hear and decide cases.

▶ STATE, DISTRICT OF COLUMBIA, AND TERRITORY COURT SYSTEMS

Each state, the District of Columbia, and each territory of the United States has its own separate court system (hereafter collectively referred to as "**state courts**"). Most state court systems include the following: *limited-jurisdiction trial courts, general-jurisdiction trial courts, intermediate appellate courts,* and a *supreme court.*

Limited-Jurisdiction Trial Courts

limited-jurisdiction trial court
A court that hears matters of a specialized or limited nature.

State **limited-jurisdiction trial courts**, which are sometimes referred to as **inferior trial courts**, hear matters of a specialized or limited nature.

Examples Traffic courts, juvenile courts, justice-of-the-peace courts, probate courts, family law courts, courts that hear misdemeanor criminal law cases, and courts that hear misdemeanor criminal law cases are limited-jurisdiction courts in many states.

Because limited-jurisdiction courts are trial courts, evidence can be introduced and testimony can be given. Most limited-jurisdiction courts keep records of their proceedings. Their decisions can usually be appealed to a general-jurisdiction court or an appellate court.

small claims court
A court that hears civil cases involving small dollar amounts.

Many states have also created **small claims courts** to hear civil cases involving small dollar amounts (e.g., $5,000 or less). Generally, the parties must appear individually and cannot have lawyers represent them. The decisions of small claims courts are often appealable to general-jurisdiction trial courts or appellate courts.

General-Jurisdiction Trial Courts

general-jurisdiction trial court
A court that hears cases of a general nature that are not within the jurisdiction of limited-jurisdiction trial courts. Testimony and evidence at trial are recorded and stored for future reference.

Every state has a **general-jurisdiction trial court**. These courts are often referred to as **courts of record** because the testimony and evidence at trial are recorded and stored for future reference. These courts hear cases that are not within the jurisdiction of limited-jurisdiction trial courts, such as felonies, civil cases over a certain dollar amount, and so on.

Some states divide their general-jurisdiction courts into two divisions, one for criminal cases and another for civil cases. Evidence and testimony are given at general-jurisdiction trial courts. The decisions handed down by these courts are appealable to an intermediate appellate court or the state supreme court, depending on the circumstances.

Intermediate Appellate Courts

intermediate appellate court
An intermediate court that hears appeals from trial courts.

In many states, **intermediate appellate courts** (also called **appellate courts** or **courts of appeals**) hear appeals from trial courts. They review the trial court record to determine whether there have been any errors at trial that would require reversal or modification of the trial court's decision. Thus, an appellate court reviews either pertinent parts or the whole trial court record from the lower court. No new evidence or testimony is permitted.

The parties usually file legal *briefs* with the appellate court, stating the law and facts that support their positions. Appellate courts usually grant a brief oral hearing to the parties. Appellate court decisions are appealable to the state's highest court. In sparsely populated states that do not have an intermediate appellate court, trial court decisions can be appealed directly to the state's highest court.

Highest State Court

Each state has a highest court in its court system. Most states call this highest court the **state supreme court**. Some states use other names for their highest courts. The function of a state's highest court is to hear appeals from intermediate appellate state courts and certain trial courts. No new evidence or testimony is heard. The parties usually submit pertinent parts of or the entire lower court record for review. The parties also submit legal briefs to the court and are usually granted a brief oral hearing. Decisions of highest state courts are final unless a question of law is involved that is appealable to the U.S. Supreme Court.

Exhibit 2.1 portrays a typical state court system. Exhibit 2.2 lists the websites for the court systems of 50 states and 4 jurisdictions associated with the United States.

state supreme court
The highest court in a state court system; it hears appeals from intermediate appellate state courts and certain trial courts.

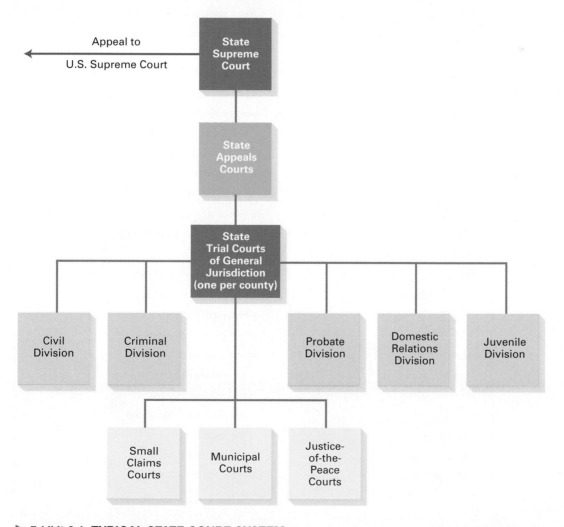

▶ **Exhibit 2.1 TYPICAL STATE COURT SYSTEM**

▶ **Exhibit 2.2 STATE COURT SYSTEMS**

State	Website
Alabama	www.judicial.state.al.us
Alaska	www.state.ak.us/courts
Arizona	www.supreme.state.az.us
Arkansas	www.courts.state.ar.us
California	www.courtinfo.ca.gov/courts
Colorado	www.courts.state.co.us
Connecticut	www.jud.state.ct.us
Delaware	www.courts.state.de.us
District of Columbia	www.dccourts.gov
Florida	www.flcourts.org
Georgia	georgiacourts.org
Guam	www.guamsupremecourt.com
Hawaii	www.courts.state.hi.us
Idaho	www.isc.idaho.gov
Illinois	www.state.il.us/court
Indiana	www.in.gov/judiciary
Iowa	www.judicial.state.ia.us
Kansas	www.kscourts.org
Kentucky	www.courts.ky.gov
Louisiana	www.lasc.org
Maine	www.courts.state.me.us
Maryland	www.courts.state.md.us
Massachusetts	www.mass.gov/courts
Michigan	www.courts.michigan.gov
Minnesota	www.courts.state.mn.us
Mississippi	www.mssc.state.ms.us
Missouri	www.courts.mo.gov
Montana	www.montanacourts.org
Nebraska	court.nol.org
Nevada	www.nvsupremecourt.us
New Hampshire	www.courts.state.nh.us
New Jersey	www.judiciary.state.nj.us
New Mexico	www.nmcourts.com
New York	www.courts.state.ny.us
North Carolina	www.nccourts.org
North Dakota	www.ndcourts.com
Ohio	www.sconet.state.oh.us
Oklahoma	www.oscn.net/oscn/schome
Oregon	www.ojd.state.or.us
Pennsylvania	www.courts.state.pa.us

► Exhibit 2.2 (*Continued*)

State	Website
Puerto Rico	www.tribunalpr.org
Rhode Island	www.courts.state.ri.us
South Carolina	www.judicial.state.sc.us
South Dakota	www.sdjudicial.com
Tennessee	www.tsc.state.tn.us
Texas	www.courts.state.tx.us
Utah	www.utcourts.gov
Vermont	www.vermontjudiciary.org
Virginia	www.courts.state.va.us
Virgin Islands	www.visuperiorcourt.org
Washington	www.courts.wa.gov
West Virginia	www.wv.gov
Wisconsin	www.wicourts.gov
Wyoming	www.courts.state.wy.us

CONTEMPORARY ENVIRONMENT

Specialized Courts Hear Commercial Disputes

In most states, business and commercial disputes are heard by the same courts that hear and decide criminal, landlord–tenant, matrimonial, medical malpractice, and other non-business-related cases. The one major exception to this standard has been the state of Delaware, where a special chancery court hears and decides business litigation. The chancery court, which deals mainly with cases involving corporate government disputes, has earned a reputation for its expertise in handling and deciding corporate matters. Perhaps the existence of this special court and a corporation code that tends to favor corporate management are the primary reasons that more than 60 percent of the corporations listed on the New York Stock Exchange are incorporated in Delaware.

Businesses tend to favor special commercial courts because the judges presiding over them are expected to have the expertise to handle complex commercial lawsuits. The courts are also expected to be more efficient in deciding business-related cases, thus saving time and money for the parties. Other states are also establishing courts that specialize in commercial matters.

► FEDERAL COURT SYSTEM

Article III of the U.S. Constitution provides that the federal government's judicial power is vested in one "Supreme Court." This court is the U.S. Supreme Court. The Constitution also authorizes Congress to establish "inferior" federal courts. Pursuant to this power, Congress has established special federal courts, the U.S. district courts, and the U.S. courts of appeals. Federal judges are appointed for life by the president, with the advice and consent of the Senate (except bankruptcy court judges, who are appointed for 14-year terms).

Special Federal Courts

special federal courts
Federal courts that hear matters of specialized or limited jurisdiction.

The **special federal courts** established by Congress have limited jurisdiction. They include the following:

- **U.S. Tax Court.** The **U.S. Tax Court** hears cases that involve federal tax laws.
- **U.S. Court of Federal Claims.** The **U.S. Court of Federal Claims** hears cases brought against the United States.
- **U.S. Court of International Trade.** The **U.S. Court of International Trade** hears appeals of rulings of the U.S. Customs offices that involve tariffs and international commercial disputes.
- **U.S. Bankruptcy Court.** The **U.S. Bankruptcy Court** hears cases that involve federal bankruptcy laws.
- **U.S. Court of Appeals for the Armed Services.** The **U.S. Court of Appeals for the Armed Services** exercises appellate jurisdiction over members of the armed services.
- **U.S. Court of Appeals for Veterans Claims.** The **U.S. Court of Appeals for Veterans Claims** exercises jurisdiction over decisions of the Department of Veterans Affairs.

U.S. District Courts

U.S. district courts
The federal court system's trial courts of general jurisdiction.

The **U.S. district courts** are the federal court system's trial courts of general jurisdiction. There are 94 U.S. district courts. There is at least one federal district court in each state and the District of Columbia, and heavily populated states have more than one district court. The geographical area served by each court is referred to as a **district**. The federal district courts are empowered to impanel juries, receive evidence, hear testimony, and decide cases. Most federal cases originate in federal district courts.

U.S. Courts of Appeals

U.S. courts of appeals
The federal court system's intermediate appellate courts.

Court of Appeals for the Federal Circuit
A U.S. Court of Appeals in Washington, DC, that has special appellate jurisdiction to review the decisions of the Court of Federal Claims, the Patent and Trademark Office, and the Court of International Trade.

The **U.S. courts of appeals** are the federal court system's intermediate appellate courts. There are 13 circuits in the federal court system. The first 12 are geographical. Eleven are designated by numbers, such as the "First Circuit," "Second Circuit," and so on. The geographical area served by each court is referred to as a **circuit**. The 12th circuit court, located in Washington, DC, is called the **District of Columbia Circuit**.

Congress created the 13th court of appeals in 1982. It is called the **Court of Appeals for the Federal Circuit** and is located in Washington, DC.[1] This court has special appellate jurisdiction to review the decisions of the Court of Federal Claims, the Patent and Trademark Office, and the Court of International Trade. This court was created to provide uniformity in the application of federal law in certain areas, particularly patent law.

As an appellate court, each of these courts hears appeals from the district courts located in its circuit as well as from certain special courts and federal administrative agencies. An appellate court reviews the record of the lower court or administrative agency proceedings to determine whether there has been any error that would warrant reversal or modification of the lower court decision. No new evidence or testimony is heard. The parties file legal briefs with the court and are given a short oral hearing. Appeals are usually heard by a three-judge panel. After a decision is rendered by the three-judge panel, a petitioner can request a review *en banc* by the full court.

Exhibit 2.3 shows a map of the 13 federal circuit courts of appeals. Exhibit 2.4 lists the websites of the 13 U.S. courts of appeals.

▶ **Exhibit 2.3 MAP OF THE FEDERAL CIRCUIT COURTS**

▶ **Exhibit 2.4 FEDERAL COURT OF APPEALS**

United States Court of Appeals	Main Office	Website
First Circuit	Boston, Massachusetts	www.ca1.uscourts.gov
Second Circuit	New York, New York	www.ca2.uscourts.gov
Third Circuit	Philadelphia, Pennsylvania	www.ca3.uscourts.gov
Fourth Circuit	Richmond, Virginia	www.ca4.uscourts.gov
Fifth Circuit	Houston, Texas	www.ca5.uscourts.gov
Sixth Circuit	Cincinnati, Ohio	www.ca6.uscourts.gov
Seventh Circuit	Chicago, Illinois	www.ca7.uscourts.gov
Eighth Circuit	St. Paul, Minnesota	www.ca8.uscourts.gov
Ninth Circuit	San Francisco, California	www.ca9.uscourts.gov
Tenth Circuit	Denver, Colorado	www.ca10.uscourts.gov
Eleventh Circuit	Atlanta, Georgia	www.ca11.uscourts.gov
District of Columbia	Washington, DC	www.dcd.uscourts.gov
Court of Appeals for the Federal Circuit	Washington, DC	www.cafc.uscourts.gov

Supreme Court of the United States, Washington, DC *The highest court in the land is the Supreme Court of the United States, located in Washington, DC. The U.S. Supreme Court decides the most important constitutional law cases and other important issues it deems ripe for review and decision. The Supreme Court's unanimous and majority decisions are precedent for all the other courts in the country.*

U.S. Supreme Court
The highest court in the United States, located in Washington, DC. The Supreme Court was created by Article III of the U.S. Constitution.

▶ UNITED STATES SUPREME COURT

The highest court in the land is the **U.S. Supreme Court**, located in Washington, DC. The Court is composed of nine justices who are nominated by the president and confirmed by the Senate. The president appoints one justice as **chief justice**, who is responsible for the administration of the Supreme Court. The other eight justices are **associate justices**.

Following is Alexis de Tocqueville's description of the Supreme Court's role in U.S. society:

> *The peace, the prosperity, and the very existence of the Union are vested in the hands of the justices of the Supreme Court. Without them, the Constitution would be a dead letter: the executive appeals to them for assistance against the encroachments of the legislative power; the legislature demands their protection against the assaults of the executive; they defend the Union from the disobedience of the states, the states from the exaggerated claims of the Union; the public interest against private interests, and the conservative spirit of stability against the fickleness of the democracy.*

CONTEMPORARY ENVIRONMENT

The Process of Choosing Supreme Court Justices

In an effort to strike a balance of power between the executive and legislative branches of government, Article II, Section 2, of the U.S. Constitution gives the president the power to appoint Supreme Court justices "with the advice and consent of the Senate." This means that the majority of the 50 senators must approve the president's nominee in order for that nominee to become a justice of the U.S. Supreme Court.

President George W. Bush, a Republican, was given the chance to cast a conservative shadow over the Court's decisions when Justice Thurgood Marshall retired in 1991. Marshall, who served 24 years, was one of the most liberal members of the Court. President Bush nominated Clarence Thomas, an African American conservative, who was confirmed by the U.S. Senate with a 52–48 vote.

The election of Bill Clinton as president swung the pendulum back to the Democrats. President Clinton, with the consent of the Senate, replaced Justice Byron White, a Democrat-appointed liberal, with Ruth Bader Ginsburg, a moderate liberal.

President George W. Bush, a Republican, became president of the United States in January 2001 and served two terms. In 2005, then presiding Chief Justice Rehnquist died. President Bush nominated John G. Roberts, Jr., to be the next chief justice of the Supreme Court. Justice Roberts, a conservative, was easily confirmed by the Senate. In the same year, Justice Sandra Day O'Connor, the centrist vote on the Court, resigned from the Supreme Court. President Bush nominated Samuel A. Alito, Jr., a conservative, to fill the vacancy. Justice Alito was confirmed by a 58–42 vote of the Senate.

President Barack Obama, who was inaugurated as president in January 2009, may have the opportunity to nominate one or more Supreme Court justices.

Jurisdiction of the U.S. Supreme Court

The Supreme Court, which is an appellate court, hears appeals from federal circuit courts of appeals and, under certain circumstances, from federal district courts, special federal courts, and the highest state courts. No new evidence or testimony is heard. As with other appellate courts, the lower court record is reviewed to determine whether there has been an error that warrants a reversal or modification of the decision. Legal briefs are filed, and the parties are granted a brief oral hearing. The Supreme Court's decision is final.

The federal court system is illustrated in Exhibit 2.5.

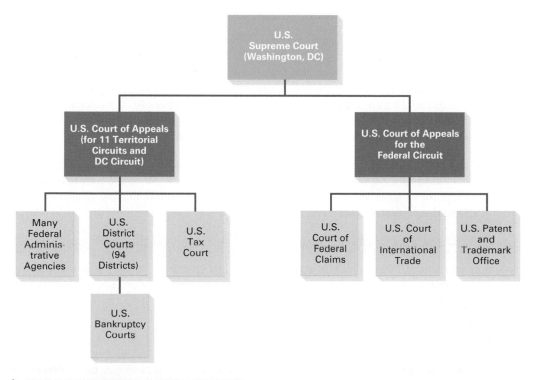

▶ **Exhibit 2.5 FEDERAL COURT SYSTEM**

Decisions of the U.S. Supreme Court

petition for certiorari
A petition asking the Supreme Court to hear a case.

writ of certiorari
An official notice that the Supreme Court will review a case.

The U.S. Constitution gives Congress the authority to establish rules for the appellate review of cases by the Supreme Court, except in the rare case in which mandatory review is required. Congress has given the Supreme Court discretion to decide what cases it will hear.[2]

A petitioner must file a **petition for certiorari**, asking the Supreme Court to hear the case. If the Court decides to review a case, it issues a **writ of certiorari**. Because the Court issues only about 100 opinions each year, writs are granted only in cases involving constitutional and other important issues.

Each justice of the Supreme Court, including the chief justice, has an equal vote. The Supreme Court can issue several types of decisions, as described in the following paragraphs.

Unanimous Decision   If all the justices voting agree as to the outcome and reasoning used to decide a case, it is a **unanimous decision**. Unanimous decisions are precedent for later cases.

Example Suppose all nine justices hear a case, and all nine agree to the outcome (e.g., the petitioner wins) and the reason why (e.g., the Equal Protection Clause of the U.S. Constitution had been violated); this is a unanimous decision. This unanimous decision becomes precedent for later cases.

Majority Decision   If a majority of the justices agree as to the outcome and reasoning used to decide a case, it is a **majority decision**. Majority decisions are precedent for later cases. A majority decision occurs if five, six, seven, or eight justices vote for the same outcome for the same reason.

Example If all nine justices hear a case, and five of them agree as to the outcome (e.g., the petitioner wins) and all of these five justices agree to the same reason why (e.g., the Equal Protection Clause of the U.S. Constitution has been violated), it is a majority opinion. The majority opinion becomes precedent for later cases and has the same force of law as a unanimous decision. The remaining four justices' vote for the respondent has no legal effect whatsoever.

Plurality Decision   If a majority of the justices agree as to the outcome of a case but not as to the reasoning for reaching the outcome, it is a **plurality decision**. A plurality decision settles the case but is not precedent for later cases.

Example If all nine justices hear a case, and five of them agree as to the outcome (e.g., the petitioner wins), but not all of these five agree to the reason why (e.g., three base their vote on a violation of the Equal Protection Clause and two base their vote on a violation of the Freedom of Speech Clause of the U.S. Constitution), it is a plurality decision. Five justices have agreed to the same outcome, but those five have not agreed for the same reason. The petitioner wins his or her case, but the decision is not precedent for later cases. The remaining four justices' votes for the respondent have no legal effect whatsoever.

Sancho: But if this is hell, why do we see no lawyers?
Clarindo: They won't receive them, lest they bring lawsuits here.
Sancho: If there are no lawsuits here, hell's not so bad.

Lope de Vega
The Star of Seville, Act 3, Scene 2

The glorious uncertainty of law.

Thomas Wilbraham
A toast at a dinner of judges and counsel at Serjeants' Inn Hall

Tie Decision   Sometimes the Supreme Court sits without all nine justices being present. This could happen because of illness, conflict of interest, or a justice not having been confirmed to fill a vacant seat on the Court. If there is a **tie decision**, the lower court decision is affirmed. Such votes are not precedent for later cases.

Example A petitioner wins her case at the U.S. Court of Appeals. At the U.S. Supreme Court, only eight justices hear the case. Four justices vote for the petitioner, and four justices vote for the respondent. This is a tie vote. The petitioner remains the winner because she won at the Court of Appeals. This decision of the Supreme Court sets no precedent for later cases.

Concurring Opinion   A justice who agrees with the outcome of a case but not the reason proffered by other justices can issue a **concurring opinion** that sets forth his or her reasons for deciding the case.

Dissenting Opinion   A justice who does not agree with a decision can file a **dissenting opinion** that sets forth the reasons for his or her dissent.

CONTEMPORARY ENVIRONMENT

"I'll Take You to the U.S. Supreme Court!"

In reality, the chance of ever having your case heard by the highest court is slim to none. Each year, more than 7,000 petitioners ask the Supreme Court to hear their cases. These petitioners usually pay big law firms from $30,000 to $200,000 or more to write the appeal petition. In recent years, the Supreme Court has accepted only fewer than 100 of these cases for full review each term.

Each of the nine Supreme Court justices has three law clerks—recent law school graduates usually chosen from elite law schools across the country—who assist them. The justices rarely read the appellate petitions but instead delegate this task to their law clerks. A clerk writes a short memorandum, discussing the key issues raised by the appeal, and recommends to the justices whether they should grant or deny a review. The justices meet once a week to discuss what cases merit review. The votes of four justices are necessary to grant an appeal and schedule an oral argument before the Court (**"rule of four"**). Written opinions by the justices are usually issued many months later.

So what does it take to win a review by the Supreme Court? The U.S. Supreme Court usually decides to hear cases involving major constitutional questions, such as freedom of speech, freedom of religion, equal protection, and due process. The Supreme Court also hears many cases involving the interpretation of statutes enacted by Congress. The Court rarely decides day-to-day legal issues such as breach of contract, tort liability, or corporations law unless they involve more important constitutional or federal law questions.

So the next time you hear someone say, "I'll take you to the U.S. Supreme Court!" just say, "Probably not!"

▶ JURISDICTION OF FEDERAL AND STATE COURTS

Federal courts and state courts each have jurisdiction to hear and decide certain types of cases.

Jurisdiction of Federal Courts

Article III, Section 2, of the U.S. Constitution sets forth the jurisdiction of federal courts. Federal courts have *limited jurisdiction* to hear cases involving a federal question or based on diversity of citizenship.

Federal Question   The federal courts have jurisdiction to hear cases involving "federal questions." **Federal question cases** are cases arising under the U.S. Constitution, treaties, and federal statutes and regulations. There is no dollar-amount limit on federal question cases that can be brought in federal court.[3]

federal question case
A case arising under the U.S. Constitution, treaties, or federal statutes and regulations.

Diversity of Citizenship   A case may be brought in federal court if there is diversity of citizenship. **Diversity of citizenship** occurs if a lawsuit involves (1) citizens of different states or (2) a citizen of a state and a citizen or subject of a foreign country. Diversity of citizenship is used to bring or maintain a lawsuit in federal court when the subject matter of the lawsuit involves a nonfederal question. A corporation is considered to be a citizen of the state in which it is incorporated and in which it has its principal place of business.

The reason for providing diversity of citizenship jurisdiction to federal courts was to prevent state court bias against nonresidents. The federal court must apply the appropriate state's law in deciding the case. The dollar amount of the controversy must exceed $75,000.[4] If this requirement is not met, action must be brought in the appropriate state court.

diversity of citizenship
A means for bringing a lawsuit in federal court that involves a nonfederal question if the parties are (1) citizens of different states or (2) a citizen of a state and a citizen or subject of a foreign country.

Exclusive Jurisdiction   Federal courts have **exclusive jurisdiction** to hear cases involving federal crimes, antitrust, bankruptcy, patent and copyright cases, suits against the United States, and most admiralty cases. State courts cannot hear these cases.

exclusive jurisdiction
Jurisdiction held by only one court.

CONCEPT SUMMARY

JURISDICTION OF FEDERAL COURTS

Type of Jurisdiction	Description
Federal question	Cases arising under the U.S. Constitution, treaties, and federal statutes and regulations. There is no dollar-amount limit in federal question cases.
Diversity of citizenship	Cases between citizens of different states or between a citizen of a state and a citizen or subject of a foreign country. Federal courts must apply the appropriate state law in such cases. The controversy must exceed $75,000 for the federal court to hear the case.

Jurisdiction of State Courts

State courts have jurisdiction to hear cases that federal courts do not have jurisdiction to hear. These usually involve state laws.

Examples Real estate, corporations, partnerships, limited liability companies, contracts, sales and lease contracts, and negotiable instruments are state law subject matters. (Remember that state law cases that involve diversity of citizenship can be heard by federal courts.)

concurrent jurisdiction
Jurisdiction shared by two or more courts.

State courts have **concurrent jurisdiction** with federal courts to hear cases involving diversity of citizenship and federal questions over which federal courts do not have exclusive jurisdiction.

If a case involving concurrent jurisdiction is brought by a plaintiff in federal court, the case remains in federal court. If the plaintiff brings a case involving concurrent jurisdiction in state court, the defendant can either let the case be decided by the state court or remove the case to federal court.

If a case does not qualify to be brought in federal court, it must be brought in the appropriate state court.

Exhibit 2.6 illustrates the jurisdiction of federal and state courts.

▶ **Exhibit 2.6 JURISDICTION OF FEDERAL AND STATE COURTS**

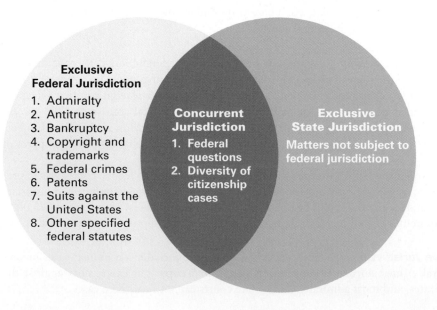

Exclusive Federal Jurisdiction

1. Admiralty
2. Antitrust
3. Bankruptcy
4. Copyright and trademarks
5. Federal crimes
6. Patents
7. Suits against the United States
8. Other specified federal statutes

Concurrent Jurisdiction

1. Federal questions
2. Diversity of citizenship cases

Exclusive State Jurisdiction

Matters not subject to federal jurisdiction

In the following case, the court had to decide which state's law applied to a case.

CASE 2.1 Jurisdiction of Courts

Bertram v. Norden, et al.

159 Ohio App.3d 171, 823 N.E.2d 478, Web 2004 Ohio App. Lexis 5500 (2004)
Court of Appeals of Ohio

"We note that Michigan is a known snowmobiling destination, and, as such, Michigan lawmakers have taken steps to deal with the liability issues that go along with the dangers of snowmobiling."

—Judge Rogers

Facts

Four friends, John Bertram, Matt Norden, Scott Olson, and Tony Harvey, all residents of Ohio, traveled to the Upper Peninsula of Michigan to go snowmobiling. On their first day of snowmobiling, after going about 135 miles, the lead snowmobiler, Olson, came to a stop sign on the snowmobile trail, where it intersected a private driveway. As Olson approached the sign, he gave the customary hand signal and stopped his snowmobile. Harvey, second in line, was going too fast to stop, so Olson pulled his snowmobile to the right side of the private driveway. Harvey, to avoid hitting Olson, pulled his snowmobile to the left and went over a five- or six-foot snow embankment. Bertram, third in line, going about 30 miles per hour, slammed on his break, turned 45 degrees, and slammed into Olson's snowmobile. Bertram was thrown from his snowmobile. Norden, fourth in line, could not stop, and his snowmobile hit Bertram's leg. Bertram's tibia and fibula were both fractured and protruded through his skin. Bertram underwent surgery to repair the broken bones.

Bertram filed a lawsuit against Olson, Harvey, and Norden in a trial court in Ohio, claiming that each of his friends was liable to him for their negligent snowmobile operation. The Ohio court held that Michigan law applied and that a Michigan statute specifically stated that snowmobilers assumed the risks associated with snowmobiling. The court therefore held that the three friends were not liable to Bertram and granted their motions for summary judgment. Ohio law did not contain an assumption of the risk rule regarding snowmobiling. Bertram appealed, alleging that Ohio law applied to the case because all of the parties were from Ohio.

Issue

Does Michigan or Ohio law apply to this case?

Language of the Court

Because the accident took place in Michigan, we must presume that Michigan law applies absent any other jurisdiction having more substantial contacts. Bertram, however, contends that Ohio law should apply, because all of the parties were residents of Ohio at the time of the accident and all consequences flowing from his injury occurred in Ohio. We disagree.

Because the snowmobiling accident took place in Michigan, the place where the conduct causing Bertram's injury occurred in Michigan and Michigan has enacted specific legislation involving the risks of snowmobiling, we find that Michigan law clearly controls in this case. While all parties are residents of and have their relationships in the State of Ohio, we are not persuaded by Bertram's argument that this issue should control.

Decision

The Court of Appeals of Ohio held that the law of the state of Michigan, where the accident occurred, and not the law of the state of Ohio, the state of the residence of the parties, should apply. The court upheld the trial court's application of Michigan assumption of the risk statute to this case and affirmed the trial court's grant of summary judgment to the three defendant friends of plaintiff Bertram.

Case Questions

Critical Legal Thinking What does the doctrine of assumption of the risk provide? Explain.

Business Ethics Was it ethical for Bertram to sue his three friends for negligence? Why or why not?

Contemporary Business Why did Bertram want Ohio law, and not Michigan law, to apply to the case?

▶ PERSONAL JURISDICTION OF COURTS

Not every court has the authority to hear all types of cases. First, to bring a lawsuit in a court, the plaintiff must have *standing to sue*. In addition, the court must have *personal jurisdiction* to hear the case, and the case must be brought in the proper *venue*. These topics are discussed in the following paragraphs.

Standing to Sue

standing to sue
Some stake in the outcome
of a lawsuit.

To bring a lawsuit, a plaintiff must have **standing to sue**. This means the plaintiff must have some stake in the outcome of the lawsuit.

Example Linda's friend Jon is injured in an accident caused by Emily. Jon refuses to sue. Linda cannot sue Emily on Jon's behalf because she does not have an interest in the result of the case.

A few states now permit investors to invest money in a lawsuit for a percentage return of any award of judgment. Courts hear and decide actual disputes involving specific controversies. Hypothetical questions will not be heard, and trivial lawsuits will be dismissed.

In Personam Jurisdiction

in personam jurisdiction
Jurisdiction over the parties to a
lawsuit.

service of process
A summons being served on the
defendant to obtain personal
jurisdiction over him or her.

Jurisdiction over a person is called *in personam* **jurisdiction**, or **personal jurisdiction**. A *plaintiff*, by filing a lawsuit with a court, gives the court *in personam* jurisdiction over himself or herself. The court must also have *in personam* jurisdiction over the *defendant*, which is usually obtained by having a summons served to that person within the territorial boundaries of the state (i.e., **service of process**). Service of process is usually accomplished by personal service of the summons and complaint on the defendant.

If personal service is not possible, alternative forms of notice, such as mailing of the summons or publication of a notice in a newspaper, may be permitted. A corporation is subject to personal jurisdiction in the state in which it is incorporated, has its principal office, and is doing business.

A party who disputes the jurisdiction of a court can make a *special appearance* in that court to argue against imposition of jurisdiction. Service of process is not permitted during such an appearance.

LANDMARK U.S. Supreme Court Case

International Shoe Company *v.* State of Washington

How far can a state go to require a person or business to defend himself or itself in a court of law in that state? That question was present to the Supreme Court of the United States in the landmark case **International Shoe Company v. State of Washington.**[5]

The International Shoe Company was a Delaware corporation that had its principal place of business in St. Louis, Missouri. The company manufactured and distributed shoes throughout the United States. The company maintained a sales force throughout the United States. In the state of Washington, its sales representative did not have a specific office but sold shoes door-to-door and sometimes at temporary locations. The sales representatives were paid commissions based on the number of shoes they sold.

The state of Washington assessed an unemployment tax on International Shoe for the sales representative it had in the state. When International Shoe failed to pay, Washington served personal service on a sales representative of the company in Washington and mailed the service of process to the company's

headquarters in St. Louis. International Shoe appeared specially to argue that it did not do sufficient business in Washington to warrant having to pay unemployment taxes in that state. The office of unemployment ruled against International Shoe, and the appeals tribunal, the superior court, and supreme court of Washington agreed. International Shoe appealed to the U.S. Supreme Court.

In its decision, the U.S. Supreme Court noted, "due process requires only that in order to subject a defendant to a judgment in personam, if he be not present within the territory of the forum, he have certain minimum contacts with it such that the maintenance of that suit does not offend 'traditional notions of fair play and substantial justice.'"

The Supreme Court stated:

Applying these standards, the activities carried on in behalf of International Shoe in the state of Washington

(case continues)

> *were neither irregular nor casual. They were systematic and continuous throughout the years in question. They resulted in a large volume of interstate business, in the course of which International Shoe received the benefits and protection of the laws of the state, including the right to resort to the courts for the enforcement of its rights. The obligation which is here sued upon arose out of those very activities. It is evident that these operations establish sufficient contacts or ties with the state of the forum to make it reasonable and just, according to our traditional conception of fair play and substantial*
>
> *justice, to permit the state to enforce the obligations which International Shoe has incurred there. Hence, we cannot say that the maintenance of the present suit in the state of Washington involves an unreasonable or undue procedure.*
>
> *Thus, the famous "minimum contacts" test and "traditional notions of fair play and substantial justice" establish when a state may subject a person or business to the walls of its courtrooms. Obviously, this is not a bright-line test, so battles of in personam jurisdiction abound to this day.*

In Rem Jurisdiction

A court may have jurisdiction to hear and decide a case because it has jurisdiction over the property of the lawsuit. This is called ***in rem* jurisdiction** ("jurisdiction over the thing"). For example, a state court would have jurisdiction to hear a dispute over the ownership of a piece of real estate located within the state. This is so even if one or more of the disputing parties live in another state or states.

in rem jurisdiction
Jurisdiction to hear a case because of jurisdiction over the property of the lawsuit.

Quasi In Rem Jurisdiction

Sometimes a plaintiff who obtains a judgment against a defendant in one state will try to collect the judgment by attaching property of the defendant that is located in another state. This is permitted under ***quasi in rem* jurisdiction**, or **attachment jurisdiction**. Under the **Full Faith and Credit Clause** of the U.S. Constitution (Article IV, Section 1), a judgment of a court of one state must be given "full faith and credit" by the courts of another state.

quasi in rem jurisdiction
Jurisdiction that allows a plaintiff who obtains a judgment in one state to try to collect the judgment by attaching property of the defendant located in another state.

CONCEPT SUMMARY

IN PERSONAM, IN REM, AND QUASI IN REM JURISDICTION

Type of Jurisdiction	Description
In personam jurisdiction	With *in personam* jurisdiction, a court has jurisdiction over the parties to the lawsuit. The plaintiff submits to the jurisdiction of the court by filing the lawsuit there. Personal jurisdiction is obtained over the defendant through *service of process* to that person.
In rem jurisdiction	With *in rem* jurisdiction, a court has jurisdiction to hear and decide a case because it has jurisdiction over the property at issue in the lawsuit (e.g., real property located in the state).
Quasi in rem jurisdiction	A plaintiff who obtains a judgment against a defendant in one state may utilize the court system of another state to attach property of the defendant that is located in the second state.

Long-Arm Statute

In most states, a state court can obtain jurisdiction over persons and businesses located in another state or country through the state's **long-arm statute**. These statutes extend a state's jurisdiction to nonresidents who were not served a summons within the state. The nonresident must have had some **minimum contact** with the state.[6] In addition, the maintenance of the suit must uphold the traditional notions of fair play and substantial justice.

long-arm statute
A statute that extends a state's jurisdiction to nonresidents who were not served a summons within the state.

The exercise of long-arm jurisdiction is generally permitted over nonresidents who have (1) committed torts within the state (e.g., caused an automobile accident in the state), (2) entered into a contract either in the state or that affects the state (and allegedly breached the contract), or (3) transacted other business in the state that allegedly caused injury to another person.

Venue

venue
A concept that requires lawsuits to be heard by the court with jurisdiction that is nearest the location in which the incident occurred or where the parties reside.

Venue requires lawsuits to be heard by the court with jurisdiction nearest the location in which the incident occurred or where the parties reside.

Example Harry, a resident of the state of Georgia, commits a felony crime in Los Angeles County, California. The California state Superior Court located in Los Angeles is the proper venue because the crime was committed there, the witnesses are probably from the area, and so on. Although Harry lives in Georgia, the state of Georgia is not the proper venue for this case.

Occasionally, pretrial publicity may prejudice jurors located in the proper venue. In such cases, a **change of venue** may be requested so that a more impartial jury can be found. The courts generally frown upon **forum shopping** (i.e., looking for a favorable court without a valid reason).

Forum-Selection and Choice-of-Law Clauses

forum-selection clause
A contract provision that designates a certain court to hear any dispute concerning nonperformance of the contract.

choice-of-law clause
A contract provision that designates a certain state's law or country's law that will be applied in any dispute concerning nonperformance of the contract.

One issue that often comes up when parties from different states have a legal dispute is which state's court will be used, or which federal courts in either of the states will hear the case. When the parties have not agreed in advance, courts must make the decision about which court has jurisdiction. Also, sometimes there is a dispute as to which state's laws apply to a case. If there is a dispute regarding the correct court to hear the case, or what law applies to the case, a court will make that decision. This will cost time and money.

Therefore, parties sometimes agree in their contract as to what state's courts, what federal courts, or what country's court will have jurisdiction to hear a legal dispute should one arise. Such clauses in contracts are called **forum-selection clauses**.

In addition to agreeing to a forum, the parties also often agree in contracts as to what state's law or country's law will apply in resolving a dispute. These clauses are called **choice-of-law clauses**.

TEST REVIEW TERMS AND CONCEPTS

Associate justice
Change of venue
Chief justice
Choice-of-law clause
Circuit
Concurrent jurisdiction
Concurring opinion
Court of Appeals for the Federal Circuit
Dissenting opinion
District
District of Columbia circuit
Diversity of citizenship
Exclusive jurisdiction
Federal question case

Forum shopping
Forum-selection clause
Full Faith and Credit Clause
General-jurisdiction trial court (court of record)
In personam jurisdiction (personal jurisdiction)
In rem jurisdiction
Intermediate appellate court (appellate court or court of appeals)
International Shoe Company v. State of Washington
Limited-jurisdiction trial court (inferior trial court)

Long-arm statute
Majority decision
Minimum contact
Petition for certiorari
Plurality decision
Quasi in rem jurisdiction (attachment jurisdiction)
"Rule of four"
Service of process
Small claims court
Special federal court
Standing to sue
State courts
State supreme court
Tie decision

Unanimous decision
U.S. Bankruptcy Court
U.S. Court of Federal Claims
U.S. Court of Appeals
U.S. Court of Appeals for the Armed Services
U.S. Court of Appeals for Veterans Claims
U.S. Court of International Trade
U.S. District Court
U.S. Supreme Court
U.S. Tax Court
Venue
Writ of certiorari

CASE PROBLEMS

2.1 Federal Question Nutrilab, Inc., manufactures and markets a product known as "Starch Blockers." The purpose of the product is to block the human body's digestion of starch as an aid in controlling weight. The U.S. FDA classified Starch Blockers as a drug and requested that it be removed from the market until the FDA approved its use. The FDA claimed that it had the right to classify new products as drugs and prevent their distribution until their safety is determined. Nutrilab disputed the FDA's decision and wanted to bring suit to halt the FDA's actions. Do the federal courts have jurisdiction to hear this case? *Nutrilab, Inc. v. Schweiker*, 713 F.2d 335, **Web** 1983 U.S. App. Lexis 25121 (United States Court of Appeals for the Seventh Circuit)

2.2 Jurisdiction   James Clayton Allison, a resident of the state of Mississippi, was employed by the Tru-Amp Corporation as a circuit breaker tester. As part of his employment, Allison was sent to inspect, clean, and test a switch gear located at the South Central Bell Telephone Facility in Brentwood, Tennessee. One day, when he attempted to remove a circuit breaker manufactured by ITE Corporation (ITE) from a bank of breakers, a portion of the breaker fell off. The broken piece fell behind a switching bank and, according to Allison, caused an electrical fire and explosion. Allison was severely burned in the accident. Allison brought suit against ITE in a Mississippi state court, claiming more than $50,000 in damages. Can this suit be removed to federal court? *Allison v. ITE Imperial Corp.*, 729 F.Supp. 45, **Web** 1990 U.S. Dist. Lexis 607 (United States District Court for the Southern District of Mississippi)

BUSINESS ETHICS CASE

2.3 Business Ethics   One day, Joshua Gnaizda, a three-year-old, received what he (or his mother) thought was a tantalizing offer in the mail from Time, Inc. The front of the envelope contained a see-through window that revealed the following statement: "Joshua Gnaizda, I'll give you this versatile new calculator watch free just for opening this envelope." Beneath the offer was a picture of the calculator watch itself. When Joshua's mother opened the envelope, she realized that the see-through window had not revealed the full text of Time's offer. Not viewable through the see-through window were the following words: "And mailing this Certificate today." The certificate required Joshua to purchase a subscription to *Fortune* magazine in order to receive the free calculator watch. Joshua (through his father, a lawyer) sued Time in a class action, seeking compensatory damages in an amount equal to the value of the calculator watch and $15 million in punitive damages. The trial court dismissed the lawsuit as being too trivial for the court to hear. Joshua appealed. Should Joshua be permitted to maintain his lawsuit against Time, Inc.? Did Time act ethically? Should Joshua's father have sued for $15 million? *Harris v. Time, Inc.*, 191 Cal.App.3d 449, 237 Cal.Rptr. 584, **Web** 1987 Cal.App. Lexis 1619 (Court of Appeals of California)

ENDNOTES

1. Federal Courts Improvement Act of 1982. Public Law 97–164, 96 Stat. 25, 28 U.S.C. Section 1292 and Section 1295.
2. Effective September 25, 1988, mandatory appeals were all but eliminated, except for reapportionment cases and cases brought under the Civil Rights Act and Voting Rights Act, antitrust laws, and the Presidential Election Campaign Fund Act.
3. Prior to 1980, there was a minimum dollar amount controversy requirement of $10,000 to bring a federal question action in federal court. This minimum amount was eliminated by the Federal Question Jurisdictional Amendment Act of 1980, Public Law 96–486.
4. The amount was raised to $75,000 by the 1996 Federal Courts Improvement Act. Title 28 U.S.C. Section 1332(a).
5. 326 U.S. 310, 66 S.Ct. 154, 90 L.Ed 95, **Web** 1945 U.S. Lexis 1447 (Supreme Court of the United States).
6. *International Shoe Co. v. Washington*, 326 U.S. 310, 66 S.Ct. 154, 90 L.Ed. 95, **Web** 1945 U.S. Lexis 1447 (Supreme Court of the United States).

3 | JUDICIAL, ALTERNATIVE, AND ONLINE DISPUTE RESOLUTION

▲ **Typical American Courtroom** *When people think of resolving disputes, courtrooms often come to mind, though there are other legal ways to resolve disputes other than trials.*

CHAPTER OBJECTIVES

After studying this chapter, you should be able to:

1. Describe the pretrial litigation process.
2. Describe how a case proceeds through trial.
3. Describe how a trial court decision is appealed.

4. Explain the use of arbitration and other nonjudicial methods of alternative dispute resolution.
5. Describe *online dispute resolution*.

CHAPTER CONTENTS

"We're the jury, dread our fury!"

William S. Gilbert
Trial by Jury

► INTRODUCTION TO JUDICIAL, ALTERNATIVE, AND ONLINE DISPUTE RESOLUTION

The process of bringing, maintaining, and defending a lawsuit is called *litigation*. This is also called *judicial dispute resolution* because courts are used to decide the case. Litigation is a difficult, time-consuming, and costly process that must comply with complex procedural rules. Although it is not required, most parties employ a lawyer to represent them when they are involved in a lawsuit.

Several forms of **nonjudicial dispute resolution** have developed in response to the expense and difficulty of bringing a lawsuit. These methods, collectively called *alternative dispute resolution*, are being used more and more often to resolve contract and commercial disputes. In addition, arbitration is often used to solve Internet and e-commerce disputes. This is called **online dispute resolution**.

This chapter discusses the judicial litigation process, alternative dispute resolution, and online dispute resolution.

► PRETRIAL LITIGATION PROCESS

The bringing, maintaining, and defense of a lawsuit are generally referred to as the *litigation process*, or **litigation**. The pretrial litigation process can be divided into the following major phases: *pleadings*, *discovery*, *dismissals and pretrial judgments*, and *settlement conference*. Each of these phases is discussed in the paragraphs that follow.

litigation
The process of bringing, maintaining, and defending a lawsuit.

► PLEADINGS

The paperwork that is filed with the court to initiate and respond to a lawsuit is referred to as the **pleadings**. The major pleadings are the *complaint*, the *answer*, the *cross-complaint*, and the *reply*.

pleadings
The paperwork that is filed with the court to initiate and respond to a lawsuit.

Complaint and Summons

To initiate a lawsuit, the party who is suing (the **plaintiff**) must file a **complaint** in the proper court. The complaint must name the parties to the lawsuit, alleges the ultimate facts and law violated, and contains a "prayer for relief" for a remedy to be awarded by the court. The complaint can be as long as necessary, depending on the case's complexity. A sample complaint appears in Exhibit 3.1.

Once a complaint has been filed with the court, the court will issue a summons. A **summons** is a court order directing the defendant to appear in court and answer the complaint. The complaint and summons are served on the defendant by a sheriff, another government official, or a private process server.

plaintiff
The party who files a complaint.

complaint
The document a plaintiff files with the court and serves on the defendant to initiate a lawsuit.

summons
A court order directing the defendant to appear in court and answer the complaint.

Answer

The defendant must file an **answer** to the plaintiff's complaint. The defendant's answer is filed with the court and served on the plaintiff. In the answer, the defendant admits or denies the allegations contained in the plaintiff's complaint. A judgment is entered against a defendant who admits all of the allegations in the complaint. The case proceeds if the defendant denies all or some of the allegations.

answer
The defendant's written response to a plaintiff's complaint that is filed with the court and served on the plaintiff.

▶ **Exhibit 3.1 SAMPLE COMPLAINT**

In the United States District Court for the District of Idaho

John Doe   Civil No. 2-1001
        Plaintiff

        v.   COMPLAINT

Jane Roe

        Defendant

The plaintiff, by and through his attorney, alleges:

1. The plaintiff is a resident of the State of Idaho, the defendant is a resident of the State of Washington, and there is diversity of citizenship between the parties.
2. The amount in controversy exceeds the sum of $75,000, exclusive of interest and costs.
3. On January 10, 2008, plaintiff was exercising reasonable care while walking across the intersection of Sun Valley Road and Main Street, Ketchum, Idaho when defendant negligently drove her car through a red light at the intersection and struck plaintiff.
4. As a result of the defendant's negligence, plaintiff has incurred medical expenses of $104,000 and suffered severe physical injury and mental distress.

WHEREFORE, plaintiff claims judgment in the amount of $1,000,000 interest at the maximum legal rate, and costs of this action.

                                            By _____
                                                Edward Lawson
                                                Attorney for Plaintiff
                                                100 Main Street
                                                Ketchum, Idaho

---

Pieces of evidence, each by itself insufficient, may together constitute a significant whole and justify by their combined effect a conclusion.

Lord Wright
Grant v. Australian Knitting Mills, Ltd. (1936)

If the defendant does not answer the complaint, a **default judgment** is entered against him or her. A default judgment establishes the defendant's liability. The plaintiff then has only to prove damages.

In addition to answering the complaint, a defendant's answer can assert **affirmative defenses**.

Examples If a complaint alleges that the plaintiff was personally injured by the defendant, the defendant's answer could state that he or she acted in self-defense. Another affirmative defense would be an assertion that the plaintiff's lawsuit is barred because the *statute of limitations* (time within which to bring the lawsuit) has expired.

Cross-Complaint and Reply

cross-complaint
A document filed by the defendant against the plaintiff to seek damages or some other remedy.

A defendant who believes that he or she has been injured by the plaintiff can file a **cross-complaint** against the plaintiff in addition to an answer. In the cross-complaint, the defendant (now the **cross-complainant**) sues the plaintiff (now the **cross-defendant**) for damages or some other remedy. The original plaintiff must file a **reply** (answer) to the cross-complaint. The reply, which can include affirmative defenses, must be filed with the court and served on the original defendant.

reply
A document filed by the original plaintiff to answer the defendant's cross-complaint.

Intervention and Consolidation

intervention
The act of others to join as parties to an existing lawsuit.

If other persons have an interest in a lawsuit, they may **intervene** and become parties to the lawsuit.

Example A bank that has made a secured loan on a piece of real estate can intervene in a lawsuit between parties who are litigating ownership of the property.

CONCEPT SUMMARY
PLEADINGS

Type of Pleading	Description
Complaint	A document filed by a plaintiff with a court and served with a *summons* on the defendant. It sets forth the basis of the lawsuit.
Answer	A document filed by a defendant with a court and served on the plaintiff. It usually denies most allegations of the complaint.
Cross-complaint and reply	A document filed and served by a defendant if he or she countersues the plaintiff. The defendant is the *cross-complainant*, and the plaintiff is the *cross-defendant*. The cross-defendant must file and serve a *reply* (answer).

If several plaintiffs have filed separate lawsuits stemming from the same fact situation against the same defendant, the court can **consolidate** the cases into one case if doing so would not cause undue prejudice to the parties.

consolidation
The act of a court to combine two or more separate lawsuits into one lawsuit.

Example If a commercial airplane crashes, killing and injuring many people, the court could consolidate all the lawsuits against the defendant airplane company. This is because the deaths and injuries all relate to the same fact situation.

INTERNET LAW & ONLINE COMMERCE
E-Filings

When litigation takes place, the clients, lawyers, and judges involved in the case are usually buried in papers. These papers include pleadings, interrogatories, documents, motions to the court, briefs, and memorandums; the list goes on and on. By the time a case is over, reams of paper are stored in dozens, if not hundreds, of boxes. In addition, court appearances, for no matter how small the matter, must be made in person.

Example Lawyers often wait hours for a 10-minute scheduling conference or other conference with a judge. The time it takes to drive to and from court also has to be taken into account, which in some areas may amount to hours.

Today, because of the Internet and other technologies, a **virtual courthouse** is being developed. Technology allows

for the electronic filing—**e-filing**—of pleadings, briefs, and other documents related to a lawsuit. E-filing includes using CD-ROMs for briefs, scanning evidence and documents into a computer for storage and retrieval, and e-mailing correspondence and documents to the court and the opposing counsel. Scheduling and other conferences with the judge or opposing counsel are held via telephone conferences and e-mail.

Many courts have instituted e-filing and electronic document filing and tracking. In some courts, e-filing is now mandatory. Companies such as Microsoft and LexisNexis have developed systems to manage e-filings of court documents.

Statute of Limitations

A **statute of limitations** establishes the period during which a plaintiff must bring a lawsuit against a defendant. If a lawsuit is not filed within this time period, the plaintiff loses his or her right to sue. A statute of limitations begins to "run" at the time the plaintiff first has the right to sue the defendant (e.g., when the accident happens or when the breach of contract occurs).

statute of limitations
A statute that establishes the period during which a plaintiff must bring a lawsuit against a defendant.

Federal and state governments have established statutes of limitations for each type of lawsuit. Most are from one to four years, depending on the type of lawsuit.

Example The state of Idaho has a two-year statute of limitations for negligence actions. On July 1, 2009, Otis negligently causes an automobile accident in Sun Valley, Idaho, in which Cha-Yen is injured. Cha-Yen has until July 1, 2011, to bring a negligence lawsuit against Otis. If she waits longer than that, she loses her right to sue him.

▶ DISCOVERY

discovery
A legal process during which each party engages in various activities to discover facts of the case from the other party and witnesses prior to trial.

The legal process provides for a detailed pretrial procedure called **discovery**. During discovery, each party engages in various activities to discover facts of the case from the other party and witnesses prior to trial. Discovery serves several functions, including preventing surprises, allowing parties to thoroughly prepare for trial, preserving evidence, saving court time, and promoting the settlement of cases. The major forms of discovery are discussed in the following paragraphs.

Deposition

deposition
Oral testimony given by a party or witness prior to trial. The testimony is given under oath and is transcribed.

deponent
A party who gives his or her deposition.

A **deposition** is the oral testimony given by a party or witness prior to trial. The person giving a deposition is called the **deponent**. A *party* to the lawsuit must give a deposition, if called upon by the other party to do so. The deposition of a *witness* can be given voluntarily or pursuant to a subpoena (court order). The deponent can be required to bring documents to the deposition. Most depositions are taken at the office of one of the attorneys. The deponent is placed under oath and then asked oral questions by one or both of the attorneys. The questions and answers are recorded in written form by a court reporter. Depositions can also be videotaped. The deponent is given an opportunity to correct his or her answers prior to signing the deposition. Depositions are used to preserve evidence (e.g., if the deponent is deceased, ill, or not otherwise available at trial) and impeach testimony given by witnesses at trial.

Interrogatories

interrogatories
Written questions submitted by one party to another party. The questions must be answered in writing within a stipulated time.

Interrogatories are written questions submitted by one party to a lawsuit to another party. The questions can be very detailed. In addition, certain documents might be attached to the answers. A party is required to answer the interrogatories in writing within a specified time period (e.g., 60 to 90 days). An attorney usually helps with the preparation of the answers. The answers are signed under oath.

Production of Documents

production of documents
A request by one party to another party to produce all documents relevant to the case prior to the trial.

Often, particularly in complex business cases, a substantial portion of a lawsuit may be based on information contained in documents (e.g., memorandums, correspondence, and company records). One party to a lawsuit may request that the other party produce all documents that are relevant to the case prior to trial. This is called **production of documents**. If the documents sought are too voluminous to be moved or are in permanent storage, or if their movement would disrupt the ongoing business of the party who is to produce them, the requesting party may be required to examine the documents at the other party's premises.

Physical or Mental Examination

physical or mental examination
A court-ordered examination of a party to a lawsuit before trial to determine the extent of the alleged injuries.

In cases that concern the physical or mental condition of a party, a court can order the party to submit to certain **physical or mental examinations** to determine the extent of the alleged injuries. This would occur, for example, where the plaintiff has been injured in an accident and is seeking damages for physical injury and mental distress.

CONCEPT SUMMARY
DISCOVERY

Type	Description
Deposition	Oral testimony given by a *deponent*, either a party or witness. Depositions are transcribed.
Interrogatories	Written questions submitted by one party to the other party of a lawsuit. They must be answered within a specified period of time.
Production of documents	Copies of all relevant documents obtained by a party to a lawsuit from another party upon order of the court.
Physical or mental examination	Court-ordered examination of a party where injuries are alleged that could be verified or disputed by such examination.

▶ DISMISSALS AND PRETRIAL JUDGMENTS

There are several **pretrial motions** that parties to a lawsuit can make to try to dispose of all or part of a lawsuit prior to trial. The two major pretrial motions are *motion for judgment on the pleadings* and *motion for summary judgment*.

pretrial motion
A motion a party can make to try to dispose of all or part of a lawsuit prior to trial.

Motion for Judgment on the Pleadings

A **motion for judgment on the pleadings** can be made by either party once the pleadings are complete. This motion alleges that if all the facts presented in the pleadings are true, the party making the motion would win the lawsuit when the proper law is applied to these facts. In deciding this motion, the judge cannot consider any facts outside the pleadings.

motion for judgment on the pleadings
A motion which alleges that if all the facts presented in the pleadings are taken as true, the party making the motion would win the lawsuit when the proper law is applied to these asserted facts.

Motion for Summary Judgment

The trier of fact (i.e., the jury or, if there is no jury, the judge) determines factual issues. A **motion for summary judgment** asserts that there are no factual disputes to be decided by the jury and that the judge should apply the relevant law to the undisputed facts and decide the case. Thus, the case can be decided before trial by a judge who comes to a conclusion and issues a summary judgment in the moving party's favor. Motions for summary judgment, which can be made by either party, are supported by evidence outside the pleadings. Affidavits from the parties and witnesses, documents (e.g., a written contract between the parties), depositions, and such are common forms of evidence.

motion for summary judgment
A motion which asserts that there are no factual disputes to be decided by the jury and that the judge can apply the proper law to the undisputed facts and decide the case without a jury. These motions are supported by affidavits, documents, and deposition testimony.

If, after examining the evidence, the court finds no factual dispute, it can decide the issue or issues raised in the summary judgment motion. This may dispense with the entire case or with part of the case. If the judge finds that a factual dispute exists, the motion will be denied, and the case will go to trial.

In the following case, the court did not grant a motion for summary judgment because it found that there were factual disputes for the jury to decide.

CASE 3.1 Summary Judgment

Toote v. Canada Dry Bottling Company of New York, Inc. and Pathmark Stores, Inc.

7 A.D.3d 251, 776 N.Y.S.2d 42, Web 2004 N.Y. App. Div. Lexis 6470 (2004)
Supreme Court of New York, Appellate Division

"Plaintiff alleges that she tripped over cases of soda that were stacked on the floor of defendant's supermarket."

—Judge Lerner

Facts

Plaintiff Phyllis Toote filed a lawsuit against Pathmark Stores, Inc., a grocery store, and Canada Dry Bottling Company of New York, a bottler and distributor of soda. In her complaint, plaintiff alleged that the defendants were liable for negligence for injuries she suffered when she fell over cases of soda that were stacked on the floor of the supermarket when she was shopping at the supermarket.

Defendant Pathmark took plaintiff Toote's deposition, in which she stated that she had entered the supermarket, and upon entering the store, she immediately walked to the soda aisle. Toote stated that she did not see the soda stacked on the floor before she fell over the soda. In the deposition, Toote stated that she did not know how long the soda had been on the floor before she tripped and fell. Pathmark made a motion for summary judgment, alleging that plaintiff Toote could not establish how long the soda had been on the floor before she fell. The motion court denied Pathmark's motion for summary judgment, finding that there were questions of fact to be decided by the jury. Pathmark appealed.

Issue

Should the motion court have granted Pathmark's motion for summary judgment?

Language of the Court

Plaintiff alleges that she tripped over cases of soda that were stacked on the floor of defendant's supermarket. It appears that at the time of the accident, the supermarket's shelves, in accordance with usual practice, were being "packed out" with soda by an employee of either defendant bottling company or defendant soda distributor. The supermarket moved for summary judgment, contending that it did not create the alleged dangerous condition and that plaintiff's deposition testimony, to the effect that she walked to the soda aisle immediately after entering the store and did not see any soda on the floor before falling, shows that she cannot establish how long the soda had been on the floor before she fell. The motion court correctly held that such testimony does not establish, prima facie, the supermarket's lack of prior actual or constructive notice of the soda on the floor, or that it may not be held liable for an independent contractor's negligence on the basis of the supermarket's non-delegable duty to keep the public areas of its premises reasonably safe.

Decision

The appellate court decided that there were issues of fact to be decided by a jury and affirmed the motion court's denial of Pathmark's motion for summary judgment.

Case Questions

Critical Legal Thinking What is a motion for summary judgment? When is a motion for summary judgment granted?

Business Ethics Was it ethical for Pathmark, the supermarket, to make a motion for summary judgment based on the facts of this case? Explain.

Contemporary Business Do you think supermarkets have to face a significant number of "faked" slip-and-fall cases?

▶ SETTLEMENT CONFERENCE

settlement conference
A hearing before a trial in order to facilitate the settlement of a case. Also called a *pretrial hearing*.

Federal court rules and most state court rules permit the court to direct the attorneys or parties to appear before the court for a **settlement conference**, or **pretrial hearing**. One of the major purposes of such hearings is to facilitate the settlement of a case. Pretrial conferences are often held informally in the judge's chambers. If no settlement is reached, the pretrial hearing is used to identify the major trial issues and other relevant factors. More than 95 percent of all cases are settled before they go to trial.

CONTEMPORARY ENVIRONMENT

Cost–Benefit Analysis of a Lawsuit

The choice of whether to bring or defend a lawsuit should be analyzed like any other business decision. This includes performing a **cost–benefit analysis** of the lawsuit. For the plaintiff, it may be wise not to sue. For the defendant, it may be wise to settle. The following factors should be considered in deciding whether to bring or settle a lawsuit:

- The probability of winning or losing
- The amount of money to be won or lost
- Lawyers' fees and other costs of litigation

- Loss of time by managers and other personnel
- The long-term effects on the relationship and reputation of the parties
- The amount of prejudgment interest provided by law
- The aggravation and psychological costs associated with a lawsuit
- The unpredictability of the legal system and the possibility of error
- Other factors peculiar to the parties and lawsuit

▶ TRIAL

Pursuant to the Seventh Amendment to the U.S. Constitution, a party to an action at law is guaranteed the right to a **jury trial** in a case in federal court.[1] Most state constitutions contain a similar guarantee for state court actions. If either party requests a jury, the trial will be by jury. If both parties waive their right to a jury, the trial will occur without a jury. The judge sits as the **trier of fact** in nonjury trials. At the time of trial, each party usually submits to the judge a **trial brief** that contains legal support for its side of the case.

A trial can last less than one day to many months, depending on the type and complexity of the case. A typical trial is divided into stages. The stages of a trial are discussed in the following paragraphs.

trier of fact
The jury in a jury trial; the judge where there is not a jury trial.

Jury Selection

The pool of potential jurors is usually selected from voter or automobile registration lists. Individuals are selected to hear specific cases through a process called **voir dire** ("to speak the truth"). Lawyers for each party and the judge can ask prospective jurors questions to determine whether they would be biased in their decisions. Biased jurors can be prevented from sitting on a particular case. Once the appropriate number of jurors is selected (usually 6 to 12 jurors), they are **impaneled** to hear the case and are sworn in. The trial is ready to begin. A jury can be **sequestered** (i.e., separated from family, etc.) in important cases. Jurors are paid fees for their service.

voir dire
The process whereby prospective jurors are asked questions by the judge and attorneys to determine whether they would be biased in their decisions.

Opening Statements

Each party's attorney is allowed to make an **opening statement** to the jury. In opening statements, an attorney usually summarizes the main factual and legal issues of the case and describes why he or she believes the client's position is valid. The information given in this statement is not considered as evidence.

The Plaintiff's Case

A plaintiff bears the **burden of proof** to persuade the trier of fact of the merits of his or her case. This is called the **plaintiff's case**. The plaintiff's attorney calls witnesses to give testimony. After a witness has been sworn in, the plaintiff's attorney examines (i.e., questions) the witness. This is called **direct examination**. Documents and other evidence can be introduced through each witness. After the plaintiff's attorney has completed his or her questions, the defendant's attorney can question the witness. This is called **cross-examination**. The defendant's attorney can ask questions only about the subjects that were brought up during the direct examination. After the defendant's attorney completes his or her questions, the plaintiff's attorney can ask questions of the witness. This is called **re-direct examination**.

Courts of appeals should be constantly alert to the trial judge's firsthand knowledge of witnesses, testimony, and issues; in other words, appellate courts should give due consideration to the first-instance decision maker's "feel" for the overall case.

Justice Ginsburg
Weisgram v. Marley Company 528 U.S. 440, 120 S.Ct. (2000)

The Defendant's Case

The **defendant's case** proceeds after the plaintiff has concluded his or her case. The defendant's case must (1) rebut the plaintiff's evidence, (2) prove any affirmative defenses asserted by the defendant, and (3) prove any allegations contained in the defendant's cross-complaint. The defendant's witnesses are examined by the defendant's attorney. The plaintiff's attorney can cross-examine each witness. This is followed by re-direct by the defendant and re-cross-examination by the plaintiff.

Rebuttal and Rejoinder

After the defendant's attorney has finished calling witnesses, the plaintiff's attorney can call witnesses and put forth evidence to rebut the defendant's case. This is called a **rebuttal**. The defendant's attorney can call additional witnesses and introduce other evidence to counter the rebuttal. This is called the **rejoinder**.

Closing Arguments

At the conclusion of the presentation of the evidence, each party's attorney is allowed to make a **closing argument** to the jury. Both attorneys try to convince the jury to render a verdict for their clients by pointing out the strengths in the client's case and the weaknesses in the other side's case. Information given by the attorneys in their closing statements is not evidence.

Jury Instructions

jury instructions
Instructions given by the judge to the jury that inform them of the law to be applied in the case.

Once the closing arguments are completed, the judge reads **jury instructions** (or **charges**) to the jury. These instructions inform the jury about what law to apply when they decide the case. For example, in a criminal trial, the judge reads the jury the statutory definition of the crime charged. In an accident case, the judge reads the jury the legal definition of *negligence*.

Jury Deliberation and Verdict

After the judge reads the jury instructions, the jury retires to the jury room to **deliberate** its findings. This can take from a few minutes to many weeks. After deliberation, the jury reaches a **verdict**. In civil cases, the jury will assess damages against the defendant if they have held in favor of the plaintiff. The jury often assesses penalties in criminal cases.

Entry of Judgment

After the jury has returned its verdict, in most cases the judge will enter a **judgment** to the successful party, based on the verdict. This is the official decision of the court.

The court may, however, overturn the verdict if it finds bias or jury misconduct. This is called a **judgment notwithstanding the verdict** or **judgment n.o.v.** or **j.n.o.v.**

In a civil case, the judge may reduce the amount of monetary damages awarded by the jury if he or she finds the jury to have been biased, emotional, or inflamed. This is called **remittitur**.

The trial court usually issues a **written memorandum** that sets forth the reasons for the judgment. This memorandum, together with the trial transcript and evidence introduced at trial, constitutes the permanent **record** of the trial court proceeding.

▶ APPEAL

appeal
The act of asking an appellate court to overturn a decision after the trial court's final judgment has been entered.

In a civil case, either party can **appeal** the trial court's decision once a **final judgment** is entered. Only the defendant can appeal in a criminal case. The appeal is made to the appropriate appellate court. A **notice of appeal** must be filed within a prescribed time after judgment is entered (usually within 60 or 90 days).

The appealing party is called the **appellant**, or **petitioner**. The responding party is called the **appellee**, or **respondent**. The appellant is often required to post a bond (e.g., one-and-one-half times the judgment) on appeal.

The parties may designate all or relevant portions of the trial record to be submitted to the appellate court for review. The appellant's attorney may file an **opening brief** with the court that sets forth legal research and other information to support his or her contentions on appeal. The appellee can file a **responding brief**, answering the appellant's contentions. Appellate courts usually permit a brief oral argument at which each party's attorney is heard.

An appellate court will reverse a lower court decision if it finds an **error of law** in the record.

An appellate court will not reverse a **finding of fact** unless such finding is unsupported by the evidence or is contradicted by the evidence. Very few trial court decisions are reversed because most findings of fact are supported by the evidence. In rare occasions, an appellate court will overturn a jury verdict if the appellate court cannot, from the record of the trial court, find sufficient evidence to support the trier of fact's findings.

appellant
The appealing party in an appeal. Also known as the *petitioner*.

appellee
The responding party in an appeal. Also known as the *respondent*.

ETHICS SPOTLIGHT

Frivolous Lawsuit

Although most lawsuits that are filed have some merit, some lawsuits do not. These are called frivolous lawsuits. Consider the following case. The Chungs are Korean residents who came to the United States in 1992. The Chungs opened a dry-cleaning store and eventually owned three dry-cleaning stores in the Washington, DC (DC) area. Roy L. Pearson was a DC administrative judge who was a customer at one of the Chungs' dry-cleaning stores. Pearson walked to the Chungs' store because he did not have a car.

The Chungs had signs in the window of their store that stated "Satisfaction Guaranteed" and "Same Day Service." Pearson claimed that the Chungs lost a pair of his pants. He sued the Chungs for $67 million in damages, alleging that they violated the DC Consumer Protection Act. Pearson later reduced his demand to $54 million. Pearson demanded $3 million for violation of the "Satisfaction Guaranteed" sign, $2 million for mental suffering and inconvenience, $500,000 in legal fees for representing himself, $6 million for 10 years of rental car fees to drive to another dry-cleaning shop, and $51 million to help similarly dissatisfied DC customers. Pearson stated that

he had no choice but to take on "the awesome responsibility" for suing the Chungs on behalf of every DC resident.

The court, in denying class action status, stated "The court has significant concerns that the plaintiff is acting in bad faith." After hearing testimony of witnesses, the trial court judge ruled in favor of the Chungs. Pearson made a motion to reconsider to the trial court, which was denied. A website was set up to accept donations for the Chungs' legal fees of $83,000, which were eventually paid by donations.

A DC commission voted against reappointing Pearson for a 10-year term as an administrative law judge in part because his lawsuit against the Chungs demonstrated a lack of "judicial temperament." Pearson lost a $100,000-per-year salary. The Chungs sold the dry-cleaning store involved in the dispute. Pearson filed a notice of appeal.

Business Ethics What is a frivolous lawsuit? Explain. Do you think Pearson's lawsuit had any merit? Do you think Pearson acted in "bad faith" in this case? How much emotional distress do you think the Chungs suffered because of this lawsuit?

▶ ALTERNATIVE DISPUTE RESOLUTION

The use of the court system to resolve business and other disputes can take years and cost thousands, or even millions, of dollars in legal fees and expenses. In commercial litigation, the normal business operations of the parties are often disrupted. To avoid or reduce these problems, businesses are increasingly turning to methods of **alternative dispute resolution (ADR)** and other aids to resolving disputes. The most common form of ADR is *arbitration*. Other forms of ADR are *negotiation, mediation, conciliation, mini-trial, fact-finding,* and using a *judicial referee*.

alternative dispute resolution (ADR)
Methods of resolving disputes other than litigation.

Negotiation

The simplest form of alternative dispute resolution is engaging in negotiations between the parties to try to settle a dispute. **Negotiation** is a procedure whereby the parties to a dispute engage in negotiations to try to reach a voluntary settlement of their dispute. Negotiation may take place either before a lawsuit is filed, after a lawsuit is filed, or before other forms of alternative dispute resolution are engaged in.

In a negotiation, the parties, who are often represented by attorneys, negotiate with each other to try to reach an agreeable solution to their dispute. During negotiation proceedings, the parties usually make offers and counteroffers to one another. The parties or their attorneys also may provide information to the other side that would assist the other side in reaching an amicable settlement.

Many courts require that the parties to a lawsuit engage in settlement discussions prior to trial to try to negotiate a settlement of the case. In such a case, the judge must be assured that a settlement of the case is not possible before he or she permits the case to go to trial. A judge may convince the parties to engage in further negotiations if he or she determines that the parties are not too far apart in the negotiations of a settlement.

If a settlement of the dispute is reached through negotiation, a settlement agreement is drafted that contains the terms of the agreement. A **settlement agreement** is an agreement that is voluntarily entered into by the parties to a dispute that settles the dispute. Each side must sign the settlement agreement for it to be effective. The settlement agreement is usually submitted to the court, and the case will be dismissed based on the execution of the settlement agreement.

Arbitration

arbitration
A form of ADR in which the parties choose an impartial third party to hear and decide the dispute.

arbitration clause
A clause in a contract that requires disputes arising out of the contract to be submitted to arbitration.

Federal Arbitration Act (FAA)
A federal statute that provides for the enforcement of most arbitration agreements.

In **arbitration**, the parties choose an impartial third party to hear and decide the dispute. This neutral party is called the **arbitrator**. Arbitrators are usually members of the American Arbitration Association (AAA) or another arbitration association. Labor union agreements, franchise agreements, leases, and other commercial contracts often contain **arbitration clauses** that require disputes arising out of the contract to be submitted to arbitration. If there is no arbitration clause, the parties can enter into a **submission agreement** whereby they agree to submit a dispute to arbitration after the dispute arises.

Congress enacted the *Federal Arbitration Act* to promote the arbitration of disputes.[2] About half of the states have adopted the **Uniform Arbitration Act**, which promotes the arbitration of disputes at the state level. Many federal and state courts have instituted programs to refer legal disputes to arbitration or another form of ADR.

LANDMARK LAW

Federal Arbitration Act

"By agreeing to arbitrate a statutory claim, a party does not forgo the substantive rights afforded by the statute, it only submits to their resolution in an arbitral, rather than a judicial, forum."

Justice White

The **Federal Arbitration Act (FAA)** was originally enacted in 1925 to reverse the long-standing judicial hostility to arbitration agreements that had existed at English common law and had been adopted by U.S. courts. The FAA provides that arbitration agreements involving commerce are valid, irrevocable, and enforceable contracts, unless some grounds exist at law or equity (e.g., fraud, duress) to revoke them. The FAA permits one party to obtain a court order to compel arbitration if the other party has failed, neglected, or refused to comply with an arbitration agreement.

Since the FAA's enactment, the courts have wrestled with the problem of which types of disputes should be arbitrated. Breach of contract cases, tort claims, and such are clearly candidates for arbitration if there is a valid arbitration agreement. In addition, the U.S. Supreme Court has enforced arbitration agreements that call for the resolution of disputes arising under federal statutes. The Supreme Court has stated, "By agreeing to arbitrate a statutory claim, a party does not forgo the substantive rights afforded by the statute, it only submits to their resolution in an arbitral, rather than a judicial, forum."[3]

Arbitration Providers   ADR services are usually provided by private organizations or individuals who qualify to hear and decide certain disputes.

Arbitration Procedure   An arbitration agreement often describes the specific procedures that must be followed for a case to proceed to and through arbitration. If one party seeks to enforce an arbitration clause, that party must give notice to the other party. The parties then select an arbitration association or arbitrator, as provided in the agreement. The parties usually agree on the date, time, and place of the arbitration (e.g., at the arbitrator's office, at a law office, or at any other agreed-upon location).

At the arbitration, the parties can call witnesses to give testimony and introduce evidence to support their case and refute the other side's case. Rules similar to those followed by federal courts are usually followed at an arbitration. Often, each party pays a filing fee and other fees for the arbitration. Sometimes the agreement provides that one party will pay all the costs of the arbitration. Arbitrators are paid by the hour, day, or other agreed-upon method of compensation.

Decision and Award   After an arbitration hearing is complete, the arbitrator reaches a decision and issues an award. The parties often agree in advance to be bound by the arbitrator's decision and remedy. This is called **binding arbitration**. In this situation, the decision and award of the arbitrator cannot be appealed to the courts. If the arbitration is not binding, the decision and award of the arbitrator can be appealed to the courts. This is called *non-binding arbitration*. Courts usually give great deference to an arbitrator's decision and award.

If an arbitrator has rendered a decision and an award, but a party refuses to abide by the arbitrator's decision, the other party may file an action in court to have the arbitrator's decision enforced.

Mediation

Mediation is a form of negotiation in which a neutral third party assists the disputing parties in reaching a settlement of their dispute. The neutral third party is called a **mediator**. The mediator is usually a person who is an expert in the area of the dispute, or a lawyer or retired judge. The mediator is selected by the parties as provided in their agreement, or as otherwise selected by the parties. Unlike an arbitrator, however, a mediator does not make a decision or an award.

A mediator's role is to assist the parties in reaching a settlement. The mediator usually acts as an intermediary between the parties. In many cases, the mediator will meet with the two parties at an agreed-upon location, often the mediator's office or one of the offices of the parties. The mediator will then meet with both parties, usually separately, to discuss each side of the case.

After discussing the facts of the case with both sides, the mediator will encourage settlement of the dispute and will transmit settlement offers from one side to the other. In doing so, the mediator points out the strengths and weaknesses of each party's case and gives his or her opinion to each side about why they should decrease or increase their settlement offers. The mediator's job is to facilitate settlement of the case.

If the parties agree to a settlement, a settlement agreement is drafted that expresses their agreement. Execution of the settlement agreement ends the dispute. The parties, of course, must perform their duties under the settlement agreement. If an agreement is not reached, the parties may proceed to a judicial resolution of their case.

> **mediation**
> A form of ADR in which the parties use a mediator to propose a settlement of their dispute.

Conciliation

Conciliation is a form of alternative dispute resolution in which an interested party, a **conciliator**, helps the parties try to reach a resolution of their dispute. Conciliation is often used when the parties do not want to face each other in an adversarial setting. The conciliator schedules meetings and appointments during which information can be transferred to the parties. A conciliator usually carries offers and counteroffers for a settlement back and forth between the disputing parties. A conciliator cannot make a decision or an award.

Although the role of a conciliator is not to propose a settlement of the case, many often do. In many cases, conciliators are neutral third parties, although in some circumstances,

> **conciliation**
> A form of ADR in which the parties use a third party to help them resolve their dispute.

the parties may select an interested third party to act as the conciliator. If the parties reach a settlement of their dispute through the use of conciliation, a settlement agreement is drafted and executed by the parties.

Mini-trial

A **mini-trial** is a voluntary private proceeding in which lawyers for each side present a shortened version of their case to the representatives of both sides. The representatives of each side who attend the mini-trial have the authority to settle the dispute. In many cases, the parties also hire a neutral third party—often someone who is an expert in the field concerning the disputed matter or a legal expert—who presides over the mini-trial. After hearing the case, the neutral third party often is called upon to render an opinion as to how the court would most likely decide the case.

During a mini-trial, the parties get to see the strengths and weaknesses of their own position and that of the opposing side. Once the strengths and weaknesses of both sides are exposed, the parties to a mini-trial often settle the case. The parties also often settle a mini-trial based on the opinion rendered by the neutral third party. If the parties settle their dispute after a mini-trial, they enter into a settlement agreement that sets forth their agreement.

Mini-trials serve a useful purpose in that they act as a substitute for a real trial, but they are much briefer and not as complex and expensive to prepare for. Because the strengths and weaknesses of both sides' cases are exposed, the parties are usually more realistic regarding their own positions and the merits of settling the case prior to an expensive, and often risky, trial.

Fact-Finding

In some situations, called **fact-finding**, the parties to a dispute employ a neutral third party to act as a fact-finder to investigate the dispute. The fact-finder is authorized to investigate the dispute, gather evidence, prepare demonstrative evidence, and prepare reports of his or her findings.

A fact-finder is not authorized to make a decision or an award. In some cases, a fact-finder will recommend settlement of the case. The fact-finder presents the evidence and findings to the parties, who may then use the information in negotiating a settlement if they wish.

Judicial Referee

If the parties agree, the court may appoint a **judicial referee** to conduct a private trial and render a judgment. Referees, who are often retired judges, have most of the same powers as trial judges, and their decisions stand as judgments of the court. The parties usually reserve their right to appeal.

In the following case, the U.S. Supreme Court addressed the issue of alternative dispute resolution.

U.S. SUPREME COURT   CASE 3.2 Arbitration

Circuit City Stores, Inc. v. Adams

532 U.S. 105, 121 S.Ct. 1302, 149 L.Ed.2d 234, Web 2001 U.S. Lexis 2459 (2001)
Supreme Court of the United States

"Congress enacted the Federal Arbitration Act (FAA) in 1925. The FAA was a response to hostility of American courts to the enforcement of arbitration agreements."

—Justice Kennedy

Facts

Saint Clair Adams was hired as a sales counselor by Circuit City Stores, Inc., a national retailer of consumer electronics.

(case continues)

Adams signed an employment contract that included the following arbitration clause:

> *I agree that I will settle any and all previously unasserted claims, disputes or controversies arising out of or relating to my application or candidacy for employment, employment and/or cessation of employment with Circuit City, exclusively by final and binding arbitration before a neutral Arbitrator. By way of example only, such claims include claims under federal, state, and local statutory or common law, such as the Age Discrimination in Employment Act, Title VII of the Civil Rights Act of 1964, the Americans with Disabilities Act, the law of contract and the law of tort.*

Two years later, Adams filed an employment discrimination lawsuit against Circuit City in court. Circuit City sought to enjoin the court proceeding and to compel arbitration, pursuant to the FAA. The U.S. District Court granted Circuit City's request. The U.S. Court of Appeals reversed, holding that employment contracts are not subject to arbitration. Adams appealed to the U.S. Supreme Court.

Issue

Are employment contracts subject to arbitration if a valid arbitration agreement has been entered into between the parties?

Language of the U.S. Supreme Court

> *Congress enacted the Federal Arbitration Act (FAA) in 1925. The FAA was a response to hostility of American courts to the enforcement of arbitration agreements. To give effect to this purpose, the FAA compels judicial enforcement of a wide range of written arbitration agreements. The FAA's coverage provision, Section 2, provides that "a written provision in any contract evidencing a transaction involving commerce to settle by arbitration a controversy thereafter arising out of such contract or transaction, or the refusal to perform the whole or any part thereof, shall be valid, irrevocable, and enforceable, save upon such grounds as exist at law or in equity for the revocation of any contract."*

Decision

The U.S. Supreme Court held that employment contracts, including the one in this case between Circuit City and Adams, are subject to arbitration if a valid arbitration agreement has been executed. The Supreme Court reversed the decision of the Court of Appeals and remanded the case for further proceedings.

Case Questions

Critical Legal Thinking What is arbitration? What does the Federal Arbitration Act provide?

Business Ethics Is it ethical for employers to include arbitration clauses in employment contracts? Or should employers face judicial litigation? Explain.

Contemporary Business Who do you think benefits most from arbitration clauses in employment contracts: employers or employees? Why?

INTERNET LAW & ONLINE COMMERCE

Online Dispute Resolution

Many ADR service providers now offer **online arbitration**. Most of these services allow a party to a dispute to register the dispute with the service and then notify the other party by e-mail of the registration of the dispute. Most online arbitration requires the registering party to submit an amount that the party is willing to accept or pay to the other party in the online arbitration. The other party is afforded the opportunity to accept the offer. If that party accepts the offer, a settlement has been reached. The other party, however, may return a counteroffer. The process continues until a settlement is reached or one or both of the parties remove themselves from the online ADR process.

Also, several websites offer **online mediation** services. In an online mediation, the parties sit before their computers and sign onto the website. Two chat rooms are assigned to each party. One chat room is used for private conversations with the online mediator, and the other chat room is for conversations between both parties and the mediator.

Online arbitration and online mediation services charge fees, but the fees are reasonable. In an online arbitration or online mediation, a settlement can be reached rather quickly, without paying lawyers' fees and court costs. The parties also act through a more objective online process rather than meet face-to-face or negotiate over the telephone, either of which could involve verbal arguments.

Federal Courthouse, Orange County, California
This is the U.S. District Court for the Central District of California, Southern Division, located in Santa Ana, California.

TEST REVIEW TERMS AND CONCEPTS

Affirmative defense
Alternative dispute
   resolution (ADR)
Answer
Appeal
Appellant (petitioner)
Appellee (respondent)
Arbitration
Arbitration clause
Arbitrator
Binding arbitration
Burden of proof
Closing argument
Complaint
Conciliation
Conciliator
Consolidation
Cost–benefit analysis
Cross-complainant
Cross-complaint
Cross-defendant
Cross-examination
Defendant's case

Default judgment
Deponent
Deposition
Direct examination
Discovery
E-filing
Error of law
Fact-finding
Federal Arbitration Act
   (FAA)
Final judgment
Finding of fact
Impaneled
Interrogatories
Intervention
Judgment
Judgment notwithstanding
   the verdict (judgment
   n.o.v. or j.n.o.v.)
Judicial referee
Jury deliberation
Jury instructions (charges)
Jury trial

Litigation
Mediation
Mediator
Mini-trial
Motion for judgment on
   the pleadings
Motion for summary
   judgment
Negotiation
Nonjudicial dispute
   resolution
Notice of appeal
Online arbitration
Online dispute resolution
Online mediation
Opening brief
Opening statement
Physical or mental
   examination
Plaintiff
Plaintiff's case
Pleadings
Pretrial motion

Production of documents
Rebuttal
Record
Re-direct examination
Rejoinder
Remittitur
Reply
Responding brief
Sequester
Settlement agreement
Settlement conference
   (pretrial hearing)
Statute of limitations
Submission agreement
Summons
Trial brief
Trier of fact
Uniform Arbitration Act
Verdict
Virtual courthouse
Voir dire
Written memorandum

CASE PROBLEMS

3.1 Long-Arm Statute   Sean O'Grady, a professional boxer, was managed by his father, Pat. Sean was a contender for the world featherweight title. Pat entered into a contract with Magna Verde Corporation, a Los Angeles–based business, to co-promote a fight between Sean and the then-current featherweight champion. The fight was scheduled to take place in Oklahoma City, Oklahoma. To promote the fight, Pat O'Grady scheduled a press conference. At the conference, Pat was involved in a confrontation with a sportswriter named Brooks. He allegedly struck Brooks in the face. Brooks brought suit against Pat O'Grady and Magna Verde Corporation in an Oklahoma state court. Court records showed that the only contact Magna Verde had with Oklahoma was that a few of its employees had taken several trips to Oklahoma to plan the title fight. The fight was never held. Oklahoma has a long-arm statute. Magna Verde was served by mail and made a special appearance in Oklahoma state court to argue that Oklahoma does not have personal jurisdiction over it. Does Oklahoma have jurisdiction over Magna Verde Corporation? *Brooks v. Magna Verde Corp.*, 1980 Ok. Civ. App. 40, 619 P.2d 1271, **Web** 1980 Okla. Civ. App. Lexis 118 (Court of Appeals of Oklahoma)

3.2 Minimum Contacts   The National Enquirer, Inc., is a Florida corporation with its principal place of business in Florida. It publishes the *National Enquirer*, a national weekly newspaper with a total circulation of more than 5 million copies. About 600,000 copies, almost twice the level in the next highest state, are sold in California. The *Enquirer* published an article about Shirley Jones, an entertainer. Jones, a California resident, filed a lawsuit in California state court against the *Enquirer* and its president, who was a resident of Florida. The suit sought damages for alleged defamation, invasion of privacy, and intentional infliction of emotional distress. Are the defendants subject to suit in California? *Calder v. Jones*, 465 U.S. 783, 104 S.Ct. 1482, 79 L.Ed.2d 804, **Web** 1984 U.S. Lexis 4 (Supreme Court of the United States)

3.3 Physical Examination   Robert Schlagenhauf worked as a bus driver for the Greyhound Corporation. One night the bus he was driving rear-ended a tractor-trailer. Seven passengers on the bus who were injured sued Schlagenhauf and Greyhound for damages. The complaint alleged that Greyhound was negligent for allowing Schlagenhauf to drive a bus when it knew that his eyes and vision "were impaired and deficient." The plaintiffs petitioned the court to order Schlagenhauf to be medically examined concerning these allegations. Schlagenhauf objected to the examination. Who wins? *Schlagenhauf v. Holder*, 379 U.S. 104, 85 S.Ct. 234, 13 L.Ed.2d 152, **Web** 1964 U.S. Lexis 152 (Supreme Court of the United States)

3.4 Interrogatories   Cine Forty-Second Street Theatre Corporation operates a movie theater in New York City's Times Square area. Cine filed a lawsuit against Allied Artists Pictures Corporation, alleging that Allied Artists and local theater owners illegally attempted to prevent Cine from opening its theater, in violation of federal antitrust law. The suit also alleged that once Cine opened the theater, the defendants conspired with motion picture distributors to prevent

Cine from exhibiting first-run, quality films. Attorneys for Allied Artists served a set of written questions concerning the lawsuit on Cine. Does Cine have to answer these questions? *Cine Forty-Second Street Theatre Corp. v. Allied Artists Pictures Corp.*, 602 F.2d 1062, **Web** 1979 U.S. App. Lexis 13586 (United States Court of Appeals for the Second Circuit)

3.5 Judgment n.o.v.   Mr. Simblest was driving a car that collided with a fire engine at an intersection in Burlington, Vermont. The accident occurred on a night on which a power blackout had left most of the state without lights. Mr. Simblest, who was injured in the accident, sued the driver of the fire truck for damages. During the trial, Simblest testified that when he entered the intersection, the traffic light was green in his favor. All the other witnesses testified that the traffic light had gone dark at least 10 minutes before the accident. Simblest testified that the accident was caused by the fire truck's failure to use any warning lights or sirens. Simblest's testimony was contradicted by four witnesses, who testified that the fire truck had used both its lights and sirens. The jury found that the driver of the fire truck had been negligent and rendered a verdict for Simblest. The defense made a motion for judgment n.o.v. Who wins? *Simblest v. Maynard*, 427 F.2d 1, **Web** 1970 U.S. App. Lexis 9265 (United States Court of Appeals for the Second Circuit)

3.6 Arbitration   AMF Incorporated and Brunswick Corporation both manufacture electric and automatic bowling center equipment. In 1983, the two companies became involved in a dispute over whether Brunswick had advertised certain automatic scoring devices in a false and deceptive manner. The two parties settled the dispute by signing an agreement that any future problems between them involving advertising claims would be submitted to the National Advertising Council for arbitration. Brunswick advertised a new product, Armor Plate 3000, a synthetic laminated material used to make bowling lanes. Armor Plate 3000 competed with wooden lanes produced by AMF. Brunswick's advertisements claimed that bowling centers could save up to $500 per lane per year in maintenance and repair costs if they switched to Armor Plate 3000 from wooden lanes. AMF disputed this claim and requested arbitration. Is the arbitration agreement enforceable? *AMF Incorporated v. Brunswick Corp.*, 621 F.Supp. 456, **Web** 1985 U.S. Dist. Lexis 14205 (United States District Court for the Eastern District of New York)

BUSINESS ETHICS CASE

3.7 Business Ethics   Dennis and Francis Burnham were married in West Virginia in 1976. In 1977, the couple moved to New Jersey, where their two children were born. In July 1987, the Burnhams decided to separate. Mrs. Burnham, who intended to move to California, was to have custody of the children. Mr. Burnham agreed to file for divorce on

grounds of irreconcilable differences. Mr. Burnham threatened to file for divorce in New Jersey on grounds of desertion. After unsuccessfully demanding that Mr. Burnham adhere to the prior agreement, Mrs. Burnham brought suit for divorce in California state court in early January 1988. In late January, Mr. Burnham visited California on a business trip. He then visited his children in the San Francisco Bay area, where his wife resided. He took the older child to San Francisco for the weekend. Upon returning the child to Mrs. Burnham's home, he was served with a California court summons and a copy of Mrs. Burnham's divorce petition. He then returned to New Jersey. Mr. Burnham made a special appearance in the California court and moved to quash the service of process. Did Mr. Burnham act ethically in trying to quash the service of process? Did Mrs. Burnham act ethically in having Mr. Burnham served on his visit to California? Is the service of process good? *Burnham v. Superior Court of California*, 495 U.S. 604, 110 S.Ct. 2105, 109 L.Ed.2d 631, **Web** 1990 U.S. Lexis 2700 (Supreme Court of the United States)

ENDNOTES

1. There is no right to a jury trial for actions in equity (e.g., injunctions, specific performance).
2. 9 U.S.C. Section 1 et seq.
3. *Gilmer v. Interstate/Johnson Lane Corporation*, 500 U.S. 20, 111 S.Ct. 1647, 114 L.Ed.2d 26, **Web** 1991 U.S. Lexis 2529 (Supreme Court of the United States).

CONSTITUTIONAL LAW FOR BUSINESS AND E-COMMERCE

4

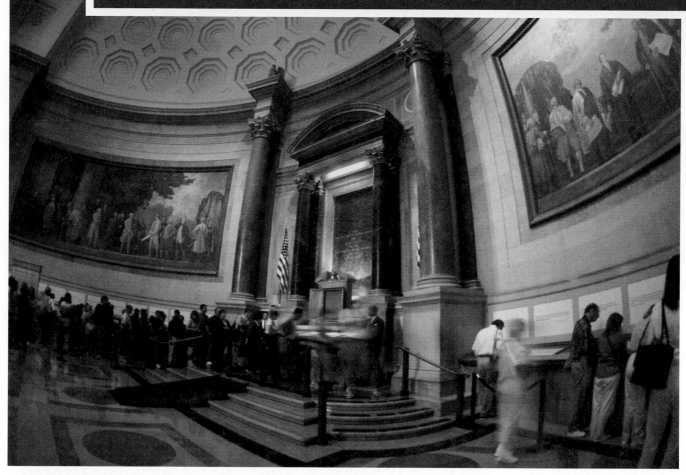

▲ **Washington D.C.** *The Constitution of the United States of America establishes the structure of the federal government, delegates powers to the federal government, and guarantees certain fundamental rights. The Constitution is a document that can be amended. The first ten amendments to the Constitution are called the "Bill of Rights" and contain some of our most important personal rights. Other amendments have also been added to the Constitution.*

CHAPTER OBJECTIVES

After studying this chapter, you should be able to:

1. Describe the concept of federalism and the doctrine of separation of powers.
2. Define and apply the Supremacy Clause of the U.S. Constitution.
3. Explain the federal government's authority to regulate foreign commerce and interstate commerce.
4. Explain how speech is protected by the First Amendment.
5. Explain the doctrines of equal protection and due process.

CHAPTER CONTENTS

"We the People of the United States, in Order to form a more perfect Union, establish Justice, insure domestic Tranquility, provide for the common defense, promote the general Welfare, and secure the Blessings of Liberty to ourselves and our Posterity, do ordain and establish this Constitution for the United States of America."

Preamble to the Constitution of the United States of America

▶ INTRODUCTION TO CONSTITUTIONAL LAW FOR BUSINESS AND E-COMMERCE

Prior to the American Revolution, each of the 13 original colonies operated as a separate sovereignty under the rule of England. In September 1774, representatives of the colonies met as a Continental Congress. In 1776, the colonies declared independence from England, and the American Revolution ensued. The **Declaration of Independence** was the document that declared independence from England.

This chapter examines the major provisions of the U.S. Constitution and the amendments that have been added to the Constitution. Of particular importance, this chapter discusses how these provisions affect the operations of business in this country. The Constitution, with amendments, is set forth as Appendix A to this book.

▶ CONSTITUTION OF THE UNITED STATES OF AMERICA

U.S. Constitution
The fundamental law of the United States of America. It was ratified by the states in 1788.

In 1778, the Continental Congress formed a **federal government** and adopted the **Articles of Confederation**. The Articles of Confederation created a federal Congress composed of representatives of the 13 new states. The Articles of Confederation was a particularly weak document that gave limited power to the newly created federal government. It did not provide Congress with the power to levy and collect taxes, to regulate commerce with foreign countries, or to regulate interstate commerce.

The **Constitutional Convention** was convened in Philadelphia in May 1787. The primary purpose of the convention was to strengthen the federal government. After substantial debate, the delegates agreed to a new **U.S. Constitution**. The Constitution was reported to Congress in September 1787. State ratification of the Constitution was completed in 1788. Many amendments, including the Bill of Rights, have been added to the Constitution since that time.

The U.S. Constitution serves two major functions:

1. It creates the three branches of the federal government (i.e., the legislative, executive, and judicial branches) and allocates powers to these branches.
2. It protects individual rights by limiting the government's ability to restrict those rights.

The Constitution itself provides that it may be amended to address social and economic changes. Some important constitutional concepts are discussed in the following paragraphs. Exhibit 4.1 shows the U.S. Constitution.

The nation's armour of defence against the passions of men is the Constitution. Take that away, and the nation goes down into the field of its conflicts like a warrior without armour.

Henry Ward Beecher
Proverbs from Plymouth Pulpit,
1887

▶ **Exhibit 4.1 THE CONSTITUTION OF THE UNITED STATES OF AMERICA**

Federalism and Delegated Powers

federalism
The U.S. form of government, in which the federal government and the 50 state governments share powers.

Our country's form of government is referred to as **federalism**. That means that the federal government and the 50 state governments share powers.

When the states ratified the Constitution, they **delegated** certain powers—called **enumerated powers**—to the federal government.

Example The federal government is authorized to deal with national and international affairs.

enumerated powers
Certain powers delegated to the federal government by the states.

Any powers that are not specifically delegated to the federal government by the Constitution are **reserved** to the state governments. State governments are empowered to deal with local affairs.

Doctrine of Separation of Powers

As mentioned previously, the federal government is divided into three branches:

legislative branch
The part of the U.S. government that makes federal laws. It is known as Congress (the Senate and the House of Representatives).

1. Article I of the Constitution establishes the **legislative branch** of government. The legislative branch is responsible for making federal law. This branch is **bicameral**; that is, it consists of the Senate and the House of Representatives. Collectively, they are referred to as **Congress**.[1] Each state has two senators. The number of representatives to the House of Representatives is determined according to the population of each state. The current number of representatives is determined by the most recent census.

executive branch
The part of the U.S. government that enforces the federal law; it consists of the president and vice president.

2. Article II of the Constitution establishes the **executive branch** of government by providing for the election of the president and vice president. The president is not elected by popular vote but instead is selected by the **electoral college**, whose representatives are appointed by state delegations.[2] The executive branch of government is responsible for enforcing federal law.

judicial branch
The part of the U.S. government that interprets the law. It consists of the Supreme Court and other federal courts.

3. Article III of the Constitution establishes the **judicial branch** of the government by establishing the U.S. Supreme Court and providing for the creation of other federal courts by Congress.[3] The judicial branch is responsible for interpreting the U.S Constitution and federal law.

Checks and Balances

checks and balances
A system built into the U.S. Constitution to prevent any one of the three branches of the government from becoming too powerful.

Certain **checks and balances** are built into the Constitution to ensure that no one branch of the federal government becomes too powerful.

Example The *judicial branch* has authority to examine the acts of the other two branches of government and determine whether those acts are constitutional.[4]

Example The *executive branch* can enter into treaties with foreign governments only with the advice and consent of the Senate.

Example The *legislative branch* is authorized to create federal courts and determine their jurisdiction and to enact statutes that change judicially made law.

CONCEPT SUMMARY

BASIC CONSTITUTIONAL CONCEPTS

Concept	Description
Federalism	The Constitution created the federal government. The federal government and the 50 state governments and Washington, DC, share powers in this country.
Delegated powers	When the states ratified the Constitution, they delegated certain powers to the federal government. These are called *enumerated powers*.
Reserved powers	Those powers not granted to the federal government by the Constitution are reserved to the state governments.

Separation of powers	Each branch of the federal government has separate powers. These powers are:
	a. Legislative branch—power to make the law.
	b. Executive branch—power to enforce the law.
	c. Judicial branch—power to interpret the law.
Checks and balances	Certain checks and balances are built into the Constitution to ensure that no one branch of the federal government becomes too powerful.

▶ SUPREMACY CLAUSE

The **Supremacy Clause** establishes that the U.S. Constitution and federal treaties, laws, and regulations are the supreme law of the land.[5] State and local laws that conflict with valid federal law are unconstitutional. The concept of federal law taking precedence over state or local law is commonly called the **preemption doctrine**.

Congress may expressly provide that a particular federal statute *exclusively* regulates a specific area or activity. No state or local law regulating the area or activity is valid if there is such a statute. More often, though, federal statutes do not expressly provide for exclusive jurisdiction. In these instances, state and local governments have *concurrent jurisdiction* to regulate the area or activity. However, any state or local law that "directly and substantially" conflicts with valid federal law is preempted under the Supremacy Clause.

In the following case, the U.S. Supreme Court applied the Supremacy Clause.

Supremacy Clause
A clause of the U.S. Constitution which establishes that the U.S. Constitution and federal treaties, laws, and regulations are the supreme law of the land.

preemption doctrine
The concept that federal law takes precedence over state or local law.

U.S. SUPREME COURT   CASE 4.1 Supremacy Clause

Rowe, Attorney General of Maine v. New Hampshire Motor Transport Association

128 S.Ct. 989, 169 L.Ed.2d 933, Web 2008 U.S. Lexis 2010 (2008)
Supreme Court of the United States

"And to allow Maine directly to regulate carrier services would permit other States to do the same. We find that federal law must preempt Maine's efforts directly to regulate carrier services."

—Justice Breyer

Facts

Prior to 1980, the trucking industry was subject to substantial federal government regulation that licensed routes, set pricing, and regulated other aspects of commercial trucking. The U.S. Congress enacted the federal Motor Carrier Act of 1980, which deregulated the trucking industry to make it competitively market oriented. In addition, Congress enacted two other federal statutes that preempted the regulation of trucking by the states.

Subsequently, the state of Maine adopted a state statute that regulated the trucking industry. One provision of the state statute forbids anyone other than a Maine-licensed tobacco retailer to accept an order for delivery of tobacco. Another provision forbids anyone knowingly to transport a tobacco product to a person in Maine unless either the sender or the receiver has a tobacco sales license issued by the state of Maine.

Several trucking associations brought a lawsuit in U.S. District Court, claiming that federal law preempted Maine's statute. The District Court held that federal law preempted the two provisions of the Maine statute. The U.S. Court of Appeals agreed. The state of Maine appealed to the U.S. Supreme Court.

Issue

Does federal law preempt the two provisions of the Maine state statute at issue in this case?

Language of the U.S. Supreme Court

The Court described Congress' overarching goal as helping assure transportation rates, routes, and services that reflect maximum reliance on competitive market forces, thereby stimulating efficiency, innovation, and low prices, as well as variety and quality. We find that federal law preempts the Maine laws at issue here. The Maine law thereby produces the very effect that the federal law sought to avoid, namely, a State's direct substitution of its own governmental commands for competitive market forces in determining the services that motor carriers will provide.

(case continues)

To allow Maine to insist that the carriers provide a special checking system would allow other States to do the same. And to interpret the federal law to permit these, and similar, state requirements could easily lead to a patchwork of state service-determining laws, rules, and regulations. That state regulatory patchwork is inconsistent with Congress' major legislative effort to leave such decisions, where federally unregulated, to the competitive marketplace. And to allow Maine directly to regulate carrier services would permit other States to do the same. We find that federal law must preempt Maine's efforts directly to regulate carrier services.

Decision

The U.S. Supreme Court affirmed the decisions of the U.S. District Court and the U.S. Court of Appeals, which held that

federal law preempted the Maine statute that regulated the trucking industry.

Case Questions

Critical Legal Thinking What is the Supremacy Clause? Explain.

Business Ethics Why do you think the state of Maine passed these laws?

Contemporary Business What would be the consequences if there were no Supremacy Clause in the U.S. Constitution? Explain.

▶ COMMERCE CLAUSE

Commerce Clause

A clause of the U.S. Constitution that grants Congress the power "to regulate commerce with foreign nations, and among the several states, and with Indian tribes."

The **Commerce Clause** of the U.S. Constitution grants Congress the power "to regulate commerce with foreign nations, and among the several states, and with Indian tribes."[6] Because this clause authorizes the federal government to regulate commerce, it has a greater impact on business than any other provision in the Constitution. Among other things, this clause is intended to foster the development of a national market and free trade among the states.

The U.S. Constitution grants the federal government the power to regulate three types of commerce:

1. Commerce with Native American tribes
2. Foreign commerce
3. Interstate commerce

Each of these is discussed in the following paragraphs.

Commerce with Native Americans

Before Europeans arrived in the "New World," the land had been occupied for thousands of years by people we now refer to as Native Americans. There were many different Native American tribes, each having its own independent and self-governing system of laws.

When the United States was first founded over 200 years ago, it consisted of the original 13 colonies, all located in the east, primarily on the Atlantic Ocean. At that time, these colonies (states), in the U.S. Constitution, delegated to the federal government the authority to regulate commerce with the Native American tribes—in both the original 13 states and the territory that was to eventually become the United States of America.

Under its Commerce Clause powers, the federal government entered into treaties with many Native American nations. Most tribes, in the face of white settlers' encroachment on their land and federal government pressure, were forced to sell their lands to the federal government. The Native Americans received money and goods for land. The federal government obtained many treaties through unscrupulous means, cheating the Native Americans of their land. These tribes were then relocated to other, smaller, pieces of land called *reservations*, often outside their typical tribal lands. The federal government eventually broke many of the treaties.

Once Native Americans came under U.S. authority, they lost much of their political power. Most tribes were allowed to keep their own governments but were placed under the "protection" of the U.S. government. In general, the United States treats Native Americans as separate nations, similarly to the way it treats Spain or France; however, it still considers Native Americans "domestic dependent" nations with limited sovereignty.

Today, many Native Americans live on reservations set aside for various tribes. Others live and work outside reservations.

Indian Gaming Regulatory Act   In the late 1980s, the federal government authorized Native American tribes to operate gaming facilities. Congress passed the **Indian Gaming Regulatory Act**,[7] which sets the terms of casino gambling and other gaming activities on tribal land. This act allows Native Americans to negotiate with the states for gaming compacts and ensures that the states do so in good faith. If a state fails to do so, the tribe can bring suit in federal court, forcing the state to comply. Today, casinos operated by Native Americans can be found in many states. Profits from the casinos have become an important source of income for members of certain tribes.

Foreign Commerce

The Commerce Clause of the U.S. Constitution gives the federal government the *exclusive power* to regulate commerce with foreign nations.

Direct and indirect regulation of foreign commerce by state or local governments that unduly burdens foreign commerce violates the Commerce Clause and is therefore unconstitutional.

In the following case, the U.S. Supreme Court struck down a state law as violating the U.S. Constitution.

U.S. SUPREME COURT   CASE 4.2 Foreign Commerce

Crosby, Secretary of Administration and Finance of Massachusetts v. National Foreign Trade Council

530 U.S. 363, 120 S.Ct. 2288, 147 L.Ed.2d 352, Web 2000 U.S. Lexis 4153 (2000)
Supreme Court of the United States

"Within the sphere defined by Congress, then, the federal statute has placed the president in a position with as much discretion to exercise economic leverage against Burma, with an eye toward national security, as our law will admit."

—Justice Souter

Facts

The military regime of the country of Myanmar (called Burma prior to 1989) has been accused of major civil rights violations, including using forced and child labor, imprisoning and torturing political opponents, and harshly repressing ethnic minorities. These inhumane actions have been condemned by human rights organizations around the world. The state legislators of the state of Massachusetts were so appalled at these actions that in June 1996, they enacted a state statute banning the state government from purchasing goods and services from any company that did business with Myanmar.

In the meantime, the U.S. Congress enacted a federal statute that delegated power to the president of the United States to regulate U.S. dealings with Myanmar. The federal statute (1) banned all aid to the government of Myanmar except for humanitarian assistance, (2) authorized the president to impose economic sanctions against Myanmar, and (3) authorized the president to develop a comprehensive multilateral strategy to bring democracy to Myanmar.

The National Foreign Trade Council—a powerful Washington, DC–based trade association with more than 500 member companies—filed a lawsuit against Massachusetts to have the state law declared unconstitutional. The council argued that the Massachusetts "anti-Myanmar" statute conflicted with the federal statute and that under the Supremacy Clause that makes federal law the "supreme law of the land" the state statute was preempted by the federal statute. The U.S. District Court and U.S. Court of Appeals ruled in favor of the council. Massachusetts appealed to the U.S. Supreme Court.

(case continues)

Issue

Did the Massachusetts anti-Myanmar state statute violate the Supremacy Clause of the U.S. Constitution?

Language of the U.S. Supreme Court

Within the sphere defined by Congress, then, the federal statute has placed the president in a position with as much discretion to exercise economic leverage against Burma, with an eye toward national security, as our law will admit. And it is just this plenitude of executive authority that we think controls the issue of preemption here. The president has been given this authority not merely to make a political statement but to achieve a political result, and the fullness of his authority shows the importance in the congressional mind of reaching that result. It is simply implausible that Congress would have gone to such lengths to empower the president if it had been willing to compromise his effectiveness by deference to every provision of state statute or local ordinance that might, if enforced, blunt the consequences of discretionary presidential action.

We find it unlikely that Congress intended both to enable the president to protect national security by giving him the flexibility to suspend or terminate federal sanctions and simultaneously to allow Massachusetts to act at odds with the president's judgment of what national security requires. And that is just what the Massachusetts Burma law would do in imposing a different, state system of economic pressure against the Burmese political regime.

Decision

The U.S. Supreme Court held that the Massachusetts anti-Myanmar law conflicted with federal law and was therefore preempted by the Supremacy Clause of the Constitution. The Supreme Court affirmed the decisions of the U.S. District Court and U.S. Court of Appeals in favor of the National Foreign Trade Council.

Case Questions

Critical Legal Thinking What does the Supremacy Clause provide? Explain.

Business Ethics Do you think companies that have goods manufactured in Myanmar violate any ethical principles? Explain.

Contemporary Business Could the federal government enact an anti-Myanmar law such as the one Massachusetts enacted?

Myanmar *The country of Myanmar (also called Burma) is ruled by a junta composed of its military generals. The country has been accused of human rights violations, including using child labor and forced labor, eliminating political dissidents, and strict censorship. The country, once a democracy, has been run by the military since 1962.*

Interstate Commerce

The Commerce Clause gives the federal government the authority to regulate **interstate commerce**. Originally, the courts interpreted this clause to mean that the federal government could only regulate commerce that moved *in* interstate commerce. The modern rule, however, allows the federal government to regulate activities that *affect* interstate commerce.

Under the **effects on interstate commerce test**, the regulated activity does not itself have to be in interstate commerce. Thus, any local (*intrastate*) activity that has an effect on interstate commerce is subject to federal regulation. Theoretically, this test subjects a substantial amount of business activity in the United States to federal regulation.

Example In the famous case *Wickard, Secretary of Agriculture v. Filburn*,[8] a federal statute limited the amount of wheat that a farmer could plant and harvest for home consumption. Filburn, a farmer, violated the law. The U.S. Supreme Court upheld the federal statute on the grounds that it involved interstate commerce because the statute was designed to prevent nationwide surpluses and shortages of wheat during the Depression. The Court reasoned that wheat grown for home consumption would affect the supply of wheat available in interstate commerce.

interstate commerce
Commerce that moves between states or that affects commerce between states.

The American Constitution is, so far as I can see, the most wonderful work ever struck off at a given time by the brain and purpose of man.

W. E. Gladstone
Kin Beyond Sea (1878)

LANDMARK U.S. SUPREME COURT CASE

Heart of Atlanta Motel v. United States

"One need only examine the evidence which we have discussed . . . to see that Congress may . . . prohibit racial discrimination by motels serving travelers, however 'local' their operations may appear."

—Justice Clark

The Heart of Atlanta Motel, which was located in the state of Georgia, had 216 rooms available to guests. The motel was readily accessible to motorists using U.S. interstate highways 75 and 85 and Georgia state highways 23 and 41. The motel solicited patronage from outside the state of Georgia through various national advertising media, including magazines of national circulation. The motel maintained more than 50 billboards and highway signs within the state of Georgia. Approximately 75 percent of the motel's registered guests were from out of state. The Heart of Atlanta Motel refused to rent rooms to blacks.

*Congress enacted the **Civil Rights Act of 1964**, which made it illegal for motels, hotels, and other public accommodations to discriminate against guests based on their race. After the act was passed, the Heart of Atlanta Motel continued to refuse to rent rooms to blacks. The owner-operator of the motel brought a declaratory relief action in U.S. District Court, **Heart of Atlanta Motel v. United States**, to have the Civil Rights Act of 1964 declared unconstitutional. The plaintiff argued that Congress, in passing the act, had exceeded its powers to regulate interstate commerce under the Commerce Clause of the U.S. Constitution. The U.S. District Court upheld the Civil Rights Act and enjoined the owner-operator of the Heart of Atlanta*

Motel from discriminating against blacks. The owner-operator of the motel appealed to the U.S. Supreme Court.

The U.S. Supreme Court held that the provisions of the Civil Rights Act of 1964 that prohibited discrimination in accommodations properly regulated interstate commerce. In reaching its decision, the U.S. Supreme Court stated:

The power of Congress over interstate commerce is not confined to the regulation of commerce among the states. It extends to those activities intrastate which so affect interstate commerce or the exercise of the power of Congress over it as to make regulation of them appropriate means to the attainment of a legitimate end, the exercise of the granted power of Congress to regulate interstate commerce.

Thus the power of Congress to promote interstate commerce also includes the power to regulate the local incidents thereof, including local activities in both the States of origin and destination, which might have a substantial and harmful effect upon that commerce. One need only examine the evidence which we have discussed above to see that Congress may—as it has—prohibit racial discrimination by motels serving travelers, however "local" their operations may appear.

The U.S. Supreme Court held that the challenged provisions of the Civil Rights Act of 1964 were constitutional as a proper exercise of the commerce power of the federal government. Heart of Atlanta Motel v. United States, 379 U.S. 241, 85 S.Ct. 348, 13 L.Ed.2d 258, Web 1964 U.S. Lexis 2187 (Supreme Court of the United States)

State Police Power

The federal government does not retain sole power to regulate business. States retain the power to regulate *intrastate* business activity and much interstate business activity that occurs within their borders. This is commonly referred to as states' **police power**.

Police power permits states (and, by delegation, local governments) to enact laws to protect or promote the *public health, safety, morals, and general welfare*. This includes the authority to enact laws that regulate the conduct of business.

police power
Power that permits states and local governments to enact laws to protect or promote the public health, safety, morals, and general walfare.

Examples Zoning ordinances, state environmental laws, corporation and partnership laws, and property laws are enacted under state police power.

Dormant Commerce Clause

If the federal government has chosen not to regulate an area of interstate commerce that it has the power to regulate under its Commerce Clause powers, this area of commerce is subject to what is referred to as the **Dormant Commerce Clause**. A state, under its police power, can enact laws to regulate that area of commerce. However, if a state enacts laws to regulate commerce that the federal government has the power to regulate but has chosen not to regulate, the Dormant Commerce Clause prohibits the state's regulation from unduly burdening interstate commerce.

unduly burden interstate commerce
A concept which says that states may enact laws that protect or promote the public health, safety, morals, and general welfare, as long as the laws do not unduly burden interstate commerce.

Example Assume that one state's corporations code permits only corporations from that state, but from no other state, to conduct business in that state. That state's law would unduly burden interstate commerce and would be unconstitutional.

INTERNET LAW & ONLINE COMMERCE

E-Commerce and the Commerce Clause

"State bans on interstate direct shipping represent the single largest regulatory barrier to expanded e-commerce in wine."

—Justice Kennedy

In this Information Age, federal and state governments have had to grapple with how to regulate the Internet and e-commerce. The federal government seems to be taking the upper hand in passing laws that regulate business conducted in cyberspace, thus creating laws that apply uniformly across the country. However, states have also enacted laws that regulate the Internet and e-commerce. State laws that unduly burden interstate e-commerce are unconstitutional, however. Consider the following case.

The state of Michigan regulates the sale of wine within its boundaries. Michigan law permits in-state wineries to sell wine directly to consumers, including by mail, Internet, and other means of sale. Michigan law prohibits out-of-state wineries from selling wine directly to Michigan consumers, including over the Internet. Michigan instead requires out-of-state wineries to sell their wine to Michigan wholesalers, who then sell the wine to Michigan retailers, who then sell the wine to Michigan consumers. Many small wineries across the country rely on the Internet to sell wine to residents in other states. Out-of-state wineries that are required by law to sell wine to Michigan wholesalers would incur a cost that in-state-wineries would not incur, thus

making it more costly and often unprofitable for out-of-state wineries to sell to Michigan consumers.

Domaine Alfred, a small winery located in San Luis Obispo, California, and several other out-of-state wineries that were prohibited from selling wine directly to Michigan consumers, sued Michigan. The plaintiff wineries alleged that the Michigan law caused an undue burden on interstate e-commerce, in violation of the Commerce Clause of the U.S. Constitution. The U.S. District Court ruled in favor of Michigan. The U.S. Court of Appeals reversed and ruled in favor of the out-of-state wineries, finding that the Michigan law caused an undue burden on interstate e-commerce. The state of Michigan appealed to the U.S. Supreme Court.

The U.S. Supreme Court held that the Michigan state law that discriminated against out-of-state wineries in favor of in-state wineries caused an undue burden on interstate e-commerce, in violation of the Commerce Clause of the U.S. Constitution. The U.S. Supreme Court stated, "Technological improvements, in particular the ability of wineries to sell wine over the Internet, have helped make direct shipments an attractive sales channel. State bans on interstate direct shipping represent the single largest regulatory barrier to expanded e-commerce in wine." In this case, the U.S. Supreme Court saved e-commerce from a discriminatory state law. *Granholm, Governor of Michigan v. Heald*, 544 U.S. 460, 125 S.Ct. 1885, 161 L.Ed.2d 796, **Web** 2005 U.S. Lexis 4174 (Supreme Court of the United States, 2005)

▶ BILL OF RIGHTS

The U.S. Constitution provides that it may be amended. In 1791, the 10 amendments that are commonly referred to as the **Bill of Rights** were approved by the states and became part of the U.S. Constitution. The Bill of Rights guarantees certain fundamental rights to natural persons and protects these rights from intrusive government action.

Bill of Rights
The first 10 amendments to the Constitution, which were added to the U.S. Constitution in 1791.

Examples Fundamental rights guaranteed in the Bill of Rights include freedom of speech, freedom to assemble, freedom of the press, freedom of religion, and such. Most of these rights have also been found applicable to so-called artificial persons (i.e., corporations).

In addition to the Bill of Rights, 17 other **amendments** have been added to the Constitution. These amendments cover a variety of issues.

Examples The additional 17 amendments to the Constitution have abolished slavery, prohibited discrimination, authorized the federal income tax, given women the right to vote, and specifically recognized that persons 18 years of age and older have the right to vote.

Originally, the Bill of Rights limited intrusive action by the *federal government* only. Intrusive actions by state and local governments were not limited until the *Due Process Clause of the Fourteenth Amendment* was added to the Constitution in 1868. The Supreme Court has applied the **incorporation doctrine** and held that most of the fundamental guarantees contained in the Bill of Rights are applicable to *state and local government* action. The amendments to the Constitution that are most applicable to business are discussed in the sections that follow.

Protest, Los Angeles, California. *The Freedom of Speech Clause of the First Amendment to the U.S. Constitution protects the right to engage in political speech. Freedom of speech is one of Americans' most highly prized rights.*

▶ FREEDOM OF SPEECH

One of the most honored freedoms guaranteed by the Bill of Rights is the **freedom of speech** of the First Amendment. Many other constitutional freedoms would be meaningless without it. The First Amendment's Freedom of Speech Clause protects speech only, not conduct. The First Amendment protects oral, written and symbolic speech.

freedom of speech
The right to engage in oral, written, and symbolic speech protected by the First Amendment.

The U.S. Supreme Court places speech into three categories: (1) *fully protected*, (2) *limited protected*, and (3) *unprotected speech*. These types of speech are discussed in the following paragraphs.

Fully Protected Speech

Fully protected speech is speech that the government cannot prohibit or regulate. The government cannot prohibit or regulate the content of fully protected speech.

I disapprove of what you say, but I will defend to the death your right to say it.

Voltaire

Example Political speech is an example of fully protected speech. Thus, the government could not enact a law that forbids citizens from criticizing the current president.

The First Amendment protects oral, written, and symbolic speech.

Limited Protected Speech

The Supreme Court has held that certain types of speech have only **limited protection** under the First Amendment. The government cannot forbid this type of speech, but it can subject this speech to *time, place, and manner restrictions*. Two types of speech are accorded limited protection: *offensive speech* and *commercial speech*.

offensive speech
Speech that is offensive to many members of society. It is subject to time, place, and manner restrictions.

Offensive Speech   **Offensive speech** is speech that offends many members of society. (It is not the same as obscene speech, however.) The Supreme Court has held that the content of offensive speech may not be forbidden but that it may be restricted by the government under time, place, and manner restrictions.

Example The Federal Communications Commission (FCC) is a federal administrative agency that regulates radio, television, and cable stations. Under its powers, the FCC has regulated the use of offensive language on television by limiting such language to time periods when children would be unlikely to be watching (e.g., late at night).

commercial speech
Speech used by businesses, such as advertising. It is subject to time, place, and manner restrictions.

Commercial Speech   **Commercial speech**, such as advertising, was once considered unprotected by the First Amendment. However, today, because of U.S. Supreme Court decisions, the content of commercial speech is protected but is also subject to time, place, and manner restrictions.

Example In *Virginia State Board of Pharmacy v. Virginia Citizens Consumer Council, Inc.*[9] the U.S. Supreme Court held that a state statute that prohibited a pharmacist from advertising the price of prescription drugs was unconstitutional because it violated the Freedom of Speech Clause. The U.S. Supreme Court held that this was commercial speech that was protected by the First Amendment.

Example A city can prohibit billboards along its highways for safety and aesthetic reasons if other forms of advertising (e.g., print media) are available. This is a lawful place restriction.

In the following case, the court had to decide whether the government properly regulated commercial speech.

CASE 4.3 Commercial Speech

Mainstream Marketing Services, Inc. v. Federal Trade Commission and Federal Communications Commission

358 F.3d 1228, Web 2004 U.S. App. Lexis 2564 (2004)
United States Court of Appeals for the Tenth Circuit

"The national do-not-call registry offers consumers a tool with which they can protect their homes against intrusions that Congress has determined to be particularly invasive."

—Judge Ebel

Facts

Pursuant to enabling statutes, two federal administrative agencies—the Federal Trade Commission (FTC) and the Federal Communications Commission (FCC)—created the national do-not-call registry. The national do-not-call registry is a list that contains the personal telephone number of telephone users who have voluntarily placed themselves on this list, indicating that they do not want to receive unsolicited calls from commercial telemarketers. Commercial telemarketers are prohibited from calling phone numbers that have been placed on the do-not-call registry. Telemarketers must pay an annual fee to access the phone numbers on the registry so that they can delete those numbers from their solicitation lists. The national do-not-call registry restrictions apply only to telemarketers' calls made by or on behalf of sellers of goods or services. Charitable and fundraising calls are exempt from the do-not-call registry's restrictions. Persons who do not voluntarily place their phone numbers on the do-not-call registry may still receive unsolicited telemarketers' calls.

Mainstream Marketing Services, Inc., and other telemarketers sued the FTC and the FCC in several lawsuits, alleging that their free speech rights were violated and that the do-not-call registry was unconstitutional. The FTC and FCC defended, arguing that unsolicited telemarketing calls constituted commercial speech that could properly be regulated by the government's do-not-call registry's restrictions. The separate lawsuits were consolidated for appeal.

Issue

Are unsolicited telemarketing calls commercial speech that is constitutionally regulated by the do-not-call registry restrictions?

Language of the Court

Four key aspects of the do-not-call registry convince us that it is consistent with First Amendment requirements. First, the list restricts only core commercial speech—i.e., commercial sales calls. Second, the do-not-call registry targets speech that invades the privacy of the home, a personal sanctuary that enjoys a unique status in our constitutional jurisprudence. Third, the do-not-call registry is an opt-in program that puts the choice of whether or not to restrict commercial calls entirely in the hands of consumers. Fourth, the do-not-call registry materially furthers the government's interests in combating the danger of abusive telemarketing and preventing the invasion of consumer privacy, blocking a significant number of the calls that cause these problems.

A number of additional features of the national do-not-call registry, although not dispositive, further demonstrate that the list is consistent with the First Amendment rights of commercial speakers. The challenged regulations do not hinder any business' ability to contact consumers by other means, such as through direct mailings or other forms of advertising. Moreover, they give consumers a number of different options to avoid calls they do not want to receive. Namely, consumers who wish to restrict some but not all commercial sales calls can do so by using company-specific do-not-call lists or by granting some businesses express permission to call. In addition, the government chose to offer consumers broader options to restrict commercial sales calls than charitable and political calls after finding that commercial calls were more intrusive and posed a greater danger of consumer abuse.

The national do-not-call registry offers consumers a tool with which they can protect their homes against intrusions that Congress has determined to be particularly invasive. Just as a consumer can avoid door-to-door peddlers by placing a "No Solicitation" sign in his or her front yard, the do-not-call registry lets consumers avoid unwanted sales pitches that invade the home via telephone, if they choose to do so. We are convinced that the First Amendment does not prevent the government from giving consumers this option.

For the reasons discussed above, the government has asserted substantial interests to be served by the do-not-call registry (privacy and consumer protection), the do-not-call registry will directly advance those interests by banning a substantial amount of unwanted telemarketing calls, and the regulation is narrowly tailored because its opt-in feature ensures that it does not restrict any speech directed at a willing listener. In other words, the do-not-call registry bears a reasonable fit with the purposes the government sought to advance. Therefore, it is consistent with the limits the First Amendment imposes on laws restricting commercial speech.

Decision

The U.S. Supreme Court held that unsolicited telemarketing calls constituted commercial speech that was subject to government regulation and that the do-not-call registry restrictions did not violate the free speech rights of the plaintiff telemarketers.

Case Questions

Critical Legal Thinking What is the do-not-call registry? How does it work?

Business Ethics Is it ethical for telemarketers to make unsolicited phone calls to persons' houses? What time are some of these calls made? Is much fraud committed by telemarketers? Explain.

Contemporary Business What is the economic effect on telemarketers of the do-not-call registry?

INTERNET LAW & ONLINE COMMERCE

Broad Free Speech Rights Granted in Cyberspace

"As the most participatory form of mass speech yet developed, the Internet deserves the highest protection from government intrusion."

—Justice Stevens

Once or twice a century, a new medium comes along that presents new problems for applying freedom of speech rights. This time it is the Internet. In 1996 Congress enacted the **Computer Decency Act**, which made it a felony to knowingly make "indecent" or "patently offensive" materials available on computer systems, including the Internet, to persons under 18 years of age. Immediately, more than 50 cyberspace providers and users filed a lawsuit, challenging the act as a violation of their free speech rights granted under the First Amendment to the Constitution. The U.S. District Court agreed with the plaintiffs and declared the act an unconstitutional violation of the Freedom of Speech Clause.

On appeal, the U.S. Supreme Court agreed and held that the act was an unconstitutional violation of free speech rights. The Supreme Court concluded that the Internet allows an individual to reach an audience of millions at almost no cost, setting it apart from TV, radio, and print media, which are prohibitively expensive to use.

The Court stated, "As the most participatory form of mass speech yet developed, the Internet deserves the highest protection from government intrusion." The Court declared emphatically that the Internet must be given the highest possible level of First Amendment free speech protection.

Proponents of the Computer Decency Act argued that the act was necessary to protect children from indecent materials. The Supreme Court reasoned that limiting the content on the Internet to what is suitable for a child resulted in unconstitutionally limiting adult speech. The Court noted that children are far less likely to trip over indecent material on the Internet than on TV or radio because the information must be actively sought out on the Internet. The Court noted that less obtrusive means for protecting children are available, such as requiring parents to regulate their children's access to materials on the Internet and placing filtering and blocking software on computers to control what their children see on the Internet. It still remains a crime under existing laws to transmit *obscene* materials over the Internet. *Reno v. American Civil Liberties Union*, 521 U.S. 844, 117 S.Ct. 2329, 138 L.Ed.2d 874, **Web** 1997 U.S. Lexis 4037 (Supreme Court of the United States)

Unprotected Speech

unprotected speech
Speech that is not protected by the First Amendment and may be forbidden by the government.

The Supreme Court has held that the following types of speech are **unprotected speech** (i.e., they are not protected by the First Amendment and may be totally forbidden by the government):

1. **Dangerous speech.**

   Example Yelling "fire" in a crowded theater when there is no fire is not protected speech.

2. **Fighting words that are likely to provoke a hostile or violent response from an average person.**[10]

   Example Walking up to a person and intentionally calling that person names because of race or ethnicity would not be protected speech if it would likely cause the person being called the names to respond in a hostile manner.

3. **Speech that incites the violent or revolutionary overthrow of the government.** However, the mere abstract teaching of the morality and consequences of such action is protected.[11]

4. **Defamatory language.**[12]

   Examples Committing libel or slander by writing or telling untrue statements about another person or committing product disparagement or trade libel by writing or telling untrue statements about a company's products or services is not protected speech, and the injured party may bring a civil lawsuit to recover damages.

5. **Child pornography.**[13]

   Example Selling material depicting children engaged in sexual activity is unprotected speech.

6. **Obscene speech.**[14]   If speech is considered **obscene speech**, it has no protection under the Freedom of Speech Clause of the First Amendment and can be banned by the government.

   Examples Movies, videos, music, and other forms of speech that are obscene are unprotected speech.

The definition of *obscenity* has plagued the courts. The definition of *obscene speech* is quite subjective. One Supreme Court justice stated, "I know it when I see it."[15] In **Miller v. California**, the U.S. Supreme Court determined that speech is obscene when:

1. The average person, applying contemporary community standards, would find that the work, taken as a whole, appeals to the *prurient interest.*
2. The work depicts or describes, in a patently offensive way, sexual conduct specifically defined by the applicable state law.
3. The work, taken as a whole, lacks serious literary, artistic, political, or scientific value.[16]

States are free to define what constitutes obscene speech. Movie theaters, magazine publishers, and so on are often subject to challenges that the materials they display or sell are obscene and therefore not protected by the First Amendment. Over the years, the content of material that has been found to be obscene has shifted to a more liberal view as the general norms of society have become more liberal. Today, fewer obscenity cases are brought than have been in the past.

▶ FREEDOM OF RELIGION

Freedom of religion is a key concept addressed by the First Amendment. The First Amendment contains two separate religion clauses, the *Establishment Clause* and the *Free Exercise Clause*. These two clauses are discussed in the following paragraphs.

Establishment Clause

The U.S. Constitution requires federal, state, and local governments to be neutral toward religion. The **Establishment Clause** prohibits the government from either establishing a government-sponsored religion or promoting one religion over another. Thus, it guarantees that there will be no state-sponsored religion.

Example The U.S. Supreme Court ruled that an Alabama statute that authorized a one-minute period of silence in school for "meditation or voluntary prayer" was invalid.[17] The Court held that the statute endorsed religion.

Free Exercise Clause

The **Free Exercise Clause** prohibits the government from interfering with the free exercise of religion in the United States. Generally, this clause prevents the government from enacting laws that either prohibit or inhibit individuals from participating in or practicing their chosen religions.

Examples Federal, state, or local governments could not enact a law that prohibits all religions. The government could not enact a law that prohibits churches, synagogues, mosques, or temples. The government could not prohibit religious practitioners from celebrating their major holidays and high holy days.

Example In *Church of Lukumi Babalu Aye, Inc. v. City of Hialeah, Florida*,[18] the U.S. Supreme Court held that a city ordinance that prohibited ritual sacrifices of chickens

obscene speech
Speech that (1) appeals to the prurient interest, (2) depicts sexual conduct in a patently offensive way, and (3) lacks serious literary, artistic, political, or scientific value.

The Constitution of the United States is not a mere lawyers' document: It is a vehicle of life, and its spirit is always the spirit of the age.

Woodrow Wilson
Constitutional Government in the United States 69 (1927)

Establishment Clause
A clause to the First Amendment that prohibits the government from either establishing a state religion or promoting one religion over another.

Free Exercise Clause
A clause to the First Amendment that prohibits the government from interfering with the free exercise of religion in the United States.

during church services violated the Free Exercise Clause and that such sacrifices should be allowed.

Of course, the right to be free from government intervention in the practice of religion is not absolute.

Example Human sacrifices are unlawful and are not protected by the First Amendment.

CONCEPT SUMMARY
FREEDOM OF RELIGION

Clause	Description
Establishment Clause	Prohibits the government from establishing a government-sponsored religion and from promoting one religion over other religions.
Free Exercise Clause	Prohibits the government from enacting laws that either prohibit or inhibit individuals from participating in or practicing their chosen religions.

▶ EQUAL PROTECTION CLAUSE

Fourteenth Amendment
An amendment added to the U.S. Constitution in 1868 that contains the Due Process, Equal Protection, and Privileges and Immunities clauses.

The **Fourteenth Amendment** was added to the U.S. Constitution in 1868. Its original purpose was to guarantee equal rights to all persons after the Civil War. The provisions of the Fourteenth Amendment prohibit discriminatory and unfair action by the government. Several of these provisions—namely, the *Equal Protection Clause*, the *Due Process Clause*, and the *Privileges and Immunities Clause*—have important implications for business. The Equal Protection Clause is discussed in this section. The Due Process Clause and the Privileges and Immunities Clause are discussed in following sections.

Federal, State, and Local Government Action

Equal Protection Clause
A clause which provides that a state cannot "deny to any person within its jurisdiction the equal protection of the laws."

The **Equal Protection Clause** provides that a state cannot "deny to any person within its jurisdiction the equal protection of the laws." Although this clause expressly applies to state and local government action, the Supreme Court has held that it also applies to federal government action.

This clause prohibits state, local, and federal governments from enacting laws that classify and treat "similarly situated" persons differently. Artificial persons, such as corporations, are also protected. Note that this clause is designed to prohibit invidious discrimination: It does not make the classification of individuals unlawful per se.

Standards of Review

The Supreme Court, over years of making decisions involving the Equal Protection Clause, has held that the government can treat people or businesses differently from one another if the government has sufficient justification for doing so. The Supreme Court has adopted three different standards of review for deciding whether the government's different treatment of people or businesses violates or does not violate the Equal Protection Clause:

strict scrutiny test
A test that is applied to classifications based on race.

1. **Strict scrutiny test.** Any government activity or regulation that classifies persons based on a *suspect class* (i.e., **race**) is reviewed for lawfulness using a **strict scrutiny test**. This means that the government must have an exceptionally important reason for treating persons differently because of their race in order for such unequal treatment to be lawful. Under this standard, many government classifications of persons based on race are found to be unconstitutional. Others are found lawful.

Example A government rule that permits persons of one race but not of another race to receive government benefits such as Medicaid would violate this test.

Example An affirmative action program that gives racial minorities a "plus factor" when considered for public university admission is lawful, as long as it does not constitute a quota system.[19]

2. **Intermediate scrutiny test.** The lawfulness of government classifications based on *protected classes* other than race (e.g., **sex**, **age**) is examined using an **intermediate scrutiny test**. This means that the government must have an important reason for treating persons differently because of their age or sex in order for such unequal treatment to be lawful. Under this standard, many government classifications of persons based on age or sex are found to be unconstitutional. Under this standard, the courts must determine whether the government classification is "reasonably related" to a legitimate government purpose.

intermediate scrutiny test
A test that is applied to classifications based on protected classes other than race (e.g., sex, age).

Examples A rule prohibiting persons over a certain age from participating in military combat is lawful. The justification is that younger members of society are generally more physically fit for military service. However, a rule prohibiting persons over a certain age from being government engineers would not be lawful.

Example The federal government's Social Security program, which pays benefits to older members of society but not to younger members of society, is lawful. The reason is that older members of society have earned this right during the course of their lifetimes.

Example The federal government's requirement that males who reach the age of 18 must register for a military draft but that females do not have to register for the draft has been found constitutional by the U.S. Supreme Court.[20]

3. **Rational basis test.** The lawfulness of all government classifications that do not involve suspect or protected classes is examined using a **rational basis test**. Under this test, the courts will uphold government regulation as long as there is a justifiable reason for the law. This standard permits much of the government regulation of business.

rational basis test
A test that is applied to classifications not involving a suspect or protected class.

Example Providing government subsidies to farmers but not to those in other occupations is permissible.

▶ DUE PROCESS CLAUSES

The Fifth and Fourteenth Amendments to the U.S. Constitution both contain **Due Process Clauses**. These clauses provide that no person shall be deprived of "life, liberty, or property" without due process of the law. The Due Process Clause of the Fifth Amendment applies to federal government action; that of the Fourteenth Amendment applies to state and local government action. It is important to understand that the government is not prohibited from taking a person's life, liberty, or property. However, the government must follow due process to do so. There are two categories of due process: *substantive* and *procedural*.

Due Process Clause
A clause which provides that no person shall be deprived of "life, liberty, or property" without due process of the law.

Substantive Due Process

The **substantive due process** category of due process requires that government statutes, ordinances, regulations, and other laws be clear on their face and not overly broad in scope. The test of whether substantive due process is met is whether a "reasonable person" could understand the law to be able to comply with it. Laws that do not meet this test are declared *void for vagueness*.

substantive due process
A category of due process which requires that government statutes, ordinances, regulations, or other laws be clear on their face and not overly broad in scope.

Example A city ordinance making it illegal for persons to wear "clothes of the opposite sex" would be held unconstitutional as void for vagueness because a reasonable person could not clearly determine whether his or her conduct violates the law.

Most government laws, although often written in "legalese," are considered not to violate substantive due process.

Procedural Due Process

procedural due process
A category of due process which requires that the government give a person proper notice and hearing of the legal action before that person is deprived of his or her life, liberty, or property.

The **procedural due process** form of due process requires that the government give a person proper *notice* and *hearing* of legal action before that person is deprived of his or her life, liberty, or property.

Example If the federal government or a state government brings a criminal lawsuit against a defendant for the alleged commission of a crime, the government must notify the person of its intent (by charging the defendant with a crime) and provide the defendant with a proper hearing (a trial).

▶ PRIVILEGES AND IMMUNITIES CLAUSE

Privileges and Immunities Clause
A clause that prohibits states from enacting laws that unduly discriminate in favor of their residents.

The purpose of the U.S. Constitution is to promote nationalism. If the states were permitted to enact laws that favored their residents over out-of-state residents, the concept of nationalism would be defeated. Both Article IV of the Constitution and the Fourteenth Amendment contain **Privileges and Immunities Clauses** that prohibit states from enacting laws that unduly discriminate in favor of their residents. Note that the Privileges and Immunities Clause applies only to citizens; it does not protect corporations.

Example A state cannot enact a law that prevents residents of other states from owning property or businesses in that state.

Courts have held that certain types of discrimination that favor state residents over nonresidents do not violate the Privileges and Immunities Clause.

Examples State universities are permitted to charge out-of-state residents higher tuition than in-state residents. States are also permitted to charge higher fees to nonresidents for hunting and fishing licenses.

United States Post Office, Alhambra, California *The United States has had many blemishes on its citizen's constitutional rights. For example, during World War II, Japanese Americans were involuntarily placed in camps. During the McCarthy hearings of the 1950s, citizens who were communists or associated with communists were "blackballed" from their occupations, most notably in the film industry. It was not until the mid-1960s that equal opportunity laws outlawed discrimination in the workplace based on race and sex.*

TEST REVIEW TERMS AND CONCEPTS

Age
Amendments
Articles of Confederation
Bicameral
Bill of Rights
Checks and balances
Civil Rights Act of 1964
Commerce Clause
Commercial speech
Computer Decency Act
Congress
Constitutional Convention
Declaration of
    Independence
Delegated
Dormant Commerce Clause

Due Process Clause
Effects on interstate
    commerce test
Electoral college
Enumerated powers
Equal Protection Clause
Establishment Clause
Executive branch
Federal government
Federalism
Fourteenth
    Amendment
Free Exercise Clause
Freedom of religion
Freedom of speech
Fully protected speech

Heart of Atlanta Motel v.
    United States
Incorporation doctrine
Indian Gaming Regulatory
    Act
Intermediate scrutiny test
Interstate commerce
Judicial branch
Legislative branch
Limited protected
    speech
Miller v. California
Obscene speech
Offensive speech
Police power
Preemption doctrine

Privileges and Immunities
    Clause
Procedural due process
Race
Rational basis test
Sex
Strict scrutiny test
Substantive due process
Supremacy Clause
Unduly burden interstate
    commerce
Unprotected speech
Wickard, Secretary of
    Agriculture v. Filburn
U.S. Constitution

CASE PROBLEMS

4.1 Separation of Powers In 1951, a dispute arose between steel companies and their employees about the terms and conditions that should be included in a new labor contract. At the time, the United States was engaged in a military conflict in Korea that required substantial steel resources from which to make weapons and other military goods. On April 4, 1952, the steelworkers' union gave notice of a nationwide strike called to begin at 12:01 A.M. on April 9. The indispensability of steel as a component in weapons and other war materials led President Dwight D. Eisenhower to believe that the proposed strike would jeopardize the national defense and that governmental seizure of the steel mills was necessary in order to ensure the continued availability of steel. Therefore, a few hours before the strike was to begin, the president issued Executive Order 10340, which directed the secretary of commerce to take possession of most of the steel mills and keep them running. The steel companies obeyed the order under protest and brought proceedings against the president. Is this seizure of the steel mills constitutional? *Youngstown Co. v. Sawyer, Secretary of Commerce*, 343 U.S. 579, 72 S.Ct. 863, 96 L.Ed.2d 1153, **Web** 1952 U.S. Lexis 2625 (Supreme Court of the United States)

4.2 Commerce and Supremacy Clauses Congress enacted a federal statute called the Ports and Waterways Safety Act that established uniform standards for the operation of boats on inland waterways in the United States. The act coordinated its provisions with those of foreign countries so that there was a uniform body of international rules that applied to vessels that traveled between countries. Pursuant to the act, a federal rule was adopted that regulated the design, length, and size of oil tankers, some of which traveled the waters of the Puget Sound area in the state of Washington. Oil tankers from various places entered Puget Sound to bring crude oil to refineries located in Washington. The state of Washington enacted a statute that established different designs, smaller lengths, and smaller sizes for oil tankers serving Puget Sound than allowed

by the federal law. Oil tankers used by the Atlantic Richfield Company (ARCO) to bring oil into Puget Sound met the federal standards but not the state standards. ARCO sued to have the state statute declared unconstitutional. Who wins? *Ray, Governor of Washington v. Atlantic Richfield Co.*, 435 U.S. 151, 98 S.Ct. 988, 55 L.Ed.2d 179, **Web** 1978 U.S. Lexis 18 (Supreme Court of the United States))

4.3 Undue Burden on Interstate Commerce Most trucking firms, including Consolidated Freightways Corporation, use 65-foot-long "double" trailer trucks to ship commodities on the highway system across the United States. Almost all states permit these vehicles on their highways. The federal government does not regulate the length of trucks that can use the nation's highways. The state of Iowa enacted a statute that restricted the length of trucks that could use highways in the state to 55 feet. This meant that if Consolidated wanted to move goods through Iowa, it needed to either use smaller trucks or detach the double trailers and shuttle them through the state separately. Its only other alternative was to divert its 65-foot doubles around Iowa. Consolidated filed suit against Iowa, alleging that the state statute was unconstitutional. Is it? *Kassel v. Consolidated Freightways Corporation*, 450 U.S. 662, 101 S.Ct. 1309, 67 L.Ed.2d 580, **Web** 1981 U.S. Lexis 17 (Supreme Court of the United States)

4.4 Privileges and Immunities Clause During a period of a booming economy in Alaska, many residents of other states moved there in search of work. Construction work on the Trans-Alaska Pipeline was a major source of employment. The Alaska legislature enacted an act called the Local Hire Statute. This act required employers to hire Alaska residents in preference to nonresidents. Is this statute constitutional? *Hicklin v. Orbeck, Commissioner of the Department of Labor of Alaska*, 437 U.S. 518, 98 S.Ct. 2482, 57 L.Ed.2d 397, **Web** 1978 U.S. Lexis 36 (Supreme Court of the United States)

4.5 Commercial Speech The city of San Diego, California, enacted a city zoning ordinance that prohibited outdoor advertising display signs—including billboards. On-site signs at a business location were exempted from this rule. The city based the restriction on traffic safety and aesthetics. Metromedia, Inc., a company in the business of leasing commercial billboards to advertisers, sued the city of San Diego, alleging that the zoning ordinance was unconstitutional. Is it? *Metromedia, Inc. v. City of San Diego*, 453 U.S. 490, 101 S.Ct. 2882, 69 L.Ed.2d 800, **Web** 1981 U.S. Lexis 50 (Supreme Court of the United States)

4.6 Substantive Due Process The village of Hoffman Estates, Illinois, enacted an ordinance regulating drug paraphernalia. The ordinance made it unlawful for any person "to sell any items, effect, paraphernalia, accessory or thing which is designed or marketed for use with illegal cannabis or drugs as defined by Illinois Revised Statutes, without obtaining a license therefore." The license fee was $150. A violation was subject to a fine of not more than $500. The Flipside, a retail store located in the village, sold a variety of merchandise, including smoking accessories, clamps, roach clips, scales, water pipes, vials, cigarette rolling papers, and other items. Instead of applying for a license, Flipside filed a lawsuit against the village, alleging that

the ordinance was unconstitutional, as a violation of substantive due process, because it was overly broad and vague. Who wins? *Village of Hoffman Estates v. Flipside, Hoffman Estates, Inc.*, 455 U.S. 489, 102 S.Ct. 1186, 71 L.Ed.2d 362, **Web** 1982 U.S. Lexis 78 (Supreme Court of the United States)

4.7 Equal Protection Clause The state of Alabama enacted a statute that imposed a tax on premiums earned by insurance companies. The statute imposed a 1 percent tax on domestic insurance companies (i.e., insurance companies that were incorporated in Alabama and had their principal office in the state). The statute imposed a 4 percent tax on the premiums earned by out-of-state insurance companies that sold insurance in Alabama. Out-of-state insurance companies could reduce the premium tax by 1 percent by investing at least 10 percent of their assets in Alabama. Domestic insurance companies did not have to invest any of their assets in Alabama. Metropolitan Life Insurance Company, an out-of-state insurance company, sued the state of Alabama, alleging that the Alabama statute violated the Equal Protection Clause of the U.S. Constitution. Who wins? *Metropolitan Life Insurance Co. v. Ward, Commissioner of Insurance of Alabama*, 470 U.S. 869, 105 S.Ct. 1676, 84 L.Ed.2d 751, **Web** 1985 U.S. Lexis 80 (Supreme Court of the United States)

BUSINESS ETHICS CASES

4.8 Business Ethics The Raiders are a professional football team and a National Football League (NFL) franchise. Each NFL franchise is independently owned. Al Davis was an owner and the managing general partner of the Raiders. The NFL establishes schedules, negotiates television contracts, and otherwise promotes NFL football, including conducting the Super Bowl each year. The Raiders play home and away games against other NFL teams.

For years, the Raiders played their home games in Oakland, California. The owners of the Raiders decided to move the team from Oakland to Los Angeles, California, to take advantage of the greater seating capacity of the Los Angeles Coliseum, the larger television market of Los Angeles, and other economic factors. The renamed team was to be known as the Los Angeles Raiders. The city of Oakland brought an eminent domain proceeding in court to acquire the Raiders as a city-owned team. Can the city of Oakland acquire the Raiders through eminent domain? Is it socially responsible for a professional sports team to move to another location? *City of Oakland, California v. Oakland Raiders*, 174

Cal.App.3d 414, 220 Cal.Rptr. 153, **Web** 1985 Cal.App. Lexis 2751 (Court of Appeal of California)

4.9 Business Ethics Congress enacted the Flag Protection Act, which made it a crime to knowingly mutilate, deface, physically defile, burn, or trample the U.S. flag. The law provided for fines and up to one year in prison upon conviction [18 U.S.C. Section 700]. Certain individuals set fire to several U.S. flags on the steps of the U.S. Capitol in Washington, DC, to protest various aspects of the federal government's foreign and domestic policy. In a separate incident, other individuals set fire to a U.S. flag to protest the act's passage. All these individuals were prosecuted for violating the act. The U.S. District Courts held the act unconstitutional, in violation of the defendants' First Amendment free speech rights, and dismissed the charges. The government appealed to the U.S. Supreme Court, which consolidated the two cases. Who wins? Does a flag burner exhibit moral behavior? *United States v. Eichman*, 496 U.S. 310, 110 S.Ct. 2404, 110 L.Ed.2d 287, **Web** 1990 U.S. Lexis 3087 (Supreme Court of the United States)

ENDNOTES

1. To be elected to Congress, an individual must be a U.S. citizen, either naturally born or granted citizenship. To serve in the Senate, a person must be 30 years of age or older. To serve in the House of Representatives, a person must be 25 years of age or older.
2. To be president, a person must be 35 years of age or older and a natural citizen of the United States. According to the Twenty-Second Amendment to the Constitution, a person can serve only two full terms as president.
3. Federal court judges and justices are appointed by the president, with the consent of the Senate.
4. The principle that the U.S. Supreme Court is the final arbiter of the U.S. Constitution evolved from *Marbury v. Madison*, 1 Cranch 137, 5 U.S. 137, 2 L.Ed. 60, **Web** 1803 U.S. Lexis 352 (Supreme Court of the United States, 1803). In that case, the Supreme Court held that a judiciary statute enacted by Congress was unconstitutional.
5. Article VI, Section 2.
6. Article I, Section 8, clause 3.
7. 25 U.S.C Sections 2701–2721.
8. 317 U.S. 111, 63 S.Ct. 82, 87 L.Ed.122, **Web** 1942 U.S. Lexis 1046 (Supreme Court of the United States).
9. 425 U.S. 748, 96 S.Ct. 1817, 48 L.Ed.2d 346, **Web** 1976 U.S. Lexis 55 (Supreme Court of the United States).
10. *Chaplinsky v. New Hampshire*, 315 U.S. 568, 62 S.Ct. 766, 86 L.Ed. 1031, **Web** 1942 U.S. Lexis 851 (Supreme Court of the United States).
11. *Brandenburg v. Ohio*, 395 U.S. 444, 89 S.Ct. 1827, 23 L.Ed.2d 430, **Web** 1969 U.S. Lexis 1367 (Supreme Court of the United States).
12. *Beauharnais v. Illinois*, 343 U.S. 250, 72 S.Ct. 725, 96 L.Ed. 919, **Web** 1952 U.S. Lexis 2799 (Supreme Court of the United States).
13. *New York v. Ferber*, 458 U.S. 747, 102 S.Ct. 334, 73 L.Ed.2d 1113, **Web** 1982 U.S. Lexis 12 (Supreme Court of the United States).
14. *Roth v. United States*, 354 U.S. 476, 77 S.Ct. 1304, 1 L.Ed.2d 1498, **Web** 1957 U.S. Lexis 587 (Supreme Court of the United States).
15. Justice Stewart in *Jacobellis v. Ohio*, 378 U.S. 184, 84 S.Ct. 1676, 12 L.Ed.2d 793, **Web** 1964 U.S. Lexis 822 (Supreme Court of the United States).
16. 413 U.S. 15, 93 S.Ct. 2607, 37 L.Ed.2d 419, **Web** 1973 U.S. Lexis 149 (Supreme Court of the United States).
17. *Wallace v. Jaffree*, 472 U.S. 38, 105 S.Ct. 2479, 86 L.Ed.2d 29, **Web** 1985 U.S. Lexis 91 (Supreme Court of the United States).
18. 508 U.S. 520, 113 S.Ct. 2217, 124 L.Ed.2d 472, **Web** 1993 U.S. Lexis 4022 (Supreme Court of the United States).
19. *Grutter v. Bollinger and the University of Michigan Law School*, 539 U.S. 306, 123 S.Ct. 2325, 156 L.Ed.2d 304, **Web** 2003 U.S. Lexis 4800 (Supreme Court of the United States, 2003).
20. *Rostker v. Goldberg*, 453 U.S. 57, 101 S.Ct. 2646, 69 L.Ed.2d 478, Web 1981 U.S. Lexis 126 (Supreme Court of the United States).

Part II

TORTS, CRIMES, AND INTELLECTUAL PROPERTY

PRIVATE

PROPERTY

NO
TRESSPASSING

5 | INTENTIONAL TORTS AND NEGLIGENCE

▲ **Children's Ride.** *In this children's "thrill" ride, the children are strapped in with their feet left dangling. The car goes up a 100-foot tower and then free-falls down, giving the riders a feeling of weightlessness. Operators of thrill rides carry liability insurance.*

CHAPTER OBJECTIVES

After studying this chapter, you should be able to:

1. List and describe intentional torts against persons.
2. List and explain the elements necessary to prove negligence.
3. Describe special negligence doctrines.
4. Describe assumption of the risk and other defenses to a charge of negligence.
5. Describe and apply the doctrine of strict liability.

CHAPTER CONTENTS

"Negligence is not actionable unless it involves the invasion of a legally protected interest, the violation of a right. Proof of negligence in the air, so to speak, will not do."

—Chief Judge Cardozo
Palsgraf v. Long Island Railroad Co., 248 N.Y. 339, 162 N.E. 99, 1928 N.Y. Lexis 1269 (1928)

▶ INTRODUCTION TO INTENTIONAL TORTS AND NEGLIGENCE

Tort is the French word for a "wrong." The law provides remedies to persons and businesses that are injured by the tortuous actions of others. Under tort law, an injured party can bring a *civil lawsuit* to seek compensation for a wrong done to the party or to the party's property. Many torts have their origin in common law. The courts and legislatures have extended tort law to reflect changes in modern society.

Tort damages are monetary damages that are sought from the offending party. They are intended to compensate the injured party for the injury suffered. Such injury may consist of past and future medical expenses, loss of wages, pain and suffering, mental distress, and other damages caused by the defendant's tortious conduct. If the victim of a tort dies, his or her beneficiaries can bring a *wrongful death action* to recover damages from the defendant. *Punitive damages*, which are awarded to punish the defendant, may be recovered in intentional tort and strict liability cases. Other remedies, such as injunctions, may be available, too.

This chapter discusses intentional torts, negligence, and defenses to tort actions.

tort
A wrong. There are three categories of torts: (1) intentional torts, (2) unintentional torts (negligence), and (3) strict liability.

▶ INTENTIONAL TORTS AGAINST PERSONS

The law protects a person from unauthorized touching, restraint, or other contact. In addition, the law protects a person's reputation and privacy. Violations of these rights are actionable as torts. **Intentional torts** against persons are discussed in the paragraphs that follow.

intentional tort
A category of torts that requires that the defendant possessed the intent to do the act that caused the plaintiff's injuries.

Assault

Assault is (1) the threat of immediate harm or offensive contact or (2) any action that arouses reasonable apprehension of imminent harm. Actual physical contact is unnecessary. Threats of future harm are not actionable.

Examples Suppose a 6-foot-5-inch, 250-pound person makes a fist and threatens to punch a 5-foot, 100-pound person. If the threatened person is afraid that he or she will be physically harmed, that person can sue the threatening person to recover damages for the assault. If the threatened person is a black-belt karate champion and laughs at the threat, there is no assault because the threat does not cause any apprehension.

assault
(1) The threat of immediate harm or offensive contact or (2) any action that arouses reasonable apprehension of imminent harm. Actual physical contact is unnecessary.

Battery

Battery is unauthorized and harmful or offensive physical contact with another person that causes injury. Basically, the interest protected here is each person's reasonable sense of dignity and safety. Direct physical contact, such as intentionally hitting someone with a fist, is battery.

Indirect physical contact between the victim and the perpetrator is also battery, as long as injury results.

Examples Throwing a rock, shooting an arrow or a bullet, knocking off a hat, pulling a chair out from under someone, and poisoning a drink are all instances of actionable battery. The victim need not be aware of the harmful or offensive contact (e.g., it may take place while the victim is asleep).

Assault and battery often occur together, although they do not have to (e.g., the perpetrator hits the victim on the back of the head without any warning).

battery
Unauthorized and harmful or offensive direct or indirect physical contact with another person that causes injury.

Transferred Intent Doctrine   Sometimes a person acts with the intent to injure one person but actually injures another. The **transferred intent doctrine** applies to such situations. Under this doctrine, the law transfers the perpetrator's intent from the target to the actual victim of the act. The victim can then sue the defendant.

False Imprisonment

false imprisonment
The intentional confinement or restraint of another person without authority or justification and without that person's consent.

The intentional confinement or restraint of another person without authority or justification and without that person's consent constitutes **false imprisonment**. The victim may be restrained or confined by physical force, barriers, threats of physical harm, or the perpetrator's false assertion of legal authority (i.e., false arrest). A threat of future harm or moral pressure is not considered false imprisonment. The false imprisonment must be complete.

Examples   Locking one's doors in a house or automobile and not letting the other person leave is false imprisonment. Merely locking one door to a building when other exits are not locked is not false imprisonment. However, a person is not obliged to risk danger or an affront to his or her dignity by attempting to escape.

Shoplifting and Merchant Protection Statutes

merchant protection statutes
Statutes that allow merchants to stop, detain, and investigate suspected shoplifters without being held liable for false imprisonment if (1) there are reasonable grounds for the suspicion, (2) suspects are detained for only a reasonable time, and (3) investigations are conducted in a reasonable manner.

Shoplifting causes substantial losses to retail and other merchants each year. Oftentimes, suspected shoplifters are stopped by the store employees, and their suspected shoplifting is investigated. These stops sometimes lead to the merchant being sued for false imprisonment because the merchant detained the suspect.

Almost all states have enacted **merchant protection statutes**, also known as the **shopkeeper's privilege**. These statutes allow merchants to stop, detain, and investigate suspected shoplifters without being held liable for false imprisonment if:

1. There are *reasonable grounds* for the suspicion.
2. Suspects are detained for only a *reasonable time*.
3. Investigations are conducted in a *reasonable manner*.

Proving these elements is sometimes difficult. The following case applies the merchant's protection statute.

CASE 5.1   False Imprisonment

Wal-Mart Stores, Inc. v. Cockrell

61 S.W.3d 774, Web 2001 Tex. App. Lexis 7992 (2001)
Court of Appeals of Texas

"He made me feel like I was scum. That I had no say-so in the matter, that just made me feel like a little kid on the block, like the bully beating the kid up. . . ."

—Karl Cockrell

Facts

Karl Cockrell and his parents went to the layaway department at a Wal-Mart store. Cockrell stayed for about five minutes and decided to leave. As he was going out the front door, Raymond Navarro, a Wal-Mart loss-prevention officer, stopped him and requested that Cockrell follow him to the manager's office. Once in the office, Navarro told him to pull his pants down. Cockrell put his hands between his shorts and underwear, pulled them out, and shook them. Nothing fell out. Next Navarro told him to take off his shirt. Cockrell raised his shirt, revealing a large bandage which covered a surgical wound on the right side of his abdomen. Cockrell had recently had a liver transplant. Navarro asked him to take off the bandage, despite Cockrell's explanation that the bandage maintained a sterile environment around his surgical wound. On Navarro's insistence Cockrell took down the bandage, revealing the wound. Afterwards Navarro apologized and let Cockrell go. Cockrell sued Wal-Mart to recover damages for false imprisonment. Wal-Mart defended, alleging that the shopkeeper's privilege protected it from liability. The trial court found in favor of Cockrell and awarded Cockrell $300,000 for his mental anguish. Wal-Mart appealed.

Issue

Does the shopkeeper's privilege protect Wal-Mart from liability under the circumstances of the case?

Language of the Court

Neither Raymond Navarro nor any other store employee saw Cockrell steal merchandise. However Navarro claimed he had reasons to suspect Cockrell of shoplifting. He said that Cockrell was acting suspiciously, because he saw him in the women's department standing very close to a rack of clothes and looking around. Later he saw Cockrell looking around and walking slowly by the cigarette aisle and then "pass out of the store." We conclude that a rational jury could have found that Navarro did not "reasonably believe" a theft had occurred and therefore lacked authority to detain Cockrell.

The extent to which Wal-Mart searched Cockrell compels us to address the reasonable manner of the detention. Navarro's search was unreasonable in scope, because he had no probable cause to believe that Cockrell had hidden any merchandise under the bandage. Removal of the bandage compromised the sterile environment surrounding the wound.

Evidence of Cockrell's mental anguish comes largely from the following testimony: Counsel asked Cockrell to describe his demeanor when he took down his bandage in the manager's office. He stated that Navarro: "Made me feel like I was scum. That I had no say-so in the matter, that just made me feel like a little kid on the block, like the bully beating the kid up and saying, 'Well, I didn't catch you with nothing; but I'm going to humiliate him, twist a knife a little bit more into them.'"

Cockrell testified that after Navarro let him go he was shaking, crying, nervous, scared, and looking around to make sure no one else was trying to stop him. Cockrell's parents saw him in the Wal-Mart store immediately after he was let go. They said he was upset, nervous, had tears in his eyes, and looked scared, pale, and badly shaken up. When he arrived at home he was crying, nervous, and still "pretty well shook up." His mother said that he stayed upset for a "long time" and would not go out of the house.

Decision

The court of appeals upheld the trial court's finding that Wal-Mart had falsely imprisoned Cockrell and had not proved the shopkeeper's privilege. The court of appeals upheld the trial court's judgment that awarded Cockrell $300,000 for mental anguish.

Case Questions

Critical Legal Thinking What is the tort of false imprisonment? Explain.

Business Ethics Did Navarro, the Wal-Mart employee, act responsibly in this case? Did Wal-Mart act ethically in denying liability in this case?

Contemporary Business What does the shopkeeper's privilege provide? What are the elements necessary to prove the shopkeeper's privilege? Do you think Wal-Mart had a good chance of proving the shopkeeper's privilege in this case?

Misappropriation of the Right to Publicity

Each person has the exclusive legal right to control and profit from the commercial use of his or her name and identity during his or her lifetime. This is a valuable right, particularly to well-known persons such as sports figures and movie stars. Any attempt by another person to appropriate a living person's name or identity for commercial purposes is actionable. The wrongdoer is liable for the **tort of misappropriation of the right to publicity** (also called the **tort of appropriation**).

In such cases, the plaintiff can (1) recover the unauthorized profits made by the offending party and (2) obtain an injunction preventing further unauthorized use of his or her name or identity. Many states provide that the right to publicity survives a person's death and may be enforced by the deceased's heirs.

tort of misappropriation of the right to publicity
An attempt by another person to appropriate a living person's name or identity for commercial purposes.

Example Brad Pitt is a famous movie star. If an advertising agency places Brad Pitt's likeness (e.g., photo) on a billboard advertising a product without Brad Pitt's permission, it has engaged in the tort of misappropriation of the right to publicity. Brad Pitt could sue and recover the profits made by the offending party as well as obtain an injunction to prevent unauthorized use of his likeness by the offending party.

Invasion of the Right to Privacy

The law recognizes each person's right to live his or her life without being subjected to unwarranted and undesired publicity. A violation of this right constitutes the tort of **invasion of the right to privacy**. If a fact is public information, there is no claim to privacy.

However, a fact that was once public (e.g., commission of a crime) may become private after the passage of time.

Examples Secretly taking photos of another person with a cell phone camera in a men's or women's locker room would constitute invasion of the right to privacy. Reading someone else's mail, wiretapping someone's telephone, and reading someone else's e-mail without authorization to do so are also examples of invasion of the right to privacy.

Placing someone in a "false light" constitutes an invasion of privacy.

Example Sending an objectionable telegram to a third party and signing another's name would place the purported sender in a false light in the eyes of the receiver.

Defamation of Character

A person's reputation is a valuable asset. Therefore, every person is protected from false statements made by others during his or her lifetime. This protection ends upon a person's death. The tort of **defamation of character** requires a plaintiff to prove that:

1. The defendant made an *untrue statement of fact* about the plaintiff.
2. The statement was intentionally or accidentally *published* to a third party. In this context, *publication* simply means that a third person heard or saw the untrue statement. It does not require appearance in newspapers, magazines, or books.

A false statement that appears in writing or other fixed medium is **libel**. The name for an oral defamatory statement is **slander**.

Examples False statements that appear in a letter, newspaper, magazine, book, photograph, movie, video, and the like would be libel. Most courts hold that defamatory statements in radio and television broadcasts are considered libel because of the permanency of the media.

The publication of an untrue statement of fact is not the same as the publication of an *opinion*. The publication of opinions is usually not actionable. Because defamation is defined as an untrue statement of fact, truth is an absolute defense to a charge of defamation.

Examples The statement "My lawyer is lousy" is an opinion and is not defamation. The statement "My lawyer has been disbarred from the practice of law," when she has not been disbarred, is an untrue statement of fact and is actionable as defamation.

Public Figures as Plaintiffs   In *New York Times Co. v. Sullivan*,[1] the U.S. Supreme Court held that *public officials* cannot recover for defamation unless they can prove that the defendant acted with "actual malice." Actual malice means that the defendant made the false statement knowingly or with reckless disregard of its falsity. This requirement has since been extended to *public figure* plaintiffs such as movie stars, sports personalities, and other celebrities.

---

defamation of character
False statement(s) made by one person about another. In court, the plaintiff must prove that (1) the defendant made an untrue statement of fact about the plaintiff and (2) the statement was intentionally or accidentally published to a third party.

libel
A false statement that appears in a letter, newspaper, magazine, book, photograph, movie, video, and so on.

slander
Oral defamation of character.

Hard cases make bad law.

Legal Maxim

CONTEMPORARY ENVIRONMENT

Eminem's Rap Song Is Not Slander

"It is therefore this court's ultimate position that Eminem is entitled to summary disposition."

—Judge Servitto

Eminem is a famous hip-hop artist and rapper who won a Grammy award for his music in the movie *8-Mile* in which he starred. Eminem's lyrics often contain references to his personal experiences. In "Brain Damage," a song from his 1999 CD *The Slim Shady LP*, Eminem sang lyrics he had written about his childhood experiences with DeAngelo Bailey. The lyrics read in part:

> *Way before my baby daughter Hailey*
> *I was harassed daily by this fat kid named D'Angelo Bailey . . .*
> *He banged my head against the urinal til he broke my nose . . .*
> *Soaked my clothes in blood, grabbed me and choked my throat*

DeAngelo Bailey sued Eminem for $1 million, alleging that the lyrics were untrue and slanderous. Eminem's mother publicly defended her son's account of the bullying by Bailey. Under questioning, Bailey admitted that when he was in the fourth grade, he was part of a group at school that did "bully type things" such as pushing Eminem down. Bailey described what was done to Eminem as "jokes, play games, you know, like we probably like—I mean this is kid stuff, so I'm saying." Bailey also testified that he was present when his friends pushed Eminem and that he would personally bump into Eminem by throwing a "little shove." Bailey offered no evidence to refute Eminem's claims in his deposition that Bailey was bigger than him, shoved him into walls, called him names, took his orange juice, and knocked over his books.

After hearing all the evidence, trial judge Deborah Servitto granted summary disposition in favor of Eminem. She wrote in her opinion:

> *Mr. Bailey complains that his rap is trash*
> *So he's seeking compensation in the form of cash.*
> *Bailey thinks he's entitled to some money gain*
> *Because Eminem used his name in vain.*
> *The lyrics are stories no one would take as fact*
> *They're an exaggeration of a childish act.*
> *It is therefore this court's ultimate position*
> *That Eminem is entitled to summary disposition.*

On appeal, the court of appeals of Michigan upheld the trial court's decision. *DeAngelo Bailey v. Marshall Bruce Mathers, III a/k/a/ Eminem*, 2005 Mich.App. Lexis 930 (Court of Appeals of Michigan, 2005)

Disparagement or Trade Libel

Business firms rely on their reputation and the quality of their products and services to attract and keep customers. That is why state unfair-competition laws protect businesses from disparaging statements made by competitors or others. A disparaging statement is an untrue statement made by one person or business about the products, services, property, or reputation of another business.

To prove **disparagement**, which is also called **trade libel**, **product disparagement**, and **slander of title**, the plaintiff must show that the defendant (1) made an untrue statement about the plaintiff's products, services, property, or business reputation; (2) published that untrue statement to a third party; (3) knew the statement was not true; and (4) made the statement maliciously (i.e., with intent to injure the plaintiff).

All slander must still be strangled in its birth, or time will soon conspire to make it strong enough to overcome the truth.

Sir William D'Avenant

product disparagement
False statements about a competitor's products, services, property, or business reputation. Also known as *trade libel*, *product disparagement*, and *slander of title*.

Intentional Misrepresentation (Fraud)

One of the most pervasive business torts is **intentional misrepresentation**. This tort is also known as **fraud** or **deceit**. It occurs when a wrongdoer deceives another person out of money, property, or something else of value. A person who has been injured by intentional misrepresentation can recover damages from the wrongdoer. Four elements are required to find fraud:

1. The wrongdoer made a false representation of material fact.
2. The wrongdoer had knowledge that the representation was false and intended to deceive the innocent party.
3. The innocent party justifiably relied on the misrepresentation.
4. The innocent party was injured.

Item 2, which is called **scienter**, includes situations in which the wrongdoer recklessly disregards the truth in making a representation that is false. Intent or recklessness can be inferred from the circumstances.

intentional misrepresentation
The intentional defrauding of a person out of money, property, or something else of value. Also known as *fraud* or *deceit*.

He that's cheated twice by the same man, is an accomplice with the Cheater.

Thomas Fuller
Gnomologia (1732)

Intentional Infliction of Emotional Distress

intentional infliction of emotional distress
A tort that says a person whose extreme and outrageous conduct intentionally or recklessly causes severe emotional distress to another person is liable for that emotional distress. Also known as the *tort of outrage*.

In some situations, a victim may suffer mental or emotional distress without first being physically harmed. The *Restatement (Second) of Torts* provides that a person whose *extreme and outrageous* conduct intentionally or recklessly causes severe emotional distress to another is liable for that emotional distress.[2] This is called the tort of **intentional infliction of emotional distress**, or the **tort of outrage**.

The plaintiff must prove that the defendant's conduct was "so outrageous in character and so extreme in degree as to go beyond all possible bounds of decency, and to be regarded as atrocious and utterly intolerable in a civilized society."[3] The tort does not require any publication to a third party or physical contact between the plaintiff and defendant.

An indignity, an annoyance, rough language, or an occasional inconsiderate or unkind act does not constitute outrageous behavior. However, repeated annoyances or harassment coupled with threats are considered outrageous.

The mental distress suffered by the plaintiff must be severe. Many states require that this mental distress be manifested by some form of physical injury, discomfort, or illness, such as nausea, ulcers, headaches, or miscarriage. This requirement is intended to prevent false claims. Some states have abandoned this requirement.

Examples Shame, humiliation, embarrassment, anger, fear, and worry constitute severe mental distress.

Malicious Prosecution

malicious prosecution
A lawsuit in which the original defendant sues the original plaintiff. In the second lawsuit, the defendant becomes the plaintiff and vice versa.

Businesses and individuals often believe they have a reason to sue someone to recover damages or other remedies. If the plaintiff has a legitimate reason to bring the lawsuit and does so, but the plaintiff does not win the lawsuit, he or she does not have to worry about being sued by the person whom he or she sued. But a losing plaintiff does have to worry about being sued by the defendant in a second lawsuit for **malicious prosecution** if certain elements are met. In a lawsuit for malicious prosecution, the original defendant sues the original plaintiff. In this second lawsuit, which is a *civil* action for damages, the original defendant is the plaintiff and the original plaintiff is the defendant. To succeed in a malicious prosecution lawsuit, the courts require the plaintiff to prove all of the following:

1. The plaintiff in the original lawsuit (now the defendant) instituted or was responsible for instituting the original lawsuit.
2. There was no *probable cause* for the first lawsuit (i.e., it was a frivolous lawsuit).
3. The plaintiff in the original action brought it with *malice*. (Caution: This is a very difficult element to prove.)
4. The original lawsuit was terminated in favor of the original defendant (now the plaintiff).
5. The current plaintiff suffered injury as a result of the original lawsuit.

Negligence is the omission to do something which a reasonable man would do, or doing something which a prudent and reasonable man would not do.

B. Alderson Blyth v. Birmingham Waterworks Co. *(1856)*

The courts do not look favorably on malicious prosecution lawsuits because they feel such lawsuits inhibit the original plaintiff's incentive to sue.

▶ UNINTENTIONAL TORTS (NEGLIGENCE)

unintentional tort
A doctrine that says a person is liable for harm that is the foreseeable consequence of his or her actions. Also known as *negligence*.

Under the doctrine of **unintentional tort**, commonly referred to as **negligence**, a person is liable for harm that is the *foreseeable consequence* of his or her actions. *Negligence* is defined as "the omission to do something which a reasonable man would do, or doing something which a prudent and reasonable man would not do."[4]

To be successful in a negligence lawsuit, the plaintiff must prove that (1) the defendant owed a *duty of care* to the plaintiff, (2) the defendant *breached* this duty of care, (3) the plaintiff suffered *injury*, (4) the defendant's negligent act *caused* the plaintiff's injury and (5) the defendant's negligent act was the proximate cause of the plaintiff's injuries. Each of these elements is discussed in the paragraphs that follow.

CONCEPT SUMMARY

ELEMENTS OF NEGLIGENCE

1. The defendant owed a *duty of care* to the plaintiff.

2. The defendant *breached this duty*.

3. The plaintiff suffered *injury*.

4. The defendant's negligent act was the *actual cause* (or *causation in fact*) of the plaintiff's injuries.

5. The defendant's negligent act was the *proximate cause* (or *legal cause*) of the plaintiff's injuries. The defendant is liable only for the *foreseeable* consequences of his or her negligent act.

Duty of Care

To determine whether a defendant is liable for negligence, it must first be ascertained whether the defendant owed a **duty of care** to the plaintiff. *Duty of care* refers to the obligation people owe each other—that is, the duty not to cause any unreasonable harm or risk of harm.

duty of care
The obligation people owe each other not to cause any unreasonable harm or risk of harm.

Examples Each person owes a duty to drive his or her car carefully, not to push or shove on escalators, not to leave skateboards on the sidewalk, and the like. Businesses owe a duty to make safe products, not to cause accidents, and so on.

The courts decide whether a duty of care is owed in specific cases by applying a *reasonable person standard*. Under this test, the courts attempt to determine how an *objective, careful, and conscientious person would have acted in the same circumstances* and then measure the defendant's conduct against that standard. The defendant's subjective intent ("I did not mean to do it") is immaterial in assessing liability. Certain impairments do not affect the reasonable person standard.

No court has ever given, nor do we think ever can give, a definition of what constitutes a reasonable or an average man.

Lord Goddard C.J.R. v. McCarthy
(1954)

Defendants with a particular expertise or competence are measured against a *reasonable professional standard*. This standard is applied in much the same way as the reasonable person standard.

Breach of Duty

Once a court finds that the defendant actually owed the plaintiff a duty of care, it must determine whether the defendant breached that duty. A **breach of the duty of care** is the failure to exercise care. In other words, it is the failure to act as a reasonable person would act. A breach of this duty may consist of an action.

breach of the duty of care
A failure to exercise care or to act as a reasonable person would act.

Example Throwing a lit match on the ground in the forest and causing a fire is a breach of a duty of care.

A breach of duty may also consist of a failure to act when there is a duty to act.

Example A firefighter who refuses to put out a fire when her safety is not at stake breaches her duty of care for failing to act when she has a duty to act.

Passersby are generally not expected to rescue others gratuitously to save them from harm. However, most states require certain relatives—parents to children, children to parents if the children are old enough—to try to save their relatives from harm.

CONTEMPORARY ENVIRONMENT

Ouch! McDonald's Coffee Is Too Hot!

McDonald's Corporation found itself embroiled in one of the most famous negligence cases of modern times. Many studies have shown that people care less about how good their coffee tastes than whether it is hot. So restaurants, coffee shops, and other sellers make their coffee hot. McDonald's, however, discovered that it was in hot water for making its coffee too hot.

Stella Liebeck, a 79-year-old resident of Albuquerque, New Mexico, visited a drive-through window of a McDonald's restaurant with her grandson Chris. Her grandson, the driver of the vehicle, placed the order for breakfast. When breakfast came at the drive-through window, Chris handed a hot cup of coffee to Stella. Because there were no cup holders in the vehicle, Chris pulled over so that Stella could put cream and sugar in her coffee. Stella took the lid off the coffee cup she held in her lap and the hot coffee spilled in her lap. The coffee spilled all over Stella, who suffered third-degree burns on her legs, thighs, groin, and buttocks. Stella was driven to the emergency room and was hospitalized for seven days. She required medical treatment and later returned to the hospital to have skin grafts. She suffered permanent scars from the incident.

Stella's medical costs were $11,000. Stella asked McDonald's to pay her $20,000 to settle the case, but McDonald's offered only $800. Stella refused this settlement and sued McDonald's in court for negligence for selling coffee that was too hot and for failing to warn her of the danger of the hot coffee it served. McDonald's went to trial.

At trial, McDonald's denied that it had been negligent and asserted that Stella's own negligence—opening a hot coffee cup on her lap—had caused her injuries. The jury heard evidence that McDonald's enforces a quality-control rule that requires its restaurants and franchises to serve coffee at 180 to 190 degrees Fahrenheit. Third-degree burns occur on skin in just two to five seconds when coffee is served at 185 degrees. Evidence at trial showed that McDonald's coffee temperature was 20 degrees hotter than coffee served by competing restaurant chains and approximately 40 to 50 degrees hotter than normal house-brewed coffee. Evidence also showed that McDonald's had received more than 700 prior complaints of people who had been scalded by McDonald's coffee, but McDonald's had failed to place a warning on its cups to alert patrons that the coffee it served would scald skin.

Based on this evidence, the jury turned its anger on McDonald's and concluded that McDonald's acted recklessly and awarded Stella $200,000 compensatory damages (reduced by $40,000 for her own negligence) and $2.7 million punitive damages. The trial court judge reduced the amount of punitive damages to $480,000, which was three times the amount of compensatory damages. McDonald's has not turned down the temperature of its coffee, but it does place warnings on its coffee cups. *Liebeck v. McDonald's Restaurants, P.T.S., Inc.* (New Mexico District Court, Bernalillo County, New Mexico, 1994)

In the following case, the court had to determine whether the defendant was liable for negligence.

CASE 5.2 Negligence

James v. Meow Media, Inc.

300 F.3d 683, Web 2002 U.S. App. Lexis 16185 (2002)
United States Court of Appeals for the Sixth Circuit

"Our inquiry is whether the deaths of James, Steger, and Hadley were the reasonably foreseeable result of the defendants' creation and distribution of their games, movie, and Internet sites."

—Judge Boggs

Facts

Michael Carneal was a 14-year-old freshman student at Heath High School in Paducah, Kentucky. Carneal regularly played the violent interactive video and computer games "Doom," "Quake," "Castle Wolfenstein," "Rampage,"

"Nightmare Creatures," "Mech Warrior," "Resident Evil," and "Final Fantasy." These games involved the player shooting virtual opponents with computer guns and other weapons. Carneal also watched videotaped movies, including one called *The Basketball Diaries*, in which a high-school-student protagonist dreams of killing his teacher and several of his fellow classmates. On December 1, 1997, Carneal took a .22-caliber pistol and five shotguns into the lobby of Heath High School and shot several of his fellow students, killing three and wounding many others. The three students killed were Jessica James, Kayce Steger, and Nicole Hadley.

The parents of the three dead children ("James") sued the producers and distributors of the violent video games and movies that Carneal had watched previous to the shooting. The parents sued to recover damages for wrongful death, alleging that the defendants were negligent in producing and distributing such games and movies to Carneal. The U.S. District Court applied Kentucky law and held that the defendants did not owe or breach a duty to the plaintiffs and therefore were not liable for negligence. The plaintiffs appealed.

Issue

Did the defendant video and movie producers and distributors owe a duty of care to the plaintiffs by selling and licensing violent video games and movies to Carneal, who killed the three children?

Language of the Court

Kentucky courts have held that the determination of whether a duty of care exists is whether the harm to the plaintiff resulting from the defendant's negligence was "foreseeable." Kentucky courts have struggled with the formless nature of this inquiry. Our inquiry is whether the deaths of James, Steger, and Hadley were the reasonably foreseeable result of the defendants' creation and distribution of their games, movie, and Internet sites.

It appears simply impossible to predict that these games, movie, and Internet sites would incite a young person to violence. We find that it is simply too far a leap from shooting characters on a video screen (an activity undertaken by millions) to shooting people in a classroom (an activity undertaken by a handful, at most) for Carneal's actions to have been reasonably foreseeable to the manufacturers of the media that Carneal played and viewed. Carneal's reaction was not a normal reaction. Indeed, Carneal is not a normal person. Individuals are generally entitled to assume that third parties will not commit intentional criminal acts.

Decision

The Court of Appeals held that the defendant video game and movie producers and distributors did not owe a duty of care to the plaintiffs by selling and licensing violent video games and movies to Carneal, who murdered the three children.

Case Questions

Critical Legal Thinking How do the courts define *foreseeability*? Did the Court of Appeals use a narrow, middle, or broad interpretation of foreseeability in deciding this case? Explain.

Business Ethics Do producers and distributors of video games and movies owe a duty of care to society not to produce and distribute violent games and movies?

Contemporary Business What would have been the consequences for the video game and movie industries if the court had held in favor of the plaintiffs? Are any free speech issues involved in this case? Explain.

Injury to Plaintiff

Even though a defendant's negligent act may have breached a duty of care owed to the plaintiff, this breach is not actionable unless the plaintiff suffers **injury** or injury to his or her property. That is, the plaintiff must have suffered some injury before he or she can recover any damages.

The damages recoverable depend on the effect of the injury on the plaintiff's life or profession.

Examples Suppose that a man injures his hand when a train door malfunctions. The train company is found negligent. If the injured man is a star professional basketball player who makes $5 million per year, with an expected seven years of good playing time left, this plaintiff can recover multiple millions of dollars because he can no longer play professional basketball. If the injured man is a college professor with 15 years until retirement who is making only one-fortieth per year of what the basketball player makes, he can recover some money for his injuries. Because he makes a lot less per year than the professional basketball player and because he can continue working, albeit with more difficulty, the professor can recover much less for the same injury.

Actual Cause

A defendant's negligent act must be the **causation in fact**, or **actual cause**, of the plaintiff's injuries. The test is this: "But for" the defendant's conduct, would the accident

injury
A plaintiff's personal injury or damage to his or her property that enables him or her to recover monetary damages for the defendant's negligence.

actual cause
The actual cause of negligence. A person who commits a negligent act is not liable unless actual cause can be proven. Also called *causation in fact*.

have happened? If the defendant's act caused the plaintiff's injuries, there is causation in fact.

Examples Suppose a corporation negligently pollutes the plaintiff's drinking water. The plaintiff dies of a heart attack unrelated to the polluted water. Although the corporation has acted negligently, it is not liable for the plaintiff's death. There were a negligent act and an injury, but there was no cause-and-effect relationship between them. If, instead, the plaintiff had died from the polluted drinking water, there would have been causation in fact, and the polluting corporation would have been liable.

If two (or more) persons are liable for negligently causing the plaintiff's injuries, both (or all) can be held liable to the plaintiff if each of their acts is a substantial factor in causing the plaintiff's injuries.

Proximate Cause

proximate cause
A point along a chain of events caused by a negligent party after which this party is no longer legally responsible for the consequences of his or her actions. Also called *legal cause*.

Under the law, a negligent party is not necessarily liable for all damages set in motion by his or her negligent act. Based on public policy, the law establishes a point along the damage chain after which the negligent party is no longer responsible for the consequences of his or her actions. This limitation on liability is referred to as **proximate cause**, or **legal cause**. The general test of proximate cause is *foreseeability*. A negligent party who is found to be the actual cause—but not the proximate cause—of the plaintiff's injuries is not liable to the plaintiff. Situations are examined on a case-by-case basis.

LANDMARK LAW

Palsgraf v. The Long Island Railroad Company

"Negligence is not actionable unless it involves the invasion of a legally protected interest, the violation of a right. Proof of negligence in the air, so to speak, will not do."

—Justice Cardozo

The landmark case establishing the doctrine of proximate cause is *Palsgraf v. The Long Island Railroad Company*, a New York case decided in 1928. Helen Palsgraf was standing on a platform, waiting for a passenger train. The Long Island Railroad Company owned and operated the trains and employed the station guards. As a man carrying a package wrapped in a newspaper tried to board the moving train, railroad guards tried to help him. In doing so, the package was dislodged from the man's arm, fell to the railroad tracks, and exploded. The package contained hidden fireworks. The explosion shook the railroad platform, causing a scale located on the platform to fall on Helen Palsgraf, injuring her.

Palsgraf sued the railroad for negligence. Justice Cardozo eloquently addressed the issue of proximate cause:

> The conduct of the defendant's guard, if a wrong in its relation to the holder of the package, was not a wrong in its relation to the plaintiff, standing far away. Relatively to her it was not negligence at all. Nothing in

the situation gave notice that the falling package had in it the potency of peril to persons thus removed. Negligence is not actionable unless it involves the invasion of a legally protected interest, the violation of a right. Proof of negligence in the air, so to speak, will not do. In every instance, before negligence can be predicated on a given act, in back of the act must be sought and found a duty to the individual complaining, the observance of which would have averted or avoided the injury.

> The argument for the plaintiff is built upon the shifting meanings of such words as "wrong" and "wrongful," and shares their instability. What the plaintiff must show is "a wrong" to herself, i.e., a violation of her own right, and not merely a wrong to some one else, nor conduct "wrongful" because unsocial. The risk reasonably to be perceived defines the duty to be obeyed, and risk imports relation; it is risk to another or to others within the range of apprehension. Here, by concession, there was nothing in the situation to suggest to the most cautious mind that the parcel wrapped in newspaper would spread wreckage through the station. If the guard had thrown it down knowingly and willfully, he would not have threatened the plaintiff's safety, so far as appearances could warn him.

His conduct would not have involved, even then, an unreasonable probability of invasion of her bodily security. Liability can be no greater where the act is inadvertent.

Negligence, like risk, is thus a term of relation. Negligence in the abstract, apart from things related, is surely not a tort, if indeed it is understandable at all. One who seeks redress at law does not make out a cause of action by showing without more that there has been damage to his person. If the harm was not willful, *he must show that the act as to him had possibilities of danger so many and apparent as to entitle him to be protected against the doing of it though the harm was unintended.*

Justice Cardozo denied Palsgraf's recovery, finding that the railroad company was not the proximate cause of her injuries. *Palsgraf v. The Long Island Railroad Company*, 248 N.Y. 339, 162 N.E. 99, **Web** 1928 N.Y. Lexis 1269 (Court of Appeals of New York, 1928)

Automobiles, Las Vegas, Nevada *Most automobile and other vehicle drivers drive safely and are not often involved in accidents. However, vehicular accidents are a primary cause of injury and death. In the United States there are more than 40,000 fatalities of passenger car and SUV occupants, pedestrians, and cyclists each year. More than 4,000 motor cycle fatalities also occur each year.*

▶ SPECIAL NEGLIGENCE DOCTRINES

The courts have developed many *special negligence doctrines*. The most important of these are discussed in the paragraphs that follow.

Professional Malpractice

Professionals, such as doctors, lawyers, architects, accountants, and others, owe a duty of ordinary care in providing their services. This duty is known as the *reasonable professional standard*. A professional who breaches this duty of care is liable for the injury his or her negligence causes. This liability is commonly referred to as **professional malpractice**.

Examples A doctor who amputates a wrong leg is liable for *medical malpractice*. A lawyer who fails to file a document with the court on time, causing the client's case to be dismissed, is liable for *legal malpractice*. An accountant who fails to use reasonable care, knowledge, skill, and judgment in providing auditing and other accounting services to a client is liable for *accounting malpractice*.

professional malpractice
The liability of a professional who breaches his or her duty of ordinary care.

Negligent Infliction of Emotional Distress

Some jurisdictions have extended the tort of emotional distress to include the **negligent infliction of emotional distress**.

negligent infliction of emotional distress
A tort that permits a person to recover for emotional distress caused by the defendant's negligent conduct.

Example The most common example of negligent infliction of emotional distress involve bystanders who witness the injury or death of a loved one that is caused by another's negligent conduct. Under this tort, the bystander, even though not personally physically injured, can sue the negligent party for his or her own mental suffering.

Generally, to be successful in this type of case, the plaintiff must prove that (1) a close relative was killed or injured by the defendant, (2) the plaintiff suffered severe emotional distress, and (3) the plaintiff's mental distress resulted from a sensory and contemporaneous observance of the accident. Some states require that the plaintiff's mental distress be manifested by some physical injury; other states have eliminated this requirement.

Negligence per Se

Statutes often establish duties owed by one person to another. The violation of a statute that proximately causes an injury is **negligence per se**. The plaintiff in such an action must prove that (1) a statute existed, (2) the statute was enacted to prevent the type of injury suffered, and (3) the plaintiff was within a class of persons meant to be protected by the statute.

negligence per se
A tort in which the violation of a statute or an ordinance constitutes the breach of the duty of care.

Example Most cities have an ordinance that places the responsibility for fixing public sidewalks in residential areas on the homeowners whose homes front the sidewalks. A homeowner is liable if he or she fails to repair a damaged sidewalk in front of his or her home and a pedestrian trips and is injured because of the damage. The injured party does not have to prove that the homeowner owed the duty because the statute establishes that.

Res Ipsa Loquitur

If a defendant is in control of a situation in which a plaintiff has been injured and has superior knowledge of the circumstances surrounding the injury, the plaintiff might have difficulty proving the defendant's negligence. In such a situation, the law applies the doctrine of *res ipsa loquitur* (Latin for "the thing speaks for itself"). This doctrine raises a presumption of negligence and switches the burden to the defendant to prove that he or she was not negligent. *Res ipsa loquitur* applies in cases where the following elements are met:

res ipsa loquitur
A tort in which the presumption of negligence arises because (1) the defendant was in exclusive control of the situation and (2) the plaintiff would not have suffered injury but for someone's negligence. The burden switches to the defendant to prove that he or she was not negligent.

1. The defendant had exclusive control of the instrumentality or situation that caused the plaintiff's injury.
2. The injury would not have ordinarily occurred but for someone's negligence.

Examples Haeran goes in for major surgery and is given anesthesia to put her to sleep during the operation. Sometime after the operation, it is discovered that a surgical instrument was left in Haeran during the operation. She suffers severe injury because of the left-in instrument. Haeran has no way to identify which doctor or nurse carelessly left the instrument in her body. In this case, the court can apply the doctrine of *res ipsa loquitur* and place the presumption of negligence on the defendants. Any defendant who can prove he or she did not leave the instrument in Haeran escapes liability; any defendant who does not disprove his or her negligence is liable. Other typical *res ipsa loquitur* cases involve commercial airplane crashes, falling elevators, and the like.

Good Samaritan Laws

In the past, liability exposure made many doctors, nurses, and other medical professionals reluctant to stop and render aid to victims in emergency situations, such as highway accidents. Almost all states have enacted **Good Samaritan laws** that relieve medical professionals from liability for injury caused by their ordinary negligence in such circumstances. Good Samaritan laws protect medical professionals only from liability for their *ordinary negligence*, not for injuries caused by their gross negligence or reckless or intentional conduct. Most Good Samaritan laws protect licensed doctors, nurses, and laypersons who have been certified in CPR. Laypersons not trained in CPR are not generally protected by

Good Samaritan law
A statute that relieves medical professionals from liability for ordinary negligence when they stop and render aid to victims in emergency situations.

Good Samaritan statutes—that is, they are liable for injuries caused by their ordinary negligence in rendering aid.

Examples Sam is injured in an automobile accident and is unconscious in his automobile alongside the road. Doctor Pamela Heathcoat, who is driving by the scene of the accident, stops, pulls Sam from the burning wreckage, and administers first aid. In doing so, Pamela negligently breaks Sam's shoulder. If Pamela's negligence is ordinary negligence, she is not liable to Sam because the Good Samaritan law protects her from liability; if Pamela was grossly negligent or reckless in administering aid to Sam, she is liable to him for the injuries she caused. It is a question of fact for the jury to decide whether a doctor's conduct was ordinary negligence or gross negligence or recklessness.

Every unjust decision is a reproach to the law or the judge who administers it. If the law should be in danger of doing injustice, then equity should be called in to remedy it. Equity was introduced to mitigate the rigour of the law.

Lord Denning
M.R. Re Vandervell's Trusts (1971)

▶ DEFENSES AGAINST NEGLIGENCE

A defendant in a negligence lawsuit may raise several defenses to the imposition of liability. These defenses are discussed in the following paragraphs.

Superseding or Intervening Event

Under negligence, a person is liable only for foreseeable events. Therefore, an original negligent party can raise a **superseding event** or an **intervening event** as a defense to liability.

Example Assume that an avid golfer negligently hits a spectator with a golf ball, knocking the spectator unconscious. While lying on the ground, waiting for an ambulance to come, the spectator is struck by a bolt of lightning and killed. The golfer is liable for the injuries caused by the golf ball. He is not liable for the death of the spectator, however, because the lightning bolt was an unforeseen intervening event.

superseding or intervening event
An event for which a defendant is not responsible. The defendant is not liable for injuries caused by the superseding or intervening event.

Assumption of the Risk

If a plaintiff knows of and voluntarily enters into or participates in a risky activity that results in injury, the law recognizes that the plaintiff assumed, or took on, the risk involved. Thus, the defendant can raise the defense of **assumption of the risk** against the plaintiff. This defense assumes that the plaintiff (1) had knowledge of the specific risk and (2) voluntarily assumed that risk.

Example Under assumption of the risk, a race-car driver assumes the risk of being injured or killed in a crash.

assumption of the risk
A defense a defendant can use against a plaintiff who knowingly and voluntarily enters into or participates in a risky activity that results in injury.

In the following case, the court had to decide whether the plaintiff had assumed the risk.

CASE 5.3 Assumption of the Risk

Lilya v. The Greater Gulf State Fair, Inc.
855 So.2d 1049, Web 2003 Ala. Lexis 57 (2003)
Supreme Court of Alabama

"Here, the only evidence of danger stemming from the mechanical bull ride is the most open and obvious characteristic of the ride: the possibility of falling off the mechanical bull."

—Judge Houston

Facts
The Greater Gulf State Fair, Inc., operated the Gulf State Fair in Mobile County, Alabama. One of the events at the fair was a mechanical bull ride for which participants paid money to ride the mechanical bull. A mechanical bull is a

ride where the rider sits on a motorized device shaped like a real bull, and the ride simulates a real bull ride as the mechanical bull turns, twists, and bucks. The challenge is to stay on the bull and not be thrown off the bull. A large banner above the ride read "Rolling Thunder."

John Lilya and a friend watched as a rider was thrown from the mechanical bull. Lilya also watched as his friend paid and rode the bull and also was thrown off. Lilya then paid the $5 admission charge and signed a release agreement that stated:

> *I acknowledge that riding a mechanical bull entails known and unanticipated risks which could result in physical or emotional injury, paralysis, death, or damage to myself, to property, or to third parties. I expressly agree and promise to accept and assume all of the risks existing in this activity. My participation in this activity is purely voluntary, and I elect to participate in spite of the risks.*

Lilya boarded the mechanical bull and was immediately thrown off onto a soft pad underneath the bull. Lilya reboarded the bull for a second ride. The bull ride began again and became progressively faster, spinning and bucking to the left and right until Lilya fell off the bull. On the fall, Lilya landed on his head and shoulders, and he suffered a fractured neck. Lilya sued Gulf State Fair to recover damages for his severe injuries. The trial court granted summary judgment to Gulf State Fair, finding that Lilya had voluntarily assumed an open and obvious danger. Lilya appealed.

Issue
Was riding a mechanical bull an open and obvious danger for which Lilya had voluntarily assumed the risk when he rode the mechanical bull?

Language of the Court
As the landowner, Gulf State Fair would owe Lilya, its invitee, the duty to use reasonable care. The owner of premises has no duty to warn an invitee of open and obvious defects in the premises which the invitee is aware of or should be aware of in the exercise of reasonable care. Here, the only evidence of danger stemming from the mechanical bull ride is the most open and obvious characteristic of the

ride: the possibility of falling off the mechanical bull. Lilya was aware that the two riders who had ridden the mechanical bull immediately before he rode it had fallen off. He noticed the thick floor mat, and he knew that the mat was there to protect riders when they fell. Also, he signed a release that explicitly stated that riding the mechanical bull involved inherent risks and that the risks included falling off or being thrown from the bull which could result in head, neck, and back injuries. Additionally, the very name of the ride—"Rolling Thunder"—hanging on a banner above the ride, gives a somewhat graphic indication of what is the very nature of bull riding: an extremely turbulent, ride the challenge of which is to hang on and not fall off. The entertainment value—and, indeed, the concept—of bull riding becomes meaningless without the inherent possibility of falling off. "Volenti non fit injuria" (a person who knowingly and voluntarily risks danger cannot recover for any resulting injury).

Decision
The supreme court of Alabama held that riding a mechanical bull and being thrown and injured by the bull is an open and obvious danger and that Lilya had voluntarily assumed the risk when he rode the bull and was thrown and injured. The supreme court affirmed the trial court's grant of summary judgment in favor of Gulf State Fair.

Case Questions

Critical Legal Thinking What does the doctrine of assumption of the risk provide? Do you think the doctrine of assumption of the risk should be recognized by the law? Explain.

Business Ethics Did Gulf State Fair act ethically by making money from such a dangerous activity as mechanical bull riding? Did Lilya act ethically in suing for damages?

Contemporary Business What public purpose does the defense of assumption of the risk serve? What would be the consequences if this defense were not available? Explain.

Contributory Negligence

contributory negligence
A doctrine that says a plaintiff who is partially at fault for his or her own injury cannot recover against the negligent defendant.

Sometimes a plaintiff is partially liable for causing his or her own injuries. Under the common law doctrine of **contributory negligence**, a plaintiff who is partially at fault for his or her own injury cannot recover against the negligent defendant. Many states follow this rule.

Example Suppose a driver who is driving over the speed limit negligently hits and injures a pedestrian who is jaywalking. Suppose the jury finds that the driver is 80 percent responsible for the accident, and the jaywalker is 20 percent responsible. The pedestrian suffered

$100,000 in injuries. Under the doctrine of contributory negligence, the pedestrian cannot recover any damages from the driver.

Last Clear Chance Rule   There is one major exception to the doctrine of contributory negligence: The defendant has a duty under the law to avoid the accident if at all possible. This rule is known as the *last clear chance rule.*

Example A driver who sees a pedestrian walking across the street against a "Don't Walk" sign must avoid hitting him or her if possible. When deciding cases involving this rule, the courts consider the attentiveness of the parties and the amount of time each had to respond to the situation.

Comparative Negligence

The application of the doctrine of contributory negligence could reach an unfair result where a party only slightly at fault for his or her injuries could not recover from an otherwise negligent defendant. Many states have replaced the doctrine of contributory negligence with the doctrine of **comparative negligence**, also called **comparative fault**. Under this doctrine, damages are apportioned according to fault.

comparative negligence
A doctrine under which damages are apportioned according to fault.

Example When the comparative negligence rule is applied to the previous example, the result is much fairer. The plaintiff-pedestrian, who was 20 percent at fault for causing his own injuries, can recover 80 percent of his damages (or $80,000) from the defendant-driver. This is an example of **pure comparative negligence**.

Several states have adopted **partial comparative negligence**, which provides that a plaintiff must be less than 50 percent responsible for causing his or her own injuries to recover under comparative negligence; otherwise, contributory negligence applies.

▶ STRICT LIABILITY

Strict liability, another category of torts, is *liability without fault.* That is, a participant in a covered activity will be held liable for any injuries caused by the activity, even if he or she was not negligent. This doctrine holds that (1) there are certain activities that can place the public at risk of injury even if reasonable care is taken and (2) the public should have some means of compensation if such injury occurs.

strict liability
Liability without fault.

Strict liability was first imposed for **abnormally dangerous activities**, such as crop dusting, blasting, fumigation, burning of fields, storage of explosives, and the keeping of wild animals as pets.

District of Shinjuku in Tokyo, Japan *Each country has developed its own civil law system. In Japan, for example, no class actions or contingency fee arrangements are allowed. Plaintiffs must pay their lawyers an upfront fee of up to eight percent of the damages sought, plus a nonrefundable filing fee to the court of one-half of one percent of the damages sought. No discovery is permitted. Even if the plaintiff wins the lawsuit, damage awards are low. Therefore, most legal disputes in Japan are decided by private arbitrators.*

TEST REVIEW TERMS AND CONCEPTS

Abnormally dangerous
   activities
Actual cause (causation in
   fact)
Assault
Assumption of the risk
Battery
Breach of the duty of care
Comparative negligence
   (comparative fault)
Contributory negligence
Defamation of character
Disparagement (trade libel,
   product disparagement,
   or slander of title)

Duty of care
False imprisonment
Good Samaritan law
Injury
Intentional infliction of
   emotional distress (tort
   of outrage)
Intentional
   misrepresentation (fraud
   or deceit)
Intentional tort
Intervening event
Invasion of the right to
   privacy
Libel

Malicious prosecution
Merchant protection statute
   (shopkeeper's privilege)
Misappropriation of the
   right to publicity (tort of
   appropriation)
Negligence (unintentional
   tort)
Negligence per se
Negligent infliction of
   emotional distress
*New York Times Co. v.
   Sullivan*
*Palsgraf v. The Long Island
   Railroad Company*

Partial comparative
   negligence
Professional malpractice
Proximate cause (legal
   cause)
Pure comparative
   negligence
Res ipsa loquitur
Scienter
Slander
Strict liability
Superseding event
Tort
Tort of appropriation
Transferred intent doctrine

CASE PROBLEMS

5.1 Intentional Tort   The Baltimore Orioles, a professional baseball team, visited Boston's Fenway Park to play the Boston Red Sox, another professional baseball team. Ross Grimsley was a pitcher for the visiting Baltimore club. During one period of the game, Grimsley was warming up in the bullpen, throwing pitches to a catcher. During this warm-up, Boston spectators in the stands heckled Grimsley. After Grimsley had completed warming up, Grimsley wound up as if he were going to throw the ball in his hand at the plate but then turned and threw the ball at one of the hecklers in the stand. The ball traveled at about 80 miles an hour, passed through a wire fence protecting the spectators, missed the heckler that Grimsley was aiming at, and hit another spectator, David Manning, Jr., causing injury. Manning sued Grimsley and the Baltimore Orioles. Are the defendants liable? *Manning v. Grimsley*, 643 F.2d 20, **Web** 1981 U.S. App. Lexis 19782 (United States Court of Appeals for the First Circuit)

5.2 Merchant Protection Statute   At about 7:30 P.M., Deborah A. Johnson entered a Kmart store located in Madison, Wisconsin, to purchase some diapers and several cans of motor oil. She took her small child along to enable her to purchase the correct size diapers, carrying the child in an infant seat that she had purchased at Kmart two or three weeks previously. A large Kmart price tag was still attached to the infant seat. Johnson purchased the diapers and oil and some children's clothes. She was in a hurry to leave because it was 8:00 P.M., her child's feeding time, and she hurried through the checkout lane. She paid for the diapers, the oil, and the clothing. Just after leaving the store, she heard someone ask her to stop. She turned around and saw a Kmart security officer. He showed her a badge and asked her to come back into the store, which she did. The man stated, "I have reason to believe that you have stolen this car seat." Johnson explained that she had purchased the seat previously. She demanded to see the manager, who was called to the scene. When Johnson pointed out that the seat had cat hairs, food crumbs, and milk stains on it, the man said, "I'm really sorry, there's been a terrible mistake. You can go." Johnson looked at the clock, which read 8:20 P.M., when she left. Johnson sued Kmart for false imprisonment. Is Kmart liable? *Johnson v. K-Mart Enterprises, Inc.*, 98 Wis.2d 533, 297 N.W.2d 74, **Web** 1980 Wisc.App. Lexis 3197 (Court of Appeals of Wisconsin)

5.3 Negligence   George Yanase was a paying guest at the Royal Lodge-Downtown Motel in San Diego, California. Yanase was a member of the Automobile Club of Southern California. The Auto Club publishes a "Tourbook" in which it lists hotels and motels and rates the quality of their services, including the cleanliness of rooms, quality of the restaurant, level of personal service, and the like. Yanase had selected the Royal from the Tourbook. On the night of his stay at the Royal, Yanase was shot in the parking lot adjacent to the motel and died as a result of his injuries. Yanase's widow sued the Auto Club for negligence. Is the Auto Club liable? *Yanase v. Automobile Club of Southern California*, 212 Cal.App.3d 468, 260 Cal.Rptr. 513, **Web** 1989 Cal.App. Lexis 746 (Court of Appeal of California)

5.4 Causation   W. L. Brown purchased a new large Chevrolet truck from Days Chevrolet. The truck had been manufactured by General Motors Corporation. One month later, an employee of Brown's was operating the truck when it ceased to function in rush-hour traffic on Interstate Highway 75 in the Atlanta suburbs. A defect within the alternator had caused a complete failure of the truck's electrical system. The defect was caused by General Motors's negligence in manu-facturing the truck. When the alternator failed to operate, the truck came to rest in the right-hand lane of two north-bound lanes of freeway traffic. Because of the electrical failure, no blinking lights could be used to warn traffic of the danger. The driver, however, tried to motion traffic around the truck. Sometime later, when the freeway traffic had returned to nor-mal, the large Chevrolet truck was still motionless on the freeway. At approximately 6:00 P.M., a panel truck approached the stalled truck in the right-hand lane of traffic at freeway speed. Immediately behind the panel truck, Mr. Davis, driv-ing a Volkswagen fastback, was unable to see the stalled truck. At the last moment, the driver of the panel truck saw the stalled truck and swerved into another lane to avoid it. Mr. Davis drove his Volkswagen into the stalled truck at freeway speed, causing his death. Mr. Davis's wife brought a wrongful death action based on negligence against General Motors. Is there causation linking the negligence of the defendant to the fatal accident? *General Motors Corporation v. Davis*, 141 Ga.App. 495, 233 S.E.2d 825, **Web** 1977 Ga.App. Lexis 1961 (Court of Appeals of Georgia)

5.5 Negligence Per Se   Julius Ebanks set out from his home in East Elmhurst, Queens, New York, en route to his employ-ment in the downtown district of Manhattan. When Ebanks reached Bowling Green subway station, he boarded an escala-tor owned and operated by the New York City Transit Authority. While the escalator was ascending, Ebanks's left foot became caught in a two-inch gap between the escalator step on which he was standing and the side wall of the escala-tor. Ebanks was unable to free himself. When he reached the top of the escalator, he was thrown to the ground, fracturing his hip and causing other serious injuries. The two-inch gap exceeded the three-eighths-inch standard required by the city's building code. Ebanks sued the Transit Authority to recover damages for his injuries. Who wins? *Ebanks v. New York City Transit Authority*, 70 N.Y.2d 621, 518 N.Y.S.2d 776, **Web** 1987 N.Y. Lexis 17294 (Court of Appeals of New York)

5.6 Emotional Distress   Gregory and Demetria James, brother and sister, were riding their bicycles north on 50th Street in Omaha, Nebraska. Spaulding Street intersects 50th Street. A garbage truck owned by Watts Trucking Service, Inc., and driven by its employee, John Milton Lieb, was back-ing up into the intersection of 50th and Spaulding streets. The truck backed into the intersection, through a stop sign, and hit and ran over Demetria, killing her. Gregory helplessly watched the entire accident but was not in danger himself. As a result of watching his sister's peril, Gregory suffered severe emotional distress. Gregory sued Watts and Lieb to recover damages for his emotional distress. Who wins? *James v. Watts Trucking Service, Inc.*, 221 Neb. 47, 375 N.W.2d 109, **Web** 1985 Neb. Lexis 1209 (Supreme Court of Nebraska)

5.7 Defense   The New York Yankees professional baseball team played the Chicago White Sox at Shea Stadium, New York. Elliot Maddox played center field for the Yankees that night. It had rained the day before, and the previous night's game had been canceled because of bad weather. On the evening of the game, the playing field was still wet, and Maddox commented on this fact several times to the club's manager but continued to play. In the ninth inning, when Maddox was attempting to field a ball in center field, he slipped on a wet spot, fell, and injured his right knee. Maddox sued the City of New York, which owned Shea Stadium; the Metropolitan Baseball Club, Inc., as lessee; the architect; the consulting engineer; and the American Baseball League. Maddox alleged that the parties were negligent in causing the field to be wet and that the injury ended his professional career. Who wins? *Maddox v. City of New York*, 66 N.Y.2d 270, 487 N.E.2d 553, 496 N.Y.S.2d 726, **Web** 1985 N.Y. Lexis 17254 (Court of Appeals of New York)

BUSINESS ETHICS CASES

5.8 Business Ethics   Radio station KHJ was a successful Los Angeles broadcaster of rock music that commanded a 48 percent market share of the teenage audience in the Los Angeles area. KHJ was owned and operated by RKO General, Inc. KHJ inaugurated a promotion titled "The Super Summer Spectacular." As part of this promotion, KHJ had a disc jockey known as "The Real Don Steele" ride around the Los Angeles area in a conspicuous red automobile. Periodically KHJ would announce to its radio audience Steele's location. The first listener to thereafter locate Steele and answer a question received a cash prize and participated in a brief interview on the air with Steele. One KHJ broadcast identified Steele's next des-tination as Canoga Park. Robert Sentner, 17 years old, heard the broadcast and immediately drove to Canoga Park. Marsha Baime, 19 years old, also heard the broadcast and drove to Canoga Park. By the time Sentner and Baime located Steele, someone else had already claimed the prize. Without the knowledge of the other, Sentner and Baime each decided to fol-low Steele to the next destination and to be first to "find" him.

Steele proceeded onto the freeway. For the next few miles Sentner and Baime tried to jockey for position closest to the Steele vehicle, reaching speeds of up to 80 miles per hour. There is no evidence that the Steele vehicle exceeded the speed limit. When Steele left the freeway at the Westlake off ramp, Sentner and Baime tried to follow. In their attempts to do so, they knocked another vehicle, driven by Mr. Weirum, into the center divider of the freeway, where it overturned. Mr. Weirum died in the accident. Baime stopped to report the accident. Sentner, after pausing momentarily to relate the tragedy to a passing police officer, got back into his car, pur-sued and successfully located Steele, and collected the cash prize. The wife and children of Mr. Weirum brought a wrongful death negligence action against Sentner, Baime, and

RKO General. Who wins? Did RKO General, Inc., act responsibly in this case? *Weirum v. RKO General, Inc.*, 15 Cal.3d 40, 539 P.2d 36, 123 Cal.Rptr. 468, **Web** 1975 Cal. Lexis 220 (Supreme Court of California)

5.9 Business Ethics   Guy Portee, a seven-year-old, resided with his mother in an apartment building in Newark, New Jersey. Edith and Nathan Jaffee owned and operated the building. One day, Guy became trapped in the building's elevator, between its outer door and the wall of the elevator shaft. When someone activated the elevator, the boy was dragged up to the third floor. Another child who saw the accident ran to seek help. Soon afterward, Renee Portee, the boy's mother, and Newark Police Department officers arrived. The officers worked for hours, trying to release the boy, during which time the mother watched as her son moaned, cried out, and flailed his arms. The police contacted the Atlantic Elevator Company, which was responsible for the installation and maintenance of the elevator, and requested that the company send a mechanic to assist in the effort to free the boy. Apparently no one came. The boy suffered multiple bone fractures and massive internal hemorrhaging. He died while still trapped, his mother a helpless observer.

After her son's death, Renee became severely distressed and seriously self-destructive. Three years after the incident, she attempted to take her own life. She survived, and the wound was repaired by surgery, but thereafter she required considerable physical therapy. She had received extensive counseling and psychotherapy to help overcome the mental and emotional problems associated with her son's death. Renee sued the Jaffees and Atlantic to recover damages for her emotional distress. Who wins? Did either of the defendants act unethically in this case? *Portee v. Jaffee*, 84 N.J. 88, 417 A.2d 521, **Web** 1980 N.J. Lexis 1387 (Supreme Court of New Jersey)

ENDNOTES

1. 376 U.S. 254, 84 S.Ct. 710, 11 L.Ed.2d 686, Web 1964 U.S. Lexis 1655 (Supreme Court of the United States, 1964).

2. *Restatement (Second) of Torts*, Section 46.

3. *Restatement (Second) of Torts*, Section 46, Comment d.

4. Justice B. Anderson, *Blyth v. Birmingham Waterworks Co.*, 11 Exch. 781, 784 (1856).

▲ **Hot Dog Stand** *The sellers of goods, including food, can be held liable under the doctrines of negligence and strict liability for injuries caused by the products they sell.*

CHAPTER OBJECTIVES

After studying this chapter you should be able to:

1. Describe and distinguish among the several legal theories of product liability.
2. Define the doctrine of *strict liability*.
3. Identify and describe defects in manufacture and design.
4. Identify and describe defects of failure to warn and in packaging.
5. Describe the damages recoverable in a product liability lawsuit.

CHAPTER CONTENTS

"A manufacturer is strictly liable in tort when an article he places on the market, knowing that it is to be used without inspection for defects, proves to have a defect that causes injury to a human being."

—Greenman v. Yuba Power Products, Inc.
59 Cal.2d 57, 27 Cal.Rptr. 697, 1963 Cal. Lexis 140 (1963)

▶ INTRODUCTION TO STRICT LIABILITY AND PRODUCT LIABILITY

If a product defect causes injury or death to purchasers, lessees, users, or bystanders, the injured party or the heirs of a deceased person may bring legal actions and recover damages under certain tort doctrines. These tort doctrines include negligence, misrepresentation, and the modern theory of strict liability. The liability of manufacturers, sellers, lessors, and others for injuries caused by defective products is commonly referred to as **product liability**. If a violation of strict liability has been found, the plaintiff may also recover punitive damages if the defendant's conduct has been reckless or intentional.

The various tort principles that permit injured parties to recover damages caused by defective products are discussed in this chapter.

▶ NEGLIGENCE AND MISREPRESENTATION

Depending on the circumstances of the case, persons who are injured by defective products may be able to recover damages under the tort theories of *negligence* and *misrepresentation*. Both theories require the defendant to be *at fault* for causing the plaintiff's injuries. These theories are discussed in the paragraphs that follow.

Negligence

A person injured by a defective product may bring an action for **negligence** against the negligent party. To be successful, the plaintiff must prove that the defendant breached a duty of due care to the plaintiff and thereby caused the plaintiff's injuries. In other words, the plaintiff must prove that the defendant was at fault for causing his injuries.

Failure to exercise due care includes failing to assemble a product carefully, negligent product design, negligent inspection or testing of a product, negligent packaging, failure to warn of the dangerous propensities of a product, and such. It is important to note that in a negligence lawsuit, only a party who was actually negligent is liable to the plaintiff.

Example Assume that the purchaser of a motorcycle is injured in an accident. The accident occurred because a screw was missing from the motorcycle. How does the buyer prove who was negligent? Was it the manufacturer, which left the screw out during the assembly of the motorcycle? Was it the retailer, who negligently failed to discover the missing screw while preparing the motorcycle for sale? Was it the mechanic, who failed to replace the screw after repairing the motorcycle? Negligence remains a viable, yet difficult, theory on which to base a product liability action.

Misrepresentation

A buyer or lessee who is injured because a seller or lessor fraudulently misrepresented the quality of a product can sue the seller for the tort of **intentional misrepresentation**,

---

product liability
The liability of manufacturers, sellers, and others for the injuries caused by defective products.

negligence
A tort related to defective products in which the defendant has breached a duty of due care and caused harm to the plaintiff.

An injustice anywhere is an injustice everywhere.

Samuel Johnson

intentional misrepresentation
A tort in which a seller or lessor fraudulently misrepresents the quality of a product and a buyer is injured thereby. Also known as *fraud*.

or **fraud**. Recovery is limited to persons who were injured because they relied on the misrepresentation.

Intentional misrepresentation occurs when a seller or lessor either (1) affirmatively misrepresents the quality of a product or (2) conceals a defect in it. Because most reputable manufacturers, sellers, and lessors do not intentionally misrepresent the quality of their products, fraud is not often used as the basis for product liability actions.

▶ STRICT LIABILITY

In the landmark case *Greenman v. Yuba Power Products, Inc.,*[1] the California Supreme court adopted the **doctrine of strict liability in tort** as a basis for product liability actions. Most states have now adopted this doctrine as a basis for product liability actions. The doctrine of strict liability removes many of the difficulties for the plaintiff associated with other theories of product liability. This section examines the scope of the strict liability doctrine.

Liability Without Fault

Unlike negligence, strict liability does not require the injured person to prove that the defendant breached a duty of care. **Strict liability** is **liability without fault**. A seller can be found strictly liable even though he or she has exercised all possible care in the preparation and sale of his or her product. Strict liability may not be disclaimed.

The doctrine of strict liability applies to sellers and lessors of products who are engaged in the business of selling and leasing products. Casual sales and transactions by nonmerchants are not covered. Thus, a person who sells a defective product to a neighbor in a casual sale is not strictly liable if the product causes injury.

Strict liability applies only to products, not services. In hybrid transactions that involve both services and products, the dominant element of the transaction dictates whether strict liability applies. For example, in a medical operation that requires a blood transfusion, the operation would be the dominant element, and strict liability would not apply. Strict liability may not be disclaimed.

strict liability
A tort doctrine that makes manufacturers, distributors, wholesalers, retailers, and others in the chain of distribution of a defective product liable for the damages caused by the defect, *irrespective of fault.*

All in the Chain of Distribution Are Liable

All parties in the **chain of distribution** of a defective product are strictly liable for the injuries caused by that product. Thus, all manufacturers, distributors, wholesalers, retailers, lessors, and subcomponent manufacturers may be sued under the doctrine of strict liability in tort. This view is based on public policy. Lawmakers presume that sellers and lessors will insure against the risk of a strict liability lawsuit and spread the cost to their consumers by raising the price of products.

chain of distribution
All manufacturers, distributors, wholesalers, retailers, lessors, and subcomponent manufacturers involved in a transaction.

Example Suppose a subcomponent manufacturer produces a defective tire and sells it to a truck manufacturer. The truck manufacturer places the defective tire on one of its new-model trucks. The truck is distributed by a distributor to a retail dealer. Ultimately, the retail dealer sells the truck to a buyer. The defective tire causes an accident in which the buyer is injured. All the parties in the tire's chain of distribution can be sued by the injured party; in this case, the liable parties are the subcomponent manufacturer, the truck manufacturer, the distributor, and the retailer.

Exhibit 6.1 compares the doctrines of negligence and strict liability.

A defendant who has not been negligent but who is made to pay a strict liability judgment can bring a separate action against the negligent party in the chain of distribution to recover its losses.

▶ **Exhibit 6.1 NEGLIGENCE AND STRICT LIABILITY COMPARED**

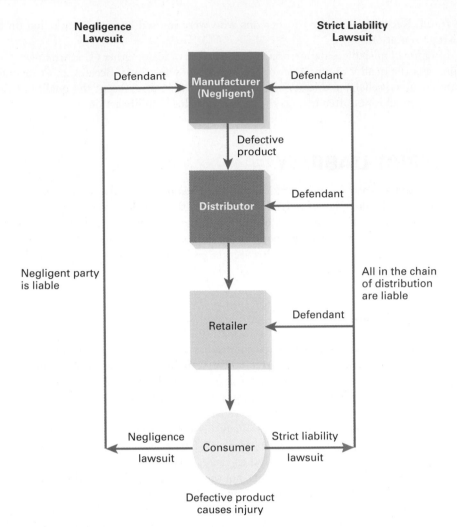

LANDMARK LAW

Restatement of Torts Definition of Strict Liability

Restatement (Second) of Torts

The most widely recognized articulation of the doctrine of strict liability in tort is found in *Section 402A* of the *Restatement (Second) of Torts*, which provides:

1. One who sells any product in a defective condition unreasonably dangerous to the user or consumer or to his property is subject to liability for physical harm thereby caused to the ultimate user or consumer, or to his property, if
   a. the seller is engaged in the business of selling such a product, and
   b. it is expected to and does reach the user or consumer without substantial change in the condition in which it is sold.
2. The rule stated in Subsection (1) applies although
   a. the seller has exercised all possible care in the preparation and sale of his product, and
   b. the user or consumer has not bought the product from or entered into any contractual relation with the seller.

Restatement (Third) of Torts

In 1997, the American Law Institute (ALI) adopted the *Restatement (Third) of Torts: Product Liability*. This new *Restatement* includes the following definition of *defect*:

A product is defective when, at the time of sale or distribution, it contains manufacturing defect, is defective in design, or is defective because of inadequate instructions or warnings.

A product:
a. contains a manufacturing defect when the product departs from its intended design even though all possible care was exercised in the preparation and marketing of the product;
b. is defective in design when the foreseeable risks of harm posed by the product could have been reduced or avoided by the adoption of a reasonable alternative design by the seller or other distributor, or a predecessor in the commercial chain of distribution, and the omission of the alternative design renders the product not reasonably safe;

c. is defective because of inadequate instructions or warnings when the foreseeable risks of harm posed by the product could have been reduced or avoided by the provision of reasonable instructions or warnings by the seller or other distributor, or a predecessor in the commercial chain of distribution, and the omission of the instructions or warnings renders the product not reasonably safe.

Parties Who Can Recover for Strict Liability

Because strict liability is a tort doctrine, *privity of contract* between the plaintiff and the defendant is not required. In other words, the doctrine applies even if the injured party had no contractual relations with the defendant. Thus, manufacturers, distributors, sellers, and lessors of a defective product are liable to the consumer who purchased the product and any user of the product. Users include the purchaser or lessee, family members, guests, employees, customers, and persons who passively enjoy the benefits of the product (e.g., passengers in automobiles).

The manufacturer, distributor, seller, and lessor of a defective product are also liable to third-party bystanders injured by the defective product. The courts have stated that bystanders who are injured by a defective product should be entitled to the same protection as a consumer or user. Bystanders and non-users do not even have the opportunity to inspect products for defects and to limit their purchases to articles manufactured by reputable manufacturers and sold by reputable retailers.

Nobody has a more sacred obligation to obey the law than those who make the law.

Sophocles

Damages Recoverable for Strict Liability

The damages recoverable in a strict liability action vary by jurisdiction. Damages for personal injuries are recoverable in all jurisdictions that have adopted the doctrine of strict liability, although some jurisdictions limit the dollar amount of the award. Property damage is recoverable in most jurisdictions, but economic loss (e.g., lost income) is recoverable in only a few jurisdictions.

Punitive damages, which are monetary damages awarded to punish the defendant, are generally allowed if the plaintiff can prove that the defendant either intentionally injured her or acted with reckless disregard for her safety.

▶ DEFECTIVE PRODUCT

To recover for strict liability, the injured party must first show that the product that caused the injury was somehow *defective*. (Remember that the injured party does not have to prove who caused the product to become defective.) Plaintiffs can allege multiple **product defects** in one lawsuit. A product can be found to be defective in many ways. The most common types of defects are:

- Defect in manufacture
- Defect in design
- Failure to warn
- Defect in packaging
- Failure to provide adequate instructions

These defects are discussed in the following paragraphs.

product defect
Something wrong, inadequate, or improper in the manufacture, design, packaging, warning, or instructions about a product.

▶ DEFECT IN MANUFACTURE

A **defect in manufacture** occurs when the manufacturer fails to (1) properly assemble a product, (2) properly test a product, or (3) adequately check the quality of a product.

defect in manufacture
A defect that occurs when a manufacturer fails to (1) properly assemble a product, (2) properly test a product, or (3) adequately check the quality of the product.

Example American Ladder Company designs, manufactures, and sells ladders. American Ladder Company manufactures a ladder, but a worker at the company fails to insert one of the screws that would support one of the steps of the ladder. The ladder is sold to Weingard Distributor, a wholesaler, which sells it to Reynolds Hardware Store, which sells the ladder to Heather, a consumer. When Heather is on the ladder painting her house, the step of the ladder breaks because of the missing screw, and Heather falls and is injured. The missing screw is an example of a defect in manufacture. Under the doctrine of strict liability, American Ladder Company, Weingard Distributor, and Reynolds Hardware Store are liable to Heather.

The following case is a classic example involving a defect in manufacture.

CASE 6.1 Defect in Manufacture

Shoshone Coca-Cola Bottling Company v. Dolinski

82 Nev. 439, 420 P.2d 855, Web 1966 Nev. Lexis 260 (1966) Supreme Court of Nevada

"In the case at hand, Shoshone contends that insufficient proof was offered to establish that the mouse was in the bottle of 'Squirt' when it left Shoshone's possession."

—Judge Thompson

Facts

Leo Dolinski purchased a bottle of Squirt, a soft drink, from a vending machine at a Sea and Ski plant, his place of employment. Dolinski opened the bottle and consumed part of its contents. He immediately became ill. Upon examination, it was found that the bottle contained the decomposed body of a mouse, mouse hair, and mouse feces. Dolinski visited a doctor and was given medicine to counteract nausea. Dolinski suffered physical and mental distress from consuming the decomposed mouse and thereafter possessed an aversion to soft drinks. The Shoshone Coca-Cola Bottling Company (Shoshone) had manufactured and distributed the Squirt bottle. Dolinski sued Shoshone, basing his lawsuit on the doctrine of strict liability. The state of Nevada had not previously recognized the doctrine of strict liability. However, the trial court adopted the doctrine of strict liability, and the jury returned a verdict in favor of the plaintiff. Shoshone appealed.

Issue

Should the state of Nevada judicially adopt the doctrine of strict liability? If so, was there a defect in the manufacture of the Squirt bottle that caused the plaintiff's injuries?

Language of the Court

In our view, public policy demands that one who places upon the market a bottled beverage in a condition dangerous for use must be held strictly liable to the ultimate user for injuries resulting from such use, although the seller has exercised all reasonable care.

Our acceptance of strict tort liability against the manufacturer and distributor of a bottled beverage does not mean that the plaintiff is relieved of the burden of proving a case. He must still establish that his injury was caused by a defect in the product and that such defect existed when the product left the hands of the defendant.

In the case at hand, Shoshone contends that insufficient proof was offered to establish that the mouse was in the bottle of "Squirt" when it left Shoshone's possession. The plaintiff offered the expert testimony of a toxicologist who examined the bottle and contents on the day the plaintiff drank from it. It was his opinion that the mouse "had been dead for a long time" and that the dark stains (mouse feces) that he found on the bottom of the bottle must have been there before the liquid was added. The jury apparently preferred the latter evidence that traced cause to the defendant.

Decision

The supreme court of Nevada adopted the doctrine of strict liability and held that the evidence supported the trial court's finding that there was a defect in manufacture. The supreme court affirmed the trial court's decision in favor of plaintiff Dolinski.

Case Questions

Critical Legal Thinking Describe the doctrine of strict liability. How does it differ from negligence? Explain.

Business Ethics Was it ethical for Shoshone to argue that it was not liable to Dolinski? Could this case have been "faked"?

Contemporary Business Should all parties in the chain of distribution of a defective product—even parties that are not responsible for the defect—be held liable under the doctrine of strict liability? Or should liability be based only on fault?

▶ DEFECT IN DESIGN

A **defect in design** can support a strict liability action. Design defects that have supported strict liability awards include toys that are designed with removable parts that could be swallowed by children, machines and appliances designed without proper safeguards, and trucks and other vehicles designed without warning devices to let people know that the vehicle is backing up. A defect in design occurs when a product is designed incorrectly. In this case, not just one item but all of the defectively designed products can cause injury.

In evaluating the adequacy of a product's design, the courts apply a risk–utility analysis. This requires the court to consider the gravity of the danger posed by the design, the likelihood that injury will occur, the availability and cost of producing a safer alternative design, the social utility of the product, and other factors.

In the following case, the courts had to decide whether there was a design defect.

defect in design
A defect that occurs when a product is improperly designed.

CASE 6.2 Design Defect

Higgins v. Intex Recreation Corporation
123 Wn.App. 821, 99 P.3d 421, Web 2004 Wash.App. Lexis 2424 (2004)
Court of Appeals of Washington

"Now, the ride down a snow-covered hill backward at 30 miles per hour may be a thrill. But it has very little social value when compared to the risk of severe injury."

—Judge Sweeney

Facts

Intex Recreation Corporation designed and sold the Extreme Sno-Tube II. This snow tube is ridden by a user down snow-covered hills and can reach speeds of 30 miles per hour. The snow tube has no steering device, and therefore a rider may end up spinning and going down a hill backward.

Dan Falkner bought an Extreme Sno-Tube II and used it sledding the same day. During Falkner's second run, the tube rotated him backward about one-quarter to one-third of the way down the hill. A group of parents, including Tom Higgins, stood near the bottom of the hill. Higgins saw seven-year-old Kyle Potter walking in the path of Falkner's speeding Sno-Tube. Higgins ran and grabbed Potter to save him from harm, but while he was doing so, the Sno-Tube hit Higgins and threw him into the air. Higgins landed on his forehead, which snapped his head back. The impact severed Higgins's spinal cord and left him quadriplegic.

Higgins sued Intex for damages based on strict liability. Evidence was introduced at trial that showed that the Sno-Tube could rotate while going downhill and that it had no guiding mechanism and no steering device. Evidence also showed that Intex made a Sno-Boggan that went just as fast but did not rotate because of ridges on the bottom of the device. The jury found a design defect in the Sno-Tube and held Intex liable for 35 percent of Higgins's damages.

Issue

Was the Extreme Sno-Tube II defectively designed, thus supporting the judgment against Intex?

Language of the Court

There are two tests for determining whether a product is defective. The risk–utility test requires a showing that the likelihood and seriousness of harm outweigh the burden on the manufacturer to design a product that would have prevented that harm and would not have impaired the product's usefulness. The consumer-expectation test requires a showing that the product is more dangerous than the ordinary consumer would expect. This test focuses on the reasonable expectation of the consumer.

A plaintiff can satisfy its burden of proving an alternative design by showing that another product more safely serves the same function as the challenged product. There is evidence in this record from which a jury could conclude that the placement of ribs or ridges on the bottom of the Sno-Tube, like those used on Intex's Sno-Boggan, would keep the rider from facing downhill. The rider could then see obstacles and direct the tube. All this could be done without sacrificing speed. This is enough to prove an alternative safer design. Now, the ride down a snow-covered hill backward at 30 miles per hour may be a thrill. But it has very little social value when compared to the risk of severe injury. We do not think the Sno-Tube is a product that is necessary regardless of the risks involved to the user. We find ample evidence to support this verdict, applying the risk–utility test.

We next take up Intex's assertion that the tube was not unsafe to an extent beyond that which would be

(case continues)

contemplated by the ordinary consumer. Again, we find ample evidence in this record to support the Higgins's assertion to the contrary. And a reasonable jury could easily infer that the average consumer may expect the Sno-Tube to rotate. But he or she might not expect that it would continue in a backward position. Here, the Sno-Tube is inexpensive. But so is Intex's Sno-Boggan. And the Sno-Boggan provides a fast ride but not a blind high-speed ride. A jury could then find that a reasonable consumer would expect that a snow sliding product would not put him or her in a backward, high-speed slide. We find ample evidence in favor of the plaintiffs applying the consumer-expectation test.

Decision

The court of appeals held that the Sno-Tube was defectively designed and affirmed the judgment in favor of Higgins against Intex.

Case Questions

Critical Legal Thinking What is a design defect? Explain.

Business Ethics Should Intex have placed a ridge on the bottom of the Sno-Tube or equipped it with a steering device to make it safer? Would you have found for or against Intex in this case? Why or why not?

Contemporary Business What does the risk–utility test require? What does the consumer-expectation test require? How do these two tests differ?

Crashworthiness Doctrine

crashworthiness doctrine
A doctrine that says automobile manufacturers are under a duty to design automobiles so they take into account the possibility of harm from a person's body striking something inside the automobile in the case of a car accident.

Often, when an automobile is involved in an accident, the driver or passengers are not injured by the blow itself. Instead, they are injured when their bodies strike something inside their own automobile (e.g., the dashboard, the steering wheel). This is commonly referred to as the "second collision." The courts have held that automobile manufacturers are under a duty to design automobiles to take into account the possibility of this second collision. This is called the **crashworthiness doctrine**. Failure to design an automobile to protect occupants from foreseeable dangers caused by a second collision subjects the manufacturer and dealer to strict liability.

▶ FAILURE TO WARN

failure to warn
A defect that occurs when a manufacturer does not place a warning on the packaging of products that could cause injury if the danger is unknown.

Certain products are inherently dangerous and cannot be made any safer and still accomplish the task for which they are designed. Many such products have risks and side effects caused by their use. Manufacturers and sellers owe a duty to warn consumers and users about the dangers of using these products. A proper and conspicuous warning placed on the product insulates the manufacturer and others in the chain of distribution from strict liability. **Failure to warn** of these dangerous propensities is a defect that will support a strict liability action.

Example The Universal Drug Corporation develops a new prescription drug that has tremendous success in preventing and treating a certain type of cancer. The drug, however, has a three percent probability of causing an increased risk of heart disease in patients who take the drug. The drug cannot be made any safer and still possess its cancer treatment effects. The Universal Drug Corporation owes a duty to warn potential users of its drug of these heart-related risks. If it failed to do so and a user suffered a heart attack because of using the drug, the Universal Drug Corporation would be held strictly liable for failure to warn.

In the following case, the court had to decide whether there was a failure to warn.

CASE 6.3 Failure to Warn

Bunch v. Hoffinger Industries, Inc.

123 Cal.App.4th 1278, 20 Cal.Rptr.3d 780, Web 2004 Cal.App. Lexis 1869 (2004)
Court of Appeal of California

"We find that the danger of diving into a shallow above-ground pool is not open and obvious to an 11 year old as a matter of law."

—Judge Raye

Facts

Joe and Loretta Frank, husband and wife, received a used frame for an aboveground swimming pool as a gift. The pool frame measured 33 feet long, 18 feet wide, and 4 feet deep. The Franks purchased a pool liner from McMasker Enterprises, Inc. (McMasker), a swimming pool supplier. Hoffinger Industries, Inc. (Hoffinger) manufactured the pool liner.

The Franks placed the pool in the yard of their house. Mr. Frank built a deck around the pool at the level of the pool frame and built a wooden bench on the deck next to the pool. Hoffinger did not place warning labels on their pool liners about the dangers of diving into the shallow pool. Instead, Hoffinger provided consumers with labels and instructions on how to place the labels on the pool liner. The warning label stated: "Caution—no diving—shallow water." The warning label was 0.75 inch wide and 5.25 inches long. The Franks testified that they affixed a warning label to the pool liner.

Leesa Bunch, 11 years old, and her brother Eric, 9 years old, were using the Franks' pool. Mrs. Frank told the children "not to dive" into the pool and went into the house. Leesa had watched the summer Olympics and tried to imitate the shallow racing dives of the Olympic swimmers. Leesa dove from the bench into the pool. Eric then saw Leesa curled up and floating in the pool, and he jumped in and dragged her to the edge of the pool. Leesa was rendered a quadriplegic by the dive.

Leesa Bunch sued McMasker and Hoffinger for strict liability for failure to adequately warn her of the danger of diving into the pool. Evidence at trial proved that during the past 17 years, there had been 47 prior incidents of persons becoming quadriplegic from diving into Hoffinger pools. McMasker settled with Leesa for $1 million. At trial, the jury found that Hoffinger had provided inadequate warnings of the dangers of diving into the pool and awarded Leesa $12,526,890 in damages plus costs. Hoffinger appealed.

Issue

Did Hoffinger adequately warn Leesa, an 11-year old girl, about the dangers of diving into a 4-foot-deep pool?

Language of the Court

We find that the danger of diving into a shallow above-ground pool is not open and obvious to an 11 year old as a matter of law. In the context of products liability actions, the plaintiff must prove that the defective products supplied by the defendant were a substantial factor in bringing about his or her injury. The court instructed that the jury must find "that the design of the warning system for the pool liner was a substantial factor in causing harm to the plaintiff." The court also instructed that the jury must find a "lack of sufficient warnings was a substantial factor in causing plaintiff's harm."

Bunch presented testimony by Ross Buck, Ph.D., a professor of communication sciences and psychology at the University of Connecticut. According to Buck, effective warnings "act as brakes to stop dangerous behaviors." Buck outlined the components of an effective persuasive warning: it must command attention, galvanize memory, evoke emotion, contain an explicit instruction, and show a consequence. This kind of warning is especially important for children under the age of 12. Dr. Buck testified that a young diver standing at the edge of an aboveground pool cannot necessarily judge the depth of the pool. Warnings act as "brakes to stop dangerous behaviors." Warnings to children between the ages of seven and 12 must be concrete and spell out the dangers and consequences of actions in order to be effective. Buck found the labels supplied with the Hoffinger pool liner neither adequate nor effective. The labels failed to spell out any consequences of diving into shallow water.

Dr. Johnson, another of Bunch's experts, testified that based on his experience and research, the risk of spinal paraplegia was not readily apparent to an 11 year old. Many people who dive into pools are unable to gauge the depth of the water. After reviewing the facts, Johnson opined that Bunch was attempting a shallow racing dive and was unaware of the possible consequences of that dive.

Given the testimony of Bunch and her two expert witnesses, we find sufficient evidence to support the conclusion

(case continues)

that the lack of an adequate warning label was neither a negligible nor theoretical contribution to Bunch's injury. The evidence presented at trial revealed that the lack of a persuasive label outlining the consequences of diving into the pool was a substantial factor in causing the injury.

Decision

The court of appeal of California affirmed the trial court's finding that Hoffinger failed to adequately warn Leesa of the dangers of diving into the four-foot-deep pool. The court of appeal upheld the monetary judgment in favor of Leesa against Hoffinger.

Case Questions

Critical Legal Thinking Describe the doctrine of defect by failure to warn.

Business Ethics Based upon the previous 47 cases in which users of Hoffinger pools were rendered quadriplegic, should the warning on the pool liner in this case have been stronger?

Contemporary Business After the judgment of the trial court was issued, Hoffinger filed for bankruptcy. What are the consequences to Leesa of Hoffinger's filing for bankruptcy?

▶ DEFECT IN PACKAGING

defect in packaging
A defect that occurs when a product has been placed in packaging that is insufficiently tamperproof.

Manufacturers owe a duty to design and provide safe packages for their products. This duty requires manufacturers to provide packages and containers that are tamperproof or that clearly indicate whether they have been tampered with. Certain manufacturers, such as drug manufacturers, owe a duty to place their products in containers that cannot be opened by children. A manufacturer's failure to meet this duty—a **defect in packaging**—subjects the manufacturer and others in the chain of distribution of the product to strict liability.

Food Counter *Should sellers of foods that are not packaged but are easily tampered with be held liable if a consumer is injured by eating such tainted food?*

▶ OTHER DEFECTS

failure to provide adequate instructions
A defect that occurs when a manufacturer does not provide detailed directions for safe assembly and use of a product.

Sellers are responsible to provide adequate instructions for the safe assembly and use of the products they sell. **Failure to provide adequate instructions** for the safe assembly and use of a product is a defect that subjects the manufacturer and others in the chain of distribution to strict liability.

Example Mother buys her four-year-old daughter Lia a tricycle manufactured by Bicycle Corporation. The tricycle comes in a box with many parts that need to be assembled. The instructions for assembly are vague and hard to follow. Mother puts together the tricycle, using these instructions. The first time that Lia uses the tricycle, the handlebar becomes loose, and Lia's tricycle goes into the street, where she is hit and injured by an automobile. In this case, Mother could sue Bicycle Corporation on behalf of Lia for strict liability to recover damages for failing to provide adequate instructions.

Other defects that support a finding of product liability based on strict liability include inadequate testing of products, inadequate selection of component parts or materials, and improper certification of the safety of a product. The concept of "defect" is an expanding area of the law.

▶ PUNITIVE DAMAGES

In product liability cases, a court can award **punitive damages** if it finds that the defendant's conduct was committed with intent or with reckless disregard for human life. Punitive damages are meant to punish the defendant and to send a message to the defendant (and other companies) that such behavior will not be tolerated.

punitive damages
Monetary damages that are awarded to punish a defendant who either intentionally or recklessly injured the plaintiff.

▶ DEFENSES TO PRODUCT LIABILITY

Defendants in strict liability or negligence actions may raise several defenses to the imposition of liability. These defenses are discussed in the paragraphs that follow.

Generally Known Dangers

Certain products are inherently dangerous and are known to the general population to be so. Sellers are not strictly liable for failing to warn of **generally known dangers**.

Example It is a known fact that guns shoot bullets. Manufacturers of guns do not have to place a warning on the barrel of a gun warning of this generally known danger.

generally known dangers
A defense that acknowledges that certain products are inherently dangerous and are known to the general population to be so.

Government Contractor Defense

Many defense and other contractors manufacture products (e.g., rockets, airplanes) to government specification. Most jurisdictions recognize a **government contractor defense** to product liability actions. To establish this defense, a government contractor must prove that (1) the precise specifications for the product were provided by the government, (2) the product conformed to those specifications, and (3) the contractor warned the government of any known defects or dangers of the product.

government contractor defense
A defense that says a contractor who was provided specifications by the government is not liable for any defect in the product that occurs as a result of those specifications.

Assumption of the Risk

Theoretically, the traditional doctrine of **assumption of the risk** is a defense to a product liability action. For this defense to apply, the defendant must prove that (1) the plaintiff knew and appreciated the risk and (2) the plaintiff voluntarily assumed the risk. In practice, the defense assumption of the risk is narrowly applied by the courts.

Misuse of the Product

Sometimes users are injured when they misuse a product. If a user brings a product liability action, the defendant-seller may be able to assert **misuse** as a defense. Whether the

misuse
A defense that relieves a seller of product liability if the user *abnormally* misused the product. Products must be designed to protect against *foreseeable* misuse.

defense is effective depends on whether the misuse was foreseeable. The seller is relieved of product liability if the plaintiff has **abnormally misused** the product—that is, if there has been an **unforeseeable misuse** of the product. However, the seller is liable if there has been a **foreseeable misuse** of the product. This reasoning is intended to provide an incentive for manufacturers to design and manufacture safer products.

Correction of a Product Defect

A manufacturer that produces a defective product and later discovers said defect must (1) notify purchasers and users of the defect and (2) **correct the defect**. Most manufacturers faced with this situation recall the defective product and either repair the defect or replace the product.

The seller must make reasonable efforts to notify purchasers and users of the defect and the procedure to correct it. Reasonable efforts normally consist of sending letters to known purchasers and users and placing notices in newspapers and magazines of general circulation. If a user ignores such notice and fails to have the defect corrected, the seller may raise this as a defense against further liability with respect to the defect. Many courts have held that reasonable notice is effective even against users who did not see the notice.

Supervening Event

supervening event or intervening event
An alteration or a modification of a product by a party in the chain of distribution that absolves all prior sellers from strict liability.

For a seller to be held strictly liable, the product it sells must reach the consumer or user "without substantial change" in its condition. Under the doctrine of **supervening event** or **intervening event**, the original seller is not liable if the product is materially altered or modified after it leaves the seller's possession and the alteration or modification causes an injury. A supervening or intervening event absolves all prior sellers in the chain of distribution from strict liability.

Example A manufacturer produces a safe piece of equipment. It sells the equipment to a distributor, which removes a safety guard from the equipment. The distributor sells it to a retailer, who sells it to a buyer. The buyer is injured because of the removal of the safety guard. The manufacturer can raise the defense of supervening event against the imposition of liability. However, the distributor and retailer are strictly liable for the buyer's injuries.

Statute of Limitation

statute of limitations
A statute that requires an injured person to bring an action within a certain number of years from the time that he or she was injured by a defective product.

Most states have **statutes of limitations** that require an injured person to bring an action within a certain number of years from the time that he or she was injured by a defective product. This limitation period varies from state to state. Failure to bring an action within the appropriate time relieves the defendant of liability.

In most jurisdictions, the statute of limitations does not begin to run until the plaintiff suffers an injury. This subjects sellers and lessors to exposure for an unspecified period of time because a defective product may not cause an injury for years, or even decades, after it was sold.

Statute of Repose

statute of repose
A statute that limits the seller's liability to a certain number of years from the date when the product was first sold.

Some states have enacted **statutes of repose**, which limit the seller's liability to a certain number of years from the date when the product was first sold. The period of repose varies from state to state.

CONCEPT SUMMARY

STATUTE OF LIMITATION AND STATUTE OF REPOSE

Statute	Begins to Run
Statute of limitations	When the plaintiff suffers injury
Statute of repose	When the product is first sold

Contributory Negligence and Comparative Fault

Sometimes a person who is injured by a defective product is negligent and contributes to his or her own injuries. The defense of **contributory negligence** bars an injured plaintiff from recovering from the defendant in a negligence action. However, this doctrine generally does not bar recovery in strict liability actions.

Many states have held that the doctrine of **comparative fault** applies to strict liability actions. Under this doctrine, a plaintiff who is contributorily negligent for his or her injuries is responsible for a *proportional share* of the damages. In other words, the damages are apportioned between the plaintiff and the defendant.

Examples An automobile manufacturer produces a car with a hidden defect, and a consumer purchases the car from an automobile dealer. The consumer is injured in an automobile accident in which the defect is found to be 75 percent responsible for the accident, and the consumer's reckless driving is found to be 25 percent responsible. The plaintiff suffers $1 million worth of injuries. Under the doctrine of *contributory negligence*, the plaintiff would recover nothing from the defendants. Under the doctrine of *comparative negligence*, the plaintiff would recover $750,000 from the defendants (75 percent of $1 million).

contributory negligence
A defense that says a person who is injured by a defective product but has been negligent and has contributed to his or her own injuries cannot recover from the defendant.

comparative fault
A doctrine that applies to strict liability actions that says a plaintiff who is contributorily negligent for his or her injuries is responsible for a proportional share of the damages.

CONCEPT SUMMARY
CONTRIBUTORY NEGLIGENCE AND COMPARATIVE FAULT

Doctrine	Description
Contributory negligence	A person who is partially responsible for causing his or her own injuries may not recover anything from the manufacturer or seller of a defective product.
Comparative fault	A person who is partially responsible for causing his or her own injuries is responsible for a proportional share of the damages. The manufacturer or seller of the defective product is responsible for the remainder of the plaintiff's damages.

South Korean Currency
Many countries have developed laws that permit lawsuits based on product defects. The Republic of Korea has enacted the Product Liability Act (PLA), which imposes strict liability on all parties along the chain of manufacture of a defective product, which would include the manufacturer of the product, an assembling manufacturer, and a manufacturer of defective component parts. Distributors, wholesalers, and the retailers that distribute defective products can be held liable if the manufacturer of the defective product cannot be found. Strict liability is imposed on importers of defective products.

TEST REVIEW TERMS AND CONCEPTS

Abnormal misuse
(unforeseeable misuse)
Assumption of the risk
Chain of distribution
Comparative fault
Contributory negligence
Correction of a product
defect
Crashworthiness doctrine

Defect in design
Defect in manufacture
Defect in packaging
Doctrine of strict liability in
tort
Failure to provide adequate
instructions
Failure to warn
Foreseeable misuse

Generally known dangers
*Greenman v. Yuba Power
Products, Inc.*
Government contractor
defense
Intentional
misrepresentation (fraud)
Intervening event
Misuse of the product

Negligence
Product defect
Product liability
Punitive damages
Statute of limitations
Statute of repose
Strict liability (liability
without fault)
Supervening event

CASE PROBLEMS

6.1 Strict Liability Jeppesen and Company produces charts that graphically display approach procedures for airplanes landing at airports. These charts are drafted from tabular data supplied by the Federal Aviation Administration (FAA), a federal agency of the U.S. government. By law, Jeppesen cannot construct charts that include information different from that supplied by the FAA. One day, the pilot of an airplane owned by World Airways was on descent to land at the Cold Bay, Alaska, airport. The pilot was using an instrument approach procedure chart published by Jeppesen. The airplane crashed into a mountain near Cold Bay, killing all six crew members and destroying the aircraft. Evidence showed that the FAA data did not include the mountain. The heirs of the deceased crew members and World Airways brought a strict liability action against Jeppesen. Does the doctrine of strict liability apply to this case? Is Jeppesen liable? *Brocklesby v. Jeppesen and Company*, 767 F.2d 1288, **Web** 1985 U.S. App. Lexis 21290 (United States Court of Appeals for the Ninth Circuit)

6.2 Failure to Warn The Emerson Electric Co. manufactures and sells a product called the Weed Eater XR-90. The Weed Eater is a multipurpose weed-trimming and brush-cutting device. It consists of a handheld gasoline-powered engine connected to a long drive shaft, at the end of which can be attached various tools for cutting weeds and brush. One such attachment is a 10-inch circular saw blade capable of cutting through growth up to 2 inches in diameter. When this saw blade is attached to the Weed Eater, approximately 270 degrees of blade edge are exposed when in use. The owner's manual contained the following warning: "Keep children away. All people and pets should be kept at a safe distance from the work area, at least 30 feet, especially when using the blade." Donald Pearce, a 13-year-old boy, was helping his uncle clear an overgrown yard. The uncle was operating a Weed Eater XR-90 with the circular saw blade attachment. When Pearce stooped to pick up something off the ground about 6 to 10 feet behind and slightly to the left of where his uncle was operating the Weed Eater, the saw blade on the Weed Eater struck something near the ground. The Weed Eater kicked back to the left and cut off Pearce's right

arm to the elbow. Pearce, through his mother, Charlotte Karns, sued Emerson to recover damages under strict liability. Is Emerson liable? *Karns v. Emerson Electric Co.*, 817 F.2d 1452, **Web** 1987 U.S. App. Lexis 5608 (United States Court of Appeals for the Tenth Circuit)

6.3 Crashworthiness Doctrine One night Verne Prior, while driving on U.S. 101 under the influence of alcohol and drugs at speeds of 65 to 85 miles per hour, crashed his automobile into the left rear of a Chevrolet station wagon stopped on the shoulder of the freeway because of a flat tire. Christine Smith was sitting in the passenger seat of the parked car when the accident occurred. In the crash, the Chevrolet station wagon was knocked into a gully, where its fuel tank ruptured. The vehicle caught fire, and Smith suffered severe burn injuries. The Chevrolet station wagon was manufactured by General Motors Corporation. Evidence showed that the fuel tank was located in a vulnerable position in the back of the station wagon, outside the crossbars of the frame. Evidence further showed that if the fuel tank had been located underneath the body of the station wagon, between the crossbars of the frame, it would have been well protected in the collision. Smith sued General Motors for strict liability. Is the Chevrolet station wagon a defective product? *Smith v. General Motors Corporation*, 42 Cal.App.3d 1, 116 Cal.Rptr. 575, **Web** 1974 Cal.App. Lexis 1199 (Court of Appeal of California)

6.4 Failure to Warn Virginia Burke purchased a bottle of "Le Domaine" champagne that was manufactured by Almaden Vineyards, Inc. At home, she removed the wine seal from the top of the bottle but did not remove the plastic cork. She set the bottle on the counter, intending to serve it in a few minutes. Shortly thereafter, the plastic cork spontaneously ejected from the bottle, ricocheted off the wall, and struck Burke in the left lens of her eyeglasses, shattering the lens and driving pieces of glass into her eye. The champagne bottle did not contain any warning of this danger. Evidence showed that Almaden had previously been notified of the spontaneous ejection of the cork from its champagne bottles. Burke sued Almaden to recover damages for strict liability. Is Almaden liable? *Burke v. Almaden Vineyards, Inc.*, 86 Cal.App.3d 768,

150 Cal.Rptr. 419, **Web** 1978 Cal.App. Lexis 2123 (Court of Appeal of California)

6.5 Assumption of Risk   Lillian Horn was driving her Chevrolet station wagon, which was designed and manufactured by General Motors Corporation, down Laurel Canyon Boulevard in Los Angeles, California. Horn swerved to avoid a collision when a car coming toward her crossed the center line and was coming at her. In doing so, her hand knocked the horn cap off the steering wheel, which exposed the area underneath the horn cap, including three sharp prongs that had held the horn cap to the steering wheel. A few seconds later, when her car hit an embankment, Horn's face was impaled on the three sharp exposed prongs, causing her severe facial injuries. Horn sued General Motors for strict liability. General Motors asserted the defense of assumption of the risk against Horn. Who wins? *Horn v. General Motors Corporation*, 17 Cal.3d 359, 551 P.2d 398, 131 Cal.Rptr. 78, **Web** 1976 Cal. Lexis 283 (Supreme Court of California)

6.6 Misuse   The Wilcox-Crittendon Company manufactured harnesses, saddles, bridles, leads, and other items commonly used for horses, cattle, and other ranch and farm animals. One such item was a stallion or cattle tie, a five-inch-long iron hook with a one-inch ring at one end. The tongue on the ring opened outward to allow the hook to be attached to a rope or another object. A purchasing agent for United Airlines, who was familiar with this type of hook because of his previous experience on a farm, purchased one of these hooks from Keystone Brothers, a harness and saddlery wares outlet located in San Francisco, California. Four years later Edward Dosier, an employee of United Airlines, was working to install a new grinding machine at a United Airlines maintenance plant. As part of the installation process, Dosier attached the hook to a 1,700-pound counterweight and raised the counterweight into the air. While the counterweight was suspended in the air, Dosier reached under the counterweight to retrieve a missing bolt. The hook broke, and the counterweight fell and crushed Dosier's arm. Dosier sued Wilcox-Crittendon for strict liability. Who wins? *Dosier v. Wilcox-Crittendon Company*, 45 Cal.App.3d. 74, 119 Cal.Rptr. 135, **Web** 1975 Cal.App. Lexis 1665 (Court of Appeal of California).

BUSINESS ETHICS CASE

6.7 Business Ethics   Celestino Luque lived with his cousins Harry and Laura Dunn in Millbrae, California. The Dunns purchased a rotary lawn mower from Rhoads Hardware. The lawn mower was manufactured by Air Capital Manufacturing Company and was distributed by Garehime Corporation. Neighbors asked Luque to mow their lawn. While Luque was cutting the lawn, he noticed a small carton in the path of the lawn mower. Luque left the lawn mower in a stationary position with its motor running and walked around the side of the lawn mower to remove the carton. As he did so, he slipped on the wet grass and fell backward. Luque's left hand entered the unguarded hole of the lawn mower and was caught in its revolving blade, which turns at 175 miles per hour and 100 revolutions per second. Luque's hand was severely mangled and lacerated. The word *Caution* was printed above the unguarded hole on the lawn mower. Luque sued Rhoads Hardware, Air Capital, and Garehime Corporation for strict liability. The defendants argued that strict liability does not apply to *patent* (obvious) defects. Was it ethical for the defendants to argue that they were not liable for patent defects? Would patent defects ever be corrected if the defendants' contention was accepted by the court? Who wins? *Luque v. McLean, Trustee*, 8 Cal.3d 136, 501 P.2d 1163, 104 Cal.Rptr. 443, **Web** 1972 Cal. Lexis 245 (Supreme Court of California)

ENDNOTE

1. 59 Cal.2d 57, 377 P.2d 897, 27 Cal.Rptr. 697, Web 1963 Cal. Lexis 140 (Supreme Court of California). For the complete opinion of this case, go to www.prenhall.com/cheeseman/.

INTELLECTUAL PROPERTY AND CYBER PIRACY

▲ **Children's Books in French and German** *Companies of the United States and other countries conduct business internationally. Intellectual property rights—which include trade secrets, patents, copyrights, trademarks, and information technology—have significant value and require protection worldwide. The United States, India, and other counties have signed international treaties providing for the protection of intellectual property rights.*

CHAPTER OBJECTIVES

After studying this chapter, you should be able to:

1. Describe the business tort of misappropriating a trade secret.
2. Describe how an invention can be patented under federal patent laws and the penalties for patent infringement.
3. List the items that can be copyrighted and describe the penalties of copyright infringement.
4. Define *trademarks* and *service marks* and describe the penalties for trademark infringement.
5. Define *cyber piracy* and describe the penalties for engaging in cyber infringement of intellectual property rights.

CHAPTER CONTENTS

"The Congress shall have the power . . . to promote the Progress of Science and useful Arts, by securing for limited Times to Authors and Inventors the exclusive Right to their respective Writings and Discoveries."
Article 1, Section 8, Clause 8 of the U.S. Constitution

▶ INTRODUCTION TO INTELLECTUAL PROPERTY AND CYBER PIRACY

The U.S. economy is based on the freedom of ownership of property. In addition to real estate and personal property, **intellectual property rights** have value to both businesses and individuals. This is particularly the case in the modern era of the Information Age, computers, and the Internet.

Trade secrets form the basis of many successful businesses, and they are protected from misappropriation. State law imposes civil damages and criminal penalties against persons who **misappropriate trade secrets**. Federal law provides protections for intellectual property rights, such as patents, copyrights, and trademarks. Certain federal statutes provide for either civil damages or criminal penalties, or both, to be assessed against infringers of patents, copyrights, and trademarks.

This chapter discusses trade secrets, patents, copyrights and trademarks and protecting them from infringement, misappropriation and cyber piracy.

intellectual property rights
Patents, copyrights, trademarks, and trade secrets. Federal and state laws protect intellectual property rights from misappropriation and infringement.

▶ TRADE SECRET

Many businesses are successful because their **trade secrets** set them apart from their competitors. Trade secrets may be product formulas, patterns, designs, and compilations of data, customer lists, or other business secrets. Many trade secrets do not qualify to be—or simply are not—patented, copyrighted, or trademarked. Many states have adopted the **Uniform Trade Secrets Act** to give statutory protection to trade secrets.

State unfair competition laws allow the owner of a trade secret to bring a lawsuit for *misappropriation* against anyone who steals a trade secret. For the lawsuit to be actionable, the defendant (often an employee of the owner or a competitor) must have obtained the trade secret through unlawful means, such as theft, bribery, or industrial espionage. No tort has occurred if there is no misappropriation.

The owner of a trade secret is obliged to take all reasonable precautions to prevent that secret from being discovered by others. If the owner fails to take such actions, the secret is no longer subject to protection under state unfair competition laws. Precautions to protect a trade secret may include fencing in buildings, placing locks on doors, hiring security guards, and the like.

A competitor can lawfully discover a trade secret by performing **reverse engineering** (i.e., taking apart and examining a rival's product or re-creating a secret recipe). The competitor who has reversed engineered the previous trade secret can use the trade secret but not the trademarked name used by the original creator for the trade secret.

trade secret
A product formula, pattern, design, compilation of data, customer list, or other business secret.

Everything that can be invented has been invented.

Charles H. Duell

Civil Trade Secret Law: Misappropriation of a Trade Secret

The owner of a trade secret can bring a **civil lawsuit** under state law against anyone who has obtained the trade secret through unlawful means, such as theft, bribery, or industrial espionage. Generally, a successful plaintiff in a trade secret action can (1) recover the *profits* made by the offender from the use of the trade secret, (2) recover for *damages*, and (3) obtain an *injunction* prohibiting the offender from divulging or using the trade secret.

Criminal Trade Secret Law: Economic Espionage Act of 1996

Congress enacted the federal **Economic Espionage Act** of 1996,[1] which makes it a **federal crime** to steal another's trade secrets. Under the Espionage Act, it is a federal crime for any person to convert a trade secret to his or her benefit or for the benefit of others, knowing or intending that the act would cause injury to the owner of the trade secret. The definition of *trade secret* under the Espionage Act is very broad and parallels the definition used under the civil laws of misappropriating a trade secret.

One of the major reasons for the passage of the Espionage Act was to address the ease of stealing trade secrets through computer espionage and using the Internet. The Espionage Act is a very important weapon in addressing computer and Internet espionage and penalizing those who commit it.

The Espionage Act provides for severe criminal penalties. The act imposes prison terms on individuals of up to 15 years per criminal violation. An organization can be fined up to $10 million per criminal act. The criminal prison term for individuals and the criminal fine for organizations can be increased if the theft of a trade secret was made to benefit a foreign government.

ETHICS SPOTLIGHT

Coca-Cola Employee Tries to Sell Trade Secret to Pepsi-Cola

"What if you knew the markets they [Coca-Cola] were going to move into and out of . . . and beat them to the punch."

—Letter to PepsiCo

In February 2007, former Coca-Cola secretary Joya Williams was convicted by a federal jury of conspiring to steal trade secrets and attempting to sell them to archrival PepsiCo for $1.5 million. Along with Williams, two other co-conspirators were arrested and pled guilty.

Federal prosecutors asserted that Williams was in deep debt, unhappy with her job, and seeking a big payday. She was fired as a secretary in Coca-Cola's global branding department when the initial allegations came to light. Two of the more damaging pieces of evidence the jury considered were a letter written by a co-conspirator to PepsiCo, trying to sell the stolen items and FBI surveillance videotape of Williams smuggling out secret documents.

The conspiracy was initially foiled when rival PepsiCo produced a letter sent to them by one of the co-conspirators that offered Coca-Cola trade secrets to the highest bidder. "What if you knew the markets they [Coca-Cola] were going to move into and out of . . . and beat them to the punch," the letter stated. PepsiCo notified Coca-Cola officials and federal authorities, who initiated an FBI investigation into the matter.

During trial, prosecutors produced videotape of Williams putting confidential documents into her bag as well as samples of Coke products that were still in development. According to Court records, the stolen materials included details of an upcoming Coke product code-named Project Lancelot. Coke's 120-year-old "secret formula" recipe was not involved.

After the members of the jury initially instructed the Court that they were deadlocked, U.S. District Judge J. Owen Forrester ordered them to try again, and they returned with the guilty verdict. Referring to several witnesses that testified on Williams's behalf that she did not pose a risk to society, Judge Forrester said, "We never really know people." The judge sentenced Williams to eight years in jail. In handing down the decision, the judge stated, "This is the kind of offense that cannot be tolerated in our society."

The U.S. Court of Appeals upheld the decision. The Court stated that the sentence was justified based on the harm that Coca-Cola could have suffered if Williams and her co-conspirators had succeeded in selling its trade secrets to a rival and the danger to the U.S. economy these crimes pose. *United States v. Williams*, **Web** 2008 U.S. App. Lexis 6073 (United States Court of Appeals for the Eleventh Circuit, 2008)

Business Ethics   Did Williams act loyally in this case? Did PepsiCo engage in ethical conduct in this case? What was the probability that PepsiCo would have paid Williams and her co-conspirators the money they demanded? Explain.

▶ PATENT

When drafting the Constitution of the United States of America, the founders of the United States provided for protection of the work of inventors and writers. Article I, Section 8 of the Constitution provides, "The Congress shall have Power . . . To promote the Progress of Science and useful Arts, by securing for limited Times to Authors and Inventors the exclusive Right to their respective Writings and Discoveries."

Federal Patent Statute

Pursuant to the express authority granted in the U.S. Constitution, Congress enacted the **Federal Patent Statute** of 1952 to provide for obtaining and protecting **patents**.[2] This law is intended to provide an incentive for inventors to invent and make their inventions public and to protect patented inventions from infringement. Federal patent law is exclusive; there are no state patent laws. Applications for patents must be filed with the **United States Patent and Trademark Office (PTO)** in Washington, DC.

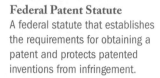

Federal Patent Statute
A federal statute that establishes the requirements for obtaining a patent and protects patented inventions from infringement.

U.S. Court of Appeals for the Federal Circuit

The **U.S. Court of Appeals for the Federal Circuit** in Washington, DC, was created in 1982. This is a special federal appeals court that hears patent appeals from federal courts concerning patent issues. This Court was created to promote uniformity in patent law.

Patent Period

In 1995, in order to bring the U.S. patent system into harmony with the patent systems of the majority of other developed nations, Congress made the following important changes in U.S. patent law:

• Patents for inventions are valid for *20 years* (instead of the previous term of 17 years). Design patents are valid for 14 years.
• The patent term begins to run from the date the patent application is *filed* (instead of when the patent is issued, as was previously the case).

The United States still follows the *first-to-invent rule* rather than the *first-to-file rule* followed by some other countries. Thus, in the United States, the first person to invent an item or a process is given patent protection over another party who was first to file a patent application.

After the patent period runs out, the invention or design enters the *public domain*, which means that anyone can produce and sell the invention without paying the prior patent holder.

Patent Application

A **patent application** must contain a written description of the invention and be filed with the PTO in Washington, DC. Patent applications are complicated. An inventor should hire a patent attorney to assist in obtaining a patent for an invention. If a patent is granted, the invention is assigned a **patent number**. Patent holders usually affix the word *patent* or *pat.* and the patent number to the patented article. If a patent application is filed but a patent has not yet been issued, the applicant usually places the words **patent pending** on the article. Any party can challenge either the issuance of a patent or the validity of an existing patent.

Only certain subject matter can be patented. Federal patent law recognizes categories of innovation that can be patented. These include:

- Machines
- Processes
- Compositions of matter
- Improvements to existing machines, processes, or compositions of matter
- Designs for an article of manufacture
- Asexually reproduced plants
- Living material invented by a person.

Abstractions and scientific principles cannot be patented unless they are part of the tangible environment.

Example Einstein's Theory of Relativity ($E = mc^2$) cannot be patented.

For centuries, most patents involved tangible inventions and machines, such as the telephone and the light bulb. Next, chemical and polymer inventions were patented. Then biotechnology patents were granted. Now, business methods involving the computer, Internet, and e-commerce have been added to what can be patented.

Requirements for Obtaining a Patent

To be patented, an invention must be (1) *novel, (2) useful*, and (3) *non-obvious*. To be patented, an invention must meet all three of these requirements. If an invention is found to not meet any one of these requirements, it cannot be patented:

1. **Novel.**   An invention is **novel** if it is new and has not been invented and used in the past. If the invention has been used in "prior art," it is not novel and cannot be patented.
2. **Useful.**   An invention is **useful** if it has some practical purpose. If an invention has only theoretical benefit, and no useful purpose, it cannot be patented.
3. **Non-obvious.**   If an invention is **non-obvious**, it qualifies for a patent; if it is obvious, then it does not qualify for a patent.

One-Year "On Sale" Doctrine

Under the **one-year "on sale" doctrine**, also called the **public use doctrine**, a patent may not be granted if the invention was used by the public for more than one year prior to the filing of a patent application. This doctrine forces inventors to file their patent applications at the proper time.

Example Suppose Cindy invents a new invention on January 10, 2010. She allows the public to use this invention and does not file a patent application until February 10, 2011. Thus, Cindy has lost the right to patent her invention because she has waited over

The patent system added the fuel of interest to the fire of genius.

Abraham Lincoln
*Lectures on Discoveries, Inventions, and Improvements
(1859)*

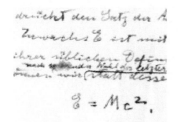

Einstein's Notes on the Theory of Relativity

one-year "on sale" doctrine
A doctrine that says a patent may not be granted if the invention was used by the public for more than one year prior to the filing of the patent application.

one year after her product has been used by the public before attempting to patent her invention.

The American Inventors Protection Act

In 1999, Congress enacted the **American Inventors Protection Act**. This statute does the following:

1. Permits an inventor to file a **provisional application** with the PTO, pending the preparation and filing of a final and complete patent application. This part of the law grants "provisional rights" to an inventor for three months, pending the filing of a final application.
2. Requires the PTO to issue a patent within three years after the filing of a patent application, unless the applicant engages in dilatory activities.
3. Provides that non–patent holders may challenge a patent as being overly broad by requesting a contested reexamination of the patent application by the PTO. This provides that the reexamination will be within the confines of the PTO; the decision of the PTO can be appealed to the U.S. Court of Appeals for the Federal Circuit in Washington, DC.

American Inventors Protection Act
A federal statute that permits an inventor to file a *provisional application* with the U.S. Patent and Trademark Office three months before the filing of a final patent application, among other provisions.

INTERNET LAW & ONLINE COMMERCE
Patenting Internet and E-Commerce Business Method Models

We know that patents can be obtained for mechanical, scientific, and chemical innovations. However, the U.S. Court of Appeals for the Federal Circuit has recently held that patents may also be obtained for business plans and models. The case that heralded this change is **State Street Bank & Trust Co. v. Signature Financial Group, Inc.** The facts were as follows: Signature Financial Group, Inc. (Signature), filed for and was granted a patent for a computerized accounting system that determines share prices through a series of mathematical calculations and is then used to manage mutual funds (U.S. Patent No. 5193056).

State Street Bank, another financial institution that wanted to offer a similar mutual fund investment program to clients, sued to have Signature's patent declared invalid. Signature defended, arguing that its intangible financial business model was a "process" that was protected under federal patent law. The U.S. Court of Appeals for the Federal Circuit, to which patent appeals are brought, upheld the patent as a "practical application of a mathematical algorithm, formula, or calculation, because it produces a useful, concrete and tangible result." Thus, a patent may be obtained for a business method as long as it produces a useful, concrete, and tangible result. The business method must also meet the same tests as any other invention—that is, it needs to be novel, useful, and non-obvious.

Taking the lead from the *State Street* case, many persons and businesses have and are filing for patents with the U.S. Patent and Trademark Office (PTO) for business method models. Most of the business method patents sought have been in the fields of the Internet and e-commerce. Methods of doing business that involve the use of a computer, such as data processing involving finance, accounting, electronic shopping, inventory management, business practice, and management areas, qualify for business method patents. Because this is such a new area of the law, the PTO is experiencing delays in processing most business method patents.

The granting of business model patents reflects the evolution in patent law into the Information Age. *State Street Bank & Trust Co. v. Signature Financial Group, Inc.*, 149 F.3d 1368, **Web** 1998 U.S. App. Lexis 16869 (United States Court of Appeals for the Federal Circuit)

Patent Infringement

Patent holders own exclusive rights to use and exploit their patents. **Patent infringement** occurs when someone makes unauthorized use of another's patent. In a suit for patent infringement, a successful plaintiff can recover (1) money damages equal to a reasonable royalty rate on the sale of the infringed articles, (2) other damages caused by the infringement (e.g., loss of customers), (3) an order requiring the destruction of the infringing article, and (4) an injunction preventing the infringer from such action in the future. The Court has the discretion to award up to treble damages if the infringement was intentional.

patent infringement
Unauthorized use of another's patent. A patent holder may recover damages and other remedies against a patent infringer.

ETHICS SPOTLIGHT

Patent Infringement: Inventor Wipes Windshields Clean

Robert Kearns, a professor at Wayne State University in Detroit, Michigan, patented his design for the electronic intermittent-speed windshield wiper for automobiles and other vehicles. He peddled his invention around to many automobile manufacturers but never reached a licensing deal with any of them. Two years later, automobile manufacturers began producing cars using Kearns's intermittent-speed windshield wiper invention. Virtually all cars sold in the United States today now have these wipers as standard equipment. Kearns filed patent infringement lawsuits against virtually all automobile manufacturers.

The Ford case went to trial first. Ford alleged that Kearns's patents were not valid because of obviousness and prior art. The Court disagreed with Ford, finding that the intermittent-speed windshield wipers were not obvious and did not appear in the prior art. The Court held that Kearns's patents were valid and that Ford had engaged in patent infringement. Ford settled by paying Kearns $10.2 million and agreeing to drop all appeals. This represented 50¢ per Ford vehicle that used the wiper system.

In the Chrysler case, Kearns fired his lawyers and represented himself. Kearns won a second victory: The jury found that Chrysler had infringed Kearns's patents and awarded him $11.3 million. Kearns received over $21 million from Chrysler, which amounted to 90¢ for every vehicle sold by Chrysler with the wiper system.

Over the next two years, the Court dismissed Kearns's lawsuits against 23 other automobile manufacturers, including General Motors, Porsche, Nissan, Toyota, and Honda because Kearns failed to comply with Court orders to disclose documents. This ended Kearns's legal battle with the automobile industry.

Business Ethics Did the automobile manufacturers act ethically by using Kearns's invention without paying him? Do you think that intermittent-speed windshield wipers were obvious or non-obvious? Explain. *Kearns v. Chrysler Corporation*, 32 F.3d 1541, **Web** 1994 U.S. App. Lexis 21272 (United States Court of Appeals for the Federal Circuit)

► COPYRIGHT

Copyright Revision Act

A federal statute that (1) establishes the requirements for obtaining a copyright and (2) protects copyrighted works from infringement.

Article I, Section 8 of the Constitution of the United States of America authorizes Congress to enact statutes to protect the works of writers for limited times.

Pursuant to this authority, Congress has enacted **copyright** laws. The **Copyright Revision Act** of 1976 currently governs copyright law.[3] The act establishes the requirements for obtaining a copyright and protects copyrighted works from infringement. Federal copyright law is exclusive; there are no state copyright laws. Federal copyright law protects the work of authors and other creative persons from the unauthorized use of their copyrighted materials and provides a financial incentive for authors to write, thereby increasing the number of creative works available in society.

Only **tangible writings**—writings that can be physically seen—are subject to copyright registration and protection. The term *writing* has been broadly defined.

Examples Books, periodicals, and newspapers; lectures, sermons, addresses, and poems; musical compositions; plays, motion pictures, and radio and television productions;

maps; works of art, including paintings, drawings, sculpture, jewelry, glassware, tapestry, and lithographs; architectural drawings and models, photographs, including prints, slides, and filmstrips, greeting cards, and picture postcards; photoplays, including feature films, cartoons, newsreels, travelogues, and training films; and sound recordings published in the form of tapes, cassettes, compact discs, and MP3 files qualify for copyright protection.

Exhibit 7.1 shows a copyrighted poem.

> Like oceans, we have spent
> this time together before.
> In galley slave pits you fed me
> water and removed my slivers.
> Riding Ch'u dynasty chariots
> we perished on Mongol swords.
> We toiled rocks in chains
> and built Stonehenge,
> drank with King Arthur
> and danced with Black Elk.
> We fled, hand-in-hand, dodging
> Hitler's bullets, and
> I carried you over the border
> to have our baby in freedom.
> During past full moons, the sun set
> the seas in orbit
> and as driftwood we tumbled
> onto the shores of Los Angeles.
> Another life together, my love?
>
> Henry Cheeseman

▶ **Exhibit 7.1**
COPYRIGHTED POEM

Registration of Copyrights

To be protected under federal copyright law, a work must be the original work of the author. A copyright is created when an author produces his or her work. For example, when a student writes a term paper for his class, he owns a copyright to his work.

Published and unpublished works may be registered with the **United States Copyright Office** in Washington, DC. **Registration of a copyright** is permissive and voluntary and can be affected at any time during the term of the copyright.

In 1989, the United States signed the **Berne Convention**, an international copyright treaty. This law eliminated the need to place the symbol © or the word *copyright* or *copr.* on a copyrighted work.

The **Sonny Bono Copyright Term Extension Act** of 1998 extended copyright protection to the following:

1. Individuals are granted copyright protection for their life plus 70 years.
2. Copyrights owned by businesses are protected for the shorter of either:
   a. 95 years from the year of first publication
   b. 120 years from the year of creation

After the copyright period runs out, the work enters the **public domain**, which means that anyone can publish the work without paying the prior copyright holder.

CONCEPT SUMMARY
COPYRIGHT PERIOD

Type of Holder	Copyright Period
Individual	Life of the author plus 70 years beyond the author's life
Business	The shorter of either 95 years from the year of first publication or 120 years from the year of creation

The law in respect to literature ought to remain upon the same footing as that which regards the profits of mechanical inventions and chemical discoveries.

William Wordsworth
Letter (1838)

copyright infringement
An infringement that occurs when a party copies a substantial and material part of a plaintiff's copyrighted work without permission. A copyright holder may recover damages and other remedies against the infringer.

Copyright Infringement

Copyright infringement occurs when a party copies a substantial and material part of the plaintiff's copyrighted work without permission. The copying does not have to be either word for word or the entire work. A plaintiff can bring a civil action against the alleged infringer and, if successful, recover (1) the profit made by the defendant from the copyright infringement, (2) damages suffered by the plaintiff, (3) an order requiring the impoundment and destruction of the infringing works, and (4) an injunction preventing the defendant from infringing in the future. The Court, in its discretion, can award statutory damages for willful infringement in lieu of actual damages.

The following case involves peer-to-peer software file-sharing of music.

CASE 7.1 Copyright Infringement and Internet File-Sharing of Music
BMG Music v. Gonzalez
430 F.3d 888, Web 2005 U.S. App. Lexis 26903 (2005)
United States Court of Appeals for the Seventh Circuit

"Nor can she defend by observing that other persons were greater offenders; Gonzalez's theme that she obtained 'only 30' (or 'only 1,300') copyrighted songs is no more relevant than a thief's contention that he shoplifted 'only 30' compact discs, planning to listen to them at home and pay later for any he liked."

—Judge Easterbrook

Facts
Cecilia Gonzalez downloaded 1,370 copyrighted songs on her computer using the Kazaa file-sharing network during a few weeks, and she kept them on her computer until she was caught. BMG Music sued Gonzalez for copyright infringement of 30 of these songs. Gonzalez defended, arguing that her downloading of these copyrighted songs was lawful. The U.S. District Court granted summary judgment in favor of BMG Music, assessed $22,500 in damages against Gonzalez, and issued an injunction against Gonzalez, enjoining her from further copyright infringement. Gonzalez appealed.

Issue
Did Gonzalez engage in copyright infringement?

Language of the Court
Gonzalez's position is that she was just sampling music to determine what she liked enough to buy at retail. Instead of erasing songs that she decided not to buy, she retained them. A copy downloaded, played, and retained on one's hard drive for future use is a direct substitute for a purchased copy. Gonzalez was not engaged in a nonprofit use; she downloaded (and kept) whole copyrighted songs and she did this despite the fact that these works often are sold per song as well as per album.

As she tells the tale, downloading on a try-before-you-buy basis is good advertising for copyright proprietors, expanding the value of their inventory. As file sharing has increased, the sales of recorded music have dropped. The events likely are related. Music downloaded for free from the Internet is a close substitute for purchased music; many people are bound to keep the downloaded files without buying originals. That is exactly what Gonzalez did for at least 30 songs.

Licensed Internet sellers, such as the iTunes Music Store, offer samples—but again they pay authors a fee for the right to do so, and the teasers are just a portion of the original. Other intermediaries (Yahoo! Music Unlimited and Real Rhapsody but also the revived Napster) offer licensed access to large collections of music; customers may rent the whole library by the month or year, sample them all, and purchase any songs they want to keep. New technologies, such as SNOCAP, enable authorized trials over peer-to-peer systems. Authorized previews share the feature of evanescence: if a listener decides not to buy (or stops paying the rental fee), no copy remains behind.

Nor can she defend by observing that other persons were greater offenders; Gonzalez's theme that she obtained "only 30" (or "only 1,300") copyrighted songs is no more relevant than a thief's contention that he shoplifted "only 30" compact discs, planning to listen to them at home and pay later for any he liked.

Decision

The U.S. Court of Appeals held that Gonzalez had engaged in copyright infringement. The Court of Appeals affirmed the judgment of the U.S. District Court in favor of BMG Music and the award of $22,500 in damages and the injunction against Gonzalez.

Case Questions

Critical Legal Thinking   What is copyright infringement? Did Gonzalez engage in copyright infringement in this case?

Business Ethics   Do you think that Gonzalez knew that she was engaging in copyright infringement when she copied the music onto her computer?

Contemporary Business   Have you ever downloaded music using a peer-to-peer file-sharing program without paying the musician or the music company? Have you ever violated copyright law in any other way?

INTERNET LAW & ONLINE COMMERCE
File-Sharing Programs

"The ease of copying songs or movies using software like Grokster's or StreamCast's is fostering distain for copyright protection."

—Justice Souter

Federal copyright law can assess *secondary liability* on parties who knowingly contribute to another party's copyright infringement. That is, a party may be held liable for **contributory copyright infringement** if it assists another party in engaging in copyright infringement. The most famous case where contributory copyright infringement was found was the landmark U.S. Supreme Court decision *Metro-Goldwyn-Mayer Studios v. Grokster, Ltd. and StreamCast Networks, Inc.*

Many students and other parties who engage in copyright infringement by downloading copyrighted music do so by using software—file-sharing programs—specifically designed to assist in copyright infringement. Two companies that provided file-sharing software for free were Grokster, Ltd., and StreamCast Networks, Inc. Their free software allows computer users to share electronic files through peer-to-peer networks where users' computers communicate directly with each other. These peer-to-peer networks are primarily used to share copyrighted music and video files without authorization of the copyright holder. Thus, music and video files stored on one computer can be downloaded onto another computer using Grokster's and StreamCast's software. Grokster and StreamCast could provide their software for free and encouraged users to infringe copyrighted material. Grokster and StreamCast made their money by streaming advertising to their users; the more users they had, the more advertising money they made.

Statistical evidence shows that nearly 90 percent of the files available for download were copyrighted works. The parties downloading the copyrighted music and videos using the file-sharing programs were obviously liable for copyright infringement.

Metro-Goldwyn-Mayer Studios, Inc., and other owners of copyrighted music and movies (collectively MGM) sued Grokster and StreamCast, alleging that they were secondarily liable for contributing to acts of infringement by third parties using their peer-to-peer software. The case was eventually appealed to the U.S. Supreme Court. The

Supreme Court held that a party who distributes a device with the object of promoting its use to infringe copyrighted works is secondarily liable for the resulting acts of infringement by third parties using such device. The U.S. Supreme Court held that both Grokster and StreamCast were secondarily liable for contributing to copyright infringement. The Supreme Court reasoned:

> *MGM's evidence gives reason to think that the vast majority of users' downloads are acts of infringement, and because well over 100 million copies of the software in question are known to have been downloaded, and billions of files shared across the networks each month, the probable scope of copyright infringement is staggering. The ease of copying songs or movies using software like Grokster's and StreamCast's is fostering distain for copyright protection.*

The Supreme Court vacated the judgment of the U.S. Court of Appeals and remanded the case for further proceedings, consistent with the Court's decision. *Metro-Goldwyn-Mayer Studios v. Grokster, Ltd. and StreamCast Networks, Inc.*, 545 U.S. 913, 125 S.Ct. 2764, 162 L.Ed.2d 781, **Web** 2005 U.S. Lexis 5212 (Supreme Court of the United States, 2005)

Business Ethics Do you think Grokster and StreamCast knew that their software was being used to facilitate copyright infringement? Who suffers financial loss from the illegal downloading of music and videos? How big do you think this loss is?

FBI Warning *Movies and television programs are copyrighted. An FBI warning concerning copyright infringement usually appears at the beginning of a DVD, before the feature movie or program is shown.*

The Fair Use Doctrine

fair use doctrine

A doctrine that permits certain limited use of a copyright by someone other than the copyright holder without the permission of the copyright holder.

A copyright holder's rights in a work are not absolute. The law permits certain limited unauthorized use of copyrighted materials under the **fair use doctrine**. The following uses are protected under this doctrine: (1) quotation of the copyrighted work for review or criticism or in a scholarly or technical work, (2) use in a parody or satire, (3) brief quotation in a news report, (4) reproduction by a teacher or student of a small part of the work to illustrate a lesson, (5) incidental reproduction of a work in a newsreel or broadcast of an event being reported, and (6) reproduction of a work in a legislative or judicial proceeding. The copyright holder cannot recover for copyright infringement where fair use is found.

Criminal Copyright Infringement: The No Electronic Theft Act (NET Act)

In 1997, Congress enacted the **No Electronic Theft Act (NET Act)**, which criminalizes certain copyright infringement. The NET Act prohibits any person from willfully infringing a copyright for the purpose of either commercial advantage or financial gain, or by reproduction or distribution, even without commercial advantage or financial gain, including by electronic means, where the retail value of the copyrighted work exceeds $1,000. Criminal penalties for violating the act include imprisonment for up to five years and fines of up to $100,000.

The creation of the NET Act adds a new law the federal government can use to criminally attack copyright infringement and curb digital piracy.

No Electronic Theft Act (NET Act)
A federal statute that makes it a crime for a person to willfully infringe on a copyright work that exceeds $1,000 in retail value.

Digital Millennium Copyright Act (DMCA)
A federal statute that prohibits unauthorized access to copyrighted digital works by circumventing encryption technology or the manufacture and distribution of technologies designed for the purpose of circumventing encryption protection of digital works.

INTERNET LAW & ONLINE COMMERCE

Digital Millennium Copyright Act (DMCA)

The Internet makes it easier than ever before for people to illegally copy and distribute copyrighted works. To combat this, software and entertainment companies have developed "wrappers" and **encryption technology** to protect their copyrighted works from unauthorized access. Not to be outdone, software pirates and other Internet users have devised ways to crack these wrappers and protection devices. Software and entertainment companies lobbied Congress to enact federal legislation to make the cracking of their wrappers and selling of technology to do so illegal. In response, Congress enacted the **Digital Millennium Copyright Act (DMCA)**,[4] a federal statute that does the following:

- Prohibits unauthorized access to copyrighted *digital works* by circumventing the wrapper or encryption technology that protects the intellectual property. This "black box" protection prohibits simply accessing the protected information and does not require that the accessed information be misused.
- Prohibits the manufacture and distribution of technologies, products, or services primarily designed for the purpose of circumventing wrappers or encryption technology protecting digital works. However, multipurpose devices that can be used in ways other than for cracking wrappers or encryption technology can be manufactured and sold without violating the DMCA.

Congress granted exceptions to DMCA liability to (1) software developers to achieve compatibility of their software with the protected work; (2) federal, state, and local law enforcement agencies conducting criminal investigations; (3) parents who are protecting children from pornography or other harmful materials available on the Internet; (4) Internet users who are identifying and disabling cookies and other identification devices that invade their personal privacy rights; and (5) nonprofit libraries, educational institutions, and archives that access a protected work to determine whether to acquire the work.

The DMCA imposes civil and criminal penalties. A successful plaintiff in a civil action can recover actual damages from first-time offenders and treble damages from repeat offenders, costs and attorneys' fees, an order for the destruction of illegal products and devices, and an injunction against future violations by the offender. As an alternative to actual damages, a plaintiff can recover statutory damages of not less than $2,500 and up to $25,000 per act of circumvention. The following criminal penalties can be assessed for willful violations committed for "commercial advantage" or "private financial gain":

- First time violators can be fined and imprisoned for up to 5 years.
- Subsequent violators can be fined and imprisoned for up to 10 years.

▶ TRADEMARK

Businesses often develop company names, as well as advertising slogans and commercial logos, to promote the sale of their goods and services. Companies such as Nike, Microsoft, Louis Vuitton, and McDonald's spend millions of dollars annually to gain market recognition from consumers. The U.S. Congress has enacted trademark laws to provide legal protection for these names, slogans, and logos.

Federal Lanham Trademark Act

Lanham Act
An amended federal statute that (1) establishes the requirements for obtaining a federal mark and (2) protects marks from infringement.

In 1946, Congress enacted the **Lanham Act**[5] to provide federal protection to trademarks, service marks, and other marks. This act, as amended, is intended to (1) protect the owner's investment and goodwill in a **mark** and (2) prevent consumers from being confused as to the origin of goods and services.

mark
The collective name for trademarks, service marks, certification marks, and collective marks that can be trademarked.

Trademarks are registered with the United States PTO in Washington, DC. The original registration of a mark is valid for 10 years, and it can be renewed for an unlimited number of 10-year periods.

The registration of a trademark, which is given nationwide effect, serves as constructive notice that the mark is the registrant's personal property. The registrant is entitled to use the registered trademark symbol ® in connection with a registered trademark or service mark. Use of the symbol is not mandatory. Note that the frequently used notations "TM" and "SM" have no legal significance.

An applicant can register a mark if it has been used in commerce (e.g., actually used in the sale of goods or services). An applicant can also register a mark six months prior to its proposed use in commerce, but if the mark is not used within this period, the applicant loses the mark (the applicant may file for a six-month extension to use the mark in commerce). A party other than the registrant can submit an *opposition* to a proposed registration of a mark or the *cancellation* of a previously registered mark.

Marks That Can Be Trademarked

The word *mark* collectively refers to *trademarks, service marks, certification marks*, and *collective marks*:

trademark
A distinctive mark, symbol, name, word, motto, or device that identifies the goods of a particular business.

- **Trademarks.** A **trademark** is a distinctive mark, symbol, name, word, motto, or device that identifies the *goods* of a particular business.

Examples *Coca-Cola* (The Coca-Cola Company), *Big Mac* (McDonald's Corporation), *Mac* (Apple Computer), *Intel inside* (Intel Corporation), and *Better Ingredients. Better Pizza.* (Pizza Hut) are trademarks.

service mark
A mark that distinguishes the services of the holder from those of its competitors.

- **Service marks.** A **service mark** is used to distinguish the *services* of the holder from those of its competitors.

Examples *FedEx* (FedEx Corporation), *The Friendly Skies* (United Air Lines, Inc.), *Big Brown* (UPS Corporation), and *Weight Watchers* are service marks.

- **Certification marks.** A **certification mark** is a mark that is used to certify that a good or service is of a certain quality or originates from a particular geographical area. The owner of the mark is usually a nonprofit corporation that licenses producers that meet standards or conditions to use the mark.
- **Collective marks.** A **collective mark** is owned by an organization (such as an association) whose members use it to identify themselves with a level of quality or accuracy, geographical origin, or other characteristic set by the organization.

Examples *Washington Apple* (Washington Apple Commission), *FTD Florist* (FTD, Inc.), and *Grown in Idaho* (The Idaho Potato Commission) are examples of collective marks.

Certain marks cannot be registered. They include (1) the flag or coat of arms of the United States, any state, municipality, or foreign nation; (2) marks that are immoral or scandalous; (3) geographical names standing alone (e.g., "South"); (4) surnames standing alone (note that a surname can be registered if it is accompanied by a picture or fanciful name, such as *Smith Brothers cough drops*); and (5) any mark that resembles a mark already registered with the federal PTO.

Napa Valley, California *A certification mark is a mark that is used to certify that goods and services are of a certain quality or originate from particular geographical areas. This certification mark designates California cheese manufacturers.*

Distinctiveness of a Mark

To qualify for federal protection, a mark must be either (1) **distinctive** or (2) have acquired a **secondary meaning**. A distinctive mark would be a word or design that is unique. Ordinary words that are descriptive can qualify as a mark if they have taken on a secondary meaning. Words that are descriptive but have no secondary meaning cannot be trademarked.

Examples Marks such as *Xerox* and *Acura* are distinctive. Nike, Inc., has trademarked its *Just Do It* slogan, which takes on a secondary meaning.

distinctive
Being unique and fabricated.

"secondary meaning"
A brand name that has evolved from an ordinary term.

Trademark Infringement

The owner of a mark can sue a third party for the unauthorized use of a mark. To succeed in a **trademark infringement** case, the owner must prove that (1) the defendant infringed the plaintiff's mark by using it in an unauthorized manner and (2) such use is likely to cause confusion, mistake, or deception of the public as to the origin of the goods or services.

A successful plaintiff can recover (1) the profits made by the infringer through the unauthorized use of the mark, (2) damages caused to the plaintiff's business and reputation, (3) an order requiring the defendant to destroy all goods containing the unauthorized mark, and (4) an injunction preventing the defendant from such infringement in the future. The court has discretion to award up to *treble* damages where intentional infringement is found.

In the following case, the court had to decide whether there was a trademark.

trademark infringement
Unauthorized use of another's mark. The holder may recover damages and other remedies from the infringer.

CASE 7.2 Trademark

Menashe v. Victoria's Secret Stores, Inc.

409 F.Supp.2d 412, Web 2006 U.S. Dist. Lexis 7763 (2006)
United States District Court for the Southern District of New York

"I find that because Victoria's Secret made bona fide trademark use of 'SEXY LITTLE THINGS' in commerce before Plaintiffs.... Victoria's Secret has acquired priority in the Mark."

—Judge Baer

Facts

As early as Fall 2002, Victoria's Secret, a woman's lingerie manufacturer and retailer, began to develop the concept and making of a line of lingerie named "SEXY LITTLE THINGS." Victoria's Secret rolled out its "SEXY LITTLE THINGS" collection in its stores. Victoria Secret first used the term "SEXY LITTLE THINGS" in commerce on July 28, 2004.

In June 2004, Ronit Menashe and Audrey Quock ("Menashe"), embarked on a joint venture to produce and launch a line of women's underwear. In late July or early August 2004, Menashe came up with the phrases "SEXY LITTLE THING" and "SEXY LITTLE THINGS" for a line of lingerie. On September 13, 2004, Menashe filed an intent-to-use (ITU) application with the United States Patent and Trademark Office (PTO) for these two names for lingerie. On November 11, 2004, Victoria's Secret applied to register "SEXY LITTLE THINGS" for lingerie on the PTO's Principal Register based on its first use in commerce dating from July 28, 2004. At that time Victoria's Secret learned of Menashe's ITU application for "SEXY LITTLE THING" and "SEXY LITTLE THINGS."

Victoria's Secret immediately sent Menashe and Quock a cease-and-desist letter, informing them that Victoria's Secret had been using "SEXY LITTLE THINGS" as a trademark for lingerie since prior to the filing date of Menashe's ITU application. The letter demanded that Menashe cease and desist from using "SEXY LITTLE THING" and "SEXY LITTLE THINGS" and abandon the ITU application.

Menashe halted the production of the underwear project and filed a lawsuit against Victoria's Secret, seeking a declaratory judgment that asked the Court to order that she had not infringed Victoria's Secret's claimed trademark in "SEXY LITTLE THINGS." Menashe sought damages from Victoria's Secret. The PTO suspended further action on Victoria's Secret's trademark application, pending the disposition of the case. At trial, both Menashe and Quock denied any knowledge that Victoria's Secret had been using the term "SEXY LITTLE THINGS" when they filed their ITU application with the PTO.

Issue

Should Menashe be granted a declaratory judgment of trademark non-infringement for using the terms "SEXY LITTLE THING" and "SEXY LITTLE THINGS" for their lingerie?

Language of the Court

At trial—while it stretches credulity—Menashe testified that since the time she received the cease and desist letter, she has not been in a Victoria's Secret store to see whether Victoria's Secret was selling merchandise under the name "SEXY LITTLE THINGS." Quock testified that she did not visit a Victoria's Secret store until some time after receipt of the cease and desist letter, when she walked into a Victoria's Secret store and saw a display for "SEXY LITTLE THINGS."

Plaintiffs' determination fails to overcome the overwhelming evidence that Victoria's Secret used "SEXY LITTLE THINGS" as a trademark in commerce beginning on July 28, 2004. I find that because Victoria's Secret made bona fide trademark use of "SEXY LITTLE THINGS" in commerce before Plaintiffs filed their ITU application, and has continued to use that Mark in commerce, Victoria's Secret has acquired priority in the Mark. Consequently, Plaintiffs are not entitled to a declaratory judgment of non-infringement under the Lanham Act.

Decision

The U.S. District Court held that Victoria's Secret had obtained priority in the mark "SEXY LITTLE THINGS." The District Court dismissed Menashe's petition for declaratory judgment and dismissed the case against Victoria's Secret.

Case Questions

Critical Legal Thinking Did Victoria's Secret use the term "SEXY LITTLE THINGS" in commerce before Menashe and Quock decided to use the same term? What was the significance of this fact?

Business Ethics Do you think Menashe and Quock had knowledge of Victoria's Secret's use of the term "SEXY LITTLE THINGS" before they filed their application with the PTO?

Contemporary Business Do you think name "SEXY LITTLE THINGS" is a valuable trademark?

Generic Names

When filing for a trademark, if a word, name, or slogan is too generic, it cannot be registered as a trademark. If a word is not generic, it can be trademarked.

Example The word *apple* cannot be trademarked because it is a generic name. However, the brand name *Apple Computer* is permitted to be trademarked because it is not a generic name.

Example The word *secret* cannot be trademarked because it is a generic name. However, the brand name *Victoria's Secret* is permitted to be trademarked because it is not a generic name.

Once a company has been granted a trademark or service mark, the company usually uses the mark as a brand name to promote its goods or services. However, sometimes a company may be *too* successful in promoting a mark, and at some point in time the public begins to use the brand name as a common name to denote the type of product or service being sold rather than as the trademark or service mark of the individual seller. A trademark that becomes a common term for a product line or type of service is called a **generic name**. Once a trademark becomes a generic name, the term loses its protection under federal trademark law.

Exhibit 7.2 lists names that at one time were trademarked but lost trademark protection because the trademarked name became overused and generic. Exhibit 7.3 lists trademarked names that are at some risk of becoming generic names.

generic name
A term for a mark that has become a common term for a product line or type of service and therefore has lost its trademark protection.

▶**Exhibit 7.2 GENERIC NAMES**

> **The following once-trademarked names have been so overused to designate an entire class of products that they have been found to be generic and have lost their trademark status.**
>
> | | |
> |---|---|
> | Windsurfer | Frisbee |
> | Laser | Trampoline |
> | Escalator | Cornflakes |
> | Kerosene | Yo-yo |
> | Formica | Raisin brand |
> | Thermos | Tollhouse cookies |
> | Linoleum | Nylon |

▶**Exhibit 7.3 NAMES AT RISK OF BECOMING GENERIC NAMES**

Certain trademark and service marks are often used improperly and have some risk in the future of becoming generic names. Several of these marks are listed below, with their proper use and typical misuse also noted:

Mark	Proper Use	Misuse
Xerox	"Copy this document on a Xerox brand copier."	"Go xerox this."
Google	"Use the Google search engine to find information about him."	"Just google him."
FedEx	"Use FedEx overnight delivery service to send this package."	"Please fedex this."
Rollerblade	"Let's go inline skating on our Rollerblade inline skates."	"Let's go rollerblading."

CONCEPT SUMMARY

TYPES OF INTELLECTUAL PROPERTY PROTECTED BY FEDERAL LAW

Type	Subject Matter	Term
Patent	Inventions (e.g., machines; processes; compositions of matter; designs for articles of manufacture; and improvements to existing machines and processes). Invention must be novel, useful, and nonobvious. *Public use doctrine:* Patent will not be granted if the invention was used in public for more than one year prior to the filing of the patent application.	Patents on articles of manufacture and processes: 20 years; design patents: 14 years.
Copyright	Tangible writing (e.g., books, magazines, newspapers, lectures, operas, plays, screenplays, musical compositions, maps, works of art, lithographs, photographs, postcards, greeting cards, motion pictures, newsreels, sound recordings, computer programs, and mask works fixed to semiconductor chips). Writing must be the original work of the author. The *fair use doctrine* permits the use of copyrighted material without consent for limited uses (e.g., scholarly work, parody or satire, and brief quotation in news reports).	Individual holder: life of author plus 70 years. Corporate holder: the shorter of either 120 years from the year of creation or 95 years from the year of first publication
Trademark	Marks (e.g., name, symbol, word, logo, or device). Marks include trademarks, service marks, certification marks, and collective marks. Mark must be distinctive or have acquired a secondary meaning. *Generic name*: A mark that becomes a common term for a product line or type of service loses its protection under federal trademark law.	Original registration: 10 years. Renewal registration: unlimited number of renewals for 10-year terms.

Federal Dilution Act

Many companies that own trademarks spend millions of dollars each year advertising and promoting the quality of the goods and services sold under their names. Many of these become household names that are recognized by millions of consumers, such as Coca-Cola, McDonald's, Microsoft, and Nike.

Traditional trademark law protected these marks where an infringer used the mark and confused consumers as to the source of the goods or services.

Example If a knockoff company sold athletic shoes and apparel under the name "Nike," there would be trademark infringement.

Federal Dilution Act
A federal statute that protects famous marks from dilution, erosion, blurring, or tarnishing.

Often, however, a party would use a name similar to, but not exactly identical to, a holder's trademark. Congress enacted the **Federal Dilution Act** of 1995 to protect *famous marks* from dilution. The Federal Dilution Act provides that owners of marks have a valuable property right in their marks that should not be *eroded, blurred, tarnished,* or *diluted* in any way by another. The Federal Dilution Act has three fundamental requirements:

1. The mark must be famous.
2. The use by the other party must be commercial.
3. The use must cause dilution of the distinctive quality of the mark.

Dilution is broadly defined as the lessening of the capacity of a famous mark to identify and distinguish its holder's goods and services, regardless of the presence or absence of competition between the owner of the mark and the other party.

Example Someone other than Nike having a website titled www.mynike.com or www.nikeathletesrun.com would be unlawful dilution.

Congress enacted the **Trademark Dilution Revision Act**, which became law in 2006. This act provides that a dilution plaintiff does not need to show that it has suffered actual harm to prevail in its dilution lawsuit. The act also lists factors that help in defining *dilution*, *blurring*, and *tarnishing*. The act permits truthful comparative advertising and provides a "fair use" defense for parodying someone else's famous mark.

Hong Kong *These counterfeit knockoff goods are an example of how companies' trademarks and copyrights are being infringed around the world. Knockoff goods cause a huge monetary loss to the owners' intellectual property rights.*

TEST REVIEW TERMS AND CONCEPTS

American Inventors
    Protection Act
Berne Convention
Certification mark
Civil lawsuit
Collective mark
Contributory copyright
    infringement
Copyright
Copyright infringement
Copyright Revision Act
Digital Millennium
    Copyright Act (DMCA)
Distinctive
Economic Espionage Act
Encryption technology
Fair use doctrine

Federal crime
Federal Dilution Act
Federal Patent Statute
Generic name
Intellectual property rights
Lanham Act
Mark
*Metro-Goldwyn-Mayer
    Studios v. Grokster, Ltd.
    and StreamCast
    Networks, Inc.*
Misappropriation of a trade
    secret
No Electronic Theft Act
    (NET Act)
Non-obvious
Novel

One-year "on sale" doctrine
    (public use doctrine)
Patent
Patent application
Patent infringement
Patent number
Patent pending
Provisional application
Public domain
Registration of a
    copyright
Reverse engineering
Secondary meaning
Service mark
*State Street Bank & Trust
    Co. v. Signature Financial
    Group, Inc.*

Sonny Bono Copyright
    Term Extension Act
Tangible writings
Trademark
Trademark Dilution
    Revision Act
Trademark infringement
Trade secret
Uniform Trade Secrets Act
United States Copyright
    Office
United States Court of
    Appeals for the Federal
    Circuit
United States Patent and
    Trademark Office (PTO)
Useful

CASE PROBLEMS

7.1 Trade Secret   CRA-MAR Video Center, Inc., sells electronic equipment and videocassettes, as does its competitor, Koach's Sales Corporation. Both CRA-MAR and Koach's purchased computers from Radio Shack. CRA-MAR used the computer it purchased to store customer lists, movie lists, personnel files, and financial records. Because the computer was new to CRA-MAR, Randall Youts, Radio Shack's salesman and programmer, agreed to modify CRA-MAR's programs when needed, including the customer list program. At one point, CRA-MAR decided to send a mailing to everyone on its customer list. The computer was unable to perform the function, so Youts took the disks containing the customer lists to the Radio Shack store to work on the program. Somehow Koach's came into possession of CRA-MAR's customer lists and sent advertising mailings to the parties on the lists. When CRA-MAR discovered this fact, it sued Koach's, seeking an injunction against any further use of its customer lists. Is a customer list a trade secret that can be protected from misappropriation? *Koach's Sales Corp. v. CRA-MAR Video Center, Inc.*, 478 N.E.2d 110, **Web** 1985 Ind. App. Lexis 2432 (Court of Appeals of Indiana)

7.2 Patent Patent No. 3,397,928 (928) was issued to Edward M. Galle, an executive of Hughes Tool Company. Galle assigned the patent, and other related patents, to Hughes. The patent was for an O-ring rubber seal that was used to seal bearings in the cone of a rock bit that rotated to drill holes in rocks in order to drill oil wells. Hughes did not license its 928 patent, which was a substantial commercial success. Smith International, Inc., was Hughes's major competitor in this industry. For 13 years, Smith made more than 460,000 rock bits (reaping sales of about $1.3 billion) that contained rubber seals that infringed on Hughes's patents. Hughes sued Smith for patent infringement and requested $1.2 billion in lost royalties and interest. Smith offered $20 million to $60 million in settlement. The case went to trial, and the Court found Smith liable for patent infringement. How much should Hughes be awarded in damages? *Smith Internat'l, Inc. v. Hughes Tool Co.*, 759 F.2d 1572, **Web** 1985 U.S. App. Lexis 14777 (United States Court of Appeals for the Federal Circuit)

7.3 Copyright When Spiro Agnew resigned as vice president of the United States, President Richard M. Nixon appointed Gerald R. Ford as vice president. Amid growing controversy surrounding the Watergate scandal, President Nixon resigned, and Vice President Ford acceded to the presidency. As president, Ford pardoned Nixon for any wrongdoing regarding the Watergate affair and related matters. Ford served as president until he was defeated by Jimmy Carter in the presidential election. Ford entered into a contract with Harper & Row Publishers, Inc., to publish his memoirs in book form. The memoirs were to contain significant unpublished materials concerning the Watergate affair and Ford's personal reflections on that time in history. The publisher instituted security measures to protect the confidentiality of the manuscript. Several weeks before the book was to be released, an unidentified person secretly brought a copy of the manuscript to Victor Navasky, editor of *The Nation*, a weekly political commentary magazine. Navasky, knowing that his possession of the purloined manuscript was not authorized, produced a 2,250-word piece titled "The Ford Memoirs" and published it in an issue of *The Nation*. Verbatim quotes of between 300 and 400 words from Ford's manuscript, including some of the most important parts, appeared in the article. Harper & Row sued the publishers of *The Nation* for copyright infringement. Who wins? *Harper & Row, Publishers, Inc. v.*

Nation Enterprises, 471 U.S. 539, 105 S.Ct. 2218, 85 L.Ed.2d 588, **Web** 1985 U.S. Lexis 17 (Supreme Court of the United States)

7.4 Fair Use Doctrine Once in the past, when the City of New York teetered on the brink of bankruptcy, on the television screens of America there appeared an image of a top-hatted Broadway showgirl, backed by an advancing phalanx of dancers, chanting: "I-I-I-I-I Love New Yo-o-o-o-o-o-rk." As an ad campaign for an ailing city, it was an unparalleled success. Crucial to the campaign was a brief but exhilarating musical theme written by Steve Karmin called "I Love New York." Elsmere Music, Inc., owned the copyright to the music. The success of the campaign did not go unnoticed. The popular weekly variety program *Saturday Night Live (SNL)* performed a comedy sketch over National Broadcasting Company's network (NBC). In the sketch, the cast of *SNL*, portraying the mayor and members of the chamber of commerce of the biblical city of Sodom, were seen discussing Sodom's poor public image with out-of-towners and its effect on the tourist trade. In an attempt to recast Sodom's image in a more positive light, a new advertising campaign was revealed, with the highlight of the campaign being a song "I Love Sodom" sung a cappella by a chorus line of *SNL* regulars to the tune of "I Love New York." Elsmere Music did not see the humor of the sketch and sued NBC for copyright infringement. Who wins? *Elsmere Music, Inc. v. National Broadcasting Co., Inc.*, 623 F.2d 252, **Web** 1980 U.S. App. Lexis 16820 (United States Court of Appeals for the Second Circuit)

7.5 Trademark Clairol Incorporated manufactures and distributes hair tinting, dyeing, and coloring preparations. Clairol embarked on an extensive advertising campaign to promote the sale of its "Miss Clairol" hair-color preparations that included advertisements in national magazines, on outdoor billboards, on radio and television, in mailing pieces, and on point-of-sale display materials to be used by retailers and beauty salons. The advertisements prominently displayed the slogans "Hair Color So Natural Only Her Hairdresser Knows for Sure" and "Does She or Doesn't She?" Clairol registered these slogans as trademarks. During the next decade, Clairol spent more than $22 million on advertising materials, resulting in more than a billion separate audio and visual impressions using the slogans. Roux Laboratories, Inc., a manufacturer of hair-coloring products and a competitor of Clairol's, filed an opposition to Clairol's registration of the slogans as trademarks. Do the slogans qualify for trademark protection? *Roux Laboratories, Inc. v. Clairol Inc.*, 427 F.2d 823, **Web** 1970 CCPA Lexis 344 (United States Court of Customs and Patent Appeals)

7.6 Trademark Mead Data Central, Inc., has provided computer-assisted legal research services to lawyers and others under the trademark "Lexis." Lexis is based on *lex*, the Latin word for "law," and *IS*, for "information systems." Through extensive sales and advertising, Mead has made Lexis a strong mark in the computerized legal research field, particularly among lawyers. However, Lexis is recognized by only one percent of the general population, with almost half of this one percent being attorneys. Toyota Motor Corporation has for many years manufactured automobiles, which it markets in the United States through its subsidiary Toyota Motor Sales, U.S.A., Inc. Toyota announced a new line of luxury automobiles to be called Lexus. Toyota planned on spending almost $20 million for marketing and advertising Lexus during the first nine months of 1989. Mead filed suit against Toyota, alleging that Toyota's use of the name Lexus violated New York's anti-dilution statute and would cause injury to the business reputation of Mead and a dilution of the distinctive quality of the Lexis mark. Who wins? *Mead Data Central, Inc. v. Toyota Motor Sales, U.S.A., Inc.*, 875 F.2d 1026, **Web** 1989 U.S. App. Lexis 6644 (United States Court of Appeals for the Second Circuit)

7.7 Generic Name   The Miller Brewing Company, a national brewer, produces a reduced-calorie beer called Miller Lite. Miller began selling beer under this name and spent millions of dollars promoting the Miller Lite brand name on television, in print, and via other forms of advertising. Falstaff Brewing Corporation had brewed and distributed a reduced-calorie beer called "Falstaff Lite." Miller brought suit under the Lanham Act, seeking an injunction to prevent Falstaff from using the term *Lite*. Is the term *Lite* a generic name that does not qualify for trademark protection? *Miller Brewing Co. v. Falstaff Brewing Corp.*, 655 F.2d 5, **Web** 1981 U.S. App. Lexis 11345 (United States Court of Appeals for the First Circuit)

BUSINESS ETHICS CASES

7.8 Business Ethics   Integrated Cash Management Services, Inc. (ICM), designs and develops computer software programs and systems for banks and corporate financial departments. ICM's computer programs and systems are not copyrighted, but they are secret. After Alfred Sims Newlin and Behrouz Vafa completed graduate school, they were employed by ICM as computer programmers. They worked at ICM for several years, writing computer programs. They left ICM to work for Digital Transactions, Inc. (DTI). Before leaving ICM, however, they copied certain ICM files onto computer disks. Within two weeks of starting to work at DTI, they created prototype computer programs that operated in substantially the same manner as comparable ICM programs and were designed to compete directly with ICM's programs. ICM sued Newlin, Vafa, and DTI for misappropriation of trade secrets. Are the defendants liable? Did the defendants act ethically in this case? *Integrated Cash Management Services, Inc. v. Digital Transactions, Inc.*, 920 F.2d 171, **Web** 1990 U.S. App. Lexis 20985 (United States Court of Appeals for the Second Circuit)

7.9 Business Ethics   John W. Carson was the host and star of *The Tonight Show*, a well-known nightly television talk show broadcast by the National Broadcasting Company (NBC). Carson also appeared as an entertainer in theaters and night clubs around the country. For the 30 years he hosted *The Tonight Show*, he had been introduced on the show each night with the phrase "Here's Johnny." The phrase "Here's Johnny" was generally associated with Carson by a substantial segment of the television-viewing public. Carson had licensed the use of the phrase to a chain of restaurants, a line of toiletries, and other business ventures. Johnny Carson Apparel, Inc. (apparel) manufactured and marketed men's clothing to retail stores. Carson, president of Apparel and owner of 20 percent of its stock, had licensed Apparel to use the phrase "Here's Johnny" on labels for clothing and in advertising campaigns. The phrase had never been registered by Carson or Apparel as a trademark or service mark.

Earl Broxton was the owner and president of Here's Johnny Portable Toilets, Inc. (Toilets), a Michigan corporation that engaged in the business of renting and selling "Here's Johnny" portable toilets. Broxton was aware when he formed the corporation that the phrase "Here's Johnny" was the introductory slogan for Carson on *The Tonight Show*. Broxton indicated that he coupled the phrase "Here's Johnny" with a second one, "The World's Foremost Commodian," to make a good play on the phrase. Shortly after Toilets went into business in 1976, Carson and Apparel sued Toilets, seeking an injunction prohibiting the further use of the phrase "Here's Johnny" as a corporate name for or in connection with the sale or rental of its portable toilets. Who wins? Did Broxton act ethically by appropriating the phrase "Here's Johnny" to promote the sale and rental of portable toilets? *Carson v. Here's Johnny Portable Toilets, Inc.*, 698 F.2d 831, **Web** 1983 U.S. App. Lexis 30866 (United States Court of Appeals for the Sixth Circuit)

ENDNOTES

1. 18 U.S.C. Sections 1831–1839.
2. 35 U.S.C. Section 10 et seq.
3. 17 U.S.C. Section 101 et seq.

4. 17 U.S.C. 1201.
5. 15 U.S.C. Section 1114 et seq.

▲ **New York Police Department Times Square, New York City** *Criminal cases make up a large portion of cases tried in courts of this country. Criminal cases are bought against persons for violating federal, state, and local laws. Suspected criminals are provided many rights by the U.S. Constitution and state constitutions. Parties in this country are free from unreasonable searches and seizures of evidence, and any evidence obtained illegally is considered "tainted" evidence and cannot be used in court. People who are suspected of a criminal act may assert their right of privilege against self-incrimination and may choose not to testify at any pretrial proceedings or at trial. Parties have a right to a public trial by a jury of their peers. In addition, if convicted of a crime, the criminal is free from cruel and unusual punishment.*

CHAPTER OBJECTIVES

After studying this chapter, you should be able to:

1. List and describe the essential elements of a crime.
2. Describe criminal procedure, including arrest, indictment, arraignment, and the criminal trial.
3. Define major white-collar crimes, such as *embezzlement*, *bribery*, and *criminal fraud*.
4. List and describe laws involving domestic and international business crimes.
5. Explain the constitutional safeguards provided by the Fourth, Fifth, Sixth, and Eighth Amendments to the U.S. Constitution.

CHAPTER CONTENTS

"It is better that ten guilty persons escape, than that one innocent suffer."
—Sir William Blackstone

▶ INTRODUCTION TO CRIMINAL LAW AND CYBER CRIMES

For members of society to peacefully coexist and commerce to flourish, people and their property must be protected from injury by other members of society. Federal, state, and local governments' **criminal laws** are intended to afford this protection by providing an incentive for persons to act reasonably in society and imposing penalties on persons who violate them.

The United States has one of the most advanced and humane criminal law systems in the world. It differs from other criminal law systems in several respects. A person charged with a crime in the United States is *presumed innocent until proven guilty*. The *burden of proof* is on the government to prove that the accused is guilty of the crime charged. Further, the accused must be found guilty **beyond a reasonable doubt**. Conviction requires unanimous jury vote. Under many other legal systems, a person accused of a crime is presumed guilty unless the person can prove he or she is not. A person charged with a crime in the United States is also provided with substantial constitutional safeguards during the criminal justice process.

Many crimes are referred to as *white-collar crimes* because they are most often committed by business managers and employees. These crimes include fraud, bribery, and other such crimes. In addition, in the Information Age, many cyber crimes are committed using computers and the Internet.

This chapter discusses criminal procedure, white-collar crimes, business crimes, cyber crimes, and the constitutional safeguards afforded criminal defendants.

▶ DEFINITION OF A CRIME

A **crime** is defined as any act done by an individual in violation of those duties that he or she owes to society and for the breach of which the law provides that the wrongdoer shall make amends to the public. Many activities have been considered crimes through the ages, whereas other crimes are of recent origin.

crime
A violation of a statute for which the government imposes a punishment.

Penal Codes and Regulatory Statutes

Statutes are the primary source of criminal law. Most states have adopted comprehensive **penal codes** that define in detail the activities considered to be crimes within their jurisdictions and the penalties that will be imposed for their commission. A comprehensive federal criminal code defines federal crimes.[1]

In addition, state and federal **regulatory statutes** often provide for criminal violations and penalties. The state and federal legislatures are continually adding to the list of crimes.

penal code
A collection of criminal statutes.

regulatory statutes
Statutes such as environmental laws, securities laws, and antitrust laws that provide for criminal violations and penalties.

The penalty for committing a crime may consist of the imposition of a fine, imprisonment, both, or some other form of punishment (e.g., probation). Generally, imprisonment is imposed to (1) incapacitate the criminal so he or she will not harm others in society, (2) provide a means to rehabilitate the criminal, (3) deter others from similar conduct, and (4) inhibit personal retribution by the victim.

Parties to a Criminal Action

In a criminal lawsuit, the government (not a private party) is the **plaintiff**. The government is represented by a lawyer called the **prosecutor**. The accused, which is usually an individual or a business, is the **defendant**. The accused is represented by a **defense attorney**. Sometimes the accused will hire a private attorney to represent him if he can afford to do so. If the accused cannot afford a private defense lawyer, the government will provide one free of charge. This government defense attorney is often called a **public defender**. (See Exhibit 8.1.)

▶**Exhibit 8.1 PARTIES AND ATTORNEYS INVOLVED IN A CRIMINAL CASE**

PARTIES TO A CRIMINAL LAWSUIT

Government	**Person or Business**
(plaintiff)	(defendant)

ATTORNEYS REPRESENTING THE PARTIES

Prosecutor	**Defense Attorney**
(government attorney)	(private attorney or public defender)

Law cannot persuade, where it cannot punish.

Thomas Fuller
Gnomologia (1732)

A crime is generally classified as a *felony*, *misdemeanor*, or *violation*.

Felony

felony
The most serious type of crime; inherently evil crime. Most crimes against persons and some business-related crimes are felonies.

Felonies are the most serious kinds of crimes. Felonies include crimes that are *mala in se*—that is, inherently evil. Most crimes against persons (e.g., murder, rape) and certain business-related crimes (e.g., embezzlement, bribery) are felonies in most jurisdictions. Felonies are usually punishable by imprisonment. In some jurisdictions, certain felonies (e.g., first-degree murder) are punishable by death. Federal law[2] and some state laws require mandatory sentencing for specified crimes. Many statutes define different degrees of crimes (e.g., first-, second-, and third-degree murder). Each degree earns different penalties. Serious violations of regulatory statutes are also felonies.

Misdemeanor

misdemeanor
A less serious crime; not inherently evil but prohibited by society. Many crimes against property are misdemeanors.

Misdemeanors are less serious than felonies. They are crimes *mala prohibita*; that is, they are not inherently evil but are prohibited by society. Many crimes against property, such as robbery, burglary, and less serious violations of regulatory statutes, are included in this category. Misdemeanors carry lesser penalties than felonies. They are usually punishable by fines and/or imprisonment for one year or less.

Violation

violation
A crime that is neither a felony nor a misdemeanor that is usually punishable by a fine.

Crimes such as traffic violations, jaywalking, and such are neither felonies nor misdemeanors. These crimes, which are called **violations**, are generally punishable by fines. Occasionally, a few days of imprisonment are imposed.

CONCEPT SUMMARY
CLASSIFICATION OF CRIMES

Classification	Description
Felony	The most serious kinds of crimes. They are *mala in se* (inherently evil), and they are usually punishable by imprisonment.
Misdemeanor	Crimes that are less serious than felonies. They are *mala prohibita* (prohibited by society), and they are usually punishable by fine and/or imprisonment for less than one year.
Violation	Crimes that are neither felonies nor misdemeanors. Violations are generally punishable by a fine.

Intent Crimes

Most crimes require criminal intent to be proven before the accused can be found guilty of the defined crime. Two elements must be proven for a person to be found guilty of an intent crime: (1) criminal act (*actus reus*) and (2) criminal intent (*mens rea*).

Criminal Act (Actus Reus)   The defendant must have actually performed the prohibited act. The actual performance of the criminal act is called the **actus reus** (guilty act). Sometimes, the omission of an act can constitute the requisite *actus reus*.

actus reus
"Guilty act"—the actual performance of a criminal act.

Example Killing someone without legal justification constitutes a criminal act (*actus reus*). This is because the law forbids persons from killing one another.

Example If a taxpayer who is under a legal duty to file income tax returns and pay income taxes that are due the government fails to do so, there is the requisite criminal act (*actus reus*).

Criminal Intent (Mens Rea)   To be found guilty of an intent crime, the accused must be found to have possessed the requisite state of mind (i.e., specific or general intent) when the act was performed. This is called **mens rea** (evil intent). **Specific intent** is found where the accused purposefully, intentionally, or with knowledge commits a prohibited act. **General intent** is found where there is a showing of recklessness or a lesser degree of mental culpability. Individual criminal statutes state whether the crime requires a showing of specific or general intent. Juries may infer an accused's intent from the facts and circumstances of the case.

mens rea
"Evil intent"—the possession of the requisite state of mind to commit a prohibited act.

Merely thinking about committing a crime is not a crime because no action has been taken. Thus, merely thinking about killing someone or evading taxes and not actually doing so is not a crime.

CONCEPT SUMMARY
ELEMENTS OF AN INTENT CRIME

Element	Description
Actus reus	Guilty act.
Mens rea	Evil intent.

Non-Intent Crimes

Most states provide for certain **non-intent crimes**. The crime of **involuntary manslaughter** is often imposed for reckless or grossly negligent conduct.

non-intent crime
A crime that imposes criminal liability without a finding of *mens rea* (intent).

The magnitude of a crime is proportionate to the magnitude of the injustice which prompts it. Hence, the smallest crimes may be actually the greatest.

Aristotle
The Rhetoric, Book 1, Chapter XIV

Criminal Acts as the Basis for Tort Actions

An injured party may bring a *civil tort action* against a wrongdoer who has caused the party injury during the commission of a criminal act. Civil lawsuits are separate from the government's criminal action against the wrongdoer. In a civil lawsuit, the plaintiff usually wants to recover monetary damages from the wrongdoer. In many cases, a person injured by a criminal act will not sue the criminal to recover civil damages. This is because the criminal is often **judgment proof**—that is, the criminal does not have the money to pay a civil judgment.

CONCEPT SUMMARY

CIVIL AND CRIMINAL LAW COMPARED

Issue	Civil Law	Criminal Law
Party who brings the action	The plaintiff	The government
Trial by jury	Yes, except actions for equity	Yes
Burden of proof	Preponderance of the evidence	Beyond a reasonable doubt
Jury vote	Judgment for plaintiff requires specific jury vote (e.g., 9 of 12 jurors)	Conviction requires unanimous jury vote
Sanctions and penalties	Monetary damages and equitable remedies (e.g., injunction, specific performance)	Imprisonment, capital punishment, fine, probation

▶ CRIMINAL PROCEDURE

The procedure for initiating and maintaining a criminal action is quite detailed. It includes both pretrial procedures and the actual trial.

Arrest

arrest warrant
A document for a person's detainment, based upon a showing of probable cause that the person committed a crime.

Before the police can **arrest** a person for the commission of a crime, they usually must obtain an **arrest warrant** based on a showing of probable cause. The police go before a judge and present the evidence they have for arresting the suspect. If the judge finds that there is probable cause to issue the warrant, she will do so. The police will then use the arrest warrant to arrest the suspect. **Probable cause** is defined as the substantial likelihood that a person either committed or is about to commit a crime.

If there is no time for the police to obtain a warrant, the police may still arrest the suspect without obtaining an arrest warrant. Warrantless arrests are judged by the probable cause standard.

Examples The police can make a warrantless arrest if they arrive during the commission of a crime, when a person is fleeing from the scene of a crime, or when it is likely that evidence will be destroyed.

Example In *Atwater v. Lago Vista, Texas,*[3] the U.S. Supreme Court held that a police officer may make a warrantless arrest pursuant to a minor criminal offense. Gail Atwater was driving her pickup truck in Lago Vista, Texas, with her three-year-old son and five-year-old daughter in the front seat. None of them were wearing seat belts. Bart Turek, a Lago Vista police officer, observed the seat belt violation and pulled Atwater over. A friend of Atwater's arrived at the scene and took charge of the children. Turek handcuffed Atwater, placed her in his squad car, and drove her to the police station. Atwater was booked, her mug shot was taken, and she was placed in a jail cell for about one hour, until she was released on $310 bond. Atwater ultimately pleaded no contest to the misdemeanor seat belt offenses and paid a $50 fine. Atwater sued the City of Lago Vista and the police officer for compensatory and punitive damages for allegedly violating her Fourth Amendment right to be free from unreasonable seizure. The U.S. Supreme Court ruled against Atwater, finding that the Fourth Amendment permits police officers to make a warrantless arrest pursuant to a minor criminal offense.

After a person is arrested, he or she is taken to the police station to be booked. **Booking** is the administrative procedure for recording an arrest, fingerprinting the suspect, taking a photograph of the suspect (often called a "mug shot"), and so on.

Bail Bond

When a person is arrested, a **bail** amount is usually set. If the arrested person "posts" bail, he can be released from prison until the date of his trial. The arrested person can post the bail himself or pay a bail bonds person to post the bond. Bail will not be set if the crime is substantial (e.g., murder) or if the arrestee is a flight risk who might not later show up for trial.

Most arrestees (or their relatives or friend) pay a professional bail bonds person who operates a bail bonds business to post the bond. Bail bonds persons usually require payment of 10% of the bail in order to post bond. If the bail is set at $100,000, then the amount for payment of the bail bond is $10,000. The bail bonds person keeps this $10,000 payment. The bail bonds person guarantees the court that he will pay the court $100,000 if the arrestee does not show up for trial. If this happens, the bail bonds person will attempt to obtain the amount of the bond from the arrestee. Bail bonds persons often require collateral (e.g., title to an automobile, second mortgage on a house) before they issue a bail bond.

Bail Bond *When a person is arrested, a bail amount is usually set by the court. If the arrested person posts bail, either by paying the bail amount or by paying a bail bond company to post the bail, he or she can be released from prison until the date of trial. Bail will not be set if the alleged crime is heinous (e.g., murder) or if the arrestee is a flight risk who might not later show up for trial.*

Indictment or Information

An accused person must be formally charged with a crime before he or she can be brought to trial. This is usually done through the issuance of a **grand jury indictment** or a **magistrate's information statement**.

Evidence of serious crimes, such as murder, is usually presented to a **grand jury**. Most grand juries comprise between 6 and 24 citizens who are charged with evaluating the evidence presented by the government. Grand jurors sit for a fixed period of time, such as one year. If the grand jury determines that there is sufficient evidence to hold the accused for trial, it issues an **indictment**. Note that the grand jury does not determine guilt. If an indictment is issued, the accused will be held for later trial.

For lesser crimes (e.g., burglary, shoplifting), the accused will be brought before a **magistrate** (judge). A magistrate who finds that there is enough evidence to hold the accused for trial will issue **information** statement.

The case against the accused is dismissed if neither an indictment nor information statement is issued.

Arraignment

If an indictment or information is issued, the accused is brought before a court for an **arraignment** proceeding, during which the accused is (1) informed of the charges against him and (2) asked to enter a **plea**. The accused may plead **guilty** or **not guilty**.

Nolo Contendere   A party may also enter a plea of ***nolo contendere***, whereby the accused agrees to the imposition of a penalty but does not admit guilt. The government has the option of accepting a *nolo contendere* plea or requiring the defendant to plead guilty or not guilty. If the government agrees to accept the *nolo contendere* plea, the accused and the government usually enter into a plea bargain in which the accused agrees to the imposition of a penalty but does not admit guilt. A *nolo contendere* plea cannot be used as evidence of liability against the accused at a subsequent civil trial. Corporate defendants often enter this plea.

Plea Bargaining

Sometimes the accused and the government enter into a **plea bargaining agreement**. The government engages in plea bargaining to save costs, avoid the risks of a trial, and prevent further overcrowding of the prisons. This type of arrangement allows the accused to admit to a lesser crime than charged. In return, the government agrees to impose a lesser penalty or sentence than might have been obtained had the case gone to trial. Over 90 percent of criminal cases are settled and do not go to trial.

The Criminal Trial

At a criminal trial, all jurors must *unanimously* agree before the accused is found *guilty* of the crime charged. If even one juror disagrees (i.e., has reasonable doubt) about the guilt of the accused, the accused cannot be found guilty of the crime charged. If all the jurors agree that the accused did not commit the crime, the accused is found *not guilty* of the crime charged. After trial, the following rules apply:

- If the defendant is found guilty, he or she may appeal.
- If the defendant is found not guilty, the government cannot appeal.
- If the jury cannot come to a **unanimous decision** about the defendant's guilt one way or the other, the jury is considered a **hung jury**. The government may choose to retry the case before a new judge and jury.

▶ COMMON CRIMES

Many **common crimes** are committed against persons and property. Some of the most important common crimes against persons and property are discussed in the following paragraphs.

Murder

Murder is defined as the unlawful killing of a human being by another with aforethought of malice. In most states there are several degrees of murder—such as **first-**

---

indictment
The charge of having committed a crime (usually a felony), based on the judgment of a grand jury.

information
The charge of having committed a crime (usually a misdemeanor), based on the judgment of a judge (magistrate).

arraignment
A hearing during which the accused is brought before a court and is (1) informed of the charges against him or her and (2) asked to enter a plea.

plea bargain
An agreement in which the accused admits to a lesser crime than charged. In return, the government agrees to impose a lesser sentence than might have been obtained had the case gone to trial.

There can be no equal justice where the kind of trial a man gets depends on the amount of money he has.

Justice Black
Griffin v. Illinois (1956)

hung jury
A jury that cannot come to a unanimous decision about the defendant's guilt. In the case of a hung jury, the government may choose to retry the case.

degree murder, second-degree murder, third-degree murder—depending on the cicumstances of the case.

Felony Murder Rule

Sometimes a murder is committed during the commission of another crime even though the perpetrator did not originally intend to committ murder. Most states hold the perpetrator liable for the crime of murder in addition to the other crime. This is called the **felony murder rule**. The intent to commit the murder is inferred from the intent to commit the other crime. Many states also hold accomplices liable under this doctrine.

In the following case, the court found that the accused had committed murder.

CASE 8.1 Murder

State of Ohio v. Wilson

2004 Ohio 2838, Web 2004 Ohio App. Lexis 2503 (2004) Court of Appeals of Ohio

"In determining whether a verdict is against the manifest weight of the evidence, the appellate court acts as a 'thirteenth juror.'"

—Judge Sadler

Facts

Gregory O. Wilson, who had been arguing earlier in the day with his girlfriend, Melissa Spear, approached a parked car within which Ms. Spear was seated, and poured gasoline from a beer bottle over her head. When Ms. Spear exited the car, Wilson ignited her with his cigarette lighter, setting her body on fire. As Ms. Spear became engulfed in flames, and while bystanders tried to assist her, Wilson walked away and down the street as if nothing had happened.

Paramedics arrived at the scene. One paramedic described Ms. Spear's burns as the worst he had ever seen. A witness described her after the fire as "totally black, no hair, laying there with her skin melted off of her, the flesh looked like was melted. She was black, looked up at me saying 'help me.'"

Ms. Spear was transported from the scene to the hospital. When she arrived, she had third-degree burns on her face, neck, trunk, arms, hands, and thighs. She was put in a medically induced coma and placed on a respirator. She remained in a coma for 45 days, during which time she underwent 10 surgeries that excised her burn wounds and placed synthetic skin dressing or skin grafts onto her wound sites. Ms. Spear was transferred to a rehabilitation facility. Upon her release from the rehabilitation facility, she received continual treatment and medicine for pain, infection, and depression. Nine months after the incident occurred, and five days before her 30th birthday, Ms. Spear's seven-year-old son found her lying dead in her bed.

The state of Ohio brought criminal charges against Wilson. He was convicted by a jury of aggravated murder and was sentenced to prison for 30 years to life. Mr. Wilson appealed his conviction.

Issue

Was there sufficient causation between Wilson's act of setting Ms. Spear on fire and Ms. Spear's death nine months later to warrant a conviction for murder?

Language of the Court

Wilson argues that the evidence was insufficient to support his conviction for aggravated murder, and that the verdict on this charge was against the manifest weight of the evidence. He contends that the state failed to prove the element of causation beyond a reasonable doubt. Specifically, appellant argues that the nine-month lapse of time between his act of setting Ms. Spear on fire and her eventual death render the verdict of guilty beyond a reasonable doubt on the aggravated murder charge unsupported by the manifest weight and sufficiency of the evidence.

An appellate court's function when reviewing the sufficiency of the evidence to support a criminal conviction is to examine the evidence admitted at trial to determine whether such evidence, if believed, would convince the average mind of the defendant's guilt beyond a reasonable doubt. In determining whether a verdict is against the manifest weight of the evidence, the appellate court acts as a "thirteenth juror." Under this standard of review, the appellate court weighs the evidence in order to determine whether the trier of fact clearly lost its way and created such a manifest miscarriage of justice that the conviction must be reversed and a new trial ordered.

A causal connection between the criminal agency and the cause of death is an essential element in a conviction for murder. Thus, the state must produce evidence to support each link in the chain of causation between the defendant's criminal act and the eventual death of the victim.

Proximate causation is the strongest if the victim dies immediately or shortly after being injured by the defendant. However, a defendant is not relieved of culpability for the natural consequences of inflicting serious wounds on another merely because the victim later died of complications brought on by the injury. The passing of nine months between appellant's act of setting Ms. Spear on fire and her eventual death does not, alone, render appellant's conviction for aggravated murder reversible. The evidence sufficiently demonstrates that the physical maladies that brought about the death of Ms. Spear were the natural, probable and foreseeable results of appellant's conduct. In short, there was sufficient evidence presented upon which the jury could have rationally concluded that appellant's act of setting Melissa Spear ablaze was the direct and proximate

cause of both of the physical conditions that the coroner determined precipitated her death.

Decision

The court of appeals affirmed the trial court's conviction of Wilson of the crime of the murder of Ms. Spear. The court of appeals remanded the case to the trial court to permit Wilson to make a statement on his behalf prior to sentencing.

Case Questions

Critical Legal Thinking What is murder? Is it easy to define?

Business Ethics Do you think Wilson's legal argument on appeal was justified? Why or why not?

Contemporary Business If you were a juror in this case, would you have voted for the death penalty? Do you think the death penaly should be used or abolished? Why or why not?

Robbery

robbery
The taking of personal property from another person by the use of fear or force.

In common law, **robbery** is defined as the taking of personal property from another person or business by the use of fear or force. Robbery with a deadly weapon is generally considered aggravated robbery (or armed robbery) and carries a harsher penalty.

Examples If a person threatens another person with the use of a gun unless the victim gives her purse to that person, this is the crime of robbery. If a person pick pockets somebody's wallet, it is not robbery because there has been no use of force or fear. This is a theft.

Burglary

burglary
The taking of personal property from another's home, office, or commercial or other type of building.

In common law, **burglary** is defined as "breaking and entering a dwelling at night" with the intent to commit a felony. Modern penal codes have broadened this definition to include daytime thefts from homes, offices, commercial, and other buildings. In addition, the "breaking in" element has been abandoned by most modern definitions of burglary. Thus, unauthorized entering of a building through an unlocked door is sufficient. Aggravated burglary (or armed burglary) carries stiffer penalties.

Larceny

larceny
The taking of another's personal property other than from his or her person or building.

In common law, **larceny** is defined as the wrongful and fraudulent taking of another person's personal property that is not robbery or burglary. Most personal property—including tangible property, trade secrets, computer programs, and other business property—is subject to larceny. Neither the use of force nor the entry of a building is required.

Examples Stealing of automobiles and car stereos, pick pocketing, and such are larcenies. Some states distinguish between grand larceny and petit larceny. This distinction depends on the value of the property taken.

Theft

Some states have dropped the distinction among the crimes of robbery, burglary, and larceny. Instead, these states group these crimes under the general crime of **theft**. Most of these states distinguish between grand theft and petit theft. The distinction depends on the value of the property taken.

Receiving Stolen Property

It is a crime for a person to (1) knowingly **receive stolen property** and (2) intend to deprive the rightful owner of that property. Knowledge and intent can be inferred from the circumstances. The stolen property can be any tangible property (e.g., personal property, money, negotiable instruments, stock certificates).

receiving stolen property
To (1) knowingly receive stolen property and (2) intend to deprive the rightful owner of that property.

Arson

In common law, **arson** is defined as the malicious or willful burning of the dwelling of another person. Modern penal codes have expanded this definition to include the burning of all types of private, commercial, and public buildings.

arson
The willful or malicious burning of a building.

Examples An owner of a motel burns down the motel to collect fire insurance proceeds. The owner is guilty of the crime of arson. In this case, the insurance company does not have to pay the proceeds of any insurance policy on the burned property to the arsonist-owner. On the other hand, if a third party arsonist burned down the motel without the knowledge or assistance of the owner, than the owner is entitled to recover the proceeds of any fire insurance he had on the property.

▶ WHITE-COLLAR CRIME

Certain types of crimes, often referred to as **white-collar crimes**, are prone to being committed by businesspersons. These crimes usually involve cunning and deceit rather than physical force. Many of the most important white-collar crimes are discussed in the paragraphs that follow.

Forgery

The crime of **forgery** occurs if a written document is fraudulently made or altered and that change affects the legal liability of another person. Counterfeiting, falsifying public records, and materially altering legal documents are examples of forgery.

forgery
The fraudulent making or alteration of a written document that affects the legal liability of another person.

Example Signing another person's signature to a check or changing the amount of a check without the owner's permission is forgery.

Note that signing another person's signature without intent to defraud is not forgery.

Example Forgery has not been committed if one spouse signs the other spouse's payroll check for deposit in a joint checking or savings account at the bank.

Embezzlement

Unknown in common law, the crime of **embezzlement** is not a statutory crime. Embezzlement is the fraudulent conversion of property by a person to whom that property was entrusted. Typically, embezzlement is committed by an employer's employees, agents, or representatives (e.g., accountants, lawyers, trust officers, treasurers). Embezzlers often try to cover their tracks by preparing false books, records, or entries.

embezzlement
The fraudulent conversion of property by a person to whom that property was entrusted.

The key element here is that the stolen property was *entrusted* to the embezzler. This differs from robbery, burglary, and larceny, where property is taken by someone not entrusted with the property.

Examples A bank entrusted a teller to take deposits from its customers and deposit them into the customers' accounts at the bank. Instead, the bank teller absconds with money.

This is embezzlement. A lawyer who steals money from a trust fund that has been entrusted to him to administer commits the crime of embezzlement.

Bribery

bribery
A crime in which one person gives another person money, property, favors, or anything else of value for a favor in return. A bribe is often referred to as a *payoff* or *kickback*.

Bribery is one of the most prevalent forms of white-collar crime. A bribe can be money, property, favors, or anything else of value. The crime of commercial bribery entails the payment of bribes to private persons and businesses. This type of bribe is often referred to as a **kickback**, or **payoff**. Intent is a necessary element of this crime. The offeror of a bribe commits the crime of bribery when the bribe is tendered. The offeree is guilty of the crime of bribery when he or she accepts the bribe. The offeror can be found liable for the crime of bribery even if the person to whom the bribe is offered rejects the bribe.

Example Harriet Landers is the purchasing agent for the ABC Corporation and is in charge of purchasing equipment to be used by the corporation. Neal Brown, the sales representative of a company that makes equipment that can be used by the ABC Corporation, offers to pay her a 10% kickback if she buys equipment from him. She accepts the bribe and orders the equipment. Both parties are guilty of bribery.

In common law, the crime of bribery is defined as the giving or receiving of anything of value in corrupt payment for an "official act" by a public official. Public officials include legislators, judges, jurors, witnesses at trial, administrative agency personnel, and other government officials. Modern penal codes also make it a crime to bribe public officials. For example, a developer who is constructing an apartment building cannot pay the building inspector to overlook a building code violation.

INTERNATIONAL LAW
Foreign Corrupt Practices Act

It is well known that the payment of bribes is pervasive in conducting international business. To prevent U.S. companies from engaging in this type of conduct, the U.S. Congress enacted the **Foreign Corrupt Practices Act (FCPA)** of 1977.[4] The FCPA makes it illegal for U.S. companies, or their officers, directors, agents, or employees, to bribe a foreign official, a foreign political party official, or a candidate for foreign political office. A bribe is illegal only where it is meant to influence the awarding of new business or the retention of a continuing business activity.

The FCPA imposes criminal liability where a person pays an illegal bribe himself or herself or supplies a payment to a third party or an agent, knowing that it will be used as a bribe. A firm can be fined up to $2 million, and an individual can be fined up to $100,000 and imprisoned for up to five years for violations of the FCPA.

There are two defenses. One excuses a firm or person charged with bribery under the FCPA if the firm or person can show that the payment was lawful under the written laws of that country. The other allows a defendant to show that a payment was a reasonable and bona fide expenditure related to the furtherance or execution of a contract. This latter exemption is difficult to interpret.

Some people argue that U.S. companies are placed at a disadvantage in international markets where commercial bribery is commonplace and firms from other countries are not hindered by laws similar to the FCPA.

Extortion

extortion
A threat to expose something about another person unless that other person gives money or property. Often referred to as *blackmail*.

The crime of **extortion** involves the obtaining of property from another, with his or her consent, induced by wrongful use of actual or threatened force, violence, or fear. Extortion occurs when a person threatens to expose something about another person unless that other person gives money or property. The truth or falsity of the information is immaterial. Extortion of private persons is commonly referred to as **blackmail**. Extortion of public officials is called **extortion under color of official right**.

Criminal Fraud

Obtaining title to property through deception or trickery constitutes the crime of **false pretenses**. This crime is commonly referred to as **criminal fraud** or **deceit**.

Example Bob Anderson, a stockbroker, promises Mary Greenberg, a prospective investor, that he will use any money she invests to purchase interests in oil wells. Based on this promise, Ms. Greenberg decides to make the investment. Mr. Anderson never intended to invest the money. Instead, he used the money for his personal needs. This is criminal fraud.

Mail Fraud, Wire Fraud, and Internet Fraud   Federal law prohibits the use of mails or wires (e.g., telegraphs, telephone, the Internet) to defraud another person. These crimes are called **mail fraud**[5] and **wire fraud**,[6] respectively. The government often prosecutes a suspect under these statutes if there is insufficient evidence to prove the real crime that the criminal was attempting to commit or did commit. The maximum penalty for mail, wire, and Internet fraud is 20 years in prison.

In the following case, the Court found wire fraud and mail fraud.

> **criminal fraud**
> A crime that involves obtaining title to property through deception or trickery. Also known as *false pretenses* or *deceit*.

CASE 8.2 Internet Fraud

United States of America v. Deppe

509 F.3d 54, Web 2007 U.S. App. Lexis 28562 (2007)
United States Court of Appeals for the First Circuit

"The circus impresario, P.T. Barnum, is famously reputed to have said that 'there's a sucker born every minute.'"

—Judge Selya

Facts

Michael R. Deppe, 21 years old, offered Rolex watches for sale over the Internet in exchange for funds wire-transferred directly to his bank account. He engaged in 27 transactions and snared approximately $115,000 in payments. But there was just one hitch: Deppe did not send a single customer a watch. Instead, he sent them packages that contained crumpled newspaper. Two weeks before a Super Bowl championship professional football game, Deppe and another person offered to sell over the Internet nonexistent tickets to the Super Bowl. This scheme netted nearly $263,000 for tickets that Deppe and his business partner did not possess.

A federal grand jury indicted Deppe of wire fraud and mail fraud, which are federal criminal violations. Deppe pled guilty regarding his Rolex fraud. The Super Bowl ticket scheme went to trial in U.S. District Court. The jury convicted Deppe, and the District Court judge sentenced Deppe to 78 months in jail. The court also fined Deppe $520,375. Deppe appealed his sentence, arguing that his sentence should have been reduced because he accepted responsibility for his crimes.

Issue

Did the District Court err in not reducing Deppe's jail sentence?

Language of the Court

The circus impresario, P.T. Barnum, is famously reputed to have said that "there's a sucker born every minute." That droll commentary on the human condition, whether or not fairly attributed to Barnum, appears to be as insightful in cyber-commerce as in face-to-face business transactions. This conclusion is borne out by the case at hand, which involves an Internet fraud. In the appeal proper, we are asked to consider allegations of sentencing error. The overarching themes are those of chicanery and greed.

When a defendant proceeds to trial and puts the government to its proof, a credit for acceptance of responsibility normally will not be available. The district court concluded: "The defendant did not truthfully admit the conduct of the offensive conviction and did not truthfully admit and has falsely denied other relevant conduct." The court also spoke about the appellant's failure to accept full responsibility, the need for deterrence, and the unfortunate hallmarks of the appellant's crimes (cynicism, brazenness, greed, and deliberateness). The short of it is that the sentencing court provided a logical explanation for the 78-month sentence and—given the nature of the crimes committed and the characteristics of the criminal—that sentence represents a sensible punishment.

Decision

The U.S. Court of Appeals held that defendant Deppe did not deserve a sentence reduction. The Court of Appeals upheld the District Court's sentencing of Deppe to 78 months in prison.

Case Questions

Critical Legal Thinking What is wire fraud? Explain. What is mail fraud? Explain.

Business Ethics Did Deppe act ethically in using the Internet to perpetrate his frauds?

Contemporary Business Does the Internet make it easier for crooks to commit fraud? Explain.

ETHICS SPOTLIGHT

Identity Theft

The advent of the computer and the Internet has made one type of crime—identity theft—easier to commit. Identity theft was around long before the computer was invented, but the computer and the Internet have made it much easier for criminals to obtain the information they need to commit identity theft. In **Identity theft**—or **ID theft**—one person steals information about another person to pose as that person and take the innocent person's money or property or to purchase goods and services using the victim's credit information.

To commit ID theft, thieves must first obtain certain information about you. This could be your name, Social Security number, credit card numbers, bank account information, and other personal information. The **Federal Trade Commission (FTC)**, the federal administrative agency primarily charged with handling ID theft matters, lists the following methods thieves use to obtain your personal information:

- **Dumpster diving.** Thieves rummage through trash, looking for bills or other paper with your personal information on it.
- **Skimming.** Thieves steal credit and debit card numbers by using a special storage device when processing your card.
- **Phishing.** Thieves pretend to be financial institutions or companies and send spam or pop-up messages to you online to get you to reveal your personal information.
- **Changing your address.** Thieves divert your billing statements to another location by completing a change-of-address form.
- **Old-fashioned stealing.** Thieves steal wallets and purses; mail, including bank and credit card statements; preapproved credit offers; and new checks or tax information. They steal personnel records or bribe employees who have access to such records.
- **Pretexting.** Thieves use false pretenses to obtain your personal information from financial institutions, telephone companies, and other sources.

Credit card fraud is one of the crimes most commonly committed by identity thieves. A thief may open new credit card accounts in your name and purchase goods and services with these credit cards. Or the thief may change the billing address on your existing credit cards so that you no longer receive bills, and the thief then runs up charges on your account. Because your bills are now sent to a different address, it may be some time before you realize there's a problem. When the thief uses the cards and doesn't pay the bills, the delinquent accounts appear on your credit report.

A victim of identity theft often does not find out about the ID theft until a debt collection agency contacts the victim about overdue debts, when the victim applies for a car loan or a home mortgage and it is discovered when

DETER·DETECT·DEFEND

the bank or creditor conducts a credit check, or when the victim receives something in the mail about an apartment he never rented, a house he did not buy, or a job he never had.

If you are a victim of ID theft, you could lose your money or property to the thieves. It is often impossible to trace the identity of the thieves or to recover your money or property if the thief is found. In addition, ID theft often destroys your credit rating and makes it difficult to obtain credit in the future.

If you are a victim of ID theft, there are several things you should do. You should file an **identity theft report** with the police, cancel certain credit cards, change bank accounts, change security and stock accounts, notify the credit reporting agencies of the items on your credit report that are not yours and that have been created by ID thieves, and have an extended fraud alert placed on your credit report so that credit agencies will notify you of questionable activity. In some cases of ID theft, the victim may not suffer much loss and may not have to do much work to repair his or her credit rating after the ID theft. In other cases, the victim may suffer substantial financial loss and have to spend thousands of dollars and countless hours trying to straighten out his or her credit history and financial life.

Business Ethics Have you ever been a victim of identity theft? Do you know anyone who has been a victim of ID theft?

Money Laundering

When criminals make money from illegal activities, they are often faced with the problem of having large sums of money and no record of how this money was earned. This could easily tip the government off to their illegal activities. In order to "wash" the money and make it look as though it was earned legitimately, many criminals purchase legitimate businesses and run the money through those businesses to "clean" it before they receive the money. The legitimate business has "cooked" books, showing faked expenditures and receipts, in which the illegal money is buried. Restaurants, motels, and other cash businesses make excellent money laundries.

To address the problem of **money laundering**, the federal government enacted the **Money Laundering Control Act**.[7] This act makes it a crime to:

- Knowingly engage in a *monetary transaction* through a financial institution involving property from an unlawful activity worth more than $10,000.

Examples Examples of monetary transactions through a financial institution are making deposits, making withdrawals, conducting transactions between accounts, or obtaining monetary instruments such as cashiers' checks, money orders, and travelers' checks from a bank or other financial institution for more than $10,000.

- Knowingly engage in a *financial transaction* involving the proceeds of an unlawful activity.

Examples Examples of financial transactions involving the proceeds of an illegal activity include buying real estate, automobiles, personal property, intangible assets, or anything else of value with money obtained from illegal activities.

Thus, money laundering itself is now a federal crime. The money that is washed could have been made from illegal gambling operations, drug dealing, fraud, and other crimes, including white-collar crimes. Persons convicted of money laundering can be fined up to $500,000 or twice the value of the property involved, whichever is greater, and sentenced to up to 20 years in federal prison. In addition, violation of the act subjects any property involved in or traceable to the offense to forfeiture to the government.

Money Laundering Control Act
A federal statute that makes it a crime to (1) knowingly engage in a *money transaction* through a financial institution involving property from an unlawful activity worth more than $10,000 and (2) knowingly engage in a *financial transaction* involving the proceeds of an unlawful activity.

Criminal Conspiracy

A **criminal conspiracy** occurs when two or more persons enter into an *agreement* to commit a crime. To be liable for a criminal conspiracy, a person must commit an *overt act* to further the crime. The crime itself does not have to be committed, however. The government usually brings criminal conspiracy charges if (1) the defendants have been thwarted in their efforts to commit the substantive crime or (2) there is insufficient evidence to prove the substantive crime.

Example Two securities brokers agree over the telephone to commit a securities fraud. They obtain a list of potential victims and prepare false financial statements necessary for the fraud. Because they entered into an agreement to commit a crime and took an overt act, the brokers are guilty of the crime of criminal conspiracy, even if they never carry out the securities fraud.

criminal conspiracy
A crime in which two or more persons enter into an agreement to commit a crime and an overt act is taken to further the crime.

Corporate Criminal Liability

A *corporation* is a fictitious legal person that is granted legal existence by the state after certain requirements are met. A corporation cannot act on its own behalf. Instead, it must act through *agents*, such as managers, representatives, and employees.

The question of whether a corporation can be held criminally liable has intrigued legal scholars for some time. Originally, under the common law, it was generally held that corporations lacked the criminal mind (*mens rea*) to be held criminally liable. Modern courts,

corporate criminal liability
Criminal liability of corporations for actions of their officers, employees, or agents.

Racketeer Influenced and Corrupt Organizations Act (RICO)
A federal act that provides for both criminal and civil penalties for racketeering.

however, impose **corporate criminal liability**. These courts have held that corporations are criminally liable for the acts of their managers, agents, and employees. In any event, because corporations cannot be put in prison, they are usually sanctioned with fines, loss of a license or franchise, and the like.

Corporate directors, officers, and employees are individually liable for crimes that they personally commit, whether for personal benefit or on behalf of the corporation. In addition, under certain circumstances, a corporate manager can be held criminally liable for the criminal activities of his or her subordinates. To be held criminally liable, the manager must have failed to supervise the subordinates appropriately. This is an evolving area of the law.

LANDMARK LAW

Racketeer Influenced and Corrupt Organizations Act (RICO)

There are some frauds so well conducted that it would be stupidity not to be deceived by them.

—C. C. Colton, *Lacon, Volume 1 (1820)*

Organized crime has a pervasive influence on many parts of the U.S. economy. In 1980, Congress enacted the Organized Crime Control Act. The **Racketeer Influenced and Corrupt Organizations Act (RICO)** is part of this act.[8] Originally, RICO was intended to apply only to organized crime. However, the broad language of the RICO statute has been used against non–organized crime defendants as well. RICO, which provides for both criminal and civil penalties, is one of the most important laws affecting business today.

Criminal Rico
RICO makes it a federal crime to acquire or maintain an interest in, use income from, or conduct or participate in the affairs of an enterprise through a pattern of racketeering activity. An *enterprise* is defined as a corporation, a partnership, a sole proprietorship, another business or organization, or the government.

Racketeering activity consists of a number of specifically enumerated federal and state crimes, including such activities as gambling, arson, robbery, counterfeiting,

and dealing in narcotics. Business-related crimes, such as bribery, embezzlement, mail fraud, and wire fraud, are also considered racketeering. To prove a *pattern of racketeering*, at least two of these acts must be committed by the defendant within a 10-year period. Commission of the same crime twice within this 10-year period constitutes **criminal RICO** as well.

Individual defendants found criminally liable for RICO violations can be fined, imprisoned for up to 20 years, or both. In addition, RICO provides for the *forfeiture* of any property or business interests (even interests in a legitimate business) that were gained because of RICO violations. This provision allows the government to recover investments made with monies derived from racketeering activities. The government may also seek civil penalties for RICO violations. These include injunctions, orders of dissolution, reorganization of business, and divestiture of the defendant's interest in an enterprise.

Civil Rico
Persons injured by a RICO violation can bring a private **civil RICO** action against the violator to recover for injury to business or property. A successful plaintiff may recover *treble damages* (three times actual loss) plus attorneys' fees.

---

unreasonable search and seizure
Any search and seizure by the government that violates the Fourth Amendment.

search warrant
A warrant issued by a court that authorizes the police to search a designated place for specified contraband, articles, items, or documents. A search warrant must be based on probable cause.

▶ PROTECTION AGAINST UNREASONABLE SEARCH AND SEIZURE

In many criminal cases, the government relies on information obtained from searches of individuals and businesses. The **Fourth Amendment** to the U.S. Constitution protects persons and corporations from overzealous investigative activities by the government. It protects the rights of the people from **unreasonable search and seizure** by the government. It permits people to be secure in their persons, houses, papers, and effects.

Reasonable search and seizure by the government is lawful. **Search warrants** based on probable cause are necessary in most cases. Such a warrant specifically states the place and scope of the authorized search. General searches beyond the specified area are forbidden. *Warrantless searches* are permitted only (1) incident to arrest, (2) where evidence is in "plain view," or (3) where it is likely that evidence will be destroyed. Warrantless searches are judged by the probable cause standard.

Exclusionary Rule

Evidence obtained from an unreasonable search and seizure is considered tainted evidence ("fruit of a tainted tree"). Under the **exclusionary rule**, such evidence can generally be prohibited from introduction at a trial or an administrative proceeding against the person searched. However, this evidence is freely admissible against other persons. The U.S. Supreme Court created a *good faith exception* to the exclusionary rule.[9] This exception allows evidence otherwise obtained illegally to be introduced as evidence against the accused if the police officers who conducted the unreasonable search reasonably believed that they were acting pursuant to a lawful search warrant.

The following case examines the reach of the Fourth Amendment's protection against unreasonable search and seizure.

exclusionary rule
A rule that says evidence obtained from an unreasonable search and seizure can generally be prohibited from introduction at a trial or an administrative proceeding against the person searched.

U.S. SUPREME COURT   CASE 8.3 Search

Kyllo v. United States

533 U.S. 27, 121 S.Ct. 2038, 150 L.Ed.2d 94, Web 2001 U.S. Lexis 4487 (2001)
Supreme Court of the United States

"At the very core of the Fourth Amendment stands the right of a man to retreat into his own home and there be free from unreasonable government intrusion."

—Justice Scalia

Facts

Government agents suspected that marijuana was being grown in the home of Danny Kyllo, which was part of a triplex building in Florence, Oregon. Indoor marijuana growth typically requires high-intensity lamps. In order to determine whether an amount of heat was emanating from Kyllo's home consistent with the use of such lamps, federal agents used a thermal imager to scan the triplex. Thermal imagers detect infrared radiation and produce images of the radiation. The scan of Kyllo's home, which was performed from an automobile on the street, showed that the roof over the garage and a side wall of Kyllo's home were "hot." The agents used this scanning evidence to obtain a search warrant authorizing a search of Kyllo's home. During the search, the agents found an indoor growing operation involving more than 100 marijuana plants.

Kyllo was indicted for manufacturing marijuana, a violation of federal criminal law. Kyllo moved to suppress the imaging evidence and the evidence it led to, arguing that it was an unreasonable search that violated the Fourth Amendment to the U.S. Constitution. The U.S. District Court disagreed with Kyllo and let the evidence be introduced and considered at trial. Kyllo then entered a conditional guilty plea and appealed the trial court's failure to suppress the challenged evidence to the U.S. Court of Appeals. The U.S. Court of Appeals affirmed the trial court's decision to admit the evidence. Kyllo appealed to the U.S. Supreme Court.

Issue

Is the use of a thermal-imaging device aimed at a private home from a public street to detect relative amounts of heat

within the home a "search" within the meaning of the Fourth Amendment?

Language of the U.S. Supreme Court

At the very core of the Fourth Amendment stands the right of a man to retreat into his own home and there be free from unreasonable government intrusion. With few exceptions, the question whether a warrantless search of a home is reasonable and hence constitutional must be answered no. The present case involves officers on a public street engaged in more than naked-eye surveillance of a home. The question we confront today is what limits there are upon this power of technology to shrink the realm of guaranteed privacy. We think that obtaining by sense-enhancing technology any information regarding the interior of the home that could not otherwise have been obtained without physical intrusion into a constitutionally protected area. This assures preservation of that degree of privacy against government that existed when the Fourth Amendment was adopted. On the basis of this criterion, the information obtained by the thermal imager in this case was the product of a search.

Decision

The U.S. Supreme Court held that the use of a thermal-imaging device aimed at a private home from a public street to detect relative amounts of heat within the home is a "search" within the meaning of the Fourth Amendment. The Supreme Court reversed the decision of the U.S. Court of Appeals and remanded the case for further proceedings.

Case Questions

Critical Legal Thinking What does the Fourth Amendment's prohibition against unreasonable search and seizure provide? Explain.

Business Ethics Did the police act ethically in obtaining the evidence in this case? Did Kyllo act ethically in trying to suppress the evidence?

Contemporary Business Is selling illegal drugs a big business in this country? How can the government catch entrepreneurs such as Kyllo?

Web Exercise Go to www.dailybreeze.com/ci_9009312 and read the ruling regarding searches of computers at the borders of the United States.

The criminal is to go free because the constable has blundered.

Chief Judge Cardozo
People v. Defore (1926)

Searches of Business Premises

Generally, the government does not have the right to search business premises without a search warrant.[10] Certain hazardous and regulated industries—such as sellers of firearms and liquor, coal mines, and the like—are subject to warrantless searches if proper statutory procedures are met.

▶ PRIVILEGE AGAINST SELF-INCRIMINATION

The **Fifth Amendment** to the U.S. Constitution provides that no person "shall be compelled in any criminal case to be a witness against himself." Thus, a person cannot be compelled to give testimony against himself or herself, although nontestimonial evidence (e.g., fingerprints, body fluids) may be required. A person who asserts this right is described as having "taken the Fifth." This protection applies to federal cases and is extended to state and local criminal cases through the Due Process Clause of the Fourteenth Amendment.

The protection against **self-incrimination** applies only to natural persons who are accused of crimes. Therefore, artificial persons (such as corporations and partnerships) cannot raise this protection against incriminating testimony.[11] Thus, business records of corporations and partnerships are not generally protected from disclosure, even if they incriminate individuals who work for the business. However, certain "private papers" of businesspersons (e.g., personal diaries) are protected from disclosure.

self-incrimination
A person being a witness against himself or herself. The Fifth Amendment prevents self-incrimination in any criminal case.

At the present time in this country there is more danger that criminals will escape justice than that they will be subjected to tyranny.

Justice Holmes, Dissenting
Kepner v. United States (1904)

***Miranda* rights**
Rights that a suspect must be informed of before being interrogated, so that the suspect will not unwittingly give up his or her Fifth Amendment right.

Miranda Rights

Most people have not read and memorized the provisions of the U.S. Constitution. The U.S. Supreme Court recognized this fact when it decided the landmark case *Miranda v. Arizona* in 1966.[12] In that case, the Supreme Court held that the Fifth Amendment privilege against self-incrimination is not useful unless a criminal suspect has knowledge of this right. Therefore, the Supreme Court required that the following warning—colloquially called the *Miranda* rights—be read to a criminal suspect before he or she is interrogated by the police or other government officials:

Miranda Rights

- You have the right to remain silent.

- Anything you say can and will be used against you in a court of law.

- You have the right to speak to an attorney and to have an attorney present during any questioning.

- If you cannot afford a lawyer, one will be provided for you at government expense.

Many police departments read an accused a more detailed version of the *Miranda* rights (see page 145). This is designed to cover all issues that a detainee might encounter while in police custody. A detainee may be asked to sign a statement acknowledging that the *Miranda* rights have been read to him or her.

Miranda Rights

- You have the right to remain silent and refuse to answer questions. Do you understand?

- Anything you do say may be used against you in a court of law. Do you understand?

- You have the right to consult an attorney before speaking to the police and to have an attorney present during questioning now or in the future. Do you understand?

- If you cannot afford an attorney, one will be appointed for you before any questioning if you wish. Do you understand?

- If you decide to answer questions now without an attorney present, you will still have the right to stop answering at any time until you talk to an attorney. Do you understand?

- Knowing and understanding your rights as I have explained them to you, are you willing to answer my questions without an attorney present?

Any statements or confessions obtained from a suspect prior to being read his or her *Miranda* rights can be excluded from evidence at trial. In 2000, the U.S. Supreme Court upheld *Miranda* in *Dickerson v. United States*.[13] In that opinion, Chief Justice Rehnquist stated, "We do not think there is justification for overruling *Miranda*. *Miranda* has become embedded in routine police practice to the point where the warnings have become part of our national culture."

Attorney–Client Privilege and Other Privileges

To obtain a proper defense, an accused person must be able to tell his attorney facts about his case without fear that the attorney will be called as a witness against him. The **attorney–client privilege** is protected by the Fifth Amendment. Either the client or the attorney can raise this privilege. For the privilege to apply, the information must be told to the attorney in his or her capacity as an attorney, and not as a friend or neighbor or such.

The Fifth Amendment has also recognized the following privileges under which an accused may keep the following individuals from being witnesses against him:

attorney–client privilege
A rule that says a client can tell his or her lawyer anything about the case without fear that the attorney will be called as a witness against the client.

- **Psychiatrist/psychologist–patient privilege** (so that the accused may tell the truth in order to seek help for his condition)
- **Priest/rabbi/minister/imam–penitent privilege** (so that the accused may tell the truth in order to repent, obtain help, and seek forgiveness for his deed)
- **Spouse–spouse privilege** (so that the family will remain together)
- **Parent–child privilege** (so that the family will remain together)

A spouse or child who is injured by a spouse or parent (e.g., domestic abuse) may testify against the accused. In addition, if the accused discloses that he is planning to commit a crime in the future (e.g., murder), the accused's lawyer; psychiatrist or psychologist; or priest, rabbi, minister, or imam is required to report this to the police or other relevant authorities.

The U.S. Supreme Court has held that there is no accountant–client privilege under federal law.[14] Thus, an accountant could be called as a witness in cases involving federal securities laws, federal mail or wire fraud, or other federal crimes. Nevertheless, approximately 20 states have enacted special statutes that create an **accountant–client privilege**. An accountant cannot be called as a witness against a client in a court action in a state where these statutes are in effect. Federal courts do not recognize these laws, however.

Immunity from Prosecution

On occasion, the government may want to obtain information from a suspect who has asserted his or her Fifth Amendment privilege against self-incrimination. The government

immunity from prosecution
The government's agreement not to use against a person granted immunity any evidence given by that person.

can often achieve this by offering the suspect **immunity from prosecution**. Immunity from prosecution means that the government agrees not to use against a person granted immunity any evidence given by that person. Once immunity is granted, the suspect loses the right to assert his or her Fifth Amendment privilege.

Grants of immunity are often given when the government wants a suspect to give information that will lead to the prosecution of other, more important, criminal suspects. Partial grants of immunity are also available. A suspect must agree to a partial grant of immunity in order for it to occur.

In serious cases, the government can place a witness in a government protective program whereby after the trial the witness and her family are permanently moved to an undisclosed location, given a new identity, and provided monetary assistance. Such a witness is also usually protected prior to trial.

▶ OTHER CONSTITUTIONAL PROTECTIONS

Besides those already discussed in this chapter, there are many other provisions in the U.S. Constitution and its amendments that guarantee and protect certain other rights in the criminal process. Several of these additional rights are described in the paragraphs that follow.

Fifth Amendment Protection Against Double Jeopardy

Double Jeopardy Clause
A clause of the Fifth Amendment that protects persons from being tried twice for the same crime.

The **Double Jeopardy Clause** of the Fifth Amendment protects persons from being tried twice for the same crime.

Example If a state tries a suspect for the crime of murder, and the suspect is found not guilty, the state cannot bring another trial against the accused for the same crime. This is so even if more evidence later surfaces that would lead to conviction. The government is given the opportunity to bring its case against an accused once and cannot keep retrying the same case.

However, if the same criminal act involves several different crimes, the accused may be tried for each of the crimes separately without violating the Double Jeopardy Clause. If the same act violates the laws of two or more jurisdictions, each jurisdiction may try the accused.

Example Suppose an accused kills two people during a robbery. The accused may be tried for two murders and the robbery.

Example If an accused kidnaps a person in one state and brings the victim across a state border into another state, the act violates the laws of two states and the federal government. Thus, three jurisdictions can prosecute the accused without violating the Double Jeopardy Clause.

If an accused is tried once and the jury reaches a *hung jury*—that is, the verdict is not unanimous for either guilty or not guilty—the government can retry the case against the accused without violating the Double Jeopardy Clause.

Sixth Amendment Right to a Public Jury Trial

The **Sixth Amendment** guarantees certain rights to criminal defendants. These rights are (1) to be tried by an impartial jury of the state or district in which the alleged crime was committed, (2) to confront (cross-examine) the witnesses against the accused, (3) to have the assistance of a lawyer, and (4) to have a speedy trial.[15]

Eighth Amendment Protection Against Cruel and Unusual Punishment

The **Eighth Amendment** protects criminal defendants from **cruel and unusual punishment**. For example, it prohibits the torture of criminals. However, this clause does not prohibit capital punishment.[16] The U.S. Supreme Court has held that in capital punishment cases, death by lethal injection is not cruel and unusual punishment.[17]

TEST REVIEW TERMS AND CONCEPTS

Accountant–client privilege
Actus reus
Arraignment
Arrest
Arrest warrant
Arson
Attorney–client privilege
Bail
Beyond a reasonable doubt
Booking
Bribery
Burglary
Civil RICO
Common Crimes
Corporate criminal liability
Credit card fraud
Crime
Criminal conspiracy
Criminal fraud (false
   pretenses or deceit)
Criminal laws
Criminal RICO
Cruel and unusual
   punishment
Defendant
Defense attorney
Double Jeopardy Clause

Eighth Amendment
Embezzlement
Exclusionary rule
Extortion (blackmail)
Extortion under color of
   official right
Federal Trade Commission
   (FTC)
Felony
Felony murder rule
Fifth Amendment
First-degree murder
Foreign Corrupt Practices
   Act (FCPA)
Forgery
Fourth Amendment
General intent
Grand jury
Grand jury indictment
Guilty
Hung jury
Identity theft (ID theft)
Identity theft report
Immunity from prosecution
Indictment
Information
Internet fraud

Involuntary manslaughter
Judgment proof
Kickback (payoff)
Larceny
Magistrate
Magistrate's information
   statement
Mail fraud
Mala in se
Mala prohibita
Mens rea
Miranda rights
Misdemeanor
Money laundering
Money Laundering Control
   Act
Nolo contendere
Non-intent crime
Not guilty
Parent–child privilege
Penal code
Plaintiff
Plea
Plea bargaining agreement
Priest/rabbi/minister/imam–
   penitent privilege
Probable cause

Prosecutor
Psychiatrist/psychologist–
   patient privilege
Public defender
Racketeer Influenced and
   Corrupt Organizations
   Act (RICO)
Reasonable search and
   seizure
Receiving stolen
   property
Regulatory statutes
Robbery
Search warrant
Second-degree murder
Self-incrimination
Specific intent
Sixth Amendment
Spouse–spouse privilege
Theft
Third-degree murder
Unanimous decision
Unreasonable search and
   seizure
Violation
White-collar crime
Wire fraud

CASE PROBLEMS

8.1 Criminal Liability of Corporations Representatives of hotels, restaurants, hotel and restaurant supply companies, and other businesses located in Portland, Oregon, organized an association to attract conventions to their city. Members were asked to make contributions equal to one percent of their sales to finance the association. To aid collections, hotel members, including Hilton Hotels Corporation, agreed to give preferential treatment to suppliers who paid their assessments and to curtail purchases from those who did not. This agreement violated federal antitrust laws. The United States sued the members of the association, including Hilton Hotels, for the crime of violating federal antitrust laws. Can a corporation be held criminally liable for the acts of its representatives? If so, what criminal penalties can be assessed against the corporation? *United States v. Hilton Hotels Corp.*, 467 F.2d 1000, **Web** 1972 U.S. App. Lexis 7414 (United States Court of Appeals for the Ninth Circuit)

8.2 Forgery Evidence showed that there was a burglary in which a checkbook belonging to Mary J. Harris, doing business as The Report Department, and a check encoder machine were stolen. Two of the checks from that checkbook were cashed at the Citizens & Southern National Bank branch office in Riverdale, Georgia, by Joseph Leon Foster, who was accompanied by a woman identified as Angela Foxworth. The bank teller who cashed the checks testified that the same man and woman cashed the checks on two different occasions at her drive-up window at the bank and that on both occasions, they were in the same car. Each time the teller wrote the license tag number of the car on the back of the check. The teller testified that both times, the checks and the driver's license used to identify the woman were passed to her by the man driving and that the man received the money from her. What crime has been committed? *Foster v. State of Georgia*, 193 Ga. App. 368, 387 S.E.2d 637, **Web** 1989 Ga.App. Lexis 1456 (Court of Appeals of Georgia)

8.3 Extortion The victim (Mr. X) went to the premises at 42 Taylor Terrace in New Milford, Connecticut, where his daughter and her husband lived. Lisa Percoco, who was Gregory Erhardt's girlfriend, was at the residence. Mr. X and Percoco were in the bedroom, partially dressed, engaging in sexual activity, when Erhardt entered the room and photographed them. He then informed Mr. X that unless he procured $5,000 and placed it in a mailbox at a designated address by 8 P.M. that night, Erhardt would show the photographs to

Mr. X's wife. Mr. X proceeded to make telephone arrangements for the procurement and placement of the money according to Erhardt's instructions. If the money were paid, what crime would have been committed? *State of Connecticut v. Erhardt*, 17 Conn.App. 359, 553 A.2d 188, **Web** 1989 Conn. App. Lexis 21 (Appellate Court of Connecticut)

8.4 Criminal Fraud   Miriam Marlowe's husband purchased a life insurance policy on his own life, naming his wife as the beneficiary. Three years later, after Marlowe's husband died in a swimming accident, Marlowe received payment on the life insurance policy. Marlowe later met John Walton, a friend of a friend. He convinced her and her representative that he had a friend who worked for the State Department and had access to gold in Brazil and that the gold could be purchased in Brazil for $100 an ounce and sold in the United States for $300 an ounce. Walton convinced Miriam to invest $25,000. Instead of investing the money in gold in Brazil, Walton opened an account at Tracy Collins Bank in the name of Jeffrey McIntyre Roberts and deposited Miriam's money in the account. He later withdrew the money in cash. What crime is Walton guilty of? *State of Utah v. Roberts*, 711 P.2d 235, **Web** 1985 Utah Lexis 872 (Supreme Court of Utah)

8.5 Bribery   The city of Peoria, Illinois, received federal funds from the Department of Housing and Urban Development (HUD) to be used for housing rehabilitation assistance. The city of Peoria designated United Neighborhoods, Inc. (UNI), a corporation, to administer the funds. Arthur Dixon was UNI's executive director, and James Lee Hinton was its housing rehabilitation coordinator. In these capacities, they were responsible for contracting with suppliers and tradespeople to provide the necessary goods and services to rehabilitate the houses. Evidence showed that Dixon and Hinton used their positions to extract 10 percent payments back on all contracts they awarded. What crime have they committed? *Dixon and Hinton v. United States*, 465 U.S. 482, 104 S.Ct. 1172, 79 L.Ed.2d 458, **Web** 1984 U.S. Lexis 35 (Supreme Court of the United States)

8.6 Administrative Search   Lee Stuart Paulson owned a liquor license for My House, a bar in San Francisco. The California Department of Alcoholic Beverage Control is the administrative agency that regulates bars in that state. The California Business and Professions Code, which the department administers, prohibits "any kind of illegal activity

on licensed premises." An anonymous informer tipped the department that narcotics sales were occurring on the premises of My House and that the narcotics were kept in a safe behind the bar on the premises. A special department investigator entered the bar during its hours of operation, identified himself, and informed Paulson that he was conducting an inspection. The investigator, who did not have a search warrant, opened the safe without seeking Paulson's consent. Twenty-two bundles of cocaine, totaling 5.5 grams, were found in the safe. Paulson was arrested. At his criminal trial, Paulson challenged the lawfulness of the search. Was the warrantless search of the safe a lawful search? *People v. Paulson*, 216 Cal.App.3d 1480, 265 Cal.Rptr. 579, **Web** 1990 Cal.App. Lexis 10 (Court of Appeal of California)

8.7 Search Warrant   The Center Art Galleries–Hawaii sells artwork. Approximately 20 percent of its business involves art by Salvador Dalí. The federal government, which suspected the center of fraudulently selling forged Dalí artwork, obtained identical search warrants for six locations controlled by the center. The warrants commanded the executing officer to seize items that were "evidence of violations of federal criminal law." The warrants did not describe the specific crimes suspected and did not stipulate that only items pertaining to the sale of Dalí's work could be seized. There was no evidence of any criminal activity unrelated to that artist. Are these search warrants valid? *Center Art Galleries–Hawaii, Inc. v. United States*, 875 F.2d 747, **Web** 1989 U.S. App. Lexis 6983 (United States Court of Appeals for the Ninth Circuit)

8.8 Privilege Against Self-Incrimination   John Doe is the owner of several sole proprietorship businesses. During the course of an investigation of corruption in awarding county and municipal contracts, a federal grand jury served several subpoenas on John Doe, demanding the production of certain business records. The subpoenas demanded the production of the following records: (1) general ledgers and journals, (2) invoices, (3) bank statements and canceled checks, (4) financial statements, (5) telephone company records, (6) safe deposit box records, and (7) copies of tax returns. John Doe filed a motion in federal court, seeking to quash the subpoenas, alleging that producing these business records would violate his Fifth Amendment privilege of not testifying against himself. Must John Doe disclose the records? *United States v. John Doe*, 465 U.S. 605, 104 S.Ct. 1237, 79 L.Ed.2d 552, **Web** 1984 U.S. Lexis 169 (Supreme Court of the United States)

BUSINESS ETHICS CASES

8.9 Business Ethics   Leo Shaw, an attorney, entered into a partnership agreement with three other persons to build and operate an office building. From the outset, it was agreed that Shaw's role was to manage the operation of the building. Management of the property was Shaw's contribution

to the partnership; the other three partners contributed the necessary capital. Ten years later, the other partners discovered that the loan on the building was in default and that foreclosure proceedings were imminent. Upon investigation, they discovered that Shaw had taken approximately $80,000 from the partnership's checking account. After heated discussions, Shaw repaid $13,000. When no further payment was forthcoming, a partner filed a civil suit against Shaw and notified the police. The state filed a criminal complaint against Shaw. Subsequently, Shaw repaid the remaining funds as part of a civil settlement. At his criminal trial, Shaw argued that the repayment of the money was a defense to the crime of embezzlement. Did Shaw act ethically in this case? Would your answer be different if Shaw had really only "borrowed" the money and had intended to return it? *People v. Shaw*, 10 Cal.App. 4th 969, 12 Cal.Rptr.2d 665, **Web** 1992 Cal.App. Lexis 1256 (Court of Appeal of California)

8.10 Business Ethics   Ronald V. Cloud purchased the Cal-Neva Lodge, a hotel and casino complex located in the Lake Tahoe area near the California–Nevada border, for $10 million. Cloud was a sophisticated 68-year-old entrepreneur who was experienced in buying and selling real estate and had real estate holdings valued at more than $65 million. He also had experience in banking and finance, having been the founder and chairman of Continental National Bank of Fresno. After two years of mounting operation losses, Cloud closed the Cal-Neva Lodge and actively began seeking a new buyer. Cloud met with Jon Perroton and orally agreed to transfer the lodge to Perroton for approximately $17 million. Perroton met with an executive of Hibernia Bank (Hibernia) to discuss a possible loan to finance the purchase of the lodge. Perroton made multiple false representations and presented false documents to obtain a $20 million loan from Hibernia. In particular, Perroton misrepresented the sale price for the lodge ($27.5 million) and stated that $7.5 million had already been paid to Cloud. An escrow account was opened with Transamerica Title Company (Transamerica).

Cloud and his attorney and Perroton met at Transamerica to sign mutual escrow instructions. Cloud reviewed the instructions and noticed that the sale price and down payment figures were incorrectly stated at $27.5 million and $7.5 million, respectively, and that the Hibernia loan was for $20 million, almost $3 million above what he knew to be the true sale price. Cloud signed the escrow instructions. Later, Cloud signed a settlement statement containing the same false figures and signed a grant deed to the property. The sale closed on January 23, 1985, with Hibernia making the $20 million loan to Perroton. Subsequently, when the loan went into default, Continental Insurance Company (Continental) paid Hibernia its loss of $7.5 million on the bank's blanket bond insurance policy. The United States sued Cloud for aiding and abetting a bank fraud in violation of federal law (18 U.S.C. Sections 2 and 1344). The jury convicted Cloud of the crime and ordered him to make restitution of $7.5 million to Continental. Cloud appealed. Did cloud act ethically in this case? Explain. Is Cloud guilty of aiding and abetting a bank fraud? *United States v. Cloud*, 872 F.2d 846, **Web** 1989 U.S. App. Lexis 4534 (United States Court of Appeals for the Ninth Circuit)

ENDNOTES

1. Title 18 of the U.S. Code contains the federal criminal code.
2. Sentencing Reform Act of 1984, 18 U.S.C. Section 3551 et seq.
3. 532 U.S. 318, 121 S.Ct. 1536, 149 L.Ed.2d 549, Web 2001 U.S. Lexis 3366 (Supreme Court of the United States, 2001).
4. 15 U.S.C. Section 78m.
5. 18 U.S.C. Section 1341.
6. 18 U.S.C. Section 1343.
7. 18 U.S.C. Section 1957.
8. 18 U.S.C. Sections 1961–1968.
9. *United States v. Leon*, 468 U.S. 897, 104 S.Ct. 3405, 82 L.Ed.2d 677, Web 1984 U.S. Lexis 153 (Supreme Court of the United States).
10. *Marshall v. Barlow's Inc.*, 436 U.S. 307, 98 S.Ct. 1816, 56 L.Ed.2d 305, Web 1978 U.S. Lexis 26 (Supreme Court of the United States).
11. *Bellis v. United States*, 417 U.S. 85, 94 S.Ct. 2.179, 40 L.Ed.2d 678, Web 1974 U.S. Lexis 58 (Supreme Court of the United States)
12. 384 U.S. 436, 86 S.Ct. 1602, 16 L.Ed.2d 694, Web 1966 U.S. Lexis 2817 (Supreme Court of the United States).
13. 530 U.S. 428, 120 S.Ct. 2326, 147 L.Ed.2d 405, Web 2000 U.S. Lexis 4305 (Supreme Court of the United States).
14. 409 U.S. 322, 93 S.Ct. 611, 34 L.Ed.2d 548, Web 1973 U.S. Lexis 23 (Supreme Court of the United States).
15. The Speedy Trial Act requires that a criminal defendant be brought to trial within 70 days after indictment [18 U.S.C. Section 316(c) (1)]. Continuances may be granted by the court to serve the "ends of justice."
16. *Baldwin v. Alabama*, 472 U.S. 372, 105 S.Ct. 2727, 86 L.Ed.2d 300, Web 1985 U.S. Lexis 106 (Supreme Court of the United States).
17. *Baze v. Rees*, 128 S.Ct. 1520, 170 L.Ed.2d 420, Web 2008 U.S. Lexis 3476 (Supreme Court of the United States, 2008).

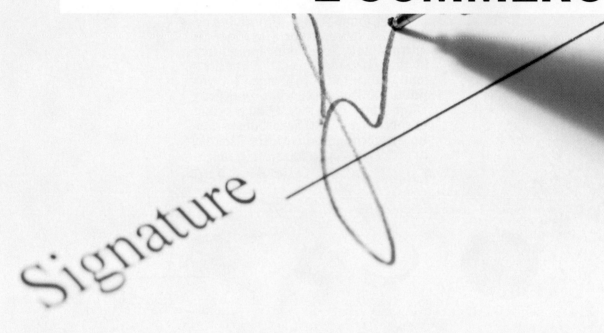

Part III

CONTRACTS AND E-COMMERCE

9 | NATURE OF TRADITIONAL AND E-CONTRACTS

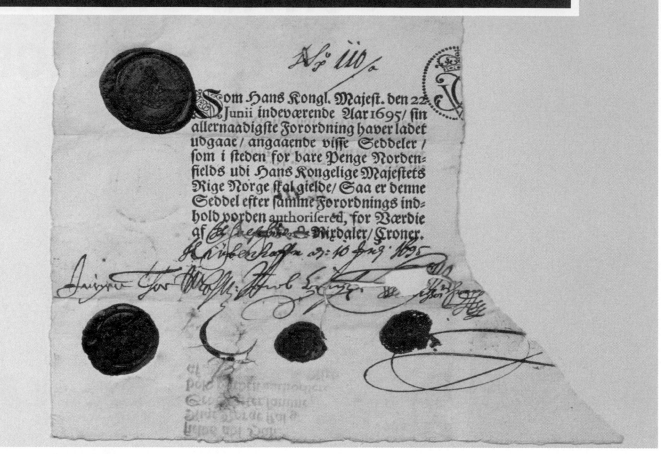

▲ **Norwegian Merchant's Note, with Four Red Seals** *Written contracts have long been used in business to ensure mutual understanding. In many societies, seals such as the ones in this photo were required to establish the document's authenticity.*

CHAPTER OBJECTIVES

After studying this chapter, you should be able to:

1. Define *contract*.
2. List the elements necessary to form a valid contract.
3. Distinguish between bilateral and unilateral contracts.
4. Describe and distinguish between express and implied-in-fact contracts.
5. Describe and distinguish among valid, void, voidable, and unenforceable contracts.

CHAPTER CONTENTS

"The movement of the progressive societies has hitherto been a movement from status to contract."

—Sir Henry Maine
Ancient Law, Chapter 5

▶ INTRODUCTION TO NATURE OF TRADITIONAL AND E-CONTRACTS

Contracts are the basis of many of our daily activities. They provide the means for individuals and businesses to sell and otherwise transfer property, services, and other rights. The purchase of goods, such as books and automobiles, is based on sales contracts; the hiring of employees is based on service contracts; the lease of an apartment is based on a rental contract; and the sale of goods and services over the Internet is based on electronic contracts. The list is almost endless. Without enforceable contracts, commerce would collapse.

Contracts are voluntarily entered into by parties. The terms of a contract become *private law* between the parties. One court has stated that "the contract between parties is the law between them and the courts are obliged to give legal effect to such contracts according to the true interests of the parties."[1]

Nevertheless, most contracts are performed without the aid of the court system. This is usually because the parties feel a moral duty to perform as promised. Although some contracts, such as illegal contracts, are not enforceable, most are **legally enforceable**.[2] This means that if a party fails to perform a contract, the other party may call upon the courts to enforce the contract.

This chapter introduces the study of **traditional law** and **e-contract law**. Such topics as the definition of *contract*, requirements for forming a contract, sources of contract law, and the various classifications of contracts are discussed.

> **legally enforceable contract**
> A contract in which if one party fails to perform as promised, the other party can use the court system to enforce the contract and recover damages or other remedy.

▶ DEFINITION OF A CONTRACT

A **contract** is an agreement that is enforceable by a court of law or equity. A simple and widely recognized definition of *contract* is provided by the *Restatement (Second) of Contracts*: "A contract is a promise or a set of promises for the breach of which the law gives a remedy or the performance of which the law in some way recognizes a duty."[3]

Parties to a Contract

Every contract involves at least two parties. The **offeror** is the party who makes an offer to enter into a contract. The **offeree** is the party to whom the offer is made (see Exhibit 9.1). In making an offer, the offeror promises to do—or to refrain from doing—something. The offeree then has the power to create a contract by accepting the offeror's offer. A contract is created if the offer is accepted. No contract is created if the offer is not accepted.

> **offeror**
> The party who makes an offer to enter into a contract.
>
> **offeree**
> The party to whom an offer to enter into a contract is made.

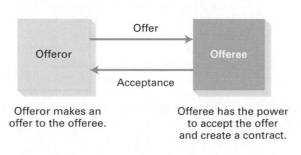

Offer

Offeror

Offeree

Acceptance

Offeror makes an offer to the offeree.

Offeree has the power to accept the offer and create a contract.

▶ **Exhibit 9.1 PARTIES TO A CONTRACT**

Contracts must not be the sports of an idle hour, mere matters of pleasantry and badinage, never intended by the parties to have any serious effect whatever.

Lord Stowell
Dalrymple v. Dalrymple (1811)

Elements of a Contract

For a contract to be enforceable, the following four basic requirements must be met:

1. **Agreement.**   To have an enforceable contract, there must be an **agreement** between the parties. This requires an **offer** by the offeror and an **acceptance** of the offer by the offeree. There must be mutual assent by the parties.
2. **Consideration.**   The promise must be supported by a bargained-for **consideration** that is legally sufficient. Money, personal property, real property, provision of services, and such qualify as consideration.
3. **Contractual capacity.**   The parties to a contract must have **contractual capacity** for the contract to be enforceable against them. Contracts cannot be enforced against parties who lacked contractual capacity when they entered into a contract.
4. **Lawful object.**   The object of the contract must be lawful. Most contracts have a **lawful object.** However, contracts that have an illegal object are void and will not be enforced.

CONCEPT SUMMARY

ELEMENTS OF A CONTRACT

1. Agreement

2. Consideration

3. Contractual capacity

4. Lawful object

Defenses to the Enforcement of a Contract

Two *defenses* may be raised to the enforcement of contracts:

1. **Genuineness of assent.**   The consent of the parties to create a contract must be **genuine**. If the consent is obtained by duress, undue influence, or fraud, there is no real consent.
2. **Writing and form.**   The law requires that certain contracts be in **writing** or in a certain **form**. Failure of such a contract to be in writing or to be in proper form may be raised against the enforcement of the contract.

The requirements to form an enforceable contract and the defenses to the enforcement of contracts are discussed in this chapter and the following chapters on contract law.

CONTEMPORARY ENVIRONMENT

The Evolution of the Modern Law of Contracts

The use of contracts originally developed in ancient times. The common law of contracts developed in England around the fifteenth century. U.S. contract law evolved from the English common law.

At first, the United States adopted a *laissez-faire* approach to the law of contracts. The central theme of this theory was *freedom of contract*. The parties (e.g., consumers, shopkeepers, farmers, traders) generally dealt with one another face-to-face, had equal knowledge and bargaining power, and had the opportunity to inspect goods prior to

sale. Contract terms were openly negotiated. There was little, if any, government regulation of the right to contract. This "pure law," or **classical law of contracts** produced objective rules, which, in turn, produced certainty and predictability in the enforcement of contracts. It made sense until the Industrial Revolution.

The Industrial Revolution changed many of the underlying assumptions of pure contract law. For example, as large corporations developed and gained control of crucial resources, the traditional balance of parties' bargaining power shifted: Large corporations now had the most power. The chain of distribution for goods also changed because (1) buyers did not have to deal face-to-face with sellers and (2) there was not always an opportunity to inspect the goods prior to sale.

Eventually sellers began using **form contracts** that offered their goods to buyers on a take-it-or-leave-it basis. That is, the consumer has no ability to negotiate the terms of the contract with the seller. The majority of contracts in this country today are form contracts.

Examples Automobile sales contracts, automobile leases, mortgages, and sales contracts for consumer goods, credit card agreements, and software licenses usually use form contracts.

Although the phrase "freedom to contract" is often used, in many situations there is not an absolute ability of freedom of contract. Both federal and state governments have enacted statutes that regulate contracts. Many of these laws are intended to protect consumers, debtors, and others from unfair contracts. Today, under this modern law of contracts, there is substantial **government regulation** of the right to contract.

Examples Federal labor laws protect the rights of workers to unionize and negotiate collective bargaining agreements with their employers. Consumer protection laws protect consumers from certain unscrupulous contracts. Equal opportunity in employment laws protect employees from contracts that attempt to discriminate against them based on race, sex, age, disability, and other protected categories. E-contracts are regulated by federal and state laws that govern transactions over the Internet.

▶ SOURCES OF CONTRACT LAW

There are several sources of contract law in the United States, including the *common law of contracts*, the *Uniform Commercial Code*, and the *Restatement (Second) of Contracts*. The following paragraphs explain these sources in more detail.

Common Law of Contracts

A major source of contract law is the **common law of contracts**, which developed from early court decisions that became precedent for later decisions. There is a limited federal common law of contracts that applies to contracts made by the federal government. The larger and more prevalent body of common law has been developed from state court decisions. Thus, although the general principles remain the same throughout the country, there is some variation from state to state.

common law of contracts
Contract law developed primarily by state courts.

Uniform Commercial Code (UCC)
A comprehensive statutory scheme which includes laws that cover aspects of commercial transactions.

LANDMARK LAW

Uniform Commercial Code (UCC)

A major source of contract law is the **Uniform Commercial Code (UCC).** The UCC, which was first drafted by the National Conference of Commissioners on Uniform State Laws in 1952, has been amended several times. Its goal is to create a uniform system of commercial law among the 50 states. The provisions of the UCC normally take precedence over the common law of contracts. (The provisions of the UCC are discussed in other chapters in this book.)

The UCC is divided into nine main articles. Every state has adopted at least part of the UCC. In the area of contract law, two of the major provisions of the UCC are:

· **Article 2 (Sales).** Article 2 (Sales) prescribes a set of uniform rules for the creation and enforcement of contracts for the sale of goods. These contracts are often referred to as **sales contracts**.

Examples The sale of equipment, automobiles, computers, clothing, and such involve sales contracts subject to Article 2 of the UCC.

· **Article 2A (Leases).** Article 2A (Leases) prescribes a set of uniform rules for the creation and enforcement of contracts for the lease of goods. These contracts are referred to as **lease contracts**.

Examples Leases of automobiles, leases of aircraft, and other leases involving goods are subject to Article 2A of the UCC.

The Restatement of the Law of Contracts

Restatement of the Law of Contracts
A compilation of model contract law principles drafted by legal scholars. The *Restatement* is not law.

In 1932, the American Law Institute, a group comprising law professors, judges, and lawyers, completed the **Restatement of the Law of Contracts**. The *Restatement* is a compilation of contract law principles, as agreed upon by the drafters. The *Restatement*, which is currently in its second edition, is cited in this book as the **Restatement (Second) of Contracts**. Note that the *Restatement* is not law. However, lawyers and judges often refer to it for guidance in contract disputes because of its stature.

▶ OBJECTIVE THEORY OF CONTRACTS

objective theory of contracts
A theory that says the intent to contract is judged by the reasonable person standard and not by the subjective intent of the parties.

The **objective theory of contracts** holds that the intent to enter into an express or implied-in-fact contract is judged by the **reasonable person standard**. Would a hypothetical reasonable person conclude that the parties intended to create a contract after considering (1) the words and conduct of the parties and (2) the surrounding circumstances? For example, no valid contract results from offers that are made in jest, anger, or undue excitement. Under the objective theory of contracts, the subjective intent of a party to enter into a contract is irrelevant.

▶ E-COMMERCE

As we entered the twenty-first century, a new economic shift brought the United States and the rest of the world into the Information Age. Computer technology and the use of the Internet increased dramatically. A new form of commerce—**electronic commerce, or e-commerce**—is flourishing. All sorts of goods and services are now sold over the Internet. You can purchase automobiles and children's toys, participate in auctions, purchase airline tickets, make hotel reservations, and purchase other goods and services over the Internet.

Uniform Computer Information Transactions Act (UCITA)
A model act that establishes uniform legal rules for the formation and enforcement of electronic contracts and licenses.

Much of the new cyberspace economy is based on electronic contracts and the licensing of computer information. E-commerce created problems for forming **e-contracts** over the Internet, enforcing e-contracts, and providing consumer protection. In many situations, traditional contract rules apply to e-contracts. Many states have adopted rules that specifically regulate e-commerce transactions. The federal government has also enacted several laws that regulate e-contracts. Contract rules that apply to e-commerce will be discussed in this and the following chapters.

INTERNET LAW & ONLINE COMMERCE

Uniform Computer Information Transactions Act (UCITA)

The National Conference of Commissioners on Uniform State Laws (a group of lawyers, judges, and legal scholars) drafted the **Uniform Computer Information Transactions Act (UCITA).**

The UCITA establishes uniform legal rules for the formation and enforcement of electronic contracts and licenses. The UCITA addresses most of the legal issues that are encountered while conducting e-commerce over the Internet.

The UCITA is a model act that does not become law until a state legislature adopts it as a statute for the state. Although most states have not adopted the UCITA, the UCITA has served as a model for states that have enacted their own statutes that govern e-commerce. Because of the need for uniformity of e-commerce rules, states are attempting to adopt uniform laws to govern the creation and enforcement of cyberspace contracts and licenses.

▶ CLASSIFICATIONS OF CONTRACTS

There are several types of contracts. Each differs somewhat in formation, enforcement, performance, and discharge. The different types of contracts are discussed in the following paragraphs.

Bilateral and Unilateral Contracts

Contracts are either *bilateral* or *unilateral*, depending on what the offeree must do to accept the offeror's offer. A contract is **bilateral** if the offeror's promise is answered with the offeree's promise of acceptance. In other words, a bilateral contract is a "promise for a promise." This exchange of promises creates an enforceable contract. No act of performance is necessary to create a bilateral contract.

Example Mary, the owner of the Chic Dress Shop, says to Peter, a painter, "If you promise to paint my store by July 1, I will pay you $3,000." Peter says "I promise to do so." A *bilateral contract* was created at the moment Peter promised to paint the dress shop (a promise for a promise). If Peter fails to paint the shop, Mary can sue Peter and recover whatever damages result from his breach of contract. Similarly, Peter can sue Mary if she refuses to pay him after he has performed as promised.

A contract is **unilateral** if the offeror's offer can be accepted only by the performance of an act by the offeree. There is no contract until the offeree performs the requested act. An offer to create a unilateral contract cannot be accepted by a promise to perform. It is a "promise for an act."

Example Mary, the owner of the Chic Dress Shop, says to Peter, a painter, "If you paint my shop by July 1, I will pay you $3,000." This offer creates a *unilateral contract*. The offer can be accepted only by the painter's performance of the requested act. If Peter does not paint the shop by July 1, there has been no acceptance, and Mary cannot sue Peter for damages. If Peter paints the shop by July 1, Mary owes Peter $3,000. If Mary refuses to pay, Peter can sue Mary to collect payment.

The language of the offeror's promise must be carefully scrutinized to determine whether it is an offer to create a bilateral contract or an offer to create a unilateral contract. If there is any ambiguity as to which it is, it is presumed to be a bilateral contract.

Incomplete or Partial Performance   Problems can arise if the offeror in a unilateral contract attempts to revoke an offer after the offeree has begun performance. Generally, an offer to create a unilateral contract can be revoked by the offeror any time prior to the offeree's performance of the requested act. However, the offer cannot be revoked if the offeree has begun or has substantially completed performance.

Example Suppose Alan Matthews tells Sherry Levine that he will pay her $5,000 if she finishes the Boston Marathon. Alan cannot revoke the offer once Sherry starts running the marathon.

Formal and Informal Contracts

Contracts may be classified as either *formal* or *informal*.

Formal contracts   **Formal contracts** are contracts that require a special form or method of creation. The *Restatement (Second) of Contracts* identifies the following types of formal contracts[4]:

- **Negotiable instruments. Negotiable instruments**, which include checks, drafts, notes, and certificates of deposit, are special forms of contracts recognized by the UCC. They require a special form and language for their creation and must meet certain requirements for transfer.
- **Letters of credit. A letter of credit** is an agreement by the issuer of the letter to pay a sum of money upon the receipt of an invoice and other documents. Letters of credit are governed by the UCC.
- **Recognizance.** In a recognizance, a party acknowledges in court that he or she will pay a specified sum of money if a certain event occurs.
- **Contracts under seal.** This type of contract is one to which a seal (usually a wax seal) is attached. Although no state currently requires contracts to be under seal, a few states provide that no consideration is necessary if a contract is made under seal.

bilateral contract
A contract entered into by way of exchange of promises of the parties; "a promise for a promise."

unilateral contract
A contract in which the offeror's offer can be accepted only by the performance of an act by the offeree; a "promise for an act."

Justice is the end of government. It is the end of civil society. It ever has been, and ever will be pursued, until it be obtained, or until liberty be lost in the pursuit.

James Madison
The Federalist No. 51 (1788)

A man must come into a court of equity with clean hands.

C.B. Eyre
Dering v. Earl of Winchelsea (1787)

formal contract
A contract that requires a special form or method of creation.

informal contract
A contract that is not formal. Valid informal contracts are fully enforceable and may be sued upon if breached.

Informal Contracts   All contracts that do not qualify as formal contracts are called **informal contracts** (or **simple contracts**). The term is a misnomer. Valid informal contracts (e.g., leases, sales contracts, service contracts) are fully enforceable and may be sued upon if breached. They are called informal contracts only because no special form or method is required for their creation. Thus, the parties to an informal contract can use any words they choose to express their contract. The majority of the contracts entered into by individuals and businesses are informal contracts.

Valid, Void, Voidable, and Unenforceable Contracts

Contract law places contracts in the following categories:

valid contract
A contract that meets all the essential elements to establish a contract; a contract that is enforceable by at least one of the parties.

1. **Valid contract.**   A **valid contract** meets all the essential elements to establish a contract. In other words, it (1) consists of an agreement between the parties, (2) is supported by legally sufficient consideration, (3) is between parties with contractual capacity, and (4) accomplished a lawful object. A valid contract is enforceable by at least one of the parties.

void contract
A contract that has no legal effect; a nullity.

2. **Void contract.**   A **void contract** has no legal effect. It is as if no contract had ever been created. A contract to commit a crime is void. If a contract is void, neither party is obligated to perform the contract, and neither party can enforce the contract.

voidable contract
A contract in which one or both parties have the option to avoid their contractual obligations. If a contract is avoided, both parties are released from their contractual obligations.

3. **Voidable contract.**   A **voidable contract** is a contract in which at least one party has the *option* to avoid his or her contractual obligations. If the contract is avoided, both parties are released from their obligations under the contract. If the party with the option chooses to ratify the contract, both parties must fully perform their obligations.

   With certain exceptions, contracts may be voided by minors; insane persons; intoxicated persons; persons acting under duress, undue influence, or fraud; and in cases involving mutual mistake.

unenforceable contract
A contract in which the essential elements to create a valid contract are met but there is some legal defense to the enforcement of the contract.

4. **Unenforceable contract.**   With an **unenforceable contract**, there is some legal defense to the enforcement of the contract. If a contract is required to be in writing under the Statute of Frauds but is not, the contract is unenforceable. The parties may voluntarily perform a contract that is unenforceable.

Executed and Executory Contracts

executed contract
A contract that has been fully performed on both sides; a completed contract.

A completed contract—that is, one that has been fully performed on both sides—is called an **executed contract**. A contract that has not been performed by both sides is called an **executory contract**. Contracts that have been fully performed by one side but not by the other are classified as executory contracts.

executory contract
A contract that has not been fully performed by either or both sides.

Examples Suppose Elizabeth signs a contract to purchase a new BMW automobile from Ace Motors. She has not yet paid for the car and Ace Motors has not yet delivered the car to Elizabeth. This is an executory contract because the contract has not yet been performed. If Elizabeth has paid for the car but Ace Motors has not yet delivered the car to Elizabeth, there is an executory contract because Ace Motors has not performed the contract. If Elizabeth has paid for the car and Ace Motors has delivered the car to Elizabeth, the contract has been fully performed by both parties and is an executed contract.

▶ EXPRESS AND IMPLIED CONTRACTS

An **actual contract** may be either *express* or *implied-in-fact*.

Express Contract

express contract
An agreement that is expressed in written or oral words.

An **express contract** is stated in oral or written words. Most personal and business contracts are express contracts. A contract that is oral or written is an express contract.

Examples A written agreement to buy an automobile from a dealership is an express contract because it is in written words. An oral agreement to purchase a neighbor's bicycle is an express contract because it is in oral words.

Implied-in-Fact Contract

Implied-in-fact contracts are implied from the conduct of the parties. The following elements must be established to create an implied-in-fact contract:

1. The plaintiff provided property or services to the defendant.
2. The plaintiff expected to be paid by the defendant for the property or services and did not provide the property or services gratuitously.
3. The defendant was given an opportunity to reject the property or services provided by the plaintiff but failed to do so.

> **implied-in-fact contract**
> A contract in which agreement between parties has been inferred from their conduct.

In the following case, the court had to decide whether the plaintiffs could sue a defendant for breach of an implied-in-fact contract.

CASE 9.1 Implied-in-Fact Contract

Wrench LLC v. Taco Bell Corporation

256 F.3d 446, Web 2001 U.S. App. Lexis 15097 (2001)
United States Court of Appeals for the Sixth Circuit

"The district court found that appellants produced sufficient evidence to create a genuine issue of material fact regarding whether an implied-in-fact contract existed between the parties."

—Judge Graham

Facts

Thomas Rinks and Joseph Shields created the "Psycho Chihuahua" cartoon character, which they promote, market, and license through their company, Wrench LLC. Psycho Chihuahua is a clever, feisty, cartoon character dog with an attitude, a self-confident, edgy, cool dog who knows what he wants and will not back down. Rinks and Shields attended a licensing trade show in New York City, where they were approached by two Taco Bell employees, Rudy Pollak, a vice president, and Ed Alfaro, a creative services manager. Taco Bell owns and operates a nationwide chain of fast-food Mexican restaurants. Pollak and Alfaro expressed interest in the Psycho Chihuahua character for Taco Bell advertisements because they thought his character would appeal to Taco Bell's core consumers, males aged 18 to 24. Pollak and Alfaro obtained some Psycho Chihuahua materials to take back with them to Taco Bell's headquarters.

Later, Alfaro contacted Rinks and asked him to create art boards combining Psycho Chihuahua with the Taco Bell name and image. Rinks and Shields prepared art boards and sent them to Alfaro, along with Psycho Chihuahua t-shirts, hats, and stickers. Alfaro showed these materials to Taco Bell's vice president of brand management as well as to Taco Bell's outside advertising agency. Alfaro tested the Psycho Chihuahua marketing concept with focus groups. Rinks suggested to Alfaro that instead of using the cartoon

version of Psycho Chihuahua in its advertisements, Taco Bell should use a live Chihuahua dog manipulated by computer graphic imaging that had the personality of Psycho Chihuahua and a love for Taco Bell food. Rinks and Shields gave a formal presentation of this concept to Taco Bell's marketing department. One idea presented by Rinks and Shields was a commercial in which a male Chihuahua dog passed by a female Chihuahua dog in order to get to Taco Bell food. Taco Bell did not enter into an express contract with Wrench LLC, Rinks, or Shields.

Just after Rinks' and Shields' presentation, Taco Bell hired a new outside advertising agency, Chiat/Day. Taco Bell gave Chiat/Day materials received from Rinks and Shields regarding Psycho Chihuahua. Three months later, Chiat/Day proposed using a Chihuahua in Taco Bell commercials. One commercial had a male Chihuahua passing up a female Chihuahua to get to a person seated on a bench eating Taco Bell food. Chiat/Day says that it conceived these ideas by itself. In July 1997, Taco Bell aired its first Chihuahua commercial in the United States, and it became an instant success and the basis of its advertising. Taco Bell paid nothing to Wrench LLC or to Rinks and Shields. Plaintiffs Wrench LLC, Rinks, and Shields sued defendant Taco Bell to recover damages for breach of an implied-in-fact contract. On this issue, the District Court agreed with the plaintiffs. The decision was appealed.

Issue

Did the plaintiffs Wrench LLC, Rinks, and Shields state a cause of action for the breach of an implied-in-fact contract?

Language of the Court

The district court found that appellants produced sufficient evidence to create a genuine issue of material fact

(case continues)

regarding whether an implied-in-fact contract existed between the parties. On appeal, Taco Bell argues that this conclusion was erroneous, and asserts that the record contains no evidence of an enforceable contract. We agree with the district court's finding that appellants presented sufficient evidence to survive summary judgment on the question of whether an implied-in-fact contract existed under Michigan law.

Decision

The U.S. Court of Appeals held that the plaintiffs had stated a proper cause of action against defendant Taco Bell for breach of an implied-in-fact contract. The Court of Appeals remanded the case for trial.

Note The U.S. Supreme Court denied review of the decision in this case. In 2003 a federal court jury ordered Taco Bell to pay $30 million to plaintiffs Thomas Rinks and Joseph Shields for stealing their idea for the Psycho Chihuahua commercials. Later, the court awarded an additional

$11.8 million in prejudgment interest, bringing the total award to over $42 million.

Case Questions

Critical Legal Thinking What does the doctrine of implied-in-fact contract provide? Explain.

Business Ethics Did Taco Bell act ethically in this case? Did Chiat/Day act ethically in this case?

Contemporary Business What is the purpose of recognizing implied-in-fact contracts? Do you think there was an implied-in-fact contract in this case? If so, what damages should have been awarded to the plaintiffs?

Web Exercise Go to **http://transcripts.cnn.com/ TRANSCRIPTS/0306/05/se.03.html** to read about the jury awarding the plaintiffs $30 million. Go to **www.youtube.com/watch?v=B0oEw0IMLXI** for a video clip of Taco Bell's Chihuahua commercial.

Implied-in-Law Contract (Quasi-Contract)

quasi-contract (implied-in-law contract)

An equitable doctrine whereby a court may award monetary damages to a plaintiff for providing work or services to a defendant even though no actual contract existed. The doctrine is intended to prevent unjust enrichment and unjust detriment.

The equitable doctrine of **quasi-contract**, also called **implied-in-law contract**, allows a court to award monetary damages to a plaintiff for providing work or services to a defendant even though no actual contract existed between the parties. Recovery is generally based on the reasonable value of the services received by the defendant.

The doctrine of quasi-contract is intended to prevent **unjust enrichment** and **unjust detriment.** It does not apply where there is an enforceable contract between the parties. A quasi-contract is imposed where (1) one person confers a benefit on another, who retains the benefit, and (2) it would be unjust not to require that person to pay for the benefit received.

Example Heather is driving her automobile when she is involved in a serious automobile accident in which she is knocked unconscious. She is rushed to Metropolitan Hospital, where the doctors and other staff perform the necessary medical procedures to save her life. Heather comes out of her coma, and after recovering is released from the hospital. Subsequently, Metropolitan Hospital sends Heather a bill for its services. The charges are reasonable. Under the doctrine of quasi-contract, Heather is responsible for any charges that are not covered by her insurance coverage.

In the following case, the court found a quasi-contract.

CASE 9.2 Quasi-Contract

Powell v. Thompson-Powell

Web 2006 Del. C.P. Lexis 10 (2006) Court of Common Pleas of Delaware

"A contract implied in law permits recovery of that amount by which the defendant has benefited at the expense of the plaintiff in order to preclude unjust enrichment."

—Judge Trader

Facts

Samuel E. Powell, Jr., and Susan Thompson-Powell, husband and wife, borrowed $37,700 from Delaware Farm Credit and gave a mortgage to Delaware Farm Credit that pledged two pieces of real property as collateral for the loan. The first piece of property was 2.7 acres of land owned as marital property. Susan had inherited the other piece of property and owned it. Eight years later, Samuel Jr. and Susan defaulted on the mortgage. Samuel Jr. went to his father, Samuel E. Powell, Sr., and orally agreed that if his father would pay the mortgage and the back taxes, he would pay his father back. Samuel Sr. paid off the mortgage and the back taxes owed on the properties. Susan was not a party to this agreement.

Two years later, Samuel Jr. and Susan were divorced. The divorce court ordered that the 2.7 acres of marital real property be sold and the sale proceeds to be divided 50 percent to each party. When the property was sold, Samuel Jr. paid Samuel Sr. one-half of the monies he had previously borrowed from his father. Samuel Sr. sued Susan to recover the other half of the money. Susan defended, alleging that she was not a party to the contract between Samuel Jr. and Samuel Sr. and therefore was not bound by it. Samuel Sr. argued that Susan was liable to him for one-half of the money based on the doctrine of quasi-contract.

Issue

Is Susan liable for one-half the money borrowed by Samuel Jr. from Samuel Sr. under the doctrine of quasi-contract?

Language of the Court

The primary issue in this case is whether the plaintiff can recover from Susan Thompson-Powell on the theory of contract implied in law. A contract implied in law permits recovery of that amount by which the defendant has benefited at the expense of the plaintiff in order to preclude unjust enrichment. To claim restitution, the plaintiff must show that the defendant was unjustly enriched and secured a benefit that it would be unconscionable to allow her to retain.

The essential elements of a quasi-contract are a benefit conferred upon the defendant by the plaintiff, appreciation

or realization of the benefit by the defendant, and acceptance and retention by the defendant of such benefit under such circumstances that it would be inequitable to retain without paying the value thereof.

In the case before me the plaintiff paid the mortgage of the son and daughter-in-law at a time when the bank was about to foreclose on the mortgage. If the property had been sold at a foreclosure sale, neither Samuel E. Powell, Jr. nor Susan Thompson-Powell would have received any benefit from the sale of the marital property. Additionally, payment of the mortgage protected Susan Thompson-Powell's inherited property. Thus, because of the plaintiff's acts in preserving the real estate from foreclosure Susan Thompson-Powell received a substantial benefit at the plaintiff's expense. Since the retention of the benefit in this case is unjust, she must repay her share of the money advanced by the plaintiff.

Decision

The court held that Samuel E. Powell, Sr., was entitled to recover from Susan Thompson-Powell one-half of the money advanced for her benefit.

Case Questions

Critical Legal Thinking What does the doctrine of quasi-contract provide? Explain.

Business Ethics Was it unethical for Susan Thompson-Powell to not pay back half of the money borrowed from Samuel E. Powell, Sr.?

Contemporary Business What is the doctrine of quasi-contract designed to prevent? Explain.

Web Exercise Go to **www.oscn.net/applications/oscn/ DeliverDocument.asp?CiteID=74212** to read a jury instruction on the issue of quasi-contract.

CONCEPT SUMMARY

CLASSIFICATIONS OF CONTRACTS

Formation

1. **Bilateral contract.** A promise for a promise.

2. **Unilateral contract.** A promise for an act.

3. **Express contract.** A contract expressed in oral or written words.

4. **Implied-in-fact contract.** A contract inferred from the conduct of the parties.

5. **Quasi-contract.** A contract implied by law to prevent unjust enrichment.

6. **Formal contract.** A contract that requires a special form or method of creation.

7. **Informal contract.** A contract that requires no special form or method of creation.

Enforceability   1. **Valid contract.** A contract that meets all the essential elements of establishing a contract.

2. **Void contract.** No contract exists.

3. **Voidable contract.** A contract for which at least one party has the option of voiding the contract.

4. **Unenforceable contract.** A contract that cannot be enforced because of a legal defense.

Performance   1. **Executed contract.** A contract that is fully performed on both sides.

2. **Executory contract.** A contract that is not fully performed by one or both parties.

▶ EQUITY

equity
A doctrine that permits judges to make decisions based on fairness, equality, moral rights, and natural law.

Recall that two separate courts developed in England: the courts of law and the Chancery Court (or courts of equity). The equity courts developed a set of maxims based on fairness, equality, moral rights, and natural law that were applied in settling disputes. **Equity** was resorted to when (1) an award of money damages "at law" would not be the proper remedy or (2) fairness required the application of equitable principles. Today, in most states of the United States, the courts of law and equity have been merged into one court. In an action "in equity," the judge decides the equitable issue; there is no right to a jury trial in an equitable action. The doctrine of equity is sometimes applied in contract cases.

ETHICS SPOTLIGHT

Equity Saves Contracting Party

"There is only minimal delay in giving notice, the harm to the lessor is slight, and the hardship to the lessee is severe."
—Judge Abbe

The courts usually interpret a valid contract as a solemn promise to perform. This view of the sanctity of a contract can cause an ethical conflict. Consider the following case.

A landlord leased a motel he owned to lessees for a 10-year period. The lessees had an option to extend the lease for an additional 10 years. To do so, they had to give written notice to the landlord three months before the first 10-year lease expired. The lease provided for forfeiture of all furniture, fixtures, and equipment installed by the lessees, free of any liens, upon termination of the lease.

For almost 10 years, the lessees devoted most of their assets and a great deal of their energy building up the business. During this time, they transformed a disheveled, unrated motel into a AAA three-star operation. With the landlord's knowledge, the lessees made extensive long-term improvements that greatly increased the value of both the property and the business. The landlord knew that the lessees had obtained long-term financing for the improvements that would extend well beyond the first 10-year term of the lease. The landlord also knew that the only source of income the lessees had to pay for these improvements was the income generated from the motel business. The lessees told the landlord orally in a conversation that they intended to extend the lease.

The lessees had instructed their accountant to exercise the option on time. Despite reminders from the lessees, the accountant failed to give the written notice within three months of the expiration of the lease. As soon as they discovered the mistake, the lessees personally delivered written notice of renewal of the option to the landlord, 13 days too late. The landlord rejected it as late and instituted a lawsuit for unlawful detainer to evict the lessees.

The trial and appellate courts held in favor of the lessees. They rejected the landlord's argument for strict adherence to the deadline for giving written notice of renewal of the lease. Instead, the courts granted **equitable relief** and permitted the late renewal notice. The court reasoned that "there is only minimal delay in giving notice, the harm to the lessor is slight, and the hardship to the lessee is severe." *Romasanta v. Mitton*, 189 Cal.App.3d 1026, 234 Cal.Rptr. 729, **Web** 1987 Cal.App. Lexis 1428 (Court of Appeal of California)

Business Ethics   Did the landlord act ethically in this case? Should the court have applied equity and saved the lessees from their mistake? Why or why not?

INTERNATIONAL LAW

United Nations Convention on Contracts for the International Sale of Goods (CISG)

The **United Nations Convention on Contracts for the International Sale of Goods (CISG)** is a model act for international sales contracts. The CISG is the work of many countries and several international organizations. There are now approximately 70 signatory countries to the CISG. In adopting the CISG, the United Nations stated in its preamble:

PREAMBLE

The State Parties to this Convention,
    Considering that the development of international trade on the basis of equality and mutual benefit is an important element in promoting friendly relations among States,
    Being of the opinion that the adoption of uniform rules which govern contracts for the international sale of goods and take into account the different social, economic and legal systems would contribute to the removal of legal barriers in international trade and promote the development of international trade,
    Have agreed as follows:

The text of the CISG follows the Preamble. The CISG provides legal rules that govern the formation, performance, and enforcement of international sales contracts entered into between international businesses.

Many of its provisions are remarkably similar to those of the U.S. Uniform Commercial Code (UCC). The CISG incorporates rules from all the major legal systems. It has, accordingly, received widespread support from developed, developing, and Communist countries.

The CISG applies to contracts for the international sale of goods. The buyer and seller must have their places of business in different countries. In order for the CISG to apply to an international sales contract, either (1) both of the nations must be parties to the convention or (2) the contract may specify that the CISG controls. The contracting parties may agree to exclude (i.e., opt out of) or modify the application of the CISG.

India *The economy of India is growing at over eight percent per year. This once-socialist-inspired country is becoming a major economic power. The second-largest country in the world—with over one billion in population—is transforming itself from an economy based on agriculture and handcrafted goods to an industrial and white-collar economy. Although per capita income remains low, sectors of the Indian economy—such as software engineering, telecommunications, biotechnology, and the provision of back office services—are growing rapidly. International contracts are necessary for India to conduct international trade.*

TEST REVIEW TERMS AND CONCEPTS

Acceptance
Actual contract
Agreement
Article 2 (Sales)
Article 2A (Leases)
Bilateral contract
Classical law of contracts
Common law of contracts
Consideration
Contract
Contractual capacity
E-contract
E-contract law
Electronic commerce
    (e-commerce)
Equitable relief
Equity
Executed contract

Executory contract
Express contract
Formal contract
Form contract
Genuineness of assent
Government regulation
Implied-in-law contract
Informal contract (simple
    contract)
Implied-in-fact contract
Laissez-faire
Lawful object
Lease contract
Legally enforceable
Letter of credit
Negotiable instrument
Objective theory of
    contracts

Offer
Offeree
Offeror
Quasi-contract (implied-
    in-law contract)
Reasonable person standard
Restatement of the Law of
    Contracts
Restatement (Second) of
    Contracts
Sales contract
Traditional law
United Nations Convention
    on Contracts for the
    International Sale of
    Goods (CISG)
Unenforceable contract

Uniform Commercial Code
    (UCC)
Uniform Computer
    Information Transactions
    Act (UCITA)
Unilateral contract
Unjust detriment
Unjust enrichment
Valid contract
Void contract
Voidable contract
Writing and form

CASE PROBLEMS

9.1 Bilateral or Unilateral Contract   G. S. Adams, Jr., vice president of the Washington Bank & Trust Co., met with Bruce Bickham. An agreement was reached whereby Bickham agreed to do his personal and corporate banking business with the bank, and the bank agreed to loan Bickham money at 7½ percent interest per annum. Bickham would have 10 years to repay the loans. For the next two years, the bank made several loans to Bickham at 7½ percent interest. Adams then resigned from the bank. The bank notified Bickham that general economic changes made it necessary to charge a higher rate of interest on both outstanding and new loans. Bickham sued the bank for breach of contract. Was the contract a bilateral or a unilateral contract? Does Bickham win? *Bickham v. Washington Bank & Trust Company*, 515 So.2d 457, **Web** 1987 La.App. Lexis 10442 (Court of Appeal of Louisiana)

9.2 Implied-in-Fact Contract   For six years, Lee Marvin, an actor, lived with Michelle Marvin. They were not mar-

ried. At the end of six years, Lee Marvin compelled Michelle Marvin to leave his household. He continued to support her for another year but thereafter refused to provide further support. During their time together, Lee Marvin earned substantial income and acquired property, including motion-picture rights worth over $1 million. Michelle Marvin brought an action against Lee Marvin, alleging that an implied-in-fact contract existed between them and that she was entitled to half of the property that they had acquired while living together. She claimed that she had given up a lucrative career as an entertainer and singer to be a full-time companion, homemaker, housekeeper, and cook. Can an implied-in-fact contract result from the conduct of unmarried persons who live together? *Marvin v. Marvin*, 18 Cal.3d 660, 557 P.2d 106, 134 Cal.Rptr. 815, **Web** 1976 Cal. Lexis 377 (Supreme Court of California)

 ## BUSINESS ETHICS CASES

9.3 Business Ethics   The Lewiston Lodge of Elks sponsored a golf tournament at the Fairlawn Country Club in Poland, Maine. For promotional purposes, Marcel Motors, an automobile dealership, agreed to give any golfer who shot a hole-in-one a new Dodge automobile. Fliers advertising the tournament were posted in the Elks Club and sent to potential participants. On the day of the tournament, the new Dodge automobile was parked near the clubhouse, with one of the posters conspicuously displayed

on the vehicle. Alphee Chenard, Jr., who had seen the promotional literature regarding the hole-in-one offer, registered for the tournament and paid the requisite entrance fee. While playing the 13th hole of the golf course, in the presence of the other members of his foursome, Chenard shot a hole-in-one. When Marcel Motors refused to tender the automobile, Chenard sued for breach of contract. Was the contract a bilateral or a unilateral contract? Does Chenard win? Was it ethical for Marcel Motors to refuse to give the automobile to Chenard? *Chenard v. Marcel Motors*,

387 A.2d 596, **Web** 1978 Me. Lexis 911 (Supreme Judicial Court of Maine)

9.4 Business Ethics   Loren Vranich, a doctor practicing under the corporate name Family Health Care, P.C., entered into a written employment contract to hire Dennis Winkel. The contract provided for an annual salary, insurance benefits, and other employment benefits. Another doctor, Dr. Quan, also practiced with Dr. Vranich. About nine months later, when Dr. Quan left the practice, Vranich and Winkel entered into an oral modification of their written contract whereby Winkel was to receive a higher salary and a profit-sharing bonus. During the next year, Winkel received the increased salary. However, a disagreement arose, and Winkel sued to recover the profit-sharing bonus. Under Montana law, a written contract can be altered only in writing or by an executed oral agreement. Dr. Vranich argued that the contract could not be enforced because it was not in writing. Does Winkel receive the profit-sharing bonus? Did Dr. Vranich act ethically in raising the defense that the contract was not in writing? *Winkel v. Family Health Care, P.C.*, 205 Mont. 40, 668 P.2d 208, **Web** 1983 Mont. Lexis 785 (Supreme Court of Montana)

ENDNOTES

1. *Rebstock v. Birthright Oil & Gas Co.*, 406 So.2d 636, Web 1981 La. App. Lexis 5242 (Court of Appeal of Louisiana).
2. *Restatement (Second) of Contracts*, Section 1.
3. *Restatement (Second) of Contracts*, Section 1.
4. *Restatement (Second) of Contracts*, Section 6.

▲ **Lost Dog Sign** *Offers to pay a reward for finding and returning things lead to interesting contract law questions. Someone who found the dog referred to in this photograph would have to have had knowledge of the reward in order to be entitled to collect it.*

CHAPTER OBJECTIVES

After studying this chapter, you should be able to:

1. Define *agreement*, *offer*, and *acceptance*.
2. Describe the required terms of an offer and describe the terms that can be implied in an offer.
3. Describe special forms of offers, including Internet auctions.

4. Define *counteroffer* and describe the effects of a counteroffer.
5. Describe how offers are terminated by acts of the parties and the operation of law.

CHAPTER CONTENTS

"When I use a word," Humpty Dumpty said, in rather a scornful tone, "it means just what I choose it to mean--neither more nor less."

"The question is," said Alice, "whether you can make words mean so many different things."

"The question is," said Humpty Dumpty, "which is to be master-- that's all."

--Lewis Carroll
Alice's Adventures in Wonderland (1865)

▶ INTRODUCTION TO AGREEMENT

Contracts are voluntary agreements between the parties; that is, one party makes an offer that is accepted by the other party. Without **mutual assent**, there is no contract. Assent may be expressly evidenced by the oral or written words of the parties or implied from the conduct of the parties. This chapter discusses offer and acceptance.

▶ AGREEMENT

Agreement is the manifestation by two or more persons of the substance of a contract. It requires an *offer* and an *acceptance*. The process of reaching an agreement usually proceeds as follows. Prior to entering into a contract, the parties may engage in preliminary negotiations about price, time of performance, and such.

At some point during these negotiations, one party makes an *offer*. The person who makes the offer is called the **offeror**, and the person to whom the offer is made is called the **offeree**. The offer sets forth the terms under which the offeror is willing to enter into the contract. The offeree has the power to create an agreement by accepting the offer.

In the following case, the court applied the adage "A contract is a contract is a contract."

agreement
The manifestation by two or more persons of the substance of a contract.

offeror
The party who makes an offer.

offeree
The party to whom an offer has been made.

CASE 10.1 Contract

Marder v. Jennifer Lopez
450 F.3d 445, Web 2006 U.S. App. Lexis 14330 (2006)
United States Court of Appeals for the Ninth Circuit

"**Though in hindsight the agreement appears to be unfair to Marder--she only received $2,300 in exchange for a release of all claims relating to a movie that grossed over $150 million. . . .**"

--Judge Pregerson

Facts

The movie *Flashdance* tells a story of a woman construction worker who performs at night as an exotic dancer. She performs an innovative form of dancing that includes a chair dance. Her goal is to obtain formal dance training at a university. The movie is based on the life of Maureen Marder, a nightclub dancer. Paramount Pictures Corporation used information from Marder to create the screenplay for the movie. Paramount paid

Marder $2,300, and Marder signed a general release contract that provided that Marder "releases and discharges Paramount Picture Corporation of and from each and every claim, demand, debt, liability, cost and expense of any kind or character which have risen or are based in whole or in part on any matters occurring at any time prior to the date of this Release." Marder also released Paramount from claims "arising out of or in any way connected with either directly or indirectly, any and all arrangements in connection with the preparation of screenplay material and the production, filming and exploitation of *Flashdance*."

Paramount released the movie *Flashdance*, which grossed over $150 million in domestic box office receipts and is still shown on television and distributed through

(case continues)

DVD rentals. Subsequently, Sony Music Entertainment paid Paramount for release of copyright and produced a music video for the Jennifer Lopez song "I'm Glad." The video featured Lopez's performance as a dancer and singer. Marder believed that the video contains re-creations of many well-known scenes from *Flashdance*.

Marder brought a lawsuit in U.S. District Court against Paramount, Sony, and Lopez. Marder sought a declaration that she had rights as a co-author of *Flashdance* and a co-owner with Paramount of the copyright to *Flashdance*. She sued Sony and Lopez for allegedly violating her copyright in *Flashdance*. The District Court dismissed Marder's claims against Paramount, Sony, and Lopez. Marder appealed.

Issue

Was the general release Marder signed an enforceable contract?

Language of the Court

The Release's language is exceptionally broad and we hold that it is fatal to each of Marder's claims against Paramount. Such a release of "each and every claim" covers all claims within the scope of the language. Accordingly, the law imputes to Marder an intention corresponding to the reasonable meaning of her words and acts. Here, Marder released a broad array of claims relating to any assistance she provided during the creation of a Hollywood movie. Thus, the only reasonable interpretation of the Release is that it encompasses the various copyright claims she asserts in the instant suit.

Though in hindsight the agreement appears to be unfair to Marder--she only received $2,300 in exchange for a release of all claims relating to a movie that grossed over $150 million--there is simply no evidence that her consent was obtained by fraud, deception, misrepresentation, duress, or undue influence.

We also affirm the district court's dismissal of claims against Sony and Lopez. As we held above, under the terms of the Release, Marder cannot sue Paramount to assert a co-ownership in Flashdance. It is therefore impossible for her to establish a prima facie case of copyright infringement against Sony and Lopez.

Decision

The U.S. Court of Appeals held that the general release Marder signed was an enforceable contract. The Court of Appeals affirmed the judgment of the District Court that dismissed Marder's complaint against Paramount, Sony, and Lopez.

Case Questions

Critical Legal Thinking What is an agreement? Explain.

Business Ethics Did Marder act ethically in bringing this lawsuit? Should Paramount have paid Marder more money after the movie *Flashdance* became a success?

Contemporary Business What does the adage "A contract is a contract is a contract" mean? Was it applied in this case?

▶ OFFER

offer
"The manifestation of willingness to enter into a bargain, so made as to justify another person in understanding that his assent to that bargain is invited and will conclude it." (Section 24 of the *Restatement (Second) of Contracts*)

Section 24 of the *Restatement (Second) of Contracts* defines an **offer** as "the manifestation of willingness to enter into a bargain, so made as to justify another person in understanding that his assent to that bargain is invited and will conclude it." The following three elements are required for an offer to be effective:

1. The offeror must *objectively intend* to be bound by the offer.
2. The terms of the offer must be definite or reasonably *certain*.
3. The offer must be *communicated* to the offeree.

The making of an offer is shown in Exhibit 10.1.

▶ **Exhibit 10.1 OFFER**

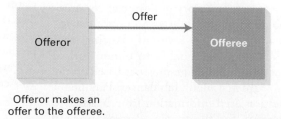

Offeror makes an
offer to the offeree.

Objective Intent

The intent to enter into a contract is determined using the **objective theory of contracts**-- that is, whether a reasonable person viewing the circumstances would conclude that the parties intended to be legally bound.

Example The statement "I will buy your building for $2 million" is a valid offer because it indicates the offeror's present intent to contract.

Example A statement such as "Are you interested in selling your building for $2 million?" is not an offer. It is an invitation to make an offer or an invitation to negotiate.

Offers that are made in jest, anger, or undue excitement do not include the necessary objective intent.

Example The owner of Company A has lunch with the owner of Company B. In the course of their conversation, Company A's owner exclaims in frustration, "For $200, I'd sell the whole computer division!" An offer such as that cannot result in a valid contract.

objective theory of contracts
A theory that says the intent to contract is judged by the reasonable person standard and not by the subjective intent of the parties.

Express Terms

The terms of an offer must be clear enough for the offeree to be able to decide whether to accept or reject the terms of the offer. To be considered definite, an offer (and contract) generally must contain the following terms: (1) identification of the parties, (2) identification of the subject matter and quantity, (3) consideration to be paid, and (4) time of performance. Complex contracts usually state additional terms.

Most offers and contracts set forth express terms that identify the parties, the subject matter of the contract, the consideration to be paid by the parties, and the time of performance, as well as other terms of the offer and contract.

If the terms are indefinite, the courts usually cannot enforce the contract or determine an appropriate remedy for its breach. However, the law permits some terms to be implied.

A contract is a mutual promise.

William Paley
*The Principles of Moral and
Political Philosophy (1784)*

Implied Terms

The common law of contracts required an exact specification of contract terms. If one essential term was omitted, the courts held that no contract had been made. This rule was inflexible.

The modern law of contracts is more lenient. The *Restatement (Second) of Contracts* merely requires that the terms of the offer be "reasonably certain."[1] Accordingly, the court can supply a missing term if a reasonable term can be implied.[2] The definition of *reasonable* depends on the circumstances. Terms that are supplied in this way are called **implied terms**.

Generally, time of performance can be implied. Price can be implied if there is a market or source from which to determine the price of the item or service (e.g., the "blue book" for an automobile price).

The parties or subject matter of the contract usually cannot be implied if an item or a service is unique or personal, such as the construction of a house or the performance of a professional sports contract.

implied term
A term in a contract that can reasonably be supplied by the courts.

Communication

An offer cannot be accepted if it is not communicated to the offeree by the offeror or a representative or an agent of the offeror.

All things obey fixed laws.

Lucretius (Titus Lucretius
Carus)

Example Mr. Jones, the CEO of Ace Corporation, wants to sell a manufacturing division to Baker Corporation. He puts the offer in writing, but he does not send it. Mr. Griswald, the CFO of Baker Corporation, visits Mr. Jones and sees the written offer lying on Jones's desk. Griswald tells his CEO about the offer. Because Mr. Jones never communicated the offer to Baker Corporation, there is no offer to be accepted.

▶ SPECIAL OFFERS

There are several special types of offers. These include advertisements, rewards, and auctions. These special types of offers are discussed in the following paragraphs.

Advertisements

advertisement
An invitation to make an offer, or an actual offer.

As a general rule, **advertisements** for the sale of goods, even at specific prices, generally are treated as **invitations to make an offer**. This rule is intended to protect advertiser-sellers from the unwarranted breach of contract suits for nonperformance that would otherwise arise if the seller ran out of the advertised goods.

There is one exception to this rule: An advertisement is considered an offer if it is so definite or specific that it is apparent that the advertiser has the present intent to bind himself or herself to the terms of the advertisement.

Rewards

reward
An award given for performance of some service or attainment. To collect a reward, the offeree must (1) have knowledge of the reward offer prior to completing the requested act and (2) perform the requested act.

An offer to pay a **reward** (e.g., for the return of lost property or the capture of a criminal) is an offer to form a unilateral contract. To be entitled to collect the reward, the offeree must (1) have knowledge of the reward offer prior to completing the requested act and (2) perform the requested act.

Example John Anderson accidentally leaves a briefcase containing $500,000 in negotiable bonds on a subway train. He places newspaper ads stating "$5,000 reward for return of briefcase left on a train in Manhattan on January 10, 2011, at approximately 10 A.M. Call 212-555-6789." Helen Smith, who is unaware of the offer, finds the briefcase. She reads the luggage tag containing Anderson's name, address, and telephone number, and she returns the briefcase to him. She is not entitled to the reward money because she did not know about it when she performed the requested act.

Auctions

auction with reserve
An auction in which the seller retains the right to refuse the highest bid and withdraw the goods from sale. Unless expressly stated otherwise, an auction is an auction with reserve.

auction without reserve
An auction in which the seller expressly gives up his or her right to withdraw the goods from sale and must accept the highest bid.

At an **auction**, the seller offers goods for sale through an auctioneer. Unless otherwise expressly stated, an auction is considered an **auction with reserve**--that is, it is an invitation to make an offer. The seller retains the right to refuse the highest bid and withdraw the goods from sale. A contract is formed only when the auctioneer strikes the gavel down or indicates acceptance by some other means. The bidder may withdraw his or her bid prior to that time.

If an auction is expressly announced to be an **auction without reserve**, the participants reverse the roles: The seller is the offeror, and the bidders are the offerees. The seller must accept the highest bid and cannot withdraw the goods from sale. However, if the auctioneer has set a minimum bid that it will accept, the auctioneer has to sell the item only if the highest bid is equal to or greater than the minimum bid.

In the following case, the court addressed the issue of an Internet auction.

CASE 10.2 Internet Auction

Lim v. The.TV Corporation International

99 Cal.App.4th 684, 121 Cal.Rptr.2d 323,
Web 2002 Cal. App. Lexis 4315 (2002)
Court of Appeal of California

"Defendant put the name 'Golf.tv' up for public auction, and plaintiff bid on that name and no other. That was an offer and acceptance, and formed a contract."

--Judge Epstein

Facts

The island nation of Tuvalu was awarded the top-level domain name "tv." Thus, Tuvalu controlled who could use domain names with the suffix "tv" on the Internet. For example, if a person named Jones acquired the suffix tv, her domain name on the Internet could be "jones.tv." Tuvalu hired The.TV Corporation International, a California corporation doing business under the name dotTV, to sell Internet names bearing the top-level domain name "tv." In April 2000, dotTV posted the name "golf.tv" for sale on its website, to be sold to the highest bidder. Je Ho Lim, a resident of South Korea, submitted the highest bid of $1,010 and authorized dotTV to charge his credit card for the amount of the bid. dotTV sent the following e-mail to Lim confirming the sale:

> DotTV--The New Frontier on the Internet
> E-Mail Invoice for Domain Registration
> NAME: Je Ho Lim
> Congratulations!
> You have won the auction for the following domain name:
> DOMAIN NAME: --golf
> SUBSCRIPTION LENGTH: 2 years, starts from activation date
> Amount (US$): $1,010 (first year registration fee)
> Please remember that the annual registration fee increases by 5 annually.
> You have the guaranteed right to renew the registration indefinitely.
> DotTV expects to charge your card and activate the registered domain name by May 15, 2000.
> See ya on the new frontier of the Internet!
> Lou Kerner CEO, dotTV Corporation www.TV

Shortly thereafter, dotTV sent another e-mail to Lim that stated "we have decided to release you from your bid" and that Lim should disregard the prior e-mail because of "an e-mail error that occurred." Later, dotTV publicly offered the domain name "golf.tv" with a beginning bid of $1 million. DotTV claimed that its original e-mail to Lim concerned a different domain name, "--golf," instead of "golf." Lim countered that characters such as two dashes ("--") are not recognized on the Internet and therefore the name "--golf" is an invalid domain name. When dotTV refused to transfer the domain name "golf.tv" to Lim, Lim sued dotTV for breach of contract. The trial court dismissed Lim's case against dotTV. Lim appealed.

Issue

Did Lim properly state a cause of action for breach of contract against dotTV?

Language of the Court

Defendant put the name "Golf.tv" up for public auction, and plaintiff bid on that name and no other. That was an offer and acceptance, and formed a contract. The distinction between "Golf.tv" and "--Golf.tv" comes from the acceptance e-mail sent by defendant. Certainly the hyphens preceding the name "golf" could not defeat the existence of an already formed contract. Defendant was accepting plaintiff's bid; it plainly was not making a counteroffer, particularly since, according to the pleading, the name "--Golf" did not "compute"; it did not qualify as a domain name. The e-mail must be read as an acknowledgment of plaintiff's winning bid and acceptance of the contract.

Decision

The court of appeal held that plaintiff Lim had properly pleaded a cause of action against defendant dotTV for breach of contract and reinstated Lim's case against dotTV.

Case Questions

Critical Legal Thinking What is the difference between an auction with reserve and an auction without reserve. Which type is presumed if there is no other statement to the contrary?

Business Ethics Did dotTV act ethically in this case? Why do you think that dotTV reneged on its e-mail confirmation to Lim?

Contemporary Business Are Internet domain names valuable? How do you register an Internet domain name?

Web Exercise Go to **www.golf.tv**. What types of goods or services are offered on this website? Think up an Internet domain name you would like to have. Go to the Network Solutions website, at **www.networksolutions.com**, and see if that name is available with the top-level domains .com, .org. or .net.

CONCEPT SUMMARY
TYPES OF AUCTIONS

Type	Does the seller offer the goods for sale
Auction with reserve	No. It is an invitation to make an offer. Because the bidder is the offeror, the seller (the offeree) may refuse to sell the goods. An auction is with reserve unless otherwise stated.
Auction without reserve	Yes. The seller is the offeror and must sell the goods to the highest bidder (the offeree). An auction is without reserve only if it is stipulated as such.

▶ TERMINATION OF AN OFFER BY ACT OF THE PARTIES

An offer may be terminated by certain **acts of the parties**. The acts of the parties that terminate an offer are discussed in the following paragraphs.

Revocation of an Offer by the Offeror

revocation
Withdrawal of an offer by the offeror which terminates the offer.

Under the common law, an offeror may revoke (i.e., withdraw) an offer any time prior to its acceptance by the offeree. Generally, an offer can be so revoked even if the offeror promised to keep the offer open for a longer time. The **revocation** may be communicated to the offeree by the offeror or by a third party and made by (1) the offeror's express statement (e.g., "I hereby withdraw my offer") or (2) an act of the offeror that is inconsistent with the offer (e.g., selling the goods to another party). Most states provide that a revocation is not effective until it is actually received by the offeree or the offeree's agent.

Offers made to the public may be revoked by communicating the revocation by the same means used to make the offer.

Example If a reward offer for a lost watch was published in two local newspapers each week for four weeks, notice of revocation must be published in the same newspapers for the same length of time. The revocation is effective against all offerees, even those who saw the reward offer but not the notice of revocation.

CONTEMPORARY ENVIRONMENT
Option Contract

An offeree can prevent the offeror from revoking his or her offer by paying the offeror compensation to keep the offer open for an agreed-upon period of time. This creates what is called an **option contract**. In other words, the offeror agrees not to sell the property to anyone except the offeree during the option period. An option contract is a contract in which the original offeree pays consideration (usually money) in return for the original offeror giving consideration (time of the option period). The death or incompetency of either party does not terminate an option contract unless the contract is for the performance of a personal service.

Example Anne offers to sell a piece of real estate to Hal for $1 million. Hal wants time to investigate the property for possible environmental problems and to arrange financing if he decides to purchase the property, so he pays Anne $20,000 to keep her offer open to him for six months. At any time during the option period, Hal may exercise his option and pay Anne the $1 million purchase price. If Hal lets the option expire, however, Anne may keep the $20,000 and sell the property to someone else. Often option contracts are written so that if the original offeree purchases the property, the option amount is applied to the sale price.

Rejection of an Offer by the Offeree

rejection
Express words or conduct by the offeree that rejects an offer. Rejection terminates the offer.

An offer is terminated if the offeree **rejects** it. Any subsequent attempt by the offeree to accept the offer is ineffective and is construed as a new offer that the original offeror (now the offeree) is free to accept or reject. A rejection may be evidenced by the offeree's express words (oral or written) or conduct. Generally, a rejection is not effective until it is actually received by the offeror.

Example Ji Eun, a sales manager at Apple Computer, Inc., offers to sell 4,000 iMac computers to Ted, the purchasing manager of General Motors Corporation, for $4,000,000. The offer is made on August 1. Ted telephones Ji Eun to say that he is not interested. This rejection terminates the offer. If Ted later decides that he wants to purchase the computers, an entirely new contract must be formed.

Counteroffer by the Offeree

A **counteroffer** by the offeree simultaneously terminates the offeror's offer and creates a new offer. Offerees' making of counteroffers is the norm in many industries. A counteroffer terminates the existing offer and puts a new offer into play. The previous offeree becomes the new offeror, and the previous offeror becomes the new offeree.

Example Fei says to Harold, "I will sell you my house for $700,000." Harold says, "I think $700,000 is too high; I will pay you $600,000." Harold has made a counteroffer. Fei's original offer is terminated, and Harold's counteroffer is a new offer that Fei is free to accept or reject.

counteroffer
A response by an offeree that contains terms and conditions different from or in addition to those of the offer. A counteroffer terminates the previous offer.

CONCEPT SUMMARY
TERMINATION OF AN OFFER BY ACT OF THE PARTIES

Action	Description
Revocation	The offeror *revokes* (withdraws) the offer any time prior to its acceptance by the offeree.
Rejection	The offeree rejects the offer by his or her words or conduct.
Counteroffer	A counteroffer by the offeree creates a new offer and terminates the offeror's offer.

▶ TERMINATION OF AN OFFER BY OPERATION OF LAW

An offer can be terminated by **operation of law**. The ways that an offer can be terminated by operation of law are discussed in the following paragraphs.

Destruction of the Subject Matter

An offer terminates if the subject matter of the offer is destroyed through no fault of either party prior to the offer's acceptance.

Death or Incompetency of the Offeror or Offeree

Prior to acceptance of an offer, the death or incompetency of either the offeror or the offeree terminates an offer. Notice of the other party's death or incompetence is not a requirement.

Example Suppose that on June 1, Shari offers to sell her house to Damian for $1,000,000, provided that Damian decides on or before June 15 that he will buy it. Shari dies on June 7, before Damian has made up his mind. The offer automatically terminates on June 7 when Shari dies.

Supervening Illegality

If the object of an offer is made illegal prior to the acceptance of the offer, the offer terminates. This situation, which usually occurs when a statute is enacted or the decision of a court is announced that makes the object of the offer illegal, is called a **supervening illegality**.

Example Suppose City Bank offers to loan ABC Corporation $5 million at an 18 percent interest rate. Prior to ABC's acceptance of the offer, the state legislature enacts a statute that sets a usury interest rate of 12 percent. City Bank's offer to ABC Corporation is automatically terminated when the usury statute became effective.

Where law ends, there tyranny begins.

William Pitt, first Earl of Chatham
Case of Wilkes (speech)

supervening illegality
The enactment of a statute, regulation, or court decision that makes the object of an offer illegal. This action terminates the offer.

Lapse of Time

lapse of time
A stated time period after which an offer terminates. If no time is stated, an offer terminates after a reasonable time.

An offer expires at the **lapse of time** of an offer. An offer may state that it is effective only until a certain date. Unless otherwise stated, the time period begins to run when the offer is actually received by the offeree and terminates when the stated time period expires.

Example If an offer states "This offer is good for 10 days," the offer expires at midnight of the 10th day after the offer was made. If an offer states "This offer must be accepted by January 1, 2012," the offer expires on midnight of January 1, 2012.

If no time is stated in the offer, the offer terminates after a "reasonable time" dictated by the circumstances. A reasonable time to accept an offer to purchase stock traded on a national stock exchange may be a few moments, but a reasonable time to accept an offer to purchase a house may be a week. Unless otherwise stated, an offer made face-to-face or during a telephone call usually expires when the conversation ends.

CONCEPT SUMMARY
TERMINATION OF AN OFFER BY OPERATION OF LAW

Action	Description
Destruction of the subject matter	The subject matter of an offer is destroyed prior to acceptance through no fault of either party.
Death or incompetency	Prior to acceptance of an offer, either the offeror or the offeree dies or becomes incompetent.
Supervening illegality	Prior to the acceptance of an offer, the object of the offer is made illegal by statute, regulation, court decision, or other law.
Lapse of time	An offer terminates upon the expiration of a stated time in the offer. If no time is stated, the offer terminates after a "reasonable time."

▶ ACCEPTANCE

acceptance
"A manifestation of assent by the offeree to the terms of the offer in a manner invited or required by the offer as measured by the objective theory of contracts." (Section 50 of the *Restatement (Second) of Contracts*)

Acceptance is "a manifestation of assent by the offeree to the terms of the offer in a manner invited or required by the offer as measured by the objective theory of contracts."[3] Recall that generally (1) unilateral contracts can be accepted only by the offeree's performance of the required act and (2) a bilateral contract can be accepted by an offeree who promises to perform (or, where permitted, by performance of) the requested act.

Who Can Accept an Offer?

Only the offeree has the legal power to accept an offer and create a contract. Third persons usually do not have the power to accept an offer. If an offer is made individually to two or more persons, each has the power to accept the offer. Once one of the offerees accepts the offer, it terminates as to the other offerees. An offer that is made to two or more persons jointly must be accepted jointly.

The acceptance of an offer is illustrated in Exhibit 10.2.

▶ **Exhibit 10.2**
ACCEPTANCE OF AN OFFER

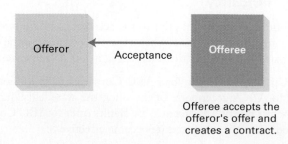

Offeree accepts the offeror's offer and creates a contract.

Unequivocal Acceptance

An offeree's acceptance must be **unequivocal**. For an acceptance to exist, the offeree must accept the terms as stated in the offer. This is called the **mirror image rule**.

Example Abraham says to Caitlin, "I will sell you my iPhone for $300." Caitlin says, "Yes, I will buy your iPhone at that price." This is an unequivocal acceptance that creates a contract.

Usually, even a "grumbling acceptance" is a legal acceptance.

Example Jordan offers to sell his computer to Taryn for $450. Taryn says "Okay, I'll take the computer, but I sure wish you would make me a better deal." This grumbling acceptance creates an enforceable contract because it was not a rejection or a counteroffer.

An equivocal response by the offeree does not create a contract.

Example Halim offers to sell his iMac computer to Nicole for $400. Nicole says "I think I would like it, but I'm not sure." This is equivocation and does not amount to an acceptance.

In the following case, the court had to decide whether there had been an acceptance of the offer.

mirror image rule
A rule which states that for an acceptance to exist, the offeree must accept the terms as stated in the offer.

CASE 10.3 Mirror Image Rule

Montgomery v. English

902 So.2d 836, Web 2005 Fla.App. Lexis 4704 (2005)
Court of Appeal of Florida

"**Florida employs the 'mirror image rule' with respect to contracts. Under this rule, in order for a contract to be formed, an acceptance of an offer must be absolute, unconditional, and identical with the terms of the offer.**"

--Judge Palmer

Facts

Norma English made an offer to purchase a house owned by Michael and Lourie Montgomery (Montgomery) for $272,000. English included in her offer a request to purchase several items of Montgomery's personal property, including paving stones and a fireplace screen. After Montgomery received English's offer, Montgomery made several changes to the offer, including (1) deleting certain items, including the paving stones and fireplace screen, from the personal property section of the offer; (2) deleting a provision regarding latent defects; (3) deleting a provision regarding building inspections; and (4) adding a specific "AS IS" rider. Montgomery signed their counteroffer and delivered it to English. English initialed most of Montgomery's changes except she did not initial the change that deleted the paving stones and fireplace screen --which were worth about $100--from the deal. Montgomery, relying on the "mirror image rule," notified English that she had not completely accepted their offer and that they were therefore withdrawing their offer to sell their house to English. That same day Montgomery signed a contract to sell their house to another buyer for $285,000. English sued Montgomery for specific performance of the

contract. The trial court held in favor of English and ordered specific performance. Montgomery appealed.

Issue

Was an enforceable contract made between English and Montgomery?

Language of the Court

Montgomery argue that the trial court erred in denying their motion for summary judgment because the record demonstrated that there had been no meeting of the minds between the parties as to the essential terms of the contract. We agree. Florida employs the "mirror image rule" with respect to contracts. Under this rule, in order for a contract to be formed, an acceptance of an offer must be absolute, unconditional, and identical with the terms of the offer. Applying the mirror image rule to these undisputed facts we hold that, as a matter of law, the parties failed to reach an agreement on the terms of the contract and, therefore, no enforceable contract was created.

Decision

The court of appeal held that because of the mirror image rule, no contract had been created between the parties. The court of appeal reversed the trial court's order of specific performance and remanded the case to the trial court, with instructions to enter summary judgment in favor of Montgomery.

(case continues)

Case Questions

Critical Legal Thinking What does the mirror image rule provide? Explain.

Business Ethics Did Montgomery act ethically when they backed out of selling the house? Did English act ethically by trying to force the sale of the house to her?

Contemporary Business Does the mirror image rule add certainty to contracting? Explain.

Web Exercise English appealed to the supreme court of Florida. Go to English's "Petitioner's Jurisdictional Brief" at **www.floridasupremecourt.org/clerk/briefs/2005/ 1001-1200/ 05-1186_JurisIni.pdf.** Scroll to the bottom of page 9 and read "II Strict Application of the 'Mirror Image Rule' Produces Harsh and Inequitable Results" on pages 9 and 10, and the "Conclusion" on page 10. The supreme court of Florida denied English's appeal to review the case.

Silence as Acceptance

Silence usually is not considered acceptance, even if the offeror states that it is. This rule is intended to protect offerees from being legally bound to offers because they failed to respond. Nevertheless, silence *does* constitute acceptance in the following situations:

1. The offeree has indicated that silence means assent.

   Example "If you do not hear from me by Friday, ship the order."

2. The offeree signed an agreement indicating continuing acceptance of delivery until further notification.

   Example Book-of-the-month and CD-of-the-month club memberships are examples of such acceptances.

3. Prior dealings between the parties indicate that silence means acceptance.

   Example A fish wholesaler who delivers 30 pounds of fish to a restaurant each Friday for several years and is paid for the fish can continue the deliveries with expectation of payment until notified otherwise by the restaurant.

4. The offeree takes the benefit of goods or services provided by the offeror even though the offeree (a) has an opportunity to reject the goods or services but fails to do so and (b) knows the offeror expects to be compensated.

   Example A homeowner who stands idly by and watches a painter whom she has not hired mistakenly paint her house owes the painter for the work.

The law has outgrown its primitive stage of formalism when the precise word was the sovereign talisman, and every slip was fatal. It takes a broader view today. A promise may be lacking, and yet the whole writing may be "instinct with an obligation," imperfectly expressed.

Judge Cardozo
Wood v. Duff-Gordon (1917)

CONCEPT SUMMARY

OFFER AND ACCEPTANCE

Type of Communication	Effective When
Offer	Received by offeree
Revocation of offer	Received by offeree
Rejection of offer	Received by offeror
Counteroffer	Received by offeror
Acceptance of offer in bilateral contract	Dispatched by offeree

Time of Acceptance

Under the common law of contracts, acceptance of a bilateral contract occurs when the offeree *dispatches* the acceptance by an authorized means of communication. This rule is called the **acceptance-upon-dispatch rule** or, more commonly, the **mailbox rule**. Under this rule, the acceptance is effective when it is dispatched, even if it is lost in transmission. If an offeree first dispatches a rejection and then sends an acceptance, the mailbox rule does not apply to the acceptance.[4]

The problem of lost acceptances can be minimized by expressly altering the mailbox rule. The offeror can do this by stating in the offer that acceptance is effective only upon actual receipt of the acceptance.

mailbox rule
A rule that states that an acceptance is effective when it is dispatched, even if it is lost in transmission. Also known as the *acceptance-upon-dispatch rule*.

Mailbox *The mailbox rule provides that an acceptance is effective when it is dispatched.*

Mode of Acceptance

An acceptance must be **properly dispatched**. The acceptance must be properly addressed, packaged in an appropriate envelope or container, and have prepaid postage or delivery charges. Under common law, if an acceptance is not properly dispatched, it is not effective until it is actually received by the offeror.

Generally, an offeree must accept an offer by an *authorized* means of communication. The offer can stipulate that acceptance must be by a specified means of communication (e.g., registered mail, telegram). Such stipulation is called **express authorization**. If the offeree uses an unauthorized means of communication to transmit the acceptance, the acceptance is not effective, even if it is received by the offeror within the allowed time period, because the means of communication was a condition of acceptance.

Most offers do not expressly specify the means of communication required for acceptance. The common law recognizes certain implied means of communication. **Implied authorization** may be inferred from what is customary in similar transactions, usage of trade, or prior dealings between the parties. Section 30 of the *Restatement (Second) of Contracts* permits implied authorization "by any medium reasonable in the circumstances."

proper dispatch
The proper addressing, packaging, and posting of an acceptance.

express authorization
A stipulation in an offer that says the acceptance must be by a specified means of communication.

implied authorization
A mode of acceptance that is implied from what is customary in similar transactions, usage of trade, or prior dealings between the parties.

TEST REVIEW TERMS AND CONCEPTS

Acceptance	Auction without reserve	Mirror image rule	Option contract
Acceptance-upon-dispatch rule (mailbox rule)	Counteroffer	Mutual assent	Properly dispatched
	Express authorization	Objective theory of contracts	Rejection of an offer
Act of the parties	Implied authorization	Offer	Revocation of an offer
Advertisements	Implied terms	Offeree	Reward
Agreement	Invitation to make an offer	Offeror	Supervening illegality
Auction	Lapse of time	Operation of law	Unequivocal acceptance
Auction with reserve			

CASE PROBLEMS

10.1 Objective Theory of Contracts   While A.H. and Ida Zehmer, husband and wife, were drinking with W.O. Lucy, Mr. Zehmer made a written offer to sell a 471-acre farm the Zehmers owned to Lucy for $50,000. Zehmer contends that his offer was made in jest and that he only wanted to bluff Lucy into admitting that he did not have $50,000. Instead, Lucy appeared to take the offer seriously, offered $5 to bind the deal, and had Mrs. Zehmer sign it. When the Zehmers refused to perform the contract, Lucy brought this action to compel specific performance of the contract. Is the contract enforceable? *Lucy v. Zehmer* 196 Va. 493, 84 S.E.2d 516, **Web** 1954 Va. Lexis 244 (Supreme Court of Virginia)

10.2 Terms of a Contract   Ben Hunt and others operated a farm under the name S.B.H. Farms. Hunt went to McIlory Bank and Trust and requested a loan to build hog houses, buy livestock, and expand farming operations. The bank agreed to loan S.B.H. Farms $175,000, for which short-term promissory notes were signed by Hunt and the other owners of S.B.H. Farms. At that time, oral discussions were held with the bank officer regarding long-term financing of S.B.H.'s farming operations; no dollar amount, interest rate, or repayment terms were discussed. When the owners of S.B.H. Farms defaulted on the promissory notes, the bank filed for foreclosure on the farm and other collateral. S.B.H. Farms counterclaimed for $750,000 damages, alleging that the bank breached its oral contract to provide long-term financing. Was there an oral contract for long-term financing? *Hunt v. McIlory Bank and Trust*, 2 Ark.App. 87, 616 S.W.2d 759, **Web** 1981 Ark.App. Lexis 716 (Court of Appeals of Arkansas)

10.3 Implied Terms   MacDonald Group, Ltd. (MacDonald), is the managing general partner of Fresno Fashion Square, a regional shopping mall in Fresno, California. The mall has several major anchor tenants and numerous smaller stores and shops, including Edmond's of Fresno, a jeweler. Edmond's signed a lease with MacDonald that provided that "there shall not be more than two jewelry stores" located in the mall. Nine years later, MacDonald sent Edmond's notice that it intended to expand the mall and lease space to other jewelers. The lease was silent as to the coverage of additional mall space. Edmond's sued MacDonald, arguing that the lease applied to mall additions. Who wins? *Edmond's of Fresno v. MacDonald Group, Ltd.*, 171 Cal.App.3d 598, 217 Cal.Rptr. 375, **Web** 1985 Cal.App. Lexis 2436 (Court of Appeal of California)

10.4 Implied Terms   Howard R. Wright hired John W. Cerdes to construct a home for him at a price of $43,150. The contract was silent regarding the time of completion. Construction was not completed after nine months. At that time, Wright obtained an injunction ordering Cerdes to stop work. Wright hired other contractors to complete the building. Cerdes sued Wright for breach of contract, claiming that he was due the contract price. How long should Cerdes have had to complete the house? *Cerdes v. Wright*, 408 So.2d 926, **Web** 1981 La.App. Lexis 5531 (Court of Appeal of Louisiana)

10.5 Reward   Rudy Turilli operated the Jesse James Museum in Stanton, Missouri. He contends that the man who was shot, killed, and buried as the notorious desperado Jesse James in 1882 was an impostor and that Jesse James lived for many years thereafter under the alias J. Frank Dalton and last lived with Turilli at his museum until the 1950s. Turilli appeared before a nationwide television audience and stated that he would pay $10,000 to anyone who could prove that his statements were wrong. After hearing this offer, Stella James, a relative of Jesse James, produced affidavits of persons related to and acquainted with the Jesse James family, constituting evidence that Jesse James was killed as alleged in song and legend on April 3, 1882. When Turilli refused to pay the reward, James sued for breach of contract. Who wins? *James v. Turilli*, 473 S.W.2d 757, **Web** 1971 Mo.App. Lexis 585 (Court of Appeals of Missouri)

10.6 Counteroffer   Glende Motor Company (Glende), an automobile dealership that sold new cars, leased premises from certain landlords. One day, fire destroyed part of the leased premises, and Glende restored the leasehold premises. The landlords received payment of insurance proceeds for the fire. Glende sued the landlords to recover the insurance proceeds. Ten days before the trial was to begin, the defendants jointly served on Glende a document titled "Offer to Compromise Before Trial," which was a settlement offer of $190,000. Glende agreed to the amount of the settlement but made it contingent upon the execution of a new lease. The next day, the defendants notified Glende that they were revoking the settlement offer. Glende thereafter tried to accept the original settlement offer. Has there been a settlement of the lawsuit? *Glende Motor Company v. Superior Court*, 159 Cal.App.3d 389, 205 Cal.Rptr. 682, **Web** 1984 Cal.App. Lexis 2435 (Court of Appeal of California)

10.7 Acceptance   Peter Andrus owned an apartment building that he had insured under a fire insurance policy sold by J. C. Durick Insurance (Durick). Two months prior to the expiration of the policy, Durick notified Andrus that the building should be insured for $48,000 (or 80 percent of the building's value), as required by the insurance company. Andrus replied that (1) he wanted insurance to match the amount of the outstanding mortgage on the building (i.e., $24,000) and (2) if Durick could not sell this insurance, he would go elsewhere. Durick sent a new insurance policy in the face amount of $48,000, with the notation that the policy was automatically accepted unless Andrus notified him to the contrary. Andrus did not reply. However, he did not pay the premiums on the policy. Durick sued Andrus to recover these premiums. Who wins? *J. C. Durick Insurance v. Andrus*, 139 Vt. 150, 424 A.2d 249, **Web** 1980 Vt. Lexis 1490 (Supreme Court of Vermont)

10.8 Mailbox Rule   William Jenkins and Nathalie Monk owned a building in Sacramento, California. They leased the building to Tuneup Masters for five years. The lease provided that Tuneup Masters could extend the lease for an additional five years if it gave written notice of its intention to do so by certified or registered mail at least six months prior to the expiration of the term of the lease.

Six months and three days before the expiration of the lease, Larry Selditz, vice president of Tuneup Masters, prepared a letter exercising the option, prepared and sealed an envelope with the letter in it, prepared U.S. Postal Service Form 3800, and affixed the certified mail sticker on the envelope, and had his secretary deliver the envelope to the Postal Service annex located on the ground floor of the office building. Postal personnel occupied the annex only between the hours of 9 and 10 A.M. At the end of each day, between 5 and 5:15 P.M., a postal employee picked up outgoing mail. The letter to the landlords was lost in the mail. The landlords thereafter refused to renew the lease and brought an unlawful detainer action against Tuneup Masters. Was the notice renewing the option effective? *Jenkins v. Tuneup Masters*, 190 Cal.App.3d 1, 235 Cal.Rptr. 214, **Web** 1987 Cal.App. Lexis 1475 (Court of Appeal of California)

BUSINESS ETHICS CASES

10.9 Business Ethics   Kortney Dempsey took a cruise on a ship operated by Norwegian Cruise Line (Norwegian). In general, suits for personal injuries arising out of maritime torts are subject to a three-year statute of limitations. However, Congress permits this period to be reduced to one year by contract. The Norwegian passenger ticket limited the period to one year. Evidence showed that the cruise line ticket contained the notation "Important Notice" in a bright red box in the bottom-right corner of each of the first four pages of the ticket. The information in the box stated that certain pages of the ticket contain information that "affect[s] important legal rights." In addition, at the top of page 6 of the ticket, where the terms and conditions begin, it is stated in bold letters: "Passengers are advised to read the terms and conditions of the Passenger Ticket Contract set forth below." The clause at issue, which appears on page 8, clearly provides that suits must be brought within one year of injury. More than one year after Dempsey had taken the cruise (but within three years), she filed suit against Norwegian, seeking damages for an alleged injury suffered while on the cruise. Dempsey asserted that the one-year limitations period had not been reasonably communicated to her. Did Dempsey act ethically in suing when she did? Did Norwegian act ethically in reducing the limitations period to one year? Who wins the lawsuit? *Dempsey v. Norwegian Cruise Line*, 972 F.2d 998, **Web** 1992 U.S. App. Lexis 10939 (United States Court of Appeals for the Ninth Circuit)

10.10 Business Ethics   Genaro Munoz owned property that he leased to Goodwest Rubber Corporation (Goodwest) for five years. The lease granted Goodwest the option to buy the property at a fair market value. Goodwest sought to exercise the option to purchase the property and tendered $80,000 to Munoz. When Munoz rejected this offer, Goodwest filed suit, seeking specific performance of the option agreement. The court was presented with a single issue for review: Was a price designation of "fair market value" definite enough to support an action for specific performance? Do you think Munoz acted ethically in refusing to honor the option? Who wins? *Goodwest Rubber Corp. v. Munoz*, 170 Cal.App.3d 919, 216 Cal.Rptr. 604, **Web** 1985 Cal.App. Lexis 2288 (Court of Appeal of California)

ENDNOTES

1. Restatement (Second) of Contracts, Section 204.
2. Section 87(2) of the Restatement (Second) of Contracts states that an offer which the offeror should reasonably expect to induce action or forbearance of a substantial character on the part of the offeree before acceptance and which does induce such action or forbearance is binding as an option contract to the extent necessary to avoid injustice.
3. Restatement (Second) of Contracts, Section 50(1).
4. Restatement (Second) of Contracts, Section 40.

11 | CONSIDERATION AND PROMISSORY ESTOPPEL

▲ **The Inns of Court, London** *The Inns of Court in London are the professional associations to one of which every barrister in England and Wales (and those judges who were formerly barristers) must belong. England follows the common law; that is, cases have been decided throughout centuries, and these cases have become precedent for future cases. The United States modeled its court system on the English system. English courts and U.S. courts hear and decide cases involving international contracts. International contracts support the conduct of trade, business, and e-commerce worldwide. For example, a company in the United States could enter into a contract to purchase goods from a company in England. This would be an international contract. The parties usually agree in their contract which country's courts will hear any cases that arise and which country's laws will be applied in settling the disputes.*

CHAPTER OBJECTIVES

After studying this chapter, you should be able to:

1. Define *consideration* and describe the requirements of consideration.
2. Define a *gift promise* and identify whether gift promises are enforceable.
3. Describe contracts that lack consideration, such as those involving illegal consideration, an illusory promise, a preexisting duty, or past consideration.
4. Define an accord and satisfaction of a disputed claim.
5. Define and apply the equitable doctrine of *promissory estoppel*.

CHAPTER CONTENTS

"The law has outgrown its primitive stage of formalism when the precise word was the sovereign talisman, and every slip was fatal. It takes a broader view today. A promise may be lacking, and yet the whole writing may be "instinct with an obligation," imperfectly expressed."

—Justice Cardozo
Wood v. Duff-Gordon, 222 N.Y.88, 91 (1917)

▶ INTRODUCTION TO CONSIDERATION AND PROMISSORY ESTOPPEL

To be enforceable, a contract must be supported by *consideration*, which is broadly defined as something of legal value. In general, this means that each side to a contract must give something of value for the contract to be enforceable. The consideration can consist of money, property, the provision of services, the forbearance of a right, or anything else of value. Most contracts are supported by consideration.

Contracts that are not supported by consideration are usually not enforceable. This means that a party who has not given consideration cannot enforce the contract. The parties may, however, voluntarily perform a contract that is lacking in consideration. If a contract that was lacking in consideration is performed by the parties, the parties cannot thereafter raise lack of consideration to undo the performed contract. *Promissory estoppel* is an equity doctrine that permits a court to order enforcement of a contract that lacks consideration.

This chapter discusses consideration, promises that lack consideration, and equity doctrines that permit promises that lack consideration to be enforced.

▶ CONSIDERATION

Consideration must be given before a contract can exist. **Consideration** is defined as something of legal value given in exchange for a promise. Consideration can come in many forms. The most common types consist of either a tangible payment (e.g., money, property) or the performance of an act (e.g., providing legal services). Less usual forms of consideration include the forbearance of a legal right (e.g., accepting an out-of-court settlement in exchange for dropping a lawsuit) and non-economic forms of consideration (e.g., refraining from "drinking, using tobacco, swearing, or playing cards or billiards for money"[1] for a specified time period).

consideration
Something of legal value given in exchange for a promise.

Written contracts are presumed to be supported by consideration. This rebuttable presumption, however, may be overcome by sufficient evidence. A few states provide that contracts made under seal cannot be challenged for lack of consideration.

Requirements of Consideration

Consideration consists of two elements: (1) Something of legal value must be given (i.e., either a legal benefit must be received or legal detriment must be suffered) and

(2) there must be a bargained-for exchange. Each of these is discussed in the paragraphs that follow:

1. **Legal value.**   Under the modern law of contracts, a contract is considered supported by **legal value** if (1) the promisee suffers a *legal detriment* or (2) the promisor receives a *legal benefit*.
2. **Bargained-for exchange.**   To be enforceable, a contract must arise from a **bargained-for exchange**. In most business contracts, the parties engage in such exchanges. The commercial setting in which business contracts are formed leads to this conclusion.

legal value
Support for a contract when either (1) the promisee suffers a legal detriment or (2) the promisor receives a legal benefit.

bargained-for exchange
Exchange that parties engage in that leads to an enforceable contract.

In the following case, the court had to decide whether there was consideration.

CASE 11.1 Consideration

In the Matter of Wirth

14 A.D.3d 572, 789 N.Y.S.2d 69, Web 2005 N.Y.App. Div. Lexis 424 (2005)
Supreme Court of New York, Appellate Division

"The Pledge Agreement further stated: 'I acknowledge that Drexel's promise to use the amount pledged by me shall constitute full and adequate consideration for this pledge.'"

—Judge Schmidt

Facts

Raymond P. Wirth signed a pledge agreement which stated that in consideration of his interest in education, and "intending to be legally bound," he irrevocably pledged and promised to pay Drexel University the sum of $150,000. The pledge agreement provided that an endowed scholarship would be created in Wirth's name. Wirth died two months after signing the pledge but before any money had been paid to Drexel. When the estate of Wirth refused to honor the pledge, Drexel sued the estate to collect the $150,000. The estate alleged that the pledge was unenforceable because of lack of consideration. The surrogate court denied Drexel's motion for summary judgment and dismissed Drexel's claim against the estate. Drexel appealed.

Issue

Was the pledge agreement supported by consideration and therefore enforceable against the estate of Wirth?

Language of the Court

Pursuant to Pennsylvania's Uniform Written Obligations Act: "A written release or promise, hereafter made and signed by the person releasing or promising, shall not be invalid or unenforceable for lack of consideration, if the writing also contains an additional express statement, in any form or language, that the signer intends to be legally bound." Pursuant to this statute, the Pledge Agreement does not fail for lack of consideration, as the decedent expressly stated his intent to be legally bound by the pledge.

Moreover, even if we were to determine that the decedent, as promisor, anticipated consideration in return for his promise, there was no failure of consideration. The Pledge Agreement, which also was executed by representatives of Drexel, provided that the pledged sum "shall be used by" Drexel to create an endowed scholarship fund in the decedent's name, per the terms of the attached Letter of Understanding. The Pledge Agreement further stated: "I acknowledge that Drexel's promise to use the amount pledged by me shall constitute full and adequate consideration for this pledge."

In our view, pursuant to the terms of the Pledge Agreement, Drexel provided sufficient consideration by expressly accepting the terms of the Pledge Agreement and by promising to establish the scholarship fund in the decedent's name. The fact that the decedent died before the initial gift was transferred into a special account set up by Drexel and therefore the scholarship fund was not yet implemented, did not negate the sufficiency of the promise as consideration to set up the fund.

Decision

The appellate court held that the pledge agreement was supported by consideration and was therefore enforceable against the estate of Wirth. The appellate court reversed the decision of the surrogate court and granted Drexel's motion for summary judgment against the estate of Wirth.

Case Questions

Critical Legal Thinking What is consideration? What happens if there is lack of consideration supporting a promise? Explain.

Business Ethics Was it ethical for the estate of Wirth to try to back out of the pledge agreement Wirth made before he died?

Contemporary Business What special statute did Pennsylvania enact that solves the issue of lack of consideration in many contracts? Does such a statute take precedent over the common law contract rule of consideration? Explain.

▶ GIFT PROMISE

Gift promises, also called **gratuitous promises**, are unenforceable because they lack consideration. To change a gift promise into an enforceable promise, the promisee must offer to do something in exchange—that is, in consideration—for the promise. Gift promises cause considerable trouble for persons who do not understand the importance of consideration.

gift promise
A promise that is unenforceable because it lacks consideration. Also known as a *gratuitous promise*.

Example On May 1, Mrs. Colby promises to give her son $10,000 on June 1. When June 1 arrives Mrs. Colby refuses to pay the $10,000. The son cannot recover the $10,000 because it was a gift promise that lacked consideration. If, however, Mrs. Colby promises to pay her son $10,000 if he earns an "A" in his business law course and the son earns the "A," the contract is enforceable and the son can recover the $10,000.

A completed gift promise cannot be rescinded for lack of consideration.

Example On May 1, Mr. Smith promises to give his granddaughter $10,000 on June 1. If on or before June 1 Mr. Smith actually gives the $10,000 to his granddaughter, it is a completed gift promise. Mr. Smith cannot thereafter recover the money from his granddaughter, even if the original promise lacked consideration.

The case that follows involves the issue of whether a giver can recover gifts that he made.

CASE 11.2 Gifts

Cooper v. Smith

800 N.E.2d 372, Web 2003 Ohio App. Lexis 5446 (2003)
Court of Appeals of Ohio

"Many gifts are made for reasons that sour with the passage of time. Unfortunately, gift law does not allow a donor to recover/revoke a gift simply because his or her reasons for giving it have soured."

—Judge Harsha

Facts

Lester Cooper suffered serious injuries that caused him to be hospitalized for an extended period of time. While he was hospitalized, Julie Smith, whom Cooper had met the year before, and Janet Smith, Julie's mother, made numerous trips to visit him. Although Julie was married to another man at the time, a romantic relationship developed between Cooper and Julie. While in the hospital, Cooper proposed marriage to Julie, and she accepted. Julie obtained a divorce from her husband. Cooper ultimately received an $180,000 settlement for his injuries.

After being released from the hospital, Cooper moved into Janet's house and lived with Janet and Julie. Over the next couple months, Cooper purchased a number of items for Julie, including a diamond engagement ring, a car, a computer, a tanning bed, and horses. On Julie's request, Cooper paid off Janet's car. Cooper also paid for various improvements to Janet's house, such as having a new furnace installed and having wood flooring laid in the kitchen. Several months later, the settlement money had run out, and Julie had not yet married Cooper. About six months later, Julie and Cooper had a disagreement, and Cooper moved out of the house. Julie returned the engagement ring to Cooper. Cooper sued Julie and Janet to recover the gifts or the value of the gifts he had given them. The magistrate who heard the case dismissed Cooper's case, and the trial court affirmed the dismissal of the case. Cooper appealed.

(case continues)

Issue
Can Cooper recover the gifts or the value of the gifts he gave to Julie and Janet Smith?

Language of the Court

Unless the parties have agreed otherwise, the donor is entitled to recover the engagement ring (or its value) if the marriage does not occur, regardless of who ended the engagement. While we are willing to imply a condition concerning the engagement ring, we are unwilling to do so for other gifts given during the engagement period. Unlike the engagement ring, the other gifts have no symbolic meaning. Rather, they are merely "tokens of love and affection" which the donor bore for the donee. Many gifts are made for reasons that sour with the passage of time. Unfortunately, gift law does not allow a donor to recover/revoke a gift simply because his or her reasons for giving it have soured.

Generally, a completed gift is absolute and irrevocable. We believe the best approach is to treat gifts exchanged during the engagement period (excluding the engagement ring) as absolute and irrevocable gifts unless the donor has expressed intent that the gift be conditioned on the subsequent marriage. Cooper offered no evidence establishing that he gave the gifts on the express condition that they be returned to him if the engagement ended. Thus, the gifts are irrevocable gifts and Cooper is not entitled to their return.

Decision
The court of appeals held that the gifts made by Cooper to Julie (other than the engagement ring) and to Janet were irrevocable gifts that he could not recover simply because his engagement with Julie ended. The court of appeals affirmed the judgment of the trial court, allowing Julie and Janet Smith to keep these gifts.

Case Questions

Critical Legal Thinking Do you agree with the law that requires an engagement ring to be returned to the giver, no matter who breaks off the engagement? Explain.

Business Ethics Did Julie and Janet Smith act ethically in keeping the gifts Cooper had given them? Did Cooper act ethically in trying to get the gifts back?

Contemporary Business Why is there a different rule regarding the returning of engagement rings than for other gifts?

Web Exercise Go to www.nytimes.com/2006/03/05/business/05goodie.html to read about gifts to movie stars.

▶ CONTRACTS LACKING CONSIDERATION

Some contracts seem as though they are supported by consideration even though they are not. The contracts described in the following paragraphs fall into this category.

Illegal Consideration

A contract cannot be supported by a promise to refrain from doing an illegal act because that is **illegal consideration**. Contracts based on illegal consideration are void.

Example The statement "I will burn your house down unless you agree to pay me $10,000," to which the homeowner agrees, is not an enforceable contract because the consideration given—not to burn down a house—is illegal consideration. Thus, the extortionist cannot enforce the contract against the homeowner.

Illusory Promise

If parties enter into a contract but one or both of the parties can choose not to perform their contractual obligations, the contract lacks consideration. Such promises, which are known as **illusory promises** (or **illusory contracts**), are unenforceable.

Example A contract which provides that one of the parties has to perform only if he or she chooses to do so is an illusory contract.

Moral Obligation

Promises made out of a sense of **moral obligation**, or honor, are generally unenforceable on the grounds that they lack consideration. In other words, moral consideration is not treated as legal consideration. A minority of states hold that moral obligations are enforceable.

illegal consideration
A promise to refrain from doing an illegal act. Such a promise will not support a contract.

illusory promise
A contract into which both parties enter but one or both of the parties can choose not to perform their contractual obligations. Thus, the contract lacks consideration. Also known as an illusory contract.

moral obligation
A sense of honor that prompts a person to make a promise. Promises made out of a sense of moral obligation lack consideration.

Preexisting Duty

A promise lacks consideration if a person promises to perform an act or do something he is already under an obligation to do. This is called a **preexisting duty**. The promise is unenforceable because no new consideration has been given.

Example Many states have adopted statutes that prohibit police officers from demanding money for investigating and apprehending criminals or that prohibit fire fighters from demanding payment for fighting fires. If a person agrees to such a demand, she does not have to pay it because there was no new consideration; public servants are under a preexisting duty to perform their functions.

In the private sector, the preexisting duty rule often arises when one of the parties to an existing contract seeks to change the terms of the contract during the course of its performance. Such midstream changes are unenforceable: The parties have a preexisting duty to perform according to the original terms of the contract.

Sometimes a party to a contract runs into substantial *unforeseen difficulties* while performing his or her contractual duties. If the parties modify their contract to accommodate these unforeseen difficulties, the modification will be enforced even though it is not supported by new consideration.

Past Consideration

Problems of **past consideration** often arise when a party promises to pay someone some money or other compensation for work done in the past. Past consideration is not consideration for a new promise; therefore, a promise based on past consideration is not enforceable.

Example Felipe, who has worked in management for the Acme Corporation for 30 years, is retiring. The president of Acme says, "Because you were such a loyal employee, Acme will pay you a bonus of $100,000." Subsequently, the corporation refuses to pay the $100,000. Unfortunately for Felipe, he has already done the work for which he has been promised to be paid. The contract is unenforceable against Acme because it is based on past consideration.

In the following case, the court held that there was lack of consideration and there was fraud, and it refused to enforce the contract.

preexisting duty
Something a person is already under an obligation to do. A promise lacks consideration if a person promises to perform a preexisting duty.

There is grim irony in speaking of freedom of contract of those who, because of their economic necessities, give their service for less than is needful to keep body and soul together.

Harlan Fiske Stone
Morehead v. N.Y. ex rel. Tipaldo (1936)

past consideration
A prior act or performance. Past consideration (e.g., prior acts) will not support a new contract. New consideration must be given.

CASE 11.3 Lack of Consideration

West America Housing Corporation v. Pearson
2007 WY 184, 171 P.3d 539, Web 2007 Wyo. Lexis 196 (2007)
Supreme Court of Wyoming

"The district court stated on the record that he found Joelson's testimony to be wildly unbelievable and likely perjury."
—Justice Hill

Facts

Donald Pearson was 80 years of age and living in an assisted living facility. Jeanne Joelson, whom Pearson knew, convinced Pearson to purchase the Wrangler Road Property, to pay $75,755 as the down payment, and to borrow $279,200 from a lender who retained a mortgage on the property. Joelson told Pearson that she, Bobbie Charles Craver, and West America Housing Corporation (WAHC), which was

owned by Joelson, Craver, and Sheena Shoopman, Joelson's daughter, would pay the mortgage payments on the property.

WAHC made the mortgage payments and paid the insurance and property taxes on the property for approximately four years. Joelson then asked Pearson to deed the property to Larry Oltman, Joelson's brother, which Joelson claimed Pearson did. There was a quitclaim deed with Pearson's signature on it that transferred the property to Oltman. The deed transferred ownership of the property to Oltman and indicated that Pearson had received $75,755 "in hand paid" as consideration for the transaction. Oltman subsequently deeded the property to WAHC.

(case continues)

Pearson sued Joelson, Craver, Shoopman, and WAHC, alleging that the transfer of the property from Pearson to Oltman lacked consideration and therefore was a voidable transfer. Pearson also alleged that the transfer of the property from Oltman to WAHC was a fraudulent transfer that was void. Pearson testified that he did not complete or sign the deed transferring the property to Oltman and that he did not receive the consideration indicated on the deed. Joelson testified that she paid Pearson $75,755 in cash that she brought to Pearson in a shoebox at the time of the sale to Oltman. However, Joelson could not produce any withdrawal slip from a bank or any other evidence of the source of the cash. The district court quieted title to the property to Pearson. Joelson, Craver, Shoopman, and WAHC appealed.

Issue

Did the transfer of the Wrangler Road Property from Pearson to Oltman lack consideration and was the transfer of the property from Oltman to WAHC a fraudulent transfer?

Language of the Court

The district court stated on the record that he found Joelson's testimony to be wildly unbelievable and likely perjury. The evidence is at best equivocal that Pearson actually signed the quitclaim deed to Oltman. The only evidence to support the element of consideration was Joelson's "wildly unbelievable" tale of delivering the consideration to Pearson on an unknown date, in the form of cash in a shoe box, for which she obtained no receipt. It was not plain error for the district court to conclude that the deed at issue was void for lack of consideration, despite the language on the face of the deed. It flows virtually without need for discussion that the succeeding deeds were also void. The district court's findings are not clearly erroneous, and its application of the law is not in error.

Decision

The supreme court of Wyoming held that there was no consideration to support the transfer of the deed from Pearson to Oltman. The court also held that the transfer of the property from Oltman to the defendants was fraudulent. The supreme court upheld the district court's decision that quieted title to the property to Pearson.

Case Questions

Critical Legal Thinking   What is the result if lack of consideration for a contract is found? Do you think that there was lack of consideration in this case? Explain.

Business Ethics   Did Joelson act ethically in this case? Did Oltman act ethically in this case?

Contemporary Business   Do you think that there was fraud in this case? Why or why not? Do you think elderly people are often targets of fraud?

Web Exercise   Go to **www.fraud.org/elderfraud/hangup. htm.** Read the article "Five Steps to Help Seniors Targeted by Telemarketing Fraud."

CONCEPT SUMMARY
PROMISES LACKING CONSIDERATION

Type of Consideration	Description of Promise
Illegal consideration	Promise to refrain from doing an illegal act.
Illusory promise	Promise in which one or both parties can choose not to perform their obligation.
Moral obligation	Promise made out of a sense of moral obligation, honor, love, or affection. Some states enforce these types of contracts.
Preexisting duty	Promise based on the preexisting duty of the promisor to perform.
Past consideration	Promise based on the past performance of the promisee.

CONTEMPORARY ENVIRONMENT

Special Business Contracts

Generally, the courts tolerate a greater degree of uncertainty as to the issue of consideration in business contracts than in personal contracts, under the premise that sophisticated parties know how to protect themselves when negotiating contracts. The law imposes an obligation of good faith on the performance of the parties to requirements and output contracts.

The following paragraphs describe special types of business contracts that allow a greater-than-usual degree of uncertainty concerning consideration.

Output Contract

In an **output contract**, the seller agrees to sell all of its production to a single buyer. Output contracts serve the legitimate business purposes of (1) assuring the seller of a purchaser for all its output and (2) assuring the buyer of a source of supply for the goods it needs.

Example Organic Foods Inc. is a company that operates farms that produce organically grown grains and vegetables. Urban Food Markets is a grocery store chain that sells organically grown foods. Urban Food Markets contracts with Organic Foods Inc. to purchase all the organic foods grown by Organic Foods Inc. this year. This is an example of an output contract: Organic Foods Inc. must sell all of its output to Urban Foods Market.

Requirements Contract

A **requirements contract** is one in which a buyer contracts to purchase all of its requirements for an item from one seller. Such contracts serve the legitimate business purposes of

(1) assuring the buyer of a uniform source of supply and (2) providing the seller with reduced selling costs.

Example The Goodyear Tire & Rubber Company manufactures tires that are used on automobiles. Ford Motor Company manufactures automobiles on which it must place tires before the automobiles can be sold. Assume Ford Motor Company enters into a contract with Goodyear Tire & Rubber Company to purchase all of the tires it will need this year from Goodyear. This is an example of a requirements contract: Ford Motor Company has agreed to purchase all of the tires it will need from Goodyear. Goodyear may sell tires to other purchasers, however.

Best-Efforts Contract

A **best-efforts contract** is a contract that contains a clause that requires one or both of the parties to use their *best efforts* to achieve the objective of the contract. The courts generally have held that the imposition of the best-efforts duty provides sufficient consideration to make a contract enforceable.

Example Real estate listing contracts often require a real estate broker to use his or her best efforts to find a buyer for the listed real estate. Contracts often require underwriters to use their best efforts to sell securities on behalf of their corporate clients. Both of these contracts would be enforceable. Of course, a party can sue another company for failing to use its promised best efforts.

▶ SETTLEMENT OF CLAIMS

The law promotes the voluntary settlement of disputed claims. Settlement saves judicial resources and serves the interests of the parties entering into the settlement.

In some situations, one of the parties to a contract believes that he or she did not receive what he or she was due. This party may attempt to reach a compromise with the other party (e.g., by paying less consideration than was provided for in the contract). If the two parties agree to a compromise, a settlement of the claim has been reached. The settlement agreement is called an **accord**. If the accord is performed, it is called a **satisfaction**. This type of settlement is called an **accord and satisfaction** or a **compromise**. If the accord is not satisfied, the other party can sue to enforce either the accord or the original contract.

accord
An agreement whereby the parties agree to accept something different in satisfaction of the original contract.

satisfaction
The performance of an accord.

Example A contract stipulated that the cost of a computer and software system that keeps track of inventory, accounts receivable, and so on is $300,000. After it is installed, the computer system does not perform as promised. To settle the dispute, the parties agree that $200,000 is to be paid as full and final payment for the computer. This accord is enforceable even though no new consideration is given because reasonable persons would disagree as to the worth of the computer system that was actually installed.

► EQUITY: PROMISSORY ESTOPPEL

promissory estoppel
An equitable doctrine that prevents the withdrawal of a promise by a promisor if it will adversely affect a promisee who has adjusted his or her position in justifiable reliance on the promise.

The courts have developed the equitable doctrine of **promissory estoppel** or (**detrimental reliance**) to avoid injustice. This doctrine is a broad policy-based doctrine. It is used to provide a remedy to a person who has relied on another person's promise when that person withdraws his or her promise and is not subject to a breach of contract action because one of the two elements contract requirements (i.e., agreement or consideration) is lacking.

The doctrine of promissory estoppel *estops* (prevents) the promisor from revoking his or her promise. Therefore, the person who has *detrimentally relied* on the promise for performance may sue the promisor for performance or other remedy the court feels is fair to award in the circumstances.

For the doctrine of promissory estoppel to be applied, the following elements must be shown:

- The promisor made a promise.
- The promisor should have reasonably expected to induce the promisee to reply on the promise.
- The promisee actually relied on the promise and engaged in an action or forbearance of a right of a definite and substantial nature.
- Injustice would be caused if the promise were not enforced.

Now equity is no part of the law, but a moral virtue, which qualifies, moderates, and reforms the rigor, hardness, and edge of the law, and is a universal truth.

Lord Cowper
Dudley v. Dudley (1705)

Example XYZ Construction Company, a general contractor, requests bids from subcontractors for work to be done on a hospital building that XYZ plans to submit a bid to build. Bert Plumbing Company, a plumbing subcontractor, submits the lowest bid for the plumbing work, and XYZ incorporates Bert's low bid in its own bid for the general contract. Based on all of the subcontractor's bids, XYZ submits the lowest overall bid to build the hospital and is awarded the contract. Bert Plumbing plans to withdraw its bid. However, the doctrine of promissory estoppel prevents Bert from withdrawing its bid. Since XYZ has been awarded the contract to build the hospital based partially upon Bert's plumbing subcontractor bid, XYZ can enforce Bert's promise to perform under the doctrine of promissory estoppel. Allowing Bert to withdraw its bid would cause injustice.

Courthouse, Santa Barbara, California *This courthouse in Santa Barbara, California, was built in 1929 and is patterned after a Spanish–Moorish palace. The court hears cases, including cases to enforce contracts. To be enforceable, a contract must be supported by consideration. If a contract is lacking consideration, the court will not enforce the contract. However, an exception to this rule is that a court can enforce a contract that is otherwise lacking consideration, using the equitable doctrine of promissory estoppel.*

TEST REVIEW TERMS AND CONCEPTS

Accord

Accord and satisfaction
  (compromise)

Bargained-for exchange

Best-efforts contract

Consideration

Gift promise (gratuitous
  promise)

Illegal consideration

Illusory promise (illusory
  contract)

Legal value

Moral obligation

Output contract

Past consideration

Preexisting duty

Promissory estoppel
  (detrimental reliance)

Requirements contract

Satisfaction

CASE PROBLEMS

11.1 Consideration   Clyde and Betty Penley were married. Eighteen years later, Clyde operated an automotive tire business, and Betty owned an interest in a Kentucky Fried Chicken (KFC) franchise. That year, when Betty became ill, she requested that Clyde begin spending additional time at the KFC franchise to ensure its continued operation. Subsequently, Betty agreed that if Clyde would devote full time to the KFC franchise, they would operate the business as a joint enterprise, share equally in the ownership of its assets, and divide its returns equally. Pursuant to this agreement, Clyde terminated his tire business and devoted his full time to the KFC franchise. Twelve years later, Betty abandoned Clyde and denied him any rights in the KFC franchise. Clyde sued to enforce the agreement with Betty. Is the agreement enforceable? *Penley v. Penley*, 314 N.C. 1, 332 S.E.2d 51, **Web** 1985 N.C. Lexis 1706 (Supreme Court of North Carolina)

11.2 Forbearance to Sue   When John W. Frasier died, he left a will that devised certain of his community and separate property to his wife, Lena, and their three children. These devises were more valuable to Lena than just her interest in the community property that she would otherwise have received without the will. The devises to her, however, were conditioned upon the filing of a waiver by Lena of her interest in the community property, and if she failed to file the waiver, she would then receive only her interest in the community property and nothing more. Lena hired her brother, D.L. Carter, an attorney, to represent her. Carter failed to file the waiver on Lena's behalf, thus preventing her from taking the devises under the will. Instead, she received her interest in the community property, which was $19,358 less than she would have received under the will. Carter sent Lena the following letter:

> *This is to advise and confirm our agreement—that in the event the J. W. Frasier estate case now on appeal is not terminated so that you will receive settlement equal to your share of the estate as you would have done if your waiver had been filed in the estate in proper time, I will make up any balance to you in payments as suits my convenience and will pay interest on your loss at 6 percent.*

The appeal was decided against Lena. When she tried to enforce the contract against Carter, he alleged that the contract was not enforceable because it was not supported by valid consideration. Who wins? *Frasier v. Carter*, 92 Idaho 79, 437 P.2d 32, **Web** 1968 Ida. Lexis 249 (Supreme Court of Idaho)

11.3 Past Consideration   A. J. Whitmire and R. Lee Whitmire were brothers. R. Lee Whitmire married Lillie Mae Whitmire. For 4 years, A. J. performed various services for his brother and sister-in-law. During this time, R. Lee and Lillie Mae purchased some land. Fifteen years later, in the presence of Lillie Mae, R. Lee told A. J., "When we're gone, this land is yours" At that time, A. J. had not done any work for R. Lee or Lillie Mae for 16 years, and none was expected or provided in the future. Thirty years later, after both R. Lee and Lillie Mae had died, A. J. filed a claim with the estate of Lillie Mae, seeking specific performance of the earlier promise to give him the land. Does A. J. get the property? *Whitmire v. Watkins*, 245 Ga. 713, 267 S.E.2d 6, **Web** 1980 Ga. Lexis 908 (Supreme Court of Georgia)

11.4 Preexisting Duty   Robert Chuckrow Construction Company (Chuckrow) was employed as the general contractor to build a Kinney Shoe Store. Chuckrow employed Ralph Gough to perform the carpentry work on the store. The contract with Gough stipulated that he was to provide all labor, materials, tools, equipment, scaffolding, and other items necessary to complete the carpentry work. Gough's employees erected 38 trusses at the job site. The next day, 32 of the trusses fell off the building. The reason for the trusses having fallen was unexplained, and evidence showed that it was not due to Chuckrow's fault or a deficiency in the building plans. Chuckrow told Gough that he would pay him to reerect the trusses and continue work. When the job was complete, Chuckrow paid Gough the original contract price but refused to pay him for the additional cost of reerecting the trusses. Gough sued Chuckrow for this expense. Can Gough recover? *Robert Chuckrow Construction Company v. Gough*, 117 Ga. App. 140, 159 S.E.2d 469, **Web** 1968 Ga.App. Lexis 1007 (Court of Appeals of Georgia)

11.5 Illegal Consideration   In 1972, Marna Balin was involved in two automobile accidents in which she suffered severe injuries. She hired Norman H. Kallen, an attorney, to represent her. Kallen filed lawsuits on behalf of Balin, seeking damages for her injuries. Kallen repeatedly urged Balin to settle the lawsuits for $25,000. In late 1974, when she became disappointed with Kallen's representation, she retained another attorney, Samuel P. Delug, and instructed him to obtain her legal files from Kallen. The California Rules of Professional Conduct for attorneys provide that an attorney may not retain a client's files [Rule 2-111 (A)(2)]. However, Kallen refused to release the files until Delug agreed to give Kallen 40 percent of the attorneys' fees recovered in the case. The cases were ultimately settled for $810,000, resulting in attorneys' fees of $324,000. When Delug refused to pay Kallen 40 percent of these fees, Kallen sued Delug. Was the fee-splitting agreement between Kallen and Delug supported by legal consideration? *Kallen v. Delug*, 157 Cal.App.3d 940, 203 Cal.Rptr. 879, **Web** 1984 Cal.App. Lexis 2257 (California Court of Appeal)

11.6 Promissory Estoppel   Nalley's, Inc. (Nalley's), was a major food distributor with its home office in the state of Washington. Jacob Aronowicz and Samuel Duncan approached Nalley's about the possibility of its manufacturing a line of sliced meat products to be distributed by Nalley's. When Nalley's showed considerable interest, Aronowicz and Duncan incorporated as Major Food Products, Inc. (Major). Meetings to discuss the proposal continued at length with Charles Gardiner, a vice president and general manager of the Los Angeles division of Nalley's. Gardiner delivered a letter to Major, agreeing to become the exclusive Los Angeles and Orange Country distributor for Major's products, but he stated in the letter "that should we determine your product line is not representative or is not compatible with our operation we are free to terminate our agreement within 30 days." Nalley's was to distribute the full production of products produced by Major.

Based on Gardiner's assurances, Major leased a plant, modified the plant to its specifications, purchased and installed equipment, signed contracts to obtain meat to be processed, and hired personnel. Both Aronowicz and Duncan resigned from their positions at other meat processing companies to devote full time to the project. Financing was completed when Aronowicz and Duncan used their personal fortunes to purchase the stock of Major. Gardiner and other representatives of Nalley's visited Major's plant and expressed satisfaction with the premises. Major obtained the necessary government approvals regarding health standards and immediately achieved full production. Because Nalley's was to pick up the finished products at Major's plant, Nalley's drivers visited Major's plant to acquaint themselves with its operations.

Gardiner sent the final proposal regarding the Nalley's–Major relationship to Nalley's home office for final approval. One week later, Nalley's home office in Washington made a decision not to distribute Major's products. Nalley's refused to give any reason to Major for its decision. No final agreement was ever executed between the parties. Immediate efforts by Major to secure other distribution for its products proved unsuccessful. Further, because Major owned no trucks itself and had no sales organization, it could not distribute the products itself. In less than six months, Major had failed, and Aronowicz's and Duncan's stock in Major was worthless. Major, Aronowicz, and Duncan sued Nalley's for damages under the doctrine of promissory estoppel. Do they win? *Aronowicz v. Nalley's. Inc.*, 30 Cal.App.3d 27, 106 Cal.Rptr. 424, **Web** 1972 Cal.App. Lexis 667 (Court of Appeal of California)

BUSINESS ETHICS CASE

11.7 Business Ethics   Ocean Dunes of Hutchinson Island Development Corporation (Ocean Dunes) was a developer of condominium units. Prior to the construction, Albert and Helen Colangelo entered into a purchase agreement to buy one of the units and paid a deposit to Ocean Dunes. A provision in the purchase agreement provided that:

If Developer shall default in the performance of its obligations pursuant to this agreement, Purchaser's only remedy shall be to terminate this agreement, whereupon the Deposit shall be refunded to Purchaser and all rights and obligations thereunder shall thereupon become null and void.

The purchase agreement provided that if the buyer defaulted, the developer could retain the buyer's deposit or sue the buyer for damages and any other legal or equitable remedy. When Ocean Dunes refused to sell the unit to the Colangelos, they sued, seeking a decree of specific performance to require Ocean Dunes to sell them the unit. Ocean Dunes alleged that the above-quoted provision prevented the

plaintiffs from seeking any legal or equitable remedy. Was the defendant's duty under the contract illusory? Was it ethical for Ocean Dunes to place the provision at issue in the contract? *Ocean Dunes of Hutchinson Island Development Corporation v. Colangelo*, 463 So.2d 437, **Web** 1985 Fla.App. Lexis 12298 (Court of Appeal of Florida)

11.8 Business Ethics   Red Owl Stores, Inc., a Minnesota corporation with its home office at Hopkins, Minnesota, owned and operated grocery supermarkets and granted franchises to franchisees to also operate such stores. Joseph Hoffman, who operated a bakery with his wife in Wautoma, Wisconsin, was interested in obtaining a Red Owl franchise to operate a grocery store in Wisconsin. Hoffman contacted a representative of Red Owl and had numerous conversations regarding this proposal. Ten months later, Mr. Lukowitz became Red Owl's representative for the territory comprising upper Michigan and most of Wisconsin. Hoffman mentioned to Lukowitz that he had the capital to invest, and Lukowitz assured him that it would be sufficient to open a Red Owl franchise.

To gain experience in the grocery store business, and upon the advice of Lukowitz and other Red Owl representatives, Hoffman bought a small grocery store in Wautoma. After three months of operating this store, a Red Owl representative came in and took inventory, checked operations, and found that the store was operating at a profit. Lukowitz advised Hoffman to sell the store to his manager and assured Hoffman that Red Owl would find a larger store for him elsewhere. Although Hoffman was reluctant to sell at that time because it meant losing the summer tourist business, he sold on the assurance that he would be operating a Red Owl store at a new location by the fall. Again, Lukowitz assured Hoffman that the capital he had was sufficient to open a Red Owl franchise.

Red Owl had selected a site in Chilton, Wisconsin, for the proposed store. On Red Owl's insistence, Hoffman obtained an option to purchase the site. Hoffman and his wife rented a house in Chilton. Hoffman met with Lukowitz, who assured him, "Everything is ready to go. Get your money together and we are set." Lukowitz told Hoffman that he must sell his bakery business and building in Wautoma and that this was the only "hitch" in the entire plan. Hoffman sold his bakery building but retained the equipment to be used in the proposed Red Owl store. During the next two months, Red Owl prepared various financial projections for the proposed site. Hoffman met with Lukowitz and the credit manager for Red Owl, who demanded that Hoffman have more capital to invest in the store. Hoffman contacted his father-in-law, who agreed to provide the additional money. A week later, Red Owl sent Hoffman a telegram, demanding that he have more capital to invest. When Hoffman could not raise the additional money, the transaction fell through. Hoffman did not purchase the store site in Chilton and forfeited the option payment. The parties had never entered into a final agreement regarding the franchise.

Hoffman sued Red Owl under the doctrine of promissory estoppel, seeking damages for the money lost on the option payment on the Chilton property and the lease payments on the house in Chilton. Did the representatives of Red Owl Stores, Inc., act ethically in this case? Should the equitable doctrine of promissory estoppel apply in this case? *Hoffman v. Red Owl Stores, Inc.*, 26 Wis.2d 683, 133 N.W.2d 267, **Web** 1965 Wisc. Lexis 1026 (Supreme Court of Wisconsin)

ENDNOTE

1. *Hamer v. Sidwa*, 124 N.Y. 538, 27 N.E. 256, **Web** 1891 N.Y. Lexis 1396 (Court of Appeal of New York).

12 | CAPACITY AND LEGALITY

▲ **Las Vegas, Nevada** *Gambling is illegal in many states. However, the state of Nevada permits lawful gambling. A casino must obtain a license from the Nevada Gaming Commission before it can engage in the gambling business.*

CHAPTER OBJECTIVES

After studying this chapter, you should be able to:

1. Define and describe the infancy doctrine.
2. Define *legal insanity* and *intoxication* and explain how they affect contractual capacity.
3. Identify illegal contracts that are contrary to statutes and those that violate public policy.
4. Describe covenants not to compete and exculpatory clauses and identify when they are lawful.
5. Define *unconscionable contract* and determine when such contracts are unlawful.

CHAPTER CONTENTS

An unconscionable contract is one which no man in his senses, not under delusion, would make, on the one hand, and which no fair and honest man would accept on the other.

—Hume v. United States
132 U.S. 406, 10 S.Ct. 134, 1889 U.S. Lexis 1888 (1889)

▶ INTRODUCTION TO CAPACITY AND LEGALITY

Generally, the law presumes that the parties to a contract have the requisite **contractual capacity** to enter into the contract. Certain persons do not have this capacity, however, including minors, insane persons, and intoxicated persons. The common law of contracts and many state statutes protect persons who lack contractual capacity from having contracts enforced against them. The party asserting incapacity or his or her guardian, conservator, or other legal representative bears the burden of proof.

An essential element for the formation of a contract is that the object of the contract be lawful. A contract to perform an illegal act is called an *illegal contract*. Illegal contracts are void. That is, they cannot be enforced by either party to the contract. The term *illegal contract* is a misnomer, however, because no contract exists if the object of the contract is illegal. In addition, courts hold that *unconscionable contracts* are unenforceable. An unconscionable contract is one that is so oppressive or manifestly unfair that it would be unjust to enforce it.

Capacity to contract and the lawfulness of contracts are discussed in this chapter.

▶ MINORS

Minors do not always have the maturity, experience, or sophistication needed to enter into contracts with adults. Common law defines minors as females under the age of 18 and males under the age of 21. In addition, many states have enacted statutes that specify the **age of majority**. The most prevalent age of majority is 18 years of age for both males and females. Any age below the statutory age of majority is called the **period of minority**.

minor
A person who has not reached the age of majority.

Infancy Doctrine

To protect minors, the law recognizes the **infancy doctrine**, which gives minors the right to *disaffirm* (or *cancel*) most contracts they have entered into with adults. This right is based on public policy which reasons that minors should be protected from the unscrupulous behavior of adults. In most states, the infancy doctrine is an objective standard. If a person's age is below the age of majority, the court will not inquire into his or her knowledge, experience, or sophistication. Generally, contracts for the necessaries of life, which we discuss later in this chapter, are exempt from the scope of this doctrine.

infancy doctrine
A doctrine that allows minors to disaffirm (cancel) most contracts they have entered into with adults.

Under the infancy doctrine, a minor has the option of choosing whether to enforce a contract (i.e., the contract is **voidable** by a minor). The adult party is bound to the minor's decision. If both parties to a contract are minors, both parties have the right to disaffirm the contract.

If performance of the contract favors the minor, the minor will probably enforce the contract. Otherwise, he or she will probably disaffirm the contract. A minor may not affirm one part of a contract and disaffirm another part.

Disaffirmance

A minor can expressly **disaffirm** a contract orally, in writing, or through his or her conduct. No special formalities are required. The contract may be disaffirmed at any time prior to the person's reaching the age of majority plus a "reasonable time." The designation of a reasonable time is determined on a case-by-case basis.

disaffirmance
The act of a minor to rescind a contract under the infancy doctrine. Disaffirmance may be done orally, in writing, or by the minor's conduct.

Minor's Duty of Restoration

If a minor's contract is executory and neither party has performed, the minor can simply disaffirm the contract: There is nothing to recover because neither party has given the other party anything of value. If the parties have exchanged consideration and partially or fully performed the contract by the time the minor disaffirms the contract, however, the issue becomes one of what consideration or restitution must be made. The following rules apply:

- **Minor's duty of restoration.** Generally, a minor is obligated only to return the goods or property he or she has received from the adult in the condition it is in at the time of disaffirmance (subject to several exceptions, discussed later in this chapter), even if the item has been consumed, lost, or destroyed or has depreciated in value by the time of disaffirmance. This rule, called the **minor's duty of restoration**, is based on the rationale that if a minor had to place the adult in status quo upon disaffirmance of a contract, there would be no incentive for an adult not to deal with a minor.
- **Competent party's duty of restitution.** If a minor has transferred consideration—money, property, or other valuables—to a competent party before disaffirming the contract, that party must place the minor in status quo. That is, the minor must be restored to the same position he or she was in before the minor entered into the contract. This restoration is usually done by returning the consideration to the minor. If the consideration has been sold or has depreciated in value, the competent party must pay the minor the cash equivalent. This action is called the **competent party's duty of restitution**.

Most states provide that the minor must put the adult in status quo upon disaffirmance of the contract if the minor's intentional, reckless, or grossly negligent conduct caused the loss of value to the adult's property. This rule is called the **minor's duty of restitution**.

On occasion, minors might misrepresent their age to adults when entering into contracts. Most state laws provide that minors who misrepresent their age must place the adult in status quo if they disaffirm the contract.

Ratification

If a minor does not disaffirm a contract either during the period of minority or within a reasonable time after reaching the age of majority, the contract is considered ratified (accepted). Hence, the minor (who is now an adult) is bound by the contract; the right to disaffirm the contract is lost. Note that any attempt by a minor to ratify a contract while still a minor can be disaffirmed just as the original contract can be disaffirmed.

The **ratification**, which relates back to the inception of the contract, can be by express oral or written words or implied from the minor's conduct (e.g., after reaching the age of majority, the minor remains silent regarding the contract).

Parents' Liability for Their Children's Contracts

Generally, parents owe a legal duty to provide food, clothing, shelter, and other necessaries of life for their minor children. Parents are liable for their children's contracts for necessaries of life if they have not adequately provided such items.

The parental duty of support terminates if a minor becomes *emancipated*. **Emancipation** occurs when a minor voluntarily leaves home and lives apart from his or her parents. The courts consider factors such as getting married, setting up a separate household, or joining the military in determining whether a minor is emancipated. Each situation is examined on its merits.

Necessaries of Life

Minors are obligated to pay for the **necessaries of life** that they contract for. Otherwise, many adults would refuse to sell these items to them. There is no standard definition of what is a necessary of life. The minor's age, lifestyle, and status in life influence what is considered necessary.

---

minor's duty of restoration
A rule which states that a minor is obligated only to return the goods or property he or she has received from the adult in the condition it is in at the time of disaffirmance.

competent party's duty of restitution
A rule which states that if a minor has transferred money, property, or other valuables to the competent party before disaffirming the contract, that party must place the minor in status quo.

The right of a minor to disaffirm his contract is based upon sound public policy to protect the minor from his own improvidence and the overreaching of adults.

Justice Sullivan
Star Chevrolet v. Green (1985)

ratification
The act of a minor after the minor has reached the age of majority by which he or she accepts a contract entered into when he or she was a minor.

emancipation
The act or process of a minor voluntarily leaving home and living apart from his or her parents.

necessaries of life
Food, clothing, shelter, medical care, and other items considered necessary to the maintenance of life. Minors must pay the reasonable value of necessaries of life for which they contract.

Examples Items such as food, clothing, shelter, and medical services are generally understood to be necessities of life.

Examples Goods and services such as automobiles, tools of trade, education, and vocational training have also been found to be necessaries of life in some situations.

The seller's recovery is based on the equitable doctrine of **quasi-contract** rather than on the contract itself. Under this theory, the minor is obligated only to pay the reasonable value of the goods or services received. Reasonable value is determined on a case-by-case basis.

CONTEMPORARY ENVIRONMENT
Special Types of Minors' Contracts

Based on public policy, many states have enacted statutes that make certain specified contracts enforceable against minors—that is, minors cannot assert the infancy doctrine against enforcement for these contracts. These usually include contracts for:

- Medical, surgical, and pregnancy care
- Psychological counseling
- Health insurance
- Life insurance
- The performance of duties related to stock and bond transfers, bank accounts, and the like

- Educational loan agreements
- Contracts to support children
- Contracts to enlist in the military
- Artistic, sports, and entertainment contracts that have been entered into with the approval of the court.

Many statutes mandate that a certain portion of the wages and fees earned by a minor (e.g., 50 percent) based on an artistic, sports, or entertainment contract be put in trust until the minor reaches the age of majority.

▶ MENTALLY INCOMPETENT PERSONS

Mental incapacity may arise because of mental illness, brain damage, mental retardation, senility, and the like. The law protects people suffering from substantial mental incapacity from enforcement of contracts against them because such persons may not understand the consequences of their actions in entering into a contract.

To be relieved of his or her duties under a contract, a person must have been legally insane at the time of entering into the contract. This state is called **legal insanity**. Most states use the *objective cognitive "understanding" test* to determine legal insanity. Under this test, the person's mental incapacity must render that person incapable of understanding or comprehending the nature of the transaction. Mere weakness of intellect, slight psychological or emotional problems, or delusions does not constitute legal insanity.

The law has developed two standards concerning contracts of mentally incompetent persons: (1) adjudged insane and (2) insane but not adjudged insane.

legal insanity
A state of contractual incapacity, as determined by law.

Adjudged Insane

In certain cases, a relative, a loved one, or another interested party may institute a legal action to have someone declared legally (i.e., adjudged) insane. If after hearing the evidence at a formal judicial or administrative hearing the person is **adjudged insane**, the court will make that person a ward of the court and appoint a guardian to act on that person's behalf. Any contract entered into by a person who has been adjudged insane is **void**. That is, no contract exists. The court-appointed guardian is the only one who has the legal authority to enter into contracts on behalf of the person.

adjudged insane
Declared legally insane by a proper court or administrative agency. A contract entered into by a person adjudged insane is *void*.

Insane but Not Adjudged Insane

If no formal ruling has been made about a person's sanity but the person suffers from a mental impairment that makes him or her legally insane—that is, the person is **insane but**

insane but not adjudged insane
Being insane but not having been adjudged insane by a court or an administrative agency. A contract entered into by such person is generally *voidable*. Some states hold that such a contract is void.

Insanity vitiates all acts.

Sir John Nicholl
Countess of Portsmouth v. Earl of Portsmouth (1828)

not adjudged insane—any contract entered into by this person is voidable by the insane person. Unless the other party does not have contractual capacity, he or she does not have the option to void the contract.

Some people have alternating periods of sanity and insanity. Any contracts made by such persons during a lucid interval are enforceable. Contracts made while the person was not legally sane can be disaffirmed.

A person who has dealt with an insane person must place that insane person in status quo if the contract is either void or voided by the insane person. Most states hold that a party who did not know he or she was dealing with an insane person must be placed in status quo upon avoidance of the contract. Insane persons are liable in *quasi-contract* to pay the reasonable value for the necessaries of life they receive.

CONCEPT SUMMARY

DISAFFIRMANCE OF CONTRACTS BASED ON LEGAL INSANITY

Type of Legal Insanity	Disaffirmance Rule
Adjudged insane	Contract is void. Neither party can enforce the contract.
Insane but not adjudged insane	Contract is voidable by the insane person; the competent party cannot void the contract.

▶ INTOXICATED PERSONS

intoxicated person
A person who is under contractual incapacity because of ingestion of alcohol or drugs to the point of incompetence.

Men intoxicated are sometimes stunned into sobriety.

Lord Mansfield
R. v. Wilkes (1770)

Most states provide that contracts entered into by certain **intoxicated persons** are voidable by those persons. The intoxication may occur because of alcohol or drugs. The contract is not voidable by the other party if that party had contractual capacity.

Under the majority rule, the contract is voidable only if the person was so intoxicated when the contract was entered into that he or she was incapable of understanding or comprehending the nature of the transaction. In most states, this rule holds even if the intoxication was self-induced. Some states allow the person to disaffirm the contract only if the person was forced to become intoxicated or did so unknowingly.

The amount of alcohol or drugs that must be consumed for a person to be considered legally intoxicated to disaffirm contracts varies from case to case. The factors that are considered include the user's physical characteristics and his or her ability to "hold" intoxicants.

A person who disaffirms a contract based on intoxication generally must be returned to the status quo. In turn, the intoxicated person generally must return the consideration received under the contract to the other party and make restitution that returns the other party to status quo. After becoming sober, an intoxicated person can ratify the contracts he or she entered into while intoxicated. Intoxicated persons are liable in *quasi-contract* to pay the reasonable value for necessaries they receive.

▶ LEGALITY

illegal contract
A contract that has an illegal object. Such contracts are *void*.

One requirement to have an enforceable contract is that the object of the contract must be lawful. Most contracts that individuals and businesses enter into are **lawful contracts** that are enforceable. These include contracts for the sale of goods, services, real property, and intangible rights; the lease of goods; property leases; licenses; and other contracts.

Some contracts have illegal objects. A contract with an illegal object is *void* and therefore unenforceable. These contracts are called **illegal contracts**. The following paragraphs discuss various illegal contracts.

Contracts Contrary to Statutes

Both federal and state legislatures have enacted statutes that prohibit certain types of conduct. Contracts to perform activities that are prohibited by statute are illegal contracts.

Examples An agreement between two companies to engage in price fixing in violation of federal antitrust statutes is illegal and therefore void. Thus, neither company to this illegal contract can enforce the contract against the other company.

Usury Laws

State **usury laws** set an upper limit on the annual interest rate that can be charged on certain types of loans. The limits vary from state to state. Lenders who charge a higher rate than the state limit are guilty of usury. These laws are intended to protect unsophisticated borrowers from loan sharks and others who charge exorbitant rates of interest.

Most states provide criminal and civil penalties for making usurious loans. Some states require lenders to remit the difference between the interest rate charged on the loan and the usury rate to the borrower. Other states prohibit lenders from collecting any interest on the loan. Still other states provide that a usurious loan is a void contract, permitting the borrower not to have to pay the interest or the principal of the loan to the lender.

Most usury laws exempt certain types of lenders and loan transactions involving legitimate business transactions from the reach of the law. These exemptions usually include loans made by banks and other financial institutions, loans above a certain dollar amount, and loans made to corporations and other businesses.

usury law
A law that sets an upper limit on the interest rate that can be charged on certain types of loans.

Contracts to Commit Crimes

Contracts to commit criminal acts are void. If the object of a contract becomes illegal after the contract is entered into because the government has enacted a statute that makes it unlawful, the parties are discharged from the contract. The contract is not an illegal contract unless the parties agree to go forward and complete it.

In the following case, the court had to determine whether a contract was illegal.

CASE 12.1 Illegal Contract

Parente v. Pirozzoli
87 Conn.App. 235, 866 A.2d 629, Web 2005 Conn.App. Lexis 25 (2005)
Appellate Court of Connecticut

"Thus, in the case of a contract whose inherent purpose is to violate the law, if both parties thereto are *in pari delicto*, the law will leave them where it finds them."
—Judge Lavery

Facts

Andrew Parente had a criminal record. He and Mario Pirozzoli, Jr., formed a partnership to open and operate the Speak Easy Café in Berlin, Connecticut, which was a bar that would serve alcohol. The owners were required to obtain a liquor license from the state of Connecticut before operating the bar. Because the state of Connecticut usually would not issue a liquor license to anyone with a criminal record, it was agreed that Pirozzoli would form a corporation called Centerfolds, Inc., to own the bar, sign the real estate lease for the bar in his name, and file for the liquor license in his name only. Pirozzoli did all of these things. Parente and Pirozzoli signed a partnership agreement that acknowledged that

Parente was an equal partner in the business. The state of Connecticut granted the liquor license, and the bar opened for business. Parente and Pirozzoli shared the profits of the bar.

Six years later, Pirozzoli terminated the partnership and kept the business. Parente sued Pirozzoli for breach of the partnership agreement to recover the value of his alleged share of the business. Pirozzoli defended, arguing that the partnership agreement was an illegal contract that should not be enforced against him. The trial court held that the partnership agreement had been breached and awarded Parente $138,000 in damages. Pirozzoli appealed.

Issue

Was the partnership agreement an illegal contract that was void and unenforceable by the court?

Language of the Court

Here, the partnership agreement was not offensive on its face, but had an illegal, ulterior purpose, namely, to

(case continues)

evade the strictures of the liquor control laws. Because the partnership agreement was made to facilitate, foster, or support patently illegal activity, we conclude that it is illegal as against public policy and, consequently, that the court's enforcement of it was improper.

Although the end result of holding the partnership agreement illegal may be to allow Pirozzoli a windfall at Parente's expense, this result is common and necessary in many cases in which contracts are deemed unenforceable on the grounds of furthering overriding policies. It is in order to effectuate an underlying public policy, rather than sanction a party seeking to enforce an illegal contract, that courts refuse to lend assistance to those who have contributed to the illegality that taints the contract. Thus, in the case of a contract whose inherent purpose is to violate the law, if both parties thereto are in pari delicto, *the law will leave them where it finds them. Knowing that they will receive no help from the courts and must trust completely to each other's good faith, the parties are less likely to enter an illegal arrangement in the first place.*

Decision

The appellate court held that the partnership agreement between Parente and Pirozzoli was an illegal contract that was void and unenforceable. The appellate court reversed the judgment of the trial court, found that Pirozzoli was not liable to Parente, and held that Pirozzoli could keep the $138,000 windfall.

Case Questions

Critical Legal Thinking What is an illegal contract? Explain.

Business Ethics Did Parente act ethically in this case? Was it honorable for Pirozzoli to argue that his partnership agreement with Parente was an illegal contract?

Contemporary Business What is the result of a court finding that a contract is illegal? Explain. Was it fair for Pirozzoli to receive the windfall in this case?

Gambling Statutes

gambling statutes
Statutes that make certain forms of gambling illegal.

All states either prohibit or regulate gambling, wagering, lotteries, and games of chance via **gambling statutes**. States provide various criminal and civil penalties for illegal gambling. There are many exceptions to wagering laws. Many states have enacted statutes that permit games of chance under a certain dollar amount, bingo games, lotteries conducted by religious and charitable organizations, and the like. Many states also permit and regulate horse racing, harness racing, dog racing, and state-operated lotteries.

Effect of Illegality

effect of illegality
A doctrine which states that the courts will refuse to enforce or rescind an illegal contract and will leave the parties where it finds them.

Because illegal contracts are void, the parties cannot sue for nonperformance. Further, if an illegal contract is executed, the court will generally leave the parties where it finds them.

Certain situations are exempt from the general rule of the effect of finding an illegal contract. If an exception applies, the innocent party may use the court system to sue for damages or to recover consideration paid under the illegal contract. Persons who can assert an exception are:

- Innocent persons who were justifiably ignorant of the law or fact that made the contract illegal.

Example A person who purchases insurance from an unlicensed insurance company may recover insurance benefits from the unlicensed company.

- Persons who were induced to enter into an illegal contract by fraud, duress, or undue influence.

Example A shop owner who pays $5,000 "protection money" to a mobster so that his store will not be burned down by the mobster can recover the $5,000.

- Persons who entered into an illegal contract who withdraw before the illegal act is performed.

Example If the president of New Toy Corporation pays $10,000 to an employee of Old Toy Corporation to steal a trade secret from his employer but reconsiders and tells the employee not to do it before he has done it, the New Toy Corporation may recover the $10,000.

• Persons who were less at fault than the other party for entering into the illegal contract. At common law, parties to an illegal contract were considered *in pari delicto* (in equal fault). Some states have changed this rule and permit the less-at-fault party to recover restitution of the consideration they paid under an illegal contract from the more-at-fault party.

in pari delicto
A situation in which both parties are equally at fault in an illegal contract.

ETHICS SPOTLIGHT

Illegal Gambling Contract

"The trial court could not have compelled Ryno to honor his wager by delivering the BMW to Tyra. However, Ryno did deliver the BMW to Tyra and the facts incident to that delivery are sufficient to establish a transfer by gift of the BMW from Ryno to Tyra."

—Judge Farris

R. D. Ryno, Jr., owned Bavarian Motors, an automobile dealership in Fort Worth, Texas. One day, Lee Tyra discussed purchasing a BMW M-1 from Ryno for $125.000. Ryno then suggested a double-or-nothing coin flip, to which Tyra agreed. If the Ryno won the coin flip, Tyra would have to pay $250,000 for the car; if Tyra won the coin flip, he would get the car for free. The coin was flipped, and Tyra won the coin flip. Ryno said, "It's yours," and handed Tyra the keys, title, and possession to the car. Tyra drove away in the BMW. A lawsuit ensued as to the ownership of the car.

The court held that when Tyra won the coin toss and Ryno voluntarily gave the keys, title, and possession of the BMW to Tyra, this was a performed illegal gambling contract. There was sufficient evidence to find that Ryno intended to transfer to Tyra his ownership interest in the BMW at the time he delivered the documents, keys, and possession of the automobile to Tyra. The court left the parties where it found them: Tyra had the keys, title, and possession of the BMW; Ryno did not have either the car or payment for the car.

Note: If, when Tyra won the coin toss, Ryno had refused to give the BMW to Tyra, the result of this case would have been different. Tyra could not have compelled Ryno to honor his wager. This is because courts will not enforce an executory illegal gambling contract. The court would again have left the parties where it found them: Ryno would have had ownership and possession of the car and refused to honor the wager; Tyra would have won the coin toss but could not obtain the car from Ryno. *Ryno v. Tyra*, 752 S.W.2d 148, **Web** 1988 Tex. App. Lexis 1646 (Court of Appeals of Texas)

Business Ethics Did Ryno act ethically in this case? Did Tyra act ethically in this case? Should the court have lent its help to Ryno to recover the BMW from Tyra? Why or why not?

Kewadin Casino, Michigan *This sign advertises an Indian gaming casino operated in the Upper Peninsula of Michigan. In 1988, Congress enacted the* **Indian Gaming Regulatory Act (IGRA)**[1] *that established the framework for permitting and regulating Indian gaming. There are more than 400 Indian gaming establishments in the country operated by more than 200 federally recognized tribes. Federal law permits Indian casino gambling only if the state permits such gambling. The Kewadin Casino in Brevort Township, Michigan, is operated by the Sault Ste. Marie Tribe of Chippewa Indians.*

Contracts Contrary to Public Policy

contract contrary to public policy
A contract that has a negative impact on society or that interferes with the public's safety and welfare.

Certain contracts are illegal because they are **contrary to public policy**. Such contracts are void. Although *public policy* eludes precise definition, the courts have held contracts to be contrary to public policy if they have a negative impact on society or interfere with the public's safety and welfare.

immoral contract
A contract whose objective is the commission of an act that is society considers immoral.

Immoral contracts—that is, contracts whose objective is the commission of an act that society considers immoral—may be found to be against public policy. Judges are not free to define morality based on their individual views. Instead, they must look to the practices and beliefs of society when defining immoral conduct.

Example A contract that is based on sexual favors is an immoral contract and void as against public policy.

ETHICS SPOTLIGHT

Murder, She Wrote

Ellen and Richard Alvin Flood, who were married, lived in a mobile home in Louisiana. Richard worked as a maintenance man, and Ellen was employed at an insurance agency. Ellen was unhappy with her marriage. Ellen took out a life insurance policy on the life of her husband and named herself as beneficiary. The policy was issued by Fidelity & Guaranty Life Insurance Company (Fidelity).

Thereafter, Richard became unexpectedly ill. He was taken to the hospital, where his condition improved. After a visit at the hospital from his wife, however, Richard died. Ellen was criminally charged with the murder of her husband by poisoning. Evidence showed that six medicine bottles at the couple's home, including Tylenol and paregoric bottles, contained arsenic. The court found that Ellen had fed Richard ice cubes laced with arsenic at the hospital. Ellen was tried and convicted of the murder of her husband.

Subsequently, Ellen, as the beneficiary of Richard's life insurance policy, requested Fidelity to pay her the benefits. Fidelity refused to pay the benefits and returned all premiums paid on the policy. A lawsuit followed. Does Fidelity have to pay Ellen the life insurance proceeds for Richard's death?

The court held that Fidelity did not have to pay Ellen the life insurance proceeds from her husband Richard's death because a beneficiary named in a life insurance policy is not entitled to the proceeds of the insurance if the beneficiary kills the insured. The enforcement of such a contract would violate public policy. The court stated, "Louisiana follows the majority rule that holds, as a matter of public policy, that a beneficiary named in a life insurance policy is not entitled to the proceeds of the insurance if the beneficiary feloniously kills the insured." *Flood v. Fidelity & Guaranty Life Insurance Company*, 394 So.2d 1311, **Web** 1981 La.App. Lexis 3538 (Court of Appeal of Louisiana)

Business Ethics Did Ellen Flood act ethically by trying to recover the life insurance proceeds from her husband's death? What would be the consequences if persons could recover insurance proceeds for losses caused by their illegal activities, such as murder?

▶ SPECIAL BUSINESS CONTRACTS

The issue of the lawfulness of contracts applies to several special business contracts. These include contracts that restrain trade; contracts to provide services that require a government license, exculpatory clauses, and covenants not to compete. These contracts are discussed in the following paragraphs.

Contract in Restraint of Trade

contract in restraint of trade
A contract that unreasonably restrains trade.

The general economic policy of this country favors competition. At common law, **contracts in restraint of trade**—that is, contracts that unreasonably restrain trade—are held to be unlawful.

Example It would be an illegal restraint of trade for Toyota, General Motors, and Ford Motor to agree to fix the prices of the automobiles they sell. Their contract would be void and could not be enforced by any of the parties against the other parties.

Licensing Statute

All states have **licensing statutes** that require members of certain professions and occupations to be licensed by the state in which they practice. Lawyers, doctors, real estate agents, insurance agents, certified public accountants, teachers, contractors, hairdressers, and such are among them. In most instances, a license is granted to a person who demonstrates that he or she has the proper schooling, experience, and moral character required by the relevant statute. Sometimes, a written examination is also required.

Problems arise if an unlicensed person tries to collect payment for services provided to another under a contract. Some statutes expressly provide that unlicensed persons cannot enforce contracts to provide these services. If the statute is silent on the point, enforcement depends on whether it is a *regulatory statute* or a *revenue raising statute*:

- **Regulatory statute.** Licensing statutes enacted to protect the public are called **regulatory statutes**. Generally, unlicensed persons cannot recover payment for services that a regulatory statute requires a licensed person to provide.

Example State law provides that legal services can be provided only by lawyers who have graduated from law school and passed the appropriate bar exam. Nevertheless, suppose Marie, a first-year law student, agrees to draft a will for Randy for a $350 fee. Because Marie is not licensed to provide legal services, she has violated a regulatory statute. She cannot enforce the contract and recover payment from Randy. Randy, even though receiving services by having his will drafted, does not have to pay Marie $350.

- **Revenue-raising statute.** Licensing statutes enacted to raise money for the government are called **revenue-raising statutes**. A person who provides services pursuant to a contract without the appropriate license required by such a statute can enforce the contract and recover payment for services rendered.

Example A state licensing statute requires licensed attorneys to pay an annual $500 renewal fee without requiring continuing education or other new qualifications. If a lawyer provides legal services but has not paid the annual licensing fee, the lawyer can still recover for her services.

Exculpatory Clause

An **exculpatory clause** (also called a **release of liability clause**) is a contractual provision that relieves one (or both) of the parties to a contract from tort liability. An exculpatory clause can relieve a party of liability for ordinary negligence. It cannot be used in a situation involving willful conduct, intentional torts, fraud, recklessness, or gross negligence. Exculpatory clauses are often found in leases, sales contracts, sporting event ticket stubs, parking lot tickets, service contracts, and the like. Such clauses do not have to be reciprocal (i.e., one party may be relieved of tort liability, whereas the other party is not).

Example Jim Jackson voluntarily enrolled in a parachute jump course and signed a contract containing an exculpatory clause that relieved the parachute center of liability. After receiving proper instruction, he jumped from an airplane. Unfortunately, Jim was injured when he could not steer his parachute toward the target area. He sued the parachute center for damages. Here, the court would usually enforce the exculpatory clause, reasoning that parachute jumping was a voluntary choice and did not involve an essential service.

Exculpatory clauses that either affect the public interest or result from superior bargaining power are usually found to be void as against public policy. Although the outcome varies with the circumstances of the case, the greater the degree to which the party serves the general public, the greater the chance that the exculpatory clause will be struck down as

licensing statute
A statute that requires a person or business to obtain a license from the government prior to engaging in a specified occupation or activity.

regulatory statute
A licensing statute enacted to protect the public.

revenue-raising statute
A licensing statute with the primary purpose of raising revenue for the government.

exculpatory clause
A contractual provision that relieves one (or both) of the parties to a contract from tort liability for ordinary negligence. Also known as a *release of liability clause*.

illegal. The courts will consider such factors as the type of activity involved; the relative bargaining power, knowledge, experience, and sophistication of the parties; and other relevant factors.

Covenant Not to Compete

covenant not to compete
A contract which provides that a seller of a business or an employee will not engage in a similar business or occupation within a specified geographical area for a specified time following the sale of the business or termination of employment. Also called a *noncompete clause.*

Entrepreneurs and others often buy and sell businesses. The sale of a business includes its "goodwill," or reputation. To protect this goodwill after the sale, the seller often enters into an agreement with the buyer not to engage in a similar business or occupation within a specified geographic area for a specified period of time following the sale. This agreement is called a **covenant not to compete**, or a **noncompete clause**.

Employers often do not want an employee who resigns or is terminated to work in a position that competes with the employer for a certain length of time after the employee is gone from the employer. Employers often require an employee, usually before he or she is hired, to sign a noncompete clause, agreeing not to work for another employer or for themselves in a position that would compete with their prior employer for a certain period of time after the employee has left or been terminated by the employer.

Covenants not to compete that are *ancillary* to a legitimate sale of a business or employment contract are lawful if they are reasonable in three aspects: (1) the line of business protected, (2) the geographic area protected, and (3) the duration of the restriction. A covenant that is found to be unreasonable is not enforceable as written. The reasonableness of covenants not to compete is examined on a case-by-case basis. If a covenant not to compete is unreasonable, the courts may either refuse to enforce it or change it so that it is reasonable. Usually, the courts choose the first option.

Examples Stacy is a certified public accountant (CPA) with a lucrative accounting practice in Providence, Rhode Island. Her business includes a substantial amount of goodwill with her clients. Stacy sells her accounting practice to Gregory. When she sells her practice to Gregory, Stacy agrees not to open another accounting practice in the state of Rhode Island for a 20-year period. This covenant not to compete is reasonable in the line of business protected but is unreasonable in geographic scope and duration. It will not be enforced by the courts as written. The covenant not to compete would be reasonable and enforceable if it prohibited Stacy only from practicing as a CPA in the city of Providence for 3 years.

▶ UNCONSCIONABLE CONTRACTS

The general rule of freedom of contract holds that if the object of a contract is lawful and the other elements for the formation of a contract are met, the courts will enforce a contract according to its terms. Although it is generally presumed that parties are capable of protecting their own interests when contracting, it is a fact of life that dominant parties sometimes take advantage of weaker parties.

In addition, many contracts that consumers sign are **contracts of adhesion**—that is, they are preprinted forms whose terms the consumer cannot negotiate and which they must sign in order to obtain a product or service. Most adhesion contracts are lawful even though there is a disparity in power of contracting.

Examples Automobile sales contracts and leases, mortgages, and apartment leases are usually contracts of adhesion.

unconscionable contract
A contract that courts refuse to enforce in part or at all because it is so oppressive or manifestly unfair as to be unjust.

However, when a contract is so oppressive or manifestly unfair as to be unjust, the law has developed the equity doctrine of unconscionability to prevent the enforcement of such contracts. The doctrine of unconscionability is based on public policy. A contract found to be unconscionable under this doctrine is called an **unconscionable contract**.

The courts are given substantial discretion in determining whether a contract or contract clause is unconscionable. There is no single definition of *unconscionability*. This doctrine may not be used merely to save a contracting party from a bad bargain.

Elements of Unconscionability

The following elements must be shown to prove that a contract or a clause in a contract is unconscionable:

- The parties possessed severely unequal bargaining power.
- The dominant party unreasonably used its unequal bargaining power to obtain oppressive or manifestly unfair contract terms.
- The adhering party had no reasonable alternative.

A good judge decides fairly, preferring equity to strict law.

Legal maxim

Unconscionable contracts are sometimes found where there is a consumer contract that takes advantage of uneducated, poor, or elderly people who have been persuaded to enter into an unfair contract. This often involves door-to-door sales and sales over the telephone. If the court finds that a contract or contract clause is unconscionable, it may (1) refuse to enforce the contract, (2) refuse to enforce the unconscionable clause but enforce the remainder of the contract, or (3) limit the applicability of any unconscionable clause so as to avoid any unconscionable result. The appropriate remedy depends on the facts and circumstances of each case. Note that because unconscionability is a matter of law, the judge may opt to decide the case without a jury trial.

Example Suppose a door-to-door salesperson sells a poor family a freezer full of meat and other foods for $3,000, with monthly payments for 60 months at 20 percent interest. If the actual cost of the freezer and the food is $1,000, this contract could be found to be unconscionable. The court could either find the entire contract unenforceable or rewrite the contract so that it has reasonable terms.

In the following case, the court found a contract clause to be unconscionable.

CASE 12.2 Unconscionable Contract

Muhammad, on Her Own Behalf and All Others Similarly Situated v. County Bank of Rehoboth Beach

189 N.J. 1, 912 A.2d 88, Web 2006 N.J. Lexis 1154 (2006)
Supreme Court of New Jersey

"By permitting claimants to band together, class actions equalize adversaries and provide a procedure to remedy a wrong that might otherwise go unredressed."

—Judge LaVecchia

Facts

Jaliyah Muhammad was a part-time student at Berkeley College in Paramus, New Jersey. Muhammad obtained a short-term single advance, unsecured loan of $200 from County Bank of Rehoboth Beach (County Bank). County Bank charged a finance charge of $60 for the loan. The loan rate was 608.33 percent. The loan was due in 21 days. Muhammad obtained two similar loans from County Bank.

To obtain the loans, Muhammad had to complete and sign three pages of standard form contracts. These loan documents contained an agreement that all disputes regarding the loan were subject to arbitration and could not be brought in court and that the borrower could not bring, join, or participate in class actions as to any disputes regarding the loans. The agreement to arbitrate and the agreement not to

bring, join, or participate in class actions were conspicuously stated in capital letters in the loan documents.

Muhammad filed a class action lawsuit in New Jersey superior court against County Bank, alleging that County Bank charged illegal rates of interest, in violation of New Jersey law. Muhammad sought restitution, damages, penalties, and costs from County Bank. Muhammad argued that the arbitration agreement was unconscionable based on the class action waiver. County Bank made a motion to compel arbitration. The trial court and the appellate court held that Muhammad's claims were subject to arbitration. Muhammad appealed.

Issue

Was the class action waiver in the arbitration agreement unconscionable?

Language of the Court

It is well settled that courts may refuse to enforce contracts that are unconscionable. The unconscionability issue in this matter centers on access to class-action proceeding in the

(case continues)

arbitral setting. By permitting claimants to band together, class actions equalize adversaries and provide a procedure to remedy a wrong that might otherwise go unredressed. If each victim were remitted to an individual suit, the remedy would be illusory, for the individual loss may be too small to warrant a suit. A class-action proceeding can aid the efficient administration of justice by avoiding the expense, in both time and money, of relitigating similar claims. In sum, the class-action mechanism is recognized to be valuable to litigants, to the courts, and to the public interest.

We hold, therefore, that the presence of the class-action waiver in Muhammad's consumer arbitration agreement renders that agreement unconscionable. As a matter of generally applicable state contract law, it was unconscionable for County Bank to deprive Muhammad of the mechanism of a class-wide action, whether in arbitration or in court litigation. Finally, although we find that the class-arbitration waivers in Muhammad's arbitration agreements are unconscionable, we find that the waivers are severable. Once the waivers are removed, the remainder of the arbitration agreement is enforceable.

Decision

The supreme court of New Jersey held that the class action waiver clause in County Bank's arbitration agreement was unconscionable. The court further held that this clause could be severed from the arbitration clause and that Muhammad's class action would be heard by an arbitration panel.

Case Questions

Critical Legal Thinking What is a contract of adhesion? Have you ever signed one? What is an unconscionable contract? Explain.

Business Ethics Did County Bank act ethically in placing the class action waiver in its loan documents? Why do you think County Bank included the class action waiver clause in its loan documents?

Contemporary Business Were the terms of the loans—the interest rate and finance charge—for County Bank's loans unconscionable?

Web Exercise Go to **www.bankrate.com/brm/news/cc/20020320a.asp** to read about credit card interest rates.

China *Since 1976, Chinese leaders have opened the country to economic reform. Since taking over the island of Macau from the Portuguese in 1999, China has made Macau into one of the world's premiere gambling centers. Gambling revenues from Macau's casinos now exceed those of Las Vegas casinos. The Sands Macau, Wynn Macau, Venetian Macau, and MGM Grand Macau have opened on the island.*

TEST REVIEW TERMS AND CONCEPTS

Adjudged insane	Contract contrary to public policy	Contractual capacity	Effect of illegality
Age of majority	Contract in restraint of trade	Covenant not to compete (noncompete clause)	Emancipation
Competent party's duty of restitution	Contract of adhesion	Disaffirm	Exculpatory clause (release of liability clause)

Gambling statute
Illegal contract
Immoral contract
Indian Gaming Regulatory
    Act (IGRA)
Infancy doctrine
In pari delicto

Insane but not adjudged
    insane
Intoxicated person
Lawful contract
Legal insanity
Licensing statute
Minor

Minor's duty of restitution
Minor's duty of restoration
Necessaries of life
Period of minority
Quasi-contract
Ratification
Regulatory statute

Revenue-raising statute
Unconscionable contract
Usury law
Void
Voidable contract

CASE PROBLEMS

12.1 Infancy Doctrine James Halbman, Jr., a minor, entered into a contract to purchase an Oldsmobile from Michael Lemke. Halbman paid $1,000 cash and agreed to make weekly payments until the full purchase price was paid. Five weeks later, a connecting rod on the vehicle's engine broke, and Halbman took the car to a garage, where it was repaired at a cost of $637.40. Halbman refused to pay for the repairs, disaffirmed the contract with Lemke, and notified Lemke where the car was located. When Lemke refused to pick up the car and pay the repair bill, the garage legally satisfied its garageman's lien by removing the vehicle's engine. It then towed the car to Halbman's residence. Halbman notified Lemke to remove the car, but Lemke refused to do so. The car was subsequently vandalized, making it worthless and unsalvageable. Halbman sued to disaffirm the contract and recover the consideration from Lemke. Lemke argued that Halbman must make full restitution. Who is correct? *Halbman v. Lemke*, 99 Wis.2d 241, 298 N.W.2d 562, **Web** 1980 Wisc. Lexis 2825 (Supreme Court of Wisconsin)

12.2 Ratification Charles Edwards Smith, a minor, purchased an automobile from Bobby Floars Toyota (Toyota). Smith executed a security agreement to finance part of the balance due on the purchase price, agreeing to pay off the balance in 30 monthly installments. Smith turned 18, which was the age of majority in his state. Smith made 10 monthly payments after turning 18. He then decided to disaffirm the contract and stopped making the payments. Smith claims that he may disaffirm the contract entered into when he was a minor. Toyota argues that Smith has ratified the contract since attaining the age of majority. Who is correct? *Bobby Floars Toyota, Inc. v. Smith*, 48 N.C.App. 580, 269 S.E.2d 320, **Web** 1980 N.C.App. Lexis 3263 (Court of Appeals of North Carolina)

12.3 Adjudged Insane Manzelle Johnson, who had been adjudicated insane, executed a quitclaim and warranty deed conveying real estate she owned to her guardian, Obbie Neal. Neal subsequently conveyed the real estate to James R. Beavers by warranty deed. Charles L. Weatherly, Johnson's present guardian, brought this action, seeking a decree of the court that title to the real estate be restored to Johnson because of her inability to contract. Should Johnson be allowed to void the contract? *Beavers v. Weatherly*, 250 Ga. 546, 299 S.E.2d 730, **Web** 1983 Ga. Lexis 581 (Supreme Court of Georgia)

12.4 Intoxication Betty Galloway, an alcoholic, signed a settlement agreement upon her divorce from her husband, Henry Galloway. Henry, in Betty's absence in court, stated that she had lucid intervals from her alcoholism, had been sober for two months, and was lucid when she signed the settlement agreement. Betty moved to vacate the settlement agreement, after she had retained present legal counsel. Four months later, Betty was declared incompetent to handle her person and her affairs, and a guardian and conservator was appointed. Betty, through her guardian, sued to have the settlement agreement voided. Who wins? *Galloway v. Galloway*, 281 N.W.2d 804, **Web** 1979 N.D. Lexis 279 (Supreme Court of North Dakota)

12.5 Licensing Statute The state of Hawaii requires a person who wants to practice architecture to meet certain educational requirements and to pass a written examination before being granted a license to practice. After receiving the license, an architect must pay an annual license fee of $15. Ben Lee Wilson satisfied the initial requirements and was granted an architecture license. Four years later, Wilson failed to renew his license by paying the required annual fee. Wilson contracted with Kealakekua Ranch, Ltd., and Gentry Hawaii (defendants) to provide architectural services for the Kealakekua Ranch Center project. Wilson provided $33,994 of architectural services to the defendants. The defendants refused to pay this fee because Wilson did not have an architectural license. Wilson sued to collect his fees. Who wins? *Wilson v. Kealakekua Ranch, Ltd., and Gentry Hawaii*, 57 Haw. 124, 551 P.2d 525, **Web** 1976 Haw. Lexis 119 (Supreme Court of Hawaii)

12.6 Covenant Not to Compete Gerry Morris owned a silk screening and lettering shop in Tucson, Arizona. Morris entered into a contract to sell the business to Alfred and Connie Gann. The contract contained the following covenant not to compete: "Seller agrees not to enter into silk screening or lettering shop business within Tucson and a 100-mile radius of Tucson, for a period of ten (10) years from the date of this agreement and will not compete in any manner whatsoever with buyers, and seller further agrees that he will refer all business contracts to buyers." Morris opened a silk screening and lettering business in competition with the Ganns and in violation of the noncompete clause. The Ganns brought this action against Morris for breach of contract and to enforce the covenant not to compete. Is the covenant not to compete valid and enforceable in this case? *Gann v. Morris*,

122 Ariz. 517, 596 P.2d 43, **Web** 1979 Ariz.App. Lexis 487 (Court of Appeals of Arizona)

12.7 Exculpatory Clause   Grady Perkins owned the Raleigh Institute of Cosmetology (Institute), and Ray Monk and Rovetta Allen were employed as instructors there. The school trained students to do hair styling and coloring, cosmetology, and other beauty services. The students received practical training by providing services to members of the public under the supervision of the instructors. Francis I. Alston went to Institute to have her hair colored and styled by a student who was under the supervision of Monk and Allen. Before receiving any services, Alston signed a written release form that released Institute and its employees from liability for their negligence. While coloring Alston's hair, the student negligently used a chemical that caused Alston's hair to fall out. Alston sued Institute, Perkins, Monk, and Allen for damages. The defendants asserted that the release form signed by Alston barred her suit. Is the exculpatory clause valid? *Alston*

v. Monk, 92 N.C.App.59, 373 S.E.2d 463, **Web** 1988 N.C. App. Lexis 987 (Court of Appeals of North Carolina)

12.8 Exculpatory Clause   Wilbur Spaulding owned and operated the Jacksonville racetrack at the Morgan Country Fairgrounds, where automobile races were held. Lawrence P. Koch was a flagman at the raceway. One day when Koch arrived at the pit shack at the raceway, he was handed a clipboard on which was a track release and waiver of liability form that released the racetrack from liability for negligence. Koch signed the form and took up his position as flagman. During the first race, the last car on the track lost control and slid off the end of the track, striking Koch. Koch suffered a broken leg and other injuries and was unable to work for 14 months. Koch sued Spaulding for damages for negligence. Spaulding asserted that the release form signed by Koch barred his suit. Is the exculpatory clause valid against Koch? *Koch v. Spaulding*, 174 Ill.App.3d 692, 529 N.E.2d. 19, **Web** 1988 Ill. App. Lexis 1427 (Appellate Court of Illinois)

BUSINESS ETHICS CASES

12.9 Business Ethics   Joe Plumlee owned and operated an ambulance company. He alleged that the law firm Paddock, Loveless & Roach agreed to pay him an up-front fee and a percentage of the law firm's fees generated from personal injury case referrals. When the law firm did not pay Plumlee, he sued to recover damages for breach of contract. Texas law prohibits lawyers from sharing fees with laypersons [Tex. Penal Code Section 38.12; supreme court of Texas]. A disciplinary rule also forbids such activity [State Bar Rules Art. X, Section 9]. The law firm asserted that the contract could not be enforced because it would be an illegal contract. Who wins? Did Plumlee act ethically in this case? If the contract existed, did the lawyers act ethically? *Plumlee v. Paddock, Loveless, and Roach*, 832 S.W.2d 757, **Web** 1992 Tex.App. Lexis 1544 (Court of Appeals of Texas)

12.10 Business Ethics   Richard Zientara was friends with Chester and Bernice Kaszuba. All three were residents of Indiana. Bernice, who was employed in an Illinois tavern where Illinois state lottery tickets were sold, had previously obtained lottery tickets for Zientara because Indiana did not have a state lottery. One day, Zientara requested that Kaszuba purchase an Illinois lottery ticket for him. He gave Kaszuba the money for the ticket and the numbers 6–15–16–23–24–37. Kaszuba purchased the ticket, but when it turned out to be the winning combination worth $1,696,800, she refused to give the ticket to Zientara and unsuccessfully tried to collect the money. Zientara filed suit against Kaszuba in Indiana, claiming the ticket and proceeds thereof. Was the contract legal? Did the Kaszubas act ethically in this case? *Kaszuba v. Zientara*, 506 N.E.2d 1, **Web** 1987 Ind. Lexis 874 (Supreme Court of Indiana)

ENDNOTE

1.   25 U.S.C. Section 2701 et seq.

▲ **Used Car Dealership** *The history of car sales has generated many cases of contracts tainted by mistakes and fraud.*

CHAPTER OBJECTIVES

After studying this chapter, you should be able to:

1. Explain genuineness of assent.
2. Explain how mutual mistake of fact excuses performance.
3. Describe intentional misrepresentation (fraud).
4. Describe duress.
5. Define *equitable doctrine of undue influence*.

CHAPTER CONTENTS

"Freedom of contract begins where equality of bargaining power begins."

—Oliver Wendell Holmes, Jr.
June 4, 1928

▶ INTRODUCTION TO GENUINENESS OF ASSENT AND UNDUE INFLUENCE

Voluntary *assent* by the parties is necessary to create an enforceable contract. Assent is determined by the relevant facts surrounding the negotiation and formation of a contract. Assent may be manifested in any manner sufficient to show agreement, including express words or conduct of the parties.

A contract may not be enforced if the assent of one or both of the parties to the contract was not genuine or real. *Genuine assent* may be missing because a party entered into a contract based on mistake, fraudulent misrepresentation, or duress. A court may permit the rescission of a contract based on the equitable doctrine of *undue influence*. Problems concerning **genuineness of assent** are discussed in this chapter.

genuineness of assent
The requirement that a party's assent to a contract be genuine.

▶ MISTAKE

A **mistake** occurs where one or both of the parties to a contract have an erroneous belief about the subject matter, value, or some other aspect of the contract. Mistakes may be either *unilateral* or *mutual*. The law permits **rescission** of some contracts made in mistake.

rescission
An action to undo a contract.

Unilateral Mistake

Unilateral mistakes occur when only one party is mistaken about a material fact regarding the subject matter of the contract. In most cases of unilateral mistake, the mistaken party will not be permitted to rescind the contract. The contract will be enforced on its terms.

There are three types of situations in which a contract may not be enforced due to a unilateral mistake:

unilateral mistake
A mistake in which only one party is mistaken about a material fact regarding the subject matter of a contract.

1. One party makes a unilateral mistake of fact, and the other party knew (or should have known) that a mistake was made.
2. A unilateral mistake occurs because of a clerical or mathematical error that is not the result of gross negligence.
3. The mistake is so serious that enforcing the contract would be unconscionable.[1]

Words are chameleons, which reflect the color of their environment.

Justice L. Hand
Commissioner v. National Carbide Co. (1948)

Example Suppose Trent wants to purchase a new car from the showroom floor. He looks at several models. Although he decides to purchase a car with a sunroof, he does not tell the salesperson about his preference. The model named in the contract he signs does not have this feature, although he believes it does. Trent's unilateral mistake will not relieve him of his contractual obligation to purchase the car.

In the following case, the court had to decide whether to allow a party to rescind a contract because of the party's unilateral mistake.

CASE 13.1 Unilateral Mistake

Wells Fargo Credit Corporation v. Martin
650 So.2d 531, Web 1992 Fla.App. Lexis 9927 (1992)
Court of Appeal of Florida

"We accept the trial court's conclusion that the amount of the sale was grossly inadequate. This inadequacy, however, occurred due to an avoidable, unilateral mistake by an agent of Wells Fargo."

—Judge Altenbernd

Facts

Wells Fargo Credit Corporation (Wells Fargo) obtained a judgment of foreclosure on a house owned by Mr. and Mrs. Clevenger. The total indebtedness stated in the judgment was $207,141. The foreclosure sale was scheduled for

11:00 A.M. July 12, 1991, at the west front door of the Hillsborough County Courthouse.

Wells Fargo was represented by a paralegal, who had attended more than 1,000 similar sales. Wells Fargo's handwritten instruction sheet informed the paralegal to make one bid at $115,000, the tax-appraised value of the property. Because the first "1" in the number was close to the "$," the paralegal misread the bid instruction as $15,000 and opened the bidding at that amount.

Harley Martin, who was attending his first judicial sale, bid $20,000. The county clerk gave ample time for another bid and then announced, "$20,000 going once, $20,000 going twice, sold to Harley. . . ." The paralegal screamed, "Stop, I'm sorry. I made a mistake!" The certificate of sale was issued to Martin. Wells Fargo filed suit to set aside the judicial sale based on its unilateral mistake. The trial court held for Martin. Wells Fargo appealed.

Issue

Does Wells Fargo's unilateral mistake constitute grounds for setting aside the judicial sale?

Language of the Court

We accept the trial court's conclusion that the amount of the sale was grossly inadequate. This inadequacy, however, occurred due to an avoidable, unilateral mistake by an *agent of Wells Fargo. As between Wells Fargo and a good faith purchaser at the judicial sale, the trial court had the discretion to place the risk of this mistake upon Wells Fargo.*

Thus, we affirm the trial court's orders denying relief to Wells Fargo. We are certain that this result seems harsh to Wells Fargo. Nevertheless, Mr. Martin's bid was accepted when the clerk announced "sold." Without ruling that a unilateral mistake by the complaining party could never justify relief, we hold that the trial court had the discretion under these facts to make Wells Fargo suffer the loss.

Decision

The appellate court held that Wells Fargo's unilateral mistake did not entitle it to relief from the judicial sale.

Case Questions

Critical Legal Thinking What is a unilateral mistake? Explain.

Business Ethics Did Martin act ethically in trying to enforce the judicial sale after being informed of the mistake? What would you have done in similar circumstances?

Contemporary Business Should a contract be allowed to be rescinded because of a unilateral mistake? What would be the danger if the assertion of unilateral mistakes could undo contracts?

Mutual Mistake of Fact

A party may rescind a contract if there has been a **mutual mistake of a past or existing material fact**.[2] A **material fact** is a fact that is important to the subject matter of a contract. An ambiguity in a contract may constitute a mutual mistake of a material fact. An ambiguity occurs where a word or term in the contract is susceptible to more than one logical interpretation. If there has been a mutual mistake, the contract may be rescinded on the grounds that no contract has been formed because there has been no "meeting of the minds" between the parties.

mutual mistake of fact
A mistake made by both parties concerning a material fact that is important to the subject matter of a contract.

Example In the celebrated case *Raffles v. Wichelhaus*,[3] which has become better known as the case of the good ship *Peerless*, the parties agreed on a sale of cotton that was to be delivered from Bombay by the ship. There were two ships named *Peerless*, however, and each party, in agreeing to the sale, was referring to a different ship. Because the sailing time of the two ships was materially different, neither party was willing to agree to shipment by the other *Peerless*. The court ruled that there was no binding contract because each party had a different ship in mind when the contract was formed.

Mutual Mistake of Value

A **mutual mistake of value** exists if both parties know the object of the contract but are mistaken as to its value. Here, the contract remains enforceable by either party because the identity of the subject matter of the contract is not at issue. If the rule were different, almost all contracts could later be rescinded by the party who got the "worst" of the deal.

mutual mistake of value
A mistake that occurs if both parties know the object of the contract but are mistaken as to its value.

Example Helen cleans her attic and finds a red and green silkscreen painting of a tomato soup can. She has no use for the painting, so she offers to sell it to Qian for $100. Qian, who thinks that the painting is "cute," accepts the offer and pays Helen $100. It is latter discovered that the painting is worth $2 million because it was painted by the famous American pop artist Andy Warhol. Neither party knew this at the time of contracting. It is a mistake of value. Helen cannot recover the painting.

▶ FRAUD

A misrepresentation occurs when an assertion is made that is not in accord with the facts.[4] An intentional misrepresentation occurs when one person consciously decides to induce another person to rely and act on a misrepresentation. Intentional misrepresentation is commonly referred to as **fraudulent misrepresentation**, or **fraud**. When fraudulent misrepresentation is used to induce another to enter into a contract, the innocent party's assent to the contract is not genuine, and the contract is voidable by the innocent party.[5] The innocent party can either rescind the contract and obtain restitution or enforce the contract and sue for contract damages.

Proving Fraud

To prove fraud, the following elements must be shown:

- The wrongdoer made a false representation of material fact.
- The wrongdoer intended to deceive the innocent party.
- The innocent party justifiably relied on the misrepresentation.
- The innocent party was injured.

Each of these elements is discussed in the following paragraphs.

Material Misrepresentation of Fact   A **misrepresentation** may occur by words (oral or written) or by the conduct of a party. To be actionable as fraud, the misrepresentation must be of a past or existing *material fact*. This means that the misrepresentation must have been a significant factor in inducing the innocent party to enter into the contract. It does not have to have been the sole factor. Statements of opinion or predictions about the future generally do not form the basis for fraud.

Intent to Deceive   To prove fraud, the person making the misrepresentation must have either had knowledge that the representation was false or made it without sufficient knowledge of the truth. This is called **scienter** ("**guilty mind**"). The misrepresentation must have been made with the **intent to deceive** the innocent party. Intent can be inferred from the circumstances.

Reliance on the Misrepresentation   A misrepresentation is not actionable unless the innocent party to whom the misrepresentation was directed acted on it. Further, an innocent party who acts in **reliance on a misrepresentation** must justify his or her reliance. Justifiable reliance is generally found unless the innocent party knew that the misrepresentation was false or was so extravagant as to be obviously false.

Injury to the Innocent Party   To recover damages, the innocent party must prove that the fraud caused him or her economic **injury**. The measure of damages is the difference between the value of the property as represented and the actual value of the property. This measure of damages gives the innocent party the "benefit of the bargain." In the alternative, the buyer can rescind the contract and recover the purchase price.

Individuals must be on guard in their commercial and personal dealings not to be taken by fraud. Basically, something sounding "too good to be true" is a signal that the situation might be fraudulent. Although the law permits a victim of fraud to rescind the contract and recover damages from the wrongdoer, often the wrongdoer cannot be found or the money has been spent.

---

fraudulent misrepresentation
An event that occurs when one person consciously decides to induce another person to rely and act on a misrepresentation. Also called *fraud*.

scienter
Knowledge that a representation is false or that it was made without sufficient knowledge of the truth.

A charge of fraud is such a terrible thing to bring against a man that it cannot be maintained in any court unless it is shown that he had a wicked mind.

M. R. Lord Esher
Le Lievre v. Gould (1732)

Fraud in the Inception

Fraud in the inception, or **fraud in the factum**, occurs if a person is deceived as to the nature of his or her act and does not know what he or she is signing. Contracts involving fraud in the inception are void rather than just voidable.

Example Heather brings her professor a grade card to sign. The professor signs the grade card on the front without reading the grade card. On the front, however, are contract terms that transfer all of the professor's property to Heather. Here, there is fraud in the inception. The contract is void.

fraud in the inception
Fraud that occurs if a person is deceived as to the nature of his or her act and does not know what he or she is signing. Also known as fraud in the factum.

Fraud in the Inducement

Many fraud cases concern **fraud in the inducement**. Here, the innocent party knows what he or she is signing or doing but has been fraudulently induced to enter into the contract. Such contracts are voidable by the innocent party.

Example Lyle tells Candice that he is forming a partnership to invest in drilling for oil in an oil field and invites her to invest in this venture. In reality, though, there is no oil field, and Lyle intends to use whatever money he receives from Candice for his personal expenses. Candice relies on Lyle's statements and invests $30,000 with Lyle. Lyle absconds with Candice's $30,000 investment. Here, there has been fraud in the inducement. Candice has been induced to give Lyle $30,000 based on Lyle's misrepresentation of fact. Candice can rescind the contract and recover the money from Lyle, if she can find him and locate his money or property.

fraud in the inducement
Fraud that occurs when the party knows what he or she is signing but has been fraudulently induced to enter into the contract.

Fraud by Concealment

Fraud by concealment occurs when one party takes specific action to conceal a material fact from another party.[6]

Example Steel Inc. contracts to buy used manufacturing equipment from United Inc. United Inc. does not show Steel Inc. the repair invoices for repairs to the equipment even though Steel Inc. has asked to see all of the repair invoices for the equipment. Relying on the knowledge that the equipment is in good condition and has never had been repaired, Steel Inc. purchases the equipment from United Inc. If Steel Inc. subsequently discovers that a significant repair record has been concealed by United Inc., Steel Inc. can sue United Inc. for fraud by concealment.

fraud by concealment
Fraud that occurs when one party takes specific action to conceal a material fact from another party.

Silence as Misrepresentation

Generally, neither party to a contract owes a duty to disclose all the facts to the other party. Ordinarily, such **silence** is not a misrepresentation unless (1) nondisclosure would cause bodily injury or death, (2) there is a fiduciary relationship (i.e., a relationship of trust and confidence) between the contracting parties, or (3) federal and state statutes require disclosure. The *Restatement (Second) of Contracts* specifies a broader duty of disclosure: Nondisclosure is a misrepresentation if it would constitute a failure to act in "good faith."[7]

Misrepresentation of Law

Usually, a **misrepresentation of law** is not actionable as fraud. The innocent party cannot generally rescind the contract because each party to a contract is assumed to know the law that applies to the transaction, either through his or her own investigation or by hiring a lawyer. There is one major exception to this rule: The misrepresentation will be allowed as grounds for rescission of the contract if one party to the contract is a professional who should know what the law is and intentionally misrepresents the law to a less sophisticated contracting party.[8]

Whoever is detected in a shameful fraud is ever after not believed even if they speak the truth.

Phaedrus (Thrace of Macedonia)

Innocent Misrepresentation

innocent misrepresentation
Fraud that occurs when a person makes a statement of fact that he or she honestly and reasonably believes to be true even though it is not.

An **innocent misrepresentation** occurs when a person makes a statement of fact that he or she honestly and reasonably believes to be true even though it is not. Innocent misrepresentation is not fraud. If an innocent misrepresentation has been made, the aggrieved party may rescind the contract but may not sue for damages. Often, innocent misrepresentation is treated as a mutual mistake.

In the following case, the court found fraud and awarded punitive damages.

CASE 13.2 Fraud

Krysa v. Payne

176 S.W.3d 150, Web 2005 Mo.App. Lexis 1680 (2005)
Court of Appeals of Missouri

"Punitive damages differ from compensatory damages in that compensatory damages are intended to redress the concrete loss that the plaintiff has suffered by reason of the defendant's wrongful conduct, while the well-established purpose of punitive damages is to inflict punishment and to serve as an example and a deterrent to similar conduct."

—Judge Ellis

Facts

Frank and Shelly Krysa were shopping for a truck to pull their 18-foot trailer. During the course of their search, they visited Payne's Car Company, a used car dealership owned by Emmett Payne. Kemp Crane, a used car salesman, showed the Krysas around the car lot. The Krysas saw an F-350 truck that they were interested in purchasing. Crane told the Krysas that the truck would tow their trailer, that the truck would make it to 400,000 miles, and that it was "a one-owner trade-in." The Krysas took the truck for a test drive and decided to purchase the truck. The Krysas, who had to borrow some of the money from Mrs. Krysas's mother, paid for the truck and took possession.

Later that day, the Krysas noticed that the power locks did not work on the truck. A few days later, the truck took three hours to start. The heater was not working. Mr. Krysa tried to fix some problems and noticed that the radiator was smashed up, the radiator cap did not have a seal, and the thermostat was missing. Mr. Krysa noticed broken glass on the floor underneath the front seats and that the driver's side window had been replaced. Shortly thereafter, Mr. Krysa attempted to tow his trailer, but within 2 miles, he had his foot to the floor trying to get the truck to pull the trailer. A large amount of smoke was pouring out of the back of the truck. Mr. Krysa also noticed that the truck was consuming a lot of oil. Mr. Krysa obtained a CARFAX report for the truck, which showed that the truck had had 13 prior owners. Evidence proved that the truck was actually two halves of different trucks that had

been welded together. An automobile expert told the Krysas not to drive the truck because it was unsafe.

Mr. Krysa went back to the dealership to return the truck and get his money back. Payne told Krysa that he would credit the purchase price of the truck toward the purchase of one of the other vehicles on the lot but that he would not give Krysa his money back. Krysa could not find another vehicle on Payne's used car lot that would suit his needs. The Krysas sued Payne for fraudulent nondisclosure and fraudulent misrepresentation, and they sought to recover compensatory and punitive damages. The jury returned a verdict for the Krysas and awarded them $18,449 in compensatory damages and $500,000 in punitive damages. Payne appealed the award of punitive damages.

Issue

Did Payne engage in fraudulent nondisclosure, fraudulent misrepresentation, and reckless disregard for the safety of the Krysas and the public to support the award of $500,000 in punitive damages?

Language of the Court

Punitive damages differ from compensatory damages in that compensatory damages are intended to redress the concrete loss that the plaintiff has suffered by reason of the defendant's wrongful conduct, while the well-established purpose of punitive damages is to inflict punishment and to serve as an example and a deterrent to similar conduct. While the damage actually sustained by the Krysas was relatively small and was economic in nature, the record clearly supports a finding that Payne acted indifferently to or in reckless disregard of the safety of the Krysas in selling them a vehicle that he knew or should have known was not safe to drive and that the potential harm to the Krysas was much greater than the harm that was actually incurred.

The evidence also supported a finding that the harm sustained by Krysas was the result of intentional malice, trickery, or deceit, and was not merely an accident. Payne had a significant amount of work done to the vehicle to make it appear to be in good shape. This included, among numerous other repairs, straightening both the bed and cab of the truck. Payne's salesman, Crane, lied to the Krysas on several occasions about the condition of the truck, its origin, and its capabilities. This evidence, in addition to other evidence previously described, sufficiently established that Payne affirmatively misrepresented the condition of the F-350 to the Krysas in an attempt to trick them into buying the vehicle.

In sum, while the harm actually sustained by the Krysas in this case was economic as opposed to physical, Payne's conduct did pose a significant risk to the physical welfare of Respondents and evinced an indifference to or reckless disregard of the health or safety of Krysas and the general public as well. Furthermore, the conduct was consistent with Payne's regular business practices and was not an isolated incident, involved acts of intentional trickery and deceit, and targeted victims that were financially vulnerable. Thus, in society's eyes, viewing the totality of the circumstances, Payne's conduct can only be seen as exhibiting a very high degree of reprehensibility.

Payne contends that the ratio between the actual damages awarded, $18,449.53, and the punitive award, $500,000, is grossly excessive, in that the ratio of punitive to actual damages is approximately 27:1. The initial problem with Payne's argument is that it fails to consider the evidence of the potential harm that could have been sustained by the Krysas. In this case, given the relatively small amount of actual damages awarded, the egregious nature of Payne's acts, Payne's open refusal to alter his behavior, and the magnitude of the potential harm that could have been sustained had the structural problems with the truck not been discovered by the Krysas's expert, the ratio of the punitive to actual damages does not, in and of itself, offend due process.

Decision

The court of appeals found that Payne's fraudulent concealment, fraudulent misrepresentation, and reckless disregard for the safety of the Krysas and the public justified the award of $500,000 of punitive damages to the Krysas.

Case Questions

Critical Legal Thinking What is fraudulent concealment? What is fraudulent misrepresentation?

Business Ethics Did Payne, the used car dealer, act ethically in this case? Should punitive damages have been awarded in this case? Why or why not?

Contemporary Business Do you have any apprehension about purchasing a car from a used car dealership? Why or why not?

CONCEPT SUMMARY

TYPES OF MISREPRESENTATION

	Legal Party May: Consequences—Innocent for	
Type of Misrepresentation	Sue for Damages	Rescind Contract
Fraud in the inception	Yes	Yes
Fraud in the inducement	Yes	Yes
Fraud by concealment	Yes	Yes
Silence as misrepresentation	Yes	Yes
Misrepresentation of law	Usually no	Usually no
Innocent misrepresentation	No	Yes

▶ DURESS

Duress occurs when one party threatens to do some wrongful act unless the other party enters into a contract. If a party to a contract has been forced into making the contract, the assent is not voluntary. Such a contract is not enforceable against the innocent party. If someone threatens to physically harm another person unless that person signs a contract, this is *physical duress*. If the victim of the duress signs the contract, it cannot be enforced against the victim.

duress
A situation in which one party threatens to do a wrongful act unless the other party enters into a contract.

The threat to commit extortion unless someone enters into a contract constitutes duress. So does a threat to bring (or not drop) a criminal lawsuit. Such threats are duress even if the criminal lawsuit is well founded.[9] A threat to bring (or not drop) a civil lawsuit, however, does not constitute duress unless such a suit is frivolous or brought in bad faith.

▶ EQUITY: UNDUE INFLUENCE

The courts may permit the rescission of a contract based on the equitable doctrine of **undue influence**. Undue influence occurs when one person (the **dominant party**) takes advantage of another person's mental, emotional, or physical weakness and unduly persuades that person (the **servient party**) to enter into a contract. The persuasion by the wrongdoer must overcome the free will of the innocent party. A contract that is entered into because of undue influence is voidable by the innocent party.[10]

The following elements must be shown to prove undue influence:

- A fiduciary or confidential relationship must have existed between the parties.
- The dominant party must have unduly used his or her influence to persuade the servient party to enter into a contract.

If there is a confidential relationship between persons—such as a lawyer and a client, a doctor and a patient, a psychiatrist and a patient—any contract made by the servient party that benefits the dominant party is presumed to be entered into under undue influence. This rebuttable presumption can be overcome through proper evidence.

Example Mr. Johnson, 70 years old, has a stroke and is partially paralyzed. He is required to use a wheelchair, and he needs constant nursing care. Prior to his stroke, Mr. Johnson had executed a will, leaving his property upon his death equally to his four grandchildren. Edward, a licensed nurse, is hired to care for Mr. Johnson on a daily basis, and Mr. Johnson relies on Edward's care. Edward works for Mr. Johnson for 2 years before Mr. Johnson passes away. It is later discovered that Mr. Johnson had executed a written contract with Edward three months before he died, deeding a valuable piece of real estate to Edward. If it is shown that Edward has used his dominant and fiduciary position to unduly influence Mr. Johnson to enter into this contract, then the contract is invalid. If no undue influence is shown, the contract with Edward is valid, and Edward will receive the property deeded to him by Mr. Johnson.

undue influence
A situation in which one person takes advantage of another person's mental, emotional, or physical weakness and unduly persuades that person to enter into a contract; the persuasion by the wrongdoer must overcome the free will of the innocent party.

The meaning of words varies according to the circumstances of and concerning which they are used.

Justice Blackburn
Allgood v. Blake (1873)

Mongolia *In Mongolia, many contracts are oral agreements where a person's word is as good as a bond. In countries where the nomadic form of living is prevalent, herders graze their animals on land owned by the government. Mongolia is a country where a large proportion of the country's residents still live the nomadic lifestyle. They have little access to lawyers or courts, so contract disputes are settled by members of the nomadic society.*

TEST REVIEW TERMS AND CONCEPTS

Dominant party	Genuineness of assent	Misrepresentation of law	Rescission
Duress	Injury to the innocent party	Mistake	Scienter ("guilty mind")
Fraud by concealment	Innocent misrepresentation	Mutual mistake of a past or	Servient party
Fraud in the inception	Intent to deceive	existing material fact	Silence as misrepresentation
(fraud in the factum)	Material fact	Mutual mistake of value	Undue influence
Fraud in the inducement	Material misrepresentation	Reliance on a	Unilateral mistake
Fraudulent	of fact	misrepresentation	
misrepresentation (fraud)			

CASE PROBLEMS

13.1 Unilateral Mistake Mrs. Chaney died, leaving a house in Annapolis, Maryland. The representative of her estate listed the property for sale with a real estate broker, stating that the property was approximately 15,650 square feet. Drs. Steele and Faust made an offer of $300,000 for the property, which was accepted by the estate. A contract for the sale of the property was signed by all the parties. When a subsequent survey (done before the deed was transferred) showed that the property had an area of 22,047 square feet, the estate requested the buyers to pay more money for the property. When the estate refused to transfer the property to the buyers, they sued for specific performance. Can the estate rescind the contract? *Steele v. Goettee*, 313 Md. 11, 542 A.2d 847, **Web** 1988 Md. Lexis 91 (Court of Appeals of Maryland)

13.2 Unilateral Mistake The County of Contra Costa, California, held a tax sale in which it offered for sale a vacant piece of property located in the city of El Cerrito. Richard J. Schultz, a carpenter, saw the notice of the pending tax sale and was interested in purchasing the lot to build a house. Prior to attending the tax sale, Schultz visited and measured the parcel, examined the neighborhood and found the houses there to be "very nice," and had a title search done that turned up no liens or judgments against the property. Schultz did not, however, check with the city zoning department regarding the zoning of the property.

Schultz attended the tax sale and, after spirited bidding, won with a bid of $9,100 and received a deed to the property. Within one week of the purchase, Schultz discovered that the city's zoning laws prevented building a residence on the lot. In essence, the lot was worthless. Schultz sued to rescind the contract. Can the contract be rescinded? *Schultz v. County of Contra Costa, California*, 157 Cal.App.3d 242, 203 Cal.Rptr. 760, **Web** 1984 Cal.App. Lexis 2198 (Court of Appeal of California)

13.3 Mutual Mistake Ron Boskett, a part-time coin dealer, purchased a dime purportedly minted in 1916 at the Denver Mint; he paid nearly $450. The fact that the "D" on the coin signified Denver mintage made the coin rare and valuable. Boskett sold the coin to Beachcomber Coins, Inc. (Beachcomber), a retail coin dealer, for $500. A principal of Beachcomber examined the coin for 15 to 45 minutes prior to

its purchase. Soon thereafter, Beachcomber received an offer of $700 for the coin, subject to certification of its genuineness by the American Numismatic Society. When this organization labeled the coin counterfeit, Beachcomber sued Boskett to rescind the purchase of the coin. Can Beachcomber rescind the contract? *Beachcomber Coins, Inc. v. Boskett*, 166 N.J. Super. 442, 400 A.2d 78, **Web** 1979 N.J. Super Lexis 659 (Superior Court of New Jersey)

13.4 Fraud Robert McClure owned a vehicle salvage and rebuilding business. He listed the business for sale and had a brochure printed that described the business and stated that the business grossed $581,117 and netted $142,727 the prior year. Fred H. Campbell saw the brochure and inquired about buying the business. Campbell hired a CPA to review McClure's business records and tax returns, but the CPA could not reconcile them with the income claimed for the business in the brochure. When Campbell asked McClure about the discrepancy, McClure stated that the business records did—and tax returns did not—accurately reflect the cash flow or profits of the business because it was such a high-cash operation, with much of the cash not being reported to the Internal Revenue Service on tax returns. McClure signed a warranty which stated that the true income of the business was as represented in the brochure.

Campbell bought the business based on McClure's representations. However, the business, although operated in substantially the same manner as when owned by McClure, failed to yield a net income similar to that warranted by McClure. Evidence showed that McClure's representations were substantially overstated. Campbell sued McClure for damages for fraud. Who wins? *Campbell v. McClure*, 182 Cal.App.3d 806, 227 Cal.Rptr. 450, **Web** 1986 Cal. App.Lexis 1751 (Court of Appeal of California)

13.5 Fraud James L. "Skip" Deupree, a developer, was building a development of townhouses called Point South in Destin, Florida. All the townhouses in the development were to have individual boat slips. Sam and Louise Butner, husband and wife, bought one of the townhouses. The sales contract between Deupree and the Butners provided that a boat slip would be built and was included in the price of the townhouse. The contract stated that permission from the Florida

Department of Natural Resources (DNR) had to be obtained to build the boat slips. It is undisputed that a boat slip adds substantially to the value of the property and that the Butners relied on the fact that the townhouse would have a boat slip.

Prior to the sale of the townhouse to the Butners, the DNR had informed Deupree that it objected to the plan to build the boat slips and that permission to build them would probably not be forthcoming. Deupree did not tell the Butners this information but instead stated that there would be "no problem" getting permission from the state to build the boat slips. The Butners purchased the townhouse. When the DNR would not approve the building of the boat slips for the Butners' townhouse, they sued for damages for fraud. Who wins? *Deupree v. Butner*, 522 So.2d 242, **Web** 1988 Ala. Lexis 55 (Supreme Court of Alabama)

13.6 Innocent Misrepresentation W. F. Yost, who owned the Red Barn Barbecue Restaurant (Red Barn), listed it for sale. Richard and Evelyn Ramano of Rieve Enterprises, Inc. (Rieve), were interested in buying the restaurant. After visiting and conducting a visual inspection of the premises, Rieve entered into a contract to purchase the assets and equipment of Red Barn, as well as the five-year lease of, and option to buy, the land and the building. Prior to the sale, the restaurant had been cited for certain health violations that Yost had corrected. In the contract of sale, Yost warranted that "the premises will pass all inspections" to conduct the business.

Rieve took possession immediately after the sale and operated the restaurant. After two weeks, when the Board of Health conducted a routine inspection, it cited 52 health code violations and thereupon closed the restaurant. Rieve sued to rescind the purchase agreement. Evidence established that Yost's misrepresentations were innocently made. Can Rieve rescind the contract? *Yost v. Rieve Enterprises, Inc.*, 461 So.2d 178, **Web** 1984 Fla.App. Lexis 16490 (Court of Appeals of Florida)

13.7 Duress Judith and Donald Eckstein were married and had two daughters. Years later, Judith left the marital abode in the parties' jointly owned Volkswagen van with only the clothes on her back. She did not take the children, who were six and eight years old at the time. She had no funds, and the husband promptly closed the couple's bank account. The wife was unemployed. Shortly after she left, the husband discovered her whereabouts and the location of the van and seized and secreted the van. The husband refused the wife's request to visit or communicate with her children and refused to give her clothing. He told her that she could see the children and take her clothes only if she signed a separation agreement prepared by his lawyer. The wife contacted Legal Aid but was advised that she did not qualify for assistance.

The wife was directed to go to her husband's lawyer's office. A copy of a separation agreement was given to her to read. The separation agreement provided that the wife (1) give custody of the children to her husband, (2) deed her interest in their jointly owned house to the husband, (3) assign her interest in a jointly owned new Chevrolet van to her husband, and (4) waive alimony, support, maintenance, court costs, attorneys' fees, and any right to inheritance in her husband's estate. By the agreement, she was to receive $1,100 cash, her clothes, the Volkswagen van, and any furniture she desired. The wife testified that her husband told her over an interoffice phone in the lawyer's office that if she did not sign the separation agreement, he would get her for desertion, that she would never see her children again, and that she would get nothing—neither her clothes nor the van—unless she signed the agreement. The wife signed the separation agreement. Immediately thereafter, her clothes were surrendered to her, and she was given $1,100 cash and the keys to the Volkswagen van. The husband filed for divorce. The wife filed an answer seeking to rescind the separation agreement. Can she rescind the separation agreement? *Eckstein v. Eckstein*, 38 Md.App. 506, 379 A.2d 757, **Web** 1978 Md.App. Lexis 324. (Court of Special Appeals of Maryland)

13.8 Undue Influence Conrad Schaneman, Sr., had eight sons and five daughters. He owned an 80-acre farm in the Scotts Bluff area of Nebraska. Conrad was born in Russia and could not read or write English. All of his children had frequent contact with Conrad and helped with his needs. Subsequently, however, his eldest son, Lawrence, advised the other children that he would henceforth manage his father's business affairs. After much urging by Lawrence, Conrad deeded the farm to Lawrence for $23,500. Evidence showed that at the time of the sale, the reasonable fair market value of the farm was between $145,000 and $160,000.

At the time of the conveyance, Conrad was over 80 years old, had deteriorated in health, suffered from heart problems and diabetes, had high and uncontrollable blood sugar levels, weighed almost 300 pounds, had difficulty breathing, could not walk more than 15 feet, and had to have a jackhoist lift him in and out of the bathtub. He was for all purposes an invalid, relying on Lawrence for most of his personal needs, transportation, banking, and other business matters. After Conrad died, the conservators of the estate brought an action to cancel the deed transferring the farm to Lawrence. Can the conservators cancel the deed? *Schaneman v. Schaneman*, 206 Neb. 113, 291 N.W.2d 412, **Web** 1980 Neb. Lexis 823 (Supreme Court of Nebraska)

BUSINESS ETHICS CASES

13.9 Business Ethics The First Baptist Church of Moultrie, Georgia, invited bids for the construction of a music, education, and recreation building. The bids were to be accompanied by a bid bond of five percent of the bid amount. Barber Contracting Company (Barber Contracting) submitted a bid in the amount of $1,860,000. A bid bond in the amount of five percent of the bid—$93,000—was issued by The American Insurance Company. The bids were opened by the church, and Barber Contracting was the lowest bid.

On the next day, Albert W. Barber, the president of Barber Contracting, informed the church that his company's bid was in error and should have been $143,120 higher. The error was caused in totaling the material costs on Barber Contracting's estimate worksheets. The church had not been provided these worksheets. Barber Contracting sent a letter to the church, stating that it was withdrawing its bid. The next day, the church sent a construction contract to Barber Contracting, containing the original bid amount. When Barber Contracting refused to sign the contract and refused to do the work for the original contract price, the church signed a contract with the second-lowest bidder, H & H Construction and Supply Company, Inc., to complete the work for $1,919,272. The church sued Barber Contracting and The American Insurance Company, seeking to recover the amount of the bid bond. Who wins? Did Barber act ethically in trying to get out of the contract? Did the church act ethically in trying to enforce Barber's bid? *First Baptist Church of Moultrie v. Barber Contracting Co.*, 189 Ga.App. 804, 377 S.E.2d 717, **Web** 1989 Ga.App. Lexis 25 (Court of Appeals of Georgia)

13.10 Business Ethics Lockheed Missiles & Space Company, Inc. (Lockheed), sent out a request to potential subcontractors, seeking bids for the manufacture of 124 ballast cans for the Trident II nuclear submarines it was building for the U.S. Navy. In February 1989, Lockheed received eight bids, including one from Sulzer Bingham Pumps, Inc. (Sulzer). Sulzer was the lowest bidder, at $6,544,055. The next lowest bid was $10,176,670, and the bids ranged up to $17,766,327. Lockheed itself estimated that the job would cost at least $8.5 million. Lockheed's employees were shocked by Sulzer's bid and thought it was surprisingly low.

Lockheed then inspected Sulzer's Portland facility to evaluate Sulzer's technical capabilities. The inspection revealed that Sulzer would have to make many modifications to its existing facility in order to complete the contract.

Lockheed did not reveal its findings to Sulzer. In addition, it never notified Sulzer that its bid was significantly lower than the next lowest bid and lower than Lockheed's own estimate of the cost of the job as well. Finally, Sulzer was never told that Lockheed suspected that the contract could not be completed at the bid price.

Lockheed accepted Sulzer's bid, and Sulzer started work. Nine months later, Sulzer revised its estimate of the cost of the job and asked Lockheed for an additional $2,110,000 in compensation. When Lockheed rejected this request, Sulzer sued Lockheed, asking the court to either increase the price of the contract to $8,645,000 or, alternatively, to rescind its bid. Did Lockheed act ethically in this case by not notifying Sulzer of the suspected mistake? Did Sulzer act ethically by trying to get out of the contract because of its own economic misjudgments? Legally, who wins? *Sulzer Bingham Pumps, Inc. v. Lockheed Missiles & Space Company, Inc.*, 947 F.2d 1362, **Web** 1991 U.S. App. Lexis 24966 (United States Court of Appeals for the Ninth Circuit)

ENDNOTES

1. *Restatement (Second) of Contracts*, Section 153.
2. *Restatement (Second) of Contracts*, Section 152.
3. 59 Eng. Rep. 375 (1864).
4. *Restatement (Second) of Contracts*, Section 159.
5. *Restatement (Second) of Contracts*, Sections 163 and 164.
6. *Restatement (Second) of Contracts*, Section 160.
7. *Restatement (Second) of Contracts*, Section 161.
8. *Restatement (Second) of Contracts*, Section 170.
9. *Restatement (Second) of Contracts*, Section 177.
10. *Restatement (Second) of Contracts*, Section 176.

14 | STATUTE OF FRAUDS AND EQUITABLE EXCEPTIONS

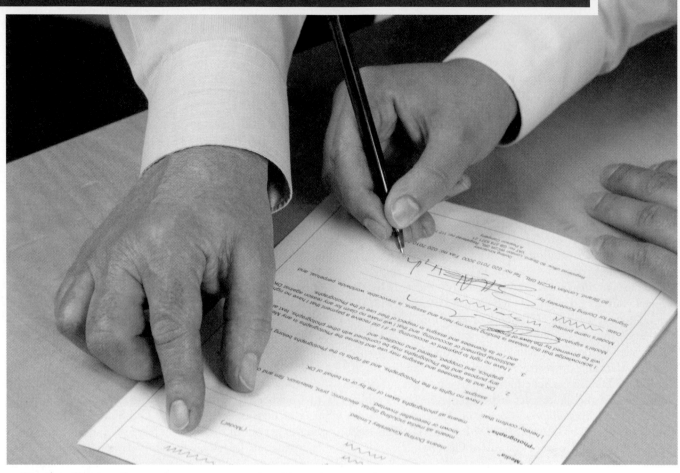

▲ **Contract Signing** *Even written contracts can be subject to interpretation.*

CHAPTER OBJECTIVES

After studying this chapter, you should be able to:

1. List the contracts that must be in writing under the Statute of Frauds.
2. Explain the effect of noncompliance with the Statute of Frauds.
3. Describe how the Statute of Frauds is applicable to the sale of goods.

4. Describe the formality of the writing of contracts and the parol evidence rule.
5. Apply the equity doctrines of *part performance* and *promissory estoppel*.

CHAPTER CONTENTS

"A verbal contract isn't worth the paper it's written on."

—Samuel Goldwyn

▶ INTRODUCTION TO STATUTE OF FRAUDS AND EQUITABLE EXCEPTIONS

Certain types of contracts must be in writing pursuant to the Statute of Frauds. Other issues regarding the form of a contract may arise, such as the form of signature that is required on a written contract, whether a contract can be created by the integration of several documents, whether any previous oral or written agreements between the parties can be given effect, and how contract language should be interpreted. Also, there are several equitable exceptions to the Statute of Frauds—namely the part performance exception and the doctrine of promissory estoppel.

Issues regarding the Statute of Frauds, the formality of the writing of contracts and equitable doctrines that allow exceptions to the Statute of Frauds are discussed in this chapter.

▶ STATUTE OF FRAUDS

In 1677, the English Parliament enacted a statute called "An Act for the Prevention of Frauds and Perjuries." This act required that certain types of contracts had to be in writing and signed by the party against whom enforcement was sought. Today, every U.S. state has enacted a **Statute of Frauds** that requires certain types of contracts to be in *writing*. This statute is intended to ensure that the terms of important contracts are not forgotten, misunderstood, or fabricated. One court stated about the Statute of Frauds, "It is the purpose of the Statute of Frauds to suppress fraud, i.e., cooked-up claims of agreement, sometimes fathered by wish, sometimes imagined in the light of subsequent events, and sometimes simply conjured up."[1]

Statute of Frauds
A state statute that requires certain types of contracts to be in writing.

Writing Requirement

Although the statutes vary slightly from state to state, most states require the following types of contracts to be in writing.[2]

Statute of Frauds: That unfortunate statute, the misguided application of which has been the cause of so many frauds.

Bacon, Viscount
Morgan v. Worthington (1878)

- Contracts involving interests in real property
- Contracts that by their own terms cannot possibly be performed within one year
- Collateral contracts in which a person promises to answer for the debt or duty of another
- Promises made in consideration of marriage
- Contracts for the sale of goods for $500 or more
- Contracts for the lease of goods with payments of $1,000 or more
- Real estate agents' contracts
- Agents' contracts where the underlying contract must be in writing
- Promises to write a will
- Contracts to pay debts barred by the statute of limitations or discharged in bankruptcy
- Contracts to pay compensation for services rendered in negotiating the purchase of a business
- Finder's fee contracts

Generally, an **executory contract** that is not in writing even though the Statute of Frauds requires it to be is unenforceable by either party. The Statute of Frauds is usually raised by one party as a defense to the enforcement of the contract by the other party.

If an oral contract that should have been in writing under the Statute of Frauds is already executed, neither party can seek to **rescind** the contract on the ground of noncompliance with the Statute of Frauds. That is, the contract may be voluntarily performed by the parties.

Don't get it right, just get it written.

James Thurber

Generally, contracts listed in the Statute of Frauds must be in writing to be enforceable. There are several equity exceptions to this rule. The contracts that must be in writing pursuant to the Statute of Frauds and the exceptions to this rule are discussed in the following paragraphs.

Contracts Involving Interests in Real Property

real property
The land itself, as well as buildings, trees, soil, minerals, timber, plants, crops, fixtures and other things permanently affixed to the land or buildings.

Under the Statute of Frauds, any contract that transfers an ownership interest in **real property** must be in writing to be enforceable. Real property includes the land itself, buildings, trees, soil, minerals, timber, plants, crops, fixtures, and things permanently affixed to the land or buildings. Certain items of personal property that are permanently affixed to the real property are fixtures that become part of the real property.

Example Built-in cabinets in a house are *fixtures* that become part of the real property.

Other contracts that transfer an ownership interest in land must be in writing under the Statute of Frauds. These interests include the following:

mortgage
An interest in real property given to a lender as security for the repayment of a loan.

- **Mortgages.** Borrowers often give a lender an interest in real property as security for the repayment of a loan. This action must be done through the use of a written **mortgage** or **deed of trust**.

Example Ida purchases a house for $1 million. She pays $400,000 toward the payment of the house and borrows $600,000 of the purchase price from CityBank. CityBank requires that the house be collateral for the loan and takes a mortgage on the house. Here, the mortgage between Ida and CityBank must be in writing to be enforceable.

lease
The transfer of the right to use real property for a specified period of time.

life estate
An interest in real property for a person's lifetime; upon that person's death, the interest will be transferred to another party.

easement
A right to use someone else's land without owning or leasing it.

- **Leases.** A **lease** is the transfer of the right to use real property for a specified period of time. Most Statutes of Frauds require leases for a term over one year to be in writing.
- **Life estates.** On some occasions, a person is given a **life estate** in real property. In other words, the person has an interest in the real property for the person's lifetime, and the interest will be transferred to another party on that person's death. A life estate is an ownership interest that must be in writing under the Statute of Frauds.
- **Easements.** An **easement** is a given or required right to use another person's land without owning or leasing it. Easements may be either express or implied. Express easements must be in writing to be enforceable, while implied easements need not be written.

One-Year Rule

one-year rule
A rule which states that an executory contract that cannot be performed by its own terms within one year of its formation must be in writing.

According to the Statute of Frauds, an executory contract that cannot be performed by its own terms within one year of its formation must be in writing.[3] This **one-year rule** is intended to prevent disputes about contract terms that may otherwise occur toward the end of a long-term contract. If the performance of the contract is possible within the one-year period, the contract may be oral.

The extension of an oral contract might cause the contract to violate the Statute of Frauds if the original term and the extension period exceed one year.

Example Frederick, the owner of a store, hires Anna as the store manager for 6 months. Assume that after 3 months Frederick and Anna agree to extend the contract for an additional 11 months. At the time of the extension, the contract would be for 14 months (the 3 left on the original contract plus 11 months added by the extension). The modification would have to be in writing because it exceeds the one-year rule.

In the following case, the court held that the one-year rule prohibited the enforcement of an oral contract.

basis during a two-year period. The loan process was informal: Gulf Coast Motors set up a ledger account and recorded each loan made to Glenn, and Glenn would sign the ledger "I agree to pay Jerry Sellers as above." At various times, Glenn would make small payments toward his account, but he would thereafter borrow more money. At the times the loans were made, Glenn was not working and had no assets in his own name. There was no evidence as to what Glenn used the loan proceeds for, but evidence showed that he had a gambling problem.

Sellers testified that toward the end of the two-year period of making loans to Glenn, he telephoned Mary R. Page, Glenn's wife, and Mary orally guaranteed to repay Glenn's loans. Mary had significant assets of her own. Mary denied that she had promised to pay any of Glenn's debt, and she denied that Sellers had asked her to pay Glenn's debt. Gulf Coast Motors sued Glenn and Mary to recover payment for the unpaid loans. The trial court entered judgment in the amount of $23,020 in favor of Gulf Coast Motors. Mary appealed.

Issue

Was Mary's alleged oral promise to guarantee her husband's debts an enforceable guaranty contract?

Language of the Court

A promise to pay the debt of another is barred by the Statute of Frauds unless it is in writing. It is not disputed that Mary did not sign a note, guaranty, or any other writing promising to pay any part of Glenn's debts. Therefore, if the purported agreement to pay Glenn's debt is within the Statute of Frauds, Mary is not liable even if the trial court found Seller's testimony to be credible. Mary's alleged oral promises are not enforceable under the Statute of Frauds. We conclude that Mary's alleged promises to guaranty or repay Glenn's debts were within the Statute of Frauds and, therefore, were not enforceable.

Decision

The court of civil appeals held that Mary's alleged oral promises to guarantee her husband's debts were not in writing, as required by the Statute of Frauds. The court remanded the case to the trial court to enter judgment in Mary's favor.

Case Questions

Critical Legal Thinking What is a guaranty contract? Explain.

Business Ethics Did Glenn act ethically in this case? Would Mary have acted unethically if she had actually orally guaranteed to repay her husband's debts and then raised the Statute of Frauds to prevent enforcement of the oral promises?

Contemporary Business Are guaranty contracts often used in business? Can you think of a situation in which a guaranty contract would be required?

Contract for the Sale of Goods

Section 2-201(1) of the Uniform Commercial Code (UCC) is the basic Statute of Frauds provision for **sales contracts**. It states that contracts for the sale of goods costing *$500 or more* must be in writing to be enforceable. If the contract price of an original sales contract is below $500, it does not have to be in writing under the **UCC Statute of Frauds**. However, if a modification of the sales contract increases the sales price to $500 or more, the *modification* has to be in writing to be enforceable.

Example Echo enters into an oral contract to sell James her used car for $10,000, with the delivery date to be May 1. When May 1 comes and James tenders $10,000 to Echo, Echo refuses to sell her car to James. The contract will not be enforced against Echo because it was an oral contract for the sale of goods costing $500 or more, and it should have been in writing.

The most recent revision to UCC 2-201 requires that contracts for the sale of goods costing *$5,000 or more* must be in writing to be enforceable. A state must adopt this amendment for it to become effective.

Contract for the Lease of Goods

Section 2A-201(1) of the Uniform Commercial Code (UCC) is the Statute of Frauds provision that applies to the lease of goods. It states that **lease contracts** involving payments of $1,000 or more must be in writing. If a lease payment of an original lease contract is below $1,000, it does not have to be in writing under the UCC Statute of Frauds. However, if a modification of the lease contract increases the lease payment to $1,000 or more, the *modification* has to be in writing to be enforceable.

UCC Statute of Frauds Section 2-201(1)
A section of the Uniform Commercial Code which states that sales contracts for the sale of goods costing $500 or more must be in writing.

To break an oral agreement which is not legally binding is morally wrong.

Bava Metzi'a
The Talmud

UCC Statute of Frauds Section 2A-201(1)
A section of the Uniform Commercial Code which states that lease contracts involving payments of $1,000 or more must be in writing.

Agents' Contracts

equal dignity rule
A rule which says that agents' contracts to sell property covered by the Statute of Frauds must be in writing to be enforceable.

Many state Statutes of Frauds require that **agents' contracts** to sell real property covered by the Statute of Frauds be in writing to be enforceable. The requirement is often referred to as the **equal dignity rule**.

Example Barney hires Cynthia, a licensed real estate broker, to sell his house. Because a contract to sell real estate must be in writing pursuant to the Statute of Frauds, the equal dignity rule requires that the real estate agents' contract be in writing as well. Some state Statutes of Frauds expressly state that the real estate broker and agents' contracts must be in writing.

Promises Made in Consideration of Marriage

Under the Statute of Frauds, a unilateral promise to pay money or property in consideration for a promise to marry must be in writing.

Example A **prenuptial agreement**, which is a contract entered into by parties prior to marriage that defines their ownership rights in each other's property, must be in writing.

▶ EQUITY: PART PERFORMANCE

part performance
An equitable doctrine that allows the court to order an oral contract for the sale of land or transfer of another interest in real property to be specifically performed if it has been partially performed and performance is necessary to avoid injustice.

If an oral contract for the sale of land or transfer of another interest in real property has been partially performed, it may not be possible to return the parties to their *status quo*. To solve this problem, the courts have developed the equitable doctrine of **part performance**. This doctrine allows the court to order such an oral contract to be specifically performed if performance is necessary to avoid injustice. For this performance exception to apply, most courts require that the purchaser either pay part of the purchase price and take possession of the property or make valuable improvements on the property.

ETHICS SPOTLIGHT

Equity: Part Performance

"The doctrine of part performance by the purchaser is a well-recognized exception to the Statute of Frauds as applied to contracts for the sale of real property."

—Judge Kline, P. J.

Arlene and Donald Warner inherited a home at 101 Molimo Street in San Francisco. The Warners obtained a $170,000 loan on the property. Donald Warner and Kenneth Sutton were friends. Donald Warner proposed that Sutton and his wife purchase the residence. His proposal included a $15,000 down payment toward the purchase price of $185,000. The Suttons were to pay all the mortgage payments and real estate taxes on the property for five years, and at any time during the five-year period, they could purchase the house. All this was agreed to orally.

The Suttons paid the down payment and cash payments equal to the monthly mortgage to the Warners. The Suttons paid the annual property taxes on the house. The Suttons also made improvements to the property. Four and one-half years later, the Warners reneged on the oral sales/option agreement. At that time, the house had risen in value to between $250,000 and $320,000. The Suttons sued for specific performance of the sales agreement. The Warners defended, alleging that the oral promise to sell

real estate had to be in writing under the Statute of Frauds and was therefore unenforceable.

The trial court applied the equitable doctrine of part performance and ordered the Warners to specifically perform the oral contract. The court of appeal, which agreed, stated:

The doctrine of part performance by the purchaser is a well-recognized exception to the Statute of Frauds as applied to contracts for the sale of real property. The actions taken by the Suttons in reliance upon the oral agreement, when considered together with the Warners' admission that there was an oral agreement of some duration, satisfy the elements of the part performance doctrine.

The court of appeal held that the equitable doctrine of part performance made the oral contract for the sale of real property in this case enforceable. *Sutton v. Warner*, 12 Cal.App.4th 415, 15 Cal.Rptr.2d 632, **Web** 1993 Cal.App. Lexis 22 (Court of Appeal of California)

Business Ethics   What does the equitable doctrine of part performance provide? Did the Statute of Frauds give the Warners a justifiable reason not to go through with the deal?

► FORMALITY OF THE WRITING

Some written commercial contracts are long, detailed documents that have been negotiated by the parties and drafted and reviewed by their lawyers. Others are preprinted forms with blanks that can be filled in to fit the facts of a particular situation.

A written contract does not, however, have to be either drafted by a lawyer or formally typed to be legally binding. Generally, the law only requires a writing containing the essential terms of the parties' agreement. Thus, any writing—including letters, telegrams, invoices, sales receipts, checks, and handwritten agreements written on scraps of paper—can be an enforceable contract under this rule.

Required Signature

The Statute of Frauds and the UCC require a written contract, whatever its form, to be signed *by the party against whom enforcement is sought*. The signature of the person who is enforcing the contract is not necessary. Thus, a written contract may be enforceable against one party but not the other party.

Generally, the signature may appear anywhere on the writing. In addition, it does not have to be a person's full legal name. The person's last name, first name, nickname, initials, seal, stamp, engraving, or other symbol or mark (e.g., an *X*) that indicates the person's intent can be binding. The signature may be affixed by an authorized agent.

If a signature is suspected of being forged, the victim can hire handwriting experts and use modern technology to prove it is not his or her signature.

Integration of Several Writings

Both the common law of contracts and the UCC permit several writings to be **integrated** to form a single written contract. That is, the entire writing does not have to appear in one document to be an enforceable contract.

Integration may be by an *express reference* in one document that refers to and incorporates another document within it. This procedure is called **incorporation by reference**. Thus, what may often look like a simple one-page contract may actually be hundreds of pages long when all of the documents incorporated by reference are considered.

Example Credit card contracts often incorporate by express reference such documents as the master agreement between the issuer and cardholders, subsequent amendments to the agreement, and such.

Several documents may be integrated to form a single written contract if they are somehow physically attached to each other to indicate a party's intent to show integration. Attaching several documents together with a staple, paper clip, or some other means may indicate integration. Placing several documents in the same container (e.g., an envelope) may also indicate integration. Such an action is called *implied integration*.

Interpreting Contract Words and Terms

When contracts are at issue in a lawsuit, courts are often called upon to interpret the meaning of certain contract words or terms. The parties to a contract may define the words and terms used in their contract. Many written contracts contain a detailed definition section—usually called a **glossary**—that defines many of the words and terms used in the contract.

If the parties have not defined the words and terms of a contract, the courts apply the following **standards of interpretation**:

• *Ordinary* words are given their usual meaning according to the dictionary.
• *Technical words* are given their technical meaning, unless a different meaning is clearly intended.

Most of the disputes in the world arise from words.

Lord Mansfield, C. J.
Morgan v. Jones (1773)

integration of several writings
The combination of several writings to form a single contract.

incorporation by reference
Integration made by express reference in one document that refers to and incorporates another document within it.

Counsel Randle Jackson: In the book of nature, my lords, it is written—
—Lord Ellenborough: Will you have the goodness to mention the page, sir, if you please?

Lord Campbell
Lives of the Chief Justices (1857)

- *Specific terms* are presumed to qualify *general terms*. For example, if a provision in a contract refers to the subject matter as "corn," but a later provision refers to the subject matter as "feed corn" for cattle, this specific term qualifies the general term.
- If both parties are members of the same trade or profession, words will be given their meaning as used in the trade (i.e., *usage of trade*). If the parties do not want trade usage to apply, the contract must indicate that.
- Where a preprinted form contract is used, *typed words* in a contract prevail over *preprinted words*. *Handwritten words* prevail over both preprinted and typed words.
- If there is an ambiguity in a contract, the ambiguity will be resolved against the party who drafted the contract.

▶ PAROL EVIDENCE RULE

parol evidence
Any oral or written words outside the four corners of a written contract.

By the time a contract is reduced to writing, the parties usually have engaged in prior or contemporaneous discussions and negotiations or exchanged prior writings. Any oral or written words outside the *four corners* of the written contract are called **parol evidence**. *Parol* means "word."

parol evidence rule
A rule that says if a written contract is a complete and final statement of the parties' agreement, any prior or contemporaneous oral or written statements that alter, contradict, or are in addition to the terms of the written contract are inadmissible in court regarding a dispute over the contract. There are several exceptions to this rule.

The **parol evidence rule** was originally developed by courts as part of the common law of contracts. The UCC has adopted the parol evidence rule for sales and lease contracts.[6] The parol evidence rule states that if a written contract is a complete and final statement of the parties' agreement (i.e., a **complete integration**), any prior or contemporaneous oral or written statements that alter, contradict, or are in addition to the terms of the written contract are inadmissible in any court proceeding concerning the contract.[7] In other words, a completely integrated contract is viewed as the best evidence of the terms of the parties' agreement.

Merger, or Integration, Clause

merger clause
A clause in a contract that stipulates that it is a complete integration and the exclusive expression of the parties' agreement. Also known as an *integration clause*.

The parties to a written contract may include a clause stipulating that the contract is a complete integration and the exclusive expression of their agreement and that parol evidence may not be introduced to explain, alter, contradict, or add to the terms of the contract. This type of clause, called a **merger clause**, or an **integration clause**, expressly reiterates the parol evidence rule.

Exceptions to the Parol Evidence Rule

There are several major exceptions to the parol evidence rule. Parol evidence may be admitted in court if it:

- Shows that a contract is void or voidable (e.g., evidence that the contract was induced by fraud, misrepresentation, duress, undue influence, or mistake).
- Explains ambiguous language.
- Concerns *a prior course of dealing or course of performance* between the parties or a *usage of trade*.[8]
- *Fills in the gaps* in a contract (e.g., if a price term or time of performance term is omitted from a written contract, the court can hear parol evidence to imply the reasonable price or time of performance under the contract).
- Corrects an obvious clerical or typographical error. The court can *reform* the contract to reflect the correction.

The meaning of words varies according to the circumstances of and concerning which they are used.

Justice Blackburn
Allgood v. Blake (1873)

▶ EQUITY: PROMISSORY ESTOPPEL

promissory estoppel
An equitable doctrine that permits enforcement of oral contracts that should have been in writing. It is applied to avoid injustice. Also known as *equitable estoppel*.

The doctrine of **promissory estoppel**, or **equitable estoppel**, is another equitable exception to the strict application of the Statute of Frauds. The version of promissory estoppel in the *Restatement (Second) of Contracts* provides that if parties enter into an oral contract that should be in writing under the Statute of Frauds, the oral promise is enforceable against the promisor if three conditions are met: (1) The promise induces action or forbearance of action by another, (2) the reliance on the oral promise was foreseeable, and (3) injustice can be avoided only by enforcing the oral promise.[9] Where this doctrine applies, the promisor is *estopped* (*prevented*) from raising the Statute of Frauds as a defense to the enforcement of the oral contract.

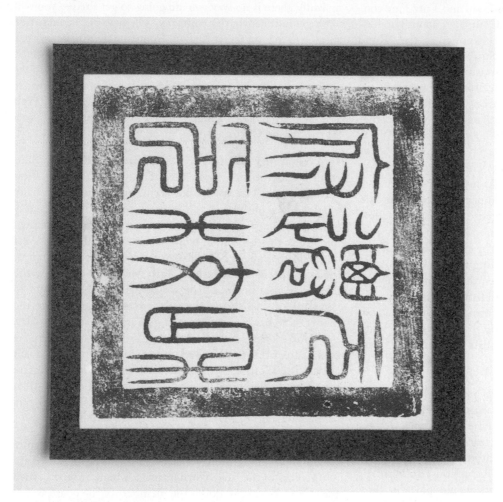

Impression Made by an Eighteenth-Century Chinese Civil Service Seal *In China, Vietnam, Japan, and other countries of Asia, individuals often follow the age-old tradition of using a stamp as their signature. Government organizations and businesses have to use stamps on contracts and other documents of official business. The stamp is a character or set of characters carved onto one end of a cylinder-shaped piece—made out of ivory, jade, agate, gold, animal's horn, wood, or plastic. The owner places the end bearing the characters in ink and then applies this end to the document to be signed, leaving an ink imprint that serves as the owner's signature. The ink is red—thus the saying "red head" document. In China it is called a chop, in Japan it is called a hanko, and in Vietnam it is called a seal. These seals are registered with the government. Younger persons in these countries are increasingly using hand-applied signatures instead of traditional seals.*

TEST REVIEW TERMS AND CONCEPTS

Agents' contract
Complete integration
Easement
Equal dignity rule
Executory contract
Glossary
Guarantor
Guaranty contract
Incorporation by reference
Integration of several writings

Lease
Lease contract
Life estate
Main purpose exception (leading object exception)
Merger clause (integration clause)
Mortgage (deed of trust)
One-year rule

Original contract (primary contract)
Parol evidence
Parol evidence rule
Part performance
Prenuptial agreement
Promissory estoppel (equitable estoppel)
Real property
Rescission

Sales contract
Section 2-201(1) of the Uniform Commercial Code (UCC)
Section 2A-201(1) of the Uniform Commercial Code (UCC)
Standards of interpretation
Statute of Frauds
UCC Statute of Frauds

CASE PROBLEMS

14.1 Statute of Frauds   Fritz Hoffman and Fritz Frey contracted the Sun Valley Company (Company) about purchasing a 1.64-acre piece of property known as the "Ruud Mountain Property," located in Sun Valley, Idaho, from Company. Mr. Conger, a representative of Company, was authorized to sell the property, subject to the approval of the executive committee of Company. Conger reached an agreement on the telephone with Hoffman and Frey, whereby they would purchase the property for $90,000, payable at 30 percent down, with the balance to be payable quarterly at an annual interest rate of 9.25 percent. The next day, Hoffman sent Conger a letter confirming the conversation.

The executive committee of Company approved the sale. Sun Valley Realty prepared the deed of trust, note, seller's closing statement, and other loan documents. However, before the documents were executed by either side, Sun Valley Company sold all its assets, including the Ruud Mountain property, to another purchaser. When the new owner refused to sell the Ruud Mountain lot to Hoffman and Frey, they brought this action for specific performance of the oral contract. Who wins? *Hoffman v. Sun Valley Company*, 102 Idaho 187, 628 P.2d 218, **Web** 1981 Ida. Lexis 320 (Supreme Court of Idaho)

14.2 Real Property   Robert Briggs and his wife purchased a home located at 167 Lower Orchard Drive, Levittown, Pennsylvania. They made a down payment and borrowed the balance on a 30-year mortgage. Six years later, when Mr. and Mrs. Briggs were behind on their mortgage payments, they entered into an oral contract to sell the house to Winfield and Emma Sackett if the Sacketts would pay the three months' arrearages on the loan and agree to make the future payments on the mortgage. Mrs. Briggs and Mrs. Sackett were sisters. The Sacketts paid the arrearages, moved into the house, and continued to live there. Fifteen years later, Robert Briggs filed an action to void the oral contract as in violation of the Statute of Frauds and evict the Sacketts from the house. Who wins? *Briggs v. Sackett*, 275 Pa. Super. 13, 418 A.2d 586, **Web** 1980 Pa.Super. Lexis 2034 (Superior Court of Pennsylvania)

14.3 One-Year Contract   Robert S. Ohanian was vice president of sales for the West Region of Avis Rent a Car System, Inc. (Avis). Officers of Avis testified that Ohanian's performance in the West Region was excellent, and, in a depressed economic period, Ohanian's West Region stood out as the one region that was growing and profitable. In the fall of 1980, when Avis's Northeast Region was doing badly, the president of Avis asked Ohanian to take over that region. Ohanian was reluctant to do so because he and his family liked living in San Francisco, and he had developed a good team in the West Region, was secure in his position, and feared the politics of the Northeast Region. Ohanian agreed to the transfer only after the general manager of Avis orally told him "unless you screw up badly, there is no way you are going to get fired— you will never get hurt here in this company." Ohanian did a commendable job in the Northeast Region. Approximately one year later, at the age of 47, Ohanian was fired without cause by Avis. Ohanian sued Avis for breach of the oral lifetime contract. Avis asserted the Statute of Frauds against this claim. Who wins? *Ohanian v. Avis Rent a Car System, Inc.*, 779 F.2d 101, **Web** 1985 U.S. App. Lexis 25456 (United States Court of Appeals for the Second Circuit)

14.4 Guaranty Contract   David Brown met with Stan Steele, a loan officer with the Bank of Idaho (now First Interstate Bank) to discuss borrowing money from the bank to start a new business. After learning that he did not qualify for the loan on the basis of his own financial strength, Brown told Steele that his former employers, James and Donna West of California, might be willing to guarantee the payment of the loan. Steele talked to Mr. West, who orally stated on the telephone that he would personally guarantee the loan to Brown. Based on this guaranty, the bank loaned Brown the money. The bank sent a written guarantee to Mr. and Mrs. West for their signatures, but it was never returned to the bank. When Brown defaulted on the loan, the bank filed suit against the Wests to recover on their guaranty contract. Are the Wests liable? *First Interstate Bank of Idaho, N.A. v. West*, 107 Idaho 851, 693 P.2d 1053, **Web** 1984 Ida. Lexis 600 (Supreme Court of Idaho)

14.5 Guaranty Contract   Six persons, including Benjamin Rosenbloom and Alfred Feiler, were members of the board of directors of the Togs Corporation. A bank agreed to loan the corporation $250,000 if the members of the board would personally guarantee the payment of the loan. Feiler objected to signing the guaranty to the bank because of other pending personal financial negotiations that the contingent liability of the guaranty might adversely affect. Feiler agreed with Rosenbloom and the other board members that if they were held personally liable on the guaranty, he would pay his one-sixth share of that amount to them directly. Rosenbloom and the other members of the board signed the personal guaranty with the bank, and the bank made the loan to the corporation. When the corporation defaulted on the loan, the five guarantors had to pay the loan amount to the bank. When they attempted to collect a one-sixth share from Feiler, he refused to pay, alleging that his oral promise had to be in writing under the Statute of Frauds. Does Feiler have to pay the one-sixth share to the other board members? *Feiler V. Rosenbloom*, 46 Md.App. 297, 416 A.2d 1345, **Web** 1980 Md.App. Lexis 328 (Court of Special Appeals of Maryland)

14.6 Agent's Contract   Paul L. McGirr operated an Enco service station in Los Angeles that sold approximately 25,000 to 35,000 gallons of gasoline a month. McGirr telephoned Gulf Oil Corporation (Gulf) regarding an advertisement for dealers. McGirr met with Theodore Marks, an area representative of Gulf, to discuss the possibility of McGirr's operating a Gulf service station. McGirr asked Marks if Gulf had any good, high-producing units available. Marks replied that he had a station at the corner of Figueroa and Avenue 26 that sold about 200,000 gallons of gasoline a month. Marks told McGirr that this station would not be available for about 90 days because Gulf had to terminate the arrangement with the current operator of the station. Marks told McGirr that he could have the Figueroa station only if he also took a "dog" station on Garvey Avenue. Marks agreed to take this station only if he also was assured he would get the Figueroa station. Marks assured him he would. When McGirr asked Marks for this assurance in writing, Marks stated that he did not have to put it in writing because he was the "kingpin in his territory." So they shook hands on the deal.

McGirr terminated his arrangement with Enco and moved to the Garvey Avenue station. He signed a written lease for the Garvey station, which was signed by Max Reed, Gulf's regional sales manager. Under the Statute of Frauds, the lease for a service station must be in writing. Nothing in writing was ever signed by the parties regarding the Figueroa station. A few months later, Marks was transferred to a different territory, and Gulf refused to lease the Figueroa station to McGirr. McGirr sued Marks and Gulf for breach of an oral contract. Is Marks or Gulf liable? *McGirr v. Gulf Oil Corporation*, 41 Cal.App. 3d 246, 115 Cal.Rptr. 902, **Web** 1974 Cal.App. Lexis 783 (Court of Appeal of California)

14.7 Promissory Estoppel   The Atlantic Wholesale Co., Inc. (Atlantic), located in Florence, South Carolina, was in the business of buying and selling gold and silver for customers' accounts. Gary A. Solondz, a New York resident, became a customer of Atlantic and thereafter made several purchases through Atlantic. One day, Solondz telephoned Atlantic and received a quotation on silver bullion. Solondz then bought 300 ounces of silver for a total price of $12,978. Atlantic immediately contracted United Precious Metals in Minneapolis and purchased the silver for Solondz. The silver was shipped to Atlantic, which paid for it.

Atlantic placed the silver in its vault while it waited for payment from Solondz. When Atlantic telephoned Solondz about payment, he told Atlantic to continue to hold the silver in its vault until he decided whether to sell it. Meanwhile, the price of silver had fallen substantially and continued to fall. When Solondz refused to pay for the silver, Atlantic sold it for $4,650, sustaining a loss of $8,328. When Atlantic sued Solondz to recover this loss, Solondz asserted that the Statute of Frauds prevented enforcement of his oral promise to buy the silver. Does the doctrine of promissory estoppel prevent the application of the Statute of Frauds in this case? *Atlantic Wholesale Co., Inc. v. Solondz*, 283 S.C. 36, 320 S.E.2d 720, **Web** 1984 S.C. App. Lexis 555 (Court of Appeals of South Carolina)

14.8 Sufficiency of a Writing   Irving Levin and Harold Lipton owned the San Diego Clippers Basketball Club, a professional basketball franchise. Levin and Lipton met with Philip Knight to discuss the sale of the Clippers to Knight. After the meeting, they all initialed a three-page handwritten memorandum that Levin had drafted during the meeting. The memorandum outlined the major terms of their discussion, including subject matter, price, and the parties to the agreement. Levin and Lipton forwarded to Knight a letter and proposed sale agreement. Two days later, Knight informed Levin that he had decided not to purchase the Clippers. Levin and Lipton sued Knight for breach of contract. Knight argued in defense that the handwritten memorandum was not enforceable because it did not satisfy the Statute of Frauds. Is he correct? *Levin v. Knight*, 865 F.2d 1271, **Web** 1989 U.S. App. Lexis 458 (United States Court of Appeals for the Ninth Circuit)

BUSINESS ETHICS CASES

14.9 Business Ethics   American Broadcasting Company Merchandising, Inc., a subsidiary of American Broadcasting Company, Inc. (collectively, ABC), entered into a written contract with model Cheryl Tiegs, whereby ABC would pay Tiegs $400,000 per year for the right to be the exclusive agent to license the merchandising of goods under her name. When ABC was unsuccessful in attracting licensing arrangements for Tiegs, a representative of ABC contacted Paul Sklar, who had previous experience in marketing apparel and licensing labels. Sklar enlisted the help of Mark Blye, and together they introduced ABC and Tiegs to Sears, Roebuck and Company (Sears). This introduction led to an agreement between Sears, ABC, and Tiegs, whereby Sears marketed a line of "Cheryl Tiegs" female apparel through Sears department stores and catalog sales. Blye and Sklar sued ABC for a finder's fee for introducing ABC and Tiegs to Sears. Because there was no express written or oral contract between ABC and Blye and Sklar, they alleged that there was an implied-in-fact contract between the parties. Section 5-701(a)(10) of the New York Statute of Frauds requires a finder's fee contract of the type in this case to be in writing. Who wins? Did ABC act ethically in this case? *Blye v. American Broadcasting Company Merchandising, Inc.*, 102 A.D.2d 297, 476 N.Y.S.2d 874, **Web** 1984 N.Y. App. Div. Lexis 18341 (Supreme Court of New York)

14.10 Business Ethics   Adolfo Mozzetti, who owned a construction company, orally promised his son, Remo, that if Remo would manage the family business for their mutual benefit and would take care of him for the rest of his life, he would leave the family home to Remo. Section 2714 of the Delaware Code requires contracts for the transfer of land to be in writing. Section 2715 of the Delaware Code requires testamentary transfers of real property to be in writing. Remo performed as requested: He managed the family business and took care of his father until the father died. When the father died, his will devised the family home to his daughter, Lucia M. Shepard. Remo brought an action to enforce his father's oral promise that the home belonged to him. The daughter argued that the will should be upheld. Who wins? Did the daughter act ethically in trying to defeat the father's promise to leave the property to the son? Did the son act ethically in trying to defeat his father's will? *Shepard v. Mozzetti*, 545 A.2d 621, **Web** 1988 Del. Lexis 217 (Supreme Court of Delaware)

ENDNOTES

1. *Elias v. George Sahely & Co.*, 1983 App. Cas. (P.C.) 646, 655.
2. *Restatement (Second) of Contracts*, Section 110.
3. *Restatement (Second) of Contracts*, Section 130.
4. *Restatement (Second) of Contracts*, Section 112.
5. *Restatement (Second) of Contracts*, Section 116.
6. UCC Section 2-202 and UCC Section 2A-202.
7. *Restatement (Second) of Contracts*, Section 213.
8. UCC Sections 1-205, 2-202, and 2–208.
9. *Restatement (Second) of Contracts*, Section 139.

▲ **Professional Baseball Player** *Professional athletes' contracts often provide that their personal service can be assigned.*

CHAPTER OBJECTIVES

After studying this chapter, you should be able to:

1. Describe assignment of contract rights and what contract rights are assignable.
2. Define *intended beneficiary* and describe this person's rights under a contract.
3. Define *covenant.*
4. Distinguish between conditions precedent, conditions subsequent, and concurrent conditions.
5. Explain when the performance of a contract is excused because of objective impossibility or commercial impracticability.

CHAPTER CONTENTS

"An honest man's word is as good as his bond."

—Don Quixote

▶ INTRODUCTION TO THIRD-PARTY RIGHTS AND DISCHARGE

privity of contract
The state of two specified parties being in a contract.

The parties to a contract are said to be in **privity of contract**. Contracting parties have a legal obligation to perform the duties specified in their contract. A party's duty of performance may be discharged by agreement of the parties, excuse of performance, or operation of law. If one party fails to perform as promised, the other party may enforce the contract and sue for breach.

With two exceptions, third parties do not acquire any rights under other people's contracts. The exceptions are (1) *assignees* to whom rights are subsequently transferred and (2) *intended third-party beneficiaries* to whom the contracting parties intended to give rights under the contract at the time of contracting.

This chapter discusses the rights of third parties under a contract, conditions to performance, and ways of discharging the duty of performance.

▶ ASSIGNMENT OF A RIGHT

assignment
The transfer of contractual rights by an obligee to another party.

In many cases, the parties to a contract can transfer their rights under the contract to other parties. The transfer of contractual rights is called an **assignment of rights** or just an **assignment**.

Form of Assignment

assignor
An obligee who transfers a right.

assignee
A party to whom a right has been transferred.

A party who owes a duty of performance is called the **obligor**. A party who is owed a right under a contract is called the **obligee**. An obligee who transfers the right to receive performance is called an **assignor**. The party to whom the right has been transferred is called the **assignee**. The assignee can assign the right to yet another person (called a **subsequent assignee**, or **subassignee**). Exhibit 15.1 illustrates these relationships.

▶ **Exhibit 15.1**
ASSIGNMENT OF A RIGHT

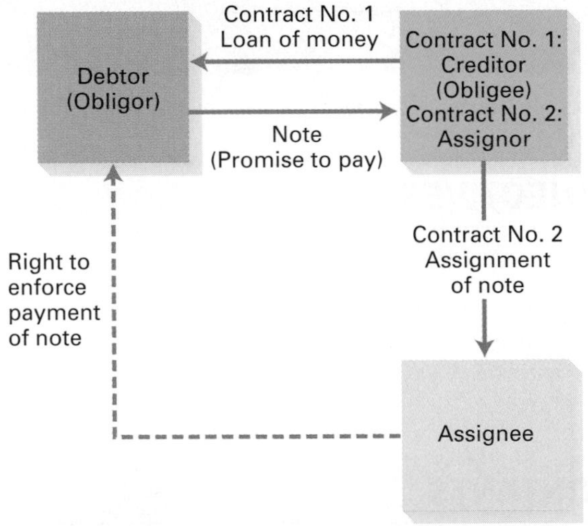

Generally, no formalities are required for a valid assignment of rights. Although the assignor often uses the word *assign*, other words or terms, such as *sell*, *transfer*, *convey*, and *give*, are sufficient to indicate intent to transfer a contract right.

Example A retail clothing store purchases $5,000 worth of goods on credit from a manufacturer. Payment is due in 120 days. If the manufacturer needs cash before the 120-day period expires, the manufacturer (assignor) can sell its right to collect the money to another party (assignee) for some price, let's say $4,000. If the retail store is given proper notice of the assignment, it must pay $5,000 to the assignee when the 120-day period is reached.

In the United States, public policy favors a free flow of commerce. Hence, most contract rights are assignable, including sales contracts and contracts for the payment of money. The following paragraphs discuss types of contracts that present special problems for assignment.

Personal Service Contract

Contracts for the provision of personal services are generally not assignable.[1]

Example If Angie Warhol, a famous artist, contracts to paint Jay-Z's portrait, Angie cannot assign this contract to another artist and send that artist to do the painting without the prior approval of Jay-Z. Jay-Z can reject this assignment and refuse to have his painting done by any artist except Angie Warhol.

The parties may agree that a **personal service contract** may be assigned.

Example Professional athletes often sign contracts with professional teams which provide that their personal service contract can be assigned.

Assignment of a Future Right

Usually, a person cannot assign a currently nonexistent right that he or she expects to have in the future (i.e., a **future right**).

Example Henrietta, an heiress worth millions of dollars, signs a will, leaving all her property to her granddaughter Brittany. Brittany has only an expected future right, and not a current right, to the money. Brittany cannot lawfully assign her expected future right to receive her inheritance. The assignment would be invalid.

Contract Where an Assignment Would Materially Alter the Risk

A contract cannot be assigned if the assignment would materially alter the risk or duties of the obligor.

Example Laura, who has a safe driving record, purchases automobile insurance from an insurance company. Laura cannot assign her rights to be insured to another driver because the assignment would materially alter the risk and duties of the insurance company.

Assignment of Legal Action

The right to sue another party for a violation of personal rights cannot usually be assigned.

Example Donald is severely injured by Alice in an automobile accident caused by Alice's negligence. Donald can sue Alice for the tort of negligence to recover monetary damages for his injuries. Donald's right to sue Alice is a personal right that cannot be assigned to another person.

A legal right that arises out of a breach of contract may be assigned.

Example Andrea borrows $10,000 from Country Bank with an 8% interest rate. The loan is to be repaid in equal monthly installments over a five-year period. If Andrea defaults on the loan, Country Bank may sue Andrea to collect the unpaid amount of the loan. Instead, Country Bank may sell (assign) its legal right to a collection agency to recover the money Andrea still owes on the loan. In this case, Country Bank is the assignor, and the collection agency is the assignee.

If a man will improvidently bind himself up by a voluntary deed, and not reserve a liberty to himself by a power of revocation, this court will not loose the fetters he hath put upon himself, but he must lie down under his own folly.

Lord Chancellor Lord
Nottingham
Villers v. Beaumont (1682)

Effect of an Assignment of a Right

*Make fair agreements and stick
to them.*

Confucius

Where there has been a valid assignment of rights, the assignee "stands in the shoes of the assignor." That is, the assignor is entitled to performance from the obligor. The unconditional assignment of a contract right extinguishes all the assignor's rights, including the right to sue the obligor directly for nonperformance.[2] An assignee takes no better rights under the contract than the assignor had.

Example If the assignor has a right to receive $10,000 from a debtor, the right to receive this $10,000 is all that the assignor can assign to the assignee.

An obligor can assert any defense he or she had against the assignor or the assignee. An obligor can raise the defenses of fraud, duress, undue influence, minority, insanity, illegality of the contract, mutual mistake, or payment by worthless check of the assignor, against enforcement of the contract by the assignee. The obligor can also raise any personal defenses (e.g., participation in the assignor's fraudulent scheme) he or she may have directly against the assignee.

Notice of Assignment

When an assignor makes an assignment of a right under a contract, the assignee is under a duty to notify the obligor that (1) the assignment has been made and (2) performance must be rendered to the assignee. If the assignee fails to provide **notice of assignment** to the obligor, the obligor may continue to render performance to the assignor, who no longer has a right to it. The assignee cannot sue the obligor to recover payment because the obligor has performed according to the original contract. The assignee's only course of action is to sue the assignor for damages.

*That what is agreed to be done,
must be considered as done.*

Lord Chancellor Lord
Hardwicke
Guidot v. Guidot (1745)

The result changes if the obligor is notified of the assignment but continues to render performance to the assignor. In such situations, the assignee can sue the obligor and recover payment. The obligor will then have to pay twice: once wrongfully to the assignor and then rightfully to the assignee. The obligor's only recourse is to sue the assignor for damages.

Anti-Assignment Clause

anti-assignment clause
A clause that prohibits the assignment of rights under the contract.

Some contracts contain an **anti-assignment clause** that prohibits the assignment of rights under the contract. Such clauses may be used if the obligor does not want to deal with or render performance to an unknown third party. Anti-assignment clauses are usually given effect.

Approval Clause

Some contracts contain an **approval clause**. Such clauses require that the obligor approve any assignment of a contract. Where there is an approval clause, many states prohibit the obligor from unreasonably withholding approval.

ETHICS SPOTLIGHT

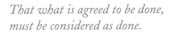
Successive Assignment of the Same Right

An obligee (the party who is owed performance, money, a right, or another thing of value) has the right to assign a contract right or a benefit to another party. If the obligee fraudulently or mistakenly makes successive assignments of the same right to a number of assignees, which assignee has the legal right to the assigned right? To answer this question, the following rules apply:

American rule (New York Rule)
The **American rule** (or **New York Rule**) provides that the first assignment *in time* prevails, regardless of notice. Most states follow this rule.

English rule
The **English rule** provides that the first assignee to *give notice* to the obligor (the person who owes the

performance, money, duty, or other thing of value) prevails.

Possession of Tangible Token Rule
The **possession of tangible token rule** provides that under either the American or English rule, if the assignor makes successive assignments of a contract right that is represented by a tangible token, such as a stock certificate

or a savings account passbook, the first assignee who receives delivery of the tangible token prevails over subsequent assignees.

Business Ethics Why does an assignor attempt to assign a contract right more than once? How can a first assignee protect his rights?

▶ DELEGATION OF A DUTY

Unless otherwise agreed, the parties to a contract can generally transfer the performance of their duties under the contract to other parties. This transfer is called the **delegation of a duty**, or just **delegation**.

An obligor who transfers his or her duty is called a **delegator**. The party to whom the duty is transferred is the **delegatee**. The party to whom the duty is owed is the *obligee*. Generally, no special words or formalities are required to create a delegation of duties. Exhibit 15.2 illustrates the parties to a delegation of a duty.

delegation of duties
A transfer of contractual duties by an obligor to another party for performance.

delegator
An obligor who has transferred his or her duty.

delegatee
A party to whom a duty has been transferred.

▶ **Exhibit 15.2 DELEGATION OF A DUTY**

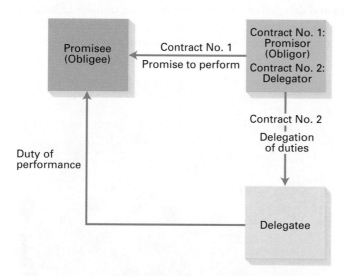

Duties That Can and Cannot Be Delegated

If an obligee has a substantial interest in having an obligor perform the acts required by a contract, these duties cannot be transferred.[3] This restriction includes obligations under the following types of contracts:

1. Personal service contracts calling for the exercise of personal skills, discretion, or expertise

   Example If P Diddy is hired to give a concert on a college campus, the Dixie Chicks cannot appear in his place.

2. Contracts whose performance would materially vary if the obligor's duties were delegated

   Example If a person hires an experienced surgeon to perform a complex surgery, a recent medical school graduate cannot be substituted to perform the operation.

Often, contracts are entered into with companies or firms rather than with individuals. In such cases, a firm may designate any of its qualified employees to perform the contract.

"If there's no meaning in it," said the King, "that saves a world of trouble, you know, we needn't try to find any."

Lewis Carroll
Alice in Wonderland, Chapter 12

Example If a client retains a firm of lawyers to represent her, the firm can **delegate** the duties under the contract to any qualified member of the firm.

Effect of Delegation of Duties

assumption of duties
A situation in which a delegation of duties contains the term *assumption, I assume the duties,* or other similar language. In such a case, the delegatee is legally liable to the obligee for nonperformance.

Where a valid delegation of duties contains the term *assumption* or other similar language, there is an **assumption of duties** by the delegatee. Here, the obligee can sue the delegatee and recover damages for nonperformance or negligent performance by the delegatee. In addition, the delegator remains legally liable for the performance of the contract. Thus, if the delegatee does not perform properly, the obligee can sue the obligor-delegator for any resulting damages caused by the delegatee's nonperformance or negligent conduct.

Anti-Delegation Clause

anti-delegation clause
A clause that prohibits the delegation of duties under the contract.

The parties to a contract can include an **anti-delegation clause** indicating that the duties cannot be delegated. Anti-delegation clauses are usually enforced. Some courts, however, have held that duties that are totally impersonal in nature—such as the payment of money—can be delegated despite such clauses.

Assignment and Delegation

An **assignment and delegation** occurs when there is a transfer of both rights and duties under a contract. If the transfer of a contract to a third party contains only language of assignment, the modern view holds that there is corresponding delegation of the duties of the contract.[4]

Morocco *The negotiation and enforcement of contracts differs in various cultures of the world.*

▶ THIRD-PARTY BENEFICIARY

Third parties sometimes claim rights under others' contracts; these parties are called **third-party beneficiaries**. Such third parties are either *intended* or *incidental beneficiaries*. Each of these designations is discussed here.

Intended Beneficiary

intended third-party beneficiary
A third party who is not in privity of contract but who has rights under the contract and can enforce the contract against the promisor.

When parties enter into a contract, they can agree that the performance of one of the parties should be rendered to or directly benefit a third party. Under such circumstances, the third party is called an **intended third-party beneficiary**. An intended third-party beneficiary can enforce the contract against the party who promised to render performance.[5]

Examples The beneficiary may be expressly named in a contract from which he or she is to benefit ("I leave my property to my son Ben") or may be identified by another means ("I leave my property to all my children, equally").

Intended third-party beneficiaries may be classified as either *donee* or *creditor* beneficiaries. These terms are defined in the following paragraphs. The *Restatement (Second) of Contracts* and many state statutes have dropped this distinction, however, and now refer to both collectively as *intended beneficiaries*.[6]

Donee Beneficiary   The first type of intended beneficiary is the *donee beneficiary*. When a person enters into a contract with the intent to confer a benefit or gift on an intended third party, the contract is called a **donee beneficiary contract**. The three persons involved in such a contract are:

donee beneficiary contract
A contract entered into with the intent to confer a benefit or gift on an intended third party.

1. The **promisee** (the contracting party who directs that the benefit be conferred on another)
2. The **promisor** (the contracting party who agrees to confer performance for the benefit of the third person)
3. The **donee beneficiary** (the third person on whom the benefit is to be conferred)

If the promisor fails to perform the contract, the donee beneficiary can sue the promisor directly.

donee beneficiary
A third party on whom a benefit is to be conferred.

Example Nina goes to Life Insurance Company and purchases a $2 million life insurance policy on her life. Nina names her husband John as the beneficiary of the life insurance policy—that is, he is to be paid the $2 million if Nina dies. John is an intended beneficiary of the Nina–Life Insurance Company contract. Nina makes the necessary premium payments to Life Insurance Company. She dies in an automobile accident. Life Insurance Company does not pay the $2 million life insurance benefits to John. John, as an intended beneficiary, can sue Life Insurance Company to recover the life insurance benefits. Here, John has rights as an intended third-party beneficiary to enforce the Nina–Life Insurance Company contract. (See Exhibit 15.3.)

He who derives the advantage ought to sustain the burden.

Legal maxim

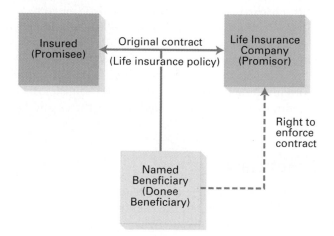

▶ **Exhibit 15.3 DONEE BENEFICIARY CONTRACT**

Creditor Beneficiary   The second type of intended beneficiary is the *creditor beneficiary*. A **creditor beneficiary contract** usually arises in the following situation:

1. A debtor (promisor) borrows money from a creditor (promisee) to purchase some item.
2. The debtor signs an agreement to pay the creditor the amount of the loan plus interest.
3. The debtor sells the item to another party before the loan is paid.
4. The new buyer (new promisor) promises the original debtor (new promisee) that he will pay the remainder of the loan amount to the original creditor.

The original creditor is now the creditor beneficiary of this second contract.[7] The parties to the second contract are the original debtor (promisee of the second contract) and the

creditor beneficiary contract
A contract that arises in the following situation: (1) a debtor borrows money, (2) the debtor signs an agreement to pay back the money plus interest, (3) the debtor sells the item to a third party before the loan is paid off, and (4) the third party promises the debtor that he or she will pay the remainder of the loan to the creditor.

creditor beneficiary
An original creditor who becomes a beneficiary under the debtor's new contract with another party.

new party (promisor of the second contract). The original creditor is the **creditor beneficiary** of the second contract. (See Exhibit 15.4.)

If the new debtor (promisor) fails to perform according to the second contract, the creditor beneficiary may either (1) enforce the original contract against the original debtor-promisor or (2) enforce the new contract against the new debtor-promisor. However, the creditor can collect only once.

▶ **Exhibit 15.4 CREDITOR BENEFICIARY CONTRACT**

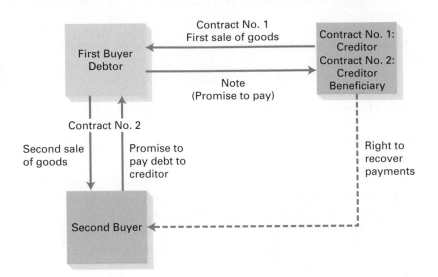

Example Big Hotels obtains a loan from City Bank to build an addition to a hotel it owns in Atlanta, Georgia. The parties sign a promissory note requiring Big Hotels (promisor) to pay off the loan in equal monthly installments over a period of 10 years to City Bank (promisee). With six years left before the loan would be paid, Big Hotels sells the hotel to Palace Hotels, another chain of hotels. Palace Hotels (new promisor) agrees with Big Hotels (new promisee) to complete the payments due to City Bank on the loan. If Palace Hotels fails to pay the loan, City Bank has two options: It can sue Big Hotels on the original promissory note to recover the unpaid loan amount, or it can use its status as a creditor beneficiary to sue and recover the unpaid loan amount from Palace Hotels.

Incidental Beneficiary

incidental beneficiary
A party who is unintentionally benefited by other people's contracts.

In many instances, the parties to a contract unintentionally benefit a third party when a contract is performed. In such situations, the third party is referred to as an **incidental beneficiary**. An incidental beneficiary has no rights to enforce or sue under other people's contracts.

Example Heather owns a house on Residential Street. Her house, which is somewhat older, needs a new exterior coat of paint. Her neighbor John owns the house next door. If Heather has her house painted, John will benefit by having a nicer-looking house next door that may actually raise housing values on the street. Heather contracts with George, a painting contractor, to paint her house. George breaches the contract and does not paint Heather's house. Although John may have benefitted if Heather's house had been painted, he is merely an incidental beneficiary to the Heather–George contract and has no cause of action to sue George for not painting Heather's house. Heather, of course, can sue George for breach of contract.

Generally, the public and taxpayers are only incidental beneficiaries to contracts entered into by the government on their behalf. As such, they acquire no right to enforce government contracts or to sue parties who breach these contracts.

▶ COVENANT

In contracts, parties make certain promises to each other. A **covenant** is an *unconditional* promise to perform. Nonperformance of a covenant is a breach of contract that gives the other party the right to sue. The majority of provisions in contracts are covenants.

Example Seed Company borrows $400,000 from Rural Bank and signs a promissory note to repay the $400,000 plus 10 percent interest in one year. This promise is a covenant. That is, it is an unconditional promise to perform.

covenant
An unconditional promise to perform.

▶ CONDITIONS

Some contract provisions are conditions rather than covenants. A **conditional promise** (or qualified promise) is not as definite as a covenant. The promisor's duty to perform or not perform arises only if the **condition** does or does not occur.[8] It becomes a covenant if the condition is met, however.

Generally, contractual language such as *if, on condition that, provided that, when, after,* and *as soon as* indicates a condition. A single contract may contain numerous conditions that trigger or excuse performance.

There are three primary types of conditions: *conditions precedent, conditions subsequent,* and *concurrent conditions.* Each of these are discussed in the following paragraphs.

condition
A qualification of a promise that becomes a covenant if it is met. There are three types of conditions: conditions precedent, conditions subsequent, and concurrent conditions.

Condition Precedent

If a contract requires the occurrence (or nonoccurrence) of an event *before* a party is obligated to perform a contractual duty, this is a **condition precedent**. The happening (or non-happening) of the event triggers the contract or duty of performance. If the event does not occur, no duty to perform the contract arises because there is a failure of condition.

condition precedent
A condition that requires the occurrence of an event before a party is obligated to perform a duty under a contract.

Condition Precedent Based on Satisfaction Some contracts reserve the right to a party to pay for services provided by the other only if the services meet the first party's "satisfaction." The courts have developed two tests—the *personal satisfaction test* and the *reasonable person test*—to determine whether this special form of condition precedent has been met:

1. **Personal satisfaction test.** The **personal satisfaction test** is a *subjective* test that applies if the performance involves personal taste and comfort (e.g., contracts for interior decorating, contracts for tailoring clothes). The only requirement is that the person given the right to reject the contract acts in good faith.

   Example Gretchen employs an artist to paint her daughter's portrait. The contract provides that Gretchen does not have to accept and pay for the portrait unless she is personally satisfied with it. This is a condition precedent based upon the personal satisfaction test. Gretchen rejects the painting because she personally dislikes it. This rejection is lawful because it is based on the personal satisfaction test.

personal satisfaction test
A subjective test that applies to contracts involving personal taste and comfort.

2. **Reasonable person test.** The **reasonable person test** is an *objective* test that is used to judge contracts involving mechanical fitness and most commercial contracts. Most contracts that require the work to meet the satisfaction of a third person (e.g., engineer, architect) are judged by this standard.

   Example E-Commerce Company hires Einstein to install a state-of-the-art Internet webpage ordering system that will handle its order entry and record-keeping functions. Einstein installs a state-of-the-art Internet webpage ordering system that meets current industry standards. E-Commerce Company rejects the contract as not meeting its personal satisfaction. This is a breach of contract because the personal satisfaction test does not apply to this contract. Instead, the objective reasonable person test applies, and a reasonable e-commerce company in the same situation would have accepted the system.

reasonable person test
An objective test that applies to commercial contracts and contracts involving mechanical fitness.

CONTEMPORARY ENVIRONMENT
"Time Is of the Essence"

Generally, there is a breach of contract if a contract is not performed when due. Nevertheless, if the other party is not jeopardized by the delay, most courts treat the delay as a minor breach and give the nonperforming party additional time to perform.

Conversely, if a contract expressly provides that **"time is of the essence"** or similar language, performance by the stated time is an express condition. There is a breach of contract if the contracting party does not perform by the stated date.

Freedom of contracts begins where equality of bargaining power begins.

Oliver Wendell Holmes, Jr.
(1928)

condition subsequent
A condition whose occurrence or nonoccurrence of a specific event automatically excuses the performance of an existing contractual duty to perform.

concurrent condition
A condition that exists when the parties to a contract must render performance simultaneously; each party's absolute duty to perform is conditioned on the other party's absolute duty to perform.

implied-in-fact condition
A condition that can be implied from the circumstances surrounding a contract and the parties' conduct.

Condition Subsequent

A **condition subsequent** exists when there is a condition in a contract which provides that the occurrence or nonoccurrence of a specific event automatically excuses the performance of an existing duty to perform. That is, failure to meet the condition subsequent relieves the other party from obligation under the contract.

Note that the *Restatement (Second) of Contracts* eliminates the distinction between conditions precedent and conditions subsequent. Both are referred to as "conditions."[9]

Concurrent Conditions

Concurrent conditions arise when the parties to a contract agree to render performance simultaneously—that is, when each party's absolute duty to perform is conditioned on the other party's absolute duty to perform.

Example A contract by Samantha's Club to purchase goods from Kid's Toys Inc. provides that payment is due upon delivery of the goods. In other words, Samantha's Club's duty to pay and Kid's Toys Inc.'s duty to deliver the goods are concurrent conditions. Recovery of damages is available if one party fails to respond to the other party's performance.

Implied Condition

Any of the previous types of conditions may be further classified as either express or implied conditions. An *express condition* exists if the parties expressly agree on it. An **implied-in-fact-condition** is one that can be implied from the circumstances surrounding a contract and the parties' conduct.

Example A contract in which a buyer agrees to purchase grain from a farmer implies that there are proper street access to the delivery site, proper unloading facilities, and the like.

CONCEPT SUMMARY
TYPES OF CONDITIONS

Type of Condition	Description
Condition precedent	A specified event must occur or not occur before a party is obligated to perform contractual duties.
Condition subsequent	The occurrence or nonoccurrence of a specified event excuses the performance of an existing contractual duty to perform.
Concurrent condition	The parties to a contract are obligated to render performance simultaneously. Each party's duty to perform is conditioned on the other party's duty to perform.
Implied condition	An implied-in-fact condition is implied from the circumstances surrounding a contract and the parties' conduct.

▶ DISCHARGE OF PERFORMANCE

A party's duty to perform under a contract may be discharged by *mutual agreement* of the parties, by *impossibility of performance*, or by *operation of law*. These methods of discharge are discussed in the paragraphs that follow.

Men keep agreements when it is to the advantage of neither to break them.

Solon

Discharge by Agreement

In many situations, the parties to a contract mutually decide to **discharge** their contractual duties. The parties can do so by *mutual rescission, substituted contract, novation,* and *accord and satisfaction.* The different types of mutual agreement are discussed in the following paragraphs:

Mutual Rescission   If a contract is wholly or partially executory on both sides, the parties can agree to rescind (i.e., cancel) the contract. **Mutual rescission** requires parties to enter into a second agreement that expressly terminates the first one.

Unilateral rescission of a contract by one of the parties without the other party's consent is not effective. Unilateral rescission of a contract constitutes a breach of that contract.

Substituted Contract   The parties to a contract may enter into a new contract that revokes and discharges an existing contract. The new contract is called a **substituted contract**.

If one of the parties fails to perform his or her duties under a substituted contract, the nonbreaching party can sue to enforce its terms against the breaching party. The prior contract cannot be enforced against the breaching party because it has been discharged.

Novation   A **novation agreement** (commonly called **novation**) substitutes a third party for one of the original contracting parties. The new substituted party is obligated to perform the contract. All three parties must agree to the substitution. In a novation, the exiting party is relieved of liability on the contract.

novation agreement
An agreement that substitutes a new party for one of the original contracting parties and relieves the exiting party of liability on the contract. Also known as simply a *novation.*

Accord and Satisfaction   The parties to a contract may agree to settle a contract dispute by an **accord and satisfaction**. The agreement whereby the parties agree to accept something different in satisfaction of the original contract is called an *accord*.[10] The performance of an accord is called a *satisfaction*.

An accord does not discharge the original contract. It only suspends it until the accord is performed. Satisfaction of the accord discharges both the original contract and the accord. If an accord is not satisfied when it is due, the aggrieved party may enforce either the accord or the original contract.

accord and satisfaction
The settlement of a contract dispute.

Discharge by Impossibility

Under certain circumstances, the nonperformance of contractual duties is excused—that is, discharged—because of *impossibility of performance*. **Impossibility of performance** (or **objective impossibility**) occurs if a contract becomes impossible to perform.[11] The impossibility must be objective impossibility ("it cannot be done") rather than subjective impossibility ("I cannot do it"). The following types of objective impossibility excuse nonperformance:

impossibility of performance
Nonperformance that is excused if a contract becomes impossible to perform. It must be objective impossibility, not subjective.

• The death or incapacity of the promisor prior to the performance of a personal service contract[12]

Example If a professional athlete dies prior to or during a contract period, his or her contract with the team is discharged.

• The destruction of the subject matter of a contract prior to performance[13]

Example If a building is destroyed by fire, the lessees are discharged from further performance unless otherwise provided in the lease.

- A supervening illegality that makes performance of the contract illegal[14]

Example An art dealer contracts to purchase native art found in a foreign country. The contract is discharged if the foreign country enacts a law forbidding native art from being exported from the country before the contract is performed.

In the following case, the court had to decide whether impossibility existed that excused performance.

CASE 15.1 Impossibility of Performance

Parker v. Arthur Murray, Inc.
295 N.E.2d 487, Web 1973 Ill.App. Lexis 2760 (1973)
Appellate Court of Illinois

"Although neither party to a contract should be relieved from performance on the ground that good business judgment was lacking, a court will not place upon language a ridiculous construction."

—Judge Stamos

Facts

Ryland S. Parker, a 37-year-old college-educated bachelor, went to the Arthur Murray Studios (Arthur Murray) in Oak Park, Illinois, to redeem a certificate entitling him to three free dancing lessons. At that time, he lived alone in a one-room attic apartment. During the free lessons, the instructor told Parker that he had "exceptional potential to be a fine and accomplished dancer." Parker thereupon signed a contract for more lessons. Parker attended lessons regularly and was praised and encouraged by his instructors despite his lack of progress. Contract extensions and new contracts for additional instructional hours were executed, which Parker prepaid. Each written contract contained the bold-type words "NONCANCELABLE CONTRACT." Two years after having started to take dancing lessons, Parker was severely injured in an automobile accident, rendering him incapable of continuing his dancing lessons. At that time, he had contracted for a total of 2,734 hours of dance lessons, for which he had prepaid $24,812. When Arthur Murray refused to refund any of the money, Parker sued to rescind the outstanding contracts. The trial courts held in favor of Parker and ordered Arthur Murray to return the prepaid contract payments. Arthur Murray appealed.

Issue

Does the doctrine of impossibility excuse Parker's performance of the personal service contracts?

Language of the Court

Plaintiff was granted rescission on the grounds of impossibility of performance. Defendants do not deny that the doctrine of impossibility of performance is generally applicable to the case at bar. Rather they assert that certain contract provisions bring the case within the Restatement's limitation that the doctrine is inapplicable if "the contract indicates a contrary intention." It is contended that such bold-type phrases as "NON-CANCELLABLE CONTRACT," NON-CANCELLABLE NEGOTIABLE CONTRACT," and "I UNDERSTAND THAT NO REFUNDS WILL BE MADE UNDER THE TERMS OF THIS CONTRACT" manifest the parties' mutual intent to waive their respective rights to invoke the doctrine of impossibility.

This is a construction that we find unacceptable. Courts engage in the construction and interpretation of contracts with the sole aim of determining the intention of the parties. We need rely on no construction aids to conclude that plaintiff never contemplated that by signing a contract with such terms as "NON-CANCELLABLE" and "NO REFUNDS," he was waiving a remedy expressly recognized by Illinois courts. Although neither party to a contract should be relieved from performance on the ground that good business judgment was lacking, a court will not place upon language a ridiculous construction. We conclude that plaintiff did not waive his right to assert the doctrine of impossibility.

Suffice it to say that overwhelming evidence supported plaintiff's contention that he was incapable of continuing his lessons.

Decision

The appellate court held that the doctrine of impossibility of performance excused Parker's performance of the personal service contracts. The appellate court affirmed the trial court's judgment that ordered Arthur Murray to return the prepaid contract payments.

Case Questions

Critical Legal Thinking What does the doctrine of impossibility of performance provide? Explain.

Business Ethics Did Arthur Murray act ethically in not returning Parker's money? Did Arthur Murray act ethically by allowing Parker to sign up for and prepay for over 2,700 hours of dance lessons?

Contemporary Business Should the doctrine of impossibility excuse parties from performance of their contracts? Why or why not?

Force Majeure Clause

The parties may agree in a contract that certain events will excuse nonperformance of the contract. These clauses are called *force majeure* **clauses**.

Example A *force majeure* clause usually excuses nonperformance caused by natural disasters such as floods, tornadoes, earthquakes, and such. Modern clauses also often excuse performance due to labor strikes, shortages of raw materials, and the like.

> *force majeure* **clause**
> A clause in a contract in which the parties specify certain events that will excuse nonperformance.

Commercial Impracticability

Many states recognize the doctrine of **commercial impracticability** as an excuse for nonperformance of contracts. Commercial impracticability excuses performance if an unforeseeable event makes it impractical for the promisor to perform. This doctrine has not yet been fully developed by the courts. It is examined on a case-by-case basis.

Example A utility company enters into a contract to purchase uranium for its nuclear-powered generator from a uranium supplier at a fixed price of $1 million per year for five years. Suppose a new uranium cartel is formed worldwide, and the supplier must pay $5 million for uranium to supply the utility with each year's supply. It is not impossible for the supplier to satisfy the contract: The supplier can purchase the uranium for $5 million and resell it to the utility company for $1 million (losing $4 million per year). However, in this situation, the court would likely allow the supplier to rescind its contract with the utility based on commercial impracticability.

> **commercial impracticability**
> Nonperformance that is excused if an extreme or unexpected development or expense makes it impractical for the promisor to perform.

Statute of Limitations

Certain legal rules discharge parties from performing contractual duties. Every state has a **statute of limitations** that applies to contract actions. Although the time periods vary from state to state, the usual period for bringing a lawsuit for breach of contract is one to five years. The UCC provides that a cause of action based on a breach of sales or lease contract must be brought within four years after the cause of action accrues.[15]

> **statute of limitations**
> A statute that establishes the time period during which a lawsuit must be brought; if the lawsuit is not brought within this period, the injured party loses the right to sue.

Bankruptcy

Bankruptcy, which is governed by federal law, is a means of allocating the debtor's nonexempt property to satisfy his or her debts. Debtors may also reorganize in bankruptcy. In most cases, the debtor's assets are insufficient to pay all the creditors' claims. In this case, the debtor receives a **discharge** of the unpaid debts. The debtor is then relieved of legal liability to pay the discharged debts.

TEST REVIEW TERMS AND CONCEPTS

Accord and satisfaction	Approval clause	Assignment of right (assignment)	Concurrent condition
American rule (New York Rule)	Assignee	Assignor	Condition
Anti-assignment clause	Assignment and delegation	Assumption of duties	Conditional promise
Anti-delegation clause	Assignment of future right	Commercial impracticability	Condition precedent
			Condition subsequent

Covenant
Creditor beneficiary
Creditor beneficiary contract
Delegate
Delegatee
Delegator
Delegation of a duty
  (delegation)
Discharge by agreement
Discharge in bankruptcy

Donee beneficiary
Donee beneficiary contract
English rule
Force majeure clause
Implied-in-fact-condition
Impossibility of performance
  (objective impossibility)
Incidental beneficiary
Intended third-party
  beneficiary

Mutual rescission
Notice of assignment
Novation agreement
  (novation)
Obligee
Obligor
Personal satisfaction test
Personal service contract
Possession of tangible token
  rule

Privity of contract
Promisee
Promisor
Reasonable person test
Statute of limitation
Subsequent assignee
  (subassignee)
Substituted contract
Third-party beneficiary
"Time is of the essence"

CASE PROBLEMS

15.1 Third-Party Beneficiary   Eugene H. Emmick hired L. S. Hamm, an attorney, to draft his will. The will named Robert Lucas and others (Lucas) as beneficiaries. When Emmick died, it was discovered that the will was improperly drafted, violated state law, and was therefore ineffective. Emmick's estate was transferred pursuant to the state's intestate laws. Lucas did not receive the $75,000 he would have otherwise received had the will been valid. Lucas sued Hamm for breach of the Emmick–Hamm contract to recover what he would have received under the will. Who wins? *Lucas v. Hamm*, 56 Cal.2d 583, 364 P.2d 685, 15 Cal.Rptr. 821, **Web** 1961 Cal. Lexis 321 (Supreme Court of California)

15.2 Third-Party Beneficiary   Angelo Boussiacos hired Demetrios Sofias, a general contractor, to build a restaurant for him. Boussiacos entered into a loan agreement with Bank of America (B of A) whereby B of A would provide the construction financing to build the restaurant. The loan agreement provided that loan funds would be periodically disbursed by B of A to Boussiacos at different stages of construction, as requested by Boussiacos. Problems arose in the progress of the construction. When Boussiacos did not pay Sofias for certain work that had been done, Sofias sued B of A for breach of contract to collect payment directly from B of A. Can Sofias maintain the lawsuit against B of A? *Sofias v. Bank of America*, 172 Cal.App.3d 583, 218 Cal.Rptr. 388, **Web** 1985 Cal.App. Lexis 2545 (Court of Appeal of California)

15.3 Assignment   William John Cunningham, a professional basketball player, entered into a contract with Southern Sports Corporation, which owned the Carolina Cougars, a professional basketball team. The contract provided that Cunningham was to play basketball for the Cougars for a three-year period. The contract contained a provision that it could not be assigned to any other professional basketball franchise without Cunningham's approval. Subsequently, Southern Sports Corporation sold its assets, including its franchise and Cunningham's contract, to the Munchak Corporation (Munchak). There was no change in the location of the Cougars after the purchase. When Cunningham refused to play for the new owners, Munchak sued to enforce Cunningham's contract. Is Cunningham's contract assignable to the new owner? *Munchak Corporation v. Cunningham*, 457 F.2d 721, **Web** 1972 U.S. App. Lexis 10272 (United States Court of Appeals for the Fourth Circuit)

15.4 Assignment   Berlinger Foods Corporation (Berlinger), pursuant to an oral contract, became a distributor for Häagen-Dazs ice cream. Over the next decade, both parties flourished as the marketing of high-quality, high-priced ice cream took hold. Berlinger successfully promoted the sale of Häagen-Dazs to supermarket chains and other retailers in the Baltimore–Washington, DC, area. Ten years later, the Pillsbury Company acquired Häagen-Dazs. Pillsbury adhered to the oral distribution agreement and retained Berlinger as a distributor for Häagen-Dazs ice cream. Two years later, Berlinger entered into a contract and sold its assets to Dreyers, a manufacturer of premium ice cream that competed with Häagen-Dazs. Dreyers ice cream had previously been sold primarily in the western part of the United States. Dreyers attempted to expand its market to the east by choosing to purchase Berlinger as a means to obtain distribution in the mid-Atlantic region. When Pillsbury learned of the sale, it advised Berlinger that its distributorship for Häagen-Dazs was terminated. Berlinger, which wanted to remain a distributor for Häagen-Dazs, sued Pillsbury for breach of contract, alleging that the oral distribution agreement with Häagen-Dazs and Pillsbury was properly assigned to Dreyers. Who wins? *Berlinger Foods Corporation v. The Pillsbury Company*, 633 F.Supp. 557, **Web** 1986 U.S. Dist. Lexis 26431 (United States District Court for the District of Maryland)

15.5 Anti-Assignment Clause   The city of Vancouver, Washington, contracted with B & B Contracting Corporation (B & B) to construct a well pump at a city-owned water station. The contract contained the following anti-assignment clause: "The contractor shall not assign this contract or any part thereof, or any moneys due or to become due thereunder." The work was not completed on time, and the city withheld $6,510 as liquidated damages from the contract price. B & B assigned the claim to this money to Portland Electric and Plumbing Company (PEPCo). PEPCo, as the assignee, filed suit against the City of Vancouver, alleging that the city had breached its contract with B & B by wrongfully refusing to pay $6,510 to B & B. Can PEPCo maintain the lawsuit against the City of Vancouver? *Portland Electric and Plumbing Company v. City of Vancouver*, 29 Wn.App. 292, 627 P.2d 1350, **Web** 1981 Wash.App. Lexis 2295 (Court of Appeals of Washington)

15.6 Delegation of Duties   C.W. Milford owned a registered Quarterhorse named Hired Chico. Milford sold the horse to Norman Stewart. Recognizing that Hired Chico was a good stud, Milford included the following provision in the written contract that was signed by both parties: "I, C.W. Milford, reserve 2 breedings each year on Hired Chico registration #403692 for the life of this stud horse regardless of whom the horse may be sold to." The agreement was filed with the County Court Clerk of Shelby County, Texas. Stewart later sold Hired Chico to Sam McKinnie. Prior to purchasing the horse, McKinnie read the Milford–Stewart contract and testified that he understood the terms of the contract. When McKinnie refused to grant Milford the stud services of Hired Chico, Milford sued McKinnie for breach of contract. Who wins? *McKinnie v. Milford*, 597 S.W.2d 953, **Web** 1980 Tex.App. Lexis 3345 (Court of Appeals of Texas)

15.7 Condition   Shumann Investments, Inc. (Shumann), hired Pace Construction Corporation (Pace), a general contractor, to build "Outlet World of Pasco Country." In turn, Pace hired OBS Company, Inc. (OBS), a subcontractor, to perform the framing, drywall, insulation, and stucco work on the project. The contract between Pace and OBS stipulated:

"Final payment shall not become due unless and until the following conditions precedent to final payment have been satisfied . . . (c) receipt of final payment for subcontractor's work by contractor from owner." When Shumann refused to pay Pace, Pace refused to pay OBS. OBS sued Pace to recover payment. Who wins? *Pace Construction Corporation v. OBS Company, Inc.*, 531 So.2d 737, **Web** 1988 Fla.App. Lexis 4020 (Court of Appeal of Florida)

15.8 Excuse of Condition   Maco, Inc. (Maco), a roofing contractor, hired Brian Barrows as a salesperson. Barrows was assigned a geographical territory and was responsible for securing contracts for Maco within his territory. The employment contract provided that Barrows was to receive a 26 percent commission on the net profits from roofing contracts that he obtained. The contract contained the following provision: "To qualify for payment of the commission, the salesperson must sell and supervise the job; the job must be completed and paid for; and the salesperson must have been in the continuous employment of Maco, Inc., during the aforementioned period." Barrows obtained a $129,603 contract with the Board of Education of Cook County for Maco to make repairs to the roof of the Hoover School in Evanston, Illinois. During the course of the work, Barrows visited the site more than 60 times. Before the work was completed, Maco fired Barrows. Later, Maco refused to pay Barrows the commission when the project was completed and paid for. Barrows sued Maco to recover the commission. Who wins? *Barrows v. Maco, Inc.*, 94 Ill.App.3d 959, 419 N.E.2d 634, **Web** 1981 Ill. App. Lexis 2371 (Appellate Court of Illinois)

BUSINESS ETHICS CASES

15.9 Business Ethics   Pabagold, Inc. (Pabagold), a manufacturer and distributor of suntan lotions, hired Mediasmith, an advertising agency, to develop an advertising campaign for Pabagold's Hawaiian Gold Pabatan suntan lotion. In the contract, Pabagold authorized Mediasmith to enter into agreements with third parties to place Pabagold advertisements for the campaign and to make payments to these third parties for the Pabagold account. Pabagold agreed to pay Mediasmith for its services and to reimburse it for expenses incurred on behalf of Pabagold. The Pabagold–Mediasmith contract provided for arbitration of any dispute arising under the contract.

Mediasmith entered into a contract with Outdoor Services, Inc. (Outdoor Services), an outdoor advertising company, to place Pabagold ads on billboards owned by Outdoor Services. Outdoor Services provided the agreed-upon work and billed Mediasmith $8,545 for its services. Mediasmith requested payment of this amount from Pabagold so it could pay Outdoor Services. When Pabagold refused to pay, Outdoor

Services filed a demand for arbitration, as provided in the Pabagold–Mediasmith contract. Pabagold defended, asserting that Outdoor Services could not try to recover the money because it was not in privity of contract with Pabagold.

Did Pabagold act ethically in refusing to pay Outdoor Services? From an ethical perspective, does it matter that Outdoor Services and Pabagold were not in privity of contract? Who wins? *Outdoor Services, Inc. v. Pabagold, Inc.*, 185 Cal.App.3d 676, 230 Cal.Rptr. 73, **Web** 1986 Cal.App. Lexis 2030 (Court of Appeal of California)

15.10 Business Ethics   Indiana Tri-City Plaza Bowl (Tri-City) leased a building from Charles H. Glueck for use as a bowling alley. The lease provided that Glueck was to provide adequate paved parking for the building. The lease gave Tri-City the right to approve the plans for the construction and paving of the parking lot. When Glueck submitted paving plans to Tri-City, it rejected the plans and withheld its approval. Tri-City argued that the plans were required to meet its personal satisfaction before it had to approve them.

Evidence showed that the plans were commercially reasonable in the circumstances. A lawsuit was filed between Tri-City and Glueck. Who wins? Was it ethical for Tri-City to reject the plans? *Indiana Tri-City Plaza Bowl, Inc. v. Estate of Glueck*, 422 N.E.2d 670, **Web** 1981 Ind.App. Lexis 1506 (Court of Appeals of Indiana)

ENDNOTES

1. *Restatement (Second) of Contracts*, Sections 311 and 318.
2. *Restatement (Second) of Contracts*, Section 317.
3. *Restatement (Second) of Contracts*, Section 318(2).
4. *Restatement (Second) of Contracts*, Section 328.
5. *Restatement (Second) of Contracts*, Section 302.
6. *Restatement (Second) of Contracts*, Section 302(1)(b).
7. *Restatement (Second) of Contracts*, Section 302(1)(a).
8. *The Restatement (Second) of Contracts*, Section 224, defines *condition* as "an event, not certain to occur, which must occur, unless its nonperformance is excused, before performance under a contract is due."
9. *Restatement (Second) of Contracts*, Section 224.
10. *Restatement (Second) of Contracts*, Section 281.
11. *Restatement (Second) of Contracts*, Section 261.
12. *Restatement (Second) of Contracts*, Section 262.
13. *Restatement (Second) of Contracts*, Section 263.
14. *Restatement (Second) of Contracts*, Section 264.
15. UCC Section 2-725 and UCC Section 2A-506.

▲ **Jewelry Store** *Many persons get engaged and most engagements result in a marriage. However, sometimes an engagement is broken off. Under the objective rule, the person who gave the engagement ring is entitled to the return of the ring and may bring a lawsuit to recover the ring if it is not voluntarily returned. Under the objective rule, the engagement ring must be returned, no matter which party broke off the engagement.*

CHAPTER OBJECTIVES

After studying this chapter, you should be able to:

1. Describe complete, substantial, and inferior performance of contractual duties.
2. Describe compensatory, consequential, and nominal damages awarded for the breach of traditional and e-contracts.
3. Explain rescission and restitution.
4. Define the equitable remedies of specific performance, reformation, and injunction.
5. Describe torts associated with contracts.

CHAPTER CONTENTS

> "Contracts must not be sports of an idle hour, mere matters of pleasantry and badinage, never intended by the parties to have any serious effect whatsoever."
>
> —Lord Stowell
> *Dalrymple v. Dalrymple, 2 Hag. Con. 54, at 105 (1811)*

▶ INTRODUCTION TO REMEDIES FOR BREACH OF TRADITIONAL AND E-CONTRACTS

breach of contract
A contracting party's failure to perform an absolute duty owed under a contract.

There are three levels of performance of a contract: *complete*, *substantial*, and *inferior*. Complete (or strict) performance by a party discharges that party's duties under the contract. Substantial performance constitutes a minor breach of the contract. Inferior performance constitutes a material breach that impairs or destroys the essence of the contract. Various remedies may be obtained by a nonbreaching party if a **breach of contract** occurs— that is, if a contracting party fails to perform an absolute duty owed under a contract.[1]

The most common remedy for a breach of contract is an award of *monetary damages*, often called the "law remedy." If a monetary award does not provide adequate relief, however, the court may order any one of several *equitable remedies*, including specific performance, reformation, and injunction. Equitable remedies are based on the concept of fairness.

This chapter discusses breach of contract and the remedies available to the nonbreaching party.

▶ PERFORMANCE AND BREACH

Men keep their agreements when it is an advantage to both parties not to break them.

Solon
(c. 600 B.C.)

If a contractual duty has not been discharged (i.e., terminated) or excused (i.e., relieved of legal liability), the contracting party owes an absolute duty (i.e., covenant) to perform the duty. As mentioned in the chapter introduction, there are three types of performance of a contract: (1) *complete performance*, (2) *substantial performance* (or minor breach), and (3) *inferior performance* (or material breach). These concepts are discussed in the following paragraphs.

Complete Performance

complete performance
A situation in which a party to a contract renders performance exactly as required by the contract. Complete performance discharges that party's obligations under the contract.

Most contracts are discharged by the **complete performance**, or **strict performance**, of the contracting parties. Complete performance occurs when a party to a contract renders performance exactly as required by the contract. A fully performed contract is called an **executed contract**.

tender of performance
An unconditional and absolute offer by a contracting party to perform his or her obligations under a contract. Also known as *tender*.

Tender of performance also discharges a party's contractual obligations. **Tender** is an unconditional and absolute offer by a contracting party to perform his or her obligations under the contract.

Example Ashley, who owns a women's retail store, contracts to purchase high-fashion blue jeans from a manufacturer for $75,000. At the time of performance, Ashley tenders the $75,000. Ashley has performed her obligation under the contract once she tenders the $75,000 to the manufacturer. The manufacturer fails to deliver the blue jeans. There is no completed contract, and Ashley can sue the manufacturer for breach of contract.

Substantial Performance: Minor Breach

substantial performance
Performance by a contracting party that deviates only slightly from complete performance.

Substantial performance occurs when there has been a **minor breach** of contract. In other words, it occurs when a party to a contract renders performance that deviates slightly from complete performance. The nonbreaching party may try to convince the breaching party to

minor breach
A breach that occurs when a party renders substantial performance of his or her contractual duties.

elevate his or her performance to complete performance. If the breaching party does not correct the breach, the nonbreaching party can sue to recover *damages* by (1) deducting the cost to repair the defect from the contract price and remitting the balance to the breaching party or (2) suing the breaching party to recover the cost to repair the defect if the breaching party has already been paid (see Exhibit 16.1).

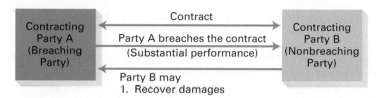

▶ **Exhibit 16.1 REMEDY WHERE THERE HAS BEEN SUBSTANTIAL PERFORMANCE (MINOR BREACH)**

No cause of action arises from a bare promise.

Legal maxim

Examples Donald Trump contracts with Big Apple Construction Co. to have Big Apple construct an office building for $100 million. The architectural plans call for installation of three-ply windows in the building. Big Apple constructs the building exactly to plan except that it installs two-ply windows. There has been substantial performance. It would cost $5 million to install the correct windows. If Big Apple agrees to replace the windows and does so, its performance is elevated to complete performance, and Trump must pay the entire contract price. However, if Trump has to hire someone else to replace the windows, he may deduct this cost of repair of $5 million from the contract price of $100 million and remit the difference of $95 million to Big Apple.

Inferior Performance: Material Breach

A **material breach** of a contract occurs when a party renders **inferior performance** of his or her contractual obligations that impairs or destroys the essence of the contract. There is no clear line between a minor breach and a material breach. A determination is made on a case-by-case basis.

Where there has been a material breach of contract, the nonbreaching party may *rescind* the contract and seek restitution of any compensation paid under the contract to the breaching party. The nonbreaching party is discharged from any further performance under the contract.[2] Alternatively, the nonbreaching party may treat the contract as being in effect and sue the breaching party to recover *damages* (see Exhibit 16.2).

material breach
A breach that occurs when a party renders inferior performance of his or her contractual duties.

inferior performance
A situation in which a party fails to perform express or implied contractual obligations and impairs or destroys the essence of a contract.

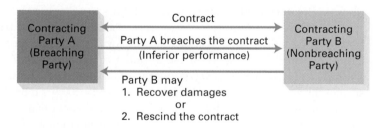

▶ **Exhibit 16.2 REMEDIES WHERE THERE HAS BEEN INFERIOR PERFORMANCE (MATERIAL BREACH)**

Example A university contracts with a general contractor to build a new three-story classroom building with classroom space for 1,000 students. The contract price is $100 million. However, the completed building cannot support more than 500 students because the contractor used inferior materials. The defect cannot be repaired without rebuilding the entire structure. Because this is a material breach, the university may rescind the contract, recover any money that it has paid to the contractor, and require the contractor to remove the building. The university is discharged of any obligations under the contract and is free to employ another contractor to rebuild the building. However, the building does meet building codes so that it can be used as an administration building of the university. Thus, as an alternative remedy, the university could accept the building as an administration building, which has a value of $20 million. The university would owe this amount—$20 million—to the contractor.

CONCEPT SUMMARY
TYPES OF PERFORMANCE

Type of Performance	Legal Consequence
Complete performance	The contract is discharged.
Substantial performance (minor breach)	The nonbreaching party may recover damages caused by the breach.
Inferior performance (material breach)	The nonbreaching party may either (1) rescind the contract and recover restitution or (2) affirm the contract and recover damages.

Anticipatory Breach

anticipatory breach
A breach that occurs when one contracting party informs the other that he or she will not perform his or her contractual duties when due.

Anticipatory breach (or **anticipatory repudiation**) of contract occurs when a contracting party informs the other party in advance that he or she will not perform his or her contractual duties when due. This type of material breach can be expressly stated or implied from the conduct of the repudiator. Where there is an anticipatory repudiation, the nonbreaching party's obligations under the contract are discharged immediately. The nonbreaching party also has the right to sue the repudiating party when the anticipatory breach occurs; there is no need to wait until performance is due.[3]

▶ MONETARY DAMAGES

monetary damages
An award of money.

A nonbreaching party may recover **monetary damages** from a breaching party. Monetary damages are available whether the breach was minor or material. Several types of monetary damages may be awarded. These include *compensatory, consequential, liquidated,* and *nominal damages.*

Compensatory Damages

compensatory damages
An award of money intended to compensate a nonbreaching party for the loss of the bargain. Compensatory damages place the nonbreaching party in the same position as if the contract had been fully performed by restoring the "benefit of the bargain."

Compensatory damages are intended to compensate a nonbreaching party for the loss of the bargain. In other words, they place the nonbreaching party in the same position as if the contract had been fully performed by restoring the "benefit of the bargain."

Examples Lederle Laboratories enters into a written contract to employ Wei as a chief operations officer (COO) of the company for three years, at a salary of $20,000 per month. After one year at work, Lederle informs Wei that her employment is terminated. This is a material breach of the contract. If Wei is unable to find a comparable job, Wei can sue Lederle Laboratiories and recover $480,000 (24 months × $20,000) as compensatory damages. If after six months Wei finds a comparable job that pays $20,000 per month, Wei can recover $360,000 from Laderle (18 months × $20,000) as compensatory damages. In these examples, the damages awarded to Wei place her in the same situation as if her contract with Lederle had been performed.

The amount of compensatory damages that will be awarded for breach of contract depends on the type of contract involved and which party breached the contract. The award of compensatory damages in some special types of contracts is discussed in the following paragraphs.

It is a vain thing to imagine a right without a remedy: for want of right and want of remedy are reciprocal.

Lord Chief Justice Holt
Ashby v. White (1703)

Sale of a Good   Compensatory damages for a breach of a sales contract involving goods are governed by the Uniform Commercial Code (UCC). The usual measure of damages for a breach of a sales contract is the difference between the contract price and the market price of the goods at the time and place the goods were to be delivered.[4]

Example Revlon, Inc., contracts to buy a piece of equipment from Greenway Supply Co. for $80,000. Greenway does not deliver the equipment to Revlon when it is required to do so. Revlon purchases the equipment from another vendor but has to pay $100,000 because the current market price for the equipment has risen. Revlon can recover $20,000 from

Greenway—the difference between the market price paid ($100,000) and the contract price ($80,000)—in compensatory damages.

Construction Contract   A construction contract arises when the owner of real property contracts to have a contractor build a structure or do other construction work. The compensatory damages recoverable for a breach of a construction contract vary with the stage of completion of the project when the breach occurs.

A contractor may recover the profits he or she would have made on the contract if the owner breaches the construction contract before construction begins.

Examples RXZ Corporation contracts to have Ace Construction Company build a factory building for $1,200,000. It will cost Ace $800,000 in materials and labor to build the factory for RXZ. If RXZ Corporation breaches the contract before construction begins, Ace can recover $400,000 in "lost profits" from RXZ as compensatory damages.

Example Entel Corporation contracts to have the Beta Construction Company build a factory building for Entel for $1,200,000. It will cost Beta Construction Company $800,000 to construct the building. Thus, Beta Corporation will make $400,000 profit on the contract. Beta begins construction and has spent $300,000 on materials and labor before Entel breaches the contract by terminating Beta. Here, Beta can recover $700,000, which is comprised of $400,000 lost profits ($1,200,000 − $800,000) plus $300,000 expended on materials and labor. The $700,000 of compensatory damages will make Beta Construction Company "whole."

If the builder breaches a construction contract, either before or during construction, the owner can recover the increased cost above the contract price that he or she has to pay to have the work completed by another contractor.

Example Ethenol Corporation contracts to have the Sherry Construction Company build a factory building for Ethenol for $1,200,000. Just before Sherry Construction Company is to begin work, it breaches the contract by withdrawing from the project. Ethenol seeks new bids, and the lowest bid to construct the building is $1,700,000. Here, Ethenol can recover $500,000 in compensatory damages from Sherry Construction Company (the $1,700,000 new contract price − $1,200,000 Sherry Construction's original price).

Employment Contract   An employee whose employer breaches an employment contract can recover lost wages or salary as compensatory damages. If the employee breaches the contract, the employer can recover the costs to hire a new employee plus any increase in salary paid to the replacement.

Mitigation of Damages

If a contract has been breached, the law places a duty on the innocent nonbreaching party to make reasonable efforts to **mitigate** (i.e., avoid or reduce) the resulting damages. The extent of mitigation required depends on the type of contract involved.

If an employer breaches an employment contract, the employee owes a duty to mitigate damages by trying to find substitute employment. The employee is only required to accept *comparable employment*. The courts consider such factors as compensation, rank, status, job description, and geographical location in determining the comparability of jobs.

Consequential Damages

A nonbreaching party can sometimes recover **consequential damages**, or **special damages**, from the breaching party. Consequential damages are **foreseeable damages** that arise from circumstances outside a contract. To be liable for consequential damages, the breaching party must know or have reason to know that the breach will cause special damages to the other party.

Example W-Mart, a major retailer, contracts with Maytell, a major manufacturer of toys, to purchase 1,000,000 of the new "G.I. Barby Dolls" produced by Maytell at $20 per doll. W-Mart plans to sell these dolls in its stores nationwide at $50 per doll, and Maytell is

Every unjust decision is a reproach to the law or the judge who administers it. If the law should be in danger of doing injustice, then equity should be called in to remedy it. Equity was introduced to mitigate the rigor of the law.

Lord Denning, Master of
the Rolls
Re: Vandervell's Trusts (1974)

mitigation
A nonbreaching party's legal duty to avoid or reduce damages caused by a breach of contract.

consequential damages
Foreseeable damages that arise from circumstances outside a contract. To be liable for these damages, the breaching party must know or have reason to know that the breach will cause special damages to the other party.

aware that W-Mart intends to resell the dolls. The popularity of Barby Dolls guarantees that all the dolls purchased by W-Mart will be sold. If Maytell breaches this contract and fails to deliver the dolls to W-Mart, W-Mart cannot purchase the dolls elsewhere because Maytell holds the copyright and trademark on the doll. Therefore, W-Mart can recover the lost profits on each lost sale as consequential damages from Maytell—that is, the difference between the would-be sales price of the dolls ($50) and the purchase price of each doll ($20), or $30 lost profit per doll. In total, W-Mart can recover $30 million in consequential damages from Maytell ($50 − $20 = $30 × 1,000,000).

Liquidated Damages

> *The very definition of a good award is that it gives dissatisfaction to both parties.*
>
> Sir Thomas Plumer, Master of the Rolls
> *Goodman v. Sayers* (1820)

liquidated damages
Damages that parties to a contract agree in advance should be paid if the contract is breached.

Under certain circumstances, the parties to a contract may agree in advance to the amount of damages payable upon a breach of contract. These damages are called **liquidated damages**. To be lawful, the actual damages must be difficult or impracticable to determine, and the liquidated amount must be reasonable in the circumstances.[5] An enforceable liquidated damages clause is an exclusive remedy, even if actual damages are later determined to be different.

A liquidated damages clause is considered a **penalty** if actual damages are clearly determinable in advance or if the liquidated damages are excessive or unconscionable. If a liquidated damages clause is found to be a penalty, it is unenforceable. The nonbreaching party may then recover actual damages.

ETHICS SPOTLIGHT

Liquidated Damages at Trump World Tower

"In his affidavit Donald Trump stated that he sought 25% down payments from preconstruction purchasers at the Trump World Tower because of the substantial length of time between contract signing and closing, and because of the obvious associated risks."

—Judge Mazzarelli

The Trump World Tower is a luxury condominium building constructed at 845 United Nations Plaza in Manhattan, New York. Donald Trump is managing general partner of the building, which is New York City's highest residential building. 845 UN Limited Partnership (845 UN) began selling condominiums at the building before the building was constructed. The condominium offering plan required a nonrefundable down payment of 25 percent of the purchase price. The purchase contract provided that if a purchaser defaulted and did not complete the purchase, 845 UN could keep the 25 percent down payment as liquidated damages.

Cem Uzan and Hakan Uzan, brothers and Turkish billionaires, each contracted to purchase two condominium units on the top floors of the building. Cem and Hakan were both represented by attorneys. Over the course of two years, while the building was being constructed, the brothers paid the 25 percent nonrefundable down payment of $8 million. On September 11, 2001, before the building was complete, terrorists attacked New York City by flying two planes into the World Trade Center, the city's two tallest buildings, murdering thousands of people. Cem and Hakan sent letters to 845 UN, rescinding their purchase agreements because of the terrorist attack that occurred on September 11.

That day, 845 UN sent Cem and Hakan default letters, notifying them that they had 30 days to cure their default. Upon the expiration of the cure period, 845 UN terminated the four purchase agreements and kept the 25 percent down payments on the four condominiums as liquidated damages. Cem and Hakan sued 845 UN, alleging that the 25 percent nonrefundable down payment liquidated damages clause was an unenforceable and unconscionable penalty and that the money should be returned to them. 845 UN defended, arguing that the 25 percent nonrefundable down payment was an enforceable liquidated damages clause. The issue for the court was: Is the 25 percent nonrefundable down payment an enforceable liquidated damages clause, or is it an unconscionable and unenforceable penalty?

The supreme court of New York, appellate division, sided with 845 UN and held that Cem and Hakan had breached their contract with 845 UN and that 845 UN was entitled to keep the 25 percent down payment as liquidated damages. The court stated:

It is clear that plaintiffs are not entitled to a return of any portion of their down payment. Here the 25% down payment was a specifically negotiated element of the contracts. There is no question that this was an arm's length transaction. The parties were sophisticated businesspeople, represented by counsel, who spent two months at the bargaining table before executing the amended purchase agreements. The detailed provision concerning the nonrefundable deposit was integral to the transaction. Clearly, plaintiffs were fully aware of and accepted the requirement of a nonrefundable 25%

down payment for these luxury preconstruction condominiums. If plaintiffs were dissatisfied with the 25% nonrefundable down payment provision in the purchase agreements, the time to have voiced objection was at the bargaining table.

The appellate court held that the 25 percent nonrefundable down payment was an enforceable liquidated damages clause and not an unconscionable penalty. The appellate court, as a matter of law, granted 845 UN's motion for summary judgment, allowing 845 UN to keep

Cem and Hakan's down payments and dismissed their complaint. *Uzan v. 845 UN Limited Partnership*, 10 A.D.3d 230, 778 N.Y.S.2d 171, **Web** 2004 N.Y.App. Div. Lexis 8362 (Supreme Court of New York, Appellate Division)

Business Ethics   Should sophisticated businesspersons be held to their bargains? Was it ethical for Cem and Hakan to try to back out of the purchase agreements and get their money back? Was it ethical for Donald Trump and 845 UN not to pay Cem and Hakan their money back?

Nominal Damages

A nonbreaching party can sue a breaching party to a contract for nominal damages even if no financial loss resulted from the breach. **Nominal damages** are usually awarded in a small amount, such as $1. Cases involving nominal damages are usually brought on principle. Most courts disfavor nominal damages lawsuits because they use valuable court time and resources.

Example Mary enters into an employment contract with Microhard Corporation. It is a three-year contract, and Mary is to be paid $100,000 per year. After Mary works for one year, Microhard Corporation fires Mary. The next day, Mary finds a better position at Microsoft Corporation, in the same city, paying $125,000 per year on a two-year contract. Mary has suffered no monetary damages but could bring a civil lawsuit against Microhard Corporation because of its breach and recover nominal damages ($1).

nominal damages
Damages awarded when the nonbreaching party sues the breaching party even though no financial loss has resulted from the breach. Nominal damages are usually $1 or some other small amount.

CONCEPT SUMMARY

TYPES OF MONETARY DAMAGES

Type of Damage	Description
Compensatory	Damages that compensate a nonbreaching party for the loss of a bargain. It places the nonbreaching party in the same position as if the contract had been fully performed.
Consequential	Damages that compensate a nonbreaching party for foreseeable special damages that arise from circumstance outside a contract. The breaching party must have known or should have known that these damages would result from the breach.
Liquidated	An agreement by the parties in advance that sets the amount of damages recoverable in case of breach. These damages are lawful if they do not cause a penalty.
Nominal	Damages awarded against the breaching party even though the nonbreaching party has suffered no financial loss because of the breach. A small amount (e.g., $1) is usually awarded.

Enforcement of Remedies

If a nonbreaching party brings a successful lawsuit against a breaching party to a contract, the court will enter a **judgment** in his or her favor. This judgment must then be collected. If the breaching party refuses to pay the judgment, the court may:

- **Issue a writ of attachment.** A **writ of attachment** orders the sheriff or other government officer to seize property in the possession of the breaching party that he or she owns and to sell the property at auction to satisfy the judgment.
- **Issue a writ of garnishment.** A **writ of garnishment** orders that wages, bank accounts, or other property of the breaching party that is in the hands of third parties be paid over to the nonbreaching party to satisfy the judgment. Federal and state laws limit the amount of the breaching party's wages or salary that can be garnished.

writ of attachment
An order of the court that enables a government officer to seize property of the breaching party and sell it at auction to satisfy a judgment.

writ of garnishment
An order of the court that orders that wages, bank accounts, or other property of the breaching party held by third persons be paid to the nonbreaching party to satisfy a judgment.

▶ RESCISSION AND RESTITUTION

rescission
An action to rescind (undo) a contract. Rescission is available if there has been a material breach of contract, fraud, duress, undue influence, or mistake.

restitution
The return of goods or property received from the other party to rescind a contract. If the actual goods or property are not available, a cash equivalent must be made.

Rescission is an action to undo a contract. It is available where there has been a material breach of contract, fraud, duress, undue influence, or mistake. Generally, to rescind a contract, the parties must make **restitution** of the consideration they received under the contract.[6] Restitution consists of returning the goods, property, money, or other consideration received from the other party. If possible, the actual goods or property must be returned. If the goods or property have been consumed or are otherwise unavailable, restitution must be made by conveying a cash equivalent. The rescinding party must give adequate notice of the rescission to the breaching party. Rescission and restitution restore the parties to the positions they occupied prior to the contract.

Example Pralene's Store contracts to purchase $1,000,000 of goods from a clothing manufacturer. Pralene's pays $100,000 as a down payment, and the first $200,000 of goods are delivered. The goods are materially defective, and the defect cannot be cured. This breach is a material breach. Pralene's can rescind the contract. Pralene's is entitled to receive its $100,000 down payment back from the manufacturer, and the manufacturer is entitled to receive the goods back from Pralene's.

In the following case, the court had to decide whether to order the rescission of a contract.

CASE 16.1 Rescission of a Contract

Hickman v. Bates

889 So.2d 1249, Web 2004 La.App. Lexis 3076 (2004)
Court of Appeal of Louisiana

"The Court finds that Keith's failure to inform his young, limited, first cousin was intentional and was done to obtain an advantage over her. That is, of divesting her interest in 45 acres in Bienville Parish and 236 acres in Madison Parish for a pittance."

—Judge Caraway

Facts

Patricia Dianne Hickman inherited one-half interests to two pieces of real property when her mother died. One of the properties, in Bienville Parish, Louisiana, contained 45 acres of woodland. The second property, in Madison Parish, Louisiana, contained approximately 236 acres of land and a house. Patricia was 20 years old and had a mental condition that required medication. Patricia, who lived separately from her parents, received a telephone call from her father, Joe Hickman, to come and visit him. Joe was ill with cancer and lived with his sister Christine Bates and her husband, who are parents of Keith Bates, Patricia's first cousin.

The day after Patricia arrived, Joe informed Patricia that an important concern of his was for her to sell her interests in the two pieces of property to Keith Bates and his wife Sheila (the Bates). Joe expressed his doubts that Patricia would be able to maintain the properties and his interest in keeping the property in the family. Patricia agreed to sell the properties to the Bates for $500. Patricia signed legal documents that had been drawn by an attorney prior to her arrival.

Subsequently, through a friend, Patricia sued the Bates to rescind the contracts that sold her interest in the two pieces of property to them, alleging fraud. Expert testimony at trial valued the Madison Parish property at $259,000 and the Bienville Parish property at $20,700. The trial court found fraud and rescinded the contracts. The trial court did not, however, award Patricia attorneys' fees. Both sides appealed.

Issue

Should the sales contracts be rescinded because of fraud, and should Patricia be awarded attorneys' fees?

Language of the Court

A contract is formed by the consent of the parties. However, consent may be vitiated by error, fraud, or duress. Fraud is a misrepresentation or a suppression of the truth made with the intention either to obtain an unjust advantage for one party or to cause a loss or inconvenience to the other. Fraud need only be proven by a preponderance of the evidence and may be established by circumstantial evidence. In its very thorough and well-reasoned oral ruling, the trial court made the following findings of fact concerning its determination of fraud:

> *The court finds that Patricia's intellectual abilities are limited, both from her lack of education and from her mental condition that requires medicine. Considering her situation, her youth, she was then*

20 years old, and her limited abilities, as well as her lack of prior knowledge of the purpose of the visit, and her father's illness, and the fact that she trusted her father and her cousin, the Court finds that Keith had a responsibility to make sure Patricia was informed fully about the transactions and make sure that she understood everything she was doing and the import of everything she was doing, including the fact that she would own nothing, and including the price considerations involved before she signed those documents. The Court finds that Keith's failure to inform his young, limited, first cousin was intentional and was done to obtain an advantage over her. That is, of divesting her interest in 45 acres in Bienville Parish and 236 acres in Madison Parish for a pittance.

We can discern no manifest error in these determinations. Accordingly, we find that the trial court committed no error in rescinding the sales on the ground of fraud.

Decision

The court of appeal affirmed the trial court's finding of fraud and its judgment rescinding the sales contracts by which Patricia sold her interests in the two properties to the Bates. The court of appeal reversed the trial court's denial of an award of attorneys' fees to Patricia and awarded $12,000 in attorneys' fees to Patricia.

Case Questions

Critical Legal Thinking Describe the rescission of a contract. When can a contract be rescinded? Explain.

Business Ethics Did Patricia's father, Joe Hickman, and her first cousin, Keith Bates, act ethically in this case? Did Patricia need the court's help in this case?

Contemporary Business Describe a fraud. Do you think people take advantage of their relatives very often?

▶ EQUITABLE REMEDIES

Equitable remedies are available if there has been a breach of contract that cannot be adequately compensated through a legal remedy. They are also available to prevent unjust enrichment. The most common equitable remedies are *specific performance*, *reformation*, and *injunction*, discussed in the following paragraphs.

Specific Performance

An award of **specific performance** orders the breaching party to perform the acts promised in a contract. The courts have the discretion to award this remedy if the subject matter of the contract is unique.[7] Specific performance is available to enforce land contracts because every piece of real property is considered to be unique. Works of art, antiques, and items of sentimental value, rare coins, stamps, heirlooms, and such also fit the requirement for uniqueness. Most other personal property does not.

Specific performance of personal service contracts is not granted because the courts would find it difficult or impracticable to supervise or monitor performance of such a contract.

The court had to decide whether to issue an order of specific performance in the following case.

specific performance
A remedy that orders the breaching party to perform the acts promised in the contract. Specific performance is usually awarded in cases in which the subject matter is unique, such as in contracts involving land, heirlooms, and paintings.

CASE 16.2 Specific Performance

Alba v. Kaufmann

27 A.D.3d 816, 810 N.Y.S.2d 539, Web 2006 N.Y.App. Div. Lexis 2321 (2006)
Supreme Court of New York, Appellate Division

"The case law reveals that the equitable remedy of specific performance is routinely awarded in contract actions involving real property, on the premise that each parcel of real property is unique."

—Judge Crew

Facts

Jean-Claude Kaufmann owned approximately 37 acres of real property located in the town of Stephentown, Rensselaer County, New York. The property is located in a wooded area and is improved with a nineteenth-century

(case continues)

farmhouse. Kaufmann and his spouse, Christine Cacace, reside in New York City and use the property as a weekend or vacation home. After Kaufmann and Cacace lost their jobs, their financial situation prompted Kaufmann to list the property for sale for $350,000.

Richard Alba and his spouse (Albas) looked at the property and offered Kaufmann the full asking price. The parties executed a contract for sale, and the Albas paid a deposit, obtained a mortgage commitment, and procured a satisfactory home inspection and title insurance. A date for closing the transaction was set. Prior to closing, Cacace sent the Albas an e-mail, indicating that she and Kaufmann had "a change of heart" and no longer wished to go forward with the sale. Albas sent a reply e-mail, stating their intent to go forward with the scheduled closing. Cacace responded with another e-mail, informing the Albas that she had multiple sclerosis and alleging that the "remorse and dread" over the impending sale was making her ill. When Kaufmann refused to close, the Albas sued, seeking specific performance, and moved for summary judgment. The supreme court denied the motion. The Albas appealed.

Issue

Was an order of specific performance of the real estate contract warranted in this case?

Language of the Court

In order to establish their entitlement to summary judgment, the Albas were required to demonstrate that they substantially performed their contractual obligations and were ready, willing and able to fulfill their remaining obligations, that Kaufmann was able but unwilling to convey the property and that there is no adequate remedy at law. The Albas plainly discharged that burden here. In short, the record demonstrates that the Albas were ready, willing and able to close and, but for Kaufmann's admitted refusal to do so, would have consummated the transaction.

As to the remedy the Albas seek, the case law reveals that the equitable remedy of specific performance is routinely awarded in contract actions involving real property, on the premise that each parcel of real property is unique. Moreover, volitional unwillingness, as distinguished from good faith inability, to meet contractual obligations furnishes neither a ground for cancellation of the contract nor a defense against its specific performance.

Even accepting, for purposes of this discussion, that the alleged exacerbation of Cacace's symptoms is both genuine and causally related to the proposed sale of property, as she is not a party to the contract, her connection to the transaction is simply too attenuated for Kaufmann to claim undue hardship. Simply put, permitting a defendant to raise an undue hardship defense under the circumstances present here would place a nearly impossible burden upon potential purchasers of real property namely, to ascertain whether any of the signatories' relatives had any potential objection to the sale in question.

Decision

The appellate court reversed the supreme court's denial of Alba's motion for summary judgment. The appellate court, as a matter of law, granted the Albas' motion for summary judgment and ordered Kaufmann to specifically perform the real estate contract.

Case Questions

Critical Legal Thinking What does the doctrine of specific performance provide? Explain.

Business Ethics Was it ethical for Kaufman to try to back out of the contract? Once the Albas were aware of Cacace's health prroblems, should they have withdrawn their contract?

Contemporary Business Should a seller be permitted to cancel a contract for the sale of real estate because he or she has "seller's remorse"?

Reformation

reformation
An equitable doctrine that permits the court to rewrite a contract to express the parties' true intentions.

Reformation is an equitable doctrine that permits the court to rewrite a contract to express the parties' true intentions. Reformation is usually available to correct clerical errors in contracts. For example, suppose a clerical error is made during the typing of a contract, and both parties sign the contract without discovering the error. If a dispute later arises, the court can reform the contract to correct the clerical error to read as the parties originally intended.

Injunction

injunction
A court order that prohibits a person from doing a certain act.

An **injunction** is a court order that prohibits a person from doing a certain act. To obtain an injunction, the requesting party must show that he or she will suffer irreparable injury if the injunction is not issued.

CONCEPT SUMMARY
TYPES OF EQUITABLE REMEDIES

Type of Equitable Remedy	Description
Specific performance	A court orders the breaching party to perform the acts promised in the contract. The subject matter of the contract must be unique.
Reformation	A court rewrites a contract to express the parties' true intentions. This remedy is usually used to correct clerical errors.
Injunction	A court prohibits a party from doing a certain act. Injunctions are available in contract actions only in limited circumstances.

▶ TORTS ASSOCIATED WITH CONTRACTS

The recovery for breach of contract is usually limited to contract damages. A party who can prove a contract-related **tort**, however, may also recover tort damages. Tort damages include compensation for personal injury, pain and suffering, emotional distress, and possibly punitive damages.

Generally, punitive damages are not recoverable for breach of contract. They are recoverable, however, for certain tortious conduct that may be associated with the non-performance of a contract.

The major torts associated with contracts are *intentional interference with contractual relations* and *breach of the implied covenant of good faith and fair dealing*. These torts are discussed in the following paragraphs.

Intentional Interference with Contractual Relations

A party to a contract may sue any third person who intentionally interferes with the contract and causes that party injury. The third party does not have to have acted with malice or bad faith. This tort, which is known as the tort of **intentional interference with contractual relations**, usually arises when a third party induces a contracting party to breach a contract with another party. The following elements must be shown:

1. A valid, enforceable contract between the contracting parties
2. Third-party knowledge of this contract
3. Third-party inducement to breach the contract

A third party can contract with the breaching party without becoming liable for this tort if a contracting party has already breached the contract and thus the third party cannot be held to have induced a breach of the other parties' contract.

intentional interference with contractual relations
A tort that arises when a third party induces a contracting party to breach the contract with another party.

Breach of the Implied Covenant of Good Faith and Fair Dealing

Several states have held that a **covenant of good faith and fair dealing** is implied in certain types of contracts. Under this covenant, the parties to a contract are not only held to the express terms of the contract but are also required to act in "good faith" and deal fairly in all respects in obtaining the objective of the contract. A breach of this implied covenant is a tort for which tort damages are recoverable. This tort, which is sometimes referred to as the **tort of bad faith**, is an evolving area of the law.

covenant of good faith and fair dealing
An implied covenant under which the parties to a contract not only are held to the express terms of the contract but are also required to act in "good faith" and deal fairly in all respects in obtaining the objective of the contract.

ETHICS SPOTLIGHT

Bad Faith Tort

"Where an insurer is pursued for its refusal to settle a claim, 'bad faith' lies in an insurer's failure to give at least equal consideration to the insured's interests when the insurer arrives at a decision on whether to settle the claim."

—Judge Clyde L. Kuehn

On Halloween Day, Christine Narvaez drove her automobile onto the parking lot of a busy supermarket. Narvaez had her two-year-old grandchild with her. The youngster was riding, unconstrained, in a booster seat. Narvaez saw a friend and decided to stop for a brief chat. She parked the car and exited the car, leaving the keys in the ignition and the motor running. The youngster crawled behind the wheel, slipped the car into gear, and set it in motion. The car struck Marguerite O'Neill, a woman in her 80s, pinned her between the Narvaez car and another car and slowly crushed the woman's trapped body.

O'Neill was pried loose and airlifted to a hospital trauma center. O'Neill suffered a crushed hip, a broken arm, and four cracked ribs, and she lost more than 40 percent of her blood supply as a result of internal bleeding. She spent one month in the hospital intensive care unit and had to be placed in a nursing home and was deprived of the ability to live independently.

Narvaez carried the $20,000 minimum amount of liability insurance allowed by law. She was insured by Gallant Insurance Company. O'Neill's medical bills totaled $105,000. O'Neill sued Narvaez and her insurance company, Gallant. O'Neill's attorney demanded the policy limit of $20,000 from Gallant in settlement of O'Neill's claim and offered a complete release from liability for Narvaez. Three Gallant insurance adjusters, its claims manager, and the lawyer of the law firm representing Gallant for the case all stated to John Moss, Gallant's executive vice president, that Gallant should accept the settlement offer. Moss rejected their advice and refused to settle the case.

One year later, on the eve of trial, Moss offered to settle for the $20,000 policy limit, but O'Neill then refused. The case went to trial, and the jury returned a verdict against Narvaez of $731,063. Gallant paid $20,000 of this amount, closed its file, and left Narvaez liable for the $711,063 excess judgment. To settle her debt to O'Neill, Narvaez assigned her claims against Gallant to O'Neill. O'Neill then sued Gallant for a bad faith tort for breaching the implied covenant of good faith and fair dealing that Gallant owed to Narvaez to settle the case. The jury found Gallant liable for a bad faith tort and awarded O'Neill $710,063 ($1,000 short of the judgment in the first trial) in actual damages and $2.3 million in punitive damages. The appellate court agreed. The court stated:

> Where an insurer is pursued for its refusal to settle a claim, "bad faith" lies in an insurer's failure to give at least equal consideration to the insured's interests when the insurer arrives at a decision on whether to settle the claim. The jury's finding of bad faith was not against the manifest weight of the evidence. We must side with O'Neill and against Gallant on the extent to which the evidence established the existence of reprehensible conduct on the part of Narvaez's insurance provider.

The appellate court held that Gallant was liable for a bad faith tort and upheld the trial court's judgment, awarding O'Neill $710,063 in actual damages and $2.3 million in punitive damages. *O'Neill v. Gallant Insurance Company*, 769 N.E.2d 100, **Web** 2002 Ill.App. Lexis 311 (Appellate Court of Illinois)

Business Ethics Did Gallant act ethically in this case? Will the implied covenant of good faith and fair dealing make insurance companies act more ethically toward their customers?

TEST REVIEW TERMS AND CONCEPTS

Anticipatory breach (anticipatory repudiation)
Breach of contract
Compensatory damages
Complete performance (strict performance)
Consequential damages (special damages or foreseeable damages)

Covenant of good faith and fair dealing
Equitable remedies
Executed contract
Inferior performance
Injunction
Intentional interference with contractual relations
Judgment

Liquidated damages
Material breach
Minor breach
Mitigation of damages
Monetary damages
Nominal damages
Penalty
Reformation
Rescission

Restitution
Specific performance
Substantial performance
Tender of performance (tender)
Tort
Tort of bad faith
Writ of attachment
Writ of garnishment

CASE PROBLEMS

16.1 Performance Louis Haeuser, who owned several small warehouses, contracted with Wallace C. Drennen, Inc. (Drennen), to construct a road to the warehouses. The contract price was $42,324. After Drennen completed the work, some cracks appeared in the road, causing improper drainage. In addition, "birdbaths" that accumulated water appeared in the road. When Haeuser refused to pay, Drennen sued to recover the full contract price. Haeuser filed a cross complaint to recover the cost of repairing the road. Who wins? *Wallace C. Drennen, Inc. v. Haeuser*, 402 So.2d 771, **Web** 1981 La. App. Lexis 4453 (Court of Appeal of Louisiana)

16.2 Anticipatory Repudiation Muhammad Ali (Ali), a professional heavyweight boxer, successfully defended his heavyweight boxing championship of the world by defeating Ken Norton. Shortly after the fight, Ali held a press conference and, as he had done on several occasions before, announced his retirement from boxing. At that time, Ali had beaten every challenger except Duane Bobick, whom he had not yet fought. Subsequently, Madison Square Garden Boxing, Inc. (MSGB), a fight promoter, offered Ali $2.5 million if he would fight Bobick. Ali agreed, stating, "We are back in business again." MSGB and Ali signed a fighters' agreement, and MSGB paid Ali a $125,000 advance payment. The fight was to take place in Madison Square Garden. Three months before the fight was to take place, Ali told MSGB that he was retiring from boxing and would not fight Bobick in February. Must MSGB wait until the date performance is due to sue Ali for breach of contract? *Madison Square Garden Boxing, Inc. v. Muhammad Ali*, 430 F.Supp. 679, **Web** 1977 U.S. Dist. Lexis 16101 (United States District Court for the Northern District of Illinois)

16.3 Damages Hawaiian Telephone Company entered into a contract with Microform Data Systems, Inc. (Microform), for Microform to provide a computerized assistance system that would handle 15,000 calls per hour with a one-second response time and with a "nonstop" feature to allow automatic recovery from any component failure. The contract called for installation of the host computer no later than mid-February of the next year. Microform was not able to meet the initial installation date, and at that time, it was determined that Microform was at least nine months away from providing a system that met contract specifications. Hawaiian Telephone canceled the contract and sued Microform for damages. Did Microform materially breach the contract? Can Hawaiian Telephone recover damages? *Hawaiian Telephone Co. v. Microform Data Systems Inc.*, 829 F.2d 919, **Web** 1987 U.S. App. Lexis 13425 (United States Court of Appeals for the Ninth Circuit)

16.4 Damages Raquel Welch was a movie actress who appeared in about 30 films over a 15-year period. She was considered a sex symbol, and her only serious dramatic role was as a roller derby queen in *Kansas City Bomber*. During that time period, Michael Phillips and David Ward developed a film package based on the John Steinbeck novella *Cannery Row*. Metro-Goldwyn-Mayer Film Company (MGM) accepted to produce the project and entered into a contract with Welch to play the leading female character, a prostitute named Suzy. At 40 years of age, Welch relished the chance to direct her career toward more serious roles. Welch was to receive $250,000 from MGM, with payment being divided into weekly increments during filming. Filming began, but three weeks later, MGM fired Welch and replaced her with another actress, Debra Winger. Welch sued MGM to recover the balance of $194,444 that remained unpaid under the contract. Who wins? *Welch v. Metro-Goldwyn-Mayer Film Co.*, 207 Cal.App.3d 164, 254 Cal.Rptr. 645, **Web** 1988 Cal.App. Lexis 1202 (Court of Appeal of California)

16.5 Damages Ptarmigan Investment Company (Ptarmigan), a partnership, entered into a contract with Gundersons, Inc. (Gundersons), a South Dakota corporation in the business of golf course construction. The contract provided that Gundersons would construct a golf course for Ptarmigan for a contract price of $1,294,129. Gundersons immediately started work and completed about one-third of the work by about three months later, when bad weather forced cessation of most work. Ptarmigan paid Gundersons for the work to that date. In the following spring, Ptarmigan ran out of funds and was unable to pay for the completion of the golf course. Gundersons sued Ptarmigan and its individual partners to recover the lost profits that it would have made on the remaining two-thirds of the contract. Can Gundersons recover these lost profits as damages? *Gundersons, Inc. v. Ptarmigan Investment Company*, 678 P.2d 1061, **Web** 1983 Colo.App. Lexis 1133 (Court of Appeals of Colorado)

16.6 Liquidated Damages H. S. Perlin Company, Inc. (Perlin), and Morse Signal Devices of San Diego (Morse) entered into a contract whereby Morse agreed to provide burglar and fire alarm service to Perlin's coin and stamp store. Perlin paid $50 per month for this service. The contract contained a liquidated damages clause limiting Morse's liability to $250 for any losses incurred by Perlin based on Morse's failure of service. Six years after the burglary system was installed, a burglary occurred at Perlin's store. Before entering the store, the burglars cut a telephone line that ran from the burglar system in Perlin's store to Morse's central location. When the line was cut, a signal indicated the interruption of service at Morse's central station. Inexplicably, Morse took no further steps to investigate the interruption of service at Perlin's store. The burglars stole stamps and coins with a wholesale value of $958,000, and Perlin did not have insurance against this loss. Perlin sued Morse to recover damages. Is the liquidated damages clause enforceable? *H. S. Perlin Company, Inc. v. Morse Signal Devices of San Diego*, 209

Cal.App.3d 1289, 258 Cal.Rptr. 1, **Web** 1989 Cal.App. Lexis 400 (Court of Appeal of California)

16.7 Liquidated Damages   United Mechanical Contractors, Inc. (UMC), an employer, agreed to provide a pension plan for its unionized workers. UMC was to make monthly payments into a pension fund administered by the Idaho Plumbers and Pipefitters Health and Welfare Fund (Fund). Payments were due by the 15th of each month. The contract between UMC and Fund contained a liquidated damages clause which provided that if payments due from UMC were received later than the 20th of the month, liquidated damages of 20 percent of the required contribution would be assessed against UMC. In one month, Fund received UMC's payment on the 24th. Fund sued UMC to recover $9,245.23 in liquidated damages. Is the liquidated damages clause enforceable? *Idaho Plumbers and Pipefitters Health and Welfare Fund v. United Mechanical Contractors, Inc.*, 875 F.2d 212, **Web** 1989 U.S. App. Lexis 14528 (United States Court of Appeals for the Ninth Circuit)

16.8 Specific Performance   Liz Claiborne, Inc. (Claiborne), is a large maker of sportswear in the United States and a well-known name in fashion, with sales of over $1 billion per year. Claiborne distributes its products through 9,000 retail outlets in the United States. Avon Products, Inc. (Avon), is a major producer of fragrances, toiletries, and cosmetics, with annual sales of more than $3 billion per year. Claiborne, which desired to promote its well-known name on perfumes and cosmetics, entered into a joint venture with Avon whereby Claiborne would make available its names, trademarks, and marketing experience and Avon would engage in the procurement and manufacture of the fragrances, toiletries, and cosmetics. The parties would equally share the financial requirements of the joint venture. During its first year of operation, the joint venture had sales of more than $16 million. In the second year, sales increased to $26 million, making it one of the fastest-growing fragrance and cosmetic lines in the country. One year later, Avon sought to "uncouple" the joint venture. Avon thereafter refused to procure and manufacture the line of fragrances and cosmetics for the joint venture. When Claiborne could not obtain the necessary fragrances and cosmetics from any other source for the fall/Christmas season, Claiborne sued Avon for breach of contract, seeking specific performance of the contract by Avon. Is specific performance an appropriate remedy in this case? *Liz Claiborne, Inc. v. Avon Products, Inc.*, 141 A.D.2d 329, 530 N.Y.S.2d 425, **Web** 1988 N.Y.App. Div. Lexis 6423 (Supreme Court of New York)

16.9 Injunction   Anita Baker, a then-unknown singer, signed a multiyear recording contract with Beverly Glen Music, Inc. (Beverly Glen). Baker recorded for Beverly Glen a record album that was moderately successful. After having some difficulties with Beverly Glen, Baker was offered a considerably more lucrative contract by Warner Communications, Inc. (Warner). Baker accepted the Warner offer and informed Beverly Glen that she would not complete their contract because she had entered into an agreement with Warner. Beverly Glen sued Baker and Warner, and it sought an injunction to prevent Baker from performing as a singer for Warner. Is an injunction an appropriate remedy in this case? *Beverly Glen Music, Inc. v. Warner Communications, Inc.*, 178 Cal.App.3d 1142, 224 Cal.Rptr. 260, **Web** 1986 Cal.App. Lexis 2729 (Court of Appeal of California)

16.10 Intentional Interference with Contractual Relations   Pacific Gas and Electric Company (PG & E) entered into a contract with Placer County Water Agency (Agency) to purchase hydroelectric power generated by Agency's Middle Fork American River Project. The contract was not terminable until 2013. As energy prices rose during the 1970s, the contract became extremely valuable to PG & E. The price PG & E paid for energy under the contract was much lower than the cost of energy from other sources. Ten year later, Bear Stearns & Company (Bear Stearns), an investment bank and securities underwriting firm, learned of Agency's power contract with PG & E. Bear Stearns offered to assist Agency in an effort to terminate the power contract with PG & E in exchange for a share of Agency's subsequent profits and the right to underwrite any new securities issued by Agency. Bear Stearns also agreed to pay the legal fees incurred by Agency in litigation concerning the attempt to get out of the PG & E contract. Who wins and why? *Pacific Gas and Electric Company v. Bear Stearns & Company*, 50 Cal.3d 1118, 791 P.2d 587, 270 Cal.Rptr. 1, **Web** 1990 Cal. Lexis 2119 (Supreme Court of California)

BUSINESS ETHICS CASES

16.11 Business Ethics   Walgreen Company began operating a pharmacy in the Southgate Mall in Milwaukee when the mall opened. It had a lease for a 30-year term that contained an exclusivity clause in which the landlord, Sara Creek Property Company (Sara Creek), promised not to lease space in the mall to anyone else who wanted to operate a pharmacy or a store containing a pharmacy. With 11 years left on the Walgreen–Sara Creek lease, after its anchor tenant went broke, Sara Creek informed Walgreen that it intended to lease the anchor tenant space to Phar-Mor Corporation. Phar-Mor, a "deep discount" chain, would occupy 100,000 square feet, of which 12,000 square feet would be occupied by a pharmacy the same size as Walgreen's. The entrances to the two stores would be within a few hundred feet of each other. Walgreen sued Sara Creek for breach of contract and sought a permanent injunction against Sara Creek's leasing the anchor premises to Phar-Mor. Do the facts of this case justify the issuance of a permanent injunction? Did Sara Creek act ethically in not living up to the contract with Walgreen? *Walgreen Co. v. Sara Creek Property Co.*, 966 F.2d 273, **Web** 1992 U.S. App. Lexis 14847 (United States Court of Appeals for the Seventh Circuit)

16.12 Business Ethics   Rosina Crisci owned an apartment building in which Mrs. DiMare was a tenant. One day while DiMare was descending a wooden staircase on the outside of the apartment building, she fell through the staircase and was left hanging 15 feet above the ground until she was rescued. Crisci had a $10,000 liability insurance policy on the building from the Security Insurance Company (Security) of New Haven, Connecticut. DiMare sued Crisci and Security for $400,000 for physical injuries and psychosis suffered from

the fall. Prior to trial, DiMare agreed to take $10,000 in settlement of the case. Security refused this settlement offer. DiMare reduced her settlement offer to $9,000, of which Crisci offered to pay $2,500. Security again refused to settle the case. The case proceeded to trial, and the jury awarded DiMare and her husband $110,000. Security paid $10,000, pursuant to the insurance contract, and Crisci had to pay the difference. Crisci, a widow of 70 years of age, had to sell her assets, became dependent on her relatives, declined in physical health, and suffered from hysteria and suicide attempts. Crisci sued Security for tort damages for breach of the implied covenant of good faith and fair dealing. Did Security act in bad faith? *Crisci v. Security Insurance Company of New Haven, Connecticut*, 66 Cal.App.2d 425, 426 P.2d 173, 58 Cal.Rptr. 13, **Web** 1967 Cal. Lexis 313 (Supreme Court of California)

ENDNOTES

1. *Restatement (Second) of Contracts*, Section 235(2).
2. *Restatement (Second) of Contracts*, Section 241.
3. *Restatement (Second) of Contracts*, Section 253; UCC Section 2-610.
4. UCC Sections 2-708 and 2-713.
5. *Restatement (Second) of Contracts*, Section 356(1).
6. *Restatement (Second) of Contracts*, Section 370.
7. *Restatement (Second) of Contracts*, Section 359.

17 | INTERNET LAW AND E-COMMERCE

▲ **Internet Law** *The development of the Internet and electronic commerce has required courts to apply existing law to online commerce transactions and spurred the federal Congress and state legislatures to enact new laws that govern the formation and enforcement of e-contracts and protect Internet users from invasion of privacy and other cyber crimes.*

CHAPTER OBJECTIVES

After studying this chapter, you should be able to:

1. Describe Internet domain names and how domain names are protected by the Anticybersquatting Consumer Protection Act.
2. Define *e-contract* and a *software license*.
3. Describe the provisions of the Uniform Computer Information Transactions Act (UCITA).
4. Describe the provisions of the Electronic Signatures in Global and National Commerce Act (E-Sign Act).
5. Describe the federal laws that protect against cyber crimes.

CHAPTER CONTENTS

▶ **INTRODUCTION TO INTERNET LAW AND E-COMMERCE**
▶ **INTERNET**
▶ **E-MAIL AND WEBSITES**
Internet Law & Online Commerce · *Controlling the Assault of Non-Solicited Pornography and Marketing Act (CAN-SPAM)*

Internet Law & Online Commerce · *Electronic Communications Privacy Act (ECPA)*
▶ **DOMAIN NAMES**
Internet Law & Online Commerce · *Anticybersquatting Consumer Protection Act (ACPA)*

> **"Through the use of chat rooms, any person with a phone line can become a town crier with a voice that resonates farther than it could from any soapbox. Through the use of Web pages, mail exploders, and newsgroups, the same individual can become a pamphleteer."**
>
> —Justice Stevens
> *Reno v. American Civil Liberties Union, 521 U.S. 844 (1997)*

► INTRODUCTION TO INTERNET LAW AND E-COMMERCE

The use of the Internet and the World Wide Web, and the sale of goods and services through **e-commerce**, have exploded. Large and small businesses sell goods and services over the Internet through **websites** and registered *domain names*. Consumers and businesses can purchase almost any good or service they want over the Internet, using such sites as Amazon.com, eBay, and others. Businesses and individuals may register domain names to use on the Internet. Anyone who infringes on these rights may be stopped from doing so and is liable for damages.

> **e-commerce**
> The sale of goods and services by computer over the Internet.

In addition, software and information may be licensed either by physically purchasing the software or information and installing it on a computer or by merely downloading the software or information directly into a computer.

Many legal scholars and lawyers argued that traditional rules of contract law do not adequately meet the needs of Internet transactions and software and information licensing. These concerns led to an effort to create new contract law for electronic transactions. After much debate, the National Conference of Commissioners on Uniform State Laws developed the *Uniform Computer Information Transactions Act (UCITA)*. This model act provides uniform and comprehensive rules for contracts involving computer information transactions and software and information licenses.

The federal government has also enacted many federal statutes that regulate the Internet and e-commerce. Federal law has been passed that regulates the Internet and protects personal rights while using the Internet. In addition, many new federal criminal statutes have been enacted to protect against cyber crimes.

This chapter covers Internet law, domain names, e-contracts, licensing of software, privacy laws, and criminal laws that regulate the Internet and online commerce.

► INTERNET

The **Internet**, or **Net,** is a collection of millions of computers that provide a network of electronic connections between the computers. Hundreds of millions of computers

> **Internet**
> A collection of millions of computers that provide a network of electronic connections between the computers.

are connected to the Internet. The Internet's evolution helped usher in the Information Age. Individuals and businesses use the Internet for communication of information and data.

World Wide Web

World Wide Web
An electronic connection of millions of computers that support a standard set of rules for the exchange of information.

The **World Wide Web** consists of millions of computers that support a standard set of rules for the exchange of information called Hypertext Transfer Protocol (HTTP). Web-based documents are formatted using common coding languages. Businesses and individuals can access the web by registering with a service such as America Online (AOL).

Individuals and businesses can have their own websites. A website is composed of electronic documents known as webpages. Websites and webpages are stored on servers throughout the world, which are operated by **Internet service providers (ISPs)**. They are viewed by using web-browsing software such as Microsoft Internet Explorer and Netscape Navigator. Each website has a unique online address.

The web has made it extremely attractive to conduct commercial activities online. Companies such as Amazon.com and eBay are e-commerce powerhouses that sell all sorts of goods and services. Existing brick-and-mortar companies, such as Wal-Mart, Merrill Lynch, and Dell Computers, sell their goods and services online as well. E-commerce over the web will continue to grow dramatically each year.

▶ E-MAIL AND WEBSITES

electronic mail (e-mail)
Electronic written communication between individuals using computers connected to the Internet.

Electronic mail, or **e-mail**, is one of the most widely used applications for communication over the Internet. Using e-mail, individuals around the world can instantaneously communicate in electronic writing with one another. Each person can have an e-mail address that identifies him or her by a unique address. E-mail will continue to grow in use in the future as it replaces some telephone and paper correspondence and increases new communication between persons.

INTERNET LAW & ONLINE COMMERCE

Controlling the Assault of Non-Solicited Pornography and Marketing Act (CAN-SPAM)

Americans are being bombarded in their e-mail accounts by "spam"—unsolicited commercial advertising. Spammers try to sell people literally anything. Spam accounts for approximately three-quarters of all business e-mail traffic. In addition, many spam messages are fraudulent and deceptive, including misleading subject lines. It takes time and money to sort through, review, and discard unwanted spam.

In 2003, Congress enacted the federal **Controlling the Assault of Non-Solicited Pornography and Marketing Act (CAN-SPAM Act)**.[1] The act (1) prohibits spammers from using falsified headers in e-mail messages, including the originating domain name and e-mail address, (2) prohibits deceptive subject lines that mislead a recipient of the contents or subject matter of the message, (3) requires that recipients of spam be given the opportunity to opt out and not have the spammer send e-mail to the recipient's address, and (4) requires spammers who send sexually

oriented e-mail to properly label it as such. The Federal Trade Commission (FTC), a federal administrative agency, is empowered to enforce the CAN-SPAM Act.

In effect, the CAN-SPAM Act does not can spam but instead approves businesses to use spam as long as they do not lie. The act expressly provides that victims of spam do not have a right to bring civil lawsuits against spammers. The CAN-SPAM Act does not regulate spam sent internationally to Americans from other countries. In essence, the CAN-SPAM Act is very weak in helping consumers ward off the spam that deluges them daily.

In 2004, the FTC adopted a rule which requires that sexually explicit spam e-mail contain a warning on the subject line reading "SEXUALLY EXPLICIT." The FTC rule also prohibits the messages themselves from containing graphic material. The graphic material can appear only after the recipient has opened the e-mail message.

Internet Service Provider (ISP)

Internet service providers (ISP) are companies that provide consumers and businesses with access to the Internet. ISPs provide e-mail accounts to users, Internet access, and storage on the Internet. ISPs offer a variety of access devices and services, including dial-up, cable, DSL, broadband wireless, Ethernet, satellite Internet access, and other services to connect users to the Internet. There are also web-hosting services that allow users to create their own websites and provide storage space for website users.

A provision in the federal **Communications Decency Act** of 1996 provides: "No provider or user of an interactive computer service shall be treated as the publisher or speaker of any information provided by another information content provider."[2] Thus, ISPs are not liable for the content transmitted over their networks by e-mail users and websites.

INTERNET LAW & ONLINE COMMERCE

Electronic Communications Privacy Act (ECPA)

E-mail, computer data, and other electronic communications are sent daily by millions of people, using computers and the Internet. Recognizing that the use of computer and other electronic communications raise special issues of privacy, the federal government enacted the **Electronic Communications Privacy Act (ECPA)**.[3]

The ECPA makes it a crime to intercept an electronic communication at the point of transmission, while in transit, when stored by a router or server, or after receipt by the intended recipient. An electronic communication includes any transfer of signals, writings, images, sounds, data, or intelligence of any nature. The ECPA makes it illegal to access stored e-mail as well as e-mail in transmission.

The ECPA provides that stored electronic communications may be accessed without violating the law by the following:

1. The party or entity providing the electronic communication service. The primary example would be an employer who can access stored e-mail communications of employees using the employer's service.
2. Government and law enforcement entities that are investigating suspected illegal activity. Disclosure would be required only pursuant to a validly issued warrant.

The ECPA provides for criminal penalties. In addition, the ECPA provides that an injured party may sue for civil damages for violations of the ECPA.

▶ DOMAIN NAMES

Most businesses conduct e-commerce by using websites on the Internet. Each website is identified by a unique Internet **domain name**.

Examples The domain name for the publisher of this book—Prentice Hall Publishing Company—is **www.prenhall.com.** The domain name for Microsoft Corporation is **www.microsoft.com.** The domain name for McDonald's Corporation is **www.mcdonalds.com.**

Domain names can be registered. The first step in registering a domain name is to determine whether any other party already owns the name. For this purpose, InterNIC maintains a "Whois" database that contains the domain names that have been registered. The InterNIC website is located online at **www.internic.net.**

Domain names can also be registered at Network Solutions, Inc.'s, website, which is located at **www.networksolutions.com**, as well as at other sites. An applicant must complete a registration form, which can be done online. It usually costs less than $50 to register a domain name for one year, and the fee may be paid by credit card online. Some country-specific domain names are more expensive to register.

The most commonly used top-level extensions for domain names are set forth in Exhibit 17.1.

domain name
A unique name that identifies an individual's or company's website.

▶ **Exhibit 17.1 COMMONLY USED TOP-LEVEL EXTENSIONS FOR DOMAIN NAMES**

It will be of little avail to the people, that the laws are made by men of their own choice, if the laws be so voluminous that they cannot be read, or so incoherent that they cannot be understood.

Alexander Hamilton
The Federalist Papers (1788)

.com	This extension represents the word *commercial* and is the most widely used extension in the world. Most businesses prefer a .com domain name because it is a highly recognized business symbol.
.net	This extension represents the word *network*, and it is most commonly used by ISPs, Web-hosting companies, and other business that are directly involved in the infrastructure of the Internet. Some businesses also choose domain names with a .net extension.
.org	This extension represents the word *organization* and is primarily used by nonprofit groups and trade associations.
.info	This extension signifies a resource website. It is an unrestricted global name that may be used by businesses, individuals, and organizations.
.biz	This extension is used for small-business websites.
.us	This extension is for U.S. websites. Many businesses choose this extension, which is a relatively new extension.
.cc	This extension was originally the country code for Coco Keeling Islands, but it is now unrestricted and may be registered by anyone from any country. It is often registered by businesses.
.bz	This extension was originally the country code for Belize, but it is now unrestricted and may be registered by anyone from any country. It is commonly used by small businesses.
.name	This extension is for individuals, who can use it to register personalized domain names.
.museum	This extension enables museums, museum associations, and museum professionals to register websites.
.coop	This extension represents the word *cooperative* and may be used by cooperative associations around the world.
.aero	This extension is exclusively reserved for the aviation community. It enables organizations and individuals in that community to reserve websites.
.pro	This extension is available to professionals, such as doctors, lawyers, and consultants.
.edu	This extension is for educational institutions.

There are other domain name extensions available. Countries have country-specific extensions assigned to the country. Some countries make these domain names extensions available for private purchase.

INTERNET LAW & ONLINE COMMERCE

Anticybersquatting Consumer Protection Act (ACPA)

In November 1999, the U.S. Congress enacted, and the president signed, the **Anticybersquatting Consumer Protection Act (ACPA)**.[4] The act was specifically aimed at cybersquatters who register Internet domain names of famous companies and people and hold them hostage by demanding ransom payments from the famous company or person.

In the past, trademark law was of little help in this area, either because the famous person's name was not trademarked or because, even if the name was trademarked, trademark laws required distribution of goods or services to find infringement, and most cybersquatters did not distribute goods or services but merely sat on the Internet domain names.

The 1999 act has two fundamental requirements: (1) The name must be famous and (2) the domain name must have been registered in bad faith. Thus, the law prohibits the act of cybersquatting itself if it is done in **bad faith**.

The first issue in applying the statute is whether the domain name is someone else's famous name. Trademarked names qualify; nontrademarked names— such as those of famous actors, actresses, singers, sports stars, politicians, and such—are also protected. In determining bad faith, the law provides that courts may consider the extent to which the domain name resembles the holder's name or the famous person's name, whether goods or services are sold under the name, the holder's offer to sell or transfer the name, and whether the holder has acquired multiple Internet domain names of famous companies and persons.

The act provides for the issuance of cease-and-desist orders and injunctions by the court. In addition, the law adds monetary penalties: A plaintiff has the option of seeking statutory damages in lieu of proving damages. The Anticybersquatting Consumer Protection Act gives owners of trademarks and persons with famous names a new weapon to attack the kidnapping of Internet domain names by cyberpirates.

Example The Academy Award–winning actress Julia Roberts won back the domain name **juliaroberts.com** because it had been registered in bad faith by another party not named Julia Roberts. The singer Sting was not so fortunate because the word *sting* is generic, allowing someone else to originally register and keep the domain name **sting.com**.

In the following case, the court applied the federal anticybersquatting act.

CASE 17.1 Domain Name

E. & J. Gallo Winery v. Spider Webs Ltd.

286 F.3d 270, Web 2002 U.S. App. Lexis 5928 (2002)
United States Court of Appeals for the Fifth Circuit

"Spider Webs has no intellectual property rights or trademark in the name 'ernestandjuliogallo,' aside from its registered domain name."

—Judge Jolly

Facts

Ernest & Julio Gallo Winery (Gallo) is a famous maker of wines that is located in California. The company registered the trademark "Ernest & Julio Gallo" in 1964 with the United States Patent and Trademark Office. The company has spent over $500 million promoting its brand name and has sold more than 4 billion bottles of wine. Its name has taken on a secondary meaning as a famous trademark name. Steve, Pierce, and Fred Thumann created Spider Webs Ltd., a limited partnership, to register Internet domain names. Spider Webs registered more than 2,000 Internet domain names, including **ernestandjuliogallo. com.** Spider Webs is in the business of selling domain names. Gallo filed suit against Spider Webs Ltd. and the Thumanns, alleging violation of the federal Anticybersquatting Consumer Protection Act (ACPA). The U.S. District Court held in favor of Gallo and ordered Spider Webs to transfer the domain name **ernestandjuliogallo. com** to Gallo. Spider Webs Ltd. appealed.

Issue

Did Spider Webs Ltd. and the Thumanns act in bad faith in registering the Internet domain name **ernestandjuliogallo .com**?

Language of the Court

Spider Webs does not appeal the holdings that Gallo had a valid registration in its mark, that the mark is famous and distinctive, and that the domain name registered by Spider Webs is identical or confusingly similar to Gallo's mark. However, Spider Webs argues that they did not act with a "bad faith intent to profit," as required by the ACPA.

Spider Webs has no intellectual property rights or trademark in the name "ernestandjuliogallo," aside from its registered domain name. The domain name does not contain the name of Spider Webs or any of the other defendants. Spider Webs had no prior use or any current use of the domain name in connection with the bona fide offering of goods or services. Steve Thumann admitted that the domain name was valuable and that they hoped Gallo would contact them so that they could "assist" Gallo in some way. There is uncontradicted evidence that Spider Webs was engaged in commerce in the selling of

(case continues)

domain names and that they hoped to sell this domain name some day.

There was evidence presented that Gallo's mark is distinctive and famous. Further, Gallo registered the mark, which is a family name, thirty-eight years ago, and other courts have found that "'Gallo' has clearly become associated with wine in the United States such that its evolution to 'secondary meaning' status may not be seriously questioned." The circumstances of this case all indicate that Spider Webs knew Gallo had a famous mark in which Gallo had built up goodwill, and that they hoped to profit from this by registering "ernestandjuliogallo.com" and waiting for Gallo to contact them so they could "assist" Gallo. In sum, the factors strongly support a finding of bad faith.

Decision

The U.S. Court of Appeals held that the name Ernest and Julio Gallo was a famous trademark name and that Spider

Web Ltd. and the Thumanns acted in bad faith when they registered the Internet domain name **ernestandjuliogallo. com.** The U.S. Court of Appeals upheld the U.S. District Court's decision, ordering the defendants to transfer the domain name to plaintiff E. & J. Gallo Winery.

Case Questions

Critical Legal Thinking What does the Anticybersquatting Consumer Protection Act (ACPA) provide? Explain.

Business Ethics Did the defendants act ethically in registering so many Internet domain names? What was the motive of the defendants?

Contemporary Business How valuable is a company's trademark name? Does the ACPA protect that value? Explain.

INTERNET LAW & ONLINE COMMERCE
Domain Names Sold for Millions

What is a domain name worth? In some case, plenty. Take the case of the domain name **www.business.com**. This name, which was originally registered as a domain name for less than $50, was sold to another purchaser for $150,000 in 1996. Many people at the time thought this was an outrageous sum to pay for a domain name—that is, until the second purchaser turned around and resold the name to ECompanies for $7.5 million. Subsequently, **www. business.com** was sold to RH Donnelley for $350 million. RH Donnelly beat out the *New York Times* and Dow Jones in the bidding for the domain name. The sale was in stock.

Other domain names have been sold at high prices, too. The domain name **www.wine.com** sold for $3 million,

www.bingo.com for $1.1 million, **www.wallstreet.com** for $1 million, **www.drugs.com** for $800,000, **www.pizza.com** for $2.6 million, and **www.vip.com** for $1.4 million. Gary Kremen, who had purchased the domain name **www.sex .com** in 1996 for next to nothing, sold the name to Escom in 2006 for $14 million.

As commerce over the Internet increases, unregistered memorable domain names become harder to find. The sale of the better domain names has increased, with multimillion-dollar price tags being paid for the most desirable names—which were originally registered for less than $50.

▶ E-CONTRACTS

e-mail and web contracts
Contracts that are entered into by e-mail and over the World Wide Web.

E-mail and the web have exploded as means of personal and business communication. In the business environment, e-mail and the web are sometimes the methods used to negotiate and agree on contract terms and to send and agree to an e-contract. Are e-contracts enforceable? Assuming that all the elements to establish a contract are present, an **e-mail contract** or **web contract** is valid and enforceable. The main problem in a lawsuit seeking to enforce an e-mail or web contract is evidence, but this problem, which exists in almost all lawsuits, can be overcome by printing out the e-mail or web contract and its prior e-mail or web negotiations, if necessary.

LANDMARK LAW

Electronic Signatures in Global and National Commerce Act (E-SIGN Act)

In 2000, the federal government enacted the **Electronic Signatures in Global and National Commerce Act (E-SIGN Act)**.[5] This act is a federal statute enacted by Congress and therefore has national reach. The act is designed to place the world of electronic commerce on a par with the world of paper contracts in the United States.

Writing Requirement of the Statute of Frauds Met
One of the main features of the E-SIGN Act is that it recognizes electronic contracts as meeting the writing requirement of the Statute of Frauds for most contracts. Statutes of Frauds are state laws that require certain types of contracts to be in writing. The 2000 federal act provides that electronically signed contracts cannot be denied effect because they are in electronic form or delivered electronically. The act also provides that record retention requirements are satisfied if the records are stored electronically.

The federal law was passed with several provisions to protect consumers. First, consumers must consent to receiving electronic records and contracts. Second, to receive electronic records, consumers must be able to demonstrate that they have access to the electronic records. Third, businesses must tell consumers that they have the right to receive hard-copy documents of their transaction.

E-Signatures Recognized as Valid
In the past, signatures have been hand-applied by the person signing a document. No more. In the electronic commerce world, it is now "What is your mother's maiden name?" "Slide your smart card in the sensor," or "Look into the iris scanner." But are electronic signatures sufficient to form an enforceable contract? The federal E-SIGN Act made the answer clear.

The E-SIGN Act recognizes an **electronic signature**, or **e-signature**. The act gives an e-signature the same force and effect as a pen-inscribed signature on paper. The act is technology neutral, however, in that the law does not define or decide which technologies should be used to create a legally binding signature in cyberspace. Loosely defined, a **digital signature** is some electronic method that identifies an individual. The challenge is to make sure that someone who uses a digital signature is the person he or she claims to be. The act provides that a digital signature can basically be verified in one of three ways:

1. By something the signatory knows, such as a secret password, pet's name, and so forth
2. By something a person has, such as a smart card, which looks like a credit card and stores personal information
3. By biometrics, which uses a device that digitally recognizes fingerprints or the retina or iris of the eye

The verification of electronic signatures is creating a need for the use of scanners and methods for verifying personal information.

▶ E-LICENSING

Much of the new cyberspace economy is based on electronic contracts and the licensing of computer software and information. E-commerce created problems for forming contracts over the Internet, enforcing e-commerce contracts, and providing consumer protection. To address these problems, in 1999 the National Conference of Commissioners on Uniform State Laws (a group of lawyers, judges, and legal scholars) drafted the **Uniform Computer Information Transactions Act (UCITA)**.

Uniform Computer Information Transactions Act (UCITA)
A model state law that creates contract law for the licensing of information technology rights.

CONTEMPORARY ENVIRONMENT

Uniform Computer Information Transactions Act (UCITA)

The Uniform Computer Information Transactions Act (UCITA) is a model act that establishes a uniform and comprehensive set of rules that govern the creation, performance, and enforcement of computer information transactions. A computer information transaction is an agreement to create, transfer, or license computer information or information rights [UCITA § 102(a)(11)].

The UCITA does not become law until a state's legislature enacts it as a state statute. Most states have adopted e-commerce and licensing statutes that are similar to many of the provisions of the UCITA as their law for computer transactions and the licensing of software and informational rights. The UCITA will be used as the basis for discussing state laws that affect computer, software, and licensing contracts.

Unless displaced by the UCITA, state law and equity principles, including principal and agent law, fraud, duress, mistake, trade secret law, and other state laws, supplement the UCITA [UCITA § 114]. Any provisions of the UCITA that are preempted by federal law are unenforceable to the extent of the preemption [UCITA § 105(a)].

The unique provisions of the UCITA as they apply to e-licensing are discussed in the sections of this chapter and the special "Internet Law & Online Commerce" features that follow.

Licensing

Intellectual property and information rights are extremely important assets of many individuals and companies. Patents, trademarks, copyrights, trade secrets, data, software programs, and such constitute valuable intellectual property and information rights.

The owners of intellectual property and information rights often wish to transfer limited rights in the property or information to parties for specified purposes and limited duration. The agreement that is used to transfer such limited rights is called a **license**, which is defined as follows [UCITA § 102(a)(40)]:

> *License means a contract that authorizes access to, or use, distribution, performance, modification, or reproduction of, information or information rights, but expressly limits the access or uses authorized or expressly grants fewer than all rights in the information, whether or not the transferee has title to a licensed copy. The term includes an access contract, a lease of a computer program, and a consignment of a copy.*

The parties to a license are the licensor and the licensee. The **licensor** is the party who owns the intellectual property or information rights and obligates him- or herself to transfer rights in the property or information to the licensee. The **licensee** is the party who is granted limited rights in or access to the intellectual property or information [UCITA § 102(a)(41), (42)]. A **licensing** arrangement is illustrated in Exhibit 17.2.

license
A contract that transfers limited rights in intellectual property and informational rights.

licensor
An owner of intellectual property or informational rights who transfers rights in the property or information to the licensee.

licensee
A party who is granted limited rights in or access to intellectual property or informational rights owned by a licensor.

▶ **Exhibit 17.2 LICENSING ARRANGEMENT**

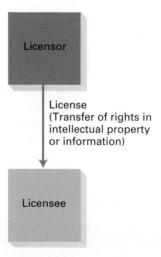

License
(Transfer of rights in intellectual property or information)

A license grants the contractual rights expressly described in the license and the right to use any information rights within the licensor's control that are necessary to exercise the expressly described rights [UCITA § 307(a)]. A license can grant the licensee the exclusive rights to use the information. An **exclusive license** means that for the specified duration of the license, the licensor will not grant to any other person rights in the same information [UCITA § 307(f)(2)].

exclusive license
A license that grants the licensee exclusive rights to use informational rights for a specified duration.

INTERNET LAW & ONLINE COMMERCE
Click-Wrap Licenses

In the past, most business and consumer contracts consisted of written agreements signed by both parties. With the advent of the Internet, many online contracts no longer fit this traditional mode. Take click-wrap licenses, for example. A **click-wrap license** is a contract used by many software companies to sell their software over the Internet or in physical packages where the software is later installed on a computer.

The software company, called the licensor, typically displays a series of dialog boxes on the computer screen that state the terms of the agreement before the software is downloaded or installed by the potential licensee. The terms of a software click-wrap license are typically not negotiable, and the licensee (the person who is granted the license) indicates his or her acceptance by clicking on a prompt button on the screen labeled "I accept" or "I agree." Click-wrap licenses contain terms of the agreement, disclaimers of warranties, guarantees for the protection of trademarks and trade secrets, and other provisions that would normally be contained in a paper license. Click-wrap agreements provide a fast, inexpensive, and convenient way for licensors to mass market their software to users without requiring paper contracts or physical signatures.

A question recently presented to the courts is whether click-wrap licenses are enforceable. The courts have held that a party is considered to have manifested her consent to enter into a contract by her physical action of using a mouse to click the "I Agree" prompt button for the click-wrap license.

The Uniform Computer Information Transactions Act (UCITA) specifically provides that a licensee who has the opportunity to review the terms of the license is bound by those terms if the licensee "manifests assent" before or during the party's initial use of or access to the licensor's software [UCITA § 210(a)]. Thus, under the modern e-commerce interpretation of the law of contracts, popular click-wrap licenses are enforceable contracts between software licensors and user licensees.

Licensing Agreement

A licensor and a licensee usually enter into a written **licensing agreement** that expressly states the terms of their agreement. Licensing agreements tend to be very detailed and comprehensive contracts. This is primarily because of the nature of the subject matter and the limited uses granted in the intellectual property or informational rights.

licensing agreement
A detailed and comprehensive written agreement between a licensor and a licensee that sets forth the express terms of their agreement.

Breach of License Agreement

The parties to a contract for the licensing of information owe a duty to perform the obligations stated in the contract. If a party fails to perform as required, there is a breach of the contract. Breach of contract by one party to a licensing agreement gives the non-breaching party certain rights, including the right to recover damages or other remedies [UCITA § 701].

Each party to a license agreement expects to receive due performance from the other party. If any reasonable grounds arise prior to the performance date that make one party think that the other party might not deliver performance when due, the aggrieved party may demand adequate assurance of due performance from the other party. Until such assurance is received, the aggrieved party may, if commercially reasonable, suspend performance until assurance is received. Failure to provide assurance within 30 days permits the aggrieved party to repudiate the contract [UCITA § 708].

If a licensor tenders a copy that is a material breach of the contract, the nonbreaching party to whom tender is made may either (1) refuse the tender, (2) accept the tender, or (3) accept any commercially reasonable units and refuse the rest [UCITA § 704].

If a licensee has accepted tender of a copy where the nonconformity is a material breach, the licensee may later revoke his or her acceptance if (1) acceptance was made because discovery was difficult at the time of tender but was then later discovered or (2) the nonconformity was discovered at the time of tender but the licensor agreed to cure the defect, and the defect has not been reasonably cured [UCITA § 707].

Our legal system faces no theoretical dilemma but a single continuous problem: how to apply to ever changing conditions the never changing principles of freedom.

Earl Warren
(1995)

INTERNET LAW & ONLINE COMMERCE
Consumers Saved from Electronic Errors

The UCITA provides that consumers are not bound by their unilateral **electronic errors** if a consumer:

1. Promptly upon learning of the error notifies the licensor of the error
2. Does not use or receive any benefit from the information or make the information or benefit available to a third party
3. Delivers all copies of the information to the licensor or destroys all copies of the information, pursuant to reasonable instructions from the licensor
4. Pays all shipping, reshipping, and processing costs of the licensor [UCITA § 217]

The UCITA does not relieve a consumer of his or her electronic error if the other party provides a reasonable method to detect and correct or avoid the error. Thus, many sellers establish methods whereby the buyer must verify the information and purchase order a second time before an electronic order is processed. This procedure strips the consumer of the defense of UCITA Section 217. Section 217 of the UCITA applies only to consumers who make electronic errors in contracting. Electronic errors by non-consumers are handled under the common law of contracts or the Uniform Commercial Code (UCC), whichever applies.

Example Kai, a consumer, intends to order 10 copies of a video game over the Internet from Cybertendo, a video game producer. In fact, Kai makes an error and orders 110 games. The electronic agent maintaining Cybertendo's website's ordering process electronically disburses 110 games. The next morning Kai discovers his mistake and immediately e-mails Cybertendo, describing the mistake and offering to return or destroy the copies at his expense. When Kai receives the games, he returns the 110 copies unused. Under the UCITA, Kai has no contract obligation for 110 copies but bears the cost of returning them to Cybertendo or destroying them if Cybertendo instructs him to do so. However, if Cybertendo's website's electronic ordering system had asked Kai to confirm his order of 110 copies of the purchase order, and Kai had confirmed the original order of 110 copies, Kai would have had to pay for the 110 copies, even if his confirmation had been in error.

Remedies

> *You must remember that some things that are legally right are not morally right."*
>
> Abraham Lincoln
> (1840)

The UCITA provides certain *remedies* to an aggrieved party upon the breach of a licensing agreement. A party may not recover more than once for the same loss, and his or her remedy (other than liquidated damages) may not exceed the loss caused by the breach [UCITA § 801]. The UCITA provides that a cause of action must be commenced within one year after the breach was or should have been discovered but not more than five years after the breach actually occurred [UCITA § 805]. Remedies are discussed in the following paragraphs.

cancellation
The termination of a contract by a contracting party upon the material breach of the contract by the other party.

Cancellation   If there has been a material breach of a contract that has not been cured or waived, the aggrieved party may cancel the contract. **Cancellation** is effective when the canceling party notifies the breaching party of the cancellation. Upon cancellation, the breaching party in possession or control of copies, information, documentation, or other materials that are the property of the other party must use commercially reasonable efforts to return them or hold them for disposal on instructions from the other party. All obligations that are executory on both sides at the time of cancellation are discharged [UCITA § 802(a) and (b)].

Upon cancellation of a license, the licensor has the right to have all copies of the licensed information returned by the licensee and to prevent the licensee from continuing to use the licensed information.

licensor's damages
Monetary damages that a licensor may recover from a licensee who breaches a contract.

Licensor's Damages   If a licensee breaches a contract, the licensor may recover **licensor's damages**. The licensor may sue and recover from the licensee monetary damages caused by the breach, plus any consequential and incidental damages [UCITA § 808]. A licensor can recover *lost profits* caused by the licensee's failure to accept or complete performance of the contract. Lost profits is a proper measure of damages in this case because the licensor has effectively unlimited capability to make access available to others so there will be no license to substitute to reduce damages owed by the breaching licensee.

Example iSuperSoftware.com licenses a master disk of its software program to Distributors, Inc., to make and distribute 10,000 copies of the software. This is a nonexclusive license, and the license fee is $1 million. It costs iSuperSoftware.com $15 to produce the disk. If Distributors, Inc., refuses the disk and breaches the contract, iSuperSoftware.com can recover $1 million less $15 as damages for the profits lost on the transaction.

INTERNET LAW & ONLINE COMMERCE
Electronic Self-Help Permitted to Licensor

Just like normal contracts, electronic licenses can be breached by licensees. If such a breach occurs, the licensor can resort to remedies provided in the UCITA. Sections 815 and 816 of the UCITA provide that a licensor can resort to **electronic self-help** if a breach occurs—for example, if the licensee fails to pay the license fee. Such electronic self-help can consist of activating disabling bugs and time bombs that have been embedded in the software or information that will prevent the licensee from further using the software or information.

Section 816 provides that a licensor is entitled to use electronic self-help only if the following requirements are met:

1. The licensee must specifically agree to the inclusion in the license of self-help as a remedy. There must be a specific self-help option to which the licensee assents.

2. The licensor must give the licensee at least 15 days' notice prior to the disabling action. The notice period allows the licensee to make lawful adjustments to minimize the effects of the licensor's self-help or to seek a judicial remedy to combat the use of the self-help.

3. The licensor may not use self-help if doing so would cause a breach of the peace, risk personal injury, cause significant damage or injury to information other than the licensee's information, result in injury to the public health or safety, or cause grave harm to national security.

A licensor who violates these provisions and uses self-help improperly is liable for damages. This liability cannot be disclaimed.

Licensee's Damages   When a licensor breaches a contract, the licensee may sue and recover monetary damages from the licensor. The amount of the damages depends on the facts of the situation. This is called the **licensee's damages**. Upon the licensor's breach, the licensee may either (1) cover by purchasing other electronic information from another source and recover the difference between the value of the promised performance from the licensor and the cost of cover or (2) not cover and recover the value of the performance from the licensor. **Cover** involves engaging in a commercially reasonable substitute transaction. The licensee may obtain an award of consequential and incidental damages in either case. A licensee cannot obtain excessive or double recovery [UCITA § 809].

Limitation of Remedies   The UCITA provides that the parties to an agreement may **limit the remedies** available for breach of the contract. This is done by including provisions in the contract. Remedies may be restricted to the return of copies and repayment of the licensing fee or limited to the repair or replacement of the nonconforming copies. Limitations of remedies in licenses subject to the UCITA are enforceable unless they are unconscionable [UCITA § 803].

▶ CYBER CRIMES

The advent of the computer and the Internet created an ability of persons to engage in a new form of crimes called *cyber crimes*. New technologies have allowed criminals to commit existing crimes using a new medium.

Fraud can now be perpetrated over the Internet. In addition, the Internet has allowed criminals to engage in new crimes. The police, law enforcement agencies, Congress, and the courts have had to address these new cyber crimes. In response, Congress has enacted several new federal statutes that define criminal behavior using computers and the Internet. The courts have had to interpret and apply these new statutes, as well as apply existing criminal statutes to this new medium of crime.

licensee's damages
Monetary damages that a licensee may recover from a licensor who breaches a contract.

cover
A licensee's right to engage in a commercially reasonable substitute transaction after the licensor has breached the contract.

The 'Net is a waste of time, and that's exactly what's right about it.

William Gibson

INTERNET LAW & ONLINE COMMERCE

Counterfeit Access Device and Computer Fraud and Abuse Act (CFAA)

The **Counterfeit Access Device and Computer Fraud and Abuse Act (CFAA)** of 1984, as amended, makes it a federal crime to access a computer knowingly to obtain (1) restricted federal government information, (2) financial records of financial institutions, and

(3) consumer reports of consumer reporting agencies. The act also makes it a crime to use counterfeit or unauthorized access devices, such as cards or code numbers, to obtain things of value, transfer funds, or traffic in such devices.[6]

INTERNET LAW & ONLINE COMMERCE

Electronic Funds Transfer Act (EFTA)

The **Electronic Funds Transfer Act (EFTA)** regulates the payment and deposit of funds using electronic funds transfers, such as direct deposit of payroll and Social Security checks in financial institutions, transactions using automated teller machines (ATMs), and such. The act

makes it a federal crime to use, furnish, sell, or transport a counterfeit, stolen, lost, or fraudulently obtained ATM card, code number, or other device used to conduct electronic funds transfers. The act imposes criminal penalties of imprisonment and the assessment of criminal fines.[7]

INTERNET LAW & ONLINE COMMERCE

Cyber Identity Fraud

For centuries, some people—for various purposes, mostly financial in nature—have attempted to take the identities of other persons. Today, stealing the identity of another can be extremely lucrative, earning the spoils of another's credit cards, bank accounts, Social Security benefits, and such. The use of new technology—computers and the Internet—has made such "identity fraud" easier than ever before. But a victim of such fraud may be left with funds stolen, a dismantled credit history, and thousands of dollars in costs trying to straighten out the mess. Identity fraud is the fastest-growing financial fraud in America.

To combat identity fraud, Congress passed the **Identity Theft and Assumption Deterrence Act** of 1998.[8] This act criminalizes identity fraud, making it a federal felony punishable with prison sentences ranging from 3 to 25 years. The act also appoints a federal administrative agency, the Federal Trade Commission (FTC), to help victims restore their credit and erase the impact of the imposter.

Law enforcement officials suggest the following steps to protect against identity fraud: Never put your Social Security number on any document unless it is legally required, obtain and review copies of your credit report at least twice each year, and use safe passwords (e.g., other than family names and birthdays) on bank accounts and other accounts that require personal identification numbers (PINs).

DETER·DETECT·DEFEND

AVOID THEFT

INTERNET LAW & ONLINE COMMERCE

Information Infrastructure Protection Act (IIP Act)

The Internet and Information Age ushered in a whole new world for education, business and consumer transactions. But what followed was a rash of cyber crimes. Prosecutors and courts wrestled over how to apply existing laws written in a nondigital age to new Internet-related abuses.

In 1996, Congress responded by enacting the **Information Infrastructure Protection Act (IIP Act)**.[9] In this federal law, Congress addressed computer-related crimes as distinct offenses. The IIP Act provides protection for any computer attached to the Internet.

The IIP Act makes it a federal crime for anyone to intentionally access and acquire information from a protected computer without authorization. The IIP Act does not require that the defendant accessed a protected computer for commercial benefit. Thus, persons who transmit a computer virus over the Internet or hackers who trespass into Internet-connected computers may be criminally prosecuted under the IIP Act. Even merely observing data on a protected computer without authorization is sufficient to meet the requirement that the defendant has accessed a protected computer. Criminal penalties for violating the IIP Act include imprisonment and fines.

The IIP Act gives the federal government a much-needed weapon for directly prosecuting cyber-crooks, hackers, and others who enter, steal, destroy, or look at others' computer data without authorization.

State Criminal Laws

Often, larceny statutes cover only the theft of tangible property. Because computer software, programs, and data are intangible property, they are not covered by some existing state criminal statutes. To compensate for this, many states have either modernized existing laws to include computer crime or amended existing penal codes to make certain abuses of computers a criminal offense. Computer trespass, the unauthorized use of computers, tampering with computers, and the unauthorized duplication of computer-related materials are usually forbidden by these acts.[10]

Our growing reliance on computers has made us more aware of the risks associated with losing the data stored on them. As a result, it is likely that the safety of the nation's ever-expanding computer networks will be legislated even more in the future.

ETHICS SPOTLIGHT

Computer Hacker Found Guilty of Cyber Crime

In "techie" circles, Kevin D. Mitnick became the underground icon of computer hackers. During a decade's reign, Mitnick terrorized the federal government, universities, and such high-tech companies as Sun Microsystems, Novell Corporation, MCI Communications, Digital Equipment Corporation, and others by breaking into their computer systems. Mitnick used his computer skills to penetrate his victims' computer systems to steal secret information and wreak havoc with their software and data.

Mitnick, a self-taught computer user, has a history of computer-related crime. As a 17-year-old, he was placed on probation for stealing computer manuals from a Pacific Bell Telephone switching center in Los Angeles. Mitnick was next accused of breaking into federal government and military computers. He has also been accused of breaking into the nation's telephone and cellular telephone networks, stealing thousands of data files and trade secrets from corporate targets, obtaining at least 20,000 credit card numbers of some of the country's richest persons, and sabotaging government, university, and private computer systems around the nation. Mitnick was arrested and convicted of computer crimes and served time in prison.

Upon release from prison, he was put on probation and placed in a medical program to treat his compulsive addiction to computers, which included a court order to not touch a computer or modem. Mitnick dropped out of sight and evaded federal law enforcement officials for several years as he continued a life of computer crime.

Mitnick's next undoing came when he broke into the computer of Tsutomu Shimomura, a researcher at the San Diego Supercomputer Center. Shimomura, a cybersleuth who advises the FBI and major companies on computer and Internet security, made it his crusade to catch the hacker who broke into his computer. Shimomura watched electronically as Mitnick invaded other computers across the country, but he could not physically locate Mitnick because he disguised his whereabouts by breaking into telephone company computers and rerouting all his computer calls. Eventually, Shimomura's patient watching paid off, as he traced the electronic burglar to Raleigh, North Carolina. Shimomura flew to Raleigh, where he used a cellular-frequency-direction-finding antenna to locate Mitnick's apartment. The FBI was notified, and an arrest warrant was obtained from a judge at his home. The FBI arrested Mitnick at his apartment. Mitnick was placed in jail without bail, pending the investigation of his case.

Mitnick's computer crimes spree has been estimated to have cost his victims several hundreds of millions of dollars in losses. Mitnick has not been accused of benefiting financially from his deeds. Mitnick entered into a plea agreement with federal prosecutors. The U.S. District Court judge sentenced Kevin Mitnick to 46 months in prison, including time served, and ordered him to pay

$4,125 in restitution to the companies he victimized. The judge called this a token amount but did not order a larger restitution because she believed Mitnick would not be able to pay more. After serving his time in jail, Mitnick was released from prison. As part of the sentencing, Mitnick cannot use electronic devices, from PCs to cellular telephones, during an additional probationary period following his release from prison. Mitnick is now acting as a consultant to businesses, advising them how to protect themselves from computer hackers.

Business Ethics Do you think hackers cause much economic loss? Should Mitnick have been given a greater sentence in this case? Why or why not?

Siem Reap, Cambodia *The world is connected by the Internet and World Wide Web.*

TEST REVIEW TERMS AND CONCEPTS

Anticybersquatting Consumer Protection Act (ACPA)
Bad faith
Cancellation
Click-wrap license
Communications Decency Act
Controlling the Assault of Non-Solicited Pornography and Marketing Act (CAN-SPAM Act)
Counterfeit Access Device and Computer Fraud and Abuse Act (CFAA)

Cover
Digital signature
Domain name
Electronic commerce (E-commerce)
Electronic Communications Privacy Act (ECPA)
Electronic errors
Electronic Funds Transfer Act (EFTA)
Electronic mail (e-mail)
Electronic self-help
Electronic signature (e-signature)
Electronic Signatures in Global and National

Commerce Act (E-SIGN Act)
E-mail contract
Exclusive license
Identity Theft and Assumption Deterrence Act
Information Infrastructure Protection Act (IIP Act)
Internet (Net)
Internet service provider (ISP)
License
Licensee

Licensee's damages
Licensing
Licensing agreement
Licensor
Licensor's damages
Limitation of remedies
Uniform Computer Information Transactions Act (UCITA)
Web contract
Website
World Wide Web

CASE PROBLEMS

17.1 Domain Name Francis Net, a freshman in college and a computer expert, browses websites for hours each day. One day, she thinks to herself, "I can make money registering domain names and selling them for a fortune." She has recently seen an advertisement for Classic Coke, a cola drink produced and marketed by Coca-Cola Company. Coca-Cola Company has a famous trademark on the term *Classic Coke* and has spent millions of dollars advertising this brand and making the term famous throughout the United States and the world. Francis goes to the website **www.networksolutions.com**, an

Internet domain name registration service, to see if the Internet domain name **classiccoke.com** has been taken. She discovers that it is available, so she immediately registers the Internet domain name **classiccoke.com** for herself and pays the $70 registration fee with her credit card. Coca-Cola Company decides to register the Internet domain name **classiccoke.com,** but when it checks at Network Solutions, Inc.'s, website, it discovers that Francis Net has already registered the Internet domain name. Coca-Cola Company contacts Francis, who demands $500,000 for the name. Coca-Cola Company sues Francis to prevent Francis from using the Internet domain name **classiccoke.com** and to recover it from her under the federal ACPA. Who wins?

17.2 E-Mail Contract The Little Steel Company is a small steel fabricator that makes steel parts for various metal machine shop clients. When Little Steel Company receives an order from a client, it must locate and purchase 10 tons of a certain grade of steel to complete the order. The Little Steel Company sends an e-mail message to West Coast Steel Company, a large steel company, inquiring about the availability of 10 tons of the described grade of steel. The West Coast Steel Company replies by e-mail that it has available the required 10 tons of steel and quotes $450 per ton. The Little Steel Company's purchasing agent replies by e-mail that the Little Steel Company will purchase the 10 tons of described steel at the quoted price of $450 per ton. The e-mails are signed electronically by the Little Steel Company's purchasing agent and the selling agent of the West Coast Steel Company. When the steel arrives at the Little Steel Company's plant, the Little Steel Company rejects the shipment, claiming the defense of the Statute of Frauds. The West Coast Steel Company sues the Little Steel Company for damages. Who wins?

17.3 Contract Einstein Financial Analysts, Inc. (EFA), has developed an electronic database that has recorded the number of plastic pails manufactured and sold in the United States since plastic was first invented. Using this data and a complicated patented software mathematical formula developed by EFA, a user can predict with 100 percent accuracy (historically) how the stock of each of the companies of the Dow Jones Industrial Average will perform on any given day of the year. William Buffet, an astute billionaire investor, wants to increase his wealth, so he enters into an agreement with EFA whereby he is granted the sole right to use the EFA data (updated daily) and its financial model for the next five years. Buffet pays EFA $100 million for the right to the data and mathematical formula. After using the data and software formula for one week, Buffet discovers that EFA has also transferred the right to use the EFA plastic pail database and software formula to his competitor. Buffet sues EFA. What type of arrangement has EFA and Buffet entered into? Who wins?

17.4 License An Internet firm called Info.com, Inc., licenses computer software and electronic information over the Internet. Info.com has a website, **Info.com**, where users can license Info.com software and electronic information. The website is operated by an electronic agent; a potential user enters Info.com's website and looks at available software and electronic information that is available from Info.com. Mildred Hayward pulls up the Info.com website on her computer and decides to order a certain type of Info.com software. Hayward enters the appropriate product code and description; her name, mailing address, and credit card information; and other data needed to complete the order for a three-year license at $300 per month. The electronic agent has Hayward verify all the information a second time. When Hayward has completed verifying the information, she types at the end of her order, "I accept this electronic software only if after I have used it for two months I still personally like it." Info.com's electronic agent delivers a copy of the software to Hayward, who downloads the copy of the software onto her computer. Two weeks later, Hayward sends the copy of the software back to Info.com, stating, "Read our contract: I personally don't like this software; cancel my license." Info.com sues Hayward to recover the license payments for three years. Who wins?

17.5 Electronic Signature David Abacus uses the Internet to place an order to license software for his computer from Inet.License, Inc. (Inet), through Inet's electronic website ordering system. Inet's webpage order form asks David to type in his name, mailing address, telephone number, e-mail address, credit card information, computer location information, and personal identification number. Inet's electronic agent requests that David verify the information a second time before it accepts the order, which David does. The license duration is two years, at a license fee of $300 per month. Only after receiving the verification of information does Inet's electronic agent place the order and send an electronic copy of the software program to David's computer, where he installs the new software program. David later refuses to pay the license fee due Inet because he claims his electronic signature and information were not authentic. Inet sues David to recover the license fee. Is David's electronic signature enforceable against him?

17.6 License Tiffany Pan, a consumer, intends to order three copies of a financial software program from iSoftware, Inc. Tiffany, using her computer, enters iSoftware's website **isoftware.com** and places an order with the electronic agent taking orders for the website. The license provides for a duration of three years at $300 per month for each copy of the software program. Tiffany enters the necessary product code and description; her name, mailing address, and credit card information; and other data necessary to place the order. When the electronic order form prompts Tiffany to enter the number of copies of the software program she is ordering, Tiffany mistakenly types in "30." iSoftware's electronic agent places the order and ships 30 copies of the software program to Tiffany. When Tiffany receives the 30 copies of the software program, she ships them back to iSoftware with a note stating, "Sorry, there has been a mistake. I only meant to order

3 copies of the software, not 30." When iSoftware bills Tiffany for the license fees for the 30 copies, Tiffany refuses to pay. iSoftware sues Tiffany to recover the license fees for 30 copies. Who wins?

17.7 License   Silvia Miofsky licenses a software program from Accura.com, Inc., to sort information from a database to be used in Silvia's financial planning business. The license is for three years, and the license fee is $500 per month. The new software program from Accura.com will be run in conjunction with other software programs and databases used by Silvia in her business. The licensing agreement between Accura.com and Silvia and the label on the software package state that the copy of the licensed software program has been tested by Accura.com and will run without error. Silvia installs the copy of Accura.com's software, but every fifth or sixth time the program is run, it fails to operate properly and shuts down Silvia's computer and other programs. Silvia sends the software, marked *defective*, back to Accura.com. When Accura.com bills Silvia for the unpaid license fees for the

three years of the license, Silvia refuses to pay. Accura.com sues Silvia to recover the license fees under the three year license. Who wins?

17.8 License   Metatag, Inc., is a developer and distributor of software and electronic information rights over the Internet. Metatag produces a software program called Virtual 4-D Links; a user of the program merely types in the name of a city and address anywhere in the world, and the computer transports the user there and creates a four-dimensional space and a sixth sense unknown to the world before. The software license is nonexclusive, and Metatag licenses its Virtual 4-D Link to millions of users worldwide. Nolan Bates, who has lived alone with his mother too long, licenses the Virtual 4-D Link program for five years for a license fee of $350 per month. Bates uses the program for two months before his mother discovers why he has had a smile on his face lately. Bates, upon his mother's urging, returns the Virtual 4-D Link software program to Metatag, stating that he is canceling the license. Metatag sues Bates to recover the unpaid license fees. Who wins?

BUSINESS ETHICS CASES

17.9 Business Ethics   BluePeace.org is a new environmental group that has decided that expounding its environmental causes over the Internet is the best and most efficient way to spend its time and money to advance its environmental causes. To draw attention to its websites, BluePeace.org comes up with catchy Internet domain names. One is **macyswearus.org,** another is **exxonvaldezesseals.org,** and another is **generalmotorscrashesdummies.org.** The **macyswearus.org** website first shows beautiful women dressed in mink fur coats sold by Macy's Department Stores and then goes into graphic photos of minks being slaughtered and skinned and made into the coats. The **exxonvaldezesseals.org** website first shows a beautiful, pristine bay in Alaska, with the *Exxon Valdez* oil tanker quietly sailing through the waters, and then it shows photos of the ship breaking open and spewing forth oil and then seals who are gooed with oil, suffocating and dying on the shoreline. The website **generalmotorscrashesdummies.org** shows a General Motors automobile involved in normal crash tests with dummies followed by photographs of automobile accident scenes where people and children lay bleeding and dying after an accident involving General Motors automobiles. Macy's Department Stores, the Exxon Oil Company, and the General Motors Corporation sue BluePeace.org for violating the federal ACPA. Who wins? Has BluePeace.org acted unethically in this case?

17.10 Business Ethics   Apricot.com is a major software developer that licenses software to be used over the Internet. One of its programs, called Match, is a search engine that searches personal ads on the Internet and provides a match for users for potential dates and possible marriage partners. Nolan Bates subscribes to the Match software program from Apricot.com. The license duration is five years, with a license fee of $200 per month. For each subscriber, Apricot.com produces a separate webpage that shows photos of the subscriber and personal data. Bates places a photo of himself with his mother, with the caption, "Male, 30 years old, lives with mother, likes quiet nights at home." Bates licenses the Apricot.com Match software and uses it 12 hours each day, searching for his Internet match. Bates does not pay Apricot.com the required monthly licensing fee for any of the three months he uses the software. After using the Match software but refusing to pay Apricot.com its licensing fee, Apricot.com activates the disabling bug in the software and disables the Match software on Bates' computer. Apricot.com does this with no warning to Bates. It then sends a letter to Bates stating, "Loser, the license is canceled!" Bates sues Apricot.com for disabling the Match software program. Who wins? Did Bates act ethically? Did Apricot.com act ethically?

ENDNOTES

1.   15 U.S.C. Sections 7701–7713.
2.   47 U.S.C. Section 230 (c)(1).
3.   18 U.S.C. Section 2510.
4.   15 U.S.C. Section 1125(d).
5.   15 U.S.C. Chapter 96.
6.   18 U.S.C. Section 1030.
7.   15 U.S.C. Section 1693.
8.   18 U.S.C. Section 1028.
9.   18 U.S.C. Section 1030.
10. See New York Session Laws, 1986, Chapter 514.

Part IV

DOMESTIC AND INTERNATIONAL SALES AND LEASE CONTRACTS

▲ **Retail Store** *The sale and lease of goods—consumer goods, automobiles, computers, electronics, business equipment, and such—makes up a considerable part of the United States economy. A special law—the Uniform Commercial Code (UCC)—contains rules that apply to contracts for the sale and lease of goods. The UCC is a model act that many states have adopted in whole or in part as their commercial code. Article 2 of the UCC covers sales of goods and Article 2A of the UCC covers the lease of goods. Under the UCC, the sale of goods that exceeds $500 sales price must be in writing to be enforceable.*

CHAPTER OBJECTIVES

After studying this chapter, you should be able to:

1. Describe sales contracts governed by Article 2 of the UCC.
2. Describe lease contracts governed by Article 2A of the UCC.
3. Describe the formation of sales and lease contracts.
4. Define the UCC's firm offer rule, additional terms rule, and written confirmation rule.
5. Describe how Revised Article 2 (Sales) and Article 2A (Leases) permit electronic contracting.

CHAPTER CONTENTS

▶ **INTRODUCTION TO FORMATION OF SALES AND LEASE CONTRACTS**

▶ **UNIFORM COMMERCIAL CODE (UCC)**
Landmark Law · *The Uniform Commercial Code (UCC)*

▶ **ARTICLE 2 (SALES)**
Case 18.1 · Brandt v. Boston Scientific Corporation and Sarah Bush Lincoln Health Center

▶ **ARTICLE 2A (LEASES)**

"Commercial law lies within a narrow compass, and is far purer and freer from defects than any other part of the system."

Henry Peter Brougham
House of Commons, February 7, 1828

▶ INTRODUCTION TO FORMATION OF SALES AND LEASE CONTRACTS

Most tangible items—such as books, clothing, and tools—are considered *goods*. In medieval times, merchants gathered at fairs in Europe to exchange such goods. Over time, certain customs and rules evolved for enforcing contracts and resolving disputes. These customs and rules, which were referred to as the *Law Merchant*, were enforced by "fair courts" established by the merchants. Eventually, the customs and rules of the Law Merchant were absorbed into the common law.

Toward the end of the 1800s, England enacted a statute (the Sales of Goods Act) that codified the common law rules of commercial transactions. In the United States, laws governing the sale of goods also developed. In 1906, the **Uniform Sales Act** was promulgated in the United States and enacted in many states. It was quickly outdated, however, as mass production and distribution of goods developed in the twentieth century.

In 1949, the National Conference of Commissioners on Uniform State Laws promulgated a comprehensive statutory scheme called the *Uniform Commercial Code (UCC)*. The UCC covers most aspects of commercial transactions.

Article 2 (Sales) and *Article 2A (Leases)* of the UCC govern personal property sales and leases. These articles are intended to provide clear, easy-to-apply rules that place the risk of loss of the goods on the party most able to either bear the risk or insure against it. The common law of contracts governs if either Article 2 or Article 2A is silent on an issue. Article 2 (Sales) and Article 2A (Leases) have been revised. Revised Article 2 (Sales) and Revised Article 2A (Leases) recognize the importance of electronic contracting and have established rules for e-contracts for the sale and lease of goods.

This chapter discusses the formation of sales and lease contracts. Subsequent chapters cover the performance, enforcement, breach, and remedies for the breach of sales and lease contracts, as well as sales and lease contract warranties.

▶ UNIFORM COMMERCIAL CODE (UCC)

One of the major frustrations of businesspersons conducting interstate business is that they are subject to the laws of each state in which they operate. To address this problem, in 1949 the National Conference of Commissioners on Uniform State Laws promulgated the **Uniform Commercial Code (UCC)**.

Uniform Commercial Code (UCC)
A model act that includes comprehensive laws that cover most aspects of commercial transactions. All the states have enacted all or part of the UCC as statutes.

LANDMARK LAW
The Uniform Commercial Code (UCC)

The UCC is a **model act** drafted by the American Law Institute and the National Conference of Commissioners on Uniform State Laws. This model act contains uniform rules that govern commercial transactions. For the UCC or any part of the UCC to become law in a state, that state needs to enact the UCC as its commercial law statute. Every state (except Louisiana, which has adopted only parts of the UCC) has enacted the UCC or the majority of the UCC as a commercial statute.

The UCC is divided into articles, with each article establishing uniform rules for a particular facet of commerce in this country. The articles of the UCC are:

Article 1	General Provisions
Article 2	Sales
Revised Article 2	Sales
Article 2A	Leases
Revised Article 2A	Leases
Article 3	Negotiable Instruments
Article 4	Bank Deposits and Collections

Article 4A	Funds Transfers
Article 5	Letters of Credit
Article 6	Bulk Transfers
Article 7	Documents of Title
Article 8	Investment Securities
Article 9	Secured Transactions
Revised Article 9	Secured Transactions

These articles of the UCC are discussed in the chapters in this section of this book.

The UCC is continually being revised to reflect changes in modern commercial practices and technology. Article 2, which establishes rules that govern the sale of goods, was recently revised. Article 2A, which governs leases of personal property, was recently revised. Article 4A was added to regulate the use of wire transfers in the banking system. Articles 3 and 4, which cover the creation and transfer of negotiable instruments and the clearing of checks through the banking system, were substantially amended. Article 9, which covers secured transactions in personal property, was also revised.

▶ ARTICLE 2 (SALES)

Article 2 (Sales)
An article of the UCC that governs sale of goods.

All states except Louisiana have adopted some version of **Article 2 (Sales)** of the UCC. Article 2 is also applied by federal courts to sales contracts governed by federal law. Article 2 has recently been revised. This article, referred to as *Revised Article 2*, has been adopted by some states. Article 2 (Sales) is set forth as Appendix B to this book.

What Is a Sale?

sale
The passing of title of goods from a seller to a buyer for a price.

Article 2 of the UCC applies to transactions in goods [UCC 2-102]. All states have held that Article 2 applies to the sale of goods. A **sale** consists of the passing of title of goods from a seller to a buyer for a price [UCC 2-106(1)].

Example The purchase of a computer is a sale subject to Article 2, whether the computer was paid for using cash, credit card, or another form of consideration (see Exhibit 18.1).

▶ **Exhibit 18.1 SALES TRANSACTION**

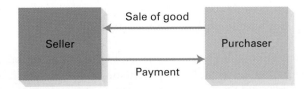

What Are Goods?

goods
Tangible things that are movable at the time of their identification to a contract.

Goods are defined as tangible things that are movable at the time of their identification to a contract [UCC 2-105(1)]. Specially manufactured goods and the unborn young of animals are examples of goods. Certain items are not considered goods and are not subject to Article 2. They include:

• Money and intangible items are not tangible goods.

Examples Stocks, bonds, and patents are not tangible goods.

• Real estate is not a tangible good because it is not movable [UCC 2-105(1)]. Minerals, structures, growing crops, and other things that are severable from real estate may be classified as goods subject to Article 2, however.

Examples The sale and removal of a chandelier in a house is a sale of goods subject to Article 2 because its removal would not materially harm the real estate. The sale and removal of the furnace, however, would be a sale of real property because its removal would cause material harm [UCC 2-107(2)].

Goods Versus Services

Contracts for the provision of services—including legal services, medical services, and den tal services—are not covered by Article 2. Sometimes, however, a sale involves both the provision of a service and a good in the same transaction. This sale is referred to as a **mixed sale**. Article 2 applies to mixed sales only if the goods are the predominant part of the transaction. Whether the sale of goods is the predominant part of a mixed sale is decided by courts on a case-by-case basis.

In the following case, the court had to decide whether a sale was of a good or a service.

mixed sale
A sale that involves the provision of a service and a good in the same transaction.

CASE 18.1 Good or Service

Brandt v. Boston Scientific Corporation and Sarah Bush Lincoln Health Center

204 Ill.2d 640, 792 N.E.2d 296, Web 2003 Ill. Lexis 785 (2003)
Supreme Court of Illinois

"**Where there is a mixed contract for goods and services, there is a transaction in goods only if the contract is predominantly for goods and incidentally for services.**"

—Justice Garman

Facts

Brenda Brandt was admitted to Sarah Bush Lincoln Health Center (Health Center) to receive treatment for urinary incontinence. During the course of an operation, the doctor surgically implanted a ProteGen Sling (sling) in Brandt. Subsequently, the manufacturer of the sling, Boston Scientific Corporation, issued a recall of the sling because it was causing medical complications in some patients. Brandt suffered serious complications and had the sling surgically removed.

Brandt sued Boston Scientific Corporation and the Health Center for breach of the implied warranty of merchantability included in Article 2 (Sales) of the Uniform Commercial Code (UCC). Health Center filed a motion with the court to have the case against it dismissed. Health Center argued that it was a provider of services and not a merchant that sold goods, and because the UCC (Sales) applies to the sale of goods, Health Center was not subject to the UCC. The trial court agreed with Health Center, found that the transaction was predominantly the provision of services and not the sale of goods, and dismissed Brandt's case against Health Center. The appellate court affirmed the decision. Brandt appealed.

Issue

Was the transaction between Brandt and Health Center predominantly the provision of services or the sale of goods?

Language of the Court

Article 2 of the UCC imposes the implied warranty of merchantability. To succeed on a claim of breach of implied warranty of merchantability, a plaintiff must allege and prove: (1) a sale of goods (2) by a merchant of those goods, and (3) the goods were not of merchantable quality. Where there is a mixed contract for goods and services, there is a transaction in goods only if the contract is predominantly for goods and incidentally for services.

We now apply the predominant purpose test to the facts of this case. In this case, Brandt's bill from the Health Center reflects that of the $11,174.50 total charge for her surgery, a charge of $1,659.50, or 14.9%, was for the sling and its surgical kit; a charge of $5,428.50, or 48.6%, was for all movable goods, including pharmaceuticals, medical supplies, and sterile supplies. The remainder of the charges were for various services, including the hospital and operating rooms and various kinds of medical testing and treatment. A charge for the implantation of the sling by the surgeon was not included in the bill. A majority of the charges, 51.4%, were for services rather than goods. Only a small fraction of the total charge was for the sling, the goods at issue in this case.

These services, the medical treatment, were the primary purpose of the transaction between Brandt and the

(case continues)

Health Center, and the purchase of the sling was incidental to the treatment. Brandt can seek recovery from the manufacturer of the sling.

Decision

The supreme court of Illinois held that the provision of services, and not the sale of goods, was the predominant feature of the transaction between Brandt and Health Center and that Health Center was not liable under Article 2 (Sales) of the UCC. The supreme court of Illinois affirmed the decision of the trial court and appellate court that dismissed Brandt's lawsuit against Health Center.

Case Questions

Critical Legal Thinking   What is a good? Where there is a mixed contract for goods and services, what does the predominant purpose test provide?

Business Ethics   Why do you think Brandt sued Health Center for violation of UCC Article 2 (Sales)?

Contemporary Business   Is Boston Scientific Corporation subject to a UCC Article 2 lawsuit in this case? Why or why not?

Who Is a Merchant?

merchant
A person who (1) deals in the goods of the kind involved in a transaction or (2) by his or her occupation holds himself or herself out as having knowledge or skill peculiar to the goods involved in the transaction.

Generally, Article 2 of the UCC applies to all sales contracts, whether they involve merchants or not. However, Article 2 contains several provisions that either apply only to merchants or impose a greater duty on merchants. UCC 2-104(1) defines a **merchant** as (1) a person who deals in the goods of the kind involved in the transaction or (2) a person who by his or her occupation holds himself or herself out as having knowledge or skill peculiar to the goods involved in the transaction.

Examples   A sporting goods dealer is a merchant with respect to the sporting goods he sells. This sporting goods dealer is not a merchant concerning the sale of his lawn mower to a neighbor.

Automobile Showroom
Many people and businesses lease their automobiles and other vehicles from dealers and other vehicle providers. Automobile and vehicle leases are subject to the rules of Article 2A (Leases) of the Uniform Commercial Code.

▶ ARTICLE 2A (LEASES)

Article 2A (Leases)
An article of the UCC that governs leases of goods.

Personal property leases are a billion-dollar industry. Consumer leases of automobiles or equipment and commercial leases of such items as aircraft and industrial machinery fall into this category. **Article 2A (Leases)** of the UCC directly addresses personal property leases [UCC 2A-101]. It establishes a comprehensive, uniform law covering the formation, performance, and default of leases in goods [UCC 2A-102, 2A-103(h)].

Article 2A is similar to Article 2. In fact, many Article 2 provisions were simply adapted to reflect leasing terminology and practices that carried over to Article 2A.

Definition of *Lease*

A **lease** is a transfer of the right to the possession and use of named goods for a set term in return for certain consideration [UCC 2A-103(1)(i)(x)]. Leased goods can be anything from a hand tool leased to an individual for a few hours to a complex line of industrial equipment leased to a multinational corporation for a number of years.

In an ordinary lease, the **lessor** is the person who transfers the right of possession and use of goods under the lease [UCC 2A-103(1)(p)]. The **lessee** is the person who acquires the right to possession and use of goods under a lease [UCC 2A-103(1)(n)].

Example Ingersoll-Rand Corporation, which manufactures robotic equipment, enters into a lease to lease robotic equipment to Dow Chemical. Ingersoll-Rand is the lessor, and Dow Chemical is the lessee (see Exhibit 18.2).

lease
A transfer of the right to the possession and use of named goods for a set term in return for certain consideration.

lessor
A person who transfers the right of possession and use of goods under a lease.

lessee
A person who acquires the right to possession and use of goods under a lease.

▶ **Exhibit 18.2 LEASE**

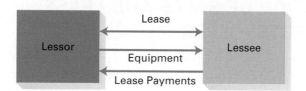

Finance Lease

A **finance lease** is a three-party transaction consisting of a lessor, a lessee, and a **supplier** (or vendor). The lessor does not select, manufacture, or supply the goods. Instead, the lessor acquires title to the goods or the right to their possession and use in connection with the terms of the lease [UCC 2A-103(1)(g)].

finance lease
A three-party transaction consisting of a lessor, a lessee, and a supplier.

Example JetGreen Airways, a commercial air carrier, decides to lease a new airplane that is manufactured by Boeing. To finance the airplane acquisition, JetGreen goes to City Bank. City Bank purchases the airplane from Boeing, and City Bank then leases the airplane to JetGreen. Boeing is the supplier, City Bank is the lessor, and JetGreen is the lessee. City Bank does not take physical delivery of the airplane; the airplane is delivered by Boeing directly to JetGreen (see Exhibit 18.3).

▶ **Exhibit 18.3 FINANCE LEASE**

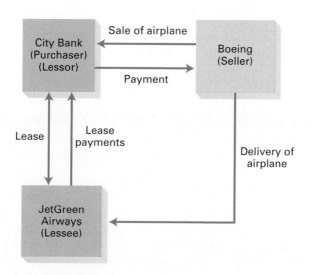

LANDMARK LAW

Revised Article 2 (Sales) and Revised Article 2A (Leases)

After years of study and debate, in 2003 **Revised Article 2 (Sales)** and **Revised Article 2A (Leases)** were promulgated by the National Conference of Commissioners on Uniform State Laws and the American Law Institute.

The modifications to Article 2 and Article 2A include changes to provisions that have been controversial in the past, as well as the addition of new provisions to recognize changes in the commercial environment. The revised Articles 2 and 2A are considered to be the most modern and efficient rules governing the sales and leases of goods.

In addition, the revised Articles 2 and 2A contain many new provisions and rules that recognize the importance of

electronic contracting for the sale and lease of goods. The revised articles provide rules for the creation and enforcement of electronic contracts for the sale and lease of goods.

Since the release of Revised UCC Article 2 (Sales) and Revised UCC Article 2A (Leases) in 2003, states have been studying whether to enact these revised articles as UCC statutes. It is expected that after sufficient study, many states will do so.

This and the following chapters on sales and lease contracts note the changes and differences that Revised Articles 2 and 2A have made to current UCC sales and lease laws.

> *Laws made by common consent must not be trampled on by individuals.*
>
> George Washington

▶ FORMATION OF SALES AND LEASE CONTRACTS: OFFER

As with general contracts, the formation of sales and lease contracts requires an offer and an acceptance. The UCC-established rules for each of these elements often differ considerably from common law.

A contract for the sale or lease of goods may be made in any manner sufficient to show agreement, including conduct by both parties that recognizes the existence of a contract [UCC 2-204(1), 2A-204(1)]. Under the UCC, an agreement sufficient to constitute a contract for the sale or lease of goods may be found even though the moment of its making is undetermined [UCC 2-204(2), 2A-204(2)].

Open Terms

Sometimes the parties to a sales or lease contract leave open a major term in the contract. The UCC is tolerant of open terms. According to UCC 2-204(3) and 2A-204(3), a contract does not fail because of indefiniteness if (1) the parties intended to make a contract and (2) there is a reasonably certain basis for giving an appropriate remedy. In effect, certain **open terms** are permitted to be "read into" a sales or lease contract. This rule is commonly referred to as the **gap-filling rule**. Some examples of terms that are commonly left open are discussed in the following paragraphs.

gap-filling rule
A rule that says an open term can be "read into" a contract.

Open Price Term   If a sales contract does not contain a specific price (**open price term**), a "reasonable price" is implied at the time of delivery.

Example A contract may provide that a price is to be fixed by a market rate, such as a commodities market rate.

Example A contract may provide that a price will be set or recorded by a third person or an agency, such as a government agency. For example, the federal government sets minimum prices for milk products.

A contract may provide that the price will be set by another standard, either upon delivery or on a set date. If the agreed-upon standard is unavailable when the price is to be set, a reasonable price is implied at the time of delivery of the goods [UCC 2-305(1)]. A seller or buyer who reserves the right to fix a price must do so in good faith [UCC 2-305(2)]. When one of the parties fails to fix an open price term, the other party may opt either (1) to treat the contract as canceled or (2) to fix a reasonable price for the goods [UCC 2-305(3)].

Open Payment Term   If the parties to a sales contract do not agree on payment terms, payment is due at the time and place at which the buyer is to receive the goods.

If delivery is authorized and made by way of document of title, payment is due at the time and place at which the buyer is to receive the document of title, regardless of where the goods are to be received [UCC 2-310].

Open Delivery Term   If the parties to a sales contract do not agree to the time, place, and manner of delivery of the goods, the place for delivery is the seller's place of business. If the seller does not have a place of business, delivery is to be made at the seller's residence.

If identified goods are located at some other place, and both parties know of this fact at the time of contracting, that place is the place of delivery [UCC 2-308].

If goods are to be shipped but the shipper is not named, the seller is obligated to make the shipping arrangements. Such arrangements must be made in good faith and within limits of commercial reasonableness [UCC 2-311(2)].

Open Time Term   If the parties to a sales contract do not set a specific time of performance for any obligation under the contract, the contract must be performed within a reasonable time.

If a sales contract provides for successive performance over an unspecified period of time, the contract is valid for a reasonable time [UCC 2-309].

Open Assortment Term   If the assortment of goods to a sales contract is left open, the buyer is given the option of choosing those goods. The buyer must make the selection in good faith and within limits set by commercial reasonableness [UCC 2-311(2)].

The foundation of justice is good faith.

Cicero
De Officiis, Book 1, Chapter VII

CONTEMPORARY ENVIRONMENT

UCC Firm Offer Rule

Recall that the common law of contracts allows the offeror to revoke an offer any time prior to its acceptance. The UCC recognizes an exception to this rule, which is called the **firm offer rule**. This rule states that a *merchant* who (1) offers to buy, sell, or lease goods and (2) gives a written and signed assurance on a separate form that the offer will be held open cannot revoke the offer for the time stated or, if no time is stated, for a reasonable time. The maximum amount of time permitted under this rule is three months [UCC 2-205, 2A-205].

Example On June 1, Sophisticated LLC, a BMW automobile dealer, offers to sell a BMW M3 coupe to Mandy for $60,000. Sophisticated LLC signs a written assurance to keep that offer open to Mandy until July 15. On July 5, Sophisticated LLC sells the car to another buyer. On July 15, Mandy tenders $60,000 for the car. Sophisticated LLC is a merchant subject to the firm offer rule. Sophisticated LLC is liable to Mandy for breach of contract. Thus, if Mandy has to pay $70,000 for the car at another dealership, she can recover $10,000 from Sophisticated LLC.

Consideration

The formation of sales and lease contracts requires consideration. However, the UCC changes the common law rule that requires the modification of a contract to be supported by new consideration. An agreement modifying a sales or lease contract needs no consideration to be binding [UCC 2-209(1), 2A-208(1)].

Modification of a sales or lease contract must be made in good faith [UCC 1-203]. As in the common law of contracts, modifications are not binding if they are obtained through fraud, duress, extortion, and such.

▶ FORMATION OF SALES AND LEASE CONTRACTS: ACCEPTANCE

Both common law and the UCC provide that a contract is created when the offeree (i.e., the buyer or lessee) sends an acceptance to the offeror (seller or lessor), not when the offeror receives the acceptance.

Examples A sales or lease contract is made when the acceptance letter is delivered to the post office. The contract remains valid even if the post office loses the letter. An e-contract is made when the offeree sends an e-mail or another electronic document to the offeror.

Method and Manner of Acceptance

Law must be stable and yet it cannot stand still.

Roscoe Pound
Interpretations of Legal History
(1923)

Unless otherwise unambiguously indicated by language or circumstance, an offer to make a sales or lease contract may be accepted in any manner and by any reasonable medium of acceptance [UCC 2-206(1)(a), 2A-206(1)].

Example A seller sends a telegram to a proposed buyer, offering to sell the buyer certain goods. The buyer responds by mailing a letter of acceptance to the seller. In most circumstances, mailing the letter of acceptance would be considered reasonable. If the goods were extremely perishable or if the market for the goods were very volatile, however, a faster means of acceptance (e.g., a telegram) might be warranted.

If an order or other offer to buy goods requires prompt or current shipment, the offer is accepted if the seller (1) promptly promises to ship the goods or (2) promptly ships either conforming or nonconforming goods [UCC 2-206(1)(b)]. The shipment of conforming goods signals acceptance of the buyer's offer.

Acceptance of goods occurs after the buyer or lessee has a reasonable opportunity to inspect them and signifies that (1) the goods are conforming, (2) he or she will take or retain the goods in spite of their nonconformity, or (3) he or she fails to reject the goods within a reasonable time after tender or delivery [UCC 2-513(1), 2A-515(1)].

CONTEMPORARY ENVIRONMENT

UCC Permits Additional Terms

Under common law's **mirror image rule**, an offeree's acceptance must be on the same terms as the offer. The inclusion of **additional terms** in the acceptance is considered a **counteroffer** rather than an acceptance. Thus, a counteroffer extinguishes the offeror's original offer.

UCC 2-207(1) is more liberal than the mirror image rule. It permits definite and timely expression of acceptance or written confirmation to operate as an acceptance even though they contain terms that are additional to or different from the offered terms, unless the acceptance is expressly conditional on assent to such terms. This rule differs for merchants and nonmerchants.

If one or both parties to a sales contract are nonmerchants, any additional terms are considered **proposed additions** to the contract. The proposed additions do not constitute a counteroffer or extinguish

the original offer. If the offeree's proposed additions are accepted by the original offeror, they become part of the contract. If they are not accepted, the sales contract is formed on the basis of the terms of the original offer [UCC 2-207(2)].

Example A salesperson at a Lexus dealership offers to sell a coupe to a buyer for $65,000. The buyer replies, "I accept your offer, but I would like to have a satellite radio in the car." The satellite radio is a proposed addition to the contract. If the salesperson agrees, the contract between the parties consists of the terms of the original offer plus the additional term regarding the satellite radio. If the salesperson rejects the proposed addition, the sales contract consists of the terms of the original offer because the buyer made a definite expression of acceptance.

Accommodation Shipment

accommodation

A shipment that is offered to a buyer as a replacement for the original shipment when the original shipment cannot be filled.

A shipment of nonconforming goods does not constitute an acceptance if the seller reasonably notifies the buyer that the shipment is offered only as an **accommodation** to the buyer [UCC 2-206(1)(b)].

Example A buyer offers to purchase 500 red umbrellas from a seller. The seller's red umbrellas are temporarily out of stock. The seller sends the buyer 500 green umbrellas and notifies the buyer that these umbrellas are being sent as an accommodation. The seller did not accept (or breach) the contract. The accommodation is a counteroffer from the seller to the buyer. The buyer is free either to accept or to reject the counteroffer.

CONTEMPORARY ENVIRONMENT

"Battle of the Forms"

When merchants negotiate sales contracts, they often exchange preprinted forms. These "boilerplate" forms usually contain terms that favor the drafter. Thus, an offeror who sends a standard form contract as an offer to the offeree may receive an acceptance drafted on the offeree's own form contract. This scenario—commonly called the **battle of the forms**—raises important questions: Is there a contract? If so, what are its terms? The UCC provides guidance in answering these questions.

Under UCC 2-207(2), if both parties are merchants, any additional terms contained in an acceptance become part of the sales contract unless (1) the offer expressly limits acceptance to the terms of the offer, (2) the additional terms materially alter the terms of the original contract, or (3) the offeror notifies the offeree that he or she objects to the additional terms within a reasonable time after receiving the offeree's modified acceptance.

The most important point in the battle of the forms is that there is no contract if the additional terms so materially alter the terms of the original offer that the parties cannot agree on the contract. This fact-specific determination is made by the courts on a case-by-case basis.

▶ UCC STATUTE OF FRAUDS

The UCC includes **Statute of Frauds** provisions that apply to all sales and lease contracts. These provisions are:

- All contracts for the *sale of goods* costing *$500 or more* must be in writing [UCC 2-201(1)].
- *Lease* contracts involving payments of *$1,000 or more* must be in writing [UCC 2A-201(1)].

The writing must be sufficient to indicate that a contract has been made between the parties. Except as discussed in the paragraphs that follow, the writing must be signed by the party against whom enforcement is sought or by his or her authorized agent or broker. If a contract falling within these parameters is not written, it is unenforceable.

Example A seller orally agrees to sell her computer to a buyer for $550. When the buyer tenders the purchase price, the seller asserts the Statute of Frauds and refuses to sell the computer to him. The seller is correct. The contract must be in writing to be enforceable because the contract price for the computer exceeds $499.99.

UCC Statute of Frauds
A rule that requires all contracts for the sale of goods costing $500 or more and lease contracts involving payments of $1,000 or more to be in writing.

Exceptions to the Statute of Frauds

In three situations, a sales or lease contract that would otherwise be required to be in writing is enforceable even if it is not in writing [UCC 2-201(3), UCC 2A-201(4)]:

1. **Specially manufactured goods.**   Buyers and lessees often order **specially manufactured goods**. If a contract to purchase or lease such goods is oral, the buyer or lessee may not assert the Statute of Frauds against the enforcement of the contract if (1) the goods are not suitable for sale or lease to others in the ordinary course of the seller's or the lessor's business and (2) the seller or lessor has made either a substantial beginning of the manufacture of the goods or commitments for their procurement.
2. **Admissions in pleadings or court.**   If the party against whom enforcement of an oral sales or lease contract is sought admits in pleadings, testimony, or otherwise in court that a contract for the sale or lease of goods was made, the oral contract is enforceable against that party. However, the contract is enforceable only as to the quantity of goods admitted.
3. **Part acceptance.**   An oral sales or lease contract that should otherwise be in writing is enforceable to the extent to which the goods have been received and accepted by the buyer or lessee.

The prince is not above the laws, but the laws above the prince.

Pliny the Younger
(Caius Caecilius Secundus)

Example A lessor orally contracts to lease 20 automobiles to a lessee. The lessee accepts the first 8 automobiles tendered by the lessor. This action is part acceptance. The lessee refuses to take delivery of the remaining 12 automobiles. Here, the lessee must pay for the 8 automobiles it originally received and accepted. The lessee does not have to accept or pay for the remaining 12 automobiles.

CONTEMPORARY ENVIRONMENT

UCC Written Confirmation Rule

It both parties to an oral sales or lease contract are merchants, the Statute of Frauds writing requirement can be satisfied if (1) one of the parties to an oral agreement sends a written confirmation of the sale or lease within a reasonable time after contracting and (2) the other merchant does not give written notice of an objection to the contract within 10 days after receiving the confirmation. This situation is true even though the party receiving the written confirmation has not signed it. The only stipulations are that the confirmation is sufficient and that the party to whom it was sent has reason to know its contents [UCC 2-201(2)].

Example A merchant-seller in Chicago orally contracts by telephone to sell goods to a merchant-buyer in Phoenix for $100,000. Within a reasonable time after contracting, the seller sends a sufficient written confirmation to the buyer of the agreed-upon transaction. The buyer, who has reason to know the contents of the written confirmation, fails to object to the contents of the confirmation in writing within 10 days after receiving it. Under the UCC, the Statute of Frauds has been met, and the buyer cannot thereafter raise it against enforcement of the contract.

When Written Modification Is Required

Oral modification of a contract is not enforceable if the parties agree that any modification of the sales or lease contract must be signed in writing [UCC 2-209(2), 2A-208(2)]. In the absence of such an agreement, oral modifications to sales and lease contracts are binding if they do not violate the Statute of Frauds. If the oral modification brings the contract within the Statute of Frauds, it must be in writing to be enforceable.

Example A lessor and lessee enter into an oral lease contract for the lease of goods at a rent of $450. Subsequently, the contract is modified by raising the rent to $550. Because the modified contract rent is more than $499.99, the contract comes under the UCC Statute of Frauds, and the modification must be in writing to be enforceable.

Parol Evidence

parol evidence rule
A rule which says that if a written contract is a complete and final statement of the parties' agreement, any prior or contemporaneous oral or written statements that alter, contradict, or are in addition to the terms of the written contract are inadmissible in court regarding a dispute over the contract.

The **parol evidence rule** states that when a sales or lease contract is evidenced by a writing that is intended to be a final expression of the parties' agreement or a confirmatory memorandum, the terms of the writing may not be contradicted by evidence of (1) a prior oral or written agreement or (2) a contemporaneous oral agreement (i.e., parol evidence) [UCC 2-202, 2A-202]. This rule is intended to ensure certainty in written sales and lease contracts.

Occasionally, the express terms of a written contract are not clear on their face and must be interpreted. In such cases, reference may be made to certain sources outside the contract. These sources are construed together when they are consistent with each other. If that is unreasonable, they are considered in descending order of priority [UCC 2-208(2), 2A-207(2)]:

1. **Course of performance.** The previous conduct of the parties regarding the contract in question
2. **Course of dealing.** The conduct of the parties in prior transactions and contracts
3. **Usage of trade.** Any practice or method of dealing that is regularly observed or adhered to in a place, a vocation, a trade, or an industry

Example A cattle rancher contracts to purchase 3,000 bushels of "corn" from a farmer. The farmer delivers feed corn to the rancher. The rancher rejects this corn and demands delivery of corn that is fit for human consumption. If the parties did not have any prior course of performance or course of dealing that would indicate otherwise, usage of trade would be used to interpret the word *corn*. Thus, the delivery of feed corn would be assumed and become part of the contract.

CONCEPT SUMMARY

COMPARISON OF CONTRACT LAW AND THE LAW OF SALES

Topic	Common Law of Contract	UCC Law of Sales
Definiteness	Contract must contain all the material terms of the parties' agreement.	The UCC gap-filling rule permits terms to be implied if the parties intended to make a contract and there is a reasonably certain basis for giving an appropriate remedy [UCC 2-204].
Irrevocable offers	Option contracts.	Option contracts. Firm offers by merchants to keep an offer open are binding up to three months without any consideration [UCC 2-205].
Counteroffers	Acceptance must be a mirror image of the offer. A counter-offer rejects and terminates the offeror's original offer.	Additional terms of an acceptance become part of the contract if (1) they do not materially alter the terms of the offer and (2) the offeror does not object within a reasonable time after reviewing the acceptance [UCC 2-207].
Statute of Frauds	Writing must be signed by the party against whom enforcement is sought.	Writing may be enforced against a party who has not signed a contract if (1) both parties are merchants, (2) one party sends a written confirmation of oral agreement within a reasonable time after contracting, and (3) the other party does not give written notice of objection within 10 days after receiving the confirmation [UCC 2-201].
Modification	Consideration is required.	Consideration is not required [UCC 2-209].

INTERNET LAW & ONLINE COMMERCE

Revised Article 2 (Sales) and Article 2A (Leases)

Recognize the Importance of Electronic Contracting

Revised Article 2 (Sales) and Revised Article 2A (Leases) contain provisions that recognize the importance of electronic contracting in sales and lease transactions. The revised articles contain new definitions that apply to sales and lease contracts. The following are some of the new definitions for electronic commerce and their implications:

- *Electronic* means relating to technology having electrical, digital, magnetic, wireless, optical, electromagnetic, or similar capabilities [Revised UCC 2-103(1)(f), Revised UCC 2A-103(1)(h)]. This term, as used throughout Revised Articles 2 and 2A, extends many of the provisions and rules of the UCC to cover electronic contracting of sales and lease contracts.
- *Electronic agent* means a computer program or an electronic or other automated means used independently to initiate an action or respond to electronic records or performances in whole or in part, without review or action by an individual [Revised UCC 2-103(1)(g), Revised UCC 2A-103(1)(i)]. This definition, as used in many of the provisions of UCC Article 2 and 2A, allows for the contracting for the sale and lease of

goods over the Internet, using websites to order or lease goods.

- *Electronic record* means a record created, generated, sent, communicated, received, or stored by electronic means [Revised UCC 2-103(1)(h), Revised UCC 2A-103(1)(j)]. This term is often used in Revised Articles 2 and 2A to replace the word *writing* and thus recognizes that UCC contracts and other information may be sent or stored by electronic means rather than in tangible writings.
- *Record* means information that is inscribed on a tangible medium or that is stored in an electronic or other medium and is retrievable in perceivable form [Revised UCC 2-103(1)(m), Revised UCC 2A-103(1)(cc)]. The term *record* is now used in many of the provisions of Revised Article 2 and 2A in place of the term *writing* and thus further recognizes the importance of electronic contracting.

These terms are used throughout the provisions of Revised Article 2 (Sales) and Revised Article 2A (Leases). These definitions expand the coverage of the provisions of UCC Article 2 and Article 2A to electronic contracting of sales and lease contracts.

TEST REVIEW TERMS AND CONCEPTS

Accommodation
Additional terms
Article 2 (Sales)
Article 2A (Leases)
Battle of the forms
Counteroffer
Finance lease
Firm offer rule

Gap-filling rule
Goods
Lease
Lessee
Lessor
Merchant
Mirror image rule
Mixed sale

Model act
Open price term
Open term
Parol evidence
Parol evidence rule
Proposed additions
Revised Article 2 (Sales)
Revised Article 2A (Leases)

Sale
Specially manufactured
   goods
Supplier
UCC Statute of Frauds
Uniform Commercial Code
   (UCC)
Uniform Sales Act

CASE PROBLEMS

18.1 Merchant   Mark Hemphill was a football player at Southern Illinois State University. As a member of the team, Hemphill was furnished with a uniform and helmet. He was injured while playing football for the school. Hemphill claimed that his helmet was defective and contributed to his injuries. Hemphill's attorneys suggested that he sue the university's athletic director, Sayers, and the head football coach, Shultz. The attorneys told Hemphill that he may be able to recover for his injuries based on several provisions of the Uniform Commercial Code. The attorneys specifically suggested that he use the UCC provisions that impose certain obligations upon merchants. Hemphill brought suit against Sayers and Shultz. Does Article 2 apply to this case? *Hemphill v. Sayers*, 552 F.Supp. 685, **Web** 1982 U.S. Dist. Lexis 16240 (United States District Court for the Southern District of Illinois)

18.2 Good or Service   Mr. Gulash lived in Shelton, Connecticut. He wanted an above-ground swimming pool installed in his backyard. Gulash contacted Stylarama, Inc. (Stylarama), a company specializing in the sale and construction of pools. The two parties entered into a contract that called for Stylarama to "furnish all labor and materials to construct a Wavecrest brand pool, and furnish and install a pool with vinyl liners." The total cost for materials and labor was $3,690. There was no breakdown in the contract of costs between labor and materials. After the pool was installed, its sides began bowing out, the 2" × 4" wooden supports for the pool rotted and misaligned, and the entire pool became tilted. Gulash brought suit, alleging that Stylarama had violated several provisions of Article 2 of the UCC. Is this transaction one involving goods, making it subject to Article 2? *Gulash v. Stylarama*, 33 Conn.Supp. 108, 364 A.2d 1221, **Web** 1975 Conn.Super. Lexis 209 (Superior Court of Connecticut)

18.3 Unconscionable Contract   Jane Wilson leased a Toyota pickup truck from World Omni Leasing, Inc. (Omni), Wilson had experience in business and had signed contracts before. In the past, Wilson had read the contracts

before signing them. When signing the contract for the lease of the truck, however, Wilson did not take the opportunity to read the lease. However, she signed a statement declaring that she had read and understood the lease. The lease contained a provision that made Wilson responsible for payments on the truck even if the truck was destroyed. Several months after leasing the truck, Wilson was involved in a two-vehicle collision. The pickup truck was destroyed. Omni demanded to be paid for the balance of the lease. Wilson refused, claiming that the lease was unconscionable. Is the lease unconscionable? *Wilson v. World Omni Leasing, Inc.*, 540 So.2d 713, **Web** 1989 Ala. Lexis 41 (Supreme Court of Alabama)

18.4 Statute of Frauds   St. Charles Cable TV (St. Charles) was building a new cable television system in Louisiana. It contacted Eagle Comtronics, Inc. (Eagle), by phone and began negotiating to buy descrambler units for its cable system. These units would allow St. Charles's customers to receive the programs they had paid for. Although no written contract was ever signed, St. Charles ordered several thousand descramblers. The descramblers were shipped to St. Charles, along with a sales acknowledgment form. St. Charles made partial payment for the descramblers before discovering that some of the units were defective. Eagle accepted a return of the defective scramblers. St. Charles then attempted to return all the descramblers, asking that they be replaced by a newer model. When Eagle refused to replace all the old descramblers, St. Charles stopped paying Eagle. Eagle sued St. Charles, claiming that no valid contract existed between the parties. Is there a valid sales contract? *St. Charles Cable TV v. Eagle Comtronics, Inc.*, 687 F.Supp. 820, **Web** 1988 U.S. Dist. Lexis 4566 (United States District Court for the Southern District of New York)

18.5 Firm Offer   Gordon Construction Company (Gordon) was a general contractor in the New York City area. Gordon planned on bidding for the job of constructing two buildings for the Port Authority of New York. In anticipation of its own bid, Gordon sought bids from subcontractors.

E. A. Coronis Associates (Coronis), a fabricator of structured steel, sent a signed letter to Gordon. The letter quoted a price for work on the Port Authority project and stated that the price could change, based upon the amount of steel used. The letter contained no information other than the price Coronis would charge for the job. One month later, Gordon was awarded the Port Authority project. Four days later, Coronis sent Gordon a telegram, withdrawing its offer. Gordon replied that it expected Coronis to honor the price that it had previously quoted to Gordon. When Coronis refused, Gordon sued. Gordon claimed that Coronis was attempting to withdraw a firm offer. Who wins? *E. A. Coronis Associates v. Gordon Construction Co.*, 90 N.J.Super. 69, 216 A.2d 246, **Web** 1966 N.J.Super. Lexis 368 (Superior Court of New Jersey)

18.6 Battle of the Forms   Dan Miller was a commercial photographer who had taken a series of photographs that had appeared in the *New York Times. Newsweek* magazine wanted to use the photographs. When a *Newsweek* employee named Dwyer phoned Miller, he was told that 72 images were available. Dwyer said that he wanted to inspect the photographs and offered a certain sum of money for each photo *Newsweek* used. The photos were to remain Miller's property. Miller and Dwyer agreed to the price and the date for delivery. *Newsweek* sent a courier to pick up the photographs. Along with the photos, Miller gave the courier a delivery memo that set out various conditions for the use of the photographs. The memo included a clause that required *Newsweek* to pay $1,500 each if any of the photos were lost or destroyed. After *Newsweek* received the package, it decided it no longer needed Miller's work. When Miller called to have the photos returned, he was told that they had all been lost. Miller demanded that *Newsweek* pay him $1,500 for each of the 72 lost photos. Assuming that the court finds Miller and *Newsweek* to be merchants, are the clauses in the delivery memo part of the sales contract? *Miller v. Newsweek, Inc.*, 660 F.Supp. 852, **Web** 1987 U.S. Dist. Lexis 4338 (United States District Court for the District of Delaware)

18.7 Open Terms   Alvin Cagle was a potato farmer in Alabama who had had several business dealings with the H. C. Schmieding Produce Co. (Schmieding). Several months before harvest, Cagle entered into an oral sales contract with Schmieding. The contract called for Schmieding to pay the market price at harvest time for all the red potatoes that Cagle grew on his 30-acre farm. Schmieding asked that the potatoes be delivered during the normal harvest months. As Cagle began harvesting his red potatoes, he contacted Schmieding to arrange delivery. Schmieding told the farmer that no contract had been formed because the terms of the agreement were too indefinite. Cagle demanded that Schmieding buy his crop. When Schmieding refused, Cagle sued to have the contract enforced. Has a valid sales contract been formed? *H. C. Schmieding Produce Co. v. Cagle*, 529 So.2d 243, **Web** 1988 Ala. Lexis 284 (Supreme Court of Alabama)

18.8 Statute of Frauds   Collins was a sales representative of Donzi Marine Corp. (Donzi), a builder of light speedboats. Collins met Wallach, the owner of a retail boat outlet, at a marine trade show. Collins offered him a Donzi dealership, which would include the right to purchase and then market Donzi speedboats. Wallach tendered a check for $50,000 to Collins. Collins accepted the check, but neither party ever signed a written contract. Wallach ordered several boats. Donzi terminated the dealership because it had found another boat dealer willing to pay more for the franchise. Wallach sued Donzi for breach of contract. Is the contract enforceable under the UCC? *Wallach Marine Corp. v. Donzi Marine Corp.*, 675 F.Supp. 838, **Web** 1987 U.S. Dist. Lexis 11762 (United States District Court for the Southern District of New York)

BUSINESS ETHICS CASES

18.9 Business Ethics   Kurt Perschke was a grain dealer in Indiana. Perschke phoned Ken Sebasty, the owner of a large wheat farm, and offered to buy 14,000 bushels of wheat for $1.95 per bushel. Sebasty accepted the offer. Perschke said that he could send a truck for the wheat on a stated date six months later. On the day of the phone call, Perschke's office manager sent a memorandum to Sebasty, stating the price and quantity of wheat that had been contracted for. One month before the scheduled delivery, Perschke called Sebasty to arrange for the loading of the wheat. Sebasty stated that no contract had been made. When Perschke brought suit, Sebasty claimed that the contract was unenforceable because of the Statute of Frauds. Was it ethical for Sebasty to raise the Statute of Frauds as a defense? Assuming that both parties are merchants, who wins the suit? *Sebasty v. Perschke*, 404 N.E.2d 1200, **Web** 1980 Ind.App. Lexis 1489 (Court of Appeals of Indiana)

18.10 Business Ethics   Alex Abatti was the sole owner of A&M Produce Company (A&M), a small farming company located in California's Imperial Valley. Although Abatti had never grown tomatoes, he decided to do so. He sought the advice of FMC Corporation (FMC), a large, diversified manufacturer of farming and other equipment, as to what kind of equipment he would need to process the tomatoes. An FMC representative recommended a certain type of machine, which A&M purchased from FMC pursuant to a form sales contract provided by FMC. Within the fine print, the contract contained one clause that disclaimed any warranty liability by FMC and a second clause that stated that FMC would not be liable for consequential damages if the machine malfunctioned.

A&M paid $10,680 down toward the $32,041 purchase price, and FMC delivered and installed the machine. A&M immediately began experiencing problems with the machine, which did not process the tomatoes quickly enough. Tomatoes began piling up in front of the belt that separated the tomatoes for weight-sizing. Overflow tomatoes had to be sent through the machine at least twice, causing damage to them. Fungus spread through the damaged crop. Because of these problems, the machine had to be continually started and stopped, which significantly reduced processing speed.

A&M tried on several occasions to get additional equipment from FMC, but on each occasion, its request was rejected. Because of the problems with the machine, A&M closed its tomato operation. A&M finally stated, "Let's call the whole thing off" and offered to return the machine if FMC would refund A&M's down payment. When FMC rejected this offer and demanded full payment of the balance due, A&M sued to recover its down payment and damages. It alleged breach of warranty caused by defect in the machine. In defense, FMC pointed to the fine print of the sales contract, stating that the buyer waived any rights to sue it for breach of warranty or to recover consequential damages from it.

Was it ethical for FMC to include waiver of liability and waiver of consequential damage clauses in its form contract? Did A&M act morally in signing the contract and then trying to get out from under its provisions? Legally, are the waiver clauses so unconscionable as to not be enforced? *A&M Produce Co. v. FMC Corp.*, 135 Cal.App.3d 473, 186 Cal.Rptr. 114, **Web** 1982 Cal.App. Lexis 1922 (Court of Appeal of California)

▲ **A Couple Watches a Container Ship** *The title and risk of loss of the goods on this ship are governed by the shipping terms used by the parties to the international contract for the sale of the goods or as otherwise agreed to by the parties.*

CHAPTER OBJECTIVES

After studying this chapter, you should be able to:

1. Identify when title to goods passes in shipment and destination contracts.
2. Define shipment and delivery terms.
3. Describe who bears the risk of loss when goods are lost or damaged in shipment.
4. Identify who bears the risk of loss when goods are stolen and resold.
5. Define *good faith purchaser for value* and *buyer in the ordinary course of business.*

CHAPTER CONTENTS

"A lawyer without history or literature is a mechanic, a mere working mason: if he possesses some knowledge of these, he may venture to call himself an architect."

—Sir Walter Scott
Guy Mannering, Chapter 37 (1815)

▶ INTRODUCTION TO TITLE TO GOODS AND RISK OF LOSS

Under common law, the rights and obligations of the buyer, the seller, and third parties were determined based on who held technical title to the goods. Article 2 of the Uniform Commercial Code (UCC) establishes precise rules for determining the *passage of title* in sales contracts. Other provisions of Article 2 apply, irrespective of title, except as otherwise provided [UCC 2-401].

Common law placed the **risk of loss** to goods on the party who held title to the goods. Article 2 of the UCC rejects this notion and adopts concise rules for risk of loss that are not tied to title. It also gives the parties to a sales contract the right to *insure* the goods against loss if they have an "insurable interest" in the goods.

Article 2A (Leases) of the UCC establishes rules regarding title and risk of loss for leased goods. It also gives the parties to the lease contract the right to *insure* the goods against loss if they have an "insurable interest" in the goods.

Title, risk of loss, and insurable interest for the sale and lease of goods are discussed in this chapter.

▶ IDENTIFICATION OF GOODS AND PASSAGE OF TITLE

Decided cases are the anchors of the law, as laws are of the state.

Francis Bacon

The *identification of goods* is rather simple. It means distinguishing the goods named in a contract from the seller's or lessor's other goods. The seller or lessor retains the risk of loss of the goods until he or she identifies them to a sales or lease contract. Further, UCC 2-401(1) and 2-501 prevent title to goods from passing from the seller to the buyer unless the goods are identified to the sales contract. In a lease transaction, title to the leased goods remains with the lessor or a third party. It does not pass to the lessee.

The identification of goods and passage of title are discussed in the following paragraphs.

Identification of Goods

identification of goods
Distinguishing the goods named in a contract from the seller's or lessor's other goods.

Identification of goods can be made at any time and in any manner explicitly agreed to by the parties of a contract. In the absence of such an agreement, the UCC mandates when identification occurs [UCC 2-501(1), 2A-217].

Already existing goods are identified when a contract is made and names the specific goods sold or leased.

Examples A piece of farm machinery, a car, or a boat is identified when its serial number is listed on a sales or lease contract.

Goods that are part of a larger mass of goods are identified when the specific merchandise is designated.

Example If a food processor contracts to purchase 150 cases of oranges from a farmer who has 1,000 cases of oranges, the buyer's goods are identified when the seller explicitly separates or tags the 150 cases for that buyer.

Future goods are goods not yet in existence.

Examples Unborn young animals (such as unborn cattle) are identified when the young are conceived. Crops to be harvested are identified when the crops are planted or otherwise become growing crops.

Future goods other than crops and unborn young are identified when the goods are shipped, marked, or otherwise designated by the seller or lessor as the goods to which the contract refers.

future goods
Goods not yet in existence (e.g., ungrown crops, unborn stock animals).

Passage of Title

Once the goods that are the subject of a contract exist and have been identified, title to the goods may be transferred from the seller to the buyer. Article 2 of the UCC establishes precise rules for determining the **passage of title** in sales contracts. (As mentioned earlier, lessees do not acquire title to the goods they lease.)

Under UCC 2-401(1), **title** to goods passes from the seller to the buyer in any manner and on any conditions explicitly agreed upon by the parties. If the parties do not agree to a specific time, title passes to the buyer when and where the seller's performance with reference to the physical delivery is completed. This point in time is determined by applying the rules discussed in the following paragraphs [UCC 2-401(2)].

title
Legal, tangible evidence of ownership of goods.

Shipment and Destination Contracts

A **shipment contract** requires the seller to ship the goods to the buyer via a common carrier. The seller is required to (1) make proper shipping arrangements and (2) deliver the goods into the carrier's hands. Title passes to the buyer at the time and place of shipment [UCC 2-401(2)(a)].

A **destination contract** requires the seller to deliver the goods either to the buyer's place of business or to another destination specified in the sales contract. Title passes to the buyer when the seller tenders delivery of the goods at the specified destination [UCC 2-401(2)(b)].

shipment contract
A contract that requires the seller to ship the goods to the buyer via a common carrier.

destination contract
A contract that requires the seller to deliver the goods either to the buyer's place of business or to another destination specified in the sales contract.

Delivery of Goods Without Moving Them

Sometimes a sales contract authorizes goods to be delivered without requiring the seller to move them. In other words, the buyer might be required to pick up goods from the seller. In such situations, the time and place of the passage of title depends on whether the seller is to deliver a **document of title** (i.e., a warehouse receipt or bill of lading) to the buyer. If a document of title is required, title passes when and where the seller delivers the document to the buyer [UCC 2-401(3)(a)].

document of title
An actual piece of paper, such as a warehouse receipt or bill of lading, that is required in some transactions of pickup and delivery.

Example If the goods named in a sales contract are located at a warehouse, title passes when the seller delivers to the buyer a warehouse receipt representing the goods.

If (1) no document of title is needed and (2) the goods are identified at the time of contracting, title passes at the time and place of contracting [UCC 2-401(3)(b)].

Example If a buyer signs a sales contract to purchase bricks from a seller, and the contract stipulates that the buyer will pick up the bricks at the seller's place of business, title passes when the contract is signed by both parties. This situation is true even if the bricks are not picked up until a later date.

CONTEMPORARY ENVIRONMENT

Shipping Terms

Often, goods subject to a sales contract are shipped by a common carrier such as a trucking company, a ship, or a railroad. Many sales contracts contain shipping terms that have different legal meanings and consequences. The following are commonly used shipping terms:

- **F.O.B. (free on board) *point of shipment*** requires the seller to arrange to ship the goods and put the goods in the carrier's possession. The buyer bears the shipping expense and risk of loss while the goods are in transit [UCC 2-319(1)(a)].

Example If a shipment contract specifies "F.O.B. Anchorage, Alaska," and the goods are shipped from New Orleans, Louisiana, the buyer bears the shipping expense and risk of loss while the goods are in transit to Anchorage, Alaska.

- **F.A.S. (free alongside ship)** or **F.A.S. (*vessel*) port of shipment** requires the seller to deliver and tender the goods alongside the named vessel or on the dock designated and provided by the buyer. The seller bears the expense and risk of loss until this is done [UCC 2-319(2)(a)]. The buyer bears shipping costs and the risk of loss during transport.

Example If a contract specifies "F.A.S. *The Gargoyle*, New Orleans," and the goods are to be shipped to Anchorage, Alaska, the seller bears the expense and risk of loss until it delivers the goods into the hands of the vessel *The Gargoyle* in New Orleans. Once this is done, the buyer pays the shipping costs and the risk of loss passes to the buyer during transport to Anchorage, Alaska.

- **C.I.F. (cost, insurance, and freight)** is a pricing term that means that the price includes the cost of the goods and the costs of insurance and freight. C.&F. (cost and freight) is a pricing term that means that the price includes the cost of the goods and the cost of freight. In both cases the seller must at his own expense and risk put the goods into the possession of a carrier. The buyer bears the risk of loss during transportation [UCC 2-320(1)(3)].

Example If a contract specifies "C.I.F. *The Gargoyle*, New Orleans, Louisiana" or "C.&F. *The Gargoyle*, New Orleans, Louisiana," and the goods are to be shipped to Anchorage, Alaska, the seller bears the expense and risk of loss until it delivers the goods into the hands of the vessel *The Gargoyle* in New Orleans. Once this is done, the risk of loss passes to the buyer during transport from New Orleans to Anchorage, Alaska.

- **F.O.B. (free on board) *place of destination*** requires the seller to bear the expense and risk of loss until the goods are tendered to the buyer at the place of destination [UCC 2-319(1)(b)].

Example If a destination contract specifies "F.O.B. Anchorage, Alaska," and the goods are shipped from New Orleans, Louisiana, the seller bears the expense and risk of loss before and while the goods are in transit until the goods are tendered to the buyer at the port of Anchorage, Alaska.

- **Ex-ship (from the carrying vessel)** requires the seller to bear the expense and risk of loss until the goods are unloaded from the ship at its port of destination [UCC 2-322(1)(b)].

Example If a contract specifies "Ex-ship, *The Gargoyle*, Anchorage, Alaska," and the goods are shipped from New Orleans, Louisiana, the seller bears the expense and risk of loss before and until the goods are unloaded from *The Gargoyle* at the port in Anchorage, Alaska.

- **No-arrival, no-sale contract** requires the seller to bear the expense and risk of loss of the goods during transportation. However, the seller is under no duty to deliver replacement goods to the buyer because there is no contractual stipulation that the goods will arrive at the appointed destination [UCC 2-324(a),(b)].

▶ RISK OF LOSS: NO BREACH OF SALES CONTRACT

In the case of sales contracts, common law placed the risk of loss of goods on the party who had title to the goods. Article 2 of the UCC rejects this notion and allows the parties to a sales contract to agree among them who will bear the risk of loss if the goods subject to the contract are lost or destroyed. If the parties do not have a specific agreement concerning the assessment of the risk of loss, the UCC mandates who will bear the risk.

Where there has been no breach of the sales contract, the UCC provides the following rules regarding title and risk of loss.

Carrier Cases: Movement of Goods

Unless otherwise agreed, goods that are shipped via carrier (e.g., railroad, ship, truck) are considered to be sent pursuant to a *shipment contract* or a *destination contract*. Absent any indication to the contrary, sales contracts are presumed to be shipment contracts rather than destination contracts.

A **shipment contract** requires the seller to deliver goods conforming to the contract to a carrier. The risk of loss passes to the buyer when the seller delivers the conforming goods to the carrier. The buyer bears the risk of loss of the goods during transportation [UCC 2-509(1)(a)]. Shipment contracts are created in two ways. The first method requires the use of the term *shipment contract*. The second requires the use of one of the following delivery terms: F.O.B., point of shipment, F.A.S., C.I.F., or C.&F.

A sales contract that requires the seller to deliver conforming goods to a specific destination is a **destination contract**. Such a contract requires the seller to bear the risk of loss of the goods during their transportation. Thus, with the exception of a no-arrival, no-sale contract, the seller is required to replace any goods lost in transit. The buyer does not have to pay for destroyed goods. The risk of loss does not pass until the goods are tendered to the buyer at the specified destination [UCC 2-509(1)(b)].

Unless otherwise agreed, destination contracts are created in two ways. The first method requires the use of the term *destination contract*. The alternative method requires the use of the following delivery terms: F.O.B. *place of destination*, ex-ship, or no-arrival, no-sale contract.

Noncarrier Cases: No Movement of Goods

Sometimes a sales contract stipulates that the buyer is to pick up the goods at either the seller's place of business or another specified location. This type of arrangement raises a question: Who bears the risk of loss if the goods are destroyed or stolen after the contract date but before the buyer picks up the goods from the seller? The UCC provides two different rules for this situation. One applies to *merchant-sellers* and the other to *nonmerchant-sellers* [UCC 2-509(3)].

Merchant-Seller   If the seller is a merchant, the risk of loss does not pass to the buyer until the goods are received. In other words, a merchant-seller bears the risk of loss between the time of contracting and the time the buyer picks up the goods.

Nonmerchant-Seller   Nonmerchant-sellers pass the risk of loss to the buyer upon "tender of delivery" of the goods. Tender of delivery occurs when the seller (1) places or holds the goods available for the buyer to take delivery and (2) notifies the buyer of this fact.

Goods in the Possession of a Bailee

Goods sold by a seller to a buyer are sometimes in the possession of a **bailee** (e.g., a warehouse). If such goods are to be delivered to the buyer without the seller moving them, the risk of loss passes to the buyer when (1) the buyer receives a negotiable document of title (such as a warehouse receipt or bill of lading) covering the goods, or (2) the bailee acknowledges the buyer's right to possession of the goods, or (3) the buyer receives a nonnegotiable document of title or other written direction to deliver *and* has a reasonable time to present the document or direction to the bailee and demand the goods. If the bailee refuses to honor the document or direction, the risk of loss remains on the seller [UCC 2-509(2)].

► RISK OF LOSS: CONDITIONAL SALES

Sellers often entrust possession of goods to buyers on a trial basis. These transactions are classified as *sales on approval*, *sales or returns*, and *consignment* transactions [UCC 2-326]. Title and risk of loss in these types of **conditional sales** are discussed in the following paragraphs.

Sale on Approval

In a **sale on approval**, there is no sale unless and until the buyer accepts the goods. A sale on approval occurs when a merchant allows a customer to take the goods for a specified

shipment contract
The buyer bears the risk of loss during transportation.

destination contract
The seller bears the risk of loss during transportation.

The law is not a series of calculating machines where definitions and answers come tumbling out when the right levers are pushed.

William O. Douglas
The Dissent, A Safeguard of Democracy (1948)

bailee
A holder of goods who is not a seller or a buyer (e.g., a warehouse).

sale on approval
A type of sale in which there is no actual sale unless and until the buyer accepts the goods.

period of time to see if they fit the customer's needs. The prospective buyer may use the goods to try them out during this time.

Acceptance of the goods occurs if the buyer (1) expressly indicates acceptance, (2) fails to notify the seller of rejection of the goods within the agreed-upon trial period (or, if no time is agreed upon, a reasonable time), or (3) uses the goods inconsistently with the purpose of the trial (e.g., a customer resells a computer to another person).

In a sale on approval, the risk of loss and title to the goods remain with seller. They do not pass to the buyer until acceptance [UCC 2-327(1)]. The goods are not subject to the claims of the buyer's creditors until the buyer accepts them.

Sale or Return

sale or return contract
A contract in which the seller delivers goods to a buyer with the understanding that the buyer may return them if they are not used or resold within a stated or reasonable period of time.

In a **sale or return contract**, the seller delivers goods to a buyer with the understanding that the buyer may return them if they are not used or resold within a stated period of time (or within a reasonable time, if no specific time is stated). The sale is considered final if the buyer fails to return the goods within the specified time or within a reasonable time, if no time is specified. The buyer has the option of returning all the goods or any commercial unit of the goods.

Example Louis Vuitton delivers 10 women's handbags to a Fashion Boutique Store on a sale or return basis. The boutique pays $10,000 ($1,000 per handbag). If Fashion Boutique Store sells 6 handbags but fails to sell the other 4 handbags within a reasonable time, such as three months, it may return the unsold handbags to Louis Vuitton. Fashion Boutique Store can recover the compensation it paid to Louis Vuitton for the 4 returned handbags ($4,000).

In a sale or return contract, the risk of loss and title to the goods pass to the buyer when the buyer takes possession of the goods [UCC 2-327(2)]. Goods sold pursuant to a sale or return contract are subject to the claims of the buyer's creditors while the goods are in the buyer's possession.

Example In the previous example, title and risk of loss transferred to Fashion Boutique Store when it took possession of the Louis Vuitton handbags. If the Louis Vuitton handbags are destroyed while in the possession of Fashion Boutique Store, the store is responsible for their loss. It cannot recover the value of the handbags from Louis Vuitton.

Consignment

consignment
An arrangement in which a seller (the consignor) delivers goods to a buyer (the consignee) to sell.

In a **consignment**, a seller (the **consignor**) delivers goods to a buyer (the **consignee**) to sell. The consignee is paid a fee if he or she sells the goods on behalf of the consignor.

A consignment is treated as a sale or return under the UCC; that is, title and risk of loss of the goods pass to the consignee when the consignee takes possession of the goods.

Whether goods are subject to the claims of a buyer's creditors usually depends on whether the seller files a financing statement, as required by Article 9 of the UCC. If the seller files a financing statement, the goods are subject to the claims of the seller's creditors. If the seller fails to file such statement, the goods are subject to the claims of the buyer's creditors [UCC 2-326(3)].

▶ RISK OF LOSS: BREACH OF SALES CONTRACT

Special risk of loss rules apply to situations in which there has been a breach of a sales contract [UCC 2-510]. These rules are discussed in the following paragraphs.

Seller in Breach of a Sales Contract

A seller breaches a sales contract if he or she tenders or delivers nonconforming goods to the buyer. If the goods are so nonconforming that the buyer has the right to reject them, the risk of loss remains on the seller until (1) the defect or nonconformity is cured or (2) the buyer accepts the nonconforming goods.

Example A buyer orders 1,000 talking dolls from a seller. The contract is a shipment contract, which normally places the risk of loss during transportation on the buyer. However, the seller ships to the buyer totally nonconforming dolls that cannot talk. This switches the risk of loss to the seller during transit. The goods are destroyed in transit. The seller bears the risk of loss because he breached the contract by shipping nonconforming goods.

Laws are not masters but servants, and he rules them who obeys them.

Henry Ward Beecher
*Proverbs from Plymouth Pulpit
(1887)*

Buyer in Breach of a Sales Contract

A buyer breaches a sales contract if he or she (1) refuses to take delivery of conforming goods, (2) repudiates the contract, or (3) otherwise breaches the contract. A buyer who breaches a sales contract before the risk of loss would normally pass to him bears the risk of loss of any goods identified to the contract. The risk of loss rests on the buyer for only a commercially reasonable time. The buyer is liable only for any loss in excess of insurance recovered by the seller.

▶ RISK OF LOSS: LEASE CONTRACTS

The parties to a lease contract are the party who leases the goods (the **lessor**) and the party who receives the goods (the **lessee**). The lessor and the lessee may agree as to who will bear the risk of loss of the goods if they are lost or destroyed. If the parties do not so agree, the UCC supplies the following risk of loss rules:

*Faith, I have been a truant in the law
And never yet could frame my will to it,
And therefore frame the law unto my will.*

William Shakespeare
King Henry the Sixth, Part I

1. In the case of an **ordinary lease**, if the lessor is a merchant, the risk of loss passes to the lessee on the receipt of the goods [UCC 2A-219].
2. If the lease is a **finance lease** and the supplier is a merchant, the risk of loss passes to the lessee on the receipt of the goods [UCC 2A-219]. A finance lease is a three-party transaction consisting of a lessor, a lessee, and a supplier (or vendor).
3. If a tender of delivery of goods fails to conform to the lease contract, the risk of loss remains with the lessor or supplier until cure or acceptance [UCC 2A-220(1)(a)].

CONTEMPORARY ENVIRONMENT

Insuring Against Loss of Goods

To protect against financial loss that would occur if goods were damaged, destroyed, lost, or stolen, the parties to sales and lease contracts should purchase insurance against such loss. If the goods are then lost or damaged, the insured party receives reimbursement from the insurance company for the loss.

To purchase insurance, a party must have an *insurable interest* in the goods. A seller has an insurable interest in goods as long as he or she retains title or has a security interest in the goods. A lessor retains an insurable interest in the goods during the term of the lease. A buyer or lessee obtains an insurable interest in the goods when they are identified in the sales or lease contract. Both the buyer and seller, or the lessee and lessor, can have an insurable interest in the goods at the same time [UCC 2-501, 2A-218].

To obtain and maintain proper insurance coverage on goods, a contacting party should:

- Determine the value of goods subject to the sales or lease contract.
- Purchase insurance from a reputable insurance company to cover the goods subject to the contract.
- Maintain the insurance by paying the premiums when they are due.
- Immediately file the proper claim and supporting documentation with an insurance company if the goods are damaged, destroyed, lost, or stolen.

void title
A situation in which a thief acquires no title to goods he or she steals. Also known as a *void leasehold interest*.

voidable title
A title that a purchaser has if the goods were obtained by (1) fraud, (2) a check that is later dishonored, or (3) impersonation of another person. Also known as *voidable leasehold interest*.

good faith purchaser for value
A person to whom good title can be transferred from a person with voidable title. The real owner cannot reclaim goods from a good faith purchaser for value.

good faith subsequent lessee
A person to whom a lease interest can be transferred from a person with voidable title. The real owner cannot reclaim the goods from the subsequent lessee until the lease expires.

buyer in the ordinary course of business
A person who in good faith and without knowledge that the sale violates the ownership or security interests of a third party buys goods in the ordinary course of business from a person in the business of selling goods of that kind. A buyer in the ordinary course of business takes the goods free of any third-party security interest in the goods.

▶ SALES BY NONOWNERS

Sometimes people sell goods even though they do not hold valid title to them. The UCC anticipated many of the problems this situation could cause and established rules concerning the title, if any, that could be transferred to purchasers.

Stolen Goods: Void Title

In a case in which a buyer purchases goods or a lessee leases goods from a thief who has stolen them, the purchaser does not acquire title to the goods, and the lessee does not acquire any leasehold interest in the goods. The real owner can reclaim the goods from the purchaser or lessee [UCC 2-403(1)]. This is called **void title** or **void leasehold interest**.

Example Jack steals a truckload of Sony high-definition television sets that are owned by Electronics Store. The thief resells the televisions to City-Mart, which does not know that the goods were stolen. If Electronics Store finds out where the televisions are, it can reclaim them. This is because the thief had no title in the goods, so title was not transferred to City-Mart. There is void title. City-Mart's only recourse is against the thief, if he or she can be found.

Sales or Lease of Goods to Good Faith Purchasers for Value: Voidable Title

A seller or lessor has **voidable title**, or **voidable leasehold interest**, to goods if the goods were obtained by fraud, if a check is later dishonored, or if he or she impersonates another person.

A person with voidable title to goods can transfer good title to a **good faith purchaser for value** or a **good faith subsequent lessee**. A good faith purchaser or lessee for value is someone who pays sufficient consideration or rent for the goods to the person he or she honestly believes has good title to those goods [UCC 2-201(1), 1-201(44)(d)]. The real owner cannot reclaim goods from such a purchaser or lessee [UCC 2-403(1)].

Example Max buys a Rolex watch from his neighbor Dorothy for nearly fair market value. It is later discovered that Dorothy obtained the watch from Jewelry Store with a "bounced check"—that is, a check for which there were insufficient funds to pay for the Rolex watch. Jewelry Store cannot reclaim the watch from Max because Max, the second purchaser, purchased the watch in good faith and for value.

CONTEMPORARY ENVIRONMENT

Entrustment Rule

If an owner **entrusts** the possession of his or her goods to a merchant who deals in goods of that kind, the merchant has the power to transfer all rights (including title) in the goods to a **buyer in the ordinary course of business** [UCC 2-403(2)]. The real owner cannot reclaim the goods from this buyer. This is called the **entrustment rule**.

Example Kim brings her diamond ring to Ring Store to be repaired. Ring Store both sells and repairs jewelry. Kim leaves (entrusts) her ring at the store until it is repaired. Ring Store sells Kim's ring to Harold, who is going to propose marriage to Gretchen. Harold, a buyer in the ordinary course of business, acquires title to the ring.

Kim cannot reclaim her ring from Harold (or Gretchen). Her only recourse is to sue Ring Store.

The entrustment rule also applies to leases. If a lessor entrusts the possession of his or her goods to a lessee who is a merchant who deals in goods of that kind, the merchant-lessee has the power to transfer all the lessor's and lessee's rights in the goods to a buyer or sublessee in the ordinary course of business [UCC 2A-305(2)].

In the following entrustment case, the court had to decide whether a purchaser was a buyer in the ordinary course of business.

CASE 19.1 Entrustment

Lindholm v. Brant

283 Conn. 65, 925 A.2d 1048, Web 2007 Conn. Lexis 264 (2007)
Supreme Court of Connecticut

"Any entrusting of possession of goods to a merchant who deals in goods of that kind gives him power to transfer all rights of the entruster to a buyer in ordinary course of business."

—Judge Rogers

Facts

In 1962, Andy Warhol, a famous artist, created a silkscreen on canvas titled *Red Elvis*. *Red Elvis* consists of 36 identical faces of Elvis Presley, with a red background, and is approximately 5.75 feet in height and 4.35 feet in width. Kerstin Lindholm was an art collector who, for 30 years, had been represented by Anders Malmberg, an art dealer. In 1987, with the assistance and advice of Malmberg, Lindholm purchased *Red Elvis* for $300,000

In 1996, the Guggenheim Museum in New York City decided to sponsor an Andy Warhol exhibition. The staff of the Guggenheim contacted Malmberg to see if Lindholm was willing to lend *Red Elvis* to the exhibition. Lindholm agreed, and *Red Elvis* was placed in the Guggenheim's exhibition. When the Guggenheim exhibition was completed in 2000, Malmberg told Lindholm that he could place *Red Elvis* on loan to the Louisiana Museum in Denmark if Lindholm agreed. By letter dated March 20, 2000, Lindholm agreed and gave permission to Malmberg to obtain possession of *Red Elvis* from the Guggenheim Museum and place it on loan to the Louisiana Museum. Instead of placing *Red Elvis* on loan to the Louisiana Museum, Malmberg, claiming ownership to *Red Elvis*, immediately contracted to sell *Red Elvis* to Peter M. Brant, an art collector, for $2.9 million. Brant had his lawyer do a UCC lien search and a search of the Art Loss Registry related to *Red Elvis*. These searches revealed no claims or liens against *Red Elvis*. Brant paid $2.9 million to Malmberg and received an invoice of sale and possession of *Red Elvis*.

Subsequently, Lindholm made arrangements to sell *Red Elvis* to a Japanese buyer for $4.6 million. Shortly thereafter, Lindholm discovered the fraud. Lindholm brought a civil lawsuit in the state of Connecticut against Brant to recover *Red Elvis*. Brant argued that he was a buyer in the ordinary course of business because he purchased *Red Elvis* from an art dealer to whom Lindholm had entrusted *Red Elvis*, and he had a claim that was superior to Lindholm's claim of ownership. The superior court of Connecticut issued a memorandum opinion that awarded *Red Elvis* to Brant.

Issue

Was Brant a buyer in the ordinary course of business who had a claim of ownership to *Red Elvis* that was superior to that of the owner Lindholm?

Language of the Court

The Brant defendants have pleaded a special defense to all counts that Brant is a buyer in the ordinary course pursuant to Conn. Gen. Stat. Sections 42a-2-403(2) and (3). A person with voidable title has power to transfer a good title to a good faith purchaser for value. Any entrusting of possession of goods to a merchant who deals in goods of that kind gives him power to transfer all rights of the entruster to a buyer in ordinary course of business. "Entrusting" includes any delivery and any acquiescence in retention of possession regardless of any condition expressed between the parties to the delivery or acquiescence and regardless of whether the procurement of the entrusting or the possessor's disposition of the goods have been such as to be larcenous under the criminal law.

That statutory provision sets forth the circumstances in which an innocent, good faith purchaser of goods who acquires them from a dealer in goods of that kind has a right to the goods superior to the rights of the owner/entrustor of the goods. This special defense requires the Brant defendants to show that Brant was a buyer in the ordinary course. K. Lindholm's March 20, 2000 letter constituted an entrustment of Red Elvis to a merchant, Malmberg. Once K. Lindholm entrusted Red Elvis to Malmberg she gave him the power to transfer all of her rights as the entruster to a buyer in the ordinary course.

After considering all of the evidence, the court finds that pursuant to Conn. Gen. Stat. Section 42a-2-403 Brant took good title to Red Elvis. Specifically, Brant purchased Red Elvis from Malmberg in good faith and in the ordinary course of business. Brant honestly believed Malmberg owned Red Elvis when he purchased the painting from him. Brant also observed reasonable commercial standards of fair dealing in the art industry when he purchased Red Elvis from Malmberg. Accordingly, because Brant has proven his special defense of being a buyer in the ordinary course, judgment will enter in favor of the defendants on all counts.

Decision

The trial court held that Brant was a buyer in the ordinary course of business who obtained ownership to *Red*

(case continues)

Elvis when he purchased the stolen *Red Elvis* from Malmberg. The court held that Brant's claim of ownership as a buyer in the ordinary course of business was superior to Lindholm's claim of ownership because she had entrusted *Red Elvis* to an art dealer who sold the stolen *Red Elvis* to Brant.

Note: Lindholm appealed the decision of the trial court to the supreme court of Connecticut, which affirmed the decision of the trial court and awarded the *Red Elvis* to Brant. A court in Sweden convicted Malmberg of criminal fraud and sentenced him to three years in prison. A Swedish court awarded Lindholm $4.6 in damages against Malmberg.

Case Questions

Critical Legal Thinking What is the entrustment rule? Explain. What does the rule of ordinary buyer in the course of business provide regarding the purchase of stolen property? Explain.

Business Ethics Did Malmberg act ethically in this case? Did he act criminally? Did Brandt have any ethical duty to return *Red Elvis* to its original owner, Lindholm?

Contemporary Business What are the possible consequences of an owner of a good entrusting the good to a merchant who sells the type of property that is entrusted to him?

CONCEPT SUMMARY

PASSAGE OF TITLE BY NONOWNER THIRD PARTIES

Type of Transaction	Title Possessed by Seller	Innocent Purchaser	Purchaser Acquires Title to Goods
Goods acquired by theft are resold.	Void title	Good faith purchaser for value	No. Original owner may reclaim the goods.
Goods acquired by fraud or dishonored check are resold.	Voidable title	Good faith purchaser for value	Yes. Purchaser takes goods, free of claim of original owner.
Goods entrusted by owner to merchant who deals in that type of good are resold.	No title	Buyer in the ordinary course of business	Yes. Purchaser takes goods, free of claim of original owner.

INTERNET LAW & ONLINE COMMERCE

Revised Article 2 (Sales) and Revised Article 2A (Leases)

Establish Rules for Electronic Contracts and Signatures

Written contracts and written signatures are given effect by Article 2 (Sales) and Article 2A (Leases) of the UCC. The UCC has also established rules for written communications concerning contracts for the sale and lease of goods. Revised Article 2 (Sales) and Revised Article 2A (Leases) add new rules regarding the recognition of signatures and communications concerning electronic contracts. The following are several of these rules:

- A record or signature may not be denied legal effect or enforcement solely because it is in electronic form [Revised UCC 2-211(1), Revised UCC 2A-222(1)]. This provision states that electronic contracts and electronic signatures are to be given legal effect and can be enforced against contracting parties.

- An **electronic record** or **electronic signature** is attributable to a person if it was the act of the person or the person's **electronic agent** [Revised UCC 2-212, Revised UCC 2A-223]. This provision permits a person to conduct business himself or through electronic agents, using electronic records and electronic signatures.

- If the receipt of an **electronic communication** has a legal effect, it has that effect even if no individual is aware of its receipt [Revised UCC 2-213(1), Revised UCC 2A-224(1)]. This rule acknowledges the legal effect of electronic communications that are received by electronic agents such as Internet websites.

- Receipt of an **electronic acknowledgment** of an electronic communication establishes that the communication was received but, in itself, does not establish that the content sent corresponds to the content received [Revised UCC 2-213(2), Revised UCC 2A-224(2)]. Thus, an electronic acknowledgement of the receipt of an electronic communication proves that the electronic communication was received.

This acknowledgment does not, in itself, establish what the content of the electronic communication was, however. That must come from other evidence.

These rules place electronic signatures on par with written signatures. They also establish special conditions regarding the receipt of electronic communications.

INTERNATIONAL LAW
Letters of Credit in International Trade

The major risks in any business transaction involving the sale of goods are (1) that the seller will not be paid after delivering the goods and (2) that the buyer will not receive the goods after paying for them. These risks are especially acute in international transactions, where the buyer and seller may not know each other, the parties are dealing at long distance, and the judicial systems of the parties' countries may not have jurisdiction to decide a dispute if one arises. The irrevocable **letter of credit** has been developed to manage these risks in international sales. The function of a letter of credit is to substitute the credit of a recognized international bank for that of the buyer.

Example Suppose a buyer in one country and a seller in another country enter into a contract for the sale of goods. The buyer goes to his or her bank and pays the bank a fee to issue a letter of credit in which the bank agrees to pay the amount of the letter (which is the amount of the

purchase price of the goods) to the seller's bank if certain conditions are met. These conditions are usually the delivery of documents indicating that the seller has placed the goods in the hands of a shipper. The buyer is called the **account party**, the bank that issues the letter of credit is called the **issuing bank**, and the seller is called the **beneficiary** of the letter of credit.

Article 5 (Letters of Credit) of the Uniform Commercial Code governs letters of credit unless otherwise agreed by the parties. The International Chamber of Commerce has promulgated the **Uniform Customs and Practices for Documentary Credits (UCP)**, which contains rules governing the formation and performance of letters of credit. Although the UCP is neither a treaty nor a legislative enactment, most banks incorporate the terms of the UCP in letters of credit they issue.

Japanese Currency *Japan and the United States have two of the largest economies in the world. There is significant trade between the two countries. Irrevocable letters of credit are used in conducting international trade to ensure that a seller located in one country will be paid for the goods it has sold to a buyer who is located in another country.*

TEST REVIEW TERMS AND CONCEPTS

Account party

Article 5 (Letters of Credit)

Bailee

Beneficiary

Buyer in the ordinary course of business

C.&F. (cost and freight)

C.I.F. (cost, insurance, and freight)

Conditional sale

Consignee

Consignment

Consignor

Destination contract

Document of title

Electronic acknowledgment

Electronic agent

Electronic communication

Electronic record (electronic signature)

Entrust

Entrustment rule

Ex-ship (from the carrying vessel)

F.A.S. (free alongside ship)

F.A.S. (*vessel*) *port of shipment*

Finance lease

F.O.B. (free on board) *place of destination*

F.O.B. (free on board) *point of shipment*

Future goods

Good faith purchaser for value

Good faith subsequent lessee

Identification of goods

Issuing bank

Lessee

Lessor

Letter of credit

No-arrival, no-sale contract

Ordinary lease

Passage of title

Risk of loss

Sale on approval

Sale or return contract

Shipment contract

Title

Uniform Customs and Practices for Documentary Credits (UCP)

Void title (void leasehold interest)

Voidable title (voidable leasehold interest)

CASE PROBLEMS

19.1 Identification of Goods The Big Knob Volunteer Fire Company (Fire Co.) agreed to purchase a fire truck from Hamerly Custom Productions (Hamerly), which was in the business of assembling various component parts into fire trucks. Fire Co. paid Hamerly $10,000 toward the price two days after signing the contract. Two weeks later, it gave Hamerly $38,000 more toward the total purchase price of $53,000. Hamerly bought an engine chassis for the new fire truck on credit from Lowe and Meyer Garage (Lowe and Meyer). After installing the chassis, Hamerly painted the Big Knob Fire Department's name on the side of the cab. Hamerly never paid for the engine chassis, and the truck was repossessed by Lowe and Meyer. Fire Co. sought to recover the fire truck from Lowe and Meyer. Although Fire Co. was the buyer of a fire truck, Lowe and Meyer questioned whether any goods had ever been identified in the contract. Are they? *Big Knob Volunteer Fire Co. v. Lowe and Meyer Garage*, 338 Pa.Super. 257, 487 A.2d 953, **Web** 1985 Pa.Super. Lexis 5540 (Superior Court of Pennsylvania)

19.2 Passage of Title New England Yacht Sales (Yacht Sales) sold a yacht to Robert Pease. Pease paid for the yacht in full, and Yacht Sales delivered to him a marine bill of sale. The marine bill of sale stated that Yacht Sales was transferring "all of its right, title, and interest" in the yacht to Pease. The yacht never left the Connecticut shipyard that Yacht Sales rented. During the winter, Yacht Sales did repair work on the yacht. In the spring, Yacht Sales delivered the yacht to Pease in Rhode Island. At issue in this case was when the sales tax was due to the state of Connecticut—on the date of sale or on the date of delivery. When does the title actually pass? *New England Yacht Sales v. Commissioner of Revenue Services*, 198 Conn. 624, 504 A.2d 506, **Web** 1986 Conn. Lexis 719 (Supreme Court of Connecticut)

19.3 Stolen Goods John Torniero was employed by Micheals Jewelers, Inc. (Micheals). During the course of his employment, Torniero stole pieces of jewelry, including several diamond rings, a sapphire ring, a gold pendant, and several loose diamonds. Over a period of several months, Torniero sold individual pieces of the stolen jewelry to G&W Watch and Jewelry Corporation (G&W). G&W had no knowledge of how Torniero obtained the jewels. Torniero was arrested when Micheals discovered the thefts. After Torniero admitted that he had sold the stolen jewelry to G&W, Micheals attempted to recover it from G&W. G&W claimed title to the jewelry as a good faith purchaser for value. Micheals challenged G&W's claim to title in court. Who wins? *United States v. Micheals Jewelers, Inc.*, 42 UCC Rep.Serv. 141, **Web** 1985 U.S. Dist. Lexis 15142 (United States District Court for the District of Connecticut)

19.4 Passage of Title J.A. Coghill owned a Rolls Royce Corniche automobile, which he sold to a man claiming to be Daniel Bellman. Bellman gave Coghill a cashier's check for $94,500. When Coghill tried to cash the check, his bank informed him that the check had been forged. Coghill reported the vehicle as stolen. Subsequently, Barry Hyken responded to a newspaper ad listing a Rolls Royce Corniche for sale. Hyken went to meet the seller of the car, the man who claimed to be Bellman, in a parking lot. When Hyken asked why the car was advertised as a 1980 model when it was in fact a 1979, Bellman replied that it was a newspaper mistake. Hyken agreed to pay $62,000 for the car. When Hyken asked to see Bellman's identification, Bellman provided documents with two different addresses. Bellman explained that he was in the process of moving. Although there seemed to be some irregularities in the title documents to the car, Hyken took possession anyway. Three weeks later, the Rolls Royce

Corniche was seized by the police. Hyken sued to get it back. Who wins? *Landshire Food Service, Inc. v. Coghill,* 709 S.W.2d 509, **Web** 1986 Mo.App. Lexis 3961 (Court of Appeals of Missouri)

19.5 Passage of Title   Cherry Creek Dodge, Inc. (Cherry Creek), sold a 1985 Dodge Ramcharger to Executive Leasing of Colorado (Executive Leasing). Executive Leasing, which was in the business of buying and selling cars, paid for the Dodge with a draft. Cherry Creek maintained a security interest in the car until the draft cleared. The same day that Executive Leasing bought the Dodge, it sold the car to Bruce and Peggy Carter. The Carters paid in full for the Dodge with a cashier's check, and the vehicle was delivered to them. The Carters had no knowledge of the financial arrangement between Executive Leasing and Cherry Creek. The draft that Executive Leasing gave Cherry Creek was worthless. Cherry Creek attempted to recover the vehicle from the Carters. Who wins? *Cherry Creek Dodge, Inc. v. Carter,* 733 P.2d 1024, **Web** 1987 Wyo. Lexis 408 (Supreme Court of Wyoming)

19.6 Entrustment Rule   Fuqua Homes, Inc. (Fuqua), is a manufacturer of prefabricated houses. MMM, a dealer of prefabricated homes, was a partnership created by two men named Kirk and Underhill. On seven occasions before the disputed transactions occurred, MMM had ordered homes from Fuqua. MMM was contacted by Kenneth Ryan, who wanted to purchase a 55-foot modular home. MMM called Fuqua and ordered a prefabricated home that met Ryan's specifications. Fuqua delivered the home to MMM and retained a security interest in it until MMM paid the purchase price. MMM installed the house on Ryan's property and collected full payment from Ryan. Kirk and Underhill then disappeared, taking Ryan's money with them. Fuqua was never paid for the prefabricated home it had manufactured. Ryan had no knowledge of the dealings between MMM and Fuqua. Fuqua claimed title to the house based upon its security interest. Who has title to the home? *Fuqua Homes, Inc. v. Evanston Bldg. & Loan Co.,* 52 OhioApp. 2d 399, 370 N.E.2d 780, **Web** 1977 OhioApp. Lexis 6968 (Court of Appeals of Ohio)

19.7 Risk of Loss   All America Export-Import Corp. (All America) placed an order for several thousand pounds of yarn with A. M. Knitwear (Knitwear). On June 4, All America sent Knitwear a purchase order. The purchase order stated the terms of the sale, including language that stated that the price was F.O.B. the seller's plant. A truck hired by All America arrived at Knitwear's plant. Knitwear turned the yarn over to the carrier and notified All America that the goods were now on the truck. The truck left Knitwear's plant and proceeded to a local warehouse. Sometime during the night, the truck was hijacked, and all the yarn was stolen. All America had paid for the yarn by check but stopped payment on it when it learned

that the goods had been stolen. Knitwear sued All America, claiming that it must pay for the stolen goods because it bore the risk of loss. Who wins? *A. M. Knitwear v. All America, Etc.,* 41 N.Y.2d 14, 359 N.E.2d 342, 390 N.Y.S.2d 832, **Web** 1976 N.Y. Lexis 3201 (Court of Appeals of New York)

19.8 Risk of Loss   Mitsubishi International Corporation (Mitsubishi) entered into a contract with Crown Door Company (Crown) that called for Mitsubishi to sell 12 boxcar loads of plywood to Crown. According to the terms of the contract, Mitsubishi would import the wood from Taiwan and deliver it to Crown's plant in Atlanta. Mitsubishi had the wood shipped from Taiwan to Savannah, Georgia. At Savannah, the plywood was loaded onto trains and hauled to Atlanta. When the plywood arrived in Atlanta, it was discovered that the railroad had been negligent in loading the train. The negligent loading had caused the cargo to shift during the trip, and the shifting had caused extensive damage to the wood. Who bears the risk of loss? *Georgia Port Authority v. Mitsubishi International Corporation,* 156 Ga.App. 304, 274 S.E.2d 699, **Web** 1980 Ga.App. Lexis 2952 (Court of Appeals of Georgia)

19.9 Risk of Loss   Martin Silver ordered two rooms of furniture from Wycombe, Meyer & Co., Inc. (Wycombe), a manufacturer and seller of custom-made furniture. On February 23, 1982, Wycombe sent invoices to Silver, advising him that the furniture was ready for shipment. Silver tendered payment in full for the goods and asked that one room of furniture be shipped immediately and that the other be held for shipment on a later date. Before any instructions were received as to the second room of furniture, it was destroyed in a fire. Silver and his insurance company attempted to recover the money he had paid for the destroyed furniture. Wycombe refused to return the payment, claiming that the risk of loss was on Silver. Who wins? *Silver v. Wycombe, Meyer & Co., Inc.,* 124 Misc.2d 717, 477 N.Y.S.2d 288, **Web** 1984 N.Y.Misc. Lexis 3319 (Civil Court of the City of New York)

19.10 Insurable Interest   Donald Hayward signed a sales contract with Dry Land Marina, Inc. (Dry Land). The contract was for the purchase of a 30-foot Revel Craft Playmate Yacht for $10,000. The contract called for Dry Land to install a number of options on Hayward's yacht and then deliver it to him. Before taking delivery of the yacht, Hayward signed a security agreement in favor of Dry Land and a promissory note. Several weeks later, a fire swept through Dry Land's showroom. Hayward's yacht was among the goods destroyed in the fire. Who has an insurable interest in the yacht? *Hayward v. Potsma,* 31 Mich.App. 720, 188 N.W.2d 31, **Web** 1971 Mich.App. Lexis 2150 (Court of Appeals of Michigan)

BUSINESS ETHICS CASES

19.11 Business Ethics Raceway Auto Auction (Raceway), New York, sold an Oldsmobile automobile to Triangle Auto Sales (Triangle). Triangle paid for the car with a check. Raceway delivered possession of the car to Triangle. Thereafter, Triangle's check bounced because of insufficient funds. In the meantime, Triangle sold the car to Campus Auto Sales (Campus), Rhode Island, which sold it to Charles Motor Co., Inc. (Charles), Rhode Island, which sold it to Lee Oldsmobile-Cadillac, Inc. (Lee Oldsmobile), Maine, which sold it to Stephanie K. LeBlanc of Augusta, Maine. When Triangle's check bounced, Raceway reported the car as stolen. Four months after she purchased the car, Stephanie was stopped by the Maine police, who seized the car. To maintain good relations with its customer, Lee Oldsmobile paid Raceway to obtain the certificate of title to the automobile and then sued Charles to recover. Did Triangle Auto Sales act ethically in this case? Does Charles Motor Co. obtain valid title to the automobile? *Lee Oldsmobile-Cadillac, Inc. v. Labonte*, 30 UCC Rep.Serv. 74, **Web** 1980 R.I.Super. Lexis 190 (Superior Court of Rhode Island)

19.12 Business Ethics Executive Financial Services, Inc. (EFS), purchased three tractors from Tri-County Farm Company (Tri-County), a John Deere dealership owned by Gene Mohr and James Loyd. The tractors cost $48,000, $19,000, and $38,000. EFS did not take possession of the tractors but instead left the tractors on Tri-County's lot. EFS leased the tractors to Mohr-Loyd Leasing (Mohr-Loyd), a partnership between Mohr and Loyd, with the understanding and representation by Mohr-Loyd that the tractors would be leased out to farmers. Instead of leasing the tractors, Tri-County sold them to three different farmers. EFS sued and obtained judgment against Tri-County, Mohr-Loyd, and Mohr and Loyd personally for breach of contract. Because that judgment remained unsatisfied, EFS sued the three farmers who bought the tractors to recover the tractors from them. Did Mohr and Loyd act ethically in this case? Who owns the tractors, EFS or the farmers? *Executive Financial Services, Inc. v. Pagel*, 238 Kan. 809, 715 P.2d 381, **Web** 1986 Kan. Lexis 290 (Supreme Court of Kansas)

▲ **Forklift** *A seller or lessor is under a duty to deliver conforming goods, but the UCC gives a seller or lessor who delivers nonconforming goods an opportunity to cure the nonconformity.*

CHAPTER OBJECTIVES

After studying this chapter, you should be able to:

1. Describe the performance of sales and lease contracts.
2. List and describe the seller's remedies for the buyer's breach of a sales contract.
3. List and describe the buyer's remedies for the seller's breach of a sales contract.
4. List and describe the lessor's remedies for the lessee's breach of a lease contract.
5. List and describe the lessee's remedies for the lessor's breach of a lease contract.

CHAPTER CONTENTS

> "Trade and commerce, if they were not made of Indian rubber,
> would never manage to bounce over the obstacles which
> legislators are continually putting in their way."
> —Henry D. Thoreau
> *Resistance to Civil Government (1849)*

▶ INTRODUCTION TO REMEDIES FOR BREACH OF SALES AND LEASE CONTRACTS

obligation
An action a party to a sales or lease contract is required by law to carry out.

breach
Failure of a party to perform an obligation in a sales or lease contract.

Usually, the parties to a sales or lease contract owe a duty to perform the **obligations** specified in their agreement [UCC 2-301, 2A-301]. The seller's or lessor's general obligation is to transfer and deliver the goods to the buyer or lessee. The buyer's or lessee's general obligation is to accept and pay for the goods.

When one party **breaches** a sales or lease contract, the UCC provides the injured party with a variety of prelitigation and litigation remedies. These remedies are designed to place the injured party in as good a position as if the breaching party's contractual obligations were fully performed [UCC 1-106(1), 2A-401(1)]. The best remedy depends on the circumstances of the particular case.

The performance of obligations and remedies available for breach of sales and lease contracts are discussed in this chapter.

▶ SELLER'S AND LESSOR'S PERFORMANCE

tender of delivery
The obligation of a seller to transfer and deliver goods to the buyer or lessee in accordance with a sales or lease contract.

The seller's or lessor's basic obligation is the **tender of delivery**, or the transfer and delivery of goods to the buyer or lessee in accordance with a sales or lease contract [UCC 2-301]. Tender of delivery requires the seller or lessor to (1) put and hold conforming goods at the buyer's or lessee's disposition and (2) give the buyer or lessee any notification reasonably necessary to enable delivery of goods. The parties may agree as to the time, place, and manner of delivery. If there is no special agreement, tender must be made at a reasonable hour, and the goods must be kept available for a reasonable period of time.

Example The seller cannot telephone the buyer at 12:01 A.M. and say that the buyer has 15 minutes to accept delivery [UCC 2-503(1), 2A-508(1)].

Unless otherwise agreed or unless the circumstances permit either party to request delivery in lots, the goods named in a contract must be tendered in a single delivery. Payment of a sales contract is due upon tender of delivery unless an extension of credit between the parties has been arranged. If the goods are rightfully delivered in lots, the payment is apportioned for each lot [UCC 2-307]. Lease payments are due in accordance with the terms of the lease contract.

Place of Delivery

Many sales and lease contracts state where the goods are to be delivered. Often, the contract will say that the buyer or lessee must pick up the goods from the seller or lessor. If the contract does not expressly state the **place of delivery**, the UCC stipulates place of delivery on the basis of whether a carrier is involved.

Noncarrier Cases

A legal decision depends not on the teacher's age, but on the force of his argument.

The Talmud

Unless otherwise agreed, the place of delivery is the seller's or lessor's place of business. If the seller or lessor has no place of business, the place of delivery is the seller's or lessor's residence. If the parties have knowledge at the time of contracting that identified goods are located in some other place, that place is the place of delivery.

Example If parties contract regarding the sale of wheat that is located in a silo, the silo is the place of delivery [UCC 2-308].

Sometimes goods are in the possession of a bailee (e.g., a warehouse) and are to be delivered without being moved. In such cases, tender of delivery occurs when the seller either (1) tenders to the buyer a negotiable document of title covering the goods, (2) produces acknowledgment from the bailee of the buyer's right to possession of the goods, or (3) tenders a nonnegotiable document of title or a written direction to the bailee to deliver the goods to a buyer. The seller must deliver all such documents in correct form [UCC 2-503(4), 2-503(5)].

Carrier Cases

Unless the parties have agreed otherwise, if delivery of goods to a buyer is to be made by carrier, the UCC establishes different rules for *shipment contracts* and *destination contracts*. These rules are described in the paragraphs that follow.

Shipment Contracts   Sales contracts that require the seller to send the goods to the buyer, but not to a specifically named destination, are called **shipment contracts**. Under such contracts, the seller must do the following [UCC 2-504]:

1. Put the goods in the carrier's possession and contract for the proper and safe transportation of the goods.
2. Obtain and promptly deliver or tender in correct form any documents (a) necessary to enable the buyer to obtain possession of the goods, (b) required by the sales contract, or (c) required by usage of trade.
3. Promptly notify the buyer of the shipment.

shipment contract
A sales contract that requires the seller to send the goods to the buyer but not to a specifically named destination.

The buyer may reject the goods if a material delay or loss is caused by the seller's failure to make a proper contract for the shipment of goods or properly notify the buyer of the shipment. If a shipment contract involves perishable goods and the seller fails to ship the goods via a refrigerated carrier, the buyer may rightfully reject the goods if they spoil during transit.

Destination Contracts   A sales contract that requires the seller to deliver goods to the buyer's place of business or another specified destination is a **destination contract**. Unless otherwise agreed, destination contracts require delivery to be tendered at the buyer's place of business or other location specified in the sales contract. Delivery must occur at a reasonable time, in a reasonable manner, and with proper notice to the buyer. Appropriate documents of title must be provided by the seller to enable the buyer to obtain the goods from the carrier [UCC 2-503].

destination contract
A sales contract that requires the seller to deliver the goods to the buyer's place of business or another specified destination.

Perfect Tender Rule

A seller or lessor is under a duty to deliver conforming goods. If the goods or tender of delivery fails in any respect to conform to the contract, the buyer or lessee may opt either (1) to reject the whole shipment, (2) to accept the whole shipment, or (3) to reject part and accept part of the shipment. This option is referred to as the **perfect tender rule** [UCC 2-601, 2A-509]. If a buyer accepts nonconforming goods, the buyer may seek remedies against the seller.

perfect tender rule
A rule that says if the goods or tender of a delivery fail in any respect to conform to the contract, the buyer may opt either (1) to reject the whole shipment, (2) to accept the whole shipment, or (3) to reject part and accept part of the shipment.

Example A sales contract requires the Lawn Mower Company to deliver 100 lawn mowers to Outdoor Store. When the buyer inspects the delivered goods, it is discovered that 80 lawn mowers conform to the contract, and 20 lawn mowers do not conform. Pursuant to the perfect tender rule, the buyer Outdoor Store may reject the entire shipment of lawn mowers. In the alternative, the buyer Outdoor Store can accept the 80 conforming lawn mowers and reject the 20 nonconforming lawn mowers. As another alternative, the buyer Outdoor Store may accept the whole shipment, both the conforming and nonconforming lawn mowers, and seek remedies from the seller Lawn Mower Company for the 20 nonconforming lawn mowers.

Exceptions to the Perfect Tender Rule

The UCC alters the perfect tender rule in the following situations:

*The buyer needs a hundred eyes,
the seller not one.*

George Herbert
Jacula Prudentum (1651)

cure
An opportunity to repair or replace
defective or nonconforming goods.

1. **Agreement of the parties.**   The parties to a sales or lease contract may agree to limit the effect of the perfect tender rule. For example, they may decide that (1) only the defective or nonconforming goods may be rejected, (2) the seller or lessor may replace nonconforming goods or repair defects, or (3) the buyer or lessee will accept nonconforming goods with appropriate compensation from the seller or lessor.
2. **Substitution of carriers.**   The UCC requires the seller to use a commercially reasonable substitute if (1) the agreed-upon manner of delivery fails or (2) the agreed-upon type of carrier becomes unavailable [UCC 2-614(1)].

CONTEMPORARY ENVIRONMENT

Opportunity to Cure

The UCC gives a seller or lessor who delivers nonconforming goods an opportunity to **cure** the nonconformity. Although the term *cure* is not defined by the UCC, it generally means an opportunity to repair or replace defective or nonconforming goods [UCC 2-508, 2A-513].

A cure may be attempted if the time for performance has not expired and the seller or lessor notifies the buyer or lessee of his or her intention to make a conforming delivery within the contract time.

Example A lessee contracts to lease a BMW 750i automobile from a lessor for delivery July 1. On June 15, the lessor delivers a BMW 550i to the lessee, and the lessee rejects it as nonconforming. The lessor has until July 1 to cure the nonconformity by delivering the BMW 750i specified in the contract.

A cure may also be attempted if the seller or lessor had reasonable grounds to believe the nonconforming delivery would be accepted. The seller or lessor may have a further reasonable time to substitute a conforming tender.

Example A buyer contracts to purchase 500 red dresses from a seller for delivery July 1. On July 1, the seller delivers 100 blue dresses to the buyer. In the past, the buyer has accepted different-colored dresses than those ordered. This time, though, the buyer rejects the blue dresses as nonconforming. The seller has a reasonable time after July 1 to deliver conforming red dresses to the buyer.

Installment Contracts

installment contract
A contract that requires or
authorizes goods to be delivered
and accepted in separate lots.

An **installment contract** is a contract that requires or authorizes goods to be delivered and accepted in separate lots. Such a contract must contain a clause that states "each delivery in a separate lot" or equivalent language.

Example A contract in which the buyer orders 1,000 widgets, to be delivered in four equal installments of 250 items, is an installment contract.

The UCC alters the perfect tender rule with regard to installment contracts. The buyer or lessee may reject the entire contract only if the nonconformity or default with respect to any installment or installments substantially impairs the value of the entire contract. The buyer or lessee may reject any nonconforming installment if the value of the installment is impaired and the defect cannot be cured. Thus, in each case, the court must determine whether the nonconforming installment impairs the value of the entire contract or only that installment [UCC 2-612, 2A-510].

Destruction of Goods

*This is the kind of order which
makes the administration of
justice stink in the nostrils of
commercial men.*

A. L. Smith
*L. J. Graham v. Sutton, Carden &
Company (1897)*

The UCC provides that if goods identified in a sales or lease contract are totally destroyed without the fault of either party before the risk of loss passes to the buyer or the lessee, the contract is void. Both parties are then excused from performing the contract.

If the goods are only partially destroyed, the buyer or lessee may inspect the goods and then choose either to treat the contract as void or to accept the goods. If the buyer or lessee opts to accept the goods, the purchase price or rent will be reduced to compensate for damages [UCC 2-613, 2A-221].

Example A buyer contracts to purchase a sofa from a seller. The seller agrees to deliver the sofa to the buyer's home. The truck delivering the sofa is hit by an automobile, and the sofa is totally destroyed. Because the risk of loss has not passed to the buyer, the contract is voided, and the buyer does not have to pay for the sofa.

ETHICS SPOTLIGHT

Good Faith and Reasonableness

Generally, the common law of contracts only obligates the parties to perform their contracts according to the **express terms** of their contract. There is no breach of contract unless the parties fail to meet these terms.

Recognizing that certain situations may develop that are not expressly provided for in a contract or that strict adherence to the terms of a contract without doing more may not be sufficient to accomplish the contract's objective, the Uniform Commercial Code (UCC) adopts two broad principles that govern the performance of sales and lease contracts: **good faith** and **reasonableness**.

UCC 1-203 states, "Every contract or duty within this Act imposes an obligation of good faith in its performance or enforcement." Thus, both parties owe a duty of good faith to perform a sales or lease contract. Nonmerchants are held to the subjective standard of honesty in fact. Merchants are held to a higher standard of good faith than nonmerchants. Merchants are held to the objective standard of fair dealing in the trade [UCC 2-103(1)(b)].

The words *reasonable* and *reasonably* are used throughout the UCC to establish the duties of performance by the parties to sales and lease contracts. For example,

unless otherwise specified, the parties must act within a "reasonable" time [UCC 1-204(1)(2)]. As another example, if a seller does not deliver the goods as contracted, the buyer may make "reasonable" purchases to cover (i.e., obtain substitute performance) [UCC 2-712(1)]. The term **commercial reasonableness** is used to establish certain duties of merchants under the UCC. Articles 2 and 2A of the UCC do not specifically define the terms *reasonable* and *commercial reasonableness*. Instead, these terms are defined by reference to the course of performance or the course of dealing between the parties, usage of trade, and such.

Note that the concepts of good faith and reasonableness extend to the "spirit" of a contract as well as the contract terms. The underlying theory is that the parties are more apt to perform properly if their conduct is to be judged against these principles. This is a major advance in the law of contracts.

Business Ethics Do the concepts of *good faith* and *reasonableness* that are contained in the Uniform Commercial Code (UCC) promote ethical behavior?

▶ BUYER'S AND LESSEE'S PERFORMANCE

The buyer or lessee to a sales or lease contract owes certain duties of performance under the contract. These duties are either specified in the contract itself or are created by UCC Articles 2 and 2A. Once the seller or lessor has properly tendered delivery, the buyer or lessee is obligated to accept and pay for the goods in accordance with the sales or lease contract. If there is no agreement, the provisions of the UCC control.

Right of Inspection

Unless otherwise agreed, the buyer or lessee has the **right to inspect** goods that are tendered, delivered, or identified in a sales or lease contract prior to accepting or paying for them. If the goods are shipped, the inspection may take place after their arrival. If the inspected goods do not conform to the contract, the buyer or lessee may reject them without paying for them [UCC 2-513(1), 2A-515(1)]. If the goods are rejected for nonconformance, the cost of inspection can be recovered from the seller [UCC 2-513(2)].

The parties may agree as to the time, place, and manner of inspection. If there is no such agreement, the inspection must occur at a reasonable time and place and in a reasonable

Nobody has a more sacred obligation to obey the law than those who make the law.

Sophocles

manner. Reasonableness depends on the circumstances of the case, common usage of trade, prior course of dealing between the parties, and such. If the goods conform to the contract, the buyer pays for the inspection.

Buyers who agree to **C.O.D. (cash on delivery) shipments** are not entitled to inspect the goods before paying for them. In certain sales contracts (e.g., cost, insurance, and freight [C.I.F.] contracts), payment is due from the buyer upon receipt of documents of title, even if the goods have not yet been received. In such a case, the buyer is not entitled to inspect the goods before paying for them [UCC 2-513(3)].

C.O.D. shipment
A type of shipment contract in which the buyer agrees to pay the shipper cash upon the delivery of the goods.

Payment

Goods that are accepted must be paid for [UCC 2-607(1)]. Unless the parties to a contract agree otherwise, **payment** is due from a buyer when and where the goods are delivered, even if the place of delivery is the same as the place of shipment. Buyers often purchase goods on credit extended by the seller. Unless the parties agree to other terms, the credit period begins to run from the time the goods are shipped [UCC 2-310]. A lessee must pay lease payments in accordance with the lease contract [UCC 2A-516(1)].

The goods can be paid for in any manner currently acceptable in the ordinary course of business (e.g., check, credit card) unless the seller demands payment in cash or unless the contract names a specific form of payment. If the seller requires cash payment, the buyer must be given an extension of time necessary to procure the cash. If the buyer pays by check, payment is conditional on the check being honored (paid) when it is presented to the bank for payment [UCC 2-511].

A proceeding may be perfectly legal and may yet be opposed to sound commercial principles.

Lord Justice Lindley
Verner v. General and Commercial Trust (1894)

Acceptance

Acceptance occurs when the buyer or lessee takes any of the following actions after a reasonable opportunity to inspect the goods: (1) signifies to the seller or lessor in words or by conduct that the goods are conforming or that the buyer or lessee will take or retain the goods despite their nonconformity or (2) fails to effectively reject the goods within a reasonable time after their delivery or tender by the seller or lessor. Acceptance also occurs if a buyer acts inconsistently with the seller's ownership rights in the goods. Acceptance occurs if the buyer resells the goods delivered by the seller [UCC 2-606(1), 2A-515(1)].

Buyers and lessees may only accept delivery of a *commercial unit*—a unit of goods that commercial usage deems is a single whole for purpose of sale. Acceptance of a part of any commercial unit is acceptance of the entire unit [UCC 2-606(2), 2A-515(2)].

acceptance
An act that occurs when a buyer or lessee takes any of the following actions after a reasonable opportunity to inspect the goods: (1) signifies to the seller or lessor in words or by conduct that the goods are conforming or that the buyer or lessee will take or retain the goods despite their nonconformity or (2) fails to effectively reject the goods within a reasonable time after their delivery or tender by the seller or lessor. Acceptance also occurs if a buyer acts inconsistently with the seller's ownership rights in the goods.

Example A commercial unit may be a single article (e.g., a machine), a set of articles (e.g., a suite of furniture or an assortment of sizes), a quantity (e.g., a bale, a gross, or a carload), or any other unit treated in use or in the relevant market as a single whole.

Revocation of Acceptance

A buyer or lessee who has accepted goods may subsequently revoke his or her acceptance if (1) the goods are nonconforming, (2) the nonconformity substantially impairs the value of the goods to the buyer or lessee, and (3) one of the following factors is shown: (a) the seller's or lessor's promise to timely cure of the nonconformity is not met, (b) the goods were accepted before the nonconformity was discovered and the nonconformity was difficult to discover, or (c) the goods were accepted before the nonconformity was discovered and the seller or lessor assured the buyer or lessee that the goods were conforming.

Revocation of acceptance is not effective until the seller or lessor is so notified. In addition, the revocation must occur within a reasonable time after the buyer or lessee discovers or should have discovered the grounds for the revocation. The revocation, which must be of a lot or commercial unit, must occur before there is any substantial change in the condition of the goods (e.g., before perishable goods spoil) [UCC 2-608(1), 2A-517(1)].

revocation of acceptance
Reversal of acceptance.

Rodeo Drive, Beverly Hills, California *This is Rodeo Drive in Beverly Hills, California, one of the premiere shopping streets in the United States. The Uniform Commercial Code (UCC) provides for various remedies if a seller or buyer breaches a sales contract or if a lessor or lessee breaches a lease contract.*

▶ SELLER'S AND LESSOR'S REMEDIES

Oftentimes, a buyer or lessee may breach a sales or lease contract. The UCC provides various remedies to sellers and lessors if a buyer or lessee *breaches a contract*. The remedies available to sellers and lessors if a buyer or lessee breaches a sales or lease contract are discussed in the following paragraphs.

Right to Withhold Delivery

A seller or lessor may withhold delivery of goods in his or her possession when the buyer or lessee breaches the contract. The **right to withhold delivery** is available if the buyer or lessee wrongfully rejects or revokes acceptance of the goods, fails to make a payment when due, or repudiates the contract. If part of the goods under the contract have been delivered when the buyer or lessee materially breaches the contract, the seller or lessor may withhold delivery of the remainder of the affected goods [UCC 2-703(a), 2A-523(1)(c)].

A seller or lessor who discovers that the buyer or lessee is insolvent before the goods are delivered may refuse to deliver as promised unless the buyer or lessee pays cash for the goods [UCC 2-702(1), 2A-525(1)]. Under the UCC, a person is insolvent when he or she (1) ceases to pay his or her debts in the ordinary course of business, (2) cannot pay his or her debts as they become due, or (3) is insolvent within the meaning of federal bankruptcy law [UCC 1-201(23)].

right to withhold delivery
A seller's or lessor's right to refuse to deliver goods to a buyer or lessee upon breach of a sales or lease contract by the buyer or lessee or the insolvency of the buyer or lessee.

Right to Stop Delivery of Goods in Transit

Often, sellers and lessors employ common carriers and other bailees (e.g., warehouses) to hold and deliver goods to buyers and lessees. The goods are considered to be *in transit* while they are in possession of these carriers or bailees.

A seller or lessor has the **right to stop delivery of goods in transit** if while the goods are in transit (1) the buyer or lessee repudiates the contract, (2) the buyer or lessee fails to make payment when due, or (3) the buyer or lessee otherwise gives the seller or lessor some other right to withhold or reclaim the goods. In these circumstances, the delivery can be stopped only if it constitutes a carload, a truckload, a planeload, or a larger express or freight shipment [UCC 2-705(1), 2A-526(1)]. A seller or lessor who learns of the buyer's or lessee's insolvency while the goods are in transit has the right to stop delivery of the goods transit, regardless of the size of the shipment. The seller or lessor is responsible for all expenses borne by the bailee in stopping the goods [UCC 2-705(3), 2A-526(3)].

right to stop delivery of goods in transit
The right of a seller or lessor to stop delivery of goods in transit if he or she learns of the buyer's or lessee's insolvency or if the buyer or lessee repudiates the contract, fails to make payment when due, or gives the seller or lessor some other right to withhold the goods.

The seller or lessor must give sufficient notice to allow the bailee, by reasonable diligence, to prevent delivery of the goods. After receipt of notice, the bailee must hold and deliver the goods according to the directions of the seller or lessor. Goods may be stopped in transit until the buyer or lessee obtains possession of the goods or the carrier or other bailee acknowledges that it is holding the goods for the buyer or lessee [UCC 2-705(2), 2A-526(2)].

Right to Reclaim Goods

right to reclaim goods
The right of a seller or lessor to demand the return of goods from the buyer or lessee under specified situations.

In certain situations, a seller or lessor may demand the return of the goods it sold or leased that are already in the possession of the buyer or lessee. In a sale transaction, the seller or lessor has the **right to reclaim goods** in two situations. If the goods are delivered in a credit sale and the seller then discovers that the buyer was insolvent, the seller has 10 days within which to demand that the goods be returned [UCC 2-507(2)]. If the buyer misrepresented his or her solvency in writing within three months before delivery [UCC 2-702(2)] or paid for goods in a cash sale with a check that bounces [UCC 2-507(2)], the seller may reclaim the goods at any time.

A lessor may reclaim goods in the possession of the lessee if the lessee is in default of the contract [UCC 2A-525(2)].

To exercise a right of reclamation, the seller or lessor must send the buyer or lessee a written notice demanding return of the goods. The seller or lessor may not use self-help to reclaim the goods if the buyer or lessee refuses to honor his or her demand. Instead, appropriate legal proceedings must be instituted.

Right to Dispose of Goods

right to dispose of goods
The right to dispose of goods in a good faith and commercially reasonable manner. A seller or lessor who is in possession of goods at the time the buyer or lessee breaches or repudiates a contract may in good faith resell, release, or otherwise dispose of the goods in a commercially reasonable manner and recover damages, including incidental damages, from the buyer or lessee.

incidental damages
Reasonable expenses incurred in stopping delivery, transportation charges, storage charges, sales commissions, and so on.

If a buyer or lessee breaches or repudiates a sales or lease contract before the seller or lessor has delivered the goods, the seller or lessor may resell or release the goods and recover damages from the buyer or lessee [UCC 2-703(d), 2-706(1), 2A-523(1)(e), 2A-527(1)]. The **right to dispose of goods** also arises if the seller or lessor has reacquired the goods after stopping them in transit.

The seller or lessor may recover any damages incurred on the disposition of the goods. In the case of a sales contract, damages are defined as the difference between the disposition price and the original contract price. In the case of a lease contract, damages are the difference between the disposition price and the rent the original lessee would have paid. Any profit made on the resale or release of the goods does not revert to the original buyer or lessee if the seller or lessor disposes of the goods at a higher price than the buyer or lessee contracted to pay.

The seller or lessor may also recover any **incidental damages** (reasonable expenses incurred in stopping delivery, transportation charges, storage charges, sales commission, and the like [UCC 2-710, 2A-530]) incurred on the disposition of the goods [UCC 2-706(1), 2A-527(2)].

The disposition of goods by the seller or lessor must be made in good faith and in a commercially reasonable manner. The goods may be disposed of as a unit or in parcels in a public or private transaction. The seller or lessor must give the buyer or lessee reasonable notification of his or her intention to dispose of goods unless the goods threaten to quickly decline in value or are perishable. The party who buys or leases the goods in good faith for value takes the goods, free of any rights of the original buyer or lessee [UCC 2-706(5), 2A-527(4)].

Unfinished Goods

Sometimes a sales or lease contract is breached or repudiated before the goods are finished. In a case of **unfinished goods**, the seller or lessor may choose either (1) to cease manufacturing the goods and resell them for scrap or salvage value or (2) to complete the manufacture of the goods and resell, release, or otherwise dispose of them to another party [UCC 2-704(2), 2A-524(2)]. The seller or lessor may recover damages from the breaching buyer or lessee.

Right to Recover the Purchase Price or Rent

In certain circumstances, the UCC provides that a seller or lessor may sue the buyer or lessee to recover the purchase price or rent stipulated in a sales or lease contract. The seller or lessor has the **right to recover the purchase price or rent** in the following situations:

1. The buyer or lessee accepts the goods but fails to pay for them when the price or rent is due.
2. The buyer or lessee breaches the contract after the goods have been identified in the contract and the seller or lessor cannot resell or dispose of them.
3. The goods are damaged or lost after the risk of loss passes to the buyer or lessee [UCC 2-709(1), 2A-529(1)].

To recover the purchase price or rent, the seller or lessor must hold the goods for the buyer or lessee. If resale or other disposition of the goods becomes possible prior to the collection of the judgment, however, the seller or lessor may resell or dispose of them. In such situations, the net proceeds of any disposition must be credited against the judgment [UCC 2-709(2), 2A-529(2), 2A-529(3)]. The seller or lessor may also recover incidental damages from the buyer or lessee.

right to recover the purchase price or rent
A seller's or lessor's right to recover the contracted-for purchase price or rent from the buyer or lessee (1) if the buyer or lessee fails to pay for accepted goods, (2) if the buyer or lessee breaches the contract and the seller or lessor cannot dispose of the goods, or (3) if the goods are damaged or lost after the risk of loss passes to the buyer or lessee.

Right to Recover Damages for Breach of Contract

If a buyer or lessee repudiates a sales or lease contract or wrongfully rejects tendered goods, the seller or lessor may sue to **recover the damages** caused by the buyer's or lessee's breach. Generally, the amount of damages is calculated as the difference between the contract price (or rent) and the market price (or rent) of the goods at the time and place the goods were to be delivered to the buyer or lessee plus incidental damages [UCC 2-708(1), 2A-528(1)].

If the preceding measure of damages will not put the seller or lessor in as good a position as performance of the contract would have, the seller or lessor has the **right to recover any lost profits** that would have resulted from the full performance of the contract plus an allowance for reasonable overhead and incidental damages [UCC 2-708(2), 2A-528(2)].

right to recover damages for breach of contract
A seller's or lessor's right to recover damages measured as the difference between the contract price (or rent) and the market price (or rent) at the time and place the goods were to be delivered, plus incidental damages, from a buyer or lessee who repudiates the contract or wrongfully rejects tendered goods.

Right to Cancel a Contract

A seller or lessor has the right to cancel a contract if the buyer or lessee breaches the contract by rejecting or revoking acceptance of the goods, failing to pay for the goods, or repudiating all or any part of the contract. The cancellation may refer only to the affected goods or to the entire contract if the breach is material [UCC 2-703(f), 2A-523(1)(a)].

A seller or lessor who rightfully cancels a sales or lease contract by notifying the buyer or lessee is discharged of any further obligations under that contract. The buyer's or lessee's duties are not discharged, however. The seller or lessor retains the right to seek damages for the breach [UCC 2-106(4), 2A-523(3)].

seller's or lessor's cancellation
A seller or lessor has the right to cancel a sales or lease contract if the buyer or lessee rejects or revokes acceptance of the goods, fails to pay for the goods, or repudiates the contract in part or in whole.

CONTEMPORARY ENVIRONMENT

Lost Volume Seller

Should a seller be permitted to recover the profits it lost on a sale to a defaulting buyer if the seller sold the goods to another buyer? It depends. If the seller had only one item or a limited number of items and could produce no more, the seller cannot recover lost profits from the defaulting buyer. This is because the seller made profits on the sale of the item to the new buyer.

If, however, the seller could have produced more of the item, the seller is a **lost volume seller**. In this situation,

the seller can make the profit from the sale of the item to the new buyer and sue the defaulting buyer to recover the profit it would have made from that sale. This is because the seller would have realized profits from two sales—the sale to the first buyer who defaulted and the second sale to the new buyer.

CONCEPT SUMMARY

SELLER'S AND LESSOR'S REMEDIES

Possession of Goods at the Time of the Buyer's or Lessee's Breach	Seller's or Lessor's Remedies

Goods in the possession of the seller or lessor	1. Withhold delivery of the goods [UCC 2-703(a), 2A-523(1)(c)].
	 2. Demand payment in cash if the buyer is insolvent [UCC 2-702(1), 2A-525(1)].
	 3. Resell or release the goods and recover the difference between the contract or lease price and the resale or release price [UCC 2-706, 2A-527].
	 4. Sue for breach of contract and recover as damages either of the following:
	    a. The difference between the market price and the contract price [UCC 2-708(1), 2A-528(1)].
	    b. Lost profits [UCC 2-708(2), 2A-528(2)].
	 5. Cancel the contract [UCC 2-703(f), 2A-523(1)(a)].
	
	 1. Stop goods in transit [UCC 2-705(1), 2A-526(1)].
	    a. Carload, truckload, planeload, or larger shipment if the buyer is solvent.
	    b. Any size shipment if the buyer is insolvent.

Goods in the possession of the buyer or lessee	1. Sue to recover the purchase price or rent [UCC 2-709(1), 2A-529(1)].
	 2. Reclaim the goods [UCC 2-507(2), 2A-525(2)].
	    a. The seller delivers goods in cash sale, and the buyer's check is dishonored.
	    b. The seller delivers goods in a credit sale, and the goods are received by an insolvent buyer.

▶ BUYER'S AND LESSEE'S REMEDIES

If a seller or lessor breaches a sales or lease contract, the UCC provides a variety of remedies to the buyer or lessee for the seller's or lessor's breach. These remedies are discussed in the following paragraphs.

Right to Reject Nonconforming Goods or Improperly Tendered Goods

right to reject nonconforming goods or improperly tendered goods
A situation in which a buyer or lessee rejects goods that do not conform to the contract. If the goods or the seller's or lessor's tender of delivery fails to conform to the contract, the buyer or lessee may (1) reject the whole, (2) accept the whole, or (3) accept any commercial unit and reject the rest.

If the contracted-for goods or the seller's or lessor's tender of delivery fails to conform to a sales or lease contract in any way, the buyer or lessee may (1) reject the whole, (2) accept the whole, or (3) accept any commercial unit and reject the rest. Nonconforming or improperly tendered goods must be rejected within a reasonable time after their delivery or tender. The seller or lessor must be notified of the **rejection**. The buyer or lessee must hold any rightfully rejected goods with reasonable care for a reasonable time [UCC 2-602(2), 2A-512(1)].

If the buyer or lessee chooses to reject the goods, he or she must identify defects that are ascertainable by reasonable inspection. Failure to do so prevents the buyer or lessee from relying on those defects to justify the rejection of the contract if the defect could have been cured had the seller or lessor received notification in a timely manner [UCC 2-601, 2A-509].

If a buyer or lessee is a merchant and the seller or lessor has no agent or place of business at the market where the goods are rejected, the merchant-buyer or merchant-lessee must follow any reasonable instructions received from the seller or lessor with respect to the rejected goods [UCC 2-603, 2A-511]. If the seller or lessor gives no instructions and the rejected goods are perishable or will quickly decline in value, the buyer or lessee may make reasonable efforts to sell them on the seller's or lessor's behalf [UCC 2-604, 2A-512].

Any buyer or lessee who rightfully rejects goods is entitled to reimbursement from the seller or lessor for reasonable expenses incurred in holding, storing, reselling, shipping, and otherwise caring for the rejected goods.

Right to Recover Goods from an Insolvent Seller or Lessor

If a buyer or lessee makes partial or full payment for goods before they are received and the seller or lessor becomes insolvent within 10 days after receiving the first payment, the buyer or lessee has the **right to recover the goods from the insolvent seller or lessor**. To do so, the buyer or lessee must tender the unpaid portion of the purchase price or rent due under the sales or lease contract. Only conforming goods that are identified in the contract may be recovered [UCC 2-502, 2A-522]. This remedy is often referred to as **capture**.

right to recover goods from an insolvent seller or lessor
The right of a buyer or lessee who has wholly or partially paid for goods before they are received to recover the goods from a seller or lessor who becomes insolvent within 10 days after receiving the first payment; the buyer or lessee must tender the remaining purchase price or rent due under the contract.

Right to Obtain Specific Performance

If goods are unique or the remedy at law is inadequate, a buyer or lessee has the **right to obtain specific performance** of a sales or lease contract. A decree of **specific performance** orders the seller or lessor to perform the contract. Specific performance is usually used to obtain possession of works of art, antiques, rare coins, and other unique items [UCC 2-716(1), 2A-521(1)].

specific performance
A decree of the court that orders a seller or lessor to perform his or her obligations under the contract; usually occurs when the goods in question are unique, such as art or antiques.

Example A buyer enters into a sales contract to purchase a specific Rembrandt painting from a seller for $25 million. When the buyer tenders payment, the seller refuses to sell the painting to the buyer. The buyer may bring an equity action to obtain a decree of specific performance from the court, which orders the seller to sell the painting to the buyer.

right to cover
The right of a buyer or lessee to purchase or lease substitute goods if a seller or lessor fails to make delivery of the goods or repudiates the contract or if the buyer or lessee rightfully rejects the goods or justifiably revokes their acceptance.

CONTEMPORARY ENVIRONMENT

Right to Cover

A buyer or lessee has the **right to cover** by purchasing or renting substitute goods if the seller or lessor fails to make delivery of the goods or repudiates the contract or if the buyer or lessee rightfully rejects the goods or justifiably revokes their acceptance. The buyer's or lessee's cover must be made in good faith and without unreasonable delay. If the exact commodity is not available, the buyer or lessee may purchase or lease any commercially reasonable substitute.

A buyer or lessee who rightfully covers may sue the seller or lessor to recover as damages the difference between the cost of cover and the contract price or rent. The buyer or lessee may also recover incidental and consequential damages, less expenses saved (such as delivery costs) [UCC 2-712, 2A-518].

Example University contracts to purchase 1,000 ePhones from Orange Store for $500 each to be used by its faculty members. Orange Store breaches the contract and does not deliver the ePhones to University. University covers and contracts with Apple Store to purchase 1,000 ePhones at the price of $600 per phone. Here, University may recover $100,000 from Orange Store ($600 cover price − $500 contract price = $100 × 1,000 phones).

The UCC does not require a buyer or lessee to cover when a seller or lessor breaches a sales or lease contract. Failure of the buyer or lessee to cover does not bar the buyer from other remedies against the seller.

Right to Replevy Goods

A buyer or lessee has the **right to replevy (recover) goods** from a seller or lessor who is wrongfully withholding the goods. The buyer or lessee must show that he or she was unable to cover or that attempts at cover will be unavailing. Thus, the goods must be scarce but not unique. **Replevin** actions are available only as to goods identified in a sales or lease contract [UCC 2-716(3), 2A-521(3)].

replevin
An action by a buyer or lessor to recover scarce goods wrongfully withheld by a seller or lessor.

buyer's or lessee's cancellation
A buyer or lessee has the right to cancel a sales or lease contract if the seller or lessor fails to deliver conforming goods or repudiates the contract or if the buyer or lessee rightfully rejects the goods or justifiably revokes acceptance of the goods.

Right to Cancel a Contract

If a seller or lessor fails to deliver conforming goods or repudiates the contract, the buyer or lessee may cancel the sales or lease contract. The buyer or lessee can also cancel a sales or lease contract if the buyer or lessee rightfully rejects the goods or justifiably revokes acceptance of the goods. The contract may be canceled with respect to the affected goods, or, if there is a material breach, the whole contract may be canceled. A buyer or lessee who rightfully cancels a contract is discharged from any further obligations on the contract and retains his or her rights to other remedies against the seller or lessor [UCC 2-711(1), 2A-508(1)(a)].

Right to Recover Damages for Nondelivery or Repudiation

damages
Damages a buyer or lessee recovers from a seller or lessor who fails to deliver the goods or repudiates the contract. Damages are measured as the difference between the contract price (or original rent) and the market price (or rent) at the time the buyer or lessee learned of the breach.

If a seller or lessor fails to deliver the goods or repudiates the sales or lease contract, the buyer or lessee has the **right to recover damages for nondelivery or repudiation**. The measure of **damages** is the difference between the contract price (or original rent) and the market price (or rent) at the time the buyer or lessee learned of the breach. Incidental and consequential damages, less expenses saved, can also be recovered [UCC 2-713, 2A-519].

Right to Recover Damages for Accepted Nonconforming Goods

A buyer or lessee may accept nonconforming goods from a seller or lessor. Even with acceptance, the buyer or lessee still has the **right to recover damages for accepted nonconforming goods** and any loss resulting from the seller's or lessor's breach. Incidental and consequential damages may also be recovered. The buyer or lessee must notify the seller or lessor of the nonconformity within a reasonable time after the breach was or should have been discovered. Failure to do so bars the buyer or lessee from any recovery. If the buyer or lessee accepts nonconforming goods, he or she may deduct all or any part of damages resulting from the breach from any part of the purchase price or rent still due under the contract [UCC 2-714(1), 2A-516(1)].

CONCEPT SUMMARY

BUYER'S AND LESSEE'S REMEDIES

Situation	Buyer's or Lessee's Remedy
Seller or lessor refuses to deliver the goods or delivers nonconforming goods that the buyer or lessee does not want.	1. Reject nonconforming goods [UCC 2-601, 2A-509]. 2. Revoke acceptance of nonconforming goods [UCC 2-608, 2A 517(1)]. 3. Cover [UCC 2-712, 2A-518]. 4. Sue for breach of contract and recover damages [UCC 2-713, 2A-519]. 5. Cancel the contract [UCC 2-711(1), 2A-508(1)(a)].
Seller or lessor tenders nonconforming goods and the buyer or lessee accepts them.	1. Sue for ordinary damages [UCC 2-714(1), 2A-516(1)]. 2. Deduct damages from the unpaid purchase or rent price [UCC 2-714(1), 2A-516(1)].
Seller or lessor refuses to deliver the goods and the buyer or lessee wants them.	1. Sue for specific performance [UCC 2-716(1), 2A-521(1)]. 2. Replevy the goods [UCC 2-716(3), 2A-521(3)]. 3. Recover the goods from an insolvent seller or lessor [UCC 2-502, 2A-522].

▶ ADDITIONAL PERFORMANCE ISSUES

UCC Articles 2 (Sales) and 2A (Leases) contain several other provisions that affect the parties' performance of a sales or lease contract. These provisions are discussed in the following paragraphs.

Assurance of Performance

Each party to a sales or lease contract expects that the other party will perform his or her contractual obligations. If one party to a contract has reasonable grounds to believe that the other party either will not or cannot perform his or her contractual obligations, an **adequate assurance of performance** may be demanded in writing. If it is commercially reasonable to do so, the party making the demand may suspend his or her performance until adequate assurance of due performance is received from the other party [UCC 2-609, 2A-401].

adequate assurance of performance
Adequate assurance of performance from the other party if there is an indication that the contract will be breached by that party.

Example A buyer contracts to purchase 1,000 bushels of wheat from a farmer. The contract requires delivery on September 1. In July, the buyer learns that floods have caused substantial crop loss in the area of the seller's farm. The farmer receives the buyer's written demand for adequate assurance on July 15. The farmer fails to give adequate assurance of performance. The buyer may suspend performance and treat the sales contract as having been repudiated.

Anticipatory Repudiation

Occasionally, a party to a sales or lease contract repudiates the contract before his or her performance is due under the contract. If the repudiation impairs the value of the contract to the aggrieved party, it is called **anticipatory repudiation**. Mere wavering on performance does not meet the test for anticipatory repudiation.

anticipatory repudiation
The repudiation of a sales or lease contract by one of the parties prior to the date set for performance.

If an anticipatory repudiation occurs, the aggrieved party can (1) await performance by the repudiating party for a commercially reasonable time (e.g., until the delivery date or shortly thereafter) or (2) treat the contract as having been breached at the time of the anticipatory repudiation, which gives the aggrieved party an immediate cause of action. In either case, the aggrieved party may suspend performance of his or her obligations under the contract [UCC 2-610, 2A-402].

An anticipatory repudiation may be retracted before the repudiating party's next performance is due if the aggrieved party has not (1) canceled the contract, (2) materially changed his or her position (e.g., purchased goods from another party), or (3) otherwise indicated that the repudiation is considered final. The retraction may be made by any method that clearly indicates the repudiating party's intent to perform the contract [UCC 2-611, 2A-403].

Statute of Limitations

The **UCC statute of limitations** provides that an action for breach of any written or oral sales or lease contract must commence within four years after the cause of the action accrues. The parties may agree to reduce the limitations period to one year, but they cannot extend it beyond four years.

UCC statute of limitations
A rule which provides that an action for breach of any written or oral sales or lease contract must commence within four years after the cause of action accrues. The parties may agree to reduce the limitations period to one year.

Agreements Affecting Remedies

The parties to a sales or lease contract may agree on remedies in addition to or in substitution for the remedies provided by the UCC. The parties may limit the buyer's or lessee's remedies to repair and replacement of defective goods or parts or to the return of the goods and repayment (refund) of the purchase price or rent.

The remedies agreed upon by the parties are in addition to the remedies provided by the UCC unless the parties expressly provide that they are exclusive. If an exclusive remedy fails in its essential purpose (e.g., there is an exclusive remedy of repair, but there are no repair parts available), any remedy may be had, as provided in the UCC.

Liquidated Damages

The UCC permits parties to a sales or lease contract to establish in advance in their contract the damages that will be paid upon a breach of the contract. Such preestablished

Convenience is the basis of mercantile law.

Lord Mansfield
Medcalf v. Hall (1782)

liquidated damages
Damages that will be paid upon a breach of contract that are established in advance.

damages, called **liquidated damages**, substitute for actual damages. In a sales or lease contract, liquidated damages are valid if they are reasonable in light of the anticipated or actual harm caused by the breach, the difficulties of proof of loss, and the inconvenience or nonfeasibility of otherwise obtaining an adequate remedy [UCC 2-718(1), 2A-504].

ETHICS SPOTLIGHT

Unconscionable Contracts

UCC Article 2 (Sales) and Article 2A (Leases) have adopted the equity doctrine of **unconscionability**. Under this doctrine, a court may determine as a matter of law that a contract is unconscionable. To prove unconscionability, there must be proof that the parties had substantially unequal bargaining power, that the dominant party misused its power in contracting, and that it would be manifestly unfair or oppressive to enforce the contract. This sometimes happens where a dominant party uses a preprinted form contract and the terms of the contract are unfair or oppressive.

If a court finds that a contract or any clause in a contract is unconscionable, the court may refuse to enforce the contract, or it may enforce the remainder of the contract without the unconscionable clause, or it may so limit the application of any unconscionable clause as to avoid any unconscionable result [UCC 2-302, 2A-108]. Unconscionability is sometimes found in a consumer lease if the consumer has been induced by unconscionable conduct to enter into the lease. The doctrine of unconscionability applies to online contracts as well as traditional contracts.

Business Ethics What does the doctrine of unconscionability provide? Explain. Does the doctrine of unconscionability encourage ethical behavior?

TEST REVIEW TERMS AND CONCEPTS

Acceptance
Adequate assurance of
   performance
Anticipatory repudiation
Breach
Buyer's or lessee's cancellation
Capture
C.O.D. (cash on delivery)
   shipment
Commercial reasonableness
Cure
Damages
Destination contract
Express terms
Good faith
Incidental damages

Installment contract
Liquidated damages
Lost volume seller
Obligations
Payment
Perfect tender rule
Place of delivery
Reasonableness
Replevin
Revocation of acceptance
Right of inspection
Right to cancel a contract
Right to cover
Right to dispose of goods
Right to obtain specific
   performance

Right to reclaim goods
Right to recover damages
   for accepted
   nonconforming goods
Right to recover damages
   for nondelivery or
   repudiation
Right to recover goods from
   an insolvent seller or lessor
Right to recover lost profit
Right to recover the
   purchase price or rent
Right to reject
   nonconforming goods or
   improperly tendered
   goods

Right to replevy (recover)
   goods
Right to stop delivery of
   goods in transit
Right to withhold
   delivery
Seller's or lessor's
   cancellation
Shipment contract
Specific performance
Tender of delivery
UCC statute of
   limitations
Unconscionability
Unfinished goods

CASE PROBLEMS

20.1 Nonconforming Goods   The Jacob Hartz Seed Company, Inc. (Hartz), bought soybeans for use as seed from E. R. Coleman. Coleman certified that the seed had an 80 percent germination rate. Hartz paid for the beans and picked them up from a warehouse in Card, Arkansas. After the seed was transported to Georgia, a sample was submitted for testing to the Georgia Department of Agriculture. When the department reported a germination level of only 67 percent,

Coleman requested that the seed be retested. The second set of tests reported a germination rate of 65 percent. Hartz canceled the contract after the second test, and Coleman reclaimed the seed. Hartz sought a refund of the money it had paid for the seed, claiming that the soybeans were nonconforming goods. Who wins? *Jacob Hartz Seed Co. v. Coleman*, 271 Ark. 756, 612 S.W.2d 91, **Web** 1981 Ark. Lexis 1153 (Supreme Court of Arkansas)

20.2 Right to Cure   Connie R. Grady purchased a new Chevrolet Chevette from Al Thompson Chevrolet (Thompson). Grady gave Thompson a down payment on the car and financed the remainder of the purchase price through General Motors Acceptance Corporation (GMAC). Grady picked up the Chevette. The next day, the car broke down and had to be towed back to Thompson. Grady picked up the repaired car one day later. The car's performance was still unsatisfactory in that the engine was hard to start, the transmission slipped, and the brakes had to be pushed to the floor to function. Two weeks later, Grady again returned the Chevette for servicing. When she picked up the car that evening, the engine started, but the engine and brake warning lights came on. This pattern of malfunction and repair continued for another two months. Grady wrote a letter to Thompson, revoking the sale. Thompson repossessed the Chevette. GMAC sued Grady to recover its money. Grady sued Thompson to recover her down payment. Thompson claimed that Grady's suit was barred because the company was not given adequate opportunity to cure. Who wins? *General Motors Acceptance Corp. v. Grady*, 27 OhioApp.3d 321, 501 N.E.2d 68, **Web** 1985 OhioApp. Lexis 10353 (Court of Appeals of Ohio)

20.3 Revocation of Acceptance   Roy E. Farrar Produce Company (Farrar) was a packer and shipper of tomatoes in Rio Arribon County, New Mexico. Farrar contacted Wilson, an agent and salesman for International Paper Company (International), and ordered 21,500 tomato boxes for $0.64 per box. The boxes were to each hold between 20 and 30 pounds of tomatoes for shipping. When the boxes arrived at Farrar's plant, 3,624 of them were immediately used to pack tomatoes. When the boxes were stacked, they began to collapse and crush the tomatoes contained within them. The produce company was forced to repackage the tomatoes and store the unused tomato boxes. Farrar contacted International and informed it that it no longer wanted the boxes because they could not perform as promised. International claimed that Farrar had accepted the packages and must pay for them. Who wins? *International Paper Co. v. Farrar*, 102 N.M. 739, 700 P.2d 642, **Web** 1985 N.M. Lexis 2000 (Supreme Court of New Mexico)

20.4 Commercial Impracticality   Charles C. Campbell was a farmer who farmed some 600 acres in the vicinity of Hanover, Pennsylvania. In the spring, Campbell entered into a contract with Hostetter Farms, Inc. (Hostetter), a grain dealer with facilities in Hanover. The sales agreement called for Campbell to sell Hostetter 20,000 bushels of No. 2 yellow corn at $1.70 per bushel. Delivery was made five months later, in the fall. Unfortunately, the summer was an unusually rainy one, and Campbell could not plant part of his crop because of the wet ground. After the corn was planted, part of the crop failed due to the excessive rain. As a result, Campbell delivered only 10,417 bushels. Hostetter sued Campbell for breach of contract. Campbell asserted the defense of commercial impracticability. Who wins? *Campbell v. Hostetter Farms, Inc.*, 251 Pa.Super. 232, 380 A.2d 463, **Web** 1977 Pa.Super. Lexis 2699 (Superior Court of Pennsylvania)

20.5 Right to Reclaim Goods   Archer Daniels Midland Company (Archer) sold ethanol for use in gasoline. Archer sold 80,000 gallons of ethanol on credit to Charter International Oil Company (Charter). The ethanol was shipped to Charter's facility in Houston. Charter became insolvent sometime during that period. Archer sent a written notice to Charter, demanding the return of the ethanol. At the time Charter received the reclamation demand, it had only 12,000 gallons of ethanol remaining at its Houston facility. When Charter refused to return the unused ethanol, Archer sued to recover the ethanol. Who wins? *Archer Daniels Midland v. Charter International Oil Company*, 60 B.R. 854, **Web** 1986 U.S. Dist. Lexis 25828 (United States District Court for the Middle District of Florida)

20.6 Right to Resell Goods   Meuser Material & Equipment Company (Meuser) was a dealer in construction equipment. Meuser entered into an agreement with Joe McMillan for the sale of a bulldozer to McMillan. The agreement called for Meuser to deliver the bulldozer to McMillan's residence in Greeley, Colorado. McMillan paid Meuser with a check. Before taking delivery, McMillan stopped payment on the check. Meuser entered into negotiations with McMillan in an attempt to get McMillan to abide by the sales agreement. During this period, Meuser paid for the upkeep of the bulldozer. When it became apparent that further negotiations would be fruitless, Meuser began looking for a new buyer. Fourteen months after the original sale was supposed to have taken place, the bulldozer was resold for less than the original contract price. Meuser sued McMillan to recover the difference between the contract price and the resale price as well as for the cost of upkeep on the bulldozer for 14 months. Who wins? *McMillan v. Meuser Material & Equipment Company*, 260 Ark. 422, 541 S.W.2d 911, **Web** 1976 Ark. Lexis 1814 (Supreme Court of Arkansas)

20.7 Right to Recover Purchase Price   C. R. Daniels, Inc. (Daniels), entered into a contract for the design and sale of grass catcher bags for lawn mowers to Yazoo Manufacturing Company, Inc. (Yazoo). Daniels contracted to design grass catcher bags that would fit the "S" series mower made by Yazoo. Yazoo provided Daniels with a lawn mower to design the bag. After Yazoo approved the design of the bags, it issued a purchase order for 20,000 bags. Daniels began to ship the bags. After accepting 8,000 bags, Yazoo requested that the shipments stop. Officials of Yazoo told Daniels that it would resume accepting shipments in a few months. Despite several attempts, Daniels could not get Yazoo to accept delivery of the remaining 12,000 bags. Daniels sued Yazoo to recover the purchase price of the grass bags still in its inventory. Who wins? *C. R. Daniels, Inc. v. Yazoo Mfg. Co., Inc.*, 641 F.Supp. 205, **Web** 1986 U.S. Dist. Lexis 23550 (United States District Court for the Southern District of Mississippi)

20.8 Right to Recover Lost Profits   Saber Energy, Inc. (Saber), entered into a sales contract with Tri-State Petroleum Corporation (Tri-State). The contract called for Saber to sell Tri-State 110,000 barrels of gasoline per month for six months. Saber was to deliver the gasoline through the colonial pipeline in Pasadena, Texas. The first 110,000 barrels were delivered on time. On August 1, Saber was informed that Tri-State was canceling the contract. Saber sued Tri-State for breach of contract and sought to recover its lost profits as damages. Tri-State admitted its breach but claimed that lost profits is an inappropriate measure of damages. Who wins? *Tri-State Petroleum Corporation v. Saber Energy, Inc.* 845 F.2d 575, **Web** 1988 U.S. App. Lexis 6819 (United States Court of Appeals for the Fifth Circuit)

20.9 Specific Performance   Dr. and Mrs. Sedmak (Sedmaks) were collectors of Chevrolet Corvettes. The Sedmaks saw an article in *Vette Vues* magazine concerning a new limited-edition Corvette. The limited edition was designed to commemorate the selection of the Corvette as the official pace car of the Indianapolis 500. Chevrolet was manufacturing only 6,000 of these pace cars. The Sedmaks visited Charlie's Chevrolet, Inc. (Charlie's), a local Chevrolet dealer. Charlie's was to receive only one limited-edition car, which the sales manager agreed to sell to the Sedmaks for the sticker price of $15,000. When the Sedmaks went to pick up and pay for the car, they were told that because of the great demand for the limited edition, it was going to be auctioned to the highest bidder. The Sedmaks sued the dealership for specific performance. Who wins? *Sedmak v. Charlie's Chevrolet, Inc.*, 622 S.W.2d. 694, **Web** 1981 Mo.App. Lexis 2911 (Court of Appeals of Missouri)

20.10 Right to Cover   Kent Nowlin Construction, Inc. (Nowlin), was awarded a contract by the state of New Mexico to pave a number of roads. After Nowlin was awarded the contract, it entered into an agreement with Concrete Sales & Equipment Rental Company, Inc. (C&E). C&E was to supply 20,000 tons of paving material to Nowlin. Nowlin began paving the roads, anticipating C&E's delivery of materials. On the delivery date, however, C&E shipped only 2,099 tons of paving materials. Because Nowlin had a deadline to meet, the company contracted with Gallup Sand and Gravel Company (Gallup) for substitute material. Nowlin sued C&E to recover the difference between the higher price it had to pay Gallup for materials and the contract price C&E had agreed to. C&E claims that it is not responsible for Nowlin's increased costs. Who wins? *Concrete Sales & Equipment Rental Company, Inc. v. Kent Nowlin Construction, Inc.*, 106 N.M. 539, 746 P.2d 645, **Web** 1987 N.M. Lexis 3808 (Supreme Court of New Mexico)

BUSINESS ETHICS CASES

20.11 Business Ethics   Ruby and Carmen Ybarra purchased a new double-wide mobile home from Modern Trailer Sales, Inc. (Modern). Modern delivered the mobile home to the Ybarras. A few days after delivery, portions of the floor began to rise and bubble, creating an unsightly and troublesome situation for the Ybarras. The Ybarras complained to Modern about the floor as soon as they discovered the defects. Modern sent repairmen to cure the defective floor on at least three occasions, but each time they were unsuccessful. The Ybarras continued to complain about the defects. The Ybarras continued to rely on Modern's assurances that it was able and willing to repair the floor. After four years of complaints, the Ybarras sued to revoke their acceptance of the sales contract. Did the Ybarras properly revoke their acceptance of the sales contract? Did Modern act ethically in this case? Did the Ybarras? *Ybarras v. Modern Trailer Sales, Inc.*, 94 N.W. 249, 609 P.2d 331, **Web** 1980 N.M. Lexis 2676 (Supreme Court of New Mexico)

20.12 Business Ethics   Allsopp Sand and Gravel (Allsopp) and Lincoln Sand and Gravel (Lincoln) were both in the business of supplying sand to construction companies. In March, Lincoln's sand dredge became inoperable. To continue in business, Lincoln negotiated a contract with Allsopp to purchase sand over the course of a year. The contract called for the sand to be loaded on Lincoln's trucks during Allsopp's regular operating season (March through November). Loading at other times was to be done by "special arrangement." By the following November, Lincoln had taken delivery of one-quarter of the sand it had contracted for. At that point, Lincoln requested that several trucks of sand be loaded in December. Allsopp informed Lincoln that it would have to pay extra for this special arrangement. Lincoln refused to pay extra, pointing out that the sand was already stockpiled at Allsopp's facilities. Allsopp also offered to supply an employee to supervise the loading. Negotiations between the parties broke down, and Lincoln informed Allsopp that it did not intend to honor the remainder of the contract. Allsopp sued Lincoln. Was it commercially reasonable for Lincoln to demand delivery of sand during December? Did Lincoln act ethically in this case? *Allsopp Sand and Gravel v. Lincoln Sand and Gravel*, 171 Ill.App.3d 532, 525 N.E.2d 1185, **Web** 1988 Ill.App. Lexis 939 (Appellate Court of Illinois)

▲ **Warranty** *Many goods—automobiles, motorcycles, electronics, computers, business equipment, and consumer goods—come with manufacturers' warranties. The manufacturer's warranty usually warrants that the product will last a certain period of time or for a certain number of uses. If the warranty is not met the manufacturer will either repair the product, replace the product, or take some other action that it has warranted.*

CHAPTER OBJECTIVES

After studying this chapter, you should be able to:

1. Identify and describe express warranties.
2. Describe the implied warranty of merchantability.
3. Describe the implied warranty of fitness for a particular purpose.

4. Identify warranty disclaimers and determine when they are unlawful.
5. Describe the warranties of good title and no infringements.

CHAPTER CONTENTS

> "When a manufacturer engages in advertising in order to bring his goods and their quality to the attention of the public and thus to create consumer demand, the representations made constitute an express warranty running directly to a buyer who purchases in reliance thereon. The fact that the sale is consummated with an independent dealer does not obviate the warranty."
>
> —Justice Francis
> *Henningsen v. Bloomfield Motors, Inc.*

▶ INTRODUCTION TO SALES AND LEASE WARRANTIES

warranty
A seller's or lessor's express or implied assurance to a buyer or lessee that the goods sold or leased meet certain quality standards.

The doctrine of *caveat emptor*—"let the buyer beware"—governed the law of sales and leases for centuries. Finally, the law recognized that consumers and other purchasers and lessees of goods needed greater protection. Article 2 of the Uniform Commercial Code (UCC), adopted in whole or in part by all 50 states, establishes certain **warranties** that apply to the sale of goods. Article 2A of the UCC, adopted in almost all states, establishes warranties that apply to lease transactions.

Warranties are the buyer's or lessee's assurance that the goods meet certain standards. Warranties, which are based on contract law, may be either *expressly* stated or *implied* by law. If the seller or lessor fails to meet a warranty, the buyer or lessee can sue for breach of warranty.

Sales and lease warranties are discussed in this chapter.

▶ EXPRESS WARRANTY

express warranty
A warranty that is created when a seller or lessor makes an affirmation that the goods he or she is selling or leasing meet certain standards of quality, description, performance, or condition.

Express warranties, which are the oldest form of warranty, are created when a seller or lessor affirms that the goods he or she is selling or leasing meet certain standards of quality, description, performance, or condition [UCC 2-313(1), 2A-210(1)]. Express warranties can be either written, oral, or inferred from the seller's conduct.

It is not necessary to use formal words such as *warrant* or *guarantee* to create an express warranty. Express warranties can be made by mistake because the seller or lessor does not have to specifically intend to make the warranty [UCC 2-313(2), 2A-210(2)].

Sellers and lessors are not required to make express warranties. Generally, express warranties are made to entice consumers and others to buy or lease their products. That is why these warranties are often found in advertisements, brochures, catalogs, pictures, illustrations, diagrams, blueprints, and so on.

An express warranty is created when a seller or lessor indicates that the goods will conform to:

1. All *affirmations of fact or promise* made about the goods.

   Examples Promises are statements such as "This car will go 100 miles per hour" or "This house paint will last at least five years."

2. Any *description* of the goods.

   Examples Descriptions of goods include terms such as *Idaho potatoes* and *Michigan cherries*.

3. Any *model* or *sample* of the goods.

   Example A model of an oil-drilling rig or a sample of wheat taken from a silo creates an express warranty.

Basis of the Bargain

Buyers and lessees can recover for a breach of an express warranty if the warranty was a contributing factor—not necessarily the sole factor—that induced the buyer to purchase the product or the lessee to lease the product. This is known as the **basis of the bargain** [UCC 2-313(1), 2A-210(1)]. The UCC does not define the term *basis of the bargain*, so this test is broadly applied by the courts. Generally, all statements by the seller or lessor prior to or at the time of contracting are presumed to be part of the basis of the bargain unless good reason is shown to the contrary. Postsale statements that modify the contract are part of the basis of the bargain.

Generally, a retailer is liable for the express warranties made by manufacturers of goods it sells. A manufacturer is not liable for express warranties made by wholesalers and retailers unless the manufacturer authorizes or ratifies a warranty.

Warranties are favored in law, being a part of a man's assurance.

Coke First Institute

Statement of Opinion

Many express warranties arise during the course of negotiations between a buyer and a seller or a lessor and a lessee. The seller's or lessor's **statement of opinion** (i.e., **puffing**) or commendation of the goods does not create an express warranty. It is often difficult to determine whether a seller's statement is an affirmation of fact (which creates an express warranty) or a statement of opinion (which does not create a warranty). An affirmation of the *value* of goods does not create an express warranty [UCC 2-313(2), 2A-210(2)].

statement of opinion
A commendation of goods, made by a seller or lessor, that does not create an express warranty. Also known as *puffing*.

Examples A used car salesperson's saying "This is the best used car available in town" does not create an express warranty because it is an opinion and mere puffing. However, a statement such as "This car has been driven only 20,000 miles" is an express warranty because it is a statement of fact.

Examples Statements such as "This painting is worth a fortune" or "Others would gladly pay $20,000 for this car" do not create an express warranty because these are statements of value and not statements of fact.

ETHICS SPOTLIGHT

Express Warranty

"We conclude that Ashe's description of the goods was more than his opinion; rather, he intended it to be a statement of a fact."

—Judge Whiting

W. Hayes Daughtrey consulted Sidney Ashe, a jeweler, about the purchase of a diamond bracelet as a Christmas present for his wife. Ashe showed Daughtrey a diamond bracelet that he had for sale for $15,000. When Daughtrey decided to purchase the bracelet, Ashe completed and signed an appraisal form that stated that the diamonds were "H color and v.v.s. quality." (v.v.s. is one of the highest ratings in a jeweler's quality classification.) After Daughtrey paid for the bracelet, Ashe put the bracelet and the appraisal form in a box. Daughtrey gave the bracelet to his wife as a Christmas present. One year later, when another jeweler looked at the bracelet, Daughtrey discovered that the diamonds were of substantially lower grade than v.v.s. Daughtrey filed a specific performance suit against Ashe to compel him to replace the bracelet with one mounted with v.v.s. diamonds or pay appropriate damages.

Was an express warranty made by Ashe regarding the quality of the diamonds in the bracelet? The trial court said no and held that the term *v.v.s. quality* was a mere opinion and not an express warranty. The supreme court of Virginia reversed, finding that the term *v.v.s. quality* created an

express warranty that the jeweler gave when he sold the bracelet to Daughtrey. The supreme court stated:

The trial court contends that Ashe's statement of the grade of the diamonds is a mere opinion and, thus, cannot qualify as an express warranty. It is not necessary to the creation of an express warranty that the seller use formal words such as "warrant" or "guarantee" or that he have a specific intention to make a warranty. Here, Ashe did more than give a mere opinion of the value of the goods; he specifically described them as diamonds of "H color and v.v.s. quality." We conclude that Ashe's description of the goods was more than his opinion; rather, he intended it to be a statement of a fact.

The supreme court of Virginia held that an express warranty had been created. The trial court's decision was reversed, and the case was remanded for a determination of appropriate damages to be awarded to Daughtrey. *Daughtrey v. Ashe*, 243 Va. 73, 413 S.E.2d 336, **Web** 1992 Va. Lexis 152 (Supreme Court of Virginia)

Business Ethics Do you think that Daughtrey relied on the term *v.v.s. quality* when he purchased the diamond bracelet? Did Ashe act ethically in denying that his statement created an express warranty?

Damages Recoverable for Breach of Warranty

compensatory damages
Damages that are generally equal to the difference between the value of the goods as warranted and the actual value of the goods accepted at the time and place of acceptance.

Where there has been a breach of warranty, the buyer or lessee may sue the seller or lessor to recover **compensatory damages**. The amount of recoverable compensatory damages is generally equal to the difference between (1) the value of the goods as warranted and (2) the actual value of the goods accepted at the time and place of acceptance [UCC 2-714(2), 2A-508(4)]. A purchaser or lessee can recover for personal injuries that are caused by a breach of warranty.

Example A used car salesperson warrants that a used car has been driven only 20,000 miles. If true, that would make the car worth $20,000. The salesperson gives the buyer a "good deal" and sells the car for $16,000. Unfortunately, the car was worth only $10,000 because it was actually driven 100,000 miles. The buyer discovers the breach of warranty and sues the salesperson for damages. The buyer can recover $10,000 ($20,000 warranted value minus $10,000 actual value). The contract price ($16,000) is irrelevant to this computation.

Example Frances purchases new tires for her car, and the manufacturer expressly warrants the tires against blowout for 50,000 miles. One of the tires blows out after being used only 20,000 miles, causing severe injury to Frances. She can recover personal injury damages from the manufacturer because of the breach of warranty.

▶ IMPLIED WARRANTY OF MERCHANTABILITY

In addition to express warranties made by a manufacturer or seller, the law sometimes *implies* warranties in the sale or lease of goods. Implied warranties are not expressly stated in the sales or lease contract but instead are **implied by law**. One such warranty is the *implied warranty of merchantability*.

implied warranty of merchantability
Unless properly disclosed, a warranty that is implied that sold or leased goods are fit for the ordinary purpose for which they are sold or leased, as well as other assurances.

If a seller or lessor of a good is a merchant with respect to goods of that kind, the sales contract or lease contract contains an **implied warranty of merchantability** of the good unless this implied warranty is properly disclaimed [UCC 2-314(1), 2A-212(1)]. This implied warranty requires that the following standards be met:

Law should be like death, which spares no one.

Charles de Montesquieu

- The goods must be fit for the ordinary purposes for which they are used.

Examples A chair must be able to safely perform the function of a chair. If a normal-sized person sits in a chair that has not been tampered with, and the chair collapses, there has been a breach of the implied warranty of merchantability. If, however, the same person is injured because he or she uses the chair as a ladder and it tips over, there is no breach of implied warranty because serving as a ladder is not the ordinary purpose of a chair.

- The goods must be adequately contained, packaged, and labeled.

Example The implied warranty of merchantability applies to a milk bottle as well as to the milk inside the bottle.

- The goods must be of an even kind, quality, and quantity within each unit.

Example All the goods in a carton, package, or box must be consistent.

- The goods must conform to any promise or affirmation of fact made on the container or label.

Example The goods must be capable of being used safely in accordance with the instructions on the package or label.

- The quality of the goods must pass without objection in the trade.

Example Other users of the goods would not object to quality of the goods.

- Fungible goods must meet a fair average or middle range of quality.

Example To be classified as a certain grade, such as pearl millet grain (*Pennisetum glaucum*) or iron ore (magnetite Fe_3O_4), goods must meet the average range of quality of that grade.

Note that the implied warranty of merchantability does not apply to sales or leases by nonmerchants or casual sales.

Examples The implied warranty of merchantability applies to the sale of a lawn mower that is sold by a merchant who is in the business of selling lawn mowers. The implied warranty of merchantability does not apply when one neighbor sells a lawn mower to another neighbor.

The following case raised the issue of implied warranty of merchantability.

CASE 21.1 Implied Warranty of Merchantability

Denny v. Ford Motor Company

87 N.Y.2d 248, 662 N.E.2d 730, 639 N.Y.S.2d 250, Web 1995 N.Y. Lexis 4445 (1995)
Court of Appeals of New York

"The law implies a warranty by a manufacturer that places its product on the market that the product is reasonably fit for the ordinary purpose for which it was intended."

—Judge Titone

Facts

Nancy Denny purchased a Bronco II, a small sport-utility vehicle (SUV) that was manufactured by Ford Motor Company. Denny testified that she purchased the Bronco for use on paved city and suburban streets and not for off-road use. When Denny was driving the vehicle on a paved road, she slammed on the brakes in an effort to avoid a deer that had walked directly into her SUV's path. The Bronco II rolled over, and Denny was severely injured. Denny sued Ford Motor Company to recover damages for breach of the implied warranty of merchantability.

Denny alleged that the Bronco II presented a significantly higher risk of occurrence of rollover accidents than did ordinary passenger vehicles. Denny introduced evidence at trial that showed that the Bronco II had a low stability index because of its high center of gravity, narrow tracks, and shorter wheelbase, as well as the design of its suspension system. Ford countered that the Bronco II was intended as an off-road vehicle and was not designed to be used as a conventional passenger automobile on paved streets. The trial court found Ford liable and awarded Denny $1.2 million in damages. Ford appealed.

Issue

Did Ford Motor Company breach the implied warranty of merchantability?

Language of the Court

Plaintiff introduced a Ford marketing manual that predicted many buyers would be attracted to the Bronco II because utility vehicles were suitable to "contemporary lifestyles" and were "considered fashionable" in some suburban areas. According to this manual, the sales presentation of the Bronco II should take into account the vehicle's

"suitability for commuting and for suburban and city driving." Additionally, the vehicle's ability to switch between two-wheel and four-wheel drive would "be particularly appealing to women who may be concerned about driving in snow and ice with their children." Plaintiff testified that the perceived safety benefits of its four-wheel drive capacity was what attracted her to the Bronco II. She was not at all interested in its off-road use.

The law implies a warranty by a manufacturer that places its product on the market that the product is reasonably fit for the ordinary purpose for which it was intended. If it is, in fact, defective and not reasonably fit to be used for its intended purpose, the warranty is breached. Plaintiff's proof focused on the sale of the Bronco II for suburban driving and everyday road travel. Plaintiff also adduced proof that the Bronco II's design characteristics made it unusually susceptible to rollover accidents when used on paved roads. All of this evidence was useful in showing that routine highway and street driving was the "ordinary purpose" for which the Bronco II was sold and that it was not "fit"—or safe—for that purpose. Thus, under the evidence in this case, a rational fact finder could have concluded that the vehicle was not safe for the "ordinary purpose" of daily driving for which it was marketed and sold.

Decision

The court of appeals held that Ford had breached the implied warranty of merchantability and upheld the jury award for the plaintiff.

Case Questions

Critical Legal Thinking What is an implied warranty of merchantability? Explain.

Business Ethics Did Ford act ethically in defending that the Bronco II was sold only as an off-road vehicle? Was this argument persuasive?

Contemporary Business Do you think that SUVs such as the Bronco II have a higher rollover danger than normal passenger automobiles?

Implied Warranty of Fitness for Human Consumption

implied warranty of fitness for human consumption
A warranty that applies to food or drink consumed on or off the premises of restaurants, grocery stores, fast-food outlets, and vending machines.

The common law implied a special warranty—the **implied warranty of fitness for human consumption**—to food products. The UCC incorporates this warranty within the implied warranty of merchantability, and it applies to food and drink consumed on or off the seller's premises. Restaurants, grocery stores, fast-food outlets, and vending-machine operators are all subject to this warranty. States use one of the following two tests in determining whether there has been a breach of the implied warranty of fitness for human consumption:

foreign substance test
A test to determine merchantability based on foreign objects found in food.

1. **Foreign substance test.** Under the **foreign substance test**, a food product is unmerchantable if a foreign object in that product causes injury to a person.

   Examples Under this test, the implied warranty would be breached if a person were injured by eating a nail in a cherry pie. This is because a nail is a foreign object in the cherry pie. The implied warranty would not be breached if a person were injured by eating a cherry pit in the pie. This is because the cherry pit is not a foreign object in the cherry pie.

consumer expectation test
A test to determine merchantability based on what the average consumer would expect to find in food products.

2. **Consumer expectation test.** The majority of states have adopted the modern **consumer expectation test** to determine the merchantability of food products. Under this test, the court asks what a consumer would expect to find or not find in food or drink that he or she consumes.

   Examples Under this test, the implied warranty would be breached if a person were injured by a chicken bone while eating a chicken salad sandwich. This is because a consumer would expect that the food producer would have removed all bones from the chicken. Under this test, the implied warranty would not be breached if a person were injured by a chicken bone while eating fried chicken. This is because a consumer would expect to find bones in fried chicken.

Restaurant, Sault Ste. Marie, Michigan *The implied warranty of fitness for human consumption is an implied warranty that food and drink served by restaurants, bars, fast-food outlets, coffee shops, vending machines, and other purveyors of food and drink be safe for human consumption. Each state applies one of two tests in determining whether there has been a breach of the implied warranty of fitness for human consumption: (1) the foreign substance test or (2) the consumer expectation test. Most states use the consumer expectation test.*

implied warranty of fitness for a particular purpose
A warranty that arises where a seller or lessor warrants that the goods will meet the buyer's or lessee's expressed needs.

▶ IMPLIED WARRANTY OF FITNESS FOR A PARTICULAR PURPOSE

The UCC contains an **implied warranty of fitness for a particular purpose**. This implied warranty attaches to the sale or lease of goods if the seller or lessor has made statements that the goods will meet the buyer's or lessee's needs or purpose. This implied warranty is breached if the goods do not meet the buyer's or lessee's expressed needs. The warranty applies to both merchant and nonmerchant sellers and lessors.

The warranty of fitness for a particular purpose is implied at the time of contracting if [UCC 2-315, 2A-213]:

- The seller or lessor has reason to know the particular purpose for which the buyer is purchasing the goods or the lessee is leasing the goods.
- The seller or lessor makes a statement that the goods will serve this purpose.
- The buyer or lessee relies on the seller's or lessor's skill and judgment and purchases or leases the goods.

Example Susan wants to buy lumber to build a small deck in her backyard. She goes to Joe's Lumber Yard to purchase the lumber and describes to Joe, the owner of the lumber yard, the size of the deck she intends to build. Susan also tells Joe that she is relying on him to select the right lumber for the project. Joe selects the lumber and states that the lumber will serve Susan's purpose. Susan buys the lumber and builds the deck. Unfortunately, the deck collapses because the lumber was not strong enough to support it. Susan can sue Joe for breach of the implied warranty of fitness for a particular purpose

CONCEPT SUMMARY

EXPRESS AND IMPLIED WARRANTIES OF QUALITY

Type of Warranty	How Created	Description
Express warranty	Made by the seller or lessor.	Affirms that the goods meet certain standards of quality, description, performance, or condition [UCC 2-313(1), 2A-210(1)].
Implied warranty of merchantability	Implied by law if the seller or lessor is a merchant.	Implies that the goods: 1. Are fit for the ordinary purposes for which they are used. 2. Are adequately contained, packaged, and labeled. 3. Are of an even kind, quality, and quantity within each unit. 4. Conform to any promise or affirmation of fact made on the container or label. 5. Pass without objection in the trade. 6. Meet a fair average, or middle range of quality for fungible goods [UCC 2-314(1), 2A-212(1)].
Implied warranty of fitness for a particular purpose	Implied by law.	Implies that the goods are fit for the purpose for which the buyer or lessee acquires the goods if: 1. The seller or lessor has reason to know the particular purpose for which the goods will be used. 2. The seller or lessor makes a statement that the goods will serve that purpose. 3. The buyer or lessee relies on the statement and buys or leases the goods [UCC 2-315, UCC 2A-213].

▶ WARRANTY DISCLAIMERS

Warranties can be **disclaimed**, or limited. If an *express warranty* is made, it can be limited only if the **warranty disclaimer** and the warranty can be reasonably construed with each

warranty disclaimer
A statement that negates express and implied warranties

other. All implied warranties of quality may be disclaimed. The rules for disclaiming implied warranties are:

- **"As is" disclaimer.** Expressions such as *as is*, *with all faults*, or other language that makes it clear to the buyer that there are no implied warranties disclaims all implied warranties. This type of disclaimer is often included in sales contracts for used products.
- **Disclaimer of the implied warranty of merchantability.** If the "as is" type of disclaimer is not used, disclaimers of the *implied warranty of merchantability* must specifically mention the term *merchantability* for the implied warranty of merchantability to be disclaimed. These disclaimers may be oral or written.
- **Disclaimer of the implied warranty of fitness for a particular purpose.** If the "as is" type of disclaimer is not used, the *implied warranty of fitness for a particular purpose* may be disclaimed in general language, without specific use of the term *fitness*. The disclaimer has to be in writing.

Conspicuous Display of Disclaimer

conspicuous
A requirement that warranty disclaimers be noticeable to the reasonable person.

Written disclaimers must be conspicuously displayed to be valid. The courts construe **conspicuous** as noticeable to a reasonable person [UCC 2-316, 2A-214]. A heading printed in uppercase letters or a typeface that is larger or in a different style than the rest of the body of a sales or lease contract is considered to be conspicuous. Different-color type is also considered conspicuous.

INTERNET LAW & ONLINE COMMERCE

Warranty Disclaimers in Software Licenses

Most software companies license their software to users. A software license is a complex contract that contains the terms of the license. Most software licenses contain warranty disclaimer and limitation on liability clauses that limit the licensor's liability if the software malfunctions. Disclaimer of warranty and limitation on liability clauses that are included in a typical software license appear below.

SOFTWARE.COM, INC.
LIMITATION AND WAIVERS OF WARRANTIES,
REMEDIES, AND CONSEQUENTIAL DAMAGES

Limited Warranty.   Software.com, Inc. warrants that (a) the software will perform substantially in accordance with the accompanying written materials for a period of 90 days from the date of receipt, and (b) any hardware accompanying the software will be free from defects in materials and workmanship under normal use and service for a period of one year from the date of the receipt. Any implied warranties on the software and hardware are limited to 90 days and one (1) year, respectively. Some states do not allow limitations on duration of an implied warranty, so the above limitation may not apply to you.

Customer Remedies.   Software.com, Inc.'s entire liability and your exclusive remedy shall be, at Software.com, Inc.'s option, either (a) return of the price paid or (b) repair or replacement of the software or hardware that does not meet Software.com, Inc.'s Limited Warranty and that is returned to Software.com, Inc. with a copy of your receipt. This Limited Warranty is void if failure of the software or hardware has resulted from accident, abuse, or misapplication. Any replacement software will be warranted for the remainder of the original warranty or 30 days, whichever is longer. These remedies are not available outside the United States of America.

No Other Warranties.   Software.com, Inc. disclaims all other warranties, either express or implied, including but not limited to implied warranties of merchantability and fitness for a particular purpose, with respect to the software, the accompanying written materials, and any accompanying hardware. This Limited Warranty gives you specific legal rights. You may have others, which vary from state to state.

No Liability for Consequential Damages.   In no event shall Software.com, Inc. or its suppliers be liable for any damages whatsoever (including, without limitation, damages for loss of business profits, business interruption, loss of business information, or other pecuniary loss) arising out of the use of or inability to use this Software.com, Inc. product, even if Software.com, Inc. has been advised of the possibility of such damages. Because some states do not allow the exclusion or limitation of liability for consequential or incidental damages, the above limitation may not apply to you.

► MAGNUSON-MOSS WARRANTY ACT

In 1975, Congress enacted the **Magnuson-Moss Warranty Act**, which covers written warranties related to *consumer products*.[1] This federal act is administered by the Federal Trade Commission (FTC). Consumer transactions, but not commercial and industrial transactions, are governed by the act.

Magnuson-Moss Warranty Act
A federal statute that regulates written warranties on consumer products.

LANDMARK LAW
Magnuson-Moss Warranty Act Protects Consumers

The Magnuson-Moss Warranty Act does not require a seller or lessor to make an *express* written warranty. However, sellers or lessors who do make express warranties are subject to the provisions of the act. If a warrantor chooses to make an express warranty, the Magnuson-Moss Warranty Act requires that the warranty be labeled as either "full" or "limited." The fact that a warranty is full or limited must be conspicuously displayed. The disclosures must be in "understandable language":

· **Full warranty.** For a warranty to qualify as a **full express warranty**, the warrantor must guarantee free repair or replacement of the defective product. The warrantor must indicate whether there is a time limit on the full warranty (e.g., "full 36-month warranty").
· **Limited warranty.** In a **limited express warranty**, the warrantor limits the scope of a full warranty in some way (e.g., a return of the purchase price).

Violations of the Magnuson-Moss Warranty Act

A consumer may bring a *civil action* against a defendant for violating the provisions of the Magnuson-Moss Warranty Act. A successful plaintiff can recover damages, attorneys' fees, and other costs incurred in bringing the action. The act authorizes warrantors to establish an informal dispute resolution procedure. The procedure must be conspicuously described in the written warranty. Aggrieved consumers must assert their claims through this procedure before they can take legal action.

Note that the act does not create any implied warranties. The act does, however, modify the state law of implied warranties in one crucial respect: Sellers or lessors who make express written warranties related to *consumer products* are forbidden from disclaiming or modifying the implied warranties of merchantability and fitness for a particular purpose. A seller or lessor may set a time limit on implied warranties, but this time limit must correspond to the duration of any express warranty.

In the following case, the court addressed the issue of a breach of an express warranty.

CASE 21.2 Magnuson-Moss Warranty Act
Milicevic v. Fletcher Jones Imports, Ltd. and Mercedes-Benz USA
402 F.3d 912, Web 2005 U.S. App. Lexis 4905 (2005)
United States Court of Appeals for the Ninth Circuit

"I feel like I am stranded. I cannot feel comfortable to take the car on a trip. I do not feel comfortable to drive because I don't know what next will come. Every day is a new problem."

—Marina Milicevic, consumer

Facts
Marina Milicevic purchased a new Mercedes-Benz S500 automobile from Fletcher Jones Imports, Ltd., a car dealership, for $98,722. The automobile had been imported into the United States by Mercedes-Benz USA. (Fletcher Jones and Mercedes-Benz are collectively referred to as Mercedes.) Mercedes advertised the car as the "best car in the world." Mercedes made a new car limited express warranty that warranted to the owner that authorized Mercedes-Benz Centers would make any repairs or replacements necessary to correct defects in material or workmanship for the duration of the warranty.

(case continues)

From day one, Milicevic's car exhibited a number of aesthetic and mechanical problems. Within the first seven months, the following repairs were made: All four brake rotors were warped and required replacement at 6,000 miles; after locking Milicevic out of the car, the remote entry system was replaced; the motor for the passenger side window was replaced; the passenger side mirror was replaced; and the rear window seal and molding were unsuccessfully repaired three times. All repairs were covered and paid for under the Mercedes-Benz limited warranty. By the end of seven months, the car had spent 55 days at the Fletcher Jones repair shop. The rear window deformity and the problem with the brakes were never corrected.

At that point, Milicevic notified Mercedes that she wanted Mercedes to replace the car or take the car back and reimburse her for the purchase price. When Mercedes did not respond, Milicevic sued Mercedes-Benz and Fletcher Jones for breach of an express limited warranty, to rescind the purchase of the automobile, and to recover the value of the car, damages, and attorneys' fees. Milicevic testified at trial: "I feel like I am stranded. I cannot feel comfortable to take the car on a trip. I do not feel comfortable to drive because I don't know what next will come. Every day is a new problem."

The U.S. District Court found that the defendants had breached the written warranty between the parties. Milicevic was awarded $93,423—the purchase price of the car, including taxes and fees, less an amount that represented her reasonable use of the automobile. The Court also awarded Milicevic costs and attorneys' fees. The defendants appealed.

Issue
Was there a breach of the express warranty by Mercedes that would permit Milicevic to rescind the purchase of the Mercedes-Benz automobile and recover the value of the car and damages?

Language of the Court
As defined in the Magnuson-Moss Warranty Act, a written warranty is a writing made by the supplier of a product relating to the nature of the material or workmanship of the product, which warranty promises that the product is defect free or will meet a certain level of performance for a given period of time, or a writing in which the supplier agrees to refund, repair, replace, or take other remedial action in the event that the product fails to meet its specifications. Here, Mercedes supplied such a limited written warranty which by its terms "warrants to the original and each subsequent owner of a new Mercedes-Benz passenger car that any authorized Mercedes-Benz Center will make any repairs or replacements necessary to correct defects in material or workmanship" at no charge for parts or labor.

The district court did not clearly err in finding that two significant nonconformities—the rear window seal and the brakes—were not corrected. Milicevic testified the brakes still did not work properly. The district court also found that all of the defects, conditions and nonconformities complained of by Milicevic, which Fletcher Jones was unable to repair, were covered by Mercedes-Benz's said warranty. Thus, when Mercedes failed to correct the defects in the rear window seal and brakes, Mercedes breached the terms of its limited written warranty. Having made out a claim for relief under the Magnuson-Moss Warranty Act, Milicevic may be awarded reasonable costs and attorneys' fees.

Decision
The U.S. Court of Appeals affirmed the U.S. District Court's judgment, which found that Mercedes had breach the express limited warranty, thus permitting Milicevic to rescind the contract and recover the value of the car, damages, costs, and attorneys' fees.

Case Questions
Critical Legal Thinking What types of contracts are covered by the Magnuson-Moss Warranty Act? What does the act provide if a dealer who made an express warranty cannot repair the defect in a reasonable time?

Business Ethics Did Mercedes-Benz or Fletcher Jones act ethically in this case? What do you think Mercedes-Benz and Fletcher Jones should have done in this case? Explain.

Contemporary Business Why do you think they fought this case to the appellate level? Was this "good business"? What do you think was the amount of Mercedes's legal fees?

▶ SPECIAL WARRANTIES OF TITLE AND POSSESSION

No man is above the law and no man is below it; nor do we ask any man's permission when we ask him to obey it.

Theodore Roosevelt

The UCC imposes special warranties on sellers and lessors of goods. These include a *warranty of good title*, a *warranty of no security interests*, a *warranty against infringements*, and a *warranty of no interference*. These warranties are discussed in the following paragraphs.

Warranty of Good Title

Unless they properly disclaim warranties, sellers of goods warrant that they have valid title to the goods they are selling and that the transfer of title is rightful [UCC 2-312(1)(a)]. This is called the **warranty of good title**. Persons who transfer goods without proper title breach this warranty.

Example Ingersoll-Rand owns a heavy-duty crane. A thief steals the crane and sells it to Turner Construction. Turner Construction does not know that the crane is stolen. If Ingersoll-Rand discovers that Turner Construction has the equipment, it can reclaim it. Turner Construction, in turn, can recover against the thief for breach of the warranty of title. This is because the thief impliedly warranted that he had good title to the equipment and that the transfer of title to Turner Construction was rightful.

warranty of good title
A warranty in which the seller warrants that he or she has valid title to the goods being sold and that the transfer of title is rightful.

Warranty of No Security Interests

Under the UCC, sellers of goods automatically warrant that the goods they sell are delivered free from any third-party security interests, liens, or encumbrances that are unknown to the buyer [UCC 2-312(1)(b)]. This is called the **warranty of no security interests**.

Example Albert purchases a refrigerator on credit from Appliance World, an appliance store. The store takes back a security interest in the refrigerator. Before completely paying off the refrigerator, Albert sells it to Monica for cash. Monica has no knowledge of the store's security interest in the refrigerator. After Albert misses several payments, the appliance store discovers that Monica has the refrigerator and repossesses the refrigerator. Monica can recover against Albert based on his breach of warranty of no security interests in the goods [UCC 2-312(1)(b)].

warranty of no security interests
A warranty in which sellers of goods warrant that the goods they sell are delivered free from any third-party security interests, liens, or encumbrances that are unknown to the buyer.

The warranties of good title and no security interests may be excluded or modified by specific language [UCC 2-312(2)]. For example, specific language such as "seller hereby transfers only those rights, title, and interest as he or she has in the goods" is sufficient to disclaim these warranties. General language such as "as is" or "with all faults" is not specific enough to be a disclaimer to the warranties of good title and no security interests. The special nature of certain sales (e.g., sheriffs' sales) tells the buyer that the seller is not giving title warranties with the sale of the goods.

Warranty Against Infringements

Unless otherwise agreed, a seller or lessor who is a merchant regularly dealing in goods of the kind sold or leased automatically warrants that the goods are delivered free of any third-party patent, trademark, or copyright claim [UCC 2-312(3), 2A-211(2)]. This is called the **warranty against infringement**.

Example Adams Company, a manufacturer of machines that make shoes, sells a machine to Smith & Franklin, a shoe manufacturer. Subsequently, Nerdette claims that she has a patent on the machine. Nerdette proves her patent claim in court. Nerdette notifies Smith & Franklin that the machine can no longer be used without her permission and the payment of a fee to her. Smith & Franklin may rescind the sales contract with Adams Company based on the breach of the warranty against infringement.

warranty against infringements
An automatic warranty of a seller or lessor who is a merchant who regularly deals in goods of the kind sold or leased which warrants that the goods are delivered free of any third-party patent, trademark, or copyright claim.

Warranty of No Interference

When goods are leased, the lessor warrants that no person holds a claim or an interest in the goods that arose from an act or omission of the lessor that will interfere with the lessee's enjoyment of his leasehold interest [UCC 2A-211(1)]. This is referred to as the **warranty against interference** or the **warranty of quiet possession**.

Example Occi-Petroleum, as lessor, leases a piece of heavy equipment to Aztec Drilling. Occi-Petroleum later gives a security interest in the equipment to CityBank as collateral

warranty against interference
A warranty in which the lessor warrants that no person holds a claim or an interest in the goods that arose from an act or omission of the lessor that will interfere with the lessee's enjoyment of his or her leasehold interest. Also known as the *warranty of quiet possession*.

for a loan. If Occi-Petroleum defaults on the loan to CityBank and CityBank repossesses the equipment from Aztec, Aztec can recover damages from Occi-Petroleum for breach of the warranty of no interference.

Delhi, India *Many countries have developed warranty law that applies to the sale or lease of goods. For example, India's Sale of Goods Act of 1930 includes laws regarding making express warranties, the creation of implied warranties, and disclaiming of warranties.*

TEST REVIEW TERMS AND CONCEPTS

Basis of the bargain
Caveat emptor
Compensatory damages
Conspicuous
Consumer expectation test
Disclaimed
Express warranty
Foreign substance test

Full express warranty
Implied by law
Implied warranty of fitness
    for human consumption
Implied warranty of fitness
    for a particular purpose
Implied warranty of
    merchantability

Limited express warranty
Magnuson-Moss Warranty
    Act
Statements of opinion
    (puffing)
Warranty
Warranty against
    infringement

Warranty against
    interference (warranty
    of quiet possession)
Warranty disclaimer
Warranty of good title
Warranty of no security
    interests

CASE PROBLEMS

21.1 Warranty of Title   When James Redmond wanted to purchase an automobile, he spoke to a salesman at Bill Branch Chevrolet, Inc. (Bill Branch). The salesman offered to sell Redmond a blue Chevrolet Caprice for $6,200. The car was to be delivered to Redmond's residence. Redmond gave the salesman $1,000 cash and received a receipt in return. The next day, the salesman delivered the car to Redmond, and Redmond paid the remaining amount due. The salesman gave Redmond a printed sales contract that reflected the payments made, with no balance due. One month later, Redmond called

Bill Branch and asked for the title papers to the car. Redmond was told that the car had been reported stolen prior to the sale and that he could not receive title until he contacted Bill Branch's insurance company. Redmond sued Bill Branch Chevrolet, Inc. Is Bill Branch liable? *Bill Branch Chevrolet v. Redmond*, 378 So.2d 319, **Web** 1980 Fla.App. Lexis 15413 (Court of Appeal of Florida)

21.2 Express Warranty   Gloria Crandell purchased a used Coronado clothes dryer from Larkin and Jones Appliance

Company (Larkin and Jones). The dryer, which was displayed on the sales floor, had a tag affixed to it that described the machine as a "quality reconditioned unit" that was "tag tested" and "guaranteed." In addition to these written statements, a salesman assured Crandell that the dryer carried a 90-day guarantee for "workmanship, parts, and labor." Crandell bought the dryer because of the guarantee and the low price. Two weeks after the machine was delivered, Crandell asked her son to put a blanket in the dryer to dry. Twenty minutes later, she noticed smoke pouring into her bedroom. By the time Crandell reached the laundry room, the machine was engulfed in flames. A defect in the clothes dryer had caused the fire. Crandell sued Larkin and Jones for breach of an express warranty. Is there an express warranty? *Crandell v. Larkin and Jones Appliance Company*, 334 N.W.2d 31, **Web** 1983 S.D. Lexis 326 (Supreme Court of South Dakota)

21.3 Statement of Fact or Opinion Jack Crothers went to Norm's Auto Sales (Norm's) to buy a used car. Maurice Boyd, a salesman at Norm's, showed Crothers a Dodge automobile. While running the car's engine, Boyd told Crothers that the Dodge "had a rebuilt carburetor" and "was a good runner." After listening to the sales pitch, Crothers bought the car. As Crothers was driving the Dodge the next day, the car suddenly went out of control and crashed into a tree. Crothers was seriously injured. The cause of the crash was an obvious defect in the Dodge's accelerator linkage. Crothers sued Norm's. Who wins? *Crothers v. Norm's Auto Sales*, 384 N.W.2d 562, **Web** 1986 Minn.App. Lexis 4202 (Court of Appeals of Minnesota)

21.4 Implied Warranty of Merchantability Geraldine Maybank took a trip to New York City to visit her son and her two-year-old grandson. She borrowed her daughter's camera for the trip. Two days before leaving for New York, Maybank purchased a package of G. T. E. Sylvania Blue Dot flashcubes at a Kmart store, owned by the S. S. Kresge Company. On the carton of the package were words to the effect that each bulb was safety coated. Upon arriving in New York, Maybank decided to take a picture of her grandson. She opened the carton of flashcubes and put one on the camera. When Maybank pushed down the lever to take a picture, the flashcube exploded. The explosion knocked her glasses off and caused cuts to her left eye. Maybank was hospitalized for eight days. Maybank sued S. S. Kresge Company. Who wins? *Maybank v. S. S. Kresge Company*, 46 N.C.App. 687, 266 S.E.2d 409, **Web** 1980 N.C.App. Lexis 2927 (Court of Appeals of North Carolina)

21.5 Implied Warranty of Fitness for Human Consumption Tina Keperwes went to a Publix Supermarket (Publix) in Florida and bought a can of Doxsee brand clam chowder. Keperwes opened the can of soup and prepared it at home. While eating the chowder, she bit down on a clamshell and injured one of her molars. Keperwes filed suit against Publix and Doxsee for breach of an implied warranty. In the lawsuit, Keperwes alleged that the clam chowder "was not fit for use as

food, but was defective, unwholesome, and unfit for human consumption" and "was in such condition as to be dangerous to life and health." At the trial, Doxsee's general manager testified as to the state-of-the-art methods Doxsee uses in preparing its chowder. Are Publix and Doxsee liable for the injury to Keperwes's tooth? *Keperwes v. Publix Supermarkets. Inc.*, 534 So.2d 872, **Web** 1988 Fla.App. Lexis 5306 (Court of Appeal of Florida)

21.6 Disclaimer of Warranty Automatic Sprinkler Corporation of America (Automatic Sprinkler) wished to purchase a dry chemical fire protection system from Ansul Company (Ansul). An Ansul representative gave Automatic Sprinkler a proposal on the company's behalf. The proposal was a document five pages long. Each page included printed information describing the fire extinguisher system. Only the fifth and last page had printing on the back. The information on the back of page 5 contained a limited five-year warranty that covered only the replacement of defective parts. The limited warranty concluded with this statement: "This warranty is in lieu of all other warranties express or implied."

Automatic Sprinkler purchased the system and installed it in a client's building. Several years later, a fire broke out in the building, and the Ansul fire extinguisher system failed to discharge. Automatic Sprinkler sued Ansul for a breach of an implied warranty of merchantability. Ansul claimed that all warranties except the limited five-year warranty were disclaimed. Is Ansul's disclaimer enforceable? *Insurance Company of North America v. Automatic Sprinkler*, 67 Ohio St.2d 91, 423 N.E.2d 151, **Web** 1981 Ohio Lexis 554 (Supreme Court of Ohio)

21.7 Disclaimer of Warranty Cole Energy Development Company (Cole Energy) wanted to lease a gas compressor for use in its business of pumping and selling natural gas and began negotiating with the Ingersoll-Rand Company (Ingersoll-Rand). On December 5, 1983, the two parties entered into a lease agreement for a KOA gas compressor. The lease agreement contained a section labeled "WARRANTIES." Part of the section read:

THERE ARE NO IMPLIED WARRANTIES OF MERCHANTABILITY OR FITNESS FOR A PARTI-CULAR PURPOSE CONTAINED HEREIN.

The gas compressor that was installed failed to function properly. As a result, Cole Energy lost business. Cole Energy sued Ingersoll-Rand for the breach of an implied warranty of merchantability. Is Ingersoll-Rand liable? *Cole Energy Development Company v. Ingersoll-Rand Company*, 678 F.Supp. 208, **Web** 1988 U.S. Dist. Lexis 923 (United States District Court for the Central District of Illinois)

21.8 Disclaimer of Warranty Edward Cate owned and operated an automotive repair shop. Cate wanted to purchase a set of automotive lifts (i.e., the devices used to elevate vehicles for repair work). Cate purchased a set of Rotary Brand lifts, manufactured by Dover Corporation (Dover). The contract for the lifts contained a five-year written warranty covering the repair of all defective parts returned to the factory. The warranty section of the contract, printed in black ink, also contained a separate paragraph stating:

> *This warranty is exclusive and in lieu of all other warranties express or implied including any implied warranty of merchantability or implied warranty of fitness for a particular purpose.*

The entire warranty section was framed by double blue lines, and the word "Warranty" was printed in solid blue letters. After the lifts were installed in Cate's shop, they began to malfunction. Cars would suddenly fall off the lifts. Dover's employees made several unsuccessful repair attempts. Rather than send the lifts back to the factory, Cate sued Dover for breach of implied warranty of merchantability. Who wins? *Cate v. Dover Corporation*, 776 S.W.2d 680, **Web** 1989 Tex. App. Lexis 2086 (Court of Appeals of Texas)

BUSINESS ETHICS CASES

21.9 Business Ethics   Brian Keith, an actor, attended a boat show in Long Beach, California. At the boat show, Keith obtained sales literature on a sailboat called the "Island Trader 41" from a sales representative of James Buchanan, a seller of sailboats. One sales brochure described the vessel as "a picture of sure-footed seaworthiness." Another brochure called the sailboat "a carefully well-equipped and very seaworthy live-aboard vessel." One month later, Keith purchased an Island Trader 41 sailboat from Buchanan for a total purchase price of $75,610. After delivery of the sailboat, a dispute arose in regard to the seaworthiness of the vessel. Keith sued Buchanan for breach of warranty. Buchanan defended, arguing that no warranty had been made. Is it ethical for Buchanan to try to avoid being held accountable for statements of quality about the product that were made in the sales brochures given to Keith? Should sales "puffing" be considered to create an express warranty? Why or why not? Who wins this case? *Keith v. Buchanan*, 173 Cal.App.3d 13, 220 Cal.Rptr. 392, **Web** 1985 Cal.App. Lexis 2603 (Court of Appeal of California)

21.10 Business Ethics   Peter Troy, president and owner of Troy's Custom Smoking Co., Inc. (Troy's), contacted Peter Bader, president of Swan Island Sheet Metal Works, Inc. (Swan Island), and asked Bader if Swan Island could manufacture two stainless steel gas-burner crab cookers for Troy's. Troy explained to Bader the planned use of the cookers and some of the special needs a crab cooker must satisfy—that is, a crab is cooked by dropping it into boiling water, allowing the water to recover to a rolling boil, and boiling the crab for 10 minutes. If the recovery time exceeds 10 minutes, or if the cooker cannot sustain a rolling boil, the crab is immersed too long in hot water, and the finished product is unpalatable. Troy and Bader were equally unknowledgeable about gas-burner cookers, but Bader assured Troy that he would hire an expert to assist in manufacturing a crab cooker to meet Troy's needs.

Bader sent Troy a brochure illustrating the type of burner the expert had selected to meet Troy's needs. Troy ordered the cooker, which was delivered to Troy's Beaverton, Oregon, store. Within two weeks after delivery, Troy complained to Swan Island about the cooker's performance. The cooker cooked too slowly, and the pilot light and burner were difficult to light and keep lit. Swan Island attempted but could not correct the defects. For four months, Troy's cooked crab in the Swan Island cooker. Because of the poor performance of the cooker, Troy's ruined a substantial amount of crab and had to obtain cooked crab from another outlet to serve its customers. Troy's notified Swan Island to pick up the crab cooker. Swan Island sued Troy's to recover the purchase price of the cooker. Troy's filed a counterclaim against Swan Island to rescind the contract and recover damages. Did Swan Island breach an implied warranty of fitness for a particular purpose? Did Swan Island act ethically in denying liability in this case? *Swan Island Sheet Metal Works, Inc. v. Troy's Custom Smoking Co., Inc.*, 49 Ore.App. 469, 619 P.2d 1326, **Web** 1980 Ore.App. Lexis 3731 (Court of Appeals of Oregon)

ENDNOTE

1. 15 U.S.C. Sections 2301-2312.

Part V
NEGOTIABLE INSTRUMENTS AND E-MONEY

▲ **Check** *A negotiable instrument must be in writing, permanent, and portable. However, it need not be on paper. In the past, creative check writers have written checks on odd items such as shirts. There is a rumor about a farmer who tried to write a check on a cow, but this story appears to be an urban legend.*

CHAPTER OBJECTIVES

After studying this chapter, you should be able to:

1. Distinguish between negotiable and nonnegotiable instruments.
2. Describe drafts and checks and identify the parties to these instruments.
3. Describe promissory notes and certificates of deposit and identify the parties to these instruments.
4. List the formal requirements of a negotiable instrument.
5. Distinguish between instruments payable to order and instruments payable to bearer.

CHAPTER CONTENTS

▶ **INTRODUCTION TO THE CREATION OF NEGOTIABLE INSTRUMENTS**

▶ **NEGOTIABLE INSTRUMENTS**

Landmark Law · *Revised Article 3 (Negotiable Instruments) of the UCC*

▶ **TYPES OF NEGOTIABLE INSTRUMENTS**

"The great object of the law is to encourage commerce."

—Judge Chambre
Beale v. Thompson (1803)

▶ INTRODUCTION TO THE CREATION OF NEGOTIABLE INSTRUMENTS

Negotiable instruments (or **commercial paper**) are important for the conduct of business and personal affairs. In this country, modern commerce could not continue without them. Examples of negotiable instruments include checks (e.g., the one that may have been used to pay for this book) and promissory notes (e.g., a note executed by a borrower of money to pay for tuition). The term **instrument** means negotiable instrument [UCC 3-104(b)]. These terms are often used interchangeably.

The types of negotiable instruments and their creation are discussed in this chapter.

negotiable instrument
A special form of contract that satisfies the requirements established by Article 3 of the UCC. Also called *commercial paper* or *instrument*.

The borrower runs in his own debt.

Ralph Waldo Emerson

▶ NEGOTIABLE INSTRUMENTS

To qualify as a negotiable instrument, a document must meet certain requirements established by Article 3 of the Uniform Commercial Code (UCC). If these requirements are met, a transferee who qualifies as a **holder in due course (HDC)** takes the instrument free of many defenses that can be asserted against the original payee. In addition, the document is considered an ordinary contract that is subject to contract law.

The concept of **negotiation** is important to the law of negotiable instruments. The primary benefit of a negotiable instrument is that it can be used as a substitute for money. As such, it must be freely transferable to subsequent parties. Technically, a negotiable instrument is negotiated when it is originally issued. The term *negotiation*, however, is usually used to describe the transfer of negotiable instruments to subsequent transferees.

Functions of Negotiable Instruments

Negotiable instruments serve the following functions:

1. **Substitute for money.**   Merchants and consumers often do not carry cash for fear of loss or theft. Further, it would be almost impossible to carry enough cash for large purchases (e.g., a car, a house). Thus certain forms of negotiable instruments—for example, checks—serve as *substitutes for money*.
2. **Act as credit devices.**   Some forms of negotiable instruments extend credit from one party to another. A seller may sell goods to a customer on a customer's promise to pay for the goods at a future time, or a bank may lend money to a buyer who signs a note promising to repay the money. Both of these examples represent *extensions of credit*. Without negotiable instruments, the "credit economy" of the United States and other modern industrial countries would not be possible.
3. **Act as record-keeping devices.**   Negotiable instruments often serve as *record-keeping devices*. Banks may return canceled checks to checking-account customers each month. These act as a record-keeping device for the preparation of financial statements, tax returns, and the like.

LANDMARK LAW

Revised Article 3 (Negotiable Instruments) of the UCC

Although negotiable instruments have been used in commerce since medieval times, the English law courts did not immediately recognize their validity. To compensate for this failure, the merchants developed rules governing their use. These rules, which were enforced by local private merchant courts, became part of what was called the **Law Merchant**. Eventually, in 1882, England enacted the Bills of Exchange Act, which codified the rules of the Law Merchant. In 1886, the National Conference of Commissioners of Uniform State Laws promulgated the **Uniform Negotiable Instruments Law (NIL)** in the United States. By 1920, all of the states had enacted the NIL as law, but the rapid development of commercial paper soon made the law obsolete.

Article 3 (Commercial Paper) of the UCC, which was promulgated in 1952, established rules for the creation of, transfer of, enforcement of, and liability on negotiable instruments. All the states and the District of Columbia have replaced the NIL with Article 3 of the UCC.

In 1990, the American Law Institute and the National Conference of Commissioners on Uniform State Laws repealed Article 3 and replaced it with **Revised Article 3 of the UCC**. The new article, which is called "Negotiable Instruments" instead of "Commercial Paper," is a comprehensive revision of Article 3. Revised Article 3 is used as the basis for this and the following chapters on negotiable instruments.

Article 3 of the UCC
A model code that establishes rules for the creation of, transfer of, enforcement of, and liability on negotiable instruments.

Revised Article 3
A comprehensive revision of the UCC law of negotiable instruments that reflects modern commercial practices.

draft
A three-party instrument that is an unconditional written order by one party that orders a second party to pay money to a third party.

drawer of a draft
The party who writes an order for a draft.

drawee of a draft
The party who must pay the money stated in a draft. Also called the *acceptor* of a draft.

payee of a draft
The party who receives the money from a draft.

time draft
A draft payable at a designated future date.

sight draft
A draft payable on sight. Also called a *demand draft*.

trade acceptance
A sight draft that arises when credit is extended (by a seller to a buyer) with the sale of goods. The seller is both the drawer and the payee, and the buyer is the drawee.

▶ TYPES OF NEGOTIABLE INSTRUMENTS

Revised Article 3 recognizes four kinds of negotiable instruments: drafts, checks, promissory notes, and certificates of deposit. Each of these is discussed in the following paragraphs.

Draft

A **draft**, which is a three-party instrument, is an unconditional written order by one party (the **drawer**) that orders a second party (the **drawee**) to pay money to a third party (the **payee**) [UCC 3-104(e)]. The drawee must be obligated to pay the drawer money before the drawer can order the drawee to pay this money to a third party (the payee).

For the drawee to be liable on a draft, the drawee must accept the drawer's written order to pay it. Acceptance is usually shown by the written word *accepted* on the face of the draft, along with the drawee's signature and the date. The drawee is called the **acceptor** of the draft because his or her obligation changes from that of having to pay the drawer to that of having to pay the payee. After the drawee accepts the draft, it is returned to the drawer or the payee. The drawer or the payee, in turn, can freely transfer it as a negotiable instrument to another party.

Example Mary owes Hector $1,000. Hector wants Mary to pay the money to Cindy instead of to him. Hector writes out a draft that orders Mary to pay the $1,000 to Cindy. Mary agrees to this change of obligation and writes the word "accepted" on the draft and signs the draft. Hector is the drawer, Mary is the drawee and acceptor of the draft, and Cindy is the payee. Mary is now obligated to pay Cindy $1,000.

A draft can be either a time draft or a sight draft. A **time draft** is payable at a designated future date. Language such as "pay on January 1, 2011" or "pay 120 days after date" creates a time draft (see Exhibit 22.1). A **sight draft** is payable on sight. A sight draft is also called a **demand draft**. Language such as "on demand pay" or "at sight pay" creates a sight draft. A draft can be both a time draft and a sight draft. Such a draft would provide that it is payable at a stated time after sight. This type of draft is created by language such as "payable 90 days after sight."

Trade Acceptance   A **trade acceptance** is a sight draft that arises when credit is extended with the sale of goods. With this type of draft, the seller is both the drawer and the payee. The buyer to whom credit is extended is the drawee. Even though only two actual parties are involved, it is considered a three-party instrument because three legal positions are involved.

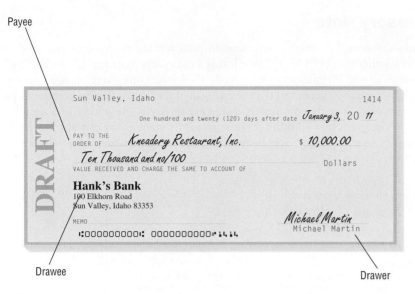

Payee

Drawee

Drawer

▶ **Exhibit 22.1 TIME DRAFT**

Check

A **check** is a distinct form of draft. It is unique in that it is drawn on a financial institution (the drawee) and is payable on demand [UCC 3-104(f)]. In other words, a check is an *order to pay* (see Exhibit 22.2). Most businesses and many individuals have checking accounts at financial institutions. Like other drafts, a check is a three-party instrument. A customer who has a checking account and writes (draws) a check is the **drawer**. The financial institution upon which the check is written is the **drawee**. And the party to whom the check is written is the **payee**.

check
A distinct form of draft drawn on a financial institution and payable on demand.

drawer of a check
The checking account holder and writer of a check.

drawee of a check
The financial institution where the drawer of a check has his or her account.

payee of a check
The party to whom a check is written.

▶ **Exhibit 22.2 CHECK**

Payee

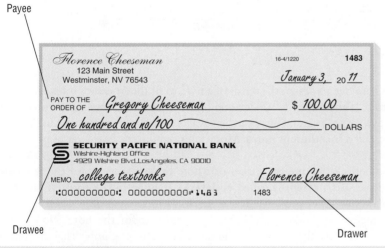

Drawee

Drawer

CONCEPT SUMMARY

TYPES OF ORDERS TO PAY

Order to Pay	Parties	Description
Draft	Drawer	Person who issues a draft.
	Drawee	Person who owes money to a drawer; person who is ordered to pay a draft and accepts the draft.
	Payee	Person to whom a draft is made payable.
Check	Drawer	Owner of a checking account at a financial institution; person who issues a check.
	Drawee	Financial institution where drawer's checking account is located; party who is ordered to pay a check.
	Payee	Person to whom a check is made payable.

promissory note
A two-party negotiable instrument that is an unconditional written promise by one party to pay money to another party.

maker of a note
The party who makes a promise to pay (borrower).

payee of a note
The party to whom a promise to pay is made (lender).

▶ **Exhibit 22.3**
PROMISSORY NOTE

Promissory Note

A **promissory note** (or **note**) is an unconditional written promise by one party to pay money to another party [UCC 3-104(e)]. It is a two-party instrument (see Exhibit 22.3), not an order to pay. Promissory notes usually arise when one party borrows money from another. The note is evidence of (1) the extension of credit and (2) the borrower's promise to repay the debt. A party who makes a promise to pay is the **maker** of a note (i.e., the borrower). The party to whom the promise to pay is made is the **payee** (i.e., the lender). A promissory note is a negotiable instrument that the payee can freely transfer to other parties.

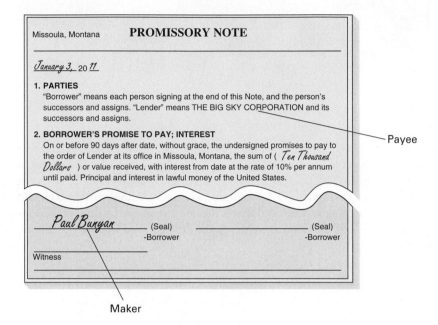

The parties are free to design the terms of a note to fit their needs. Notes can be payable at a specific time (**time notes**) or on demand (**demand notes**). Notes can be made payable to a named payee or to "bearer." They can be payable in a single payment or in installments. The latter are called **installment notes**. Most notes require the borrower to pay interest on the principal.

Lenders sometimes require the maker of a note to post security for the repayment of the note. This security, which is called **collateral**, may be in the form of automobiles, houses, securities, or other property. If a maker fails to repay a note when it is due, the lender can foreclose and take the collateral as payment for the note. Notes are often named after the security that underlies the note. For example, notes that are secured by real estate are called **mortgage notes**, and notes that are secured by personal property are called **collateral notes**.

time note
A note payable at a specific time.

demand note
A note payable on demand.

collateral
Security against repayment of a note that lenders sometimes require; can be a car, a house, or other property.

certificate of deposit (CD)
A two-party negotiable instrument that is a special form of note created when a depositor deposits money at a financial institution in exchange for the institution's promise to pay back the amount of the deposit plus an agreed-upon rate of interest upon the expiration of a set time period agreed upon by the parties.

maker of a CD
The financial institution that issues a CD (borrower).

payee of a CD
The party to whom a CD is made payable; usually the depositor (lender).

Certificate of Deposit

A **certificate of deposit (CD)** is a special form of note that is created when a depositor deposits money at a financial institution in exchange for the institution's promise to pay back the amount of the deposit plus an agreed-upon rate of interest upon the expiration of a set time period agreed upon by the parties [UCC 3-104(j)].

The financial institution is the borrower (the **maker**), and the depositor is the lender (the **payee**). A CD is a two-party instrument (see Exhibit 22.4). Note that a CD is a promise to pay, not an order to pay. Unlike a regular passbook savings account, a CD is a negotiable instrument. CDs under $100,000 are commonly referred to as **small CDs**. CDs of $100,000 or more are usually called **jumbo CDs**.

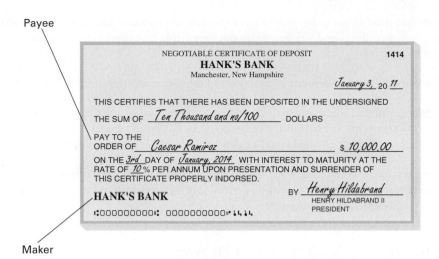

Payee

Maker

CONCEPT SUMMARY

TYPES OF PROMISES TO PAY

Promise to Pay	Parties	Description
Promissory note	Maker	Party who issues a promissory note; this is usually the borrower.
	Payee	Party to whom a promissory note is made payable; this is usually the lender.
Certificate of deposit (CD)	Maker	Financial institution that issues a CD.
	Payee	Party to whom a CD is made payable; this is usually the depositor.

▶ CREATING A NEGOTIABLE INSTRUMENT

According to UCC 3-104(a), a negotiable instrument must:

- Be in writing.
- Be signed by the maker or drawer.
- Be an unconditional promise or order to pay.
- State a fixed amount of money.
- Not require any undertaking in addition to the payment of money.
- Be payable on demand or at a definite time.
- Be payable to order or to bearer.

These requirements must appear on the *face* of the instrument. If they do not, the instrument does not qualify as negotiable. Each of these requirements is discussed in the paragraphs and sections that follow.

Writing

A negotiable instrument must be (1) in **writing** and (2) permanent and portable. Often, the requisite writing is on a preprinted form, but typewritten, handwritten, or other tangible agreements are also acceptable [UCC 1-201(46)]. In addition, the instrument can be a combination of different kinds of writing.

Example A check is often a preprinted form on which the drawer handwrites the amount of the check, the name of the payee, and the date of the check. Oral promises do not qualify as negotiable instruments because they are not clearly transferable in a manner that will prevent fraud. Most writings on paper meet the **permanency requirement**. However, a

Money can't buy friends but it can get you a better class of enemy.

Spike Milligan

permanency requirement
A requirement of negotiable instruments that says they must be in a permanent state, such as written on ordinary paper.

writing that is on tissue paper would not meet this requirement because of its impermanence. Tape recordings and videotapes are not negotiable instruments because they are not considered writings.

The **portability requirement** is intended to ensure free transfer of an instrument.

portability requirement
A requirement of negotiable instruments that says they must be able to be easily transported between areas.

Examples A promise to pay chiseled in a tree would not qualify as a negotiable instrument because the tree is not freely transferable in commerce. Writing the same promise or order to pay on a small block of wood could qualify as a negotiable instrument, however.

The best practice is to place a written promise or order to pay on traditional paper. This method ensures that the permanency and portability requirements are met so that transferees will readily accept the instrument.

Signed by the Maker or the Drawer

signature requirement
A requirement which states that a negotiable instrument must be signed by the drawer or maker. Any symbol executed or adopted by a party with a present intent to authenticate a writing qualifies as his or her signature.

The UCC **signature requirement** requires that a negotiable instrument must be *signed* by the maker if it is a note or CD and by the drawer if it is a check or draft. The maker or drawer is not liable on the instrument unless his or her signature appears on it. The signature can be placed on the instrument by the maker or drawer or by an authorized agent [UCC 3-401(a)]. Although the signature of the maker, drawer, or agent can be located anywhere on the face of the negotiable instrument, it is usually placed in the lower-right corner.

The UCC broadly defines **signature** as any symbol executed or adopted by a party with a present intent to authenticate a writing [UCC 1-201(39)]. A signature is made by the use of any name, including a trade or assumed name, or by any word or mark used in lieu of a written signature [UCC 3-401(b)].

Examples The requisite signature can be the maker's or drawer's formal name (Henry Richard Cheeseman), informal name (Hank Cheeseman), initials (HRC), or nickname (The Big Cheese). Any other symbol or device (e.g., an *X* or a thumbprint) adopted by the signer as his or her signature also qualifies. The signer's intention to use the symbol as his or her signature is controlling. Typed, printed, lithographed, rubber-stamped, and other mechanical means of signing instruments are recognized as valid by the UCC.

CONTEMPORARY ENVIRONMENT

Authorized Representative's Signature

A maker or drawer can appoint an *agent* to sign a negotiable instrument on his or her behalf. For example, corporations and other organizations use agents, usually corporate officers or employees, to sign the corporation's negotiable instruments. Individuals can also appoint agents to sign their negotiable instruments.

A maker or drawer is liable on a negotiable instrument signed by an authorized agent. The agent is not personally liable on the negotiable instrument if his or her signature properly unambiguously discloses (1) his or her agency status and (2) the identity of the maker or drawer [UCC 3-402(b)]. In the case of an organization, the agent's

signature is proper if the organization's name is preceded or followed by the name of the authorized agent.

▶ UNCONDITIONAL PROMISE OR ORDER TO PAY

To be a negotiable instrument under the requirements of UCC 3-104, a writing must contain either an **unconditional order to pay** (draft or check) or an **unconditional promise to pay** (note or CD). The term *unconditional*, which is discussed in the following paragraphs, is the key.

unconditional promise or order to pay requirement
A requirement that says a negotiable instrument must contain either an *unconditional promise to pay* (note or CD) or an *unconditional order to pay* (draft or check).

Order to Pay

To be negotiable, a *draft* or *check* must contain the drawer's unconditional **order to pay** a payee. An order is a direction for the drawee to pay and must be more than an authorization or a request to pay. The language of the order must be precise and contain the word *pay*.

order to pay
A drawer's unconditional order to a drawee to pay a payee.

Examples The words *Pay to the order of* are usually used on a check or draft. The printed word *pay* on a check is a proper order that is sufficient to make a check negotiable. The order can be in a courteous form, such as "please pay" or "kindly pay." A mere request or acknowledgment, such as "I wish you would pay," is not sufficient because it lacks a direction to pay.

An order can be directed to one or more parties jointly, such as "to A *and* B," or in the alternative, such as "to A *or* B." An order to pay a draft or check must identify the drawee, the financial institution, who is directed to make the payment. The name of the drawee's financial institution that is preprinted on a check is sufficient.

Promise to Pay

To be negotiable, a *promissory note* must contain the maker's unconditional and affirmative **promise to pay**. The mere acknowledgment of a debt is not sufficient to constitute a negotiable instrument. In other words, an implied promise to pay is not negotiable, but an expressly stated promise to pay is negotiable.

promise to pay
A maker's (borrower's) unconditional and affirmative undertaking to repay a debt to a payee (lender).

Examples The statement "I owe you $100" is merely an I.O.U. It acknowledges a debt, but it does not contain an express promise to repay the money. If the I.O.U. used language such as "I promise to pay" or "the undersigned agrees to pay," however, a negotiable instrument would be created because the note would contain an affirmative obligation to pay.

Certificates of deposit (CDs) are an exception to this rule. CDs do not require an express promise to pay because the bank's acknowledgment of the payee's bank deposit and other terms of the CD clearly indicate the bank's promise to repay the certificate holder. Nevertheless, most CDs contain an express promise to pay.

Unconditional Promise or Order

To be negotiable, a promise or order must be **unconditional** [UCC 3-104(a)]. A promise or an order that is **conditional** on another promise or event is not negotiable because the risk of the other promise or event not occurring would fall on the person who held the instrument. A conditional promise is not a negotiable instrument and is therefore subject to normal contract law.

unconditional
Not conditional or limited. Promises to pay and orders to pay must be unconditional in order for them to be negotiable.

Example American Airlines buys a $50 million airplane from Boeing. American signs a promissory note that promises to pay Boeing if it is "satisfied" with the airplane. This promise is a conditional promise. The condition—that American is satisfied with the airplane—destroys the negotiability of the note.

A promise or an order is conditional and, therefore, not negotiable if it states (1) an express condition to payment, (2) that the promise or order is subject to or governed by another writing, or (3) the rights or obligations with respect to the promise or order are stated in another writing. The mere reference to a different writing does not make a promise or an order conditional [UCC 3-106(a)].

Examples Dow Chemical purchases equipment from Illinois Tool Works and signs a sales contract. Dow Chemical borrows the purchase price from Citibank and executes a promissory note evidencing this debt and promising to repay the borrowed money plus interest to Citibank. The note contains the following reference: "Sales contract—purchase of equipment." This reference does not affect the negotiability of the note. The note would not be negotiable, however, if the reference stated, "This note hereby incorporates by this reference the terms of the sales contract between Dow Chemical and Illinois Tool Works of this date."

A promise or an order remains unconditional even if it refers to a different writing for a description of rights to collateral, prepayment, or acceleration.

Example "See collateral agreement dated January 15, 2004."

A promise or an order may also stipulate that payment is limited to a particular fund or source, and still remain unconditional [UCC 3-106(b)].

Example "Payable out of the proceeds of the Tower Construction Contract."

CONTEMPORARY ENVIRONMENT

Payable to Order or to Bearer

Because negotiable instruments are primarily intended to act as a substitute for money, they must be freely transferable to other persons or entities. The UCC requires that negotiable instruments be either **payable to order** or **payable to bearer** [UCC 3-104(a)(1)]. Promises or orders to pay that do not meet this requirement are not negotiable. They may, however, be assignable under contract law.

Order Instruments

An instrument is an **order instrument** if it is payable (1) to the order of an identified person or (2) to an identified person or order [UCC 3-109(b)].

Examples An instrument that states "payable to the order of IBM" or "payable to IBM or order" is negotiable. It would not be negotiable if it stated either "payable to IBM" or "pay to IBM" because it is not payable to *order*.

An instrument can be payable to the order of the maker, the drawer, the drawee, the payee, two or more payees together, or, alternatively, to an office, an officer by his or her title, a corporation, a partnership, an unincorporated association, a trust, an estate, or another legal entity. A party to which an instrument is payable may be identified in any way, including by name, identifying number, office, or account number. An instrument is payable to the party intended by the signer of the instrument even if that party is identified in the instrument by a name or another identification that is not that of the intended party [UCC 3-110].

Examples An instrument made "payable to the order of Lovey" is negotiable. The identification of "Lovey" may be determined by evidence. On the other hand, an instrument made "payable to the order of my loved ones" is not negotiable because the payees are not ascertainable with reasonable certainty.

Bearer Instruments

A **bearer instrument** is payable to anyone in physical possession of the instrument who presents it for payment when it is due. The person in possession of the instrument is called the **bearer**. **Bearer paper** results when the drawer or maker does not make the instrument payable to a specific payee.

Examples An instrument is payable to bearer when any of the following language is used: "payable to the order of bearer," "payable to bearer," "payable to Xerox or bearer," "payable to cash," or "payable to the order of cash." In addition, any other indication that does not purport to designate a specific payee creates bearer paper [UCC 3-109(a)]. For example, an instrument "payable to my dog Fido" creates a bearer instrument.

▶ FIXED AMOUNT OF MONEY

To be negotiable, an instrument must contain a promise or an order to pay a **fixed amount of money** [UCC 3-104(a)]. The **fixed amount requirement** ensures that the value of the instrument can be determined with certainty. The principal amount of the instrument must appear on the face of the instrument.

An instrument does not have to be payable with interest, but if it is, the amount of interest being charged may be expressed as either a *fixed* or *variable* rate. The amount or rate of interest may be stated or described in the instrument or may require reference to information not contained in the instrument. If an instrument provides for interest, but the amount of interest cannot be determined from the description, interest is payable at the judgment rate (legal rate) in effect at the place of payment of the instrument [UCC 3-112].

Example A note that contains a promise to pay $10,000 in one year at a stated rate of 10 percent interest is a negotiable instrument because the value of the note can be determined at any time. A note that contains a promise to pay in goods or services is not a negotiable instrument because the value of the note would be difficult to determine at any given time.

fixed amount of money
A requirement that a negotiable instrument contain a promise or an order to pay a fixed amount of money.

fixed amount requirement
A requirement of a negotiable instrument that ensures that the value of the instrument can be determined with certainty.

Payable in Money

UCC 3-104(a) provides that the fixed amount of a negotiable instrument must be **payable in money**. The UCC defines **money** as a "medium of exchange authorized or adopted by a domestic or foreign government as part of its currency" [UCC 1-201(24)].

Examples An instrument that is "payable in $10,000 U.S. currency" is a negotiable instrument.

Instruments that are fully or partially payable in a medium of exchange other than money are not negotiable.

Examples An instrument that is "payable in $10,000 U.S. gold" is not negotiable. Although the stated amount is a fixed amount, it is not payable in a medium of exchange of the U.S. government.

Example Instruments that are payable in diamonds, commodities, goods, services, stocks, bonds, and such do not qualify as negotiable instruments.

money
A "medium of exchange authorized or adopted by a domestic or foreign government" [UCC 1-201(24)].

Variable Interest Rate Loan

Many lending institutions offer **variable interest rate loans**. These loans tie the interest rate to some set measure, such as a major bank's prime rate (e.g., Citibank's prime) or another well-known rate (e.g., the Freddie Mac rate). Thus, the interest changes during the life of the loan. Some lenders make loans that are fixed for a period of time (i.e., the first seven years) and become variable for the remaining period of the loan.

Revised Article 3 of the UCC expressly provides that variable interest rate notes are negotiable instruments. UCC 3-112(b) provides: "Interest may be stated in an instrument as a fixed or variable amount of money or it may be expressed as a fixed or variable rate or rates." UCC 3-112(b) also provides that the amount or rate of interest may be determined by reference to information not contained in the instrument.

Bad money drives out good money.

Sir Thomas Gresham
(1560)

Not Require Any Undertaking in Addition to the Payment of Money

To qualify as a negotiable instrument, a promise or an order to pay cannot state any other undertaking by the person promising or ordering payment to do any act in addition to the payment of money [UCC 3-104(a)(3)].

Example If a note required the maker to pay a stated amount of money *and* perform some type of service, it would not be negotiable.

A promise or an order may include authorization or power to protect collateral, dispose of collateral, and waive any law intended to protect the obligee.

▶ PAYABLE ON DEMAND OR AT A DEFINITE TIME

For an instrument to be negotiable, it is necessary to know when the maker, drawee, or acceptor is required to pay it. UCC 3-104(a)(2) requires the instrument to be either **payable on demand or payable at a definite time,** as noted on the face of the instrument.

payable on demand or at a definite time requirement
A requirement that a negotiable instrument be payable either *on demand* or *at a definite time.*

demand instrument
An instrument payable on demand.

Payable on Demand

Instruments that are payable on demand are called **demand instruments**. Demand instruments are created by (1) language such as "payable on demand," "payable at sight," or "payable on presentment" or (2) silence regarding when payment is due [UCC 3-108(a)]. By definition, checks are payable on demand [UCC 3-104(f)]. Other instruments, such as notes, CDs, and drafts, can be, but are not always, payable on demand.

Payable at a Definite Time

time instrument
An instrument payable (1) at a fixed date, (2) on or before a stated date, (3) at a fixed period after sight, or (4) at a time readily ascertainable when the promise or order is issued.

Instruments that are payable at a definite time are called **time instruments**. UCC 3-108(b) and 3-108(c) states that an instrument is payable at a definite time if it is payable:

1. At a fixed date.

   Example "Payable on January 1, 2011."

2. On or before a stated date.

   Example "Payable on or before January 1, 2011." In this case, the maker or drawee has the option of paying the note before—but not after—the stated maturity date.

3. At a fixed period after sight. Drafts often contain this type of language. The holder must formally present this type of instrument for acceptance so that the date of sight can be established.

   Example "Payable 60 days after sight."

4. At a time readily ascertainable when the promise or order is issued.

   Example "Payable 60 days after January 1, 2011."

   Instruments that are payable upon an uncertain act or event are not negotiable.

Example Sarah's father executes a promissory note stating, "I promise to pay to the order of my daughter, Sarah, $100,000 on the date she marries Bobby Boggs." This note is non-negotiable because the act and date of marriage are uncertain.

Prepayment, Acceleration, and Extension Clauses

The inclusion of prepayment, acceleration, or extension clauses in an instrument does not affect its negotiability. Such clauses are commonly found in promissory notes.

A **prepayment clause** permits the maker to pay the amount due prior to the due date of the instrument. An **acceleration clause** allows the payee or holder to accelerate payment of the principal amount of an instrument, plus accrued interest, upon the occurrence of an event (e.g., default). An **extension clause** is the opposite of an acceleration clause: It allows the date of maturity of an instrument to be extended to some time in the future.

CONCEPT SUMMARY

FORMAL REQUIREMENTS FOR A NEGOTIABLE INSTRUMENT

Requirement	Description
Writing	Writing must be permanent and portable. Oral or implied instruments are nonnegotiable [UCC 3-104(d)].
Signed by maker or drawer	Signature must appear on the face of the instrument. It may be any mark intended by the signer to be his or her signature. Signature may be by an authorized representative [UCC 3-104(a)].
Unconditional promise or order to pay	Instrument must be an unconditional promise or order to pay [UCC 3-104(a)]. Permissible notations listed in UCC 3-106(a) do not affect the instrument's negotiability. If payment is conditional on the performance of another agreement, the instrument is nonnegotiable.
Fixed amount of money	1. *Fixed amount.* The amount required to discharge an instrument must be on the face of the instrument [UCC 3-104(a)]. The amount may include payment of interest and costs of collection. Revised Article 3 provides that variable interest rate notes are negotiable instruments. 2. *In money.* The amount must be payable in U.S. or foreign country's currency. If payment is to be made in goods, services, or non-monetary items, the instrument is nonnegotiable [UCC 3-104(a)].
Cannot require any undertaking in addition to the payment of money	A promise or an order to pay cannot state any other undertaking to do an act in addition to the payment of money [UCC 3-104(a)(3)]. A promise or an order may include authorization or power to protect collateral, dispose of collateral, waive any law intended to protect the obligee, and the like.
Payable on demand or at a definite time	1. *Payable on demand.* Payable at sight, upon presentation, or when no time for payment is stated [UCC 3-108(a)]. 2. *Payable at a definite time.* Payable at a definite date or before a stated date, a fixed period after a stated date, or at a fixed period after sight [UCC 3-108(b), 3-108(c)]. An instrument payable only upon the occurrence of an uncertain act or event is nonnegotiable.

Negotiable Instruments Payable in Foreign Currency

The UCC expressly provides that an instrument may state that it is **payable in foreign currency** [UCC 3-107].

Example An instrument "payable in 10,000 yen in Japanese currency" is a negotiable instrument that is governed by Article 3 of the UCC.

Unless the instrument states otherwise, an instrument that is payable in foreign currency can be satisfied by the equivalent in U.S. dollars, as determined on the due date. The conversion rate is the current bank-offered spot rate at the place of payment on the due date. The instrument can expressly provide that it is payable only in the stated foreign currency. In that case, the instrument cannot be paid in U.S. dollars.

▶ NONNEGOTIABLE CONTRACT

If a promise or an order to pay does not meet one of the previously discussed requirements of negotiability, it is a **nonnegotiable contract** and is therefore not subject to the provisions of UCC Article 3. A promise or an order that conspicuously states that it is not negotiable or is not subject to Article 3 is not a negotiable instrument [UCC 3-104(d)] and is therefore a nonnegotiable contract.

A nonnegotiable contract is not rendered either nontransferable or nonenforceable. A nonnegotiable contract can be enforced under normal contract law. If the maker or drawer of a nonnegotiable contract fails to pay it, the holder of the contract can sue the nonperforming party for breach of contract.

nonnegotiable contract
A contract that fails to meet the requirements of a negotiable instrument and, therefore, is not subject to the provisions of UCC Article 3.

TEST REVIEW TERMS AND CONCEPTS

Acceleration clause
Acceptor of a draft
Article 3 (Commercial
    Paper) of the UCC
Bearer
Bearer instrument
Bearer paper
Certificate of deposit (CD)
Check
Collateral
Collateral note
Conditional
Demand instrument
Demand note
Draft
Drawee of a check
Drawee of a draft
Drawer of a check
Drawer of a draft

Extension clause
Fixed amount of money
Fixed amount requirement
Holder in due course (HDC)
Installment note
Jumbo CD
Law Merchant
Maker of a CD
Maker of a note
Money
Mortgage note
Negotiable instrument
    (commercial paper or
    instrument)
Negotiation
Nonnegotiable contract
Order instrument
Order to pay
Payable in foreign currency

Payable in money
Payable on demand or at a
    definite time requirement
Payable to bearer
Payable to order
Payee of a CD
Payee of a check
Payee of a draft
Payee of a note
Permanency requirement
Portability requirement
Prepayment clause
Promise to pay
Promissory note (note)
Revised Article 3
    (Negotiable Instruments)
    of the UCC
Sight draft (demand draft)
Signature

Signature requirement
Small CD
Time draft
Time instrument
Time note
Trade acceptance
Unconditional
Unconditional order
    to pay
Unconditional promise
    to pay
Uniform Negotiable
    Instruments Law
    (NIL)
Variable interest rate
    loan
Writing requirement

CASE PROBLEMS

22.1 Type of Negotiable Instrument Marcus Wiley, James Tate, and James Irby were partners engaged in buying and selling used cars under the trade name Wiley, Tate & Irby. Over an extended period of time, the partnership sold a number of automobiles to Billy Houston, a sole proprietor doing business as Houston Auto Sales (Houston). In connection with each purchase, Houston executed and delivered to the partnership a negotiable instrument drawn on the Peoples Bank and Trust Company of Tupelo, Mississippi. Upon delivery of each negotiable instrument, the automobiles were delivered to Houston. Each of the instruments involved in these transactions contained a number of variations in text and form. However, each of them was similar in that each was drawn on a bank, signed by the maker, and contained an unconditional order to pay a sum certain on the demand of the payee. What type of negotiable instrument is involved in these transactions? *Wiley v. Peoples Bank and Trust Company*, 438 F.2d 513, **Web** 1971 U.S. App. Lexis 11917 (United States Court of Appeals for the Fifth Circuit)

22.2 Note Sandra McGuire and her husband entered into a contract to purchase the inventory, equipment, accounts receivable, and name of "Becca's Boutique" from Pascal and Rebecca Tursi. Becca's Boutique was a clothing store that was owned as a sole proprietorship by the Tursis. The McGuires agreed to purchase the store for $75,000, with a down payment of $10,000 and the balance to be paid at a specified date in the future. The promissory note signed by the McGuires read: "For value received, Thomas J. McGuire and Sandra A. McGuire, husband and wife, do promise to pay to the order of Pascal and Rebecca Tursi the sum of $65,000." Is the note an order to pay or a promise to pay? *P. P. Inc. v. McGuire*, 509

F.Supp. 1079, **Web** 1981 U.S. Dist. Lexis 17984 (United States District Court for the District of New Jersey)

22.3 Negotiable Instrument William H. Bailey, M.D., executed a note payable to California Dreamstreet, a joint venture that solicited investments for a cattle breeding operation. Bailey's promissory note read: "Dr. William H. Bailey hereby promises to pay to the order of California Dreamstreet the sum of $329,800." Four years later, Dreamstreet negotiated the note to Cooperatieve Centrale Raiffeisen-Boerenleenbank B.A. (Cooperatieve), a foreign bank. A default occurred, and Cooperatieve filed suit against Bailey to recover on the note. Is the note executed by Bailey a negotiable instrument? *Cooperatieve Centrale Raiffeisen-Boerenleenbank B.A. v. Bailey*, 710 F.Supp. 737, **Web** 1989 U.S. Dist. Lexis 4488 (United States District Court for the Central District of California)

22.4 Bearer or Order Instrument Broadway Management Corporation (Broadway) owned and operated the American Nursing Center. Conan Briggs had received services from the center and had executed an instrument to pay for those services. The instrument read, in relevant part, "Ninety days after date, I, we, or either of us, promises to pay to the order of $3,498.45." Briggs refused to pay on the note. Broadway claimed that this note was bearer paper and as such was payable to the holder. Briggs claimed that the note was order paper and was therefore payable only to a named payee. Can Broadway, as its bearer, collect on this note? *Broadway Management Corporation v. Briggs*, 30 Ill.App.3d 403, 332 N.E.2d 131, **Web** 1975 Ill.App. Lexis 2625 (Appellate Court of Illinois)

22.5 Formal Requirements   Mr. Higgins operated a used car dealership in the state of Alabama. Higgins purchased a Chevrolet Corvette. He paid for the car with a draft on his account at the First State Bank of Albertville. Soon after, Higgins resold the car to Mr. Holsonback. To pay for the car, Holsonback signed a check that was printed on a standard-sized envelope. The reason the check was printed on an envelope is that this practice made it easier to transfer title and other documents from the seller to the buyer. The envelope on which the check was written contained a certificate of title, a mileage statement, and a bill of sale. Does a check printed on an envelope meet the formal requirements to be classified as a negotiable instrument under the UCC? *Holsonback v. First State Bank of Albertville*, 394 So.2d 381, **Web** 1980 Ala. Civ. App. Lexis 1208 (Court of Civil Appeals of Alabama)

22.6 Unconditional Promise   M.S. Horne executed a $100,000 note in favor of R. C. Clark. The note stipulated that it could not be transferred, pledged, or assigned without Horne's consent. Along with the note, Horne signed a letter authorizing Clark to use the note as collateral for a loan. Clark pledged the note as collateral for a $50,000 loan from First State Bank of Gallup (First State). First State telephoned Horne to confirm that Clark could pledge the note, and Horne indicated that it was okay. Clark eventually defaulted on the loan. First State attempted to collect on the note, but Horne refused to pay. Does the restriction written on Horne's promissory note cause it to be nonnegotiable despite the letter of authorization? *First State Bank of Gallup v. Clark and Horne*, 91 N.M. 117, 570 P.2d 1144, **Web** 1977 N.M. Lexis 1093 (Supreme Court of New Mexico)

22.7 Demand Instrument   Stewart P. Blanchard borrowed $50,000 from Progressive Bank & Trust Company (Progressive) to purchase a home. As part of the transaction, Blanchard signed a note secured by a mortgage. The note provided for a 10 percent annual interest rate. Under the terms of the note, payment was "due on demand, if no demand is made, then $600 monthly" beginning at a specified date. Blanchard testified that he believed Progressive could demand immediate payment only if he failed to make the monthly installments. After one year, Blanchard received notice that the rate of interest on the note would rise to 11 percent. Despite the notice, Blanchard continued to make $600 monthly payments. One year later, Progressive notified Blanchard that the interest rate on the loan would be increased to 12.75 percent. Progressive requested that Blanchard sign a form consenting to the interest rate adjustment. When Blanchard refused to sign the form, Progressive demanded immediate payment of the note balance. Progressive sued Blanchard to enforce the terms of the note. Is the note a demand instrument? *Blanchard v. Progressive Bank & Trust Company*, 413 So.2d 589, **Web** 1982 La.App. Lexis 7213 (Court of Appeal of Louisiana)

22.8 Order to Pay   Sana Travel Services, Ltd. (Sana), is a travel agency located in New York. Sana was negotiating with Al-Bank Turismo, a Brazilian company, to secure additional business in that country. To expedite negotiations, one of Sana's directors, Attaullah Paracha, made out a check for $33,000 payable to the order of "Jamil Ahmed Kahn, Al-Bank Turismo." On the check Paracha wrote "Just to hold for the security of future business." Paracha then sent the check to Kahn in Brazil. Kahn, Al-Bank's owner, indorsed the check and sold it to Jurandi Carador, a Brazilian citizen. Carador then arranged for the check to be presented to the National Bank of Pakistan, Sana's New York bank. When the bank received the check, it telephoned Sana, which directed the bank to dishonor the check. Sana claims that the notation on the check "Just to hold" rendered the instrument conditional and made it a nonnegotiable instrument. Is the check a negotiable instrument? *Carador v. Sana Travel Services, Ltd.*, 876 F.2d 890, **Web** 1989 U.S. App. Lexis 10488 (United States Court of Appeals for the Second Circuit)

22.9 Reference to Another Document   J. Monte Williamson was the owner of a 16.65 percent interest in Lake Manor Associates, a partnership. Williamson agreed to sell his interest to H. Louis Salomonsky and Tiffany H. Armstrong in exchange for shares of a certain stock valued at $15 per share and a non-interest-bearing note in the amount of $4,000 for the balance. The notes were executed and contained the following notation: "For value received, the undersigned promises to pay to the order of J. Monte Williamson the principal sum of $4,000 payable as set forth in that certain agreement, an executed copy of which is attached hereto."

The agreement referred to in the notes listed conditions that had to be met to cause the notes to become due. Five years after the notes were executed, Salomonsky and Armstrong claimed that because the notes were negotiable instruments, the statute of limitations on the enforcement of the notes has run. Are these notes negotiable instruments? *Salomonsky v. Kelly*, 232 Va. 261, 349 S.E.2d 358, **Web** 1986 Va. Lexis 253 (Supreme Court of Virginia)

22.10 Reference to Another Agreement   Holly Hill Acres, Ltd. (Holly Hill), purchased land from Rogers and Blythe. As part of its consideration, Holly Hill gave Rogers and Blythe a promissory note and purchase money mortgage. The note read, in part, "This note with interest is secured by a mortgage on real estate made by the maker in favor of said payee. The terms of said mortgage are by reference made a part hereof." Rogers and Blythe assigned this note and mortgage to Charter Bank of Gainesville (Charter Bank) as security in order to obtain a loan from the bank. Within a few months, Rogers and Blythe defaulted on their obligation to Charter Bank. Charter Bank sued to recover on Holly Hill's note and mortgage. Does the reference to the mortgage in the note cause it to be nonnegotiable? *Holly Hill Acres, Ltd. v. Charter Bank of Gainesville*, 314 So.2d 209, **Web** 1975 Fla.App. Lexis 13715 (Court of Appeal of Florida)

BUSINESS ETHICS CASES

22.11 Business Ethics   Mullins Enterprises, Inc. (Mullins), was a business operating in the state of Kentucky. To raise capital, Mullins obtained loans from Corbin Deposit Bank & Trust Company (Corbin). During the course of four years, Corbin made eight loans to Mullins. Mullins executed a promissory note setting out the amount of the debt, the dates and times of installment payments, and the date of final payment and delivered it to the bank each time a loan was made. The notes were signed by an officer of Mullins. Several years later, a dispute arose between Mullins and Corbin as to the proper interpretation of the language contained in the notes. The bank contended that the notes were demand notes. Mullins claimed that the notes were time instruments. Did Corbin or Mullins act unethically in this case? Or was this just a legal dispute? Who wins? *Corbin Deposit Bank & Trust Co. v. Mullins Enterprises, Inc.*, 641 S.W.2d 760, **Web** 1982 Ky.App. Lexis 264 (Court of Appeals of Kentucky)

22.12 Business Ethics   Mike J. Rogers, owner of Arkansas Parts and Equipment Company (Arkansas Parts), invited Paul Mollenhour to be an officer of the business. Rogers wanted Mollenhour to join the business because his strong financial position would allow Rogers to more easily secure operating financing. With Mollenhour's assistance, Arkansas Parts secured financing. Arkansas Parts executed a revolving credit note with State First National Bank of Texarkana (State First) in the amount of $150,000. The note was signed as follows:

/s/Mike Rogers

Mike Rogers, Individually

/s/Dave Mollenhour, V. Pres.

Dave Mollenhour, Individually

ARKANSAS PARTS AND EQUIPMENT CO., INC.

by: /s/Mike Rogers

Mike Rogers, President

by: /s/Dave Mollenhour, V. Pres.

Dave Mollenhour, Vice President and Secretary

The note stipulated that the parties were jointly and severally obligated to State First. After Arkansas Parts defaulted on the note, State First sued Arkansas Parts and Rogers and Mollenhour individually. Mollenhour claimed that he is not liable because his signature indicated his representative capacity. Did Mollenhour act ethically in this case? Who wins? *Mollenhour v. State First National Bank of Texarkana*, 27 Ark.App. 176, 769 S.W.2d 28, **Web** 1989 Ark.App. Lexis 197 (Court of Appeals of Arkansas)

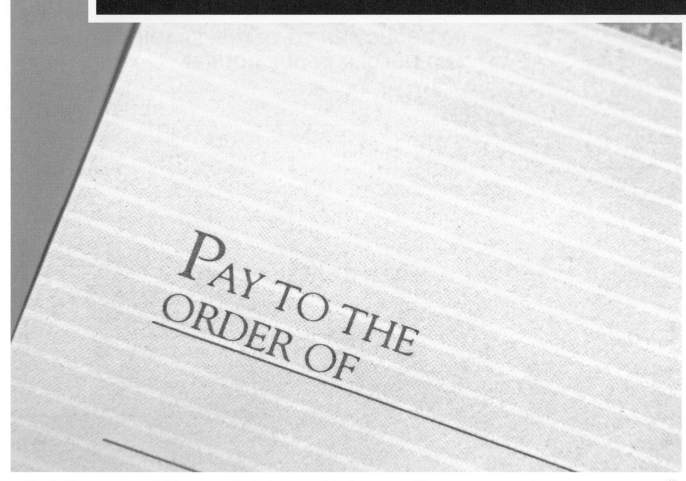

▲ **Check** *There are several different ways of indorsing a negotiable instrument. When a negotiable instrument is transferred to a holder in due course (HDC), the holder takes it free of many claims and defenses that can be asserted by other parties.*

CHAPTER OBJECTIVES

After studying this chapter, you should be able to:

1. Describe how negotiable instruments are indorsed and transferred.
2. Describe how order and bearer paper are negotiated.
3. Distinguish between blank, special, qualified, and restrictive indorsements.

4. Define *holder* and *holder in due course*.
5. Identify and apply the requirements for becoming a holder in due course.

CHAPTER CONTENTS

"A negotiable bill or note is a courier without luggage."

—Chief Justice Gibson
Overton v. Tyler (1846)

▶ INTRODUCTION TO TRANSFERABILITY AND HOLDER IN DUE COURSE

Once created, a negotiable instrument can be transferred to subsequent parties by *negotiation*. This is accomplished by placing an *indorsement* on the instrument. There are several types of indorsements, each with its own requirements and effect.

Recall that the primary purpose of commercial paper is to act as a substitute for money. For this to occur, the holder of a negotiable instrument must qualify as a *holder in due course (HDC)*. Commercial paper held by an HDC is virtually as good as money because HDCs take an instrument free of all claims and most defenses that can be asserted by other parties.

This chapter discusses the negotiation of an instrument, types of indorsements, and the requirements that must be met to qualify as an HDC.

▶ TRANSFER BY ASSIGNMENT

An **assignment** is the transfer of rights under a contract. It transfers the rights of the transferor (**assignor**) to the transferee (**assignee**). Because normal contract principles apply, the assignee acquires only the rights that the assignor possessed. Thus, any defenses to the enforcement of the contract that could have been raised against the assignor can also be raised against the assignee.

An assignment occurs when a nonnegotiable contract is transferred. In the case of a negotiable instrument, assignment occurs when the instrument is transferred but the transfer fails to qualify as a negotiation under Article 3. In this case, the transferee is an *assignee* rather than a *holder*.

assignment
The transfer of rights under a contract.

assignor
A transferor in an assignment situation.

assignee
A transferee in an assignment situation.

Money speaks sense in a language all nations understand.

Aphra Behn
The Rover

▶ **Exhibit 23.1 ASSIGNMENT**

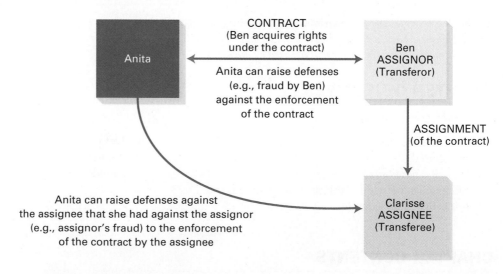

▶ TRANSFER BY NEGOTIATION

Negotiation is the transfer of a negotiable instrument by a person other than the issuer. The person to whom the instrument is transferred becomes the holder [UCC 3-201(a)]. The **holder** receives at least the rights of the transferor and may acquire even greater rights than the transferor if he or she qualifies as a holder in due course (HDC) [UCC 3-302].

negotiation
The transfer of a negotiable instrument by a person other than the issuer to a person who thereby becomes a *holder*.

An HDC has greater rights because he or she is not subject to some of the defenses that could otherwise have been raised against the transferor.

The proper method of negotiation depends on whether the instrument involved is order paper or bearer paper, as discussed in the following paragraphs.

Negotiating Order Paper

An instrument that is payable to a specific payee or indorsed to a specific indorsee is **order paper**. Order paper is negotiated by delivery with the necessary indorsement [UCC 3-201(b)]. Thus, for order paper to be negotiated, there must be delivery and indorsement.

Example Sam Bennett receives a weekly payroll check from his employer, Ace Corporation, made "Payable to the Order of Sam Bennett." Sam takes the check to a local store, signs his name on the back of the check (indorsement), gives the check to the cashier (delivery), and receives cash for the check. Sam has negotiated the check to the store. Delivery and indorsement have occurred.

order paper
An instrument that is negotiated by (1) delivery and (2) indorsement.

Negotiating Bearer Paper

An instrument that is not payable to a specific payee or indorsee is **bearer paper**. Bearer paper is negotiated by *delivery*; indorsement is not necessary [UCC 3-201(b)]. Substantial risk is associated with the loss or theft of bearer paper.

Example Mary draws from her checking account a $1,500 check made out to "pay to cash" and gives it to Peter. This is a bearer instrument because the check has not been made out to a named payee. There has been a negotiation because Mary delivered a bearer instrument (the check) to Peter. Subsequently, Carmen steals the check from Peter. There has not been a negotiation because the check was not voluntarily delivered. But Carmen physically possesses the bearer instrument. The negotiation is complete if Carmen delivers the check to an innocent third party, Ida. Ida is a holder and may qualify as a holder in due course (HDC) with all the rights in the check [UCC 3-302]. If the holder, Ida, is an HDC, she can deposit the check in her account, and Mary's checking account will be debited $1,500. Peter's only recourse is to recover the $1,500 from Carmen, the thief.

bearer paper
An instrument that is negotiated by delivery; indorsement is not necessary.

The case that follows demonstrates the danger of possessing bearer paper.

CASE 23.1 Bearer Paper

Gerber & Gerber, P.C. v. Regions Bank
266 Ga.App. 8, 596 S.E.2d 174, Web 2004 Ga.App. Lexis 206 (2004)
Court of Appeals of Georgia

"**Accordingly, when here the payees of the cashier's checks indorsed the checks in blank, the checks then became bearer paper and could—similar to cash—be transferred by possession alone.**"

—Judge Miller

Facts

Cynthia Stafford worked as a real estate closing secretary at Gerber & Gerber, P.C. (G&G), a law firm. Over a period of two years, Stafford stole cashier's checks from G&G that were made payable to named payees who in turn indorsed these checks in blank, which created bearer paper. Stafford blank-indorsed the bearer cashier's checks and deposited them in her personal bank account at Regions Bank. The total loss was $180,000. G&G had bank accounts at Regions Bank to which thousands of checks were deposited, amounting to $150 million to $200 million annually.

Stafford confessed to the theft. She pleaded guilty to criminal charges and received a five-year jail sentence. Stafford claimed to have spent the money. G&G sued Regions Bank to recover for the checks paid to Stafford, alleging that the bank was negligent in accepting the checks from Stafford. Regions Bank moved for summary judgment, arguing that it had acted properly under the Uniform Commercial Code (UCC) in accepting the bearer blank-indorsed checks from Stafford. The trial court granted Regions Bank summary judgment as to the bearer paper. G&G appealed.

(case continues)

Issue

Did Regions Bank properly accept the blank-indorsed bearer cashier's checks from Stafford?

Language of the Court

The holder of an instrument is a person entitled to enforce the instrument, even though the person is in wrongful possession of the instrument. A person is a holder of a negotiable instrument if that person possesses the instrument and the instrument is payable to bearer. An instrument is deemed payable to bearer if it is indorsed in blank (i.e., not specially indorsed). When indorsed in blank, an instrument becomes payable to bearer and may be negotiated by transfer of possession alone until specially indorsed. Accordingly, when here the payees of the cashier's checks indorsed the checks in blank, the checks then became bearer paper and could—similar to cash—be transferred by possession alone. Sanford Gerber even admitted to this well-known fact in his deposition. Thus, Regions Bank

quite properly accepted the indorsed-in-blank cashier's checks from the person in possession of them and deposited the checks into that person's account.

Decision

The court of appeals held that Regions Bank was not negligent in accepting the blank-indorsed bearer cashier's checks from Stafford and placing the money in Stafford's personal account. The court of appeals upheld the trial court's grant of summary judgment to Regions Bank.

Case Questions

Critical Legal Thinking Describe a bearer instrument. How does it differ from an order instrument?

Business Ethics Did Ms. Stafford act ethically in this case? Did G&G act ethically in suing Regions Bank to recover for Stafford's thefts?

Contemporary Business Should a business ever permit instruments to be bearer instruments?

CONTEMPORARY ENVIRONMENT

Converting Order and Bearer Paper

An instrument can be converted from order paper to bearer paper and vice versa many times until the instrument is paid [UCC 3-109(c)]. The deciding factor is the type of indorsement placed on the instrument at the time of each subsequent transfer. Follow the indorsements in the example shown here to determine whether order or bearer paper has been created.

Pay to Haeran Park
Nikki Nguyen

Vivian Chou

Pay to Linda Matsubara
Vivian Chou

The front side of the original check, drawn by Henry Cheeseman, was drawn "Pay to the Order of Nikki Nguyen."

Endorsements

First endorsement: creates order paper (Nikki Nguyen transfers the check to Haeran Park)

Second endorsement: converts instrument to bearer paper (Haeran Park transfers the check to Vivian Chou)

Third endorsement: converts instrument to order paper (Vivian Chou transfers the check to Linda Matsubara)

▶ INDORSEMENT

An **indorsement** is the signature of a signer (other than as a maker, a drawer, or an acceptor) that is placed on an instrument to negotiate it to another person. The signature may (1) appear alone, (2) name an individual to whom the instrument is to be paid, or (3) be accompanied by other words [UCC 3-204(2)]. The person who indorses an instrument is called the **indorser**. If the indorsement names a payee, this person is called the **indorsee**.

Indorsements are usually placed on the reverse side of the instrument, such as on the back of a check (see Exhibit 23.2). If there is no room on the instrument, the indorsement may be written on a separate piece of paper called an **allonge**. The allonge must be affixed (e.g., stapled, taped) to the instrument [UCC 3-204(a)].

Indorsements are required to negotiate order paper, but they are not required to negotiate bearer paper [UCC 3-201(b)]. For identification purposes and to impose liability on the transferor, however, the transferee often requires the transferor to indorse bearer paper at negotiation.

indorsement
The signature (and other directions) written by or on behalf of the holder somewhere on an instrument.

indorser
A person who indorses a negotiable instrument.

indorsee
A person to whom a negotiable instrument is indorsed.

allonge
A separate piece of paper attached to an instrument on which an indorsement is written.

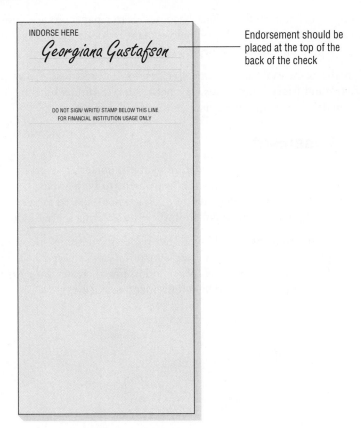

Endorsement should be placed at the top of the back of the check

▶ **Exhibit 23.2 PLACEMENT OF AN INDORSEMENT**

▶ TYPES OF INDORSEMENTS

There are four categories of indorsements:

1. Blank indorsement
2. Special indorsement
3. Qualified indorsement
4. Restrictive indorsement

These types of indorsements are discussed in the following paragraphs.

The first principle of contract negotiation is don't remind them of what you did in the past; tell them what you're going to do in the future.

Stan Musial

Blank Indorsement

A **blank indorsement** does not specify a particular indorsee. It may consist of a mere signature [UCC 3-205(b)].

blank indorsement
An indorsement that does not specify a particular indorsee. It creates *bearer paper*.

Example Harold Green draws a check "pay to the order of Victoria Rudd" and delivers the check to Victoria. Victoria indorses the check in blank by writing her signature "Victoria Rudd" on the back of the check (see Exhibit 23.3).

▶ Exhibit 23.3 BLANK INDORSEMENT

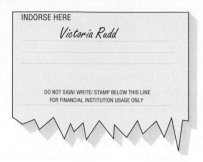

Order paper that is indorsed in blank becomes bearer paper. As mentioned earlier, bearer paper can be negotiated by delivery; indorsement is not required. Thus, a lost bearer paper can be presented for payment or negotiated to another holder.

Example If in the prior example, assume that Victoria Rudd lost the check she had indorsed in blank and Mary Smith finds the check. Mary Smith, who is in possession of bearer paper, can deliver it to another person without indorsing it.

Special Indorsement

special indorsement
An indorsement that contains the signature of the indorser and specifies the person (indorsee) to whom the indorser intends the instrument to be payable. It creates *order paper*.

A **special indorsement** contains the signature of the indorser and specifies the person (indorsee) to whom the indorser intends the instrument to be payable [UCC 3-205(a)]. Words of negotiation (e.g., "pay to the order of . . .") are not required for a special indorsement. Words such as "pay Emily Ingman" are sufficient to form a special indorsement.

Example A special indorsement would be created if Betsy McKenny indorsed her check and then wrote "pay to Dan Jones" above her signature (see Exhibit 23.4). The check is negotiated when Betsy gives it to Dan. A special indorsement creates *order paper*. As mentioned earlier, order paper is negotiated by indorsement and delivery.

▶ Exhibit 23.4 SPECIAL INDORSEMENT

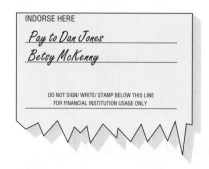

To prevent the risk of loss from theft, a special indorsement (which creates order paper) is preferred over a blank indorsement (which creates bearer paper). A holder can convert a blank indorsement into a special indorsement by writing any contract instructions consistent with the character of the indorsement over the signature of the indorser in blank [UCC 3-205(c)]. Words such as "pay to John Jones" written above the indorser's signature are enough to convert bearer paper to order paper.

Qualified Indorsement

Generally, an indorsement is a promise by the indorser to pay the holder or any subsequent indorser the amount of the instrument if the maker, drawer, or acceptor defaults on it. This promise is called an **unqualified indorsement**. Unless otherwise agreed, the order and liability of the indorsers is presumed to be the order in which they indorse the instrument [UCC 3-415(a)].

Example Cindy draws a check payable to the order of John. John (indorser) indorses the check and negotiates it to Steve (indorsee). When Steve presents the check for payment, there are insufficient funds in Cindy's account to pay the check. John, as an **unqualified indorser**, is liable on the check. John can recover from Cindy.

The UCC permits **qualified indorsements**—that is, indorsements that disclaim or limit liability on the instrument. A **qualified indorser** does not guarantee payment of the instrument if the maker, drawer, or acceptor defaults on it. A qualified indorsement is created by placing a notation such as "without recourse" or other similar language that disclaims liability as part of the indorsement [UCC 3-415(b)]. A qualified indorsement protects only the indorser who wrote an indorsement on the instrument. Subsequent indorsers must also place a qualified indorsement on the instrument to be protected from liability. An instrument containing a qualified indorsement can be further negotiated. A qualified indorsement is often used by persons who sign instruments in a representative capacity.

Example Suppose an insurance company that is paying a claim makes out a check payable to the order of the attorney representing the payee. The attorney can indorse the check to his client (the payee) with the notation "without recourse." This notation ensures that the attorney is not liable as an indorser if the insurance company fails to pay the check.

A qualified indorsement can be either a special qualified indorsement or a blank qualified indorsement. A *special qualified indorsement* creates order paper that can be negotiated by indorsement and delivery. A *blank qualified indorsement* creates bearer paper that can be further negotiated by delivery without indorsement (see Exhibit 23.5).

unqualified indorsement
An indorsement whereby the indorser promises to pay the holder or any subsequent indorser the amount of the instrument if the maker, drawer, or acceptor defaults on it.

unqualified indorser
An indorser who signs an unqualified indorsement to an instrument.

qualified indorsement
An indorsement that includes the notation "without recourse" or similar language that disclaims liability of the indorser.

qualified indorser
An indorser who signs a qualified indorsement to an instrument.

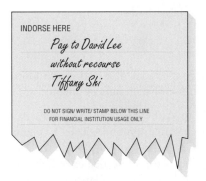

► **Exhibit 23.5 QUALIFIED INDORSEMENTS**

Restrictive Indorsement

Most indorsements are *nonrestrictive*. **Nonrestrictive indorsements** do not have any instructions or conditions attached to the payment of the funds.

Example An indorsement is nonrestrictive if the indorsee merely signs his or her signature to the back of an instrument or includes a notation to pay a specific indorsee ("pay to Sam Smith").

Occasionally, an indorser includes some form of instruction in an indorsement. This instruction is called a **restrictive indorsement**. A restrictive indorsement restricts the indorsee's rights in some manner. An indorsement that purports to prohibit further negotiation of an instrument does not destroy the negotiability of the instrument.

Example A check that is indorsed "pay to Sarah Stein only" can still be negotiated to other transferees. Because of its ineffectiveness, this type of restrictive indorsement is seldom used.

nonrestrictive indorsement
An indorsement that has no instructions or conditions attached to the payment of the funds.

restrictive indorsement
An indorsement that contains some sort of instruction from the indorser.

UCC 3-206 recognizes the following types of restrictive indorsements:

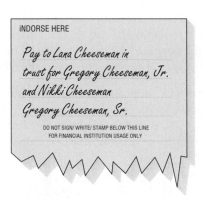

- **Indorsement for deposit or collection.** An indorser can indorse an instrument so as to make the indorsee his or collecting agent. Such indorsement—called an **indorsement for deposit or collection**—is often done when an indorser deposits a check or another instrument for collection at a bank. Words such as *for collection*, *for deposit only*, and *pay any bank* create this type of indorsement. Banks use this type of indorsement in the collection process.
- **Indorsement in trust.** An indorsement can state that it is for the benefit or use of the indorser or another person.

indorsement for deposit or collection

An indorsement that makes the indorsee the indorser's collecting agent (e.g., "for deposit only").

Example Checks are often indorsed to attorneys, executors of estates, real estate agents, and other fiduciaries in their representative capacity for the benefit of clients, heirs, or others. These indorsements are called **indorsements in trust** or **agency indorsements** (see Exhibit 23.6). The indorser is not personally liable on the instrument if there is a proper trust or agency indorsement.

▶ **Exhibit 23.6 TRUST INDORSEMENT**

INDORSE HERE

Pay to Lana Cheeseman in trust for Gregory Cheeseman, Jr. and Nikki Cheeseman

Gregory Cheeseman, Sr.

DO NOT SIGN/ WRITE/ STAMP BELOW THIS LINE
FOR FINANCIAL INSTITUTION USAGE ONLY

An indorsee who does not comply with the instructions of a restrictive indorsement is liable to the indorser for all losses that occur because of such noncompliance.

Example Suppose a check is drawn "payable to Anne Spencer, Attorney, in trust for Joseph Watkins." If Spencer indorses the check to an automobile dealer in payment for a car that she purchases personally, the automobile dealer (indorsee) has not followed the instructions of the restrictive indorsement. The automobile dealer is liable to Joseph Watkins for any losses that arise because of the dealer's noncompliance with the restrictive indorsement.

CONCEPT SUMMARY
TYPES OF INDORSEMENTS

Type of Indorsement	Description
Blank	Does not specify a particular indorsee (e.g., /s/Mary Jones). This indorsement creates bearer paper.
Special	Specifies the person to whom the indorser intends the instrument to be payable (e.g., "Pay to the order of John Smith" /s/Mary Jones). This indorsement creates order paper. (If it is not payable to order [e.g., "Pay to John Smith" /s/Mary Jones], it can be converted to order paper [e.g., "Pay to the order of Fred Roe" /s/John Smith].)
Unqualified	Does not disclaim or limit liability. The indorsee is liable on the instrument if it is not paid by the maker, acceptor, or drawer.

Qualified	Disclaims or limits the liability of the indorsee. There are two types: 1. Special qualified indorsement (e.g., "Pay to the order of John Smith, without recourse" /s/Mary Jones). 2. Blank qualified indorsement (e.g., "Without recourse" /s/Mary Jones).
Nonrestrictive	No instructions or conditions are attached to the payment of funds (e.g., "Pay to John Smith or order" /s/Mary Jones).
Restrictive	Conditions or instructions restrict the indorsee's rights. There are three types: 1. Indorsement prohibiting further indorsement (e.g., "Pay to John Smith only" /s/Mary Jones). 2. Indorsement for deposit or collection (e.g., "For deposit only" /s/Mary Jones). 3. Indorsement in trust (e.g., "Pay to John Smith, trustee" /s/Mary Jones).

Misspelled or Wrong Name

Where the name of the payee or indorsee is misspelled in a negotiable instrument, the payee or indorsee can indorse the instrument using the misspelled name, the correct name, or both.

Example If Susan Worth receives a check payable to "Susan Wirth," she can indorse the check "Susan Wirth" or "Susan Worth" or both. A person paying or taking the instrument for value or collection may require a signature in both the misspelled and the correct versions [UCC 3-204(d)].

A negotiable bill or note is a courier without luggage.

Chief Justice Gibson
Overton v. Tyler (1846)

CONTEMPORARY ENVIRONMENT

Multiple Payees or Indorsees

Drawers, makers, and indorsers often make checks, promissory notes, and other negotiable instruments payable to two or more payees or indorsees. The question then arises: Can the instrument be negotiated by the signature of one payee or indorsee, or are all of their signatures required to negotiate the instrument?

Section 3-110(d) of Revised Article 3 of the UCC and cases that have interpreted that section establish the following rules:

• If an instrument is **payable jointly** using the word *and*, both persons' indorsements are necessary to negotiate the instrument.

Example "Pay to Shou-Yi Kang and Min-Wer Chen." Here, the indorsement signatures of *both* Shou-Yi Kang and Min-Wer Chen are required to negotiate the instrument. The indorsement signature of only one of the named persons is not sufficient to negotiate the instrument.

• If the instrument is **payable in the alternative** using the word *or*, either person's indorsement signature alone is sufficient to negotiate the instrument.

Example "Pay to Shou-Yi Kang or Min-Wer Chen." Here, *either* Shou-Yi Kang or Min-Wer Chen can individually indorse and negotiate the instrument without the other's signature.

• If a **virgule**—a slash mark (/)—is used, courts have held that the instrument is *payable in the alternative*—that is, the instrument is treated as if the / is an "or." Thus, if a virgule is used, either person may individually negotiate the instrument.

Example "Pay to Shou-Yi Kang/Min-Wer Chen." Here, the virgule (/) is treated as an "or," and either Shou-Yi Kang or Min-Wer Chen can individually indorse and negotiate the instrument without the other's indorsement.

▶ HOLDER IN DUE COURSE (HDC)

Two of the most important concepts of the law of negotiable instruments are the concepts of *holder* and *holder in due course*. A **holder** is a person in possession of an instrument that is payable to bearer or an identified person who is in possession of an instrument payable to

holder
A person who is in possession of a negotiable instrument that is drawn, issued, or indorsed to him or his order, or to bearer, or in blank.

that person [UCC 1-201(20)]. The holder of a negotiable instrument has the same rights as an assignee of an ordinary nonnegotiable contract. That is, the holder is subject to all the claims and defenses that can be asserted against the transferor.

The concept of holder in due course is unique to the area of negotiable instruments. A **holder in due course (HDC)** is a holder who takes an instrument for value, in good faith, and without notice that it is defective or overdue. An HDC takes a negotiable instrument free of all claims and most defenses that can be asserted against the transferor of the instrument. Only **universal defenses**—and not **personal defenses**—may be asserted against an HDC. (Defenses are discussed in Chapter 24, the next chapter). Thus, an HDC can acquire greater rights than a transferor.

holder in due course (HDC)
A holder who takes a negotiable instrument for value, in good faith, and without notice that it is defective or overdue.

Example John purchases an automobile from Shannen. At the time of sale, Shannen tells John that the car has had only one previous owner and has been driven only 20,000 miles. John, relying on these statements, purchases the car. He pays 10 percent down and signs a promissory note to pay the remainder of the purchase price, with interest, in 12 equal monthly installments. Shannen transfers the note to Patricia. Then John discovers that the car has actually had four previous owners and has been driven 100,000 miles. If Patricia were a holder (but not an HDC) of the note, John could assert Shannen's fraudulent representations against enforcement of the note by Patricia. John could rescind the note and refuse to pay Patricia. Patricia's only recourse would be against Shannen.

Example If in the prior example Patricia qualified as an HDC, the result would be different. John could not assert Shannen's fraudulent conduct against enforcement of the note by Patricia because this type of fraud is a *personal defense* that cannot be raised against an HDC. Therefore, Patricia could enforce the note against John. John's only recourse would be against Shannen, if she could be found.

The way to wealth is as plain as the way to market. It depends chiefly on two words, industry and frugality: that is, waste neither time nor money, but make the best use of both. Without industry and frugality nothing will do, and with them everything.

Benjamin Franklin

▶ REQUIREMENTS FOR HDC STATUS

To qualify as an HDC, a transferee must meet the requirements established by the Uniform Commercial Code (UCC): The person must be the *holder* of a negotiable instrument that was taken (1) for value; (2) in good faith; (3) without notice that it is overdue, dishonored, or encumbered in any way; and (4) bearing no apparent evidence of forgery, alterations, or irregularity [UCC 3-302]. These requirements are discussed in the paragraphs that follow. Exhibit 23.7 illustrates the HDC doctrine.

▶ **Exhibit 23.7 HOLDER IN DUE COURSE**

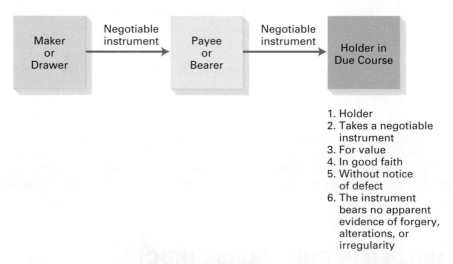

1. Holder
2. Takes a negotiable instrument
3. For value
4. In good faith
5. Without notice of defect
6. The instrument bears no apparent evidence of forgery, alterations, or irregularity

taking for value requirement
A requirement that says a holder must give value for a negotiable instrument in order to qualify as an HDC.

Taking for Value Requirement

Under the UCC **taking for value requirement**, the holder must have *given value* for the negotiable instrument in order to qualify as an HDC [UCC 3-302(a)(2)(i)].

Example Ted draws a check "payable to the order of Mary Smith" and delivers the check to Mary. Mary indorses it and gives it as a gift to her daughter. Mary's daughter cannot qualify as an HDC because she has not given value for it. The purchaser of a limited interest in a negotiable instrument is an HDC only to the extent of the interest purchased.

Under the UCC, value has been given if the holder [UCC 3-303]:

- Performs the agreed-upon promise.
- Acquires a security interest in or lien on the instrument.
- Takes the instrument in payment of or as security for an antecedent claim.
- Gives a negotiable instrument as payment.
- Gives an irrevocable obligation as payment.

If a person promises to perform but has not yet done so, no value has been given, and he or she is not an HDC.

Example Karen executes a note payable to Fred for $3,000 for goods she purchased from him. Fred transfers the note to Amy for her promise to pay the note in 90 days. Before Amy pays the note, Karen discovers that the goods she purchased from Fred are defective. Karen can raise this defect against enforcement of the note by Amy because no value has yet been given for the note. If Amy had already paid for the note, she would qualify as an HDC, and Karen could not raise the issue of defect against enforcement of the note by Amy.

Taking in Good Faith Requirement

Under the UCC **taking in good faith requirement**, a holder must *take* an instrument in *good faith* to qualify as an HDC [UCC 3-302(a)(2)(ii)]. **Good faith** means honesty in fact in the conduct or transaction concerned [UCC 1-201(19)]. *Honesty in fact* is a subjective test that examines the holder's actual belief. A holder's subjective belief can be inferred from the circumstances.

Example If a holder acquires an instrument from a stranger under suspicious circumstances and at a deep discount, it could be inferred that the holder did not take the instrument in good faith. A naïve person who acquired the same instrument at the same discount, however, may be found to have acted in good faith and thereby qualify as an HDC. Each case must be reviewed individually.

Note that the good faith test applies only to the holder. It does not apply to the transferor of the instrument.

Example A thief steals a negotiable instrument and transfers it to Harry. Harry does not know that the instrument is stolen. Harry meets the good faith test and qualifies as an HDC.

Taking Without Notice of Defect Requirement

Under the UCC **taking without notice of defect requirement**, a person cannot qualify as an HDC if he or she has notice that the instrument is defective in any of the following ways [UCC 3-302(a)(2)]:

- It is overdue.
- It has been dishonored.
- It contains an unauthorized signature or has been altered.
- There is a claim to it by another person.
- There is a defense against it.

Overdue Instruments   If a **time instrument** is not paid on its expressed due date, it becomes **overdue** the next day. When an instrument is not paid when due, there is some defect to its payment.

taking in good faith requirement
A requirement that says a holder must take the instrument in good faith in order to qualify as an HDC.

good faith
Honesty in fact in the conduct or transaction concerned. The good faith test is subjective.

taking without notice of defect requirement
A requirement that says a person cannot qualify as an HDC if he or she has notice that the instrument is defective in certain ways.

time instrument
An instrument that specifies a definite date for payment of the instrument.

Example Suppose a promissory note is due June 15, 2011. To qualify as an HDC, a purchaser must acquire the note by 11:59 P.M. on June 15, 2011. A purchaser who acquired the note on June 16, 2011, or later is only a holder, not an HDC.

Often, a debt is payable in installments or in a series of notes. If a maker misses an installment payment or fails to pay one note in a series of notes, the purchaser of the instruments is on notice that it is overdue [UCC 3-304(b)].

demand instrument
An instrument payable on demand.

A **demand instrument** is payable on demand. A purchaser cannot be an HDC if the instrument is acquired either (1) after demand or (2) at an unreasonable length of time after its issue. A "reasonable time" for presenting a check for payment is presumed to be 90 days. Business practices and the circumstances of the case determine a reasonable time for the payment of other demand instruments [UCC 3-304(a)].

dishonored instrument
An instrument that is presented for payment and payment is refused.

Dishonored Instruments An instrument is **dishonored** when it is presented for payment and payment is refused. A holder who takes the instrument with notice of its dishonor cannot qualify as an HDC.

Example A person who takes a check that has been marked by the payer bank "payment refused—not sufficient funds" cannot qualify as an HDC.

Red Light Doctrine A holder cannot qualify as an HDC if he or she has notice that an instrument contains an unauthorized signature or has been altered or that there is any adverse claim against or defense to its payment. This rule is commonly referred to as the **red light doctrine**.

red light doctrine
A doctrine that says a holder cannot qualify as an HDC if he or she has notice of an unauthorized signature or an alteration of the instrument or any adverse claim against or defense to its payment.

Notice of a defect is given when the holder (1) has actual knowledge of the defect, (2) has received a notice or notification of the defect, or (3) has reason to know from the facts and circumstances that the defect exists [UCC 1-201(25)]. The filing of a public notice does not of itself constitute notice unless the person actually reads the public notice [UCC 3-302(b)].

No Evidence of Forgery, Alteration, or Irregularity Requirement

no evidence of forgery, alteration, or irregularity requirement
A requirement that says a holder cannot become an HDC to an instrument that is apparently forged or altered or is so otherwise irregular or incomplete as to call into question its authenticity.

The UCC has a **no evidence of forgery, alteration, or irregularity requirement**. Under this rule, a holder does not qualify as an HDC if at the time the instrument was issued or negotiated to the holder, it bore apparent evidence of forgery or alteration or was otherwise so irregular or incomplete as to call into question its authenticity [UCC 3-302(a)(1)].

Clever and undetectable forgeries and alterations are not classified as obvious irregularities. Determining whether a forgery or an alteration is apparent and whether the instrument is so irregular or incomplete that its authenticity should be questioned are issues of fact that must be decided on a case-by-case basis.

Payee as an HDC Requirement

Payees generally do not meet the requirements for being HDCs because they know about any claims or defenses against the instrument. In a few situations, however, a payee who does not have such knowledge would qualify as an HDC.

Example Kate purchases an automobile from Jake for $5,000. Jake owes Sherry Smith $5,000 from another transaction. Jake has Kate make out the $5,000 check for the automobile "payable to the order of Sherry Smith." Jake gives the check to Sherry. The car Jake sold to Kate is defective, and she wants to rescind the purchase. Sherry (payee), who did not have notice of the defect in the car, is an HDC. Sherry can therefore enforce the check against Kate, and Kate's only recourse is to recover from Jake.

CONTEMPORARY ENVIRONMENT

Shelter Principle

A holder who does not qualify as a holder in due course in his or her own right becomes a holder in due course if he or she acquires the instrument through a holder in due course. This is called the **shelter principle**.

Example Jason buys a used car from Debbie. He pays 10 percent down and signs a negotiable promissory note, promising to pay Debbie the remainder of the purchase price, with interest, in 36 equal monthly installments. At the time of sale, Debbie materially misrepresented the mileage of the automobile. Later, Debbie negotiates the note to Eric, who has no notice of the misrepresentation. Eric, an HDC, negotiates the note to Jaime. Assume that Jaime does not qualify as an HDC in her own right. She becomes an HDC,

however, because she acquired the note through an HDC (Eric). Jaime can enforce the note against Jason.

To qualify as an HDC under the shelter principle, the following rules apply:

• The holder does not have to qualify as an HDC in his or her own right.
• The holder must acquire the instrument from an HDC or be able to trace his or her title back to an HDC.
• The holder must not have been a party to a fraud or an illegality affecting the instrument.
• The holder cannot have notice of a defense or claim against the payment of the instrument.

TEST REVIEW TERMS AND CONCEPTS

Allonge
Assignee
Assignment
Assignor
Bearer paper
Blank indorsement
Demand instrument
Dishonored instrument
Good faith
Holder
Holder in due course (HDC)

Indorsee
Indorsement
Indorsement for deposit or collection
Indorsement in trust (agency indorsement)
Indorser
Negotiation
No evidence of forgery, alteration, or irregularity requirement

Nonrestrictive indorsement
Order paper
Overdue instrument
Payable in the alternative
Payable jointly
Personal defenses
Qualified indorsement
Qualified indorser
Red light doctrine
Restrictive indorsement
Shelter principle

Special indorsement
Taking for value requirement
Taking in good faith requirement
Taking without notice of defect requirement
Time instrument
Universal defenses
Unqualified indorsement
Unqualified indorser
Virgule

CASE PROBLEMS

23.1 Indorsement   Katherine Warnock purchased a cashier's check in the amount of $53,541, payable to her order and drawn on the Pueblo Bank and Trust Company (Pueblo Bank). At some time during the next two weeks, Warnock indorsed "Katherine Warnock" on the reverse side of the check. Eventually the check came into the hands of Warnock's attorney, Jerry Quick. Quick added the words *for deposit only* under her indorsement and then had the check deposited into his trust account at the La Junta State Bank. Warnock died two years later. The executor of her estate suspected that Quick had illegally converted Warnock's funds into his own account. The executor claimed that the cashier's check that Quick deposited should have been payable only to Warnock because it was made to a named payee. When the executor discovered that Quick's trust account had been liquidated, the executor sued La Junta State Bank, where the deposit had been

made. Who wins? *La Junta State Bank v. Travis 727* P.2d 48, **Web** 1986 Colo. Lexis 640 (Colorado Supreme Court)

23.2 Indorsement   Charles Pribus owed $126,500 to Ford and Mary Williams (Williams). At Pribus's request, his mother, Helen Pribus, executed a promissory note for $126,500 in favor of Williams. Within a few months, Williams bought Philip L. Bush's option to purchase an apartment complex in Texas. As partial payment for the option, Williams gave Bush the promissory note they had received from Helen Pribus. A letter, which was signed by Williams, was stapled to the note. It read: "For valuable consideration, the undersigned do hereby assign the attached note to Philip L. Bush." There was sufficient space on the note itself to write an indorsement and the words contained in the letter. When Bush went to collect on the note, Helen Pribus refused to pay. Bush sued Pribus to enforce the note. Has the note been properly indorsed? *Pribus v. Bush*, Rep 118 Cal.App.3d 1003, 173 Cal.Rptr. 747, **Web** 1981 Cal.App. Lexis 1724 (Court of Appeal of California)

23.3 Indorsement   Wilson was the office manager of Palmer and Ray Dental Supply Company of Abilene, Inc. (Dental Supply). Each workday, James Frank Ray, the president of Dental Supply, would take the checks received from customers and place them on Wilson's desk. Wilson was authorized to (1) indorse these checks through the use of a rubber stamp reading "Palmer & Ray Dental Supply, Inc., of Abilene, Box 2894, 3110 B.N. 1st, Abilene, Texas 79603" and (2) deposit the indorsed checks into the company's account at the First National Bank of Abilene (First National Bank). After several years of working at Dental Supply, Wilson began to embezzle money from the company. Her scheme involved indorsing the checks made payable to Dental Supply with the rubber stamp and drawing cash on them instead of making a deposit. The bank cashed these checks without requiring any further indorsement. Is the bank liable? *Palmer & Ray Dental Supply of Abilene, Inc, v. First National Bank of Abilene*, 477 S.W.2d 954, **Web** 1972 Tex.App. Lexis 2071 (Court of Civil Appeals of Texas)

23.4 Order or Bearer Paper   Samuel C. Mazilly wrote a personal check that was drawn on Calcasieu-Marine National Bank of Lake Charles, Inc. (CMN Bank). The check was made payable to the order of Lee St. Mary and was delivered to him. St. Mary indorsed the check in blank and delivered it to Leland H. Coltharp, Sr., in payment for some livestock. Coltharp accepted the check and took it to the City Savings Bank & Trust Company (City Savings) to deposit it. He indorsed the check as follows: "Pay to the order of City Savings Bank & Trust Company, DeRidder, Louisiana." City Savings accepted the check and forwarded it to CMN Bank for payment. The check never arrived at CMN Bank. Some unknown person stole the check while it was in transit and presented it directly to CMN Bank for payment. The teller at CMN Bank cashed the check without indorsement of the person who presented it. At the time CMN Bank accepts the check, is it order or bearer paper? *Caltharp v. Calcasieu-Marine National Bank of Lake Charles, Inc.*, 199 So.2d 568, **Web** 1967 La.App. Lexis 5203 (Court of Appeal of Louisiana)

23.5 Taking for Value   Betty Ellis and her then husband W.G. Ellis executed and delivered to the Standard Finance Company (Standard) a promissory note in the amount of $2,800. After receiving the note, Standard issued a check to the couple for $2,800. The check was made payable to "W.G. Ellis and Betty Ellis." The check was cashed after both parties indorsed it. Shortly thereafter, the Ellises were divorced. Mrs. Ellis claims that (1) she never saw or used the money and (2) Standard understood that all the money went to her ex-husband. W.G. Ellis was declared bankrupt. When the note became due four years later, Betty Ellis refused to pay it. Standard sued her, seeking payment as a holder in due course. She claimed that Standard was not a holder in due course in regard to her because she never received consideration for the note and, therefore, Standard did not take the note for value. Who wins? *Standard Finance Company, Ltd. v. Ellis*, 3 Haw. App. 614, 657 P.2d 1056, **Web** 1983 Haw.App. Lexis 83 (Intermediate Court of Appeals of Hawaii)

23.6 Holder in Due Course   National Financial Services (National) issued a check to Patrick J. Doherty for $62,812.36. The check was drawn on National's account at the Bank of New England. The next day, Doherty took the check to his bank, the M & I Marshall & Ilsley Bank (M & I), and properly indorsed it. The bank gave Doherty $1,350 in cash and deposited the remainder of the funds into his checking account at the bank. As soon as the check was deposited, M & I froze these funds to help offset a $90,000 overdraft in Doherty's account. When Doherty learned of this action, he contacted National and asked them to stop payment on the check. Although National agreed to do so, it refused to issue a new check until the original check was returned. In the meantime, M & I forwarded the check for payment to the Bank of New England. The Bank of New England returned the check to M & I, stamped "payment stopped." When M & I received the dishonored check, it sent it to Doherty, who forwarded it to National. National then issued Doherty a new check. M & I sued National to recover on the first check. M & I claims it was a holder in due course and that National could not stop payment on the check. Who wins? *M & I Marshall & Ilsley Bank v. National Financial Services Corporation*, 704 F.Supp. 890, **Web** 1989 U.S. Dist. Lexis. 1233 (United States District Court for the Eastern District of Wisconsin)

23.7 Holder in Due Course   Royal Insurance Company Ltd. (Royal) issued a draft in the amount of $12,000 payable through the Morgan Guaranty Trust Company (Morgan Guaranty). The draft was made payable to Gary E. Terrell in settlement of a claim in an insurance policy for fire damage to premises located at 3031 North 11th Street, Kansas City, Kansas. On May 9, the attorney for Mr. and Mrs. Louis Wexler notified Royal that Terrell's clients had an insurable interest in the damaged property. As a result, Royal immediately stopped payment on the draft. On the same day, the draft was indorsed by Gary E. Terrell and deposited in his account at the UAW-CIO Local #31 Federal Credit Union (Federal). Over the next two days, Terrell withdrew $9,000 from this account. Immediately upon receiving the draft, Federal indorsed it and forwarded it to Morgan Guaranty for payment. The draft was returned to Federal on May 14, with the notation "payment stopped." When Royal refused to pay Federal the amount of the draft, Federal sued. The basis of the suit was whether Federal was a holder in due course. Who wins? *UAW-CIO Local #31 Federal Credit Union v. Royal Insurance Company, Ltd.*, 594 S.W.2d 276, **Web** 1980 Mo. Lexis 446 (Supreme Court of Missouri)

BUSINESS ETHICS CASES

23.8 Business Ethics Anthony and Dolores Angelini entered into a contract with Lustro Aluminum Products, Inc. (Lustro). Under the contract, Lustro agreed to replace exterior veneer on the Angelini home with Gold Bond Plasticrylic avocado siding. The cash price for the job was $3,600, and the installment plan price was $5,363.40. The Angelinis chose to pay on the installment plan and signed a promissory note as security. The note's language provided that it would not mature until 60 days after a certificate of completion was signed. Ten days after the note was executed, Lustro assigned it for consideration to General Investment Corporation (General), an experienced home improvement lender. General was aware that Lustro (1) was nearly insolvent at the time of the assignment and (2) had engaged in questionable business practices in the past. Lustro never completed the installation of siding at the Angelini home. General, as a holder in due course, demanded payment of the note from the Angelinis. Who wins? *General Investment Corporation v. Angelini,* 278 A.2d 193, **Web** 1971 N.J. Lexis 263 (Supreme Court of New Jersey)

23.9 Business Ethics Murray Walter, Inc. (Walter, Inc.), was a general contractor for the construction of a waste treatment plant in New Hampshire. Walter, Inc., contracted with H. Johnson Electric, Inc. (Johnson Electric), to install the electrical system in the treatment plant. Johnson Electric purchased its supplies for the project from General Electric Supply (G.E. Supply). Walter, Inc., issued a check payable to "Johnson Electric and G.E. Supply" in the amount of $54,900, drawn on its account at Marine Midland Bank (Marine Midland). Walter, Inc., made the check payable to both the subcontractor and its material supplier, to be certain that the supplier was paid by Johnson Electric. Despite this precautionary measure, Johnson Electric negotiated the check without G.E. Supply's indorsement, and the check was paid by Marine Midland. Johnson Electric never paid G.E. Supply. G.E. Supply then demanded payment from Walter, Inc. When Walter, Inc., learned that Marine Midland had paid the check without G.E. Supply's indorsement, it demanded to be reimbursed. When Marine Midland refused, Walter, Inc., sued Marine Midland to recover for the check. Was Johnson Electric's indorsement sufficient to legally negotiate the check to Marine Midland Bank? Did any party act unethically in this case? *Murray Walter, Inc. v. Marine Midland Bank,* 103 A.D.2d 466, 480 N.Y.S.2d 631, **Web** 1984 N.Y. App. Div. Lexis 19962 (Supreme Court of New York)

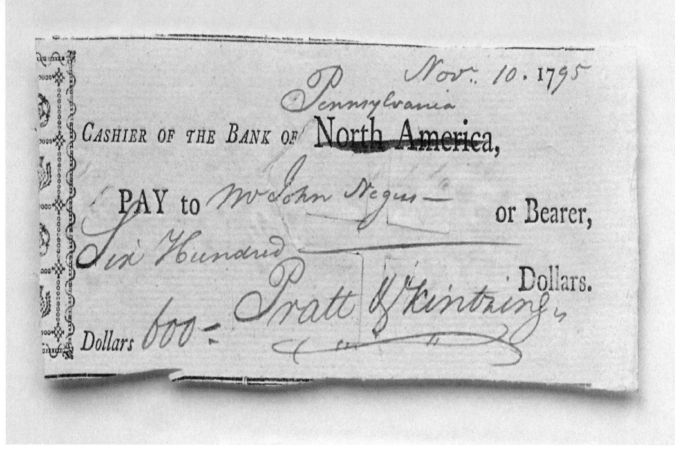

▲ **American Check from 1795** *A person's signature is required before that person can be held contractually liable on a negotiable instrument.*

CHAPTER OBJECTIVES

After studying this chapter, you should be able to:

1. Describe the signature liability of makers, drawees, drawers, acceptors, and accommodation parties.
2. List the transfer and presentment warranties and describe the liability of parties for breaching them.
3. Identify universal (real) defenses that can be asserted against a holder in due course.
4. Describe the Federal Trade Commission rule that prohibits the holder in due course rule in consumer transactions.
5. Describe how parties are discharged from liability on negotiable instruments.

CHAPTER CONTENTS

▶ **INTRODUCTION TO LIABILITY, DEFENSES, AND DISCHARGE**
▶ **SIGNATURE LIABILITY**
▶ **PRIMARY LIABILITY**
▶ **SECONDARY LIABILITY**
  Contemporary Environment · *Accommodation Party*
▶ **FORGED INDORSEMENT**

Ethics Spotlight · *Imposter Rule*
Ethics Spotlight · *Fictitious Payee Rule*
▶ **TRANSFER AND PRESENTMENT WARRANTIES**
▶ **UNIVERSAL (REAL) DEFENSES**
▶ **PERSONAL DEFENSES**
  Landmark Law · *FTC Rule Limits HDC Status*
▶ **DISCHARGE**

"If one wants to know the real value of money, he needs but to borrow some from his friends."

Confucius
Analects (c. 500 B.C.)

▶ INTRODUCTION TO LIABILITY, DEFENSES, AND DISCHARGE

If payment is not made on a negotiable instrument when it is due, the holder can use the court system to enforce the instrument. Various parties, including both signers and non-signers, may be liable on it. Some parties are primarily liable on the instrument, while others are secondarily liable. Accommodation parties (i.e., guarantors) can also be held liable.

Once a holder qualifies as a holder in due course (HDC), the HDC takes an instrument free of most **defenses** that can be asserted against other parties. However, several defenses, called *universal defenses*, can be raised against the payment of the instrument to the HDC. The Uniform Commercial Code (UCC) also specifies when and how certain parties are discharged from liability on negotiable instruments.

This chapter discusses the liability of parties to pay a negotiable instrument, the defenses that can be raised against an HDC, and the discharge of liability on a negotiable instrument.

▶ SIGNATURE LIABILITY

A person cannot be held contractually liable on a negotiable instrument unless his or her signature appears on it [UCC 3-401(a)]. Therefore, this type of liability is often referred to as **signature liability**, or **contract liability**. A signature on a negotiable instrument identifies who is obligated to pay it. If it is unclear who the signer is, parol evidence can identify the signer. This liability does not attach to bearer paper because no indorsement is needed.

Signers of instruments sign in many different capacities, including as makers of notes or certificates of deposit, drawers of drafts or checks, drawees who certify or accept checks or drafts, indorsers who indorse instruments, agents who sign on behalf of others, and accommodation parties. The location of the signature on an instrument generally determines the signer's capacity. A signature in the lower-right corner of a check indicates that the signer is the drawer of the check. A signature in the lower-right corner of a promissory note indicates that the signer is the maker of the note. The signature of the drawee named in a draft on the face of the draft or another location on the draft indicates that the signer is an acceptor of the draft.

Most indorsements appear on the back or reverse side of an instrument. Unless the instrument clearly indicates that such a signature is made in some other capacity, it is presumed to be that of the indorser. Every party that signs a negotiable instrument (except qualified indorsers and agents that properly sign the instrument) is either primarily or secondarily liable on the instrument. The following discussion outlines the particular liability of signers.

Signature Defined

The **signature** on a negotiable instrument can be any name, word, or mark used in lieu of a written signature [UCC 3-401(b)]. In other words, a signature is any symbol that is (1) handwritten, typed, printed, stamped, or made in almost any other manner and (2) executed or adopted by a party to authenticate a writing [UCC 1-201(39)]. This rule permits trade names and other assumed names to be used as signatures on negotiable instruments.

signature liability
Liability in which a person cannot be held contractually liable on a negotiable instrument unless his or her signature appears on the instrument. Also called *contract liability*.

signer
A person signing an instrument who acts in the capacity of (1) a maker of notes or certificates of deposit, (2) a drawer of drafts or checks, (3) a drawee who certifies or accepts checks or drafts, (4) an indorser who indorses an instrument, (5) an agent who signs on behalf of others, or (6) an accommodation party.

signature
Any name, word, or mark used in lieu of a written signature; any symbol that is (1) handwritten, typed, printed, stamped, or made in almost any other manner and (2) executed or adopted by a party to authenticate a writing.

The unauthorized signature of a person on an instrument is ineffective as that person's signature. It is effective as the signature of the unauthorized signer in favor of an HDC, however. A person who forges a signature on a check may be held liable to an HDC. An unauthorized signature may be ratified [UCC 3-403(a)].

▶ PRIMARY LIABILITY

primary liability
Absolute liability to pay a negotiable instrument, subject to certain universal (real) defenses.

Makers of promissory notes and certificates of deposit have **primary liability** for the instruments. Upon signing a promissory note, the maker unconditionally promises to pay the amount stipulated in the note when it is due. A maker is absolutely liable to pay the instrument, subject only to certain universal (real) defenses. The holder need not take any action to give rise to this obligation. Generally, the maker is obligated to pay a note according to its original terms. If the note was incomplete when it was issued, the maker is obligated to pay the note as completed, as long as he or she authorized the terms as they were filled in [UCC 3-412].

A draft or a check is an order from a drawer to pay the instrument to a payee (or other holder) according to its terms. No party is primarily liable when the draft or check is issued because such instruments are merely orders to pay. Thus, a drawee that refuses to pay a draft or a check is not liable to the payee or holder. If there has been a wrongful dishonor of the instrument, the drawee may be liable to the drawer for certain damages.

On occasion, a drawee is requested to accept a draft or check. Acceptance of a draft occurs when the drawee writes the word *accepted* across the face of the draft. The acceptor—that is, the drawee—is primarily liable on the instrument. A check, which is a special form of draft, is accepted when it is certified by a bank. The bank's certification discharges the drawer and all prior indorsers from liability on the check. Note that the bank may choose to refuse to certify the check without liability. The issuer of a cashier's check is also primarily liable on the instrument [UCC 3-411].

▶ SECONDARY LIABILITY

secondary liability
Liability on a negotiable instrument that is imposed on a party only when the party primarily liable on the instrument defaults and fails to pay the instrument when due.

Under the UCC's *indorsers' liability* rules, drawers of checks and drafts and unqualified indorsers of negotiable instruments have **secondary liability** on the instruments. This liability is similar to that of a guarantor of a simple contract. It arises when the party primarily liable on the instrument defaults and fails to pay the instrument when due.

If an unaccepted draft or check is dishonored by the drawee or acceptor, the drawer is obliged to pay it according to its terms, either when it is issued or, if incomplete when issued, when it is properly completed [UCC 3-414(a)].

Example Elliot draws a check on his checking account at City Bank "payable to the order of Phyllis Jones." When Phyllis presents the check for payment, City Bank refuses to pay it. Phyllis can collect the amount of the check from Elliot because Elliot—the drawer—is secondarily liable on the check when it is dishonored.

Unqualified Indorser

unqualified indorsers
Those who are secondarily liable on negotiable instruments they endorse.

An **unqualified indorser** has secondary liability on negotiable instruments. In other words, he or she must pay any dishonored instrument to the holder or to any subsequent indorser according to its terms, when issued or properly completed. Unless otherwise agreed, indorsers are liable to each other in the order in which they indorsed the instrument [UCC 3-415(a)].

Example Dara borrows $10,000 from Todd and signs a promissory note, promising to pay Todd this amount plus 10% interest in one year. Todd indorses the note and negotiates it to Frank. Frank indorses the note and negotiates it to Linda. Linda presents the note to Dara for payment when the note is due. Dara refuses to pay the note. Because Frank became secondarily liable on the note when he indorsed it to Linda, he must pay the amount of the note—$11,000—to Linda. Frank can then require Todd to pay the note to Frank because Todd (as payee) became secondarily liable on the note when he indorsed it to Frank. Todd can then enforce the note against Dara. Linda could have skipped over Frank and required the payee, Todd, to pay the note. In this instance, Frank would have been relieved of any further liability because he indorsed the instrument after the payee.

Qualified Indorser

A **qualified indorser** (i.e., an indorser who indorse instruments "without recourse" or similar language that disclaims liability) is not secondarily liable on an instrument because he or she has expressly disclaimed liability [UCC 3-415(b)]. The drawer can disclaim all liability on a draft (but not a check) by drawing the instrument "without recourse." In this instance, the drawer becomes a qualified drawer [UCC 3-414(e)]. Many payees, however, will not accept a draft or check that has been drawn without recourse.

qualified indorsers
Those who disclaim liability and are not secondarily liable on instruments they endorse.

Requirements for Imposing Secondary Liability

A party is secondarily liable on a negotiable instrument only if the following requirements are met:

- **The instrument is properly presented for payment. Presentment** is a demand for acceptance or payment of an instrument made upon the maker, acceptor, drawee, or other payer by or on behalf of the holder. Presentment may be made by any commercially reasonable means, including oral, written, or electronic communication. Presentment is effective when it is received by the person to whom presentment is made [UCC 3-501].
- **The instrument is dishonored.** An instrument is *dishonored* when acceptance or payment of the instrument is refused or cannot be obtained from the party required to accept or pay the instrument within the prescribed time after presentment is duly made [UCC 3-502].
- **Notice of the dishonor is timely given to the person to be held secondarily liable on the instrument.** A secondarily liable party cannot be compelled to accept or pay an instrument unless proper **notice of dishonor** has been given. Notice may be given by any commercially reasonable means. The notice must reasonably identify the instrument and indicate that it has been dishonored. Return of an instrument given to a bank for collection is sufficient notice of dishonor. Banks must give notice of dishonor before midnight of the next banking day following the day that presentment is made. Others must give notice of dishonor within 30 days following the day on which the person receives notice of dishonor [UCC 3-503].

presentment
A demand for acceptance or payment of an instrument made upon the maker, acceptor, drawee, or other payer by or on behalf of the holder.

notice of dishonor
The formal act of letting the party with secondary liability to pay a negotiable instrument know that the instrument has been dishonored.

accommodation party
A party who signs an instrument and lends his or her name (and credit) to another party to the instrument.

guarantee of payment
A form of accommodation in which the accommodation party guarantees *payment* of a negotiable instrument; the accommodation party is *primarily liable* on the instrument.

CONTEMPORARY ENVIRONMENT

Accommodation Party

A party who signs an instrument for the purpose of lending his or her name (and credit) to another party to the instrument is the **accommodation party**. The accommodation party, who may sign an instrument as maker, drawer, acceptor, or indorser, is obliged to *pay* the instrument in the capacity in which he or she signs [UCC 3-419(a), 3-419(b)]. An accommodation party who pays an instrument can recover reimbursement from the accommodated party and enforce the instrument against him or her [UCC 3-419(e)].

There are two types of liability of an accommodation party:

1. **Guarantee of payment.** An accommodation party who signs an instrument **guaranteeing payment** is *primarily liable* on the instrument. That is, the debtor can seek payment on the instrument directly from the accommodation maker without first seeking payment from the maker.

Example Sonny, a college student, wants to purchase an automobile on credit from ABC Motors. He does not have a sufficient income or credit history to justify the extension of credit to him alone. Sonny asks his mother to cosign the note to ABC Motors, which she does. Sonny's mother is an accommodation maker and is primarily liable on the note.

2. **Guarantee of collection.** An accommodation party may sign an instrument **guaranteeing collection** rather than payment of an instrument. In this situation, the accommodation indorser is only *secondarily liable* on the instrument. To reserve this type of liability, the signature of the accommodation party must be accompanied by

words indicating that he or she is guaranteeing collection rather than payment of the obligation.

An accommodation party who guarantees collection is obliged to pay the instrument only if (1) execution of judgment against the other party has been returned unsatisfied, (2) the other party is insolvent or in an insolvency proceeding, (3) the other party cannot be served with process, or (4) it is otherwise apparent that payment cannot be obtained from the other party [UCC 3-419(d)].

guarantee of collection
A form of accommodation in which the accommodation party guarantees *collection* of a negotiable instrument; the accommodation party is *secondarily liable* on the instrument.

CONCEPT SUMMARY

LIABILITY OF ACCOMMODATION MAKER AND ACCOMMODATION INDORSER COMPARED

Accommodation Party	Contract Liability
Accommodation maker	Primarily liable on the instrument
Accommodation indorser	Secondarily liable on the instrument

Agent's Signature

A person may either sign a negotiable instrument him- or herself or authorize a representative to sign the instrument on his or her behalf [UCC 3-401(a)]. The representative is the **agent**, and the represented person is the **principal**. The authority of an agent to sign an instrument is established under general agency law. No special form of appointment is necessary. If an authorized agent signs an instrument with either the principal's name or the agent's own name, the principal is bound as if the signature were made on a simple contract. It does not matter whether the principal is identified in the instrument [UCC 3-402(2)].

agent
A person who has been authorized to sign a negotiable instrument on behalf of another person.

principal
A person who authorizes an agent to sign a negotiable instrument on his or her behalf.

Example Suppose Anderson is the agent for Puttkammer. The following signatures on a negotiable instrument would bind Puttkammer on the instrument:

1. Puttkammer, by Anderson, agent
2. Puttkammer
3. Puttkammer, Anderson
4. Anderson

An authorized agent's personal liability on an instrument he or she signs on behalf of a principal depends on the information disclosed in the signature. The agent has no liability if the signature shows unambiguously that it is made on behalf of a principal who is identified in the instrument [UCC 3-402(b)(1)].

Example Signature number 1 above ("Puttkammer, by Anderson, agent") satisfies this requirement.

If the authorized agent's signature does not show unambiguously that the signature was made in a representative capacity and the agent cannot prove that the original parties did not intend him or her to be liable, the agent is liable (1) to an HDC who took the instrument without notice that the agent was not intended to be liable on the instrument and (2) to any other person other than an HDC [UCC 3-402(b)(2)].

A trader is trusted upon his character, and visible commerce, that credit enables him to acquire wealth.

Lord Mansfield
Worseley v. Demattos (1758)

Example Signature number 2 above ("Puttkammer") does not show unambiguously that the signature was made in a representative capacity.

Examples Signatures number 3 above ("Puttkammer, Anderson") and 4 ("Anderson") place the agent at risk of personal liability to an HDC that does not have notice that the agent was not intended to be liable on the instrument. To avoid liability to a non-HDC for these signatures, the agent would have to prove that the third-party non-HDC did not intend to hold the agent liable on the instrument.

There is one exception to these rules: If an agent signs his or her name as the drawer of a check without indicating the agent's representative status and the check is payable from the account of the principal who is identified on the check, the agent is not liable on the check [UCC 3-402(c)].

Unauthorized Signature

An **unauthorized signature** is a signature made by a purported agent without authority from the purported principal. Such a signature arises if (1) a person signs a negotiable instrument on behalf of a person for whom he or she is not an agent or (2) an authorized agent exceeds the scope of his or her authority. An unauthorized signature by a purported agent does not act as the signature of the purported principal. The purported agent is liable to any person who in good faith pays the instrument or takes it for value [UCC 3-403(a)]. The purported principal is liable if he or she ratifies the unauthorized signature [UCC 3-403(a)].

unauthorized signature
A signature made by a purported agent without authority from the purported principal.

Example Max, a purported agent, signs a contract and promissory note to purchase a building for ViVi, a purported principal. Suppose that ViVi, the purported principal, likes the deal and accepts it. ViVi has ratified the transaction and is liable on the note.

▶ FORGED INDORSEMENT

Article 3 of the UCC establishes certain rules for assessing liability when a negotiable instrument has been paid over a **forged indorsement**. With few exceptions, an unauthorized indorsement is wholly inoperative as the indorsement of the person whose name is signed [UCC 3-401(a)]. Where an indorsement on an instrument has been forged or is unauthorized, the general rule is that the loss falls on the party who first takes the forged instrument after the forgery.

forged indorsement
The forged signature of a payee or holder on a negotiable instrument.

Example Andy draws a check payable to the order of Mallory. Leslie steals the check from Mallory, forges Mallory's indorsement, and cashes the check at a liquor store. The liquor store is liable. Andy, the drawer, is not. The liquor store can recover from Leslie, the forger (if she can be found).

There are two exceptions to this rule: where a drawer or maker bears the loss and where an indorsement is forged. The rules governing these circumstances—(1) the *imposter rule* and (2) the *fictitious payee rule*—are discussed in the following Ethics Spotlight features.

ETHICS SPOTLIGHT

Imposter Rule

For purposes of the imposter rule, an *imposter* is someone who impersonates a payee and induces the maker or drawer to issue an instrument in the payee's name and give the instrument to the imposter. If the imposter forges the indorsement of the named payee, the drawer or maker is liable on the instrument to any person who, in good faith, pays the instrument or takes it for value or for collection [UCC 3-404(a)]. This rule is called the **imposter rule**.

Example Fred purchases goods by telephone from Cynthia. Fred has never met Cynthia. Beverly goes to Fred and pretends to be Cynthia. Fred draws a check payable to the order of Cynthia and gives the check to Beverly, believing her to be Cynthia. Beverly forges Cynthia's indorsement and cashes the check at a liquor store. Under the imposter rule, Fred is liable and the liquor store is not because Fred was in the best position to have prevented the forged indorsement.

The imposter rule does not apply if the wrongdoer poses as the agent of the payee.

Example Suppose in the preceding example that Beverly lies to Fred and says that she is Cynthia's agent. Believing this, Fred draws the check payable to the order of Cynthia and gives it to Beverly. Beverly forges Cynthia's indorsement and cashes the check at a liquor store. Here, the store is liable because the imposter rule does not apply. The liquor store may recover from Beverly, if she can be found.

Business Ethics   What does the imposter rule provide? Explain. Who is liable under the imposter rule? What is the public policy underlying the imposter rule? Does an imposter act ethically?

ETHICS SPOTLIGHT
Fictitious Payee Rule

A drawer or maker is liable on a forged or unauthorized indorsement under the **fictitious payee rule**. This rule applies when a person signing as or on behalf of a drawer or maker intends the named payee to have no interest in the instrument or when the person identified as the payee is a fictitious person [UCC 3-404(b)].

Example Marcia is the treasurer of the Weld Corporation. As treasurer, Marcia makes out and signs the payroll checks for the company. Marcia draws a payroll check payable to the order of her neighbor Harold Green, who does not work for the company. Marcia does not intend Harold to receive this money. She indorses Harold's name on the check and names herself as the indorsee. She cashes the check at a liquor store. Under the fictitious payee rule, Weld Corporation is liable because it was in a better position than the liquor store to have prevented the fraud.

The fictitious payee rule also applies if an agent or employee of the drawer or maker supplies the drawer or maker with the name of a fictitious payee [UCC 3-405(c)].

Example Elizabeth is an accountant for the Baldridge Corporation. She is responsible for drawing up a list of employees who are to receive payroll checks. The treasurer of Baldridge Corporation actually signs the checks. Elizabeth places the name "Annabelle Armstrong" (a fictitious person) on the list. Baldridge Corporation issues a payroll check to this fictitious person. Elizabeth indorses the instrument "Annabelle Armstrong" and names herself as indorsee. She cashes the check at a liquor store. Under the fictitious payee rule, Baldridge Corporation is liable; the liquor store is not.

Business Ethics   What does the fictitious payee rule provide? Explain. What is the public policy underlying the fictitious payee rule? Does a fictitious payee act ethically?

▶ TRANSFER AND PRESENTMENT WARRANTIES

implied warranties
Certain warranties that the law implies on transferors of negotiable instruments. There are two types of implied warranties: transfer and presentment warranties.

In addition to signature liability, transferors can be held liable for breaching certain **implied warranties** when negotiating instruments. **Warranty liability** is imposed whether or not the transferor signed the instrument. Note that a transferor makes an implied warranty; implied warranties are not made when the negotiable instrument is originally issued.

There are two types of implied warranties: *transfer warranties* and *presentment warranties*. Transfer and presentment warranties shift the risk of loss to the party who was in the best position to prevent the loss. This party is usually the one who dealt face-to-face with the wrongdoer. These implied warranties are discussed in the paragraphs that follow.

Transfer Warranties

transfer
Any passage of an instrument other than its issuance and presentment for payment.

Any passage of an instrument other than its issuance and presentment for payment is considered a **transfer**. Any person who transfers a negotiable instrument for consideration makes the following five warranties to the transferee. If the transfer is by indorsement, the transferor also makes these warranties to any subsequent transferee [UCC 3-416(a)]:

1. The transferor has good title to the instrument or is authorized to obtain payment or acceptance on behalf of one who does have good title.
2. All signatures are genuine or authorized.
3. The instrument has not been materially altered.
4. No defenses of any party are good against the transferor.
5. The transferor has no knowledge of any insolvency proceeding against the maker, the acceptor, or the drawer of an unaccepted instrument.

Transfer warranties cannot be disclaimed with respect to checks, but they can be disclaimed with respect to other instruments. An indorsement that states "without recourse" disclaims the transfer warranties [UCC 3-419(c)]. A transferee who took the instrument in good faith may recover damages for breach of transfer warranty from the warrantor equal to the loss suffered. The amount recovered cannot exceed the amount of the instrument plus expenses and interest [UCC 3-416(b)].

Example Jill signs a promissory note to pay $1,000 to Adam. Adam cleverly raises the note to $10,000 and negotiates the note to Nick. Nick indorses the note and negotiates it to Matthew. When Matthew presents the note to Jill for payment, she has to pay only the original amount of the note, $1,000. Matthew can collect the remainder of the note ($9,000) from Nick, based on a breach of the transfer warranty. If Nick is lucky, he can recover the $9,000 from Adam.

Presentment Warranties

Any person who presents a draft or check for payment or acceptance makes the following **presentment warranties** to a drawee or an acceptor who pays or accepts the instruments in good faith [UCC 3-417(a)]:

1. The presenter has good title to the instrument or is authorized to obtain payment or acceptance of the person who has good title.
2. The instrument has not been materially altered.
3. The presenter has no knowledge that the signature of the maker or drawer is unauthorized.

A drawee who pays an instrument may recover damages for breach of presentment warranty from the warrantor. The amount that can be recovered is limited to the amount paid by the drawee less the amount the drawee received or is entitled to receive from the drawer because of the payment plus expenses and interest [UCC 3-147(b)].

Example Maureen draws a $1,000 check on City Bank "payable to the order of Paul." Paul cleverly raises the check to $10,000 and indorses and negotiates the check to Neal. Neal presents the check for payment to City Bank. As the presenter of the check, Neal makes the presentment warranties of UCC 3-417(a) to City Bank. City Bank pays the check as altered ($10,000) and debits Maureen's account. When Maureen discovers the alteration, she demands that the bank recredit her account, which the bank does. City Bank can recover against the presenter (Neal), based on breach of the presentment warranty that the instrument was not altered when it was presented. Neal can recover against the wrongdoer (Paul), based on breach of the transfer warranty that the instrument was not altered.

▶ UNIVERSAL (REAL) DEFENSES

The creation of negotiable instruments may give rise to defenses against their payment. Many of these defenses arise from the underlying transactions. There are two general types of defenses: (1) universal (real) defenses and (2) personal defenses. An HDC (or a holder through an HDC) takes an instrument free from personal defenses but not universal

transfer warranties
Any of the following five implied warranties: (1) The transferor has good title to the instrument or is authorized to obtain payment or acceptance on behalf of one who does have good title; (2) all signatures are genuine or authorized; (3) the instrument has not been materially altered; (4) no defenses of any party are good against the transferor; and (5) the transferor has no knowledge of any insolvency proceeding against the maker, the acceptor, or the drawer of an unaccepted instrument.

presentment warranties
Three warranties that a person who presents a draft or check for payment or acceptance makes to a drawee or an acceptor who pays or accepts the instrument in good faith: (1) The presenter has good title to the instrument or is authorized to obtain payment or acceptance of the person who has good title; (2) the instrument has not been materially altered; and (3) the presenter has no knowledge that the signature of the maker or drawer is unauthorized.

defenses. Personal and universal defenses can be raised against a normal holder of a negotiable instrument. Universal (real) defenses are discussed in this section. (Personal defenses are discussed in a subsequent section of this chapter.)

universal defense
A defense that can be raised against both holders and HDCs. Also called a *real defense*.

Universal defenses (also called **real defenses**) can be raised against both holders and HDCs [UCC 3-305(b)]. If a universal defense is proven, the holder or HDC cannot recover on the instrument. Universal defenses are discussed in the following paragraphs.

Minority

Infancy, or **minority**, is a universal defense to a negotiable instrument to the extent that it is a defense to a simple contract [UCC 3-305(a)(1)(i)]. In most states, a minor who does not misrepresent his or her age can disaffirm contracts, including negotiable instruments. Usually, minors must pay the reasonable value of necessaries of life.

Extreme Duress

Extreme duress is a universal defense against the enforcement of a negotiable instrument by a holder or an HDC [UCC 3-305(a)(1)(ii)]. Extreme duress usually requires some form of force or violence (e.g., a promissory note signed at gunpoint). Ordinary duress is a personal defense (discussed later in this chapter).

Mental Incapacity

Adjudicated **mental incompetence** is a universal defense that can be raised against holders and HDCs [UCC 3-305(a)(1)(ii)]. A person adjudicated mentally incompetent cannot issue a negotiable instrument; the instrument is void from its inception. Nonadjudicated mental incompetence, which is usually a personal defense, is discussed later in this chapter.

Illegality

Money is better than poverty, if only for financial reasons.

Woody Allen

If an instrument arises out of an illegal transaction, the **illegality** is a universal defense if the law declares the instrument void [UCC 3-305(a)(1)(ii)].

Example Assume that a state's law declares gambling to be illegal and gambling contracts to be void. Gordon wins $1,000 from Jerry in an illegal poker game. He signs a promissory note, promising to pay Gordon this amount plus interest in 30 days. Gordon negotiates this note to Dawn, an HDC. When Dawn presents the note to Jerry for payment, Jerry can raise the universal defense of illegality against the enforcement of the note. Dawn's recourse is against Gordon. If the law makes an illegal contract voidable instead of void, it is a personal defense. (This situation is discussed later in this chapter.)

Discharge in Bankruptcy

Bankruptcy law is intended to relieve debtors of burdensome debts, including obligations to pay negotiable instruments. Thus, **discharge in bankruptcy** is a universal defense against the enforcement of a negotiable instrument by a holder or an HDC [UCC 3-305(a)(1)(iv)].

Example Hunt borrows $10,000 from Amy and signs a note promising to pay Amy this amount plus interest in one year. Amy negotiates the note to Richard, an HDC. Before the note is due, Hunt declares bankruptcy and receives a discharge of his unpaid debts. Richard cannot thereafter enforce the note against Hunt, but he can recover against Amy.

Fraud in the Inception

Fraud in the inception (also called the **fraud in the factum** or **fraud in the execution**) is a universal defense against the enforcement of a negotiable instrument by a holder or an

HDC [UCC 3-305(a)(1)(iii)]. It occurs when a person is deceived into signing a negotiable instrument, thinking that it is something else.

Example Sam, a door-to-door salesman, convinces Lance, an illiterate consumer, to sign a document purported to be an agreement to use a plasma TV set on a 90-day trial basis. In actuality, the document is a promissory note in which Lance has agreed to pay $5,000 for the plasma TV set. Sam negotiates the note to Stephanie, an HDC. Lance can raise the universal defense of fraud in the inception against the enforcement of the note by Stephanie. Stephanie, in turn, can recover from Sam.

A person is under a duty to use reasonable efforts to ascertain what he or she is signing. The court inquires into a person's age, experience, education, and other factors before allowing fraud in the inception to be asserted as a universal defense to defeat an HDC. Fraud in the inducement (discussed later) is a personal defense.

One cannot help regretting that where money is concerned it is too much the rule to overlook moral obligations.

Vice Chancellor Malins
Ellis v. Houston (1878)

Forgery

Forgery is a universal defense to the payment of a negotiable instrument. The unauthorized signature of a maker, a drawer, or an indorser is wholly inoperative as that of the person whose name is signed unless that person either ratifies it or is precluded from denying it. In the latter case, a person can be estopped from raising the defense of forgery if his or her negligence substantially contributes to the forgery. A forged signature operates as the signature of the forger. Thus, the forger is liable on the instrument [UCC 3-403(a)].

Material Alteration

An instrument that has been fraudulently and materially altered cannot be enforced by an ordinary holder. **Material alteration** consists of adding to any part of a signed instrument, removing any part of a signed instrument, making changes in the number or relations of the parties, or completing an incomplete instrument without having the authority to do so.

Under the UCC rule that words control figures, correcting the figure on a check to correspond to the written amount on the check is not a material alteration [UCC 3-118(c)]. If an alteration is not material, the instrument can be enforced by a holder for the original amount in which the drawer wrote the check [UCC 3-407(b)].

Material alteration of a negotiable instrument is only a partial defense against an HDC. Subsequent HDCs can enforce any instrument, including an altered instrument, according to its original terms, if the alteration is not apparent. An obvious change puts the holder on notice of the alteration and disqualifies him or her as an HDC [UCC 3-407(c)].

CONCEPT SUMMARY
UNIVERSAL (REAL) DEFENSES

Defense	Effect
Universal defenses:	Universal defenses can be raised against a holder in due course and ordinary holders.
1. Minority	A minor who does not misrepresent his or her age can disaffirm negotiable instruments.
2. Extreme duress	If the use of force or violence was used to issue or have issued a negotiable instrument, then it is unenforceable.
3. Mental incapacity	A person adjudicated mentally incompetent cannot issue a negotiable instrument; the instrument is void from is inception.
4. Illegality	If an instrument arises out of an illegal transaction it is unenforceable.

5. Discharge in bankruptcy	Bankruptcy law allows for obligations to pay negotiable instruments to be discharged and therefore unenforceable.
6. Fraud in the inception	If a person is deceived into signing a negotiable instrument, thinking that it is something else, it is unenforceable.
7. Forgery	The unauthorized signature of a maker, a drawer, or an indorser is wholly inoperative as that of the person whose name is signed.
8. Material alteration	An instrument that has been fraudulently and materially altered cannot be enforced by an ordinary holder.

▶ PERSONAL DEFENSES

personal defense
A defense that can be raised against enforcement of a negotiable instrument by an ordinary holder but not against an HDC.

Personal defenses cannot be raised against an HDC. Personal defenses can, however, be raised against enforcement of a negotiable instrument by an ordinary holder. Personal defenses are discussed in the paragraphs that follow.

Breach of Contract

Breach of contract is one of the most common defenses raised by a party to a negotiable instrument. This personal defense is effective only against an ordinary holder.

Example When Brian purchases a used car on credit from Karen, he signs a note, promising to pay Karen the $10,000 purchase price plus interest, in 36 equal monthly installments. The sales agreement warrants that the car is in perfect working condition. A month later, the car's engine fails; the cost of repair is $3,000. Brian, the maker of the note, can raise breach of contract as a defense against enforcement of the note by Karen.

Example The outcome would be different if Karen negotiated the promissory note to Max (an HDC) immediately after the car was sold to Brian. Max would be an HDC, and Brian could not raise the breach of contract defense against him. Max could enforce the note against Brian. Brian's only recourse would be to seek recovery for breach of warranty from Karen.

Fraud in the Inducement

Fraud in the inducement occurs when a wrongdoer makes a false statement (i.e., misrepresentation) to another person to lead that person to enter into a contract with the wrongdoer. Negotiable instruments often arise out of such transactions. Fraud in the inducement is a personal defense that is not effective against HDCs. It is effective against ordinary holders, however.

The great source of the flourishing state of this kingdom is its trade, and commerce, and paper currency, guarded by proper regulations and restrictions, is the life of commerce.

Justice Ashhurst
Jordaine v. Lashbrooke (1798)

Example Morton represents to investors that he will accept funds to drill for oil and that the investors will share in the profits from the oil wells. He plans to use these funds himself, however. Relying on Morton's statements, Mimi draws a $50,000 check payable to him. Morton absconds with the funds. Because Morton is an ordinary holder, Mimi can raise the personal defense of fraud in the inducement and, if she stops payment on the check before Morton receives payment, not pay the check.

Example If in the previous example Morton had negotiated the check to Tim, an HDC, Tim could enforce the check against Mimi. Because personal defenses are not effective against Tim (an HDC), Mimi's only recourse is to recover against the wrongdoer (Morton), if he can be found.

Additional Personal Defenses

The following additional personal defenses can be raised against enforcement of a negotiable instrument by an ordinary holder:

- Mental illness that makes a contract voidable instead of void (usually a nonadjudicated mental illness)
- Illegality of a contract that makes the contract voidable instead of void
- Ordinary duress or undue influence [UCC 3-305(a)(1)(ii)]
- Discharge of an instrument by payment or cancellation [UCC 3-602, 3-604]

CONCEPT SUMMARY
PERSONAL DEFENSES

Defense	Effect
Personal defenses:	Personal defenses cannot be raised against a holder in due course, only against ordinary holders.
1. Breach of contract	If there is a breach of contract, the negotiable instrument may be deemed unenforceable against an ordinary holder.
2. Fraud in the inducement	Occurs when a wrongdoer makes a false statement to another person to lead that person to enter into a contract with the wrongdoer. Only effective against ordinary holders, however.
3. Mental illness that makes a contract voidable instead of void (usually a nonadjudicated mental illness)	If found to make a contract voidable then the negotiable instrument is unenforceable.
4. Illegality of a contract that makes the contract voidable instead of void	If a contract is found to be illegal then the negotiable instrument is unenforceable.
5. Ordinary duress or undue influence [UCC 3-305(a)(1)(ii)]	If a person is wrongfully influenced or threatened to enter into a negotiable instrument it is unenforceable.
6. Discharge of an instrument by payment or cancellation	If an instrument is discharged by payment or cancellation it is unenforceable.

LANDMARK LAW
FTC Rule Limits HDC Status

In certain situations, the HDC rule can cause a hardship for the consumer.

Example Greg, a consumer, purchases a stereo on credit from Lou's Stereo. He signs a note, promising to pay the purchase price plus interest to Lou's Stereo in 12 equal monthly installments. Lou's Stereo immediately negotiates the note at a discount to City Bank for cash. City Bank is an HDC. The stereo is defective. Greg would like to stop paying on it, but the HDC rule prevents him from asserting any personal defenses against City Bank. Under the UCC, Greg's only recourse is to sue Lou's Stereo. However, this is often an unsatisfactory result because Greg has no leverage against Lou's Stereo,

and bringing a court action is expensive and time-consuming.

To correct this harsh result, the Federal Trade Commission (FTC), a federal administrative agency in charge of consumer protection, adopted the **FTC rule** pursuant to its federal statutory powers. The FTC rule *eliminates HDC status* with regard to negotiable instruments arising out of certain *consumer* credit transactions. [16 C.F.R. 433.2 (1987)]. This federal law takes precedence over any state's UCC.

Thus, sellers of goods and services are prevented from separating the consumer's duty to pay the credit and the seller's duty to perform. This subjects the HDC of a consumer credit instrument to *all* the defenses and claims of the consumer.

Example In the prior example, Greg can raise the defect in the stereo as a defense against enforcement of the promissory note by City Bank, an HDC.

The FTC rules applies to consumer credit transactions in which (1) the buyer signs a sales contract that includes a promissory note, (2) the buyer signs an installment sales contract that contains a waiver of defenses clause, and (3) the seller arranges consumer financing with a third-party lender. Note that payment for goods and services with a check is not covered by this rule because it is not a credit transaction.

The FTC rule requires that the following clause be included in bold type in covered consumer credit sales and installment contracts:

Notice. *Any holder of this consumer credit contract is subject to all claims and defenses which the debtor could assert against the seller of the goods or services obtained pursuant hereto or with the proceeds hereof. Recovery hereunder by the debtor shall not exceed amounts paid by the debtor hereunder.*

A consumer creditor may assert the FTC rule to prevent enforcement of a note that arose from a covered transaction. The FTC can impose monetary fines for violations.

▶ DISCHARGE

discharge
Actions or events that relieve certain parties from liability on negotiable instruments. There are three methods of discharge: (1) payment of the instrument; (2) cancellation; and (3) impairment of the right of recourse.

The UCC specifies when and how certain parties are **discharged** (relieved) from liability on negotiable instruments. Generally, all parties to a negotiable instrument are discharged from liability if (1) the party primarily liable on the instrument pays it in full to the holder of the instrument or (2) a drawee in good faith pays an unaccepted draft or check in full to the holder. When a party other than a primary obligor (e.g., an indorser) pays a negotiable instrument, that party and all subsequent parties to the instrument are discharged from liability [UCC 3-602].

The holder of a negotiable instrument can discharge the liability of any party to the instrument by **cancellation** [UCC 3-604]. Cancellation can be accomplished by (1) any manner apparent on the face of the instrument or the indorsement (e.g., writing *canceled* on the instrument) or (2) destruction or mutilation of a negotiable instrument with the intent of eliminating the obligation.

Intentionally striking out the signature of an indorser cancels that party's liability on the instrument and the liability of all subsequent indorsers. Prior indorsers are not discharged from liability. The instrument is not canceled if it is destroyed or mutilated by accident or by an unauthorized third party. The holder can bring suit to enforce the destroyed or mutilated instrument.

impairment of right of recourse
A situation in which certain parties (holders, indorsers, accommodation parties) are discharged from liability on an instrument if the holder (1) releases an obligor from liability or (2) surrenders collateral without the consent of the parties who would benefit by it.

A party to a negotiable instrument sometimes posts collateral as security for the payment of the obligation. Other parties (e.g., holders, indorsers, accommodation parties) look to the credit standing of the party primarily liable on the instrument, the collateral (if any) that is posted, and the liability of secondary parties for the payment of the instrument when it is due. A holder owes a duty not to impair the rights of others when seeking recourse against the liable parties or the collateral. Thus, a holder who either (1) releases an obligor from liability or (2) surrenders the collateral without the consent of the parties who would benefit thereby discharges those parties from their obligation on the instrument [UCC 3-605(e)]. This discharge is called **impairment of the right of recourse**.

TEST REVIEW TERMS AND CONCEPTS

Accommodation party
Agent
Breach of contract
Cancellation
Defenses
Discharge
Discharge in bankruptcy
Extreme duress
Federal Trade Commission rule (FTC rule)
Fictitious payee rule
Forged indorsement

Forgery
Fraud in the inception (fraud in the factum or fraud in the execution)
Fraud in the inducement
Guarantee of collection
Guarantee of payment
Illegality
Impairment of the right of recourse
Implied warranty
Imposter rule

Material alteration
Mental incompetence
Minority
Notice of dishonor
Personal defense
Presentment
Presentment warranty
Primary liability
Principal
Qualified indorser
Secondary liability
Signature

Signature liability (contract liability)
Signer
Transfer
Transfer warranty
Unauthorized signature
Universal defense (real defense)
Unqualified indorser
Warranty liability

CASE PROBLEMS

24.1 Principal's Liability John Smith was the corporate secretary for Carriage House Mobile Homes, Inc. (Carriage House). Smith signed a series of checks totaling $13,900 made payable to Danube Carpet Mills (Danube). The checks were in payment for carpet ordered by Carriage House. Each check was signed in the following manner: "Carriage House Mobile homes, Inc., General Account, By: /s/John Smith." When Danube presented the checks for payment to the drawee bank, the First State Bank of Phil Campbell, Alabama (First State Bank), payment was refused. The reason for the refusal was that the checks were drawn against uncollected funds. The holder of the checks, Southeastern Financial Corporation, sued Smith and Carriage House to recover the $13,900. Who is liable on the checks? *Southeastern Financial Corporation v. Smith*, 397 F.Supp. 649, **Web** 1975 U.S. Dist. Lexis 12624 (United States District Court for the District of Alabama)

24.2 Drawer's Liability Carlisle Distributing Company, Inc. (Carlisle), owed William Paladino $10,000. To pay this debt, Carlisle delivered a $10,000 check drawn on an Arkansas bank made payable to Paladino. Paladino indorsed the check and delivered it to Wildman Stores, Inc. (Wildman), as security for an $8,000 loan he had received from that company. Seventeen months after receiving the check, Wildman presented it for payment at the bank upon which it had been drawn. The payer bank dishonored the check due to insufficient funds. Wildman informed Carlisle of the dishonor and demanded payment of the $10,000. Carlisle refused Wildman's demand. Wildman sued Carlisle to collect the $10,000. The statute of limitations for enforcing a negotiable instrument in Arkansas is five years. Who wins? *Wildman Stores, Inc. v. Carlisle Distributing Co., Inc.*, 15 Ark.App. 11, 688 S.W.2d 748, **Web** 1985 Ark.App. Lexis 1926 (Court of Appeals of Arkansas)

24.3 Maker's Liability James Wright (Wright) met with Jones, the president of The Community Bank (Community Bank), to request a loan of $7,500. Because Wright was already obligated on several existing loans, he was informed that his request would have to be reviewed by the bank's loan committee. Jones suggested that this delay could be avoided if the loan were made to Mrs. Wright. Wright asked his wife to go to the bank and "indorse" a note for him. Mrs. Wright went to the bank and spoke to Jones. Although she claims that Jones told her that she was merely indorsing the note, the language of the note clearly indicated that she would be liable in the case of default. Mrs. Wright signed the instrument in its lower-right corner. Wright did not sign the instrument. The $7,500 was deposited directly into Wright's business account. The Wrights were subsequently separated. Following the separation, Mrs. Wright received notice that she was in default on the note. The notice indicated that she was solely obligated to repay the instrument. Is Mrs. Wright obligated to repay the note? *The Community Bank v. Wright*, 221 Va. 172, 267 S.E.2d 158, **Web** 1980 Va. Lexis 229 (Supreme Court of Virginia)

24.4 Accommodation Party Dr. Michael P. Cooper and his wife, Georgia, moved to Oakley, Kansas. Dr. Cooper was a chiropractor and intended to establish a practice in Oakley. In order to obtain funds to purchase equipment and remodel an office, Dr. Cooper approached the Farmers Bank of Oakley (Farmers Bank). Farmers Bank agreed to loan Cooper $5,000 if the bank received some sort of security for the money. Dr. Cooper offered professional equipment, household items, and his automobile as collateral. The president of Farmers Bank decided that these items were not enough to secure the loan completely. When Dr. Cooper learned of the bank's decision, he asked his father, Paul A. Cooper, to cosign the loan. Paul Cooper agreed to do so, and a promissory note was executed to the bank. The note was signed by Michael P. Cooper, Georgia

Cooper, and Paul A. Cooper. When the note was in default, the bank sued Paul A. Cooper to recover on the note. Who wins? *Farmers State Bank of Oakley v. Cooper*, 227 Kan. 547, 608 P.2d 929, **Web** 1980 Kan. Lexis 262 (Supreme Court of Kansas)

24.5 Transfer Warranty   David M. Fox was a distributor of tools manufactured and sold by Matco Tools Corporation (Matco). Cox purchased tools from Matco, using a credit line that he repaid as the tools were sold. The credit line was secured by Cox's Matco tool inventory. In order to expedite payment on Cox's line of credit, Matco decided to authorize Cox to deposit any customer checks that were made payable to "Matco Tools" or "Matco" into Cox's own account. Matco's controller sent Cox's bank, Pontiac State Bank (Pontiac), a letter stating that Cox was authorized to make such deposits. Several years later, some Matco tools were stolen from Cox's inventory. The Travelers Indemnity Company (Travelers), which insured Cox against such a loss, sent Cox a settlement check in the amount of $24,960. The check was made payable to "David M. Cox and Matco Tool Co." Cox indorsed the check and deposited it in his account at Pontiac. Pontiac forwarded the check through the banking system for payment by the drawee bank. Cox never paid Matco for the destroyed tools. Matco sued Pontiac for accepting the check without the proper indorsements. Is Pontiac liable? *Matco Tools Corporation v. Pontiac State Bank.* 614 F.Supp. 1059, **Web** 1985 U.S. Dist. Lexis 17234 (United States District Court for the Eastern District of Michigan)

24.6 Presentment Warranty   John Waddell Construction Company (Waddell) maintained a checking account at the Longview Bank & Trust Company (Longview Bank). Waddell drafted a check from this account, made payable to two payees, Engineered Metal Works (Metal Works) and E. G. Smith Construction (Smith Construction). The check was sent to Metal Works, which promptly indorsed the check and presented it to the First National Bank of Azle (Bank of Azle) for payment. The Bank of Azle accepted the check with only Metal Works's indorsement and credited Metal Works's account. The Bank of Azle subsequently presented the check to Longview Bank through the Federal Reserve System. Longview Bank accepted and paid the check. When Waddell received the check along with its monthly checking statements from Longview Bank, a company employee noticed the missing indorsement and notified Longview Bank. Longview Bank returned the check to the Bank of Azle, and the Bank of Azle's account was debited the amount of the check at the Federal Reserve. Has the Bank of Azle breached its warranty of good title? *Longview Bank & Trust Company v. First National Bank of Azle*, 750 S.W.2d 297, **Web** 1988 Tex.App. Lexis 1377 (Court of Appeals of Texas)

24.7 Authorized Agent's Liability   Richard G. Lee was the president of Village Homes, Inc. (Village Homes). Village Homes had several loans from Farmers & Merchants National Bank of Hattan, North Dakota (Farmers Bank), that were in default. Lee and Farmers Bank worked out an arrangement to consolidate the delinquent loans and replace them with a new loan. The new loan would be secured by a promissory note. The parties drafted a note in the amount of $85,000, with a 17 percent annual interest rate. Lee signed the note without indicating that he was signing as an agent of Village Homes. The name "Village Homes, Inc." did not appear on the note. Six months after the note was signed, Village Homes defaulted on it. Farmers Bank sued Lee, seeking to hold him personally liable for the note. Who wins? *Farmers & Merchants National Bank of Hattan, North Dakota v. Lee*, 333 N.W.2d 792, **Web** 1983 N.D. Lexis 289 (Supreme Court of North Dakota)

24.8 Liability of Accommodation Maker   John Valenti wanted to operate an Amoco service station. He contracted with American Oil Company (Amoco), the licensor of Amoco service stations, to lease a service station, and he became a dealer of Amoco products. The documents that made up the lease agreement included a promissory note and guaranty. Because Valenti had no established credit history, Amoco required that his father be a cosigner. Both Valentis signed the lease and note. After about one year, the younger Valenti abandoned the operation. Amoco sued both Valentis to recover on the note and guaranty. The suit against the son was dropped when Amoco learned that he had no assets from which to satisfy a judgment. The father claimed that Amoco could not go after him because it was not suing his son. Who wins? *American Oil Company v. Valenti*, 179 Conn. 349, 426 A.2d 305, **Web** 1979 Conn. Lexis 973 (Supreme Court of Connecticut)

24.9 Imposter Rule   Allan Q. Mowatt was employed as a bookkeeper at the law firm of McCarthy, Kenney & Reidy, P.C. The law firm maintained a primary checking account at First National Bank of Boston (Bank of Boston) and two smaller accounts at other banks to pay operating expenses. One of the law firm's secondary accounts, with Union Bank of Lowell, was under the name Clement McCarthy, the name of the firm's senior partner. It was funded by checks drawn on the Bank of Boston account and payable to "Clement McCarthy." The checks used to fund the secondary account were signed by any of four attorneys who had check-writing authority. When either of the two accounts was running low, Mowatt would make a check payable to "Clement McCarthy" and have it signed by one of the authorized attorneys. In addition to drawing checks needed to fund the secondary account, Mowatt began making out extra checks on the Bank of Boston account payable to Clement McCarthy. Mowatt would explain that the extra checks were needed to maintain funds in the secondary accounts. Mowatt then forged the indorsement of Clement McCarthy to the extra checks and deposited them into his own bank account. Who is liable for the loss caused by this forgery? *McCarthy, Kenney & Reidy, P.C. v. First National Bank of Boston*, 402 Mass. 630, 524 N.E.2d 390, **Web** 1988 Mass. Lexis. 173 (Supreme Judicial Court of Massachusetts)

24.10 Fraud in the Inception   Marvin L. Rose was an experienced real estate developer. One of his projects was Rosewood, a tract of land located in Illinois. To finance this project, Rose and his wife obtained two loans from Belleville National Bank for the aggregate amount of $879,000. The Roses executed promissory notes to the bank for each loan. The Roses claimed that officers of the bank led them to believe that the two loans were five-year-term notes with fixed interest rates. Despite this, each note stipulated that it was payable "on demand or if no demand be made, due and payable five (5) years after date." The Roses claimed that they were not aware of this language because they did not read the documents. A year and a half after the notes were executed, the bank informed the Roses that they must renew the loans, or the notes would be called. The Roses claimed that their signatures were obtained by fraud in the inception because they thought they were signing term notes and not demand notes. Did the Roses act ethically in alleging that the demand note should not be enforced against them because they had not read the note? Who wins? *Belleville National Bank v. Rose*, 456 N.E.2d 281, **Web** 1983 Ill.App. Lexis 2435 (Illinois Appellate Court.)

BUSINESS ETHICS CASES

24.11 Business Ethics   John Wade was employed by Mike Fazzari. Fazzari was an immigrant who was unable to speak or read English. Wade prepared a promissory note in the amount of $400. The instrument was payable at the Glen National Bank, Watkins Glen, New York. Wade took the note to Fazzari and told him that the document was a statement of wages earned by Wade during the course of his employment. Fazzari signed the instrument after Wade told him it was necessary for income tax purposes. Fazzari was not in debt to Wade, and there was no consideration given for the note. Four months later, the note was presented to the First National Bank of Odessa by Wellington Doane, a customer of the bank and an indorsee of the payee, Wade. Doane indorsed the check in blank and accepted a $400 cashier's check in exchange for the note. Fazzari and Glen National Bank refused payment of the note. Did Wade act ethically in this case? Can the First National Bank of Odessa enforce payment of the note as a holder in due course? *First National Bank of Odessa v. Fazzari*, 10 N.Y.2d 394, 179 N.E.2d 493, 223 N.Y.S. 2d 483, **Web** 1961 N.Y. Lexis 857 (Court of Appeals of New York)

24.12 Business Ethics   J. H. Thompson went to the Central Motor Company (Central), an automobile dealership, to purchase a car. With the assistance of Central's sales manager, Ed Boles, Thompson selected an automobile. Boles drew up a loan agreement that stipulated 35 monthly installments and a final installment of $5,265. Under this agreement, Thompson would be charged an annual interest rate of 8 percent. Boles assured Thompson that when the $5,265 installment became due, he would be allowed to sign a second note to cover that amount. Thompson was told that the interest rate on this second note would also be 8 percent. With this assurance, Thompson signed the original loan agreement and note and made all the payments except the final one. When Thompson went to Central to sign the second note, he was told that the interest rate on the second installment note would be 12 percent, not 8 percent. Thompson refused to sign the second note or make the balloon payment on the original note. Instead, he returned the car. Did Central act ethically in this case? Central was able to sell the car, but it sued Thompson to recover a deficiency judgment. Who wins? *Central Motor Company v. J.H. Thompson*, 465 S.W.2d 405, **Web** 1971 Tex.App. Lexis 2634 (Court of Civil Appeals of Texas)

24.13 Business Ethics   Warren and Kristina Mahaffey were approached by a salesman from the Five Star Solar Screens Company (Five Star). The salesman offered to install insulation in their home at a cost of $5,289. After being told that the insulation would reduce their heating bills by 50 percent, the Mahaffeys agreed to the purchase. To pay for the work, the Mahaffeys executed a note promising to pay the purchase price with interest, in installments. The note, which was secured by a deed of trust on the Mahaffeys' home, contained the following language: "Notice: Any holder of this consumer credit contract is subject to all claims and defenses which the debtor could assert against the seller of goods or services obtained pursuant hereto or with the proceeds thereof." Several days after Five Star finished working at the home, it sold the installment note to Mortgage Finance Corporation (Mortgage Finance).

There were major defects in the way the insulation was installed in the Mahaffeys' home. Large holes were left in the walls, and heater blankets and roof fans were never delivered, as called for in the purchase contract. Because of these defects, the Mahaffeys refused to make the payments due on the note. Mortgage Finance instituted foreclosure proceedings to collect the money owed. The Mahaffeys alleged that the Federal Trade Commission rule protects them and allows them to assert the defense of breach of contract by Five Star against the enforcement of the note by Mortgage Finance. Did Five Star Solar Screens Company act ethically in this case? Can the Mahaffeys successfully assert the defense of breach of contract by Five Star against the enforcement of the note by Mortgage Finance? *Mahaffey v. Investor's National Security Company*, 103 Nev. 615, 747 P.2d 890, **Web** 1987 Nev. Lexis 1875 (Supreme Court of Nevada)

25 | CHECKS, THE BANKING SYSTEM, AND E-MONEY

▲ **Hong Kong** *Hong Kong is one of the world's great banking centers. Hong Kong was a Crown colony and a territory of the United Kingdom until it was turned over to the People's Republic of China (PRC) in 1997. Hong Kong is home to large domestic banks and offices of foreign banks from around the world. Banks in Honk Kong provide a wide range of financial services, including retail banking, deposit taking, trade financing, interbank wholesale transfers, and foreign exchange.*

CHAPTER OBJECTIVES

After studying this chapter, you should be able to:

1. Describe the difference between certified and cashier's checks.
2. Describe the system of processing and collecting checks through the banking system.
3. Identify when a bank engages in a wrongful dishonor of a check.
4. Describe electronic banking and e-money.
5. Define *commercial wire transfer* and describe the use of wire transfers in commerce.

CHAPTER CONTENTS

▶ **INTRODUCTION TO CHECKS, BANKING SYSTEM, AND E-MONEY**

▶ **THE BANK–CUSTOMER RELATIONSHIP**

Landmark Law · *Uniform Commercial Code (UCC) Articles Related to Checks and Banking*

▶ **ORDINARY CHECKS**

"Bankers have no right to establish a customary law among themselves, at the expense of other men."

—Justice Foster
Hankey v. Trotman (1746)

▶ INTRODUCTION TO CHECKS, BANKING SYSTEM, AND E-MONEY

Checks are the most common form of negotiable instrument used in this country. More than 70 billion checks are written annually. Checks act both as substitutes for money and as record-keeping devices, but they do not serve a credit function. There are many special forms of checks, including certified checks and cashier's checks. The banking system, with the assistance of the Federal Reserve System, processes and honors checks. Sometimes there are problems, such as forged or altered checks.

This chapter discusses the various forms of checks, the procedure for paying and collecting on checks through the banking system, the collection process for checks, electronic funds transfers, e-banking and e-money.

Money is a good servant, but a dangerous master.

Dominique Bouhours

▶ THE BANK–CUSTOMER RELATIONSHIP

When a customer makes a deposit into a bank, a **creditor–debtor relationship** is formed. The customer is the creditor, and the bank is the debtor. In effect, the customer is loaning money to the bank.

A **principal–agent relationship** is created if (1) the deposit is a check that the bank must collect for the customer or (2) the customer writes a check against his or her account. The customer is the principal, and the bank is the agent. The bank is obligated to follow the customer's order to collect or pay the check. The rights and duties of a bank and a checking account customer are contractual. The signature card and other bank documents signed by the customer form the basis of the contract.

creditor–debtor relationship
A relationship that is created when a customer deposits money into the bank; the customer is the creditor, and the bank is the debtor.

Article 3 of the UCC
An article of the UCC that sets forth the requirements for negotiable instruments, including checks.

Revised Article 3
A revision of Article 3 of the UCC.

LANDMARK LAW

Uniform Commercial Code (UCC) Articles Related to Checks and Banking

Various articles of the Uniform Commercial Code (UCC) establish rules for creating, collecting, and enforcing checks and wire transfers. These articles are:

· **Article 3 (Commercial Paper)** establishes the requirements for negotiable instruments. Because a check is a negotiable instrument, the provisions of

Article 3 apply. **Revised Article 3 (Negotiable Instruments)** was promulgated in 1990. The provisions of Revised Article 3 serve as the basis of the discussion of Article 3 in this chapter.

· **Article 4 (Bank Deposits and Collections)** establishes the rules and principles that regulate bank deposit and collection procedures for checking accounts offered by commercial banks, NOW (negotiable order of withdrawal) accounts, and other check-like accounts offered by savings and loan associations, savings banks, credit unions, and other financial institutions. Article 4 controls when the provisions of Articles 3 and 4 conflict [UCC 4-102(a)]. Article 4 was substantially amended in 1990. The amended Article 4 serves as the basis of the discussion of Article 4 in this chapter.

· **Article 4A (Funds Transfers)** establishes rules that regulate the creation and collection of and liability for wire transfers. Article 4A was added to the UCC in 1989.

Article 4 of the UCC
An article of the UCC that establishes the rules and principles that regulate bank deposit and collection procedures.

Article 4A of the UCC
An article of the UCC that establishes rules regulating the creation and collection of and liability for wire transfers.

check
An order by a drawer to a drawee bank to pay a specified sum of money from the drawer's checking account to the named payee (or holder).

drawer of a check
The checking account holder and writer of a check.

drawee of a check
The bank where a check drawer has his or her account.

payee of a check
The party to whom a check is written.

▶ ORDINARY CHECKS

Most adults and businesses have at least one checking account at a bank. A customer opens a checking account by going to a bank, completing the necessary forms (including a signature card), and making a **deposit** to the account. The bank issues checks to the customer. The customer then uses the checks to purchase goods and services.

Parties to a Check

UCC 3-104(f) defines a **check** as an order by the drawer to the drawee bank to pay a specified sum of money from the drawer's checking account to the named payee (or holder). There are three parties to an **ordinary check**:

1. **Drawer.** The **drawer** is the customer who maintains the checking account and writes (draws) checks against the account.
2. **Drawee (or payer bank).** The **drawee** is the bank on which a check is drawn.
3. **Payee.** The **payee** is the party to whom a check is written.

Example The Kneadery Restaurant, Inc., has a checking account at Mountain Bank. Mike Mortin, the president of the Kneadery Restaurant writes a check for $1,000 from this account, payable to Sun Valley Bakery, to pay for food supplies. The Kneadery Restaurant is the drawer, Mountain Bank is the drawee, and Sun Valley Bakery is the payee. Mountain Bank is obligated to pay the check when it is presented for payment if the Kneadery Restaurant's checking account has sufficient funds to cover the amount of the check at the time of presentment. (See Exhibit 25.1.)

▶ **Exhibit 25.1 ORDINARY CHECK**

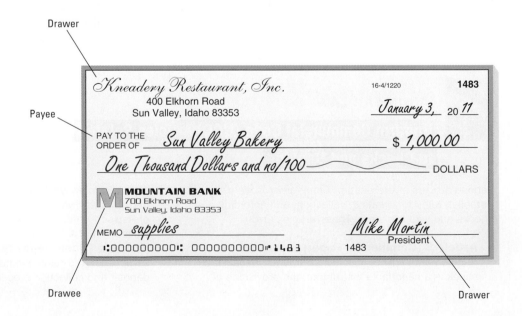

Indorsement of a Check

The payee is the *holder* of a check. As such, the payee has the right to either (1) demand payment of the check or (2) **indorse** the check to another party by signing the back of the check. This latter action is called **indorsement** of a check. The payee is the **indorser**, and the person to whom the check is indorsed is the **indorsee**. The indorsee in turn becomes a holder who can either demand payment of the check or indorse it to yet another party. Any subsequent holder can demand payment of the check or further transfer the check [UCC 3-204(a)].

Example Referring to the previous example, upon receipt of the check, the payee, Sun Valley Bakery, may either (1) present the Kneadery Restaurant's check to Mountain Bank for payment or (2) indorse the check to another party. Assume that Sun Valley Bakery indorses the check to Flour Company by signing the back of the check "Pay to the order of Flour Company, Sun Valley Bakery, John Baker, president" in payment for flour purchased from the Flour Company; Sun Valley Bakery is the indorser, and the Flour Company is the indorsee. The Flour Company may either present the check to Mountain Bank for payment or indorse it to another party, and so on.

▶ SPECIAL TYPES OF CHECKS

If a payee fears there may be insufficient funds in the drawer's account to pay a check when it is presented for payment or that the drawer has stopped payment of the check, the payee may be unwilling to accept an ordinary check from the drawer. However, the payee might be willing to accept a **bank check**—that is, a certified check or a cashier's check. These types of checks are usually considered "as good as cash" because the bank is solely or primarily liable for payment. These forms of checks are discussed in the following paragraphs.

Certified Checks

When a bank **certifies a check**, it agrees in advance (1) to accept the check when it is presented for payment and (2) to pay the check out of funds set aside from the customer's account and either placed in a special certified check account or held in the customer's account. Certified checks do not become stale. Thus, they are payable at any time from the date they are issued.

A check is a **certified check** when the bank writes or stamps the word *certified* across the face of an ordinary check. The certification should also contain the date and the amount being certified and the name and title of the person at the bank who certifies the check. Note that a bank is not obligated to certify a check. A bank's refusal to do so is not a dishonor of a check [UCC 3-409(d)]. The drawer cannot stop payment on a certified check. (See Exhibit 25.2.)

Cashier's Checks

A person can purchase a **cashier's check** from a bank by paying the bank the amount of the check plus a fee for issuing the check. Usually, a specific payee is named. The purchaser does not have to have a checking account at the bank. The check is a noncancellable negotiable instrument upon issue.

indorsement of a check
A payee's signing of the back of a check in order to turn it over to another party.

indorser of a check
A payee who indorses a check to another party.

indorsee of a check
A party to whom a check is indorsed.

bank check
A certified check or a cashier's check, the payment for which a bank is solely or primarily liable.

certification
A process in which the accepting bank writes or stamps the word *certified* on an ordinary check of an account holder and sets aside funds from that account to pay the check.

certified check
A type of check for which a bank agrees in advance (*certifies*) to accept the check when it is presented for payment.

cashier's check
A check issued by a bank for which the customer has paid the bank the amount of the check and a fee. The bank guarantees payment of the check.

▶ **Exhibit 25.2 CERTIFIED CHECK**

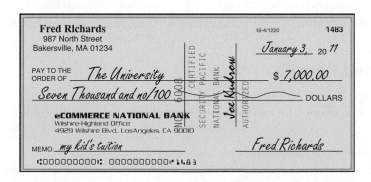

A cashier's check is a two-party check for which (1) the issuing bank serves as both the drawer and the drawee and (2) the holder serves as payee [UCC 3-104(g)]. The bank, which has been paid for the check, guarantees its payment. When the check is presented for payment, the bank debits its own account [UCC 3-412]. (See Exhibit 25.3.)

▶ **Exhibit 25.3 CASHIER'S CHECK**

eCOMMERCE NATIONAL BANK		10341504	16-4/1220
Bank Check Accounting Services			
Brea, California 92621-6398	OFFICE NUMBER		
	142	DATE: January 3, 2011	

PAY TO THE ORDER OF * * * * * * * * * * HELEN PITTS * * * * * * * * * * $ 1,000.00

EXACTLY 1,000 AND 00

($100,000 AND OVER REQUIRES TWO SIGNATURES)   **DOLLARS**

CASHIER'S CHECK

Dg Lotten   *Kerry Fields*
AUTHORIZED SIGNATURE   AUTHORIZED SIGNATURE

⑈ ⑉0341504⑈ ⑊⑉22000043⑊928⑈917016⑈

An obligated bank that wrongfully refuses to pay a cashier's check is liable to the person who asserts the right to enforce the check for expenses, loss of interest resulting from non-payment, and consequential damages [UCC 3-411].

▶ HONORING CHECKS

honor
To pay a drawer's properly drawn check.

When a customer opens a checking account at a bank, the customer impliedly agrees to keep sufficient funds in the account to pay any checks written against it. Thus, when the drawee bank receives a properly drawn and payable check, the bank is under a duty to **honor** the check and charge (debit) the drawer's account the amount of the check if there are sufficient funds in the customer's checking account at the bank [UCC 4-401(a)].

Stale Checks

stale check
A check that has been outstanding for more than six months.

Occasionally, a payee or another holder in possession of a check fails to present the check immediately to the payer bank for payment. A check that has been outstanding for more than six months is considered stale, and the bank is under no obligation to pay it. A bank that pays a **stale check** in good faith may charge the drawer's account [UCC 4-404].

Incomplete Checks

Drawers sometimes write checks that omit certain information, such as the amount of the check or the payee's name, either on purpose or by mistake. In such cases, the payee or any holder can complete the check, and the payer bank that in good faith makes payment on the completed check can charge the customer's account the amount of the completed check unless it has notice that the completion was improper [UCC 3-407(c), 4-401(d)(2)]. The UCC places the risk of loss of an incomplete item on the drawer.

The love of money is the root of all evil.

I Timothy 6:10
The Bible

Example Richard, who owes Sarah $500, draws a check payable to Sarah on his checking account at City Bank. Richard signs the check but leaves the amount blank. Sarah fraudulently fills in $1,000 and presents the check to City Bank, which pays it. City Bank can charge Richard's account $1,000. Richard's only recourse is to sue Sarah.

Postdated Checks

postdated check
A check that a drawer does not want cashed until sometime in the future.

On occasion, a drawer of a check does not want a check he or she writes to be cashed until sometime in the future. This is called a **postdated check**. Under UCC 4-401(c), to require a bank to abide by a postdated check, the drawer must take the following steps:

1. The drawer must postdate the check to some date in the future.
2. The drawer must give *separate written notice* to the bank, describing the check with reasonable certainty and notifying the bank not to pay the check until the date on the check.

If these steps are taken and the bank pays the check before its date, the bank is liable to the drawer for any losses resulting from its act.

Stop-Payment Orders

A **stop-payment order** is an order by a drawer of a check to the payer bank not to pay or certify a check. Only the drawer can order a stop-payment order. A stop-payment order can be given orally or in writing. An *oral order* is binding on the bank for only 14 calendar days, unless confirmed in writing during this time. A *written order* is effective for six months. It can be renewed in writing for additional six-month periods [UCC 4-403]. If the payer bank fails to honor a valid stop-payment order, it must recredit the customer's account.

stop-payment order
An order by a drawer of a check to the payer bank not to pay or certify a check.

Overdrafts

If the drawer does not have enough money in his or her account when a properly payable check is presented for payment, the payer bank can either (1) dishonor the check or (2) honor the check and create an overdraft in the drawer's account [UCC 4-401(a)]. The bank notifies the drawer of the dishonor and returns the check to the holder, marked **insufficient funds**. The holder often resubmits the check to the bank, hoping that the drawer has deposited more money into the account and the check will clear. If the check does not clear, the holder's recourse is against the drawer of the check.

If the bank chooses to pay the check even though there are insufficient funds in the drawer's account, it can later charge the drawer's account for the amount of the **overdraft** [UCC 4-401(a)] because there is an implied promise that the drawer will reimburse the bank for paying checks the drawer orders the bank to pay. If the drawer does not fulfill this commitment, the bank can sue him or her to recover payment for the overdrafts and overdraft fees. Many banks offer optional expressly agreed-upon overdraft protection to their customers.

overdraft
The amount of money a drawer owes a bank after it has paid a check despite the drawer's account having insufficient funds.

Wrongful Dishonor

If a bank does not honor a check when there are sufficient funds in the drawer's account to pay a properly payable check, it is liable for **wrongful dishonor**. The payer bank is liable to the drawer for damages proximately caused by the wrongful dishonor as well as for consequential damages, damages caused by criminal prosecution, and such. A payee or holder cannot sue the bank for damages caused by the wrongful dishonor of a drawer's check. The only recourse for the payee or holder is to sue the drawer to recover the amount of the check [UCC 4-402].

wrongful dishonor
A situation in which there are sufficient funds in a drawer's account to pay a properly payable check, but the bank does not do so.

LANDMARK LAW
Federal Currency Reporting Law

The **Federal Currency Reporting Law** requires financial institutions and other entities (such as retailers, car and boat dealers, antiques dealers, jewelers, travel agencies, and real estate brokers) to file a **Currency Transaction Report (CTR)** with the Internal Revenue Service (IRS), reporting:

• The receipt in a single transaction or a series of related transactions of cash in an amount greater than $10,000. "Cash" is not limited to currency but includes cashier's checks, bank drafts, traveler's checks, and money orders (but not ordinary checks) [26 U.S.C. Section 60501].

• Suspected criminal activity by bank customers involving a financial transaction of $1,000 or more in funds [12 C.F.R. Section 21.11(b)(3)].

The law also stipulates that it is a crime to structure or assist in structuring any transaction for the purpose of evading these reporting requirements [31 U.S.C. Section 5324]. Financial institutions and entities may be fined for negligent violations of the currency reporting requirements. Fines may be levied for a pattern of negligent violations. Willful failure to file reports may subject the violator to civil money penalties, charges of aiding and abetting the criminal activity, and prosecution for violating money-laundering statutes.

India *India has one of the fastest-growing economies in the world. However, this fast-growing economy is hindered by an antiquated banking system. True to its socialist roots, most of the banking system in India is bureaucratic and inefficient state-controlled banks. Some private banks operate in India. Only one bank—the State Bank of India—is among the top 250 banks in the world. Large foreign banks have entered the market and are now providing sophisticated banking and financial services to growing service and production sectors. The government of India has promised to overhaul its banking system so that it is comparable to its growing business sector and to support the country's economic growth.*

▶ FORGED SIGNATURES AND ALTERED CHECKS

Major problems associated with checks are that (1) signatures are sometimes forged and (2) a check itself may have been altered prior to presentment for payment. The UCC rules that apply to these situations are discussed in the following paragraphs. These rules apply to all types of negotiable instruments but are particularly important concerning checks.

Forged Signature of the Drawer

When a check is presented to the payer bank for payment, the bank is under a duty to verify the drawer's signature. This is usually done by matching the signature on the signature card on file at the bank to the signature on the check.

forged instrument
A check with a forged drawer's signature on it.

A check with a *forged drawer's signature* is called a **forged instrument**. A forged signature is wholly inoperative as the signature of the drawer. The check is not properly payable because it does not contain an order of the drawer. The payer bank cannot charge the customer's account if it pays a check over the forged signature. If the bank has charged the customer's account, it must recredit the account, and the forged check must be dishonored [UCC 3-401].

The bank can recover from the party who presented the check to it for payment only if that party had knowledge that the signature of the drawer on the check was unauthorized [UCC 3-417(a)(3)]. The forger is liable on the check because the forged signature acts as the forger's signature [UCC 3-403(a)]. Although the payer bank can sue the forger, the forger usually cannot be found or is judgment-proof.

Example Gregory has a checking account at Country Bank. Mildred steals one of Gregory's checks, completes it by writing in $10,000 as the amount of the check, adding her name as the payee, and forges Gregory's signature. Mildred indorses the check to Sam, who knows that Gregory's signature has been forged. Sam indorses the check to Barbara, who is innocent and does not know of the forgery. Barbara presents the check to Country Bank, the payer bank, which pays the check. Country Bank may recover from the original forger, Mildred, and from Sam, who knew of the forgery. It cannot recover from Barbara because she did not have knowledge of the forgery.

Altered Checks

Sometimes a check is altered before it is presented for payment. This is an unauthorized change in the check that modifies the legal obligation of a party [UCC 3-407(a)]. The payer bank can dishonor an **altered check** if it discovers the alteration. If the payer bank pays the altered check, it can charge the drawer's account for the **original tenor** of the check but not the altered amount [UCC 3-407(c), 4-401(d)(1)].

If the payer bank has paid the altered amount, it can recover the difference between the altered amount and the original tenor from the party who presented the altered check for payment. This is because the presenter of the check for payment and each prior transferor *warrant* that the check has not been altered [UCC 3-417(a)(2)]. This is called the **presentment warranty**. If there has been an alteration, each party in the chain of collection can recover from the preceding transferor based on a breach of this warranty. The ultimate loss usually falls on the party that first paid the altered check because that party was in the best position to identify the alteration. The forger is liable for the difference between the original tenor and the altered amount—if he or she can be found and is not judgment-proof.

Example Father draws a $100 check on City Bank made payable to his daughter. The daughter alters the check to read "$1,000" and cashes the check at a liquor store. The liquor store presents the check for payment to City Bank. City Bank pays the check. Father is liable only for the original tenor of the check ($100), and City Bank can charge the father's account this amount. City Bank is liable for the $900 difference, but it can recover this amount from the liquor store for breach of presentment warranty. This is because the liquor store was in the best position to identify the alteration. The liquor store can seek to recover the $900 from the daughter.

One-Year Rule

The drawer's failure to report a forged or altered check to the bank within *one year* of receiving the bank statement and canceled checks containing it relieves the bank of any liability for paying the instrument [UCC 4-406(3)]. Thus, the payer bank is not required after this time to recredit the customer's account for the amount of the forged or altered check, even if the customer later discovers the forgery or alteration.

Series of Forgeries

If the same wrongdoer engages in a *series of forgeries* or *alterations* on the same account, the customer must report that to the payer bank within a reasonable period of time, not exceeding 30 days from the date that the bank statement was made available to the customer [UCC 4-406(d)(2)]. The customer's failure to do so discharges the bank from liability on all similar forged or altered checks after this date and prior to notification.

The Federal Bureau of Investigation (FBI) is authorized to investigate forgeries, bank fraud, and other financial crimes.

altered check
A check that has been altered without authorization and thus modifies the legal obligation of a party.

original tenor
The original amount for which the drawer wrote a check.

presentment warranty
A guarantee in which each prior transferor warrants that a check has not been altered.

A banker so very careful to avoid risk would soon have no risk to avoid.

Lord MacNaghten
Bank of England v. Vaglliano Brothers (1891)

In the following case, the court held against a checking account holder that had not reviewed its bank statements in time to catch a series of forgeries by an employee.

CASE 25.1 Bank Statements

Spacemakers of America, Inc. v. SunTrust Bank

271 Ga.App. 335, 609 S.E.2d 683, Web 2005 Ga.App. Lexis 43 (2005)
Court of Appeals of Georgia

"In this case, the undisputed evidence showed that Spacemakers hired as a bookkeeper a twice-convicted embezzler who was on probation, then delegated the entire responsibility of reviewing and reconciling its bank statements to her while failing to provide any oversight on these essential tasks."

—Judge Ellington

Facts

Spacemakers of America, Inc., employed Jenny Triplett as its bookkeeper. Spacemakers did not inquire about any prior criminal record or conduct a criminal background check of Triplett. If it had taken those steps, it would have discovered that Triplett was on probation for 13 counts of forgery and had been convicted of theft by deception. All convictions were the result of Triplett forging checks of previous employers.

Spacemakers hired Triplett as a bookkeeper and delegated to her sole responsibility from maintaining the company's checkbook, reconciling the checkbook with monthly bank statements, and preparing financial reports. Triplett also handled the company's accounts payable and regularly presented checks to Dennis Rose, the president of Spacemakers, so he could sign them.

On January 20, 2000, just weeks after starting her job at Spacemakers, Triplett forged Rose's signature on a check for $3,000 made payable to her husband's company, "Triple M Entertainment Group," which was not a vendor for Spacemakers. By the end of the first full month of employment, Triplett had forged 5 more checks totaling $22,320, all payable to Triple M. Over the next nine months, Triplett forged 59 more checks totaling approximately $475,000. All checks were drawn against Spacemakers's bank account at SunTrust Bank. No one except Triplett reviewed the company's bank statements.

On October 13, 2000, a SunTrust loss prevention employee visually inspected a $30,670 check. She became suspicious of the signature and called Rose. The SunTrust employee faxed a copy of the check to Rose, which was made payable to "Triple M." Rose knew that Triple M was not one of the company's vendors, and a Spacemakers employee reminded Rose that Triplett's husband owned Triple M. Rose immediately called the police, and Triplett was arrested.

Spacemakers sent a letter to SunTrust Bank, demanding that the bank credit $523,106 to its account for the forged checks. The bank refused, contending that Spacemakers's failure to provide the bank with timely notice of the forgeries barred Spacemakers's claim. Spacemakers sued SunTrust for negligence and unauthorized payment of forged items. The trial court granted SunTrust's motion for summary judgment. Spacemakers appealed.

Issue

Did Spacemakers's failure to uncover the forgeries and failure to provide SunTrust with timely notice of the forgeries bar its claim against SunTrust?

Language of the Court

Spacemakers claims the trial court erred in applying Georgia Commercial Code OCGA Section 11-4-406 to the facts of this case. This rule imposes upon a bank customer the duty to promptly examine its monthly statements and notify the bank of any unauthorized transaction. If the customer fails to report the first forged item within 30 days, it is precluded from recovering for that transaction and for any additional items forged by the same wrongdoer. The underlying justification for this provision is simple: one of the most serious consequences of the failure of a customer to timely examine its statement is that it gives the wrongdoer the opportunity to repeat his misdeeds. Clearly, the customer is in the best position to discover and report small forgeries before the same wrongdoer is emboldened and attempts a larger misdeed.

In this case, the undisputed evidence showed that Spacemakers hired as a bookkeeper a twice-convicted embezzler who was on probation, then delegated the entire responsibility of reviewing and reconciling its bank statements to her while failing to provide any oversight on these essential tasks. The bookkeeper started forging checks within weeks of taking control of the company's checkbook and, by the end of January 2000, had forged six checks totaling $25,320. Triplett made all of the checks payable to her husband's company, which had never been a Spacemakers vendor. There is every reason to believe that, if Spacemakers had simply reviewed its bank statement for January 2000, it would have discovered the forgeries. More importantly, it would have been able to timely notify the bank of its discovery and avoided its subsequent losses of almost $475,000. Clearly, Spacemakers' extensive and unnecessary loss due to forgery is precisely the scenario

(case continues)

that the duties created by OCGA Section 11–4–406 were designed to prevent. Accordingly, we find that Spacemakers is precluded as a matter of law from asserting claims based upon the forgeries in this case.

Decision

The court of appeals held that Spacemakers had failed to give timely notice to SunTrust Bank as required by the Georgia Uniform Commercial Code and was therefore barred from recovering the value of the forged checks from SunTrust. The court of appeals affirmed the trial court's grant of summary judgment to SunTrust.

Case Questions

Critical Legal Thinking What is a bank account holder's duty regarding reviewing bank statements? Explain.

Business Ethics Did Triplett act ethically in this case? Would Spacemakers have hired her if it had known her prior history? Should Spacemakers have sued SunTrust to try to recover its losses from the forgeries?

Contemporary Business Could Spacemakers have prevented the forgeries in this case? Explain.

▶ THE COLLECTION PROCESS

A bank is under a duty to accept deposits into a customer's account. This includes collecting checks that are drawn on other banks and made payable or indorsed to the depositor. The collection process, which may involve several banks, is governed by Article 4 of the UCC.

When a payee or holder receives a check, he or she can either go to the drawer's bank (the **payer bank**) and present the check for payment in cash or—as is more common—deposit the check into a bank account at his or her own bank, called the **depository bank**. (The depository bank may also serve as the payer bank if both parties have accounts at the same bank.)

The depository bank must present a check to the payer bank for collection. At this point in the process, the Federal Reserve System (discussed next) and other banks may be used in the collection of a check. The depository bank and these other banks are called **collecting banks**. Banks in the collection process that are not the depository or payer bank are called **intermediary banks**. A bank can have more than one role during the collection process [UCC 4-105]. The check collection process is illustrated in Exhibit 25.4.

payer bank
The bank where the drawer has a checking account and on which a check is drawn.

depository bank
The bank where the payee or holder has an account.

collecting bank
The depository bank and other banks in the collection process (other than the payer bank).

intermediary bank
A bank in the collection process that is not the depository bank or the payer bank.

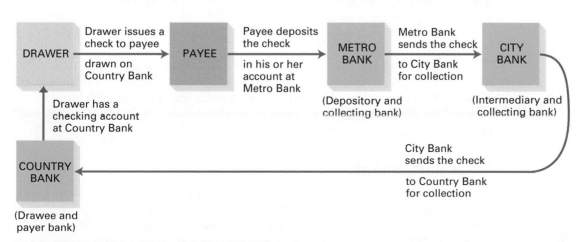

▶ **Exhibit 25.4 CHECK COLLECTION PROCESS**

CONTEMPORARY ENVIRONMENT

The Federal Reserve System

The **Federal Reserve System**, which consists of 12 regional Federal Reserve banks located in different geographical areas of the country, assists banks in the collection of checks. Rather than send a check directly to another bank for collection, member banks may submit paid checks to the Federal Reserve banks for collection.

Most banks in this country have accounts at the regional Federal Reserve banks. The Federal Reserve banks debit and credit the accounts of these banks daily to reflect the collection and payment of checks. Banks pay the Federal Reserve banks a fee for this service. In large urban areas, private clearinghouses may provide similar services [UCC 4-110, 4-213(a)].

Federal Reserve System
A system of 12 regional Federal Reserve banks that assist other banks in the collection of checks.

deferred posting rule
A rule that allows banks to fix an afternoon hour of 2:00 P.M. or later as a cutoff hour for the purpose of processing items.

provisional credit
A situation in which a collecting bank gives credit to a check in the collection process prior to its final settlement. Provisional credits may be reversed if the check does not clear.

final settlement
A situation in which a payer bank (1) pays a check in cash, (2) settles for a check without having a right to revoke the settlement, or (3) fails to dishonor a check within certain statutory time periods.

Deferred Posting

The **deferred posting rule** applies to all banks in the collection process. This rule allows banks to fix an afternoon hour of 2:00 P.M. or later as a cutoff hour for the purpose of processing checks and deposits. Any check or deposit of money received after this cutoff hour is treated as being received on the next banking day [UCC 4-108]. Saturdays, Sundays, and holidays are not banking days unless the bank is open to the public for carrying on substantially all banking functions [UCC 4-104(a)(3)].

Provisional Credits

When a customer deposits a check into a checking account for collection, the depository bank does not have to pay the customer the amount of the check until the check "clears"—that is, until final settlement occurs. The depository bank may **provisionally credit** the customer's account. Each bank in the collection process provisionally credits the account of the prior transferor [UCC 4-201(a)]. If the check is dishonored by the payer bank (e.g., for insufficient funds, a stop-payment order, or a closed account), the check is returned to the payee or holder, and the provisional credits are reversed. The collecting bank must either return the check to the prior transferor or notify that party within a reasonable time that provisional credit is being revoked. If the collecting bank fails to do this, it is liable for any losses caused by its delay [UCC 4-214].

Depository banks often allow their customers to withdraw the funds prior to final settlement. If the bank later learns that a check was dishonored, it can debit the customer's account for the amount withdrawn. If this is not possible (e.g., the payee or holder does not have sufficient funds in his or her account or has closed the account), the depository bank can sue the customer to recover the funds.

Final Settlement

A check is finally paid when the payer bank (1) pays the check in cash, (2) settles for the check without having a right to revoke the settlement, or (3) fails to dishonor the check within certain statutory time periods. These time periods are discussed in the following paragraphs. When a check is finally settled, the provisional credits along the chain of collecting banks "firm up" and become **final settlements** [UCC 4-215(a)].

"On Us" Checks

If the drawer and the payee or holder have accounts at the *same* bank, the depository bank is also the payer bank. The check is called an **"on us" item** when it is presented for payment by the payee or holder. In this case, the bank has until the opening of business on the second banking day following the receipt of the check to dishonor it. If it fails to do so, the check is considered paid. The payee or holder can withdraw the funds at this time [UCC 4-215(e)(2)].

Example Christine and Jim both have checking accounts at Country Bank. On Tuesday morning, Christine deposits a $1,000 check from Jim into her account. Country Bank issues a provisional credit to Christine's account for this amount. On Thursday morning when the bank opens for business, the check is considered honored.

"on us" item
A check that is presented for payment where the depository bank is also the payer bank. That is, the drawer and payee or holder have accounts at the same bank.

"On Them" Checks

If a drawer and a payee or holder have accounts at *different* banks, the payer bank and depository bank are not the same bank. In this case, the check is called an **"on them" item**.

Except for the collecting bank, each bank in the collection process, including the payer bank, must take proper action on an "on them" check prior to its midnight deadline. The **midnight deadline** is the midnight of the next banking day following the banking day on which the bank received an "on them" check for collection [UCC 4-104(a)(10)]. A collecting bank is permitted to act within a reasonably longer time, but the bank then has the burden of establishing the timeliness of its action [UCC 4-202(b)].

This deadline is of particular importance to the payer bank: If the payer bank does not dishonor a check by its midnight deadline, the bank is *accountable* (liable) for the face amount of the check. It does not require that the check be properly payable or not [UCC 4-302(a)].

Example If on Wednesday morning, a payer bank receives an "on them" check drawn on an account at the bank, it has until midnight of the next banking day, Thursday, to dishonor the check. If it does not, the check is considered paid by the bank. This deadline does not apply to "on us" checks, which clear when the bank opens on the second business day following receipt of the checks (unless they are dishonored).

Instead of depositing an "on them" check for collection, a depositor can physically present the check for payment at the payer bank. This is called **presentment across the counter**. In this case, the payer bank has until the end of that banking day to dishonor the check. If it fails to do so, it must pay the check [UCC 4-301(a)].

"on them" item
A check presented for payment by a payee or holder where the depository bank and the payer bank are not the same bank.

midnight deadline
The midnight of the next banking day following the banking day on which the bank received an "on them" check for collection.

presentment across the counter
A situation in which a depositor physically presents a check for payment at the payer bank instead of depositing an "on them" check for collection.

Deposit of Cash

A deposit of cash to an account becomes available for withdrawal at the opening of the next banking day following the deposit [UCC 4-215(a)].

Failure to Examine Bank Statements in a Timely Manner

Ordinarily, banks send their checking account customers monthly statements of account. The canceled checks usually accompany the statement, although banks are not required to send them. If the canceled checks are not sent to the customer, the statement of account must provide sufficient information to allow the customer to identify the checks paid (e.g., check number, amount and date of payment) [UCC 4-406(a)]. In addition, if the checks are not returned to the customer, the bank must retain either the original checks or legible copies for seven years. A customer may request a check or a copy of it during this period [UCC 4-406(b)].

The customer owes a duty to examine the statements (and canceled checks, if received) promptly and with reasonable care to determine whether any payment was not authorized because of alteration of a check or a forged signature. The customer must

A bank is a place that will lend you money if you can prove that you don't need it.

Bob Hope

promptly notify the bank of unauthorized payments [UCC 4-406(c)]. The customer is liable if the payer bank suffers a loss because of the customer's failure to perform these duties [UCC 4-406(d)(1)].

Most banks provide images of checks online.

CONTEMPORARY ENVIRONMENT

FDIC Insurance of Bank Deposits

The **Federal Deposit Insurance Corporation (FDIC)** is a government agency that insures deposits at most banks and savings institutions ("insured bank") in the United States. Each insured bank pays assessed yearly premiums based on the size of its deposits to the FDIC. If an FDIC-insured bank fails and the insured bank does not have sufficient assets to pay its depositors back their money, the FDIC will pay the depositors their lost deposits, up to certain limits.

FDIC insurance covers savings accounts, checking accounts, money market accounts, certificates of deposit, IRAs and retirement accounts, and other types of deposits received at an insured bank. The FDIC does not insure money invested in stocks, bonds, mutual funds, life insurance policies, annuities, and other investment accounts.

FDIC insurance per insured bank is: (1) $250,000 per single account owned by one person, (2) $250,000 per co-owner for joint accounts owned by two or more persons; and (3) $250,000 per corporation, partnership, and unincorporated association accounts.[1] IRAs and retirement accounts are insured up to $250,000 per owner. Accounts at separate banks are each insured to these amounts.

If the FDIC is unable to cover the insured deposits, the *full faith and credit* of the U.S. government backs the FDIC. Thus, if there are major failures of several large banks or many small banks, and the FDIC insurance fund is insufficient to cover all of the depositors' losses, then the U.S. government will pay the depositors the money owed by the FDIC. To show whether it is covered by FDIC insurance, a bank or savings institution will display the official FDIC sign.

► E-BANKING AND E-MONEY

electronic funds transfer system (EFTS)

Computer and electronic technology that makes it possible for banks to offer electronic payment and collection systems to bank customers. E-banking and e-money consists of:

1. Automated teller machines (ATMs)
2. Point-of-sale terminals
3. Direct deposit and withdrawal
4. Online banking
5. Debit cards

Men such as they are, very naturally seek money or power; and power because it is as good as money.

Ralph Waldo Emerson

Computers and electronic technology have made it possible for banks to offer electronic payment and collection systems to bank customers. This technology is collectively referred to as the **electronic funds transfer system (EFTS)**. EFTS is supported by contracts among and between customers, banks, private clearinghouses, and other third parties.

Automated Teller Machine

An **automated teller machine (ATM)** is an electronic machine that is located either on a bank's premises or at some other convenient location, such as a shopping center or super-market. These devices are connected online to the bank's computers. Each bank customer is issued a secret personal identification number (PIN) to access his or her bank accounts through ATMs.

ATMs are commonly used when a bank is not open. They are also used as an alternative means of conducting banking when the bank is open. They are used to withdraw cash from bank accounts, cash checks, make deposits to checking or savings accounts, and make payments owed to the bank.

Point-of-Sale Terminal

Many banks issue **debit cards** to customers. Debit cards replace checks in that customers can use them to make purchases. No credit is extended. Instead, the customer's bank account is immediately debited for the amount of a purchase.

Debit cards can be used at merchants that have **point-of-sale (POS) terminals** at the checkout counters. These terminals are connected online to a bank's computers. To make a purchase, a customer inserts a debit card into the terminal for the amount of the purchase. If there are sufficient funds in the customer's account, the transaction will debit the customer's account and credit the merchant's account for the amount of the purchase. If there are insufficient funds in the customer's account, the purchase is rejected unless the customer has overdraft protection. At many POS terminals, customers can also obtain cash back above the amount of their purchase.

Direct Deposit and Withdrawal

Many banks provide the service of paying recurring payments and crediting recurring deposits on behalf of customers. These payments are commonly for utilities, insurance premiums, mortgage payments, and the like. Social Security checks, wages, and dividend and interest checks are examples of recurring deposits. To provide this service, the customer's bank and the payee's bank must belong to the same clearinghouse.

Online Banking

Many banks permit customers to check their bank statements online and pay bills from their bank accounts by using personal computers and the Internet. To do so, a customer must enter his or her PIN and account name or number, the amount of the bill to be paid, and the account number of the payee to whom the funds are to be transferred. Internet banking has increased dramatically.

A man is usually more careful of his money than he is of his principles.

Edgar Watson Howe

INTERNET LAW & ONLINE COMMERCE

Electronic Funds Transfer Act

Computers have made it much easier and faster for banks and their customers to conduct banking transactions. Congress enacted the **Electronic Funds Transfer Act** [15 U.S.C. Section 1693 et seq.] to regulate consumer electronic funds transfers. The Federal Reserve Board, which is empowered to enforce the provisions of the act, adopted **Regulation E** to further interpret it. Regulation E has the force of law. The Electronic Funds Transfer Act and Regulation E establish the following consumer rights:

- **Unsolicited cards.** A bank can send unsolicited EFTS debit cards to a consumer only if the cards are not valid for use. Unsolicited cards can be validated for use by a consumer's specific request.
- **Lost or stolen debit cards.** Debit cards are sometimes lost or stolen. If a customer notifies the issuing bank within 2 days of learning that his or her debit card has been lost or stolen, the customer is liable for only $50 for unauthorized use. If a customer does not notify the bank within this 2-day period, the customer's liability increases to $500. If the customer fails to notify the bank within 60 days after an unauthorized use appears on the customer's bank statement, the customer can

be held liable for more than $500. Federal law allows states to impose a lesser liability on customers for lost or stolen debit cards.
- **Evidence of transaction.** Other than for a telephone transaction, a bank must provide a customer with a written receipt of a transaction made through a computer terminal. This receipt is *prima facie* evidence of the transaction.
- **Bank statements.** A bank must provide a monthly statement to an electronic funds transfer customer at the end of the month in which the customer conducts a transaction. Otherwise, a quarterly statement must be provided to the customer. The statement must include the date and amount of the transfer, the name of the retailer, the location and identification of the terminal, and the fees charged for the transaction. Bank statements must also contain the address and telephone number where inquiries or errors can be reported.

A bank is liable for wrongful dishonor when it fails to pay an electronic funds transfer when there are sufficient funds in the customer's account to do so.

► ELECTRONIC WIRE TRANSFERS

commercial wire transfer
An electronic transfer of funds from one party to another party. Also known as a *wholesale wire transfer*.

Commercial wire transfers, or **wholesale wire transfers**, are electronic transfers of funds from a bank to another party. They are often used to transfer payments between businesses and financial institutions. For example, a customer of a bank may request the bank to pay another party by wiring funds (money) to that party's bank account.

Trillions of dollars per day are transferred over the two principal wire payment systems—the **Federal Reserve Wire Network (Fedwire)** and the **Clearing House Interbank Payments System (CHIPS)**. A wire transfer often involves a large amount of money (multimillion-dollar transactions are commonplace). The benefits of using wire transfers are their speed—most transfers are completed on the same day—and low cost. Banks sometimes require a customer to pay for a funds transfer in advance. On other occasions, however, a bank will extend credit to a customer and pay for the funds transfer. The customer is liable to pay the bank for any properly paid funds transfer.

INTERNET LAW & ONLINE COMMERCE

UCC Article 4A (Funds Transfers)

UCC Article 4A (Funds Transfers), which was promulgated in 1989, governs commercial wire transfers. Most states have adopted this article. Where adopted, Article 4A governs the rights and obligations between parties to a funds transfer unless they have entered into a contrary agreement. Article 4A applies only to **commercial electronic funds transfers**; consumer electronic funds transfers subject to the Electronic Funds Transfer Act are not subject to Article 4A. Funds transfers are not complex transactions.

Example Boeing wants to pay Pittsburgh Steel for supplies it purchased. Instead of delivering a check to Pittsburgh Steel, Boeing instructs its bank, Washington Bank, to wire the funds to Pittsburgh Steel's bank, Liberty Bank, with instructions to credit Pittsburgh Steel's account. Boeing's order is called a *payment order*, Boeing is the *originator* of

the wire transfer, and Pittsburgh Steel is the *beneficiary*. Washington Bank is called the *originator's bank*, and Liberty Bank is called *beneficiary's bank*. In more complex transactions, there may be one or more additional banks, known as *intermediary banks*, between the originator's bank and the beneficiary's bank [UCC 4A-103(a)].

If a receiving bank mistakenly pays a greater amount to the beneficiary than ordered, the originator is liable for only the amount he or she instructed to be paid. The receiving bank that erred has the burden of recovering any overpayment from the beneficiary [UCC 4A-303(a)]. If a wrong beneficiary is paid, the originator is not obliged to pay his or her payment order. The bank that issued the erroneous payment order has the burden of recovering the payment from the improper beneficiary [UCC 4A-303(c)].

Funds Transfer Procedures

Banks and customers usually establish security procedures (e.g., codes, identifying numbers, words) to prevent unauthorized electronic payment orders. To protect the bank from liability for unauthorized payment orders, the security procedure must be commercially reasonable. If the bank verifies the authenticity of a payment order by complying with such a security procedure and pays the order, the customer is bound to pay the order, even if it was not authorized [UCC 4A-202]. The customer is not liable if it can prove that the unauthorized order was not initiated by an employee or another agent or by a person who obtained that information from a source controlled by the customer [UCC 4A-203].

The Bahamas *This office building is located in the Bahamas. There are many offices in this building that act as "banks" for offshore money. This is primarily because the Bahamas offers bank secrecy laws and tax shelter laws. There are other bank secrecy hideouts and tax evasion haven countries around the world, including Bermuda in the Caribbean, the countries of Liechtenstein and Monaco in Europe, the Isle of Man off of Great Britain, the micro-islands of Niue and Vanuatu in the South Pacific, and the Philippines, just to name a few. Tax evaders, money launderers, drug cartels, criminal organizations, corrupt government officials, white-collar criminals, terrorist groups, and others who want anonymity use these offshore banking countries to hide their money.*

TEST REVIEW TERMS AND CONCEPTS

Altered check
Article 3 (Commercial Paper) of the UCC
Article 4 (Bank Deposits and Collections) of the UCC
Article 4A (Funds Transfers) of the UCC
Automated teller machine (ATM)
Bank check
Cashier's check
Certification
Certified check
Check
Clearing House Interbank Payments System (CHIPS)
Collecting bank
Commercial electronic funds transfers

Commercial wire transfer (wholesale wire transfer)
Creditor–debtor relationship
Currency Transaction Report (CTR)
Debit card
Deferred posting rule
Deposit
Depository bank
Drawee of a check
Drawer of a check
Electronic Funds Transfer Act
Electronic funds transfer system (EFTS)
Federal Currency Reporting Law
Federal Deposit Insurance Corporation (FDIC)

Federal Reserve System
Federal Reserve Wire Network (Fedwire)
Final settlement
Forged instrument
Honor
Indorse
Indorsee of a check
Indorsement of a check
Indorser of a check
Insufficient funds
Intermediary bank
Midnight deadline
"On them" item
"On us" item
Ordinary check
Original tenor
Overdraft
Payee of a check
Payer bank

Point-of-sale (POS) terminal
Postdated check
Presentment across the counter
Presentment warranty
Principal–agent relationship
Provisional credit
Regulation E
Revised Article 3 (Negotiable Instruments) of the UCC
Stale check
Stop-payment order
Wrongful dishonor

CASE PROBLEMS

25.1 Cashier's Check Dr. Graham Wood purchased a cashier's check in the amount of $6,000 from Central Bank of the South (Bank). The check was made payable to Ken Walker and was delivered to him. Eleven months later, Bank's branch manager informed Wood that the cashier's check was still outstanding. Wood subsequently signed a form, requesting that payment be stopped and a replacement check issued. He also agreed to indemnify Bank for any damages resulting from the issuance of the replacement check. Bank issued a replacement check to Wood. Seven months later, Walker deposited the original cashier's check in his bank, which was paid by Bank. Bank requested that Woods repay the bank $6,000. When he refused, Bank sued Woods to recover this amount. Who wins? *Wood v. Central Bank of the South*, 435 So.2d 1287, **Web** 1982 Ala. Civ. App. Lexis 1362 (Court of Civil Appeals of Alabama)

25.2 Overdraft Louise Kalbe maintained a checking account at the Pulaski State Bank (Bank) in Wisconsin. Kalbe made out a check for $7,260, payable in cash. Thereafter, she misplaced it but did not report the missing check to the bank or stop payment on it. One month later, some unknown person presented the check to a Florida bank for payment. The Florida bank paid the check and sent it to Bank for collection. Bank paid the check even though it created a $6,542.12 overdraft in Kalbe's account. Bank requested Kalbe pay this amount. When she refused, Bank sued Kalbe to collect the overdraft. Who wins? *Pulaski State Bank v. Kalbe*, 122 Wis.2d 663, 364 N.W.2d 162, **Web** 1985 Wisc.App. Lexis 3034 (Court of Appeals of Wisconsin)

25.3 Wrongful Dishonor Larry J. Goodwin and his wife maintained a checking and savings account at City National Bank of Fort Smith (Bank). Bank also had a customer named Larry K. Goodwin. Two loans of Larry K. Goodwin were in default. Bank mistakenly took money from Larry J. Goodwin's checking account to pay the loans. At the end of the month, the Goodwins received written notice that four of their checks, which were written to merchants, had been dishonored for insufficient funds. When the Goodwins investigated, they discovered that their checking account balance was zero, and the bank had placed their savings account on hold. After being informed of the error, Bank promised to send letters of apology to the four merchants and to correct the error. Bank, however, subsequently "bounced" several other checks of the Goodwins. Eventually, Bank notified all the parties of its error. One month later, the Goodwins closed their accounts at Bank and were paid the correct balances due. They sued the bank for consequential and punitive damages for wrongful dishonor. Who wins? *City National Bank of Fort Smith v. Goodwin*, 301 Ark. 182, 783 S.W.2d 335, **Web** 1990 Ark. Lexis 49 (Supreme Court of Arkansas)

25.4 Stale Check Charles Ragusa & Son (Ragusa), a partnership consisting of Charles and Michael Ragusa, issued a check in the amount of $5,000, payable to Southern Masonry, Inc. (Southern). The check was drawn on Community State Bank (Bank). Several days later, Southern informed Ragusa that the check had been lost. Ragusa issued a replacement check for the same amount and sent it to Southern, and that check was cashed. At the same time, Ragusa gave a verbal stop-payment order to Bank regarding the original check. Three years later, the original check was deposited by Southern into its account at the Bank of New Orleans. When the check was presented to Bank, it paid it and charged $5,000 against Ragusa's account. The partnership was not made aware of this transaction until one month later, when it received its monthly bank statement. Ragusa demanded that Bank recredit its account $5,000. When Bank refused to do so, Ragusa sued. Who wins? *Charles Ragusa & Son v. Community State Bank*, 360 So.2d 231, **Web** 1978 La.App. Lexis 3435 (Court of Appeal of Louisiana)

25.5 Postdated Check David Siegel maintained a checking account with the New England Merchants National Bank (Bank). On September 14, Siegel drew and delivered a $20,000 check payable to Peter Peters. The check was dated November 14. Peters immediately deposited the check in his own bank, which forwarded it for collection. On September 17, Bank paid the check and charged it against Siegel's account. Siegel discovered that the check had been paid when another of his checks was returned for insufficient funds. Siegel informed Bank that the check to Peters was postdated November 14 and requested that the bank return the $20,000 to his account. When Bank refused, Siegel sued for wrongful debit of his account. Must Bank recredit Siegel's account? *Siegel v. New England Merchants National Bank*, 386 Mass. 672, 437 N.E.2d 218, **Web** 1982 Mass. Lexis 1559 (Supreme Judicial Court of Massachusetts)

25.6 Stop Payment Dynamite Enterprises, Inc. (Dynamite), a corporation doing business in Florida, maintained a checking account at Eagle National Bank of Miami (Bank). Dynamite drew a check on this account, payable to one of its business associates. Before the check had been cashed or deposited, Dynamite issued a written stop-payment order to Bank. Bank informed Dynamite that it would not place a stop-payment order on the check because there were insufficient funds in the account to pay the check. Several weeks later, the check was presented to Bank for payment. By this time, sufficient funds had been deposited in the account to pay the check. Bank paid the check and charged Dynamite's account. When Dynamite learned that the check had been paid, it requested Bank to recredit its account. When Bank refused, Dynamite sued to recover the amount of the check. Who wins? *Dynamite Enterprises, Inc. v. Eagle National Bank of Miami*, 517 So.2d 112, **Web** 1987 Fla.App. Lexis 11791 (Court of Appeal of Florida)

25.7 Examining Bank Statements Mr. Gennone maintained a checking account at Peoples National Bank & Trust Company of Pennsylvania (Bank). Gennone noticed that he was not receiving his bank statements and canceled checks. When Gennone contacted Bank, he was informed that the statements had been mailed to him. Bank agreed to hold future statements so that he could pick them up in person. Gennone picked up the statements but did not reconcile the balance of the account. As a result, it was not until two years later that he discovered that beginning over one year earlier, his wife had forged his signature on 25 checks. Gennone requested Bank to reimburse him for the amount of these checks. When Bank refused, Gennone sued Bank to recover. Who wins? *Gennone v. Peoples National Bank & Trust Co.*, 9 U.C.C. Rep.Serv. 707, **Web** 1971 Pa. Dist. & Cnty. Dec. Lexis 551, 51 Pa. D. & C.2d 529 (Common Pleas Court of Montgomery County, Pennsylvania)

25.8 Deferred Posting   Dr. Robert L. Pracht received a check in the amount of $6,571.25 from Northwest Feedyards in payment for three loads of corn. The check was drawn on a checking account at Oklahoma State Bank (Bank). Pracht also maintained an account at Bank. On Friday, Pracht indorsed the check and gave it to an associate to deposit to Pracht's account at the bank. When the associate arrived at the bank around 3:00 P.M., he discovered that the bank's doors were locked. After gaining the attention of a bank employee, the associate was allowed into the bank, where he gave the check and deposit slip to a teller. Because the bank's computer had shut down at 3:00 P.M., the teller put the check aside. The associate testified that several bank employees were working at their desks as he left the bank. The bank was not open on Saturday or Sunday. Three days later, Bank dishonored the check due to insufficient funds. Pracht sued to recover the amount of the check from Bank. Who wins? *Pracht v. Oklahoma State Bank*, 1979 OK 43, 592 P.2d 976, **Web** 1979 Okla. Lexis 209 (Supreme Court of Oklahoma)

BUSINESS ETHICS CASES

25.9 Business Ethics   Actors Equity, a union that represents 37,000 stage actors, sought to hire a new comptroller. A man named Nicholas Scotti applied for the position and submitted an extensive resume, showing that he was currently employed by Paris Maintenance Company as its comptroller. Scotti also stated that he had held various financial positions with Equitable Life Assurance Society and the Investors Funding Corporation. Officers of Actors Equity interviewed Scotti and offered him the job. No attempt was made to verify Scotti's background or prior employment history.

Actors Equity maintained a checking account at the Bank of New York. During his first six months as comptroller, Scotti forged the signature of the appropriate company employee on four Actors Equity checks totaling $100,000. The checks were made payable to N. Piscotti and were cashed by Scotti and paid by the Bank of New York. The forged signatures were of professional quality. After Scotti resigned as comptroller, the forgeries were discovered. Subsequent investigation revealed that Scotti's real name was Piscotti, that the information on his resume was false, and that he had an extensive criminal record. Actors Equity sued the drawee bank to recover the $100,000. Did Scotti act ethically in this case? Should Actors Equity have sued the bank to recover on the forged checks? Who wins? *Fireman's Fund Insurance Co. v.*

The Bank of New York, 146 A.D.2d 95, 539 N.Y.S.2d 339, **Web** 1989 N.Y. App. Div. Lexis 4172 (Supreme Court of New York)

25.10 Business Ethics   Golden Gulf, Inc. (Golden Gulf), opened a checking account at AmSouth Bank, N.A. (AmSouth). Golden Gulf entered into a subscription agreement wherein Albert M. Rossini agreed to pay $250,000 for stock in the company. Rossini tendered a check drawn on the Mark Twain Bank in Kansas City, Missouri, to Golden Gulf for that amount. Golden Gulf deposited the check in its checking account at AmSouth. Three days later, Golden Gulf contacted AmSouth and asked if the funds were "available." AmSouth said the funds were available for use. Golden Gulf requested AmSouth to wire transfer the funds to it in New York for use in that state. AmSouth complied with the request. Five days later, AmSouth received notice from the Mark Twain Bank that Rossini's check would not be paid due to insufficient funds. On the next day, AmSouth notified Golden Gulf that the check had been dishonored. AmSouth revoked the credit it had given to Golden Gulf's account, resulting in an overdraft of $248,965.69. AmSouth sued to recover this amount. Did Golden Gulf act ethically in this case? Who wins? *Golden Gulf, Inc. v. AmSouth Bank, N.A.*, 565 So.2d 114, **Web** 1990 Ala. Lexis 436 (Supreme Court of Alabama)

ENDNOTE

1. Prior to October 3, 2008, FDIC deposit insurance was $100,000 for each account owner. In response to the 2008 banking crisis in the United States, the federal government increased the amount of FDIC insurance to $250,000 for each account owner for the period October 3, 2008 until December 31, 2009.

Part VI

CREDIT, SECURED TRANSACTIONS, AND BANKRUPTCY

SOLD

26 | CREDITOR'S AND DEBTOR'S RIGHTS

▲ **House with "For Sale" Sign** *Approximately two-thirds of American families and individuals own their own homes. Some of these homeowners own their home outright, while other homeowners have borrowed money from banks and other lenders. The lender has a mortgage on the home, which means that in most cases the lender can foreclose and obtain the house if the homeowner defaults on the loan. Falling home prices and aggressive lending practices were important factors in the housing crisis that began in 2007. In 2008, Zillow.com, a provider of home valuations on the Internet, reported that almost one-third of U.S. homeowners who had bought in the previous five years owed more than their homes were worth.*

CHAPTER OBJECTIVES

After studying this chapter, you should be able to:

1. Distinguish between unsecured and secured credit.
2. Describe security interests in real property, such as mortgages and deeds of trust.
3. Explain how recording statutes and the process of foreclosure work.
4. Describe surety and guaranty arrangements.
5. List and describe federal debtor protection statutes.

CHAPTER CONTENTS

▶ **INTRODUCTION TO CREDITOR'S AND DEBTOR'S RIGHTS**
▶ **CREDIT**

▶ **SECURITY INTEREST IN REAL PROPERTY**
   Contemporary Environment · *Mechanic's Lien*

▶ **SURETY AND GUARANTY ARRANGEMENTS**
▶ **DEBTOR PROTECTION LAWS**

Landmark Law · *Truth-in-Lending Act*
▶ **COLLECTION REMEDIES**

"Creditors have better memories than debtors."

Benjamin Franklin
Poor Richard's Almanack (1758)

▶ INTRODUCTION TO CREDITOR'S AND DEBTOR'S RIGHTS

The U.S. economy is a **credit** economy. Consumers borrow money to make major purchases (e.g., homes, automobiles, appliances) and use credit cards (e.g., Visa, MasterCard) to purchase goods and services at clothing stores, restaurants, and other businesses. Businesses use credit to purchase equipment, supplies, and other goods and services. In a credit transaction, the borrower is the *debtor*, and the lender is the *creditor*.

Because lenders are sometimes reluctant to lend large sums of money simply on the borrower's promise to repay, many of them take a *security interest* in the property purchased or some other property of the debtor. The property in which the security interest is taken is called **collateral**. If the debtor does not pay the debt, the creditor can foreclose on and recover the collateral.

A lender who is unsure whether a debtor will have sufficient income or assets to repay a loan may require another person to guarantee payment. If the borrower fails to repay the loan, that person is responsible for paying it. This responsibility is called *suretyship*.

In many credit transactions, particularly consumer credit transactions, the lender is an institution or party that has greater leverage than the borrower. In the past, this sometimes led to lenders taking advantage of debtors. To rectify this problem, the federal government has enacted several major statutes that protect debtors from abusive, deceptive, and unfair credit practices.

This chapter discusses types of credit, security interests in real property, suretyship, and debtor protection laws. (Secured transactions in personal property are covered in the following chapter.)

▶ CREDIT

Credit may be extended on either an *unsecured* or a *secured* basis. The following paragraphs discuss these types of credit.

Debtor and Creditor

In a transaction involving the extension of credit (either unsecured or secured), there are two parties. The party extending the credit, the **lender**, is called the **creditor**. The party borrowing the money, the **borrower**, is called the **debtor** (see Exhibit 26.1).

Example Prima Company goes to Urban Bank and borrows $100,000. In this case, Prima Company is the borrower-debtor, and Urban Bank is the lender-creditor.

creditor
The lender in a credit transaction.

debtor
The borrower in a credit transaction.

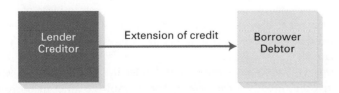

▶ **Exhibit 26.1 DEBTOR AND CREDITOR**

Unsecured Credit

unsecured credit
Credit that does not require any security (collateral) to protect the payment of the debt.

Unsecured credit does not require any security (collateral) to protect the payment of the debt. Instead, the creditor relies on the debtor's promise to repay the principal (plus any interest) when it is due. If the debtor fails to make the payments, the creditor may bring legal action and obtain a judgment against him or her. If the debtor is **judgment-proof** (i.e., has little or no property or no income that can be garnished), the creditor may never collect.

Secured Credit

secured credit
Credit that requires security (collateral) that secures payment of the loan.

To minimize the risk associated with extending unsecured credit, a creditor may require a security interest in the debtor's property (collateral). The collateral secures payment of the loan. This type of credit is called **secured credit**. Security interests may be taken in real, personal, intangible, and other property. If the debtor fails to make the payments when due, the collateral may be repossessed to recover the outstanding amount. Generally, if the sale of the collateral is insufficient to repay the loan (plus interest), the creditor may bring a lawsuit against the debtor to recover a deficiency judgment for the difference.

▶ SECURITY INTEREST IN REAL PROPERTY

Owners of real estate can create **security interests** in their property. This occurs if an owner borrows money from a lender and pledges real estate as security for repayment of the loan.

Mortgage

mortgage
A collateral arrangement in which a property owner borrows money from a creditor, who uses real estate as collateral for repayment of the loan.

mortgagor
The owner-debtor in a mortgage transaction.

mortgagee
The creditor in a mortgage transaction.

A person who owns a piece of real property has an ownership interest in that property. A property owner who borrows money from a creditor may use his or her real estate as collateral for repayment of the loan. This type of collateral arrangement, known as a **mortgage**, is a *two-party instrument*. The **owner-debtor** is the **mortgagor**, and the **creditor** is the **mortgagee**. The parties to a mortgage are illustrated in Exhibit 26.2.

Example General Electric purchases a manufacturing plant for $10 million, pays $2 million cash as a down payment, and borrows the remaining $8 million from City Bank. General Electric is the debtor, and City Bank is the creditor. To secure the loan, General Electric gives a mortgage on the plant to City Bank. This is a secured loan, with the plant being collateral for the loan. General Electric is the mortgagor, and City Bank is the mortgagee. If General Electric defaults on the loan, the bank may take action under state law to foreclose and take the property.

▶ **Exhibit 26.2 MORTGAGE**

Note and Deed of Trust

note
An instrument that evidences a borrower's debt to the lender.

deed of trust
An instrument that gives a creditor a security interest in the debtor's property that is pledged as collateral.

Some states' laws provide for the use of a *deed of trust and note* in place of a mortgage. The **note** is the instrument that evidences the borrower's debt to the lender; the **deed of trust** is the instrument that gives the creditor a security interest in the debtor's property that is pledged as collateral.

A deed of trust is a *three-party instrument*. Under it, legal title to the real property is placed with a **trustee** (usually a trust corporation) until the amount borrowed has been paid. The **owner-debtor** is called the **trustor**. Although legal title is vested in the trustee, the trustor has full legal rights to possession of the real property. The **creditor** is called the **beneficiary**. Exhibit 26.3 illustrates the relationship between the parties.

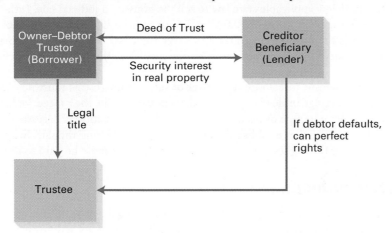

▶ **Exhibit 26.3 NOTE AND DEED OF TRUST**

When the loan is repaid, the trustee files a **written reconveyance** with the county recorder's office, which transfers title to the real property to the borrower-debtor. If the loan is not repaid, the trustee can deed the property to the lender-creditor beneficiary or sell the property through **foreclosure** proceeding, depending on state law.

Debt is the prolific mother of folly and of crime.

Benjamin Disraeli
Henrietta Temple (1837)

Recording Statute

Most states have enacted **recording statutes** that require a mortgage or deed of trust to be recorded in the county recorder's office in the county in which the real property is located. These filings are public record and alert the world that a mortgage or deed of trust has been recorded against the real property. This record gives potential lenders or purchasers of real property the ability to determine whether there are any existing liens (mortgages) on the property.

The **nonrecordation of a mortgage** or deed of trust does not affect either the legality of the instrument between the mortgagor and the mortgagee or the rights and obligations of the parties. In other words, the mortgagor is obligated to pay the amount of the mortgage according to the terms of the mortgage, even if the document is not recorded. However, an improperly recorded document is not effective against either (1) subsequent purchasers of the real property or (2) other mortgagees or lienholders who have no notice of the prior mortgages.

recording statute
A statute that requires a mortgage or deed of trust to be recorded in the county recorder's office of the county in which the real property is located.

Example Eileen purchases a house for $500,000. She borrows $400,000 from Boulevard Bank and gives the bank a mortgage on the house for this amount. Boulevard Bank fails to record the mortgage. Eileen then applies to borrow $400,000 from Advance Bank. Advance Bank reviews the real estate recordings and finds no mortgage recorded against the property, so it lends Eileen $400,000. Advance Bank records its mortgage. Later, Eileen defaults on both loans. In this case, Advance Bank can foreclose on the house because it recorded its mortgage. Boulevard Bank, even though it made the first loan to Eileen, does not get the house and can only sue Eileen to recover the unpaid loan.

By no means run in debt.

George Herbert
The Temple (1633)

Foreclosure Sale

All states permit **foreclosure sales**. Under this method, the debtor's defaulting may trigger a legal court action for foreclosure. Any party having an interest in the property—including owners of the property and other mortgagees or lienholders—must be named as defendants. If the mortgagee's case is successful, the court will issue a judgment that orders the real property to be sold at a judicial sale. The procedures for a foreclosure action and sale are mandated by state statute. Any surplus must be paid to the mortgagor.

foreclosure sale
A legal procedure by which a secured creditor causes the judicial sale of the secured real estate to pay a defaulted loan.

Example Christine borrows $500,000 from Country Bank to buy a house. Christine (mortgagor) gives a mortgage to Country Bank (mortgagee), making the house collateral to secure the loan. Later, Christine defaults on the loan. Country Bank can foreclose on the property and follow applicable state law to sell the house at a judicial sale. If the house sells for $575,000, the bank keeps $500,000 and must remit $75,000 to Christine. Most state statutes permit the mortgagee-lender to recover the costs of the foreclosure and judicial sale from the sale proceeds before remitting the surplus to the mortgagor-borrower.

power of sale
A power stated in a mortgage or deed that permits foreclosure without court proceedings and sale of the property through an auction.

Most states permit foreclosure by **power of sale**, although this must be expressly conferred in the mortgage or deed of trust. Under a power of sale, the procedure for that sale is contained in the mortgage or deed of trust itself. No court action is necessary. Some states have enacted statutes that establish the procedure for conducting the sale. Such a sale must be by auction for the highest price obtainable. Any surplus must be paid to the mortgagor.

Deficiency Judgment

deficiency judgment
A judgment of a court that permits a secured lender to recover other property or income from a defaulting debtor if the collateral is insufficient to repay the unpaid loan.

Some states permit a mortgagee to bring a separate legal action to recover a deficiency from the mortgagor. If the mortgagee is successful, the court will award a **deficiency judgment** that entitles the mortgagee to recover the amount of the judgment from the mortgagor's other property.

Example Kaye buys a house for $800,000. She puts $200,000 down and borrows $600,000 from a bank, which takes a mortgage on the property to secure the loan. Kaye defaults, and when the bank forecloses on the property, it is worth only $500,000. There is a deficiency of $100,000 ($600,000 loan − $500,000 foreclosure sale price).The bank can recover the $100,000 deficiency from Kaye's other property. The bank has to bring a legal action against Kaye to do so.

Antideficiency Statutes

antideficiency statute
A statute that prohibits deficiency judgments regarding certain types of mortgages, such as those on residential property.

Several states have enacted statutes that prohibit deficiency judgments regarding certain types of mortgages, such as loans for the original purchase of residential property. These statutes are called **antideficiency statutes**. Antideficiency statutes usually apply only to **first purchase money mortgages** (i.e., mortgages that are taken out to purchase houses). Second mortgages and other subsequent mortgages, even mortgages that refinance the first mortgage, usually are not protected by antideficiency statutes.

Example Assume that a house is located in a state that has an antideficiency statute. Qian buys the house for $800,000. She puts $200,000 down and borrows $600,000 of the purchase price from First Bank, which takes a mortgage on the property to secure the loan. This is a first purchase money mortgage. Subsequently, Qian borrows $100,000 from Second Bank and gives a second mortgage to Second Bank to secure the loan. Qian defaults on both loans, and when she defaults, the house is worth only $500,000. Both banks bring foreclosure proceedings to recover the house. First Bank can recover the house worth $500,000 at foreclosure. However, First Bank has a deficiency of $100,000 ($600,000 loan − $500,000 foreclosure sale price). Because of the state's antideficiency statute, First Bank cannot recover this deficiency from Qian; First Bank can only recover the house in foreclosure and must write off the $100,000 loss. Second Bank's loan, a second loan, is not covered by the antideficiency statute. Therefore, Second Bank can sue Qian to recover its $100,000 deficiency from Qian's other property.

Right of Redemption

right of redemption
A right that allows the mortgagor to redeem real property after default and before foreclosure. It requires the mortgagor to pay the full amount of the debt incurred by the mortgagee because of the mortgagor's default.

The common law and many state statutes give the mortgagor the right to redeem real property after default and before foreclosure. This right, which is called the **right of redemption**, requires the mortgagor to pay the full amount of the debt—that is, principal, interest, and other costs—incurred by the mortgagee because of the mortgagor's default.

Redemption of a partial interest is not permitted. Upon redemption, the mortgagor receives title to the property, free and clear of the mortgage debt.

Some states allow the mortgagor to redeem real property for a specified period (usually six months or one year) after foreclosure. This is called the **statutory period of redemption**. If this right exists, the deed to the real property is not delivered to the purchaser at the foreclosure sale until after the statutory period of redemption has expired.

Most state laws provide that any party in interest—such as a second mortgage holder or another lienholder—may redeem the property during the redemption period.

Land Sales Contract

Most states permit the transfer and sale of real property pursuant to a **land sales contract**. Here, the owner of real property agrees to sell the property to a purchaser, who agrees to pay the purchase price to the owner-seller over an agreed-upon period of time. Often, making such a loan is referred to as "carrying the paper."

Land sales contracts are often used to sell undeveloped property, farms, and the like. Under such contracts, the seller retains title to the property until the purchaser pays the purchase price (plus interest). During the period of the contract, the purchaser (1) has the legal right to possession and use of the property and (2) is responsible for the payment of insurance, taxes, and such.

If the purchaser defaults, the seller may declare forfeiture and retake possession of the property. Many states provide a statutory procedure that must be followed to foreclose on a land sales contract. These procedures are often simpler, less time-consuming, and less expensive than foreclosure on a mortgage or deed of trust. Many states give the debtor the right to redeem the real property within a specified statutory period.

land sales contract
An arrangement in which the owner of real property sells property to a purchaser and extends credit to the purchaser.

mechanic's lien
A contractor's, laborer's, and material person's statutory lien that makes the real property to which services or materials have been provided security for the payment of the services and materials.

release of lien
A written document signed by a contractor, subcontractor, laborer, or material person, waiving his or her statutory lien against real property. Also known as a *lien release*.

CONTEMPORARY ENVIRONMENT

Mechanic's Lien

Owners of real property often hire contractors and laborers (e.g., painters, plumbers, roofers, bricklayers, furnace installers) to make improvements to that property. The contractors and laborers expend the time to provide their services as well as money to provide the materials for the improvements. Their investments are protected by state statutes that permit them to file a **mechanic's lien** against the improved real property.

When a lien is properly filed, the real property to which the improvements have been made becomes security for the payment of these services and materials. In essence, the lienholder has the equivalent of a mortgage on the property. If the owner defaults, the lienholder may foreclose on the lien, sell the property, and satisfy the debt plus interest and costs out of the proceeds of the sale. Any surplus must be paid to the owner-debtor. Generally, the lien must be foreclosed on during a specific period of time (commonly six months to two years) from the date the lien is filed. Mechanic's liens are usually subject to the debtor's right of redemption.

Procedure for Obtaining a Mechanic's Lien
Although the procedures for obtaining a mechanic's lien vary from state to state, the following requirements generally must be met:

1. The lienholder must file a **notice of lien** with the county recorder's office in the county in which the real property subject to the lien is located.

2. The notice must state the amount of the claim, the name of the claimant, the name of the owner of the real property, and a description of the real property.
3. The notice must be filed within a specified time period (commonly 30 to 120 days) after the services have been performed or materials have been delivered.
4. Notice of the lien must be given to the owner of the real property.

Lien Release
Most state statutes permit an owner of real property to have contractors, subcontractors, laborers, and material persons who have provided services or materials to a real property project sign a written **release of lien** contract (also called a **lien release**) attesting to the receipt of payment and releasing any lien they might otherwise assert against the property. A lien release can be used by the property owner to defeat a statutory lienholder's attempt to obtain payment.

Example Wholesale Company, which owns an undeveloped piece of property, hires Mason Contractor, a general contractor, to build a warehouse on the property. Mason Contractor builds the warehouse and hires Roof Company, a roofer, as a subcontractor to put the roof on the warehouse. When the warehouse is complete, Wholesale Company pays Mason Contractor the full contract price for the warehouse but fails to obtain a release of lien from Roof Company. Mason Contractor fails to pay Roof Company for the roofing work. Roof Company files a mechanic's lien against the warehouse and demands payment from Wholesale Company. Here, Wholesale Company must pay Roof Company for the roofing work; if Wholesale Company does not, Roof Company can foreclose on the warehouse, have it sold, and satisfy the debt out of the proceeds of the sale. To prevent foreclosure, Wholesale Company pays Roof Company for its work. Wholesale Company ends up paying twice for the roofing work—once to Mason Contractor, the general contractor, and a second time to Roof Company, the

subcontractor. Wholesale Company's only recourse is to sue Mason Contractor to recover its payment.

Example Suppose in the preceding example that Wholesale Company obtained a lien release from Roof Company, the subcontractor, before or at the time Wholesale Company paid Mason Contractor, the general contractor. If Mason Contractor failed to pay the subcontractor Roof Company, Roof Company could not file a lien against Wholesale Company's warehouse because it had signed a lien release. In this situation, Roof Company's only recourse would be to sue Mason Contractor to recover for its services.

▶ SURETY AND GUARANTY ARRANGEMENTS

Sometimes a creditor refuses to extend credit to a debtor unless a third person agrees to become liable on the debt. The third person's credit becomes the security for the credit extended to the debtor. This relationship may be either a *surety arrangement* or a *guaranty arrangement*. These arrangements are discussed in the following paragraphs.

Surety Arrangement

surety arrangement
An arrangement in which a third party promises to be *primarily liable* with the borrower for the payment of the borrower's debt.

In a strict **surety arrangement**, a third person—known as the **surety**, or **co-debtor**—promises to be liable for the payment of another person's debt. A person who acts as a surety is commonly called an **accommodation party**, or **cosigner**. Along with the principal debtor, the surety is **primarily liable** for paying the principal debtor's debt when it is due. The principal debtor does not have to be in default on the debt, and the creditor does not have to have exhausted all its remedies against the principal debtor before seeking payment from the surety.

Guaranty Arrangement

guaranty arrangement
An arrangement in which a third party promises to be *secondarily liable* for the payment of another's debt.

In a **guaranty arrangement**, a third person, the **guarantor**, agrees to pay the debt of the principal debtor if the debtor defaults and does not pay the debt when it is due. In this type of arrangement, the guarantor is **secondarily liable** on the debt. In other words, the guarantor is obligated to pay the debt only if the principal debtor defaults and the creditor has attempted unsuccessfully to collect the debt from the debtor.

Defenses of a Surety or Guarantor

Generally, the defenses the principal debtor has against the creditor may also be asserted by a surety or guarantor.

Example If credit has been extended for the purchase of a piece of machinery that proves to be defective, the debtor and surety can both assert the defect as a defense to liability. The defenses of fraudulent inducement to enter into the surety or guaranty agreement and duress may also be cited as personal defenses to liability.

CONCEPT SUMMARY

SURETY AND GUARANTY CONTRACTS

Type of Arrangement	Party	Liability
Surety contract	Surety	Primarily liable. The surety is a co-debtor who is liable to pay the debt when it is due.
Guaranty contract	Guarantor	Secondarily liable. The guarantor is liable to pay the debt if the debtor defaults and the creditor has attempted unsuccessfully to collect the debt from the debtor.

▶ DEBTOR PROTECTION LAWS

Creditors have been known to engage in various abusive, deceptive, and unfair practices when dealing with consumer-debtors. To protect consumer-debtors from such practices, the federal government has enacted a comprehensive scheme of laws concerning the extension and collection of credit. These laws are discussed in the following sections.

Truth-in-Lending Act (TILA)
A federal statute that requires creditors to make certain disclosures to debtors in consumer transactions and real estate loans on the debtor's principal dwelling.

LANDMARK LAW
Truth-in-Lending Act

In 1968, Congress enacted the **Truth-in-Lending Act (TILA)** as part of the Consumer Credit Protection Act (CCPA) [15 U.S.C. Sections 1601–1667]. The TILA, as amended, requires creditors to make certain disclosures to debtors in consumer transactions (e.g., retail installment sales, automobile loans) and real estate loans on the debtor's principal dwelling. The TILA covers only creditors that regularly (1) extend credit for goods or services to consumers or (2) arrange such credit in the ordinary course of their business. Consumer credit is defined as credit extended to natural persons for personal, family, or household purposes.

Regulation Z
The TILA is administered by the Federal Reserve Board, which has authority to adopt regulations to enforce and interpret the act. **Regulation Z**, which sets forth detailed rules for compliance with the TILA, was adopted under this authority.[1] The TILA and Regulation Z require the creditor to disclose the following information to the consumer-debtor:

- Cash price of the product or service
- Down payment and trade-in allowance
- Unpaid cash price
- Finance charge, including interest, points, and other fees paid for the extension of credit
- **Annual percentage rate (APR)** of the finance charges
- Charges not included in the finance charge (such as appraisal fees)
- Total dollar amount financed
- Date the finance charge begins to accrue
- Number, amounts, and due dates of payments
- Description of any security interest
- Penalties to be assessed for delinquent payments and late charges
- Prepayment penalties
- Comparative costs of credit (optional)

The uniform disclosures required by the TILA and Regulation Z are intended to help consumers shop for the best credit terms.

Fair Credit Billing Act

The **Fair Credit Billing Act**[2] requires that creditors promptly acknowledge in writing consumer billing complaints and investigate billing errors. The act prohibits creditors from taking actions that adversely affect the consumer's credit standing until the investigation is completed. The act affords other protection during disputes. The amendment requires creditors to promptly post payments to the consumer's account and either refund overpayments or credit them to the consumer's account.

Regulation Z
A regulation that sets forth detailed rules for compliance with the TILA.

Consumer Leasing Act

Consumers often opt to lease consumer products, such as automobiles, rather than purchase them. The **Consumer Leasing Act (CLA)**[3] extends the TILA's coverage to lease terms in consumer leases. The CLA applies to lessors who engage in leasing or arranging leases for consumer goods in the ordinary course of their business. Casual leases (such as leases between consumers) are not subject to the CLA. Creditors that violate the CLA are subject to the civil and criminal penalties provided in the TILA.

Consumer Leasing Act (CLA)
An amendment to the TILA that extends the IILA's coverage to lease terms in consumer leases.

Fair Credit and Charge Card Disclosure Act

The **Fair Credit and Charge Card Disclosure Act**[4] of 1988 requires disclosure of credit terms on credit card and charge card solicitations and applications. The regulations adopted under the act require that any direct written solicitation to a consumer display, in tabular form, the following information: (1) the APR, (2) any annual membership fee,

Fair Credit and Charge Card Disclosure Act
An amendment to the TILA that requires disclosure of certain credit terms on credit card and charge card solicitations and applications.

(3) any minimum or fixed finance charge, (4) any transaction charge for use of the card for purchases, and (5) a statement that charges are due when the periodic statement is received by the debtor.

Equal Credit Opportunity Act

Equal Credit Opportunity Act (ECOA)

A federal statute that prohibits discrimination in the extension of credit based on sex, marital status, race, color, national origin, religion, age, or receipt of income from public assistance programs.

The **Equal Credit Opportunity Act (ECOA)**,[5] enacted in 1975, prohibits discrimination in the extension of credit based on sex, marital status, race, color, national origin, religion, age, or receipt of income from public assistance programs. The ECOA applies to all creditors that extend or arrange credit in the ordinary course of their business, including banks, savings and loan associations, automobile dealers, real estate brokers, credit card issuers, and the like.

The creditor must notify the applicant within 30 days regarding the action taken on a credit application. If the creditor takes an *adverse action* (i.e., denies, revokes, or changes the credit terms), the creditor must provide the applicant with a statement containing the specific reasons for the action. If a creditor violates the ECOA, the consumer may bring a civil action against the creditor and recover actual damages (including emotional distress and embarrassment).

Fair Credit Reporting Act

Fair Credit Reporting Act (FCRA)

An amendment to the TILA that protects a consumer who is the subject of a credit report by setting out guidelines for credit bureaus.

credit report

Information about a person's credit history that can be secured from a credit bureau reporting company.

In 1970, Congress enacted the **Fair Credit Reporting Act (FCRA)**[6] as Title VI of the TILA. This act protects a consumer who is the subject of a **credit report** by setting out guidelines for consumer reporting agencies—that is, credit bureaus that compile and sell credit reports for a fee. A consumer may request the following information at any time: (1) the nature and substance of all the information in his or her credit file, (2) the sources of this information, and (3) the names of recipients of his or her credit report.

If a consumer challenges the accuracy of pertinent information contained in a credit file, the agency may be compelled to reinvestigate. If the agency cannot find an error, despite the consumer's complaint, the consumer may file a 100-word written statement of his or her version of the disputed information. If a consumer reporting agency or user violates the FCRA, the injured consumer may bring a civil action against the violator and recover actual damages. The FCRA also provides for criminal penalties.

Fair Debt Collection Practices Act

Fair Debt Collection Practices Act (FDCPA)

A federal act that protects consumer-debtors from abusive, deceptive, and unfair practices used by debt collectors.

In 1977, Congress enacted the **Fair Debt Collection Practices Act (FDCPA)**.[7] This act protects consumer-debtors from abusive, deceptive, and unfair practices used by **debt collectors**. The FDCPA expressly prohibits debt collectors from using certain practices: (1) harassing, abusive, or intimidating tactics (e.g., threats of violence, obscene or abusive language), (2) false or misleading misrepresentations (e.g., posing as a police officer or an attorney), and (3) unfair or unconscionable practices (e.g., threatening the debtor with imprisonment).

A debt collector is not allowed to contact a debtor in some circumstances, including the following:

1. At any inconvenient time. The FDCPA provides that convenient hours are between 8:00 A.M. and 9:00 P.M., unless this time is otherwise inconvenient for the debtor (e.g., the debtor works a night shift and sleeps during the day).
2. At inconvenient places, such as at a place of worship or social events.
3. At the debtor's place of employment, if the employer objects to such contact.
4. If the debtor is represented by an attorney.
5. If the debtor gives a written notice to the debt collector that he or she refuses to pay the debt or does not want the debt collector to contact him or her again.

Credit is a system whereby a person who can't pay gets another person who can't pay to guarantee that he can pay.

Charles Dickens

The FDCPA limits the contact that a debt collector may have with third persons other than the debtor's spouse or parents. Such contact is strictly limited. Unless the court has given its approval, third parties can be consulted only for the purpose of locating a debtor, and a third party can be contacted only once. A debt collector may not inform a third person that a consumer owes a debt that is in the process of collection. A debtor may bring a civil action against a debt collector for intentionally violating the FDCPA.

▶ COLLECTION REMEDIES

The most common **collection remedies** are discussed in the following paragraphs.

Attachment

Attachment is a **prejudgment court order** that permits the seizure of a debtor's property while the lawsuit is pending. To obtain a **writ of attachment**, a creditor must follow the procedures of state law, give the debtor notice, and post a bond with the court.

Example Taryn sues Justin for fraud. Taryn lost a large sum of money to Justin when she invested in what she alleges was a fraudulent investment scheme. Because it may take over one year before the case is heard, Taryn is afraid that Justin will transfer any money or property he has to avoid having to pay a judgment if he loses at trial. Taryn can immediately make a motion to the court to have the court issue a writ of attachment ordering the seizure of Justin's property, pending the outcome of the lawsuit. The court will do so if it determines that there is some merit to Taryn's claim against Justin and there is justification to believe that Justin might dispose of his property prior to the trial.

Execution

Execution is a **postjudgment court order** that permits the seizure of the debtor's property that is in the possession of the debtor. Certain property is exempt from levy (e.g., tools of trade, clothing, homestead exemption). A **writ of execution** is a court order directing the sheriff or other government official to seize the debtor's property in the debtor's possession and authorizing a judicial sale of that property. The proceeds are used to pay the creditor the amount of the final judgment. Any surplus must be paid to the debtor.

Example Aamir wins a $25,000 judgment against Nicole. Nicole refuses to pay the amount of the judgment to Aamir. Aamir can obtain a postjudgment writ of execution from the court whereby the court directs the sheriff to seize Nicole's automobile and other property and have them sold at public auction to satisfy the judgment she owes Aamir.

Garnishment

Garnishment is a **postjudgment court order** that permits the seizure of a debtor's property that is in the possession of third parties. The creditor (also known as the **garnishor**) must go to court to seek a **writ of garnishment**. A third party in this situation is called a **garnishee**. Common garnishees are employers who possess wages due a debtor, banks in possession of funds belonging to the debtor, and other third parties in the possession of property of the debtor.

Example Yuming wins a $30,000 judgment against Lisa. Lisa refuses to pay the amount of the judgment to Yuming. Lisa works for E-Communications Company. Yuming obtains a postjudgment writ of garnishment from the court whereby the court orders E-Communications Company to pay 25 percent of Lisa's weekly disposable earnings (after taxes) directly to Yuming. Thus, after receiving this writ of garnishment, E-Communications Company must deduct the amount of the garnishment from Lisa's wages before she is paid and remit this amount to Yuming until the judgment is paid.

To protect debtors from abusive and excessive garnishment actions by creditors, Congress enacted **Title III of the Consumer Credit Protection Act**. This federal law allows debtors who are subject to a writ of garnishment to retain the greater of (1) 75 percent of their weekly disposable earnings (after taxes) or (2) an amount equal to 30 hours of work paid at federal minimum wage. State law limitations on garnishment control are often more stringent than federal law.

Beijing, China *China now has a private real estate market where buyers can purchase housing units, which are primarily condomiums as well as some single-family houses. Prior to the mid-1990s, China's 1.3 billion people lived in state-owned homes. Then the government allowed the private ownership of homes and sold off many of its residential real estate buildings. In addition, the government permits the private development of housing units, primarily the construction of condominium buildings by developers, who then sell condominium units to individuals. The government, however, continues to own the land and leases the land on long-term leases—usually for 70 years—to the homeowners.*

TEST REVIEW TERMS AND CONCEPTS

Accommodation party
    (cosigner)
Annual percentage rate (APR)
Antideficiency statute
Attachment
Beneficiary (creditor)
Collateral
Collection remedies
Consumer Leasing Act
    (CLA)
Credit
Credit report
Creditor (lender)
Debt collector
Debtor (borrower)
Deed of trust
Deficiency judgment
Equal Credit Opportunity
    Act (ECOA)

Execution
Fair Credit and Charge
    Card Disclosure Act
Fair Credit Billing Act
Fair Credit Reporting Act
    (FCRA)
Fair Debt Collection
    Practices Act
    (FDCPA)
First purchase money
    mortgage
Foreclosure
Foreclosure sale
Garnishee
Garnishment
Garnishor
Guarantor
Guaranty arrangement
Judgment-proof

Land sales contract
Mechanic's lien
Mortgage
Mortgagee (creditor)
Mortgagor (debtor)
Nonrecordation of a
    mortgage
Note
Notice of lien
Postjudgment court
    order
Power of sale
Prejudgment court
    order
Primarily liable
Recording statute
Regulation Z
Release of lien (lien
    release)

Right of redemption
Secondarily liable
Secured credit
Security interest
Statutory period of
    redemption
Surety (co-debtor)
Surety arrangement
Title III of the Consumer
    Credit Protection Act
Truth-in-Lending Act
    (TILA)
Trustee
Trustor (owner-debtor)
Unsecured credit
Writ of attachment
Writ of execution
Writ of garnishment
Written reconveyance

CASE PROBLEMS

26.1 Mechanic's Lien Ironwood Exploration, Inc. (Ironwood), owned a lease on oil and gas property located in Duchesne County, Utah. Ironwood contracted to have Lantz Drilling and Exploration Company, Inc. (Lantz), drill an oil well on the property. Thereafter, Lantz rented equipment from Graco Fishing and Rental Tools, Inc. (Graco), for use in drilling the well. Graco billed Lantz for these rentals, but Lantz did not pay. Graco filed a notice of a mechanic's lien on the well in the amount of $19,766. Ironwood, which had paid Lantz, refused to pay Graco. Graco sued to foreclose on its mechanic's lien. Who wins? *Graco Fishing and Rental Tools, Inc. v. Ironwood Exploration, Inc.*, 766 P.2d 1074, 98 Utah Adv. Rep. 28, **Web** 1988 Utah Lexis 125 (Supreme Court of Utah)

26.2 Foreclosure Atlantic Ocean Kampgrounds, Inc. (Atlantic), borrowed $60,000 from Camden National Bank (Camden National) and executed a note and mortgage on property located in Camden, Maine, securing that amount. Maine permits strict foreclosure. Atlantic defaulted on the loan, and Camden commenced strict foreclosure proceedings pursuant to state law. After the one-year period of redemption, Camden National sold the property to a third party in an amount in excess of the mortgage and costs of the foreclosure proceeding. Atlantic sued to recover the surplus from Camden National. Who wins? *Atlantic Ocean Kampgrounds, Inc. v. Camden National Bank*, 473 A.2d 884, **Web** 1984 Me. Lexis 666 (Supreme Judicial Court of Maine)

26.3 Redemption Elmer and Arletta Hans, husband and wife, owned a parcel of real property in Illinois. They borrowed $100,000 from First Illinois National Bank (First Illinois) and executed a note and mortgage to First Illinois, making the real estate security for the loan. The security agreement authorized First Illinois to take possession of the property upon the occurrence of a default and required the Hanses to execute a quitclaim deed in favor of First Illinois. The state of Illinois recognizes the doctrine of redemption. When the Hanses defaulted on the loan, First Illinois filed a lawsuit, seeking an order requiring the Hanses to immediately execute a quitclaim deed to the property. Must the Hanses execute the quitclaim deed before the foreclosure sale? *First Illinois National Bank v. Hans*, 143 Ill.App.3d 1033, 493 N.E.2d 1171, **Web** 1986 Ill.App. Lexis 2287 (Appellate Court of Illinois)

26.4 Deficiency Judgment Sally Fitch obtained a loan from Buffalo Federal Savings and Loan Association (Buffalo Federal). She signed a promissory note for $130,000 with interest at 17 percent. The loan was secured with a real estate mortgage on property owned by Fitch located in Johnson County, Wyoming. Wyoming does not have an antideficiency statute. Four years later, Fitch was in default on the note. When she was unable to pay the loan to current status, Buffalo Federal sent her a notice of foreclosure. After publication of proper public notice, the sheriff conducted the sale as advertised on the steps of the Johnson County Courthouse. The property sold for a high bid of $66,000. Buffalo Federal applied the $66,000 to the $150,209 balance on the note and sued Fitch to recover a judgment for the deficiency of $84,209. Who wins? Do antideficiency statutes serve any social purpose? *Fitch v. Buffalo Federal Savings and Loan Association*, 751 P.2d 1309, **Web** 1988 Wyo. Lexis 27 (Supreme Court of Wyoming)

26.5 Consumer Leasing Joyce Givens entered into a rental agreement with Rent-A-Center, Inc. (Rent-A-Center), whereby she rented a bar and an entertainment center. The agreement provided that she must pay in advance to keep the furniture for periods of one week or one month. Givens could terminate the agreement at any time by making arrangements for the furniture's return. Givens made payments for four months. After that, she failed to make any further payments but continued to posses the property. When Rent-A-Center became aware that Givens had moved and taken the furniture with her, in violation of the rental agreement, it filed a criminal complaint against her. Thereafter, Givens agreed to return the furniture, and Rent-A-Center dropped the charges. After Rent-A-Center recovered the furniture, Givens sued the company, claiming that the agreement she had signed violated the Consumer Leasing Act. Who wins? *Givens v. Rent-A-Center, Inc.*, 720 F.Supp. 160, **Web** 1988 U.S. Dist. Lexis 16039 (United States District Court for the Southern District of Alabama)

26.6 Fair Credit Billing Oscar S. Gray had been an American Express cardholder. Gray used his card to purchase airline tickets costing $9,312. American Express agreed that Gray could pay for the tickets in 12 equal monthly installments. In January and February, Gray made substantial prepayments of $3,500 and $1,156, respectively. When his March bill arrived, Gray was surprised because American Express had converted the deferred payment plan to a currently due charge, making the entire amount for the tickets due and payable. Gray paid the normal monthly charge under the deferred payment plan and informed American Express in April in writing of its error. In the letter, Gray identified himself, his card number, and the nature of the error. Gray did not learn of any adverse action by American Express until almost one year later, on the night of his and his wife's anniversary. When he offered his American Express card to pay for their wedding anniversary dinner, the restaurant informed Gray that American Express had canceled his account and had instructed the restaurant to destroy the card. Gray sued American Express. Did American Express violate the Fair Credit Billing Act? Who wins? *Gray v. American Express Company*, 743 F.2d 10, **Web** 1984 U.S. App. Lexis 19033 (United States Court of Appeals for the Washington, DC, Circuit)

26.7 Fair Debt Collection Stanley M. Juras was a student at Montana State University (MSU). During his four years at

MSU, Juras took out several student loans from the school under the National Direct Student Loan program. By the time Juras left MSU, he owed the school over $5,000. Juras defaulted on these loans, and MSU assigned the debt to Aman Collection Services, Inc. (Aman), for purposes of collection. Aman obtained a judgment against Juras in a Montana state court for $5,015 on the debt and $1,920 in interest and attorneys' fees. Juras, who at the time lived in California, still refused to pay these amounts. Subsequently, a vice president of Aman, Mr. Gloss, telephoned Juras twice in California before 8:00 A.M. Pacific Standard Time. Gloss told Juras that if he did not pay the debt, he would not receive a college transcript. Juras sued Aman, claiming that the telephone calls violated the Fair Debt Collection Practices Act. Gloss testified at trial that he made the calls before 8:00 A.M. because he had forgotten the difference in time zones between California and Aman's offices in South Dakota. Who wins? *Juras v. Aman Collection Services, Inc.*, 829 F.2d 739, **Web** 1987 U.S. App. Lexis 12888 (United States Court of Appeals for the Ninth Circuit)

BUSINESS ETHICS CASES

26.8 Business Ethics   Jessie Lynch became seriously ill and needed medical attention. Her sister, Ethel Sales, took her to the Forsyth Memorial Hospital in North Carolina for treatment. Lynch was admitted for hospitalization. Sales signed Lynch's admission form, which included the following section:

The undersigned, in consideration of hospital services being rendered or to be rendered by Forsyth County Memorial Hospital Authority, Inc., in Winston-Salem, N.C., to the above patient, does hereby guarantee payment to Forsyth County Hospital Authority, Inc., on demand all charges for said services and incidentals incurred on behalf of such patient.

Lynch received care and services rendered by the hospital until her discharge over 30 days later. The total bill during her hospitalization amounted to $7,977. When Lynch refused to pay the bill, the hospital instituted an action against Lynch and Sales to recover the unpaid amount. Is Sales liable? Did Sales act ethically in denying liability? Did she have a choice when she signed the contract? *Forsyth County Memorial Hospital Authority, Inc.*, 82 N.C.App. 265, 346 S.E.2d 212, **Web** 1986 N.C.App. Lexis 2432 (Court of Appeals of North Carolina)

26.9 Business Ethics   Elizabeth Valentine purchased a home in Philadelphia, Pennsylvania. She applied for and received a home loan from Salmon Building and Loan Association (Salmon) for the purpose of paneling the cellar walls and redecorating the house. Salmon took a security interest in the house as collateral for the loan. Although Salmon gave Valentine a disclosure document, nowhere on the document were finance charges disclosed. The document did notify Valentine that Salmon had a security interest in the house. Over two years later, Valentine sued Salmon (which had since merged with Influential Savings and Loan Association) to rescind the loan. Who wins? Did Salmon act ethically in this case? *Valentine v. Influential Savings and Loan Association*, 572 F.Supp. 36, **Web** 1983 U.S. Dist. Lexis 15884 (United States District Court for the Eastern District of Pennsylvania)

ENDNOTES

1. 12 C.F.R. 226.
2. 15 U.S.C. Sections 1666–1666j.
3. 15 U.S.C. Sections 1667–1667f.
4. 15 U.S.C. Sections 1637c–g.
5. 15 U.S.C. Sections 1691–1691f.
6. 15 U.S.C. Sections 1681–1681u.
7. 15 U.S.C. Sections 1692–1692f.

▲ **Stocking Wine Shelves** *Businesses often purchase goods—such as the wine here—on credit from suppliers. To secure such a loan, the supplier often takes a security interest in personal property—here, the wine—as security for repayment of the advancement of credit. If the buyer fails to pay the loan, the creditor can recover the goods.*

CHAPTER OBJECTIVES

After studying this chapter, you should be able to:

1. Describe the scope of Revised Article 9 of the UCC.
2. Describe how a security interest in personal property is created.
3. Describe the perfection of a security interest through the filing of a financing statement.

4. Explain the UCC rule for determining priority among conflicting claims.
5. Describe how Revised Article 9 provides for the electronic filing of financing statements and records.

CHAPTER CONTENTS

"Debtors are liars."

George Herbert
—*Jacula Prudentum (1651)*

▶ INTRODUCTION TO SECURED TRANSACTIONS AND ELECTRONIC FILING

Many items of *personal property* are purchased with credit rather than cash. Because lenders are reluctant to lend large sums of money simply on the borrower's promise to repay, many of them take a *security interest* in either the item purchased or some other property of the debtor. The property in which a security interest is taken is called *collateral*. When a creditor extends credit to a debtor and takes a security interest in some property of the debtor, it is called a *secured transaction*. If the debtor does not pay the debt, the creditor can foreclose on and recover the collateral.

This chapter discusses secured transactions in personal property.

▶ SECURED TRANSACTIONS

personal property
Tangible property such as equipment, vehicles, furniture, and jewelry, as well as intangible property such as securities, patents, trademarks, and copyrights.

Individuals and businesses purchase or lease various forms of tangible and intangible **personal property**. *Tangible personal property* includes equipment, vehicles, furniture, computers, clothing, jewelry, and such. *Intangible personal property* includes securities, patents, trademarks, and copyrights.

Personal property is oftentimes sold on credit. This means the purchaser-debtor borrows money from a lender-creditor to purchase the personal property. Sometimes a lender extends *unsecured credit* to a debtor to purchase personal property. In this case, the creditor takes no interest in any collateral to secure the loan but bases the decision to extend credit on the credit standing of the debtor. If the debtor defaults on the loan, the creditor must sue the debtor to try to recover the unpaid loan amount.

Revised Article 9 of the UCC
An article of the Uniform Commercial Code that governs secured transactions in personal property.

In some credit transactions, particularly those involving large or expensive items, a creditor may agree to extend credit only if the purchaser pledges some personal property as collateral for the loan. This is called *secured credit*. If the debtor defaults on the loan, the creditor may seek to recover the collateral under a lawful foreclosure action.

LANDMARK LAW
Revised Article 9—Secured Transactions

Article 9 (Secured Transactions) of the Uniform Commercial Code (UCC) governs secured transactions in personal property. Where personal property is used as collateral for a loan or the extension of credit, a resulting secured transaction is governed by Article 9 of the UCC.

After years of study and debate, **Revised Article 9 (Secured Transactions)**, as promulgated by the National Conference of Commissioners on Uniform State Laws and the American Law Institute (together "Commission"), became effective in 2001. Revised Article 9 includes modern and efficient rules that govern secured transactions in personal property. Revised Article 9

includes changes to provisions that have been controversial in the past, as well as new provisions that recognize changes in the commercial environment.

In addition, Revised Article 9 contains many new provisions and rules that recognize the importance of electronic commerce. Revised Article 9 provides rules for the creation, filing, and enforcement of electronic secured transactions.

Since its release in 2001, all states have enacted Revised Article 9 (Secured Transactions) as the UCC statute within their states. The following material in this chapter that covers secured transactions is based on the provisions of Revised Article 9.

Secured Transaction

When a creditor extends credit to a debtor and takes a security interest in some personal property of the debtor, it is called a **secured transaction**. The **secured party** is the seller, lender, or other party in whose favor there is a security interest. If the debtor defaults and does not repay the loan, generally the secured party can foreclose and recover the collateral.

Definitions important to secured transactions are listed in Exhibit 27.1.

Two-Party Secured Transaction

Exhibit 27.2 illustrates a **two-party secured transaction**. Such transactions occur, for example, when a seller sells goods to a buyer on credit and retains a security interest in the goods.

Creditor: One of a tribe of savages dwelling beyond the Financial Straits and dreaded for their desolating excursions.

Ambrose Bierce
The Devil's Dictionary (1911)

secured transaction
A transaction that is created when a creditor makes a loan to a debtor in exchange for the debtor's pledge of personal property as security.

▶ **Exhibit 27.1 DEFINITIONS IMPORTANT TO SECURED TRANSACTIONS**

Revised Article 9 contains definitions that are important for understanding secured transactions. Some of the most important definitions are described below.

1. *Debtor* – A person that has an ownership or other interest in the collateral and owes payment of a secured obligation [Revised UCC 9-102(a)(28)].

   Example A farmer who purchase a large John Deere tractor from a retail dealer on credit and gives the secured creditor an interest in the collateral is the debtor.

2. *Secured party* – A person in whose favor a security interest is created or provided under a security agreement [Revised UCC 9-102(a)(72)].

   Example In the previous example, the John Deere retail dealer is the secured creditor. [The secured party can be the seller (e.g. the John Deere retail dealer), another lender (e.g., a bank), or buyer of accounts (e.g., an investor that purchases the security interest)].

3. *Security interest* – An interest in the collateral, such as personal property or fixtures, which secures payment or performance of an obligation [UCC 1-201(b)(35)].

   Example In the previous example, the debtor-farmer gave the retail dealer-secured creditor a security interest in the John Deere tractor.

4. *Security agreement* – An agreement that creates or provides for a security interest [Revised UCC 9-102(a)(73)].

   Example In the prior example, when the farmer purchased the John Deere tractor from the retail dealer on credit, the retail dealer may require, as a condition of the sale, that the farmer sign a security agreement giving the retail dealer a secured interest in the tractor. If this is done, and the farmer defaults on the payments, the John Deere retail dealer can foreclose on its security agreement and recover the tractor.

5. *Collateral* – The property that is subject to a security agreement [Revised UCC 9-102(a)(12)].

   Example In the previous example, the John Deere tractor is the collateral for the security agreement.

6. *Financing statement* – The record of an initial financing statement or filed record relating to the initial financing statement [Revised UCC 9-102(a)(39)]. This is **Form UCC 1 (UCC Financing Statement)**. The financing statement is usually filed with the appropriate state office to give public notice of the secured party's security interest in the collateral.

   Example In the previous example, if the retail dealer (the secured creditor) files a financing statement, it has given public notice of its secured interest in the collateral, the John Deere tractor.

▶ **Exhibit 27.2 TWO-PARTY SECURED TRANSACTION**

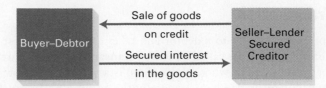

Three-Party Secured Transaction

Exhibit 27.3 illustrates a **three-party secured transaction**. This type of situation occurs when a seller sells goods to a buyer who has obtained financing from a third-party lender (e.g., bank) that takes a security interest in the goods sold.

▶ **Exhibit 27.3 THREE-PARTY SECURED TRANSACTION**

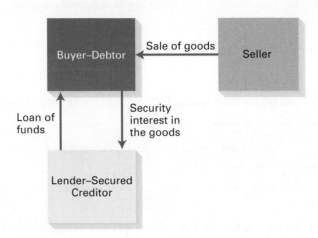

Personal Property Subject to a Security Agreement

collateral
Personal property that is subject to a security agreement.

A security interest may be given in various types of personal property that becomes **collateral** for the loan [Revised UCC 9-102(a)(12)]. Personal property that may be given as security is listed in Exhibit 27.4.

▶ **Exhibit 27.4 TYPES OF COLLATERAL**

1. **Tangible Personal Property**   All things that are movable when a security interest attaches [Revised UCC 9-102(a)(44)]. This includes:
   1. **Accessions** that are goods that are physically united with other goods in such a manner that the identity of the original goods is not lost [Revised UCC 9-102(a)(1)].

      Example GPS system that is installed in an automobile.

   2. **Consumer goods** bought or used primarily for personal, family, or household purposes [Revised UCC 9-102(a)(23)].

      Examples Household televisions, furniture, and furnishings.

   3. **Equipment** bought or used primarily for business [Revised UCC 9-102(a)(33)].

      Examples Business trucks, moving cranes, and assembly line equipment.

   4. **Farm products**, including crops, aquatic goods, livestock, and supplies produced in farming operations [Revised UCC 9-102(a)(34)].

      Examples Wheat, fish, cattle, milk, apples, and unborn calves.

5. **Inventory** held for sale or lease, including work in progress and materials [Revised UCC 9-102(a)(48)].

   Example Raw materials used in production of goods.

2. **Intangible Personal Property**   Nonphysical personal property. This includes:
   1. **Accounts** that include a right to payment of a monetary obligation (a) for personal or real property sold, leased, licensed, assigned, or otherwise disposed of, (b) services rendered or to be rendered, (c) policies of insurance, (d) secondary obligations incurred, (e) energy provided, (f) use of hire of a vessel under charter, (g) arising out of the use of a credit or charge card, (h) winnings in a state-operated or state-sponsored lottery, and (i) health-care-insurance receivables [Revised UCC 9-102(a)(1)].
   2. **Chattel paper**, which is a record that evidences both a monetary obligation and a security interest in specific goods and software used in the goods [Revised UCC 9-102(a)(11)].

      Example A security agreement. **Tangible chattel paper** is inscribed on a tangible medium [Revised UCC 9-102(a)(78)]. **Electronic chattel paper** is evidenced by information stored in an electronic medium [Revised UCC 9-102(a)(31)].

   3. **Deposit accounts** [Revised UCC 9-102(a)(29)].

      Examples Demand, time, savings, passbook, or similar account maintained at a bank.

   4. **General intangibles**, which means any personal property (other than exceptions listed in Revised UCC 9-102(a)(42)) payment intangibles, and software [Revised UCC 9-102(a)(42)].

      Examples Patents, copyrights, royalties, and the like.

   5. **Instruments**, which include negotiable instruments and any other writing that evidences a right to the payment of a monetary obligation that can ordinarily be transferred [Revised UCC 9-102(a)(47)].

      Examples Checks, notes, stocks, bonds, and other investment securities [Revised UCC 9-102(a)].

   Revised Article 9 of the UCC does not apply to transactions involving real estate mortgages, landlord's liens, artisan's or mechanic's liens, liens on wages, judicial liens, and the like. These types of liens are usually covered by other laws.

► CREATING A SECURITY INTEREST

Revised Article 9 sets forth the requirements that must be met to create a security interest in personal property. These requirements are discussed in the following paragraphs.

Security Agreement

Unless the creditor has possession of the collateral, there must be a **security agreement**. A security agreement is an agreement that creates or provides for a security interest [Revised UCC 9-102(a)(73)]. To be valid, a security agreement must (1) clearly describe the collateral so that it can be readily identified, (2) contain the debtor's promise to repay the creditor, including terms of repayment (e.g., interest rate, time of payment), (3) set forth the creditor's rights upon the debtor's default, and (4) be signed by the debtor.

security agreement
A written document signed by a debtor that creates a security interest in personal property.

Attachment

The debtor must have a current or future legal right in or the right to possession of the collateral. For example, a debtor may give a creditor a security interest in goods currently owned or in the possession of the debtor or in goods to be later acquired by the debtor. A debtor who does not have ownership or possessory rights to property cannot give a security interest in that property.

attachment
A situation in which a creditor has an enforceable security interest against a debtor and can satisfy the debt out of the designated collateral.

Cattle Pasture *The floating-lien concept provides that a security interest can attach to property that was not originally in the possession of the debtor when the security agreement was executed, such as new-born calves of a cattle herd.*

If these requirements are met, the rights of the secured party attach to the collateral. **Attachment** means that the creditor has an enforceable security interest against the debtor and can satisfy the debt out of the designated collateral (subject to the priority rules discussed later in this chapter) [Revised UCC 9-203(a)].

The Floating-Lien Concept

A security agreement may provide that the security interest attaches to property that was not originally in the possession of the debtor when the agreement was executed. This interest is usually referred to as a **floating lien**. A floating lien can attach to after-acquired property, sale proceeds, and future advances. These are discussed in the following paragraphs.

floating lien
A security interest in property that was not in the possession of the debtor when the security agreement was executed.

After-Acquired Property   Many security agreements contain a clause that gives the secured party a security interest in **after-acquired property** of the debtor. After-acquired property is property that the debtor acquires after the security agreement is executed [Revised UCC 9-204(a)].

after-acquired property
Property that a debtor acquires after a security agreement is executed.

Example Manufacturing Corporation borrows $100,000 from First Bank and gives the bank a security interest in both its current and after-acquired inventory. If Manufacturing Corporation defaults on its loan to First Bank, the bank can claim any available original inventory as well as enough after-acquired inventory to satisfy its secured claim.

Sale Proceeds   Unless otherwise stated in a security agreement, if a debtor sells, exchanges, or disposes of collateral subject to such an agreement, the secured party automatically has the right to receive the **sale proceeds** of the sale, exchange, or disposition [Revised UCC 9-102(a)(64), 9-203(f), 9-315(a)].

sale proceeds
The resulting assets from the sale, exchange, or disposal of collateral subject to a security agreement.

Rather go to bed supperless than rise in debt.

Benjamin Franklin

Example Zip, Inc., is a retail automobile dealer. To finance its inventory of new automobiles, Zip borrows money from First Bank and gives the bank a security interest in the inventory. Zip sells an automobile that is subject to the security agreement to Phyllis, who signs an installment sales contract, agreeing to pay Zip for the car in 24 equal monthly installments. If Zip defaults on its payment to First Bank, the bank is entitled to receive the remaining payments from Phyllis.

Future Advances   A debtor may establish a continuing or revolving line of credit at a bank. Certain personal property of the debtor is designated as collateral for future loans from the line of credit. A maximum limit that the debtor may borrow is set, but the debtor can draw against the line of credit at any time. Any **future advances** made against the line of credit are subject to the security interest in the collateral. A new security agreement does not have to be executed each time a future advance is taken against the line of credit [Revised UCC 9-204(c)].

future advances
Funds advanced to a debtor from a line of credit secured by collateral. Future advances are future withdrawals from a line of credit.

▶ PERFECTING A SECURITY INTEREST

The concept of **perfection of a security interest** establishes the right of a secured creditor against other creditors who claim an interest in the collateral. Perfection is a legal process. The three main methods of perfecting a security interest under the UCC are (1) perfection by filing a financing statement, (2) perfection by possession of collateral, and (3) perfection by a purchase money security interest in consumer goods. These three main methods of perfecting a security interest are discussed in the following paragraphs.

perfection of a security interest
A process that establishes the right of a secured creditor against other creditors who claim an interest in the collateral.

Perfection by Filing a Financing Statement

Often, a creditor's physical possession of collateral is impractical because it would deprive the debtor of use of the collateral (e.g., farm equipment, industrial machinery, consumer goods). At other times, it is simply impossible (e.g., accounts receivable). Filing a **financing statement** in the appropriate government office is the most common method of perfecting a creditor's security interest in such collateral [Revised UCC 9-501]. The person who files the financing statement should request the filing officer to note on his or her copy of the document the file number, date, and hour of filing. A financing statement covering fixtures is called a *fixture filing*. A financing statement can be electronically filed [Revised UCC 9-102(a)(18)]. A uniform financing statement form, UCC Form I, is used in all states [Revised UCC 9-521(a)].

financing statement
A document filed by a secured creditor with the appropriate government office that constructively notifies the world of his or her security interest in personal property.

Financing statements are available for review by the public. They serve as constructive notice to the world that a creditor claims an interest in a property. Financing statements are effective for five years from the date of filing [Revised UCC 9-515(a)]. A *continuation statement* may be filed up to six months prior to the expiration of a financing statement's five-year term. Such statements are effective for a new five-year term. Succeeding continuation statements may be filed [Revised UCC 9-515(d), 9-515(e)].

To be enforceable, a financing statement must contain the name of the debtor the name and address of the secured party or a representative of the secured party, and the collateral covered by the financing statement [Revised UCC 9-502(a)]. The secured party can file the security agreement as a financing statement. A financing statement that provides only the debtor's trade name does not sufficiently provide the name of the debtor [Revised UCC 9-503(c)].

State law specifies where a financing statement must be filed. A state may choose either the **secretary of state** or the county clerk in the county of the debtor's residence or, if the debtor is not a resident of the state, in the county where the goods are kept or in another county office or both. Most states require financing statements covering farm equipment, farm products, accounts, and consumer goods to be filed with the county clerk [Revised UCC 9-501]. Many states allow electronic filing of financing statements.

In the following case, the court had to determine whether there was a defective filing of a financing statement.

If you think nobody cares if you're alive, try missing a couple of car payments.

Earl Wilson

CASE 27.1 Financing Statement

In re FV Steel and Wire Company

310 B.R. 390, Web 2004 Bankr. Lexis 748 (2004)
United States Bankruptcy Court for the Eastern District of Wisconsin

"PSC ignored the correct legal name and filed under the trade name at its own peril."

—Judge Kelley

Facts

PSC Metals, Inc. (PSC), entered into an agreement whereby it extended credit to Keystone Consolidated Industries, Inc., and took back a security interest in personal property owned by Keystone. PSC filed a financing statement with the state, listing the debtor's trade name "Keystone Steel & Wire Co." rather than its corporate name, "Keystone Consolidated Industries, Inc." When Keystone went into bankruptcy, PSC filed a motion with the bankruptcy court to obtain the personal property securing its loan. Keystone's other creditors and the bankruptcy trustee objected, arguing that because PSC's financing statement was defectively filed, PSC did not therefore have a perfected security interest in the personal property. If this were true, then PSC would become an unsecured creditor in Keystone's bankruptcy proceeding.

Issue

Was the financing statement filed in the debtor's trade name, rather than in its corporate name, effective?

Language of the Court

In our case, a search under the true name did not reveal PSC's financing statement. The only way to find PSC's financing statement is to search under the name "Keystone" which would reveal 237 filings. PSC recognized Keystone's true corporate name in the original Agreement. PSC was obviously aware of the correct corporate name of its debtor from the beginning of the transaction, but chose to file under the trade name instead.

It is undisputed that under Revised Article 9, PSC's financing statement would be insufficient as a matter of law. Section 9-503(a) now requires the financing statement to contain the name of a corporate debtor "indicated on the public record of the debtor's jurisdiction of organization," and Section 9-503(c) expressly states: "A financing statement that provides only the debtor's trade name does not sufficiently provide the name of the debtor." One of the mantras espoused by the experts was the necessity of using the debtor's correct legal name, not a trade name or nickname. PSC knew the debtor's correct legal name. PSC ignored the correct legal name and filed under the trade name at its own peril.

Decision

The bankruptcy court held that PSC's filing of the financing statement under Keystone's trade name and not under Keystone's legal name was a defective filing. Therefore, the bankruptcy trustee could avoid PSC's unperfected security interest. PSC became an unsecured creditor for the debt owed to it by Keystone.

Case Questions

Critical Legal Thinking What is a financing statement? Where is it filed? Who files it?

Business Ethics Did PSC act ethically in arguing that its financing statement was valid? Why or why not?

Contemporary Business What is the purpose of filing a financing statement? Explain.

Perfection by Possession of Collateral

perfection by possession of the collateral
A rule that says if a secured creditor has physical possession of the collateral, no financing statement has to be filed; the creditor's possession is sufficient to put other potential creditors on notice of the creditor's secured interest in the property.

No financing statement has to be filed if the creditor has physical **possession of the collateral**. The rationale behind this rule is that if someone other than the debtor is in possession of the property, a potential creditor is on notice that another may claim an interest in the debtor's property. A secured creditor who holds the debtor's property as collateral must use reasonable care in its custody and preservation [Revised UCC 9-310, 9-312(b), 9-313].

Example Karen borrows $3,000 from Alan and gives her motorcycle to him as security for the loan. Alan does not file a financing statement. Another creditor obtains a judgment against Karen. This creditor cannot recover the motorcycle from Alan. Even though Alan has not filed a financing statement, his security interest in the motorcycle is perfected because he has possession of the motorcycle.

Perfection by a Purchase Money Security Interest in Consumer Goods

Sellers and lenders often extend credit to consumers to purchase consumer goods. **Consumer goods** include furniture, television sets, home appliances, and other goods used primarily for personal, family, or household purposes.

A creditor who extends credit to a consumer to purchase a consumer good under a written security agreement obtains a **purchase money security interest** in the consumer good. This agreement automatically perfects the creditor's security interest at the time of the sale. The creditor does not have to file a financing statement or take possession of the goods to perfect his or her security interest. This interest is called **perfection by attachment**, or the **automatic perfection rule** [Revised UCC 9-309(1)].

Example Marcia buys a $3,000 high-definition plasma television for her home on credit extended by the seller, Circuit City. Circuit City requires Marcia to sign a security agreement. Circuit City has a purchase money security interest in the television that is automatically perfected at the time of the credit sale.

We are either debtors or creditors before we have had time to look around.

Johann Wolfgang Von Goethe
Elective Affinities, Book II (1808)

purchase money security interest
An interest a creditor automatically obtains when he or she extends credit to a consumer to purchase consumer goods.

CONCEPT SUMMARY

METHODS OF PERFECTING A SECURITY INTEREST

Perfection Method	How Created
Financing statement	Creditor files a financing statement with the appropriate government office.
Possession of collateral	Creditor obtains physical possession of the collateral.
Purchase money security interest	Creditor extends credit to a debtor to purchase consumer goods and obtains a security interest in the goods.

Termination Statement

When a secured consumer debt is paid, the secured party must file a **termination statement** with each filing officer with whom the financing statement was filed. The termination statement must be filed within one month after the debt is paid or 20 days after receipt of the debtor's written demand, whichever occurs first [Revised UCC 9-513(b)]. If the affected secured party fails to file or send the termination statement as required, the secured party is liable for any other losses caused to the debtor.

termination statement
A document filed by a secured party that ends a secured interest because the debt has been paid.

▶ PRIORITY OF CLAIMS

Often, two or more creditors claim an interest in the same collateral or property. The priority of the claims is determined according to (1) whether the claim is unsecured or secured and (2) the time at which secured claims were attached or perfected.

priority of claims
The order in which conflicting claims of creditors in the same collateral are solved.

UCC Rules for Determining Priority

The UCC establishes rules for determining **priority of claims** of creditors. The UCC rules for establishing priority of claims are listed and described in Exhibit 27.5.

Buyers in the Ordinary Course of Business

A **buyer in the ordinary course of business** who purchases goods from a merchant takes the goods free of any perfected or unperfected security interest in the merchant's inventory,

buyer in the ordinary course of business
A person who in good faith and without knowledge of another's ownership or security interest in goods buys the goods in the ordinary course of business from a person in the business of selling goods of that kind.

▶ **Exhibit 27.5 UCC RULES FOR DETERMINING PRIORITY**

1. **Secured versus unsecured claims.** A creditor who has the only secured interest in the debtor's collateral has priority over unsecured interests.
2. **Competing unperfected security interests.** If two or more secured parties claim an interest in the same collateral but neither has a perfected claim, the first to attach has priority [Revised UCC 9-322(a)(3)].
3. **Perfected versus unperfected claims.** If two or more secured parties claim an interest in the same collateral but only one has perfected his or her security interest, the perfected security interest has priority [Revised UCC 9-322(a)(2)].
4. **Competing perfected security interests.** If two or more secured parties have perfected security interests in the same collateral, the first to perfect (e.g., by filing a financing statement, by taking possession of the collateral) has priority [Revised UCC 9-322(a)(1)].
5. **Perfected secured claims in fungible, commingled goods.** If a security interest in goods is perfected but the goods are later commingled with other goods in which there are perfected security interests and the goods become part of a product or mass and lose their identity, the security interests rank equally according to the ratio that the cost of goods to which each interest originally attached bears to the cost of the total product or mass [Revised UCC 9-336].

Words pay no debts.

William Shakespeare
Troilus and Cressida, Act III

even if the buyer knows of the existence of the security interest. This rule is necessary because buyers would be reluctant to purchase goods if a merchant's creditors could recover the goods if the merchant defaulted on loans owed to secured creditors [Revised UCC 9-320(a), 1-201(9)].

A buyer in the ordinary course of business is a person who buys goods in good faith, without knowledge that the sale violates the rights of another person in the goods. The buyer purchases the goods in the ordinary course from a person in the business of selling goods of that kind.

Example Central Car Sales, Inc. (Central), a new car dealership, finances all its inventory of new automobiles at First Bank. First Bank takes a security interest in Central's inventory of cars and perfects this security interest. Kim, a buyer in the ordinary course of business, purchases a car from Central for cash. The car cannot be recovered from Kim even if Central defaults on its payments to the bank.

INTERNET LAW & ONLINE COMMERCE
Revised Article 9 (Secured Transactions) Recognizes Electronic Financing Statements and Records

Revised Article 9 (Secured Transactions) contains provisions that recognize the importance of electronic records. The revised article contains new definitions that apply to secured transactions in personal property. Some of the definitions for electronic commerce and their implications are discussed here:

- **Record** means information that is inscribed on a tangible medium or that is stored in an electronic or other medium and is retrievable in perceivable form [Revised UCC 9-102(a)(69)]. The term *record* is now used in many of the provisions of Revised Article 9 in place of the term *writing*, further recognizing the importance of electronic commerce.
- **Electronic chattel paper** means chattel paper evidenced by a record or records consisting of

information stored in an electronic medium [Revised UCC 9-102(a)(31)]. This includes records initially created and executed in electronic form and tangible writings that are converted to electronic form (e.g., electronic images created from a signed writing).
- **Financing statement** means a record composed of an initial financing statement and any filed record related to the initial financing statement [Revised UCC 9-102(a)(39)]. Thus, financing statements may be in electronic form and filed and stored as electronic records.

These provisions of Revised Article 9 (Secured Transactions) recognize the importance of electronic transactions and records used in today's commercial environment.

▶ DEFAULT AND REMEDIES

Article 9 of the UCC defines the rights, duties, and remedies of the secured party and the debtor in the event of **default**. The term *default* is not defined. Instead, the parties are free to define it in their security agreement. Events such as failing to make scheduled payments when due, bankruptcy of the debtor, breach of the warranty of ownership as to the collateral, and other such events are commonly defined in security agreements as default.

Upon default by a debtor, the secured party may reduce his or her claim to judgment, foreclose, or otherwise enforce his or her security interest by any available judicial procedure [Revised UCC 9-601(a)]. The UCC provides the secured party with the remedies discussed in the following paragraphs.

default
Failure to make scheduled payments when due, bankruptcy of the debtor, breach of the warranty of ownership as to the collateral, and other events defined by the parties in a security agreement.

Taking Possession of the Collateral

Most secured parties seek to cure a default by **taking possession of the collateral**. This taking is usually done by **repossessing** the goods from the defaulting debtor. A secured party may repossess the collateral pursuant to judicial process or without judicial process if the self-help repossession of the collateral does not breach the peace [Revised UCC 9-609(b)].

After repossessing the goods, the secured party can either (1) retain the collateral, or (2) sell, lease, license, or otherwise dispose of it and satisfy the debt from the proceeds of the sale or disposition. There is one caveat: The secured party must act in good faith, with commercial reasonableness, and with reasonable care to preserve the collateral in his or her possession [Revised UCC 9-603, 9-610(a), 9-620].

repossession
A right granted to a secured creditor to take possession of the collateral upon default by the debtor.

Example Western Drilling, Inc., purchases a piece of oil-drilling equipment on credit from Haliburton, Inc. Haliburton files a financing statement covering its security interest in the equipment. If Western Drilling fails to make the required payments, Haliburton can foreclose on its lien and repossess the equipment.

Retention of Collateral

In the event of a debtor's default, a secured creditor who repossesses collateral may propose to **retain the collateral** in satisfaction of the debtor's obligation. Notice of the proposal must be sent to the debtor unless he or she has signed a written statement renouncing this right. In the case of consumer goods, no other notice need be given [Revised UCC 9-620(a)]. A secured creditor may not retain the collateral (and must dispose of the collateral) in the following two situations:

retention of collateral
A secured creditor's repossession of collateral upon a debtor's default and proposal to retain the collateral in satisfaction of the debtor's obligation.

1. **Written objection.** A secured creditor must dispose of the collateral if he or she receives a written objection to the proposal from a person entitled to receive notice within 20 days after the notice was sent [Revised UCC 9-602, 9-603, 9-610, 9-613].
2. **Consumer goods.** A secured creditor must dispose of the collateral if the debt involves consumer goods, and the debtor has paid 60 percent of the cash price or loan. In this case, the secured creditor must dispose of the goods within 90 days after taking possession of them. A consumer may renounce his or her rights in this situation [Revised UCC 9-620(e), 9-620(f)].

A secured creditor may retain the collateral as satisfaction of the debtor's obligation if neither of the preceding two situations prevents this action.

Disposition of Collateral

In the event of a debtor's default, a secured party who chooses not to retain the collateral may sell, lease, or otherwise dispose of it in its current condition or following any commercially reasonable preparation or processing. **Disposition of the collateral** may be by public or private proceedings. The method, manner, time, place, and terms of the disposition must be commercially reasonable [Revised UCC 9-610].

The secured party must notify the debtor in writing about the time and place of any public or private sale or any other intended disposition of the collateral unless the debtor

disposition of collateral
A secured creditor's repossession of collateral upon a debtor's default and selling, leasing, or otherwise disposing of it in a commercially reasonable manner.

has signed a statement renouncing or modifying his on her rights to receive such notice. In the case of consumer goods, no other notification need be sent.

The proceeds from a sale, a lease, or another disposition of collateral must be applied in the following order [Revised UCC 9-608]:

1. Reasonable expenses of retaking, holding, and preparing the collateral for sale, lease, or other disposition are paid first. Attorneys' fees and other legal expenses may be paid if provided for in the security agreement and not prohibited by law.
2. Satisfaction of the balance of the indebtedness owed by the debtor to the secured party is made next.
3. Satisfaction is made of subordinate (junior) security interests whose written notifications of demand have been received before distribution of the proceeds is completed. The secured party may require subordinate security interests to furnish reasonable proof of their interests.
4. The debtor is entitled to receive any surplus that remains.

Deficiency Judgment

Unless otherwise agreed, after a debtor's default, if the proceeds from the disposition of collateral are not sufficient to satisfy the debt to the secured party, the debtor is personally liable to the secured party for the payment of the deficiency. The secured party may bring an action to recover a **deficiency judgment** against the debtor [Revised UCC 9-608(a)(4)].

deficiency judgment
A judgment that allows a secured creditor to successfully bring a separate legal action to recover a deficiency from the debtor. It entitles the secured creditor to recover the amount of the judgment from the debtor's other property.

Example Sean borrows $15,000 from First Bank to purchase a new automobile. He signs a security agreement, giving First Bank a purchase money security interest in the automobile. Sean defaults after making payments that reduce the debt to $13,250. First Bank repossesses the automobile and sells it at a public auction for $11,000. The selling expenses and sales commission are $1,250. This amount is deducted from the proceeds. The remaining $9,750 is applied to the $13,250 balance of the debt. Sean remains personally liable to First Bank for the $3,500 deficiency ($13,250 balance − $9,750 proceeds).

Redemption Rights

In the event of a debtor's default, the debtor or another secured party may redeem the collateral before the priority lienholder has disposed of it, entered into a contract to dispose of it, or discharged the debtor's obligation by having exercised a right to retain the collateral. The right of redemption may be accomplished by payment of all obligations secured by the collateral, all expenses reasonably incurred by the secured party in retaking and holding the collateral, and any attorneys' fees and other legal expenses provided for in the security agreement and not prohibited by law [Revised UCC 9-623].

Relinquishing the Security Interest and Proceeding to Judgment on the Underlying Debt

judgment on the underlying debt
A right granted to a secured creditor to relinquish his or her security interest in the collateral and sue a defaulting debtor to recover the amount of the underlying debt.

When a debtor defaults, instead of repossessing the collateral, a secured creditor may relinquish his or her security interest in the collateral and proceed to **judgment** against the debtor to recover the underlying debt. This course of action is rarely chosen unless the value of the collateral has been reduced below the amount of the secured interest and the debtor has other assets from which to satisfy the debt [Revised UCC 9-601(a)].

Example Suppose Jack borrows $100,000 from First Bank to purchase a piece of equipment, and First Bank perfects its security interest in the equipment for this amount. Jack defaults on the loan. If the equipment has gone down in value to $60,000 at the time of default, but Jack has other personal assets to satisfy the debt, it may be in the bank's best interest to relinquish its security interest, sue Jack, and proceed to judgment on the underlying debt.

artisan's or mechanic's lien
A statutory lien given to workers on personal property to which they furnish services or materials in the ordinary course of business.

Example If the secured creditor obtains a judgment against the debtor but the debtor has no money to pay the judgment, the secured creditor can proceed to take possession of the collateral.

CONTEMPORARY ENVIRONMENT

Artisan's Lien

If a worker in the ordinary course of business furnishes services or materials to someone with respect to goods and receives a lien on the goods by statute, this **artisan's lien** prevails over all other security interests in the goods unless a statutory lien provides otherwise. Thus, such liens are often called **super-priority liens**. An artisan's lien is possessory; that is, the artisan must be in possession of the property in order to effect an artisan's lien.

Example Janice borrows money from First Bank to purchase an automobile. First Bank has a purchase money security interest in the car and files a financing statement. The automobile is involved in an accident, and Janice takes the car to Joe's Repair Shop (Joe's) to be repaired. Joe's retains an artisan's lien on the car for the amount of the repair work. When the repair work is completed, Janice refuses to pay. She also defaults on her payments to First Bank. If the car is sold to satisfy the liens, the artisan's lien is paid in full from the proceeds before First Bank is paid anything.

TEST REVIEW TERMS AND CONCEPTS

After-acquired property
Article 9 (Secured Transactions) of the Uniform Commercial Code (UCC)
Artisan's lien
Attachment
Buyer in the ordinary course of business
Collateral
Consumer goods
Default

Deficiency judgment
Disposition of collateral
Electronic chattel paper
Financing statement
Floating lien
Future advance
Judgment on the underlying debt
Perfection by attachment (automatic perfection rule)
Perfection by possession of collateral

Perfection of a security interest
Personal property
Priority of claims
Purchase money security interest
Record
Repossession
Retention of collateral
Revised Article 9 (Secured Transactions) of the UCC
Sale proceeds

Secretary of state
Secured party
Secured transaction
Security agreement
Super-priority lien
Taking possession of collateral
Termination statement
Three-party secured transaction
Two-party secured transaction

CASE PROBLEMS

27.1 Financing Statement   C&H Trucking, Inc. (C&H), borrowed $19,747.56 from S&D Petroleum Company, Inc. (S&D). S&D hired Clifton M. Tamsett to prepare a security agreement naming C&H as the debtor and giving S&D a security interest in a new Mack truck. The security agreement prepared by Tamsett declared that the collateral also secured:

any other indebtedness or liability of the debtor to the secured party direct or indirect, absolute or contingent, due or to become due, now existing or hereafter arising, including all future advances or loans which may be made at the option of the secured party.

Tamsett failed to file a financing statement or the executed agreement with the appropriate government office. C&H subsequently paid off the original debt, and S&D continued to extend new credit to C&H. Two years later, when C&H owed S&D over $17,000, S&D learned that (1) C&H was insolvent, (2) the Mack truck had been sold, and (3) Tamsett had failed to file the security agreement. Does S&D have a security interest in the Mack truck? Is Tamsett liable to S&D? *S&D Petroleum Company, Inc. v.*

Tamsett, 144 A.D.2d 849, 534 N.Y.S.2d 800, Web 1988 N.Y.App. Div. Lexis 11258 (Supreme Court of New York)

27.2 Priority of Security Agreements   World Wide Tracers, Inc. (World Wide), sold certain of its assets and properties, including equipment, furniture, uniforms, accounts receivable, and contract rights, to Metropolitan Protection, Inc. (Metropolitan). To secure payment of the purchase price, Metropolitan executed a security agreement and financing statement in favor of World Wide. The agreement, which was filed with the Minnesota secretary of state, stated that "all of the property listed on Exhibit A (equipment, furniture, and fixtures) together with any property of the debtor acquired after" the agreement was executed was collateral.

One and one-half years later, State Bank (Bank) loaned money to Metropolitan, which executed a security agreement and financing statement in favor of Bank. Bank filed the financing statement with the Minnesota secretary of state's office one month later. The financing statement contained the following language describing the collateral: "All accounts receivable and contract rights owned or hereafter acquired.

All equipment now owned and hereafter acquired, including but not limited to, office furniture and uniforms."

When Metropolitan defaulted on its agreement with World Wide six months later, World Wide brought suit, asserting its alleged security agreement in Metropolitan's accounts receivable. Bank filed a counterclaim, asserting its perfected security interest in Metropolitan's accounts receivable. Who wins? *World Wide Tracers, Inc. v. Metropolitan Protection, Inc.*, 384 N.W.2d 442, Web 1986 Minn. Lexis 753 (Supreme Court of Minnesota)

27.3 Floating Lien Joseph H. Jones and others (debtors) borrowed money from Columbus Junction State Bank (Bank) and executed a security agreement in favor of Bank. Bank perfected its security interest by filing financing statements covering "equipment, farm products, crops, livestock, supplies, contract rights, and all accounts and proceeds thereof" with the Iowa secretary of state. Four years and 10 months later, Bank filed a continuation statement with the Iowa secretary of state. Four years and 10 months after that, Bank filed a second continuation statement with the Iowa secretary of state. Two years later, the debtors filed for Chapter 7 liquidation bankruptcy. The bankruptcy trustee collected $10,073 from the sale of the debtors' crops and an undetermined amount of soybeans harvested on farmland owned by the debtors. The bankruptcy trustee claimed the funds and soybeans on behalf of the bankruptcy estate. Bank claimed the funds and soybeans as a perfected secured creditor. Who wins? *In re Jones*, 79 B.R. 839, Web 1987 Bankr. Lexis 1825 (United States Bankruptcy Court for the Northern District of Iowa)

27.4 Sale Proceeds Murphy Oldsmobile, Inc. (Murphy), operated an automobile dealership that sold new and used automobiles. General Motors Acceptance Corporation (GMAC) loaned funds to Murphy to finance the purchase of new automobiles as inventory. The loan was secured by a duly perfected security agreement in all existing and after-acquired inventory and the proceeds therefrom. Section 9-306 of the New York UCC provides that a security interest in collateral continues in "identifiable proceeds." Over the course of a week, Murphy received checks and drafts from the sale of the secured inventory in the amount of $97,888, which it deposited in a general business checking account at Norstar Bank (Bank). During that week, Murphy defaulted on certain loans it had received from Bank. Bank exercised its right of setoff and seized the funds on deposit in Murphy's checking account. GMAC sued to enforce its security claim against these funds. Who wins? *General Motors Acceptance Corporation v. Norstar Bank, N.A.*, 141 Misc.2d 349, 532 N.Y.S.2d 685, Web 1988 N.Y. Misc. Lexis 595 (Supreme Court of New York)

27.5 Priority of Security Interests Clyde and Marlys Trees (Trees), owners of the Wine Shop, Inc., borrowed money from the American Heritage Bank & Trust Company (Bank). They personally and on behalf of the corporation executed a promissory note, security agreement, and financing statement to Bank. Bank properly filed a security agreement and financing statement naming the Wine Shop's inventory, stock in trade, furniture, fixtures, and equipment "now owned or hereafter to be acquired" as collateral. Trees also borrowed money from a junior lienholder, whose promissory note was secured by the same collateral. The Wine Shop subsequently defaulted on both notes. Without informing Bank, the junior lienholder took over the assets of the Wine Shop and transferred them to a corporation, O&E, Inc. Fearing that its security interest would not be adequately protected, Bank filed a motion to enforce its security interest. Can Bank enforce its security interest even though the collateral was transferred to another party? *American Heritage Bank & Trust Company v. O&E, Inc.*, 40 Colo.App. 306, 576 P.2d 566, Web 1978 Colo. App. Lexis 667 (Court of Appeals of Colorado)

27.6 Priority of Security Interests Paul High purchased various items of personal property and livestock from William and Marilyn McGowen. To secure the purchase price, High granted the McGowens a security interest in the personal property and livestock. Two and one-half months later, High borrowed $86,695 from Nebraska State Bank (Bank) and signed a promissory note, granting Bank a security interest in all his farm products, including but not limited to all his livestock. Bank immediately perfected its security agreement by filing a financing statement with the county clerk in Dakota County, Nebraska. The McGowens perfected their security interest by filing a financing statement and security agreement with the county clerk three months after the Bank filed its financing statement. Three years later, High defaulted on the obligations owed to the McGowens and Bank. Whose security interest has priority? *McGowen v. Nebraska State Bank*, 229 Neb. 471, 427 N.W.2d 772, Web 1988 Neb. Lexis 290 (Supreme Court of Nebraska)

27.7 Purchase Money Security Interest Prior Brothers, Inc. (PBI), began financing its farming operations through Bank of California, N.A. (Bank). Bank's loans were secured by PBI's equipment and after-acquired property. Bank immediately filed a financing statement, perfecting its security interest. Two years later, PBI contacted the International Harvester dealership in Sunnyside, Washington, about the purchase of a new tractor. A retail installment contract for a model 1066 International Harvester tractor was executed. PBI took delivery of the tractor "on approval," agreeing that if it decided to purchase the tractor, it would inform the dealership of its intention and would send a $6,000 down payment. The dealership received a $6,000 check. The dealership immediately filed a financing statement concerning the tractor. Subsequently, when PBI went into receivership, the dealership filed a complaint, asking the court to declare that its purchase money security interest in the tractor had priority over Bank's security interest. Does it? *In the Matter of Prior Brothers, Inc.*, 29 Wn.App. 905, 632 P.2d 522, Web 1981 Wash.App. Lexis 2507 (Court of Appeals of Washington)

27.8 Purchase Money Security Interest Sandwich State Bank (Sandwich) made a general farm loan to David Klotz and Hinckley Grain Company. The loan was secured by the assets of Klotz's farm and after-acquired property. Sandwich filed a financing statement with the Kane County recorder to perfect its security interest. Sandwich filed the necessary continuation statements so its security interest remained in effect up to and during the time of trial. Eleven years after Sandwich State Bank made its loan, DeKalb Bank (DeKalb) loaned Klotz funds for the particular purpose of purchasing certain cattle. DeKalb immediately filed a financing statement to perfect its security interest in the cattle. The cattle in question were all purchased using funds loaned to Klotz by DeKalb. When Klotz defaulted on the loan to DeKalb, DeKalb sued to enforce its security interest and to recover possession of the cattle. Does DeKalb's security interest have priority over Sandwich's security interest? *DeKalb Bank v. Klotz*, 151 Ill.App.3d 638, 502 N.E.2d 1256, Web 1986 Ill. App. Lexis 3351 (Appellate Court of Illinois)

27.9 Buyer in the Ordinary Course of Business Heritage Ford Lincoln Mercury, Inc. (Heritage), was in the business of selling new cars. Heritage entered into an agreement with Ford Motor Credit Company (Ford), whereby Ford extended a continuing line of credit to Heritage to purchase vehicles. Heritage granted Ford a purchase money security interest in all motor vehicles it owned and thereafter acquired and in all proceeds from the sale of such motor vehicles. Ford immediately filed its financing statement with the secretary of state. When the dealership experienced financial trouble, two Heritage officers decided to double finance certain new cars by issuing dealer papers to themselves and obtaining financing for two new cars from First National Bank & Trust Company of El Dorado (Bank). The loan proceeds were deposited in the dealership's account to help with its financial difficulties. The cars were available for sale. When the dealership closed its doors and turned over the car inventory to Ford, Bank alleged that it had priority over Ford because the Heritage officers were buyers in the ordinary course of business. Who wins? *First National Bank and Trust Company of El Dorado v. Ford Motor Credit Company*, 231 Kan. 431, 646 P.2d 1057, Web 1982 Kan. Lexis 280 (Supreme Court of Kansas)

BUSINESS ETHICS CASES

27.10 Business Ethics Ozark Financial Services (Ozark) loaned money to Lonnie and Patsy Turner to purchase a tractor truck unit. The Turners signed a security agreement, giving Ozark a security interest in the tractor truck. Ozark properly filed a financing statement, giving public notice of its security interest. Two months later, the Turners took the truck to Pete & Sons Garage, Inc. (Pete & Sons), for repairs. When the Turners arrived to pick up the truck, they could not pay for the repairs. Pete & Sons returned the truck to the Turners upon their verbal agreement that if they did not pay for the repairs, they would return the truck to Pete & Sons. The Turners did not pay Pete & Sons for the repair services and defaulted on the loan payments due Ozark. Ozark brought an action to recover the truck under its security agreement. Pete & Sons asserted that it had a common law artisan's lien on the truck for the unpaid repair services and that this lien took priority over Ozark's security interest. Did the Turners act unethically in this case? Who wins? *Ozark Financial Services v. Turner*, 735 S.W.2d 374, Web 1987 Mo. App. Lexis 4273 (Court of Appeals of Missouri)

27.11 Business Ethics Harder & Sons, Inc., an International Harvester dealership in Ionia, Michigan, sold a used International Harvester 1066 diesel tractor to Terry Blaser on an installment contract. Although the contract listed Blaser's address as Ionia County, Blaser informed Harder at the time of purchase that he was going to work and live in Barry County. Blaser took delivery of the tractor at his Ionia County address three days later. On that same day, Harder filed a financing statement, which was executed by Blaser with the installment contract, in Barry County. The State of Michigan UCC requires an Article 9 financing statement to be filed in the debtor's county of residence. The contract and security agreement were immediately assigned to International Harvester Credit Corporation (International Harvester).

Blaser subsequently moved to Barry County for about three months, then to Ionia County for a few months, then to Kent County for three weeks, and then to Muskegon County, where he sold the tractor to Jay and Dale Vos. At the time of sale, Blaser informed the Vos brothers that he owned the tractor. He did not tell them that it was subject to a lien. The Vos brothers went to First Michigan Bank & Trust Company (Bank) to obtain a loan to help purchase the tractor. When the Bank checked the records of Ionia County and found that no financing statement was filed against the tractor, it made a $7,000 loan to the Vos brothers to purchase the tractor. About six months later, International Harvester filed suit to recover the tractor from the Vos brothers on the grounds that it had a prior perfected security interest. Did Blaser act ethically in this case? Who wins? *International Harvester Credit Corporation v. Vos*, 290 N.W.2d 401, 1980 Mich.App. Lexis 2430 (Michigan Court of Appeals)

BANKRUPTCY AND REORGANIZATION

▲ **"Going Out of Business" Sign** *Many of our country's original colonists were debtors fleeing the harsh laws of Britain and European countries, where debtors were often sent to debtors' prisons or were required to work off the debt owed to creditors. When the United States of America was founded, the right to declare bankruptcy was considered so important that it was included in the U.S. Constitution.*

CHAPTER OBJECTIVES

After studying this chapter, you should be able to:

1. Identify and describe the major changes to federal bankruptcy law made by the Bankruptcy Abuse Prevention and Consumer Protection Act of 2005.
2. Describe a Chapter 7 liquidation bankruptcy and the means test for filing for Chapter 7 bankruptcy.
3. Describe a Chapter 13 adjustment of debts of an individual with regular income.

4. Describe how businesses are reorganized in Chapter 11 bankruptcy.
5. Describe a Chapter 12 adjustment of debts of a family farmer or fisherman with regular income.

CHAPTER CONTENTS

> **"A trifling debt makes a man your debtor, a large one makes him your enemy."**
> —Seneca
> *Epistulae Morales and Lucilium, Letters 63–65*

▶ INTRODUCTION TO BANKRUPTCY AND REORGANIZATION

The extension of credit from creditors to debtors in commercial and personal transactions is important to the viability of the U.S. and world economies. On occasion, however, borrowers become overextended and are unable to meet their debt obligations. The goal of bankruptcy laws is to balance the rights of debtors and creditors and provide methods for debtors to be relieved of some debt in order to obtain a **fresh start**.

The founders of our country thought that the plight of debtors was so important that they included a provision in the U.S. Constitution, giving Congress the authority to establish uniform federal bankruptcy laws. Congress enacted bankruptcy laws pursuant to this power. Prior to 2005, the most recent overhaul of federal bankruptcy law occurred in 1978. The 1978 law was structured to make it easier for debtors to be relieved of much of their debt by declaring bankruptcy; it was deemed "debtor friendly" because it allowed many debtors to escape their unsecured debts.

After a decade of lobbying by credit card companies and banks, Congress enacted the **Bankruptcy Abuse Prevention and Consumer Protection Act of 2005**.[1] The 2005 act makes it much more difficult for debtors to escape their debts under federal bankruptcy law. The 2005 act, which has been criticized by consumer groups for being too "creditor friendly," has been praised by many businesses, banks, and credit card issuers.

This chapter discusses federal bankruptcy law, including how the provisions of the Bankruptcy Abuse Prevention and Consumer Protection Act of 2005 have changed bankruptcy law.

fresh start
The goal of federal bankruptcy law, to grant a debtor relief from some of his or her burdensome debts, while protecting creditors by requiring the debtor to pay more of his or her debts than would otherwise have been required prior to the 2005 act.

Bankruptcy Abuse Prevention and Consumer Protection Act of 2005
A federal act that substantially amended federal bankruptcy law. This act makes it more difficult for debtors to file for bankruptcy and have their unpaid debts discharged.

▶ BANKRUPTCY LAW

Article I, section 8, clause 4 of the U.S. Constitution provides that "The Congress shall have the power . . . to establish . . . uniform laws on the subject of bankruptcies throughout the United States." Bankruptcy law is exclusively federal law; there are no state bankruptcy laws. Congress enacted the original federal Bankruptcy Act in 1878. The **Bankruptcy Code** is contained in Title 11 of the United States Code (U.S.C.).

Bankruptcy Code
The name given to federal bankruptcy law, as amended.

LANDMARK LAW

Bankruptcy Abuse Prevention and Consumer Protection Act of 2005

Over the years, Congress has adopted various bankruptcy laws. Federal bankruptcy law was completely revised by the **Bankruptcy Reform Act of 1978** [11 U.S.C. Sections 101–1330]. The 1978 act substantially changed—and eased—the requirements for filing bankruptcy. The 1978 act made it easier for debtors to rid themselves of unsecured debt, primarily by filing for Chapter 7 liquidation bankruptcy. By 2005, more than 1 million debtors were filing for Chapter 7 liquidation bankruptcy each year.

For over a decade before 2005, credit card companies, commercial banks, and other businesses lobbied Congress to pass a new bankruptcy act that would reduce the ability of some debtors to relieve themselves of unwanted debt

through bankruptcy. In response, Congress enacted the **Bankruptcy Abuse Prevention and Consumer Protection Act of 2005** [P.L. 109-8, 119 Stat. 23 (April 20, 2005)]. The 2005 act substantially amended federal bankruptcy law, making it much more difficult for debtors to escape unwanted debt through bankruptcy.

Federal bankruptcy law, as amended, is called the *Bankruptcy Code*. The Bankruptcy Code establishes procedures for filing for bankruptcy, resolving creditors' claims, and protecting debtors' rights.

The changes made by the 2005 act are integrated throughout this chapter.

Bankruptcy Reform Act of 1978

A federal act that substantially changed federal bankruptcy law. The act made it easier for debtors to file for bankruptcy and have their unpaid debts discharged. This act was considered debtor friendly.

Types of Bankruptcy

The Bankruptcy Code is divided into chapters. Chapters 1, 3, and 5 set forth definitions and general provisions that govern case administration. The provisions of these chapters generally apply to all forms of bankruptcy.

Four special chapters of the Bankruptcy Code provide different types of bankruptcy under which individual and business debtors may be granted remedy. The four types of bankruptcies, and the filing fees established by the 2005 act, are:

Chapter	Type of Bankruptcy	Filing Fee
Chapter 7	Liquidation	$ 200
Chapter 11	Reorganization	$1,000
Chapter 12	Adjustment of Debts of a Family Farmer or Fisherman with Regular Income	$ 200
Chapter 13	Adjustment of Debts of an Individual with Regular Income	$ 150

These types of bankruptcies are covered in detail in this chapter.

Bankruptcy Courts

Congress created a system of federal **bankruptcy courts**. These special courts are necessary because the number of bankruptcies would overwhelm the federal Districts Courts. The bankruptcy courts are part of the federal court system, and one bankruptcy court is attached to each of the 94 U.S. District Courts in the country. Bankruptcy judges, specialists who hear bankruptcy proceedings, are appointed for 14-year terms. The relevant District Court has jurisdiction to hear appeals from bankruptcy courts.

Federal law establishes the office of **U.S. trustee**. A U.S. trustee is a federal government official who has responsibility for handling and supervising many of the administrative tasks associated with a bankruptcy case.[2] A U.S. trustee is empowered to perform many of the tasks that the bankruptcy judge previously performed.

bankruptcy courts
Special federal courts that hear and decide bankruptcy cases.

U.S. trustee
A federal government official who is responsible for handling and supervising many of the administrative tasks of a bankruptcy case.

▶ BANKRUPTCY PROCEDURE

The Bankruptcy Code requires that certain procedures be followed for the commencement and prosecution of a bankruptcy case. These procedures are discussed in the following paragraphs.

Pre-Petition and Post-Petition Counseling

The 2005 act added a new provision that requires an individual filing for bankruptcy to receive **pre-petition counseling** and **post-petition counseling**. A debtor must receive pre-petition credit counseling within 180 days prior to filing his or her petition for bankruptcy. This includes counseling on types of credit, the use of credit, and budget analysis. The counseling is to be provided by not-for-profit credit counseling agencies approved by the U.S. trustee.

In addition, the 2005 act requires that before an individual debtor receives a discharge in a Chapter 7 or Chapter 13 bankruptcy, the debtor must attend a personal financial management course approved by the U.S. trustee. This course is designed to provide the debtor with information on responsible use of credit and personal financial planning.

Filing a Bankruptcy Petition

A bankruptcy case is commenced when a **petition** is filed with a bankruptcy court. Two types of petitions can be filed:

1. **Voluntary petition.**   A **voluntary petition** is a petition filed by the debtor. A voluntary petition can be filed by the debtor in Chapter 7 (liquidation), Chapter 11 (reorganization), Chapter 12 (family farmer or fisherman), and Chapter 13 (adjustment of debts) bankruptcy cases. The petition has to state that the debtor has debts.
2. **Involuntary petition.**   An **involuntary petition** is a petition that is filed by a creditor or creditors and places the debtor into bankruptcy. An involuntary petition can be filed in Chapter 7 (liquidation) and Chapter 11 (reorganization) cases; an involuntary petition cannot be filed in Chapter 12 (family farmer or fisherman) or Chapter 13 (adjustment of debts) cases.

petition
A document filed with a bankruptcy court that starts a bankruptcy proceeding.

voluntary petition
A petition filed by a debtor that states that the debtor has debts.

involuntary petition
A petition filed by creditors of a debtor that alleges that the debtor is not paying his or her debts as they become due.

Neither a borrower nor a lender be,
For loan oft loses both itself and friend,
And borrowing dulleth edge of husbandry.

William Shakespeare
Hamlet Prince of Denmark
(Polonius at I, iii)

Schedules

An individual debtor must submit the following schedules upon filing a voluntary petition: a list of secured and unsecured creditors, with addresses; a list of all property owned; a statement of the financial affairs of the debtor; a statement of the debtor's monthly income; current income and expenses; evidence of payments received from employers within 60 days prior to the filing of the petition; and a copy of the debtor's federal income tax return for the most recent year ending prior to the filing of the petition.

In addition, an individual debtor must file a certificate, stating that he or she has received the required pre-petition credit counseling. All forms must be sworn under oath and signed by the debtor.

Attorney Certification

The 2005 act requires an attorney to **certify** the accuracy of the information contained in the bankruptcy petition and the schedules, under penalty of perjury. If any factual discrepancies are found, the attorney is subject to monetary fines and sanctions.

If an attorney represents a debtor in bankruptcy, the attorney has to conduct a thorough investigation of the debtor's financial position and schedules to determine the accuracy of the information contained in the petition and schedules.

Order for Relief

order for relief
An order that occurs upon the filing of either a voluntary petition or an unchallenged involuntary petition, or an order that is granted after a trial of a challenged involuntary petition.

The filing of either a voluntary petition or an unchallenged involuntary petition constitutes an **order for relief**. If the debtor challenges an involuntary petition, a trial is held to determine whether an order for relief should be granted. If an order is granted, the case is accepted for further bankruptcy proceedings. In the case of an involuntary petition, the debtor must file the same schedules filed by voluntary petition debtors.

Meeting of the Creditors

meeting of the creditors
A meeting of the creditors in a bankruptcy case that must occur within a reasonable time after an order for relief. The debtor must appear at this meeting.

Within a reasonable time after the court grants an order for relief (not less than 10 days or more than 30 days), the court must call a **meeting of the creditors** (also called the **first meeting of the creditors**). The bankruptcy judge cannot attend the meeting. The debtor must appear and submit to questioning, under oath, by creditors. Creditors may ask questions regarding the debtor's financial affairs, disposition of property prior to bankruptcy, possible concealment of assets, and such. The debtor may have an attorney present at this meeting.

Proof of Claim and Proof of Interest

proof of claim
A document required to be filed by a creditor that states the amount of his or her claim against the debtor.

proof of interest
A document required to be filed by an equity security holder that states the amount of his or her interest against the debtor.

A creditor must file a **proof of claim** stating the amount of his or her claim against the debtor. The document for filing a proof of claim is provided by the court. The proof of claim must be timely filed, which generally means within six months of the first meeting of the creditors. A secured creditor whose claim exceeds the value of the collateral may submit a proof of claim and become an unsecured claimant as to the difference. An equity security holder (e.g., a shareholder of a corporation) must file a **proof of interest**.

Bankruptcy Trustee

trustee
A legal representative of the debtor's estate.

A **trustee** must be appointed in Chapter 7 (liquidation), Chapter 12 (family farmer or family fisherman), and Chapter 13 (adjustment of debts) bankruptcy cases. A trustee may be appointed in a Chapter 11 (reorganization) case upon a showing of fraud, dishonesty, incompetence, or gross mismanagement of the affairs of the debtor by current management. Trustees, who are often lawyers, accountants, or business professionals, are entitled to receive reasonable compensation for their services and reimbursement for expenses. Once appointed, a trustee becomes the legal representative of the debtor's estate.

CONTEMPORARY ENVIRONMENT

Automatic Stay

The filing of a voluntary or an involuntary petition automatically stays—that is, suspends—certain legal actions by creditors against the debtor or the debtor's property. This is called an **automatic stay**. The stay, which applies to collection efforts of secured and unsecured creditors, is designed to prevent a scramble for the debtor's assets in a variety of court proceedings. The following creditor actions are stayed:

• Instituting or maintaining legal actions to collect pre-petition debts

• Enforcing judgments obtained against the debtor
• Obtaining, perfecting, or enforcing liens against property of the debtor
• Nonjudicial collection efforts, such as self-help activities (e.g., repossession of an automobile)

Actions to recover domestic support obligations (e.g., alimony, child support), the dissolution of a marriage, and child custody cases are not stayed in bankruptcy. Criminal actions against the debtor are also not stayed.

Discharge

In Chapter 7 (liquidation), Chapter 11 (reorganization), Chapter 12 (family farmer and family fisherman), and Chapter 13 (adjustment of debts) bankruptcies, if the requirements are met, the court grants the debtor a **discharge** of all or some of his, her, or its debts. When discharge is granted, the debtor is relieved of responsibility to pay the discharged debts. In other words, the debtor is no longer legally liable to pay the discharged debts. Discharge is one of the primary reasons a debtor files for bankruptcy. The specifics of discharge under each type of bankruptcy are discussed in this chapter.

Exceptions to Discharge   The following debts, whose dollar limits were established by the 2005 act, are not dischargeable in bankruptcy:

• Claims for income or gross receipts taxes owed to federal, state, or local governments accrued within three years prior to the filing of the petition for bankruptcy, or for such taxes for any period where the debtor made a fraudulent return or willfully attempted to evade or defeat such tax, and property taxes accrued within one year prior to the filing of the petition for bankruptcy.
• Certain fines and penalties payable to federal, state, and local governmental units.
• Claims based on the debtor's liability for causing willful or malicious injury to a person or property.
• Claims arising from fraud, larceny, or embezzlement by the debtor while acting in a fiduciary capacity.
• Domestic support obligations and alimony, maintenance, and child support payments resulting from a divorce decree or separation agreement.
• Unscheduled claims.
• Claims based on a consumer-debtor's purchase of luxury goods or services of more than $550 from a single creditor on or within 90 days of the order for relief. This is a rebuttable presumption that may be challenged by the debtor by proving that the expenses were incurred to support the debtor or dependants and were therefore not luxuries.
• Cash advances in excess of $825 obtained by a consumer-debtor by use of a revolving line of credit or credit cards on or within 70 days of the order for relief. This is also a rebuttable presumption.
• Judgments and consent decrees against the debtor for liability incurred as a result of the debtor's operation of a motor vehicle, a vessel, or an aircraft while legally intoxicated.
• A debt that would result in a benefit to the debtor that outweighs the detrimental consequences to a spouse, former spouse, or child of the debtor.
• An amount owed to a pension, profit-sharing, or stock bonus plan, and loans owed to employee retirement plans.

automatic stay
The suspension of certain legal actions by creditors against a debtor or the debtor's property.

discharge
A court order that relieves a debtor of the legal liability to pay his or her debts that were not paid in the bankruptcy proceeding.

I will pay you some, and, as most debtors do, promise you indefinitely.

William Shakespeare
Henry IV, Part 11

Creditors who have nondischargeable claims against the debtor may participate in the distribution of the bankruptcy estate. The creditor may pursue the nondischarged balance against the debtor after bankruptcy.

Reaffirmation Agreement

reaffirmation agreement
An agreement entered into by a debtor with a creditor prior to discharge, whereby the debtor agrees to pay the creditor a debt that would otherwise be discharged in bankruptcy. Certain requirements must be met for a reaffirmation agreement to be enforced.

A debtor and a creditor can enter into a **reaffirmation agreement**, whereby the debtor agrees to pay the creditor for a debt that is dischargeable in bankruptcy. This might occur if the debtor wishes to repay a debt to a family member, to a bank, or to another party. A reaffirmation agreement must be entered into before discharge is granted. A reaffirmation agreement must be filed with the court. Approval by the court is required if the debtor is not represented by an attorney. If the debtor is represented by an attorney, the attorney must certify that the debtor voluntarily entered into the reaffirmation agreement and understands the consequences of the agreement. Even if the debtor is represented by an attorney, court approval is required if the agreement will cause undue hardship on the debtor or his or her family.

▶ BANKRUPTCY ESTATE

bankruptcy estate
The debtor's property and earnings that comprise the estate of a bankruptcy proceeding.

The **bankruptcy estate** is created upon the commencement of a bankruptcy case. It includes all the debtor's legal and equitable interests in real, personal, tangible, and intangible property, wherever located, that exist when the petition is filed, and all interests of the debtor and the debtor's spouse in community property. Certain *exempt property* (as discussed later in this section) is not part of the bankruptcy estate.

Gifts, inheritances, life insurance proceeds, and property from divorce settlements that the debtor is entitled to receive within 180 days after the petition is filed are part of the bankruptcy estate. Earnings from property of the estate—such as rents, dividends, and interest payments—are property of the estate.

Earnings from services performed by an individual debtor are not part of the bankruptcy estate in a Chapter 7 liquidation bankruptcy. However, the 2005 act provides that a certain amount of post-petition earnings from services performed by the debtor that are earned for up to five years after the order for relief may be required to be paid as part of the completion of Chapter 12 (family farmer or family fisherman), Chapter 11 (reorganization), and Chapter 13 (adjustment of debts) cases.

Exempt Property

exempt property
Property that may be retained by the debtor pursuant to federal or state law that does not become part of the bankruptcy estate.

Because the Bankruptcy Code is not designed to make the debtor a pauper, certain property is exempt from the bankruptcy estate. **Exempt property** is property of the debtor that he or she can keep and that does not become part of the bankruptcy estate. The creditors cannot claim this property.

The Bankruptcy Code establishes a list of property and assets that a debtor can claim as exempt property. The federal exemptions, with the dollar limits established by the 2005 act, are listed in Exhibit 28.1.[3] Federal exemptions are adjusted every three years to reflect changes in the consumer price index.

State Exemptions

Poor bankrupt.

William Shakespeare
Romeo and Juliet

The Bankruptcy Code permits states to enact their own exemptions. States that do so may (1) give debtors the option of choosing between federal and state exemptions or (2) require debtors to follow state law. The exemptions available under state law are often more liberal than those provided by federal law.

Homestead Exemption

homestead exemption
Equity in a debtor's home that the debtor is permitted to retain.

The federal Bankruptcy Code permits homeowners to claim a **homestead exemption** of $20,200 in their principal residence. If the debtor's equity in the property (i.e., the value

▶ **Exhibit 28.1 FEDERAL EXEMPTIONS FROM THE BANKRUPTCY ESTATE**

1. Interest up to $20,200 in equity in property used as a residence and burial plots (called the "homestead exemption")
2. Interest up to $3,225 in value in one motor vehicle
3. Interest up to $525 per item in household goods and furnishings, wearing apparel, appliances, books, animals, crops, or musical instruments, up to an aggregate value of $10,775 for all items
4. Interest in jewelry up to $1,350.
5. Interest in any property the debtor chooses (including cash) up to $1,075, plus up to $10,125 of any unused portion of the homestead exemption
6. Interest up to $2,025 in value in implements, tools, or professional books used in the debtor's trade
7. Any unmatured life insurance policy owned by the debtor
8. Professionally prescribed health aids
9. Many government benefits, regardless of value, including Social Security benefits, welfare benefits, unemployment compensation, veteran's benefits, disability benefits, and public assistance benefits
10. Certain rights to receive income, including domestic support payments (e.g., alimony, child support), certain pension benefits, profit sharing, and annuity payments
11. Interests in wrongful death benefits and life insurance proceeds to the extent necessary to support the debtor or his or her dependants
12. Personal injury awards up to $20,200
13. Retirement funds that are in a fund or an account that is exempt from taxation under the Internal Revenue Code, except that an exemption for **individual retirement accounts (IRAs)** shall not exceed $1,095,000 for an individual unless the interests of justice require this amount to be increased

above the amount of mortgages and liens) exceeds the exemption limits, the trustee may sell the property to realize the excess value for the bankruptcy estate.

Example Assume that a debtor owns a principal residence worth $500,000 that is subject to a $400,000 mortgage, and the debtor therefore owns $100,000 of equity in the property. The debtor files a petition for Chapter 7 liquidation bankruptcy. The trustee may sell the home, pay off the mortgage, pay the debtor $20,200 (applying the federal exemption), and use the remaining proceeds of $79,800 for distribution to the debtor's creditors.

It is the policy of the law that the debtor be just before he be generous.

Justice Finch
Hearn 45 St. Corp. v. Jano (1940)

ETHICS SPOTLIGHT

2005 Act Limits the Homestead Exemption

The Bankruptcy Code's federal homestead exemption is $20,200. Homestead exemptions under many state laws are usually higher than the federal exemption. Most states exempt between $20,000 and $100,000 of equity in a debtor's principal residence from the bankruptcy estate.

Florida and Texas have no dollar amount limit on their homestead exemptions, although they do limit the size of the real property that qualifies for the homestead exemption. These states have been known as "debtor's havens" for wealthy debtors who file for bankruptcy. Prior to the 2005 act, many wealthy debtors from other states moved their money into principal residences in Florida and Texas to benefit from these generous homestead exemptions. Other states that

allow debtors to protect an unlimited amount of equity from claims of creditors are Iowa, Kansas, and South Dakota.

The 2005 act limits **abusive homestead exemptions**. The 2005 act provides that a debtor may not exempt an amount greater than $136,875 if the property was acquired by the debtor within 1,215 days (approximately three years and four months) before the filing of the petition for bankruptcy.

Business Ethics Why do some states adopt generous homestead exemptions for a debtor's bankruptcy estate? Will the 2005 limits on homestead exemptions reduce abusive bankruptcy behavior by wealthy debtors?

ETHICS SPOTLIGHT

Fraudulent Transfers Prior to Bankruptcy

The 2005 act gives the bankruptcy court the power to void certain **fraudulent transfers** of a debtor's property and obligations made by the debtor within two years of filing a petition for bankruptcy. To void a transfer or an obligation, the court must find that (1) the transfer was made or the obligation was incurred by the debtor with the actual intent to hinder, delay, or defraud a creditor or (2) the debtor received less than a reasonable equivalent in value. In addition, either the debtor must have been insolvent on the date the transfer was made or the obligation must have been incurred or the transfer or obligation must have been beyond the debtor's ability to pay.

Example Kathy owes her unsecured creditors $100,000. On February 9, Kathy knows that she is insolvent. Kathy owns a Mercedes-Benz automobile that is worth $55,000. On February 9, Kathy sells her Mercedes-Benz automobile

to her friend, Wei, for $35,000. Wei is a bona fide purchaser who does not know of Kathy's financial situation. On July 1, Kathy files for Chapter 7 liquidation bankruptcy while still owing the $100,000 to her unsecured creditors. The court can void Kathy's sale of her automobile to Wei as a fraudulent transfer because it occurred within two years of the petition, Kathy received less than a reasonable equivalent in value, and Kathy was insolvent at the time of the sale. Because Wei was a bona fide purchaser, the court must repay Wei the purchase price of $35,000 to recover the automobile from her.

Business Ethics Do you think there are many fraudulent transfers by debtors prior to their filing of bankruptcy petitions? What items or assets are likely to be involved in fraudulent transfers prior to bankruptcy?

---

fraudulent transfer
A transfer of a debtor's property or an obligation incurred by a debtor within two years of the filing of a petition, where (1) the debtor had actual intent to hinder, delay, or defraud a creditor or (2) the debtor received less than a reasonable equivalent in value, and the debtor was insolvent or unable to pay at the time the transfer was made or the obligation was incurred.

Poverty is not socialism. To be rich is glorious.

Deng Xiaoping
People's Republic of China

Chapter 7—liquidation
A form of bankruptcy in which the debtor's nonexempt property is sold for cash, the cash is distributed to the creditors, and any unpaid debts are discharged.

Borrowing is not much better than begging.

Ephraim Gotthold Lessing
Nathan der Weise

abusive filing
A Chapter 7 filing that is found to be an abuse of Chapter 7 liquidation bankruptcy. In such a case, the court can dismiss the case or convert the case to a Chapter 13 or Chapter 11 proceeding, with the debtor's consent.

▶ CHAPTER 7—LIQUIDATION

Chapter 7—liquidation bankruptcy (also called **straight bankruptcy**) is a familiar form of bankruptcy.[4] In this type of bankruptcy proceeding, the debtor is permitted to keep a substantial portion of his or her assets (exempt assets); the debtor's nonexempt property is sold for cash, and the cash is distributed to the creditors; and any of the debtor's unpaid debts are discharged. The debtor's future income, even if he or she becomes rich, cannot be reached to pay the discharged debt. Thus, a debtor would be left to start life anew, without the burden of his or her pre-petition debts. Prior to the 2005 act, filing for Chapter 7 bankruptcy almost became part of many persons' financial planning.

The 2005 act substantially restricts the ability of many debtors to obtain a Chapter 7 liquidation bankruptcy. The 2005 act added the *median income test* and the dollar-based *means test* that a debtor must pass before being permitted to obtain a discharge of debts under Chapter 7. The purpose of the 2005 act's changes to Chapter 7 is to force many debtors out of Chapter 7 liquidation bankruptcy and into Chapter 13 debt adjustment bankruptcy, which requires debtors to pay some of their future income over a three- or five-year period to pay off pre-petition debts. Thus, the 2005 act reduces the number of debtors who can escape their pre-petition debts entirely.

Any person, partnership, corporation, or other business entity, may be a debtor in a Chapter 7 proceeding. Voluntary and involuntary petitions may be filed. Most Chapter 7 bankruptcy petitions are voluntarily filed by individuals.

The 2005 Act's Changes to Chapter 7

Prior to the 2005 act, there was a presumption in favor of granting the relief sought by the debtor under Chapter 7. Most debtors were granted relief and a fresh start, free of their pre-petition unsecured debt.

One of the primary purposes for the enactment of the 2005 act was to make it more difficult for individual debtors to qualify for Chapter 7 liquidation bankruptcy. To do so, the 2005 act established new **simple abuse rule** and a means test to determine whether a debtor should be granted relief under Chapter 7. If a debtor fails this test, a presumption of an **abusive filing** arises, and the debtor does not qualify for Chapter 7 bankruptcy.

Thus, the goal of the 2005 act is to deny Chapter 7 discharge to debtors who have the means to pay some of their unsecured debt from post-petition earnings and to steer most of those debtors into filing for Chapter 13 bankruptcy, where they have to use a portion of their post-petition earnings to pay some of their pre-petition unsecured debt.

Test 1: Median Income Test The first step with regard to the **median income test** is to determine whether the debtor's income either exceeds or is below the **state's median family income** for a family the same size as the debtor's family. A state's median income is defined as that income where half of the state's families have income above that figure and half of the state's families have incomes below that figure.

Example If a state's median income for a family of four is $65,000, then half of the state's four-member families have incomes above $65,000, and half of the state's four-member families have incomes below $65,000.

If the debtor's family income is at or below the state's median income, there is no presumption of abuse, and the means test does not apply. The debtor may proceed with his or her Chapter 7 case and be granted discharge of his or her unsecured debts. Thus, it is important to note that for debtors at or below the state's median income, the 2005 act makes no changes in the ability to obtain Chapter 7 relief (see Exhibit 28.2).

state median income
For any size family, income for which half of the state's families of this size have incomes above this figure and half of the state's families of this size have incomes less than this figure.

▶ **Exhibit 28.2 TEST 1: MEDIAN INCOME TEST**

Top half of median family incomes. Families that have median income that is *higher* than the state's median family income. A second test, the *means test*, is applied to see if the debtor qualifies for Chapter 7 bankruptcy.

Median family income for a family in the state

Bottom half of median family incomes. Families that have median income that is *lower* than the state's median family income. There is no presumption of abuse, and the debtor qualifies for Chapter 7 bankruptcy (as long as the other requirements are met). (The means test does not apply.)

Test 2: Means Test The 2005 act makes major changes for debtors whose family income exceeds the state's median income. If the debtor's family income is above the state's median income, a new means test applies.

The **means test** is a new, complicated calculation that establishes, by law, a bright-line test to determine whether the debtor has the means to pay pre-petition debts out of post-petition income. If it is found by this calculation that the debtor has the financial means to pay some of his or her pre-petition debts out of post-petition income, the debtor is denied relief under Chapter 7.

Even if a debtor qualifies for Chapter 7 relief under the median income and means tests, the court can still deny relief if the court determines that the debtor filed the Chapter 7 petition in bad faith or because of the **totality of the circumstances** of the debtor's financial situation. This determination is made on a case-by-case basis.

means test
A new test added by the 2005 act that applies to debtors who have family incomes that exceed the state's median income for families of the same size.

Statutory Distribution of Property

If a debtor qualifies for a Chapter 7 liquidation bankruptcy, the **nonexempt property** of the bankruptcy estate must be distributed to the debtor's secured and unsecured creditors pursuant to statutory priority established by the Bankruptcy Code.

The claims of secured creditors to the debtor's nonexempt property have priority over the claims of unsecured creditors. Two situations can result:

1. **Oversecured secured creditor.** If the value of the collateral securing the secured loan exceeds the secured interest, the secured creditor is an **oversecured creditor.** In

this case, the property is usually sold, the secured creditor is paid the amount of its secured interest (i.e., principal and accrued principal and interest), and reasonable fees and costs resulting from the debtor's default. The excess becomes available to satisfy the claims of the debtor's unsecured creditors.

2. **Undersecured secured creditor.**   If the value of the collateral securing the secured loan is less than the secured interest, the secured creditor is an **undersecured creditor**. In this case, the property is usually awarded to the secured creditor. The secured creditor then becomes an unsecured creditor as to the amount still owed to it, which consists of unpaid principal and interest and reasonable fees and costs of the debtor's default.

The 2005 act added a new provision regarding **secured personal property**. Under the 2005 act, if personal property of an individual debtor secures a claim or is subject to an unexpired lease (e.g., an automobile lease) and is not exempt property, the debtor must either (1) surrender the personal property, (2) redeem the property by paying the secured lien in full, or (3) assume the unexpired lease.

Unsecured claims are to be satisfied out of the bankruptcy estate in the order of their statutory priority, as established by the Bankruptcy Code. The **statutory priority of unsecured claims**, including the changes made by the 2005 act, is set forth in Exhibit 28.3.

Small debts are like small shot; they are rattling on every side, and can scarcely be escaped without a wound; great debts are like cannon; of loud noise, but little danger.

Samuel Johnson
Letters to Joseph Simpson (1759)

▶ **Exhibit 28.3 PRIORITY OF UNSECURED CREDITOR CLAIMS**

1. Unsecured claims for domestic support obligations owed to a spouse, former spouse, or child of the debtor.
2. Fees and expenses of administering the estate, including court costs, trustee fees, attorneys' fees, appraisal fees, and other costs of administration.
3. In an involuntary bankruptcy, secured claims of "gap" creditors who sold goods or services on credit to the debtor in the ordinary course of the debtor's business between the date of the filing of the petition and the date of the appointment of the trustee or issuance of the order for relief (whichever occurred first).
4. Unsecured claims for wages, salary, commissions, severance pay, and sick leave pay earned by the debtor's employees within 180 days immediately preceding the filing of the petition, up to $10,950 per employee.
5. Unsecured claims for contributions to employee benefit plans based on services performed within 180 days immediately preceding the filing of the petition, up to $10,950 per employee.
6. Farm producers and fishermen against debtors who operate grain storage facilities or fish storage or processing facilities, respectively, up to $5,400 per claim.
7. Unsecured claims for cash deposited by a consumer with the debtor prior to the filing of the petition in connection with the purchase, lease, or rental of property or the purchases of services that were not delivered or provided by the debtor, up to $2,425 per claim.
8. Unsecured claims for unpaid income and gross receipts taxes owed to governments incurred during the three years preceding the bankruptcy petition and unpaid property taxes owed to governments incurred within one year preceding the bankruptcy petition.
9. Commitment by the debtor to maintain the capital of an insured depository institution such as a commercial bank or savings bank.
10. Claims against the debtor for personal injuries or death caused by the debtor while he or she was intoxicated from using alcohol or drugs.

Chapter 7 Discharge

In a Chapter 7 bankruptcy, the property of the estate is sold, and the proceeds are distributed to satisfy allowed claims. The remaining unpaid debts that the debtor incurred prior to the date of the order for relief are discharged. *Discharge* means that the debtor is no longer legally responsible for paying those claims. The major benefit of a **Chapter 7 discharge** is that it is granted quite soon after the petition is filed. The individual debtor is not responsible for paying pre-petition debts out of post-petition income, as would be required in other forms of bankruptcy.

Chapter 7 discharge
The termination of the legal duty of an individual debtor to pay unsecured debts that remain unpaid upon the completion of a Chapter 7 proceeding.

Example Suppose that at the time that Eric is granted Chapter 7 relief, he still owes $50,000 of unsecured debt that there is no money in the bankruptcy estate to pay. This debt is composed of credit card debt, an unsecured loan from a friend, and unsecured credit from a department store. This $50,000 of unsecured credit is discharged. This means that Eric is relieved of this debt and is not legally liable for its repayment. The unsecured creditors must write off this debt.

The 2005 act stipulates that a debtor can be granted Chapter 7 relief only after eight years following Chapter 7 or Chapter 11 relief and only after six years following Chapter 12 or Chapter 13 relief.

In the following case, the U.S. Supreme Court ruled that a debt was dischargeable in bankruptcy.

U.S. SUPREME COURT   CASE 28.1 Chapter 7 Discharge

Kawaauhau v. Geiger

523 U.S. 57, 118 S.Ct. 974, 140 L.Ed.2d 90, Web 1998 U.S. Lexis 1595
Supreme Court of the United States

"The debt is dischargeable."

—Justice Ginsburg

Facts

Margaret Kawaauhau sought treatment from Dr. Paul Geiger for a foot injury. Dr. Geiger examined Kawaauhau and admitted her to the hospital to attend to the risks of infection. Although Dr. Geiger knew that intravenous penicillin would have been a more effective treatment, he prescribed oral penicillin, explaining that he thought that his patient wished to minimize the cost of her treatment. Dr. Geiger then departed on a business trip, leaving Kawaauhau in the care of other physicians. When Dr. Geiger returned, he discontinued all antibiotics because he believed that the infection had subsided. Kawaauhau's condition deteriorated over the next few days, requiring the amputation of her right leg below the knee. Kawaauhau and her husband sued Dr. Geiger for medical malpractice. The jury found Dr. Geiger liable and awarded the Kawaauhaus $355,000 in damages. Dr. Geiger, who carried no malpractice insurance, filed for bankruptcy in an attempt to discharge the judgment. The U.S. bankruptcy court denied discharge, and the U.S. District Court agreed. The U.S. Court of Appeals reversed and allowed Dr. Geiger discharge of the damages award he owed the Kawaauhaus in his bankruptcy. The Kawaauhaus appealed to the U.S. Supreme Court.

Issue

Is a debt arising from a medical malpractice judgment that is attributable to negligent or reckless conduct dischargeable in bankruptcy?

Language of the U.S. Supreme Court

The Bankruptcy Code provides that a debt "for willful and malicious injury by the debtor to another" is not dischargeable. The question before us is whether a debt arising from a medical malpractice judgment, attributable to negligent or reckless conduct, falls within this statutory exception. We hold that it does not and that the debt is dischargeable. Had Congress meant to exempt debts resulting from unintentionally inflicted injuries, it might have selected an additional word or words, i.e., "reckless" or "negligent," to modify injury.

Decision

The U.S. Supreme Court ruled that a medical malpractice judgment based on negligent or reckless conduct—and not willful conduct—is dischargeable in bankruptcy. The U.S. Supreme Court affirmed the decision of the U.S. Court of Appeals.

Case Questions

Critical Legal Thinking Should court judgments for torts—such as a medical malpractice judgment—be permitted to be discharged in bankruptcy?

Business Ethics Was it ethical for Dr. Geiger not to carry malpractice insurance? Was it ethical for Dr. Geiger to file for bankruptcy to avoid paying the judgment to the Kawaauhaus? Do you think the result reached in this case was fair? Why or why not?

Contemporary Business Who is hurt and who is helped by this decision? What public policy is promoted by denying discharge for "willful" injurious conduct?

Acts That Bar Discharge

Any party of interest may file an objection to the discharge of a debt. The court then holds a hearing. Discharge of unsatisfied debts is denied if the debtor:

- Made false representations about his or her financial position when he or she obtained an extension of credit.
- Transferred, concealed, removed, or destroyed property of the estate with the intent to hinder, delay, or defraud creditors within one year before the date of the filing of the petition.
- Falsified, destroyed, or concealed records of his or her financial condition.
- Failed to account for any assets.
- Failed to submit to questioning at the meeting of the creditors (unless excused).
- Failed to complete an instructional course concerning personal financial management, as required by the 2005 act (unless excused).

If a discharge is obtained through fraud of the debtor, any party of interest may bring a motion to have the bankruptcy revoked. The bankruptcy court may revoke a discharge within one year after it is granted.

Beggars can never be bankrupt.

Thomas Fuller
Gnomologia (1732)

CONTEMPORARY ENVIRONMENT

Discharge of Student Loans

Upon graduation from college and professional schools, many students have borrowed money to pay tuition and living expenses. At this point in time, when a student might have large student loans and very few assets, he or she might be inclined to file for bankruptcy in an attempt to have his or her student loans discharged.

To prevent such abuse of bankruptcy law, Congress amended the Bankruptcy Code to make it more difficult for students to have their student loans discharged in bankruptcy. Student loans are defined by the Bankruptcy Code to include loans made by or guaranteed by governmental units. The 2005 act added student loans made by nongovernmental commercial institutions, such

as banks, as well as funds for scholarships, benefits, or stipends granted by educational institutions.

The Bankruptcy Code now states that student loans can be discharged in bankruptcy only if the nondischarge would cause an **undue hardship** to the debtor and his or her dependants. Undue hardship is construed strictly and is difficult for a debtor to prove unless he or she can show severe physical or mental disability or that he or she is unable to pay for basic necessities such as food or shelter for his or her family.

Cosigners (e.g., parents who guarantee their child's student loan) must also meet the heightened undue hardship test to discharge their obligation.

▶ CHAPTER 13—ADJUSTMENT OF DEBTS OF AN INDIVIDUAL WITH REGULAR INCOME

Chapter 13—adjustment of debts of an individual with regular income

A rehabilitation form of bankruptcy that permits bankruptcy courts to supervise the debtor's plan for the payment of unpaid debts in installments over the plan period.

Chapter 13—adjustment of debts of an individual with regular income is a rehabilitation form of bankruptcy for individuals.[5] Chapter 13 permits a qualified debtor to propose a plan to pay all or a portion of the debts he or she owes in installments over a specified period of time, pursuant to the requirements of Chapter 13. The bankruptcy court supervises the debtor's plan for the payment.

The debtor has several advantages under Chapter 13. These include avoiding the stigma of Chapter 7 liquidation, retaining more property than is exempt under Chapter 7, and incurring fewer expenses than in a Chapter 7 proceeding. The creditors have advantages, too: They may recover a greater percentage of the debts owed them than they would recover under a Chapter 7 bankruptcy.

Chapter 13 petitions are usually filed by individual debtors who do not qualify for Chapter 7 liquidation bankruptcy and by homeowners who want to protect nonexempt equity in their residence. Chapter 13 enables debtors to catch up on secured credit loans, such as home mortgages, and avoid repossession and foreclosure.

Filing a Chapter 13 Petition

A Chapter 13 proceeding can be initiated only through the voluntary filing of a petition by an individual debtor with regular income. A creditor cannot file an involuntary petition to institute a Chapter 13 case. An **individual with regular income** is an individual whose income is sufficiently stable and regular to enable such individual to make payments under a Chapter 13 plan. Regular income may be from any source, including wages, salary, commissions, income from investments, Social Security income, pension income, or public assistance. The debts of the individual debtor must be primarily consumer debt. **Consumer debt** means debts incurred by an individual for personal, family, or household purposes.

The petition must state that the debtor desires to effect an extension or a composition of debts, or both. An **extension** provides for a longer period of time for the debtor to pay his or her debts. A **composition** provides for the reduction of debts. The petition must be filed in good faith.

Debt rolls a man over and over, binding him hand and foot, and letting him hang upon the fatal mesh until the long-legged interest devours him.

Henry Ward Beecher
Proverbs from Plymouth Pulpit
(1887)

Limitations on Who Can File for Chapter 13 Bankruptcy

The 2005 act establishes dollar limits on the secured and unsecured debt that a debtor may have in order to qualify to file for Chapter 13 bankruptcy. Only an individual with regular income alone or with his or her spouse who owes individually or with his or her spouse (1) noncontingent, liquidated, unsecured debts of up to $336,900 and (2) secured debts up to $1,010,650 may file a petition for Chapter 13 bankruptcy. Individual debtors who exceed these dollar limits do not qualify for Chapter 13 bankruptcy. Sole proprietorships, because they are owned by individuals, may file for Chapter 13 bankruptcy.

Property of a Chapter 13 Estate

The property of a Chapter 13 estate consists of all nonexempt property of the debtor at the commencement of the case and nonexempt property acquired after the commencement of the case but before the case is closed. In addition, the property of the estate includes earnings and future income earned by the debtor after the commencement of the case but before the case is closed. This ensures that pre-petition creditors receive payments from the debtor's post-petition earnings and income.

The debtor remains in possession of all of the property of the estate during the completion of the plan except as otherwise provided by the plan. If the debtor is self-employed, the debtor may continue to operate his or her business. Alternatively, the court may order that a trustee operate the business, if necessary.

Chapter 13 Plan of Payment

The debtor's **plan of payment** must be filed not later than 90 days after the order for relief. The debtor must file information about his or her finances, including a budget of estimated income and expenses during the period of the plan. The Chapter 13 plan may be either up to three years or up to five years, depending on a complicated calculation specified in the 2005 act.

The plan must be submitted to secured creditors for acceptance. The plan is confirmed as to a secured creditor if that creditor accepts the plan. If a secured creditor does not accept the plan, the court may still confirm the plan. The plan is confirmed as to an unsecured creditor if that creditor accepts the plan. If an unsecured creditor objects to the plan, the court may still confirm the plan if the debtor agrees to commit all of his or her disposable income during the plan period to pay his or her unsecured creditors.

Bankruptcy is a legal proceeding in which you put your money in your pants pocket and give your coat to your creditors.

Joey Adams

Disposable income is defined as current monthly income less amounts reasonably necessary to be spent for the maintenance or support of the debtor and the debtor's dependants. Expenses include amounts necessary to pay domestic support obligations and charitable donations that do not exceed 15 percent of the debtor's gross income for the year the charitable donations are made. If a debtor earns more than the median income of the state, his or her expenses are determined by the objective IRS standards.

Confirmation of a Chapter 13 Plan of Payment

The court can confirm a **Chapter 13 plan of payment** if the prior requirements are met and if (1) the plan was proposed in good faith, (2) the plan passes the feasibility test (e.g., the debtor must be able to make the proposed payments), (3) the plan is in the best interests of the creditors (i.e., the present value of the payments must equal or exceed the amount that the creditors would receive in a Chapter 7 liquidation proceeding), (4) the debtor has paid all domestic support obligations owed, and (5) the debtor has filed all applicable federal, state, and local tax returns.

The debtor must begin making the planned installment payments to the trustee. The trustee is responsible for remitting these payments to the creditors. The trustee is paid for administering the plan. Payments under the plan must be made in equal monthly installments.

A Chapter 13 plan may be modified if the debtor's circumstances materially change. For example, if the debtor's income subsequently decreases, the court may decrease the debtor's payments under the plan.

Chapter 13 Discharge

Chapter 13 discharge
A discharge in a Chapter 13 case that is granted to the debtor after the debtor's plan of payment is completed (which could be up to three or up to five years).

The court grants an order discharging the debtor from all unpaid unsecured debts covered by the plan after all the payments required under the plan are completed (which could be up to three years or up to five years). This is called a **Chapter 13 discharge**. The debtor must certify that all domestic support payments have been paid before discharge is granted. Most unpaid taxes are not discharged.

A debtor cannot be granted Chapter 13 discharge if the debtor has received discharge under Chapter 7, 11, or 12 within the prior four-year period or Chapter 13 relief within the prior two-year period of the order for relief in the current Chapter 13 case.

▶ CHAPTER 11—REORGANIZATION

Chapter 11—reorganization
A bankruptcy method that allows the reorganization of the debtor's financial affairs under the supervision of the bankruptcy court.

Chapter 11 of the Bankruptcy Code provides a method for reorganizing a debtor's financial affairs under the supervision of the bankruptcy court.[6] The goal of Chapter 11 is to reorganize the debtor with a new capital structure so that the debtor emerges from bankruptcy as a viable concern. This option, which is referred to as **reorganization bankruptcy**, is often in the best interests of the debtor and its creditors.

Chapter 11 is available to individuals, partnerships, corporations, and other business entities. The majority of Chapter 11 proceedings are filed by corporations that want to reorganize their capital structure by receiving discharge of a portion of their debts, obtain relief from burdensome contracts, and emerge from bankruptcy as going concerns. A Chapter 11 petition may be filed voluntarily by a debtor or involuntarily by its creditors.

Debtor-in-Possession

debtor-in-possession
A debtor who is left in place to operate the business during the reorganization proceeding.

In most Chapter 11 cases, the debtor is left in place to operate the business during the reorganization proceeding. In such cases, the debtor is called a **debtor-in-possession**. The court may appoint a trustee to operate the debtor's business only upon a showing of cause, such as fraud, dishonesty, or gross mismanagement of the affairs of the debtor by current management.

The debtor-in-possession is empowered to operate the debtor's business during the bankruptcy proceeding. This power includes authority to enter into contracts, purchase supplies, incur debts, and so on. Credit extended by post-petition unsecured creditors in the ordinary course of business is given automatic priority as an administrative expense in bankruptcy.

Creditors' Committees

After an order for relief is granted, the court appoints a **creditors' committee** composed of representatives of the class of unsecured claims. The court may also appoint a committee of secured creditors and a committee of equity holders. Generally, the parties holding the seven largest creditor claims or equity interests are appointed to their requisite committees. Committees may appear at bankruptcy court hearings, participate in the negotiation of a plan of reorganization, assert objections to proposed plans of reorganization, and the like.

creditors' committee
A committee of unsecured creditors that is appointed by the court to represent the class of unsecured claims. The court can also appoint committees for secured creditors and for equity holders.

Automatic Stay in Chapter 11

The filing of a Chapter 11 petition stays (suspends) actions by creditors to recover the debtor's property. This **automatic stay** suspends certain legal actions against the debtor or the debtor's property, including the ability of creditors to foreclose on assets given as collateral for their loans to the debtor. This automatic stay is extremely important to a business trying to reorganize under Chapter 11 because the debtor needs to keep its assets to stay in business.

Executory Contracts and Unexpired Leases in Chapter 11

A major benefit of Chapter 11 bankruptcy is that the debtor is given the opportunity to accept or reject certain executory contracts and unexpired leases. **Executory contracts** and **unexpired leases** are contracts or leases that have not been fully performed.

executory contract or unexpired lease
A contract or lease that has not been fully performed. With the bankruptcy court's approval, a debtor may reject executory contracts and unexpired leases in bankruptcy.

Example A contract to purchase or supply goods at a later date is an executory contract; a 20-year office lease that has 8 years left until it is completed is an unexpired lease. Other executory contracts and unexpired leases may include consulting contracts, contracts to purchase or provide services, equipment leases, warehouse leases, automobile and equipment leases, leases for office and commercial space, and such.

Under the Bankruptcy Code, a debtor-in-possession (or trustee) in a Chapter 11 proceeding is given authority to assume or reject executory contracts. In general, the debtor rejects unfavorable executory contracts and assumes favorable executory contracts. The debtor is not liable for damages caused by the rejection of executory contracts and unexpired leases in bankruptcy.

Labor Union and Retiree Benefits Contracts in Chapter 11

Debtors that file for Chapter 11 reorganization sometimes have collective bargaining agreements with labor unions that require the payment of agreed-upon wages and other benefits to union member-employees for some agreed-upon period in the future. Debtors also often have contracts to pay union and nonunion retired employees and their dependants' medical, surgical, hospitalization, dental, and death benefits (retiree benefits). In a Chapter 11 case, union members and union retirees are represented by the responsible labor union. The court appoints a committee to represent nonunion retirees.

The debtor and the representatives of the union members and retirees can voluntarily agree to modify the union collective bargaining agreement and retiree benefits. If such an agreement is not reached, the debtor can petition the bankruptcy court to reject the collective bargaining agreement and to modify retiree benefits.

Chapter 11 Plan of Reorganization

plan of reorganization
A plan that sets forth a proposed new capital structure for a debtor to assume when it emerges from Chapter 11 reorganization bankruptcy.

The debtor has the exclusive right to file a **plan of reorganization** with the bankruptcy court within the first 120 days after the date of the order for relief. Under the 2005 act, this period may be extended up to 18 months. The debtor has the right to obtain creditor approval of the plan, but if the debtor fails to do so, any party of interest (e.g., a trustee, a creditor, an equity holder) may propose a plan.

The plan of reorganization sets forth the proposed new financial structure of the debtor. This includes the portion of the unsecured debts proposed to be paid by the debtor and the unsecured debt the debtor proposes to have discharged. The plan must specify the executory contracts and unexpired leases that the debtor proposes to reject that have not previously been rejected in the bankruptcy proceeding. The plan also designates how equity holders are to be treated, describes any new equity investments that are to be made in the debtor, and includes other relevant information.

The debtor must supply the creditors and equity holders with a *disclosure statement* that contains adequate information about the proposed plan of reorganization so that they can make an informed judgment about the plan.

Confirmation of a Chapter 11 Plan of Reorganization

confirmation
The bankruptcy court's approval of a plan of reorganization.

There must be **confirmation of a Chapter 11 plan of reorganization** by the bankruptcy court for the debtor to be reorganized under Chapter 11. The bankruptcy court confirms a plan of reorganization under the **acceptance method** if (1) the plan is in the best interests of the creditors because the creditors would receive at least what they would receive in a Chapter 7 liquidation bankruptcy, (2) the plan is feasible (i.e., the new reorganized company is likely to succeed), and (3) each class of creditors accepts the plan (i.e., at least one-half the number of creditors who represent at least two-thirds of the dollar amount of the debt vote to accept the plan).

acceptance method
A method whereby the court confirms a plan of reorganization if the creditors accept the plan and if other requirements are met.

If a class of creditors does not accept the plan, the plan can be confirmed by the court by using the Bankruptcy Code's **cram-down provision**. In order for the court to confirm a plan over the objection of a class of creditors, at least one class of creditors must have voted to accept the plan.

cram-down provision
A provision whereby the court confirms a plan of reorganization over an objecting class of creditors if certain requirements are met.

Example The BigDotCom Corporation has financial difficulties and has filed for Chapter 11 reorganization. At the time of filing for Chapter 11, the corporation has $100 million of secured credit, $100 million of unsecured credit, and common stockholders whose equity securities are now worthless. The corporation files a plan of reorganization whereby (1) the corporation keeps the secured assets for the business, pays the secured creditors any arrearages owed, and has the secured creditors retain their secured interests in the secured assets; (2) reduces unsecured debt by $45 million and discharges $55 million of unsecured debt; (3) eliminates the interests of the equity holders; (4) rejects specified executory contracts and unexpired leases; (5) eliminates several unprofitable product lines; (6) provides for the payment of required unpaid taxes; and (7) accepts the investment of $30 million in capital from an investment bank that wants to invest in the corporation. If this plan is approved by the court, $55 million of the corporation's unsecured debt is discharged. The corporation emerges from Chapter 11 as a reorganized going concern.

The rich ruleth over the poor, and the borrower is servant to the lender.

Proverbs 22:7
The Bible

Small Business Bankruptcy

The Bankruptcy Code permits a "small business," defined as one with total debts of less than $2,190,000, to use a simplified, fast-track form of Chapter 11 reorganization bankruptcy. **Small business bankruptcy** provides an efficient and cost-saving method for small businesses to reorganize under Chapter 11.

CONTEMPORARY ENVIRONMENT

UAL Corporation's Chapter 11 Bankruptcy

UAL Corporation is the parent company of United Air Lines, which was the largest scheduled passenger commercial airline in the world. On a daily basis, the airline offered more than 1,500 flights to 26 countries. The airline also offered regional service to domestic hubs through United Express carriers. Eventually, low-cost airlines such as Southwest Airlines began taking business from United. In response, United lowered fares to compete with the low-cost airlines. However, United's cost structure could not support its new strategy, and the company began losing substantial money on its operations.

UAL filed for Chapter 11 reorganization bankruptcy. At the time of filing the petition, UAL owned or leased airplanes, equipment, trucks and other vehicles, docking space at airports, warehouses, office space, and other assets. In many cases, UAL had borrowed the money to purchase or lease these assets. Most of the lenders took back mortgages or security interests in the assets for which they had loaned money to UAL to purchase or lease. In addition, UAL owed unsecured creditors money that it could not repay, and it had executory contracts and unexpired leases that it also could not pay.

If UAL was not in bankruptcy and defaulted on its secured loans or leases, the secured creditors could use state law and foreclose on their security interests and recover these assets as collateral. UAL would be left without most of its major assets that it would need to operate its business. When UAL filed for Chapter 11 bankruptcy, however, the automatic stay of federal bankruptcy law went into effect and prevented the secured creditors from using state law to foreclose on UAL's assets. The automatic stay also prevented unsecured creditors from using state legal procedures to collect their unsecured debts. Therefore, UAL was able to continue to operate its business while it reorganized under bankruptcy law protection.

Under bankruptcy court protection, UAL proposed a plan of reorganization that would decrease its unsecured debts to a proportion of what they were prior to its filing for bankruptcy and discharge of the unpaid unsecured debt. UAL also examined its executory contracts and unexpired leases; it kept those that were beneficial to the company's survival and rejected those it believed would be detrimental to the company's survival in the future. Bitter disputes to reduce the pay and benefits of UAL's labor unions resulted. Eventually, UAL renegotiated terms with the pilots' union, the flight attendants' union, the maintenance workers' union, and other unions.

When UAL emerged from Chapter 11 bankruptcy, it still had most of its assets. The secured creditors remained secured creditors during and after the bankruptcy reorganization but had to be paid any arrearages that UAL owed to them. UAL's unsecured credit was substantially reduced, and the unpaid portion was discharged. Also, UAL was able to reject the executory contracts and unexpired leases that it did not want. Thus, it emerged from bankruptcy a viable going concern.

The decline, insolvency, and eventual restructuring of UAL provide an example of how a company—in this case a very large corporation—can use the protection of bankruptcy law to reinvent itself into a going concern.

Family Farm, Idaho *Chapter 12 of the federal Bankruptcy Code contains special provisions for reorganizing family farmers and family fishermen.*

▶ **CHAPTER 12—FAMILY FARMER AND FAMILY FISHERMAN**

Beginning in 1986, family farmers were permitted to file for bankruptcy reorganization under Chapter 12 of the Bankruptcy Code. Chapter 12 was only a temporary part of Bankruptcy Code, however, and it needed to be periodically reenacted by Congress to remain law. The 2005 act made Chapter 12 a permanent part of the Bankruptcy Code and added family fisherman as debtors who could seek reorganization under its provisions. The 2005 act established special definitions and rules that allow family farmers and family fisherman to file for bankruptcy reorganization under **Chapter 12—adjustment of debts of a family farmer or fisherman with regular income**.[7]

Family Farmer and Family Fisherman

Chapter 12 defines a **family farmer** as an individual or an individual and spouse whose total debt does not exceed $3,544,525 and is at least 50 percent related to farming operations and whose gross income for the preceding taxable year or each of the second and third preceding taxable years was at least 50 percent earned from farming operations. A corporation or partnership that is at least 50 percent owned by one family or one family and its relatives can also file under Chapter 12 if the preceding requirements are met by the entity.

Chapter 12 defines a **family fisherman** as an individual or an individual and spouse whose total debt does not exceed $1,642,500 and is at least 80 percent related to a commercial fishing operation and whose gross income for the preceding taxable year was at least 50 percent earned from the commercial fishing operation. A corporation or partnership that is at least 50 percent owned by one family or one family and its relatives can also file under Chapter 12 if the preceding requirements are met by the entity.

Chapter 12 Procedure and Estate

Under Chapter 12, the debtor may file a voluntary petition. Creditors cannot, however, file involuntary petitions. After a debtor files for Chapter 12 bankruptcy, a trustee is appointed. The family farmer or family fisherman is a debtor-in-possession who remains in possession of the property of the estate and is permitted to operate the farming or commercial fishing operation unless cause, such as fraud, dishonesty, or gross mismanagement, is proven. Upon the filing of the petition, an automatic stay goes into place against creditors' actions (e.g., foreclosure proceedings) against the debtor.

Chapter 12 Plan of Reorganization

A family farmer or family fisherman debtor must file a *plan of reorganization* within 90 days. Generally, the plan may provide for payments to creditors over a period no longer than three years, but the court can increase the period to up to five years, based on a showing of cause. The plan of reorganization must be confirmed by the court before the plan becomes operable. A Chapter 12 plan can provide for the assumption or rejection of executory contracts and unexpired leases. The plan of reorganization can modify the rights of secured creditors and unsecured creditors.

Chapter 12 provides certain protections for secured creditors. A debtor's plan can be confirmed as to a secured creditor if (1) the holder of the claim has accepted the plan, (2) the debtor surrenders the property securing the claim to the secured creditor, or (3) the plan provides that the secured creditor retains the mortgage or lien securing the claim and the plan distributes property to the secured creditor that is not less than the allowed amount of the claim.

The debtor and an unsecured creditor can voluntarily agree to the terms for the settlement of the unsecured creditor's claim. This can take the form of reducing the amount of the claim or extending the time period for the payment of the claim. If no such agreement is reached, the plan of reorganization must provide that all of the debtor's projected disposable income for the plan period be applied to make payments under the plan.

Chapter 12—adjustment of debts of a family farmer or fisherman with regular income
A form of bankruptcy reorganization permitted to be used by family farmers and family fisherman.

family farmer
An individual, a corporation, or a partnership that engages in farming operations and meets the requirements for filing for a Chapter 12 proceeding.

family fisherman
An individual, a corporation, or a partnership that engages in commercial fishing operations and meets the requirements for filing for a Chapter 12 proceeding.

Money is indeed the most important thing in the world; and all sound and successful personal and national morality should have this fact for its basis.

George Bernard Shaw
The Irrational Knot

Confirmation of a Chapter 12 Plan

The bankruptcy court holds a hearing regarding the **confirmation of a Chapter 12 plan**. The bankruptcy court must confirm a plan if: (1) The plan has been proposed in *good faith*, (2) the plan is in the *best interests* of each of the allowed unsecured claims because the plan pays each unsecured claim at least what such claim would have received under Chapter 7 liquidation bankruptcy, and (3) the plan is *feasible*—that is, the debtor will be able to make the payments specified in the plan.

The debtor must submit all or such portion of the debtor's future earnings or other future income to the trustee as is necessary for the completion of the plan.

If a priority or nonpriority unsecured creditor objects to a Chapter 12 plan, the court can use the *cram-down provision* provided in the Bankruptcy Code and force the plan on the objecting unsecured creditors.

Poverty is no disgrace to a man, but it is confoundedly inconvenient.

Sydney Smith

Chapter 12 Discharge

When a family farmer or family fisherman debtor has completed making all payments required by the plan (which is usually three years but could be up to five years), the bankruptcy court grants the debtor discharge of all debts provided for by the plan. This is called a **Chapter 12 discharge**.

Example If a Chapter 12 plan calls for the farmer-debtor to pay 55 percent of the outstanding unsecured debt to the unsecured creditors, and this amount has been paid by the debtor during the plan period, the court grants discharge of the unpaid 45 percent of this unsecured debt.

Chapter 12 discharge
A discharge in a Chapter 12 case that is granted to a family farmer or family fisherman debtor after the debtor's plan of payment is completed (which is usually three years but could be up to five years).

China *In 2007, the Enterprise Bankruptcy Law became effective in the People's Republic of China. China's new bankruptcy law provides for the liquidation and reorganization of corporations. The law applies to the bankruptcy of both privately owned corporations and state-owned enterprises (SOEs). China's corporate bankruptcy law allows voluntary and involuntary petitions, provides for an automatic stay upon filing for bankruptcy, prohibits fraudulent transfers, allows executory contracts to be accepted or rejected, and permits the cram-down of a plan of reorganization over a dissenting class of creditors. The law makes a major change in providing that secured creditors' claims take priority over claims of workers; in the past, claims owed for wages, medical, insurance, and other compensation owed to employees took priority over secured claims. Foreign investors applaud the new law because it provides a stable legal environment for dealing with problematic investments through bankruptcy proceedings.*

TEST REVIEW TERMS AND CONCEPTS

Abusive filing
Abusive homestead
 exemption
Acceptance method
Article I, section 8, clause 4
 of the U.S. Constitution
Attorney certification
Automatic stay
Automatic stay in Chapter 11
Bankruptcy Abuse
 Prevention and
 Consumer Protection
 Act of 2005
Bankruptcy Code
Bankruptcy court
Bankruptcy estate
Bankruptcy Reform Act of
 1978
Chapter 7 discharge
Chapter 7—liquidation
 bankruptcy (straight
 bankruptcy)

Chapter 11—reorganization
 bankruptcy
Chapter 12—adjustment of
 debts of a family farmer
 or fisherman with regular
 income
Chapter 12 discharge
Chapter 13—adjustment of
 debts of an individual
 with regular income
Chapter 13 discharge
Chapter 13 plan of payment
Composition
Confirmation of a Chapter
 11 plan of reorganization
Confirmation of a Chapter
 12 plan
Consumer debt
Cram-down provision
Creditors' committee
Debtor-in-possession
Discharge

Disposable income
Executory contract
Exempt property
Extension
Family farmer
Family fisherman
Fraudulent transfer
Fresh start
Homestead exemption
Individual retirement
 account (IRA)
Individual with regular
 income
Involuntary petition
Means test
Median income test
Meeting of the creditors (first
 meeting of the creditors)
Nonexempt property
Order for relief
Oversecured creditor
Petition

Plan of payment
Plan of reorganization
Post-petition counseling
Pre-petition counseling
Proof of claim
Proof of interest
Reaffirmation agreement
Secured personal property
Simple abuse rule
Small business bankruptcy
State's median family
 income
Statutory priority of
 unsecured claims
Totality of the
 circumstances
Trustee
Undersecured creditor
Undue hardship
Unexpired lease
U.S. trustee
Voluntary petition

CASE PROBLEMS

28.1 Petition Daniel E. Beren, John M. Elliot, and Edward F. Mannino formed Walnut Street Four, a general partnership, to purchase and renovate an office building in Harrisburg, Pennsylvania. They borrowed more than $200,000 from Hamilton Bank to purchase the building and begin renovation. Disagreements among the partners arose when the renovation costs exceeded their estimates. When Beren was unable to obtain assistance from Elliot and Mannino regarding obtaining additional financing, the partnership quit paying its debts. Beren filed an involuntary petition to place the partnership into Chapter 7 bankruptcy. The other partners objected to the bankruptcy filing. At the time of the filing, the partnership owed debts of more than $380,000 and had approximately $550 in the partnership bank account. Should the petition for involuntary bankruptcy be granted? *In re Walnut Street Four*, 106 B.R. 56, **Web** 1989 Bankr. Lexis 1806 (United States Bankruptcy Court for the Middle District of Pennsylvania)

28.2 Automatic Stay James F. Kost filed a voluntary petition for relief under Chapter 11 of the Bankruptcy Code. First Interstate Bank of Greybull (First Interstate) held a first mortgage on the debtor's residence near Basin, Wyoming. Appraisals and other evidence showed that the house was worth $116,000. The debt owed to First Interstate was almost $103,000 and was increasing at a rate of $32.46 per day. The debtor had only an 11.5 percent equity cushion in the property. Further evidence showed that the (1) Greybull/Basin area was

suffering from tough economic times, (2) there were more than 90 homes available for sale in the area, (3) the real estate market in the area was declining, (4) the condition of the house was seriously deteriorating and the debtor was not financially able to make the necessary improvements, and (5) the insurance on the property had lapsed. First Interstate moved for a relief from stay so that it could foreclose on the property and sell it. Should the motion be granted? *In re Kost*, 102 B.R. 829, **Web** 1989 U.S. Dist. Lexis 8316 (United States District Court for the District of Wyoming)

28.3 Fraudulent Transfer Peter and Geraldine Tabala (Debtors), husband and wife, purchased a house in Clarkstown, New York. They purchased a Carvel ice cream business for $70,000 with a loan obtained from People's National Bank. In addition, the Carvel Corporation extended trade credit to Debtors. Two years after getting the bank loan, Debtors conveyed their residence to their three daughters, ages 9, 19, and 20, for no consideration. Debtors continued to reside in the house and to pay maintenance expenses and real estate taxes due on the property. On the date of transfer, Debtors owed obligations in excess of $100,000. Five months after conveying their residence to their daughters, Debtors filed a petition for Chapter 7 bankruptcy. The bankruptcy trustee moved to set aside Debtors' conveyance of their home to their daughters as a fraudulent transfer. Who wins? *In re Tabala*, 11 B.R. 405, **Web** 1981 Bankr. Lexis 3663 (United States Bankruptcy Court for the Southern District of New York)

28.4 Executory Contract The Record Company, Inc. (The Record Company), entered into a purchase agreement to buy certain retail record stores from Bummbusiness, Inc. (Bummbusiness). All assets and inventory were included in the deal. The Record Company agreed to pay Bummbusiness $20,000 and to pay the $380,000 of trade debt owed by the stores. In exchange, Bummbusiness agreed not to compete with the new buyer for two years within a 15-mile radius of the stores and to use its best efforts to obtain an extension of the due dates for the trade debt. The Record Company began operating the stores but shortly thereafter filed a petition for Chapter 11 bankruptcy. At the time of the bankruptcy filing, (1) The Record Company owed Bummbusiness $10,000 and owed the trade debt of $380,000, and (2) Bummbusiness was obligated not to compete with The Record Company. Can The Record Company reject the purchase agreement? *In re The Record Company*, 8 B.R. 57, **Web** 1981 Bankr. Lexis 5157 (United States Bankruptcy Court for the Southern District of Indiana)

28.5 Plan of Reorganization Richard P. Friese (Debtor) filed a voluntary petition for Chapter 11 bankruptcy. Debtor filed a plan of reorganization that divided his creditors into three classes. The first class, administrative creditors, were to be paid in full. The second class, unsecured creditors, were to receive 50 percent on their claims. The IRS was the third class; it was to receive $20,000 on confirmation and the balance in future payments. No creditors voted to accept the plan. The unsecured creditors were impaired because their legal, equitable, and contractual rights were being altered. Can the bankruptcy court confirm Debtor's plan of reorganization? *In re Friese*, 103 B.R. 90, **Web** 1989 Bankr. Lexis 1309 (United States Bankruptcy Court for the Southern District of New York)

BUSINESS ETHICS CASES

28.6 Business Ethics Donald Wayne Doyle (Debtor) obtained a guaranteed student loan to enroll in a school for training truck drivers. Due to his impending divorce, Debtor never attended the program. The first monthly installment of approximately $50 to pay the student loan became due. Two weeks later, Debtor filed a voluntary petition for Chapter 7 bankruptcy.

Debtor was a 29-year-old man who earned approximately $1,000 per month at an hourly wage of $7.70 as a truck driver, a job that he had held for 10 years. Debtor resided on a farm where he performed work in lieu of paying rent for his quarters. Debtor was paying monthly payments of $89 on a bank loan for his former wife's vehicle, $200 for his truck, $40 for health insurance, $28 for car insurance, $120 for gasoline and vehicular maintenance, $400 for groceries and meals, and $25 for telephone charges. In addition, a state court had ordered Debtor to pay $300 per month to support his children, ages four and five. Debtor's parents were assisting him by buying him $130 of groceries per month. Should Debtor's student loan be discharged in bankruptcy? *In re Doyle*, 106 B.R. 272, **Web** 1989 Bankr. Lexis 1772 (United States Bankruptcy Court for the Northern District of Alabama)

28.7 Business Ethics Scott Greig Keebler (Debtor) became indebted, and his debts exceeded his assets. The Internal Revenue Service (IRS) had levied his wages for nonpayment of taxes. Debtor was healthy and capable of earning a substantial income. Evidence showed that Debtor did not try his best to pay his debts, lived an affluent lifestyle, and determined not to pay his principal creditors. Debtor voluntarily quit his job and filed a voluntary petition for Chapter 7 bankruptcy. The petition stated that he was unemployed. Shortly after filing for bankruptcy, the petitioner resumed work. Was it ethical for Keebler to be able to file for Chapter 7 bankruptcy? *In re Keebler*, 106 B.R. 662, **Web** 1989 Bankr. Lexis 1919 (United States Bankruptcy Court for the District of Hawaii)

ENDNOTES

1. Pub.L. 109–8, 119 Stat. 23 (April 30, 2005).
2. 28 U.S.C. Sections 586–589b.
3. 11 U.S.C. Section 522d.
4. 11 U.S.C. Sections 701–784.
5. 11 U.S.C. Sections 1301–1330.
6. 11 U.S.C. Sections 1101–1174.
7. 11 U.S.C. Sections 1201–1231.

Part VII

AGENCY AND EMPLOYMENT

▲ **Real Estate Agency** *Agency is governed by a large body of common law known as agency law. Most people are familiar with many types of agencies, such as those in real estate, insurance, and travel.*

CHAPTER OBJECTIVES

After studying this chapter, you should be able to:

1. Define *agency.*
2. Identify and define a principal–independent contractor relationship.
3. Describe how express and implied agencies are created.
4. Define *apparent agency.*
5. Describe how an agency is terminated.

CHAPTER CONTENTS

"Let every eye negotiate for itself, and trust no agent."

—William Shakespeare
Much Ado About Nothing

▶ INTRODUCTION TO AGENCY FORMATION AND TERMINATION

If businesspeople had to personally conduct all their business, the scope of their activities would be severely curtailed. Partnerships would not be able to operate, corporations could not act through managers and employees, and sole proprietorships would not be able to hire employees. The use of agents (or agency), which allows one person to act on behalf of another, solves this problem.

Examples Examples of agency relationships include a salesperson selling goods for a store, an executive working for a corporation, a partner acting on behalf of a partnership, an attorney representing a client, and a real estate broker selling a house.

Agency is governed by a large body of common law known as **agency law**. The formation of agencies, the duties of principals and agents, and termination of agencies are discussed in this chapter.

agency law
The large body of common law that governs agency; a mixture of contract law and tort law.

▶ AGENCY

Agency relationships are formed by the mutual consent of a principal and an agent. Section 1(1) of the ***Restatement (Second) of Agency*** defines **agency** as a **fiduciary relationship** "which results from the manifestation of consent by one person to another that the other shall act in his behalf and subject to his control, and consent by the other so to act." The *Restatement (Second) of Agency* is the reference source for the rules of agency. A party who employs another person to act on his or her behalf is called a **principal**. A party who agrees to act on behalf of another is called an **agent**. The principal–agent relationship is commonly referred to as an *agency*. This relationship is depicted in Exhibit 29.1.

agency
The principal–agent relationship; the fiduciary relationship "which results from the manifestation of consent by one person to another that the other shall act in his behalf and subject to his control, and consent by the other so to act" [*Restatement (Second) of Agency*].

principal
A party who employs another person to act on his or her behalf.

agent
A party who agrees to act on behalf of another.

Persons Who Can Initiate an Agency Relationship

Any person who has the capacity to contract can appoint an agent to act on his or her behalf. Generally, persons who lack **contractual capacity**, such as insane persons and minors, cannot appoint agents. However, the court can appoint legal guardians or other representatives to handle the affairs of insane persons, minors, and others who lack capacity to

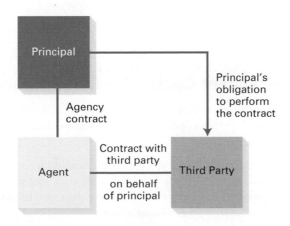

▶ **Exhibit 29.1**
PRINCIPAL–AGENT RELATIONSHIP

It isn't the people you fire who make your life miserable, it's the people you don't.

Harvey MacKay

contract. With court approval, these representatives can enter into enforceable contracts on behalf of the persons they represent.

An agency can be created only to accomplish a lawful purpose. Agency contracts that are created for illegal purposes or are against public policy are void and unenforceable.

Example A principal cannot hire an agent to kill another person.

Some agency relationships are prohibited by law.

Example Unlicensed agents cannot be hired to perform the duties of certain licensed professionals (e.g., doctors, lawyers).

Principal–Agent Relationship

principal–agent relationship
A relationship formed when an employer hires an employee and gives that employee authority to act and enter into contracts on his or her behalf.

A **principal–agent relationship** is formed when an employer hires an employee and gives that employee authority to act and enter into contracts on his or her behalf. The extent of this authority is governed by any express agreement between the parties and implied from the circumstances of the agency.

Example The president of a corporation usually has the authority to enter into major contracts on the corporation's behalf, and a supervisor on the corporation's assembly line may have the authority only to purchase the supplies necessary to keep the line running.

Employer–Employee Relationship

employer–employee relationship
A relationship that results when an employer hires an employee to perform some task or service but the employee has not been authorized to enter into contracts on behalf of his employer.

An **employer–employee relationship** exists when an employer hires an employee to perform some task or service but the employee has not been authorized to enter into contracts on behalf of his employer.

Example A welder on General Motors Corporation's assembly line is employed in an employer–employee relationship if she is not authorized to enter into contracts on behalf of her employer. She has been employed to perform a task without being given agency authority.

An employee is an agent if he or she is empowered to enter into contracts on the employer's behalf.

Example The welder in the previous example is an agent if she is given authority to enter into contracts on behalf of General Motors Corporation.

CONCEPT SUMMARY

KINDS OF EMPLOYMENT RELATIONSHIPS

Type of Relationship	Description
Principal-agent	The agent has authority to act on behalf of the principal, as authorized by the principal and implied from the agency. An employee is often the agent of his employer.
Employer-employee	An employee is hired to perform a task or service. An employee cannot enter into contracts on behalf of the employer.

Principal–Independent Contractor Relationship

independent contractor
A person or business that is not an employee but is employed by a principal to perform a certain task on behalf of the principal.

Principals often employ outsiders—that is, persons and businesses that are not employees—to perform certain tasks on their behalf. These persons and businesses are called **independent contractors**.

Examples Doctors, dentists, consultants, stockbrokers, architects, certified public accountants, real estate brokers, and plumbers are examples of those in professions and trades who commonly act as independent contractors. An independent contractor who is a professional, such as a lawyer, is called a **professional agent**.

A principal can authorize an independent contractor to enter into contracts. Principals are bound by the authorized contracts of their independent contractors. For example, if a client authorizes an attorney to settle a case within a certain dollar amount and the attorney does so, the settlement agreement is binding.

▶ FORMATION OF AN AGENCY

An agency and the resulting authority of an agent can arise in several ways, including express agency, implied agency, incidental authority, agency by ratification, and apparent agency. These types of agencies are discussed in the following paragraphs and material.

Express Agency

Express agency is the most common form of agency. In an express agency, the agent has the authority to contract or otherwise act on the principal's behalf, as expressly stated in the agency agreement. In addition, the agent may also possess certain implied or apparent authority to act on the principal's behalf (as discussed later in this chapter).

Express agency occurs when a principal and an agent expressly agree to enter into an agency agreement with each other. Express agency contracts can be either oral or written, unless the Statute of Frauds stipulates that they must be written. For example, in most states, a real estate broker's contract to sell real estate must be in writing.

If a principal and an agent enter into an **exclusive agency contract**, the principal cannot employ any agent other than the exclusive agent. If the principal does so, the exclusive agent can recover damages from the principal. If an agency is not an exclusive agency, the principal can employ more than one agent to try to accomplish a stated purpose. When multiple agents are employed, the agencies with all the agents terminate when any one of the agents accomplishes the stated purpose.

In the following case, the court had to decide whether an agency had been created.

express agency
An agency that occurs when a principal and an agent expressly agree to enter into an agency agreement with each other.

exclusive agency contract
A contract a principal and agent enter into that says the principal cannot employ any agent other than the exclusive agent.

CASE 29.1 Agency

Bosse v. Brinker Restaurant Corporation, d.b.a. Chili's Grill and Bar

Web 2005 Mass. Super. Lexis 372 (2005)
Superior Court of Massachusetts

"The evidence is insufficient to create a genuine issue whether Chili's appointed or authorized the patron to act as a posse to conduct the chase."

—Judge Sikora

Facts

Brendan Bosse and Michael Griffin were a part of a group of four teenagers eating a meal at a Chili's restaurant in Dedham, Massachusetts. Chili's is owned by Brinker Restaurant Corporation (collectively "Chili's"). The teenagers decided not to pay the $56 bill for their meal. They went out of the building, got in their car, and drove away, heading northward up Route 1.

A patron of the restaurant saw the teenagers leave without payment. He followed them in his white sport-utility vehicle (SUV). The teenagers saw him following them. A high-speed chase ensued through Dedham side streets. The patron used his cell phone to call the Chili's manager. The manager called 911 and reported the incident and the location of the car chase. The teenagers' car collided with a cement wall, and Bosse and Griffin were seriously injured. The Chili's patron drove past the crash scene and was never identified.

Bosse and Griffin sued Chili's for compensatory damages for their injuries. The plaintiffs argued that the patron was an agent of Chili's, and therefore Chili's was liable to the plaintiffs, based on the doctrine of *respondeat superior*, which holds a principal liable for the acts of its agents. Chili's filed a motion for summary judgment, arguing that the patron was not its agent.

Issue

Was the restaurant patron who engaged in the high-speed car chase an agent of Chili's?

(case continues)

Language of the Court

The plaintiffs sue under the theory of respondeat superior. They contend that the Chili's patron converted to a Chili's servant; that he conducted the chase as an agent of the restaurant; and that the restaurant should be liable for the consequences of his negligent or reckless pursuit. An agency relationship will require three elements. Most obviously, Chili's must have consented to the action of the patron on its behalf. Second, Chili's must have retained control, or the right of control, over the physical conduct of the patron in the performance of the pursuit. Third, the conduct of the agent must serve the benefit or further the interest of the principal.

The evidence is insufficient to create a genuine issue whether Chili's appointed or authorized the patron to act as a posse to conduct the chase. No information indicates any preliminary communication between the patron and restaurant manager. The events were spontaneous and fast breaking. No member of Chili's house staff joined in the pursuit. The plaintiffs argue that Chili's effectively assented to an agency relationship by acceptance of the patron's reconnaissance reports during the course of the chase; and by failure to instruct him to break off the chase. That circumstance is not enough. The patron need not have been an agent to engage in that conduct. He was pursuing petty crime. Chili's was reporting the petty crime to the police. No information indicates that Chili's had any effective control over the patron. The dominant purpose of Chili's relay of the patron's reports to the police appears to have been the public interest in the apprehension of petty criminals and not the private recovery of the unpaid bill.

Decision

The superior court held that the restaurant patron who engaged in the high-speed chase in which the plaintiffs were injured was not an agent of Chili's restaurant. The superior court granted summary judgment to Chili's.

Case Questions

Critical Legal Thinking What does the doctrine of *respondeat superior* provide? Explain.

Business Ethics Why do you think the plaintiffs sued Chili's? Do you think they had a very good chance of winning the lawsuit against Chili's?

Contemporary Business Did the elements exist to make the restaurant patron an agent of Chili's restaurant? Explain. Is the restaurant patron liable?

CONTEMPORARY ENVIRONMENT

Power of Attorney

A **power of attorney** is one of the most formal types of express agency agreements. It is often used by a principal to give an agent the power to sign legal documents, such as deeds to real estate, on behalf of the principal. There are two kinds of powers of attorney:

1. **General power of attorney**, which confers broad powers on the agent to act in any matters on the principal's behalf.

2. **Special power of attorney**, which limits the agent to those acts specifically enumerated in the agreement.

An agent with power of attorney is called an **attorney-in-fact** even though he or she does not have to be a lawyer. Powers of attorney must be written. Usually, they must also be notarized. Often, a principal makes a power of attorney a **durable power of attorney**. A durable power of attorney remains effective if the principal is incapacitated.

---

power of attorney
An express agency agreement that is often used to give an agent the power to sign legal documents on behalf of the principal.

implied agency
An agency that occurs when a principal and an agent do not expressly create an agency, but it is inferred from the conduct of the parties.

Implied Agency

In many situations, a principal and an agent do not expressly create an agency. Instead, the agency is implied from the conduct of the parties. This type of agency is referred to as an **implied agency**. The extent of the agent's authority is determined from the facts and circumstances of the particular situation. Implied authority can be conferred by either industry custom, prior dealing between the parties, the agent's position, acts deemed necessary to carry out the agent's duties, and other factors the court deems relevant. Implied authority cannot conflict with express authority or with stated limitations on express authority.

Incidental Authority

Often, even an express agency agreement does not provide enough detail to cover contingencies that may arise in the future regarding the performance of the agency. In such a case, the agent possesses certain implied authority to act beyond his express agency powers. This authority is sometimes referred to as **incidental authority**. Certain emergency situations may arise in the course of an agency. If the agent cannot contact the principal for instructions, the agent has incidental emergency powers to take all actions reasonably necessary to protect the principal's property and rights.

Example A homeowner employs a real estate broker to sell his house. The real estate broker's express powers are to advertise and market the house for sale, show the house to prospective buyers, and accept offers from persons who want to purchase the house. The homeowner goes away on a month long trip where he cannot be contacted. During this time a water pipe breaks and begins to leak water in the house. The real estate broker has incidental authority to hire a plumber to repair the pipe to stop the water leak. The homeowner is responsible for paying for the repairs.

An agent's scope of employment was at issue in the following case.

CASE 29.2 Scope of Employment

Keating v. Goldick and Lapp Roofing and Sheet Metal Company, Inc.

Web 2004 Del. Super. Lexis 102 (2004)
Superior Court of Delaware

"**There comes a point in every litigation where common sense will make some conclusions obvious.**"

—Judge Carpenter

Facts

Lapp Roofing and Sheet Metal Company, Inc., is an Ohio corporation headquartered in Dayton, Ohio. The company provides construction services in several states. Lapp Roofing sent James Goldick and other Lapp Roofing employees to work on a roofing project in Wilmington, Delaware. Lapp Roofing's company policy prohibited employees from driving company vehicles for personal purposes. Lapp Roofing entrusted Goldick, as job foreman, with a white Ford van to transport the workers to the job site and to provide transportation to meals and other necessities.

While in Wilmington, Goldick and another Lapp Roofing employee, James McNees, went to Gators Bar and Restaurant. Goldick, after eating and drinking for several hours, was ejected from the bar. Shortly thereafter, Goldick drove the company van onto the curb in front of the bar, striking two people in the parking lot and seven individuals on the curb outside the bar. Subsequently, the police stopped the van and apprehended Goldick. Goldick was arrested and pleaded guilty to criminal assault charges. Christopher M. Keating and the other injured individuals filed a personal injury lawsuit against Goldick and Lapp Roofing. Lapp Roofing defended, alleging that it was not liable because Goldick's negligent conduct was committed outside the scope of his employment.

Issue

Was Goldick's negligent conduct committed within the scope of his employment for Lapp Roofing?

Language of the Court

There comes a point in every litigation where common sense will make some conclusions obvious. If the injured plaintiffs were not involved in this litigation and were simply asked whether they believe that an individual who used an employer's truck late at night to go to a bar and consume alcohol was acting within the scope of that employer's employment, they would without hesitation say no. Logic and common sense would lead any reasonable person to the same conclusion.

One could argue that sending a work crew from Ohio with only a work truck as transportation would be sufficient deviation. To a degree, the court agrees this allows the range of covered conduct to be explained. Obviously a crew who is assigned for several days or weeks to a remote location will need to utilize the company vehicle to get meals or other necessities associated with that stay. Therefore, if this event had occurred as the employees were leaving Happy Harry's after they obtained a needed prescription or from Denny's Restaurant after a meal, the court believes these foreseeable and logical consequences of a lengthy stay away from home would bring the conduct within the scope of employment under the dual purpose rationale.

However, no reasonable person could conclude this limitation on available transportation would provide the mechanism to expand the coverage to a drunken brawl that occurred after hours and was unassociated with the

(case continues)

employee's work or associated with his stay. Such conduct is so adverse to the employer that no conceivable benefit could be derived. It is completely unrelated to the employer's business and does not advance the work for which the employees were sent to this location. Here, Goldick used the van to go drinking with another employee and drove the van in the parking lot and on the curb injuring various individuals. No jury could reasonably conclude that Goldick's conduct was actuated, even in part, by a purpose to serve his employer. This incident did not occur during working hours and Goldick decided to go to Gators and become intoxicated for purely personal reasons and not to serve Lapp Roofing's interests whatsoever.

Decision

The superior court held that Goldick was not acting within the course and scope of his employment when his negligent conduct occurred. The superior court granted summary judgment to Lapp Roofing on this issue.

Case Questions

Critical Legal Thinking Define *scope of employment*. Why is this concept important in principal–agent relationships? Explain.

Contemporary Business Why was Lapp Roofing found not liable in this case? Explain. If the negligent conduct had occurred when Goldick was driving to a restaurant for a meal, would the decision have been the same?

Business Ethics Did Lapp Roofing act ethically in denying liability for the negligent conduct of one of its employees?

Agency by Ratification

agency by ratification
An agency that occurs when (1) a person misrepresents him- or herself as another's agent when in fact he or she is not and (2) the purported principal ratifies the unauthorized act.

Agency by ratification occurs when (1) a person misrepresents himself or herself as another's agent when in fact he or she is not and (2) the purported principal ratifies (accepts) the unauthorized act. In such cases, the principal is bound to perform, and the agent is relieved of any liability for misrepresentation.

Example Bill Levine sees a house for sale and thinks his friend Sherry Maxwell would want it. Bill Levine enters into a contract to purchase the house from the seller and signs the contract "Bill Levine, agent for Sherry Maxwell." Because Bill is not Sherry Maxwell's agent, she is not bound to the contract. However, if Sherry agrees to purchase the house, there is an agency by ratification. The ratification "relates back" to the moment Bill Levine entered into the contract. Upon ratification of the contract, Sherry Maxwell is obligated to purchase the house.

▶ APPARENT AGENCY

apparent agency
Agency that arises when a principal creates the appearance of an agency that in actuality does not exist.

Apparent agency (or **agency by estoppel**) arises when a principal creates the appearance of an agency that in actuality does not exist. Where an apparent agency is established, the principal is **estopped** (stopped) from denying the agency relationship and is bound to contracts entered into by the apparent agent while acting within the scope of the apparent agency. Note that the principal's actions—not the agent's—create an apparent agency.

Example Georgia Pacific, Inc., interviews Albert Iorio for a sales representative position. Mr. Iorio, accompanied by Jane Franklin, the national sales manager, visits retail stores located in the open sales territory. While visiting one store, Jane tells the store manager, "I wish I had more sales reps like Albert." Nevertheless, Albert is not hired. If Albert later enters into contracts with the store on behalf of Georgia Pacific and Jane has not controverted the impression of Albert she left with the store manager, the company will be bound to the contract.

CONCEPT SUMMARY
FORMATION OF AGENCY RELATIONSHIPS

Type of Agency	Formation	Enforcement of the Contract
Express	Authority is expressly given to the agent by the principal.	Principal and third party are bound to the contract.

Type of Agency	Formation	Enforcement of the Contract
Implied	Authority is implied from the conduct of the parties, custom and usage of trade, or act incidental to carrying out the agent's duties.	Principal and third party are bound to the contract.
Incidental	Authority that is implied to act beyond express agency powers to take all actions reasonably necessary to protect the principal's property and rights.	Principal and third party are bound to the contract.
Apparent	Authority is created when the principal leads a third party to believe that the agent has authority.	Principal and third party are bound to the contract.
By ratification	Acts of the agent are committed outside the scope of his or her authority.	Principal and third party are not bound to the contract unless the principal ratifies the contract.

▶ PRINCIPAL'S DUTIES

A principal owes certain duties to an agent. These duties are discussed in the following paragraphs.

Principal's Duty to Compensate

A principal owes a **duty to compensate** an agent for services provided. Usually, the agency contract (whether written or oral) specifies the compensation to be paid. The principal must pay this amount either upon the completion of the agency or at some other mutually agreeable time.

If there is no agreement as to the amount of compensation, the law implies a promise that the principal will pay the agent the customary fee paid in the industry. If the compensation cannot be established by custom, the principal owes a duty to pay the reasonable value of the agent's services. There is no duty to compensate a gratuitous agent. However, gratuitous agents who agree to provide their services free of charge may be paid voluntarily.

Certain types of agents traditionally perform their services on a **contingency-fee basis**. Under this type of arrangement, the principal owes a duty to pay the agent the agreed-upon contingency fee only if the agency is completed. Real estate brokers, finders, lawyers, and salespersons often work on a contingency-fee basis.

duty to compensate
A duty that a principal owes to pay an agreed-upon amount to the agent either upon the completion of the agency or at some other mutually agreeable time.

Principal's Duties to Reimburse and to Indemnify

In carrying out an agency, an agent may spend his or her own money on the principal's behalf. Unless otherwise agreed, the principal owes a **duty to reimburse** the agent for all such expenses if they were (1) authorized by the principal, (2) within the scope of the agency, and (3) necessary to discharge the agent's duties in carrying out the agency.

Example A principal must reimburse an agent for authorized business trips taken on the principal's behalf.

A principal also owes a **duty to indemnify** the agent for any losses the agent suffers because of the principal. This duty usually arises where an agent is held liable for the principal's misconduct.

Example An agent enters into an authorized contract with a third party on the principal's behalf, the principal fails to perform on the contract, and the third party recovers a judgment against the agent. The agent can recover indemnification of this amount from the principal.

Principal's Duty to Cooperate

Unless otherwise agreed, a principal owes a **duty to cooperate** with and assist an agent in the performance of the agent's duties and the accomplishment of the agency.

Example Unless otherwise agreed, a principal who employs a real estate agent to sell her house owes a duty to allow the agent to show the house to prospective purchasers during reasonable hours.

▶ AGENT'S DUTIES

An agent owes certain duties to a principal. These duties are discussed in the following paragraphs.

Agent's Duty to Perform

duty to perform
An agent's duty to a principal that includes (1) performing the lawful duties expressed in the contract and (2) meeting the standards of reasonable care, skill, and diligence implicit in all contracts.

An agent who enters into a contract with a principal has two distinct obligations: (1) to perform the lawful duties expressed in the contract and (2) to meet the standards of reasonable care, skill, and diligence implicit in all contracts. Collectively, these duties are referred to as the agent's **duty to perform**. Normally, an agent is required to render the same standard of care, skill, and diligence that a fictitious reasonable agent in the same occupation would render in the same locality and under the same circumstances.

Examples A general medical practitioner in a rural area would be held to the standard of a reasonable general medical practitioner in rural areas. The standard might be different for a general medical practitioner in a big city. In some professions, such as accounting, a national standard of performance (e.g., "generally accepted accounting principles") is imposed. If an agent holds himself or herself as possessing higher-than-customary skills, the agent is held to that higher standard of performance. For example, a lawyer who claims to be a specialist in securities law will be held to a reasonable specialist-in-securities-law standard.

An agent who does not perform his or her express duties or fails to use the standard degree of care, skill, or diligence is liable to the principal for breach of contract. An agent who has negligently or intentionally failed to perform properly is also liable in tort to the principal.

Agent's Duty to Notify

In the course of an agency, the agent usually learns information that is important to the principal. This information may come from third parties or other sources. The agent's duty to notify the principal of such information is called the **duty to notify**. The agent is liable to the principal for any injuries resulting from a breach of this duty. Most information learned by an agent in the course of an agency is **imputed** to the principal. This means that the principal is assumed to know what the agent knows. This is so even if the agent does not tell the principal certain relevant information.

imputed knowledge
Information that is learned by an agent that is attributed to the principal.

Agent's Duty to Account

duty to account
A duty that an agent owes to maintain an accurate accounting of all transactions undertaken on the principal's behalf. Also known as the *duty of accountability*.

Unless otherwise agreed, an agent owes a duty to maintain an accurate accounting of all transactions undertaken on the principal's behalf. This **duty to account** (sometimes called the **duty of accountability**) includes keeping records of all property and money received and expended during the course of the agency. A principal has a right to demand an accounting from the agent at any time, and the agent owes a legal duty to make the accounting. This duty also requires the agent to (1) maintain a separate account for the principal and (2) use the principal's property in an authorized manner.

Any property, money, or other benefit received by the agent in the course of an agency belongs to the principal. For example, all secret profits received by an agent are the property of the principal. If an agent breaches the agency contract, the principal can sue the agent to recover damages caused by breach. The court can impose a *constructive trust* for the benefit of the principal on any property purchased with secret profits.

▶ TERMINATION OF AN AGENCY BY ACTS OF THE PARTIES

An agency contract is similar to other contracts in that it can be terminated by an act of the parties. Note that once an agency relationship is terminated, the agent can no longer represent the principal or bind the principal to contracts. The parties to an agency contract can terminate the agency contract either by agreement or by their actions. The four methods of **termination of an agency relationship by acts of the parties** are:

1. **Mutual agreement.**   As with any other contract, the parties to an agency contract can mutually agree to terminate their agreement. By doing so, the parties relieve each other of any further rights, duties, obligations, or powers provided for in the agency contract. Either party can propose the termination of an agency contract.

2. **Lapse of time.**   Agency contracts are often written for a specific period of time. When this is the case, the agency terminates when the specified time period elapses. If an agency contract does not set forth a specific termination date, the agency terminates after a reasonable time has elapsed. The courts often look to the custom of an industry in determining the reasonable time for the termination of the agency.

   Example A principal and an agent enter into an agency contract "beginning January 1, 2011, and ending December 31, 2014." The agency automatically terminates on December 31, 2014.

3. **Purpose achieved.**   A principal can employ an agent for the time it takes to accomplish a certain task, purpose, or result. Such agencies automatically terminate when they are completed.

   Example A principal employs a licensed real estate broker to sell his house. The agency terminates when the house is sold and the principal pays the broker the agreed-upon compensation.

4. **Occurrence of a specified event.**   An agency contract can specify that the agency exists until a specified event occurs. The agency terminates when the specified event happens.

   Example A principal employs an agent to take care of her dog until she returns from a trip. The agency terminates when the principal returns from the trip.

Notification Required at the Termination of an Agency

If an agency is terminated by agreement between the parties, the principal is under a **duty of notification of the termination of the agency to third parties**. Unless otherwise required, the notice can be from the principal or some other source (e.g., the agent). If an agency terminates by operation of law, there is no duty to notify third parties about the termination, however.

The termination of an agency extinguishes an agent's actual authority to act on the principal's behalf. However, if the principal fails to give the proper notice of termination to a third party, the agent still has apparent authority to bind the principal to contracts with these third parties. If this happens, the contract is enforceable against the principal. The principal's only recourse is against the agent to recover damages caused by these unauthorized contracts.

The following notification requirements must be met:

- **Parties who dealt with the agent.** Direct notice of termination must be given to all persons with whom the agent dealt. Although the notice may be either written or oral, it is better practice to give written notice.
- **Parties who have knowledge of the agency.** The principal must give direct or constructive notice to any third party who has knowledge of the agency but with whom the agent has not dealt. Direct notice is often in the form of a letter. Constructive notice usually consists of placing a notice of the termination of the agency in a newspaper serving the relevant community. This notice is effective even against persons who do not see it.
- **Parties who have no knowledge of the agency.** Generally, a principal is not obligated to give notice of termination to strangers who have no knowledge of the agency. However, a principal who has given the agent written authority to act but fails to

The way to wealth is as plain as the way to market. It depends chiefly on two words, industry and frugality: that is, waste neither time nor money, but make the best use of both. Without industry and frugality nothing will do, and with them everything.

Benjamin Franklin

Shortly his fortune shall be lifted higher;
True industry doth kindle honour's fire.

William Shakespeare

recover the writing upon termination of the agency may be liable to strangers who later rely on the writing and deal with the agent. The laws of most states provide that this liability can be avoided by giving constructive notice (e.g., newspaper announcement) of the termination of the agency.

CONTEMPORARY ENVIRONMENT

Agency Coupled with an Interest

An **agency coupled with an interest** is a special type of agency relationship that is created for the agent's benefit. This type of agency is **irrevocable** by the principal (i.e., the principal cannot terminate it). An agency coupled with an interest is commonly used in security agreements to secure loans. An agency coupled with an interest is not terminated by the death or incapacity of either the principal or the agent. It terminates only when the agent's obligations are performed. However, the parties can expressly agree that an agency coupled with an interest is terminated.

Example Heidi owns a piece of real estate. She goes to Wells Fargo Bank to obtain a loan on the property. The bank makes the loan but requires her to sign a security agreement (e.g., a mortgage) pledging the property as collateral for the loan. The security agreement contains a clause that appoints that bank as Heidi's agent and permits the bank to sell the property and recover the amount of the loan from the sale proceeds if she defaults on her payments. This agency is irrevocable by Heidi, the principal.

---

agency coupled with an interest
A special type of agency that is created for the agent's benefit and that the principal cannot revoke.

Wrongful Termination of an Agency or Employment Contract

Generally, agency and employment contracts that do not specify a definite time for their termination can be terminated at will by either the principal or the agent, without liability to the other party. When a principal terminates an agency contract, it is called a **revocation of authority**. When an agent terminates an agency, it is called a **renunciation of authority**.

Unless an agency is irrevocable, both the principal and the agent have individual power to unilaterally terminate any agency contract. Note that having the power to terminate an agency agreement is not the same as having the right to terminate it. The unilateral termination of an agency contract may be wrongful. If a principal's or an agent's termination of an agency contract breaches the contract, the other party can sue for damages for **wrongful termination**.

wrongful termination
The termination of an agency contract in violation of the terms of the agency contract. The nonbreaching party may recover damages from the breaching party.

Example A principal employs a licensed real estate agent to sell his house. The agency contract gives the agent an exclusive listing for three months. After one month, the principal unilaterally terminates the agency. The principal has the power to do so, and the agent can no longer act on behalf of the principal. However, because the principal did not have the right to terminate the contract, the agent can sue him and recover damages (i.e., lost commission) for wrongful termination.

▶ TERMINATION OF AN AGENCY BY OPERATION OF LAW

The crowning fortune of a man is to be born to some pursuit which finds him employment and happiness, whether it be to make baskets, or broad swords, or canals, or statues, or songs.

Ralph Waldo Emerson

Agency contracts can be **terminated by operation of law** as well as by agreement. The five methods of terminating an agency relationship by operation of law are:

1. **Death.**   The death of either the principal or the agent terminates an agency relationship. This rule is based on the old legal principle that because a dead person cannot act, no one can act for him or her. Note that an agency terminates even if one party is unaware of the other party's death. An agent's actions that take place after the principal's death do not bind the principal's estate.

2. **Insanity.**   The insanity of either the principal or the agent generally terminates an agency relationship. A few states have modified this rule to provide that a contract entered into by an agent on behalf of an insane principal is enforceable if (1) the insane person has not been adjudged insane, (2) the third party does not have knowledge of the principal's insanity at the time of contracting, and (3) the enforcement of the contract will prevent injustice.

3. **Bankruptcy.**   An agency relationship is terminated if the principal is declared bankrupt. Bankruptcy requires the filing of a petition for bankruptcy under federal bankruptcy law. With few exceptions, neither the appointment of a state court receiver nor the principal's financial difficulties or insolvency terminates the agency relationship. The agent's bankruptcy usually does not terminate an agency unless the agent's credit standing is important to the agency relationship.

4. **Changed circumstances.**   An agency terminates when there is an unusual change in circumstances that would lead the agent to believe that the principal's original instructions should no longer be valid.

   Example A principal employs a licensed real estate agent to sell a farm for $100,000. The agent thereafter learns that oil has been discovered on the property and makes it worth $1 million. The agency terminates because of this change in circumstances.

5. **War.**   The outbreak of a war between the principal's country and the agent's country terminates an agency relationship between the parties. Such an occurrence usually makes the performance of the agency contract impossible.

Termination by Impossibility

An agency relationship terminates if a situation arises that makes its fulfillment impossible. The following circumstances can lead to **termination by impossibility**:

• The loss or destruction of the subject matter of the agency

Example A principal employs an agent to sell his horse, but the horse dies before it is sold. The agency relationship terminates at the moment the horse dies.

• The loss of a required qualification

Example A principal employs a licensed real estate agent to sell her house, and the real estate agent's license is revoked. The agency terminates at the moment the license is revoked.

• A change in the law

Example A principal employs an agent to trap alligators. If a law is passed that makes trapping alligators illegal, the agency contract terminates when the law becomes effective.

Most are engaged in business the greater part of their lives, because the soul abhors a vacuum and they have not discovered any continuous employment for man's nobler faculties.

Henry David Thoreau

TEST REVIEW TERMS AND CONCEPTS

Agency	Duty of notification of termination of an agency	Estopped	Principal–agent relationship
Agency by ratification		Exclusive agency contract	Professional agent
Agency coupled with an interest	Duty to account (duty of accountability)	Express agency	Renunciation of authority
Agency law	Duty to compensate	Fiduciary relationship	*Restatement (Second) of Agency*
Agent	Duty to cooperate	General power of attorney	Revocation of authority
Apparent agency (agency by estoppel)	Duty to indemnify	Implied agency	Special power of attorney
Attorney-in-fact	Duty to notify	Imputed knowledge	Termination by acts of the parties
Contingency-fee basis	Duty to perform	Incidental authority	Termination by impossibility
Contractual capacity	Duty to reimburse	Independent contractor	Termination by operation of law
Durable power of attorney	Employer–employee relationship	Irrevocable agency	Wrongful termination
		Power of attorney	
		Principal	

CASE PROBLEMS

29.1 Creation of an Agency Renaldo, Inc., doing business as Baker Street, owned and operated a nightclub in Georgia. On the evening in question, plaintiff Ginn became "silly drunk" at the nightclub and was asked by several patrons and the manager to leave the premises. The police were called, and Ginn left the premises. When Ginn realized that his jacket was still in the nightclub, he attempted to reenter the premises. He was met at the door by the manager, who refused him admittance. When Ginn persisted, an unidentified patron, without the approval of the manager, pushed Ginn, who lost his balance and fell backward. To break his fall, Ginn put his hand against the door jamb. The unidentified patron slammed the door on Ginn's hand and held it shut for several minutes. Ginn, who suffered severe injuries to his right hand, sued the nightclub for damages. Is the unidentified patron an agent of the nightclub? *Ginn v. Renaldo, Inc.*, 183 Ga.App. 618, 359 S.E.2d 390, **Web** 1987 Ga.App. Lexis 2023 (Court of Appeals of Georgia)

29.2 Independent Contractor Mercedes Connolly and her husband purchased airline tickets and a tour package for a tour to South Africa from Judy Samuelson, a travel agent doing business as International Tours of Manhattan. Samuelson sold tickets for a variety of airline companies and tour operators, including African Adventurers, which was the tour operator for the Connollys' tour. Mercedes fell while trying to cross a 6-inch-deep stream while the tour group was on a walking tour to see hippopotami in a river at a game reserve. In the process, she injured her left ankle and foot. She sued Samuelson for damages. Is Samuelson liable? *Connolly v. Samuelson*, 671 F.Supp. 1312, **Web** 1987 U.S. Dist. Lexis 8308 (United States District Court for the District of Kansas)

29.3 Contract Liability Leroy Behlman and 18 other football fans from Connecticut and New York decided to attend the Super Bowl football game in New Orleans. They entered into contracts with Octagon Travel Center, Inc. (Octagon), a tour operator, and paid $399 each for transportation, lodging, and a ticket to the Super Bowl football game. They purchased the tour package through Universal Travel Agency, Inc. (Universal), a travel agency that acts as a broker for a number of airline companies and tour operators. The individual contracts, however, were between the football fans and Octagon. When they arrived in New Orleans, no tickets to the Super Bowl were forthcoming. Upon returning, they sued Universal for breach of contract. Is Universal liable? *Behlman v. Universal Travel Agency, Inc.*, 4 Conn.App. 688, 496 A.2d 962, **Web** 1985 Conn. App. Lexis 1092 (Appellate Court of Connecticut)

29.4 Power of Attorney As a result of marital problems, Howard R. Bankerd "left for the west," and Virginia Bankerd, his wife, continued to reside in their jointly owned home. Before his departure, Howard executed a power of attorney to Arthur V. King, which authorized King to "convey, grant, bargain, and/or sell" Howard's interest in the property. For the ensuing decade, Howard lived in various locations in Nevada, Colorado, and Washington but rarely contacted King. Howard made no payments on the mortgage, for taxes, or for maintenance or upkeep of the home.

Nine years later, Virginia, who was nearing retirement, requested King to exercise his power of attorney and transfer Howard's interest in the home to her. King's attempts to locate Howard were unsuccessful. He believed that Howard, who would then be 69 years of age, might be dead. King gifted Howard's interest in the property to Virginia, who sold the property for $62,500. Four years later, Howard returned and filed suit against King, alleging breach of trust and fiduciary duty. Is King liable? *King v. Bankerd*, 303 Md. 98, 492 A.2d 608, **Web** 1985 Md. Lexis 589 (Court of Appeals of Maryland)

29.5 Apparent Agency Robert Bolus was engaged in various businesses in which he sold and repaired trucks. He decided to build a truck repair facility in Bartonsville, Pennsylvania. Bolus contacted United Penn Bank (Bank) to obtain financing for the project and was referred to Emmanuel Ziobro, an assistant vice president. Ziobro orally agreed that Bank would provide funding for the project. He did not tell Bolus that he only had express authority to make loans of up to $10,000. After extending $210,000 in loans to Bolus, Bank refused to provide further financing. When Bolus defaulted on the loans, Bank pressed judgment against Bolus. Bank sought to recover Bolus's assets in payment for the loan. Bolus sued Bank for damages for breach of contract. Who wins? *Bolus v. United Penn Bank*, 363 Pa. Super. 247, 525 A.2d 1215, **Web** 1987 Pa. Super. Lexis 7258 (Superior Court of Pennsylvania)

29.6 Imputed Knowledge Iota Management Corporation entered into a contract to purchase the Bel Air West Motor Hotel in the city of St. Louis from Boulevard Investment Company. The agreement contained the following warranty: "Seller has no actual notice of any substantial defect in the structure of the Hotel or in any of its plumbing, heating, air-conditioning, electrical, or utility systems."

When the buyer inspected the premises, no leaks in the pipes were visible. Iota purchased the hotel for $2 million. When Iota removed some of the walls and ceilings during remodeling, it found evidence of prior repairs to leaking pipes and ducts, as well as devices for catching water (e.g., milk, cartons, cookie sheets, buckets). The estimate to repair these leaks was $500,000. Evidence at trial showed that Cecil Lillibridge, who was Boulevard's maintenance supervisor for the four years prior to the motor hotel's sale, had actual knowledge of these problems and had repaired some of the pipes. Iota sued Boulevard to rescind the contract. Is Boulevard liable? *Iota Management Corporation v. Boulevard Investment Company*, 731 S.W.2d 399, **Web** 1987 Mo.App. Lexis 4027 (Court of Appeals of Missouri)

BUSINESS ETHICS CASES

29.7 Business Ethics   The Hagues, husband and wife, owned a 160-acre tract that they decided to sell. They entered into a listing agreement with Harvey C. Hilgendorf, a licensed real estate broker, which gave Hilgendorf the exclusive right to sell the property for a period of 12 months. The Hagues agreed to pay Hilgendorf a commission of 6 percent of the accepted sale price if a bona fide buyer was found during the listing period.

By letter 5 months later, the Hagues terminated the listing agreement with Hilgendorf. Hilgendorf did not acquiesce to the Hagues' termination, however. One month later, Hilgendorf presented an offer to the Hagues from a buyer willing to purchase the property at the full listing price. The Hagues ignored the offer and sold the property to another buyer. Hilgendorf sued the Hagues for breach of the agency agreement. Did the Hagues act ethically in this case? Who wins the lawsuit? *Hilgendorf v. Hague*, 293 N.W.2d 272, **Web** 1980 Iowa Sup. Lexis 882 (Supreme Court of Iowa)

29.8 Business Ethics   Elizabeth Krempasky, who was 82 years old, owned a house and four certificates of deposit (CDs) at a bank. In her will, Krempasky devised her estate to her niece, Lydia Vrablova Wanamaker. Krempasky died while a patient at a hospital. Wanamaker, who was appointed executrix of the decedent's estate, could not find the CDs. Upon further inquiry, she discovered that the name of Anna A. Parana, an acquaintance of Krempasky's, had been added to the CDs on the day of the decedent's death. Evidence showed that (1) Parana prepared the forms necessary to authorize the bank to add her name to the CDs, (2) the decedent signed the forms on the day of her death sometime before dying at 2:45 P.M., and (3) Parana presented the authorization forms to the bank sometime between 3:00 P.M. and 4:00 P.M. on the same day. A transfer of CDs to joint tenancy is not effective until the bank officially makes the transfer on its records, which it did because it did not have notice of Krempasky's death. Wanamaker, as executrix of the decedent's estate, filed a petition requesting that the CDs be ordered returned to the decedent's estate. Is Anna Parana an agent of Elizabeth Krempasky? Did Parana act ethically in this case? *Estate of Krempasky*, 348 Pa. Super. 128, 501 A.2d 681, **Web** 1985 Pa. Super. Lexis 10545 (Superior Court of Pennsylvania)

30 | LIABILITY OF PRINCIPALS, AGENTS, AND INDEPENDENT CONTRACTORS

▲ **New York City** *These are taxis in New York City. If a taxi driver owns his or her vehicle, the taxi owner is liable for injuries he or she causes while driving the taxi. Many taxis, however, are owned by one party, and another party—the taxi driver—is hired to drive the taxi. In this case, the owner of the taxi is the principal, and the driver is the agent. The owner of the taxi is liable for the negligent conduct of the driver while the driver is acting within the scope of employment.*

CHAPTER OBJECTIVES

After studying this chapter, you should be able to:

1. Describe the duty of loyalty owed by an agent to a principal.
2. Identify and describe the principal's liability for the tortious conduct of an agent.
3. Describe the principal's and agent's liability on third-party contracts.
4. Describe how independent contractor status is created.
5. Describe the principal's liability for torts of an independent contractor.

CHAPTER CONTENTS

▶ **INTRODUCTION TO LIABILITY OF PRINCIPALS, AGENTS, AND INDEPENDENT CONTRACTORS**

▶ **AGENT'S DUTY OF LOYALTY TO THE PRINCIPAL**

▶ **TORT LIABILITY TO THIRD PARTIES**
Case 30.1 · Siegenthaler v. Johnson Welded Products, Inc.

Case 30.2 · American National Property and
      Casualty Company v. Farah
Ethics Spotlight · *Intentional Tort*

▶ **CONTRACT LIABILITY TO THIRD PARTIES**
▶ **INDEPENDENT CONTRACTOR**
    Ethics Spotlight · *Principal Liable for Repo Man's Tort*

"The law, wherein, as in a magic mirror, we see reflected not only our lives, but the lives of all men that have been! When I think on this majestic theme, my eyes dazzle."

—Oliver Wendell Holmes, Jr.
To the Suffolk Bar Association (1885)

▶ INTRODUCTION TO LIABILITY OF PRINCIPALS, AGENTS, AND INDEPENDENT CONTRACTORS

Principals and agents owe certain duties to each other and are liable to each other for breaching these duties. When acting for the principal, an agent often enters into contracts and otherwise deals with third parties. Agency law has established certain rules that make principals, agents, and independent contractors liable to third persons for contracts and tortious conduct.

This chapter discusses the liability of principals, agents, and independent contractors to each other and to third parties.

▶ AGENT'S DUTY OF LOYALTY TO THE PRINCIPAL

Because an agency relationship is based on trust and confidence, an agent owes the principal a **duty of loyalty** in all agency-related matters. Thus, an agent owes a fiduciary duty not to act adversely to the interests of the principal. If this duty is breached, the agent is liable to the principal. The most common types of breaches of loyalty by an agent are discussed in the following paragraphs.

agent's duty of loyalty
A fiduciary duty owed by an agent not to act adversely to the interests of the principal.

Self-Dealing

Agents are generally prohibited from undisclosed **self-dealing** with the principal.

Example A real estate agent who is employed to purchase real estate for a principal cannot secretly sell his own property to the principal. However, the deal is lawful if the principal agrees to buy the property after the agent discloses his ownership of the property.

Usurping an Opportunity

An agent cannot **usurp an opportunity** that belongs to the principal. A third-party offer to an agent must be conveyed to the principal. The agent cannot appropriate the opportunity for himself or herself unless the principal rejects it after due consideration. Opportunities to purchase real estate, businesses, products, ideas, and other property are subject to this rule.

Competing with the Principal

Agents are prohibited from **competing with the principal** during the course of an agency unless the principal agrees to the competition. The reason for this rule is that an agent cannot meet his or her duty of loyalty when his or her personal interests conflict with the principal's interests. If the parties have not entered into an enforceable covenant not to compete, the agent is free to compete with the principal when the agency has ended.

Misuse of Confidential Information

In the course of an agency, the agent often acquires confidential information about the principal's affairs (e.g., business plans, technological innovations, customer lists, trade

If we are industrious, we shall never starve; for, at the workingman's house hunger looks in, but dares not enter. Nor will the bailiff or the constable enter, for industry pays debts, while despair increaseth them.

Benjamin Franklin

No nation was ever ruined by trade.

Benjamin Franklin

secrets). The agent is under a legal duty not to disclose or **misuse confidential information** either during or after the course of the agency. There is no prohibition against using general information, knowledge, or experience acquired during the course of the agency.

Dual Agency

An agent cannot meet a duty of loyalty to two parties that have conflicting interests. **Dual agency** occurs when an agent acts for two or more different principals in the same transaction. This practice is generally prohibited unless all the parties involved in the transaction agree to it. If an agent acts as an undisclosed dual agent, he or she must forfeit all compensation received in the transaction. Some agents, such as middlemen and finders, are not considered dual agents. This is because they only bring interested parties together; they do not take part in any negotiations.

▶ TORT LIABILITY TO THIRD PARTIES

A principal and an agent are each personally liable for their own tortious conduct. The principal is liable for the tortious conduct of an agent who is acting within the scope of his or her authority. The agent, however, is liable for the tortious conduct of the principal only if he or she directly or indirectly participates in or aids and abets the principal's conduct.

The courts have applied a broad and flexible standard in interpreting scope of authority in the context of employment. Although other factors may also be considered, the courts answer the following questions to determine whether an agent's conduct occurred within the scope of his or her employment:

- Was the act specifically requested or authorized by the principal?
- Was it the kind of act that the agent was employed to perform?
- Did the act occur substantially within the time period of employment authorized by the principal?
- Did the act occur substantially within the location of employment authorized by the employer?
- Was the agent advancing the principal's purpose when the act occurred?

Where liability is found, tort remedies are available to the injured party. These remedies include recovery for medical expenses, lost wages, pain and suffering, emotional distress, and, in some cases, punitive damages. As discussed in the following paragraphs, the three main sources of **tort liability** for principals and agents are negligence, intentional torts, and misrepresentation.

Negligence

respondeat superior
A rule that says an employer is liable for the tortious conduct of its employees or agents while they are acting within the scope of its authority.

Principals are liable for the negligent conduct of agents acting within the scope of their employment. This liability is based on the common law doctrine of *respondeat superior* ("let the master answer"), which, in turn, is based on the legal theory of **vicarious liability** (liability without fault). In other words, the principal is liable because of his or her employment contract with the negligent agent, not because the principal was personally at fault.

The doctrine of **negligence** rests on the principle that if the principal expects to derive certain benefits from acting through others (i.e., an agent), that person should also bear the liability for injuries caused to third persons by the negligent conduct of an agent who is acting within the scope of his or her employment.

frolic and detour
A situation in which an agent does something during the course of his or her employment to further his or her own interests rather than the principal's.

Frolic and Detour   Agents sometimes do things during the course of their employment to further their own interests rather than the principal's. For example, an agent might take a detour to run a personal errand while on assignment for the principal. This is commonly referred to as **frolic and detour**. Negligence actions stemming from frolic and detour are examined on a case-by-case basis. Agents are always personally liable for their tortious conduct in such situations. Principals are generally relieved of liability if the agent's frolic and detour is substantial. However, if the deviation is minor, the principal is liable for the injuries caused by the agent's tortious conduct.

The following case involves frolic and detour.

CASE 30.1 Frolic and Detour

Siegenthaler v. Johnson Welded Products, Inc.

2006 Ohio 5588, Web 2006 OhioApp. Lexis 5616 (2006)
Court of Appeals of Ohio

"No reasonable finder of fact could find from this evidence that Spires was subject to the direction and control of Johnson Welded Products as to the operation of his truck at the time of the collision, while he was on his way to a friend's house for lunch."

—Judge Fain

Facts

Jesse Spires was employed as a welder by Johnson Welded Products, Inc. Johnson Welded Products provides a lunchroom equipped with a microwave, refrigerator, and vending machine for sandwiches, snacks, and drinks. Spires worked a shift that ran from 3:15 P.M. until 12:15 A.M. One day at work, Spires was on his way to a friend's house for lunch during his lunch break, driving his own pickup truck, when he collided with Donald Siegenthaler, who was riding a motorcycle. The collision, which was the result of Spires's negligence, caused injury to Siegenthaler.

Siegenthaler sued Johnson Welded Products, alleging that Spires was an agent of Johnson Welded Products at the time of the accident and that Johnson Welded Products was vicariously liable under the doctrine of *respondeat superior*. Johnson Welded Products argued that Spires was on personal business when he caused the accident. The trial court granted Johnson Welded Products's motion for summary judgment. Siegenthaler appealed.

Issue

Was Spires an agent of Johnson Welded Products, acting within the scope of his employment, at the time of the accident that injured Siegenthaler?

Language of the Court

Under the doctrine of respondeat superior, *an employer will be held liable for the negligent act of its employee if the employee was acting within the course and scope of his employment. No reasonable finder of fact could find from this evidence that Spires was subject to the direction and control of Johnson Welded Products as to the operation of his truck at the time of the collision, while he was on his way to a friend's house for lunch.*

There is nothing in this record to suggest that Spires's contract of employment with Johnson Welded Products purported to give Johnson Welded Products the right to control the manner in which Spires would drive his own vehicle to or from work, and the only reasonable inference is that Johnson Welded Products had no right to control Spires's conduct in that matter. We can see no reason why Johnson Welded Products would have any desire to control the manner in which its employees drive to or from work.

Decision

The court of appeals held that Spires was not acting within his scope of employment when he collided with and injured Siegenthaler. The court of appeals affirmed the trial court's grant of summary judgment to Johnson Welded Products.

Case Questions

Critical Legal Thinking Describe the doctrine of *respondeat superior*. What does the doctrine of frolic and detour provide?

Business Ethics Could Siegenthaler recover from Spires? If so, under what legal theory? Did Siegenthaler act ethically in bringing this case against Johnson Welded Products?

Contemporary Business How important is the element of control in determining whether an employee is acting within the scope of his or her employment?

Coming and Going Rule   Under the common law, a principal is generally not liable for injuries caused by its agents and employees while they are on their way to or from work. This rule, called the **coming and going rule**, applies even if the principal supplies the agent's automobile or other transportation or pays for gasoline, repairs, and other automobile operating expenses. This rule is quite logical. Because principals do not control where their agents and employees live, they should not be held liable for tortious conduct of agents on their way to and from work.

In the following case, the court applied the coming and going rule.

coming and going rule
A rule that says a principal is generally not liable for injuries caused by its agents and employees while they are on their way to or from work.

CASE 30.2 Coming and Going Rule

American National Property and Casualty Company v. Farah

2006 Ohio 5519, Web 2006 Ohio App. Lexis 5496 (2006)
Court of Appeals of Ohio

> "Therefore, the trial court applied the coming and going rule and determined that Morgenstern was not in the course of his company's business at the time of the accident."

—Judge Klatt

Facts

Daniel J. Morgenstern was a licensed chiropractor and owned and was the sole shareholder of Daniel J. Morgenstern, D.C., Inc., d.b.a. Morning Star Chiropractic. He treated patients in an office located in Gahanna, Ohio. One day, when he did not have any scheduled appointments, he planned on meeting his wife at her sister's house. Around 11:00 A.M., Morgenstern drove to a restaurant for lunch. After having lunch, he headed toward his sister-in-law's house. On the way, he stopped at a grocery store in Columbus, Ohio. After leaving the store, his lunch began to "weigh a little heavy" on his stomach, so he decided to go to his office to take some nutrients for his stomach. On the way, Morgenstern collided with Ayan Farah's automobile. Farah was seriously injured as a result of the collision. Farah sued Morgenstern personally as well as his company, alleging that Morgenstern's negligence caused her injuries and that the company was vicariously liable.

American National Property and Casualty Company (ANPAC) insured Morgenstern personally for $250,000 for liability and insured the company for $1 million for liability. ANPAC filed a declaratory judgment action to resolve its insurance liability. ANPAC conceded that Morgenstern's $250,000 personal liability automobile insurance policy provided Farah with coverage. ANPAC argued, however, that its $1 million commercial automobile policy on the company did not cover Farah because Morgenstern was not acting in the scope of his employment when the accident happened. ANPAC argued that the coming and going rule protected it from liability. The trial court agreed with ANPAC and entered judgment in favor of ANPAC. Farah appealed.

Issue

Did the coming and going rule protect the company, and therefore ANPAC, from liability to Farah?

Language of the Court

In determining whether an employee has a fixed place of employment, and therefore is subject to the coming and going rule, courts have focused on when and where the

employee commences his substantial employment duties. If an employee commences substantial employment duties only after arriving at a specific and identifiable work place designated by the employer, the employee has a fixed place of employment and the coming and going rule applies. In the case at bar, the trial court found that Morgenstern has a fixed place of employment. Therefore, the trial court applied the coming and going rule and determined that Morgenstern was not in the course of his company's business at the time of the accident. Consequently, there was no coverage under the company's commercial policy. We agree.

In the normal context, an employee's commute to a fixed work site bears no meaningful relation to his employment contract and serves no purpose of the employer's business. Morgenstern was driving to his office primarily because he did not feel well. Simply because he was listening to an audiotape of his lecture notes at the time of the accident does not change the fundamental character of the drive to his office. In conclusion, Morgenstern was driving to his Gahanna office at the time of the accident. That office was a fixed place of employment for Morgenstern. Thus, under the coming and going rule, he was not in the course of his company's business when he collided with appellant. Accordingly, ANPAC's commercial policy does not provide Morgenstern with coverage.

Decision

The court of appeals held that Morgenstern was not acting within the course of the company's business when he collided with Farah and that the coming and going rule applied. The court of appeals affirmed the trial court's judgment, which held that ANPAC's $1 million commercial policy insuring the company was not available to Farah's claims.

Case Questions

Critical Legal Thinking What does the coming and going rule provide? Explain. What is the public policy that supports the coming and going rule?

Business Ethics Did Morgenstern want to be found to have been acting within the scope of his company's employment when the accident happened? Why or why not? Was it unethical for ANPAC to deny coverage on its commercial insurance policy?

Contemporary Business Why did the injured victim, Farah, want Morgenstern to be found to be acting in the scope of the company's employment when the accident happened?

Dual-Purpose Mission   Sometimes, a principal requests that an agent run errands or conduct other acts on his or her behalf while the agent or employee is on personal business. In this case, the agent is on a **dual-purpose mission**. That is, he or she is acting partly for himself or herself and partly for the principal. Most jurisdictions hold both the principal and the agent liable if the agent injures someone while on such a mission.

Example Suppose a principal asks an employee to drop off a package at a client's office on the employee's way home. If the employee negligently injures a pedestrian while on this dual-purpose mission, the principal is liable to the pedestrian.

> **dual-purpose mission**
> An errand or another act that a principal requests of an agent while the agent is on his or her own personal business.

Intentional Tort

Intentional torts include such acts as assault, battery, false imprisonment, and other intentional conduct that causes injury to another person. A principal is not liable for the intentional torts of agents and employees that are committed outside the principal's scope of business.

Example If an employee attends a sporting event after working hours and gets into a fight with another spectator at the event, the employer is not liable.

However, a principal is liable under the doctrine of vicarious liability for intentional torts of agents and employees committed within the agent's scope of employment. The courts generally apply one of the following tests in determining whether an agent's intentional torts were committed within the agent's scope of employment:

- **Motivation test.** Under the **motivation test**, if the agent's motivation in committing an intentional tort is to promote the principal's business, the principal is liable for any injury caused by the tort. However, if an agent's motivation in committing the intentional tort is personal, the principal is not liable, even if the tort takes place during business hours or on business premises.

> **motivation test**
> A test that determines whether an agent's motivation in committing an intentional tort is to promote the principal's business; if so, the principal is liable for any injury caused by the tort.

Example Under the motivation test, an employer—the principal—is not liable if his employee, who is motivated by jealousy, injures on the job someone who dated her boyfriend. Here, the motivation of the employee was personal and not for the promotion of the principal's business.

- **Work-related test.** Some jurisdictions have rejected the motivation test as too narrow. These jurisdictions apply the **work-related test** instead. Under this test, if an agent commits an intentional tort within a work-related time or space—for example, during working hours or on the principal's premises—the principal is liable for any injuries caused by the agent's intentional torts. Under this test, the agent's motivation is immaterial.

> **work-related test**
> A test that determines whether an agent committed an intentional tort within a work-related time or space; if so, the principal is liable for any injury caused by the agent's intentional tort.

Example Under the work-related test, an employer—the principal—is liable if his employee, who was motivated by jealousy, injures on the work premises and during work hours someone who dated her boyfriend. Here, the motivation of the employee is not relevant. What is relevant is that the intentional tort was committed on work premises and during the employee's work hours.

ETHICS SPOTLIGHT

Intentional Tort

Kenya Massey and her fiancée, Raymond Rodriquez, entered a Starbucks coffee shop in Manhattan, New York City. The couple ordered two beverages from Starbucks employee Okang Wilson and paid for the drinks. When Massey and Rodriquez moved toward the seating area while waiting for their drinks to be prepared, Karen Morales, the shift supervisor at the store, told Massey and Rodriquez that they could not sit down because the store was closing. Massey asked Morales what time the store closed, and Morales told her that it closed at 10:00. Massey pointed at a large digital clock across the street that read 9:52. Morales responded that it was

10:00 according to her watch and that she was closing the store.

Massey, who had not yet received her drinks, informed Morales that when she received her drinks, she and Rodriquez intended to sit and enjoy them at Starbucks. Morales instructed Starbucks employee Louis Suriel to cancel Massey's beverage order and refund Massey's money. Massey asked to speak with a manager. Morales identified herself as the manager and told Massey to "get a life." Massey insisted she was not leaving until she could file a complaint about Morales's behavior.

At that point, Starbucks employee Melissa Polanco became involved in the argument. She told Massey, "I get off at ten o'clock, and we can go outside." Rodriquez suggested to Massey that they leave voluntarily, and Massey agreed. Suriel apologized to them as Morales, Polanco, and Wilson held the door open for Massey and Rodriquez as they exited. The couple walked away from the store while Massey and the employees yelled profanities at each other.

As Massey continued to walk away, Polanco ran after and caught her and punched Massey in the face. Morales then jumped on Massey's back. Massey and Morales fell into a snow bank on the sidewalk, and a physical altercation ensued. A pedestrian passerby finally separated Massey and Morales. Massey's face was bleeding when she got up.

Massey pressed criminal charges against Morales and Polanco the next morning. Morales and Polanco each pleaded guilty to assault. All three Starbucks employees who were involved in the altercation—Morales, Polanco, and Wilson—were terminated by Starbucks. Massey sued Starbucks for damages for the injuries she suffered. Starbucks moved for summary judgment, alleging that the employees were not acting within the scope of their employment when they assaulted Massey.

The U.S. District Court held against Massey and granted Starbucks's motion for summary judgment. The Court found that the Starbucks employees were acting outside the scope of their employment when they assaulted Massey on the street. The court stated:

> Massey contends that because her assault was sparked by a dispute concerning whether the store should close, the employees were acting in an employment capacity even when they chased Massey down the street. Massey fails to consider that she suffered no damages as a result of the dispute, but only as a result of the assault. Thus, the question for this court is not whether employees were acting within the scope of their employment when they first began arguing with Massey. Rather, the question is whether they were acting within the scope of their employment when they assaulted her.
>
> While the dispute may have started when the employees were acting within the scope of employment; it ended in an assault that was clearly outside of that scope. In this case, the employees did not assault Massey as part of their job. They did not attack Massey on the sidewalk to remove her from the store at closing time, or for any other employment-related purpose. In fact, the employees deliberately waited until Massey had voluntarily left the store before they assaulted her.

The U.S. District Court held that the Starbucks employees were not acting within the scope of their employment when they assaulted Massey. The U.S. District Court granted Starbucks's motion for summary judgment. *Massey v. Starbucks Corporation*, **Web** 2004 U.S. Dist. Lexis 12993 (United States District Court for the Southern District of New York, 2004)

Business Ethics   Was it ethical for Starbucks Corporation to deny liability in this case? Why or why not?

Misrepresentation

intentional misrepresentation
A deceit in which an agent makes an untrue statement that he or she knows is not true.

Intentional misrepresentations are also known as **fraud** or **deceit**. They occur when an agent makes statements that he or she knows are not true. An **innocent misrepresentation** occurs when an agent negligently makes a misrepresentation to a third party. A principal is liable for the intentional and innocent misrepresentations made by an agent acting within the scope of employment. The third party can either (1) rescind the contract with the principal and recover any consideration paid or (2) affirm the contract and recover damages.

Example Assume that (1) a car salesman is employed as an agent to sell the principal's car and (2) the principal tells the agent that the car was repaired after it was involved in a major accident. If the agent intentionally tells the buyer that the car was never involved in an accident, the agent has made an intentional misrepresentation. Both the principal and the agent are liable for this misrepresentation.

CONCEPT SUMMARY

TORT LIABILITY OF PRINCIPALS AND AGENTS TO THIRD PARTIES

Agent's Conduct	Agent Liable	Principal Liable
Negligence	Yes	The principal is liable under the doctrine of *respondeat superior* if the agent's negligent act was committed within his or her scope of employment.

Agent's Conduct	Agent Liable	Principal Liable
Intentional tort	Yes	*Motivation test*: The principal is liable if the agent's motivation in committing the intentional tort was to promote the principal's business.
	Yes	*Work-related test*: The principal is liable if the agent committed the intentional tort within work-related time and space.
Misrepresentation	Yes	The principal is liable for the intentional and innocent misrepresentations made by an agent acting within the scope of his or her authority.

▶ CONTRACT LIABILITY TO THIRD PARTIES

A principal who authorizes an agent to enter into a contract with a third party is liable on the contract. Thus, the third party can enforce the contract against the principal and recover damages from the principal if the principal fails to perform it. The agent can also be held liable on the contract in certain circumstances. Imposition of **contract liability to third parties** depends on whether the agency is classified as fully disclosed, partially disclosed, or undisclosed.

Fully Disclosed Agency

A **fully disclosed agency** results if a third party entering into a contract knows (1) that the agent is acting as an agent for a principal and (2) the actual identity of the principal.[1] The third party has the requisite knowledge if the principal's identity is disclosed to the third party by either the agent or some other source.

In a fully disclosed agency, the contract is between the principal and the third party. Thus, the principal, who is called a **fully disclosed principal**, is liable on the contract. The agent, however, is not liable on the contract because the third party relied on the principal's credit and reputation when the contract was made. An agent is liable on the contract if he or she guarantees that the principal will perform the contract.

The agent's signature on a contract entered into on the principal's behalf is important. It can establish the agent's status and, therefore, his or her liability. For instance, in a fully disclosed agency, the agent's signature must clearly indicate that he or she is acting as an agent for a specifically identified principal.

Examples Examples of proper signatures for an agent include "Allison Adams, agent for Peter Perceival," "Peter Perceival, by Allison Adams, agent," and "Peter Perceival, by Allison Adams."

Example Poran Kawamara decides to sell her house and hires Mark Robbins, a real estate broker, to list and sell the house for a price of $1 million. They agree that Mark will disclose the existence of the agency and the identity of the principal to interested third parties. This is a fully disclosed agency. Mark shows the house to Heather, a prospective buyer, and discloses to Heather that he is acting as an agent for Poran. Heather makes an offer for the house at the $1 million asking price. Mark signs the contract with Heather on behalf of Poran by signing "Mark Robbins, agent for Poran Kawamara." Poran is liable on the contract with Heather, but Mark is not liable on the contract with Heather.

Partially Disclosed Agency

A **partially disclosed agency** occurs if the agent discloses his or her agency status but does not reveal the principal's identity and the third party does not know the principal's identity from another source. The nondisclosure may be because (1) the principal instructs the agent not to disclose his or her identity to the third party or (2) the agent forgets to tell the third party the principal's identity. In this kind of agency, the principal is called a **partially disclosed principal**.

In a partially disclosed agency, both the principal and the agent are liable on a third-party contract.[2] This is because the third party must rely on the agent's reputation, integrity, and credit because the principal is unidentified. If the agent is made to pay the

fully disclosed agency
An agency in which a contracting third party knows (1) that the agent is acting for a principal and (2) the identity of the principal.

partially disclosed agency
An agency in which a contracting third party knows that the agent is acting for a principal but does not know the identity of the principal.

contract, the agent can sue the principal for indemnification. The third party and the agent can agree to relieve the agent's liability. A partially disclosed agency can be created either expressly or by mistake.

Example A principal and an agent agree that the agent will represent the principal to purchase a business and that the agent will disclose the existence of the agency and the identity of the principal to third parties; this is a fully disclosed agency. Suppose the agent finds a suitable business for the principal and contracts to purchase the business on behalf of the principal, but the agent mistakenly signs the contract with the third party "Allison Adams, agent." This is a partially disclosed agency that occurs because of mistake. The principal is liable on the contract with the third party, and the agent is also liable.

Undisclosed Agency

undisclosed agency
An agency in which a contracting third party does not know of either the existence of the agency or the principal's identity.

An **undisclosed agency** occurs when a third party is unaware of either the existence of an agency or the principal's identity. The principal is called an **undisclosed principal**. Undisclosed agencies are lawful. They are often used when the principal feels that the terms of the contract would be changed if his or her identity were known. For example, a wealthy person may use an undisclosed agency to purchase property if he thinks that the seller would raise the price of the property if his identity were revealed.

In an undisclosed agency, both the principal and the agent are liable on the contract with the third party. This is because the agent, by not divulging that he or she is acting as an agent, becomes a principal to the contract. The third party relies on the reputation and credit of the agent in entering into the contract. If the principal fails to perform the contract, the third party can recover against the principal or the agent. If the agent is made to pay the contract, he or she can recover indemnification from the principal. An undisclosed agency can be created either expressly or by mistake.

Example The Walt Disney Company wants to open a new theme park in Chicago but needs to first acquire land for the park. Disney employs an agent to work on its behalf to acquire the needed property, with an express agreement that the agent will not disclose the existence of the agency to a third-party seller. If a seller agrees to sell the needed land and the agent signs her name "Allison Adams," without disclosing the existence of the agency, it is an undisclosed agency. Disney is liable on the contract with the third-party seller, and so is the agent.

Agent Exceeding the Scope of Authority

implied warranty of authority
A warranty of an agent who enters into a contract on behalf of another party that he or she has the authority to do so.

ratification
A situation in which a principal accepts an agent's unauthorized contract.

An agent who enters into a contract on behalf of another party impliedly warrants that he or she has the authority to do so. This is called the agent's **implied warranty of authority**. If the agent exceeds the scope of his or her authority, the principal is not liable on the contract unless the principal **ratifies** it. The agent, however, is liable to the third party for breaching the implied warranty of authority. To recover, the third party must show (1) reliance on the agent's representation and (2) ignorance of the agent's lack of status.

CONCEPT SUMMARY
CONTRACT LIABILITY OF PRINCIPALS AND AGENTS TO THIRD PARTIES

Type of Agency	Principal Liable	Agent Liable
Fully disclosed	Yes	No, unless the agent (1) acts as a principal or (2) guarantees the performance of the contract
Partially disclosed	Yes	Yes, unless the third party relieves the agent's liability
Undisclosed	Yes	Yes
Nonexistent	No, unless the principal ratifies the contract	Yes, the agent is liable for breaching the implied warranty of authority.

► INDEPENDENT CONTRACTOR

Principals often employ outsiders—that is, persons and businesses that are not employees—to perform certain tasks on their behalf. These persons and businesses are called **independent contractors**. The party that employs an independent contractor is called a *principal*.

Example Lawyers, doctors, dentists, consultants, stockbrokers, architects, certified public accountants, real estate brokers, and plumbers are examples of people who commonly act as independent contractors.

Example Jamie is a lawyer who has her own law firm and specializes in real estate law. Raymond, a real estate developer, hires Jamie to represent him in the purchase of land. Raymond is the principal, and Jamie is the independent contractor.

A principal–independent contractor relationship is depicted in Exhibit 30.1.

independent contractor
"A person who contracts with another to do something for him who is not controlled by the other nor subject to the other's right to control with respect to his physical conduct in the performance of the undertaking" [*Restatement (Second) of Agency*].

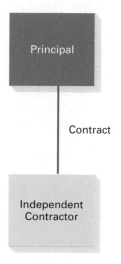

► **Exhibit 30.1**
PRINCIPAL–INDEPENDENT CONTRACTOR RELATIONSHIP

Factors for Determining Independent Contractor Status

Section 2 of the *Restatement (Second) of Agency* defines *independent contractor* as "a person who contracts with another to do something for him who is not controlled by the other nor subject to the other's right to control with respect to his physical conduct in the performance of the undertaking." Independent contractors usually work for a number of clients, have their own offices, hire employees, and control the performance of their work.

The crucial factor in determining whether someone is an independent contractor or an employee is the **degree of control** that the principal has over the agent. Critical factors in determining independent contractor status include:

- Whether the worker is engaged in a distinct occupation or an independently established business
- The length of time the agent has been employed by the principal
- The amount of time that the agent works for the principal
- Whether the principal supplies the tools and equipment used in the work
- The method of payment, whether by time or by the job
- The degree of skill necessary to complete the task
- Whether the worker hires employees to assist him or her
- Whether the employer has the right to control the manner and means of accomplishing the desired result

If an examination of these factors shows that the principal asserts little control, the person is an independent contractor. Substantial control indicates an employer–employee relationship. Labeling someone an independent contractor is only one factor in determining whether independent contractor status exists.

Liability for an Independent Contractor's Contracts

A principal can authorize an independent contractor to enter into contracts. Principals are bound by the authorized contracts of their independent contractors.

Example A client hires a lawyer as an independent contractor to represent her in a civil lawsuit against a defendant to recover monetary damages. If the client authorizes the lawyer to settle a case within a certain dollar amount and the lawyer does so, the settlement agreement is binding.

If an independent contractor enters into a contract with a third party on behalf of the principal, without express or implied authority from the principal to do so, the principal is not liable on the contract.

Liability for an Independent Contractor's Torts

Generally, a principal is not liable for the torts of its independent contractors. Independent contractors are personally liable for their own torts. The rationale behind this rule is that principals do not control the means by which the results are accomplished.

Example Qixia hires Harold, a lawyer and an independent contractor, to represent her in a court case. While driving to the courthouse to represent Qixia at trial, Harold negligently causes an automobile accident in which Mildred is severely injured. Harold is liable to Mildred because he caused the accident. Qixia is not liable to Mildred because Harold was an independent contractor when he caused the accident.

Exceptions in Which a Principal Is Liable for the Torts of an Independent Contractor

There are two exceptions in which the law imposes liability on a principal for the tortious conduct of an independent contractor he or she has hired:

1. **Inherently dangerous activities.** Principals cannot avoid strict liability for **inherently dangerous activities** assigned to independent contractors. For example, the use of explosives, clearing of land by fire, crop dusting, and such involve special risks that are shared by the principal.
2. **Negligence in the selection of an independent contractor.** A principal who hires an unqualified or known dangerous person as an independent contractor is liable if that person injures someone while on the job.

ETHICS SPOTLIGHT

Principal Liable for Repo Man's Tort

"The issue in this case is whether a secured creditor may avoid liability for breaches of the peace by using an independent contractor."

—Judge Mauzy

Yvonne Sanchez borrowed money from MBank El Paso (MBank) to purchase an automobile. She gave MBank a security interest in the vehicle to secure the loan. When Sanchez defaulted on the loan, MBank hired El Paso Recovery Service, an independent contractor, to repossess the automobile. The two men who were dispatched to

Sanchez's house found the car parked in the driveway and hooked it to a tow truck. Sanchez demanded that they cease their efforts and leave the premises, but the men nonetheless continued with the repossession. Before the men could tow the automobile into the street, Sanchez jumped into the car, locked the doors, and refused to leave. The men towed the car at a high rate of speed to the repossession yard. They parked the car in the fenced repossession yard, with Sanchez inside, and padlocked the gate. Sanchez was left in the repossession lot with a Doberman Pinscher guard dog loose in the yard. Later, she

---

Nature seems to have taken a particular care to disseminate her blessings among the different regions of the world, with an eye to their mutual intercourse and traffic among mankind, that the nations of the several parts of the globe might have a kind of dependence upon one another and be united together by their common interest.

Joseph Addison

was rescued by the police. The law prohibits the repossession of a vehicle if a breach of peace would occur. Sanchez filed suit against MBank, alleging that it was liable for the tortious conduct of El Paso Recovery Service. The trial court granted summary judgment to MBank, but the court of appeals reversed. MBank appealed.

The supreme court of Texas held that MBank, the principal, was liable for the tortious conduct of El Paso Recovery Service, an independent contractor. The court held that the act of repossessing an automobile from a defaulting debtor is an inherently dangerous activity and a nondelegable duty. The court concluded that El Paso

Recovery Service had breached the peace in repossessing the car from Sanchez and caused her physical and emotional harm. The court held that MBank, the principal, could not escape liability by hiring an independent contractor to do this task. The court found MBank liable to Sanchez. *MBank El Paso, N.A. v. Sanchez*, 836 S.W.2d 151, **Web** 1992 Tex. Lexis 97 (Supreme Court of Texas)

Business Ethics Did the independent contractor act responsibly in this case? Should the principal bank have been held liable in this case? Why or why not?

TEST REVIEW TERMS AND CONCEPTS

Agent's duty of loyalty
Coming and going rule
Competing with the
   principal
Contract liability to third
   parties
Degree of control
Dual agency
Dual-purpose mission
Frolic and detour

Fully disclosed agency
Fully disclosed principal
Implied warranty of
   authority
Independent contractor
Inherently dangerous
   activity
Innocent misrepresentation

Intentional
   misrepresentation (fraud
   or deceit)
Intentional tort
Misuse of confidential
   information
Motivation test
Negligence
Partially disclosed agency
Partially disclosed principal

Ratification
Respondeat superior
Self-dealing
Tort liability
Undisclosed agency
Undisclosed principal
Usurping an opportunity
Vicarious liability
Work-related test

CASE PROBLEMS

30.1 Fiduciary Duty After Francis Pusateri retired, he met with Gilbert J. Johnson, a stockbroker with E. F. Hutton & Co., Inc., and informed Johnson that he wished to invest in tax-free bonds and money market accounts. Pusateri opened an investment account with E. F. Hutton and checked a box stating that his objective was "tax-free income and moderate growth." During the course of a year, Johnson churned Pusateri's account to make commissions and invested Pusateri's funds in volatile securities and options. Johnson kept telling Pusateri that his account was making money, and the monthly statement from E. F. Hutton did not indicate otherwise. The manager at E. F. Hutton was aware of Johnson's activities but did nothing to prevent them. When Johnson left E. F. Hutton, Pusateri's account—which had been called the "laughingstock" of the office—had shrunk from $196,000 to $96,880. Pusateri sued E. F. Hutton for damages. Is E. F. Hutton liable? *Pusateri v. E. F. Hutton & Co., Inc.*, 180 Cal.App.3d 247, 225 Cal.Rptr. 526, **Web** 1986 Cal.App. Lexis 1502 (Court of Appeal of California)

30.2 Fiduciary Duty Boettcher DTC Building Joint Venture (Boettcher) owned an office building in which it leased space to tenants. Harmon Wilfred, an independent leasing agent, contacted Boettcher on behalf of Landmark Associates (Landmark), which was interested in leasing office space in the Boettcher building. Wilfred represented Boettcher as a special agent in the transaction. Landmark executed a 68-month lease

with Boettcher. Boettcher paid Wilfred a commission. Shortly thereafter, Landmark began negotiating with Boettcher for additional lease space. Landmark also contacted Wilfred to inquire about the availability of lease space in other buildings. When Wilfred found lease space for Landmark in another office building, Landmark vacated its premises at the Boettcher building and defaulted on its lease agreement. Boettcher sued Wilfred for damages, alleging that Wilfred had violated his fiduciary duty to Boettcher. Who wins? *Boettcher DTC Building Joint Venture v. Wilfred*, 762 P.2d 788, **Web** 1988 Colo.App. Lexis. 323 (Court of Appeals of Colorado)

30.3 Duty of Loyalty Peter Shields was the president and a member of the board of directors of Production Finishing Corporation for seven years. The company provided steel polishing services. It did most, if not all, of the polishing work in the Detroit area, except for that of the Ford Motor Company. (Ford did its own polishing.) On a number of occasions, Shields discussed with Ford, on behalf of Production Finishing, the possibility of providing Ford's steel polishing services. When Shields learned that Ford was discontinuing its polishing operation, he incorporated Flat Rock Metal and submitted a confidential proposal to Ford which provided that he would buy Ford's equipment and provide polishing services to Ford. It was not until he resigned from Production Finishing that he informed the board of directors that he was pursuing the Ford business himself. Production Finishing sued Shields. Did

Shields breach his fiduciary duty of loyalty to Production Finishing? Who wins? *Production Finishing Corporation v. Shields*, 158 Mich.App. 479, 405 N.W.2d 171, **Web** 1987 Mich.App. Lexis 2379 (Court of Appeals of Michigan)

30.4 Independent Contractor The Butler Telephone Company, Inc. (Butler), contracted with the Sandidge Construction Company to lay 18 miles of telephone cable in a rural area. In the contract, Butler reserved the right to inspect the work for compliance with the terms of the contract. Butler did not control how Sandidge performed the work. Johnnie Carl Pugh, an employee of Sandidge, was killed on the job when the sides to an excavation in which he was working caved in on top of him. Evidence disclosed that the excavation was not properly shored or sloped and that it violated general safety standards. Pugh's parents and estate brought a wrongful death action against Butler. Is Butler liable? *Pugh v. Butler Telephone Company, Inc.*, 512 So.2d 1317, **Web** 1987 Ala. Lexis 4468 (Supreme Court of Alabama)

30.5 Personal Guaranty Sebastian International, Inc. entered into a five-year lease to lease a building in Chadsworth, California. Just over two years later, with the consent of the master lessors, Sebastian sublet the building to West Valley Grinding, Inc. In conjunction with the execution of the sublease, the corporate officers of West Valley, including Kenneth E. Peck, each signed a guaranty of lease, personally ensuring the payment of West Valley's rental obligations. The guaranty contract referred to Peck in his individual capacity; however, on the signature line, he was identified as "Kenneth Peck, Vice President." Eight months later, West Valley went out of business, leaving 24 months remaining on the sublease. After unsuccessful attempts to secure another sublessee, Sebastian surrendered the leasehold back to the master lessors and brought suit against Peck to recover the unpaid rent. Peck argued that he was not personally liable because his signature was that of an agent for a disclosed principal and not that of a principal himself. Who wins? *Sebastian International, Inc. v. Peck*, 195 Cal.App.3d 803, 240 Cal.Rptr. 911, **Web** 1987 Cal. App. Lexis 2237 (Court of Appeal of California)

30.6 Contract Liability G. Elvin Grinder of Marbury, Maryland, was a building contractor who, for years, did business as an individual and traded as "Grinder Construction." Grinder maintained an open account on his individual credit, with Bryans Road Building & Supply Co., Inc. Grinder would purchase materials and supplies from Bryans on credit and later pay the invoices. G. Elvin Grinder Construction, Inc., a Maryland corporation, was formed, with Grinder personally owning 52 percent of the stock of the corporation. Grinder did not inform Bryans that he had incorporated, and he continued to purchase supplies on credit from Bryans under the name "Grinder Construction." Five years later, after certain invoices were not paid by Grinder, Bryans sued Grinder personally to recover. Grinder asserted that the debts were owed by the corporation. Bryans amended its complaint to include the corporation as a defendant. Who is liable to

Bryans? *Grinder v. Bryans Road Building & Supply Co., Inc.*, 290 Md. 687, 432 A.2d 453, **Web** 1981 Md. Lexis 246 (Court of Appeals of Maryland)

30.7 Dual Agency Chemical Bank was the primary bank for Washington Steel Corporation. As an agent for Washington Steel, Chemical Bank expressly and impliedly promised that it would advance the best interests and welfare of Washington Steel. During the course of the agency, Washington Steel provided the bank with comprehensive and confidential financial information, other data, and future business plans.

At some point during the agency, TW Corporation and others approached Chemical Bank to request a loan of $7 million to make a hostile tender offer for the stock of Washington Steel. Chemical Bank agreed and became an agent for TW. Management at Chemical Bank did not disclose to Washington Steel its adverse relationship with TW, did not request Washington Steel's permission to act as an agent for TW, and directed employees of the bank to conceal from Washington Steel the bank's involvement with TW. After TW commenced its public tender offer, Washington Steel filed suit, seeking to obtain an injunction against Chemical Bank and TW. Who wins? *Washington Steel Corporation v. TW Corporation*, 465 F.Supp. 1100, **Web** 1979 U.S. Dist. Lexis 14391 (United States District Court for the Western District of Pennsylvania)

30.8 Tort Liability Ray Johnson and his eight-year-old son, David, were waiting for a "walk" sign before crossing a street in downtown Salt Lake City. A truck owned by Newspaper Agency Corporation (NAC) and operated by its employee, Donald Rogers, crossed the intersection and jumped the curb, killing David and injuring Ray. Before reporting for work on the evening of the accident, Rogers had consumed approximately seven mixed drinks containing vodka and had chugalugged a 27-ounce drink containing two minibottles of tequila. His blood alcohol content after the accident was .18 percent.

Evidence showed that the use of alcohol and marijuana was widespread at NAC and that the company made no effort to curtail such use. Evidence further showed that NAC vehicles were returned with beer cans in them and that on one occasion, an NAC supervisor who had observed drivers smoking marijuana had told the drivers to "do it on the road." Ray Johnson sued Rogers and NAC for the wrongful death of his child, David, and physical injury to Ray. Is NAC liable? *Johnson v. Rogers*, 763 P.2d 771, 90 Utah Adv.Rep.3, **Web** 1988 Utah Lexis 81 (Supreme Court of Utah)

30.9 Tort Liability Intrastate Radiotelephone, Inc., was a public utility that supplied radiotelephone utility service to the general public for radiotelephones, pocket pagers, and beepers. Robert Kranhold, an employee of Intrastate, was authorized to use his personal vehicle on company business. One morning, when Kranhold was driving his vehicle to Intrastate's main office, he negligently struck a motorcycle being driven by Michael S. Largey, causing severe and permanent injuries to

Largey. The accident occurred at the intersection where Intrastate's main office is located. Evidence showed that Kranhold acted as a consultant to Intrastate, worked both in and out of Intrastate's offices, had no set hours of work, often attended meetings at Intrastate's offices, and went to Intrastate's offices to pick things up or drop things off. Largey sued Intrastate for damages. Is Intrastate liable? *Largey v. Radiotelephone, Inc.*, 136 Cal.App.3d 660, 186 Cal.Rptr. 520, **Web** 1982 Cal.App. Lexis 2049 (Court of Appeal of California)

30.10 Tort Liability   Donnie Joe Jackson hired Ted Green to do some remodeling work on his house. Jackson never paid Green for his work, and a dispute arose as to how much was owed to Green. Jackson worked at the Higgenbotham-Bartlett Lumber Company, a lumberyard where Green often purchased lumber and supplies. During the course of the following year, when Green went to the lumberyard to do business, Jackson verbally accosted him on at least three separate occasions. Each time, Green left the lumberyard. Green, accompanied by his son, made two trips to the facility. On the first trip, Jackson and Green had a verbal altercation. On the second trip, Jackson hit Green, knocking him unconscious and causing injuries. Green sued Jackson's employer for damages. Is the lumber company liable for the intentional tort of its agent? *Green v. Jackson*, 674 S.W.2d 395, **Web** 1984 Tex. App. Lexis 5592 (Court of Appeals of Texas)

BUSINESS ETHICS CASES

30.11 Business Ethics   William Venezio, a real estate broker, conducted his business under the trade name King Realty and had properly filed the required name certificate in the Schenectady County clerk's office. King Realty entered into a contract to purchase property located in the town of Rotterdam, Schenectady County, from Ermino Bianchi. Venezio signed the end of the contract "King Realty for Customer." Four days later, King Realty entered into a contract to sell the property to Mario Attanasio. However, Bianchi refused to sell the property to King Realty, alleging that because the original contract had failed to adequately identify the purchaser, there was not a binding contract. Venezio, d.b.a. King Realty, brought an action for specific performance against Bianchi. Was it ethical for Bianchi to try to back out of the contract? Can King Realty, as an agent for a partially disclosed principal, enforce the contract against Bianchi? *Venezio v. Bianchi*, 124 A.D.2d 933, 508 N.Y.S.2d 349, **Web** 1986 N.Y.App. Div. Lexis 62252 (Supreme Court of New York)

30.12 Business Ethics   National Biscuit Company (Nabisco) is a corporation that produces and distributes cookies and other food products to grocery stores and other outlets across the nation. Nabisco hired Ronnell Lynch as a cookie salesman-trainee and eventually assigned Lynch to his own sales territory. Lynch's duties involved making sales calls, taking orders, and making sure that shelves of stores in his territory were stocked with Nabisco products. During the first two months, Nabisco received numerous complaints from store owners in Lynch's territory that Lynch was overly aggressive and was taking for Nabisco products shelf space that was reserved for competing brands.

One day, after having been in his territory for two months, Lynch visited a grocery store that was managed by Jerome Lange. Lynch was there to place previously delivered merchandise on the store's shelves. An argument developed between Lynch and Lange. Lynch became very angry and started swearing. Lange told Lynch to stop swearing or leave the store because children were present. Lynch became uncontrollably angry and went behind the counter and dared Lange to fight. When Lange refused to fight, Lynch proceeded to viciously assault and batter Lange, causing severe injuries. When Lange sued Nabisco, Nabisco denied liability. Was it ethical for Nabisco to deny liability in this case? Do you think the prior complaints against Lynch had any effect on the decision reached in this case? Is Nabisco liable for the intentional tort (assault and battery) of its employee Ronnell Lynch? *Lange v. National Biscuit Company*, 297 Minn. 399, 211 N.W.2d 783, **Web** 1973 Minn. Lexis 1106 (Supreme Court of Minnesota)

ENDNOTES

1. *Restatement (Second) of Agency*, Section 4.

2. *Restatement (Second) of Agency*, Section 321.

▲ **Washington, DC** *Federal and state laws provide workers' compensation and occupational safety laws to protect workers in this country.*

CHAPTER OBJECTIVES

After studying this chapter, you should be able to:

1. Explain how state workers' compensation programs work and describe the benefits available.
2. Describe employers' duty to provide safe working conditions under the Occupational Safety and Health Act.
3. Describe the minimum wage and overtime pay rules of the Fair Labor Standards Act.
4. Describe the protections afforded by the Family and Medical Leave Act
5. Explain the rules governing private pensions under the Employee Retirement Income Security Act.

CHAPTER CONTENTS

"It is difficult to imagine any grounds, other than our own personal economic predilections, for saying that the contract of employment is any the less an appropriate subject of legislation than are scores of others, in dealing with which this Court has held that legislatures may curtail individual freedom in the public interest."

—Justice Stone
Dissenting Opinion, Morehead v. New York (1936), 298 U.S. 587, 56 S.Ct. 918

▶ INTRODUCTION TO EMPLOYMENT, WORKER PROTECTION, AND IMMIGRATION LAWS

Before the Industrial Revolution, the doctrine of laissez-faire governed the employment relationship in this country. Generally, this meant that employment was subject to the common law of contracts and agency law. In most instances, employees and employers had somewhat equal bargaining power.

This changed dramatically when the country became industrialized in the late 1800s. For one thing, large corporate employers had much more bargaining power than their employees. For another, the issues of child labor, unsafe working conditions, long hours, and low pay caused concern. Both federal and state legislation were enacted to protect workers' rights. Today, employment law is a mixture of contract law, agency law, and government regulation.

Today, many high-technology and other businesses rely on employees who have been issued work visas by the U.S. government to work in the United States. These workers have to meet certain qualifications to obtain foreign guest worker visas.

This chapter discusses employment law, workers' compensation, occupational safety, overtime pay, government programs, immigration law, and other laws affecting employment.

▶ WORKERS' COMPENSATION

Many types of employment are dangerous, and each year, many workers are injured on the job. Under common law, employees who were injured on the job could sue their employers for negligence. This time-consuming process placed the employee at odds with his or her employer. In addition, there was no guarantee that the employee would win the case. Ultimately, many injured workers—or the heirs of deceased workers—were left uncompensated.

Workers' compensation acts were enacted by states in response to the unfairness of that result. These acts create an administrative procedure for workers to receive compensation for injuries that occur on the job. First, the injured worker files a claim with the appropriate state government agency (often called the workers' compensation board or commission). Next, that entity determines the legitimacy of the claim. If the worker disagrees with the agency's findings, he or she may appeal the decision through the state court system. Workers' compensation benefits are paid according to preset limits established by statute or regulation. The amounts that are recoverable vary from state to state.

workers' compensation
Compensation paid to workers and their families when workers are injured in connection with their jobs.

Workers' Compensation Insurance

States usually require employers to purchase insurance from private insurance companies or state funds to cover workers' compensation claims. Some states permit employers to self-insure if they demonstrate that they have the ability to pay workers' compensation claims. Many large companies self-insure. Workers can sue their employers in court to recover damages for employment-related injuries if the employer does not carry **workers' compensation insurance** or does not self-insure if permitted to do so.

Employment-Related Injury

For an injury to be compensable under workers' compensation, the claimant must prove that the injury arose out of and in the course of his or her employment. An accident that occurs while an employee is actively working is clearly within the scope of this rule. Accidents that occur at a company cafeteria or while on a business lunch for an employer are covered. Accidents that happen while the employee is at an off-premises restaurant during his or her personal lunch hour are not covered. Many workers' compensation acts include stress as a compensable **employment-related injury**.

Poorly paid labor is inefficient labor, the world over.

Henry George

Exclusive Remedy

Workers' compensation is an **exclusive remedy**. Thus, workers cannot both receive workers' compensation and sue their employers in court for damages. There is one exception to this rule: If an employer intentionally injures a worker, the worker can collect workers' compensation benefits and sue the employer. Workers' compensation acts do not bar injured workers from suing responsible third parties to recover damages.

The following case involves workers' compensation issues.

CASE 31.1 Workers' Compensation

Medrano v. Marshall Electrical Contracting Inc.

173 S.W.3d 333, Web 2005 Mo.App. Lexis 1088 (2005)
Court of Appeals of Missouri

"In determining that Medrano's accidental death arose out of and in the course of his employment with MEC, the Commission relied on the mutual benefit doctrine."

—Judge Hardwick

Facts

Immar Medrano was employed as a journeyman electrician by Marshall Electrical Contracting, Inc. (MEC), in Marshall, Missouri. Medrano attended an electrician apprenticeship night class at a community college in Sedalia, Missouri. MEC paid Medrano's tuition and book fees. Attendance at the course required Medrano to drive 70 miles round-trip. One night, when Medrano was driving home from the class, a drunk driver crossed the centerline of U.S. Highway 65 and collided head-on with Medrano's automobile. Medrano died in the accident. His wife and two children filed a workers' compensation claim for death benefits against MEC. After a hearing, an administrative law judge (ALJ) denied the claim, determining that Medrano's death did not arise out of or within the course and scope of his employment. The Labor and Industrial Relations Commission (Commission) reversed the ALJ's decision, finding that Medrano was acting within the course and scope of his employment when he was killed, and awarded death benefits to Medrano's family. MEC appealed.

Issue

Was Medrano acting within the course and scope of his employment when he was killed in the automobile accident?

Language of the Court

In determining that Medrano's accidental death arose out of and in the course of his employment with MEC, the Commission relied on the mutual benefit doctrine. The doctrine holds that an injury suffered by an employee while performing an act for the mutual benefit of the employer and the employee is usually compensable. MEC argues that it received no benefit from Medrano's attendance at the apprenticeship class and, thus, the Commission erred in determining the death claim was compensable. However, our review of the entire record indicates there is substantial and competent evidence to support the Commission's finding that the classroom instruction was beneficial to Medrano and his employer.

Mike Mills, the owner and president of MEC, testified at the administrative hearing: "The training made the employees more valuable to MEC by improving the quality of service to customers." The record is sufficient to show that MEC derived substantial benefit from having its employees travel from Marshall to Sedalia to fully participate in the apprenticeship program. MEC encouraged employees to attend the classroom instruction and covered the costs of tuition. Even though employees like Medrano obtained personal benefits in formalizing their education, MEC mutually benefited from the program as a convenient way for MEC to train its employees and ultimately provide a better quality of service to its customers.

(case continues)

Decision

The court of appeals upheld the Commission's finding that Medrano was acting within the course and scope of his employment when he was fatally injured in the car crash. The court of appeals affirmed the Commission's award of workers' compensation death benefits to Medrano's family.

Case Questions

Critical Legal Thinking What is workers' compensation? Explain. What does the mutual benefit doctrine provide? Explain.

Business Ethics Was it ethical for MEC to argue that it did not owe workers' compensation death benefits to Medrano's surviving family?

Contemporary Business Do businesses favor workers' compensation programs? Why or why not? Do employees favor workers' compensation programs? Why or why not?

▶ OCCUPATIONAL SAFETY

In 1970, Congress enacted the **Occupational Safety and Health Act**[1] to promote safety in the workplace. Virtually all private employers are within the scope of the act, but federal, state, and local governments are exempt. Industries regulated by other federal safety legislation are also exempt.[2] The act also established the **Occupational Safety and Health Administration (OSHA)**, a federal administrative agency within the Department of Labor that is empowered to enforce the act. The act imposes record-keeping and reporting requirements on employers and requires them to post notices in the workplace, informing employees of their rights under the act.

OSHA is empowered to adopt rules and regulations to interpret and enforce the Occupational Safety and Health Act. OSHA has adopted thousands of regulations to enforce the safety standards established by the act.

Occupational Safety and Health Act
A federal act enacted in 1970 that promotes safety in the workplace.

Specific Duty Standards

Many of the OSHA standards are **specific duty standards**. For example, OSHA standards establish safety requirements for equipment (e.g., safety guards), set maximum exposure levels for hazardous chemicals, regulate the location of machinery, establish safety procedures for employees, and the like.

specific duty standard
An OSHA standard that addresses a safety problem of a specific duty nature (e.g., requirement for a safety guard on a particular type of equipment).

General Duty

The Occupational Safety and Health Act imposes a **general duty** on an employer to provide a work environment free from recognized hazards that are causing or are likely to cause death or serious physical harm to his employees. This is so even if no specific regulation applies to the situation.

OSHA is empowered to inspect places of employment for health hazards and safety violations. If a violation is found, OSHA can issue a *written citation* that requires the employer to abate or correct the situation. Contested citations are reviewed by the Occupational Safety and Health Review Commission. Its decision is appealable to the Court of Appeals for the Federal Circuit. Employers who violate the act, OSHA rules and regulations, or OSHA citations are subject to both civil and criminal penalties.

general duty
A duty that an employer has to provide a work environment free from recognized hazards that are causing or are likely to cause death or serious physical harm to employees.

ETHICS SPOTLIGHT

Company Violates OSHA's Safety Rule

"The purpose of the safety devices listed in the regulation is to provide fall protection, and a roof cannot provide fall protection if workers must operate along the perimeter."

—Judge Thornberry

Corbesco, Inc. (Corbesco), an industrial roofing and siding installation company, was hired to put metal roofing and siding over the skeletal structure of five aircraft hangars at Chennault Air Base in Louisiana. Corbesco assigned three of its employees to work on the partially completed flat roof of Hangar B, a large single-story building measuring 60 feet high, 374 feet wide, and 574 feet long. Soon after starting work, one of the workers, Roger Matthew, who was on his knees installing insulation on the roof, lost his balance and fell 60 feet to the concrete below. He was killed by the fall.

The next day, an Occupational Safety and Health Administration (OSHA) compliance officer cited Corbesco for failing to install a safety net under the work site. The officer cited an OSHA safety standard that requires that safety nets be provided when workers are more than 25 feet above the ground. Corbesco argued that the flat roof on which the employees were working served as a "temporary floor," and therefore it was not required to install a safety net. An administrative law judge (ALJ) of the **Occupational Safety and Health Review Commission (Commission)** held that Corbesco had committed a serious violation of the Occupational Safety and Health Act (Act) by failing to install a safety net at the work site. Corbesco appealed.

The U.S. Court of Appeals rejected Corbesco's argument. The Court of Appeals held that Corbesco had notice that it was required to install safety nets under its crew while they were working on the edge of a flat roof some 60 feet above a concrete floor. The Court of Appeals stated:

> Moreover, we do not believe that the Commission has abused its discretion by determining that a flat roof cannot be a temporary floor. The purpose of the safety devices listed in the regulation is to provide fall protection, and a roof cannot provide fall protection if workers must operate along the perimeter.

The Court of Appeals held that Corbesco had violated OSHA's rules by not providing a safety net below its employees who were working more than 25 feet above the ground.

Note: This case involves OSHA suing the company for a violation of a federal occupational safety rule. The dependents of the worker who was killed in this case can collect workers' compensation benefits because the worker was killed while on the job. *Corbesco, Inc. v. Dole, Secretary of Labor*, 926 F.2d 422, 1991 U.S. App. 3369 (United States Court of Appeals for the Fifth Circuit)

Business Ethics   Did Corbesco act ethically in arguing that the flat roof created a temporary floor that relieved it of the duty to install a safety net?

▶ FAIR LABOR STANDARDS ACT (FLSA)

Fair Labor Standards Act (FLSA)

A federal act enacted in 1938 to protect workers. It prohibits child labor and spells out minimum wage and overtime pay requirements.

In 1938, Congress enacted the **Fair Labor Standards Act (FLSA)** to protect workers.[3] The FLSA applies to private employers and employees engaged in the production of goods for interstate commerce. The **U.S. Department of Labor** is empowered to enforce the FLSA. Private civil actions are also permitted under the FLSA.

Child Labor

The FLSA forbids the use of oppressive **child labor** and makes it unlawful to ship goods produced by businesses that use oppressive child labor. The Department of Labor has adopted the following regulations that define lawful child labor: (1) Children under the age of 14 cannot work except as newspaper deliverers; (2) children ages 14 and 15 may work limited hours in nonhazardous jobs approved by the Department of Labor (e.g., restaurants, gasoline stations); and (3) children ages 16 and 17 may work unlimited hours in nonhazardous jobs. The Department of Labor determines which occupations are hazardous (e.g., mining, roofing, working with explosives). Children who work in agricultural employment and child actors and performers are exempt from these restrictions. Persons age 18 and older may work at any job, whether it is hazardous or not.

Minimum Wage

The FLSA establishes minimum wage and overtime pay requirements for workers. Managerial, administrative, and professional employees are exempt from the act's wage and hour provisions. The FLSA requires that most employees in the United States be paid at least the federal minimum wage for all hours worked. The federal **minimum wage** is set by Congress and can be changed. As of 2009, it was set at $7.25 per hour. The Department of Labor permits employers to pay less than the minimum wage to students and apprentices. An employer may reduce the minimum wage by an amount equal to the reasonable cost of food and lodging provided to employees.

There is a special minimum wage rule for tipped employees. An employee who earns tips can be paid $2.13 an hour by an employer if that amount plus the tips received equals at least the minimum wage. If an employee's tips and direct employer payment does not equal the minimum wage, than the employer must make up the difference.

Over half of the states have enacted minimum wage laws that set minimum wages at a rate higher than the federal rate. Some cities have enacted minimum wage requirements, usually called **living wage laws**, which also set higher minimum wage rates than the federal level.

Overtime Pay

Under the FLSA, an employer cannot require nonexempt employees to work more than 40 hours per week unless they are paid **overtime pay** of one-and-a-half times their regular pay for each hour worked in excess of 40 hours that week. Each week is treated separately.

Example If an employee works 50 hours one week and 30 hours the next, the employer owes the employee 10 hours overtime pay for the first week.

ETHICS SPOTLIGHT

Fair Labor Standards Act Pay Violation

"The relevant text describes the workday as roughly the period from 'whistle to whistle.'"

—Justice Stevens

IBP, Inc., is a large producer of fresh beef, pork, and related products. At its plant in Pasco, Washington, it employs approximately 178 workers in its slaughter division and 800 line workers. All workers must wear gear such as outer garments, hardhats, earplugs, gloves, aprons, leggings, and boots. Those who use knives must wear additional protective equipment. IBP requires employees to store their equipment and tools in company locker rooms, where the workers don and doff their equipment and protective gear.

The pay for production workers is based on time spent cutting and bagging meat. Pay begins with the first piece of meat and ends with the last piece of meat. IBP pays for four minutes of clothes-changing time. IBP employees filed a class action lawsuit against IBP to recover compensation for preproduction and postproduction work, including time spent donning and doffing protective gear and time walking

between the locker room and the production floor before and after their assigned shifts. The employees alleged that IBP violated the Fair Labor Standards Act (FLSA).

The U.S. District Court and the U.S. Court of Appeals held in favor of the workers. On appeal to the U.S. Supreme Court, IBP gave up on its claim for paying for the donning and doffing of protective gear but still alleged that it did not have to pay for the time spent by employees walking between the locker room and production area. The Supreme Court held against IBP. The Supreme Court stated:

The Department of Labor has adopted the continuous workday rule, which means that the "workday" is generally defined as the period between the commencement and completion on the same workday of an employee's principal activity or activities. The relevant text describes the workday as roughly the period from "whistle to whistle." Moreover, during a continuous workday, any walking time that occurs after the beginning of the employee's first principal activity and before the end of the employee's last principal activity is covered by the FLSA.

The U.S. Supreme Court held that the time spent by employees walking between the locker room and the production areas of the plant were compensable under the Fair Labor Standards Act. The Supreme Court confirmed the District Court's award of $3 million to the workers. *IBP,*

Inc. v. Alvarez, 546 U.S. 21, 126 S.Ct. 514, 163 L.Ed.2d 288, **Web** 2005 U.S. Lexis 8373 (Supreme Court of the United States, 2005)

Business Ethics   Did IBP act ethically in not paying the workers for the time they spent walking between the locker room and the production areas? Explain. Why do you think IBP, Inc., fought so hard against the workers' demands?

Exemptions from Minimum Wage and Overtime Pay Requirements

The FLSA establishes the following categories of exemptions from federal minimum wage and overtime pay requirements:

- **Executive exemption.** Executives who are compensated on a salary basis, who engage in management, have authority to hire employees, and regularly direct two or more employees.
- **Administrative employee exemption.** Employees who are compensated on a salary or fee basis, whose primary duty is the performance of office or non-manual work, and whose work includes the exercise of discretion and independent judgment with respect to matters of significance.
- **Learned professional exemption.** Employees compensated on a salary or fee basis who perform work that is predominantly intellectual in character, who possess advanced knowledge in a field of science or learning, and whose advanced knowledge was acquired through a prolonged course of specialized intellectual instruction.
- **Highly compensated employee exemption.** Highly compensated employees who perform office or non-manual work, are paid total annual compensation of $100,000 or more, and regularly perform at least one of the duties of an exempt executive, administrative, or professional employee.
- **Computer employee exemption.** Employees compensated either on a salary or fee basis; are employed as a computer systems analyst, computer programmer, software engineer or other similarly skilled worker in the computer field; and are engaged in the design, development, documentation, analysis, creation, testing, or modification of computer systems or programs.
- **Outside sales representative exemption.** Employees whose primary duty is making sales or obtaining orders or contracts for services, who will be paid by the client or customer, and who are customarily and regularly engaged away from the employer's place of business.

ETHICS SPOTLIGHT

Microsoft Violates Federal Employment Law

"It is our conclusion that Microsoft either exercised, or retained the right to exercise, direction over the services performed. This control establishes an employer–employee relationship."

—Judge Schwarzer

Microsoft Corporation is the world's largest provider of computer operating systems, software programs, and Internet browsers. The company has grown into one of the largest corporations in the United States, making one of its founders, Bill Gates, the richest person in the world. But

the company was caught nickel-and-diming some of its workers. The situation was brought to light by an Internal Revenue Service (IRS) investigation.

Microsoft is headquartered in the state of Washington. In addition to having regular employees, Microsoft used the services of other workers, classified as **independent contractors** (called **freelancers**) and **temporary agency employees** (called **temps**). Most of these special employees worked full time for Microsoft, doing jobs that were identical to jobs performed by Microsoft's regular employees. Microsoft paid the special employees by check as outside workers. The IRS conducted an employment tax examination and determined that Microsoft had misclassified these special workers as independent contractors and that the workers in these positions needed to be reclassified as employees for federal tax purposes.

But the IRS investigation was not the end of the story. Plaintiff Donna Vizcaino and other freelancers sued Microsoft in a class action lawsuit, alleging that they were denied employment benefits, especially employee stock options, that were paid to regular employees. Microsoft contributed 3 percent of an employee's salary to the stock option plan. The U.S. Court of Appeals agreed with the plaintiffs, citing the Internal Revenue Code, which requires such stock option plans to be available to all employees.

The Court of Appeals stated, "It is our conclusion that Microsoft either exercised, or retained the right to exercise, direction over the services performed. This control establishes an employer–employee relationship." Thus, Microsoft's attempt to define certain full-time employees as freelancers and temps was rebuffed by the courts. *Vizcaino v. United States District Court for the Western District of Washington*, 173 F.3d 713, **Web** 1999 U.S. App. Lexis 9057 (United States Court of Appeals for the Ninth Circuit)

Business Ethics   Did Microsoft act ethically in this case? Why did Microsoft classify full-time workers as freelancers and temps? Explain.

▶ OTHER WORKER PROTECTION LAWS

In addition to the statutes already discussed in this chapter, the federal government has enacted many other statutes that regulate employment relationships. These include the Consolidated Omnibus Budget Reconciliation Act (COBRA), the Family and Medical Leave Act, and the Employee Retirement Income Security Act (ERISA). These federal statutes are discussed in the following paragraphs.

Consolidated Omnibus Budget Reconciliation Act (COBRA)

The **Consolidated Omnibus Budget Reconciliation Act (COBRA)** of 1985[4] provides that an employee of a private employer or the employee's beneficiaries must be offered the opportunity to continue his or her group health insurance after the voluntary or involuntary termination of a worker's employment or the loss of coverage due to certain qualifying events defined in the law. The employer must notify covered employees and their beneficiaries of their rights under COBRA. To continue coverage, a person must pay the required group rate premium. Government employees are subject to parallel provisions found in the Public Health Service Act.

Consolidated Omnibus Budget Reconciliation Act (COBRA)
A federal law that permits employees and their beneficiaries to continue their group health insurance after an employee's employment has ended.

Family and Medical Leave Act (FMLA)
A federal act that guarantees workers up to 12 weeks of unpaid leave in a 12-month period to attend to family and medical emergencies and other specified situations.

Our children and grandchildren are not merely statistics towards which we can be indifferent.

John F. Kennedy

LANDMARK LAW
Family and Medical Leave Act

In February 1993, Congress enacted the **Family and Medical Leave Act (FMLA)**.[5] This act guarantees workers unpaid time off from work for family and medical emergencies and other specified situations. The act, which applies to companies with 50 or more workers as well as federal, state, and local governments, covers about half of the nation's workforce. To be covered by the act, an employee must have worked for the employer for at least one year and have performed more than 1,250 hours of service during the previous 12-month period.

Covered employers are required to provide up to 12 weeks of unpaid leave during any 12-month period due to:

1. The birth of and care for a child
2. The placement of a child with an employee for adoption or foster care
3. A serious health condition that makes the employee unable to perform his or her duties

4. Care for a spouse, child, or parent with a serious health problem

Leave because of the birth of a child or the placement of a child for adoption or foster care cannot be taken intermittently unless the employer agrees to such arrangement. Other leaves may be taken on an intermittent basis. The employer may require medical proof of claimed serious health conditions.

An eligible employee who takes leave must, upon returning to work, be restored to either the same or an equivalent position with equivalent employment benefits and pay. The restored employee is not entitled to the accrual of seniority during the leave period, however. A covered employer may deny restoration to a salaried employee who is among the highest-paid 10 percent of that employer's employees if the denial is necessary to prevent "substantial and grievous economic injury" to the employer's operations.

Employee Retirement Income Security Act (ERISA)

Employee Retirement Income Security Act (ERISA)
A federal act designed to prevent fraud and other abuses associated with private pension funds.

Employers are not required to establish pension plans for their employees. If they do, however, they are subject to the record-keeping, disclosure, and other requirements of the **Employee Retirement Income Security Act (ERISA)**.[6] ERISA is a complex act designed to prevent fraud and other abuses associated with private pension funds. Federal, state, and local government pension funds are exempt from its coverage. ERISA is administered by the Department of Labor and the IRS.

Among other things, ERISA requires pension plans to be in writing and to name a pension fund manager. The plan manager owes a fiduciary duty to act as a "prudent person" in managing the fund and investing its assets. No more than 10 percent of a pension fund's assets can be invested in the securities of the sponsoring employer.

Vesting occurs when an employee has a nonforfeitable right to receive pension benefits. First, ERISA provides for immediate vesting of each employee's own contributions to the plan. Second, it requires employers' contributions to be either (1) totally vested after five years (*cliff vesting*) or (2) gradually vested over a seven-year period and completely vested after that time.

▶ GOVERNMENT PROGRAMS

The U.S. government has established several programs that provide benefits to workers and their dependents. Two of these programs, unemployment compensation and Social Security, are discussed in the following paragraphs.

Unemployment Compensation

Federal Unemployment Tax Act (FUTA)
A federal act that requires employers to pay unemployment taxes; unemployment compensation is paid to workers who are temporarily unemployed.

In 1935, Congress established an **unemployment compensation** program to assist workers who are temporarily unemployed. Under the **Federal Unemployment Tax Act (FUTA)**[7] and state laws enacted to implement the program, employers are required to pay unemployment contributions (taxes). The tax rate and unemployment wage level are subject to change. Employees do not pay unemployment taxes.

State governments administer unemployment compensation programs under general guidelines set by the federal government. Each state establishes its own eligibility requirements and the amount and duration of the benefits. To collect benefits, applicants must be able and available for work and seeking employment. Workers who have been let go because of bad conduct (e.g., illegal activity, drug use on the job) or who voluntarily quit work without just cause are not eligible to receive unemployment benefits.

Social Security

Social Security
A federal system that provides limited retirement and death benefits to covered employees and their dependents.

In 1935, Congress established the federal **Social Security** system to provide limited retirement and death benefits to certain employees and their dependents. The Social Security system is administered by the **Social Security Administration**. Today, Social Security benefits include (1) retirement benefits, (2) survivors' benefits to family members of deceased workers, (3) disability benefits, and (4) medical and hospitalization benefits (Medicare).

Under the **Federal Insurance Contributions Act (FICA)**,[8] employees must make contributions (pay taxes) into the Social Security fund. An employee's employer must pay a matching amount. Social Security does not operate like a savings account. Instead, current contributions are used to fund current claims. The employer is responsible for deducting employees' portions from their wages and remitting the entire payment to the IRS.

Under the **Self-Employment Contributions Act**,[9] self-employed individuals must pay Social Security contributions, too. The amount of taxes self-employed individuals must pay is equal to the combined employer–employee amount.

Failure to submit Social Security taxes subjects the violator to interest payments, penalties, and possible criminal liability. Social Security taxes may be changed by act of Congress.

China *One reason many jobs in the United States are outsourced to other countries is because many foreign countries do not provide the workers' compensation, occupational safety, family leave rights, overtime pay, unemployment benefits, Social Security benefits, and other worker protection and security laws provided in the United States. The provision of these benefits is costly to U.S. businesses. Therefore, they outsource the production of many goods to other countries that do not have worker safety and benefits laws as substantial as those of the United States. Is it ethical for U.S. firms to outsource the manufacture of goods, knowing that the goods will be produced by foreign workers who are not provided with such benefits?*

▶ IMMIGRATION LAWS

The **Immigration Reform and Control Act of 1986 (IRCA)**[10] and the **Immigration Act of 1990**[11] are administered by the **U.S. Immigration and Customs Enforcement**. These acts make it unlawful for employers to hire illegal immigrants. Employers are required to inspect documents of prospective employees and determine that they are either U.S. citizens or otherwise qualified to work in the country (e.g., have proper work visas). Employers must maintain records and post in the workplace notices of the contents of the law. Violators are subject to both civil and criminal penalties.

For many people like myself, it can be called the Ellis Island of the 20th century.

Theodore H.M. Prudon
Describing Kennedy Airport

H-1B Foreign Guest Worker Visa

An **H-1B visa** is a non-immigrant visa that allows U.S. employers to employ in the United States foreign nationals who are skilled in specialty occupations.[12] A foreign guest worker under an H-1B visa must have a bachelor's degree or higher and have a "specialty occupation," such as engineering, mathematics, computer science, physical sciences, or medicine.

A **foreign guest worker** must be sponsored by a U.S. employer. Employers apply for H-1B visas for proposed foreign guest workers. The number of H-1B visas is limited, usually to fewer than 100,000 per year, so the competition is fierce to obtain such visas. H-1B visa holders are allowed to bring their immediate family members (i.e., spouse and children under 21) to the United States under the **H4 visa** category as dependents. An H4 visa holder may remain in the United States as long as he or she remains in legal status. An H4 visa holder is not eligible to work in the United States.

The duration of stay for a worker on an H-1B visa is three years, and this can usually be extended another three years. During this time, an employer may sponsor an H-1B holder for a green card, which if issued permits the foreign national to eventually obtain U.S. citizenship.

TEST REVIEW TERMS AND CONCEPTS

Child labor
Consolidated Omnibus
    Budget Reconciliation
    Act (COBRA)
Employee Retirement
    Income Security Act
    (ERISA)
Employment-related injury
Exclusive remedy
Fair Labor Standards Act
    (FLSA)
Family and Medical Leave
    Act (FMLA)
Federal Insurance
    Contributions Act
    (FICA)

Federal Unemployment Tax
    Act (FUTA)
Foreign guest worker
General duty
H-1B visa
H4 visa
Immigration Act of 1990
Immigration Reform and
    Control Act of 1986
    (IRCA)
Independent contractors
    (freelancers)
Living wage law

Minimum wage
Occupational Safety and
    Health Act
Occupational Safety and
    Health Administration
    (OSHA)
Occupational Safety and
    Health Review
    Commission
Overtime pay
Self-Employment
    Contributions Act
Social Security

Social Security
    Administration
Specific duty standard
Temporary agency
    employees (temps)
Unemployment
    compensation
U.S. Department of Labor
U.S. Immigration and
    Customs Enforcement
Workers' compensation
Workers' compensation
    insurance

CASE PROBLEMS

31.1 Workers' Compensation John B. Wilson was employed by the city of Modesto, California, as a police officer. He was a member of the special emergency reaction team (SERT), a tactical unit of the city's police department that is trained and equipped to handle highly dangerous criminal situations. Membership in SERT is voluntary for police officers. No additional pay or benefits are involved. To be a member of SERT, each officer is required to pass physical tests four times a year. One such test requires members to run two miles in 17 minutes. Other tests call for minimum numbers of push-ups, pull-ups, and sit-ups. Officers who do not belong to SERT are not required to undergo these physical tests. One day, Wilson completed his patrol shift, changed clothes, and drove to the Modesto Junior College track. While running there, he injured his left ankle. Wilson filed a claim for workers' compensation benefits, which was contested by his employer. Who wins? *Wilson v. Workers' Compensation Appeals Board,* 196 Cal.App.3d 902, 239 Cal.Rptr. 719, **Web** 1987 Cal.App. Lexis 2382 (Court of Appeal of California)

31.2 Workers' Compensation Joseph Albanese was employed as a working foreman by Atlantic Steel Company, Inc., for approximately 17 years. His duties included supervision of plant employees. The business was sold to a new owner. One year later, after the employees voted to unionize, friction developed between Albanese and the workers. Part of the problem was caused by management's decision to eliminate overtime work, which required Albanese to go out into the shop and prod the workers to expedite the work.

Additional problems resulted from the activities of Albanese's direct supervisor, the plant manager. On one occasion, the manager informed Albanese that the company practice of distributing Thanksgiving turkeys was to be discontinued. The following year, the manager told Albanese that the company did not intend to give the workers a Christmas bonus. The plant manager also informed Albanese that he did not intend to pay overtime wages to any worker. On each occasion, after Albanese relayed the information to the workers, the plant manager reversed his own decision.

After the last incident, Albanese became distressed and developed chest pains and nausea. When the chest pains became sharper, he went home to bed. Albanese did not work thereafter. He experienced continuing pain, sweatiness, shortness of breath, headaches, and depression. Albanese filed a claim for workers' compensation based on stress. The employer contested the claim. Who wins? *Albanese's Case*, 378 Mass. 14, 389 N.E.2d 83, **Web** 1979 Mass. Lexis 795 (Supreme Judicial Court of Massachusetts)

31.3 Occupational Safety Getty Oil Company (Getty) operates a separation facility where it gathers gas and oil from wells and transmits them to an outgoing pipeline under high pressure. Getty engineers designed and produced a pressure vessel, called a fluid booster, which was to be installed to increase pressure in the system. Robinson, a Getty engineer, was instructed to install the vessel. Robinson picked up the vessel from the welding shop without having it tested. After he completed the installation, the pressure valve was put into operation. When the pressure increased from 300 to 930 pounds per square inch, an explosion occurred. Robinson died from the explosion, and another Getty employee was seriously injured. The secretary of labor issued a citation against Getty for violating the general duty provision for worker safety contained in the Occupational Safety and Health Act. Getty challenged the citation. Who wins? *Getty Oil Company v. Occupational Safety and Health Review Commission*, 530 F.2d 1143, **Web** 1976 U.S. App. Lexis 11640 (United States Court of Appeals for the Fifth Circuit)

31.4 ERISA United Artists is a Maryland corporation doing business in the state of Texas. United Pension Fund (Plan) is a defined-contribution employee pension benefit plan sponsored by United Artists for its employees. Each employee has his or her own individual pension account, but Plan's assets are pooled for investment purposes. Plan is administered by a board of trustees. During a period of nine years, seven of the trustees used Plan to make a series of loans to themselves. The trustees did not (1) require the borrowers to submit written applications for the subject loans, (2) assess the prospective borrowers' ability to repay the loans, (3) specify a period in which the loans were to be repaid, or (4) call in the loans when they remained unpaid. The trustees also charged less than fair market value interest rates for the loans. The secretary of labor sued the trustees, alleging that they had breached their fiduciary duty, in violation of ERISA. Who wins? *McLaughlin v. Rowley*, 698 F.Supp. 1333, **Web** 1988 U.S. Dist. Lexis 12674 (United States District Court for the Northern District of Texas)

31.5 Unemployment Benefits Devon Overstreet, who worked as a bus driver for the Chicago Transit Authority (CTA) for over six years, took sick leave for six weeks. Because she had been on sick leave for more than seven days, CTA required her to take a medical examination. The blood and urine analysis indicated the presence of cocaine. A second test confirmed this finding. The CTA suspended her and placed her in the employee assistance program for substance abuse for not less than 30 days, with a chance of reassignment to a nonoperating job if she successfully completed the program. The program is an alternative to discharge and is available at the election of the employee. Overstreet filed for unemployment compensation benefits. CTA contested her claim. Who wins? *Overstreet v. Illinois Department of Employment Security*, 168 Ill.App. 3d 24, 522 N.E.2d 185, **Web** 1988 Ill.App. Lexis 269 (Appellate Court of Illinois)

BUSINESS ETHICS CASES

31.6 Business Ethics Jeffrey Glockzin was an employee of Nordyne, Inc. (Nordyne), which manufactured air-conditioning units. Sometimes Glockzin worked as an assembly line tester. The job consisted of attaching one of two wire leads with bare metal alligator-type clips leading from the testing equipment to each side of an air-conditioning unit. When the tester turned on a toggle switch, the air-conditioning unit was energized. Once a determination was made that the air-conditioning unit was working properly, the toggle switch would be turned off and the wire leads removed. One day, while testing an air-conditioning unit, Glockzin grabbed both alligator clips at the same time. He had failed to turn off the toggle switch, however. Glockzin received a 240-volt electric shock, causing his death. His heirs sued Nordyne for wrongful death and sought to recover damages for an intentional tort. Nordyne made a motion for summary judgment, alleging that workers' compensation

benefits were the exclusive remedy for Glockzin's death. Does the "intentional tort" exception to the rule that workers' compensation is the exclusive remedy for a worker's injury apply in this case? Did Nordyne's management violate its ethical duty by not providing safer testing equipment? *Glockzin v. Nordyne, Inc.*, 815 F.Supp. 1050, **Web** 1992 U.S. Dist. Lexis 8059 (United States District Court for the Western District of Michigan)

31.7 Business Ethics Whirlpool Corporation (Whirlpool) operated a manufacturing plant in Marion, Ohio, for the production of household appliances. Overhead conveyors transported appliance components throughout the plant. To protect employees from objects that occasionally fell from the conveyors, Whirlpool installed a horizontal wire-mesh guard screen approximately 20 feet above the plant floor. The mesh screen was welded to angle-iron frames suspended from the building's structural steel skeleton.

Maintenance employees spent several hours each week removing objects from the screen, replacing paper spread on the screen to catch grease drippings from the materials on the conveyors, and performing occasional maintenance work on the conveyors. To perform these duties, maintenance employees were usually able to stand on the iron frames, but sometimes they found it necessary to step onto the wire-mesh screen itself. Several employees had fallen partly through the screen. One day, a maintenance employee fell to his death through the guard screen.

The next month, two maintenance employees, Virgil Deemer and Thomas Cornwell, met with the plant supervisor to voice their concern about the safety of the screen. Unsatisfied with the supervisor's response, two days later, they met with the plant safety director and voiced similar concerns. When they asked him for the name, address, and telephone number of the local OSHA office, he told them they "had better stop and think about" what they were doing. The safety director then furnished them with the requested information, and later that day, one of the men contacted the regional OSHA office and discussed the guard screen.

The next day, Deemer and Cornwell reported for the night shift at 10:45 P.M. Their foreman directed the two men to perform their usual maintenance duties on a section of the screen. Claiming that the screen was unsafe, they refused to carry out the directive. The foreman sent them to the personnel office, where they were ordered to punch out without working or being paid for the remaining six hours of the shift. The two men subsequently received written reprimands, which were placed in their employment files.

The secretary of labor filed suit, alleging that Whirlpool's actions constituted discrimination against the two men, in violation of the Occupational Safety and Health Act. Did Whirlpool act ethically in this case? Can employees engage in self-help under certain circumstances under OSHA regulations? *Whirlpool Corporation v. Marshall, Secretary of Labor*, 445 U.S. 1, 100 S.Ct. 883, 63 L.Ed.2d 154, **Web** 1980 U.S. Lexis 81 (Supreme Court of the United States).

ENDNOTES

1. 29 U.S.C. Sections 553, 651–678.
2. For example, the Railway Safety Act and the Coal Mine Safety Act regulate workplace safety of railway workers and coal miners, respectively.
3. 29 U.S.C. Sections 201–206.
4. 26 U.S.C. Sections 1161–1169.
5. 29 U.S.C. Sections 2601, 2611–2619, 2651–2654.
6. 29 U.S.C. Sections 1001 et seq.
7. 26 U.S.C. Sections 3301–3310.
8. 26 U.S.C. Sections 3101–3125.
9. 26 U.S.C. Sections 1401–1403.
10. 29 U.S.C. Section 1802.
11. 8 U.S.C. Sections 1101 et seq.
12. 8 U.S.C. Section 101(a)(15)(H).

▲ **National Ladies Garment Workers Union** *Workers carry banners for the International Ladies Garment Workers Union during a demonstration on a city street.*

CHAPTER OBJECTIVES

After studying this chapter, you should be able to:

1. Describe how a union is organized.
2. Explain the consequences of an employer's illegal interference with a union election.
3. Describe the process of collective bargaining.
4. Describe employees' rights to strike and picket.
5. Explain state right-to-work laws.

CHAPTER CONTENTS

499

> **"Strong responsible unions are essential to industrial fair play. Without them the labor bargain is wholly one-sided."**
> —Louis D. Brandeis (1935)

▶ INTRODUCTION TO LABOR LAW AND COLLECTIVE BARGAINING

Prior to the Industrial Revolution, employees and employers had somewhat equal bargaining power. When the country became industrialized in the late 1800s, large corporate employers had much more bargaining power than their employees. In response, federal legislation was enacted that gave employees the right to form and join labor unions. Through negotiation with employers, labor unions obtained better working conditions, higher wages, and greater benefits for their members.

This chapter discusses labor unions and labor relations laws.

▶ LABOR LAW

AFL-CIO
The 1955 combination of the AFL and the CIO.

No private business monopoly, producer organization or cartel wields the market (and physical) power or commands the discipline over its members which many unions have achieved.

Gottfried Haberler
Economic Growth and Stability
(1974)

In the 1880s, few laws protected workers against employment abuses. Workers reacted by organizing unions in an attempt to gain bargaining strength. Unlike unions in many European countries, unions in the United States did not form their own political party. By the early 1900s, employers used violent tactics against workers who were trying to organize into unions. The courts generally sided with employers in such disputes.

The **American Federation of Labor (AFL)** was formed in 1886, under the leadership of Samuel Gompers. Only skilled craft workers such as silversmiths and artisans were allowed to belong. In 1935, John L. Lewis formed the **Congress of Industrial Organizations (CIO)**. The CIO permitted semiskilled and unskilled workers to become members. In 1955, the AFL and CIO combined to form the **AFL-CIO**. Individual unions (such as the United Auto Workers and United Steel Workers) may choose to belong to the AFL-CIO, but not all unions opt to join.

Today, approximately 10 percent of private-sector wage and salary workers belong to labor unions. Many government employees also belong to unions.

LANDMARK LAW
Federal Labor Union Statutes

In the early 1900s, members of the labor movement lobbied Congress to pass laws to protect their rights to organize and bargain with management. During the Great Depression of the 1930s, several statutes that were enacted gave workers certain rights and protections. Other statutes have been added since then. The major federal statutes in this area are:

- **Norris-LaGuardia Act.** Enacted in 1932, the **Norris-LaGuardia Act** stipulates that it is legal for employees to organize.[1]
- **National Labor Relations Act (NLRA).** The **National Labor Relations Act (NLRA)**, also known as the **Wagner Act**, was enacted in 1935.[2] The NLRA establishes the right of employees to form, join, and assist labor organizations; to bargain collectively with employers; and to engage in concerted activity to promote these rights.

- **Labor Management Relations Act.** In 1947, Congress enacted the **Labor Management Relations Act** (the **Taft-Hartley Act**).[3] This act (1) expands the activities that labor unions can engage in, (2) gives employers the right to engage in free-speech efforts against unions prior to a union election, and (3) gives the president of the United States the right to seek an injunction (for up to 80 days) against a strike that would create a national emergency.
- **Labor Management Reporting and Disclosure Act.** In 1959, Congress enacted the **Labor Management Reporting and Disclosure Act**, also known as the **Landrum-Griffin Act**).[4] This act regulates internal union affairs and establishes the rights of union members.
- **Railway Labor Act.** The **Railway Labor Act** of 1926, as amended in 1934, covers employees of railroad and airline carriers.[5]

National Labor Relations Board (NLRB)

The National Labor Relations Act created the **National Labor Relations Board (NLRB)**. The NLRB is an administrative body composed of five members appointed by the president and approved by the Senate. The NLRB oversees union elections, prevents employers and unions from engaging in illegal and unfair labor practices, and enforces and interprets certain federal labor laws. The decisions of the NLRB are enforceable in court.

▶ ORGANIZING A UNION

Section 7 of the NLRA gives employees the right to join together to form a union. Section 7 provides that employees shall have the right to self-organize; to form, join, or assist labor organizations; to bargain collectively through representatives of their own choosing; and to engage in other concerted activities for the purpose of collective bargaining or other mutual aid protection.

The group that a union is seeking to represent—which is called the **appropriate bargaining unit**, or **bargaining unit** —must be defined before the union can petition for an election. This group can be the employees of a single company or plant, a group within a single company (e.g., maintenance workers at all of a company's plants), or an entire industry (e.g., nurses at all hospitals in the country). Managers and professional employees may not belong to unions formed by employees whom they manage.

Types of Union Elections

If it can be shown that at least 30 percent of the employees in a bargaining unit are interested in joining or forming a union, the NLRB can be petitioned to investigate and set an election date. The following types of elections are possible:

- **Contested election.** Most union elections are contested by the employer. The NLRB is required to supervise all **contested elections**. A simple majority vote (over 50 percent) wins the election.

Example If 51 of 100 employees vote for the union, the union is certified as the bargaining agent for all 100 employees.

- **Consent election.** If management does not contest an election, a **consent election** may be held without NLRB supervision.
- **Decertification election.** If employees no longer want to be represented by a union, a **decertification election** will be held. Decertification elections must be supervised by the NLRB.

Union Solicitation on Company Property

If union solicitation is being conducted by employees, an employer may restrict solicitation activities to the employees' free time (e.g., coffee breaks, lunch breaks, before and after work). The activities may also be limited to nonworking areas, such as the cafeteria, rest room, or parking lot. Off-duty employees may be barred from union solicitation on company premises, and nonemployees (e.g., union management) may be prohibited from soliciting on behalf of the union anywhere on company property. Employers may dismiss employees who violate these rules.

An exception to this rule applies if the location of the business and the living quarters of the employees place the employees beyond the reach of reasonable union efforts to communicate with them. This so-called **inaccessibility exception** applies to logging camps, mining towns, company towns, and the like.

National Labor Relations Board (NLRB)
A federal administrative agency that oversees union elections, prevents employers and unions from engaging in illegal and unfair labor practices, and enforces and interprets certain federal labor laws.

Section 7 of the NLRA
A law that gives employees the right to join together to form a union.

Labor is discovered to be the grand conqueror, enriching and building up nations more surely than the proudest battles.

William Ellery Channing
War

inaccessibility exception
A rule that permits employees and union officials to engage in union solicitation on company property if the employees are beyond reach of reasonable union efforts to communicate with them.

In the following case, the U.S. Supreme Court addressed the issue of whether an employer had to allow nonemployee union organizers on its property.

U.S. SUPREME COURT   CASE 32.1 Organizing a Labor Union

Lechmere, Inc. v. National Labor Relations Board

502 U.S. 527, 112 S.Ct. 841, 117 L.Ed.2d 79, Web 1992 U.S. Lexis 555 (1992)
Supreme Court of the United States

"In practice, nonemployee organizational trespassing had generally been prohibited except where 'unique obstacles' prevented nontresspassory methods of communication with the employees."

—Justice Thomas

Facts

Lechmere, Inc. (Lechmere), owned and operated a retail store in the Lechmere Shopping Plaza in Newington, Connecticut. Thirteen smaller stores were located between the Lechmere store and the parking lot, which was owned by Lechmere. The United Food and Commercial Workers Union, AFL-CIO (Union), attempted to organize Lechmere's 200 employees, none of whom belonged to a union. After a full-page advertisement in a local newspaper drew little response, nonemployee Union organizers entered Lechmere's parking lot and began placing handbills on windshields of cars parked in the employee section of the parking lot. Lechmere's manager informed the organizers that Lechmere prohibited solicitation or handbill distribution of any kind on the property and asked them to leave. They did so, and Lechmere personnel removed the handbills. Union organizers renewed their handbill effort in the parking lot on several subsequent occasions, but each time, they were asked to leave, and the handbills were removed. Union filed a grievance with the NLRB. The NLRB ruled in favor of Union and ordered Lechmere to allow handbill distribution in the parking lot. The Court of Appeals affirmed this decision. Lechmere appealed to the U.S. Supreme Court.

Issue

May a storeowner prohibit nonemployee union organizers from distributing leaflets in a shopping mall parking lot owned by the store?

Language of the U.S. Supreme Court

In practice, nonemployee organizational trespassing had generally been prohibited except where "unique obstacles"

prevented nontresspassory methods of communication with the employees. The inaccessibility exception is a narrow one. It does not apply wherever nontrespassory access to employees may be cumbersome or less-than-ideally effective, but only where the location of a plant and the living quarters of the employees place the employees beyond the reach of reasonable union efforts to communicate with them.

Although the employees live in a large metropolitan area (Greater Hartford), that fact does not in itself render them "inaccessible." Their accessibility is suggested by the union's success in contacting a substantial percentage of them directly, via mailings, phone calls, and home visits. In this case, other alternative means of communication were readily available. Thus, signs (displayed, for example, from the public grassy strip adjoining Lechmere's parking lot) would have informed the employees about the union's organizational efforts. Access to employees, not success in winning them over, is the critical issue.

Decision

The U.S. Supreme Court held that under the facts of this case, Lechmere could prohibit nonemployee union organizers from distributing leaflets to employees in the store's parking lot. The Supreme Court reversed the decision of the Court of Appeals.

Case Questions

Critical Legal Thinking Should property rights take precedence over a union's right to organize employees? Explain.

Business Ethics Is it ethical for an employer to deny union organizers access to company property to conduct their organizational efforts? Is it ethical for union organizers to demand this as a right?

Contemporary Business What implication does this case have for business? Was the decision in this case a pro- or anti-business decision?

Illegal Interference with an Election

Section 8(a) of the NLRA
A law that makes it an unfair labor practice for an employer to interfere with, coerce, or restrain employees from exercising their statutory right to form and join unions.

Section 8(a) of the NLRA makes it an **unfair labor practice** for an employer to interfere with, coerce, or restrain employees from exercising their statutory right to form and join unions. Threats of loss of benefits for joining the union, statements such as "I'll close this plant if a union comes in here," and the like are unfair labor practices. Also, an employer may not form a company union.

Section 8(b) of the NLRA prohibits unions from engaging in unfair labor practices that interfere with a union election. Coercion, physical threats, and such are unfair labor practices. Where an unfair labor practice has been found, the NLRB or the courts may issue a cease-and-desist order or an injunction to restrain unfair labor practices and may set aside an election and order a new election.

The following is a classic case in which the U.S. Supreme Court found that an employer had engaged in an unfair labor practice.

U.S. SUPREME COURT   CASE 32.2 Labor Union Election

National Labor Relations Board v. Exchange Parts Company

375 U.S. 405, 84 S.Ct. 457, 11 L.Ed.2d 435, Web 1964 U.S. Lexis 2263 (1964)
Supreme Court of the United States

"The danger inherent in well-timed increases in benefits is the suggestion of a 'fist inside a velvet glove.'"

—Justice Harlan

Facts

Exchange Parts Co. (Exchange Parts) was engaged in the business of rebuilding automobile parts in Fort Worth, Texas. Its employees were not represented by a labor union. The International Brotherhood of Boilermakers, Iron Ship-builders, Blacksmiths, Forgers and Helpers, AFL-CIO (Union), advised Exchange Parts that it was going to conduct a campaign to organize the workers at the plant. After obtaining sufficient support from members of the appropriate bargaining unit, Union petitioned the NLRB to set an election date. After completing its investigation, the NLRB issued an order setting an election date. Three weeks prior to the election date, Exchange Parts held a dinner for its employees at which management announced a new company benefit allowing employees to have an extra holiday (their birthday). Two weeks before the election date, Exchange Parts sent a letter to its employees that announced new increased wages for overtime pay and an extended vacation plan for employees. Union subsequently lost the election. Union filed a complaint with the NLRB, and the NLRB held in favor of Union and ordered a new election. The Court of Appeals reversed. The NLRB appealed to the U.S. Supreme Court.

Issue

Is it an unfair practice for an employer to confer new economic benefits on its employees on the eve of a union election?

Language of the U.S. Supreme Court

The broad purpose of Section 8(a) is to establish the right of employees to organize for mutual aid without employer interference. We have no doubt that it prohibits not only *intrusive threats but also conduct immediately favorable to employees that is undertaken with the express purpose of impinging upon their freedom of choice for or against unionization and is reasonably calculated to have that effect. The danger inherent in well-timed increases in benefits is the suggestion of a "fist inside a velvet glove." Employees are not likely to miss the inference that the source of benefits now conferred is also the source from which future benefits must flow and which may dry up if it is not obliged.*

We cannot agree with the court of appeals that enforcement of the NLRB's order will have the ironic result of discouraging benefits for labor. The beneficence of an employer is likely to be ephemeral if prompted by a threat of unionization that is subsequently removed. Insulating the right of collective organization from calculated goodwill of this sort deprives employees of little that has lasting value.

Decision

The U.S. Supreme Court held that an employer's conferral of benefits on employees on the eve of a union election in an attempt to affect the outcome of that election is an unfair labor practice. The Supreme Court reversed the decision of the Court of Appeals.

Case Questions

Critical Legal Thinking Should a company be prohibited from taking away (or giving) economic benefits in its fight with a union?

Business Ethics Was it ethical for the employer in this case to increase employee benefits on the eve of the union election?

Contemporary Business Do you think the employer's conduct in this case constituted a "fist in a velvet glove"? Were the benefits conferred in this case likely to be ephemeral?

▶ COLLECTIVE BARGAINING

Once a union has been elected, the employer and the union discuss the terms of employment of union members and try to negotiate a contract that embodies these terms. The act of

collective bargaining
The act of negotiating contract terms between an employer and the members of a union.

collective bargaining agreement
The contract that results from a collective bargaining procedure.

negotiating is called **collective bargaining**, and the resulting contract is called a **collective bargaining agreement**. The employer and the union must negotiate with each other in good faith. Among other things, this prohibits making take-it-or-leave-it proposals.

The subjects of collective bargaining are classified as follows:

- **Compulsory subjects.** Wages, hours, and other terms and conditions of employment are **compulsory subjects of collective bargaining**.

Examples In addition to wages and hours, other compulsory subjects of collective bargaining include fringe benefits, health benefits, retirement plans, work assignments, safety rules, and the like.

- **Illegal subjects.** Certain topics are **illegal subjects of collective bargaining** and therefore cannot be subjects of negotiation or agreement.

Examples Subjects such as discrimination and closed shops are illegal subjects of collective bargaining.

- **Permissive subjects.** Subjects that are not compulsory or illegal are **permissive subjects of collective bargaining**. These subjects may be bargained for if the company and union agree to do so.

Examples Permissive subjects of collective bargaining include such issues as the size and composition of the supervisory force, location of plants, corporate reorganizations, and the like.

Union Security Agreements

To obtain the greatest power possible, elected unions sometimes try to install a **union security agreement**. There are two types of security agreements:

union shop
A workplace where an employee must join the union within a certain number of days after being hired.

agency shop
A workplace where an employee does not have to join the union but must pay a fee equal to the union dues.

- **Union shop.** Under a **union shop** agreement, an employee must join the union within a certain time period (e.g., 30 days) after being hired. Employees who do not join the labor union must be discharged by the employer upon receiving notice from the union. Union members pay union dues to the union. Union shops are lawful.
- **Agency shop.** Under an **agency shop** agreement, employees do not have to become union members, but they do have to pay an agency fee (an amount equal to dues) to the union. Agency shops are lawful.

Upon proper notification by the union, union and agency shop employers are required to (1) deduct union dues and agency fees from employees' wages and (2) forward these dues to the union.

CONTEMPORARY ENVIRONMENT
State Right-to-Work Laws

In 1947, Congress amended the Taft-Hartley Act by enacting Section 14(b), which provides: "Nothing in this Act shall be construed as authorizing the execution or application of agreements requiring membership in a labor organization as a condition of employment in any State or Territory in which such execution or application is prohibited by State or Territorial Law." In other words, states can enact **right-to-work laws** —either by constitutional amendment or statute—that outlaw union and agency shops.

If a state enacts a right-to-work law, individual employees cannot be forced to join a union or pay union dues and fees even though a labor union has been elected by other employees.

Right-to-work laws are often enacted by states to attract new businesses to a nonunion and low-wage environment. Unions vehemently oppose the enactment of right-to-work laws because they substantially erode union power. The remedies for violation of right-to-work laws vary from state to state but usually include damages to persons injured by the violation, injunctive relief and criminal penalties. Today, the following 22 states have enacted right-to-work laws: Alabama, Arizona, Arkansas, Florida, Georgia, Idaho, Iowa, Kansas, Louisiana, Mississippi, Nebraska, Nevada, North Carolina, North Dakota, Oklahoma, South Carolina, South Dakota, Tennessee, Texas, Utah, Virginia, and Wyoming.

New York City *In the United States, federal labor laws protect the rights of workers to form and join unions and to engage in peaceful strikes and picketing.*

▶ STRIKES

The NLRA gives union management the right to recommend that the union call a **strike** if a collective bargaining agreement cannot be reached. Before there can be a strike, though, a majority of the union's members must vote in favor of the action. In order to support a strike, union members often picket at their employer's place of business. Picketing and strikes are discussed in the following paragraphs.

strike
A cessation of work by union members in order to obtain economic benefits or correct an unfair labor practice.

Cooling-Off Period

Before a strike, a union must give a 60-day notice to the employer that the union intends to strike. It is illegal for a strike to begin during the mandatory 60-day **cooling-off period**. The 60-day time period is designed to give the employer and the union enough time to negotiate a settlement of the union grievances and avoid a strike. Any strike without a proper 60-day notice is illegal, and the employer may dismiss the striking workers.

cooling-off period
A mandatory 60 days' notice before a strike can commence.

Illegal Strikes

Several types of strikes have been held to be illegal and are not protected by federal labor law. The following are **illegal strikes**:

- **Violent strikes.** In **violent strikes**, striking employees cause substantial damage to property of the employer or a third party. Courts usually tolerate a certain amount of isolated violence before finding that the entire strike is illegal.
- **Sit-down strikes.** In **sit-down strikes**, striking employees continue to occupy the employer's premises. Such strikes are illegal because they deny the employer's statutory right to continue its operations during the strike.
- **Partial or intermittent strikes.** In **partial strikes**, or **intermittent strikes**, employees strike part of the day or workweek and work the other part. This type of strike is illegal because it interferes with the employer's right to operate its facilities at full operation.
- **Wildcat strikes.** In **wildcat strikes**, individual union members go on strike without proper authorization from the union. The courts have recognized that a wildcat strike becomes lawful if it is quickly ratified by the union.

An employer can discharge illegal strikers, who then have no rights to reinstatement.

Management and union may be likened to that serpent of the fables who on one body had two heads that fighting with poisoned fangs, killed themselves.

Peter Drucker
The New Society (1951)

No-Strike Clause

An employer and a union can agree in a collective bargaining agreement that the union will not strike during a particular period of time. The employer gives economic benefits to the union and, in exchange, the union agrees that no strike will be called for the set time. It is illegal for a strike to take place in violation of a negotiated **no-strike clause**. An employer may dismiss union members who strike in violation of a no-strike clause.

Crossover and Replacement Workers

Individual members of a union do not have to honor a strike. They may (1) choose not to strike or (2) return to work after joining the strikers for a time. Employees who choose either of these options are known as **crossover workers**.

Once a strike begins, the employer may continue operations by using management personnel and hiring **replacement workers** to take the place of the striking employees. Replacement workers can be hired on either a temporary or permanent basis. If replacement workers are given permanent status, they do not have to be dismissed when the strike is over.

Employer Lockout

If an employer reasonably anticipates a strike by some of its employees, it may prevent those employees from entering the plant or premises. This is called an **employer lockout**.

Example The National Hockey League (NHL) is a professional hockey league with teams located in Canada and the United States. The National Hockey League Players' Association, a labor union, represents the players. The NHL and the players' association negotiate and enter into collective bargaining agreements that establish working conditions and financial matters. On several occasions, the players' association has gone on strike. Therefore, in 2004, when it looked as if the players might go on strike, the NHL locked the players out before they could strike. The team owners and the union could not reach an agreement, and the 2004–2005 season was cancelled.

▶ PICKETING

Striking union members often engage in **picketing** in support of their strike. Picketing usually takes the form of the striking employees and union representatives walking in front of the employer's premises, carrying signs announcing their strike. Picketing is used to put pressure on an employer to settle a strike. The right to picket is implied from the NLRA.

Picketing is lawful unless it (1) is accompanied by violence, (2) obstructs customers from entering the employer's place of business, (3) prevents nonstriking employees from entering the employer's premises, or (4) prevents pickups and deliveries at the employer's place of business. An employer may seek an injunction against unlawful picketing.

Secondary Boycott Picketing

Unions sometimes try to bring pressure against an employer by picketing the employer's suppliers or customers. Such **secondary boycott picketing** is lawful only if it is product picketing (i.e., if the picketing is against the primary employer's product). The picketing is illegal if it is directed against the neutral employer instead of the struck employer's product.

A truly American sentiment recognizes the dignity of labor and the fact that honor lies in honest toil.

S. Grover Cleveland
Letter accepting the nomination for president

employer lockout
An act of an employer to prevent employees from entering the work premises when the employer reasonably anticipates a strike.

picketing
The action of strikers walking in front of an employer's premises, carrying signs announcing their strike.

secondary boycott picketing
A type of picketing in which a union tries to bring pressure against an employer by picketing the employer's suppliers or customers.

ETHICS SPOTLIGHT

Labor Union Conducts Mock Funeral

"Their message may have been unsettling or even offensive to someone visiting a dying relative, but unsettling and even offensive speech is not without the protection of the First Amendment."

—Chief Judge Ginsburg

The Sheet Metal Workers' International Association Local 15, AFL-CIO (Union), had a labor dispute with Massey Metals, Inc. (Massey), and Workers Temporary Staffing (WTS), which supplied nonunion labor employees to Massey, whom Massey used on its various construction projects. The Brandon Regional Medical Center (Hospital) employed Massey as the metal fabricator and installation contractor for a construction project at Hospital.

One day, Union staged a mock funeral procession in front of the Hospital. The procession consisted of four Union representatives acting as pallbearers and carrying a large coffin back and forth on the sidewalk near the entrance to Hospital. Another Union representative accompanied the procession dressed as the "Grim Reaper." The funeral procession took place about 100 feet from the hospital. Union broadcast somber funeral music over loudspeakers mounted on a flatbed trailer that was positioned nearby. Four other Union representatives, who did not impede Hospital ingress or egress, distributed to persons entering and leaving Hospital handbills that stated, "Going to Brandon Regional Hospital Should Not be a Grave Decision." The procession lasted approximately two hours and was videotaped.

The regional director of the National Labor Relations Board (NLRB) immediately filed a petition for a temporary injunction against Union's mock funeral. The NLRB alleged that Union's mock funeral procession at Hospital constituted an illegal secondary boycott picketing. The U.S. District Court agreed and issued an injunction against Union, prohibiting such mock funeral processions at Hospital. Union appealed.

On appeal, the U.S. Court of Appeals reversed, finding that the mock funeral was not coercive, threatening, restraining, or intimidating and therefore was not illegal secondary picketing or boycott. The court cited the facts that the funeral took place about 100 feet from the hospital and the union members did not impede hospital ingress or egress and were not confrontational with the patrons of the hospital. The Court of Appeals stated:

Nor was their "message"—invoking the iconography of the funeral rite and stating that "Going to Brandon Hospital Should Not Be a Grave Decision"—one by which a person of ordinary fortitude would be intimidated. Their message may have been unsettling or even offensive to someone visiting a dying relative, but unsettling and even offensive speech is not without the protection of the First Amendment. The right to free speech may not be curtailed simply because the speaker's message may be offensive to his audience.

The U.S. Court of Appeals held that Union's mock funeral procession at the hospital did not constitute illegal secondary boycott picketing because there was no coercive, threatening, restraining, or intimidating conduct by the union members. The Court of Appeals remanded the case to the NLRB for proceedings consistent with the Court's opinion. *Sheet Metal Workers' International Association, Local 15, AFL-CIO v. National Labor Relations Board*, 491 F.3d 429, **Web** 2007 U.S. App. Lexis 14361 (United States Court of Appeals for the District of Columbia Circuit, 2007)

Business Ethics For what purpose did Union hold a mock funeral procession at Hospital? Do you think that Union's conduct was ethical in this case?

▶ INTERNAL UNION AFFAIRS

Unions may adopt **internal union rules** to regulate the operation of the union, acquire and maintain union membership, and the like. The undemocratic manner in which many unions were formulating these rules prompted Congress in 1959 to enact **Title I of the Landrum-Griffin Act**. Title I, which is often referred to as **labor's "bill of rights,"** gives each union member equal rights and privileges to nominate candidates for union office, vote in elections, and participate in membership meetings. It further guarantees union members the rights of free speech and assembly, provides for due process (notice and hearing), and permits union members to initiate judicial or administrative action.

A union may discipline members for participating in certain activities, including (1) walking off the job in a nonsanctioned strike, (2) working for wages below union scale, (3) spying for an employer, and (4) any other unauthorized activity that has an adverse economic impact on the union. A union may not punish a union member for participating in a civic duty, such as testifying in court against the union.

Title I of the Landrum-Griffin Act
Labor's "bill of rights," which gives each union member equal rights and privileges to nominate candidates for union office, vote in elections, and participate in membership meetings.

Worker Adjustment and Retraining Notification (WARN) Act
A federal act that requires employers with 100 or more employees to give their employees 60 days' notice before engaging in certain plant closings or layoffs.

ETHICS SPOTLIGHT

Plant Closing Act

Often, a company would choose to close a plant without giving its employees prior notice of the closing. To remedy this situation, in 1988, Congress enacted the **Worker Adjustment and Retraining Notification (WARN) Act**, also called the **Plant Closing Act** [29 U.S.C. Section 2102]. The act requires employers with 100 or more employees to give their employees 60 days' notice before engaging in certain plant closings or layoffs.

If employees are represented by a union, the notice must be given to the union; if they are not, the notice must be given to the employees individually.

The act covers the following actions:

· **Plant closings.** A **plant closing** is a permanent or temporary shutdown of a single site that results in a loss of employment of 50 or more employees during any 30-day period.

· **Mass layoffs.** A **mass layoff** is a reduction of 33 percent of the employees or at least 50 employees during any 30-day period.

An employer is exempted from having to give such notice if:

· The closing or layoff is caused by business circumstances that were not reasonably foreseeable as of the time that the notice would have been required.
· The business was actively seeking capital or business that, if obtained, would have avoided or postponed the shutdown and the employer in good faith believed that giving notice would have precluded it from obtaining the needed capital or business.

Business Ethics What does the WARN Act provide? Was the WARN Act enacted to prevent unethical conduct by business? Explain.

TEST REVIEW TERMS AND CONCEPTS

AFL-CIO
Agency shop
American Federation of Labor (AFL)
Appropriate bargaining unit (bargaining unit)
Collective bargaining
Collective bargaining agreement
Compulsory subject of collective bargaining
Congress of Industrial Organizations (CIO)
Consent election
Contested election
Cooling-off period

Crossover worker
Decertification election
Employer lockout
Illegal strike
Illegal subjects of collective bargaining
Inaccessibility exception
Internal union rules
Labor Management Relations Act (Taft-Hartley Act)
Labor Management Reporting and Disclosure Act (Landrum-Griffin Act)
Mass layoffs

National Labor Relations Act (NLRA) (Wagner Act)
National Labor Relations Board (NLRB)
Norris-LaGuardia Act
No-strike clause
Partial (intermittent) strike
Permissive subjects of collective bargaining
Picketing
Plant closings
Railway Labor Act
Replacement worker
Right-to-work laws
Secondary boycott picketing
Section 7 of the NLRA

Section 8(a) of the NLRA
Secondary boycott picketing
Sit-down strike
Strike
Title I of the Landrum-Griffin Act (labor's "bill of rights")
Unfair labor practice
Union security agreement
Union shop
Violent strike
Wildcat strike
Worker Adjustment and Retraining Notification (WARN) Act (Plant Closing Act)

CASE PROBLEMS

32.1 Unfair Labor Practice The Teamsters Union (Teamsters) began a campaign to organize the employees at a Sinclair Company (Sinclair) plant. When the president of Sinclair learned of the Teamsters' drive, he talked with all of his employees and emphasized the results of a long strike 13 years earlier that he claimed "almost put our company out of business," and he expressed worry that the employees were forgetting the "lessons of the past." He emphasized that Sinclair was on "thin ice" financially, that the Teamsters' "only

weapon is to strike," and that a strike "could lead to the closing of the plant" because Sinclair had manufacturing facilities elsewhere. He also noted that because of the employees' ages and the limited usefulness of their skills, they might not be able to find reemployment if they lost their jobs. Finally, he sent literature to the employees stating that "the Teamsters Union is a strike happy outfit" and that they were under "hoodlum control," and included a cartoon showing the preparation of a grave for Sinclair and other headstones containing the names of other plants allegedly victimized by unions. The Teamsters lost the election 7 to 6 and then filed an unfair labor practice charge with the NLRB. Did Sinclair violate labor law? Who wins? *N.L.R.B. v. Gissel Packing Co.*, 395 U.S. 575, 89 S.Ct. 1918, 23 L.Ed.2d 547, **Web** 1969 U.S. Lexis 3172 (Supreme Court of the United States)

32.2 Right-to-Work Law   Mobil Oil Corporation (Mobil) had its headquarters in Beaumont, Texas. It operated a fleet of eight oceangoing tankers that transported its petroleum products from Texas to ports on the East Coast. A typical trip on a tanker from Beaumont to New York took about five days. No more than 10 to 20 percent of the seamen's work time was spent in Texas. The 300 or so seamen who were employed to work on the tankers belonged to the Oil, Chemical & Atomic Workers International Union, AFL-CIO (Union), which had an agency shop agreement with Mobil. The state of Texas enacted a right-to-work law. Mobil sued Union, claiming that the agency shop agreement was unenforceable because it violated the Texas right-to-work law. Who wins? *Oil, Chemical & Atomic Workers International Union, AFL-CIO v. Mobil Oil Corp.*, 426 U.S. 407, 96 S.Ct. 2140, 48 L.Ed.2d 736, **Web** 1976 U.S. Lexis 106 (Supreme Court of the United States)

32.3 Plant Closing   Arrow Automotive Industries, Inc. (Arrow), was engaged in the remanufacture and distribution of automobile and truck parts. All its operating plants produced identical product lines. Arrow was planning to open a new facility in Santa Maria, California. The employees at the Arrow plant in Hudson, Massachusetts were represented by the United Automobile, Aerospace, and Agricultural Implement Workers of America (Union). The Hudson plant had a history of unprofitable operations. Union called a strike when the existing collective bargaining agreement expired and a new agreement could not be reached. After several months, the board of directors of Arrow voted to close the striking plant. The closing gave Arrow a 24 percent increase in gross profits and freed capital and equipment for the new Santa Maria plant. In addition, the existing customers of the Hudson plant could be serviced by the Spartanburg plant, which was being underutilized. Union filed an unfair labor practice claim with the NLRB. Does Arrow have to bargain with Union over the decision to close a plant? What would have to be done if the Plant Closing Act applied to this situation? *Arrow Automotive Industries, Inc. v. N.L.R.B.*, 853 F.2d 223, **Web** 1988 U.S. App. Lexis 10091 (United States Court of Appeals for the Fourth Circuit)

32.4 Unfair Labor Practice   The Frouge Corporation (Frouge) was the general contractor on a housing project in Philadelphia. The carpenter employees of Frouge were represented by the Carpenters' International Union (Union). Traditional jobs of carpenters included taking blank wooden doors and mortising them for doorknobs, routing them for hinges, and beveling them to fit between the doorjambs. Union had entered into a collective bargaining agreement with Frouge that provided that no member of Union would handle any doors that had been fitted prior to being furnished to the job site. The housing project called for 3,600 doors. Frouge contracted for the purchase of premachined doors that were already mortised, routed, and beveled. When Union ordered its members not to hang the prefabricated doors, the National Woodwork Manufacturers Association filed an unfair labor practice charge against Union with the NLRB. Is Union's refusal to hang prefabricated doors lawful? *National Woodwork Manufacturers Association v. N.L.R.B.*, 386 U.S. 612, 87 S.Ct. 1250, **Web** 1967 U.S. Lexis 2858 (Supreme Court of the United States)

32.5 Illegal Strike   The employees of the Shop Rite Foods, Inc. (Shop Rite), warehouse in Lubbock, Texas, elected the United Packinghouse, Food and Allied Workers (Union) as its bargaining agent. Negotiations for a collective bargaining agreement began. Three months later, when an agreement had not yet been reached, Shop Rite found excessive amounts of damage to merchandise in its warehouse and concluded that it was being intentionally caused by dissident employees as a pressure tactic to secure concessions from Shop Rite. Shop Rite notified the Union representative that employees caught doing such acts would be terminated; the Union representative in turn notified the employees.

A Shop Rite manager observed an employee in the flour section—where he had no business being—making quick motions with his hands. The manager found several bags of flour that had been cut. The employee was immediately fired. Another employee (a fellow Union member) led about 30 other employees in an immediate walkout. The company discharged these employees and refused to rehire them. The employees filed a grievance with the NLRB. Can they get their jobs back? *N.L.R.B. v. Shop Rite Foods, Inc.*, 430 F.2d 786, **Web** 1970 U.S. App. Lexis 7613 (United States Court of Appeals for the Fifth Circuit)

32.6 Employer Lockout   The American Ship Building Company (American) operated a shipyard in Chicago, Illinois, where it repaired Great Lakes ships during the winter months, when freezing on the Great Lakes rendered shipping impossible. The workers at the shipyard were represented by several labor unions. The unions notified American of their intention to seek modification of the current collective bargaining agreement when it expired three months later. On five previous occasions, agreements had been preceded by strikes (including illegal strikes) that were called just after the ships had arrived in the shipyard for repairs so that the unions increased their leverage in negotiations with the company.

Based on this history, American displayed anxiety as to the unions' strike plans and possible work stoppage. On the day that the collective bargaining agreement expired, after extended negotiations, American and the unions reached an impasse in their collective bargaining. In response, American decided to lay off most of the workers at the shipyard. It sent them the following notice: "Because of the labor dispute which has been unresolved, you are laid off until further notice." The unions filed unfair labor practice charges with the NLRB. Are American's actions legal? *American Ship Building Company v. N.L.R.B.*, 380 U.S. 300, 85 S.Ct. 955, 13 L.Ed.2d 855, **Web** 1965 U.S. Lexis 2310 (Supreme Court of the United States)

32.7 Replacement Workers   The union (Union) member-employees of the Erie Resistor Company (Company) struck Company over the terms of a new collective bargaining agreement that was being negotiated between Company and Union. Company continued production operations during the strike by hiring new hires and crossover union members who were persuaded to abandon the strike and come back to work. Company promised all replacement workers superseniority. This would take the form of adding 20 years to the length of a worker's actual service for the purpose of future layoffs and recalls. Many union members accepted the offer. Union filed an unfair labor practice charge with the NLRB. Is Company's offer of the superseniority lawful? *N.L.R.B. v. Erie Resistor Co.*, 373 U.S. 221, 83 S.Ct. 1139, 10 L.Ed.2d 308, **Web** 1963 U.S. Lexis 2492 (Supreme Court of the United States)

32.8 Secondary Boycott   Safeco Title Insurance Company (Safeco) was a major insurance company that underwrote title insurance for real estate in the state of Washington. Five local title companies acted as insurance brokers that exclusively sold Safeco insurance. Local 1001 of the Retail Store Employees Union, AFL-CIO (Union), was elected as the bargaining agent for certain Safeco employees. When negotiations between Safeco and Union reached an impasse, the employees went on strike. Union did not confine its picketing to Safeco's office in Seattle but also picketed each of the five local title companies. The picketers carried signs declaring that Safeco had no contract with Union and distributed handbills, asking consumers to support the strike by canceling their Safeco insurance policies. The local title companies filed a complaint with the NLRB. Is the picketing of the neutral title insurance companies lawful? *N.L.R.B. v. Retail Store Employees Union, Local 1001, Retail Clerks International Association, AFL-CIO*, 447 U.S. 607, 100 S.Ct. 2372, 65 L.Ed.2d 377, **Web** 1980 U.S. Lexis 133 (Supreme Court of the United States)

BUSINESS ETHICS CASES

32.9 Business Ethics   The International Association of Machinists and Aerospace Workers, AFL-CIO (Union), began soliciting the employees of Whitcraft Houseboat Division, North American Rockwell Corp. (Whitcraft), to organize a union. For three days, Whitcraft management dispersed congregating groups of employees. During these three days, production was down almost 50 percent. On the third day, Whitcraft adopted the following no-solicitation rule and mailed a copy to each employee and posted it around the workplace:

As you well know working time is for work. No one will be allowed to solicit or distribute literature during our working time, that is, when he or she should be working. Anyone doing so and neglecting his work or interfering with the work of another employee will be subject to discharge.

Two days later, a manager of Whitcraft found that two employees of the company were engaged in union solicitation during working hours in a working area. Whitcraft discharged them for violating the no-solicitation rule. Is their discharge lawful? Did Whitcraft act ethically in discharging the employees? *Whitcraft Houseboat Division, North American Rockwell Corporation v. International Association of Machinists and Aerospace Workers, AFL-CIO*, 195 N.L.R.B. 1046 (N.L.R.B.), **Web** 1972 NLRB Lexis 1117 (N.L.R.B).

32.10 Business Ethics   Most musicians belonged to the American Federation of Musicians (Union), which represented more than 200,000 members in the United States. Union was divided into separate local unions (Locals) that each represented the members from a certain geographic area. Gamble Enterprises, Inc. (Gamble), owned and operated the Palace Theater in Akron, Ohio, which staged the performances of local and traveling musicians.

Union adopted the following rule: "Traveling members cannot, without the consent of a Local, play any presentation performance unless a local house orchestra is also employed." This meant that the theater owner might have to pay two bands or orchestras. Gamble's refusal to abide by this rule caused Union to block the appearances of traveling bands and orchestras. Gamble filed an unfair labor practice charge with the NLRB. Is Union's rule lawful? *N.L.R.B. v. Gamble Enterprises, Inc.*, 345 U.S. 117, 73 S.Ct. 560, 97 L.Ed. 864, **Web** 1953 U.S. Lexis 2620 (Supreme Court of the United States)

ENDNOTES

1. 29 U.S.C. Sections 101–110, 113–115.
2. 29 U.S.C. Sections 151–169.
3. 29 U.S.C. Section 141 et seq.
4. 29 U.S.C. Section 401 et seq.
5. 45 U.S.C. Sections 151–162, 181–188.

▲ **Disabled Person Parking Spot** *The federal Americans with Disabilities Act (ADA), which became law in 1990, protects persons with disabilities from discrimination in many facets of life. Title I of the ADA requires employers to make reasonable accommodations for individuals with disabilities that do not cause undue hardship to the employer. Title II requires public agencies and public transportation to be accessible to persons with disabilities. Title III requires public accommodations and commercial facilities—such as lodging and hotels, recreation, transportation, education, dining, and stores—to reasonably accommodate persons with disabilities. And Title VI requires telecommunications companies to provide functionally equivalent services to persons who are deaf or hard of hearing and persons with speech impairments.*

CHAPTER OBJECTIVES

After studying this chapter, you should be able to:

1. Describe the scope of coverage of Title VII of the Civil Rights Act of 1964.
2. Identify race, color, and national origin discrimination that violate Title VII.
3. Identify sex discrimination—including sexual harassment—that violates Title VII.

4. Describe the scope of coverage of the Age Discrimination in Employment Act.
5. Describe the protections afforded by the Americans with Disabilities Act.

CHAPTER CONTENTS

> **"What people have always sought is equality of rights before the law. For rights that were not open to all equally would not be rights."**
>
> —Cicero
> *De Officiis, Book II, Chapter XII*

▶ INTRODUCTION TO EQUAL OPPORTUNITY IN EMPLOYMENT

Under common law, employers could terminate an employee at any time and for any reason. In this same vein, employers were free to hire and promote anyone they chose without violating the law. This often created unreasonable hardship on employees and erected employment barriers to certain minority classes.

Starting in the 1960s, Congress began enacting a comprehensive set of federal laws that eliminated major forms of employment **discrimination**. These laws, which were passed to guarantee **equal employment opportunity** to all employees and job applicants, have been broadly interpreted by the federal courts, particularly the U.S. Supreme Court. States have also enacted antidiscrimination laws. Many state and local governments have adopted laws that prevent discrimination in employment.

This chapter discusses **equal opportunity in employment** laws.

equal opportunity in employment
The right of all employees and job applicants (1) to be treated without discrimination and (2) to be able to sue employers if they are discriminated against.

▶ TITLE VII OF THE CIVIL RIGHTS ACT OF 1964

Prior to the passage of major federal antidiscrimination laws in the 1960s, much discrimination in employment existed in this country. In the 1960s, Congress enacted several major federal statutes that outlawed employment discrimination against members of certain classes. These federal laws were instrumental to providing equal opportunity in employment in this country. One of the main statutes is *Title VII of the Civil Rights Act of 1964*.[1]

Title VII of the Civil Rights Act of 1964
A title of a federal statute enacted to eliminate job discrimination based on five protected classes: *race, color, religion, sex,* and *national origin*.

LANDMARK LAW

Title VII of the Civil Rights Act of 1964

After substantial debate, Congress enacted the **Civil Rights Act of 1964. Title VII of the Civil Rights Act** (called the **Fair Employment Practices Act**) was intended to eliminate job discrimination based on the following *protected classes: race, color, national origin, sex,* and *religion.*

As amended by the **Equal Employment Opportunity Act of 1972**, Section 703(a)(2) of Title VII provides, in pertinent part, that:

> It shall be an unlawful employment practice for an employer
> (1) to fail or refuse to hire or to discharge any individual, or otherwise to discriminate against any individual with respect to his compensation, terms, conditions, or privileges of employment, because of such individual's race, color, religion, sex, or national origin; or
> (2) to limit, segregate, or classify his employees or applicants for employment in any way which would deprive or tend to deprive any individual of employment opportunities or otherwise adversely affect his status as an employee, because of such individual's race, color, religion, sex, or national origin.

Scope of Coverage of Title VII

Title VII of the Civil Rights Act of 1964 applies to (1) employers with 15 or more employees, (2) all employment agencies, (3) labor unions with 15 or more members, (4) state and local governments and their agencies, and (5) most federal government employment. Native American tribes and tax-exempt private clubs are expressly excluded from coverage. Other portions of the Civil Rights Act of 1964 prohibit discrimination in housing, education, and other facets of life.

Title VII prohibits discrimination in hiring, decisions regarding promotion or demotion, payment of compensation and fringe benefits, availability of job training and apprenticeship opportunities, referral systems for employment, decisions regarding dismissal, work rules, and any other "term, condition, or privilege" of employment. Any employee of a covered employer, including undocumented aliens,[2] may bring actions for employment discrimination under Title VII.

Title VII prohibits two major forms of employment discrimination: disparate-treatment discrimination and disparate-impact discrimination.

Rights matter most when they are claimed by unpopular minorities.

J. Michael Kirby
Sydney Morning Herald,
November 30, 1985

Disparate-Treatment Discrimination   **Disparate-treatment discrimination** occurs when an employer treats a specific *individual* less favorably than others because of that person's race, color, national origin, sex, or religion. In such situations, the complainant must prove that (1) he or she belongs to a Title VII protected class (2) he or she applied for and was qualified for the employment position, (3) he or she was rejected despite this, and (4) the employer kept the position open and sought applications from persons with the complainant's qualifications.[3]

disparate-treatment discrimination
A form of discrimination that occurs when an employer discriminates against a specific individual because of his or her race, color, national origin, sex, or religion.

Example A member of a minority race applies for a promotion to a position advertised as available at his company. The minority applicant, who is qualified for the position, is rejected by the company, which hires a nonminority applicant for the position. The minority applicant sues under Title VII. He has a *prima facie* case of illegal discrimination. The burden of proof shifts to the employer to prove a nondiscriminatory reason for its decision. If the employer offers a reason, such as saying that the minority applicant lacked sufficient experience, the burden shifts back to the minority applicant to prove that this was just a *pretext* (not the real reason) for the employer's decision.

Disparate-Impact Discrimination   **Disparate-impact discrimination** occurs when an employer discriminates against an entire protected *class*. Many disparate-impact cases are brought as class action lawsuits. Often, this type of discrimination is proven through statistical data about the employer's employment practices. The plaintiff must demonstrate a *causal link* between the challenged practice and the statistical imbalance. Showing a statistical disparity between the percentages of protected class employees versus the percentage of the population that the protected class makes within the surrounding community is not enough, by itself, to prove discrimination.

disparate-impact discrimination
A form of discrimination that occurs when an employer discriminates against an entire protected class. An example would be discrimination in which a racially neutral employment practice or rule causes an adverse impact on a protected class.

Example Disparate-impact discrimination occurs when an employer adopts a work rule that is neutral on its face but is shown to cause an adverse impact on a protected class. If an employer has a rule that all applicants for an executive position must be at least 5'8" tall, this looks like a neutral rule because it applies to both males and females. However, because this rule is unrelated to the performance of an executive position and eliminates many more females than males from being hired or promoted to an executive position, it is disparate-impact sex discrimination in violation of Title VII.

Intentional Discrimination

In a case involving intentional discrimination, the aggrieved party can recover compensatory damages. A court can award **punitive damages** against an employer in a case involving an employer's malice or reckless indifference to federally protected rights. The sum of compensatory and punitive damages is capped at different amounts of money, depending on the size of the employer.

Equal Employment Opportunity Commission (EEOC)

Equal Employment Opportunity Commission (EEOC)
The federal administrative agency that is responsible for enforcing most federal antidiscrimination laws.

The **Equal Employment Opportunity Commission (EEOC)** is the federal agency responsible for enforcing most federal antidiscrimination laws. The members of the EEOC are appointed by the U.S. president. The EEOC is empowered to conduct investigations, interpret the statutes, encourage conciliation between employees and employers, and bring suit to enforce the law. The EEOC can also seek injunctive relief.

To bring an action under Title VII, a private complainant must first file a complaint with the EEOC within 180 days or 300 days (depending on the state) of the alleged discrimination.[4] This time period has been strictly construed by the U.S. Supreme Court.[5] The EEOC is given the opportunity to sue the employer on the complainant's behalf. If the EEOC chooses not to bring suit, it will issue a **right to sue letter** to the complainant. This gives the complainant the right to sue the employer.

Remedies for Violations of Title VII

A successful plaintiff in a Title VII action can recover back pay and reasonable attorneys' fees. The courts also have broad authority to grant equitable remedies. For instance, the courts can order reinstatement, grant fictional seniority, and issue injunctions to compel the hiring or promotion of protected minorities.

Racial discrimination in any form and in any degree has no justifiable part whatever in our democratic way of life. It is unattractive in any setting but it is utterly revolting among a free people who have embraced the principles set forth in the Constitution of the United States.

Justice Murphy
Dissenting opinion, Korematsu v. United States (1944)

▶ RACE, COLOR, AND NATIONAL ORIGIN DISCRIMINATION

Title VII of the Civil Rights Act of 1964 was primarily enacted to prohibit employment discrimination based on *race*, *color*, and *national origin*.

Race Discrimination

Race refers to broad categories such as African American, Caucasian, Asian, and Native American. **Race discrimination** in employment violates Title VII.

Color Discrimination

Color refers to the color of a person's skin. Discrimination by an employer based on color violates Title VII. **Color discrimination** cases are not brought as often as cases involving other forms of discrimination.

National Origin or Heritage Discrimination

National origin and heritage refers to the country of a person's ancestors, cultural characteristics, or heritage. **National origin or heritage discrimination** would include discrimination against persons of a particular nationality (e.g., persons of Irish descent), against persons who come from a certain place (e.g., the Middle East), against persons of a certain culture (e.g., Hispanics), or against persons because of their accents. Discrimination by an employer based on a person's national origin or heritage violates Title VII.

ETHICS SPOTLIGHT

Walgreen to Pay $24 Million in Race Discrimination Lawsuit

The EEOC has adopted an **E-RACE Initiative** to identify barriers that contribute to race and color discrimination in employment, to litigate cases involving such discrimination, and to educate the public about race and color discrimination in the workplace. With its adoption of its E-RACE Initiative, the EEOC has pursued many high-profile race and color discrimination cases. In one such case, the EEOC sued the Walgreen Company, which operates more than 6,000 stores throughout the country, for engaging in race and color discrimination. The charge asserted that Walgreen systematically discriminated against African American retail management and pharmacy employees in promotions, compensation, and assignments.

The EEOC filed its complaint against Walgreen in 2007. In addition, several private lawsuits had also been filed against Walgreen, charging the same violations. Walgreen Company agreed to settle all charges—the EEOC action and the private lawsuits—by agreeing to pay $24 million to a class of thousands of African American employees and former employees nationwide. The federal court overseeing the case ruled that the consent decree is fair, reasonable, and adequate. The award is one of the largest awards obtained by the EEOC in a race and color discrimination lawsuit.

The Court also issued an injunction prohibiting the Walgreen Company from engaging in similar conduct in the future. The consent decree requires Walgreen to employ outside consultants to develop standardized, nondiscriminatory store assignment and promotion standards and to review Walgreen's employment practices. The EEOC retained jurisdiction over the consent decree for five years.

An EEOC spokesperson said, "The EEOC's case is a good example of the Commission's renewed emphasis on class and systemic litigation and furthers the agency's E-RACE Initiative, which is designed to address major issues of race and color discrimination." *EEOC v. Walgreen Company* and *Tucker v. Walgreen Company, Civil No. 07-CV-172-GPM and Civil No. 05-CV-440-GPM* (United States District Court for the Southern District of Illinois, 2008)

▶ SEX DISCRIMINATION AND SEXUAL HARASSMENT

Title VII of the Civil Rights Act of 1964 prohibits job discrimination based on gender. The act, as amended, the EEOC's rules, and court decisions prohibit employment discrimination based on gender, pregnancy, and sexual orientation. In addition, sexual harassment is also prohibited.

Sex Discrimination

Title VII prohibits employment discrimination based on gender. Although the prohibition against **sex discrimination** applies equally to men and women, the overwhelming majority of Title VII sex discrimination cases are brought by women. Sex discrimination cases are brought where there is direct sex discrimination and quid pro quo sex discrimination.

sex discrimination
Discrimination against a person solely because of his or her gender.

Pregnancy Discrimination

In 1978, the **Pregnancy Discrimination Act** was enacted as an amendment to Title VII.[6] This amendment forbids employment discrimination because of "pregnancy, childbirth, or related medical conditions."

Sexual Harassment

Sometimes managers and co-workers engage in conduct that is offensive because it is sexually charged. This is often referred to as sexual harassment. The U.S. Supreme Court has held that sexual harassment that creates a **hostile work environment** violates Title VII. Conduct such as making lewd remarks, touching, intimidation, posting of indecent materials, and other verbal or physical conduct of a sexual nature constitute **sexual harassment**.[7]

To determine what conduct creates a hostile work environment, the U.S. Supreme Court has stated:

We can say that whether an environment is "hostile" or "abusive" can be determined only by looking at all the circumstances. These may include the frequency of the discriminatory conduct; its severity; whether it is physically threatening or humiliating, or a mere offensive utterance; and whether it unreasonably interferes with an employee's work performance.[8]

In the following case, the U.S. Supreme Court decided a hostile work environment issue.

sexual harassment
Lewd remarks, touching, intimidation, posting of indecent materials, and other verbal or physical conduct of a sexual nature that occurs on the job.

U.S. SUPREME COURT　CASE 33.1　Sexual Harassment

Pennsylvania State Police v. Suders

542 U.S. 129, 124 S.Ct. 2342, 159 L.Ed.2d 204, Web 2004 U.S. Lexis 4176 (2004)
Supreme Court of the United States

"Essentially, Suders presents a 'worse case' harassment scenario, harassment ratcheted up to the breaking point."

—Justice Ginsburg

Facts

The Pennsylvania State Police (PSP) hired Nancy Drew Suders as a police communications operator for the McConnellsburg barracks. Suders's supervisors were Sergeant Eric D. Easton, station commander at the McConnellsburg barracks, Patrol Corporal William D. Baker, and Corporal Eric B. Prendergast. Those three supervisors subjected Suders to a continuous barrage of sexual harassment that ceased only when she resigned from the force. Easton would bring up the subject of people having sex with animals each time Suders entered his office. He told Prendergast, in front of Suders, that young girls should be given instruction in how to gratify men with oral sex. Easton also would sit down near Suders, wearing Spandex shorts, and spread his legs apart. Baker repeatedly made an obscene gesture in Suders's presence that involved grabbing his genitals and shouting out a vulgar comment inviting oral sex. Baker made this gesture as many as 5 to 10 times per night throughout Suders's employment at the barracks. Further, Baker would rub his rear end in front of her and remark "I have a nice ass, don't I?"

Five months after being hired, Suders contacted Virginia Smith-Elliot, PSP's equal opportunity officer, stating that she was being harassed at work and was afraid. Smith-Elliot's response appeared to Suders to be insensitive and unhelpful. Two days later, Suders resigned from the force. Suders sued PSP, alleging that she had been subject to sexual harassment and constructively discharged and forced to resign. The U.S. District Court held that although the evidence was sufficient for a jury to conclude that Suders's supervisors had engaged in sexual harassment, PSP was not vicariously liable for the supervisors' conduct. The U.S. District Court granted PSP's motion for summary judgment. The U.S. Court of Appeals reversed and remanded the case for trial on the merits against PSP. PSP appealed to the U.S. Supreme Court.

Issue

Can an employer be held vicariously liable when the sexual harassment conduct of its employees is so severe that the victim of the harassment resigns?

Language of the U.S. Supreme Court

To establish hostile work environment, plaintiffs like Suders must show harassing behavior sufficiently severe or pervasive to alter the conditions of their employment. The very fact that the discriminatory conduct was so severe or pervasive that it created a work environment abusive to employees because of their gender offends Title VII's broad rule of workplace equality. Beyond that, we hold, to establish "constructive discharge," the plaintiff must make a further showing: She must show that the abusive working environment became so intolerable that her resignation qualified as a fitting response. An employer may defend against such a claim by showing both (1) that it had installed a readily accessible and effective policy for reporting and resolving complaints of sexual harassment, and (2) that the plaintiff unreasonably failed to avail herself of that employer-provided preventive or remedial apparatus. This affirmative defense will not be available to the employer, however, if the plaintiff quits in reasonable response to an employer-sanctioned adverse action officially changing her employment status or situation, for example, a humiliating demotion, extreme cut in pay, or transfer to a position in which she would face unbearable working conditions.

Essentially, Suders presents a "worse case" harassment scenario, harassment ratcheted up to the breaking point. Harassment so intolerable as to cause a resignation may be effected through co-worker conduct, unofficial supervisory conduct, or official company acts. Unlike an actual termination, which is always effected through an official act of the company, a constructive discharge need not be. A constructive discharge involves both an employee's decision to leave and precipitating conduct.

Decision

The U.S. Supreme Court agreed with the U.S. Court of Appeals that Suders's case presented genuine issues of material fact concerning Suders's hostile work environment and constructive discharge claims. The Supreme Court remanded the case for further proceedings consistent with its opinion.

Case Questions

Critical Legal Thinking What is *vicarious liability*? What is *constructive discharge*? Explain.

Business Ethics Did Suders's supervisors act responsibly in this case?

Contemporary Business Do you think very much sexual harassment occurs in the workplace?

Same-Sex Discrimination

For years, it was unclear whether same-sex sexual harassment and **same-sex discrimination** in employment were actionable under Title VII. In 1998, in ***Omcale v. Sundowner Offshore Services, Incorporated***,[9] the U.S. Supreme Court held that same-sex harassment violated Title VII. Many state and local antidiscrimination laws outlaw same-sex discrimination and harassment in the workplace.

CONTEMPORARY ENVIRONMENT

Employer's Defense to a Charge of Sexual Harassment

In two cases, ***Faragher v. City of Boca Raton*** [524 U.S. 775, 118 S.Ct. 2275, 141 L.Ed.2d 662, **Web** 1998 U.S. Lexis 4216 (Supreme Court of the United States)] and ***Burlington Industries, Inc. v. Ellerth*** [524 U.S. 742, 118 S.Ct. 2257, 141 L.Ed.2d 633, **Web** 1998 U.S. Lexis 4217 (Supreme Court of the United States)], female plaintiffs sued their employers, proving that their supervisors had engaged in unconsented physical touching and verbal sexual harassment. In each case, the female employee quit her job and sued her employer for sexual harassment in violation of Title VII. In *Faragher*, the employer had never disseminated to its employees a policy against sexual harassment. The U.S. District Court held in favor of the female employee. In *Burlington Industries*, the employer had disseminated its policy against sexual harassment to its employees and had put into place a complaint system that the female employee did not use. In this case, the U.S. District Court granted summary judgment to the company. After appeals, the U.S. Supreme Court accepted these two cases for review.

The U.S. Supreme Court, in both of these decisions, held that an employer is not strictly liable for sexual harassment. The Supreme Court held that an employer may raise an **affirmative defense** against liability by proving two elements:

1. The employer exercised reasonable care to prevent, and promptly correct, any sexual harassing behavior.
2. The plaintiff employee unreasonably failed to take advantage of any preventive or corrective opportunities provided by the employer or to otherwise avoid harm.

The defendant employer has the burden of proving this affirmative defense. In determining whether the defense has been proven, a court must consider (1) whether the employer has an anti-harassment policy, (2) whether the employer had a complaint mechanism in place, (3) whether employees were informed of the anti-harassment policy and complaint procedure, and (4) other factors that the court deems relevant.

INTERNET LAW & ONLINE COMMERCE
E-Mails That Lead to Sexual Harassment

The use of e-mail in business has dramatically increased efficiency and information sharing among employees. Managers and workers alike can communicate with each other, send documents, and keep each other appraised of business developments. In many organizations, e-mail has replaced the telephone as the most-used method of communication, and it has eliminated the need for many meetings. This is a boon for business. But the downside is that e-mail has increased the exposure of businesses to sexual and racial harassment lawsuits.

E-mail often sets the social tone of an office and has been permitted to be slightly ribald. At some point, however, e-mail conduct becomes impermissible and crosses the line to actionable sexual or racial harassment. The standard of whether e-mail creates an illegal hostile work environment is the same as that for measuring harassment in any other context: The offensive conduct must be severe and cannot consist of isolated or trivial remarks and incidents. And, as in other harassment cases, an employer may raise a defense if it meets two required elements: (1) The employer exercised reasonable care to prevent and correct the behavior and (2) the plaintiff employee unreasonably failed to take advantage of any preventive or corrective opportunities provided by the employer or to avoid the harm.

E-mail harassment differs from many other incidents of harassment because it is subtle and insidious. Unlike paper pin-up calendars in plain view, an employer does not readily see e-mail messages. Obscenity pulled off the Internet or scanned into a computer can be sent as an attachment to an e-mail message. Because e-mail is hidden, to detect offensive messages, employers must take action to review e-mail messages on its network. Courts have generally held that an employee does not have an expectation of privacy of e-mail. Stored e-mail is the property of the employer, which may review it freely. Employers can also use software to scan and filter e-mail messages that contain any of a predefined list of objectionable words or phrases or certain "to" or "from" headers. Employers can also use software programs to scan graphics and block X-rated pictures.

E-mail has increased the possibility of sexual or racial harassment on the job, and it has also become a smoking gun that undermines a company's attempt to defend such cases. Therefore, employers must adopt policies pertaining to the use of e-mail by their employees and make their employees aware that certain e-mail messages constitute sexual or racial harassment and violate the law. Employers should make periodic inspections and audits of stored e-mail to ensure that employees are complying with company anti-harassment policies.

▶ RELIGIOUS DISCRIMINATION

religious discrimination
Discrimination against a person solely because of his or her religion or religious practices.

Title VII prohibits employment discrimination based on a person's religion. *Religions* in this case includes traditional religions, other religions that recognize a supreme being, and religions based on ethical or spiritual tenets. Many **religious discrimination** cases involve a conflict between an employer's work rule and an employee's religious beliefs (e.g., when an employee is required to work on his or her religious holiday).

The right of an employee to practice his or her religion is not absolute. Under Title VII, an employer is under a duty to *reasonably accommodate* the religious observances, practices, or beliefs of its employees if doing so does not cause an *undue hardship* on the employer. The courts must apply these general standards to specific fact situations. In making their decisions, the courts must consider such factors as the size of the employer, the importance of the employee's position, and the availability of alternative workers.

Title VII expressly permits religious organizations to give preference in employment to individuals of a particular religion. For example, if a person applies for a job with a religious organization but does not subscribe to its religious tenets, the organization may refuse to hire that person.

We hold these truths to be self-evident, that all men and women are created equal.

Elizabeth Cady Stanton
(1848)

▶ DEFENSES TO A TITLE VII ACTION

Title VII and case law recognize several defenses to a charge of discrimination under Title VII. These include merit, seniority, and bona fide occupational qualification (BFOQ). These defenses are discussed in the following paragraphs.

Merit

Employers can select or promote employees based on *merit*. Merit decisions are often based on work, educational experience, and professionally developed ability tests. To be lawful under Title VII, such a requirement must be job related.

Seniority

Many employers maintain *seniority* systems that reward long-term employees. Higher wages, fringe benefits, and other preferential treatment (e.g., choice of working hours and vacation schedule) are examples of such rewards. Seniority systems provide an incentive for employees to stay with the company. Such systems are lawful if they are not the result of intentional discrimination.

Bona Fide Occupational Qualification (BFOQ)

Discrimination based on protected classes (other than race or color) is permitted if it is shown to be a **bona fide occupational qualification (BFOQ)**. Thus, an employer can justify discrimination based on gender in some circumstances. To be legal, a BFOQ must be both *job related* and a *business necessity*.

As the following U.S. Supreme Court case shows, BFOQ exceptions are narrowly interpreted by the courts.

> **bona fide occupational qualification (BFOQ)**
> A true job qualification. Employment discrimination based on a protected class (other than race or color) is lawful if it is *job related* and a *business necessity*. This exception is narrowly interpreted by the courts.

U.S. SUPREME COURT   CASE 33.2 Bona Fide Occupational Qualification (BFOQ)

International Union, United Automobile, Aerospace and Agricultural Implement Workers of America, UAW v. Johnson Controls, Inc.

499 U.S. 187, 111 S.Ct. 1196, 113 L.Ed.2d 158, Web 1991 U.S. Lexis 1715 (1991)
Supreme Court of the United States

"**The bias in Johnson Controls' policy is obvious. Fertile men, but not fertile women, are given a choice as to whether they wish to risk their reproductive health for a particular job.**"

—Justice Blackmun

Facts

Johnson Controls, Inc. (Johnson Controls), manufactures batteries. Lead is the primary ingredient in the manufacturing process. Exposure to lead entails health risks, including risk of harm to a fetus carried by a female employee. To protect unborn children from such risk, Johnson Controls adopted an employment rule that prevented pregnant women and women of childbearing age from working at jobs involving lead exposure. Only women who were sterilized or could prove they could not have children were not affected by the rule. Consequently, most female employees were relegated to lower-paying clerical jobs at the company. Several female employees filed a class action suit, challenging Johnson Controls's fetal-protection policy as sex discrimination in violation of Title VII. The U.S. District Court held that the policy was justified as a bona fide occupational qualification (BFOQ) and granted

summary judgment to Johnson Controls; the U.S. Court of Appeals affirmed the judgment. The plaintiffs appealed to the U.S. Supreme Court.

Issue

Is Johnson Controls's fetal-protection policy a BFOQ?

Language of the U.S. Supreme Court

The bias in Johnson Controls' policy is obvious. Fertile men, but not fertile women, are given a choice as to whether they wish to risk their reproductive health for a particular job. Johnson Controls' fetal-protection policy explicitly discriminates against women on the basis of their sex. The policy excludes women with childbearing capacity from lead-exposed jobs and so creates a facial classification based on gender.

The bona fide occupational qualifications (BFOQ) defense is written narrowly, and this Court has read it narrowly. We have no difficulty concluding that Johnson Controls cannot establish a BFOQ. Fertile women, as far as appears in the record, participate in the manufacture of batteries as efficiently as anyone else. Johnson Controls' professed moral and ethical concerns about the welfare of the

(case continues)

next generation do not suffice to establish a BFOQ of female sterility. Decisions about the welfare of future children must be left to the parents who conceive, bear, support, and raise them rather than to the employers who hire those parents.

Decision

The U.S. Supreme Court held that Johnson Controls's fetal-protection policy was not a BFOQ. Instead, it was sex discrimination in violation of Title VII. The Supreme Court reversed the decision of the U.S. Court of Appeals and remanded the case for further proceedings.

Case Questions

Critical Legal Thinking What is a BFOQ? Should a BFOQ exception to Title VII liability be permitted? Why or why not?

Business Ethics Did Johnson Controls's concerns about the safety and welfare of the next generation justify its actions?

Contemporary Business Does Johnson Controls have any tort liability to children who are born injured by exposure to lead? Explain.

CONCEPT SUMMARY

TITLE VII OF THE CIVIL RIGHTS ACT

Covered employers and employment decisions	1. **Employers.** Employers with 15 or more employees for 20 weeks in the current or preceding year, all employment agencies, labor unions with 15 or more members, state and local governments and their agencies and most federal government employment.
	2. **Employment decisions.** Decisions regarding hiring; promotion; demotion; payment of salaries, wages, and fringe benefits; dismissal; job training and apprenticeships; work rules; or any other term, condition, or privilege of employment. Decisions to admit partners to a partnership are also covered.
Protected classes	1. **Race.** A broad class of individuals with common characteristics (e.g., African American, Caucasian, Asian, Native American).
	2. **Color.** The color of a person's skin (e.g., light-skinned person, dark-skinned person).
	3. **National origin.** A person's country of origin or national heritage (e.g., Italian, Hispanic).
	4. **Sex.** A person's sex, whether male or female. Includes sexual harassment and discrimination against females who are pregnant.
	5. **Religion.** A person's religious beliefs. An employer has a duty to reasonably accommodate an employee's religious beliefs if doing so does not cause an undue hardship on the employer.
Types of discrimination	1. **Disparate-treatment discrimination.** Discrimination against a specific individual because that person belongs to a protected class.
	2. **Disparate-impact discrimination.** Discrimination in which an employer discriminates against a protected class. A neutral-looking employment rule that causes discrimination against a protected class is disparate-impact discrimination.
Defenses	1. **Merit.** Job-related experience, education, or unbiased ability test.
	2. **Seniority.** Length of time an employee has been employed by the employer. Intentional discrimination based on seniority is unlawful.
	3. **Bona fide occupational qualification (BFOQ).** Discrimination based on sex, religion, or national origin is permitted if it is a valid BFOQ for the position. Qualification based on race or color is not a permissible BFOQ.
Remedies	1. **Equitable remedy.** The court may order the payment of back pay, issue an injunction awarding reinstatement, grant fictional seniority, or order some other equitable remedy.
	2. **Damages.** The court can award compensatory damages in cases of intentional discrimination. The court can award punitive damages in cases involving an employer's malice or reckless indifference to federally protected rights.

LANDMARK LAW

Civil Rights Act of 1866

The **Civil Rights Act of 1866** was enacted after the Civil War. **Section 1981** of this act states that all persons "have the same right . . . to make and enforce contracts . . . as is enjoyed by white persons" [42 U.S.C. Section 1981]. This law was enacted to give African Americans, just freed from slavery, the same right to contract as whites. Section 1981 expressly prohibits racial discrimination; it has also been held to forbid discrimination based on national origin.

Employment decisions are covered by Section 1981 because the employment relationship is contractual. Although most racial and national origin employment discrimination cases are brought under Title VII, there are two reasons that a complainant would bring an action under Section 1981: (1) A private plaintiff can bring an action without going through the procedural requirements of Title VII, and (2) there is no cap on the recovery of compensatory or punitive damages under Section 1981.

▶ EQUAL PAY ACT

Discrimination often takes the form of different pay scales for men and women performing the same job. The **Equal Pay Act** of 1963 protects both sexes from pay discrimination based on sex.[10] This act covers all levels of private-sector employees and state and local government employees. Federal workers are not covered, however.

The act prohibits disparity in pay for jobs that require *equal skill* (i.e., equal experience), *equal effort* (i.e., mental and physical exertion), *equal responsibility* (i.e., equal supervision and accountability), or *similar working conditions* (e.g., dangers of injury, exposure to the elements). To make this determination, the courts examine the actual requirements of jobs to determine whether they are equal and similar. If two jobs are determined to be equal and similar, an employer cannot pay disparate wages to members of different sexes.

Employees can bring a private cause of action against an employer for violating the Equal Pay Act. Back pay and liquidated damages are recoverable. In addition, the employer must increase the wages of the discriminated-against employee to eliminate the unlawful disparity of wages. The wages of other employees may not be lowered.

Criteria That Justify a Differential in Wages

The Equal Pay Act expressly provides four criteria that justify a differential in wages. These defenses include payment systems that are based on:

- Seniority
- Merit (as long as there is some identifiable measurement standard)
- Quantity or quality of product (commission, piecework, or quality-control–based payment systems are permitted)
- "Any factor other than sex" (including shift differentials, i.e., night versus day shifts)

The employer bears the burden of proving these defenses.

▶ AGE DISCRIMINATION IN EMPLOYMENT ACT

Some employers have discriminated against employees and prospective employees based on their age. Primarily, employers have often refused to hire older workers. The **Age Discrimination in Employment Act (ADEA)**, which prohibits certain *age discrimination* practices, was enacted in 1967.[11]

The ADEA covers nonfederal employers with at least 20 employees, labor unions with at least 25 members, and all employment agencies. State and local government employees except those in policy-making positions are covered, as are employees of certain sectors of the federal government.

Civil Rights Act of 1866
A federal statute enacted after the Civil War that says all persons "have the same right . . . to make and enforce contracts . . . as is enjoyed by white persons." It prohibits racial and national origin employment discrimination.

Equal Pay Act
A federal statute that protects both sexes from pay discrimination based on sex. It extends to jobs that require equal skill, equal effort, equal responsibility, and similar working conditions.

Legislation to apply the principle of equal pay for equal work without discrimination because of sex is a matter of simple justice.

Dwight D. Eisenhower

Age Discrimination in Employment Act (ADEA) of 1967
A federal statute that prohibits age discrimination practices against employees who are 40 and older.

Older Workers Benefit Protection Act (OWBPA)
A federal statute that prohibits age discrimination in employee benefits.

By what justice can an association of citizens be held together when there is no equality among the citizens?

Cicero
De Re Publia De Legibus, I, xxxii, 49

Americans with Disabilities Act (ADA)
A federal statute that imposes obligations on employers and providers of public transportation, telecommunications, and public accommodations to accommodate individuals with disabilities.

Title I of the ADA
A title of a federal statute that prohibits employment discrimination against qualified individuals with disabilities in regard to job application procedures, hiring, compensation, training, promotion, and termination.

The ADEA prohibits age discrimination in all employment decisions, including hiring, promotions, payment of compensation, and other terms and conditions of employment. The **Older Workers Benefit Protection Act (OWBPA)** amended the ADEA to prohibit age discrimination with regard to employee benefits. Employers cannot use employment advertisements that discriminate against applicants covered by the ADEA.

Protected Age Categories

Originally, the ADEA prohibited employment discrimination against persons between the ages of 40 and 65. Later, its coverage was extended to persons up to age 70. Further amendments completely eliminated an age ceiling, so the ADEA now applies to employees who are 40 and older. As a result, covered employers cannot establish mandatory retirement ages for their employees.

Because persons under 40 are not protected by the ADEA, an employer can maintain an employment policy of hiring only workers who are 40 years of age or older without violating the ADEA. However, an employer cannot maintain an employment practice whereby it hires only persons 50 years of age and older because that would discriminate against persons aged 40 to 49.

The ADEA is administered by the EEOC. Private plaintiffs can also sue under the ADEA. A successful plaintiff in an ADEA action can recover back wages, attorneys' fees, and equitable relief, including hiring, reinstatement, and promotion. Where a violation of the ADEA is found, the employer must raise the wages of the discriminated-against employee. It cannot lower the wages of other employees.

▶ AMERICANS WITH DISABILITIES ACT

The **Americans with Disabilities Act (ADA),**[12] which was signed into law July 26, 1990, is the most comprehensive piece of civil rights legislation since the Civil Rights Act of 1964. The ADA imposes obligations on employers and providers of public transportation, telecommunications, and public accommodations to accommodate individuals with disabilities.

LANDMARK LAW
Americans with Disabilities Act

Title I of the ADA prohibits employment discrimination against qualified individuals with disabilities in regard to job application procedures, hiring, compensation, training, promotion, and termination. Title I covers employers with 15 or more employees. The United States, corporations wholly owned by the United States, and bona fide tax-exempt private membership clubs are exempt from Title I coverage.

Title I requires an employer to make reasonable accommodations to individuals with disabilities that do not cause undue hardship to the employer. **Reasonable accommodations** may include making facilities readily accessible to individuals with disabilities, providing part-time or modified work schedules, acquiring equipment or devices, modifying examination and training materials, and providing qualified readers or interpreters.

Employers are not obligated to provide accommodations that would impose an **undue burden**—that is, actions that would require significant difficulty or expense. The EEOC and the courts consider factors such as the nature and cost of accommodation, the overall financial resources of the employer, and the employer's type of operation. Obviously, what may be a significant difficulty or expense for a small employer may not be an undue hardship for a large employer.

---

qualified individual with a disability
A person who (1) has a physical or mental impairment that substantially limits one or more of his or her major life activities, (2) has a record of such impairment, or (3) is regarded as having such impairment.

Qualified Individual with a Disability

A **qualified individual with a disability** is a person who, with or without reasonable accommodation, can perform the essential functions of the job that person desires or holds. A disabled person is someone who (1) has a physical or mental impairment that substantially limits one or more of his or her major life activities, (2) has a record of such impairment, or (3) is regarded as having such impairment. Mental retardation, paraplegia, schizophrenia, cerebral palsy, epilepsy, diabetes, muscular dystrophy, multiple sclerosis, cancer, infection with HIV (human immunodeficiency virus), and visual, speech, and hearing impairments are covered under the ADA. A current user of illegal drugs or an alcoholic who uses alcohol or is under the influence of alcohol at the workplace is not covered. However, recovering alcoholics and former users of illegal drugs are protected.

Forbidden Conduct

Title I of the ADA limits an employer's ability to inquire into or test for an applicant's disabilities. Title I forbids an employer from asking a job applicant about the existence, nature, and severity of a disability. An employer may, however, inquire about the applicant's ability to perform job-related functions. Preemployment medical examinations are forbidden before a job offer. Once a job offer has been made, an employer may require a medical examination and may condition the offer on the examination results, as long as all entering employees are subject to such an examination. The information obtained must be kept confidential.

Procedure and Remedies

Title I of the ADA is administered by the EEOC. An aggrieved individual must first file a charge with the EEOC, which may take action against the employer or permit the individual to pursue a private cause of action. Relief can take the form of an injunction, hiring or reinstatement (with back pay), payment of attorneys' fees, and recovery of compensatory and punitive damages (subject to the same caps as Title VII damages).

All about me may be silence and darkness, yet within me, in the spirit, is music and brightness, and color flashes through all my thoughts.

Helen Keller
The Open Door (1957)

affirmative action
A policy which provides that certain job preferences will be given to minority or other protected-class applicants when an employer makes an employment decision.

reverse discrimination
Discrimination against a group that is usually thought of as a majority.

CONTEMPORARY ENVIRONMENT

Affirmative Action

Title VII of the Civil Rights Act of 1964 outlawed discrimination in employment based on race, color, national origin, sex, and religion. The law clearly prohibited any further discrimination based upon these protected classes. However, did the federal statute intend to grant a favorable status to the classes of persons who had been previously discriminated against? In a series of cases, the U.S. Supreme Court upheld the use of affirmative action programs to make up for egregious past discrimination, particularly based on race.

Affirmative Action Plans
Employers often adopt **affirmative action** plans, which provide that certain job preferences will be given to members of minority racial and ethnic groups, females, and other protected-class applicant when an employer makes an employment decision. Such plans can be voluntarily adopted by employers, undertaken to settle a discrimination action, or ordered by the courts.

To be lawful, an affirmative action plan must be *narrowly tailored* to achieve some *compelling interest*. Employment quotas based on a specified number or percentage of minority applicants or employees are unlawful. If a person's minority status is only one factor of many factors considered in an employment decision, that decision will usually be considered lawful.

Reverse Discrimination
Title VII not only applies to members of minority groups but also protects members of majority classes from discrimination. Lawful affirmative action plans have an effect on members of majority classes. The courts have held that if an affirmative action plan is based on preestablished numbers or percentage quotas for hiring or promoting minority applicants, then it causes illegal **reverse discrimination**. In this case, the members of the majority class may sue under Title VII and recover damages and other remedies for reverse discrimination. Some reverse discrimination cases are successful.

▶ RETALIATION

Title VII of the Civil Rights Act of 1964 expressly prohibits employers from **retaliating** against an employee for filing a charge of discrimination or participating in a discrimination proceeding regarding race, color, national origin, sex, or religious discrimination. Acts of retaliation are also forbidden for bringing and maintaining charges of age discrimina-

Rights Act of 1866. Acts of retaliation include dismissing, demoting, harassing, or other methods of retaliation.

South Korea *The United States and South Korea are signatories to the U.S.–South Korea Friendship, Commerce and Navigation Treaty. One provision of this treaty permits Korean corporations operating in the United States to select and promote executives "of their choice." This treaty is criticized because it permits South Korean companies operating in the United States to discriminate against females in the selection and promotion of executives.*

TEST REVIEW TERMS AND CONCEPTS

Affirmative action
Affirmative defense
Age Discrimination in
  Employment Act
  (ADEA)
Americans with Disabilities
  Act
Bona fide occupation
  qualification (BFOQ)
*Burlington Industries, Inc. v.
  Ellerth*
Civil Rights Act of 1866
Civil Rights Act of 1964
Color discrimination
Discrimination
Disparate-impact
  discrimination

Disparate-treatment
  discrimination
Equal employment
  opportunity
Equal Employment
  Opportunity Act of 1972
Equal Employment
  Opportunity
  Commission (EEOC)
Equal opportunity in
  employment
Equal Pay Act
E-RACE Initiative
Faragher v. City of Boca Raton
Hostile work environment
National origin or heritage
  discrimination

Older Workers Benefit
  Protection Act
  (OWBPA)
*Omcale v. Sundowner
  Offshore Services,
  Incorporated*
Pregnancy Discrimination
  Act
Punitive damages
Qualified individual with a
  disability
Race discrimination
Reasonable
  accommodations
Religious discrimination
Retaliating
Reverse discrimination

Right to sue letter
Same-sex discrimination
Section 1981 of the Civil
  Rights Act of 1866
Sex discrimination
Sexual harassment
Title I of the ADA
Title VII of the Civil
  Rights Act of 1964 (Fair
  Employment Practices
  Act)
Undue burden

CASE PROBLEMS

33.1 Equal Pay Act   For years, New York law prevented females from working at night. Therefore, Corning Glass Works employed male workers for night inspection jobs and female workers for day inspection jobs. Males working the night shift were paid higher wages than were females who worked the day shift. When the federal Equal Pay Act was enacted, Corning began hiring females for night shift jobs, but it instituted a "red circle" wage rate that permitted previously hired male night shift workers to continue to receive higher wages than newly hired night shift workers. Does this violate the Equal Pay Act? *Corning Glass Works v. Brennan, Secretary of Labor*, 417 U.S. 188, 94 S.Ct. 2223,

41 L.Ed.2d 1, **Web** 1974 U.S. Lexis 62 (Supreme Court of the United States)

33.2 Sex Discrimination   The Los Angeles Department of Water and Power maintains a pension plan for its employees that is funded by both employer and employee contributions. The plan pays men and women retirees' pensions with the same monthly benefits. However, because statistically women live, on average, several years longer than men, female employees are required to make monthly contributions to the pension fund that are 14.84 percent higher than the contributions required of male employees. Because employee contributions are withheld from paychecks, a female employee takes home less pay than a male employee earning the same salary. Does this practice violate Title VII? *City of Los Angeles Department of Water and Power v. Manhart*, 435 U.S. 702, 98 S.Ct. 1370, 55 L.Ed.2d 657, **Web** 1978 U.S. Lexis 23 (Supreme Court of the United States)

33.3 Hostile Work Environment   Shirley Huddleston became the first female sales representative of Roger Dean Chevrolet, Inc. (RDC), in West Palm Beach, Florida. Shortly after she began working at RDC, Philip Geraci, a fellow sales representative, and other male employees began making derogatory comments to and about her, expelled gas in her presence, and called her derogatory names. Many of these remarks were made in front of customers. The sales manager of RDC participated in the harassment. On several occasions, Huddleston complained about this conduct to RDC's general manager. Was Title VII violated? Who wins? *Huddleston v. Roger Dean Chevrolet, Inc.*, 845 F.2d 900, **Web** 1988 U.S. App. Lexis 6823 (United States Court of Appeals for the Eleventh Circuit)

33.4 National Origin Discrimination   The Federal Bureau of Investigation (FBI) engaged in a pattern and practice of discrimination against Hispanic FBI agents. Job assignments and promotions were areas that were especially affected. Bernardo M. Perez, a Hispanic, brought a Title VII action against the FBI. Did the FBI violate Title VII? Who wins? *Perez v. Federal Bureau of Investigation*, 714 F.Supp. 1414, **Web** 1989 U.S. Dist. Lexis 8426 (United States District Court for the Western District of Texas)

33.5 Religious Discrimination   Trans World Airlines (TWA), an airline, operated a large maintenance and overhaul base for its airplanes in Kansas City, Missouri. Because of its essential role, the stores department at the base operated 24 hours per day, 365 days per year. The employees at the base were represented by the International Association of Machinists and Aerospace Workers (Union). TWA and Union entered into a collective bargaining agreement that included a seniority system for the assignment of jobs and shifts.

TWA hired Larry Hardison to work as a clerk in the stores department. Soon after beginning work, Hardison joined the Worldwide Church of God, which does not allow its members to work from sunset on Friday until sunset on Saturday and on certain religious holidays. Hardison, who had the second lowest seniority within the stores department, did not have enough seniority to observe his Sabbath regularly. When Hardison asked for special consideration, TWA offered to allow him to take his Sabbath off if he could switch shifts with another employee-union member. None of the other employees would do so. TWA refused Hardison's request for a four-day workweek because it would have had to either hire and train a part-time worker to work on Saturdays or incur the cost of paying overtime to an existing full-time worker on Saturdays. Hardison sued TWA for religious discrimination in violation of Title VII. Did TWA's actions violate Title VII? Who wins? *Trans World Airlines v. Hardison*, 432 U.S. 63, 97 S.Ct. 2264, 53 L.Ed.2d 113, **Web** 1977 U.S. Lexis 115 (Supreme Court of the United States)

33.6 Bona Fide Occupational Qualification   At age 60, Manuel Fragante emigrated from the Philippines to Hawaii. In response to a newspaper ad, Fragante applied for an entry-level civil service clerk job with the City of Honolulu's Division of Motor Vehicles and Licensing. The job required constant oral communication with the public, either at the information counter or on the telephone. Fragante scored the highest of 731 test takers on a written examination that tested word usage, grammar, and spelling. As part of the application process, two civil service employees who were familiar with the demands of the position interviewed Fragante. They testified that his accent made it difficult to understand him. Fragante was not hired for the position, which was filled by another applicant. Fragante sued, alleging national origin discrimination in violation of Title VII. Who wins? *Fragante v. City and County of Honolulu*, 888 F.2d 591, **Web** 1989 U.S. App. Lexis 2636 (United States Court of Appeals for the Ninth Circuit)

33.7 Age Discrimination   Walker Boyd Fite was an employee of First Tennessee Production Credit Association for 19 years. He had attained the position of vice president–credit. During the course of his employment, he had never received an unsatisfactory review. On December 26, 1983, at age 57, Fite was hospitalized with a kidney stone. On January 5, 1984, while Fite was recovering at home, an officer of First Tennessee called to inform him that he had been retired as of December 31, 1983. A few days later, Fite received a letter stating that he had been retired because of poor job performance. Fite sued First Tennessee for age discrimination. Who wins? *Fite v. First Tennessee Production Credit Association*, 861 F.2d 884, **Web** 1988 U.S. App. Lexis 14759 (United States Court of Appeals for the Sixth Circuit)

BUSINESS ETHICS CASES

33.8 Business Ethics   Dianne Rawlinson, 22 years old, was a college graduate whose major course of study was correctional psychology. After graduation, she applied for a position as a correctional counselor (prison guard) with the Alabama Board of Corrections. Her application was rejected because she failed to meet the minimum 120-pound weight requirement of an Alabama statute that also established a height minimum of 5 feet 2 inches. In addition, the Alabama Board of Corrections adopted Administrative Regulation 204, which established gender criteria for assigning correctional counselors to maximum-security prisons for "contact positions." These are correctional counselor positions that require continual close physical proximity to inmates. Under this rule, Rawlinson did not qualify for contact positions with male prisoners in Alabama maximum-security prisons. Rawlinson brought a class action lawsuit against Dothard, who was the director of the Department of Public Safety of Alabama. Does either the height–weight requirement or the contact position rule consti-

tute a bona fide occupational qualification that justifies the sex discrimination in this case? Does society owe a duty of social responsibility to protect women from dangerous job positions? Or is this "romantic paternalism"? *Dothard, Director, Department of Public Safety of Alabama v. Rawlinson*, 433 U.S. 321, 97 S.Ct. 2720, 53 L.Ed.2d 786, **Web** 1977 U.S. Lexis 143 (Supreme Court of the United States)

33.9 Business Ethics   Rita Machakos, a white female, worked for the Civil Rights Division (CRD) of the Department of Justice. During her employment, she was denied promotion to certain paralegal positions. In each instance, the individual selected was a black female. Evidence showed that the CRD maintained an institutional and systematic discrimination policy that favored minority employees over white employees. Machakos sued the CRD for race discrimination under Title VII. Who wins? *Machakos v. Attorney General of the United States*, 859 F.2d 1487, **Web** 1988 U.S. App. Lexis 14672 (United States Court of Appeals for the District of Columbia Circuit)

ENDNOTES

1. 42 U.S.C. Sections 2000e–2000e-17.
2. *Equal Employment Opportunity Commission v. Tortilleria "La Mejor,"* 758 F.Supp. 585, **Web** 1991 U.S. Dist. Lexis 5754 (United States District Court for the Eastern District of California).
3. *McDonnell Douglas v. Green*, 411 U.S. 792, 93 S.Ct. 1817, 36 L.Ed.2d 668, **Web** 1973 U.S. Lexis154 (Supreme Court of the United States).
4. In some states, the complaint must be filed with the appropriate state agency rather than the EEOC.
5. *Ledbetter v. The Goodyear Tire & Rubber Company, Inc.*, 127 S.Ct. 2162, 167 L.Ed.2d 982, **Web** 2007 U.S. Lexis 6295 (Supreme Court of the United States).
6. 42 U.S.C. Section 2000e(K).
7. *Meritor Savings Bank v. Vinson,* 477 U.S. 57, 106 S.Ct. 2399, 91 L.Ed.2d 49, **Web** 1986 U.S. Lexis 108 (Supreme Court of the United States).
8. *Harris v. Forklift Systems, Inc.*, 510 U.S. 17, 114 S.Ct. 367, 126 L.Ed.2d 295, **Web** 1993 U.S. Lexis 7155 (Supreme Court of the United States).
9. 523 U.S. 75, 118 S.Ct. 998, 140 L.Ed.2d 201, **Web** 1998 U.S. Lexis 1599 (Supreme Court of the United States).
10. 29 U.S.C. Section 206(d).
11. 29 U.S.C. Sections 621–634.
12. 42 U.S.C. Section 12102–12118.

Part VIII
BUSINESS
ORGANIZATIONS
AND ETHICS

34 | SMALL BUSINESSES, ENTREPRENEURS, AND GENERAL PARTNERSHIPS

▲ **Pantry Restaurant, Los Angeles, California** *Small businesses account for the majority of businesses in the United States. The Pantry Restaurant in downtown Los Angeles has been open since 1924—'round the clock—including Thanksgiving and Christmas.*

CHAPTER OBJECTIVES

After studying this chapter, you should be able to:

1. Define *sole proprietorship*.
2. Describe the liability of a sole proprietor.
3. Define *general partnership* and describe how general partnerships are formed.

4. Explain the contract and tort liability of partners.
5. Describe how a partnership is dissolved and terminated.

CHAPTER CONTENTS

"One of the most fruitful sources of ruin to a man of the world is the recklessness or want of principle of partners, and it is one of the perils to which every man exposes himself who enters into a partnership."

—Vice Chancellor Malins
Mackay v. Douglas, 14 Eq. 106 at 118 (1872)

▶ INTRODUCTION TO SMALL BUSINESSES, ENTREPRENEURS, AND GENERAL PARTNERSHIPS

A person who wants to start a business must decide whether the business should operate as one of the major forms of business organization—*sole proprietorship, general partnership, limited partnership, limited liability partnerships, limited liability company,* and *corporation*— or under other available legal business forms. The selection depends on many factors, including the ease and cost of formation, the capital requirements of the business, the flexibility of management decisions, government restrictions, personal liability, tax considerations, and the like.

This chapter discusses **entrepreneurship**, sole proprietorship and general partnership. Limited partnership, corporation, limited liability company, limited liability partnership, franchise, and other forms of business are discussed in following chapters.

▶ ENTREPRENEURSHIP

An **entrepreneur** is a person who forms and operates a business. An entrepreneur may start a business by him- or herself or cofound a business with others. Most businesses started by entrepreneurs are small, although some grow into substantial organizations. For example, Bill Gates started Microsoft Corporation, which grew into the giant software and Internet company. Michael Dell started Dell Computers as a mail-order business; it has become a leader in computer sales. Every day, entrepreneurs in this country and elsewhere around the world create new businesses that hire employees, provide new products and services, and contribute to the growth of economies of countries.

entrepreneur

A person who forms and operates a new business either by himself or herself or with others.

Entrepreneurial Forms of Conducting Business

Entrepreneurs contemplating starting a business have many options when choosing the legal form in which to conduct the business. Each of these forms of business has advantages and disadvantages for the entrepreneurs. The major forms for conducting businesses and professions are:

It is when merchants dispute about their own rules that they invoke the law.

Judge Brett
Robinson v. Mollett (1875)

- Sole proprietorship
- General partnership
- Limited partnership
- Limited liability partnership
- Limited liability company
- Corporation

Certain requirements must be met to form and operate each of these forms of business. These requirements are discussed in this chapter and the other chapters of this Unit that follow.

CONTEMPORARY ENVIRONMENT

Entrepreneurship: The Founding of Facebook

In 2004, Facebook was launched from a dorm room at Harvard University. Facebook was the brainchild of Mark Zuckerberg, a Harvard student, computer science major Andrew McCollum, and roommates Dustin Moskovitz and Chris Hughes. At first Facebook became successful at Harvard University, with two-thirds of its students signing up in the first several weeks. The program was then spread to Stanford, Yale, and Columbia, and then to other universities.

The online social networking website became an instant success with the college crowd, and within a year, it had spread to thousands of campuses. Facebook then became popular among others, including high school students, geographical networks, and most other young people. Facebook allows a user to create a profile and post messages and photos for their friends to view—all for free. With more than 80 million users worldwide, Facebook has become the most popular website for uploading photos. More than one-half of its users return to it daily.

Facebook provides a limited and closed network. Membership can be gained only by entering an e-mail address; in addition, only individuals specifically tagged as friends are allowed to see that person's profile. Thus, Facebook is a "walled garden" in which users can post pictures and text, knowing that the general public—parents, teachers, employers, potential employers—cannot view the content. This creates a sense of privacy and has distinguished Facebook from other social networks, such as MySpace, that allow users to communicate more freely. However, most users do not realize that this "wall" does not include Facebook itself. The Facebook licensing agreement gives Facebook royalty-free, perpetual, and irrevocable rights to the content posted by the users.

In 2004, Zuckerberg's Harvard classmates Divya Narendra, Cameron Winklevoss, and Tyler Winklevoss filed a lawsuit against him. They claimed that they hired Zuckerberg to finish the source code for their website, ConnectU, and that he stole their idea and source code. Their lawsuit asserted breach of contract, misappropriation of trade secrets, and copyright infringement, and the plaintiffs sought monetary damages. Zuckerberg denied their claims. A California judge has approved the settlement of the claims.

Mark Zuckerberg, the mythic entrepreneur, has been dubbed the youngest Internet billionaire. Facebook now offers one of the most lucrative venues for advertising on the Internet, and it has drawn the interest of several potential buyers.

▶ SOLE PROPRIETORSHIP

sole proprietorship
A form of business in which the owner is actually the business; the business is not a separate legal entity.

A **sole proprietorship** is the simplest form of business organization. The owner of the business, the **sole proprietor**, is the business. There is no separate legal entity. Sole proprietorships are the most common form of business organization in the United States. Many small businesses—and a few large ones—operate in this way.

There are several major advantages to operating a business as a sole proprietorship. They include the following:

- Forming a sole proprietorship is easy and does not cost a lot.
- The owner has the right to make all management decisions concerning the business, including those involving hiring and firing employees.
- The sole proprietor owns all of the business and has the right to receive all of the business's profits.
- A sole proprietorship can be easily transferred or sold if and when the owner desires to do so; no other approval (such as from partners or shareholders) is necessary.

There are important disadvantages to this business form, too. For example, the sole proprietor's access to the capital is limited to personal funds plus any loans he or she can obtain, and the sole proprietor is legally responsible for the business's contracts and the torts he or she or any of his or her employees commit in the course of employment.

Creation of a Sole Proprietorship

The merchant has no country.

Thomas Jefferson

Creating a sole proprietorship is easy. There are no formalities, and no federal or state government approval is required. Some local governments require all businesses, including sole proprietorships, to obtain licenses to do business within the city. If no other form of business organization is chosen, the business is by default a sole proprietorship.

CONTEMPORARY ENVIRONMENT
d.b.a.—"Doing Business As"

A sole proprietorship can operate under the name of the sole proprietor or a **trade name**. For example, the author of this book can operate a sole proprietorship under the name "Henry R. Cheeseman" or under a trade name such as "The Big Cheese." Operating under a trade name is commonly designated as **d.b.a. (doing business as)** (e.g., Henry R. Cheeseman, doing business as "The Big Cheese").

Most states require all businesses that operate under a trade name to file a **fictitious business name statement** (or **certificate of trade name**) with the appropriate

government agency. The statement must contain the name and address of the applicant, the trade name, and the address of the business. Most states also require notice of the trade name to be published in a newspaper of general circulation serving the area in which the applicant does business.

These requirements are intended to disclose the real owner's name to the public. Noncompliance can result in a fine. Some states prohibit violators from maintaining lawsuits in the state's courts.

Personal Liability of Sole Proprietors

A sole proprietor bears the risk of loss of the business; that is, the owner will lose his or her entire capital contribution if the business fails. In addition, the sole proprietor has **unlimited personal liability** (see Exhibit 34.1). Therefore, creditors may recover claims against the business from the sole proprietor's personal assets (e.g., home, automobile, bank accounts).

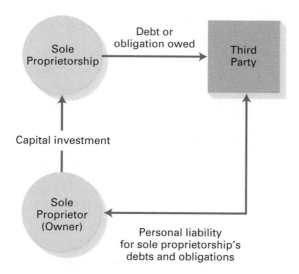

▶ **Exhibit 34.1 SOLE PROPRIETORSHIP**

Example Nathan opens a clothing store called "The Clothing Store" and operates it as a sole proprietorship. Nathan files the proper statement and publishes the necessary notice of the use of the trade name. Nathan contributes $25,000 of his personal funds to the business and borrows $100,000 from a bank in the name of the business. Assume that after several months, Nathan closes the business because it is unsuccessful. At the time it is closed, the business has no assets, owes the bank $100,000, and owes rent, trade credit, and other debits of $25,000. Here, Nathan, the sole proprietor, is personally liable to pay the bank and all the debts of the sole proprietorship from his personal assets.

In the following case, the court had to decide the liability of a sole proprietor.

CASE 34.1   Sole Proprietorship

Vernon v. Schuster, d/b/a Diversity Heating and Plumbing

179 Ill.2d 338, 688 N.E.2d 1172, Web 1997 Ill. Lexis 482 (1997)
Supreme Court of Illinois

"It is well settled that a sole proprietorship has no legal identity separate from that of the individual who owns it."

—Judge Freeman

Facts

James Schuster was a sole proprietor doing business as (d.b.a.) "Diversity Heating and Plumbing." Diversity Heating was in the business of selling, installing, and servicing heating and plumbing systems. George Vernon and others (Vernon) owned a building that needed a new boiler. Vernon hired Diversity Heating to install a new boiler in the building. Diversity Heating installed the boiler and gave a warranty that the boiler would not crack for 10 years. Four years later, James Schuster died. On that date, James's son, Jerry Schuster, inherited his father's business and thereafter ran the business as a sole proprietorship under the d.b.a "Diversity Heating and Plumbing." One year later, the boiler installed in Vernon's building broke and could not be repaired. Vernon demanded that Jerry Schuster honor the warranty and replace the boiler. When Jerry Schuster refused to do so, Vernon had the boiler replaced at a cost of $8,203 and sued Jerry Schuster to recover this amount for breach of warranty. The trial court dismissed Vernon's complaint, but the appellate court reinstated the case. Jerry Schuster appealed to the supreme court of Illinois.

Issue

Is Jerry Schuster liable for the warranty made by his father?

Language of the Court

> *Common identity of ownership is lacking when one sole proprietorship succeeds another. It is well settled that a sole proprietorship has no legal identity separate from that of the individual who owns it. The sole proprietor may do business under a fictitious name if he or she chooses.*

> *However, doing business under another name does not create an entity distinct from the person operating the business. The individual who does business as a sole proprietor under one or several names remains one person, personally liable for all his or her obligations. There is generally no continuity of existence because on the death of the sole proprietor, the sole proprietorship obviously ends.*

> *In this case, therefore, it must be remembered that "Diversity Heating" has no legal existence. Diversity Heating was only a pseudonym for James Schuster. Once he died, Diversity Heating ceased to exist. Now, Diversity Heating is only a pseudonym for the defendant, Jerry Schuster. Once sole proprietor James Schuster died, he could not be the same sole proprietor as defendant Jerry Schuster who became a sole proprietor after his father's death. James Schuster and Jerry Schuster, one succeeding the other, cannot be the same entity. Even though defendant Jerry Schuster inherited Diversity Heating from his father, defendant would not have continued his father's sole proprietorship, but rather would have started a new sole proprietorship.*

Decision

The Illinois supreme court held that Jerry Schuster, as a sole proprietor, was not liable for the warranty previously made by his father, who was also a sole proprietor. The supreme court reversed the decision of the appellate court.

Case Questions

Critical Legal Thinking Is a sole proprietorship a separate legal entity? Explain.

Business Ethics Did Jerry Schuster act unethically by failing to honor the warranty made by his father?

Contemporary Business What are the benefits and detriments of operating a sole proprietorship?

Taxation of a Sole Proprietorship

A sole proprietorship is not a separate legal entity, so it does not pay taxes at the business level. Instead, the earnings and losses from a sole proprietorship are reported on the sole proprietor's personal income tax filing. A sole proprietorship business earns income and pays expenses during the course of operating the business. A sole proprietor has to file tax returns and pay taxes to state and federal governments. For federal income tax purposes, a sole proprietor must prepare a personal income tax **Form 1040 U.S. Individual Income Tax Return** and report the income or loss from the sole proprietorship on his or her personal income tax form. The income or loss from the sole proprietorship is reported on **Schedule C (Profit or Loss from Business)**, which must be attached to the taxpayer's Form 1040.

Small Business *Many sole proprietorships are successful and provide their owners with the opportunity to make money, be their own boss, and build up a business they are proud of that supports them and their families. Sole proprietorships make up "small town" America and also account for many of the businesses in urban areas.*

▶ GENERAL PARTNERSHIP

General partnership, or **ordinary partnership**, has been recognized since ancient times. The English common law of partnerships governed early U.S. partnerships. The individual states expanded the body of partnership law.

A general partnership, or partnership, is a voluntary association of two or more persons for carrying on a business as co-owners for profit. The formation of a partnership creates certain rights and duties among partners and with third parties. These rights and duties are established in the partnership agreement and by law. **General partners**, or **partners**, are personally liable for the debts and obligations of the partnership (see Exhibit 34.2).

general partnership
An association of two or more persons to carry on as co-owners of a business for profit [UPA Section 6(1)]. Also known as an *ordinary partnership*.

general partners
Persons liable for the debts and obligations of a general partnership. Also known simply as *partners*.

▶ **Exhibit 34.2 GENERAL PARTNERSHIP**

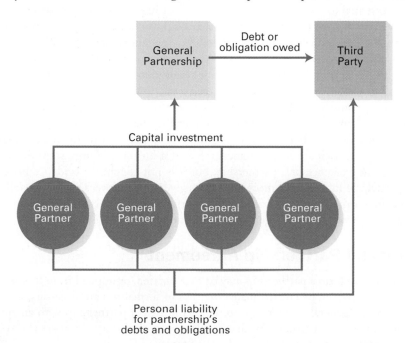

LANDMARK LAW
Uniform Partnership Act (UPA)

In 1914, the National Conference of Commissioners on Uniform State Laws (a group of lawyers, judges, and legal scholars) promulgated the **Uniform Partnership Act (UPA)**. The UPA codifies partnership law. Its goal was to establish consistent partnership law that was uniform throughout the Unites States. The UPA has been adopted in whole or in part by 48 states, the District of Columbia, Guam, and the Virgin Islands. Because it is so important, the UPA forms the basis of the study of general partnerships in this chapter.

The UPA covers most problems that arise in the formation, operation, and dissolution of ordinary partnerships. Other rules of law or equity govern if there is no applicable provision of the UPA [UPA Section 5].

Uniform Partnership Act (UPA)
A model act that codifies partnership law. Most states have adopted the UPA in whole or in part.

The partner of my partner is not my partner.

Legal maxim

General Partnership Name

An ordinary partnership can operate under the names of any one or more of the partners or under a fictitious business name. A partnership must file a fictitious business name statement—d.b.a. (doing business as)—with the appropriate government agency to operate under a trade name. The general partnership usually must publish a notice of the use of the trade name in a newspaper of general circulation where the partnership does business. The name selected by the partnership cannot indicate that it is a corporation (e.g., it cannot contain the term *Inc.*) and cannot be similar to the name used by any existing business entity.

Formation of a General Partnership

A business must meet four criteria to qualify as a partnership under the UPA [UPA Section 6(1)]. It must be (1) an association of two or more persons (2) carrying on a business (3) as co-owners (4) for profit. A partnership is a voluntary association of two or more persons. All partners must agree to the participation of each co-partner. A person cannot be forced to be a partner or to accept another person as a partner. The UPA's definition of *person* includes natural persons, partnerships (including limited partnerships), corporations, and other associations. A business—a trade, an occupation, or a profession—must be carried on. The organization or venture must have a profit motive in order to qualify as a partnership, even though the business does not actually have to make a profit.

A general partnership may be formed with little or no formality. Co-ownership of a business is essential to create a partnership. The most important factor in determining co-ownership is whether the parties share the business's profits and management responsibility.

Receipt of a share of business profits is *prima facie* evidence of a partnership because nonpartners usually are not given the right to share in a business's profits. No inference of the existence of a partnership is drawn if profits are received in payment of (1) a debt owed to a creditor in installments or otherwise; (2) wages owed to an employee; (3) rent owed to a landlord; (4) an annuity owed to a widow, widower, or representative of a deceased partner; (5) interest owed on a loan; or (6) consideration for the sale of goodwill of a business [UPA Section 7]. An agreement to share losses of a business is strong evidence of a partnership.

The right to participate in the management of a business is important evidence for determining the existence of a partnership, but it is not conclusive evidence because the right to participate in management is sometimes given to employees, creditors, and others. It is compelling evidence of the existence of a partnership if a person is given the right to share in profits, losses, and management of a business.

The General Partnership Agreement

The **agreement** to form a partnership may be oral, written, or implied from the conduct of the parties. It may even be created inadvertently. No formalities are necessary, although a few states require general partnerships to file certificates of partnership with an appropriate government agency. Partnerships that exist for more than one year or are authorized to deal in real estate must be in writing under the Statute of Frauds.

It is good practice for partners to put their partnership agreement in writing. A written document is important evidence of the terms of the agreement, particularly if a dispute arises among the partners.

A written partnership agreement is called a **partnership agreement**, or **articles of partnership**. The parties can agree to almost any terms in their partnership agreement, except terms that are illegal. The articles of partnership can be short and simple or long and complex. If the agreement fails to provide for an essential term or contingency, the provisions of the UPA control. Thus, the UPA acts as a gap-filling device to the partners' agreement.

partnership agreement
A written agreement that partners sign. Also called *articles of partnership.*

Taxation of Partnerships

Partnerships do not pay federal income taxes. Instead, the income and losses of partnership flow onto and have to be reported on the individual partners' personal income tax returns. This is called "flow-through" taxation. A partnership has to file an information return with the government, telling the government how much income was earned or losses were incurred by the partnership. This way, the government tax authorities can trace whether partners are correctly reporting their income or losses.

India *Small businesses operate throughout the world and make up a large part of the economies of many foreign countries.*

▶ RIGHTS OF GENERAL PARTNERS

The partners of a general partnership have certain rights. The rights of general partners are discussed in the following paragraphs.

Right to Participate in Management

In the absence of an agreement to the contrary, all partners have equal **rights in the conduct and management of the partnership business**. In other words, each partner has one vote, regardless of the proportional size of his or her capital contribution or share in the partnership's profits. Under the UPA, a simple majority decides most ordinary partnership matters [UPA Section 18]. If the vote is tied, the action being voted on is considered to be defeated.

right to participate in management
A situation in which, unless otherwise agreed, each partner has a right to participate in the management of a partnership and has an equal vote on partnership matters.

Right to Share in Profits

Unless otherwise agreed, the UPA mandates that a partner has the right to an equal share in the partnership's profits and losses [UPA Section 18(a)]. The **right to share in the profits** of the partnership is considered to be the right to share in the earnings from the investment of capital.

Right to Compensation and Reimbursement

Unless otherwise agreed, the UPA provides that no partner is entitled to remuneration for his or her performance in the partnership's business [UPA Section 18(f)]. Under this rule, partners are not entitled to receive a salary for providing services to the partnership unless agreed to by the partners.

Under the UPA, it is implied that partners will devote full time and service to the partnership. Thus, unless otherwise agreed, income earned by partners from providing services elsewhere belongs to the partnership [UPA Section 21]. Partners sometimes incur personal travel, business, and other expenses on behalf of the partnership. A partner is entitled to **indemnification** (i.e., reimbursement) for such expenditures if they are reasonably incurred in the ordinary and proper conduct of the business [UPA Section 18(b)].

indemnification
The right of a partner to be reimbursed for expenditures incurred on behalf of the partnership.

Right to Return of Loans and Capital

A partner who makes a loan to the partnership becomes a creditor of the partnership. The partner is entitled to repayment of the loan, but this right is subordinated to the claims of creditors who are not partners [UPA Section 40(b)]. The partner is also entitled to receive interest from the date of the loan.

Upon termination of a partnership, the partners are entitled to have their capital contributions returned to them [UPA Section 18(a)]. However, this right is subordinated to the rights of creditors, who must be paid their claims first [UPA Section 40(b)].

Right to Information

Each partner has the right to demand true and full information from any other partner of all things affecting the partnership [UPA Section 20]. The corollary to this rule is that each partner has a duty to provide such information upon the receipt of a reasonable demand. The partnership books (e.g., financial records, tax records) must be kept at the partnership's principal place of business [UPA Section 19]. The partners have an absolute right to inspect and copy these records.

▶ DUTIES OF GENERAL PARTNERS

General partners owe certain duties to each other and the partnership. The duties of partners are discussed in the following paragraphs.

Duty of Loyalty

Partners are in a **fiduciary relationship** with one another. As such, they owe each other a **duty of loyalty**. This duty is imposed by law and cannot be waived. If there is a conflict between partnership interests and personal interests, the partner must choose the interest of the partnership. Some basic forms of breach of loyalty involve:

duty of loyalty
A duty that a partner owes not to act adversely to the interests of the partnership.

- **Self-dealing. Self-dealing** occurs when a partner deals personally with the partnership, such as buying or selling goods or property to the partnership. Such actions are permitted only if full disclosure is made and consent of the other partners is obtained.

Example Dan is a partner in a partnership that is looking for a piece of real property on which to build a new store. Dan owns a desirable piece of property. To sell the property to the partnership, Dan must first disclose his ownership interest and receive his partners' consent.

It has been uniformly laid down in this Court, as far back as we can remember, that good faith is the basis of all mercantile transactions.

Justice Buller
Salomons v. Nissen (1788)

- **Usurping a partnership opportunity.** A partner who is offered an opportunity on behalf of the partnership cannot **usurp the opportunity** for himself or herself. Thus, if a third party offers a business opportunity to a partner in his partnership status, the partner cannot take the opportunity for himself before offering it to the partnership. If the partnership rejects the opportunity, the partner is free to pursue the opportunity.
- **Competing with the partnership.** A partner may not **compete with the partnership** without the permission of the other partners.

Example A partner of a general partnership that operates an automobile dealership cannot open a competing automobile dealership without his or her co-partners' permission.

• **Secret profits.** Partners may not make **secret profits** from partnership business.

Example A partner who takes a kickback from a supplier has made a secret profit. The secret profit belongs to the partnership.

• **Breach of confidentiality.** Partners owe a duty to keep partnership information confidential.

Example Trade secrets, customer lists, and other secret information are confidential. A partner who misuses this information—either himself or by transferring the information to someone else—has **breached confidentiality**.

• **Misuse of property.** Partners owe a duty not to use partnership property for personal use.

A partner who breaches the duty of loyalty must disgorge any profits made from the breach to the partnership. In addition, the partner is liable for any damages caused by the breach.

Duty of Care

A partner must use reasonable care and skill in transacting partnership business. The **duty of care** calls for the partners to use the same level of care and skill that a reasonable business manager in the same position would use in the same circumstances. Breach of the duty of care is **negligence**. A partner is liable to the partnership for any damages caused by his or her negligence. The partners are not liable for honest errors in judgment.

duty of care
The obligation partners owe to use the same level of care and skill that a reasonable person in the same position would use in the same circumstances. A breach of the duty of care is *negligence*.

Examples Tina, Eric, and Brian form a partnership to sell automobiles. Tina, who is responsible for ordering inventory, orders large, expensive SUVs that use a lot of gasoline. A war breaks out in the Middle East that interrupts the supply of oil to the United States. The demand for large SUVs drops substantially, and the partnership cannot sell its inventory. Tina is not liable because the duty of care was not breached.

Duty to Inform

Partners owe a **duty to inform** their co-partners of all information they possess that is relevant to the affairs of the partnership [UPA Section 20]. Even if a partner fails to do so, the other partners are **imputed** with knowledge of all notices concerning any matters relating to partnership affairs. Knowledge is also imputed regarding information acquired in the role of partner that affects the partnership and should have been communicated to the other partners [UPA Section 12].

duty to inform
A duty a partner owes to inform his or her co-partners of all information he or she possesses that is relevant to the affairs of the partnership.

Example Ted and Diane are partners. Ted knows that a piece of property owned by the partnership contains dangerous toxic wastes but fails to inform Diane of this fact. Even though Diane does not have actual knowledge of this fact, it is imputed to her.

Duty of Obedience

The **duty of obedience** requires partners to adhere to the provisions of the partnership agreement and the decisions of the partnership. A partner who breaches this duty is liable to the partnership for any damages caused by the breach.

duty of obedience
A duty that requires partners to adhere to the provisions of the partnership agreement and the decisions of the partnership.

Example Jodie, Bart, and Denise form a partnership to develop real property. Their partnership agreement specifies that acts of the partners are limited to those necessary to accomplish the partnership's purpose. Suppose Bart, acting alone, loses $100,000 of partnership funds in commodities trading. Bart is personally liable to the partnership for the lost funds because he breached the partnership agreement.

CONTEMPORARY ENVIRONMENT

Right to an Accounting

Partners are not permitted to sue the partnership or other partners at law. Instead, they are given the right to bring an **action for an accounting** against other partners. An action for an accounting is a formal judicial proceeding in which the court is authorized to (1) review the partnership and the partners' transactions and (2) award each partner his or her share of the partnership assets [UPA Section 24]. An action results in a money judgment for or against partners, according to the balance struck.

action for an accounting
A formal judicial proceeding in which the court is authorized to (1) review the partnership and the partners' transactions and (2) award each partner his or her share of the partnership assets.

▶ LIABILITY OF GENERAL PARTNERS

Partners must deal with third parties in conducting partnership business. This often includes entering into contracts with third parties on behalf of the partnership. Partners, employees, and agents of the partnership sometimes injure third parties while conducting partnership business. Partners of a general partnership have personal liability for the contracts and torts of the partnership. Contract and tort liability of partnerships and their partners is discussed in the following paragraphs.

Tort Liability

While acting on partnership business, a partner or an employee of the partnership may commit a tort that causes injury to a third person. This tort could be caused by a negligent act, a breach of trust (such as embezzlement from a customer's account), breach of fiduciary duty, defamation, fraud, or another intentional tort. The partnership is liable if the act is committed while the person is acting within the ordinary course of partnership business or with the authority of his or her co-partners.

joint and several liability
Tort liability of partners together and individually. A plaintiff can sue one or more partners separately. If successful, the plaintiff can recover the entire amount of the judgment from any or all of the defendant-partners who have been found liable.

Under the UPA, partners are **jointly and severally liable** for torts and breaches of trust [UPA Section 15(a)]. This is so even if a partner did not participate in the commission of the act. This type of liability permits a third party to sue one or more of the partners separately. Judgment can be collected only against the partners who are sued. The partnership and partners who are made to pay **tort liability** may seek indemnification from the partner who committed the wrongful act. A release of one partner does not discharge the liability of other partners.

Example Nicole, Jim, and Maureen form a partnership. Jim, while on partnership business, causes an automobile accident that injures Catherine, a pedestrian. Catherine suffers $100,000 in injuries. Catherine, at her option, can sue Nicole, Jim, or Maureen separately, or any two of them, or all of them.

The court applied the doctrine of joint and several liabilities in the following case.

CASE 34.2   Tort Liability of General Partners

Zuckerman v. Antenucci
124 Misc.2d 971, 478 N.Y.S.2d 578, Web 1984 N.Y. Misc. Lexis 3283 (1984)
Supreme Court of New York

"A partnership is liable for the tortious act of a partner, and a partner is jointly and severally liable for tortious acts chargeable to the partnership."
—Judge Leviss

Facts
Jose Pena and Joseph Antenucci were both medical doctors who were partners in a medical practice. Both doctors treated Elaine Zuckerman during her pregnancy. Her son, Daniel Zuckerman, was born with severe physical problems. Elaine, as Daniel's mother and natural guardian, brought a medical malpractice suit against both doctors. The jury found that Pena was guilty of medical malpractice but that Antenucci was not. The amount of the verdict totaled $4 million. The trial court entered judgment against Pena but not against Antenucci. The plaintiffs made a posttrial motion for judgment against both defendants.

Issue

Is Antenucci jointly and severally liable for the medical malpractice of his partner, Pena?

Language of the Court

A partnership is liable for the tortious act of a partner, and a partner is jointly and severally liable for tortious acts chargeable to the partnership. When a tort is committed by the partnership, the wrong is imputable to all of the partners jointly and severally, and an action may be brought against all or any of them in their individual capacities or against the partnership as an entity. Therefore, even though the jury found that defendant Antenucci was not guilty of any malpractice in his treatment of the patient, but that defendant Pena, his partner, was guilty of malpractice in his treatment of the patient, they were then *both jointly and severally liable for the malpractice committed by defendant Pena by operation of law.*

Decision

The court held that both partners were jointly and severally liable for the judgment. The supreme court reversed the decision of the trial court and held that Antenucci was liable for the tort of his partner, Pena.

Case Questions

Critical Legal Thinking What is joint and several liability? How does it differ from joint liability?

Business Ethics Is it ethical for a partner to deny liability for torts of other partners?

Contemporary Business What types of insurance should a partnership purchase? Why?

Contract Liability

As a legal entity, a partnership must act through its agents—that is, its partners. Contracts entered into with suppliers, customers, lenders, or others on the partnership's behalf are binding on the partnership.

Under the UPA, partners are **jointly liable** for the contracts and debts of the partnership [UPA Section 15(b)]. This means that a third party who sues to recover on a partnership contract or debt must name all the partners in the lawsuit. If such a lawsuit is successful, the plaintiff can collect the entire amount of the judgment against any or all of the partners. If the third party's suit does not name all the partners, the judgment cannot be collected against any of the partners or the partnership assets. Similarly, releasing any partner from the lawsuit releases them all. A partner who is made to pay more than his or her proportionate share of **contract liability** may seek indemnification from the partnership and from those partners who have not paid their share of the loss.

joint liability
Liability of partners for contracts and debts of the partnership. A plaintiff must name the partnership and all of the partners as defendants in a lawsuit.

Liability of Incoming Partners

A new partner who is admitted to a partnership is liable for the existing debts and obligations (**antecedent debts**) of the partnership only to the extent of his or her capital contribution. The **incoming partner** is personally liable for debts and obligations incurred by the partnership after becoming a partner.

Example Bubble.com is a general partnership with four partners. On May 1, Frederick is admitted as a new general partner by investing a $100,000 capital contribution. As of May 1, Bubble.com owes $800,000 of preexisting debt. After Frederick becomes a partner, the general partnership borrows $1 million of new debt. If the general partnership goes bankrupt and out of business still owing both debts, Frederick's capital contribution of $100,000 will go toward paying the $800,000 of existing debt owed by the partnership when he joined the partnership, but he is not personally liable for this debt. However, Frederick is personally liable for the $1 million of unpaid debt that the partnership borrowed after he became a partner.

▶ DISSOLUTION OF A GENERAL PARTNERSHIP

The duration of a partnership can be a fixed term (e.g., five years) or until a particular undertaking is accomplished (e.g., until a real estate development is completed), or it can be an unspecified term. A partnership with a fixed duration is called a **partnership for a term**. A partnership with no fixed duration is called a **partnership at will**.

partnership for a term
A partnership created for a fixed duration.

partnership at will
A partnership created with no fixed duration.

dissolution
The change in the relation of the partners caused by any partner ceasing to be associated in the carrying on of the business [UPA Section 29].

winding up
The process of liquidating a partnership's assets and distributing the proceeds to satisfy claims against the partnership.

wrongful dissolution
A situation in which a partner withdraws from a partnership without having the right to do so at that time.

The **dissolution** of a partnership is "the change in the relation of the partners caused by any partner ceasing to be associated in the carrying on of the business" [UPA Section 29]. A partnership that is formed for a specific time (e.g., five years) or purpose (e.g., the completion of a real estate development) dissolves automatically upon the expiration of the time or the accomplishment of the objective. Any partner of a partnership at will (i.e., one without a stated time or purpose) may rightfully withdraw and dissolve the partnership at any time.

Unless a partnership is continued, the **winding up** of the partnership follows its dissolution. The process of winding up consists of the liquidation (sale) of partnership assets and the distribution of the proceeds to satisfy claims against the partnership. The surviving partners have the right to wind up the partnership. If a surviving partner performs the winding up, he or she is entitled to reasonable compensation for his or her services [UPA Section 18(f)].

Wrongful Dissolution

A partner has the *power* to withdraw and dissolve the partnership at any time, whether it is a partnership at will or a partnership for a term. A partner who withdraws from a partnership at will has the *right* to do so and is therefore not liable for dissolving the partnership. A partner who withdraws from a partnership for a term prior to the expiration of the term does not have the right to dissolve the partnership. The partner's action causes a **wrongful dissolution** of the partnership. The partner is liable for damages caused by the wrongful dissolution of the partnership.

Notice of Dissolution

The dissolution of a partnership terminates the partners' actual authority to enter into contracts or otherwise act on behalf of the partnership. **Notice of dissolution** must be given to certain third parties. The degree of notice depends on the relationship of the third party with the partnership [UPA Section 35]:

1. Third parties who have actually dealt with the partnership must be given **actual notice** (verbal or written) of dissolution or have acquired knowledge of the dissolution from another source.
2. Third parties who have not dealt with the partnership but have knowledge of it must be given either actual or constructive notice of dissolution. **Constructive notice** consists of publishing a notice of dissolution in a newspaper of general circulation serving the area where the business of the partnership was regularly conducted.
3. Third parties who have not dealt with the partnership and do not have knowledge of it do not have to be given notice.

If proper notice is not given to a required third party after the dissolution of a partnership, and a partner enters into a contract with the third party, liability may be imposed on the previous partners on the grounds of **apparent authority**.

Distribution of Assets

After partnership assets have been liquidated and reduced to cash, the proceeds are **distributed** to satisfy claims against the partnership. The debts are satisfied in the following order [UPA Section 40(b)]:

1. Creditors (except partners who are creditors)
2. Creditor-partners
3. Capital contributions
4. Profits

Fraud is infinite in variety: sometimes it is audacious and unblushing: sometimes it pays a sort of homage to virtue, and then it is modest and retiring: it would be honesty itself, if it could only afford it.

Lord MacNaghten
Reddaway v. Banham (1896)

The partners can agree to change the priority of distributions among themselves. If the partnership cannot satisfy its creditors' claims, the partners are personally liable for the partnership's debts and obligations [UPA Sections 40(d), 40(f)]. After the proceeds are distributed, the partnership automatically terminates. Termination ends the legal existence of the partnership [UPA Section 30].

Continuation of a General Partnership After Dissolution

The surviving, or remaining, partners have the right to continue a partnership after its dissolution. It is good practice for the partners of a partnership to enter into a *continuation agreement* that expressly sets forth the events that allow for **continuation of the partnership**, the amount to be paid **outgoing partners**, and other details.

When a partnership is continued, the old partnership is dissolved, and a new partnership is created. The new partnership is composed of the remaining partners and any new partners admitted to the partnership. The creditors of the old partnership become creditors of the new partnership and have equal status with the creditors of the new partnership [UPA Section 41].

Liability of Outgoing Partners

The dissolution of a partnership does not of itself discharge the liability of outgoing partners for existing partnership debts and obligations. If a partnership is dissolved, each partner is personally liable for debts and obligations of the partnership that exist at the time of dissolution.

If a partnership is dissolved because a partner leaves the partnership and the partnership is continued by the remaining partners, the outgoing partner is personally liable for the debts and obligations of the partnership at the time of dissolution. The outgoing partner is not liable for any new debts and obligations incurred by the partnership after the dissolution, as long as proper notification of his or her withdrawal from the partnership has been given to the creditor.

No nation was ever ruined by trade.

Benjamin Franklin

CONTEMPORARY ENVIRONMENT

Right of Survivorship

A partner is a co-owner with the other partners of the specific partnership property as a **tenant in partnership** [UPA Section 25(1)]. This is a special legal status that exists only in a partnership. Upon the death of a partner, the deceased partner's right in specific partnership property vests in the remaining partner or partners; it does not pass to his or her heirs or next of kin. This is called the **right of survivorship**. Upon the death of the last surviving partner, the rights in specific partnership property vest in the deceased partner's legal representative [UPA Section 25(2)(C)]. The *value* of the deceased partner's interest in the partnership passes to his or her beneficiaries or heirs upon his or her death, however.

Example Jennifer, Harold, Shou-Ju, and Jesus form a general partnership to operate a new restaurant. After their first restaurant is successful, they expand until the partnership owns 100 restaurants. At that time, Jennifer dies. None of the partnership assets transfer to Jennifer's heirs: for example, they do not get 25 of the restaurants. Instead, under the right of survivorship, they inherit Jennifer's *ownership interest*, and her heirs now have the right to receive Jennifer's one-quarter of the partnership's profits each year.

TEST REVIEW TERMS AND CONCEPTS

Action for an accounting
Actual notice
Antecedent debt
Apparent authority
Breach of confidentiality
Competing with the
   partnership
Constructive notice
Continuation of a general
   partnership
Contract liability
d.b.a. (doing business as)

Dissolution of a general
   partnership
Distribution of assets
Duty of care
Duty of loyalty
Duty of obedience
Duty to inform
Entrepreneur
Entrepreneurship
Fictitious business name
   statement (certificate of
   trade name)

Fiduciary relationship
Form 1040 U.S. Individual
   Income Tax Return
General partner (partner)
General partnership
   (ordinary partnership)
General partnership
   agreement
Imputed knowledge
Incoming partner
Indemnification
Joint and several liability

Joint liability
Negligence
Notice of dissolution
Outgoing partner
Partnership agreement
   (articles of partnership)
Partnership at will
Partnership for a term
Right of survivorship
Right to participate in
   management
Right to share in profits

Schedule SE (Form 1040)	Sole proprietor	Trade name	Usurping a partnership
Self Employment Tax	Sole proprietorship	Uniform Partnership Act	opportunity
Secret profits	Tenant in partnership	(UPA)	Winding up
Self-dealing	Tort liability	Unlimited personal liability	Wrongful dissolution

CASE PROBLEMS

34.1 General Partnership Thomas Smithson, a house builder and small-scale property developer, decided that a certain tract of undeveloped land in Franklin, Tennessee, would be extremely attractive for development into a subdivision. Smithson contacted the owner of the property, Monsanto Chemical Company, and was told that the company would sell the property at the "right price."

Smithson did not have the funds with which to embark unassisted in the endeavor, so he contacted Frank White, a co-owner of the Andrews Realty Company, and two agents of the firm Dennis Devrow and Temple Ennis. Smithson showed them a sketch map with the proposed layout of the lots, roads, and so forth. Smithson testified that they all orally agreed to develop the property together, and in lieu of a financial investment, Smithson would oversee the engineering of the property. Subsequently, H. R. Morgan was brought into the deal to provide additional financing.

Smithson later discovered that White had contacted Monsanto directly. When challenged about this, White assured Smithson that he was still "part of the deal" but refused to put the agreement in writing. White, Devrow, Ennis, and Morgan purchased the property from Monsanto. They then sold it to H.A.H. Associates, a corporation, for a $184,000 profit. When they refused to pay Smithson, he sued to recover an equal share of the profits. Was a partnership formed between Smithson and the defendants? Who wins? *Smithson v. White*, **Web** 1988 Tenn.App. Lexis 221 (Court of Appeals of Tennessee)

34.2 General Partnership Richard Filip owned Trans Texas Properties (Trans Tex). Tracy Peoples was an employee of the company. In order to obtain credit to advertise in the *Austin American–Statesman* newspaper, which was owned by Cox Enterprises, Inc., Peoples completed a credit application that listed Jack Elliot as a partner in Trans Texas. Evidence showed that Elliot did not own an interest in Trans Texas and did not consent to or authorize Peoples to make this representation to Cox. Cox made no effort to verify the accuracy of the representation and extended credit to Trans Texas. When Trans Texas defaulted on payments owed Cox, Cox sued both Filip and Elliot to recover the debt. Is Elliot liable? *Cox Enterprises, Inc. v. Filip and Elliot*, 538 S.W.2d 836, **Web** 1976 Tex.App. Lexis 2947 (Court of Civil Appeals of Texas)

34.3 Tort Liability Charles Fial and Roger J. Steeby entered into a partnership called Audit Consultants to perform auditing services. Pursuant to the agreement, they shared equally the equity, income, and profits of the partnership. Originally, they performed the auditing services themselves, but as business increased, they engaged independent contractors to do some of the audit work. Fial's activities generated approximately 80 percent of the partnership's revenues. Unhappy with their agreement to divide the profits equally, Fial wrote a letter to Steeby 7 years later, dissolving the partnership.

Fial asserted that the clients should be assigned based on who brought them into the business. Fial formed a new business called Audit Consultants of Colorado, Inc. He then terminated the original partnership's contracts with many clients and put them under contract with his new firm. Fial also terminated the partnership's contracts with the independent-contractor auditors and signed many of these auditors with his new firm. The partnership terminated about 11 months after Fial wrote the letter to Steeby. Steeby brought an action against Fial, alleging breach of fiduciary duty and seeking a final accounting. Who wins? *Steeby v. Fial*, 765 P.2d 1081, **Web** 1988 Colo.App. Lexis 409 (Court of Appeals of Colorado)

34.4 Fiduciary Duty Edgar and Selwyn Husted, attorneys, formed Husted and Husted, a law partnership. Herman McCloud, who was the executor of his mother's estate, hired them as attorneys for the estate. When taxes were due on the estate, Edgar told McCloud to make a check for $18,000 payable to the Husted and Husted Trust Account and that he would pay the IRS from this account. There was no Husted and Husted Trust Account. Instead, Edgar deposited the check into his own personal account and converted the funds to his own personal use. When Edgar's misconduct was uncovered, McCloud sued the law firm for conversion of estate funds. Is the partnership liable for Edgar's actions? *Husted v. McCloud*, 436 N.E.2d 341, **Web** 1982 Ind.App. Lexis 1244 (Court of Appeals of Indiana)

34.5 Tort Liability Thomas McGrath was a partner in the law firm Tarbenson, Thatcher, McGrath, Treadwell & Schoonmaker. One day, at approximately 4:30 P.M., McGrath went to a restaurant-cocktail establishment in Kirkland, Washington. From that time until about 1:00 A.M., he imbibed considerable alcohol while socializing and discussing personal and firm-related business. After 11:00 P.M., McGrath did not discuss firm business but continued to socialize and drink until approximately 1:45 A.M., when he and Fredrick Hayes, another bar patron, exchanged words. Shortly thereafter, the two encountered each other outside, and after another exchange, McGrath shot Hayes. Hayes sued McGrath and the law firm for damages. Who is liable? *Hayes v. Tarbenson, Thatcher, McGrath, Treadwell & Schoonmaker*, 50 Wn.App. 505, 749 P.2d 178, **Web** 1988 Wash.App. Lexis 27 (Court of Appeals of Washington)

34.6 Notice of Dissolution   Leonard Sumter, Sr., entered into a partnership agreement with his son, Michael T. Sumter, to conduct a plumbing business in Shreveport, Louisiana, under the name Sumter Plumbing Company. The father, on behalf of the partnership, executed a credit application with Thermal Supply of Louisiana, Inc., for an open account to purchase supplies on credit. For the next four years, the Sumters purchased plumbing supplies from Thermal on credit and paid their bills without fail. Both partners and one employee signed for supplies at Thermal. In May 1980, the partnership was dissolved, and all outstanding debts to Thermal were paid in full. The Sumters did not, however, notify Thermal that the partnership had been dissolved.

A year later, the son decided to reenter the plumbing business. He used the name previously used by the former partnership, listed the same post office address for billing purposes, and hired the employee of the former partnership who signed for supplies at Thermal. The father decided not to become involved in this venture. The son began purchasing supplies on credit from Thermal on the open credit account of the former partnership. Thermal was not informed that the son was opening a new business. When the son defaulted on payments to Thermal, it sued the original partnership to recover the debt. Is the father liable for these debts? *Thermal Supply of Louisiana, Inc. v. Sumter*, 452 So.2d 312, **Web** 1984 La.App. Lexis 8975 (Court of Appeal of Louisiana)

34.7 Liability of General Partners   Pat McGowan, Val Somers, and Brent Robertson were general partners of Vermont Place, a limited partnership formed for the purpose of constructing duplexes on an undeveloped tract of land in Fort Smith, Arkansas. The general partners appointed McGowan and his company, Advance Development Corporation, to develop the project, including contracting with materials people, mechanics, and other suppliers. None of the limited partners took part in the management or control of the partnership.

Eight months later, Somers and Robertson discovered that McGowan had not been paying the suppliers. They removed McGowan from the partnership and took over the project. The suppliers sued the partnership to recover the money owed them. The partnership assets were not sufficient to pay all their claims. Who is liable to the suppliers? *National Lumber Company v. Advance Development Corporation*, 293 Ark. 1, 732 S.W.2d 840, **Web** 1987 Ark. Lexis 2225 (Supreme Court of Arkansas)

BUSINESS ETHICS CASES

34.8 Business Ethics   Harriet Hankin, Samuel Hankin, Moe Henry Hankin, Perch P. Hankin, and Pauline Hankin, and their spouses, for many years operated a family partnership composed of vast real estate holdings. Some of the properties included restaurants, industrial buildings, shopping centers, golf courses, a motel chain, and hundreds of acres of developable ground, estimated to be worth $72 million. Because of family disagreement and discontent, the Hankin family agreed to dissolve the partnership. When they could not agree on how to liquidate the partnership assets, Harriet and Samuel (collectively called Harriet) initiated an equity action.

Based on assurances from Moe and Perch that they would sell the partnership assets as quickly as possible and at the highest possible price, the court appointed them as liquidators of the partnership during the winding-up period. Based on similar assurances, the court again appointed them liquidators for the partnership. But two years later, only enough property had been sold to retire the debt of the partnership. Evidence showed that Moe and Perch had not aggressively marketed the remaining properties and that Moe wished to purchase some of the properties for himself at a substantial discount from their estimated value. Six years and three appeals to the superior court later, Harriet brought an action seeking the appointment of a receiver to liquidate the remaining partnership assets.

Did the winding-up partners breach their fiduciary duties? Should the court appoint a receiver to liquidate the remaining partnership assets? Did Moe Henry Hankin act ethically in this case? *Hankin v. Hankin*, 507 Pa. 603, 493 A.2d 675, **Web** 1985 Pa. Lexis 337 (Supreme Court of Pennsylvania)

34.9 Business Ethics   John Gilroy, an established commercial photographer in Kalamazoo, Michigan, had a small contractual clientele of schools for which he provided student portrait photographs. Robert Conway joined Gilroy's established business, and they formed a partnership called "Skylight Studios." Both partners solicited schools with success, and gross sales, which were $40,000, increased every year and amounted to over $200,000 six years later.

Conway notified Gilroy that the partnership was dissolved. Gilroy discovered that Conway had closed up the partnership's place of business and opened up his own business, had purchased equipment and supplies in preparation for opening his own business and charged them to the partnership, had taken with him the partnership's employees and most of its equipment, had personally taken over business of some customers by telling them the partnership was being dissolved, and had withdrawn partnership funds for personal use. Gilroy sued Conway for an accounting, alleging that Conway had converted partnership assets. Did Conway act ethically in this case? Who wins? *Gilroy v. Conway*, 151 Mich.App. 628, 391 N.W.2d 419, **Web** 1986 Mich.App. Lexis 2633 (Court of Appeals of Michigan)

35 | LIMITED PARTNERSHIPS AND LIMITED LIABILITY LIMITED PARTNERSHIPS

▲ **Business Partners** *Businesses that have a single purpose—movie production, investment in real estate, and such—are often formed and operated as limited partnerships.*

CHAPTER OBJECTIVES

After studying this chapter, you should be able to:

1. Define *limited partnership*.
2. Describe the process of forming a limited partnership.
3. Distinguish between limited and general partners.
4. Identify and describe the liability of general and limited partners.

5. Describe the process of dissolution and winding up of a limited partnership.

CHAPTER CONTENTS

"There are a great many of us who will adhere to that ancient principle that we prefer to be governed by the power of laws, and not by the power of men."

Woodrow Wilson
Speech, September 25, 1912

▶ INTRODUCTION TO LIMITED PARTNERSHIPS AND LIMITED LIABILITY LIMITED PARTNERSHIPS

Limited partnerships are statutory creations that have been used since the Middle Ages. They include both general (manager) and limited (investor) partners. Today, all states have enacted statutes that provide for the creation of limited partnerships. In most states, these partnerships are called *limited partnerships* or special partnerships. Limited partnerships are used for such business ventures as investing in real estate, drilling oil and gas wells, investing in movie productions, and the like. In most states, the formation, operation, and termination of limited partnerships are regulated by the *Revised Uniform Limited Partnership Act (RULPA)*. Some limited partnerships qualify as *master limited partnerships* that are traded publicly. In addition, many states now permit the formation of a special form of partnership called a *limited liability limited partnership*.

This chapter discusses the formation, operation, and dissolution of limited partnerships. Master limited partnerships and limited liability limited partnerships are also reviewed.

▶ LIMITED PARTNERSHIP

A **limited partnership**, or **special partnership**, has two types of partners: (1) **general partners**, who invest capital, manage the business, and are personally liable for partnership debts, and (2) **limited partners**, who invest capital but do not participate in management and are not personally liable for partnership debts beyond their capital contributions (see Exhibit 35.1).

limited partnership
A type of partnership that has two types of partners: (1) general partners and (2) limited partners.

general partners
Partners in a limited partnership who invest capital, manage the business, and are personally liable for partnership debts.

limited partners
Partners in a limited partnership who invest capital but do not participate in management and are not personally liable for partnership debts beyond their capital contributions.

▶ **Exhibit 35.1 LIMITED PARTNERSHIP**

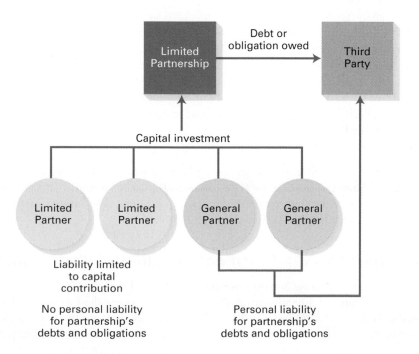

Revised Uniform Limited Partnership Act (RULPA)
A 1976 revision of the ULPA that provides a more modern, comprehensive law for the formation, operation, and dissolution of limited partnerships.

A limited partnership must have one or more general partners and one or more limited partners [RULPA Section 101(7)]. There are no upper limits on the number of general or limited partners allowed in a limited partnership. Any person—including natural persons, partnerships, limited partnerships, trusts, estates, associations, and corporations—may be a general or limited partner. A person may be both a general partner and a limited partner in the same limited partnership.

The Revised Uniform Limited Partnership Act (RULPA) permits a corporation to be the sole general partner of a limited partnership. Where this is permissible, it affects the liability of the limited partnership. This is because the limited partners are liable only to the extent of their capital contributions, and the corporation acting as general partner is liable only to the extent of its assets.

LANDMARK LAW

Revised Uniform Limited Partnership Act

In 1916, the National Conference of Commissioners on Uniform State Laws, a group of lawyers, judges, and legal scholars, promulgated the **Uniform Limited Partnership Act (ULPA)**. The ULPA contains a uniform set of provisions for the formation, operation, and dissolution of limited partnerships. Most states originally enacted this law.

In 1976, the National Conference of Commissioners on Uniform State Laws promulgated the **Revised Uniform**

Limited Partnership Act (RULPA), which provides a more modern, comprehensive law for the formation, operation, and dissolution of limited partnerships. This law supersedes the ULPA in the states that have adopted it. The RULPA provides the basic foundation for the discussion of limited partnership law in the following text. In 2001, certain **amendments** were made to the RULPA. The changes made by these amendments are noted in this chapter.

Certificate of Limited Partnership

certificate of limited partnership
A document that two or more persons must execute and sign that makes a limited partnership legal and binding.

The creation of a limited partnership is formal and requires public disclosure. The entity must comply with the statutory requirements of the RULPA or other state statutes. Under the RULPA, two or more persons must execute and sign a **certificate of limited partnership** [RULPA Sections 201, 206]. The certificate must contain the following information:

- Name of the limited partnership
- General character of the business
- Address of the principal place of business and name and address of the agent to receive service of legal process
- Name and business address of each general and limited partner
- Latest date on which the limited partnership is to dissolve
- Amount of cash, property, or services (and description of property or services) contributed by each partner and any contributions of cash, property, or services promised to be made in the future
- Any other matters that the general partners determine to include

The certificate of limited partnership must be filed with the secretary of state of the appropriate state and, if required by state law, with the county recorder in the county or counties in which the limited partnership carries on business. The limited partnership is formed when the certificate of limited partnership is filed.

Amendments to the Certificate of Limited Partnership

A limited partnership must keep its certificate of limited partnership current by filing necessary certificates of amendment at the same offices where the certificate of limited partnership is filed [RULPA Section 202(a)]. Such amendments are filed to apprise creditors and others of current information regarding the limited partnership and its partners.

A certificate of amendment must be filed within 30 days of the occurrence of the following events:

- A change in a partner's capital contribution
- The admission of a new partner
- The withdrawal of a partner
- The continuation of the business after a judicial decision dissolving the limited partnership after the withdrawal of the last general partner

Name of the Limited Partnership

The name of a limited partnership may not include the surname of a limited partner unless (1) it is also the surname of a general partner or (2) the business was carried on under that name before the admission of the limited partner [RULPA Section 102(2)]. A limited partner who knowingly permits his or her name to be used in violation of this provision becomes liable as a general partner to any creditors who extend credit to the partnership without actual knowledge of his or her true status [RULPA Section 303(d)].

Other restrictions on the name of a limited partnership are that (1) the name cannot be the same as or deceptively similar to the names of corporations or other limited partnerships, (2) states can designate words that cannot be used in limited partnership names, and (3) the name must contain, without abbreviation, the words *limited partnership* [RULPA Section 102].

It is the privilege of a trader in a free country, in all matters not contrary to law, to regulate his own mode of carrying it on according to his own discretion and choice.

Baron Alderson
Hilton v. Eckersly (1855)

Capital Contributions

Under the RULPA, the capital contributions of general and limited partners may be in cash, property, services rendered, or promissory notes or other obligations to contribute cash or property or to perform services [RULPA Section 501]. A partner or creditor of a limited partnership may bring a lawsuit to enforce a partner's promise to make a contribution [RULPA Section 502(a)].

Defective Formation

Defective formation occurs when (1) a certificate of limited partnership is not properly filed, (2) there are defects in a certificate that is filed, or (3) some other statutory requirement for the creation of a limited partnership is not met. If there is a substantial defect in the creation of a limited partnership, persons who thought they were limited partners can find themselves liable as general partners.

Partners who erroneously but in good faith believe they have become limited partners can escape liability as general partners by either (1) causing the appropriate certificate of limited partnership (or certificate of amendment) to be filed or (2) withdrawing from any future equity participation in the enterprise and causing a certificate showing this withdrawal to be filed. Nevertheless, the limited partner remains liable to any third party who transacts business with the enterprise before either certificate is filed if the third person believed in good faith that the partner was a general partner at the time of the transaction [RULPA Section 304].

Limited Partnership Agreement

Although not required by law, the partners of a limited partnership often draft and execute a **limited partnership agreement** (also called the **articles of limited partnership**) that sets forth the rights and duties of the general and limited partners; the terms and conditions regarding the operations, termination, and dissolution of the partnership; and so on. Where there is no such agreement, the certificate of limited partnership serves as the articles of limited partnership.

It is good practice to establish voting rights in a limited partnership agreement or certificate of limited partnership. The limited partnership agreement can provide which

limited partnership agreement
A document that sets forth the rights and duties of general and limited partners; the terms and conditions regarding the operation, termination, and dissolution of a partnership; and so on.

transactions must be approved by which partners (i.e., general, limited, or both). General and limited partners may be given unequal voting rights.

Share of Profits and Losses

A limited partnership agreement may specify how profits and losses from the limited partnership are to be allocated among the general and limited partners. If there is no such agreement, the RULPA provides that profits and losses from a limited partnership are shared on the basis of the value of each partner's capital contribution [RULPA Section 503].

Example There are four general partners, each of whom contributes $50,000 in capital to the limited partnership, and four limited partners, each of whom contributes $200,000 capital. The total amount of contributed capital is $1 million. The limited partnership agreement does not stipulate how profits and losses are to be allocated. Assume that the limited partnership makes $3 million in profits. Under the RULPA, each general partner would receive $150,000 profit, and each limited partner would receive $600,000 profit.

Example In the previous example, suppose that instead of making a profit, the limited partnership loses $3 million. The loss would be distributed based on the value of each partner's capital contribution. Each general partner would receive $150,000 loss and each limited partner would receive $600,000 loss.

Right to Information

It is the spirit and not the form of law that keeps justice alive.

Earl Warren
The Law and the Future (1955)

Upon reasonable demand, each limited partner has the right to obtain from the general partners true and full information regarding the state of the business, the financial condition of the limited partnership, and so on [RULPA Section 305]. In addition, the limited partnership must keep the following records at its principal office:

- A copy of the certificate of limited partnership and all amendments thereto
- A list of the full name and business address of each partner
- Copies of effective written limited partnership agreements
- Copies of federal, state, and local income tax returns
- Copies of financial statements of the limited partnership for the three most recent years

Admission of a New Partner

Once a limited partnership has been formed, a new limited partner can be added only upon the written consent of all partners, unless the limited partnership agreement provides otherwise. New general partners can be admitted only with the specific written consent of each partner [RULPA Section 401]. A limited partnership agreement cannot waive the right of partners to approve the admission of new general partners. The admission is effective when an amendment of the certificate of limited partnership reflecting that fact is filed [RULPA Section 301].

Foreign Limited Partnership

domestic limited partnership
A limited partnership in the state in which it was formed.

foreign limited partnership
A limited partnership in all other states besides the one in which it was formed.

A limited partnership is a **domestic limited partnership** in the state in which it is organized. It is a **foreign limited partnership** in all other states. Under the RULPA, the law of the state in which the entity is organized governs its organization, its internal affairs, and the liability of its limited partners [RULPA Section 901].

Before transacting business in a foreign state, a foreign limited partnership must file an application for registration with that state's secretary of state. If the application conforms with that state's law, a **certificate of registration** permitting the foreign limited partnership to transact business will be issued [RULPA Section 902].

Once registered, a foreign limited partnership may use the courts of the foreign state to enforce its contracts and other rights. Failure to register neither impairs the validity of any act or contract of the unregistered foreign limited partnership nor prevents it from defending itself in any proceeding in the courts of the foreign state. However, unregistered foreign limited partnerships may not initiate litigation in the foreign jurisdiction. The limited partner's status is not affected by whether the limited partnership is registered or unregistered. For example, if a foreign limited partnership has failed to register in a foreign state and causes an injury to someone in that state, the limited partners are not personally liable [RULPA Section 907].

certificate of registration
A document that permits a foreign limited partnership to transact business in a state.

master limited partnership
A form of limited partnership that is listed on stock exchanges and is publicly traded to provide liquidity.

CONTEMPORARY ENVIRONMENT
Master Limited Partnership

One of the major drawbacks for investors who are limited partners in a limited partnership is that their investment usually is not liquid because there is no readily available market for buying and selling limited partnership interests. Certain limited partnerships can choose to be **master limited partnerships (MLPs)**. An MLP is a limited partnership whose limited partnership interests are traded on organized securities exchanges such as the New York Stock Exchange. An investment in an MLP is liquid because it can be sold on the stock exchange. Shares of ownership in MLPs are referred to as **units**.

By law, MLPs may engage in only certain businesses, such as petroleum and natural gas extraction, businesses involving pipelines for the transportation of natural resources, financial services, and some real estate

enterprises. In most MLPs, a corporation remains the general partner of the MLP, and public investors are the limited partners. MLPs pay their investors **quarterly required distributions (QRDs)** similar to interest payments on bonds at an amount stated in the investment contract.

There are tax benefits to owning a limited partnership interest in an MLP rather than owning corporate stock. MLPs pay no income tax; partnership income and losses flow directly onto the individual partners' income tax returns. Profits and other distributions of MLPs also avoid the double taxation of corporate dividends. In addition, limited partners may deduct their prorated share of the MLP's depreciation on their personal tax returns. Thus, MLPs combine the liquidity of publicly traded securities and the tax benefits of limited partnerships.

▶ LIABILITY OF GENERAL AND LIMITED PARTNERS

The general partners of a limited partnership have **unlimited liability** for the debts and obligations of the limited partnerships. Thus, general partners have unlimited **personal liability** for the debts and obligations of the limited partnership. This liability extends to debts that cannot be satisfied with the existing capital of the limited partnership.

Generally, limited partners have **limited liability** for the debts and obligations of the limited partnership. Limited partners are liable only for the debts and obligations of the limited partnership up to their capital contributions, and they are not personally liable for the debts and obligations of the limited partnership.

personal liability of general partners
The unlimited personal liability of general partners of a limited partnership for the debts and obligations of the general partnership.

Example Gertrude and Gerald are the general partners of a limited partnership called Real Estate Development, Ltd. Lin, Leopold, Lonnie, and Lawrence are limited partners of the limited partnership and have each invested $100,000 in the limited partnership. Real Estate Development, Ltd., borrows $2 million from City Bank. After six months, the limited partnership goes bankrupt, still owing City Bank $2 million. The limited partnership has spent all of its capital and is broke. In this case, the four limited partners each lose their $100,000 capital investment but are not personally liable for the $2 million debt owed by the limited partnership to City Bank. The two general partners, however, are each personally liable to City Bank for the limited partnership's unpaid $2 million loan to City Bank.

limited liability of limited partners
The limited liability of limited partners of a limited partnership only up to their capital contributions to the limited partnership; limited partners are not personally liable for the debts and obligations of the limited partnership.

Participation in Management

Under partnership law, general partners have the right to manage the affairs of the limited partnership. On the other hand, as a trade-off for limited liability, limited partners give up their right to participate in the control and management of the limited partnership. This means, in part, that limited partners have no right to bind the partnership to contracts or other obligations.

Under the RULPA, a limited partner is liable as a general partner if his or her participation in the control of the business is substantially the same as that of a general partner, but the limited partner is liable only to persons who reasonably believed him or her to be a general partner [RULPA Section 303(a)].

Permissible Activities of Limited Partners

The RULPA clarifies the types of activities that a limited partner may engage in without losing his or her limited liability. These activities include [RULPA Sections 303(b), 303(c)]:

- Being an agent, an employee, or a contractor of the limited partnership
- Being a consultant or an advisor to a general partner regarding the limited partnership
- Acting as a surety for the limited partnership
- Approving or disapproving an amendment to the limited partnership agreement
- Voting on the following partnership matters:

  a. The dissolution and winding up of the limited partnership
  b. The sale, transfer, exchange, lease, or mortgage of substantially all of the assets of the limited partnership
  c. The incurrence of indebtedness by the limited partnership other than in the ordinary course of business
  d. A change in the nature of the business of the limited partnership
  e. The removal of a general partner

Example Laura is an investor limited partner in a limited partnership. At some time after she becomes a limited partner, Laura thinks that the general partners are not doing a very good job at managing the affairs of the limited partnership, so she participates in the management of the limited partnership. While doing so, a bank loans $1 million to the limited partnership, believing that Laura is a general partner because of her involvement in the management of the limited partnership. If the limited partnership defaults on the $1 million loan owed to the bank, Laura will be treated as a general partner and will be held personally liable for the loan along with the general partners of the limited partnership.

Example Assume that in the previous example the general partners of the limited partnership vote to make Laura, a limited partner, president of the limited partnership. Laura therefore has two distinct relationships with the limited partnership: first as an investor limited partner and second as a manager (president) of the limited partnership. In this case, Laura can lawfully participate in the management of the limited partnership without losing the limited liability shield granted by her limited partner status.

Liability on a Personal Guarantee

On some occasions, when limited partnerships apply for an extension of credit from a bank, a supplier, or another creditor, the creditor will not make the loan based on the limited partnership's credit history or ability to repay the credit. The creditor may require a limited partner to personally guarantee the repayment of the loan in order to extend credit to the limited partnership. If a limited partner personally guarantees a loan made by a creditor to the limited partnership and the limited partnership defaults on the loan, the creditor may enforce the **personal guarantee** and recover payment from the limited partner who personally guaranteed the repayment of the loan.

Let every nation know, whether it wishes us well or ill, that we shall pay any price, bear any burden, meet any hardship, support any friend, oppose any foe to assure the survival and the success of liberty.

John F. Kennedy
Inaugural speech, January 20, 1961

Four things belong to a judge: to hear courteously, to answer wisely, to consider soberly, and to decide impartially.

Socrates

CONCEPT SUMMARY
LIABILITY OF LIMITED PARTNERS OF A LIMITED PARTNERSHIP

General rule	Limited partners are not individually liable for the obligations of the partnership beyond the amount of their capital contribution.
Exceptions to the general rule	Limited partners are individually liable for the debts and obligations of the partnership in three situations:

1. *Defective formation.* There has not been substantial compliance in good faith with the statutory requirements to create a limited partnership. *Exception:* Persons who erroneously believed themselves to be limited partners either (1) caused the appropriate certificate of limited partnership or amendment thereto to be filed or (2) withdrew from any future equity participation in the profits of the partnership and caused a certificate of withdrawal to be filed.

2. *Participation in management.* The limited partner participated in the management and control of the partnership. *Exception:* The limited partner was properly employed by the partnership as a manager or an executive.

3. *Personal guarantee.* The limited partner signed an enforceable personal guarantee to guarantee the performance of the limited partnership.

CONTEMPORARY ENVIRONMENT

Control Rule

The general rule is that limited partners who take part in the management of the affairs of the limited partnership who have not been expressly elected to office to do so lose their limited liability shield and become general partners and are personally liable for the debts and obligations of the limited partnership.

The 2001 amendments to the RULPA make an important change to this "control rule." The new Section 303 eliminates this restriction and permits limited partners to participate in the management of a limited partnership without losing their limited liability shield. The limited liability partnership agreement can permit certain or all limited partners a say in how the partnership's business should be run. Section 303 places limited partners on par with shareholders of a corporation, members of a limited liability company (LLC), and the partners of a limited liability partnership (LLP) in terms of being able to participate in the management of the entity without becoming personally liable for the debts and obligations of the limited partnership.

States may adopt this change as part of their own limited liability partnership law.

▶ DISSOLUTION OF A LIMITED PARTNERSHIP

Just like a general partnership, a limited partnership may be **dissolved** and its affairs wound up. The RULPA establishes rules for the dissolution and winding up of limited partnerships. Upon the dissolution and the commencement of the winding up of a limited partnership, a **certificate of cancellation** must be filed by the limited partnership with the secretary of state of the state in which the limited partnership is organized [RULPA Section 203].

certificate of cancellation
A document that is filed with the secretary of state upon the dissolution of a limited partnership.

Causes of Dissolution

Under the RULPA, the following four events cause the dissolution of a limited partnership [RULPA Section 801]:

1. The end of the life of the limited partnership, as specified in the certificate of limited partnership (i.e., the end of a set time period or the completion of a project).
2. The written consent of all general and limited partners.

3. The withdrawal of a general partner. Withdrawal includes the retirement, death, bankruptcy, adjudged insanity, or removal of a general partner or the assignment by a general partner of his or her partnership interest. If a corporation or partnership is a general partner, the dissolution of the corporation or partnership is considered withdrawal.

4. The entry of a **decree of judicial dissolution**, which may be granted to a partner whenever it is not reasonably practical to carry on the business in conformity with the limited partnership agreement [RULPA Section 802] (e.g., if the general partners are deadlocked over important decisions affecting the limited partnership).

A limited partnership is not dissolved upon the withdrawal of a general partner if (1) the certificate of limited partnership permits the business to be carried on by the remaining general partner or partners or (2) within 90 days of the withdrawal, all partners agree in writing to continue the business (and select a general partner or partners, if necessary) [RULPA Section 801].

Winding Up

A judge is a law student who marks his own examination papers.

Henry Louis Mencken

A limited partnership must **wind up** its affairs upon dissolution. Unless otherwise provided in the limited partnership agreement, the partnership's affairs may be wound up by the general partners who have not acted wrongfully or, if there are none, the limited partners. Any partner may petition the court to wind up the affairs of a limited partnership [RULPA Section 803]. A partner who winds up the affairs of a limited partnership has the same rights, powers, and duties as a partner winding up a general partnership.

Distribution of Assets

A lawyer with his briefcase can steal more than a hundred men with guns.

Mario Puzo
The Godfather

After the assets of a limited partnership have been liquidated, the proceeds must be distributed. The RULPA provides the following order of distribution of partnership assets upon the winding up of a limited partnership [RULPA Section 804]:

1. *Creditors* of the limited partnership, including partners who are creditors (except for liabilities for distributions)
2. *Partners* with respect to:
   a. Unpaid distributions
   b. Capital contributions
   c. The remainder of the proceeds

The partners may provide in the limited partnership agreement for a different distribution among the partners, but the creditors must retain their first priority.

▶ LIMITED LIABILITY LIMITED PARTNERSHIP (LLLP)

limited liability limited partnership (LLLP)
A special type of limited partnership that has both general partners and limited partners where both the general and limited partners have limited liability and are not personally liable for the debts of the LLLP.

The 2001 amendments to the Revised Uniform Limited Partnership Act permit a new form of entity called a **limited liability limited partnership (LLLP)**. An LLLP may be organized under state law by filing **articles of limited liability limited partnership** with the secretary of state's office. If all filing documents are correct and the proper fee is paid, the state will issue a **certificate of limited liability limited partnership**. An existing limited partnership may convert to being a LLLP. In most states, an LLLP must identify itself by using "L.L.L.P." or "LLLP" after the partnership name.

Like a limited partnership, an LLLP requires at least one general partner and at least one limited partner. However, the difference between a limited partnership and an LLLP is that in an LLLP, the general partners are not jointly and severally personally liable for the debts and obligations of the LLLP. Thus, neither the general partners nor the limited partners have personal liability for the debts and obligations of the LLLP. The debts of an LLLP are solely the responsibility of the partnership.

Typically, the general partners of an LLLP manage the partnership, while the limited partners are investors who only have a financial interest in the LLLP. Thus, a general partner can manage the affairs of the LLLP but not be personally responsible for the debts of the LLLP.

Many states currently offer the ability to form LLLPs. Other states are doing so as well. An LLLP is a **domestic LLLP** in the state in which it is formed and a **foreign LLLP** in other states in which it operates. Because the LLLP is a new form of business, its use is not widespread. Most use of the LLLP form of business has been for real estate investments. Because the LLLP form of business is so new, there is very little case law in the area.

TEST REVIEW TERMS AND CONCEPTS

Amendments to the Revised Uniform Limited Partnership Act (RULPA)	Decree of judicial dissolution	Limited liability limited partnership (LLLP)	Personal liability
	Defective formation	Limited liability of limited partners	Quarterly required distributions (QRDs)
Articles of limited liability limited partnership	Dissolution of a limited partnership	Limited partner	Revised Uniform Limited Partnership Act (RULPA)
Certificate of cancellation	Domestic limited liability limited partnership	Limited partnership (special partnership)	Uniform Limited Partnership Act (ULPA)
Certificate of limited liability limited partnership	Domestic limited partnership	Limited partnership agreement (articles of limited partnership)	Unit
Certificate of limited partnership	Foreign limited liability limited partnership	Master limited partnership (MLP)	Unlimited liability
Certificate of registration	Foreign limited partnership	Personal guarantee	Winding up (wind up)
	General partner		

CASE PROBLEMS

35.1 Liability of General Partners Pat McGowan, Val Somers, and Brent Robertson were general partners of Vermont Place, a limited partnership formed for the purpose of constructing duplexes on an undeveloped tract of land in Fort Smith, Arkansas. The general partners appointed McGowan and his company, Advance Development Corporation, to develop the project, including contracting with materials people, mechanics, and other suppliers. None of the limited partners took part in the management or control of the partnership.

Eight months later, Somers and Robertson discovered that McGowan had not been paying the suppliers. They removed McGowan from the partnership and took over the project. The suppliers sued the partnership to recover the money owed them. The partnership assets were not sufficient to pay all their claims. Who is liable to the suppliers? *National Lumber Company v. Advance Development Corporation*, 293 Ark. 1, 732 S.W.2d 840, **Web** 1987 Ark. Lexis 2225 (Supreme Court of Arkansas)

35.2 Liability of Limited Partners Union Station Associates of New London (USANL) was a limited partnership formed under the laws of Connecticut. Allen M. Schultz, Anderson Nolter Associates, and the Lepton Trust were limited partners. The limited partners did not take part in the management of the partnership. The National Railroad

Passenger Association (NRPA) entered into an agreement to lease part of a railroad facility from USANL. NRPA sued USANL for allegedly breaching the lease and also named the limited partners as defendants. Are the limited partners liable? *National Railroad Passenger Association v. Union Station Associates of New London*, 643 F.Supp. 192, **Web** 1986 U.S. Dist. Lexis 22190 (United States District Court for the District of Columbia)

35.3 Liability of Limited Partners 8 Brookwood Fund (Brookwood) was a limited partnership that was formed to invest in securities. The original certificate of limited partnership was filed with the Westchester County, New York, clerk; it listed Kenneth Stein as the general partner and Barbara Stein as the limited partner. Within the next four months, additional investors joined Brookwood as limited partners. However, no certificate amending the original certificate was filed to reflect the newly admitted limited partners. The newly added partners conducted themselves at all times as limited partners.

The partnership purchased securities on margin (i.e., it borrowed a percentage of the purchase price of the securities) from the securities firms of Sloate, Weisman, Murray & Co., Inc. (Sloate), and Bear Stearns & Co., Inc. (Bear Stearns). One day, the stock market crashed, causing many of the securities that Brookwood had purchased to go down in value. The securities firms made margin calls on Brookwood to pay more money to cover the losses. When the margin calls were not met, Sloate and Bear Stearns immediately initiated arbitration proceedings to recover the balance of $1,849,183 allegedly due after Brookwood's accounts were liquidated. Nine days later, Brookwood filed a certificate amending the original certificate of limited partnership to reflect the recently added limited partners.

Upon receiving the notice of arbitration, the recently added limited partners renounced their interest in the profits of the limited partnership. Can these limited partners be held individually liable for the partnership debts owed to Sloate and Bear Stearns? *8 Brookwood Fund v. Bear Stearns & Co., Inc.*, 148 A.D.2d 661, 539 N.Y.S.2d 411, **Web** 1989 N.Y. App. Div. Lexis 4208 (Supreme Court of New York)

35.4 Liability of Limited Partners   Virginia Partners, Ltd. (Virginia Partners), a limited partnership organized under the laws of Florida, conducted business in Kentucky but failed to register as a foreign limited partnership, as required by Kentucky law. Robert Day was tortiously injured in Garrard County, Kentucky, by a negligent act of Virginia Partners. At the time of the accident, Day was a bystander observing acid being injected into an abandoned oil well by Virginia Partners. The injury occurred when a polyvinyl chloride (PVC) valve failed, causing a hose to rupture from its fitting and spray nitric acid on Day, severely injuring him. Day sued Virginia Partners and its limited partners to recover damages. Are the limited partners liable? *Virginia Partners, Ltd. v. Day*, 738 S.W.2d 837, **Web** 1987 Ky.App. Lexis 564 (Court of Appeals of Kentucky)

35.5 Liability of Partners   Raugust-Mathwig, Inc., a corporation, was the sole general partner of a limited partnership. Calvin Raugust was the major shareholder of this corporation. The three limited partners were (1) Cal-Lee Trust, (2) W.J. Mathwig, Inc., and (3) W.J. Mathwig, Inc., and Associates. All three of the limited partners were valid corporate entities. Although the limited partnership agreement was never executed and a certificate of limited partnership was not filed with the state, the parties opened a bank account and began conducting business.

John Molander, an architect, entered into an agreement with the limited partnership to design a condominium complex and professional office building to be located in Spokane, Washington. The contract was signed on behalf of the limited partnership by its corporate general partner. Molander provided substantial architectural services to the partnership, but neither project was completed because of a lack of financing. Molander sued the limited partnership, its corporate general partner, the corporate limited partners, and Calvin Raugust individually to recover payments allegedly due him. Against

whom can Molander recover? *Molander v. Raugust-Mathwig, Inc.*, 44 Wn.App. 53, 722 P.2d 103, **Web** 1986 Wash.App. Lexis 2992 (Court of Appeals of Washington)

35.6 Limited Partnership   The Courts of the Phoenix was a limited partnership that owned a building that housed several racquetball and handball courts. William Reich was its general partner. Charter Oaks Fire Insurance Company (Charter Oaks) issued a fire insurance policy that insured the building. One day, a fire caused extensive damage to the building. When the Chicago fire department found evidence of arson, Charter Oaks denied the partnership's $1.7 million-plus insurance claim. It reasoned that Reich had either set the fire or had arranged to have it set in order to liquidate a failing investment. Can the limited partnership recover on the fire insurance policy? *Courts of the Phoenix v. Charter Oaks Fire Insurance Company*, 560 F.Supp. 858, **Web** 1983 U.S. Dist. Lexis 17792 (United States District Court for the Northern District of Illinois)

35.7 Removal of General Partner   The Aztec Petroleum Corporation (Aztec) was the general partner of a limited partnership. The partnership agreement provided that it could be amended by a vote of 70 percent of the limited partnership units. More than 70 percent of these units voted to amend the partnership agreement to provide that a vote of 70 percent of the limited partnership units could remove the general partner and replace it with another general partner. Prior to this amendment, there had been no provision for the removal and substitution of a general partner. Texas law requires unanimous approval of new partners unless the partnership agreement provides otherwise.

When a vote was held, more than 70 percent of the limited partnership units voted to remove Aztec as the general partner and replace it with the MHM Company. Aztec challenged its removal. Who wins? *Aztec Petroleum Corporation v. MHM Company*, 703 S.W.2d 290, **Web** 1985 Tex. App. Lexis 12879 (Court of Appeals of Texas)

35.8 Limited Partner's Interest   When the Chrysler Credit Corporation (Chrysler Credit) extended credit to Metro Dodge, Inc. (Metro Dodge), Donald P. Peterson signed an agreement, guaranteeing to pay the debt if Metro Dodge did not pay. When Metro Dodge failed to pay, Chrysler Credit sued Peterson on the guarantee and obtained a judgment of $350,000 against him. After beginning collection efforts, Chrysler Credit learned through discovery that Peterson owned four limited partnership units in Cedar Riverside Properties, a limited partnership. Can Chrysler Credit charge Peterson's limited partnership interests? *Chrysler Credit Corporation v. Peterson*, 342 N.W.2d 170, **Web** 1984 Minn.App. Lexis 2976 (Court of Appeals of Minnesota)

BUSINESS ETHICS CASES

35.9 Business Ethics   Robert K. Powers and Lee M. Solomon were among other limited partners of the Cosmopolitan Chinook Hotel (Cosmopolitan), a limited partnership. Cosmopolitan entered into a contract to lease and purchase neon signs from Dwinell's Central Neon (Dwinell's). The contract identified Cosmopolitan as a "partnership" and was signed on behalf of the partnership, "R. Powers, President." At the time the contract was entered into, Cosmopolitan had taken no steps to file its certificate of limited partnership with the state, as required by limited partnership law. The certificate was not filed with the state until several months after the contract was signed. When Cosmopolitan defaulted on payments due under the contract, Dwinell's sued Cosmopolitan and its general and limited partners. Did the limited partners act ethically in denying liability on the contract? Are the limited partners liable? *Dwinell's Central Neon v. Cosmopolitan Chinook Hotel*, 21 Wn.App. 929, 587 P.2d 191, **Web** 1978 Wash.App. Lexis 2735 (Court of Appeals of Washington)

35.10 Business Ethics   The Second Montclair Company was a limited partnership organized under the laws of Alabama to develop an office building in Birmingham called Montclair II. Joseph Cox, Sr., and F&S were general partners, each owning a one-third interest in the limited partnership. Eleven limited partners owned equal shares of the remaining one-third interest. Cox was president of Cox Realty and Development Company (Cox Realty), which had its offices in Montclair II. Cox Realty managed Montclair II under a written agreement with the limited partnership. Evidence showed that Cox used assets of the limited partnership for personal use. F&S sued Cox, seeking dissolution and liquidation of the limited partnership and damages. Did Cox act ethically in this case? Should the limited partnership be dissolved? Should damages be awarded? *Cox v. F&S*, 489 So.2d 516, **Web** 1986 Ala. Lexis 3448 (Supreme Court of Alabama)

36 | CORPORATE FORMATION AND FINANCING

▲ **Corporate Boardroom** *Corporations have existed since medieval Europe and now are recognized as separate legal entities. Corporations are led by a board of directors and officers that form its corporate management.*

CHAPTER OBJECTIVES

After studying this chapter, you should be able to:

1. Define *corporation* and list the major characteristics of a corporation.
2. Describe the process of forming a corporation.
3. Describe promoters' liability.

4. Define *common stock* and *preferred stock*.
5. Define *S corporation* and describe the tax benefits of this form of corporation.

CHAPTER CONTENTS

▶ **INTRODUCTION TO CORPORATE FORMATION AND FINANCING**
▶ **NATURE OF THE CORPORATION**

Landmark Law · *Revised Model Business Corporation Act (RMBCA)*

▶ **INCORPORATION PROCEDURE**

"A corporation is an artificial being, invisible, intangible, and existing only in the contemplation of law. Being the mere creature of the law, it possesses only those properties which the charter of its creation confers upon it, either expressly or as incidental to its very existence. These are such as supposed best calculated to effect the object for which it was created. Among the most important are immortality, and, if the expression may be allowed, individuality; properties by which a perpetual succession of many persons are considered as the same, and may act as a single individual."

—Chief Justice John Marshall

Dartmouth College v. Woodward, 4 Wheaton 518, 636 (1819)

▶ INTRODUCTION TO CORPORATE FORMATION AND FINANCING

Corporations are the most dominant form of business organization in the United States, generating over 85 percent of the country's gross business receipts. Corporations range in size from one owner to thousands of owners. Owners of corporations are called **shareholders**.

Corporations were first formed in medieval Europe. Great Britain granted charters to certain trading companies from the 1500s to the 1700s. The English law of corporations applied in most of the colonies until 1776. After the Revolutionary War, the states of the United States developed their own corporation law.

Originally, corporate charters were individually granted by state legislatures. In the late 1700s, however, the states began enacting **general corporation statutes** that permitted corporations to be formed without the separate approval of the legislature. Today, most corporations are formed pursuant to general corporation laws of the states.

The formation and financing of corporations are discussed in this chapter.

corporation
A fictitious legal entity that is created according to statutory requirements.

▶ NATURE OF THE CORPORATION

Corporations can be created only pursuant to the laws of the state of incorporation. These laws—commonly referred to as **corporations codes**—regulate the formation, operation, and dissolution of corporations. The state legislature may amend its corporate statutes at any time. Such changes may require a corporation's articles of incorporation to be amended.

The courts interpret state corporation statutes to decide individual corporate and shareholder disputes. As a result, a body of common law has evolved concerning corporate and shareholder rights and obligations.

corporations codes
State statutes that regulate the formation, operation, and dissolution of corporations.

The Corporation as a Legal "Person"

A corporation is a separate **legal entity** (or **legal person**) for most purposes. Corporations are treated, in effect, as artificial persons created by the state that can sue or be sued in their own names, enter into and enforce contracts, hold title to and transfer property, and be found civilly and criminally liable for violations of law. Because corporations cannot be put in prison, the

limited liability of shareholders
A general rule of corporate law which provides that generally shareholders are liable only to the extent of their capital contributions for the debts and obligations of their corporation and are not personally liable for the debts and obligations of the corporation.

▶ **Exhibit 36.1**
CORPORATION

normal criminal penalty is the assessment of a fine, loss of a license, or another sanction. Corporations have unique characteristics, as discussed in the paragraphs that follow.

Limited Liability of Shareholders

As separate legal entities, corporations are liable for their own debts and obligations. Generally, the shareholders have only **limited liability**. That is, they are liable only to the extent of their capital contributions and do not have personal liability for the corporation's debts and obligations (see Exhibit 36.1).

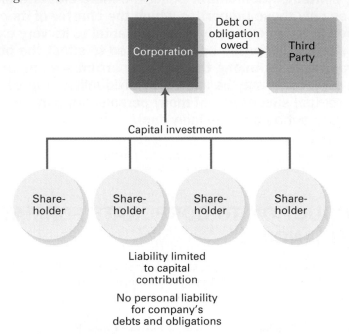

Example Tina, Vivi, and Qixia form IT.com, Inc., a corporation, and each contributes $100,000 capital. The corporation borrows $1 million from State Bank. One year later, IT.com, Inc., goes bankrupt and defaults on the $1 million loan owed to State Bank. At that time, IT.com, Inc., has only $50,000 cash left, which State Bank recovers. Tina, Vivi, and Qixia each lose their $100,000 capital contribution. However, Tina, Vivi, and Qixia are not personally liable for the $950,000 still owed to State Bank. State Bank must absorb this loss.

Free Transferability of Shares

They (corporations) cannot commit treason, nor be outlawed, nor excommunicated, for they have no souls.

Lord Edward Coke
Reports (vol. V, Case of Sutton's Hospital)

Corporate shares are freely transferable by a shareholder by sale, assignment, pledge, or gift unless they are issued pursuant to certain exemptions from securities registration. Shareholders may agree among themselves as to restrictions on the transfer of shares. National securities markets, such as the New York Stock Exchange and NASDAQ, have been developed for the organized sale of securities.

Perpetual Existence

Corporations exist in perpetuity unless a specific duration is stated in a corporation's articles of incorporation. The existence of a corporation can be voluntarily terminated by the shareholders. A corporation may be involuntarily terminated by the corporation's creditors if an involuntary petition for bankruptcy against the corporation is granted. The death, insanity, or bankruptcy of a shareholder, a director, or an officer of a corporation does not affect its existence.

Centralized Management

The **board of directors** makes policy decisions concerning the operation of a corporation. The members of the board of directors are elected by the shareholders. The directors, in turn, appoint corporate **officers** to run the corporation's day-to-day operations. Together, the directors and the officers form the **corporate management**.

LANDMARK LAW

Revised Model Business Corporation Act (RMBCA)

The Committee on Corporate Laws of the American Bar Association first drafted the **Model Business Corporation Act (MBCA)** in 1950. The model act was intended to provide a uniform law regulating the formation, operation, and termination of corporations.

In 1984, the committee completely revised the MBCA and issued the **Revised Model Business Corporation Act (RMBCA)**. Certain provisions of the RMBCA have been amended since 1984. The RMBCA arranges the provisions of the act more logically, revises the language of the act to be more consistent, and makes substantial changes in the

provisions of the model act. Many states have adopted all or part of the RMBCA. The RMBCA serves as the basis for the discussion of corporation law in this book.

There is no general federal corporations law governing the formation and operation of private corporations. Many federal laws regulate the operation of private corporations, however. These include federal securities laws, labor laws, antitrust laws, consumer protection laws, environmental protection laws, bankruptcy laws, and the like. These federal statutes are discussed in other chapters in this book.

Public and Private Corporations

Government-owned corporations (or **public corporations**) are formed to meet a specific governmental or political purpose. Public corporations are formed pursuant to state law. Most cities and towns are formed as corporations, as are most water, school, sewage, and park districts. Local government corporations are often called **municipal corporations**.

Private corporations are formed to conduct privately owned business. They are owned by private parties, not by the government. They include small one-owner corporations to large multinational corporations such as Microsoft Corporation, Starbucks Corporation, and Google, Inc.

Profit and Not-for-Profit Corporations

Private corporations can be classified as either for *profit* or *not-for-profit corporations*. **Profit corporations** are created to conduct a business for profit and can distribute profits to shareholders in the form of dividends. Most private corporations fit this definition.

Not-for-profit corporations are formed for charitable, educational, religious, or scientific purposes. Although not-for-profit corporations may make a profit, they are prohibited by law from distributing this profit to their members, directors, or officers. About a dozen states have enacted the **Model Nonprofit Corporation Act**, which governs the formation, operation, and termination of not-for-profit corporations. All other states have their own individual statutes that govern the formation, operation, and dissolution of such corporations.

Publicly Held and Closely Held Corporations

Publicly held corporations have many shareholders. Often, they are large corporations with hundreds or thousands of shareholders, and their shares are traded on organized securities markets. Wal-Mart Stores, Inc., General Motors Corporation, and IBM are examples of publicly held corporations. The shareholders rarely participate in the management of such corporations.

A **closely held** (or **close**) **corporation**, on the other hand, is one whose shares are owned by a few shareholders who are often family members, relatives, or friends. Frequently, the shareholders are involved in the management of the corporation. The shareholders sometimes enter into buy-and-sell agreements that prevent outsiders from becoming shareholders.

Professional Corporations

Professional corporations are formed by professionals such as lawyers, accountants, physicians, and dentists. The abbreviations **P.C. (professional corporation)**, **P.A. (professional**

Revised Model Business Corporation Act (RMBCA)
A 1984 revision of the MBCA that arranges the provisions of the act more logically, revises the language to be more consistent, and makes substantial changes in the provisions.

private corporation
A corporation formed to conduct privately owned business.

profit corporation
A corporation created to conduct a business for profit that can distribute profits to shareholders in the form of dividends.

publicly held corporation
A corporation that has many shareholders and whose securities are often traded on national stock exchanges.

closely held corporation
A corporation owned by one or a few shareholders. Also known as a *close corporation*.

professional corporation
A corporation formed by lawyers, doctors, or other professionals.

association), and **S.C. (service corporation)** often identify professional corporations. Shareholders of professional corporations are often called *members*. Generally, only licensed professionals may become members.

All states permit the incorporation of professional corporations, although some states allow only designated types of professionals to incorporate. Professional corporations have normal corporate attributes and are formed like other corporations. Members of a professional corporation are not usually liable for the torts committed by the corporation's agents or employees. Some states impose liability on members for the malpractice of other members of the corporation.

Domestic, Foreign, and Alien Corporations

domestic corporation
A corporation in the state in which it was formed.

foreign corporation
A corporation in any state or jurisdiction other than the one in which it was formed.

A corporation is a **domestic corporation** in the state in which it is incorporated. It is a **foreign corporation** in all other states and jurisdictions.

Example The Ford Motor Company, a major manufacturer of automobiles and other vehicles, is incorporated in Delaware. It is a domestic corporation in Delaware. The Ford Motor Company conducts business in Michigan, where its headquarters offices are located, and it distributes vehicles in Delaware as well as the other 49 states. The Ford Motor Company is a foreign corporation in these other 49 states.

A state can require a foreign corporation to *qualify* to conduct intrastate commerce within the state. Where a foreign corporation is required to qualify to conduct intrastate commerce in a state, it must obtain a **certificate of authority** from the state [RMBCA Section 15.01(a)]. This requires the foreign corporation to file certain information with the secretary of state, pay the required fees, and appoint a registered agent for service of process.

Conduct that usually constitutes "doing business" includes maintaining an office to conduct intrastate business, selling personal property in intrastate business, entering into contracts involving intrastate commerce, using real estate for general corporate purposes, and the like. Activities that are generally *not* considered doing business within the state include maintaining, defending, or settling a lawsuit or an administrative proceeding; maintaining bank accounts; effectuating sales through independent contractors; soliciting orders through the mail; securing or collecting debts; transacting any business in interstate commerce; and the like [RMBCA Sections 15.01(b), 15.01(c)].

Conducting intrastate business in a state in which it is not qualified subjects a corporation to fines. In addition, the corporation cannot bring a lawsuit in the state, although it can defend itself against lawsuits and administrative proceedings brought by others [RMBCA Section 15.02].

alien corporation
A corporation that is incorporated in another country.

An **alien corporation** is a corporation that is incorporated in another country. In most instances, alien corporations are treated as foreign corporations.

CONCEPT SUMMARY
TYPES OF CORPORATIONS

Type of Corporation	Description
Domestic	A corporation is a domestic corporation in the state in which it is incorporated.
Foreign	A corporation is a foreign corporation in states other than the one in which it is incorporated.
Alien	A corporation is an alien corporation in the United States if it is incorporated in another country.

▶ INCORPORATION PROCEDURE

Corporations are creatures of statute. Thus, the organizers of a corporation must comply with the state's corporations code to form a corporation. The procedure for *incorporating* a corporation varies somewhat from state to state. The procedure for incorporating a corporation is discussed in the following paragraphs.

Selecting a State for Incorporating a Corporation

A corporation can be incorporated in only one state, even though it can do business in all other states in which it qualifies to do business. In choosing a state for incorporation, the incorporators, directors, and/or shareholders must consider the corporation law of the states under consideration.

For the sake of convenience, most corporations (particularly small ones) choose the state in which the corporation will be doing most of its business as the state for incorporation. Large corporations generally opt to incorporate in the state with the laws that are most favorable to the corporation's internal operations (e.g., Delaware).

Selecting a Corporate Name

When starting a new corporation, the organizers must choose a name for the entity. To ensure that the name selected is not already being used by another business, the organizers should do the following [RMBCA Section 4.01]:

- Choose a name (and alternative names) for the corporation. The name must contain the word *corporation*, *company*, *incorporated*, or *limited* or an abbreviation of one of these words (i.e., *Corp., Co., Inc., Ltd.*).
- Make sure the name chosen does not contain any word or phrase that indicates or implies that the corporation is organized for any purpose other than those stated in the articles of incorporation. For example, a corporate name cannot contain the word *Bank* if it is not authorized to conduct the business of banking.
- Determine whether the name selected is federally trademarked by another company and is therefore unavailable for use. Trademark lawyers and specialized firms can conduct trademark searches for a fee.
- Determine whether the chosen name is similar to other non-trademarked names and is therefore unavailable for use. Lawyers and specialized firms can conduct such searches for a fee.
- Determine whether the name selected is available as a domain name on the Internet. If the domain name is already owned by another person or business, the new corporation cannot use this domain name to conduct e-commerce over the Internet. Therefore, it is advisable to select another corporate name.

> *The corporation is, and must be, the creature of the state, into its nostrils the state must breathe the breath of a fictitious life for otherwise it would be no animated body but individualistic dust.*
>
> Frederic William Maitland
> *Introduction to Gierke, Political Theories of the Middle Ages*

INTERNET LAW & ONLINE COMMERCE
Choosing a Domain Name

Most large corporations trademark their corporate names as well as the major brand names of their products and services. In addition, since the advent of the Internet, these corporations usually register the **domain name** of their trademarks and service marks to promote and conduct business over the World Wide Web. One such corporation that did so was Ticketmaster Corporation, which registered the name "Ticketmaster" as a mark with the U.S. Patent and Trademark Office and also registered the domain name **ticketmaster.com**.

Subsequently, a person named Brown registered three domain names—**urn2ticketmaster.com**, **urn2ticketmaster.net**, and **urn2ticketmaster.org**. Ticketmaster Corporation brought an arbitration proceeding against Brown in the World Intellectual Property Organization (WIPO), alleging a violation of the Uniform Domain Name Dispute Resolution Procedure (UDRP), by which all domain name registrants agree to abide. To recover or cancel a domain name under UDRP, the petitioner must prove that (1) the challenged domain name is identical or confusingly similar to its trademark or service mark, (2) the registrant of the domain name has no legitimate interest in the name, and (3) the domain name was registered in *bad faith*.

The arbitrator first found that the three domain names registered by Brown were confusingly similar to Ticketmaster's service mark and that the addition of the prefix "urn2" (pronounced "you are into") did nothing to reduce the domain names' similarity or confusion with

Ticketmaster's famous mark. Second, the arbitrator held that Brown had no legitimate interest in the domain names. Third, the arbitrator found that Brown had acted in bad faith in registering the domain names. The arbitrator noted that Brown had offered to sell **urn2ticketmaster.com** to Ticketmaster Corporation and had made no use of any of the names. Accordingly, the arbitrator ordered that the three domain names be canceled. *Ticketmaster Corporation v. Brown*, WIPO, No. D2001-0716 (2001)

Incorporators

incorporator
The person or persons, partnerships, or corporations that are responsible for incorporation of a corporation.

One or more persons, partnerships, domestic or foreign corporations, or other associations may act as **incorporators** of a corporation [RMBCA Section 2.01]. An incorporator's primary duty is to sign the articles of incorporation. Incorporators often become shareholders, directors, or officers of the corporation.

ETHICS SPOTLIGHT

Promoters' Liability

A **promoter** is a person who organizes and starts a corporation, finds the initial investors to finance the corporation, and so on. Promoters often enter into contracts on behalf of a corporation prior to its actual incorporation. **Promoters' contracts** include leases, sales contracts, contracts to purchase real or personal property, employment contracts, and the like. **Promoters' liability** and the corporation's liability on promoters' contracts follow these rules:

- If the corporation never comes into existence, the promoters have joint personal liability on the contract unless the third party specifically exempts them from such liability.

- If the corporation is formed, it becomes liable on a promoter's contract only if it agrees to become bound to the contract. A resolution of the board of directors binds the corporation to a promoter's contract.
- Even if the corporation agrees to be bound to the contract, the promoter remains liable on the contract unless the parties enter into a **novation**, a three-party agreement in which the corporation agrees to assume the contract liability of the promoter with the consent of the third party. After a novation, the corporation is solely liable on the promoter's contract.

promoter
A person or persons who organize and start a corporation, negotiate and enter into contracts in advance of its formation, find the initial investors to finance the corporation, and so forth.

promoters' contracts
A collective term for such things as leases, sales contracts, contracts to purchase property, and employment contracts entered into by promoters on behalf of the proposed corporation prior to its actual incorporation.

articles of incorporation
The basic governing documents of a corporation. It must be filed with the secretary of state of the state of incorporation. Also known as a *corporate charter*.

Articles of Incorporation

The **articles of incorporation** (or **corporate charter**) is the basic governing document of a corporation. It must be drafted and filed with, and approved by, the state before the corporation can be officially incorporated. Under the RMBCA, the articles of incorporation must include [RMBCA Section 2.02(a)]:

- The name of the corporation
- The number of shares the corporation is authorized to issue
- The address of the corporation's initial registered office and the name of the initial registered agent
- The name and address of each incorporator

The articles of incorporation may also include provisions concerning (1) the period of duration (which may be perpetual), (2) the purpose or purposes for which the corporation is organized, (3) limitation or regulation of the powers of the corporation, (4) regulation of the affairs of the corporation, or (5) any provision that would otherwise be contained in the corporation's bylaws.

Exhibit 36.2 illustrates sample articles of incorporation.

ARTICLES OF INCORPORATION
OF
THE BIG CHEESE CORPORATION

ONE: The name of this corporation is:

THE BIG CHEESE CORPORATION

TWO: The purpose of this corporation is to engage in any lawful act or activity for which a corporation may be organized under the General Corporation Law of California other than the banking business, the trust company business, or the practice of a profession permitted to be incorporated by the California Corporations Code.

THREE: The name and address in this state of the corporation's initial agent for service of process is:

Nikki Nguyen, Esq.
1000 Main Street
Suite 800
Los Angeles, California 90010

FOUR: This corporation is authorized to issue only one class of shares which shall be designated common stock. The total number of shares it is authorized to issue is 1,000,000 shares.

FIVE: The names and addresses of the persons who are appointed to act as the initial directors of this corporation are:

Shou-Yi Kang	100 Maple Street Los Angeles, California 90005
Frederick Richards	200 Spruce Road Los Angeles, California 90006
Jessie Quian	300 Palm Drive Los Angeles, California 90007
Richard Eastin	400 Willow Lane Los Angeles, California 90008

SIX: The liability of the directors of the corporation from monetary damages shall be eliminated to the fullest extent possible under California law.

SEVEN: The corporation is authorized to provide indemnification of agents (as defined in Section 317 of the Corporations Code) for breach of duty to the corporation and its stockholders through bylaw provisions or through agreements with the agents, or both, in excess of the indemnification otherwise permitted by Section 317 of the Corporations Code, subject to the limits on such excess indemnification set forth in Section 204 of the Corporations Code.

IN WITNESS WHEREOF, the undersigned, being all the persons named above as the initial directors, have executed these Articles of Incorporation.

Dated: January 1, 2010

▶ **Exhibit 36.2 ARTICLES OF INCORPORATION**

Amending the Articles of Incorporation

A corporation's articles of incorporation can be amended to contain any provision that could have been lawfully included in the original document [RMBCA Section 10.01]. Such an amendment must show that (1) the board of directors adopted a *resolution* recommending the amendment and (2) the shareholders voted to approve the amendment [RMBCA Section 10.03]. The board of directors of a corporation may approve an amendment to the articles of incorporation without shareholder approval if the amendment does not affect rights attached to shares [RMBCA Section 10.02]. After the shareholders approve an amendment, the corporation must file **articles of amendment** with the secretary of state of the state of incorporation [RMBCA Section 10.06].

Corporate Status

The RMBCA provides that corporate existence begins when the articles of incorporation are filed. The secretary of state's filing of the articles of incorporation is *conclusive proof* that

Did you ever expect a corporation to have a conscience, when it has no soul to be damned, and no body to be kicked?

Lord Edward Thurlow, first
Baron Thurlow

the corporation satisfied all conditions of incorporation. After that, only the state can bring a proceeding to cancel or revoke the incorporation or involuntarily dissolve the corporation. Third parties cannot thereafter challenge the existence of the corporation or assert its lack of existence as a corporation as a defense against the corporation [RMBCA Section 2.03]. The corollary to this rule is that failure to file articles of incorporation is conclusive proof of the nonexistence of a corporation.

Purpose of a Corporation

A corporation can be formed for any lawful purpose. Many corporations include a **general-purpose clause** in their articles of incorporation. Such a clause allows the corporation to engage in any activity permitted by corporation law. A corporation may choose to limit its purpose or purposes by including a **limited-purpose clause** in the articles of incorporation [RMBCA Section 3.01]. For example, a corporation may be organized "to engage in the business of real estate development."

Registered Agent

registered agent
A person or corporation that is empowered to accept service of process on behalf of a corporation.

The articles of incorporation must identify a **registered office** with a designated **registered agent** (either an individual or a corporation) in the state of incorporation [RMBCA Section 5.01]. The registered office does not have to be the same as the corporation's place of business. A statement of change must be filed with the secretary of state of the state of incorporation if either the registered office or the registered agent is changed. Attorneys often act as the registered agents of corporations.

The registered agent is empowered to accept service of process on behalf of the corporation.

Example If someone is suing a corporation, the complaint and summons are served on the registered agent. If no registered agent is named or the registered agent cannot be found at the registered office with reasonable diligence, service may be made by mail or alternative means [RMBCA Section 5.04].

Corporate Bylaws

bylaws
A detailed set of rules adopted by the board of directors after a corporation is incorporated that contains provisions for managing the business and the affairs of the corporation.

In addition to the articles of incorporation, corporations are governed by their **bylaws**. Either the incorporators or the initial directors can adopt the bylaws of the corporation. The bylaws are much more detailed than are the articles of incorporation. Bylaws may contain any provisions for managing the business and affairs of the corporation that are not inconsistent with law or the articles of incorporation [RMBCA Section 2.06]. They do not have to be filed with any government official. The bylaws are binding on the directors, officers, and shareholders of the corporation.

The bylaws govern the internal management structure of a corporation. For example, they typically specify the time and place of the annual shareholders' meeting, how special meetings of shareholders are called, the time and place of annual and monthly meetings of the board of directors, how special meetings of the board of directors are called, the notice required for meetings, the quorum necessary to hold a shareholders' or board meeting, the required vote necessary to enact a corporate matter, the corporate officers and their duties, the committees of the board of directors and their duties, where the records of the corporation are kept, directors' and shareholders' rights to inspect corporate records, the procedure for transferring shares of the corporation, and such.

Sample provisions of corporate bylaws are set forth in Exhibit 36.3.

The board of directors has the authority to amend the bylaws unless the articles of incorporation reserve that right for the shareholders. The shareholders of the corporation have the absolute right to amend the bylaws even though the board of directors may also amend the bylaws [RMBCA Section 10.20].

**BYLAWS
OF
THE BIG CHEESE CORPORATION**

ARTICLE I   Offices

Section 1. Principal Executive Office.   The corporation's principal executive office shall be fixed and located at such place as the Board of Directors (herein called the "Board") shall determine. The Board is granted full power and authority to change said principal executive office from one location to another.

Section 2. Other Offices.   Branch or subordinate offices may be established at any time by the Board at any place or places.

ARTICLE II   Shareholders

Section 1. Annual Meetings.   The annual meetings of shareholders shall be held on such date and at such time as may be fixed by the Board. At such meetings, directors shall be elected and any other proper business may be transacted.

Section 2. Special Meetings.   Special meetings of the shareholders may be called at any time by the Board, the Chairman of the Board, the President, or by the holders of shares entitled to cast not less than ten percent of the votes at such meeting. Upon request in writing to the Chairman of the Board, the President, any Vice President or the Secretary by any person (other than the Board) entitled to call a special meeting of shareholders, the officer forthwith shall cause notice to be given to the shareholders entitled to vote that a meeting will be held at a time requested by the person or persons calling the meeting, not less than thirty-five nor more than sixty days after the receipt of the request. If the notice is not given within twenty days after receipt of the request, the persons entitled to call the meeting may give the notice.

Section 3. Quorum.   A majority of the shares entitled to vote, represented in person or by proxy, shall constitute a quorum at any meeting of shareholders. If a quorum is present, the affirmative vote of a majority of the shares represented and voting at the meeting (which shares voting affirmatively also constitute at least a majority of the required quorum) shall be the act of the shareholders, unless the vote of a greater number or voting by classes is required by law or by the Articles, except as provided in the following sentence. The shareholders present at a duly called or held meeting at which a quorum is present may continue to do business until adjournment, notwithstanding the withdrawal of enough shareholders to leave less than a quorum, if any action taken (other than adjournment) is approved by at least a majority of the shares required to constitute a quorum.

ARTICLE III   Directors

Section 1. Election and term of office.   The directors shall be elected at each annual meeting of the shareholders, but if any such annual meeting is not held or the directors are not elected thereat, the directors may be elected at any special meeting of shareholders held for that purpose. Each director shall hold office until the next annual meeting and until a successor has been elected and qualified.

Section 2. Quorum.   A majority of the authorized number of directors constitutes a quorum of the Board for the transaction of business. Every act or decision done or made by a majority of the directors present at a meeting duly held at which a quorum is present shall be regarded as the act of the Board, unless a greater number be required by law or by the Articles. A meeting at which a quorum is initially present may continue to transact business notwithstanding the withdrawal of directors, if any action taken is approved by at least a majority of the required quorum for such meeting.

Section 3. Participation in Meetings by Conference Telephone.   Members of the Board may participate in a meeting through use of conference telephone or similar communications equipment, so long as all members participating in such meeting can hear one another.

Section 4. Action Without Meeting.   Any action required or permitted to be taken by the Board may be taken without a meeting if all members of the board shall individually or collectively consent in writing to such action. Such consent or consents shall have the same effect as a unanimous vote of the Board and shall be filed with the minutes of the proceedings of the Board.

▶ **Exhibit 36.3 BYLAWS**

Corporate Seal

Most corporations adopt a **corporate seal** [RMBCA Section 3.02(2)]. Generally, the seal is a design that contains the name of the corporation and the date of incorporation. It is imprinted by the corporate secretary on certain legal documents (e.g., real estate deeds) that are signed by corporate officers or directors. The seal is usually affixed using a metal stamp.

Organizational Meeting

An **organizational meeting** of the initial directors of a corporation must be held after the articles of incorporation are filed. At this meeting, the directors must adopt the bylaws, elect corporate officers, and transact such other business as may come before the meeting [RMBCA Section 2.05]. The last category includes such matters as accepting share subscriptions, approving the form of the stock certificate, authorizing the issuance of the shares, ratifying or adopting promoters' contracts, authorizing the reimbursement of promoters' expenses, selecting a bank, choosing an auditor, forming committees of the board of directors, fixing the salaries of officers, hiring employees, authorizing the filing of applications for government licenses to transact the business of the corporation, and empowering corporate officers to enter into contracts on behalf of the corporation. Exhibit 36.4 contains sample corporate resolutions from an organizational meeting of a corporation.

organizational meeting
A meeting that must be held by the initial directors of a corporation after the articles of incorporation are filed.

**MINUTES OF FIRST MEETING
OF
BOARD OF DIRECTORS
OF
THE BIG CHEESE CORPORATION
January 2, 2010
10:00 A.M.**

The Directors of said corporation held their first meeting on the above date and at the above time pursuant to required notice.

The following Directors, constituting a quorum of the Board of Directors, were present at such meeting:

Shou-Yi Kang
Frederick Richards
Jessie Quian
Richard Eastin

Upon motion duly made and seconded, Shou-Yi was unanimously elected Chairman of the meeting and Frederick Richards was unanimously elected Secretary of the meeting.

1.   Articles of Incorporation and Agent for Service of Process

The Chairman stated that the Articles of Incorporation of the Corporation were filed in the office of the California Secretary of State. The Chairman presented to the meeting a certified copy of the Articles of Incorporation. The Secretary was directed to insert the copy in the Minute Book. Upon motion duly made and seconded, the following resolution was unanimously adopted:

RESOLVED, that the agent named as the initial agent for service of process in the Articles of Incorporation of this corporation is here by confirmed as this corporation's agent for the purpose of service of process.

2.   Bylaws

The matter of adopting Bylaws for the regulation of the affairs of the corporation was next considered. The Secretary presented to the meeting a form of Bylaws, which was considered and discussed. Upon motion duly made and seconded, the following recitals and resolutions were unanimously adopted:

WHEREAS, there has been presented to the directors a form of Bylaws for the regulation of the affairs of this corporation; and
    WHEREAS, it is deemed to be in the best interests of this corporation that said Bylaws be adopted by this Board of Directors as the Bylaws of this corporation;
    NOW, THEREFORE, BE IT RESOLVED, that Bylaws in the form presented to this meeting are adopted and approved as the Bylaws of this corporation until amended or repealed in accordance with applicable law.
    RESOLVED FURTHER, that the Secretary of this corporation is authorized and directed to execute a certificate of the adoption of said Bylaws and to enter said Bylaws as so certified in the Minute Book of this corporation, and to see that a copy of said Bylaws is kept at the principal executive or business office of this corporation in California.

3.   Corporate Seal

The secretary presented for approval a proposed seal of the corporation. Upon motion duly made and seconded, the following resolution was unanimously adopted:

RESOLVED, that a corporate seal is adopted as the seal of this corporation in the form of two concentric circles, with the name of this corporation between the two circles and the state and date of incorporation within the inner circle.

4.   Stock Certificate

The Secretary presented a proposed form of stock certificate for use by the corporation. Upon motion duly made and seconded, the following resolution was unanimously adopted:

RESOLVED, that the form of stock certificate presented to this meeting is approved and adopted as the stock certificate of this corporation.

The secretary was instructed to insert a sample copy of the stock certificate in the Minute Book immediately following these minutes.

5.   Election of officers

The Chairman announced that it would be in order to elect officers of the corporation. After discussion and upon motion duly made and seconded, the following resolution was unanimously adopted:

RESOLVED, that the following persons are unanimously elected to the offices indicated opposite their names

Title	Name
Chief Executive Officer	Shou-Yi Kang
President	Frederick Richards
Secretary and Vice President	Jessie Quian
Treasurer	Richard Eastin

There being no further business to come before the meeting, on motion duly made, seconded and unanimously carried, the meeting was adjourned.

▶ **Exhibit 36.4 MINUTES OF AN ORGANIZATIONAL MEETING**

CONTEMPORARY ENVIRONMENT

Close Corporation Election Under State Corporation Law

Many of the formal rules in state corporation statutes are designed to govern the management of large, publicly held corporations. These rules may not be relevant for regulating the management of *close corporations*—that is, corporations formed by entrepreneurs with few shareholders who often work for the corporation and manage its day-to-day operations.

The **Model Statutory Close Corporation Supplement (Supplement)** was added to the RMBCA to permit entrepreneurial corporations to choose to be close corporations under state law. Only corporations with 50 or fewer shareholders may elect statutory close corporation (SCC) status. To choose this status, two-thirds of the shares of each class of shares of the corporation must approve the election. The articles of incorporation must contain a statement that the corporation is a statutory close corporation, and the share certificates must conspicuously state that the shares have been issued by a statutory close corporation.

A close corporation may dispense with some of the formalities of operating a corporation. For example, if all the shareholders approve, a close corporation may operate without a board of directors, and the articles of incorporation should contain a statement to that effect. The powers and affairs of the corporation are then managed by the shareholders. A close corporation need not adopt bylaws if the provisions required by law to be contained in bylaws are contained in the articles of incorporation or a shareholders' agreement.

A statutory close corporation need not hold annual shareholders' meetings unless one or more shareholders demand in writing that such meetings be held. The shareholders may enter into a shareholders' agreement about how the corporation will be managed. In effect, the shareholders can treat the corporation as a partnership for governance purposes [Supp. Section 20(b)(3)]. Selecting statutory close corporation status does not affect the limited liability of shareholders [Supp. Section 25].

CONTEMPORARY ENVIRONMENT

S Corporation Election for Federal Tax Purposes

A **C corporation** is a corporation that does not qualify to or does not elect to be federally taxed as an S corporation. Any corporation with more than 100 shareholders is automatically a C corporation for federal income tax purposes. A C corporation must pay federal income tax at the corporate level. In addition, if a C corporation distributes its profits to shareholders in the form of dividends, the shareholders must pay personal income tax on the dividends. This causes **double taxation**: one tax paid at the corporate level and another paid at the shareholder level.

Congress enacted the **Subchapter S Revision Act** [26 U.S.C. Sections 6242 et seq.] to allow some corporations and their shareholders to avoid double taxation by electing to be S corporations.

If a corporation elects to be taxed as an **S corporation**, it pays no federal income tax at the corporate level. As in a partnership, the corporation's income or loss flows to the shareholders' individual income tax returns. Thus, this election is particularly advantageous if (1) the corporation is expected to have losses that can be offset against other income of the shareholders or (2) the corporation is expected to make profits, and the shareholders' income tax brackets are lower than the corporation's. Profits are taxed to the shareholders even if the income is not distributed. The shares retain other attributes of the corporate form, including limited liability.

Election to Be an S Corporation
Corporations that meet the following criteria can elect to be taxed as S corporations:

- The corporation must be a domestic corporation.
- The corporation cannot be a member of an affiliated group of corporations.
- The corporation can have no more than 100 shareholders.
- Shareholders must be individuals, estates, or certain trusts. Corporations and partnerships cannot be shareholders.
- Shareholders must be citizens or residents of the United States. Nonresident aliens cannot be shareholders.
- The corporation cannot have more than one class of stock. Shareholders do not have to have equal voting rights.

An S corporation election is made by filing **Form 2553** with the Internal Revenue Service (IRS). The election can be rescinded by shareholders who collectively own at least a majority of the shares of the corporation. However, if the election is rescinded, another S corporation election cannot be made for five years.

▶ FINANCING THE CORPORATION: STOCK

A corporation needs to finance the operation of its business. The most common way to do this is by selling *equity securities* and *debt securities*. **Equity securities** (or **stocks**) represent ownership rights in the corporation. Equity securities can be *common stock* and *preferred stock*. These are discussed in the following paragraphs.

equity securities
Representation of ownership rights to a corporation. Also called *stocks*.

Common Stock

Common stock is an equity security that represents the residual value of a corporation. Common stock has no preferences. That is, creditors and preferred shareholders must receive their required interest and dividend payments before common shareholders receive anything. Common stock does not have a fixed maturity date. If a corporation is liquidated, the creditors and preferred shareholders are paid the value of their interests first, and the common shareholders are paid the value of their interests (if any) last. Corporations may issue different classes of common stock [RMBCA Sections 6.01(a), 6.01(b)].

Persons who own common stock are called **common stockholders**. A common stockholder's investment in the corporation is represented by a **common stock certificate**. Common stockholders have the right to elect directors and to vote on mergers and other important matters. In return for their investment, common stockholders receive **dividends** declared by the board of directors.

common stock
A type of equity security that represents the *residual* value of a corporation.

common stockholder
A person who owns common stock.

Preferred Stock

Preferred stock is an equity security that is given certain *preferences and rights over common stock* [RMBCA Section 6.01(c)]. The owners of preferred stock are called **preferred stockholders**. Preferred stockholders are issued **preferred stock certificates** to evidence their ownership interest in the corporation.

Preferred stock can be issued in classes or series. One class of preferred stock can be given preference over another class of preferred stock. Like common stockholders, preferred stockholders have limited liability. Preferred stockholders generally are not given the right to vote for the election of directors or such. However, they are often given the right to vote if there is a merger or if the corporation has not made the required dividend payments for a certain period of time (e.g., three years).

Preferences of preferred stock must be set forth in the articles of incorporation. Preferred stock may have any or all of the preferences or rights discussed in the following paragraphs.

preferred stock
A type of equity security that is given certain preferences and rights over common stock.

preferred stockholder
A person who owns preferred stock.

Dividend Preference   A **dividend preference** is the right to receive a **fixed dividend** at set periods during the year (e.g., quarterly). The dividend rate is usually a set percentage of the initial offering price.

dividend preference
The right to receive a fixed dividend at stipulated periods during the year (e.g., quarterly).

Example A stockholder purchases $10,000 of a preferred stock that pays an 8 percent dividend annually. The stockholder has the right to receive $800 each year as a dividend on the preferred stock.

Liquidation Preference   The right to be paid before common stockholders if the corporation is dissolved and liquidated is called a **liquidation preference**. A liquidation preference is normally a stated dollar amount.

liquidation preference
The right to be paid a stated dollar amount if a corporation is dissolved and liquidated.

Example A corporation issues a preferred stock that has a liquidation preference of $200. This means that if the corporation is dissolved and liquidated, the holder of each preferred share will receive at least $200 before the common shareholders receive anything. Note that because the corporation must pay its creditors first, there may be insufficient funds to pay this preference.

Cumulative Dividend Right   Corporations must pay a preferred dividend if they have the earnings to do so. **Cumulative preferred stock** provides that any missed dividend payments must be paid in the future to the preferred shareholders before the common shareholders can receive any dividends. The amount of unpaid cumulative dividends is called dividend **arrearages**. Usually, arrearages can be accumulated for only a limited period of time (e.g., three years).

With **noncumulative preferred stock**, there is no right of accumulation. In other words, the corporation does not have to pay any missed dividends.

cumulative preferred stock
Stock for which any missed dividend payments must be paid in the future to the preferred shareholders before the common shareholders can receive any dividends.

Example   The WindSock Corporation issues cumulative preferred stock that requires the payment of a quarterly dividend of $1.00 per share. The WindSock Corporation falls behind with six quarterly payments—$6.00 per share of preferred stock. The next quarter, the corporation makes a profit of $7.00 per share. The corporation must pay the $6.00 per share of arrearages to the preferred shareholders plus this quarter's payment of $1.00 per share. Thus, the common shareholders receive nothing.

Right to Participate in Profits   **Participating preferred stock** allows a preferred stockholder to participate in the profits of the corporation along with the common stockholders. Participation is in addition to the fixed dividend paid on preferred stock. The terms of participation vary widely. Usually, the common stockholders must be paid a certain amount of dividends before participation is allowed. **Nonparticipating preferred stock** does not give the holder a right to participate in the profits of the corporation beyond the fixed dividend rate. Most preferred stock falls into this category.

participating preferred stock
Stock that allows the preferred stockholder to participate in the profits of the corporation along with the common stockholders.

Conversion Right   **Convertible preferred stock** permits the preferred stockholders to convert their shares into common stock. The terms and exchange rate of the conversion are established when the shares are issued. The holders of convertible preferred stock usually exercise this option if the corporation's common stock significantly increases in value. Preferred stock without a conversion feature is called **nonconvertible preferred stock**. Nonconvertible stock is more common than convertible stock.

convertible preferred stock
Stock that permits the preferred stockholders to convert their shares into common stock.

Redeemable Preferred Stock

Redeemable preferred stock (or **callable preferred stock**) permits a corporation to redeem (i.e., buy back) the preferred stock at some future date. The terms of the redemption are established when the shares are issued. Corporations usually redeem the shares when the current interest rate falls below the dividend rate of the preferred shares. Preferred stock that is not redeemable is called **nonredeemable preferred stock**. Nonredeemable stock is more common than redeemable stock.

redeemable preferred stock
Stock that permits a corporation to buy back the preferred stock at some future date.

Authorized, Issued, and Outstanding Shares

The number of shares provided for in the articles of incorporation is called **authorized shares** [RMBCA Section 6.01]. The shareholders may vote to amend the articles of incorporation to increase this amount. Authorized shares that have been sold by the corporation are called **issued shares**. Not all authorized shares have to be issued at the same time. Authorized shares that have not been issued are called **unissued shares**. The board of directors can vote to issue unissued shares at any time without shareholder approval.

A corporation is permitted to repurchase its shares [RMBCA Section 6.31]. Repurchased shares are commonly called **treasury shares**. Treasury shares cannot be voted by the corporation, and dividends are not paid on these shares. Treasury shares can be reissued by the corporation. The shares that are in shareholder hands, whether originally issued or reissued treasury shares, are called **outstanding shares**. Only outstanding shares have the right to vote [RMBCA Section 6.03].

authorized shares
The number of shares provided for in the articles of incorporation.

issued shares
Shares that have been sold by a corporation.

CONCEPT SUMMARY
TYPES OF SHARES

Type of Share	Description
Authorized	Shares authorized in the corporation's articles of incorporation.
Issued	Shares sold by the corporation.
Treasury	Shares repurchased by the corporation. These shares do not have the right to vote.
Outstanding	Issued shares minus treasury shares. These shares have the right to vote.

Consideration to Be Paid for Shares

The RMBCA allows shares to be issued in exchange for any benefit to the corporation, including cash, tangible property, intangible property, promissory notes, services performed, contracts for services performed, or other securities of the corporation. In the absence of fraud, the judgment of the board of directors or shareholders as to the value of consideration received for shares is conclusive [RMBCA Sections 6.21(b), 6.21(c)].

▶ FINANCING THE CORPORATION: DEBT SECURITIES

debt securities
Securities that establish a debtor-creditor relationship in which the corporation borrows money from the investor to whom a debt security is issued.

A corporation often raises funds by issuing debt securities [RMBCA Section 3.02(7)]. **Debt securities** (also called **fixed income securities**) establish a debtor–creditor relationship in which the corporation borrows money from the investor to whom the debt security is issued. The corporation promises to pay interest on the amount borrowed and to repay the principal at some stated maturity date in the future. The corporation is the *debtor*, and the holder is the *creditor*. The three classifications of debt securities—*debentures*, *bonds*, and *notes*—are discussed in the following paragraphs.

Debenture

debenture
A long-term unsecured debt instrument that is based on a corporation's general credit standing.

A **debenture** is a *long-term* (often 30 years or more), *unsecured* debt instrument that is based on a corporation's general credit standing. If the corporation encounters financial difficulty, unsecured debenture holders are treated as general creditors of the corporation (i.e., they are paid only after the secured creditors' claims are met).

Bond

bond
A long-term debt security that is secured by some form of collateral.

A **bond** is a *long-term* debt security that is *secured* by some form of *collateral* (e.g., real estate, personal property). Thus, bonds are the same as debentures except that they are secured. Secured bondholders can foreclose on the collateral in the event of nonpayment of interest, principal, or other specified events.

Note

note
A debt security with a maturity of five years or less.

A **note** is a *short-term* debt security with a maturity of five years or less. Notes can be either *unsecured* or *secured*. They usually do not contain a conversion feature. They are sometimes made redeemable.

Indenture Agreement

indenture agreement
A contract between a corporation and a holder that contains the terms of a debt security.

The terms of a debt security are commonly contained in a contract between the corporation and the holder; this contract is known as an **indenture agreement** (or simply an indenture). The indenture generally contains the maturity date of the debt security, the required interest payment, the collateral (if any), rights to conversion into common or preferred stock, call provisions, any restrictions on the corporation's right to incur other indebtedness, the rights of holders upon default, and such. It also establishes the rights and duties of the indenture trustee. Generally, a trustee is appointed to represent the interest of the debt security holders. Bank trust departments often serve in this capacity.

CONCEPT SUMMARY
DEBT INSTRUMENTS

Debt Instrument	Description
Debenture	A *long-term, unsecured* debt instrument that is based on a corporation's general credit rating.
Bond	A *long-term* debt security that is *secured* by some form of property. The property securing the bond is called *collateral*. In the event of nonpayment of interest or principal or other specified events, bondholders can foreclose on and obtain the collateral.
Note	A *short-term* debt instrument with a maturity of five years or less. Notes can be either unsecured or secured.

CONTEMPORARY ENVIRONMENT

Delaware and Nevada Corporation Law

The **State of Delaware** is the corporate haven of the United States. More than 50 percent of the publicly traded corporations in America, including 60 percent of the Fortune 500 companies, are incorporated in Delaware. In total, more than 500,000 business corporations are incorporated in Delaware. But why?

Remember that the state in which a corporation is incorporated determines the law that applies to the corporation: The corporations code of the state of incorporation applies to such things as election of directors, requirements for a merger to occur, laws for fending off corporate raiders, and such. So, even if a corporation does no business in Delaware, it can obtain the benefits of Delaware corporation law by incorporating in Delaware.

On the legislative side, Delaware has enacted the **Delaware General Corporation Law**. This law is the most advanced corporation law in the country. And the statute is particularly written to be of benefit to large corporations. For example, the Delaware corporations code provides for the ability of corporations incorporated in Delaware to adopt "poison pills" that make it virtually impossible for another company to take over a Delaware corporation unless the board of directors of the target corporation agrees and removes such poison pills. In addition, the legislature keeps amending the corporations code as the demands of big business warrant or need such changes. For instance, the legislature has enacted a state antitakeover statute that makes it legally impossible to take over a Delaware corporation unless the corporation's directors waive the state's antitakeover law and agree to be taken over.

On the judicial side, Delaware has a special court—the **court of chancery**—that hears and decides business cases. This court has been around for over 200 years. In that time, it has interpreted Delaware corporation law

favorably to large corporations in such matters as electing corporate boards of directors, eliminating negligence liability of outside directors, upholding the antitakeover provisions of the Delaware corporations code, and such. And there are no emotional juries to worry about. The decisions of the chancery court are made by judges who are experts at deciding corporate law disputes. The court is known for issuing decisions favorable to large corporations as the court applies Delaware corporation law to decide disputes. Appeals from the court of chancery are brought directly to the supreme court of Delaware. Thus, Delaware courts have created a body of precedent of legal decisions that provides more assurance to Delaware corporations in trying to decide whether they will be sued and what the outcome will be if they do get sued.

The state of Delaware makes a substantial sum of money each year on fees charged to corporations incorporated within the state. Delaware is the "business state," providing advanced corporate laws and an expert judiciary for deciding corporate disputes.

The **State of Nevada** has become a state of choice for incorporation of corporations. The primary reason for incorporating in Nevada is tax reasons: There are no state taxes on corporate income, franchises, or personal income, and for a Nevada resident, there is no state inheritance, gift, or estate tax. In addition, the Nevada corporations code makes it virtually impossible for creditors to ever reach the assets of shareholders of Nevada corporations. Nevada has also established a business court that has expert judges who hear only corporate and business matters. Nevada has taken a lead from Delaware and established itself as a "business-friendly" state. But Nevada has aimed to attract smaller corporations, whereas Delaware still remains the choice of large publicly held corporations.

▶ CORPORATE POWERS

A corporation has the same basic rights to perform acts and enter into contracts as a physical person [RMBCA Section 3.02]. The express and implied powers of a corporation are discussed in the following paragraphs.

Express Powers

express powers
Powers given to a corporation by (1) the U.S. Constitution, (2) state constitutions, (3) federal statutes, (4) state statues, (5) articles of incorporation, (6) bylaws, and (7) resolutions of the board of directors.

A corporation's **express powers** are found in (1) the U.S. Constitution, (2) state constitutions, (3) federal statutes, (4) state statutes, (5) articles of incorporation, (6) bylaws, and (7) resolutions of the board of directors. Corporation statutes normally state the express powers granted to the corporation.

Generally, a corporation has the power to purchase, own, lease, sell, mortgage, or otherwise deal in real and personal property; make contracts; lend money; borrow money; incur liabilities; issue notes, bonds, and other obligations; invest and reinvest funds; sue and be sued in its corporate name; make donations for the public welfare or for charitable, scientific, or educational purposes; and the like. RMBCA Section 3.02 provides a list of express corporate powers.

Corporations formed under general incorporation laws cannot engage in certain businesses, such as banking, insurance, or operation of public utilities. A corporation must obtain a corporate charter under special incorporation statutes and receive approval of special government administrative agencies before engaging in these businesses.

Implied Powers

implied powers
Powers beyond express powers that allow a corporation to accomplish its corporate purpose.

Neither governing laws nor corporate documents can anticipate every act necessary for a corporation to carry on its business. **Implied powers** allow a corporation to exceed its express powers in order to accomplish its corporate purpose.

Example A corporation has implied power to open a bank account, reimburse its employees for expenses, engage in advertising, purchase insurance, and the like.

Ultra Vires Act

***ultra vires* act**
An act by a corporation that is beyond its express or implied powers.

An act by a corporation that is beyond its express or implied powers is called an ***ultra vires* act**. The following remedies are available if an *ultra vires* act is committed:

- Shareholders can sue for an injunction to prevent the corporation from engaging in the act.
- The corporation (or the shareholders, on behalf of the corporation) can sue the officers or directors who caused the act for damages.
- The attorney general of the state of incorporation can bring an action to enjoin the act or to dissolve the corporation [RMBCA Section 3.04].

▶ DISSOLUTION AND TERMINATION OF CORPORATIONS

The life of a corporation may be terminated voluntarily or involuntarily. The methods for dissolving and terminating corporations are discussed in the following paragraphs.

Voluntary Dissolution

A corporation can be voluntarily dissolved. If the corporation has not commenced business or issued any shares, it may be dissolved by a vote of the majority of the incorporators or initial directors [RMBCA Section 14.01]. After that, the corporation can be voluntarily dissolved if the board of directors recommends dissolution and a majority of shares entitled to vote (or a greater number, if required by the articles of incorporation or bylaws) votes for dissolution as well [RMBCA Section 14.02].

For a **voluntary dissolution** to be effective, **articles of dissolution** must be filed with the secretary of state of the state of incorporation. A corporation is dissolved upon the effective date of the articles of dissolution [RMBCA Section 14.03].

Administrative Dissolution

The secretary of state can obtain **administrative dissolution** of a corporation if (1) it failed to file an annual report, (2) it failed for 60 days to maintain a registered agent in the state, (3) it failed for 60 days after a change of its registered agent to file a statement of such change with the secretary of state, (4) it did not pay its franchise fee, or (5) the period of duration stated in the corporation's articles of incorporation has expired [RMBCA Section 14.20]. If the corporation does not cure the default within 60 days of being notified of it, the secretary of state issues a **certificate of dissolution** that dissolves the corporation [RMBCA Section 14.21].

Judicial Dissolution

A corporation can be involuntarily dissolved by a judicial proceeding. **Judicial dissolution** can be instituted by the attorney general of the state of incorporation if the corporation (1) procured its articles of incorporation through fraud or (2) exceeded or abused the authority conferred on it by law [RMBCA Section 14.30(1)]. If a court judicially dissolves a corporation, it enters a **decree of dissolution** that specifies the date of dissolution [RMBCA Section 14.33].

Winding Up, Liquidation, and Termination

A dissolved corporation continues its corporate existence but may not carry on any business except as required to **wind up and liquidate** its business and affairs [RMBCA Section 14.05].

In a voluntary dissolution, the liquidation is usually carried out by the board of directors. If the dissolution is involuntary or the dissolution is voluntary but the directors refuse to carry out the liquidation, a court-appointed receiver carries out the winding up and liquidation of the corporation [RMBCA Section 14.32].

Termination occurs only after the winding up of the corporation's affairs, the liquidation of its assets, and the distribution of the proceeds to the claimants. The liquidated assets are paid to claimants according to the following priority: (1) expenses of liquidation and creditors according to their respective liens and contract rights, (2) preferred shareholders according to their liquidation preferences and contract rights, and (3) common stockholders.

The dissolution of a corporation does not impair any rights or remedies available against the corporation or its directors, officers, or shareholders for any right or claim existing or incurred prior to dissolution.

voluntary dissolution
Dissolution of a corporation that has begun business or issued shares upon recommendation of the board of directors and a majority vote of the shares entitled to vote.

administrative dissolution
Involuntary dissolution of a corporation that is ordered by the secretary of state if a corporation has failed to comply with certain procedures required by law.

judicial dissolution
Dissolution of a corporation through a court proceeding instituted by the state.

winding up and liquidation
The process by which a dissolved corporation's assets are collected, liquidated, and distributed to creditors, preferred shareholders, and common shareholders.

TEST REVIEW TERMS AND CONCEPTS

Administrative dissolution
Alien corporation
Arrearages
Articles of amendment
Articles of dissolution
Articles of incorporation (corporate charter)

Authorized shares
Board of directors
Bond
Bylaws
C corporation
Certificate of authority
Certificate of dissolution

Closely held (close) corporation
Common stock
Common stock certificate
Common stockholder
Convertible preferred stock
Corporate management

Corporate seal
Corporation
Corporations code
court of chancery
Cumulative preferred stock
Debenture

Debt securities (fixed income securities)	Indenture agreement (indenture)	Nonparticipating preferred stock	Promoter
Decree of dissolution	Issued shares	Nonredeemable preferred stock	Promoters' contracts
Delaware General Corporation Law	Judicial dissolution	Note	Promoters' liability
Dividend preference	Legal entity (legal person)	Not-for-profit corporation	Publicly held corporation
Dividends	Limited liability of shareholders	Novation	Redeemable preferred stock (callable preferred stock)
Domain name	Limited-purpose clause	Officers	Registered agent
Domestic corporation	Liquidation preference	Organizational meeting	Registered office
Double taxation	Model Business Corporation Act (MBCA)	Outstanding shares	Revised Model Business Corporation Act (RMBCA)
Equity securities (stocks)		P.A. (professional association)	
Express powers	Model Nonprofit Corporation Act	Participating preferred stock	S corporation
Fixed dividend	Model Statutory Close Corporation Supplement (Supplement)	P.C. (professional corporation)	S.C. (service corporation)
Foreign corporation		Preferred stock	Shareholder
Form 2553		Preferred stockholder	Subchapter S Revision Act
General corporation statutes		Preferred stock certificate	Termination
General-purpose clause	Municipal corporation	Private corporation	Treasury shares
Government-owned (public) corporation	Nonconvertible preferred stock	Professional corporation	*Ultra vires* act
Implied powers	Noncumulative preferred stock	Profit corporation	Unissued shares
Incorporator			Voluntary dissolution
			Winding up and liquidation

CASE PROBLEMS

36.1 Legal Entity Jeffrey Sammak was the owner of a contracting business known as Senaco. Sammak decided to enter the coal reprocessing business. Sammak attended the "Coal Show" in Chicago, Illinois, at which he met representatives of the Deister Co., Inc. (Deister). Deister was incorporated under the laws of Pennsylvania. Sammak began negotiating with Deister to purchase equipment to be used in his coal reprocessing business. Deister sent Sammak literature, guaranteeing a certain level of performance for the equipment. Sammak purchased the equipment. After the equipment was installed, Sammak became dissatisfied with its performance. Sammak believed that Deister breached an express warranty and wanted to sue. Can a suit be brought against a corporation such as Deister? *Blackwood Coal v. Deister Co., Inc.*, 626 F.Supp. 727, **Web** 1985 U.S. Dist. Lexis 12767 (United States District Court for the Eastern District of Pennsylvania)

36.2 Limited Liability of Shareholders Joseph M. Billy was an employee of the USM Corporation (USM), a publicly held corporation. Billy was at work when a 4,600-pound ram from a vertical boring mill broke loose and crushed him to death. Billy's widow brought suit against USM, alleging that the accident was caused by certain defects in the manufacture and design of the vertical boring mill and the two moving parts directly involved in the accident, a metal lifting arm and the 4,600-pound ram. If Mrs. Billy's suit is successful, can the shareholders of USM be held personally liable for any judgment against USM? *Billy v. Consolidated Machine Tool. Corp.*, 51 N.Y.2d 152, 412 N.E.2d 934, 432 N.Y.S.2d 879, **Web** 1980 N.Y. Lexis 2638 (Court of Appeals of New York)

36.3 Corporation William O'Donnel and Vincent Marino worked together as executives of a shipping container repair company known as Marine Trailers. Marine Trailers's largest customer was American Export Lines (American Export). When American Export became unhappy with the owners of Marine Trailers, it let O'Donnel and Marino know that if they formed their own company, American Exports would give them its business. O'Donnel and Marino decided to take American Exports's suggestion, and they bought the majority of shares of a publicly traded corporation known as Marine Repair Services, Inc. (Repair Services). O'Donnel and Marino operated Repair Services as a container repair company at the Port of New York. The company prospered, expanding to five other states and overseas. O'Donnel and Marino's initial $12,000 investment paid off. Ten years after buying the company, each man was earning over $150,000 a year in salary alone. What type of corporation is Repair Services? *O'Donnel v. Marine Repair Services, Inc.*, 530 F.Supp. 1199, **Web** 1982 U.S. Dist. Lexis 10456 (United States District Court for the Southern District of New York)

36.4 Corporation Hutchinson Baseball Enterprises, Inc. (Hutchinson, Inc.), was incorporated under the laws of Kansas. Among the purposes of the corporation, according to its bylaws, were to "promote, advance, and sponsor baseball, which shall include Little League and Amateur baseball, in the Hutchinson, Kansas, area." The corporation was involved in a number of activities, including leasing a field for American Legion teams, furnishing instructors as coaches for Little League teams, conducting a Little League camp, and leasing a baseball field to a local junior college for a nominal fee. Hutchinson, Inc., raised money through ticket sales to amateur baseball games, concessions, and contributions. Any profits were used to improve the playing fields. Profits were never distributed to the corporation's directors or members. What type of corporation is Hutchinson, Inc.? *Hutchinson Baseball Enterprises, Inc. v. Commissioner of Internal Revenue*, 696 F.2d 757, **Web** 1982 U.S. App. Lexis 23179 (United States Court of Appeals for the Tenth Circuit)

36.5 Corporation Elmer Balvik and Thomas Sylvester formed a partnership, named Weldon Electric, for the purpose of engaging in the electrical contracting business. Balvik contributed $8,000 and a vehicle worth $2,000, and Sylvester contributed $25,000 to the partnership's assets. The parties operated the business as a partnership for several years and then decided to incorporate. Stock was issued to Balvik and Sylvester in proportion to their partnership ownership interests, with Sylvester receiving 70 percent and Balvik receiving 30 percent of the stock. Balvik and his wife and Sylvester and his wife were the four directors of the corporation. Sylvester was elected president of the corporation. Balvik was vice president. The corporation's bylaws stated that "sales of shares of stock by any shareholder shall be as set forth in a 'Buy Sell Agreement' entered into by the shareholders." What type of corporation is Weldon Electric? *Balvik v. Sylvester*, 411 N.W.2d 383, **Web** 1987 N.D. Lexis 392 (Supreme Court of North Dakota)

36.6 Corporation Leo V. Mysels was the president of Florida Fashions of Interior Design, Inc. (Florida Fashions). Florida Fashions, which was a Pennsylvania corporation, had never registered to do business in the state of Florida. While acting in the capacity of a salesman for the corporation, Mysels took an order for goods from Francis E. Barry. The transaction took place in Florida. Barry paid Florida Fashions for the goods ordered. When Florida Fashions failed to perform its obligations under the sales agreement, Barry brought suit in Florida. What type of corporation is Florida Fashions in regard to the state of Pennsylvania and to the state of Florida? Can Florida Fashions defend itself in a lawsuit? *Mysels v. Barry*, 332 So.2d 38, **Web** 1976 Fla.App. Lexis 14344 (Court of Appeal of Florida)

36.7 Promoters' Liability The Homes Corporation (Homes), a closely held corporation whose sole stockholders were Jerry and Beverly Ann Allen, purchased 10 acres of real estate near Kahaluu on the island of Oahu, Hawaii. Homes made a down payment of $50,000. The Allens intended to obtain approval for a planned unit development (PUD) from the city and county of Honolulu and then develop the property with some 60 condominium townhouses. To further this project, the Allens sought an outside investor. Herbert Hadley, a real estate developer from Texas, decided to join the Allens' project. The two parties entered an agreement whereby a new Hawaiian corporation would be formed to build the condominiums, with Handley owning 51 percent of the corporation's stock and the Allens the remaining 49 percent. The two

parties began extensive planning and design of the project. They also took out a $69,500 loan from the Bank of Hawaii. After a year had gone by, Handley informed the Allens that he was no longer able to advance funds to the project. Soon thereafter, the city and county denied their PUD zoning application. The new corporation was never formed. Who is liable for the failed condominium project's contractual obligations? *Handley v. Ching*, 2 Haw.App. 166, 627 P.2d 1132, **Web** 1981 Haw.App. Lexis 192 (Intermediate Court of Appeals of Hawaii)

36.8 Promoters' Contracts Martin Stern, Jr., was an architect who worked in Nevada. Nathan Jacobson asked Stern to draw plans for Jacobson's new hotel/casino, the Kings Castle at Lake Tahoe. Stern agreed to take on the project and immediately began preliminary work. At this time, Stern dealt directly with Jacobson, who referred to the project as "my hotel." One month later, Stern wrote to Jacobson, detailing, among other things, the architect's services and fee. The two men subsequently discussed Stern's plans and set Stern's fee at $250,000. Three months later, Jacobson formed Lake Enterprises, Inc. (Lake Enterprises), a Nevada corporation of which Jacobson was the sole shareholder and president. Lake Enterprises was formed for the purpose of owning the new casino. During this period, Stern was paid monthly by checks drawn on an account belonging to another corporation controlled by Jacobson. Stern never agreed to contract with any of these corporations and always dealt exclusively with Jacobson. When Stern was not paid the full amount of his architectural fee, he sued Jacobson to recover. Jacobson claimed that he was not personally liable for any of Stern's fee because a novation had taken place. Who wins? *Jacobson v. Stern*, 96 Nev. 56, 605 P.2d 198, **Web** 1980 Nev. Lexis 522 (Supreme Court of Nevada)

36.9 Preferred Stock Commonwealth Edison Co. (Commonwealth Edison), through its underwriters, sold 1 million shares of preferred stock at an offering price of $100 per share. Commonwealth Edison wanted to issue the stock with a dividend rate of 9.26 percent, but its major underwriter, First Boston Corporation (First Boston), advised that a rate of 9.44 percent should be paid. According to First Boston, a shortage of investment funds existed, and a higher dividend rate was necessary for a successful stock issue. Commonwealth Edison's management was never happy with the high dividend rate being paid on this preferred stock. Nine months later, Commonwealth Edison's vice chairman was quoted in the report of the annual meeting of the corporation as saying "we were disappointed at the 9.44 percent dividend rate on the preferred stock we sold last August, but we expect to refinance it when market conditions make it feasible." Commonwealth Edison, pursuant to the terms under which the stock was sold, bought back the 1 million shares of preferred stock at a price of $110 per share. What type of preferred stock is this? *The Franklin Life Insurance Company v. Commonwealth Edison Company*, 451 F.Supp. 602, **Web** 1978 U.S. Dist. Lexis 17604 (United States District Court for the Southern District of Illinois)

36.10 Debt Security United Financial Corporation of California (United Financial) was incorporated in the state of Delaware. United Financial owned the majority of a California savings and loan association as well as three insurance agencies. The next year, the original investors in United Financial decided to capitalize on an increase in investor interest in savings and loans. The first public offering of United Federal stock was made. The stock was sold as a unit, with 60,000 units being offered. Each unit consisted of two shares of United Financial stock and one $100, 5 percent interest-bearing debenture bond. This initial offering was a success. It provided $7.2 million to the corporation, of which $6.2 million was distributed as a return of capital to the original investors. What is the difference between the stock offered for sale by United Financial and the debenture bonds? *Jones v. H.F. Ahmanson & Company*, 1 Cal. 3d 93, 460 P.2d 464, 81 Cal.Rptr. 592, **Web** 1969 Cal. Lexis 195 (Supreme Court of California)

BUSINESS ETHICS CASES

36.11 Business Ethics John A. Goodman was a real estate salesman in the state of Washington. Goodman sold to Darden, Doman & Stafford Associates (DDS), a general partnership, an apartment building that needed extensive renovation. Goodman represented that he personally had experience in renovation work. During the course of negotiations on a renovation contract, Goodman informed the managing partner of DDS that he would be forming a corporation to do the work. A contract was executed in August between DDS and "Building Design and Development (In Formation), John A. Goodman, President." The contract required the renovation work to be completed by October 15. Goodman immediately subcontracted the work, but the renovation was not completed on time. DDS also found that the work that was completed was of poor quality. Goodman did not file the articles of incorporation for his new corporation until November 1. The partners of DDS sued Goodman to hold him liable for the renovation contracts. Goodman denied personal liability. Was it ethical for Goodman to deny liability? Is Goodman personally liable? *Goodman v. Darden, Doman & Stafford Associates*, 100 Wn.2d 476, 670 P.2d 648, **Web** 1983 Wash. Lexis 1776 (Supreme Court of Washington)

36.12 Business Ethics Pursuant to a public offering, Knoll International, Inc. (Knoll), issued debentures to investors. The debentures bore interest at 8.125 percent, matured in 30 years, and were subordinated, convertible into common stock at the rate of each $19.20 of principal amount for one share of common stock, and redeemable. Section 8.08 of the indenture agreement provided that no debenture holder could sue unless the holders of 35 percent of the debentures requested the trustee to sue. The indenture also gave the trustee the authority to amend the indenture agreement.

Knoll was controlled through a series of subsidiaries by Knoll International Holdings, Inc. (Holdings), which, in turn, was controlled by Marshall S. Cogan. Four years later, Knoll merged into Holdings and paid its common shareholders $12 cash per share. Knoll and the indenture trustee executed a supplemental indenture which provided that each debenture holder would receive $12 cash for each $19.20 principal amount of debentures. Simons, a debenture holder who did not own 35 percent of the debentures, brought a suit against Knoll and Cogan. Does Knoll International, Inc., or Cogan owe a fiduciary duty to the debenture holders? Did Cogan breach an ethical duty to the debenture holders? *Simons v. Cogan*, 542 A.2d 785, **Web** 1987 Del. Ch. Lexis 520 (Court of Chancery of Delaware)

▲ **Signing of the Sarbanes-Oxley Act of 2002** *George W. Bush signs the Sarbanes–Oxley Act of 2002 in the East Room of the White House. The act is designed to improve quality and transparency in financial reporting and independent audits as well as accounting services for public companies.*

CHAPTER OBJECTIVES

After studying this chapter, you should be able to:

1. Describe the functions of shareholders, directors, and officers in managing the affairs of a corporation.
2. Describe a director's and an officer's duty of care and the business judgment rule.
3. Describe a director's and an officer's duty of loyalty and how this duty is breached.

4. Define *piercing the corporate veil*, or *alter ego doctrine*.
5. Describe how the Sarbanes-Oxley Act affects corporate governance.

CHAPTER CONTENTS

▶ **INTRODUCTION TO CORPORATE GOVERNANCE AND THE SARBANES-OXLEY ACT**

▶ **SHAREHOLDERS**
Contemporary Environment · *Cumulative Voting*
Case 37.1 · *Northeast Iowa Ethanol, LLC v. Drizin*

Internet Law & Online Commerce · *Corporations Codes Recognize Electronic Communications*

▶ **BOARD OF DIRECTORS**
Ethics Spotlight · *Sarbanes-Oxley Act Imposes Duties on Audit Committee*

"Corporation: An ingenious device for obtaining individual profit without individual responsibility."

—Ambrose Bierce
The Devil's Dictionary (1911)

▶ INTRODUCTION TO CORPORATE GOVERNANCE AND THE SARBANES-OXLEY ACT

Shareholders, directors, and officers have different rights in managing a corporation. The shareholders elect the directors and vote on other important issues affecting the corporation. The directors are responsible for making policy decisions and employing officers. The officers are responsible for the corporation's day-to-day operations.

As a legal entity, a corporation can be held liable for the acts of its directors and officers and for authorized contracts entered into on its behalf. The directors and officers of a corporation have certain rights and owe certain duties to the corporation and its shareholders. A director or an officer who breaches any of these duties can be held personally liable to the corporation, to its shareholders, or to third parties. Except in a few circumstances, shareholders do not owe a fiduciary duty to other shareholders or the corporation.

Following substantial corporate fraud in the 1990s and early 2000s, Congress enacted the *Sarbanes-Oxley Act of 2002 (SOX)*. This federal statute established rules to improve corporate governance, prevent fraud, and add transparency to corporate operations. SOX has ushered in a new era of corporate governance.

This chapter discusses the rights, duties, and liability of corporate shareholders, directors, and officers. It also discusses the provisions of the Sarbanes-Oxley Act.

▶ SHAREHOLDERS

A corporation's **shareholders** own the corporation (see Exhibit 37.1). Nevertheless, they are not agents of the corporation (i.e., they cannot bind the corporation to contracts), and the only management duty they have is the right to vote on matters such as the election of directors and the approval of fundamental changes in the corporation.

▶ **Exhibit 37.1
SHAREHOLDERS**

Shareholders' Meetings

Annual shareholders' meetings are held to elect directors, choose an independent auditor, and take other actions. These meetings must be held at the times fixed in the bylaws [RMBCA Section 7.01]. If a meeting is not held within either 15 months of the last annual meeting or 6 months after the end of the corporation's fiscal year, whichever is earlier, a shareholder may petition the court to order the meeting held [RMBCA Section 7.03].

Special shareholders' meetings may be called by the board of directors, the holders of at least 10 percent of the voting shares of the corporation, or any other person authorized to do so by the articles of incorporation or bylaws (e.g., the president) [RMBCA Section 7.02]. Special meetings may be held to consider important or emergency issues, such as a merger or consolidation of the corporation with one or more other corporations, the removal of directors, amendment of the articles of incorporation, or dissolution of the corporation.

Any act that can be taken at a **shareholders' meeting** can be taken without a meeting if all the corporate shareholders sign a written consent approving the action [RMBCA Section 7.04].

annual shareholders' meeting
A meeting of the shareholders of a corporation that must be held by the corporation to elect directors and to vote on other matters.

special shareholders' meetings
Meetings of shareholders that may be called to consider and vote on important or emergency issues, such as a proposed merger or amending the articles of incorporation.

Notice of Shareholders' Meetings

A corporation is required to give the shareholders written notice of the place, day, and time of annual and special meetings. For a special meeting, the purpose of the meeting must also be stated. Only matters stated in the **notice of a meeting** can be considered at the meeting. The notice, which must be given not less than 10 days or more than 50 days before the date of the meeting, may be given in person or by mail [RMBCA Section 7.05]. If the required notice is not given or is defective, any action taken at the meeting is void.

Proxies

Shareholders do not have to attend a shareholders' meeting to vote. Shareholders may vote by *proxy*; that is, they can appoint another person (the proxy) as their agent to vote at a shareholders' meeting. The proxy may be directed exactly how to vote the shares or may be authorized to vote the shares at his or her discretion. Proxies may be in writing or posted online. The written document itself is called the **proxy** (or **proxy card**). Unless otherwise stated, a proxy is valid for 11 months [RMBCA Section 7.22].

proxy
A written document that a shareholder signs, authorizing another person to vote his or her shares at the shareholders' meetings in the event of the shareholder's absence.

Voting Requirements

At least one class of shares of stock of a corporation must have voting rights. The Revised Model Business Corporation Act (RMBCA) permits corporations to grant more than one vote per share to some classes of stock and less than one vote per share to others [RMBCA Section 6.01].

Only shareholders who own stock as of a set date may vote at a shareholders' meeting. This date, which is called the **record date**, is set forth in the corporate bylaws. The record date may not be more than 70 days before the shareholders' meeting [RMBCA Section 7.07]. The corporation must prepare a **shareholders' list** that contains the names and addresses of the shareholders as of the record date and the class and number of shares owned by each shareholder. This list must be available for inspection at the corporation's main office [RMBCA Section 7.20].

record date
A date specified in corporate bylaws that determines whether a shareholder may vote at a shareholders' meeting.

Quorum and Vote Required

Unless otherwise provided in the articles of incorporation, if a majority of shares entitled to vote are represented at a meeting in person or by proxy, there is a **quorum** to hold the meeting. Once a quorum is present, the withdrawal of shares does not affect the quorum of the meeting [RMBCA Sections 7.25(a), 7.25(b)]. The affirmative *vote* of the majority of the *voting* shares represented at a shareholders' meeting constitutes an act of the shareholders for actions other than for the election of directors [RMBCA Section 7.25(c)].

quorum
The required number of shares that must be represented in person or by proxy to hold a shareholders' meeting. The RMBCA establishes a majority of outstanding shares as a quorum.

Example A corporation has 20,000 shares outstanding. A shareholders' meeting is duly called to amend the articles of incorporation, and 10,001 shares are represented at the meeting. A quorum is present because a majority of the shares entitled to vote are represented. Suppose that 5,001 shares are voted in favor of the amendment. The amendment passes. In this example, just over 25 percent of the shares of the corporation bind the other shareholders to the action taken at the shareholders' meeting.

Straight (Noncumulative) Voting

Unless otherwise stated in a corporation's articles of incorporation, voting for the election of directors is by the **straight voting**, or **noncumulative voting**, method. This voting method is quite simple: Each shareholder votes the number of shares he or she owns on candidates for each of the positions open for election. Thus, a majority shareholder can elect the entire board of directors.

Example A corporation has 10,000 outstanding shares. Erin owns 5,100 shares (51 percent), and Michael owns 4,900 shares (49 percent). Suppose that three directors of the corporation are to be elected from a potential pool of 10 candidates. Erin casts 5,100 votes each for her three chosen candidates. Michael votes 4,900 shares for each of his three chosen candidates, who are different from those favored by Erin. Each of the three candidates whom Erin voted for wins, with 5,100 votes.

CONTEMPORARY ENVIRONMENT

Cumulative Voting

A corporation's articles of incorporation may provide for **cumulative voting** for the election of directors. Under this method, a shareholder can accumulate all of his or her votes and vote them all for one candidate or split them among several candidates. This means that each shareholder is entitled to multiply the number of shares he or she owns by the number of directors to be elected and cast the product for a single candidate or distribute the product among two or more candidates [RMBCA Section 7.28]. Cumulative voting gives a minority shareholder a better opportunity to elect someone to the board of directors.

Example Suppose Lisa owns 1,000 shares of a corporation. Assume that four directors are to be elected to the board. With cumulative voting, Lisa can multiply the number of shares she owns (1,000) by the number of directors to be elected (four). She can cast all the resulting votes (4,000) for one candidate or split them among candidates as she determines.

Examples of cumulative voting are set forth in Exhibit 37.2.

Supramajority Voting Requirement

The articles of incorporation or the bylaws of a corporation can require a greater than majority of the shares to constitute a quorum of the vote of the shareholders [RMBCA Section 7.27]. This is called a **supramajority voting requirement** (or **supermajority**). Such votes are often required to approve mergers, consolidation, the sale of substantially all the assets of a corporation, and such. To add a supramajority voting requirement, the amendment must be adopted by the number of shares of the proposed increase. For example, increasing a majority voting requirement to an 80 percent supramajority voting requirement would require an 80 percent affirmative vote.

Voting Trusts

Sometimes shareholders agree in advance as to how their shares will be voted. A **voting trust** is an arrangement whereby shareholders transfer their stock certificates to a trustee. Legal title to these shares is held in the name of the trustee. In exchange, **voting trust certificates** are issued to the shareholders. The trustee of the voting trust is empowered to vote the shares held by the trust. The trust may either specify how the trustee is to vote the

---

straight voting
A system in which each shareholder votes the number of shares he or she owns on candidates for each of the positions open. Also called *noncumulative voting*.

cumulative voting
A system in which a shareholder can accumulate all of his or her votes and vote them all for one candidate or split them among several candidates.

The law does not permit the stockholders to create a sterilized board of directors.

Justice Collins
Manson v. Curtis (1918)

supramajority voting requirement
A requirement that a greater than majority of shares constitutes a quorum of the vote of the shareholders.

voting trust
An arrangement in which the shareholders transfer their stock certificates to a trustee who is empowered to vote the shares.

Formula for Cumulative Voting. A shareholder can use the following formula to determine whether or not he or she owns a sufficient number of shares to elect a director to the board of directors using cumulative voting:

$$\frac{S \times T}{D + 1} + 1 = X$$

where X is the number of shares needed by a shareholder to elect a director to the board, S is the number of shares that actually vote at the shareholders' meeting, T is the number of directors the shareholder wants to elect, and D is the number of directors to be elected at the shareholders' meeting.

Example 1 Suppose there are 9,000 outstanding shares of a corporation. Shareholder 1 owns 1,000 shares, shareholder 2 owns 4,000 shares, and shareholder 3 owns 4,000 shares. Assume nine directors are to be elected to the board of directors. All the shares are voted. Under cumulative voting, does shareholder 1 have enough votes to elect a director to the board? The answer is yes:

$$\frac{9{,}000 \times 1}{9 + 1} + 1 = 901$$

Example 2 If a board of directors is divided into classes and elected by staggered elections, the ability of a minority shareholder to elect a director to the board is diminished. Suppose in Example 1 that the corporation staggered the election of the board of directors so that three directors are elected each year to serve three-year terms. How many shares would a shareholder have to own to elect a director to the board?

$$\frac{9{,}000 \times 1}{3 + 1} + 1 = 2{,}251$$

Because of the staggered election of the board of directors, shareholder 1 (who owns 1,000 shares) would not be able to elect a director to the board without the assistance of another shareholder.

shares or authorize the trustee to vote the shares at his or her discretion. The members of the trust retain all other incidents of ownership of the stock. A voting trust agreement must be in writing and cannot exceed 10 years. It must be filed with the corporation and is open to inspection by shareholders of the corporation [RMBCA Section 7.30].

Shareholder Voting Agreements

Two or more shareholders may enter into an agreement that stipulates how they will vote their shares for the election of directors or other matters that require a shareholder vote. **Shareholder voting agreements** are not limited in duration and do not have to be filed with the corporation. They are specifically enforceable [RMBCA Section 7.31]. Shareholder voting agreements can be either revocable or irrevocable [RMBCA Section 7.22(d)].

shareholder voting agreement
An agreement between two or more shareholders that stipulates how they will vote their shares.

Right of First Refusal

Generally, shareholders have the right to transfer their shares. Shareholders may enter into agreements with one another to prevent unwanted persons from becoming owners of the corporation [RMBCA Section 6.27]. A **right of first refusal** is an agreement that shareholders enter into whereby they grant each other the right of first refusal to purchase shares they are going to sell. A selling shareholder must offer his or her shares for sale to the other parties to the agreement before selling them to anyone else. If the shareholders do not exercise their right of first refusal, the selling shareholder is free to sell his or her shares to another party. A right of first refusal may be granted to the corporation as well.

right of first refusal
An agreement that requires a selling shareholder to offer his or her shares for sale to the other parties to the agreement before selling them to anyone else.

Buy-and-Sell Agreement

Shareholders sometimes enter into a **buy-and-sell agreement** that requires selling shareholders to sell their shares to the other shareholders or to the corporation at the price

buy-and-sell agreement
An agreement that requires selling shareholders to sell their shares to the other shareholders or to the corporation at the price specified in the agreement.

specified in the agreement. The price of the shares is normally determined by a formula that considers, among other factors, the profitability of the corporation. The purchase of shares of a deceased shareholder pursuant to a buy-and-sell agreement is often funded by proceeds from life insurance.

Preemptive Rights

preemptive rights
Rights that give existing shareholders the option of subscribing to new shares being issued in proportion to their current ownership interests.

The articles of incorporation can grant shareholders preemptive rights. **Preemptive rights** give existing shareholders the option of subscribing to new shares being issued by the corporation in proportion to their current ownership interests [RMBCA Section 6.30]. Such a purchase can prevent a shareholder's interest in the corporation from being *diluted*. Shareholders are given a reasonable period of time (e.g., 30 days) to exercise their preemptive rights. If a shareholder does not exercise his or her preemptive rights during this time, shares can then be sold to anyone.

Example The ABC Corporation has 10,000 outstanding shares, and Linda owns 1,000 shares (10 percent). Assume that the corporation plans to raise more capital by issuing another 10,000 shares of stock. With preemptive rights, Linda must be offered the option to purchase 1,000 of the 10,000 new shares before they are offered to the public. If she does not purchase them, her ownership in the corporation will be diluted from 10 percent to 5 percent.

Right to Receive Information and Inspect Books and Records

annual report
A report provided to shareholders that contains a balance sheet, an income statement, and a statement of changes in shareholder equity.

Shareholders have the right to be informed about the affairs of the corporation. A corporation must furnish its shareholders with an **annual report** that contains a balance sheet, an income statement, and a statement of changes in shareholder equity [RMBCA Section 16.20].

Shareholders have an absolute *right to inspect* the shareholders' list, the articles of incorporation, the bylaws, and the minutes of shareholders' meetings held within the past three years. To inspect accounting and tax records, minutes of board and committee meetings, and minutes of shareholders' meetings held more than three years in the past, a shareholder must demonstrate a "proper purpose," such as deciding how to vote in a shareholder election, identifying fellow shareholders to communicate with them regarding corporate matters, investigating the existence of corporate mismanagement or improper action, and the like [RMBCA Section 16.02].

Dividends

dividend
A distribution of profits of the corporation to shareholders.

Profit corporations operate to make a profit. The objective of the shareholders is to share in those profits, either through capital appreciation, the receipt of dividends, or both. **Dividends** are paid at the discretion of the board of directors [RMBCA Section 6.40]. The directors are responsible for determining when, where, how, and how much will be paid in dividends. They may opt to retain the profits in the corporation to be used for corporate purposes instead of as dividends. This authority cannot be delegated to a committee of the board of directors or to officers of the corporation.

When a corporation declares a dividend, it sets a date, usually a few weeks prior to the actual payment, that is called the *record date*. Persons who are shareholders on that date are entitled to receive the dividend, even if they sell their shares before the payment date. Once declared, a cash or property dividend cannot be revoked. Shareholders can sue to recover declared but unpaid dividends.

Stock Dividends

stock dividend
Additional shares of stock distributed as a dividend.

Corporations may use additional shares of stock as a dividend. **Stock dividends** are not a distribution of corporate assets. They are distributed in proportion to the existing ownership interests of shareholders, so they do not increase a shareholder's proportionate ownership interest.

Example Betty owns 1,000 shares (10 percent) of the 10,000 outstanding shares of ABC Corporation. If ABC Corporation declares a stock dividend of 20 percent, Betty will receive a stock dividend of 200 shares. She now owns 1,200 shares—or 10 percent—of a total of 12,000 outstanding shares.

Derivative Lawsuits

If a corporation is harmed by someone, the directors of the corporation have the authority to bring an action on behalf of the corporation against the offending party to recover damages or other relief. If the corporation fails to bring the lawsuit, shareholders have the right to bring the lawsuit on behalf of the corporation. This is called a **derivative action**, or **derivative lawsuit** [RMBCA Section 7.40].

A shareholder can bring a derivative action if he or she (1) was a shareholder of the corporation at the time of the act complained of; (2) fairly and adequately represents the interests of the corporation; and (3) made a written demand upon the corporation to take suitable actions and either the corporation rejected the demand or 90 days have expired since the date of the demand.

To bring a derivative lawsuit, a shareholder usually must make a written demand upon the corporate directors to bring the lawsuit, and if the directors fail to bring the suit, then the shareholder may pursue the lawsuit on behalf of the corporation. Oftentimes, the third party who has damaged the corporation is one or more of the corporation's own directors or officers. For example, board members or officers, or both, may have committed fraud or otherwise stolen property from or misused property of the corporation. In this case, the written demand will be excused.

A derivative lawsuit will be dismissed by the court if either a majority of independent directors or a panel of independent persons appointed by the court determines that the lawsuit is not in the best interests of the corporation. This decision must be reached in good faith and only after conducting a reasonable inquiry.

If a shareholder's derivative action is successful, any award goes into the corporate treasury. The plaintiff-shareholder is entitled to recover payment for reasonable expenses, including attorneys' fees, incurred in bringing and maintaining the derivative action. Any settlement of a derivative action requires court approval.

> **derivative lawsuit**
> A lawsuit a shareholder brings against an offending party on behalf of a corporation when the corporation fails to bring the lawsuit.

Piercing the Corporate Veil

Shareholders of a corporation generally have **limited liability** (i.e., they are liable for the debts and obligations of the corporation only to the extent of their capital contribution), and they are not personally liable for the debts and obligations of the corporation. However, if a shareholder or shareholders dominate a corporation and misuse it for improper purposes, a court of equity can *disregard the corporate entity* and hold the shareholders of the corporation personally liable for the corporation's debts and obligations. This doctrine is commonly referred to as **piercing the corporate veil**. It is often resorted to by unpaid creditors who are trying to collect from shareholders a debt owed by the corporation. The piercing the corporate veil doctrine is also called the **alter ego doctrine** because the corporation becomes the *alter ego* of the shareholder.

Courts will pierce the corporate veil if (1) the corporation has been formed without sufficient capital (i.e., *thin capitalization*) or (2) separateness has not been maintained between the corporation and its shareholders (e.g., commingling of personal and corporate assets, failure to hold required shareholders' meetings, failure to maintain corporate records and books). The courts examine this doctrine on a case-by-case basis.

The piercing the corporate veil doctrine was raised in the following case.

> **piercing the corporate veil**
> A doctrine that says if a shareholder dominates a corporation and uses it for improper purposes, a court of equity can disregard the corporate entity and hold the shareholder personally liable for the corporation's debts and obligations. Also called the *alter ego doctrine*.

CASE 37.1 Piercing the Corporate Veil

Northeast Iowa Ethanol, LLC v. Drizin

Web 2006 U.S. Dist. Lexis 4828 (2006)
United States District Court for the Northern District of Iowa

"If capital is illusory or trifling compared with the business to be done and the risk of loss, this is a ground for denying the separate entity privilege."

—Judge Jarvey

Facts

Local farmers in Manchester, Iowa, decided to build an ethanol plant in the Manchester area. An ethanol plant produces ethanol and feed grain, which can be sold at a profit exceeding that of the sale of grain. After many meetings, the local farmers invested $2,365,000 for the project. The farmers formed Northeast Iowa Ethanol, LLC (Northeast Iowa), to hold the money and develop the project. William Ethanol Service agreed to invest $1 million, and North Central Construction agreed to invest $500,000. In all, $3,865,000 was raised for the construction of the ethanol plant. The funds were placed in an escrow account. The project needed another $20 million, for which financing needed to be secured.

Jerry Drizin formed Global Syndicate International, Inc. (GSI), a Nevada corporation, with $250 capital. GSI was formed for the purpose of assisting Northeast Iowa raise the additional financing for the project. Traditional financing from banks was not available for such a project, so Drizin looked for other sources of money. Drizin talked Northeast Iowa into transferring money to a bank in south Florida to serve as security for a possible loan. Drizin commingled those funds with his own personal funds. Through an array of complex transfers orchestrated by Drizin, all of the funds of Northeast Iowa were stolen. Drizin invested some funds in a worthless gold mine and lost the rest of the money in other worthless investments.

Plaintiff Northeast Iowa sued Drizin for civil fraud to recover its funds. Drizin defended, arguing that GSI was liable but that he was not liable because he was but a shareholder of GSI. The plaintiffs alleged that the doctrine of piercing the corporate veil applied and that Drizin was therefore personally liable for the funds.

Issue

Does the doctrine of piercing the corporate veil apply in this case, thus allowing the plaintiffs to pierce the corporate veil of GSI and reach shareholder Drizin for liability for civil fraud?

Language of the Court

In every financial scam like that perpetrated on the plaintiff here, there comes a point at which the victim must make an exceedingly quick decision and seemingly, the entire fate of the project depends on taking that leap of faith. From that point on, very bad things follow and only time will tell what they are.

Generally a corporation is a distinct entity from its shareholders. This distinction usually insulates shareholders from personal liability for corporate debts. However, this protection is not absolute. Personal liability may be imposed upon shareholders in "exceptional circumstances." The corporate veil may be pierced, for example, where the corporation is a mere shell, serving no legitimate business purpose, and used primarily as an intermediary to perpetuate fraud or promote injustice.

If a corporation lacks substantial capital such that it would not be able to meet its debts, this is a ground for denying the privilege of separate entity. If capital is illusory or trifling compared with the business to be done and the risk of loss, this is a ground for denying the separate entity privilege. Secondly, if corporate funds are not segregated, there is a strong inference that they are being used by the shareholders for their individual purposes. A major corporate officer cannot avoid liability be emulating the three fabled monkeys, "hearing, seeing and speaking no evil."

Without question, this case presents the "exceptional circumstance" warranting the piercing of GSI's corporate veil and finding Mr. Drizin personally liable for GSI's misdeeds, as the sole purpose of establishing GSI was to perpetuate fraud. GSI engaged in no legitimate business transactions whatsoever. The $250.00 initial capitalization of GSI is, in fact, "trifling compared with the business to be done and the risk of loss." GSI had no errors and omissions insurance. Mr. Drizin used GSI's accounts as his own, constantly transferring money from the GSI escrow account to his personal accounts for "reimbursement" and to other accounts for "safekeeping" and "diversification." And now, GSI is a defunct corporation. Justice and equity call for piercing the corporate veil.

Drizin's actions with respect to plaintiff's money were both outrageous and malicious. As a result of Drizin's tortious conduct, good people were hurt. The evidence is clear, convincing, and satisfactory that punitive damages are appropriate in this case to punish Drizin and to deter others from engaging in similar conduct.

Decision

The U.S. District Court held that the corporate veil of GSI could be pierced to reach its shareholder Drizin. The Court

awarded the plaintiff compensatory damage of $3.8 million and punitive damages of $7.6 million against Drizin.

Case Questions

Critical Legal Thinking What is civil fraud? Explain. What does the doctrine of piercing the corporate veil provide? Explain.

Business Ethics Did Drizin act ethically in this case? Did the owners of Northeast Iowa have any responsibility for the losses they suffered in this case? Explain.

Contemporary Business Do you think that the plaintiff Northeast Iowa will recover on its $11.4 million judgment in this case?

INTERNET LAW & ONLINE COMMERCE

Corporations Codes Recognize Electronic Communications

Most state corporations codes have been amended to permit the use of electronic communications to shareholders and among directors. For example, the Delaware General Corporation Law recognizes the following uses of electronic technology:

- Delivery of notices to shareholders may be made electronically if the shareholder consents to the delivery of notices in this form.
- Proxy solicitation for shareholder votes may be made by electronic transmission.
- The shareholders list of a corporation that must be made available during the 10 days prior to a shareholders' meeting may be made available either at the principal place of business of the corporation or by posting the list on an electronic network.

- Shareholders who are not physically present at a meeting may be deemed present, participate in, and vote at the meeting by electronic communication; a meeting may be held solely by electronic communication, without a physical location.
- The election of directors of the corporation may be held by electronic transmission.
- Directors' actions by unanimous consent may be taken by electronic transmission.

The use of electronic transmissions, electronic networks, and communications by e-mail will make the operation and administration of corporate affairs more efficient.

▶ BOARD OF DIRECTORS

The **board of directors** of a corporation is elected by the shareholders of the corporation. The board of directors is responsible for formulating *policy decisions* that affect the management, supervision, control, and operation of the corporation (see Exhibit 37.3) [RMBCA Section 8.01]. Such policy decisions include deciding the business or businesses in which the corporation should be engaged, selecting and removing the top officers of the corporation, determining the capital structure of the corporation, declaring dividends, and the like.

The board may initiate certain actions that require shareholders' approval. These actions are initiated when the board of directors adopts a *resolution* that approves a transaction and recommends that it be submitted to the shareholders for a vote. Examples of such transactions include mergers, sale of substantially all of the corporation's assets outside the course of ordinary business operations, amendment of the articles of incorporation, and voluntary dissolution of the corporation.

Corporate directors are required to have access to the corporation's books and records, facilities, and premises, as well as any other information that affects the operation of the corporation. This right of inspection is absolute. It cannot be limited by the articles of incorporation, the bylaws, or board resolution.

board of directors
A panel of decision makers who are elected by the shareholders.

Compensating Directors

Originally, it was considered an honor to serve as a director. No payment was involved. Today, directors are often paid an annual retainer and an attendance fee for each meeting

▶ **Exhibit 37.3 BOARD OF DIRECTORS**

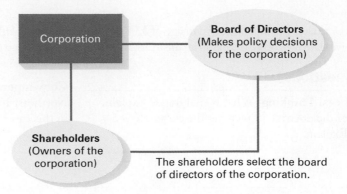

Corporation

Board of Directors (Makes policy decisions for the corporation)

Shareholders (Owners of the corporation)

The shareholders select the board of directors of the corporation.

attended. Unless otherwise provided in the articles of incorporation, the directors are permitted to fix their own compensation [RMBCA Section 8.11].

Selecting Directors

inside director
A member of the board of directors who is also an officer of the corporation.

outside director
A member of a board of directors who is not an officer of the corporation.

Boards of directors are typically composed of inside and outside directors. An **inside director** is a person who is also an officer of the corporation. For example, the president of the corporation often sits as a director of the corporation.

An **outside director** is a person who sits on the board of directors of a corporation but is not an officer of that corporation. Outside directors are often officers and directors of other corporations, bankers, lawyers, professors, and others. Outside directors are often selected for their business knowledge and expertise.

There are no special qualifications that a person must meet to be elected a director of a corporation. A director need not be a resident of the state of incorporation of the corporation or a shareholder of the corporation. The articles of incorporation or bylaws may prescribe qualifications for directors, however [RMBCA Section 8.02].

A board of directors can consist of one or more individuals. The number of initial directors is fixed by the articles of incorporation. This number can be amended in the articles of incorporation or the bylaws. The articles of incorporation or bylaws can establish a variable range for the size of the board of directors. The exact number of directors within the range may be changed from time to time by the board of directors or the shareholders [RMBCA Section 8.03].

CONCEPT SUMMARY
CLASSIFICATION OF DIRECTORS

Classification	Description
Inside director	A person who is also an officer of the corporation
Outside director	A person who is not an officer of the corporation

The director is really a watch-dog, and the watch-dog has no right, without the knowledge of his master, to take a sop from a possible wolf.

Lord Justice Bowen
Re The North Australian Territory Co. Ltd. (1891)

Term of Office

The term of a director's office expires at the next annual shareholders' meeting following his or her election, unless terms are staggered [RMBCA Section 8.05]. The RMBCA allows boards of directors that consist of nine or more members to be divided into two or three classes (each class to be as nearly equal in number as possible) that are elected to serve *staggered terms* of two or three years [RMBCA Section 8.06]. The specifics of such an arrangement must be outlined in the articles of incorporation.

Example Suppose a board of directors consists of nine directors. The board can be divided into three classes of three directors each, each class to be elected to serve a three-year term.

Only three directors of the nine-member board would come up for election each year. This nine-member board could also be divided into two classes of five and four directors, each class to be elected to a two-year term.

Vacancies on a board of directors can occur because of death, illness, the resignation of a director before the expiration of his or her term, or an increase in the number of positions on the board. Such vacancies can be filled by the shareholders or the remaining directors [RMBCA Section 8.10].

Meetings of the Board of Directors

The directors of a corporation can act only as a board. They cannot act individually on the corporation's behalf. Every director has the right to participate in any meeting of the board of directors. Each director has one vote. Directors cannot vote by proxy.

Regular meetings of a board of directors are held at the times and places established in the bylaws. Such meetings can be held without notice. The board can call **special meetings** as provided in the bylaws [RMBCA Section 8.20(a)]. Special meetings are usually convened for such reasons as issuing new shares, considering proposals to merge with other corporations, adopting maneuvers to defend against hostile takeover attempts, and the like. The board of directors may act without a meeting if all the directors sign written consents that set forth the actions taken. The RMBCA permits meetings of the board to be held via conference calls [RMBCA Section 8.20(b)].

Quorum and Voting Requirement

A simple majority of the number of directors established in the articles of incorporation or bylaws usually constitutes a **quorum** for transacting business. However, the articles of incorporation and the bylaws may increase this number. If a quorum is present, the approval or disapproval of a majority of the quorum binds the entire board. The articles of incorporation or the bylaws can require a greater than majority of directors to constitute a quorum of the vote of the board [RMBCA Section 8.24].

quorum
The number of directors necessary to hold a board meeting or transact business of the board.

ETHICS SPOTLIGHT

Sarbanes-Oxley Act Imposes Duties on Audit Committee

During the late 1990s and early 2000s, many corporations engaged in accounting fraud to report inflated earnings or to conceal losses. It was often management who perpetrated this accounting fraud, which was not detected by the board of directors. Sometimes members of the board of directors conspired or participated in the accounting fraud. In response, Congress enacted the federal *Sarbanes-Oxley Act* of 2002, which placed certain responsibilities on a corporation's **audit committee**.

A public company must have an audit committee. Members of the audit committee must be members of the board of directors and must be independent—that is, not employed by or receive compensation from the company or any of its subsidiaries for services other than as a board member and member of the audit committee. These board members are called *outside* board members because they are not employees (e.g., president, CEO) of the corporation. At least one member of the audit committee must be a financial expert, based on either education or prior experience, who is able to understand generally accepted accounting principles, preparation of financial statements, and audit committee functions.

The audit committee is responsible for the appointment of, payment of compensation for, and oversight of public accounting firms employed to audit the company. The audit committee must preapprove all audit and permissible nonaudit services to be performed by a public accounting firm. The audit committee has authority to employ independent legal counsel and other advisors.

The Sarbanes-Oxley Act requires public companies to establish and maintain adequate internal controls and procedures for financial reporting. The act requires a public company to prepare an assessment of the effectiveness of its internal controls at the end of each fiscal year. These internal audits are supervised by the audit committee.

Business Ethics Do you think there is very much fraud by boards of directors in managing corporations? Will the requirement of having only independent outside directors on the audit committee help prevent accounting fraud? Explain.

officers
Employees of a corporation who are appointed by the board of directors to manage the day-to-day operations of the corporation.

▶ **Exhibit 37.4 CORPORATE OFFICERS**

▶ CORPORATE OFFICERS

A corporation's board of directors has the authority to appoint the officers of the corporation. The **corporate officers** are elected by the board of directors at such time and by such manner as prescribed in the corporation's bylaws. The directors can delegate certain management authority to the officers of the corporation (see Exhibit 37.4).

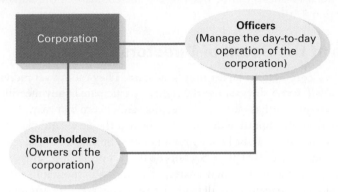

At a minimum, most corporations have the following officers: a president, one or more vice presidents, a secretary, and a treasurer. The bylaws or the board of directors can authorize duly appointed officers the power to appoint assistant officers. The same individual may simultaneously hold more than one office in the corporation [RMBCA Section 8.40]. The duties of each officer are specified in the bylaws of the corporation.

An officer of a corporation may be removed by the board of directors. The board only has to determine that the best interests of the corporation will be served by such removal [RMBCA Section 8.43(b)]. Officers who are removed in violation of an employment contract can sue the corporation for damages.

Agency Authority of Officers

History suggests that capitalism is a necessary condition for political freedom.

Milton Friedman

Officers and agents of a corporation have such authority as may be provided in the bylaws of the corporation or as determined by resolution of the board of directors [RMBCA Section 8.41]. Because they are agents, officers have authority, implied authority, and apparent authority to bind a corporation to contracts.

A corporation can *ratify* an unauthorized act of a corporate officer or agent. For example, suppose an officer acts outside the scope of his or her employment and enters into a contract with a third person. If the corporation accepts the benefits of the contract, it has ratified the contract and is bound by it. Officers are liable on an unauthorized contract if the corporation does not ratify it.

CONCEPT SUMMARY
MANAGEMENT OF A CORPORATION

Group	Function
Shareholders	Owners of the corporation. They vote on the directors and other major actions to be taken by the corporation.
Board of directors	Responsible for making policy decisions and employing the major officers for the corporation. It may initiate certain actions that require shareholders' approval.
Officers	Responsible for the day-to-day operation of the corporation, including acting as agents for the corporation, hiring other officers and employees, and the like.

FIDUCIARY DUTY: DUTY OF OBEDIENCE

The directors and officers of a corporation must act within the authority conferred upon them by the state's corporations code, the articles of incorporation, the corporate bylaws, and the resolutions adopted by the board of directors. This duty is called the **duty of obedience**. Directors and officers who either intentionally or negligently act outside their authority are personally liable for any resultant damages caused to the corporation or its shareholders.

Example Suppose the articles of incorporation of a corporation authorize the corporation to invest in real estate only. If a corporate officer invests corporate funds in the commodities markets, the officer is liable to the corporation for any losses suffered.

▶ FIDUCIARY DUTY: DUTY OF CARE

The directors and officers of a corporation owe certain **fiduciary duties** when making decisions and taking action on behalf of the corporation. One such duty is the **duty of care**. The duty of care requires corporate directors and officers to use *care and diligence* when acting on behalf of the corporation. To meet this duty of care, the directors and officers must discharge their duties (1) in good faith, (2) with the care that an *ordinary prudent person* in a like position would use under similar circumstances, and (3) in a manner they reasonably believe to be in the best interests of the corporation [RMBCA Sections 8.30(a), 8.42(a)].

A director or an officer who breaches the duty of care is personally liable to the corporation and its shareholders for any damages caused by the breach. Such breaches, which are normally caused by **negligence**, often involve a director's or an officer's failure to (1) make a reasonable investigation of a corporate matter, (2) attend board meetings on a regular basis, (3) properly supervise a subordinate who causes a loss to the corporation through embezzlement and such, or (4) keep adequately informed about corporate affairs. The courts examine breaches on a case-by-case basis.

The Business Judgment Rule

The determination of whether a corporate director or officer has met his or her duty of care is measured as of the time the decision is made; the benefit of hindsight is not a factor. Therefore, the directors and officers are not liable to the corporation or its shareholders for honest mistakes of judgment. This is called the **business judgment rule**. Were it not for the protection afforded by the business judgment rule, many high-risk but socially desirable endeavors might not be undertaken.

Example After conducting considerable research and investigation, the directors of a major automobile company decide to produce large and expensive SUVs. Three years later, when the SUVs are introduced to the public for sale, few of them are sold because of the public's interest in buying smaller, less expensive automobiles due to an economic recession and an increase in gasoline prices. Because this was an honest mistake of judgment on the part of corporate management, their judgment is shielded by the business judgment rule.

The court had to decide whether directors were protected by the business judgment rule in the following classic case.

---

duty of obedience
A duty that directors and officers of a corporation have to act within the authority conferred upon them by state corporation codes, the articles of incorporation, the corporate bylaws, and the resolutions adopted by the board of directors.

fiduciary duties
The duties of obedience, care, and loyalty owed by directors and officers to their corporation and its shareholders.

duty of care
A duty of corporate directors and officers to use care and diligence when acting on behalf of the corporation.

negligence
Failure of a corporate director or officer to exercise the duty of care while conducting the corporation's business.

business judgment rule
A rule that says directors and officers are not liable to the corporation or its shareholders for honest mistakes of judgment.

CASE 37.2 Duty of Care

Smith v. Van Gorkom

488 A.2d 858, Web 1985 Del. Lexis 421 (1985)
Supreme Court of Delaware

"**In the specific context of a proposed merger of a domestic corporation, a director has a duty, along with his fellow directors, to act in an informed and deliberate manner in determining whether to approve an agreement of merger.**"

—Judge Horsey

Facts

Trans Union Corporation (Trans Union) was a publicly traded, diversified holding company that was incorporated in Delaware. Its principal earnings were generated by its railcar leasing business. Jerome W. Van Gorkom was a

(case continues)

Trans Union officer for more than 24 years, its chief executive officer for more than 17 years, and the chairman of the board of directors for 2 years. Van Gorkom, a lawyer and certified public accountant, owned 75,000 shares of Trans Union. He was approaching 65 years of age and mandatory retirement. Trans Union's board of directors was composed of 10 members—5 inside directors and 5 outside directors.

Van Gorkom decided to meet with Jay A. Pritzker, a well-known corporate takeover specialist and a social acquaintance of Van Gorkom's, to discuss the possible sale of Trans Union to Pritzker. Van Gorkom met Pritzker at Pritzker's home on Saturday. He did so without consulting Trans Union's board of directors. At this meeting, Van Gorkom proposed a sale of Trans Union to Pritzker at a price of $55 per share. The stock was trading at about $38 in the market. On Monday, Pritzker notified Van Gorkom that he was interested in the $55 cash-out merger proposal. Van Gorkom, along with two inside directors, privately met with Pritzker on Tuesday and Wednesday. After meeting with Van Gorkom on Thursday, Pritzker notified his attorney to begin drafting the merger documents.

On Friday, Van Gorkom called a special meeting of Trans Union's board of directors for the following day. The board members were not told the purpose of the meeting. At the meeting, Van Gorkom disclosed the Pritzker offer and described its terms in a 20-minute presentation. Neither the merger agreement nor a written summary of the terms of agreement was furnished to the directors. No valuation study as to the value of Trans Union was prepared for the meeting. After two hours, the board voted in favor of the cash-out merger with Pritzker's company at $55 per share for Trans Union's stock. The board also voted not to solicit other offers. The merger agreement was executed by Van Gorkom during Saturday evening at a formal social event he hosted for the opening of the Chicago Lyric Opera's season. Neither he nor any other director read the agreement prior to its signing and delivery to Pritzker.

Trans Union's board of directors recommended that the merger be approved by its shareholders and distributed proxy materials to the shareholders, stating that the $55 per share price for their stock was fair. In the meantime, Trans Union's board of directors took steps to dissuade two other possible suitors who showed an interest in purchasing Trans Union. On February 10, 1981, 69.9 percent of the shares of Trans Union stock was voted in favor of the merger. The merger was consummated.

Alden Smith and other Trans Union shareholders sued Van Gorkom and the other directors for damages, alleging that the defendants were negligent in their conduct in selling Trans Union to Pritzker. The Delaware court of chancery held in favor of the defendants. The plaintiffs appealed.

Issue

Did Trans Union's directors breach their duty of care?

Language of the Court

In the specific context of a proposed merger of a domestic corporation, a director has a duty, along with his fellow directors, to act in an informed and deliberate manner in determining whether to approve an agreement of merger. The directors (1) did not adequately inform themselves as to Van Gorkom's role in forcing the sale of the company and in establishing the per share purchase price; (2) they were uninformed as to the intrinsic value of the company and (3) given these circumstances, at a minimum, they were grossly negligent in approving the sale of the company upon two hours' consideration, without prior notice, and without the exigency of a crisis or emergency.

Without any documents before them concerning the proposed transaction, the members of the board were required to rely entirely upon Van Gorkom's 20-minute oral presentation of the proposal. No written summary of the terms of the merger was presented; the directors were given no documentation to support the adequacy of $55 price per share for sale of the company; and the board had before it nothing more than Van Gorkom's statement of his understanding of the substance of an agreement that he admittedly had never read or that any member of the board had ever seen. Thus, the record compels the conclusion that the board lacked valuation information to reach an informed business judgment as to the fairness of $55 per share for sale of the company. We conclude that Trans Union's board was grossly negligent in that it failed to act with informed reasonable deliberation in agreeing to the Pritzker merger proposal.

Decision

The supreme court of Delaware held that the defendant directors had breached their duty of care. The supreme court reversed the judgment of the court of chancery and remanded the case to the court of chancery to conduct an evidentiary hearing to determine the fair value of the shares represented by the plaintiffs' class. If that value was higher than $55 per share, the difference was to be awarded to the plaintiffs as damages.

Case Questions

Critical Legal Thinking Describe the fiduciary duty of care owed by directors and officers. What does the business judgment rule provide? Explain.

Business Ethics Do you think Van Gorkom and the other directors had the shareholders' best interests in mind? Explain.

Contemporary Business What type of liability exposure is there for being a member of a board of directors? Explain.

▶ FIDUCIARY DUTY: DUTY OF LOYALTY

Directors and officers of a corporation owe a fiduciary duty to act honestly. This duty, called the **duty of loyalty**, requires directors and officers to subordinate their personal interests to those of the corporation and its shareholders. Justice Benjamin Cardozo defined the duty of loyalty as follows:

> [A corporate director or officer] owes loyalty and allegiance to the corporation—a loyalty that is undivided and an allegiance that is influenced by no consideration other than the welfare of the corporation. Any adverse interest of a director [or officer] will be subjected to a scrutiny rigid and uncompromising. He may not profit at the expense of his corporation and in conflict with its rights; he may not for personal gain divert unto himself the opportunities that in equity and fairness belong to the corporation.
>
> Many forms of conduct permissible in a workaday world for those acting at arm's length are forbidden to those bound by fiduciary ties. Not honesty alone, but the punctilio of an honor the most sensitive, is then the standard of behavior. As to this there has developed a tradition that is unbending and inveterate.[1]

If a director or an officer breaches his or her duty of loyalty and makes a secret profit on a transaction, the corporation can sue the director or officer to recover the secret profit. Some of the most common breaches of the duty of loyalty are discussed in the following paragraphs.

Usurping a Corporate Opportunity

Directors and officers may not personally usurp (steal) a corporate opportunity for themselves. **Usurping a corporate opportunity** constitutes a violation of a director's or an officer's duty of loyalty. If usurping is proven, the corporation can (1) acquire the opportunity from the director or officer and (2) recover any profits made by the director or officer.

The following elements must be shown to prove usurping:

- The opportunity was presented to the director or officer in his or her corporate capacity.
- The opportunity is related to or connected with the corporation's current or proposed business.
- The corporation has the financial ability to take advantage of the opportunity.
- The corporate officer or director took the corporate opportunity for him- or herself.

However, the director or officer is personally free to take advantage of a corporate opportunity if it was fully disclosed and presented to the corporation and the corporation rejected it.

Self-dealing

Under the RMBCA, a contract or transaction with a corporate director or officer is voidable by the corporation if it is unfair to the corporation [RMBCA Section 8.31]. Contracts of a corporation to purchase property from, sell property to, or make loans to corporate directors or officers where the directors or officers have not disclosed their interest in the transaction are often voided under this standard. In the alternative, the corporation can affirm the contract and recover any profits from the **self-dealing** employee. Contracts or transactions with corporate directors or officers are enforceable if their interest in the transaction has been disclosed to the corporation, and the disinterested directors or the shareholders have approved the transaction.

Competing with the Corporation

Directors and officers cannot engage in activities that **compete with the corporation** unless full disclosure is made and a majority of the disinterested directors or shareholders approve the activity. The corporation can recover any profits made by nonapproved competition and any other damages caused to the corporation.

duty of loyalty
A duty that directors and officers have not to act adversely to the interests of the corporation and to subordinate their personal interests to those of the corporation and its shareholders.

The increase of a great number of citizens in prosperity is a necessary element to the security, and even to the existence, of a civilized people.

Eugene Buret

It appears to me that the atmosphere of the temple of Justice is polluted by the presence of such things as companies.

Lord Justice James
Wilson v. Church (1879)

Making a Secret Profit

If a director or an officer breaches his or her duty of loyalty and **makes a secret profit** on a transaction, the corporation can sue the director or officer to recover the secret profit.

Example Maxine is the purchasing agent for the Roebolt Corporation. Her duties require her to negotiate and execute contracts to purchase office supplies and equipment for the corporation. Assume that Bruce, a computer salesperson, pays Maxine a $10,000 kickback to purchase from him computers needed by the Roebolt Corporation. The Roebolt Corporation can sue and recover the $10,000 secret profit from Maxine.

CONCEPT SUMMARY

FIDUCIARY DUTIES OF CORPORATION DIRECTORS AND OFFICERS

Duty	Description	Violation
Duty of obedience	Duty to act within the authority given by state corporations code, articles of incorporation, the corporate by laws and resolutions adopted by the board of directors.	Acts outside the corporate officer's or director's authority.
Duty of care	Duty to use care and diligence when acting on behalf of the corporation. This duty is discharged if an officer or a director acts: 1. In good faith 2. With the care that an ordinary prudent person in a like position would use under similar circumstances 3. In a manner he or she reasonably believes to be in the best interests of the corporation	Acts of negligence and mismanagement. Such acts include failure to: 1. Make a reasonable investigation of a corporate matter 2. Attend board meetings on a regular basis 3. Properly supervise a subordinate who causes a loss to the corporation 4. Keep adequately informed about corporate matters 5. Take other actions necessary to discharge duties
Duty of loyalty	Duty to subordinate personal interests to those of the corporation and its shareholders.	Acts of disloyalty. Such acts include unauthorized: 1. Self-dealing with the corporation 2. Usurping of a corporate opportunity 3. Competition with the corporation 4. Making of secret profit that belongs to the corporation

▶ SARBANES-OXLEY ACT

During the late 1990s and early 2000s, the U.S. economy was wracked by a number of business and accounting scandals. Companies such as Enron, Tyco, and WorldCom engaged in fraudulent conduct, leading to many corporate officers being convicted of financial crimes. Many of these companies went bankrupt, causing huge losses to their shareholders, employees, and creditors. Boards of directors were complacent, not keeping a watchful eye over the conduct of their officers and employees.

In response, Congress enacted the federal **Sarbanes-Oxley Act** of 2002. This act establishes far-reaching rules regarding corporate governance. The goals of the Sarbanes-Oxley Act are to improve corporate governance rules, eliminate conflicts of interest, and instill confidence in investors and the public that management will run public companies in the best interests of all constituents. Excerpts from the Sarbanes-Oxley Act are set forth as Appendix C to this book.

ETHICS SPOTLIGHT

Sarbanes-Oxley Act Improves Corporate Governance

The Sarbanes-Oxley Act has changed the rules of corporate governance in important respects. Several major provisions of the act regarding corporate governance are discussed in the following paragraphs.

CEO and CFO Certification

The CEO and CFO of a public company must file a statement accompanying each annual and quarterly report, certifying that the signing officer has reviewed the report, based on the officer's knowledge that the report does not contain any untrue statement of a material fact or omit to state a material fact that would make the statement misleading and that the financial statement and disclosures fairly present, in all material aspects, the operation and financial condition of the company. A knowing and willful violation is punishable by up to 20 years in prison and a fine up to $5 million.

Reimbursement of Bonuses and Incentive Pay

If a public company is required to restate its financial statements because of material noncompliance with financial reporting requirements, the CEO and CFO must reimburse the company for any bonuses, incentive pay, or securities trading profits made because of the noncompliance.

Prohibition on Personal Loans

The act prohibits public companies from making personal loans to their directors or executive officers.

Tampering with Evidence

The act makes it a crime for any person to knowingly alter, destroy, mutilate, conceal, or create any document to impair, impede, influence, or obstruct any federal investigation. A violation is punishable by up to 20 years in prison and a monetary fine.

Bar from Acting as an Officer or a Director

The Securities and Exchange Commission (SEC), a federal government agency, may issue an order prohibiting any person who has committed securities fraud from acting as an officer or a director of a public company.

Although the Sarbanes-Oxley Act applies only to public companies, private companies and nonprofit organizations are also influenced by the act's accounting and corporate governance rules.

Business Ethics   Will the CEO and CFO certification requirement reduce corporate fraudulent conduct? Explain. Will the Sarbanes-Oxley Act encourage more ethical behavior from corporate officers and directors?

TEST REVIEW TERMS AND CONCEPTS

Annual financial statement
Annual shareholders' meeting
Audit committee
Board of directors
Business judgment rule
Buy-and-sell agreement
Competing with a corporation
Corporate officer
Cumulative voting
Derivative action (derivative lawsuit)
Dividend
Duty of care

Duty of loyalty
Duty of obedience
Fiduciary duties
Inside director
Limited liability
Making a secret profit
Negligence
Notice of a shareholders' meeting
Outside director
Piercing the corporate veil (alter ego doctrine)
Preemptive rights
Proxy (proxy card)
Quorum

Record date
Regular meeting of a board of directors
Right of first refusal
Sarbanes-Oxley Act
Self-dealing
Shareholder
Shareholders' list
Shareholders' meeting
Shareholder voting agreement
Special meeting of a board of directors
Special shareholders' meeting

Stock dividend
Straight (noncumulative) voting
Supramajority voting requirement (supramajority)
Usurping a corporate opportunity
Voting trust
Voting trust certificate

CASE PROBLEMS

37.1 Shareholders' Meeting Ocilla Industries, Inc. (Ocilla), owned 40 percent of the stock of Direct Action Marketing, Inc. (Direct Action). Direct Action was a New York corporation that specialized in the marketing of products through billing inserts. Ocilla helped place Howard Katz and Joseph Esposito on Direct Action's five-member board of directors. A dispute between Ocilla and the two directors caused Ocilla to claim that Katz and Esposito wanted excess remuneration in exchange for leaving the board at the end of their terms. As a result, no shareholders' meeting was held for one and one-half years. Under the Model Business Corporations Act, can Ocilla compel Direct Action to hold the meeting earlier? *Ocilla Industries, Inc. v. Katz*, 677 F.Supp. 1291, **Web** 1987 U.S. Dist. Lexis 12741 (United States District Court for the Eastern District of New York)

37.2 Special Shareholders' Meeting Jack C. Schoenholtz was a shareholder and member of the board of directors of Rye Psychiatric Hospital Center, Inc. (Rye Hospital). Four years after the hospital was incorporated, a split had developed among the board of directors concerning the operation of the facility. Three directors stood on one side of the dispute, and three directors on the other. In an attempt to break the deadlock, Schoenholtz, who owned over 10 percent of the corporation's voting stock, asked the corporation's secretary to call a special meeting of the shareholders. In response, the secretary sent a notice to the shareholders, stating that a special meeting of the shareholders would be held "for the purpose of electing directors." The meeting was held as scheduled. Some shareholders brought suit, claiming that the special shareholders' meeting was not called properly. Who wins? *Rye Psychiatric Hospital Center, Inc. v. Schoenholtz*, 101 A.D.2d 309, 476 N.Y.S.2d 339, **Web** 1984 N.Y.App. Div. Lexis 17818 (Supreme Court of New York)

37.3 Proxy George Gibbons, William Smith, and Gerald Zollar were all shareholders in GRG Operating, Inc. (GRG). Zollar contributed $1,000 of his own funds so that the corporation could begin to do business. In exchange for this contribution, Gibbons and Smith both granted Zollar the right to vote their shares of GRG stock. They gave Zollar a signed form which stated that "Gibbons and Smith, for a period of 10 years from the date hereof, appoint Zollar as their proxy. This proxy is solely intended to be an irrevocable proxy." A year after the agreement was signed, Gibbons and Smith wanted to revoke their proxies. Can they? *Zollar v. Smith*, 710 S.W.2d 155, **Web** 1986 Tex.App. Lexis 12900 (Court of Appeals of Texas)

37.4 Right to Inspect Records Helmsman Management Services, Inc. (Helmsman), became a 25 percent shareholder of A&S Consultants, Inc. (A&S), a Delaware corporation. Helmsman paid $50,000 for its interest in A&S. At the time of the stock purchase, Helmsman was also a customer of A&S, paying the company for the use of a computer software program. After making his investment, Helmsman verified A&S's billings with a periodic review of certain of A&S's books and records. Three years later, Helmsman conducted a review of A&S's records over a six-day period. The review showed that A&S had never paid any dividends on the stock held by Helmsman and that Helmsman had never received notice of A&S's shareholder meetings. Suspecting that A&S was being mismanaged, Helmsman sent a letter to A&S, asking to inspect all of A&S's records. The letter stated several

purposes for the inspection, including to (1) determine the reasons for nonpayment of dividends and (2) gain information to be used in determining how to vote in shareholders' elections. Under the Model Business Corporations Act, should Helmsman's request be honored? *Helmsman Management Services, Inc. v. A & S Consultants, Inc.*, 525 A.2d 160, **Web** 1987 Del. Ch. Lexis 397 (Court of Chancery of Delaware)

37.5 Dividends Gay's Super Markets, Inc. (Super Markets), was a corporation formed under the laws of the state of Maine. Hannaford Bros. Company held 51 percent of the corporation's common stock. Lawrence F. Gay and his brother Carrol were both minority shareholders in Super Markets. Lawrence Gay was also the manager of the corporation's store at Machias, Maine. One day, he was dismissed from his job. At the meeting of Super Markets's board of directors, a decision was made not to declare a stock dividend for the prior year. The directors cited expected losses from increased competition and the expense of opening a new store as reasons for not paying a dividend. Lawrence Gay claims that the reason for not paying a dividend was to force him to sell his shares in Super Markets. Lawrence sued to force the corporation to declare a dividend. Who wins? *Gay v. Gay's Super Markets, Inc.*, 343 A.2d 577, **Web** 1975 Me. Lexis 391 (Supreme Judicial Court of Maine)

37.6 Duty of Loyalty Edward Hellenbrand ran a comedy club known as the Comedy Cottage in Rosemont, Illinois. The business was incorporated, with Hellenbrand and his wife as the corporation's sole shareholders. The corporation leased the premises in which the club was located. Hellenbrand hired Jay Berk as general manager of the club. Two years later, Berk was made vice president of the corporation and given 10 percent of its stock. Hellenbrand experienced health problems and moved to Nevada, leaving Berk to manage the daily affairs of the business. Four years later, the ownership of the building where the Comedy Cottage was located changed hands. Shortly thereafter, the club's lease on the premises expired. Hellenbrand instructed Berk to negotiate a new lease. Berk arranged a month-to-month lease but had the lease agreement drawn up in his name instead of that of the corporation. When Hellenbrand learned of Berk's move, he fired him. Berk continued to lease the building in his own name and opened his own club, the Comedy Company, Inc., there. Hellenbrand sued Berk for an injunction to prevent Berk from leasing the building. Who wins? *Comedy Cottage, Inc. v. Berk*, 145 Ill.App.3d 355, 495 N.E.2d 1006, **Web** 1986 Ill.App. Lexis 2486 (Appellate Court of Illinois)

37.7 Duty of Loyalty Lawrence Gaffney was the president and general manager of Ideal Tape Company (Ideal). Ideal, which was a subsidiary of Chelsea Industries, Inc. (Chelsea), was engaged in the business of manufacturing pressure-sensitive tape. Gaffney recruited three other Ideal executives to join him in starting a tape manufacturing business. The four men remained at Ideal for the two years it took them to plan the new enterprise. During this time, they used their positions at Ideal to travel around the country to gather business ideas, recruit potential customers, and purchase equipment for their business. At no time did they reveal to Chelsea their intention to open a competing business. The new business was incorporated as Action Manufacturing Company (Action). When executives at Chelsea discovered the existence of the new venture, Gaffney and the others resigned from Chelsea. Chelsea sued them for damages. Who wins? *Chelsea Industries, Inc. v. Gaffney*, 389 Mass. 1, 449 N.E.2d 320, **Web** 1983 Mass. Lexis 1413 (Supreme Judicial Court of Massachusetts)

37.8 Indemnification   William G. Young was a director of Pool Builders Supply, Inc. (Pool Builders). Pool Builders experienced financial difficulties and was forced to file for bankruptcy. Eddie Lawson was appointed the receiver for the creditors of the corporation. Lawson believed that Young had mismanaged the corporation. Lawson filed a suit against Young and Pool Builders, alleging that Young had used Pool Builders personally to obtain money, goods, and property from creditors on the credit of the corporation. Lawson's suit also alleged that Young had attempted to convert corporate assets for his own use. Young defended the suit for himself and the corporation. At trial, the judge found insufficient evidence to support Lawson's charges, and the suit was dismissed. Young then sought to have Pool Builders pay the legal fees he had incurred while defending the suit. Can Young recover this money from the corporation? *Lawson v. Young*, 21 Ohio App.3d 190, 486 N.E.2d 1177, **Web** 1984 Ohio App. Lexis 12678 (Court of Appeals of Ohio)

37.9 Derivative Shareholder Lawsuit   Four brothers—Monnie, Mechel, Merko, and Sam Dotlich—formed a partnership to run a heavy equipment rental business. One decade later, the company had been incorporated as Dotlich Brothers, Inc. Each brother owned 25 percent of the corporation's stock, and each served on the board of directors. During the course of its operation, the business acquired a 56-acre tract of land in Speedway, Indiana. This land was held in the name of Monnie Dotlich. Each of the brothers was aware of this agreement. The corporation also had purchased six other pieces of property, all of which were held in Monnie's name. Sam Dotlich was not informed that Monnie was the record owner of these other properties. Sam discovered this irregularity and requested that the board of directors take action to remedy the situation. When the board refused to do so, Sam initiated a lawsuit on behalf of the corporation. Can Sam bring this lawsuit? *Dotlich v. Dotlich*, 475 N.E.2d 331, **Web** 1985 Ind.App. Lexis 2233 (Court of Appeals of Indiana)

37.10 Piercing the Corporate Veil   M.R. Watters was the majority shareholder of several closely held corporations, including Wildhorn Ranch, Inc. (Wildhorn). All these businesses were run out of Watters's home in Rocky Ford, Colorado. Wildhorn operated a resort called the Wildhorn Ranch Resort in Teller County, Colorado. Although Watters claimed that the ranch was owned by the corporation, the deed for the property listed Watters as the owner. Watters paid little attention to corporate formalities, holding corporate meetings at his house, never taking minutes of those meetings, and paying the debts of one corporation with the assets of another. During August 1986, two guests of Wildhorn Ranch Resort drowned while operating a paddleboat at the ranch. The family of the deceased guests sued for damages. Can Watters be held personally liable? *Geringer v. Wildhorn Ranch, Inc.*, 706 F.Supp. 1442, **Web** 1988 U.S. Dist. Lexis 15701 (United States District Court for the District of Colorado)

BUSINESS ETHICS CASES

37.11 Business Ethics   Alfred S. Johnson, Inc. (Corporation), was incorporated by Alfred S. Johnson, who owned 70 shares of the corporation. Two employees of the corporation, James DeBaun and Walter Stephens, owned 20 and 10 shares, respectively. When Johnson died 10 years later, his will created a testamentary trust in which his 70 shares were placed. Johnson's will named First Western Bank and Trust Company (Bank) trustee for the trust. Several years later, Bank decided to sell the 70 shares but did not tell anyone associated with Corporation of its decision. An appraisal was obtained that valued the corporation at $326,000 as a going concern.

Three years later, Raymond J. Mattison submitted an offer to purchase the 70 shares for $250,000, payable as $50,000 in securities of companies Mattison owned and the $200,000 balance over a five-year period. Bank obtained a Dun & Bradstreet report that showed several outstanding tax liens against Mattison. Bank accepted Mattison's explanation that they were not his fault. At the time, Mattison owed Bank a judgment for fraud. Bank was also aware that Mattison owed unpaid debts and that several entities in which he was involved were insolvent. Bank did not investigate these matters. If it had, the public records of Los Angeles County would have revealed 38 unsatisfied judgments against Mattison and his entities, totaling $330,886, 54 pending lawsuits claiming damages of $373,588, and 18 tax liens aggregating $20,327. Bank agreed to sell the 70 shares to Mattison and accepted the assets of Corporation as security for the repayment of the $200,000 balance. As part of the transaction, Bank required Mattison to agree to have Corporation give its banking business to Bank.

At the time of sale, Corporation was a successful going business with a bright future. It had cash of $76,000 and other liquid assets of over $120,000. Its net worth was about $220,000. Corporation was profitable, and its trend of earnings indicated a pattern of growth. Mattison immediately implemented a systematic scheme to loot Corporation. He (1) diverted $73,000 in corporate cash to himself and a shell company he owned, (2) caused Corporation to assign all its assets, including accounts receivable, to the shell company, (3) diverted all corporate mail to a post office box and extracted incoming checks to Corporation, (4) refused to pay corporate creditors on time or at all, (5) issued payroll checks without sufficient corporate funds, and (6) removed Corporation's books and records. One year later, hopelessly insolvent, Corporation shut down operations and was placed in receivership. At that time, its debts exceeded its assets by over $200,000. DeBaun's and Stephens's shares were worthless. They sued Bank for damages, alleging that Bank, as the majority shareholder of Corporation, had breached its fiduciary duty to the minority shareholders.

Did Bank have knowledge of the dangerous situation in which it placed Corporation? Did Bank, as the controlling shareholder of Corporation, breach its fiduciary duty to the minority shareholders? *DeBaun v. First Western Bank and Trust Co.*, 46 Cal.App.3d 686, 120 Cal.Rptr. 354, **Web** 1975 Cal.App. Lexis 1801 (Court of Appeal of California)

37.12 Business Ethics   Jon-T Chemicals, Inc. (Chemicals), was an Oklahoma corporation engaged in the fertilizer and chemicals business. John H. Thomas was its majority shareholder and its president and board chairman. Chemicals incorporated Jon-T Farms, Inc. (Farms), as a wholly owned subsidiary, to engage in the farming and land-leasing business.

Chemicals invested $10,000 to establish Farms. All the directors and officers of Farms were directors and officers of Chemicals, and Thomas was its president and board chairman. In addition, Farms used officers, computers, and accountants of Chemicals without paying a fee, and Chemicals paid the salary of Farms's only employee. Chemicals made regular informal advances to pay Farms's expenses. These payments reached $7.5 million by January 1975.

Thomas and Farms engaged in a scheme whereby they submitted fraudulent applications for agricultural subsidies from the federal government under the Uplands Cotton Program. As a result of these applications, the Commodity Credit Corporation, a government agency, paid over $2.5 million in subsidies to Thomas and Farms. After discovering the fraud, the federal government obtained criminal convictions against Thomas and Farms. In a separate civil action, the federal government obtained a $4.7 million judgment against Thomas and Farms, finding them jointly and severally liable for the tort of fraud. Farms declared bankruptcy, and Thomas was unable to pay the judgment. Because Thomas and Farms were insolvent, the federal government sued Chemicals to recover the judgment. Was Farms the alter ego of Chemicals, permitting the United States to pierce the corporate veil and recover the judgment from Chemicals? Did Thomas act ethically in this case? *United States of America v. Jon-T Chemicals, Inc.*, 768 F.2d 686, **Web** 1985 U.S. App. Lexis 21255 (United States Court of Appeals for the Fifth Circuit)

ENDNOTE

1. *Meinhard v. Salmon*, 249 N.Y. 458, 164 N.E. 545, Web 1928 N.Y. Lexis 830 (Court of Appeals of New York).

▲ **Ratan Tata, Chairman of the Tata Group** *Companies around the world are now merging with or purchasing assets from U.S. companies. In 2008, India's Tata Motors purchased the storied Jaguar and Land Rover automobile brands from Ford Motor Company for $2.3 billion. Ford had bought British brand Jaguar in 1989 for $2.5 billion and British brand Land Rover in 2000 for $2.7 billion. Tata Motors is part of the Tata Group, India's largest private company. The Tata Group is a multinational company that owns approximately 100 other companies.*

CHAPTER OBJECTIVES

After studying this chapter, you should be able to:

1. Describe the process of soliciting proxies from shareholders and engaging in proxy contests.
2. Define *shareholder resolution* and identify when a shareholder can include a resolution in proxy materials.
3. Describe the process for approving a merger or share exchange.

4. Define *tender offer* and describe poison pills, greenmail, and other defensive maneuvers to prevent hostile takeover.
5. Examine the use of multinational corporations in conducting international business.

CHAPTER CONTENTS

> **"To supervise wisely the great corporations is well; but to look backward to the days when business was polite pillage and regard our great business concerns as piratical institutions carrying letters of marque and reprisal is a grave error born in the minds of little men. When these little men legislate they set the brakes going uphill."**
>
> —Elbert Hubbard
> *Notebook, page 16*

▶ INTRODUCTION TO CORPORATE ACQUISITIONS AND MULTINATIONAL CORPORATIONS

During the course of its existence, a corporation may go through certain **fundamental changes**. A corporation must seek shareholder approval for many changes. This requires the solicitation of votes or proxies from shareholders. Persons who want to take over the management of a corporation often conduct proxy contests to try to win over shareholder votes.

Corporations often engage in acquisitions of other corporations or businesses. This may occur by friendly merger or by hostile tender offer. In defense, a corporation may erect certain barriers or impediments to a hostile takeover.

Multinational corporations conduct international business around the world. This is usually done through a variety of business arrangements, including branch offices, subsidiary corporations, and such.

This chapter discusses fundamental changes to a corporation, including the solicitation of proxies, mergers, hostile tender offers, and defensive strategies of corporations to prevent hostile takeovers. This chapter also examines the use of multinational corporations in conducting international business.

▶ PROXY SOLICITATION AND PROXY CONTEST

Corporate shareholders have the right to vote on the election of directors, mergers, charter amendments, and the like. They can exercise their power to vote either in person or by proxy [RMBCA Section 7.22]. Voting by proxy is common in large corporations that have thousands of shareholders located across the country and around the world.

A **proxy** is a written document (often called a **proxy card**) that is completed and signed by a shareholder and sent to the corporation. The proxy authorizes another person—the proxy holder—to vote the shares at the shareholders' meeting as directed by the shareholder. The proxy holder is often a director or an officer of the corporation.

Federal Proxy Rules

Section 14(a) of the Securities Exchange Act of 1934 gives the Securities and Exchange Commission (SEC) the authority to regulate the solicitation of proxies.[1] The federal proxy rules promote full disclosure. In other words, management or any other party soliciting proxies from shareholders must prepare a **proxy statement** that fully describes (1) the matter for which the proxy is being solicited, (2) who is soliciting the proxy, and (3) any other pertinent information.

---

proxy
A written document signed by a shareholder that authorizes another person to vote the shareholder's shares. Also called a *proxy card*.

Section 14(a)
A provision of the Securities Exchange Act of 1934 that gives the SEC the authority to regulate the solicitation of proxies.

proxy statement
A document that fully describes (1) the matter for which a proxy is being solicited, (2) who is soliciting the proxy, and (3) any other pertinent information.

A copy of the proxy, the proxy statement, and all other solicitation material must be filed with the SEC at least 10 days before the materials are sent to the shareholders. If the SEC requires additional disclosures, the solicitation can be held up until these disclosures are made.

Antifraud Provision

Section 14(a) of the Securities Exchange Act of 1934 is an **antifraud provision** that prohibits material misrepresentations or omissions of a material fact in the proxy materials. Known false statements of facts, reasons, opinions, or beliefs in proxy solicitation materials are actionable. Violations of this rule can result in civil and criminal actions by the SEC and the Justice Department, respectively. The courts have implied a private cause of action under this provision. Thus, shareholders who are injured by a material misrepresentation or omission in proxy materials can sue the wrongdoer and recover damages. The court can also order a new election if a violation is found.

antifraud provision
Section 14(a) of the Securities Exchange Act of 1934, which prohibits misrepresentations or omissions of a material fact in the proxy materials.

Proxy Contest

Shareholders sometimes oppose the actions taken by the **incumbent directors** and management. These **insurgent shareholders** may challenge the incumbent management in a **proxy contest**, in which both sides solicit proxies from the other shareholders. The side that receives the greatest number of votes wins the proxy contest. Such contests are usually held with regard to the election of directors. Management must either (1) provide a list of shareholders to the dissenting group or (2) mail the proxy solicitation materials of the challenging group to the shareholders.

proxy contest
A contest in which opposing factions of shareholders and managers solicit proxies from other shareholders; the side that receives the greatest number of votes wins the proxy contest.

▶ SHAREHOLDER RESOLUTION

At times, shareholders may wish to submit issues for a vote of other shareholders. The Securities Exchange Act of 1934 and SEC rules permit a shareholder to submit a resolution to be considered by other shareholders if (1) the shareholder has owned at least $2,000 worth of shares of the company's stock or 1 percent of all shares of the company (2) for at least one year. The resolution cannot exceed 50 words. Such **shareholder resolutions** are usually made when the corporation is soliciting proxies from its shareholders.

If management does not oppose a resolution, it may be included in the proxy materials issued by the corporation. Even if management is not in favor of a resolution, a shareholder has a right to have the shareholder resolution included in the corporation's proxy materials if it (1) relates to the corporation's business, (2) concerns a *policy issue* (and not the day-to-day operations of the corporation), and (3) does not concern the payment of dividends. The SEC rules on whether a resolution can be submitted to shareholders.

shareholder resolution
A resolution that a shareholder who meets certain ownership requirements may submit to other shareholders for a vote. Many shareholder resolutions concern social issues.

What passes in the world for talent or dexterity or enterprise is often only a want of moral principle.

William Hazlitt

Examples Shareholder resolutions have been presented concerning protecting the environment; reducing global warming; preventing the overcutting of the rain forests in Brazil; prohibiting U.S. corporations from purchasing goods manufactured in developing countries under poor working conditions, including the use of forced and child labor; protecting human rights; and engaging in socially responsible conduct.

Most shareholder resolutions have a slim chance of being enacted because large-scale investors usually support management. They can, however, cause a corporation to change the way it does business. For example, to avoid the adverse publicity such issues can create, some corporations voluntarily adopt the changes contained in shareholder resolutions. Others negotiate settlements with the sponsors of resolutions to get the measures off the agenda before the annual shareholders' meetings.

ETHICS SPOTLIGHT

Shareholder Resolution

The E. I. du Pont de Nemours and Company (DuPont), organized under the laws of the state of Delaware, is one of the largest chemical and consumer products companies in the world. DuPont has manufacturing and production facilities located in many foreign countries. Several of these countries have been criticized because child labor and forced labor are alleged to be used to produce goods in those countries.

At its annual meeting, the International Brotherhood of Teamsters General Fund, owner of shares of DuPont common stock, proposed the following shareholder resolution to the shareholders of DuPont:

Stockholder Proposal on International Workplace Standards

RESOLVED: *That the Board of Directors of E. I. du Pont de Nemours and Company (Du Pont) shall adopt, implement and enforce the workplace Code of Conduct (Code) as based on the International Labor Organization's (ILO) Conventions on workplace human rights, which include:*

- *No use of child labor.*
- *No discrimination or intimidation in employment.*
- *All workers have the right to form and join unions and to bargain collectively.*
- *No use of forced labor.*

Stockholder's (Teamster's) Statement in support of the proposal:
The Teamsters, in support of its proposal, provided the following statement in Du Pont's annual Proxy Statement submitted to Du Pont shareholders.

As a global institution, Du Pont and its international operations and sourcing arrangements are exposed to sundry risks. Adoption of this proposal manages the risk of being a party to serious human rights violations in the workplace. Du Pont operates or has business relationships in a number of countries, including China, Indonesia, and Thailand, where the U.S. State Department, Amnesty International, and Human Rights Watch indicate law and public policy do not adequately protect human rights. To wit: Forced labor, illegal child labor, and violence against women.

The success of Du Pont's operations depends on consumer and governmental good will. Brand name is a significant asset. Du Pont benefits from adopting and enforcing the Code ensuring that it isn't associated with human rights violations. This protects Du Pont's brand names and its relationships with customers and the numerous governments under which Du Pont operates and with which it does business.

Position of the Board of Directors in Opposition to the Proposal

In response, Du Pont included the following statement in the Proxy Statement, recommending that Du Pont shareholders vote against the shareholder resolution.

Du Pont is committed to conducting its business affairs with the highest ethical standards, and works diligently to be a respected corporate citizen throughout the world. The company has had in place for many years an Ethics Policy, Mission Statement and Code of Business Conduct addressing many of the issues covered in the standards proposed for adoption. These corporate policies are applicable to all employees in all Du Pont businesses around the world.

The company is supportive of the general intent of the proposal and similar international workplace standards suggested by other organizations for adoption. The company reviews on an ongoing basis codes offered by other organizations, and examines its own policies and practices in light of the provisions of the proposed codes. The company also meets with advocates of codes to explore issues of mutual concern. These efforts will continue. The company therefore believes adoption of the proposed code is unnecessary.

The shareholder resolution for the adoption of international workplace standards was defeated by an overwhelming majority of DuPont shareholders at the annual meeting.

Business Ethics Why do you think the International Brotherhood of Teamsters introduced this shareholder resolution? Do you think the reasons DuPont asserted for recommending that its shareholders vote against the proposal were legitimate? Explain.

► MERGERS AND ACQUISITIONS

Corporations may agree to friendly acquisitions or combinations of one another. This may occur through merger, share exchange, or sale of assets. These types of combinations are discussed in the following paragraphs.

Merger

A **merger** occurs when one corporation is absorbed into another corporation and ceases to exist. The corporation that continues to exist is called the **surviving corporation**. The other corporation, which ceases to exist, is called the **merged corporation** [RMBCA Section 11.01]. The surviving corporation gains all the rights, privileges, powers, duties, obligations, and liabilities of the merged corporation. Title to property owned by the merged corporation transfers to the surviving corporation, without formality or deeds. The shareholders of the merged corporation receive stock or securities of the surviving corporation or other consideration, as provided in the plan of merger.

merger
A situation in which one corporation is absorbed into another corporation and ceases to exist.

Example Corporation A and Corporation B merge, and it is agreed that Corporation A will absorb Corporation B. Corporation A is the surviving corporation. Corporation B is the merged corporation. The representation of this merger is A + B = A (see Exhibit 38.1).

► Exhibit 38.1 MERGER

| Corporation A (Merged and surviving corporation) | + | Corporation B (Merged corporation) | = | Corporation A (Surviving corporation) |

CONTEMPORARY ENVIRONMENT

Google Takes Over YouTube

Sergery Brin and Larry Page, university students, founded Google in 1998 in a garage. They then built the company into a search engine, a giant of the Internet, and an advertising marketer. Chad Hurley and Steve Chen, who had left PayPal, subsequently started YouTube, a popular online video service where people watch and share original videos.

In 2006, Google acquired YouTube in a stock-for-stock transaction. The purchase price was $1.65 billion. YouTube shareholders will receive Google stock in return for their YouTube stock. Google, however, will take advantage of the YouTube brand name and operate YouTube independently. The deal keeps YouTube founders Chad Hurley and Steve Chen as well as YouTube's 67 employees.

At the time of the takeover, YouTube was still unprofitable. But Google sees YouTube as being at the forefront in the online video revolution. Google believes that YouTube's video sharing site will provide marketing opportunities that will increase as viewers and advertisers migrate from television to the Internet. Google believes that the combination of the two firms will continue to build the next-generation platform for serving media worldwide.

Share Exchange

One corporation can acquire all the shares of another corporation through a **share exchange**. In a share exchange, both corporations retain their separate legal existence. After the exchange, one corporation (the **parent corporation**) owns all the shares of the other corporation (the **subsidiary corporation**) [RMBCA Section 1102]. Such exchanges are often used to create holding company arrangements (e.g., bank or insurance holding companies).

share exchange
A situation in which one corporation acquires all the shares of another corporation, and both corporations retain their separate legal existence.

Example Corporation A wants to acquire Corporation B. Assume that Corporation A offers to exchange its shares for those of Corporation B and that Corporation B's shareholders approve the transaction. After the share exchange, Corporation A owns all the stock of Corporation B. Corporation A is the parent corporation, and Corporation B is the wholly owned subsidiary of Corporation A (see Exhibit 38.2).

▶ **Exhibit 38.2 SHARE EXCHANGE**

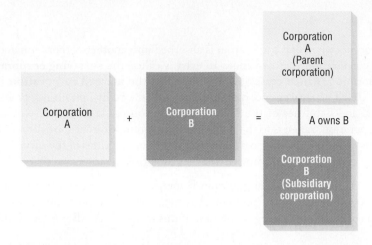

When your ship comes in, make sure you are willing to unload it.

Robert Anthony

Required Approvals for a Merger or Share Exchange

An ordinary merger or share exchange requires (1) the recommendation of the board of directors of each corporation and (2) an affirmative vote of the majority of shares of each corporation that are entitled to vote [RMBCA Section 11.03]. The articles of incorporation or corporate bylaws can require the approval of a **supramajority**, such as 80 percent of the voting shares.

The approval of the surviving corporation's shareholders is not required if the merger or share exchange increases the number of voting shares of the surviving corporation by 20 percent or less [RMBCA Section 11.03(g)]. The approved **articles of merger** or **articles of share exchange** must be filed with the secretary of state of the surviving corporation. The state normally issues a *certificate of merger or share exchange* to the surviving corporation after all the formalities are met and the requisite fees are paid [RMBCA Section 11.05].

Short-Form Merger

short-form merger
A merger between a parent corporation and a subsidiary corporation that does not require the approval of the shareholders of either corporation or the approval of the board of directors of the subsidiary corporation.

If the parent corporation owns 90 percent or more of the outstanding shares of the subsidiary corporation, a **short-form merger** procedure may be followed to merge the two corporations. A short-form merger procedure is simpler than an ordinary merger because neither the approval of the shareholders of either corporation nor the approval of the board of directors of the subsidiary corporation is needed. All that is required is the approval of the board of directors of the parent corporation [RMBCA Section 11.04].

Sale or Lease of Assets

A corporation may sell, lease, or otherwise dispose of all or substantially all of its property in other than the usual and regular course of business. Such a **sale or lease of assets** requires (1) the recommendation of the board of directors and (2) an affirmative vote of the majority of the shares of the selling or leasing corporation that are entitled to vote (unless greater vote is required) [RMBCA Section 12.02]. This rule prevents the board of directors from selling all or most of the assets of the corporation without shareholder approval.

Dissenting Shareholder Appraisal Rights

Specific shareholders sometimes object to a proposed ordinary or short-form merger, share exchange, or sale or lease of all or substantially all of the property of a corporation, even though the transaction received the required approvals. Objecting shareholders are provided a statutory right to dissent and obtain payment of the fair value of their shares [RMBCA Section 13.02]. This is referred to as a **dissenting shareholder appraisal right**, or an **appraisal right**. Shareholders have no other recourse unless the transaction is unlawful or fraudulent.

A corporation must notify shareholders of the existence of their appraisal rights before a transaction can be voted on [RMBCA Section 13.20]. To obtain appraisal rights, a dissenting shareholder must (1) deliver written notice of his or her intent to demand payment of his or her shares to the corporation before the vote is taken and (2) not vote his or her shares in favor of the proposed action [RMBCA Section 13.23]. The shareholder must deposit his or her share certificates with the corporation [RMBCA Section 13.23]. Shareholders who fail to comply with these statutory procedures lose their appraisal rights.

As soon as the proposed action is taken, the corporation must pay each dissenting shareholder the amount the corporation estimates to be the fair value of his or her shares, plus accrued interest [RMBCA Section 13.25]. If the dissenter is dissatisfied, the corporation must petition the court to determine the fair value of the shares [RMBCA Section 13.30].

After a hearing, the court will issue an order declaring the fair value of the shares. Appraisers may be appointed to help determine this value. Court costs and appraisal fees are usually paid by the corporation. However, the court can assess these costs against the dissenters if they acted arbitrarily, vexatiously, or in bad faith [RMBCA Section 13.31].

dissenting shareholder appraisal rights
The rights of shareholders who object to a proposed merger, share exchange, or sale or lease of all or substantially all of the property of a corporation to have their shares valued by the court and receive cash payment of this value from the corporation. Also called *appraisal rights*.

▶ TENDER OFFER

Recall that a merger, a share exchange, and a sale of assets all require the approval of the board of directors of the corporation whose assets or shares are to be acquired. If the board of directors of the target corporation does not agree to a merger or an acquisition, the acquiring corporation—the **tender offeror**—can make a **tender offer** for the shares directly to the shareholders of the **target corporation**. The shareholders each make an individual decision about whether to sell their shares to the tender offeror (see Exhibit 38.3). Such offers are often referred to as **hostile tender offers**.

The tender offeror's board of directors must approve the offer, although the shareholders do not have to approve. The offer can be made for all or a portion of the shares of the

tender offeror
The party that makes a tender offer.

tender offer
An offer that an acquirer makes directly to a target corporation's shareholders in an effort to acquire the target corporation.

target corporation
The corporation that is proposed to be acquired in a tender offer situation.

▶ **Exhibit 38.3 TENDER OFFER**

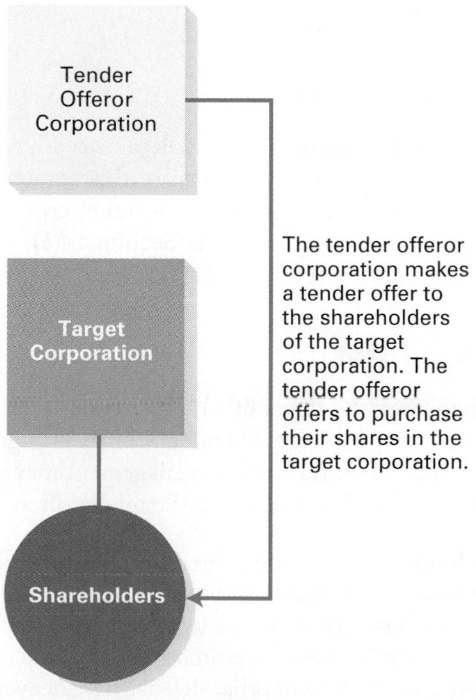

Tender Offeror Corporation

Target Corporation

Shareholders

The tender offeror corporation makes a tender offer to the shareholders of the target corporation. The tender offeror offers to purchase their shares in the target corporation.

target corporation. In a tender offer, the tendering corporation and the target corporation retain their separate legal status. However, a successful tender offer is sometimes followed by a merger of the two corporations.

Williams Act

Williams Act
An amendment to the Securities Exchange Act of 1934 made in 1968 that specifically regulates tender offers.

Prior to 1968, tender offers were not federally regulated. However, securities that were issued in conjunction with such offers had to be registered with the SEC or qualify for an exemption from registration. Tender offers made with cash were not subject to any federal disclosure requirements. In 1968, Congress enacted the **Williams Act** as an amendment to the Securities Exchange Act of 1934.[2] This act specifically regulates all tender offers, whether they are made with securities, cash, or other consideration, and it establishes certain disclosure requirements and antifraud provisions.

Tender Offer Rules

The Williams Act does not require a tender offeror to notify either the management of the target company or the SEC until the offer is made.[3] Detailed information regarding the terms, conditions, and other information concerning the tender offer must be disclosed at that time. Tender offers are governed by the following rules:

fair price rule
A rule that says any increase in price paid for shares tendered must be offered to all shareholders, even those who have previously tendered their shares.

pro rata rule
A rule that says shares must be purchased on a pro rata basis if too many shares are tendered.

- The offer cannot be closed before 20 business days after the commencement of the tender offer.
- The offer must be extended for 10 business days if the tender offeror increases the number of shares it will take or the price it will pay for the shares.
- The **fair price rule** stipulates that any increase in price paid for shares tendered must be offered to all shareholders, even those who have previously tendered their shares.
- The **pro rata rule** holds that the shares must be purchased on a pro rata basis if too many shares are tendered.

A shareholder who tenders his or her shares has the absolute right to withdraw them at any time prior to the closing of the tender offer. The dissenting shareholder appraisal rights are not available. The SEC's tender offer rules do not apply to tender offers that result in ownership of 5 percent or less of the outstanding shares of a company. These are often called **mini-tender offers**.

Antifraud Provision

Section 14(e)
A provision of the Williams Act that prohibits fraudulent, deceptive, and manipulative practices in connection with a tender offer.

Section 14(e) of the Williams Act prohibits fraudulent, deceptive, and manipulative practices in connection with a tender offer.[4] Violations of this section may result in the SEC bringing civil charges or the Justice Department bringing criminal charges. The courts have implied a private civil cause of action under Section 14(e). Therefore, a shareholder who has been injured by a violation of Section 14(e) can sue the wrongdoer for damages.

Fighting a Tender Offer

The incumbent management of the target of a hostile tender offer may not want the corporation taken over by the tender offeror. Therefore, it may engage in various activities to impede and defeat the tender offer. Incumbent management may use some of the following strategies and tactics in defending against hostile tender offers:

- **Persuasion of shareholders.** Media campaigns are often organized to convince shareholders that the tender offer is not in their best interests.
- **Delaying lawsuits.** Lawsuits may be filed, alleging that the tender offer violates securities laws, antitrust laws, or other laws. The time gained by this tactic gives management the opportunity to erect or implement other defensive maneuvers.

- **Selling a crown jewel.** Assets such as profitable divisions or real estate that is particularly attractive to outside interests—**crown jewels**—may be sold. This tactic makes the target corporation less attractive to the tender offeror.
- **Adopting a poison pill. Poison pills** are defensive strategies that are built into the target corporation's articles of incorporation, corporate bylaws, or contracts and leases. For example, contracts and leases may provide that they will expire if the ownership of the corporation changes hands. These tactics make the target corporation more expensive to the tender offeror.
- **White knight merger. White knight mergers** are mergers with friendly parties—that is, parties that promise to leave the target corporation and/or its management intact.
- **Pac-Man tender offer.** With a **Pac-Man (or reverse) tender offer**, the target corporation makes a tender offer on the tender offeror. Thus, the target corporation tries to purchase the tender offeror.
- **Issuing additional stock.** Placing additional stock on the market increases the number of outstanding shares that the tender offeror must purchase in order to gain control of the target corporation.
- **Creating an employee stock ownership plan (ESOP).** A company may create an **employee stock ownership plan (ESOP)** and place a certain percentage of the corporation's securities (e.g., 15 percent) in it. The ESOP is then expected to vote the shares it owns against the potential acquirer in a proxy contest or tender offer because the beneficiaries (i.e., the employees) have a vested interest in keeping the company intact.
- **Flip-over and flip-in rights plans.** These plans provide that existing shareholders of the target corporation may convert their shares for a greater number (e.g., twice the value) of shares of the acquiring corporation (**flip-over rights plan**) or debt securities of the target company (**flip-in rights plan**). Rights plans are triggered if the acquiring firm acquires a certain percentage (e.g., 20 percent) of the shares of the target corporation. They make it more expensive for the acquiring firm to take over the target corporation.
- **Greenmail and standstill agreements.** Most tender offerors purchase a block of stock in the target corporation before making an offer. Occasionally, the tender offeror will agree to give up its tender offer and agree not to purchase any further shares if the target corporation agrees to buy back the stock at a premium over fair market value. This payment is called **greenmail**. The agreement of the tender offeror to abandon its tender offer and not purchase any additional stock is called a **standstill agreement**.

There are many other strategies and tactics that target companies initiate and implement in defending against a tender offer.

Business Judgment Rule

The members of the board of directors of a corporation owe a fiduciary duty to the corporation and its shareholders. This duty, which requires the board to act carefully and honestly, is truly tested when a tender offer is made for the stock of the company. That is because shareholders and others then ask whether the board's initiation and implementation or defensive measures were taken in the best interests of the shareholders or to protect the board's own interests and jobs.

The legality of defensive strategies is examined using the **business judgment rule**. This rule protects the decisions of a board of directors that acts on an informed basis, in good faith, and in the honest belief that an action taken was in the best interests of the corporation and its shareholders.[5] In the context of a tender offer, the defensive measures chosen by the board must be reasonable in relation to the threat posed.[6]

▶ STATE ANTITAKEOVER STATUTES

Many states have enacted **antitakeover statutes** that are aimed at protecting from hostile takeovers corporations that are either incorporated in or do business within the state. Many of these state statutes have been challenged as being unconstitutional because they

crown jewel
A valuable asset of a target corporation that the tender offeror particularly wants to acquire in a tender offer.

The usual trade and commerce is cheating all round by consent.

Thomas Fuller
Gnomologia (1732)

greenmail
The purchase by a target corporation of its stock from an actual or perceived tender offeror at a premium.

business judgment rule
A rule that protects the decisions of a board of directors that acts on an informed basis, in good faith, and in the honest belief that the action taken was in the best interests of the corporation and its shareholders.

antitakeover statutes
Statutes enacted by a state legislature that protect against the hostile takeover of corporations incorporated in or doing business in the state.

violate the Williams Act and the Commerce Clause and the Supremacy Clause of the U.S. Constitution.

In the following case, the U.S. Supreme Court held that a state antitakeover statute was constitutional.

U.S. SUPREME COURT   CASE 38.1 State Antitakeover Statute

CTS Corporation v. Dynamics Corporation of America

481 U.S. 69, 107 S.Ct. 1637, 95 L.Ed.2d. 67, Web 1987 U.S. Lexis 1811 (1987)
Supreme Court of the United States

"The desire of the Indiana legislature to protect shareholders of Indiana corporations from this type of coercive offer does not conflict with the Williams Act. Rather, it furthers the federal policy of investor protection."

—Justice Powell

Facts

Indiana enacted the Control Share Acquisitions Chapter. This act covers corporations that (1) are incorporated in Indiana and have at least 100 shareholders, (2) have their primary place of business or substantial assets in Indiana, and (3) have either 10 percent of their shareholders in Indiana or 10 percent of their shares owned by Indiana residents. The act provides that if an entity acquires 20 percent or more of the voting shares of a covered corporation, the acquirer loses voting rights to these shares unless a majority of the disinterested shareholders of the acquired corporation vote to restore such voting rights. The acquirer can request that such vote be held within 50 days after its acquisition. If the shareholders do not restore the voting rights, the target corporation may redeem the shares from the acquirer at fair market value, but it is not required to do so.

Dynamics Corporation of America (Dynamics), a Delaware corporation, announced a tender offer for 1 million shares of CTS Corporation, an Indiana corporation covered by the act. The purchase of these shares would have brought Dynamics's voting interest in CTS to 27.5 percent. Dynamics sued in federal court, alleging that Indiana's Control Share Acquisitions Chapter was unconstitutional. The U.S. District Court held for Dynamics. The Court of Appeals affirmed. CTS appealed.

Issue

Does the Indiana Control Share Acquisitions Chapter conflict with the Williams Act or violate the Commerce Clause of the U.S. Constitution by unduly burdening interstate commerce?

Language of the U.S. Supreme Court

It is entirely possible for entities to comply with both the Williams and the Indiana acts. The statute now before the court protects the independent shareholder against the contending parties. Thus, the Indiana act furthers a basic purpose of the Williams Act, placing investors on an equal footing with the takeover bidder. The Indiana act operates on the assumption that independent shareholders faced with tender offers often are at a disadvantage. By allowing such shareholders to vote as a group, the act protects them from the coercive aspects of some tender offers. Under the Indiana act, the shareholders as a group could reject the offer although individual shareholders might be inclined to accept it. The desire of the Indiana legislature to protect shareholders of Indiana corporations from this type of coercive offer does not conflict with the Williams Act. Rather, it furthers the federal policy of investor protection.

Decision

The U.S. Supreme Court held that the Indiana Control Share Acquisitions Chapter neither conflicts with the Williams Act nor violates the Commerce Clause of the U.S. Constitution. The Supreme Court reversed the decision of the Court of Appeals.

Case Questions

Critical Legal Thinking What is a state antitakeover statute? Why would a state adopt an antitakeover statute? Explain.

Business Ethics Is it ethical for a target corporation's management to assert a state antitakeover statute?

Contemporary Business What are the economic effects of a state antitakeover statute? Whom do you think these statutes actually protect?

▶ MULTINATIONAL CORPORATIONS

Many of the largest corporations in the world are **multinational corporations**—that is, corporations that operate in many countries. These corporations are also called

transnational corporations. Some multinational corporations operate across borders by using branch offices, while others use subsidiary corporations.

Multinational corporations also include corporations that do business in other countries through a variety of means. This would include the use of agents, business alliances, strategic partnerships, franchising, and other arrangements.

INTERNATIONAL LAW

International Branch Office

A corporation can conduct business in another country by using a **branch office**. A branch office is not a separate legal entity but merely an office of the corporation. As such, the corporation is liable for the contracts of the branch office and is also liable for the torts committed by personnel of the branch office. There is no liability shield between the corporation and the branch office.

Conducting International Business Using a Branch Office

Corporation A
(in Country A)

No limited liability shield—
Corporation A in Country A is liable
for the tort and contract liabilities
of its branch office in Country B.

Branch Office
(in Country B)

The branch office
is not a separate
legal entity.

International Branch Office

INTERNATIONAL LAW

International Subsidiary Corporation

A corporation can conduct business in another country by using a subsidiary corporation. The *subsidiary corporation* is organized under the laws of the foreign country. The *parent corporation* usually owns all or the majority of the subsidiary corporation. A subsidiary corporation is a separate legal entity. Therefore, the parent corporation is not liable for the contracts of or torts committed by the subsidiary corporation. There is a liability shield between the parent corporation and the subsidiary corporation.

Conducting International Business Using a Subsidiary Corporation

Corporation A
(in Country A)

Limited liability shield—Corporation A
in Country A is not liable for the tort
and contract liabilities of its subsidiary
corporation in Country B except up to
its capital contribution in Corporation B.

Corporation B
(in Country B)

Corporation B is a
separate legal entity.

International Subsidiary Corporation

INTERNATIONAL LAW
The Exon-Florio Law

The **Exon-Florio law** of 1988, as amended, mandates the president of the United States to suspend, prohibit, or dismantle the acquisition of U.S. businesses by foreign investors if there is credible evidence that the foreign investor might take action that threatens to impair the "national security" [50 U.S.C. 2170].

The act applies to mergers, acquisitions, takeovers, stock purchases, asset purchases, joint ventures, and proxy contests that would result in foreign control of U.S. businesses engaged in interstate commerce in the United States. The U.S. business could be a corporation, a partnership, a sole proprietorship, or another business. The size of the U.S. operation is irrelevant.

Exon-Florio and the regulations adopted thereunder do not define the term *national security*. The Treasury Department has interpreted the term broadly to include not only defense contractors but also technology and other businesses. The term *control* includes any investment exceeding 10 percent ownership in a U.S. business by a foreign investor.

When a foreign investor proposes to acquire an interest in a U.S. business, it may voluntarily notify the U.S. government of its intention. If the president of the United States finds a threat to the national security, the acquisition may be prohibited. If the foreign investor does not notify the U.S. government and completes the acquisition, it remains indefinitely subject to divestment if the president subsequently determines that the acquisition threatens the national security. The president's decision is not subject to judicial review.

TEST REVIEW TERMS AND CONCEPTS

Antifraud provision
Antitakeover statute
Articles of merger
Articles of share exchange
Branch office
Business judgment rule
Crown jewel
Dissenting shareholder
    appraisal right (appraisal
    right)
Employee stock ownership
    plan (ESOP)
Exon-Florio law
Fair price rule

Flip-in rights plan
Flip-over rights plan
Fundamental change
Greenmail
Hostile tender offer
Incumbent director
Insurgent shareholder
Merged corporation
Merger
Mini-tender offer
Multinational corporation
Pac-Man (or reverse) tender
    offer
Parent corporation

Poison pill
Pro rata rule
Proxy (proxy card)
Proxy contest
Proxy statement
Sale or lease of assets
Section 14(a) of the
    Securities Exchange Act
    of 1934
Section 14(e) of the
    Williams Act
Share exchange
Shareholder resolution
Short-form merger

Standstill agreement
Subsidiary corporation
Supramajority
Surviving corporation
Target corporation
Tender offer
Tender offeror
Transnational corporation
White knight merger
Williams Act

CASE PROBLEMS

38.1 Proxy Disclosure Western Maryland Company (Western) was a timbering and mining concern. A substantial portion of its stock was owned by CSX Minerals (CSX), its parent corporation. The remaining shares were owned by several minority shareholders, including Sanford E. Lockspeiser. Western's stock was not publicly traded. The board of directors of Western voted to merge the company with CSX. Western distributed to the minority shareholders a proxy statement which stated that CSX would vote for the merger and recommended approval of the merger by the other shareholders. The proxy materials disclosed Western's natural resource holdings in terms of acreage of minerals and timber.

It also stated real property values as carried on the company's books—that is, a book value of $17.04 per share. It included an opinion of the First Boston Corporation, an investment banking firm, that the merger was fair to shareholders; First Boston did not undertake an independent evaluation of Western's physical assets. Lockspeiser sued, alleging that the proxy materials were misleading because they did not state tonnage of Western's coal reserves, timber holdings in board feet, and actual value of Western's assets. Has Lockspeiser stated a claim for relief? *Lockspeiser v. Western Maryland Company*, 768 F.2d 558, **Web** 1985 U.S. App. Lexis 20476 (United States Court of Appeals for the Fourth Circuit)

38.2 Proxy Contest The Medfield Corporation (Medfield) was a publicly held corporation engaged in operating hospitals and other health care facilities. Medfield established a date for its annual shareholders' meeting, at which time the board of directors would be elected. In its proxy statement, management proposed the incumbent slate of directors. A group known as the Medfield Shareholders Committee nominated a rival slate of candidates and also solicited proxies. Medfield sent to shareholders proxy solicitation material that:

1. Failed to disclose that Medfield had been overpaid more than $1.8 million by Blue Cross and this amount was due and owing Blue Cross.
2. Failed to disclose that Medicare funds were being withheld because of Medfield's nonpayment.
3. Failed to adequately disclose self-dealing with Medfield by one of the directors who owned part of a laboratory used by Medfield.
4. Failed to disclose that Medfield was attempting to sell two nursing homes.
5. Impugned the character, integrity, and personal reputation of one of the rival candidates by stating that he had previously been found liable for patent infringement when, in fact, the case had been reversed on appeal.

At the annual meeting, the incumbent slate of directors received 50 percent of the votes cast, against 44 percent of the insurgent slate of directors. The Gladwins, who owned voting stock, sued to have the election overturned. Who wins? *Gladwin v. Medfield Corporation*, 540 F.2d 1266, **Web** 1976 U.S. App. Lexis 6548 (United States Court of Appeals for the Fifth Circuit)

38.3 Proxy Contest The Fairchild Engine and Airplane Corporation (Fairchild) was a privately held corporation whose management proposed the incumbent slate of directors for election at its annual shareholders' meeting. An insurgent slate of directors challenged the incumbents for election to the board. After the solicitation of proxies and a hard-fought proxy contest, the insurgent slate of directors was elected. Evidence showed that the proxy contest was waged over matters of corporate policy and for personal reasons. The old board of directors had spent $134,000 out of corporate funds to wage the proxy contest. The insurgents had spent $127,000 of their personal funds in their successful proxy contest and sought reimbursement from Fairchild for this amount. The payment of these expenses was ratified by a 16-to-1 majority vote of the shareholders. Mr. Rosenfeld, an attorney who owned 25 of the 2,300,000 outstanding shares of the corporation, filed an action to recover the amounts already paid by the corporation and to prevent any further payments of these expenses. Who wins? *Rosenfeld v. Fairchild Engine and Airplane Corporation*, 309 N.Y. 168, 128 N.E.2d 291, **Web** 1955 N.Y. Lexis 947 (Court of Appeals of New York)

38.4 Shareholder Resolution The Medical Committee for Human Rights (Committee), a nonprofit corporation organized to advance concerns for human life, received a gift of shares of Dow Chemical (Dow) stock. Dow manufactured napalm, a chemical defoliant that was used during the Vietnam Conflict. Committee objected to the sale of napalm by Dow primarily because of its concerns for human life. Committee owned sufficient shares for a long enough time to propose a shareholders' resolution, as long as it met the other requirements to propose such a resolution. Committee proposed that the following resolution be included in the proxy materials circulated by management for the annual shareholders' meeting:

> RESOLVED, *that the shareholders of the Dow Chemical company request that the Board of Directors, in accordance with the law, consider the advisability of adopting a resolution setting forth an amendment to the composite certificate of incorporation of the Dow Chemical Company that the company shall not make napalm.*

Dow's management refused to include the requested resolution in its proxy materials. Committee sued, alleging that its resolution met the requirements to be included in the proxy materials. Who wins? *Medical Committee for Human Rights v. Securities and Exchange Commission*, 139 U.S. App. D.C. 226, 432 F.2d 659, **Web** 1970 U.S. App. Lexis 8284 (United States Court of Appeals for the District of Columbia Circuit)

38.5 Merger The board of directors of Plant Industries, Inc. (Plant), under the guidance of Robert B. Bregman, the chief executive officer of the corporation, embarked on a course of action that resulted in the sale of several unprofitable subsidiaries. Bregman then engaged in a course of action to sell Plant National (Quebec) Ltd., a subsidiary that constituted Plant's entire Canadian operations. This was a profitable subsidiary that comprised over 50 percent of Plant's assets, sales, and profits. Do Plant's shareholders have to be accorded voting and appraisal rights regarding the sale of this subsidiary? *Katz v. Bregman*, 431 A.2d 1274, **Web** 1981 Del. Ch. Lexis 449 (Court of Chancery of Delaware)

38.6 Dissenting Shareholder Appraisal Rights Over a period of several years, the Curtiss-Wright Corporation (Curtiss-Wright) purchased 65 percent of the stock of Dorr-Oliver Incorporated (Dorr-Oliver). Curtiss-Wright's board of directors decided that a merger with Dorr-Oliver would be beneficial to Curtiss-Wright. The board voted to approve a merger of the two companies and to pay $23 per share to the stockholders of Dorr-Oliver. The Dorr-Oliver board and 80 percent of Dorr-Oliver's shareholders approved the merger. The merger became effective. John Bershad, a minority shareholder of Dorr-Oliver, voted against the merger but thereafter tendered his 100 shares and received payment of $2,300. Bershad subsequently sued, alleging that the $23 per share paid to Dorr-Oliver shareholders was grossly inadequate. Can Bershad obtain minority shareholder appraisal rights? *Bershad v. Curtiss-Wright Corporation*, 535 A.2d 840, **Web** 1987 Del. Lexis 1313 (Supreme Court of Delaware)

38.7 Tender Offer Mobil Corporation (Mobil) made a tender offer to purchase up to 40 million outstanding common shares of stock in Marathon Oil Company (Marathon) for $85 per share in cash. It further stated its intentions to follow the purchase with a merger of the two companies. Mobil was primarily interested in acquiring Marathon's oil and mineral interests in certain properties, including the Yates Field. Marathon directors immediately held a board meeting and determined to find a white knight. Negotiations developed between Marathon and United States Steel Corporation (U.S. Steel). Two weeks later, Marathon and U.S. Steel entered into an agreement whereby U.S. Steel would make a tender offer for 30 million common shares of Marathon stock at $125 per share, to be followed by a merger of the two companies.

The Marathon–U.S. Steel agreement was subject to the following two conditions: (1) U.S. Steel was given an irrevocable option to purchase 10 million authorized but unissued shares of Marathon common stock for $90 per share (or 17 percent of Marathon's outstanding shares), and (2) U.S. Steel was given an option to purchase Marathon's interest in oil and mineral rights in Yates Field for $2.8 billion (Yates Field option). The Yates Field option could be exercised only if U.S. Steel's offer did not succeed and if a third party gained control of Marathon. Evidence showed that Marathon's interest in Yates Field was worth up to $3.6 billion. Marathon did not give Mobil either of these two options. Mobil sued, alleging that these two options violated Section 14(e) of the Williams Act. Who wins? *Mobil Corporation v. Marathon Oil Company*, 669 F.2d 366, **Web** 1981 U.S. App. Lexis 14958 (United States Court of Appeals for the Sixth Circuit)

38.8 Tender Offer   The Fruehauf Corporation (Fruehauf) is engaged in the manufacture of large trucks and industrial vehicles. The Edelman group (Edelman) made a cash tender offer for the shares of Fruehauf for $48.50 per share. The stock had sold in the low $20-per-share range a few months earlier. Fruehauf's management decided to make a competing management-led leveraged buyout (MBO) tender offer for the company in conjunction with Merrill Lynch. The MBO would be funded using $375 million borrowed from Merrill Lynch, $375 million borrowed from Manufacturers Hanover Bank, and $100 million contributed by Fruehauf. The total equity contribution to the new company under the MBO would be only $25 million: $10 million to $15 million from management and the rest from Merrill Lynch. In return for their equity contributions, management would receive between 40 and 60 percent of the new company.

Fruehauf's management agreed to pay $30 million to Merrill Lynch for brokerage fees that Merrill Lynch could keep even if the deal did not go through. Management also agreed to a no-shop clause whereby they agreed not to seek a better deal with another bidder. Incumbent management received better information about the goings-on. They also

gave themselves golden parachutes that would raise the money for management's equity position in the new company.

Edelman informed Fruehauf's management that it could top their bid, but Fruehauf's management did not give them the opportunity to present their offer. Management's offer was accepted. Edelman sued, seeking an injunction. Did Fruehauf's management violate the business judgment rule? Who wins? *Edelman v. Fruehauf Corporation*, 798 F.2d 882, **Web** 1986 U.S. App. Lexis 27911 (United States Court of Appeals for the Sixth Circuit)

38.9 Flip-Over Defense   Household International, Inc. (Household), was a diversified holding company with its principal subsidiaries engaged in financial services, transportation, and merchandising. The board of directors of Household adopted a 48-page "Rights Plan" by a 14-to-2 vote. Basically, the plan provided that Household common stockholders were entitled to the issuance of one irrevocable right per common share if any party acquired 20 percent of Household's shares. The right permitted Household shareholders to purchase $200 of the common stock of the tender offeror for $100. In essence, this forced any party interested in taking over Household to negotiate with Household's directors. Dyson-Kissner-Moran Corporation (DKM), which was interested in taking over Household, filed suit, alleging that this flip-over rights plan violated the business judgment rule. Who wins? *Moran v. Household International, Inc.*, 500 A.2d 1346, **Web** 1985 Del. Lexis 557 (Supreme Court of Delaware)

38.10 State Antitakeover Statute   The state of Wisconsin enacted an antitakeover statute that protects corporations that are incorporated in Wisconsin and have their headquarters, substantial operations, or 10 percent of their shares of shareholders in the state. The statute prevents any party that acquires a 10 percent interest in a covered corporation from engaging in a business combination (e.g., merger) with the covered corporation for three years unless approval of management is obtained in advance of the combination. Wisconsin firms cannot opt out of the law. This statute effectively eliminates hostile leveraged buyouts because buyers must rely on the assets and income of the target company to help pay off the debt incurred in effectuating the takeover.

Universal Foods (Universal) was a Wisconsin corporation covered by the statute. Amanda Acquisition Corporation (Amanda) commenced a cash tender offer for up to 75 percent of the stock of Universal. Universal asserted the Wisconsin law. Is Wisconsin's antitakeover statute lawful? *Amanda Acquisition Corporation v. Universal Foods*, 877 F.2d 496, **Web** 1989 U.S. App. Lexis 9024 (United States Court of Appeals for the Seventh Circuit)

BUSINESS ETHICS CASES

38.11 Business Ethics   MCA, Inc. (MCA), a corporate holding company, owned 92 percent of the stock of Universal Pictures Company (Universal) and 100

percent of the stock of Universal City Studios, Inc. (Universal City). These two subsidiaries merged pursuant to Delaware's short-form merger statute. The minority shareholders of Universal were offered $75 per share for their shares. Francis I.

Du Pont & Company and other minority shareholders (Plaintiffs) rejected the offer and then perfected their dissenting shareholder appraisal rights. The appraiser filed a final report in which he found the value of Universal stock to be $91.47 per share. Both parties filed exceptions to this report.

The parties' ultimate disagreement was over the value of the stock. Plaintiffs submitted that the true value was $131.89 per share; the defendant said it was $52.36. The computations were as follows:

Plaintiffs' Valuation

Value Factor	Value	Weight	Result
Earnings	$129.12	70%	$90.38
Market	144.36	20	28.87
Assets	126.46	10	12.64
Value per share			**$131.89**

Defendant's Valuation

Value Factor	Value	Weight	Result
Earnings	$51.93	70%	$36.35
Dividends	41.66	20	8.33
Assets	76.77	10	7.68
Value per share			**$52.36**

Appraiser's Valuation

Value Factor	Value	Weight	Result
Earnings	$92.89	80%	$74.31
Assets	85.82	20	17.16
Value per share			**$91.47**

The defendant took exception to the appraiser's failure to find that, in the years prior to merger, the industry was declining, and Universal was ranked near its bottom. The defendant argued that Universal was in the business of producing and distributing feature motion pictures for theatrical exhibition. It contended that such business, generally, was in a severe decline at the time of merger and that Universal, in particular, was in a vulnerable position because it had failed to diversify, its feature films were of low commercial quality, and, unlike other motion picture companies, substantially all of its film library had already been committed to distributors for television exhibition. In short, defendant Universal was a weak "wasting asset" corporation in a sick industry with poor prospects for revival.

The shareholders saw a different company. They said that Universal's business was indeed the production and distribution of feature films, but not merely for theatrical exhibition. They argued that there was a dramatic increase in the television market for such feature films at the time of the merger. This market, they contended, gave great new value to a fully amortized film library and significantly enhanced the value of Universal's current and future productions. Thus, they painted a portrait of a well-situated corporation in a rejuvenated industry.

Did the parties act ethically in arriving at their proposed values of the company? What is the value of the minority shareholders' shares of Universal Pictures Company? *Francis I. Du Pont & Company v. Universal City Studios, Inc.*, 312 A.2d 344, **Web** 1973 Del. Ch. Lexis 123 (Court of Chancery of Delaware)

38.12 Business Ethics Realist, Inc. (Realist), was a Delaware corporation with its principal place of business in Wisconsin. In March 1988, Royal Business Group, Inc. (Royal), a New Hampshire corporation, acquired 8 percent of the outstanding voting stock of Realist. Royal sent a series of letters to Realist, declaring its intention to acquire all of Realist's outstanding shares at an above-market premium. Realist repulsed Royal's overtures. Unbeknownst to Royal, Realist began negotiations to acquire Ammann Laser Technik AG (Ammann), a company based in Switzerland.

Royal instituted a proxy contest and nominated two candidates for the two Realist directorships to be filed at the annual shareholders' meeting. Realist and Royal both submitted proxy statements to Realist's shareholders.

The insurgent Royal nominees prevailed. Realist announced that it had acquired Ammann. This acquisition made Realist much less attractive as a takeover target. Royal immediately withdrew its offer to acquire Realist and sued Realist to recover the $350,000 it had spent in connection with the proxy contest. Royal alleged that Realist had engaged in fraud in violation of Section 14(a) of the Securities Exchange Act of 1934 by failing to disclose its secret negotiations with Ammann in its proxy materials. The basis of Royal's complaint was that if Realist had disclosed that it intended to acquire Ammann, Royal would not have engaged in the costly proxy contest. Is Realist liable to Royal? Did Realist act unethically in seeking to acquire Ammann to thwart Royal's takeover attempt? *Royal Business Group, Inc. v. Realist, Inc.*, 933 F.2d 1056, **Web** 1991 U.S. App. Lexis 10389 (United States Court of Appeals for the First Circuit)

ENDNOTES

1. 15 U.S.C. Section 78n(a).
2. 15 U.S.C. Sections 78n(d), 78n(e).
3. Section 13(d) of the Securities Exchange Act of 1934 requires that any party that acquires 5 percent or more of any equity security of a company registered with the SEC must report the acquisition to the SEC and disclose its intentions regarding the acquisition. This is public information.
4. 15 U.S.C. Section 78n(e).
5. *Smith v. Van Gorkom*, 488 A.2d 858, Web 1985 Del. Lexis 421 (Supreme Court of Delaware).
6. *Unocal Corporation v. Mesa Petroleum Company*, 493 A.2d 946, Web 1985 Del. Lexis 482 (Supreme Court of Delaware).

39 | LIMITED LIABILITY COMPANIES AND LIMITED LIABILITY PARTNERSHIPS

▲ **Certificate of Interest** *Various types of business forms are used throughout the world. The limited liability company form of business was developed and used extensively in the world for centuries before this form of business developed in the United States. In 1977, Wyoming became the first state in the United States to enact a limited liability company (LLC) act. In 1988, the Internal Revenue Service (IRS) issued a ruling that treated an LLC as a partnership for tax purposes. All 50 states now permit the formation of LLCs.*

CHAPTER OBJECTIVES

After studying this chapter, you should be able to:

1. Define *limited liability company (LLC)* and *limited liability partnership (LLP)*.
2. Describe the process of organizing LLCs and LLPs.
3. Describe the limited liability shield provided by LLCs and LLPs.
4. Compare member-managed LLCs and manager-managed LLCs.
5. Determine when members and managers owe fiduciary duties of loyalty and care to an LLC.

CHAPTER CONTENTS

"Justice is the end of government. It is the end of civil society. It ever has been, and ever will be pursued, until it be obtained, or until liberty be lost in the pursuit."

—James Madison
The Federalist, No. 51 (1788)

▶ INTRODUCTION TO LIMITED LIABILITY COMPANIES AND LIMITED LIABILITY PARTNERSHIPS

Owners may choose to operate a business as a *limited liability company (LLC)*. The use of LLCs as a form of conducting business in the United States is of rather recent origin. In 1977, Wyoming was the first state in the United States to enact legislation creating an LLC as a legal form for conducting business. This new form of business received little attention until the early 1990s, when several more states enacted legislation to allow the creation of LLCs. The evolution of LLCs then grew at blinding speed, with all the states having enacted LLC statutes by 1998. Most LLC laws are quite similar, although some differences do exist between these state statutes.

An LLC is an unincorporated business entity that combines the most favorable attributes of general partnerships, limited partnerships, and corporations. An LLC may elect to be taxed as a partnership, the owners can manage the business, and the owners have limited liability for debts and obligations of the partnership. Many entrepreneurs who begin new businesses choose the LLC as their legal form for conducting business.

Most states have enacted laws that permit certain types of professionals, such as accountants, lawyers, and doctors, to operate as *limited liability partnerships (LLPs)*. The owners of an LLP have limited liability for debts and obligations of the partnership.

The formation and operation of LLCs and LLPs and the liability of their owners are discussed in this chapter.

▶ LIMITED LIABILITY COMPANY (LLC)

Limited liability companies (LLCs) are creatures of state law, not federal law. An LLC can only be created pursuant to the laws of the state in which the LLC is being organized. These statutes, commonly referred to as **limited liability company codes**, regulate the formation, operation, and dissolution of LLCs. The state legislature may amend its LLC statutes at any time. The courts interpret state LLC statutes to decide LLC and member disputes.

An LLC is a separate *legal entity* (or legal person) distinct from its members [ULLCA Section 201]. LLCs are treated as artificial persons who can sue or be sued, enter into and enforce contracts, hold title to and transfer property, and be found civilly and criminally liable for violations of law.

limited liability company (LLC)
An unincorporated business entity that combines the most favorable attributes of general partnerships, limited partnerships, and corporations.

Uniform Limited Liability Company Act (ULLCA)
A model act that provides comprehensive and uniform laws for the formation, operation, and dissolution of LLCs.

LANDMARK LAW

Uniform Limited Liability Company Act

In 1996, the National Conference of Commissioners on Uniform State Laws (a group of lawyers, judges, and legal scholars) issued the **Uniform Limited Liability Company Act (ULLCA)**. The ULLCA codifies LLC law. Its goal is to establish comprehensive LLC law that is uniform throughout the United States. The ULLCA covers most problems that arise in the formation, operation, and

termination of LLCs. The ULLCA is not law unless a state adopts it as its LLC statute. Many states have adopted all or part of the ULLCA as their LLC law. The ULLCA was revised in 2006, and this revision is called the **Revised Uniform Limited Liability Company Act (RULLCA)**.

The ULLCA forms the basis of the study of limited liability companies in this chapter.

Taxation of LLCs

Under the Internal Revenue Code and regulations adopted by the Internal Revenue Service (IRS) for federal income tax purposes, an LLC is **taxed** as a partnership unless it elects to be taxed as a corporation. Thus, an LLC is not taxed at the entity level, but its income or losses "flow through" to the members' individual income tax returns. This avoids double taxation. Most LLCs accept the default status of being taxed as a partnership instead of electing to be taxed as a corporation.

Powers of an LLC

Morality cannot be legislated, but behavior can be regulated. Judicial decrees may not change the heart, but they can restrain the heartless.

Martin Luther King, Jr.
Strength to Love (1963)

An economist's guess is liable to be as good as anybody else's.

Will Rogers

An LLC has the same **powers** as an individual to do all things necessary or convenient to carry on its business or affairs, including owning and transferring personal property; selling, leasing, and mortgaging real property; making contracts and guarantees; borrowing and lending money; issuing notes and bonds; suing and being sued; and taking other actions to conduct the affairs and business of the LLC [ULLCA Section 112].

▶ FORMATION OF AN LLC

Most LLCs are organized to operate businesses, real estate developments, and such. Certain professionals, such as accountants, lawyers, and doctors, cannot operate practices as LLCs; instead, they can operate practices as limited liability partnerships (LLPs).

An LLC can be organized in only one state, even though it can conduct business in all other states. When choosing a state for organization, the members should consider the LLC codes of the states under consideration. For the sake of convenience, most LLCs, particularly small ones, choose as the state of organization the state in which the LLC will be doing most of its business.

When starting a new LLC, the organizers must choose a name for the entity. The name must contain the words *limited liability company* or *limited company* or the abbreviation *L.L.C.*, *LLC*, *L.C.*, or *LC. Limited* may be abbreviated as *Ltd.*, and *company* may be abbreviated as *Co.* [ULLCA Section 105(a)].

Articles of Organization

articles of organization
The formal documents that must be filed at the secretary of state's office of the state of organization of an LLC to form the LLC.

Because LLCs are creatures of statute, certain formalities must be taken and statutory requirements must be met to form an LLC. Under the ULLCA, an LLC may be organized by one or more persons. Some states require at least two members to organize an LLC. In states where an LLC may be organized by only one member, sole proprietors can obtain the benefit of the limited liability shield of an LLC.

An LLC is formed by delivering **articles of organization** to the office of the secretary of state of the state of organization for filing. If the articles are in proper form, the secretary of state will file the articles. The existence of an LLC begins when the articles of organization are filed. The filing of the articles of organization by the secretary of state is conclusive proof that the organizers have satisfied all the conditions necessary to create the LLC [ULLCA Section 202]. Under the ULLCA, the articles of organization of an LLC must set forth [ULLCA Section 203]:

- The name of the LLC
- The address of the LLC's initial office
- The name and address of the initial agent for service of process
- The name and address of each organizer
- Whether the LLC is a term LLC and, if so, the term specified
- Whether the LLC is to be a manager-managed LLC and, if so, the name and address of each manager
- Whether one or more of the members of the LLC are to be personally liable for the LLC's debts and obligations

The articles of organization may set forth provisions from the members' operating agreement and any other matter not inconsistent with law. A sample articles of organization is set forth in Exhibit 39.1. An LLC can amend its articles of organization at any time by filing **articles of amendment** with the secretary of state [ULLCA Section 204].

> **ARTICLES OF ORGANIZATION**
> **FOR FLORIDA LIMITED LIABILITY COMPANY**
>
> **ARTICLE I - NAME**
> The name of the Limited Liability Company is
> iCitrusSystems.com
>
> **ARTICLE II - ADDRESS**
> The mailing address and street address of the principal office of the Limited Liability Company is
>
> 3000 Dade Boulevard
> Suite 200
> Miami Beach, Florida 33139
>
> **ARTICLE III - DURATION**
> The period of duration for the Limited Liability Company shall be
> 50 years
>
> **ARTICLE IV - MANAGEMENT**
> The Limited Liability Company is to be managed by a manager and the name and address of such manager is
>
> Susan Escobar
> 1000 Collins Avenue
> Miami Beach, Florida 33141
>
> _____
> Thomas Blandford
>
> _____
> Pam Rosales

▶ **Exhibit 39.1 ARTICLES OF ORGANIZATION**

Duration of an LLC

An LLC is an **at-will LLC** (i.e., with no specified term) unless it is designated as a **term LLC** and the duration of the term is specified in the articles of organization [ULLCA Section 203(a)(5)]. The duration of a term LLC may be specified in any manner that sets forth a specific and final date for the dissolution of the LLC.

at-will LLC
An LLC that has no specified term of duration.

Examples Periods specified as "50 years from the date of filing of the articles of organizations" and "the period ending January 1, 2050" are valid to create a term LLC.

term LLC
An LLC that has a specified term of duration.

Capital Contribution to an LLC

A member's capital contribution to an LLC may be in the form of money, personal property, real property, other tangible property, intangible property (e.g., a patent), services performed, contracts for services to be performed, promissory notes, or other agreements to contribute cash or property [ULLCA Section 401].

A member's obligation to contribute capital is not excused by the member's death, disability, or other inability to perform. If a member cannot make the required contribution of property or services, he or she is obligated to contribute money equal to the value of the promised contribution. The LLC or any creditor who extended credit to the LLC in reliance on the promised contribution may enforce the promised obligation [ULLCA Section 402].

Certificate of Interest

certificate of interest
A document that evidences a member's ownership interest in an LLC.

An LLC's operating agreement may provide that a member's ownership interest may be evidenced by a **certificate of interest** issued by the LLC [ULLCA Section 501(c)]. The certificate of interest acts the same as a stock certificate issued by a corporation.

Operating Agreement

operating agreement
An agreement entered into among members that governs the affairs and business of the LLC and the relations among members, managers, and the LLC.

Members of an LLC may enter into an **operating agreement** that regulates the affairs of the company and the conduct of its business and governs relations among the members, managers, and company [ULLCA Section 103(a)]. The operating agreement may be amended by the approval of all members unless otherwise provided in the agreement. The operating agreement and amendments may be oral but are usually written.

Conversion of an Existing Business to an LLC

Many LLCs are formed by entrepreneurs to start new businesses. In addition, an existing business may want to convert to an LLC to obtain its tax benefits and limited liability shield. General partnerships, limited partnerships, and corporations may be converted to LLCs if the following requirements are met [ULLCA Section 902]:

agreement of conversion
A document that states the terms for converting an existing business to an LLC.

- An **agreement of conversion** is drafted that sets forth the terms of the conversion.
- The terms of the conversion are approved by all the parties or by the number or percentage of owners required for conversion.
- Articles of organization of the LLC are filed with the secretary of state. The articles must state that the LLC was previously another form of business and the prior business's name.

The conversion takes effect when the articles of organization are filed with the secretary of state or at any later date specified in the articles of organization. When the conversion takes effect, all property owned by the prior business vests in the LLC, and all debts, obligations, and liabilities of the prior business become those of the LLC [ULLCA Section 903].

Dividing an LLC's Profits and Losses

Unless otherwise agreed, the ULLCA mandates that a member has the right to an equal share in the LLC's profits [ULLCA Section 405(a)]. This is a default rule that the members can override by agreement and is usually a provision in their operating agreement. In many instances, the members may not want the profits of the LLC to be shared equally. This would normally occur if the capital contributions of the members were unequal. If the members of an LLC want the profits to be divided in the same proportion as their capital contributions, that should be specified in the operating agreement.

Examples Lilly and Harrison form an LLC. Lilly contributes $75,000 capital, and Harrison contributes $25,000 capital. They do not have an agreement as to how profits are to be shared. If the LLC makes $100,000 in profits, under the ULLCA, Lilly and Harrison will share the profits equally—$50,000 each. To avoid this outcome, Lilly and Harrison should agree in their operating agreement how they want the profits to be divided.

There shall be one law for the native and for the stranger who sojourns among you.

Moses
Exodus 12:49

Losses from an LLC are shared equally unless otherwise agreed. Sometimes members will not want to divide losses equally and maybe not even in the same way as their capital contributions. If the LLC has chosen to be taxed as a partnership, the losses from an LLC flow to the members' individual income tax returns. Losses from an LLC can sometimes be offset against members' gains from other sources. Therefore, the members may want to agree to divide the losses so that the members who can use them to offset other income will receive a greater share of the losses.

Profits and losses from an LLC do not have to be distributed in the same proportion.

Example A member who has the right to a 10 percent share of profits may be given in the operating agreement the right to receive 25 percent of the LLC's losses.

Distributional Interest

A member's ownership interest in an LLC is called a **distributional interest**. A member's distributional interest in an LLC is personal property and may be transferred in whole or in part [ULLCA Section 501(b)]. Unless otherwise provided in the operating agreement, a transfer of an interest in an LLC does not entitle the transferee to become a member of the LLC or to exercise any right of a member. A transfer entitles the transferee to receive only distributions from the LLC to which the transferor would have been entitled [ULLCA Section 502]. A transferee of a distributional interest becomes a member of the LLC if it is so provided in the operating agreement or if all the other members of the LLC consent [ULLCA Section 503(a)].

Example Cleveland, Heather, and Archibald are members of the Boston Tea Party LLC; each owns a one-third interest in the LLC, and the members agree to divide the distributions equally in one-third portions. The LLC's operating agreement does not provide that a transferee of a distributional interest will become a member. Cleveland sells his one-third interest to Theodore. The members do not consent to allow Theodore to become a member. The LLC makes $99,999 in profits. Theodore is entitled to receive one-third of the distributions ($33,333). Theodore is not a member of the LLC, however.

A transferor who transfers his or her distributional interest is not released from liability for the debts, obligations, and liabilities of the LLC [ULLCA Section 503(c)].

> **distributional interest**
> A member's ownership interest in an LLC that entitles the member to receive distributions of money and property from the LLC.

CONTEMPORARY ENVIRONMENT

DreamWorks SKG, LLC

Steven Spielberg, Jeffrey Katzenberg, and David Geffen formed DreamWorks SKG, which is a major movie and recording production company. Spielberg's fame and money came from directing films, Katzenberg had been a leading executive at Disney, and Geffen had built and sold a major record company. These multimillionaire multimedia giants combined their talents to create a formidable entertainment company.

DreamWorks was formed as a Delaware LLC. The organizers chose to create an LLC because it is taxed as a partnership, the profits (or losses) flow directly to the owners, and like a corporation the owners are protected from personal liability beyond their capital contributions.

DreamWorks issued several classes of interests. The three principals put up $100 million ($33.3 million each) for "SKG" stock, which grants the principals 100 percent voting control and 67 percent of the firm's profits. In addition, each principal has multiyear employment contracts plus other benefits.

DreamWorks raised the other $900 million of its $1 billion capital from other investors, who were to receive one-third of future profits. The other investors were issued the following classes of stock:

Class	Investments
A	Outside investors. Class A stock was sold to big investors with over $20 million to invest. Microsoft's cofounder, Paul Allen, purchased $500 million of Class A stock. Class A investors got seats on the board of directors.
S	Outside investors. Class S stock was issued for smallish, "strategic" investments with other companies for cross-marketing purposes.
E	Employees. Employees were granted the right to participate in an employee stock purchase plan.

▶ LIABILITY OF AN LLC

An LLC is liable for any loss or injury caused to anyone as a result of a wrongful act or omission by a member, a manager, an agent, or an employee of the LLC who commits the wrongful act while acting within the ordinary course of business of the LLC or with authority of the LLC [ULLCA Section 302].

The great can protect themselves, but the poor and humble require the arm and shield of the law.

Andrew Jackson

Example Sable, Silvia, and Samantha form SSS, LLC, to own and operate a business. Each member contributes $10,000 capital. While on LLC business, Sable drives her automobile and accidentally hits and injures Damon. Damon can recover damages for his injuries from Sable personally because she committed the negligent act. Damon can also recover damages from SSS, LLC, because Sable was acting within the scope of the ordinary business of the LLC when the accident occurred. Silvia and Samantha have limited liability only up to their capital contributions in SSS, LLC.

Liability of Managers

Managers of LLCs are not personally liable for the debts, obligations, and liabilities of the LLC they manage [ULLCA Section 303(a)].

Example An LLC that is engaged in real estate development hires Sarah Goldstein, a non-member, to be its president. While acting within the scope of her LLC authority, Sarah signs a loan agreement whereby the LLC borrows $1 million from a bank to complete the construction of an office building. If the LLC subsequently suffers financial difficulty and defaults on the bank loan, Sarah is not personally responsible for the loan. The LLC is liable for the loan, but Sarah is not because she was acting as the manager of the LLC.

▶ MEMBERS' LIMITED LIABILITY

member
An owner of an LLC.

limited liability
The liability of LLC members for the LLC's debts, obligations, and liabilities only to the extent of their capital contributions.

The owners of LLCs are usually called **members**. The general rule is that members are not personally liable to third parties for the debts, obligations, and liabilities of an LLC beyond their capital contribution. Members are said to have **limited liability** (see Exhibit 39.2). The debts, obligations, and liabilities of an LLC, whether arising from contracts, torts, or otherwise, are solely those of the LLC [ULLCA Section 303(a)].

▶ **Exhibit 39.2 LIMITED LIABILITY COMPANY (LLC)**

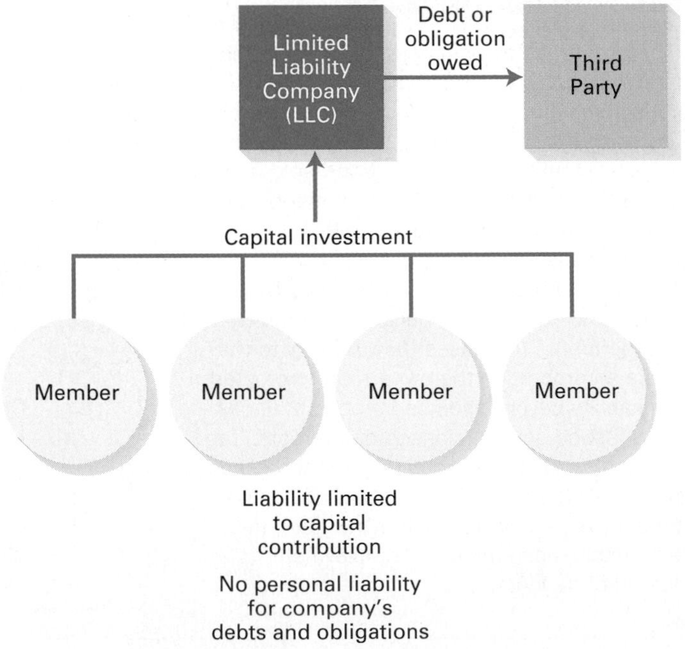

Example Jasmin, Shou-Yi, and Vanessa form an LLC, and each contributes $25,000 in capital. The LLC operates for a period of time, during which it borrows money from banks and purchases goods on credit from suppliers. After some time, the LLC experiences financial difficulty and goes out of business. If the LLC fails with $500,000 in debts, each of the members will lose her capital contribution of $25,000 but will not be personally liable for the rest of the unpaid debts of the LLC.

The failure of an LLC to observe the usual company formalities is not grounds for imposing personal liability on the members of the LLC [ULLCA Section 303(b)]. For example, if the LLC does not keep minutes of the company's meetings, the members do not become personally liable for the LLC's debts.

In the following case, the court addressed the issue of the limited liability of a member of an LLC.

CASE 39.1 Limited Liability Company

Siva v. 1138 LLC

2007 Ohio 4667, Web 2007 Ohio App. Lexis 4202 (2007)
Court of Appeals of Ohio

"**Finally, the evidence did not show that Siva was misguided as to the fact he was dealing with a limited liability company.**"

—Judge Brown

Facts

Five members—Richard Hess, Robert Haines, Lisa Hess, Nathan Hess, and Zack Shahin—formed a limited liability company called 1138 LLC. Ruthiran Siva owned a commercial building located at 1138 Bethel Road, Franklin County, Ohio. Siva entered into a written lease agreement with 1138 LLC whereby 1138 LLC leased premises in Siva's commercial building for a term of five years at a monthly rental of $4,000. 1138 LLC began operating a bar on the premises. Six months later, 1138 LLC was in default and breach of the lease agreement. Siva sued 1138 LLC and Richard Hess to recover damages. Siva received a default judgment against 1138 LLC, but there was no money in 1138 LLC to pay the judgment. Hess, who had been sued personally, defended, arguing that as a member-owner of the LLC, he was not personally liable for the debts of the LLC. The trial court found in favor of Hess and dismissed Siva's complaint against Hess. Siva appealed.

Issue

Is Richard Hess, a member-owner of 1138 LLC, personally liable for the debt owed by the LLC to Siva?

Language of the Court

Based upon the court's examination of the record, we find there was competent, credible evidence to support the trial court's determination. The evidence does not show that Hess purposely undercapitalized 1138 LLC, or that

he formed the limited liability company in an effort to avoid paying creditors. According to Hess, the bar was never profitable. Based upon the evidence presented, a reasonable trier of fact could have concluded that 1138 LLC became insolvent due to unprofitable operations. Moreover, even if the record suggests poor business judgment by Hess, it does not demonstrate that he formed 1138 LLC to defraud creditors. Finally, the evidence did not show that Siva was misguided as to the fact he was dealing with a limited liability company. Siva's counsel drafted the lease agreement and Siva acknowledged at trial he did not ask any of the owners of 1138 LLC to sign the lease in an individual capacity.

Decision

The court of appeals held that Hess, as a member-owner of 1138 LLC, was not personally liable for the debt that the LLC owed to Siva. The court of appeals affirmed the decision of the trial court that dismissed Siva's complaint against Hess.

Case Questions

Critical Legal Thinking What is the liability of an LLC for its debts? What is the liability of a member-owner of an LLC for the LLC's debts? Explain.

Business Ethics Did Hess owe an ethical duty to pay the debt owed by 1138 LLC to Siva? Did Siva act ethically by suing Hess personally to recover the debt owed by the 1138 LLC?

Contemporary Business What should Siva have done if he wanted Hess to be personally liable on the lease? Explain.

Liability of Tortfeasors

A person who intentionally or unintentionally (negligently) causes injury or death to another person is called a **tortfeasor**. A tortfeasor is personally liable to persons he or she injures and to the heirs of persons who die because of his or her conduct. This rule applies to members and managers of LLCs. Thus, if a member or a manager of an LLC negligently causes injury or death to another person, he or she is personally liable to the injured person or the heirs of the deceased person.

tortfeasor
A person who intentionally or unintentionally (negligently) causes injury or death to another person. A person liable to persons he or she injures and to the heirs of persons who die because of his or her conduct.

▶ MANAGEMENT OF AN LLC

An LLC can be either a *member-managed LLC* or a *manager-managed LLC*. An LLC is a member-managed LLC unless it is designated as a manager-managed LLC in its articles of organization [ULLCA Section 203(a) (b)]. The distinctions between these two are:

- **Member-managed LLC.** In this type of LLC, the members of the LLC have the right to manage the LLC.
- **Manager-managed LLC.** In this type of LLC, the members designate a manager or managers to manage the LLC, and by doing so, they delegate their management rights to the manager or managers, designated manager or managers have the authority to manage the LLC, and the members no longer have the right to manage the LLC.

A manager may be a member of an LLC or a nonmember. Whether an LLC is a member-managed or manager-managed LLC has important consequences on the right to bind the LLC to contracts and on determining the fiduciary duties owed by members to the LLC. These important distinctions are discussed in the paragraphs that follow.

Member-Managed LLC

member-managed LLC
An LLC that has not designated it is a manager-managed LLC in its articles of organization and is managed by its members.

In a **member-managed LLC**, each member has equal rights in the management of the business of the LLC, regardless of the size of his or her capital contribution. Any matter relating to the business of the LLC is decided by a majority vote of the members [ULLCA Section 404(a)].

Example Allison, Jaeson, Stacy, Lan-Wei, and Ivy form North West.com, LLC. Allison contributes $100,000 capital, and the other four members each contribute $25,000 capital. When deciding whether to add another line of products to the business, Stacy, Lan-Wei, and Ivy vote to add the line, and Allison and Jaeson vote against it. The line of new products is added to the LLC's business because three members voted yes, while two members voted no. It does not matter that the two members who voted no contributed $125,000 in capital collectively versus $75,000 in capital contributed by the three members who voted yes.

Manager-Managed LLC

manager-managed LLC
An LLC that has designated in its articles of organization it is a manager-managed LLC and whose nonmanager members give their management rights over to designated managers.

Laws too gentle are seldom obeyed; too severe, seldom executed.

Benjamin Franklin
Poor Richard's Almanack (1756)

In a **manager-managed LLC**, the members and nonmembers who are designated managers control the management of the LLC. The members who are not managers have no rights to manage the LLC unless otherwise provided in the operating agreement. In a manager-managed LLC, each manager has equal rights in the management and conduct of the company's business. Any matter related to the business of the LLC may be exclusively decided by the managers by a majority vote of the managers [ULLCA Section 403(b)]. A manager must be appointed by a vote of a majority of the members; managers may also be removed by a vote of the majority of the members [ULLCA Section 404(b)(3)].

Certain actions cannot be delegated to managers but must be voted on by all members of the LLC. These include (1) amending the articles of organization, (2) amending the operating agreement, (3) admitting new members, (4) consenting to dissolve the LLC, (5) consenting to merge the LLC with another entity, and (6) selling, leasing, or disposing of all or substantially all of the LLC's property [ULLCA Section 404(c)].

CONCEPT SUMMARY

MANAGEMENT OF AN LLC

Type of LLC	Description
Member-managed LLC	The members do not designate managers to manage the LLC. The LLC is managed by its members.
Manager-managed LLC	The members designate certain members or nonmembers to manage the LLC. The LLC is managed by the designated managers; nonmanager members have no right to manage the LLC.

Compensation and Reimbursement

A nonmanager member of an LLC is not entitled to remuneration for services performed for the LLC (except for winding up the business of the LLC). Managers of an LLC, whether they are members or not, are paid compensation and benefits as specified in their employment agreements with the LLC [ULLCA Section 403(d)].

An LLC is obligated to reimburse members and managers for payments made on behalf of the LLC (e.g., business expenses) and to indemnify members and managers for liabilities incurred in the ordinary course of LLC business or in the preservation of the LLC's business or property [ULLCA Section 403(a)].

Agency Authority to Bind an LLC to Contracts

The designation of an LLC as member managed or manager managed is important in determining who has authority to bind the LLC to contracts. The following rules apply:

- **Member-managed LLC.** In a member-managed LLC, all members have agency authority to bind the LLC to contracts.

Example If Theresa, Artis, and Yolanda form a member-managed LLC, each one of them can bind the LLC to a contract with a third party such as a supplier, purchaser, or landlord.

- **Manager-managed LLC.** In a manager-managed LLC, the managers have authority to bind the LLC to contracts, but nonmanager members cannot bind the LLC to contracts.

Example Alexis, Derek, Ashley, and Sadia form an LLC. They designate the LLC as a manager-managed LLC and name Alexis and Ashley as the managers. Alexis, a manager, enters into a contract to purchase goods from a supplier for the LLC. Derek, a nonmanager member, enters into a contract to lease equipment on behalf of the LLC. The LLC is bound to the contract entered into by Alexis, a manager, but is not bound to the contract entered into by Derek, a nonmanager member.

An LLC is bound to contracts that members or managers have properly entered into on its behalf in the ordinary course of business [ULLCA Section 301].

> *It is the spirit and not the form of law that keeps justice alive.*
>
> Earl Warren
> *The Law and the Future (1955)*

CONCEPT SUMMARY

AGENCY AUTHORITY TO BIND AN LLC TO CONTRACTS

Type of LLC	Agency Authority
Member-managed LLC	All members have agency authority to bind the LLC to contracts.
Manager-managed LLC	The managers have authority to bind the LLC to contracts; the nonmanager members cannot bind the LLC to contracts.

Duty of Loyalty Owed to an LLC

A member of a member-managed LLC and a manager of a manager-managed LLC owe a *fiduciary* **duty of loyalty** to the LLC. This means that these parties must act honestly in their dealings with the LLC. The duty of loyalty includes the duty not to usurp the LLC's opportunities, make secret profits, secretly deal with the LLC, secretly compete with the LLC, or represent any interests adverse to those of the LLC [ULLCA Section 409(b)].

Example Ester, Yi, Maria, and Enrique form the member-managed LLC Big.Business.com, LLC, which conducts online auctions over the Internet. Ester secretly starts a competing business to conduct online auctions over the Internet. Ester is liable for breaching her duty of loyalty to the LLC with Yi, Maria, and Enrique. Ester is liable for any secret profits she made, and her business will be shut down.

Example In the preceding example, suppose that Ester, Yi, Maria, and Enrique designated their LLC as a manager-managed LLC and named Ester and Yi managers. In this case,

duty of loyalty
A duty owed by a member of a member-managed LLC and a manager of a manager-managed LLC to be honest in his or her dealings with the LLC and to not act adversely to the interests of the LLC.

only the managers owe a duty of loyalty to the LLC, but nonmanager members do not. Therefore, Ester and Yi, the named managers, could not compete with the LLC; Maria and Enrique, nonmanager members, could compete with the LLC without any legal liability.

Limited Duty of Care Owed to an LLC

duty of care
A duty owed by a member of a member-managed LLC and a manager of a manager-managed LLC not to engage in (1) a known violation of law, (2) intentional conduct, (3) reckless conduct, or (4) grossly negligent conduct that injures the LLC.

A member of a member-managed LLC and a manager of a manager-managed LLC owe a *fiduciary* **duty of care** to the LLC not to engage in (1) a known violation of law, (2) intentional conduct, (3) reckless conduct, or (4) grossly negligent conduct that injures the LLC. A member of a member-managed LLC or a manager of a manager-managed LLC is liable to the LLC for any damages the LLC incurs because of such conduct.

This duty is a *limited duty of care* because it does not include ordinary negligence. Thus, if a covered member or manager commits an *ordinarily negligent* act that is not grossly negligent, he or she is not liable to the LLC.

Example Charlene is a member of a member-managed LLC. While engaging in LLC business, Charlene is driving an automobile and accidentally hits Zubin, a pedestrian, and severely injures him. Under agency theory, Zubin sues the LLC and recovers $1 million in damages. If the court determines that Charlene was ordinarily negligent when she caused the accident—for example, she was driving the speed limit and did not see Zubin because the sun was in her eyes—she will not be liable to the LLC for any losses caused to the LLC by her ordinary negligence. If instead the court determines that Charlene was driving 65 mph in a 35 mph zone and thus was grossly negligent, Charlene is liable to the LLC for the $1 million it was ordered to pay Zubin.

No Fiduciary Duty Owed by a Nonmanager Member

Business will be either better or worse.

Calvin Coolidge

A member of a manager-managed LLC who is not a manager owes no fiduciary duty of loyalty or care to the LLC or its other members [ULLCA Section 409(h)(1)]. Basically, a nonmanager member of a manager-managed LLC is treated equally to a shareholder in a corporation.

Example Felicia is a member of a 30-person manager-managed LLC that is engaged in buying, developing, and selling real estate. Felicia is not a manager of the LLC but is just a member-owner. If a third party approaches Felicia with the opportunity to purchase a large and valuable piece of real estate that is ripe for development, and the price is below fair market value, Felicia owes no duty to offer the opportunity to the LLC. She may purchase the piece of real estate for herself without violating any duty to the LLC.

▶ DISSOLUTION OF AN LLC

Unless an LLC's operating agreement provides otherwise, a member has the *power* to withdraw from the LLC, whether it is an at-will LLC or a term LLC [ULLCA Section 602(a)]. The disassociation of a member from an at-will LLC is not wrongful unless the power to withdraw is eliminated in the operating agreement [ULLCA Section 602(b)]. The disassociation of a member from a term LLC before the expiration of the specified term is wrongful. A member who wrongfully disassociates him- or herself from an LLC is liable to the LLC and to the other members for any damages caused by his or her **wrongful disassociation** [ULLCA Section 602(c)].

wrongful disassociation
When a member withdraws from (1) a term LLC prior to the expiration of the term or (2) an at-will LLC when the operating agreement eliminates a member's power to withdraw.

A member's disassociation from an LLC terminates that member's right to participate in the management of the LLC, act as an agent of the LLC, or conduct the LLC's business [ULLCA Section 603(b)(3)]. Disassociation also terminates the disassociating member's duties of loyalty and care to the LLC [ULLCA Section 603(b)(3)].

Payment of Distributional Interest

If a member disassociates from an at-will LLC without causing a wrongful disassociation, the LLC must purchase the disassociated member's distributional interest [ULLCA

Section 701(a)(1)]. The price and terms of a distributional interest may be fixed in the operating agreement [ULLCA Section 701(c)]. If the price is not agreed upon in the operating agreement, the LLC must pay the fair market value of the distributional interest.

If a member disassociates him- or herself from a term LLC, the LLC must only purchase the disassociating member's distributional interest on the expiration of the specified term of the LLC [ULLCA Section 701(a)(2)]. Any damages caused by wrongful withdrawal must be offset against the purchase price [ULLCA Section 701(f)].

Notice of Disassociation

For two years after a member disassociates him- or herself from an LLC that continues in business, the disassociating member has apparent authority to bind the LLC to contracts in the ordinary course of business except to parties who either (1) know of the disassociation or (2) are given notice of disassociation [ULLCA Section 703].

An LLC can give *constructive notice* of a member's disassociation by filing a **statement of disassociation** with the secretary of state, stating the name of the LLC and the name of the member disassociated from the LLC [ULLCA Section 704]. This notice is effective against any person who later deals with the disassociated member, whether the person was aware of the notice or not.

> **statement of disassociation**
> A document filed with the secretary of state that gives constructive notice that a member has disassociated from an LLC.

Example William, Jesse, and Sandy are members of a member-managed LLC that operates an automobile dealership. Jesse disassociates from the LLC. The LLC fails to file a statement of disassociation with the secretary of state. Although Jesse has no express agency authority to bind the LLC to contracts because she is no longer a member of the LLC, Jesse has apparent authority to bind the LLC to contracts in the ordinary course of business for two years after the disassociation or until the LLC files a statement of disassociation with the secretary of state. This does not apply to parties who are aware of Jesse's disassociation with the LLC or those parties who are given notice of Jesse's disassociation with the LLC.

Continuation of an LLC

At the expiration of the term of a term LLC, some of its members may want to continue the LLC. At the expiration of its term, a term LLC can be continued in two situations. First, the members of the LLC may vote prior to the expiration date to continue the LLC for an additional specified term. This requires the unanimous vote of all the members and the filing of an amendment to the articles of organization with the secretary of state, stating this fact. Second, absent the unanimous vote to continue the term LLC, the LLC may be continued as an at-will LLC by a simple majority vote of the members of the LLC [ULLCA Section 411(b)].

Winding Up an LLC's Business

If an LLC is not continued, the LLC is wound up. The **winding up** of an LLC involves preserving and selling the assets of the LLC and distributing the money and property to creditors and members.

The assets of an LLC that is being dissolved must be applied to first pay off the creditors; thereafter, the surplus amount is distributed to the members in equal shares, unless the operating agreement provides otherwise [ULLCA Section 806]. It is good practice for members to specify in the operating agreement how distributions will be made to members. After dissolution and winding up, an LLC may terminate its existence by filing **articles of termination** with the secretary of state [ULLCA Section 805].

> **articles of termination**
> The documents that are filed with the secretary of state to terminate an LLC as of the date of filing or upon a later effective date specified in the articles.

▶ LIMITED LIABILITY PARTNERSHIP (LLP)

Many states have enacted legislation to permit the creation of **limited liability partnerships (LLPs)**. In an LLP, there does not have to be a general partner who is personally liable for the debts and obligations of the partnership. Instead, *all* partners are limited partners who

> **limited liability partnership (LLP)**
> A special form of partnership in which all partners are limited partners, and there are no general partners.

stand to lose only their capital contribution if the partnership fails. None of the partners is personally liable for the debts and obligations of the partnership beyond his or her capital contribution (see Exhibit 39.3).

▶ **Exhibit 39.3 LIMITED LIABILITY PARTNERSHIP (LLP)**

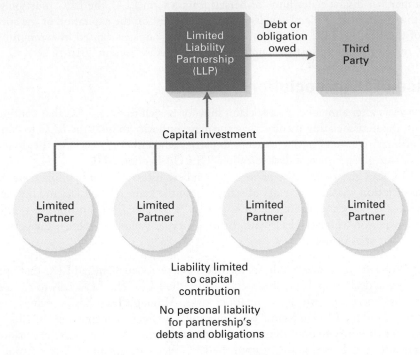

In most states, the law restricts the use of LLPs to certain types of professionals, such as accountants, lawyers, and doctors. Nonprofessionals cannot use the LLP form of partnership. LLPs enjoy the "flow-through" tax benefit of other types of partnerships—that is, there is no tax paid at the partnership level, and all profits and losses are reported on the individual partners' income tax returns.

Example Suppose Shou-Yi, Patricia, Ricardo, and Namira, all lawyers, form an LLP called Shou-Yi, Namira LLP to provide legal services. While providing legal services to the LLP's client Multi Motors, Inc., Patricia commits legal malpractice (negligence). This malpractice causes Multi Motors, Inc., a huge financial loss. In this case, Multi Motors, Inc., can sue and recover against Patricia, the negligent party, and against Shou-Yi, Namira LLP. Shou-Yi, Ricardo, and Namira can lose their capital contribution in Shou-Yi, Namira LLP but are not personally liable for the damages caused to Multi Motors, Inc. Patricia is personally liable to Multi Motors, Inc., because she was the negligent party.

Articles of Limited Liability Partnership

articles of partnership
The formal documents that must be filed at the secretary of state's office of the state of organization of an LLP to form the LLP.

An LLP is created formally by filing **articles of partnership** with the secretary of state of the state in which the LLP is organized. This is a public document. The LLP is a **domestic LLP** in the state in which it is organized. The LLP law of the state governs the operation of the LLP. An LLP may do business in other states, however. To do so, the LLP must register as a **foreign LLP** in any state in which it wants to conduct business.

LLP Liability Insurance

In most states, LLP law restricts the use of LLPs to certain types of professionals, such as accountants and lawyers. Many state laws require LLPs to carry a minimum of $1 million of liability insurance that covers negligence, wrongful acts, and misconduct by partners or employees of the LLP. This requirement guarantees that injured third parties will have compensation to recover for their injuries and is a quid pro quo for permitting partners to have limited liability.

CONTEMPORARY ENVIRONMENT

Accounting Firms Operate as LLPs

Prior to the advent of the limited liability partnership (LLP) form of doing business, accounting firms operated as general partnerships. As such, the general partners were personally liable for the debts and obligations of the general partnership. In large accounting firms, this personal liability was rarely imposed because the partnership usually carried sufficient liability insurance to cover most awards to third-party plaintiffs in lawsuits.

Under this system, when accounting firms were hit with large court judgments, the partners were personally liable. Many lawsuits were brought in conjunction with the failure of large commercial banks and other large firms that accountants had audited. Many of these firms failed because of fraud by their major owners and officers. The shareholders and creditors of these failed companies sued the auditors, alleging that the auditors had been negligent in not catching the fraud. Many juries agreed and awarded large awards against the accounting firms. Sometimes an accounting firm's liability insurance was not enough to cover a judgment, and personal liability was imposed on partners.

To address this issue, state legislatures created a new form of business, the LLP. This entity was particularly created for accountants, lawyers, and other professionals to offer their services under an umbrella of limited liability. The partners of an LLP have limited liability up to their capital contribution; the partners do not have personal liability for the debts and liabilities of the LLP, however.

Once LLPs were permitted by law, all of the "Big Four" accounting firms changed their status from general partnerships to LLPs. The signs and letterhead of each Big Four accounting firm prominently announce that the firm is an LLP. Many other accounting firms have also changed over to LLP status, as have many law firms.

TEST REVIEW TERMS AND CONCEPTS

Agreement of conversion
Articles of amendment
Articles of organization
Articles of partnership
Articles of termination
At-will LLC
Certificate of interest
Distributional interest
Domestic LLP
Duty of care

Duty of loyalty
Foreign LLP
Limited liability
Limited liability company (LLC)
Limited liability company codes
Limited liability partnership (LLP)
Manager-managed LLC

Member
Member-managed LLC
Operating agreement
Powers of an LLC
Revised Uniform Limited Liability Company Act (RULLCA)
Statement of disassociation
Taxation of LLCs
Term LLC

Tortfeasor
Uniform Limited Liability Company Act (ULLCA)
Winding up
Wrongful disassociation

CASE PROBLEMS

39.1 Liability of Members   Harold, Jasmine, Caesar, and Yuan form Microhard.com, LLC, a limited liability company, to sell computer hardware and software over the Internet. Microhard.com, LLC, hires Heather, a recent graduate of the University of Chicago and a brilliant software designer, as an employee. Heather's job is to design and develop software that will execute a computer command when the computer user thinks of the next command he or she wants to execute on the computer. Using Heather's research, Microhard.com, LLC, develops the Third Eye software program that does this. Microhard.com, LLC, sends Heather to the annual Comdex computer show in Las Vegas, Nevada, to unveil this revolutionary software. Heather goes to Las Vegas, and while there, she rents an automobile to get from the hotel to the computer show and to meet interested buyers at different locations in Las Vegas. While Heather is driving from her hotel to the site of the Comdex computer show, she negligently causes an accident in which she runs over Harold Singer, a pedestrian.

Singer, who suffers severe personal injuries, sues Microhard.com, LLC, Heather, Harold, Jasmine, Caesar, and Yuan to recover monetary damages for his injuries. Who is liable?

39.2 Liability of Members   Isabel, Koshi, and Winchester each contribute $50,000 capital to form a limited liability company called Fusion Restaurant, LLC, which operates an upscale restaurant that serves "fusion" cuisine, combining foods from cultures around the world. Fusion Restaurant, LLC, as a business, borrows $1 million from Melon Bank for operating capital. Isabel, Koshi, and Winchester are so busy cooking, serving, and running the restaurant that they forget to hold members' meetings, keep minute books, or otherwise observe any usual company formalities for the entire first year of business. After this one year of hard work, Fusion Restaurant, LLC, suffers financial difficulties and defaults on the $1 million bank loan from Melon Bank. Melon Bank sues Fusion Restaurant, LLC, Isabel, Koshi, and Winchester to recover the unpaid bank loan. Who is liable?

39.3 Personal Guarantee   Tran, Donald, and Elvira form a limited liability company called Real Estate Developers, LLC. Each of the three owners contributes $50,000 capital to the LLC, and the LLC then purchases a 400-acre parcel of vacant land 75 miles from Chicago, Illinois. Real Estate Developers, LLC, wants to build a tract of homes on the site. The owners of Real Estate Developers, LLC, go to City Bank and ask to borrow $100 million to complete the development and construction of the homes. City Bank agrees to make the loan, but only if Donald agrees to personally guarantee the LLC's loan and give security for the loan by pledging his 12-story penthouse in Manhattan, worth $100 million, as collateral for the loan. Donald agrees and signs the personal guarantee that pledges his penthouse as collateral for the loan; City Bank makes the $100 million loan to the LLC. Real Estate Developers, LLC, makes regular interest payments on the loan for one year and then defaults on the loan, with $100

million still owed to City Bank. At the time of default, Real Estate Developers, LLC's only asset is the 400-acre parcel of land that is still worth $150,000. City Bank sues Real Estate Developers, LLC, Tran, Donald, and Elvira to recover the amount of the unpaid loan. Who is liable to City Bank?

39.4 Member-Managed LLC   Jennifer, Martin, and Edsel form a limited liability company called Big Apple, LLC, to operate a bar in New York City. Jennifer, Martin, and Edsel are member-managers of the LLC. One of Jennifer's jobs as a member-manager is to drive the LLC's truck and pick up certain items of supply for the bar each Wednesday. On the way back to the bar one Wednesday after picking up the supplies for that week, Jennifer negligently runs over a pedestrian, Tilly Tourismo, on a street in Times Square. Tilly is severely injured and sues Big Apple, LLC, Jennifer, Martin, and Edsel to recover monetary damages for her injuries. Who is liable?

39.5 Contract Liability   Maria, Richard, and Dakota form a limited liability company called Ummmmm, LLC, to operate a spa in Santa Fe, New Mexico. Each member contributes $100,000 in capital to start the LLC. Ummmmm, LLC, is a member-managed LLC. Maria enters into a contract on behalf of the LLC in which she contracts to have a new hot tub installed at the spa by Hot Tubs, Inc., for $80,000. Hot Tubs, Inc., installs the hot tub and sends a bill for $80,000 to Ummmmm, LLC. When Ummmmm, LLC, fails to pay the bill, Hot Tubs, Inc., sues Ummmmm, LLC, to recover the unpaid $80,000. Is Ummmmm, LLC, liable?

39.6 Manager-Managed LLC   Juan, Min-Yi, and Chelsea form Unlimited, LLC, a limited liability company that operates a chain of women's retail clothing stores that sell eclectic women's clothing. The company is a manager-managed LLC, and Min-Yi has been designated in the articles of organization filed with the secretary of state as the manager of Unlimited, LLC. Min-Yi sees a store location on Rodeo Drive in Beverly Hills, California, that she thinks would be an excellent location for an Unlimited Store. Min-Yi enters into a five-year lease on behalf of Unlimited, LLC, with Landlord, Inc., the owner of the store building, to lease the store at $100,000 rent per year. While visiting Chicago, Chelsea sees a store location on North Michigan Avenue in Chicago that she thinks is a perfect location for an Unlimited store. Chelsea enters into a five-year lease on behalf of Unlimited, LLC, with Real Estate, Inc., the owner of the store building, to lease the store location at $100,000 rent per year. Is Unlimited, LLC, bound to either of these leases?

39.7 Division of Profits   Donna, Arnold, Jose, and Won-Suk form a limited liability company called Millennium Foods, LLC, to operate an organic foods grocery store in Portland, Oregon. Donna and Arnold each contribute $25,000 capital, Jose contributes $50,000, and Won-Suk contributes $100,000. The LLC's articles of organization are silent as to how profits and losses of the LLC are to be divided. The organic foods grocery store is an immediate success, and Millennium Foods, LLC, makes $200,000 profit the first year. Jose and Won-Suk want the profits distributed based on the amount of the members' capital contribution. Arnold and Donna think the profits should be distributed equally. Who is correct?

39.8 Distributional Interest   Daniel is one of five members of Blue Note, LLC, a limited liability company that operates a jazz club in New Orleans, Louisiana. The LLC's operating agreement provides that Daniel has the right to receive 20 percent of the LLC's profits. Daniel also owns another business as a sole proprietorship and has taken out a $100,000 loan from River Bank to operate this other business. Daniel defaults on his loan from River Bank, and River Bank sues Daniel and obtains a charging order against Daniel's ownership interest in Blue Note, LLC. What rights does River Bank have with regard to Blue Note, LLC, and Daniel's interest in Blue Note, LLC?

39.9 Duty of Loyalty   Ally is a member and a manager of a manager-managed limited liability company called Movers & You, LLC, a moving company. The main business of Movers & You, LLC, is moving large corporations from old office space to new office space in other buildings. After Ally has been a member-manager of Movers & You, LLC, for several years, she decides to join her friend Lana and form another LLC, called Lana & Me, LLC. This new LLC provides moving services that move large corporations from old office space to new office space. Ally becomes a member-manager of Lana & Me, LLC, while retaining her member-manager position at Movers & You, LLC. Ally does not disclose her new position at Lana & Me, LLC, to the other members or managers of Movers & You, LLC. Several years later, the other members of Movers & You, LLC, discover Ally's other ownership and management position at Lana & Me, LLC. Movers & You, LLC, sues Ally to recover damages for her working for Lana & Me, LLC. Is Ally liable?

39.10 Duty of Care   Jonathan is a member of a member-managed limited liability company called Custom Homes, LLC. Custom Homes, LLC, is hired by an owner of a piece of vacant land located on Hilton Head Island, South Carolina, to build a new custom home on the site. Custom Homes, LLC, begins work on the house. Jonathan is responsible for making sure that flashing warning lights are placed in front of the house while it is being constructed to mark open holes in the ground and other dangerous conditions. One night Jonathan leaves the site and forgets to place a flashing warning light marking a hole in front of the house that the LLC is building. That night, Candy, a neighbor who lives in one of the houses in the housing tract where the new house is being built, takes her dog for a walk. As Candy is walking by the unmarked area in front of the new house, she falls into the hole and is severely injured. Candy sues Custom Homes, LLC, to recover damages for her injuries. The jury finds that Jonathan was ordinarily negligent when he failed to place the flashing warning lights to mark the hole that Candy fell in and awards Candy $1 million for her injuries. Custom Homes, LLC, pays Candy the $1 million and then sues Jonathan to recover the $1 million. Is Jonathan liable?

BUSINESS ETHICS CASES

39.11 Business Ethics   Angela, Yoko, Cherise, and Serena want to start a new business that designs and manufactures toys for children. At a meeting in which the owners want to decide what type of legal form to use to operate the business, Cherise states:

> We should use a limited liability company to operate our business because this form of business provides us, the owners, with a limited liability shield, which means that if the business gets sued and loses, we the owners are not personally liable to the injured party except up to our capital contribution in the business.

The others agree and form a limited liability company called Fuzzy Toys, LLC, to conduct the member-managed business. Each of the four owners contributes $50,000 as her capital contribution to the LLC. Fuzzy Toys, LLC, purchases $800,000 of liability insurance from Allied Insurance Company and starts business. Fuzzy Toys, LLC, designs and produces "Heidi," a new toy doll and female action figure. The new toy doll is an instant success, and Fuzzy Toys, LLC, produces and sells millions of these female action figures. After a few months, however, the LLC starts getting complaints that one of the parts of the female action figure is breaking off quite regularly, and some children are swallowing the part. The concerned member-managers of Fuzzy Toys, LLC, issue an immediate recall of the female action figure, but before all of the dolls are returned for a refund, Catherine, a seven-year-old child, swallows the toy's part and is severely injured. Catherine, through her mother, sues Fuzzy Toys, LLC, Allied Insurance Company, Angela, Yoko, Cherise, and Serena to recover damages for product liability. At the time of suit, Fuzzy Toys, LLC, has $200,000 of assets. The jury awards Catherine $10 million for her injuries. Who is liable to Catherine and for how much? How much does Catherine recover? Did Angela, Yoko, Cherise, and Serena act ethically in setting up their toy business as an LLC? Explain.

39.12 Business Ethics   Christopher, Melony, Xie, and Ruth form iNet.com, LLC, a limited liability company. The four members are all Ph.D. scientists who have been working together in a backyard garage to develop a handheld wireless device that lets you receive and send e-mail, surf the Internet, use a word processing program that can print to any printer in the world, view cable television stations, and keep track of anyone you want anywhere in the world as well as zoom in on the person being tracked without that person knowing you are doing so. This new device, called Eros, costs only $29 but makes the owners $25 profit per unit sold. The owners agree that they will buy a manufacturing plant and start producing the unit in six months. Melony, who owns a one-quarter interest in iNet.com, LLC, decides she wants "more of the action" and soon, so she secretly sells the plans and drawings for the new Eros unit to a competitor for $100 million. The competitor comes out with exactly the same device, called Zeus, in one month and beats iNet.com, LLC, to market. The LLC, which later finds out about Melony's action, suffers damages of $100 million because of Melony's action. Is Melony liable to iNet.com, LLC? Explain. Did Melony act ethically in this case?

▲ **Seoul, South Korea** *This is a KFC restaurant in Seoul, South Korea. International franchising of American brands to foreign countries—and foreign countries' brands to the United States—exploded in the late twentieth century. Franchising on a global scale continues unabated in the twenty-first century.*

CHAPTER OBJECTIVES

After studying this chapter, you should be able to:

1. Define *franchise* and describe the various forms of franchises.
2. Describe the rights and duties of the parties to a franchise agreement.
3. Identify the contract tort liability of franchisors and franchisees.

4. Define *licensing* and describe how trademarks and intellectual property are licensed.
5. Describe how international franchising, joint ventures, and strategic alliances are used in global commerce.

CHAPTER CONTENTS

"It has been uniformly laid down in this Court, as far back as we can remember, that good faith is the basis of all mercantile transactions."

—Judge Buller
Salomons v. Nisson (1788)

▶ INTRODUCTION TO FRANCHISES AND SPECIAL FORMS OF BUSINESS

Franchising is an important method for distributing goods and services to the public. Originally pioneered by the automobile and soft drink industries, franchising today is used in many other forms of business. The 700,000-plus franchise outlets in the United States account for over 25 percent of retail sales and about 15 percent of the gross domestic product (GDP).

Special forms of business are used in domestic and international commerce. *Licensing* permits one business to use another business's trademarks, service marks, trade names, and other intellectual property in selling goods or services. *Joint ventures* allow two or more businesses to combine their resources to pursue a single project or transaction. *Strategic alliances* are often used to enter foreign markets.

This chapter discusses franchises, licensing, joint ventures, and strategic alliances used in domestic and international commerce.

▶ FRANCHISE

franchise
An arrangement that is established when one party (the *franchisor*) licenses another party (the *franchisee*) to use the franchisor's trade name, trademarks, commercial symbols, patents, copyrights, and other property in the distribution and selling of goods and services.

A **franchise** is established when one party (the **franchisor**, or **licensor**) licenses another party (the **franchisee**, or **licensee**) to use the franchisor's trade name, trademarks, commercial symbols, patents, copyrights, and other property in the distribution and selling of goods and services. Generally, the franchisor and the franchisee are established as separate corporations. The term *franchise* refers to both the agreement between the parties and the franchise outlet.

There are several advantages to franchising. For example, the franchisor can reach lucrative new markets, the franchisee has access to the franchisor's knowledge and resources while running an independent business, and consumers are assured of uniform product quality.

A typical franchise arrangement is illustrated in Exhibit 40.1.

▶ **Exhibit 40.1 FRANCHISE**

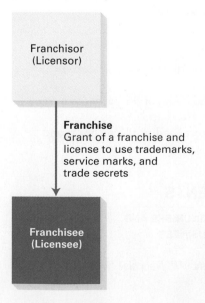

Franchisor
(Licensor)

Franchise
Grant of a franchise and license to use trademarks, service marks, and trade secrets

Franchisee
(Licensee)

Types of Franchises

There are four basic forms of franchises: (1) *distributorship franchise*, (2) *processing plant franchise*, (3) *chain-style franchise*, and (4) *area franchise*. They are discussed in the following paragraphs.

Distributorship Franchise   In a **distributorship franchise**, the franchisor manufactures a product and licenses a retail dealer to distribute a product to the public.

Example Ford Motor Company manufactures automobiles and franchises independently owned automobile dealers (franchisees) to sell them to the public.

Processing Plant Franchise   In a **processing plant franchise**, the franchisor provides a secret formula or the like to the franchisee. The franchisee then manufactures the product at its own location and distributes it to retail dealers.

Example The Coca-Cola Corporation, which owns the secret formulas for making Coca-Cola and other soft drinks, licenses regional bottling companies to manufacture and distribute soft drinks under the "Coca-Cola" name and other brand names.

Chain-Style Franchise   In a **chain-style franchise**, the franchisor licenses the franchisee to make and sell its products or services to the public from a retail outlet serving an exclusive geographical territory The product is made or the service provided by the franchise. Most fast-food franchises use this form.

Example The Pizza Hut Corporation franchises independently owned restaurant franchises to make and sell pizzas to the public under the "Pizza Hut" name.

Area Franchise   In an **area franchise**, the franchisor authorizes the franchisee to negotiate and sell franchises on behalf of the franchisor. The area franchisee is called a **subfranchisor** (see Exhibit 40.2). An area franchise is granted for a certain designated geographical area, such as a state, a region, or another agreed-upon area. Area franchises are often used when a franchisor wants to enter a market in another country.

Example If Starbucks wanted to enter the country of Vietnam to operate its coffee shops, it could grant an area franchise to a Vietnamese company, which would then choose the individual franchisees in that country.

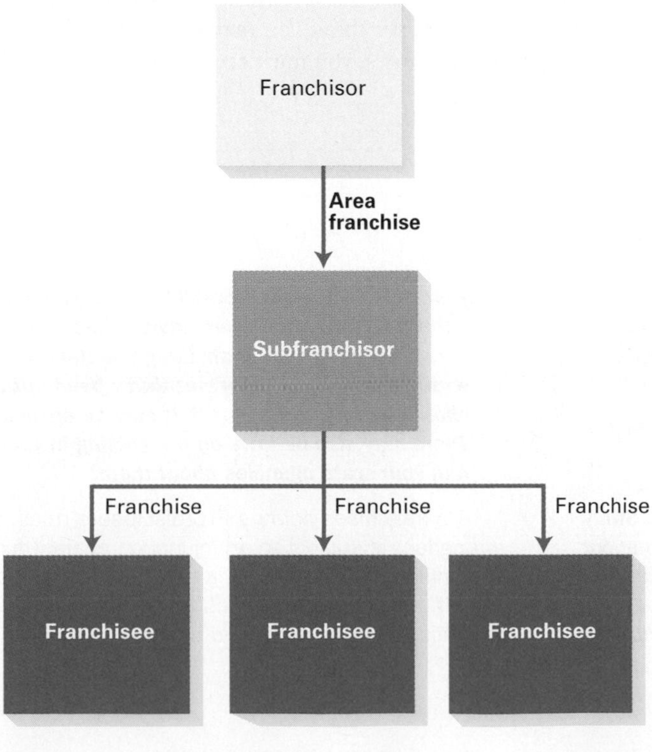

> *The jury, passing on the prisoner's life,*
> *May, in the sworn twelve, have a thief or two*
> *Guiltier than him they try.*
>
> William Shakespeare
> *Measure for Measure*

▶ **Exhibit 40.2 AREA FRANCHISE**

State Disclosure Laws

Uniform Franchise Offering Circular (UFOC)
A uniform disclosure document that requires a franchisor to make specific presale disclosures to prospective franchisees.

Most states have enacted franchise laws that require franchisors to register and deliver disclosure documents to prospective franchisees. State franchise administrators developed a uniform disclosure document called the **Uniform Franchise Offering Circular (UFOC)**.

The UFOC and state laws require a franchisor to make specific presale disclosures to prospective franchisees. Information that must be disclosed includes a description of the franchisor's business, balance sheets and income statements of the franchisor for the preceding three years, material terms of the franchise agreement, any restrictions on the franchisee's territory, reasons permitted for the termination of the franchise, and other relevant information.

FTC Franchise Rule

Federal Trade Commission (FTC)
A federal government agency that is empowered to enforce federal franchising rules.

FTC franchise rule
A rule set out by the FTC that requires franchisors to make full presale disclosures to prospective franchisees.

The **Federal Trade Commission (FTC)**, a federal administrative agency, has adopted the **FTC franchise rule**. The FTC rule requires franchisors to make full *presale* disclosures nationwide to prospective franchisees.[1] The FTC does not require the registration of the disclosure document with the FTC prior to its use. The UFOC satisfies both state regulations and the FTC. The FTC rule requires the disclosures discussed in the following paragraphs.

Disclosure of Sales or Earnings Projections Based on Actual Data   If a franchisor makes sales or earnings projections for a potential franchise location that are based on the actual sales, income, or profit figures of an existing franchise, the franchisor must disclose the following:

- The number and percentage of its actual franchises that have obtained such results.
- A cautionary statement in at least 12-point boldface type that reads, "Caution: Some outlets have sold (or earned) this amount. There is no assurance you'll do as well. If you rely upon our figures, you must accept the risk of not doing so well."

Disclosure of Sales or Earnings Projections Based on Hypothetical Data   If a franchisor makes sales or earnings projections based on hypothetical examples, the franchisor must disclose the following:

- The assumptions underlying the estimates.
- The number and percentage of actual franchises that have obtained such results.
- A cautionary statement in at least 12-point boldface print that reads, "Caution: These figures are only estimates of what we think you may earn. There is no assurance you'll do as well. If you rely upon our figures, you must accept the risk of not doing so well."

FTC notice
A statement required by the FTC to appear in at least 12-point boldface type on the cover of a franchisor's required disclosure statement to prospective franchisees.

CONTEMPORARY ENVIRONMENT

FTC Franchise Notice

The FTC requires that the following statement, called the **FTC notice,** appear in at least 12-point boldface type on the cover of a franchisor's required disclosure statement to prospective franchisees:

To protect you, we've required your franchisor to give you this information.

We haven't checked it, and don't know if it's correct. It should help you make up your mind. Study it carefully. While it includes some information about your contract, don't rely on it alone to understand your contract. Read all of your contract carefully. Buying a franchise is a complicated investment. Take

your time to decide. If possible, show your contract and this information to an adviser, like a lawyer or an accountant. If you find anything you think may be wrong or anything important that's been left out, you should let us know about it. It may be against the law. There may also be laws on franchising in your state. Ask your state agencies about them.

If a franchisor violates FTC disclosure rules, the wrongdoer is subject to an injunction against further franchise sales, civil fines, and an FTC civil action on behalf of injured franchisees to recover damages from the franchisor that were caused by the violation.

▶ FRANCHISE AGREEMENT

A prospective franchisee must apply to the franchisor for a franchise. The **franchise application** often includes detailed information about the applicant's previous employment, financial and educational history, credit status, and so on.

If an applicant is approved, the parties enter into a **franchise agreement** that sets forth the terms and conditions of the franchise. Although some states permit oral franchise agreements, most have enacted Statutes of Frauds that requires franchise agreements to be in writing. To prevent unjust enrichment, the courts occasionally enforce oral franchise agreements that violate the Statute of Frauds.

A franchise agreement often specifies the total investment that a franchisee must provide in order to be granted the franchise.

> **franchise agreement**
> An agreement that a franchisor and franchisee enter into that sets forth the terms and conditions of a franchise.

Topics Covered in a Franchise Agreement

Franchise agreements do not usually have much room for negotiation. Generally, the agreement is a standard form contract prepared by the franchisor. Franchise agreements cover the following topics:

- **Quality control standards.** The franchisor's most important assets are its name and reputation. The quality control standards set out in a franchise agreement—such as the franchisor's right to make periodic inspections of the franchisee's premises and operations—are intended to protect these assets. Failure to meet the proper standards can result in loss of the franchise.
- **Training requirements.** Franchisees and their personnel are usually required to attend training programs either on site or at the franchisor's training facilities.
- **Covenant not to compete.** Covenants not to compete prohibit franchisees from competing with the franchisor during a specific time and in a specified area after the termination of the franchise. Unreasonable (overextensive) covenants not to compete are void.
- **Arbitration clause.** Most franchise agreements contain an arbitration clause which provides that any claim or controversy arising from the franchise agreement or an alleged breach thereof is subject to arbitration. The U.S. Supreme Court has held such clauses to be enforceable.[2]
- **Other terms and conditions.** Capital requirements are included in a franchise agreement. Other terms and conditions may include restrictions on the use of the franchisor's trade name, trademarks, and logo; standards of operation; duration of the franchise; record-keeping requirements; sign requirements; hours of operation; prohibition as to the sale or assignment of the franchise; conditions for the termination of the franchise; and other specific terms pertinent to the operation of the franchise and the protection of the parties' rights.

Sample provisions of a franchise agreement are set forth in Exhibit 40.3.

> *The minute you read something that you can't understand, you can almost be sure that it was drawn up by a lawyer.*
>
> Will Rogers

Franchise Fees

Franchise fees payable by the franchisee are usually stipulated in the franchise agreement. The franchisor may require the franchisee to pay any or all of the following fees:

- **Initial license fee.** An **initial license fee** is a lump-sum payment for the privilege of being granted a franchise.
- **Royalty fees.** A **royalty fee** is a fee for the continued use of the franchisor's trade name, property, and assistance that is often computed as a percentage of the franchisee's gross sales. Royalty fees are usually paid on a monthly basis.
- **Assessment fee.** An **assessment fee** is a fee for such things as advertising and promotional campaigns and administrative costs, billed either as a flat monthly or annual fee or as a percentage of gross sales.
- **Lease fees.** **Lease fees** are payment for any land or equipment leased from the franchisor, billed either as a flat monthly or annual fee or as a percentage of gross sales or other agreed-upon amount.

> *Whatever the human law may be, neither an individual nor a nation can commit the least act of injustice against the obscurest individual without having to pay the penalty for it.*
>
> Henry David Thoreau

FRANCHISE AGREEMENT

Agreement, this 2nd day of January, 2010, between ALASKA PANCAKE HOUSE, INC., an Alaska corporation located in Anchorage, Alaska (hereinafter called the Company) and PANCAKE SYRUP COMPANY, INC., a Michigan corporation located in Detroit, Michigan (hereinafter called the Franchisee), for one KLONDIKE PANCAKE HOUSE restaurant to be located in the City of Mackinac Island, Michigan.

RECITALS

A.   The Company is the owner of proprietary and other rights and interests in various service marks, trademarks, and trade names used in its business including the trade name and service mark "KLONDIKE PANCAKE HOUSE."

B.   The Company operates and enfranchises others to operate restaurants under the trade name and service mark "KLONDIKE PANCAKE HOUSE" using certain recipes, formulas, food preparation procedures, business methods, business forms, and business policies it has developed. The Company has also developed a body of knowledge pertaining to the establishment and operation of restaurants. The Franchisee acknowledges that he does not presently know these recipes, formulas, food preparation procedures, business methods, or business policies, nor does the Franchisee have these business forms or access to the Company's body of knowledge.

C.   The Franchisee intends to enter the restaurant business and desires access to the Company's recipes, formulas, food preparation procedures, business methods, business forms, business policies, and body of knowledge pertaining to the operation of a restaurant. In addition, the Franchisee desires access to information pertaining to new developments and techniques in the Company's restaurant business.

D.   The Franchisee desires to participate in the use of the Company's rights in its service marks and trademarks in connection with the operation of one restaurant to be located at a site approved by the Company and the Franchisee.

E.   The Franchisee understands that information received from the Company or from any of its officers, employees, agents, or franchisees is confidential and has been developed with a great deal of effort and expense. The Franchisee acknowledges that the information is being made available to him so that he may more effectively establish and operate a restaurant.

F.   The Company has granted, and will continue to grant others, access to its recipes, formulas, food preparation procedures, business methods, business forms, business policies, and body of knowledge pertaining to the operation of restaurants and information pertaining to new developments and techniques in its business.

G.   The Company has and will continue to license others to use its service marks and trademarks in connection with the operation of restaurants at Company-approved locations.

H.   The Franchise Fee and Royalty constitute the sole consideration to the Company for the use by the Franchisee of its body of knowledge, systems, and trademark rights.

I.   The Franchisee acknowledges that he received the Company's franchise offering prospectus at or prior to the first personal meeting with a Company representative and at least ten (10) business days prior to the signing of this Agreement and that he has been given the opportunity to clarify provisions he did not understand and to consult with an attorney or other professional advisor. Franchisee represents he understands and agrees to be bound by the terms, conditions, and obligations of this Agreement.

J.   The Franchisee acknowledges that he understands that the success of the business to be operated by him under this Agreement depends primarily upon his efforts and that neither the Company nor any of its agents or representatives have made any oral, written, or visual representations or projections of actual or potential sales, earnings, or net or gross profits. Franchisee understands that the restaurant operated under this Agreement may lose money or fail.

AGREEMENT

Acknowledging the above recitals, the parties hereto agree as follows:

1.   Upon execution of this Agreement, the Franchisee shall pay to the Company a Franchise Fee of $30,000 that shall not be refunded in any event.

2.   The Franchisee shall also pay to the Company, weekly, a Royalty equal to eight (8%) percent of the gross sales from each restaurant that he operates throughout the term of this Agreement. "Gross sales" means all sales or revenues derived from the Franchisee's location exclusive of sales taxes.

3.   The Company hereby grants to the Franchisee:

a.   Access to the Company's recipes, formulas, food preparation procedures, business methods, business forms, business policies, and body of knowledge pertaining to the operation of a restaurant.

b.   Access to information pertaining to new developments and techniques in the Company's restaurant business.

c.   License to use of the Company's rights in and to its service marks and trademarks in connection with the operation of one restaurant to be located at a site approved by the Company and the Franchisee.

4.   The Company agrees to:

a.   Provide a training program for the operator of restaurants using the Company's recipes, formulas, food preparation procedures, business methods, business forms, and business policies. The Franchisee shall pay all transportation, lodging, and other expenses incurred in attending the program. The Franchisee must attend the training program before opening his restaurant.

b.   Provide a Company Representative that the Franchisee may call upon for consultation concerning the operation of his business.

c.   Provide the Franchise with a program of assistance that shall include periodic consultations with a Company Representative, publish a periodical advising of new developments and techniques in the Company's restaurant business, and grant access to Company personnel for consultations concerning the operation of his business.

5.   The Franchisee agrees to:

a.   Begin operation of a restaurant within 365 days. The restaurant will be at a location found by the Franchisee and approved by the Company. The Company or one of its designees will lease the premises and sublet them to the Franchisee at cost. The Franchisee will then construct and equip his unit in accordance with Company specifications contained in the Operating Manual. Upon written request from the Franchisee, the Company will grant a 180-day extension that is effective immediately upon receipt of the request. Under certain circumstances, and at the sole discretion of the Company, the Company may grant additional time in which to open the business. In all instances, the location of each unit must be approved by the Company and the Franchisee. If the restaurant is not operating within 365 days, or within any approved extensions, this Agreement will automatically expire.

b.   Operate his business in compliance with applicable laws and governmental regulations. The Franchisee will obtain at his expense, and keep in force, any permits, licenses, or other consents required for the leasing, construction, or operation of his business. In addition, the Franchisee shall operate his restaurant in accordance with the Company's Operation Manual, which may be amended from time to time as a result of experience, changes in the law, or changes in the marketplace. The Franchisee shall refrain from conducting any business or selling any products other than those approved by the Company at the approved location.

c.   Be responsible for all costs of operating his unit, including but not limited to, advertising, taxes, insurance, food products, labor, and utilities. Insurance shall include, but not be limited to, comprehensive liability insurance including products liability coverage in the minimum amount of $1,000,000. The Franchisee shall keep these policies in force for the mutual benefit of the parties. In addition, the Franchisee shall save the Company harm from any claim of any type that arises in connection with the operation of his business.

▶ **Exhibit 40.3 SAMPLE PROVISIONS OF A FRANCHISE AGREEMENT**

• **Cost of supplies.** Cost of supplies involves payment for supplies purchased from the franchisor.
• **Consulting fees and other expenses.** Many franchisors charge a monthly or annual fee for having experts from the franchisor help the franchisee to better conduct business.

Trademarks

A franchisor's ability to maintain the public's perception of the quality of the goods and services associated with its trade name, **trademarks**, and **service marks** is the essence of its success. The **Lanham Trademark Act**[3] provides for the registration of trademarks and service marks with the federal **Patent and Trademark Office** in Washington, DC, by franchisors and others. Most franchisors license the use of their trade names, trademarks, and service marks and prohibit their franchisees from misusing these marks. Anyone who uses a mark without authorization may be sued for *trademark infringement*. The trademark holder can sue to recover damages and obtain an injunction prohibiting further unauthorized use of the mark.

trademark or service mark
A distinctive mark, symbol, name, word, motto, or device that identifies the goods or services of a particular franchisor.

Trade Secrets

Franchisors are often owners of **trade secrets**, including product formulas, business plans and models, and other ideas. Franchisors license and disclose many of their trade secrets to franchisees. The misappropriation of a trade secret is called **unfair competition**. The holder of the trade secret can sue the offending party for damages and obtain an injunction to prohibit further unauthorized use of the trade secret.

trade secrets
Ideas that make a franchise successful but that do not qualify for trademark, patent, or copyright protection.

INTERNATIONAL LAW
International Franchising

The international market presently offers a great opportunity for U.S. franchisors to expand their businesses. Many U.S. franchisors view international expansion as their number-one priority. However, in addition to providing lucrative new markets, international franchising also poses difficulties and risks.

The expansion into other countries through franchising means that U.S. franchisors can expand internationally without expending the huge capital investments that would otherwise be required if the franchisors tried to penetrate those markets with company-owned stores or branches. In addition, a foreign franchisee will have knowledge about the cultural and business traditions of the foreign country that the franchisor does not have. Consequently, the franchisee will be better able to serve the consumers and customers in the particular market.

Foreign franchising is not without difficulties, however. For example, the host country's laws may differ from U.S. laws. Foreign cultures may also require different advertising, marketing, and promotional approaches. In addition, the franchisor may be subjecting itself to government regulation in the host country. Finally, different dispute settlement procedures may be in place that will have to be used if there is a dispute between the U.S. franchisor and the foreign franchisee.

U.S. franchisors are expanding to Latin America, Asia, western and eastern Europe, and other areas of the world.

Flag of Brazil *Foreign franchisors view the United States and other parts of the world as a potential market. This will provide an opportunity for U.S. entrepreneurs to become franchisees for foreign franchisors.*

▶ LIABILITY OF FRANCHISOR AND FRANCHISEE

If a franchise is properly organized and operated, the franchisor and franchisee are separate legal entities. Therefore, the franchisor deals with the franchisee as an *independent contractor*. Franchisees are liable on their own contracts and are liable for their own torts (e.g., negligence). Franchisors are liable for their own contracts and torts. Generally, neither party is liable for the contracts or torts of the other.

Example Suppose that McDonald's Corporation, a fast-food restaurant franchisor, grants a restaurant franchise to Tina Corporation. Tina Corporation opens the franchise restaurant. One day, a customer at the franchise spills a chocolate shake on the floor. The employees at the franchise fail to clean up the spilled shake, and one hour later, another customer slips on the spilled shake and suffers severe injuries. The injured customer can recover damages from the franchisee, Tina Corporation, because it was negligent. It cannot recover damages from the franchisor, McDonald's Corporation.

Example Suppose that in the preceding example, McDonald's Corporation, the franchisor, grants a franchise to Gion Corporation, the franchisee. McDonald's Corporation enters into a loan agreement with City Bank, whereby it borrows $100 million. Gion Corporation, the franchisee, is not liable on the loan. McDonald's Corporation, the franchisor and debtor, is liable on the loan.

In the case that follows, the court imposed liability on a franchisor for its own negligent conduct.

CASE 40.1 Franchisor Liability

Martin v. McDonald's Corporation

572 N.E.2d 1073, Web 1991 Ill.App. Lexis 715 (1991)
Court of Appeals of Illinois

"**The trial court correctly determined that McDonald's Corporation had a duty to protect plaintiffs Laura Martin, Maureen Kincaid, and Therese Dudek from harm.**"

—Judge McNulty

Facts

McDonald's Corporation (McDonald's) is a franchisor that licenses franchisees to operate fast-food restaurants and to use McDonald's trademarks and service marks. One such franchise, which was located in Oak Forest, Illinois, was owned and operated by McDonald's Restaurants of Illinois, the franchisee.

Recognizing the threat of armed robbery at its franchises, especially in the time period immediately after closing, McDonald's established a corporate division to deal with security problems at franchises. McDonald's prepared a manual for restaurant security operations and required its franchisees to adhere to these procedures.

Jim Carlson was the McDonald's regional security manager for the area in which the Oak Forest franchise was located. Carlson visited the Oak Forest franchise on October 31, to inform the manager of security procedures. He specifically mentioned these rules: (1) No one should

throw garbage out the backdoor after dark, and (2) trash and grease were to be taken out the side glass door at least one hour prior to closing. During his inspection, Carlson noted that the locks had to be changed at the restaurant and an alarm system needed to be installed for the backdoor. Carlson never followed up to determine whether these security measures had been taken.

On the evening of November 29, a six-woman crew, all teenagers, was working to clean up and close the Oak Forest restaurant. Laura Martin, Therese Dudek, and Maureen Kincaid were members of that crew. A person later identified as Peter Logan appeared at the back of the restaurant with a gun. He ordered the crew to open the safe and get him the money and then ordered them into the refrigerator. In the course of moving the crew into the refrigerator, Logan shot and killed Martin and assaulted Dudek and Kincaid. Dudek and Kincaid suffered severe emotional distress from the assault.

Evidence showed that Logan had entered the restaurant through the backdoor. Trial testimony proved that the work crew used the backdoor exclusively, both before and after dark, and emptied garbage and grease through the backdoor all day and all night. In addition, there was evidence that the latch on the backdoor did not work properly.

(case continues)

Evidence also showed that the crew had not been instructed about the use of the backdoor after dark, the crew had never received copies of the McDonald's security manual, and the required warning about not using the backdoor after dark had not been posted at the restaurant.

Martin's parents, Dudek, and Kincaid sued McDonald's to recover damages for negligence. The trial court awarded damages of $1,003,445 to the Martins for the wrongful death of their daughter and awarded $125,000 each to Dudek and Kincaid. McDonald's appealed.

Issue

Is McDonald's liable for negligence?

Language of the Court

The trial court correctly determined that McDonald's Corporation had a duty to protect plaintiffs Laura Martin, Maureen Kincaid, and Therese Dudek from harm. Although it did not specifically state that such duty was "assumed," there is ample support in case law and the facts of this case to support a determination that McDonald's Corporation voluntarily assumed a duty to provide security to plaintiffs and protect them from harm.

Once McDonald's Corporation assumed the duty to provide security and protection to plaintiffs, it had the obligation to perform this duty with due care and competence, and any failure to do so would lead to a finding of breach of duty. Accordingly, there was ample evidence for the jury to determine that McDonald's had breached its assumed duty to plaintiffs.

Decision

The appellate court held that McDonald's was negligent for not following up and making sure that the security deficiencies it had found at the Oak Forest franchise had been corrected. The appellate court affirmed the judgment of the trial court, holding McDonald's liable.

Case Questions

Critical Legal Thinking Should businesses be held liable for criminal actions of others? Why or why not?

Business Ethics Should McDonald's have denied liability in this case?

Contemporary Business What is the benefit to a franchisor of establishing and requiring its franchisees to adhere to security rules? Is there any potential detriment? Explain.

Apparent Agency

If a franchisee is the *actual* or *apparent agent* of the franchisor, the franchisor is responsible for the torts and contracts the franchisee committed or entered into within the scope of the agency. Actual agency is created when a franchisor expressly or implicitly makes a franchisee its agent. The franchisor is liable for the contracts entered into and torts committed by the franchisee while the franchisee is acting within the scope of the agency. Franchisors very seldom appoint franchisees as their agents.

Apparent agency is created when a franchisor leads a third person into believing that the franchisee is its agent. For example, a franchisor and franchisee who use the same trade name and trademarks and make no effort to inform the public of their separate legal status may find themselves in such a situation. However, mere use of the same name does not automatically make a franchisor liable for the franchisee's actions. The court's decision of whether an apparent agency has been created depends on the facts and circumstances of the case.

apparent agency
Agency that arises when a franchisor creates the appearance that a franchisee is its agent when in fact an actual agency does not exist.

CONTEMPORARY ENVIRONMENT

Franchisor and Apparent Agency

"Clearly, on the question of reliance, the jury had a right to conclude that appellees believed exactly what Holiday Inns, Inc. wanted them to believe—that the Fort Pierce Holiday Inn and its Rodeo Bar were part of Holiday Inn's system."
—Judge Hersey

Holiday Inns, Inc. (Holiday Inns), is a franchisor that licenses franchisees to operate hotels using its trademarks and service marks. Holiday Inns licensed Hospitality Venture to operate a franchised hotel in Fort Pierce, Florida. The Rodeo Bar, which had a reputation as the "hottest bar in town," was located in the hotel.

The Fort Pierce Holiday Inn and Rodeo Bar did not have sufficient parking, so security guards posted in the Holiday Inn parking lot required Rodeo Bar patrons to park in vacant lots that surrounded the hotel but that were not owned by the hotel. Two unarmed security guards were on duty on the night in question. One guard was drinking on the job, and the other was an untrained temporary fill-in.

The record disclosed that although the Rodeo Bar had a capacity of 240 people, the bar regularly admitted 270 to 300 people, with 50 to 75 people waiting outside. Fights occurred all the time in the bar and the parking lots, and often there were three or four fights a night. Police reports involving 58 offenses, including several weapons charges and battery and assault charges, had been filed during the previous 18 months.

On the night in question, the two groups involved in the altercation did not leave the Rodeo Bar until closing time. These individuals exchanged remarks as they moved toward their respective vehicles in the vacant parking lots adjacent to the Holiday Inn. Ultimately, a fight erupted. The evidence shows that during the course of physical combat, Mr. Carter shot David Rice, Scott Turner, and Robert Shelburne. Rice died from his injuries.

Rice's heirs, Turner, and Shelburne sued the franchisee, Hospitality Venture, and the franchisor, Holiday Inns, for damages. Were the franchisee and the franchisor liable? The trial court found Hospitality Venture

negligent for not providing sufficient security to prevent the foreseeable incident that took the life of Rice and injured Turner and Shelburne. The court also found that Hospitality Venture was the apparent agent of Holiday Inns and therefore Holiday Inns was vicariously liable for its franchisee's tortious conduct. The court of appeal affirmed the judgment. With regard to the liability of Holiday Inns under the doctrine of apparent authority, the court stated:

Clearly, this evidence shows that Holiday Inns, Inc. represented to the public that this particular hotel was a part of the national chain of Holiday Inns and that it could find a certain level of service and safety at its hotel and bar. Clearly, on the question of reliance, the jury had a right to conclude that appellees believed exactly what Holiday Inns, Inc. wanted them to believe—that the Fort Pierce Holiday Inn and its Rodeo Bar were part of Holiday Inn's system.

The court of appeal held that Hospitality Venture, the franchisee, was negligent and that the franchisee was the apparent agent of Holiday Inns. The court of appeal affirmed the judgment of the trial court that awarded Turner $3,825,000 for his injuries, Shelburne $1 million for his injuries, and Rice's interests $1 million. *Holiday Inns, Inc. v. Shelburne*, 576 So.2d 322, **Web** 1991 Fla.App. Lexis 585 (District Court of Appeal of Florida)

▶ TERMINATION OF A FRANCHISE

Most franchise agreements permit a franchisor to terminate the franchise **for cause**. For example, the continued failure of a franchisee to pay franchise fees or meet legitimate quality control standards would be deemed just cause. Unreasonably strict application of a just cause termination clause constitutes **wrongful termination**. A single failure to meet a quality control standard, for example, is not cause for termination.

wrongful termination
Termination of a franchise without just cause.

Termination-at-will clauses in franchise agreements are generally held to be void on the grounds that they are unconscionable. The rationale for this position is that the franchisee has spent time, money, and effort developing the franchise. If a franchise is terminated without just cause, the franchisee can sue the franchisor for wrongful termination. The franchisee can recover damages caused by the unlawful termination and recover the franchise.

Breach of the Franchise Agreement

A lawful franchise agreement is an enforceable contract. Each party owes a duty to adhere to and perform under the terms of the franchise agreement. If the agreement is **breached**, the aggrieved party can sue the breaching party for rescission of the agreement, restitution, and damages.

In the following case, the court held that a franchisor had properly terminated a franchisee.

CASE 40.2 Termination of a Franchise

Dunkin' Donuts of America, Inc. v. Middletown Donut Corporation

495 A.2d 66, Web 1985 N.J. Lexis 2369
Supreme Court of New Jersey

"A franchisee who gets caught with his hand in the proverbial cookie jar (or doughnut box, as the case may be) must suffer the known consequences."

—Judge Clifford

Facts

Dunkin' Donuts of America, Inc. (Dunkin' Donuts), is a franchisor that licenses franchised donuts shops throughout the United States. Gerald Smothergill, through two corporations, entered into franchise and lease agreements with Dunkin' Donuts to operate Dunkin' Donuts franchise shops in Middletown and West Long Branch, New Jersey. Smothergill paid $115,000 for the two franchises. Under each franchise agreement, Smothergill was required to keep accurate sales records, pay a basic franchise fee of 4.9 percent of gross sales, and pay an advertising fee of 2 percent of gross sales. The lease agreements were conditioned on Smothergill's remaining a franchisee in good standing under the franchise agreements.

Subsequently, Dunkin' Donuts notified Smothergill that his franchise agreements were being terminated due to his intentional underreporting of gross sales. The termination notice provided an opportunity for Smothergill to cure the breach by making prompt payment of the amounts due. Smothergill made no attempt to cure and refused to abandon his Dunkin' Donuts shops. Dunkin' Donuts sued to enforce its claimed right of termination and to collect damages. The trial court permitted Dunkin' Donuts to terminate the franchise agreements. Smothergill appealed.

Issue

Did Dunkin' Donuts properly terminate the franchise agreements for cause?

Language of the Court

At the conclusion of the trial, the trial court found as fact that Smothergill had been guilty of substantial, intentional, and long-continued underreporting of gross sales at both of his Dunkin' Donuts stores. The court determined that Smothergill had failed to keep the financial records that were required under the franchise agreements and that the failure to keep records was not the result of carelessness or incompetence. Rather, Smothergill's delinquency in recordkeeping was part of a deliberate effort to underreport sales, which in turn would result in the underpayment of franchise fees, underpayment of advertising fund fees, underpayment of rental override charges, and evasion of federal and state taxes. In short, the trial court found as a fact that Smothergill was "guilty of unconscionable cheating."

Dunkin' Donuts, as franchisor of a sizeable network of New Jersey franchises, has a real and legitimate interest in maintaining the integrity of its system. Other Dunkin' Donuts franchisees also have an interest in promoting honest reporting because a percentage of their reported gross sales are pooled in a common advertising fund that benefits all. To the extent that a franchisee such as Smothergill underreports gross sales, he cheats not only the franchisor but all other franchisees as well. Upon signing the Dunkin' Donuts franchise agreement, both franchisor and franchisee were aware of the rules of the game. Those rules seem fair. A franchisee who gets caught with his hand in the proverbial cookie jar (or doughnut box, as the case may be) must suffer the known consequences.

Decision

The supreme court of New Jersey held that Smothergill had intentionally breached the franchise agreements and that Dunkin' Donuts had properly terminated Smothergill as a franchisee. The supreme court affirmed the trial court's decision, allowing Dunkin' Donuts to terminate the franchise agreements.

Case Questions

Critical Legal Thinking Should franchisors be permitted to terminate franchises at will? Or is the rule that permits franchisors to terminate franchises for cause a better rule? Explain.

Business Ethics Did Smothergill act ethically in this case?

Contemporary Business Do you think many franchisees "cheat" when franchise royalty fees are based on gross sales?

▶ LICENSING

licensing
A business arrangement that occurs when the owner of intellectual property (the *licensor*) contracts to permit another party (the *licensee*) to use the intellectual property.

Licensing is an important business arrangement in both domestic and international markets. **Licensing** occurs when one business or party that owns trademarks, service marks, trade names, and other intellectual property (the **licensor**) contracts to permit another business or party (the **licensee**) to use its trademarks, service marks, trade names, and other intellectual property in the distribution of goods, services, software, and digital information. A licensing arrangement is illustrated in Exhibit 40.4.

▶ **Exhibit 40.4 LICENSING**

Example The Walt Disney Company owns the merchandising rights to "Winnie the Pooh" stories and all the characters associated with the Winnie the Pooh stories. The Walt Disney Company enters into an agreement whereby it permits the Beijing Merchandising Company, a business formed under Chinese law, to manufacture and distribute a line of clothing, children's toys, and other items bearing the likeness of the Winnie the Pooh characters. This is a **license**. The Walt Disney Company is the licensor, and the Beijing Merchandising Company is the licensee.

▶ JOINT VENTURE

joint venture
An arrangement in which two or more business entities combine their resources to pursue a single project or transaction.

A **joint venture** is an arrangement in which two or more business entities combine their resources to pursue a single project or transaction. The parties to a joint venture are called **joint venturers**. Joint ventures resemble partnerships, except that partnerships are usually formed to pursue ongoing business operations rather than to focus on a single project or transaction. Unless otherwise agreed, joint venturers have equal rights to manage a joint venture. Joint venturers owe each other the fiduciary duties of loyalty and care. If a joint venturer violates these duties, it is liable for the damages the breach causes.

Joint Venture Partnership

joint venture partnership
A partnership owned by two or more joint venturers that is formed to operate a joint venture.

If a joint venture is operated as a partnership, then each joint venturer is considered a partner of the joint venture. This is called a **joint venture partnership** (see Exhibit 40.5). In a joint venture partnership, each joint venturer is liable for the debts and obligations of the joint venture partnership.

Example A new oil field is discovered in northern Canada. Two large oil companies, ChevronTexaco Corporation and ConocoPhillips Corporation, would each like to drill for oil there, but neither one has sufficient resources to do so alone. They join together to form a joint venture partnership, and each contributes $100 million capital to the joint venture. If the joint venture fails and the joint venture owes $1 billion to its creditors, which it cannot

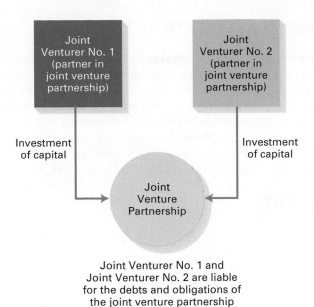

pay, ChevronTexaco and ConocoPhillips are each responsible for the joint venture's unpaid debts and obligations. This is because they are partners in the joint venture.

Joint Venture Corporation

In pursuing a joint venture, joint venturers often form a corporation to operate the joint venture. This is called a **joint venture corporation** (see Exhibit 40.6). The joint venturers are shareholders of the joint venture corporation. The joint venture corporation is liable for its debts and obligations. The joint venturers are liable for the debts and obligations of the joint venture corporation only up to their capital contributions to the joint venture corporation.

joint venture corporation
A corporation owned by two or more joint venturers that is created to operate a joint venture.

Example Suppose that in the preceding example, ChevronTexaco Corporation and ConocoPhillips Corporation form a third corporation, called Canadian Imperial Corporation, to operate the joint venture. ChevronTexaco and ConocoPhillips each contribute $100 million capital to Canadian Imperial Corporation, and each becomes a shareholder of Canadian Imperial Corporation. If the joint venture fails and Canadian Imperial Corporation owes $1 billion to its creditors, which it cannot pay, ChevronTexaco and ConocoPhillips each loses its $100 million capital contribution but is not liable for any further unpaid debts or obligations of Canadian Imperial Corporation.

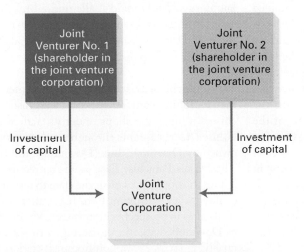

▶ STRATEGIC ALLIANCE

A **strategic alliance** is an arrangement between two or more companies in the same industry in which they agree to ally themselves to accomplish a designated objective. A strategic alliance allows the companies to reduce risks, share costs, combine technologies, and extend their markets. For example, companies often enter into strategic alliances when they decide to expand internationally into foreign countries.

Strategic alliances do not have the same protection as mergers, joint ventures, or franchising, and sometimes they are dismantled. Consideration must always be given to the fact that a strategic alliance partner is also a potential competitor.

TEST REVIEW TERMS AND CONCEPTS

Apparent agency
Area franchise
Assessment fee
Breach of a franchise
    agreement
Chain-style franchise
Cost of supplies
Distributorship franchise
Federal Trade Commission
    (FTC)
For cause termination of a
    franchise

Franchise
Franchise agreement
Franchise application
Franchisee (licensee)
Franchisor (licensor)
FTC franchise rule
FTC notice
Initial license fee
Joint venture
Joint venture corporation
Joint venture partnership
Joint venturer

Lanham Trademark Act
Lease fees
License
Licensee
Licensor
Licensing
Patent and Trademark
    Office
Processing plant franchise
Royalty fee
Service mark
Strategic alliance

Subfranchisor
Termination-at-will clause
Trademark
Trade secret
Unfair competition
Uniform Franchise Offering
    Circular (UFOC)
Wrongful termination

CASE PROBLEMS

40.1 Franchise Agreement   H&R Block, Inc. (Block), is a franchisor that licenses franchisees to provide tax preparation services to customers under the "H&R Block" service mark. June McCart was granted a Block franchise at 900 Main Street, Rochester, New York. For seven years, her husband, Robert, was involved in the operation of a Block franchise in Rensselaer, New York. After that, he assisted June in the operation of her Block franchise. All the McCarts' income during the time in question came from the Block franchises.

The Block franchise agreement that June signed contained a provision whereby she agreed not to compete (1) in the business of tax preparation (2) within 250 miles of the franchise (3) for a period of two years after the termination of the franchise. Robert did not sign the Rochester franchise agreement. Two years later, June wrote a letter to Block, giving notice that she was terminating the franchise. Shortly thereafter, the McCarts sent a letter to people who had been clients of the Rochester Block office, informing them that June was leaving Block and that Robert was opening a tax preparation service in which June would assist him. Block granted a new franchise in Rochester to another franchisee. It sued the McCarts to enforce the covenant not to compete against them. Who wins? *McCart v. H&R Block, Inc.*, 470 N.E.2d 756, **Web** 1984 Ind. App. Lexis 3039 (Court of Appeals of Indiana)

40.2 Franchise Agreement   Libby-Broadway Drive-In, Inc. (Libby), is a corporation licensed to operate a McDonald's

fast-food franchise restaurant by the McDonald's System, Inc. (McDonald's). Libby was granted a license to operate a McDonald's in Cleveland, Ohio, and was granted an exclusive territory in which McDonald's could not grant another franchise. The area was described as "bound on the north by the south side of Miles Avenue, on the west and south side by Turney Road, on the east by Warrensville Center Road." McDonald's granted a franchise to another franchisee to operate a McDonald's restaurant on the west side of Turney Road. Libby sued McDonald's, alleging a breach of the franchise agreement. Is McDonald's liable? *Libby-Broadway Drive-In, Inc. v. McDonald's System, Inc.*, 72 Ill.App.3d 806, 391 N.E.2d 1, **Web** 1979 Ill.App. Lexis 2698 (Appellate Court of Illinois)

40.3 Franchisor Disclosure   My Pie International, Inc. (My Pie), an Illinois corporation, was a franchisor that licensed franchisees to open pie shops under its trademark name. My Pie licensed 13 restaurants throughout the country, including one owned by Dowmont, Inc. (Dowmont), in Glen Ellyn, Illinois. The Illinois Franchise Disclosure Act requires a franchisor that desires to issue franchises in the state to register with the state or qualify for an exemption from registration and to make certain disclosures to prospective franchisees. My Pie granted the license to Dowmont without registering with the state of Illinois or qualifying for an exemption from registration and without making the required disclosures to Dowmont. Dowmont operated its restaurant as a "My Pie" franchise for four years, and after that, it operated it under the name "Arnold's." Dowmont paid franchise royalty fees for the four years. My Pie sued Dowmont for breach of the franchise agreement to recover royalties it claimed were due from Dowmont. Dowmont filed a counterclaim, seeking to rescind the franchise agreement and recover the royalties it paid to My Pie. Who wins? *My Pie International, Inc. v. Dowmont, Inc.*, 687 F.2d 919, **Web** 1982 U.S. App. Lexis 16537 (United States Court of Appeals for the Seventh Circuit)

40.4 Tort Liability Georgia Girl Fashions, Inc. (Georgia Girl), was a franchisor that licensed franchisees to operate women's retail clothing stores under the "Georgia Girl" trademark. Georgia Girl granted a franchise to a franchisee to operate a store on South Cobb Drive in Smyrna, Georgia. Georgia Girl did not supervise or control the day-to-day operations of the franchisee. Melanie McMullan entered the store to exchange a blouse that she had previously purchased at the store. When she found nothing that she wished to exchange the blouse for, she began to leave the store. At that time, she was physically restrained and accused of shoplifting the blouse. McMullan was taken to the local jail, where she was held until her claim of prior purchase could be verified. The store then dropped the charges against her, and she was released from jail. McMullan filed an action against the store owner and Georgia Girl to recover damages for false imprisonment. Is Georgia Girl liable? *McMullan v. Georgia Girl Fashions, Inc.*, 180 Ga.App. 228, 348 S.E.2d 748, **Web** 1986 Ga.App. Lexis 2093 (Court of Appeals of Georgia)

40.5 Tort Liability The Seven-Up Company (Seven-Up) is a franchisor that licenses local bottling companies to manufacture, bottle, and distribute soft drinks using the "7-Up" trademark. The Brooks Bottling Company (Brooks) was a Seven-Up franchisee that bottles and sells 7-Up soft drinks to stores in Michigan. Under the franchise agreement, the franchisee was required to purchase the 7-Up syrup from Seven-Up, but it could purchase its bottles, cartons, and other supplies from independent suppliers if Seven-Up approved the design of these articles.

Brooks used cartons designed and manufactured by Olinkraft, Inc., using a design that Seven-Up had approved. Sharon Proos Kosters, a customer at a Meijer Thrifty Acres Store in Holland, Michigan, removed a cardboard carton containing six glass bottles of 7-Up from a grocery store shelf, put it under her arm, and walked toward the checkout counter. As she did so, a bottle slipped out of the carton, fell on the floor, and exploded, causing a piece of glass to strike Kosters in her eye as she looked down; she was blinded in that eye. Evidence showed that the 7-Up carton was designed to be held from the top and was made without a strip on the side of the carton that would prevent a bottle from slipping out if held underneath. Kosters sued Seven-Up to recover damages for her injuries. Is Seven-Up liable? *Kosters v. Seven-Up Company*, 595 F.2d 347, **Web** 1979 U.S. App. Lexis 15945 (United States Court of Appeals for the Sixth Circuit)

40.6 Trademark The Kentucky Fried Chicken Corporation (KFC) is the franchisor of Kentucky Fried Chicken restaurants.

Franchisees must purchase equipment and supplies from manufacturers approved in writing by KFC. Equipment includes cookers, fryers, ovens, and the like; supplies include carry-out boxes, napkins, towelettes, and plastic eating utensils known as "sporks." These products are not trade secrets. KFC may not "unreasonably withhold" approval of any suppliers who apply and whose goods are tested and found to meet KFC's quality control standards. The 10 manufacturers who went through KFC's approval process were approved. KFC also sells supplies to franchisees in competition with these independent suppliers. All supplies, whether produced by KFC or the independent suppliers, must contain "Kentucky Fried Chicken" trademarks.

Upon formation, Diversified Container Corporation (Diversified) began manufacturing and selling supplies to KFC franchisees without applying for or receiving KFC's approval. All the items sold by Diversified contained KFC trademarks. Diversified represented to franchisees that its products met "all standards" of KFC and that it sold "approved supplies." Diversified even affixed KFC trademarks to the shipping boxes in which it delivered supplies to franchisees. Evidence showed that Diversified products did not meet the quality control standards set by KFC. KFC sued Diversified for trademark infringement. Who wins? *Kentucky Fried Chicken Corporation v. Diversified Container Corporation*, 549 F.2d 368, **Web** 1977 U.S. App. Lexis 14128 (United States Court of Appeals for the Fifth Circuit)

40.7 Trademark Ramada Inns, Inc. (Ramada Inns), is a franchisor that licenses franchisees to operate motor hotels using the "Ramada Inns" trademarks and service marks. In August, the Gadsden Motel Company (Gadsden), a partnership, purchased a motel in Attalla, Alabama, and entered into a franchise agreement with Ramada Inns to operate it as a Ramada Inns motor hotel. Five years later, the motel began receiving poor ratings from Ramada Inns inspectors, and Gadsden fell behind on its monthly franchise fee payments. Despite prodding from Ramada Inns, the motel never met the Ramada Inns operational standards again. One year later, Ramada Inns properly terminated the franchise agreement, citing quality deficiencies and Gadsden's failure to pay past-due franchise fees. The termination notice directed Gadsden to remove any materials or signs identifying the motel as a Ramada. Gadsden continued using Ramada Inns signage, trademarks, and service marks inside and outside the motel. In September, Ramada Inns sued Gadsden for trademark infringement. Who wins? *Ramada Inns, Inc. v. Gadsden Motel Company*, 804 F.2d 1562, **Web** 1986 U.S. App. Lexis 34279 (United States Court of Appeals for the Eleventh Circuit)

40.8 Termination of a Franchise Kawasaki Motors Corporation (Kawasaki), a Japanese corporation, manufactures motorcycles that it distributes in the United States through its subsidiary, Kawasaki Motors Corporation, U.S.A. (Kawasaki USA). Kawasaki USA is a franchisor that grants franchises to dealerships to sell Kawasaki motorcycles. Kawasaki USA granted the Kawasaki Shop of Aurora, Inc. (Dealer), a franchise to sell Kawasaki motorcycles in Aurora, Illinois. The franchise changed locations twice. Both moves were within the five-mile exclusive territory granted Dealer in the franchise agreement.

Dealer did not obtain Kawasaki USA's written approval for either move, as required by the franchise agreement. Kawasaki USA acquiesced to the first move but not the second. At the second new location, Dealer also operated Honda and Suzuki motorcycle franchises and was negotiating to operate a Yamaha franchise. The Kawasaki franchise agreement expressly permitted multiline dealerships. Kawasaki USA objected to the second move, asserting that Dealer had not received written approval for the move, as required by the franchise agreement. Evidence showed, however, that the real reason Kawasaki objected to the move was because it did not want its motorcycles to be sold at the same location as other manufacturers' motorcycles. Kawasaki terminated Dealer's franchise. Dealer sued Kawasaki USA for wrongful termination. Who wins? *Kawasaki Shop of Aurora, Inc. v. Kawasaki Motors Corporation, U.S.A.*, 188 Ill.App.3d 664, 544 N.E.2d 457, **Web** 1989 Ill.App. Lexis 1442 (Appellate Court of Illinois)

BUSINESS ETHICS CASES

40.9 Business Ethics   Southland Corporation (Southland) owns the "7-Eleven" trademark and licenses franchisees throughout the country to operate 7-Eleven stores. The franchise agreement provides for fees to be paid to Southland by each franchisee based on a percentage of gross profits. In return, franchisees receive a lease of premises, a license to use the 7-Eleven trademark and trade secrets, advertising merchandise, and bookkeeping assistance. Vallerie Campbell purchased an existing 7-Eleven store in Fontana, California, and became a Southland franchisee. The franchise was designated #13974 by Southland. As part of the purchase, she applied to the state of California for transfer of the beer and wine license from the prior owner. Southland also executed the application. California approved the transfer and issued the license to "Campbell Vallerie Southland #13974."

An employee of Campbell's store sold beer to Jesse Lewis Cope, a minor who was allegedly intoxicated at the time. After drinking the beer, Cope drove his vehicle and struck another vehicle. Two occupants of the other vehicle, Denise Wickham and Tyrone Crosby, were severely injured, and a third occupant, Cedrick Johnson, was killed. Johnson (through his parents), Wickham, and Crosby sued Southland—but not Campbell—to recover damages. Is Southland legally liable for the tortious acts of its franchisee? Is it morally responsible? *Wickham v. The Southland Corporation*, 168 Cal.App.3d 49, 213 Cal.Rptr. 825, **Web** 1985 Cal.App. Lexis 2070 (Court of Appeal of California)

40.10 Business Ethics   The Kentucky Fried Chicken Corporation (KFC), with its principal place of business in Louisville, Kentucky, is the franchisor of KFC restaurants. KFC's registered trademarks and service marks include "Kentucky Fried Chicken," "It's Finger Lickin' Good," and the portrait of Colonel Harlan Sanders. KFC grants licenses to its franchisees to use these marks in connection with the preparation and sale of "Original Recipe Kentucky Fried Chicken." Original Recipe Kentucky Fried Chicken, which is sold only by KFC franchisees, is prepared by a special cooking process featuring the use of a secret recipe seasoning known as "KFC Seasoning." This blend of seasoning was developed by KFC's founder, Colonel Harlan Sanders. As a condition of each franchise agreement, KFC requires that its franchisees use only KFC Seasoning in connection with the preparation and sale of Kentucky Fried Chicken.

KFC Seasoning is a trade secret. To make the seasoning, KFC has entered into contracts with two spice blenders, the John W. Sexton Company, Inc. (Sexton), and Strange Company (Strange). Each of these companies blends approximately one-half the spices of KFC Seasoning; neither has knowledge of the complete formulation of KFC Seasoning, and both entered into secrecy agreements to maintain the confidentiality of their formulations. After the seasoning is blended by Sexton and Strange, it is mixed together and sold directly to all KFC franchisees. KFC does not receive a royalty or other economic benefit from the sale of KFC Seasoning. KFC's relationship with Sexton and Strange has existed for more than 25 years; no other companies are licensed to blend KFC Seasoning.

Marion-Kay Company, Inc. (Marion-Kay), was a spice blender engaged in the manufacture of chicken seasoning known as "Marion-Kay Seasoning." Marion-Kay requested permission from KFC to sell its seasoning products to KFC franchisees. KFC refused the request. Four years later, KFC learned that Marion-Kay was supplying some KFC franchisees with Marion-Kay seasoning and demanded it cease this practice. When Marion-Kay refused, KFC sued it for interference with contractual relations. Marion-Kay filed a counterclaim, alleging violation of antitrust law. Who wins? Was KFC justified in preventing Marion-Kay from blending its seasonings? Did Marion-Kay act ethically in selling seasoning to KFC franchisees? *KFC Corporation v. Marion-Kay Company, Inc.*, 620 F.Supp. 1160, **Web** 1985 U.S. Dist. Lexis 14766 (United States District Court for the Southern District of Indiana)

ENDNOTES

1. 16 CFR Section 436.

2. *Southland Corporation v. Keating*, 465 U.S. 1, 104 S.Ct. 852, 79 L.Ed.2d 1, **Web** 1984 U.S. Lexis 2 (Supreme Court of the United States).

3. 15 U.S.C. Section 1114 et seq.

▲ **New York Stock Exchange** *This is the home of the New York Stock Exchange (NYSE) in New York City. The NYSE, nicknamed the "Big Board," is the premier stock exchange in the world. It lists the stocks and securities of approximately 3,000 of the world's largest companies for trading. The origin of the NYSE dates to 1792, when several stockbrokers met under a buttonwood tree on Wall Street. The NYSE is located at 11 Wall Street, which has been designated a National Historic Landmark. The NYSE is now operated by NYSE Euronext, which was formed when the NYSE merged with the fully electronic stock exchange Euronext.*

CHAPTER OBJECTIVES

After studying this chapter, you should be able to:

1. Describe the procedure for going public and how securities are registered with the Securities and Exchange Commission.
2. Describe the requirements for qualifying for private placement, intrastate, and small offering exemptions from registration.
3. Describe insider trading that violates Section 10(b) of the Securities Exchange Act of 1934.
4. Describe the liability of tippers and tippees for insider trading.
5. Describe short-swing profits that violate Section 16(b) of the Securities Exchange Act of 1934.

CHAPTER CONTENTS

▶ **INTRODUCTION TO INVESTOR PROTECTION AND ONLINE SECURITIES TRANSACTIONS**

▶ **SECURITIES LAW**
  Landmark Law · *Federal Securities Laws*

"When there is blood on the street, I am buying."

—Nathaniel Mayer Victor Rothschild, third Baron Rothschild

▶ INTRODUCTION TO INVESTOR PROTECTION AND ONLINE SECURITIES TRANSACTIONS

Prior to the 1920s and 1930s, the securities markets in this country were not regulated by the federal government. Securities were sold to investors with little, if any, disclosure. Fraud in these transactions was common. To respond to this lack of regulation, federal and state governments enacted securities statutes to regulate the securities markets. The federal and state securities statutes are designed to require disclosure of information to investors and prevent fraud. This chapter discusses federal and state securities laws and regulations that provide investor protection, as well as the sale of securities online.

▶ SECURITIES LAW

The federal and state governments have enacted statutes that regulate the issuance and trading in securities. The primary purposes of these acts is to promote full disclosure to investors and to prevent fraud in the issuance and trading of securities. These federal and state statutes are enforced by federal and state regulatory authorities, respectively.

LANDMARK LAW
Federal Securities Laws

Following the stock market crash of 1929, Congress enacted a series of statutes designed to regulate securities markets. These federal securities statutes are designed to require disclosure to investors and prevent securities fraud. The two primary securities statutes enacted by the federal government, both of which were enacted during the Great Depression years, are:

· **Securities Act of 1933.** This federal statute, enacted in 1933, primarily regulates the issue of securities by companies and other businesses. This act applies to original issue of securities, both initial public offerings (IPOs) by new public companies and sales of new securities by established companies. The primary purpose of this act is to require full and honest disclosure of information to investors at the time of the issuance of the securities. The act also prohibits fraud during the sale of issued securities. Securities are now issued online, and the 1933 act regulates the issue of securities online.

· **Securities Exchange Act of 1934.** This federal statute was enacted in 1934 to prevent fraud in the subsequent trading of securities. This act has been applied to prohibit insider trading and other frauds in the purchase and sale of securities in the after markets, such as trading on securities exchanges and other purchases and sales of securities. The act also requires continuous reporting—annual reports, quarterly reports, and other reports—to investors and the Securities Exchange Commission. Securities are now sold online and on electronic stock exchanges. The 1934 act regulates the purchase and sale of securities online.

The Securities Exchange Commission (SEC), a federal administrative agency, enacts rules and regulates to interpret and administer federal securities laws.

▶ DEFINITION OF SECURITY

Congress has enacted the Securities Act of 1933, the Securities Exchange Act of 1934, and several other securities statutes to regulate the issuance and sale of securities. For these federal statutes to apply, however, a **security** must first be found. Federal securities laws define securities as:

- **Common securities.** Interests or instruments that are commonly known as securities are securities.

Examples Common stock, preferred stock, bonds, debentures, and warrants are common securities.

- **Statutorily defined securities.** Interests or instruments that are expressly mentioned in securities acts are securities.

Examples The securities acts specifically define preorganization subscription agreements; interests in oil, gas, and mineral rights; and deposit receipts for foreign securities as securities.

- **Investment contracts.** An **investment contract** is any contract whereby an investor invests money or other consideration in a common enterprise and expects to make a profit from the significant efforts of others. The courts apply the **Howey test**[1] in determining whether an arrangement is an investment contract and therefore a security. Under this test, an arrangement is considered an investment contract if there is an investment of money by an investor in a common enterprise and the investor expects to make profits based on the sole or substantial efforts of the promoter or others.

Examples A limited partnership interest is an investment contract because the limited partner expects to make money based on the effort of the general partners. Pyramid sales schemes where persons give money to a promoter who promises them the return of their money with a promised interest or payment is an investment contract because the person who gave money to the promoter expects the promised return based on the efforts of the promoter. Investments in farm animals accompanied by care agreements have been found to be securities under this test, which is known as the *Howey test*.

> **security**
> (1) An interest or instrument that is common stock, preferred stock, a bond, a debenture, or a warrant; (2) an interest or instrument that is expressly mentioned in securities acts; and (3) an investment contract.

> *Anyone who thinks there's safety in numbers hasn't looked at the stock market pages.*
>
> Irene Peter

CONCEPT SUMMARY

DEFINITION OF *SECURITY*

Type of Security	Definition
Common securities	Interests or instruments that are commonly known as securities, such as common stock, preferred stock, debentures, and warrants.
Statutorily defined securities	Interests and instruments that are expressly mentioned in securities acts as being securities, such as interests in oil, gas, and mineral rights.
Investment contracts	A flexible standard for defining a security. Under the Howey test, a security exists if an investor invests money in a common enterprise and expects to make a profit from the significant efforts of others.

► THE SECURITIES AND EXCHANGE COMMISSION (SEC)

Securities and Exchange Commission (SEC)
The federal administrative agency that is empowered to administer federal securities laws. The SEC can adopt rules and regulations to interpret and implement federal securities laws.

The Securities Exchange Act of 1934 created the **Securities and Exchange Commission (SEC)** and empowered it to administer federal securities laws. The SEC is an administrative agency composed of five members who are appointed by the president. The major responsibilities of the SEC are:

- Adopting **rules** (also called **regulations**) that further the purpose of the federal securities statutes. These rules have the force of law.
- Investigating alleged securities violations and bringing enforcement actions against suspected violators. This may include a recommendation of criminal prosecution. Criminal prosecutions of violations of federal securities laws are brought by the U.S. Department of Justice.
- Regulating the activities of securities brokers and advisors. This includes registering brokers and advisors and taking enforcement action against those who violate securities laws.

The SEC has an electronic filing and forms system called **EDGAR**, where companies file required forms and information. The electronic filings on this system are viewable by the public.

► PRIVATE TRANSACTIONS EXEMPT FROM REGISTRATION

Certain *transactions* where securities are sold are **exempt** from registration with the SEC if they meet specified requirements. These are called **exempt transactions**. Thus, the securities sold pursuant to an exempt transaction do not have to be registered with the SEC. Exempt transactions include the *non-issuer exemption, intrastate offering exemption, private placement exemption*, and *small offering exemption*. These exempt transactions are discussed in the paragraphs that follow.

Exempt transactions that do not have to be registered with the SEC are subject to the antifraud provisions of the federal securities laws. Therefore, the issuer must provide investors with adequate information—including annual reports, quarterly reports, proxy statements, financial statements, and so on—even though a registration statement is not required.

Non-issuer Exemption

Non-issuers, such as average investors, do not have to file a registration statement prior to reselling securities they have purchased. This **non-issuer exemption** exists because the Securities Act of 1933 exempts from registration securities transactions not made by an issuer, an underwriter, or a dealer. For example, an investor who owns shares of IBM can resell those shares to another at any time without having to register with the SEC.

Intrastate Offering Exemption

intrastate offering exemption
An exemption from registration that permits local businesses to raise capital from local investors to be used in the local economy without the need to register with the SEC.

The purpose of the **intrastate offering exemption** is to permit local businesses to raise from local investors capital to be used in the local economy without the need to register with the SEC.[2] There is no limit on the dollar amount of capital that can be raised pursuant to an intrastate offering exemption. An issuer can qualify for this exemption in only one state.

Three requirements must be met to qualify for this exemption:[3]

1. The issuer must be a resident of the state for which the exemption is claimed. A corporation is a resident of the state in which it is incorporated.
2. The issuer must be doing business in that state. This requires that 80 percent of the issuer's assets be located in the state, 80 percent of its gross revenues be derived from the state, its principal office be located in the state, and 80 percent of the proceeds of the offering be used in the state.
3. The purchasers of the securities must all be residents of that state.

An intrastate offering can be made only in the one state in which all these requirements have been met. **Rule 147** stipulates that securities sold pursuant to an intrastate offering exemption cannot be sold to nonresidents for a period of nine months.

Private Placement Exemption

An issue of securities that does not involve a public offering is exempt from the registration requirements.[4] This exemption—known as the **private placement exemption**—allows issuers to raise capital from an unlimited number of accredited investors without having to register the offering with the SEC.[5] There is no dollar limit on the securities that can be sold pursuant to this exemption.

An **accredited investor** is:[6]

- Any natural person who has individual net worth or joint net worth with a spouse that exceeds $1 million.
- A natural person with income exceeding $200,000 in each of the two most recent years or joint income with a spouse exceeding $300,000 for those years and a reasonable expectation of the same income level in the current year.
- A charitable organization, a corporation, a partnership, a trust, or an employee benefit plan with assets exceeding $5 million.
- A bank, an insurance company, a registered investment company, a business development company, or a small business investment company.
- Insiders of the issuers, such as directors, executive officers, or general partner of the company selling the securities.
- A business in which all the equity owners are accredited investors.

No more than 35 **nonaccredited investors** may purchase securities pursuant to a private placement exemption. These nonaccredited investors are usually friends and family members of the insiders. Nonaccredited investors must be sophisticated investors, however, either through their own experience and education or through representatives (e.g., accountants, lawyers, business managers). General selling efforts, such as advertising to the public, are not permitted.

private placement exemption
An exemption from registration that permits issuers to raise capital from an unlimited number of accredited investors and no more than 35 nonaccredited investors without having to register the offering with the SEC.

Small Offering Exemption

Securities offerings that do not exceed a certain dollar amount are exempt from registration.[7] Rule 504 exempts from registration the sale of securities not exceeding $1 million during a 12-month period. The securities may be sold to an unlimited number of accredited and unaccredited investors, but general selling efforts to the public are not permitted. This is called the **small offering exemption**.

Rule 144 provides that securities sold pursuant to the private placement exemption or the small offering exemption must be held for one year from the date when the securities were paid for. During the second year, only limited sales can be made. After two years, the securities are no longer restricted.

small offering exemption
An exemption from registration that permits the sale of securities not exceeding $1 million during a 12-month period.

CONTEMPORARY ENVIRONMENT

Securities Exempt from Registration

Certain *securities* are exempt from registration. Once a security is exempt, it is exempt forever. It does not matter how many times the security is transferred. **Exempt securities** include:

- Securities issued by any government in the United States (e.g., municipal bonds issued by city governments).

- Short-term notes and drafts that have a maturity date that does not exceed nine months (e.g., commercial paper issued by corporations).
- Securities issued by nonprofit issuers, such as religious institutions, charitable institutions, and colleges and universities.

- Securities of financial institutions (e.g., banks and savings associations) that are regulated by the appropriate banking authorities.
- Securities issued by common carriers (railroads and trucking companies) that are regulated by the Interstate Commerce Commission (ICC).

- Insurance and annuity contracts issued by insurance companies.
- Stock dividends and stock splits.
- Securities issued in a corporate reorganization in which one security is exchanged for another security.

▶ THE SECURITIES ACT OF 1933: GOING PUBLIC

Securities Act of 1933
A federal statute that primarily regulates the issuance of securities by corporations, partnerships, associations, and individuals.

The **Securities Act of 1933** primarily regulates the issuance of securities by corporations, limited partnerships, other businesses, and individuals.[8] **Section 5 of the Securities Act of 1933** requires securities offered to the public through the use of the mails or any facility of interstate commerce to be registered with the SEC by means of a registration statement and an accompanying prospectus.

The business or party selling securities to the public is called the **issuer**. The issuer may be a relatively new company (e.g., Google, Inc.) selling securities to the public through an **initial public offering (IPO)**, or it may be an established company (e.g., Microsoft Corporation) selling new securities to the public. Many issuers of securities employ **investment bankers**, which are independent securities companies, to sell their securities to the public. Issuers pay a fee to investment bankers for this service.

Registration Statement

registration statement
A document that an issuer of securities files with the SEC that contains required information about the issuer, the securities to be issued, and other relevant information.

A covered issuer must file a written **registration statement** with the SEC. The issuer's lawyer normally prepares the statement, with the help of the issuer's management, accountants, and underwriters.

A registration statement must contain descriptions of (1) the securities being offered for sale; (2) the registrant's business; (3) the management of the registrant, including compensation, stock options and benefits, and material transactions with the registrant; (4) pending litigation; (5) how the proceeds from the offering will be used; (6) government regulation; (7) the degree of competition in the industry; and (8) any special risk factors. In addition, a registration statement must be accompanied by financial statements certified by certified public accountants.

Registration statements usually become effective 20 business days after they are filed, unless the SEC requires additional information to be disclosed. A new 20-day period begins each time a registration statement is amended. At the registrant's request, the SEC may "accelerate the *effective date*" (i.e., not require the registrant to wait 20 days after the last amendment is filed).

The SEC does not pass judgment on the merits of the securities offered. It decides only whether the issuer has met the disclosure requirements.

INTERNET LAW & ONLINE COMMERCE

Google's Internet IPO

Most computer users either use or are aware of the large Internet search engine Google. Sergey Brin, 31, and Larry Page, 32, launched Google in September 1998 in a garage in Menlo Park, California. The name of the company—Google—stands for a numeral that is a 1 followed by 100 zeros. Brin and Page raised $1 million in funding from angel investors. Google attracted several commercial clients and in 1999 raised $25 million from a venture capitalist, Sequoia Capital. Google spent five years developing and promoting its Internet search engine, turned profitable, and had approximately 2,000 employees.

Google Inc. began thinking about making an initial public offering (IPO) of its stock. In a traditional IPO, shares are set at a fixed price and then are usually sold by an investment banker and participating securities firms to their favored customers. Thus, in a desirable IPO, the small investor is left out and must wait to purchase shares in the after market, usually at a much higher price than the IPO price. The investment banks and their rich clients are the only buyers in a traditional IPO.

The owners of Google decided to conduct an IPO of their stock and filed a registration statement with the Securities and Exchange Commission (SEC). Google spurned the traditional IPO process in several ways. First, Google's IPO shares were offered over the Internet instead of being sold by investment banks. Second, Google wanted to democratize its IPO by offering shares to small and large investors alike. Third, rather than being priced beforehand, the shares were to be offered using what is called a "Dutch auction," where the auction would fix the price. In addition to the company's shares, Brin, Page, and other executives also sold some of their shares in the IPO.

Google made its prospectus available electronically. After receiving a prospectus, bidders obtained a unique bidder ID. The bidder was then free to submit bids over the Internet once Google's IPO auction started. The Dutch auction worked like this: Each bidder selected the number of shares he or she wanted to purchase and made a bid at the price he or she was willing to pay. Some bids were at $50 per share, others at $75 per share, others at $110 per share, and so on. The company then worked backward from the highest bid until all the shares it had to offer were sold. This occurred at $85 per share. Everyone who was awarded shares, including those who had bid a higher price, paid this final price. Everyone who had offered less than this price received no shares.

The Dutch auction priced Google shares at $85 per share, and 19.6 million shares were sold. Google raised $1.2 billion, and the Google insiders made $450 million. The final price was 80 times Google's per-share profit. See Exhibit 41.1 for the cover page of Google's registration statement.

▶ **Exhibit 41.1 COVER PAGE OF THE REGISTRATION STATEMENT OF GOOGLE, INC.**

As filed with the Securities and Exchange Commission on April 29, 2004 Registration No. 333-

SECURITIES AND EXCHANGE COMMISSION

Washington, D.C. 20549

FORM S-1

REGISTRATION STATEMENT

Under

The Securities Act of 1933

GOOGLE INC.

(Exact name of Registrant as specified in its charter)

Delaware	7375	77-0493581
(State or other jurisdiction of incorporation or organization)	(Primary Standard Industrial Classification Code Number)	(I.R.S. Employer Identification Number)

1600 Amphitheatre Parkway
Mountain View, CA 94043
(650) 623-4000

(Address, including zip code, and telephone number, including area code, of Registrant's principal executive offices)

Eric Schmidt

Chief Executive Officer

Google Inc.

1600 Amphitheatre Parkway

Mountain View, CA 94043

(650) 623-4000

(Name, address, including zip code, and telephone number, including area code, of agent for service)

Copies to:

Larry W. Sonsini, Esq. David J. Segre, Esq. Wilson Sonsini Goodrich & Rosati, P.C. 650 Page Mill Road Palo Alto, California 94304-1050 (650) 493-9300	David C. Drummond, Esq. Jeffery L. Donovan, Esq. Anna Itoi, Esq. Google Inc. 1600 Amphitheatre Parkway Mountain View, CA 94043 (650) 623-4000	William H. Hinman, Jr., Esq. Simpson Thacher & Bartlett LLP 3330 Hillview Avenue Palo Alto, California 94304 (650) 251-5000

Approximate date of commencement of proposed sale to the public: As soon as practicable after the effective date of this Registration Statement.

If any of the securities being registered on this Form are being offered on a delayed or continuous basis pursuant to Rule 415 under the Securities Act of 1933, as amended (the "Securities Act"), check the following box.   ☐

If this Form is filed to register additional securities for an offering pursuant to Rule 462(b) under the Securities Act, please check the following box and list the Securities Act registration number of the earlier effective registration statement for the same offering.   ☐

If this Form is a post-effective amendment filed pursuant to Rule 462(c) under the Securities Act, check the following box and list the Securities Act registration number of the earlier effective registration statement for the same offering.   ☐

If this Form is a post-effective amendment filed pursuant to Rule 462(d) under the Securities Act, check the following box and list the Securities Act registration statement number of the earlier effective registration statement for the same offering.   ☐

If delivery of the prospectus is expected to be made pursuant to Rule 434, check the following box.   ☐

CALCULATION OF REGISTRATION FEE

Title of Each Class of Securities to be Registered	Proposed Maximum Aggregate Offering Price (1)(2)	Amount of Registration Fee
Class A common stock, par value $0.001 per share	$2,718,281,828	$344,406.31

(1) Estimated solely for the purpose of computing the amount of the registration fee, in accordance with Rule 457(o) promulgated under the Securities Act of 1933.

(2) Includes offering price of shares that the underwriters have the option to purchase to cover over-allotments, if any.

The Registrant hereby amends this Registration Statement on such date or dates as may be necessary to delay its effective date until the Registrant shall file a further amendment which specifically states that this Registration Statement shall thereafter become effective in accordance with Section 8(a) of the Securities Act or until the Registration Statement shall become effective on such date as the Securities and Exchange Commission, acting pursuant to said Section 8(a), may determine.

Prospectus

A **prospectus** is a written disclosure document that must be submitted to the SEC along with the registration statement. A prospectus is used as a selling tool by the issuer. It is provided to prospective investors to enable them to evaluate the financial risk of an investment.

A prospectus must contain the following language in capital letters and boldface (usually red) type:

> *These securities have not been approved or disapproved by the Securities and Exchange Commission or any state securities commission nor has the Securities and Exchange Commission or any state securities commission passed upon the accuracy or adequacy of this prospectus. Any representation to the contrary is a criminal offense.*

prospectus
A written disclosure document that must be submitted to the SEC along with the registration statement and given to prospective purchasers of the securities.

Conditioning the Market

The **prefiling period** begins when the issuer first contemplates issuing the securities and ends when the registration statement is filed. For example, the prefiling period would begin when a board of directors first considers making a public offering of the company's securities. The prefiling period runs until the date of filing the registration statement with the SEC. During the **waiting period**, the issuer cannot **condition the market** for the upcoming securities offering.

prefiling period
A period of time that begins when the issuer first contemplates issuing securities and ends when the registration statement is filed. The issuer may not condition the market during this period.

Examples Before a planned securities offering, it is illegal for an issuer to engage in a public relations campaign (e.g., newspaper and magazine articles, advertisements) that touts the prospects of the company and the planned securities issue. However, sending annual reports to shareholders and making public announcements of factual matters (such as the settlement of a strike) are permissible because they are considered normal corporate disclosures.

Sale of Unregistered Securities

Sale of securities that should have been registered with the SEC but were not violates the Securities Act of 1933. Investors can rescind their purchase and recover damages. The U.S. government can impose criminal penalties on any person who willfully violates the Securities Act of 1933.

Regulation A Offering

Regulation A permits issuers to sell up to $5 million of securities to the public during a 12-month period, pursuant to a simplified registration process. Such offerings may have an unlimited number of purchasers who do not have to be accredited investors. Issuers with offerings exceeding $100,000 must file an **offering statement** with the SEC. An offering statement requires less disclosure than a registration statement and is less costly to prepare. Investors must be provided with an offering circular prior to the purchase of securities. There are no **resale restrictions** on the securities.

Regulation A
A regulation that permits the issuer to sell securities pursuant to a simplified registration process.

Small Corporate Offering Registration (SCOR) Form Small businesses often need to raise capital and must find public investors to buy company stock. In 1992, after years of investigation, the SEC amended Regulation A by adopting the **Small Corporate Offering Registration (SCOR) form**. The SCOR form—**Form U-7**—is a question-and-answer disclosure form that small businesses can complete and file with the SEC if they plan on raising $1 million or less from the public issue of securities. An issuer must answer the questions on Form U-7, which then becomes the offering circular that must be given to prospective investors.

Form U-7 questions are so clearly and specifically drawn that they can be answered by the issuer without the help of an expensive securities lawyer. SCOR form questions require the issuer to develop a business plan that states specific company goals and how it intends to reach them. The SCOR form is available only to domestic businesses. A SCOR form offering cannot exceed $1 million, and the offering price of the common stock or its equivalent may not be less than $5 per share. SCOR form offerings are a welcome addition for entrepreneur-owners who want to raise money through a small public offering.

Private Actions

Private parties who have been injured by violations of the Securities Act of 1933 have recourse against the violator under the following two sections:

Section 12
A provision of the Securities Act of 1933 that imposes civil liability on any person who violates the provisions of Section 5 of the act.

Section 11
A provision of the Securities Act of 1933 that imposes civil liability on persons who intentionally defraud investors by making misrepresentations or omissions of material facts in the registration statement or who are negligent for not discovering the fraud.

due diligence defense
A defense to a Section 11 action that, if proven, makes the defendant not liable.

1. **Section 12 of the Securities Act of 1933** imposes *civil liability* on any person who violates the provisions of Section 5 of the act. Violations include selling securities pursuant to an unwarranted exemption and making misrepresentations concerning the offer or sale of securities. The purchaser's remedy for a violation of Section 12 is either to rescind the purchase or to sue for damages.

2. **Section 11 of the Securities Act of 1933** provides for *civil liability* for damages when a registration statement on its effective date misstates or omits a material fact. Liability under Section 11 is imposed on those who (1) intentionally defraud investors or (2) are negligent in not discovering the fraud. Thus, the issuer, certain corporate officers (e.g., chief executive officer, chief financial officer, chief accounting officer), directors, signers of the registration statement, underwriters, and experts (e.g., accountants who certify financial statements and lawyers who issue legal opinions that are included in a registration statement) may be liable.

All defendants except the issuer may assert a **due diligence defense** against the imposition of Section 11 liability. If this defense is proven, the defendant is not liable. To establish a due diligence defense, the defendant must prove that after reasonable investigation, he or she had reasonable grounds to believe and did believe that, at the time the registration statement became effective, the statements contained therein were true and there was no omission of material facts.

Example In the classic case ***Escott v. BarChris Construction Corporation***,[9] the company was going to issue a new bond to the public. The company prepared financial statements wherein the company overstated current assets, understated current liabilities, overstated sales, overstated gross profits, overstated the backlog of orders, did not disclose loans to officers, did not disclose customer delinquencies in paying for goods, and lied about the use of the proceeds from the offering. The company gave these financial statements to its auditors, Peat, Marwick, Mitchell & Co. (Peat Marwick), who did not discover the lies. Peat Marwick certified the financial statements that became part of the registration statement filed with the SEC. The bonds were sold to the public. One year later, the company filed for bankruptcy. The bondholders sued Russo, the chief executive officer (CEO) of BarChris; Vitolo and Puglies, the founders of the business and the president and vice president, respectively; Trilling, the controller; and Peat Marwick, the auditors. Each defendant pleaded the due diligence defense. The court rejected each of the party's defenses, finding that the chief executive office, president, vice president, and controller were all in positions to either have created or discovered the misrepresentations. The court also found that the auditor, Peat Marwick, did not do a proper investigation and had not proven its due diligence defense. The court found that the defendants had violated Section 11 of the Securities Act of 1933 by submitting misrepresentations and omissions of material facts in the registration statement filed with the SEC.

SEC Actions

The SEC may (1) issue a **consent order** whereby a defendant agrees not to violate securities laws in the future but does not admit to having violated securities laws in the past, (2) bring an action in federal District Court to obtain an **injunction**, or (3) request the court to grant ancillary relief, such as *disgorgement of profits* by the defendant.

Criminal Liability

Section 24 of the Securities Act of 1933 imposes *criminal liability* on any person who *willfully* violates either the act or the rules and regulations adopted thereunder.[10] A violator may be fined or imprisoned up to five years, or both. Criminal actions are brought by the Department of Justice.

Section 24
A provision of the Securities Act of 1933 that imposes criminal liability on any person who willfully violates the 1933 act or the rules or regulations adopted thereunder.

ETHICS SPOTLIGHT

Sarbanes-Oxley Act Erects a Wall Between Investment Bankers and Securities Analysts

Investment banking is a service provided by many securities firms, whereby they assist companies in **going public** when issuing shares to the public and otherwise selling securities. The securities firms are paid lucrative fees for providing investment banking services in assisting companies to sell their securities and finding customers to purchase these securities. These same securities firms often provide securities analysis— providing investment advice and recommending securities listed on the stock exchanges and other securities to be purchased by the public.

In the late 1990s and early 2000s, many conflicts of interest were uncovered. Investment bankers and securities analysts of the same firm shared information, and the analysts were paid or pressured by the securities firms to write glowing reports of companies from which the investment bankers of the firm were earning fees.

Congress sought to remedy this problem by enacting Section 501 of the **Sarbanes-Oxley Act** of 2002. Section 501 established rules for separating the investment banking

and securities advice functions of securities firms, thus eliminating many conflicts of interest:

- Securities firms must establish structural and institutional "walls" between their investment banking and securities analysis areas. These walls must protect analysts from review, pressure, and oversight by persons employed by the investment banking area of a securities firm.
- Securities analysts must disclose in each research report or public appearance any conflicts of interest that are known or should have been known to exist at the time of publication or public appearance.

The SEC is empowered to adopt rules to enforce the provisions of Section 501.

Business Ethics Why did investment bankers of securities firms put pressure on analysts to issue positive reports on certain companies? Will the required "walls" between securities analysts and investment bankers make the analysts' information more reliable? Explain.

▶ THE SECURITIES EXCHANGE ACT OF 1934: TRADING IN SECURITIES

Unlike the Securities Act of 1933, which regulates the original issuance of securities, the **Securities Exchange Act of 1934** primarily regulates subsequent trading.[11] It provides for the registration of certain companies with the SEC, the continuous filing of periodic reports by these companies to the SEC, and the regulation of securities exchanges, brokers, and dealers. It also contains provisions that assess civil and criminal liability on violators of the 1934 act and rules and regulations adopted thereunder.

Securities Exchange Act of 1934
A federal statute that primarily regulates the trading in securities.

Section 10(b) and Rule 10b-5

Section 10(b) is one of the most important sections in the entire 1934 act.[12] It prohibits the use of manipulative and deceptive devices in contravention of the rules and regulations prescribed by the SEC. Pursuant to its rule-making authority, the SEC has adopted **Rule 10b-5**,[13] which provides:

> It shall be unlawful for any person, directly or indirectly, by use of any means or instrumentality of interstate commerce or of the mails, or of any facility of any national securities exchange,
>   a. to employ any device, scheme, or artifice to defraud,

Section 10(b)
A provision of the Securities Exchange Act of 1934 that prohibits the use of manipulative and deceptive devices in the purchase or sale of securities in contravention of the rules and regulations prescribed by the SEC.

Rule 10b-5
A rule adopted by the SEC to clarify the reach of Section 10(b) against deceptive and fraudulent activities in the purchase and sale of securities.

> b. to make any untrue statement of a material fact or to omit to state a material fact necessary in order to make the statements made, in light of the circumstances under which they were made, not misleading, or
>
> c. to engage in any act, practice, or course of business that operates or would operate as a fraud or deceit upon any person, in connection with the purchase or sale of any security.

Rule 10b-5 is not restricted to purchases and sales of securities of reporting companies.[14] All transfers of securities, whether made on a stock exchange, in the over-the-counter market, in a private sale, or in connection with a merger, are subject to this rule.[15] The U.S. Supreme Court has held that only conduct involving **scienter** (intentional conduct) violates Section 10(b) and Rule 10b-5. Negligent conduct is not a violation.[16]

Section 10(b) and Rule 10b-5 require reliance by the injured party on the misstatement. However, many sales and purchases of securities occur in open-market transactions (e.g., over stock exchanges), where there is no direct communication between the buyer and the seller.

scienter
Intentional conduct. Scienter is required for there to be a violation of Section 10(b) and Rule 10b-5.

Private Right of Action

Although Section 10(b) and Rule 10b-5 do not expressly provide for a private right of action, courts have *implied* such a right. Generally, a private plaintiff may seek rescission of the securities contract or recover damages (e.g., disgorgements of the illegal profits by the defendants). Private securities fraud claims must be brought within two years after discovery or five years after the violation occurs, whichever is shorter.

Fraud includes the pretense of knowledge when knowledge there is none.

Chief Justice Cardozo
Ultramares Corp. v. Touche (1931)

SEC Action

The SEC may investigate suspected violations of the Securities Exchange Act of 1934 and of the rules and regulations adopted thereunder. The SEC may enter into *consent orders* with defendants, seek *injunctions* in federal District Court, or seek court orders requiring defendants to *disgorge* illegally gained profits.

In 1984, Congress enacted the **Insider Trading Sanctions Act**,[17] which permits the SEC to obtain a **civil penalty** of up to three times the illegal profits gained or losses avoided on insider trading. The fine is payable to the U.S. Treasury. Under the Sarbanes-Oxley Act, the SEC may issue an order prohibiting any person who has committed securities fraud from acting as an officer or a director of a public company.

Insider Trading Sanctions Act
A federal statute that permits the SEC to obtain a civil penalty of up to three times the illegal benefits received from insider trading.

Section 32
A provision of the Securities Exchange Act of 1934 that imposes criminal liability on any person who willfully violates the 1934 act or the rules or regulations adopted thereunder.

Criminal Liability

Section 32 of the Securities Exchange Act of 1934 makes it a criminal offense to willfully violate the provisions of the act or the rules and regulations adopted thereunder.[18] Under the Sarbanes-Oxley Act of 2002, a person who willfully violates the Securities Exchange Act of 1934 can be fined up to $5 million or imprisoned for up to 25 years, or both. A corporation or another entity may be fined up to $2.5 million.

insider trading
A situation in which an insider makes a profit by personally purchasing shares of the corporation prior to public release of favorable information or by selling shares of the corporation prior to the public disclosure of unfavorable information.

Insider Trading

One of the most important purposes of Section 10(b) and Rule 10b-5 is to prevent **insider trading**. Insider trading occurs when a company employee or company advisor uses material nonpublic information to make a profit by trading in the securities of the company. This practice is considered illegal because it allows insiders to take advantage of the investing public.

In the ***Matter of Cady, Roberts & Co.***[19] the SEC announced that the duty of an insider who possesses material nonpublic information is to either (1) abstain from trading in the securities of the company or (2) disclose the information to the person on the other side of the transaction before the insider purchases the securities from or sells the securities to him or her.

The insiders here were not trading on an equal footing with the outside investors.

Judge Waterman
Securities and Exchange Commission v. Texas Gulf Sulphur Company (1968)

For purposes of Section 10(b) and Rule 10b-5, **insiders** are defined as (1) officers, directors, and employees at all levels of a company; (2) lawyers, accountants, consultants, and agents and representatives who are hired by the company on a temporary and non-employee basis to provide services or work to the company; and (3) others who owe a fiduciary duty to the company.

Example The Widger Corporation has its annual audit done by its outside CPAs, Young & Old, CPAs. Priscilla is one of the CPAs who conduct the audit. The audit discloses that the Widger Corporation's profits have doubled since last year, and Priscilla rightfully discloses this fact to Martha, the chief financial officer (CFO) of Widger Corporation. Both Martha and Priscilla are *insiders*. The earnings information is definitely *material*, and it is *nonpublic* until the corporation publicly announces its earnings in two days. Prior to the earnings information being made public, Priscilla and Martha buy stock in Widger Corporation at $100 per share. After the earnings information is made public, the stock of Widger Corporation increases to $150 per share. Both Priscilla and Martha are liable for insider trading in violation of Section 10(b) and Rule 10b-5 because they traded in the securities of Widger Corporation while insiders in possession of material nonpublic inside information. Martha and Priscilla could be held civilly liable and criminally guilty of insider trading in violation of Section 10(b) and Rule 10b-5.

Tipper–Tippee Liability

A person who discloses material nonpublic information to another person is called a **tipper**. A person who receives such information is known as a **tippee**. A tippee is liable for acting on material information that he or she knew or should have known was not public. The tipper is liable for the profits made by the tippee. If the tippee tips other persons, both the tippee (who is now a tipper) and the original tipper are liable for the profits made by these remote tippees. The remote tippees are liable for their own trades if they knew or should have known that they possessed material inside information.

In the following case, the Court found an insider criminally liable for insider trading and tipping.

tipper
A person who discloses material nonpublic information to another person.

tippee
A person who receives material nonpublic information from a tipper.

CASE 41.1 Insider Trading

United States v. Bhagat

436 F.3d 1140, Web 2006 U.S. App. Lexis 3008 (2006)
United States Court of Appeals for the Ninth Circuit

"**The fact that this evidence was all circumstantial does not lessen its sufficiency to support a guilty verdict.**"

—Judge Rawlinson

Facts

Atul Bhagat worked for NVIDIA Corporation (Nvidia). Nvidia competed for a multimillion-dollar contract to develop a video game console (the Xbox) for Microsoft Corporation. Upon receiving news that Nvidia had been awarded the contract, Nvidia's chief executive officer (CEO) sent a company-wide e-mail late Sunday night, announcing the contract award. The next morning, Nvidia sent a number of follow-up e-mails, advising Nvidia employees that the Xbox information should be kept confidential and imposing a trading blackout on the purchase of Nvidia stock by employees for several days.

On Monday morning, within roughly 20 minutes after the final e-mail was sent, Bhagat purchased a large quantity of Nvidia stock. Bhagat testified that he read the e-mails roughly 40 minutes after he purchased the stock. Bhagat also testified that upon learning of the trading blackout, he attempted to cancel his trade by contacting his broker, who advised him that it was too late. Bhagat could not remember what company he contacted nor the name or gender of the person with whom he spoke. However, there was no direct evidence that Bhagat read the e-mails prior to his purchase of the Nvidia stock.

Less than one-half hour after Bhagat made his purchase, his friend Mamat Gill purchased Nvidia stock. Bhagat denied having told anyone about the Xbox contract before the information was made public. There was no

(case continues)

direct evidence that Bhagat contacted Gill prior to Gill's purchase of Nvidia stock.

The Securities and Exchange Commission (SEC) investigated Bhagat's and Gill's purchases of Nvidia stock. Subsequently, the United States brought criminal charges against Bhagat, charging him with insider trading, tipping, and obstruction of an SEC investigation. Bhagat stuck with his story regarding his purchase of Nvidia stock and denied tipping Gill about the Xbox contract. Based on circumstantial evidence, the jury convicted Bhagat of insider trading, tipping, and obstruction of an SEC investigation. Bhagat appealed.

Issue

Was Bhagat criminally guilty of insider trading, tipping, and obstruction of an SEC investigation?

Language of the Court

Insider Trading To convict Bhagat of insider trading, the government was required to prove that he traded stock on the basis of material, nonpublic information. The government offered significant evidence to support the jury's conclusion that Bhagat was aware of the confidential X-Box information before he executed his trades. The X-Box e-mails were sent prior to his purchase. The e-mails were found on his computer. Bhagat was at his office for several hours prior to executing his trade, which provided him the opportunity to read the e-mails. Finally, Bhagat took virtually no action to divest himself of the stock, or to inform his company that he had violated the company's trading blackout. The fact that this evidence was all circumstantial does not lessen its sufficiency to support a guilty verdict.

Tipping To convict Bhagat of tipping Gill, the government was required to prove that the tipper, Bhagat, provided the tippee, Gill, with material, inside information,

prior to the tippee's purchase of stock. Viewing the evidence in the light most favorable to the prosecution, we cannot say that no reasonable trier of fact could have found Bhagat guilty. Bhagat and Gill were friends, Gill purchased stock shortly after Bhagat, and Gill's purchase was his largest purchase of the year.

Obstructing an Agency Proceeding To convict Bhagat for obstructing an agency proceeding, the government was required to prove that an agency of the United States government was conducting a proceeding; that the defendant was aware of that proceeding; and that the defendant intentionally interfered with, or obstructed the course of, that proceeding. Sufficient evidence also supports the jury's verdict on this charge. It is undisputed that there was an SEC investigative proceeding of which Bhagat was aware. The prosecution also introduced evidence that Bhagat intentionally obstructed that proceeding by providing the SEC investigators with false information to cover up his acts of insider trading and tipping and eliminate himself as a suspect.

Decision

The U.S. Court of Appeals upheld the U.S. District Court's judgment, finding Bhagat criminally guilty of insider trading, tipping, and obstruction of the SEC's investigation. The U.S. Court of Appeals remanded the case to the U.S. District Court for sentencing of Bhagat.

Case Questions

Critical Legal Thinking What is insider trading? Explain. What is tipping? Explain.

Business Ethics Do you think Bhagat committed the crimes he was convicted of? Why or why not?

Contemporary Business What percentage of insider trading do you think the government catches?

Misappropriation Theory

The courts have developed laws to address trading in securities by insiders who possess inside information. But sometimes a person who possesses inside information about a company is not an employee or a temporary insider of that company. Instead, the party may be an outsider. However, an outsider's misappropriation of information in violation of his or her fiduciary duty violates Section 10(b) and Rule 10b-5. This rule is called the **misappropriation theory**.

Aiders and Abettors

Many principal actors in a securities fraud obtain the knowing assistance of other parties to successfully complete the fraud. These other parties are known as *aiders* and *abettors*. The principal party in a securities fraud is civilly liable and criminally guilty of violating Section 10(b) and Rule 10b-5. However, whether aiders and abettors were civilly liable under Section 10(b) and Rule 10b-5 was questionable. The U.S. Supreme Court decided this issue in the following case.

U.S. SUPREME COURT   CASE 41.2 Aiding and Abetting

Stoneridge Investment Partners, LLC v. Scientific-Atlanta, Inc.

128 S.Ct. 761, 169 L.Ed.2d 627, Web 2008 U.S. Lexis 1091 (2008)
Supreme Court of the United States

"There is no private right of action for aiding and abetting a Section 10(b) violation."

—Justice Kennedy

Facts

Charter Communications, Inc. (Charter), fraudulently issued financial statements that affected the value of its securities. Charter was a cable operator that provided cable service to subscribers. Charter wanted to show increased subscriber growth and cash flow. To do so, Charter obtained the knowing assistance of two companies, Scientific-Atlanta, Inc. (Scientific), and Motorola, Inc. Scientific and Motorola supplied Charter with digital cable converters—set-top boxes—that Charter's cable subscribers needed to receive cable service.

Charter entered into a fraudulent arrangement with Scientific and Motorola whereby Charter would overpay $20 for each box it purchased from Scientific and Motorola. Charter would then capitalize these payments over years rather than expense them during the current year. In addition, the parties agreed that Scientific and Motorola would repay the overpayments by purchasing advertising from Charter at higher prices than fair value. This two-part fraudulent scheme would increase Charter's revenues and profits for the year. Charter was the primary fraudulent party, and Scientific and Motorola were aiders and abettors to Charter's fraud.

Charter gave its fraudulent financial statements to its outside auditor, Arthur Andersen LLP (Andersen), to audit. During its audit of the financial statements, Andersen was fooled and did not discover Charter's fraud. Andersen certified Charter's financial statements, which Charter filed with the Securities and Exchange Commission (SEC) and made public. The fraud was discovered, and the price of Charter's stock plummeted.

Stoneridge Investment Partners, LLC, which owned stock in Charter, brought a class action civil lawsuit against Scientific and Motorola on behalf of itself and other Charter shareholders (collectively "Stoneridge"). Stoneridge relied on the ability to bring its civil action on the implied private cause of action under Section 10(b) that previous U.S. Supreme Court decisions had created. The lawsuit alleged that Scientific and Motorola—the aiders and abettors to Charter's fraud—violated Section 10(b) and Rule 10b-5 and were liable to the plaintiffs for monetary damages. The U.S. District Court dismissed Stoneridge's lawsuit. The U.S. Court of Appeals affirmed. Stoneridge appealed to the U.S. Supreme Court.

Issue

Is there an implied private civil cause of action against aiders and abettors under Section 10(b)?

Language of the U.S. Supreme Court

We conclude the implied right of action does not reach the customer/supplier companies because the investors did not rely upon their statements or representations. At most, respondents had aided and abetted Charter's misstatement of its financial results; but, there is no private right of action for aiding and abetting a Section 10(b) violation. The Section 10(b) implied private right of action does not extend to aiders and abettors.

In all events we conclude respondents' deceptive acts, which were not disclosed to the investing public, are too remote to satisfy the requirement of reliance. It was Charter, not respondents, that misled its auditor and filed fraudulent financial statements. The petitioner invokes the private cause of action under Section 10(b) and seeks to apply it beyond the securities markets—the realm of financing business—to purchase and supply contracts—the realm of ordinary business operations. The latter realm is governed, for the most part, by state law. Concerns with the judicial creation of a private cause of action caution against its expansion. The decision to extend the cause of action is for Congress, not for us. Though it remains the law, the Section 10(b) private right should not be extended beyond its present boundaries.

Decision

The U.S. Supreme Court held that there was no implied civil private right of action under Section 10(b) against aiders and abettors of securities fraud. The U.S. Supreme Court affirmed the decision of the lower court and remanded the case for further proceedings, consistent with its opinion.

Note: Although the U.S. Supreme Court held that there was no implied private cause of action under Section 10(b) against aiders and abettors (here, Scientific and Motorola), it did not disturb the implied right of plaintiffs to bring private civil actions against the primary party who commits the securities fraud (here, Charter). Therefore, Stoneridge would have an implied civil cause of action against Charter to recover monetary damages for securities fraud in violation of Section 10(b).

Under the express right of action provided in Section 10(b), the Securities Exchange Commission (SEC) can bring civil

(case continues)

cases against aiders and abettors, and the U.S. government can bring criminal charges against aiders and abettors. An injured party (here, Stoneridge) can bring a civil common law fraud action in state court against aiders and abettors (here, Scientific and Motorola) to recover monetary damages.

If an auditor (here, Andersen) aids and abets a primary party's securities fraud (here, Charter), the auditor would stand in the same shoes as other aiders and abettors (here, Scientific and Motorola) and not be civilly liable because the U.S. Supreme Court's decision in this case eliminated an implied civil right of action against aiders and abettors under Section 10(b). However, an injured party (here, Stoneridge) could bring a civil common law action in state court against an auditor (here, Andersen) for negligence for not discovering the fraud.

Case Questions

Critical Legal Thinking What is the difference between an *express* cause of action and an *implied* cause of action? Explain.

Business Ethics Did Charter act ethically in this case? Why do you think Scientific and Motorola participated in Charter's fraud?

Contemporary Business Why do you think Stoneridge sued Scientific and Motorola? Explain.

▶ SHORT-SWING PROFITS

Section 16(a) of the Securities Exchange Act of 1934 defines any person who is an executive officer, a director, or a 10 percent shareholder of an equity security of a reporting company as a **statutory insider** for Section 16 purposes. Statutory insiders must file reports with the SEC, disclosing their ownership and trading in the company's securities.[20] These reports must be filed with the SEC and made available on the company's website within two days after the trade occurs.

Section 16(b)

Section 16(b)
A section of the Securities Exchange Act of 1934 that requires that any profits made by a statutory insider on transactions involving *short-swing profits* belong to the corporation.

Section 16(b) of the Securities Exchange Act of 1934 requires that any profits made by a statutory insider on transactions involving **short-swing profits**—that is, trades involving equity securities occurring within six months of each other—belong to the corporation.[21] The corporation may bring a legal action to recover these profits. Involuntary transactions, such as forced redemption of securities by the corporation or an exchange of securities in a bankruptcy proceeding, are exempt. Section 16(b) is a strict liability provision. Generally, no defenses are recognized. Neither intent nor the possession of inside information need be shown.

SEC Section 16 Rules

He will lie sir, with such volubility that you would think truth were a tool.

William Shakespeare
All's Well That Ends Well (1604)

The SEC has adopted the following rules under Section 16:

- It clarifies the definition of **officer** to include only executive officers who perform *policy-making* functions. Officers who run day-to-day operations but are not responsible for policy decisions are not included.

Examples Policy-making executives include the chief executive officer (CEO), the president, vice presidents in charge of business units or divisions, the chief financial officer (CFO), the principal accounting officer, and the like.

- It relieves insiders of liability for transactions that occur within six months before becoming a insider.

Example If a non-insider buys shares of a company on January 15, is hired by the company and becomes an insider March 15, and sells the shares on May 15, there is no liability.

- It continues the rule that insiders are liable for transactions that occur within six months of the last transaction engaged in while an insider.

Example If an insider buys shares in his company April 30 and leaves the company May 15, he cannot sell the shares before October 30. If he does, he violates Section 16(b).

CONCEPT SUMMARY
SECTION 10(B) AND SECTION 16(B) COMPARED

Element	Section 10(b) and Rule 10b-5	Section 16(b)
Covered securities	All securities.	Securities required to be registered with the SEC under the 1934 act.
Inside information	Defendant made a misrepresentation or traded on inside (or perhaps misappropriated) information.	Short-swing profits recoverable whether or not they are attributable to misappropriation or inside information.
Recovery	Belongs to the injured purchaser or seller.	Belongs to the corporation.

▶ STATE SECURITIES LAWS

Most states have enacted securities laws. These laws generally require the registration of certain securities, provide exemptions from registration, and contain broad antifraud provisions. State securities laws are usually applied when smaller companies are issuing securities within that state. The **Uniform Securities Act** has been adopted by many states. This act coordinates **state securities laws** with federal securities laws.

State securities laws are often referred to as **"blue-sky" laws** because they help prevent investors from purchasing a piece of the blue sky. The state that has most actively enforced its securities laws has been New York. The office of the New York state attorney has brought many high-profile criminal fraud cases in recent years. The website of the Office of the New York State Attorney is **www.oag.state.ny.us/home.html.**

TEST REVIEW TERMS AND CONCEPTS

Accredited investor
Civil penalty
Condition the market
Consent order
Due diligence defense
EDGAR
Escott v. BarChris Construction Corporation
Exempt
Exempt security
Exempt transaction
Form U-7
Going public
Howey test
Injunction
Initial public offering (IPO)
Insiders
Insider trading
Insider Trading Sanctions Act

Intrastate offering exemption
Investment banker
Investment contract
Issuer
Matter of Cady, Roberts & Co.
Misappropriation theory
Nonaccredited investor
Non-issuer exemption
Offering statement
Officer
Prefiling period
Private placement exemption
Prospectus
Registration statement
Regulation A
Resale restrictions
Rule 10b-5

Rule 144
Rule 147
Rules (regulations)
Sarbanes-Oxley Act
Scienter
Section 5 of the Securities Act of 1933
Section 10(b)
Section 11 of the Securities Act of 1933
Section 12 of the Securities Act of 1933
Section 24 of the Securities Act of 1933
Section 16(a) of the Securities Exchange Act of 1934
Section 16(b) of the Securities Exchange Act of 1934

Section 32 of the Securities Exchange Act of 1934
Securities Act of 1933
Securities and Exchange Commission (SEC)
Securities Exchange Act of 1934
Security
Short-swing profits
Small Corporate Offering Registration (SCOR) form
Small offering exemption
State securities laws ("blue-sky" laws)
Statutory insider
Tippee
Tipper
Uniform Securities Act
Waiting period

CASE PROBLEMS

41.1 Definition of *Security* Dare To Be Great, Inc. (Dare), was a Florida corporation that was wholly owned by Glenn W. Turner Enterprises, Inc. Dare offered self-improvement courses aimed at improving self-motivation and sales ability. In return for an investment of money, the purchaser received certain tapes, records, and written materials. In addition, depending on the level of involvement, the purchaser had the opportunity to help sell the Dare courses to others and to receive part of the purchase price as a commission. There were four different levels of involvement.

The task of salespersons was to bring prospective purchasers to "Adventure Meetings." The meetings, which were conducted by Dare people and not the salespersons, were conducted in a preordained format that included great enthusiasm, cheering and charming, exuberant handshaking, standing on chairs, and shouting. The Dare people and the salespersons dressed in modern, expensive clothes, displayed large sums of cash, drove new expensive automobiles, and engaged in "hard-sell" tactics to induce prospects to sign their name and part with their money. In actuality, few Dare purchasers ever attained the wealth promised. The tape recordings and materials distributed by Dare were worthless. Is this sales scheme a "security" that should have been registered with the SEC? *Securities and Exchange Commission v. Glenn W. Turner Enterprises, Inc.*, 474 F.2d 476, **Web** 1973 U.S. App. Lexis 11903 (United States Court of Appeals for the Ninth Circuit)

41.2 Definition of *Security* The Farmer's Cooperative of Arkansas and Oklahoma (Co-Op) was an agricultural cooperative that had approximately 23,000 members. To raise money to support its general business operations, Co-Op sold to investors promissory notes that were payable upon demand. Co-Op offered the notes to both members and non-members, advertised the notes as an "investment program," and offered an interest rate higher than that available on savings accounts at financial institutions. More than 1,600 people purchased the notes, worth a total of $10 million. Subsequently, Co-Op filed for bankruptcy. A class of holders of the notes filed suit against Ernst & Young, a national firm of certified public accountants that had audited Co-Op's financial statements, alleging that Ernst & Young had violated Section 10(b) of the Securities Exchange Act of 1934. Are the notes issued by Co-Op "securities"? *Reeves v. Ernst & Young*, 494 U.S. 56, 110 S.Ct. 945, 108 L.Ed.2d 47, **Web** 1990 U.S. Lexis 1051 (Supreme Court of the United States)

41.3 Intrastate Offering Exemption The McDonald Investment Company was a corporation organized and incorporated in the state of Minnesota. The principal and only place of business from which the company conducted operations was located in Rush City, Minnesota. More than 80 percent of the company's assets were located in Minnesota, and more than 80 percent of its income was derived from Minnesota. McDonald sold securities to Minnesota residents only. The proceeds from the sale were used entirely to make loans and other investments in real estate and other assets located outside the state of Minnesota. The company did not file a registration statement with the SEC. Does this offering qualify for an intrastate offering exemption from registration? *Securities and Exchange Commission v. McDonald Investment Company*, 343 F.Supp. 343, **Web** 1972 U.S. Dist. Lexis 13547 (United States District Court for the District of Minnesota)

41.4 Transaction Exemption Continental Enterprises, Inc., had 2,510,000 shares of stock issued and outstanding. Louis E. Wolfson and members of his immediate family and associates owned in excess of 40 percent of those shares. The balance was in the hands of approximately 5,000 outside shareholders. Wolfson was Continental's largest shareholder and the guiding spirit of the corporation, who gave direction to and controlled the company's officers. During the course of five months, without public disclosure, Wolfson and his family and associates sold 55 percent of their stock through six brokerage houses. Wolfson and his family and associates did not file a registration statement with the SEC with respect to these sales. Do the securities sales by Wolfson and his family and associates qualify for an exemption for registration as a sale "not by an issuer, an underwriter, or a dealer"? *United States v. Wolfson*, 405 F.2d 779, **Web** 1968 U.S. App. Lexis 4342 (United States Court of Appeals for the Second Circuit)

41.5 Insider Trading Chiarella worked as a "markup man" in the New York composing room of Pandick Press, a financial printer. Among the documents that Chiarella handled were five secret announcements of corporate takeovers. The tender offerors had hired Pandick Press to print the offers, which would later be made public, when the tender offers were made to the shareholders of the target corporations. When the documents were delivered to Pandick Press, the identities of the acquiring and target corporations were concealed by blank spaces or false names. The true names would not be sent to Pandick Press until the night of the final printing.

Chiarella was able to deduce the names of the target companies before the final printing. Without disclosing this knowledge, he purchased stock in the target companies and sold the shares immediately after the takeover attempts were made public. Chiarella realized a gain of $30,000 in the course of 14 months. The federal government indicted Chiarella for criminal violations of Section 10(b) of the Securities Exchange Act of 1934. Is Chiarella guilty? *Chiarella v. United States*, 445 U.S. 222, 100 S.Ct. 1108, 63 L.Ed.2d 348, **Web** 1980 U.S. Lexis 88 (Supreme Court of the United States)

41.6 Section 10(b) Leslie Neadeau was the president of T.O.N.M. Oil & Gas Exploration Corporation (TONM). Charles Lazzaro was a registered securities broker employed by Batemen Eichler, Hill Richards, Inc. (Bateman Eichler). The stock of TONM was traded in the over-the-counter market. Lazzaro made statements to potential investors that he had "inside information" about TONM, including that (1) vast amounts of gold had been discovered in Surinam and that TONM had options on thousands of acres in the gold-producing regions of Surinam; (2) the discovery was "not publicly known, but would be subsequently announced"; and (3) when this information was made public, TONM stock, which was then selling from $1.50 to $3.00 per share, would increase to $10.00 to $15.00 within a short period of time and might increase to $100.00 per share within a year.

The potential investors contacted Neadeau at TONM, and he confirmed that the information was not public knowledge. In reliance on Lazzaro's and Neadeau's statements, the investors purchased TONM stock. The "inside information" turned out to be false, and the shares declined substantially below the purchase price. The investors sued Lazzaro, Bateman Eichler, Neadeau, and TONM, alleging violations of Section 10(b) of the Securities Exchange Act of 1934. The defendants asserted that the plaintiffs' complaint should be dismissed because they participated in the fraud. Who wins? *Bateman Eichler, Hill Richards, Inc. v. Berner*, 472 U.S. 299, 105 S.Ct. 2622, 86 L.Ed.2d 215, **Web** 1985 U.S. Lexis 95 (Supreme Court of the United States)

41.7 Insider Trading   Donald C. Hoodes was the chief executive officer of the Sullair Corporation. As an officer of the corporation, he was regularly granted stock options to purchase stock of the company at a discount. On July 20, Hoodes sold 6,000 shares of Sullair common stock for $38,350. On July 31, Sullair terminated Hoodes as an officer of the corporation. On August 20, Hoodes exercised options to purchase 6,000 shares of Sullair stock that cost Hoodes $3.01 per share ($18,060) at the time they were trading at $4.50 per share ($27,000). Hoodes did not possess material nonpublic information about Sullair when he sold or purchased the securities of the company. The corporation brought suit against Hoodes to recover the profits Hoodes made on these trades. Who wins? *Sullair Corporation v. Hoodes*, 672 F.Supp. 337, **Web** 1987 U.S. Dist. Lexis 10152 (United States District Court for the Northern District of Illinois)

BUSINESS ETHICS CASES

41.8 Business Ethics   Stephen Murphy owned Intertie, a California company that was involved in financing and managing cable television stations. Murphy was both an officer of the corporation and chairman of the board of directors. Intertie would buy a cable television station, make a small cash down payment, and finance the remainder of the purchase price. It would then create a limited partnership and sell the cable station to the partnership for a cash down payment and a promissory note in favor of Intertie. Finally, Intertie would lease the station back from the partnership. Intertie purchased more than 30 stations and created an equal number of limited partnerships, from which it received more than $7.5 million from approximately 400 investors.

Evidence showed that most of the limited partnerships were not self-supporting but that this fact was not disclosed to investors. Intertie commingled partnership funds, taking funds generated from the sale of new partnership offerings to meet debt service obligations of previously sold cable systems; Intertie also used funds from limited partnerships that were formed but that never acquired cable systems. Intertie did not keep any records regarding the qualifications of investors to purchase the securities and also refused to make its financial statements available to investors.

Intertie suffered severe financial difficulties and eventually filed for bankruptcy. The limited partners suffered substantial losses. Did each of the limited partnership offerings alone qualify for the private placement exemption from registration? Should the 30 limited partnership offerings be integrated? *Securities and Exchange Commission v. Murphy*, 626 F.2d 633, **Web** 1980 U.S. App. Lexis 15483 (United States Court of Appeals for the Ninth Circuit)

41.9 Business Ethics   R. Foster Winans, a reporter for the *Wall Street Journal*, was one of the writers of the "Heard on the Street" column, a widely read and influential column in the *Journal*. This column frequently included articles that discussed the prospects of companies listed on national and regional stock exchanges and the over-the-counter market. David Carpenter worked as a news clerk at the *Journal*. The *Journal* had a conflict-of-interest policy that prohibited employees from using nonpublic information learned on the job for their personal benefit. Winans and Carpenter were aware of this policy.

Kenneth P. Felis and Peter Brant were stockbrokers at the brokerage house of Kidder Peabody. Winans agreed to provide Felis and Brant with information that was to appear in the "Heard" column in advance of its publication in the *Journal*. Generally, Winans would provide this information to the brokers the day before it was to appear in the *Journal*. Carpenter served as a messenger between the parties. Based on this advance information, the brokers bought and sold securities of companies discussed in the "Heard" column. During 1983 and 1984, prepublication trades of approximately 27 "Heard" columns netted profits of almost $690,000. The parties used telephones to transfer information. The *Wall Street Journal* is distributed by mail to many of its subscribers.

Eventually, Kidder Peabody noticed a correlation between the "Heard" column and trading by the brokers. After an SEC investigation, criminal charges were brought against defendants Winans, Carpenter, and Felis in U.S. District Court. Brant became the government's key witness. Winans and Felis were convicted of conspiracy to commit securities, mail, and wire fraud. Carpenter was convicted of aiding and abetting the commission of securities, mail, and wire fraud. The defendants appealed their convictions. Can the defendants be held criminally liable for conspiring to violate and aiding and abetting the violation of Section 10(b) and Rule 10b-5 of securities law? Did Winans act ethically in this case? Did Brant act ethically by turning government's witness? *United States v. Carpenter*, 484 U.S. 19, 108 S.Ct. 316, 98 L.Ed.2d 275, **Web** 1987 U.S. Lexis 4815 (Supreme Court of the United States)

ENDNOTES

1. *Securities and Exchange Commission v. W. J. Howey Co.*, 328 U.S. 293, 66 S. Ct. 1100, 90 L.Ed. 1244, Web 1946 U.S. Lexis 3159 (Supreme Court of the United States).
2. Securities Act of 1933, Section 3(a)(11).
3. SEC Rule 147.
4. Securities Act of 1933, Section 4(2).
5. SEC Rule 506.
6. SEC Rule 501.
7. Securities Act of 1933, Section 3(b).
8. 15 U.S.C. Sections 77a–77aa.
9. 283 F.Supp. 643, **Web** 1968 U.S. Dist. Lexis 3853 (United States District Court for the Southern District of New York).
10. 15 U.S.C. Section 77x.
11. 15 U.S.C. Sections 78a–78mm.
12. 15 U.S.C. Section 78j(b).
13. 17 C.F.R.240.10b-5.
14. Litigation instituted pursuant to Section 10(b) and Rule 10b-5 must be commenced within one year after the discovery of the violation and within three years after such violation. *Lampf, Pleva, Lipkind, Prupis & Petigrow v. Gilbertson*, 501 U.S. 350, 111 S.Ct. 2773, 115 L.Ed.2d 321, **Web** 1991 U.S. Lexis 3629 (Supreme Court of the United States).
15. The U.S. Supreme Court has held that the sale of a business is a sale of securities that is subject to Section 10(b). *See Gould v. Ruefenacht*, 471 U.S. 701, 105 S.Ct. 2308, 85 L.Ed.2d 708, Web 1985 U.S. Lexis 21 (Supreme Court of the United States), where 50 percent of a business was sold, and *Landreth Timber Co. v. Landreth*, 471 U.S. 681, 105 S.Ct. 2297, 85 L.Ed.2d 692, Web 1985 U.S. Lexis 20 (Supreme Court of the United States), where 100 percent of a business was sold.
16. *Ernst & Ernst v. Hochfelder*, 425 U.S. 185, 96 S.Ct. 1375, 47 L.Ed.2d 668, **Web** 1976 U.S. Lexis 2 (Supreme Court of the United States).
17. 15 U.S.C. Section 78ff.
18. P.L. 98–376.
19. 40 SEC 907 (1961).
20. 15 U.S.C. Section 78l.
21. 15 U.S.C. Section 78p(b).

▲ **Hue, Vietnam** *American companies "outsource" the production of many of the goods that are sold in America (e.g., clothing, athletic shoes, toys). The reason they do so is because they can get the goods produced at a lower cost in foreign countries and then make higher profits when they sell the goods in the United States. By having their goods made in foreign countries, U.S. companies avoid the expenses of occupational safety laws that require workplaces to be safe to work in, the cost of workers' compensation laws that pay workers if they are injured on the job, fair labor standards laws that prevent child labor and require the payment of minimum wages and overtime wages, the payment of health care and pension benefits for employees, the payment of Social Security taxes, and such. Is it ethical for U.S. companies to "export" the production of their goods to foreign workers who have none of these protections?*

CHAPTER OBJECTIVES

After studying this chapter, you should be able to:

1. Describe how law and ethics intertwine.
2. Describe the moral theories of business ethics.
3. Describe the theories of the social responsibility of business.
4. Examine the provisions of the Sarbanes-Oxley Act.
5. Describe corporate social audits.

CHAPTER CONTENTS

▶ **INTRODUCTION TO ETHICS AND SOCIAL RESPONSIBILITY OF BUSINESS**

▶ **ETHICS AND THE LAW**

▶ **BUSINESS ETHICS**
  Ethics Spotlight · *Wal-Mart Pays Big for Meal Break Violations*

"Ethical considerations can no more be excluded from the administration of justice, which is the end and purpose of all civil laws, than one can exclude the vital air from his room and live."

—John F. Dillon
Laws and Jurisprudence of England and America Lecture I (1894)

▶ INTRODUCTION TO ETHICS AND SOCIAL RESPONSIBILITY OF BUSINESS

Businesses organized in the United States are subject to its laws. They are also subject to the laws of other countries in which they operate. In addition, businesspersons owe a duty to act ethically in the conduct of their affairs, and businesses owe a social responsibility not to harm society.

Although much of the law is based on ethical standards, not all ethical standards have been enacted as law. The law establishes a minimum degree of conduct expected by persons and businesses in society. Ethics demands more. This chapter discusses business ethics and the social responsibility of business.

▶ ETHICS AND THE LAW

ethics
A set of moral principles or values that governs the conduct of an individual or a group.

Ethics precede laws as man precedes society.

Jason Alexander
Philosophy for Investors (1979)

Sometimes the rule of law and the golden rule of **ethics** demand the same response by a person confronted with a problem. For example, federal and state laws make bribery unlawful. A person violates the law if he or she bribes a judge for a favorable decision in a case. Ethics would also prohibit this conduct. However, the law may permit something that would be ethically wrong.

Example Occupational safety laws set standards for emissions of dust from toxic chemicals in the workplace. Suppose a company can reduce the emission below the legal standard by spending additional money. The only benefit from the expenditure would be better employee health. Ethics would require the extra expenditure; the law would not.

Another alternative occurs where the law demands certain conduct but a person's ethical standards are contrary.

Example Federal law prohibits employers from hiring certain illegal alien workers. Suppose an employer advertises the availability of a job and receives no response except from a person who cannot prove he or she is a citizen of this country or does not possess a required visa. The worker and his or her family are destitute. Should the employer hire him or her? The law says no, but ethics says yes (see Exhibit 42.1).

▶ **Exhibit 42.1 LAW AND ETHICS**

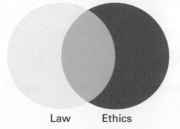

Law   Ethics

► BUSINESS ETHICS

How can ethics be measured? The answer is very personal: What is considered ethical by one person may be considered unethical by another. However, there do seem to be some universal rules about what conduct is ethical and what conduct is not. The following discussion highlights five major theories of ethics.

He who seeks equality must do equity.

Joseph Story
Equity Jurisprudence (1836)

ETHICS SPOTLIGHT

Wal-Mart Pays Big for Meal Break Violations

"At Wal-Mart, not only is there no such thing as a free lunch for employees but, in this sad case, there is no lunch at all."

—Wal-Mart Watch

In recent years, retail giant Wal-Mart has been the target of hundreds of lawsuits by employees in dozens of states, claiming the company violated wage-and-hour laws. In Colorado, Wal-Mart settled with a group of employees for $50 million because of denied meal break violations. In Oregon, workers were rewarded with nearly $2,000 each for similar violations.

A group of California Wal-Mart employees became the first in a series of class action lawsuits involving the denied meal breaks. In *Wal-Mart Stores v. S.C. (Savaglio)*, **Web** 2004 Cal. Lexis 3284 (Supreme Court of California, 2004), both current and former employees argued that Wal-Mart had violated California's meal period law. Wal-Mart fought back, saying that it didn't break any law.

The Oakland, California, jury watched four months of testimony and deliberated for three days before coming back with its verdict: 116,000 current and former Wal-Mart employees were to receive $172 million in general and punitive damages. Wal-Mart employees and community activists felt vindicated and insisted that the company fix the broken system. Wal-Mart Watch, a union-backed group that keeps a very close eye on everything the company does, commented, "At Wal-Mart, not only is there no such thing as a free lunch for employees but, in this sad case, there is no lunch at all."

Less than a year after the meal break case, Wal-Mart was in court in Pennsylvania. This time, the jury hit the company with over $78 million in damages for forcing employees to work "off the clock" and during rest breaks.

Business Ethics Did Wal-Mart act ethically in this case? Why do think Wal-Mart acted as it did in this case?

Ethical Fundamentalism

Under **ethical fundamentalism**, a person looks to an **outside source** for ethical rules or commands. This may be a book (e.g., the Bible, the Koran) or a person (e.g., Karl Marx). Critics argue that ethical fundamentalism does not permit people to determine right and wrong for themselves. Taken to an extreme, the result could be considered unethical under most other moral theories. For example, a literal interpretation of the maxim "an eye for an eye" would permit retaliation.

ethical fundamentalism
A theory of ethics that says a person looks to an outside source for ethical rules or commands.

LANDMARK LAW

The Whistleblower Statute

The Bayer Corporation (Bayer) is a U.S. subsidiary corporation of the giant German-based Bayer A.G. Bayer is a large pharmaceutical company that produces prescription drugs, including its patented antibiotic Cipro. Bayer sold Cipro to private health providers and hospitals, including Kaiser Permanente Medical Care Program, the largest health maintenance organization in the United States. Bayer also sold Cipro to the federal government's Medicaid program, which provides medical insurance to the poor. Federal law contains a "best price" rule that prohibits a company that sells a drug to Medicaid from charging

Medicaid a price higher than the lowest price for which it sells the drug to private purchasers.

Kaiser told Bayer that it would not purchase Cipro from Bayer—and would switch to a competitor's antibiotics— unless Bayer reduced the price of Cipro. Bayer's executives came up with a plan whereby Bayer would put a private label on its Cipro and not call it Cipro and sell the antibiotic to Kaiser at a 40 percent discount. Thus, Bayer continued to charge Medicaid the full price for Cipro while giving Kaiser a 40 percent discount through the private labeling program. One of Bayer's executives who negotiated this deal with Kaiser was corporate account manager George Couto.

Office of the Whistleblower Protection Program

Everything went well for Bayer until Couto attended a mandatory ethics training class at Bayer at which a video of Heige Wehmeier, then company chief executive, was shown. When the video stated that Bayer employees were to obey not only "the letter of the law but the spirit of the law as well," some of the Bayer executives laughed. Later that day, Couto attended a staff meeting at which it was disclosed that Bayer kept $97 million from Medicaid by using the discounted private labeling program for Kaiser and other health care companies. Two days later, Couto wrote a memorandum to his boss, questioning the legality of the private labeling program in light of Medicaid's "best price" law.

When he received no response to his memo, Couto contacted a lawyer. Couto filed a *qui tam* **lawsuit** under the federal **False Claims Act**—also known as the **Whistleblower Statute**—which permits private parties to sue companies for fraud on behalf of the government. The riches: The whistleblower can be awarded up to 25 percent of the amount recovered on behalf of the federal government, even if the informer has been a co-conspirator in perpetrating the fraud [31 U.S.C. Sections 3729-3733].

After the case was filed, the U.S. Department of Justice took over the case, as allowed by law, and filed criminal as well as civil charges against Bayer. After discovery was taken, Bayer pleaded guilty to one criminal felony and agreed to pay federal and state governments $257 million to settle the civil and criminal cases. Couto, age 39, died of pancreatic cancer three months prior to the settlement. Couto was awarded $34 million, which went to his three children. Did Bayer act ethically in this case? Did Couto act ethically in this case? *United States ex. rel. Estate of George Couto v. Bayer Corporation* (United States District Court for the District of Massachusetts, 2003).

Utilitarianism

utilitarianism
A moral theory that dictates that people must choose the action or follow the rule that provides the greatest good to society.

Utilitarianism is a moral theory with origins in the works of Jeremy Bentham (1748–1832) and John Stuart (1806–1873). This moral theory dictates that people must choose the actions or follow the rule that provides the **greatest good to society**. This does not mean the greatest good for the greatest number of people.

Example If an action would increase the good of 25 people by 1 unit each and an alternative action would increase the good of 1 person by 26 units, then the latter action should be taken.

Utilitarianism has been criticized because it is difficult to estimate the "good" that will result from different actions, it is hard to apply in an imperfect world, and it treats morality as if it were an impersonal mathematical calculation.

Example A company is trying to determine whether it should close an unprofitable plant located in a small community. Utilitarianism would require that the benefits to shareholders from closing the plant be compared to the benefits to employees, their families, and others in the community in keeping it open.

Kantian Ethics

Kantian ethics
A moral theory which says that people owe moral duties that are based on universal rules, such as the categorical imperative "Do unto others as you would have them do unto you." Also known as *duty ethics.*

Immanuel Kant (1724–1804) is the best-known proponent of **duty ethics**, also called **Kantian ethics**. Kant believed that people owe moral duties that are based on **universal rules**. Kant's philosophy is based on the premise that people can use reasoning to reach ethical decisions. His ethical theory would have people behave according to the *categorical imperative* "Do unto others as you would have them do unto you."

Example According to Kantian ethics, keeping a promise to abide by a contract is a moral duty even if that contract turns out to be detrimental to the obligated party.

The universal rules of Kantian ethics are based on two important principles: (1) consistency— that is, all cases are treated alike, with no exceptions—and (2) reversibility— that is, the actor must abide by the rule he or she uses to judge the morality of someone else's conduct. Thus, if you are going to make an exception for yourself, that exception becomes a universal rule that applies to all others. For example, if you rationalize that it is acceptable for you to engage in deceptive practices, it is acceptable for competitors to do so also. A criticism of Kantian ethics is that it is difficult to reach consensus as to what the universal rules should be.

In the following case, a company alleged that a competitor had engaged in false advertising.

CASE 42.1 Business Ethics

Pizza Hut, Inc. v. Papa John's International, Inc.

227 F.3d 489, Web 2000 U.S. App. Lexis 23444 (2000)
United States Court of Appeals for the Fifth Circuit

"This simple statement, 'Better Pizza.,' epitomizes the exaggerated advertising, blustering and boasting by a manufacturer upon which no consumer would reasonably rely."

—Judge Jolly

Facts

Papa John's International, Inc., is the third-largest pizza chain in the United States, with more than 2,050 locations. Papa John's adopted a new slogan—"Better Ingredients. Better Pizza."—and applied for and received a federal trademark for this slogan. Papa John's spent over $300 million building customer recognition and goodwill for this slogan. This slogan has appeared on millions of signs, shirts, menus, pizza boxes, napkins, and other items, and it has regularly appeared as the tag line at the end of Papa John's radio and television advertisements.

Pizza Hut, Inc., is the largest pizza chain in the United States, with more than 7,000 restaurants. Two years after the Papa John's advertisements began, Pizza Hut launched a new advertising campaign in which it declared "war" on poor-quality pizza. The advertisements touted the "better taste" of Pizza Hut's pizza and "dared" anyone to find a better pizza.

A few weeks later, Papa John's countered with a comparative advertising campaign that touted the superiority of Papa John's pizza over Pizza Hut's pizza. Papa John's claimed it had superior sauce and dough to Pizza Hut. Many of these advertisements were accompanied by the Papa John's slogan "Better Ingredients. Better Pizza."

Pizza Hut filed a civil action in U.S. District Court, charging Papa John's with false advertising in violation of Section 43(a) of the federal Lanham Act. The U.S. District Court found that the Papa John's slogan "Better Ingredients. Better Pizza." standing alone was mere puffery and did not constitute false advertising. The District Court found, however, that Papa John's claims of superior sauce and dough were misleading and that the Papa John's slogan "Better Ingredients. Better Pizza." became tainted because it was associated with these misleading statements. The U.S. District Court enjoined Papa John's from using the slogan "Better Ingredients. Better Pizza." Papa John's appealed.

Issue

Is the Papa John's slogan "Better Ingredients. Better Pizza." false advertising?

Language of the Court

One form of non-actionable statements of general opinion under Section 43(a) of the Lanham Act has been referred to as "puffery." Prosser and Keeton on the Law of Torts (5th edition) define "puffing" as "a seller's privilege to lie his head off, so long as he says nothing specific, on the theory that no reasonable man would believe him, or that no reasonable man would be influenced by such talk."

We turn now to consider the case before us. Reduced to its essence, the question is whether the evidence established that Papa John's slogan "Better Ingredients. Better Pizza." is misleading and violative of Section 43(a) of the Lanham Act. Bisecting the slogan "Better Ingredients. Better Pizza.," it is clear that the assertion by Papa John's that it makes a "Better Pizza." is a general statement of opinion regarding the superiority of its product over all others. Consequently, it appears indisputable that Papa John's assertion "Better Pizza." is non-actionable puffery.

Moving next to consider the phrase "Better Ingredients," the same conclusion holds true. Like "Better Pizza." it is typical puffery. Thus, it is equally clear that Papa John's assertion that it uses "Better Ingredients." is one of opinion not actionable under the Lanham Act. Consequently, the slogan as a whole is a statement of non-actionable opinion. Thus, there is no legally sufficient basis to support the jury's finding that the slogan is a "false or misleading" statement of fact.

Decision

The U.S. Court of Appeals held that the Papa John's trademarked slogan "Better Ingredients. Better Pizza." was mere puffery and a statement of opinion that was not false advertising and did not violate Section 43(a) of the Lanham Act. The U.S. Court of Appeals reversed the judgment of the U.S. District Court and remanded the case to the District Court for entry of judgment for Papa John's.

Case Questions

Critical Legal Thinking What is false advertising? What is puffery? How do they differ from one another?

Business Ethics Do businesses sometimes make exaggerated claims about their products? Are consumers smart enough to see through companies' puffery?

Contemporary Business If the Court of Appeals had found in favor of Pizza Hut, what would have been the effect on advertising in this country? Explain.

Rawls's Social Justice Theory

social contract
A moral theory that says each person is presumed to have entered into a social contract with all others in society to obey moral rules that are necessary for people to live in peace and harmony.

John Locke (1632–1704) and Jean-Jacques Rousseau (1712–1778) proposed a **social contract** theory of morality. Under this theory, each person is presumed to have entered into a social contract with all others in society to obey moral rules that are necessary for people to live in peace and harmony. This implied contract states, "I will keep the rules if everyone else does." These moral rules are then used to solve conflicting interests in society.

The leading proponent of the modern justice theory was John Rawls (1921–2002), a philosopher at Harvard University. Under **Rawls's social justice theory**, fairness is considered the essence of justice. The principles of justice should be chosen by persons who do not yet know their station in society—thus, their "veil of ignorance" would permit the fairest possible principles to be selected.

Example Under Rawls's social justice theory, the principle of equal opportunity in employment would be promulgated by people who would not yet know if they were in a favored class.

The notion that a business is clothed with a public interest and has been devoted to the public use is little more than a fiction intended to beautify what is disagreeable to the sufferers.

Justice Holmes
Tyson & Bro-United Theatre Ticket Officers v. Banton (1927)

As a caveat, Rawls also proposed that the least advantaged in society must receive special assistance in order to realize their potential. Rawls's theory of social justice is criticized for two reasons. First, establishing the blind "original position" for choosing moral principles is impossible in the real world. Second, many persons in society would choose not to maximize the benefit to the least advantaged persons in society.

Ethical Relativism

ethical relativism
A moral theory which holds that individuals must decide what is ethical based on their own feelings about what is right and wrong.

Ethical relativism holds that individuals must decide what is ethical based on their own feelings about what is right and wrong. Under this moral theory, if a person meets his or her own moral standard in making a decision, no one can criticize him or her for it. Thus, there are no universal ethical rules to guide a person's conduct. This theory has been criticized because action that is usually thought to be unethical (e.g., committing fraud) would not be unethical if the perpetrator thought it was in fact ethical. Few philosophers advocate ethical relativism as an acceptable moral theory.

CONCEPT SUMMARY
THEORIES OF ETHICS

Theory	Description
Ethical fundamentalism	Persons look to an outside source (e.g., the Bible, the Koran) or a central figure for ethical guidelines.
Utilitarianism	Persons choose the alternative that would provide the greatest good to society.
Kantian ethics	A set of universal rules establishes ethical duties. The rules are based on reasoning and require (1) consistency in application and (2) reversibility.
Rawls's social justice theory	Moral duties are based on an implied social contract. Fairness is justice. The rules are established from an original position of a "veil of ignorance."
Ethical relativism	Individuals decide what is ethical based on their own feelings as to what is right or wrong.

▶ SOCIAL RESPONSIBILITY OF BUSINESS

Businesses do not operate in a vacuum. Decisions made by businesses have far-reaching effects on society. In the past, many business decisions were based solely on a cost–benefit analysis and how they affected the "bottom line." Such decisions, however, may cause negative externalities for others. For example, the dumping of hazardous wastes from a manufacturing plant into a river affects the homeowners, farmers, and others who use the river's waters. Thus, corporations are considered to owe some degree of **social responsibility** for their actions. Four theories of the social responsibility of business are discussed in the following paragraphs.

Maximizing Profits

The traditional view of the social responsibility of business is that business should **maximize profits** for shareholders. This view, which dominated business and the law during the nineteenth century, holds that the interests of other constituencies (e.g., employees, suppliers, residents of the communities in which businesses are located) are not important in and of themselves.

Example In the famous case *Dodge v. Ford Motor Company*,[1] a shareholder sued Ford Motor Company when its founder Henry Ford introduced a plan to reduce the prices of cars so that more people would be put to work and more people could own cars. The shareholders alleged that such a plan would not increase dividends. Mr. Ford testified, "My ambition is to employ still more men, to spread the benefits of this industrial system to the greatest number, to help them build up their lives and their homes." The court sided with the shareholders and stated that:

> [Mr. Ford's] *testimony creates the impression that he thinks the Ford Motor company has made too much money, has had too large profits and that, although large profits might still be earned, a sharing of them with the public, by reducing the price of the output of the company, ought to be undertaken.*
>
> *There should be no confusion of the duties which Mr. Ford conceives that he and the stockholders owe to the general public and the duties which in law he and his codirectors owe to protesting, minority stockholders. A business corporation is organized and carried on primarily for the profit of the stockholders. The powers of the directors are to be employed for that end. The discretion of directors is to be exercised in the choice of means to attain that end and does not extend to a change in the end itself, to the reduction of profits, or to the nondistribution of profits among stockholders in order to devote them to other purposes.*

Milton Friedman, who won the Nobel Prize in economics when he taught at the University of Chicago, advocated the theory of maximizing profits for shareholders. Friedman asserted that in a free society, "there is one and only one social responsibility of business—to use its resources and engage in activities designed to increase its profits as long as it stays within the rules of the game, which is to say, engages in open and free competition without deception and fraud."[2]

In the following case, Wal-Mart was accused of unlawfully knocking off another company's product design.

The ultimate justification of the law is to be found, and can only be found, in moral considerations.

Lord MacMillan
Law and Other Things (1937)

maximizing profits
A theory of social responsibility that says a corporation owes a duty to take actions that maximize profits for shareholders.

Public policy: That principle of the law which holds that no subject can lawfully do that which has a tendency to be injurious to the public or against the public good.

Lord Truro
Egerton v. Brownlow (1853)

U.S. SUPREME COURT   CASE 42.2 Business Ethics

Wal-Mart Stores, Inc. v. Samara Brothers, Inc.

529 U.S. 205, 120 S.Ct. 1339, 146 L.Ed.2d 182, Web 2000 U.S. Lexis 2197 (2000)
Supreme Court of the United States

"Their suspicions aroused, however, Samara officials launched an investigation, which disclosed that Wal-Mart [was] selling the knockoffs of Samara's outfits."

—Justice Scalia

Facts

Samara Brothers, Inc. (Samara), is a designer and manufacturer of children's clothing. The core of Samara's business is its annual new line of spring and summer children's garments. Samara sold its clothing to retailers, who in turn sold the clothes to consumers. Wal-Mart Stores, Inc. (Wal-Mart), operates a large chain of budget warehouse stores that sell thousands of items at very low prices. Wal-Mart contacted one of its suppliers, Judy-Philippine, Inc. (JPI), about the possibility of making a line of children's clothes just like Samara's successful line. Wal-Mart sent photographs of Samara's children's clothes to JPI (the name "Samara" was readily discernible on the labels of the garments) and directed JPI to produce children's clothes exactly like those in the photographs. JPI produced a line of children's clothes for Wal-Mart that copied the designs, colors, and patterns of Samara's clothing. Wal-Mart then sold this line of children's clothing in its stores, making a gross profit of over $1.15 million on these clothes sales during the 1996 selling season.

(case continues)

Samara discovered that Wal-Mart was selling the knockoff clothes at a price that was lower than Samara's retailers were paying Samara for its clothes. After sending unsuccessful cease-and-desist letters to Wal-Mart, Samara sued Wal-Mart, alleging that Wal-Mart stole Samara's trade dress (i.e., look and feel) in violation of Section 43(a) of the Lanham Act. Although not finding that Samara's clothes had acquired a secondary meaning in the minds of the public, the U.S. District Court held in favor of Samara and awarded damages. The U.S. Court of Appeals affirmed the award to Samara. Wal-Mart appealed to the U.S. Supreme Court.

Issue

Must a product's design have acquired a secondary meaning before it is protected as trade dress?

Language of the U.S. Supreme Court

The Lanham Act, in Section 43(a), gives a producer a cause of action for the use by any person of "any word, term, name, symbol, or device, or any combination thereof which is likely to cause confusion as to the origin, sponsorship, or approval of his or her goods." The text of Section 43(a) provides little guidance as to the circumstances under which unregistered trade dress may be protected. It
does require that a producer show that the allegedly infringing feature is likely to cause confusion with the product for which protection is sought. In an action for infringement of unregistered trade dress a product's design is protectable only upon a showing of secondary meaning.

Decision

The U.S. Supreme Court held that a product's design has to have acquired a secondary meaning in the public's eye before it is protected as trade dress under Section 43(a) of the Lanham Act. The Supreme Court reversed the decision of the U.S. Court of Appeals and remanded the case for further proceedings consistent with its opinion.

Case Questions

Critical Legal Thinking What is trade dress? Should it have been protected in this case?

Business Ethics Even if Wal-Mart's conduct was ruled legal, was it ethical?

Contemporary Business What can companies like Samara do to protect themselves from similar conduct by Wal-Mart or other larger companies? Explain.

Moral Minimum

moral minimum
A theory of social responsibility that says a corporation's duty is to make a profit while avoiding causing harm to others.

Some proponents of corporate social responsibility argue that a corporation's duty is to **make a profit while avoiding causing harm to others**. This theory of social responsibility is called the **moral minimum**. Under this theory, as long as business avoids or corrects the social injury it causes, it has met its duty of social responsibility.

Example A corporation that pollutes the waters and then compensates those whom it injures has met its moral minimum duty of social responsibility.

The legislative and judicial branches of government have established laws that enforce the moral minimum of social responsibility on corporations.

Examples Occupational safety laws establish minimum safety standards for protecting employees from injuries in the workplace. Consumer protection laws establish safety requirements for products and make manufacturers and sellers liable for injuries caused by defective products.

LANDMARK LAW

Sarbanes-Oxley Act Prompts Public Companies to Adopt Codes of Ethics

In the late 1990s and early 2000s, many large corporations in the United States were found to have engaged in massive financial frauds. Many of these frauds were perpetrated by the chief executive officers and other senior officers of the companies. Financial officers, such as chief financial officers and controllers, were also found to have been instrumental in committing these frauds. In response, Congress enacted the **Sarbanes-Oxley Act** of 2002, which makes certain conduct illegal and establishes criminal penalties for violations. In addition, the Sarbanes-Oxley Act prompts companies to encourage senior officers

of public companies to act ethically in their dealings with shareholders, employees, and other constituents.

Section 406 of the Sarbanes-Oxley Act requires a public company to disclose whether it has adopted a **code of ethics** for senior financial officers, including its principal financial officer and principal accounting officer. In response, public companies have adopted codes of ethics for their senior financial officers. Many public companies have included all officers and employees in the coverage of their codes of ethics.

A typical code of ethics is illustrated in Exhibit 42.2.

Big Cheese Corporation
Code of Ethics

Big Cheese Corporation's mission includes the promotion of professional conduct in the practice of general management worldwide. Big Cheese's Chief Executive Officer (CEO), Chief Financial Officer (CFO), corporate Controller, and other employees of the finance organization and other employees of the corporation hold an important and elevated role in the corporate governance of the corporation. They are empowered and uniquely capable to ensure that all constituents' interests are appropriately balanced, protected, and preserved.

This Code of Ethics embodies principles to which we are expected to adhere and advocate. The CEO, CFO, finance organization employees, and other employees of the corporation are expected to abide by this Code of Ethics and all business conduct standards of the corporation relating to areas covered by this Code of Ethics. Any violation of the Code of Ethics may result in disciplinary action, up to and including termination of employment. All employees will:

- Act with honesty and integrity, avoiding actual or apparent conflicts of interest in their personal and professional relations.
- Provide stakeholders with information that is accurate, fair, complete, timely, objective, relevant, and understandable, including in our filings with and other submissions to the U.S. Securities and Exchange Commission.
- Comply with rules and regulations of federal, state, provincial, and local governments and other appropriate private and public regulatory agencies.
- Act in good faith, responsibly, with due care, competence, and diligence, without misrepresenting material facts or allowing one's independent judgment to be subordinated.
- Respect the confidentiality of information acquired in the course of one's work, except when authorized or otherwise legally obligated to disclose. Confidential information acquired in the course of one's work will not be used for personal advantage.
- Share knowledge and maintain professional skills important and relevant to stakeholders' needs.
- Proactively promote and be an example of ethical behavior as a responsible partner among peers, in the work environment and the community.
- Achieve responsible use, control, and stewardship over all Big Cheese's assets and resources that are employed or entrusted to us.
- Not unduly or fraudulently influence, coerce, manipulate, or mislead any authorized audit or interfere with any auditor engaged in the performance of an internal or independent audit of Big Cheese's financial statements or accounting books and records.

If you are aware of any suspected or known violations of this Code of Ethics or other Big Cheese policies or guidelines, you have a duty to promptly report such concerns either to your manager, another responsible member of management, a Human Resources representative, or the Director of Compliance or the 24-hour Business Conduct Line.

If you have a concern about a questionable accounting or auditing matter and wish to submit the concern confidentially or anonymously, you may do so by sending an e-mail to (bc.codeofethics@bigcheese.cc) or calling the Business Conduct Line 24-hour number at 1-888-666-BIGC (2442).

Big Cheese will handle all inquiries discreetly and make every effort to maintain, within the limits allowed by law, the confidentiality of anyone requesting guidance or reporting questionable behavior and/or a compliance concern.

It is Big Cheese's intention that this Code of Ethics to be its written code of ethics under Section 406 of the Sarbanes-Oxley Act of 2002 complying with the standards set forth in Securities and Exchange Commission Regulation S-K Item 406.

▶ **Exhibit 42.2 CODE OF ETHICS**

Stakeholder Interest

Businesses have relationships with all sorts of people besides their shareholders, including employees, suppliers, customers, creditors, and the local community. Under the **stakeholder interest** theory of social responsibility, a corporation must consider the effects its actions have on these *other stakeholders*. For example, a corporation would violate the stakeholder interest theory if it viewed employees solely as a means of maximizing shareholder wealth.

The stakeholder interest theory is criticized because it is difficult to harmonize the conflicting interests of stakeholders.

Example In deciding to close an unprofitable manufacturing plant, certain stakeholders would benefit (e.g., shareholders and creditors), while other stakeholders would not (e.g., current employees and the local community).

stakeholder interest
A theory of social responsibility that says a corporation must consider the effects its actions have on persons other than its shareholders.

Corporate Citizenship

The **corporate citizenship** theory of social responsibility argues that business has a responsibility to do well. That is, business is responsible for helping to solve social problems that it did little, if anything, to cause.

corporate citizenship
A theory of responsibility that says a business has a responsibility to do good.

In civilized life, law floats in a sea of ethics.

Earl Warren

Example Under corporate citizenship theory of social responsibility, corporations owe a duty to subsidize schools and help educate children.

This theory contends that corporations owe a duty to promote the same social goals as individual members of society. Proponents of this "do good" theory argue that corporations owe a debt to society to make it a better place and that this duty arises because of the social power bestowed on them. That is, this social power is a gift from society and should be used to good ends.

A major criticism of this theory is that the duty of a corporation to do good cannot be expanded beyond certain limits. There is always some social problem that needs to be addressed, and corporate funds are limited. Further, if this theory were taken to its maximum limit, potential shareholders might be reluctant to invest in corporations.

CONCEPT SUMMARY

THEORIES OF SOCIAL RESPONSIBILITY

Theory	Social Responsibility
Maximizing profits	To maximize profits for stockholders.
Moral minimum	To avoid causing harm and to compensate for harm caused.
Stakeholder interest	To consider the interests of all stakeholders, including stockholders, employees, customers, suppliers, creditors, and the local community.
Corporate citizenship	To do well and solve social problems.

CONTEMPORARY ENVIRONMENT

The Corporate Social Audit

It has been suggested that corporate audits should be extended to include not only audits of the financial health of a corporation but also of its moral health. It is expected that corporations that conduct **corporate social audits** would be more apt to prevent unethical and illegal conduct by managers, employees, and agents. The audit would examine how well employees have adhered to the company's code of ethics and how well the corporation has met its duty of social responsibility.

Such audits would focus on the corporation's efforts to promote employment opportunities for members of protected classes, worker safety, environmental protection, consumer protection, and the like. Social audits are not easy. First, it may be difficult to conceptualize just what is being audited. Second, it may be difficult to measure results. Despite these factors, a growing number of companies are expected to undertake social audits.

Companies should institute the following procedures when conducting a social audit:

- An independent outside firm should be hired to conduct the audit. This ensures autonomy and objectivity in conducting the audit.
- The company's personnel should cooperate fully with the auditing firm while the audit is being conducted.
- The auditing firm should report its findings directly to the company's board of directors.
- The board of directors should review the results of the audit. The board of directors should determine how the company can better meet its duty of social responsibility and can use the audit to implement a program to correct any deficiencies it finds.

TEST REVIEW TERMS AND CONCEPTS

Code of ethics	Greatest good to society	*Qui tam* lawsuit	Stakeholder interest
Corporate citizenship	Kantian ethics (duty ethics)	Rawls's social justice theory	Universal rules
Corporate social audit			Utilitarianism
Ethical fundamentalism	Maximizing profits	Sarbanes-Oxley Act	
Ethical relativism	Moral minimum (make a profit while avoiding causing harm to others)	Section 406	
Ethics		Social contract	
False Claims Act (Whistleblower Statute)		Social responsibility of business	
	Outside source		

CASE PROBLEMS

42.1 Fraud   The Warner-Lambert Company has manufactured and distributed Listerine antiseptic mouthwash since 1879. Its formula has never changed. Ever since Listerine's introduction, the company has represented the product as being beneficial in preventing and curing colds and sore throats. Direct advertising of these claims to consumers began in 1921. Warner-Lambert spent millions of dollars annually advertising these claims in print media and in television commercials.

After 100 years of Warner-Lambert's making such claims, the Federal Trade Commission (FTC) filed a complaint against the company, alleging that it had engaged in false advertising in violation of federal law. Four months of hearings were held before an administrative law judge that produced an evidentiary record of more than 4,000 pages of documents from 46 witnesses. After examining the evidence, the FTC issued an opinion which held that the company's representations that Listerine prevented and cured colds and sore throats were false. The U.S. Court of Appeals affirmed. Is Warner-Lambert guilty of fraud? If so, what remedies should the court impose on the company? Did Warner-Lambert act ethically in making its claims for Listerine? *Warner-Lambert Company v. Federal Trade Commission*, 183 U.S. App. D.C. 230, 562 F.2d 749, **Web** 1977 U.S. App. Lexis 11599 (United States Court of Appeals for the District of Columbia Circuit)

42.2 Liability   The Johns-Manville Corporation was a profitable company that made a variety of building and other products. It was a major producer of asbestos, which was used for insulation in buildings and for a variety of other uses. It has been medically proven that excessive exposure to asbestos causes asbestosis, a fatal lung disease. Thousands of employees of the company and consumers who were exposed to asbestos and contracted this fatal disease sued the company for damages. Eventually, the lawsuits were being filed at a rate of more than 400 per week.

In response to the claims, Johns-Manville Corporation filed for reorganization bankruptcy. It argued that if it did not, an otherwise viable company that provided thousands of jobs and served a useful purpose in this country would be destroyed and that without the declaration of bankruptcy, a few of the plaintiffs who first filed their lawsuits would win awards of hundreds of millions of dollars, leaving nothing for the remainder of the plaintiffs. Under the bankruptcy court's protection, the company was restructured to survive. As part of the release from bankruptcy, the company contributed money to a fund to pay current and future claimants. The fund was not large enough to pay all injured persons the full amounts of their claims.

Is Johns-Manville liable for negligence? Was it ethical for Johns-Manville to declare bankruptcy? Did it meet its duty of social responsibility in this case? *In re Johns-Mansville Corporation*, 36 B.R. 727, **Web** 1984 Bankr. Lexis 6384 (United States Bankruptcy Court for the Southern District of New York)

BUSINESS ETHICS CASES

42.3 Fraud   The Reverend Leon H. Sullivan, a Baptist minister from Philadelphia who was also a member of the board of directors of General Motors Corporation, proposed a set of rules to guide American-owned companies doing business in the Republic of South Africa. The *Sullivan Principles*, as they became known, call for the nonsegregation of races in South Africa. They call for employers to (a) provide equal and fair employment practices for all employees and (b) improve the quality of employees' lives outside the work environment in such areas as housing, education, transportation, recreation, and health facilities. The principles also require signatory companies to report regularly and to be graded on their conduct in South Africa.

Eventually, the Sullivan Principles were subscribed to by several hundred U.S. corporations with affiliates doing business in South Africa. Which of the following theories of social responsibility are the companies that subscribed to the Sullivan Principles following?

1. Maximizing profits
2. Moral minimum
3. Stakeholder interest
4. Corporate citizenship

To put additional pressure on the government of the Republic of South Africa to end apartheid, Reverend Sullivan called for the complete withdrawal of all U.S. companies from doing business in or with South Africa. Very few companies agreed to do so. Do companies owe a social duty to withdraw from South Africa? Should universities divest themselves of investments in companies that do not withdraw from South Africa?

42.4 Business Ethics   Kaiser Aluminum & Chemical Corporation entered into a collective bargaining agreement with the United Steelworkers of America, a union that represented employees at Kaiser's plants. The agreement contained an affirmative-action program to increase the representation of minorities in craft jobs. To enable plants to meet these goals, on-the-job training programs were established to teach unskilled production workers the skills necessary to become craft workers. Assignment to the training program was based on seniority, except that the plan reserved 50 percent of the openings for black employees.

Thirteen craft trainees were selected from Kaiser's Gramercy plant for the training program. Of these, 7 were black and 6 white. The most senior black trainee selected had less seniority than several white production workers who had applied for the positions but were rejected. Brian Weber, one of the white rejected employees, instituted a class action lawsuit, alleging that the affirmative action plan violated Title VII of the Civil Rights Act of 1964, which made it "unlawful to discriminate because of race" in hiring and selecting apprentices for training programs. The U.S. Supreme Court upheld the affirmative-action plan in this case. The decision stated:

> *We therefore hold that Title VII's prohibition against racial discrimination does not condemn all private, voluntary, race-conscious affirmative action plans. At the same time, the plant does not unnecessarily trammel the interests of the white employees. Moreover, the plan is a temporary measure; it is not intended to maintain racial balance, but simply to eliminate a manifest racial imbalance.*

Do companies owe a duty of social responsibility to provide affirmative-action programs? *United Steelworkers of America v. Weber*, 443 U.S. 193, 99 S.Ct. 2721, 61 L.Ed.2d 480, **Web** 1979 U.S. Lexis 40 (Supreme Court of the United States)

42.5 Business Ethics   Iroquois Brands, Ltd., a Delaware corporation, had $78 million in assets, $141 million in sales, and $6 million in profits. As part of its business, Iroquois imported pâté de foie gras (goose pâté) from France and sold it in the United States. Iroquois derived only $79,000 in revenues from sales of such pâté. The French force-fed the geese from which the pâté was made. Peter C. Lovenheim, who owned 200 shares of Iroquois common stock, proposed to include a shareholder proposal in Iroquois's annual proxy materials to be sent to shareholders. His proposal criticized the company because the force-feeding caused "undue stress, pain and suffering" to the geese and requested that shareholders vote to have Iroquois discontinue importing and selling pâté produced by this method.

Iroquois refused to allow the information to be included in its proxy materials. Iroquois asserted that its refusal was based on the fact that Lovenheim's proposal was "not economically significant" and had only "ethical and social" significance. The company reasoned that because a corporation is an economic entity, only an economic test applied to its activities, and Iroquois was therefore not subject to an ethical or a social responsibility test. Is Iroquois correct? That is, should only an economic test be applied in judging the activities of a corporation? Or should a corporation also be subject to an ethical or a social responsibility test? *Lovenheim v. Iroquois Brands, Ltd.*, 618 F.Supp. 554, **Web** 1985 U.S. Dist. Lexis 21259 (United States District Court for the District of Columbia)

ENDNOTES

1. 204 Mich. 459, 170 N.W. 668, Web 1919 Mich. Lexis 720 (Supreme Court of Michigan).

2. Milton Friedman, "The Social Responsibility of Business Is to Increase Its Profits," *New York Times Magazine*, September 13, 1970.

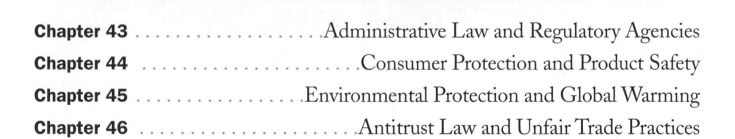

Part IX

GOVERNMENT

REGULATION

43 | ADMINISTRATIVE LAW AND REGULATORY AGENCIES

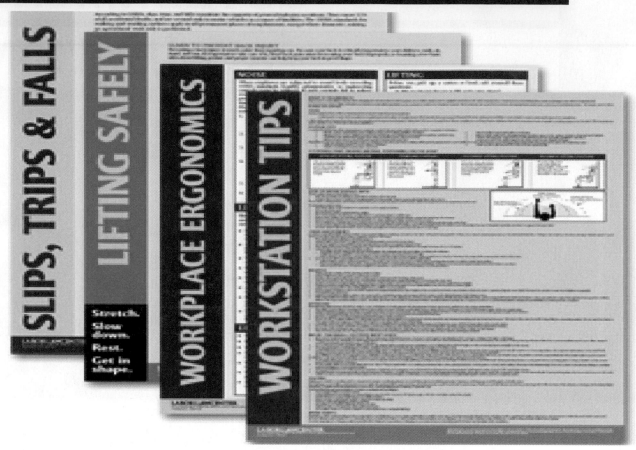

▲ **OSHA Poster** *The Occupational Safety and Health Administration (OSHA) is an agency of the U.S. Department of Labor. It is one of many government agencies that regulate businesses and industries.*

CHAPTER OBJECTIVES

After studying this chapter, you should be able to:

1. Describe the types of government regulation of business.
2. Define *administrative law*.
3. List and explain the functions of administrative agencies.

4. Describe the provisions of the Administrative Procedure Act.
5. Explain the procedure for judicial review of administrative agency decision.

CHAPTER CONTENTS

"Good government is an empire of laws."

—John Adams
Thoughts on Government (1776)

▶ INTRODUCTION TO ADMINISTRATIVE LAW AND REGULATORY AGENCIES

Federal and state governments enact laws that regulate business. The legislative and executive branches of government have created numerous administrative agencies to assist in implementing and enforcing these laws. The operation of these administrative agencies is governed by a body of *administrative law*. Because of their importance, administrative agencies are informally referred to as the "fourth branch of government."

This chapter examines administrative agencies and administrative law.

▶ SOURCES OF ADMINISTRATIVE AGENCIES

Administrative agencies are created by federal, state, and local governments. They range from large, complex federal agencies, such as the federal Department of Health and Human Services, to local zoning boards. At the federal government level, the **legislative branch (Congress)** and the **executive branch (the president)** have created more than 100 administrative agencies. Thousands of other administrative agencies have been created by state and local governments.

When Congress enacts a statute, it often creates an administrative agency to administer and enforce the statute (see Exhibit 43.1). When Congress enacts some statutes, it authorizes an existing administrative agency to administer and enforce the new statute.

administrative agencies
Agencies that the legislative and executive branches of federal and state governments establish.

▶ **Exhibit 43.1**
ADMINISTRATIVE AGENCY

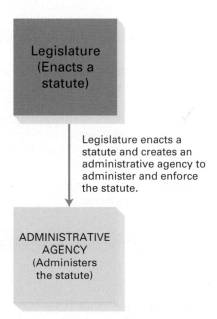

Legislature
(Enacts a statute)

Legislature enacts a statute and creates an administrative agency to administer and enforce the statute.

ADMINISTRATIVE AGENCY
(Administers the statute)

Example When Congress enacted the Securities Act of 1933 and the Securities Exchange Act of 1934, it created the Securities and Exchange Commission (SEC), a federal administrative agency, to administer and enforce those statutes.

General Government Regulation

Many administrative agencies, and the laws they enforce, regulate businesses and industries collectively. That is, most of the industries and businesses in the United States are subject to these laws.

Examples The federal National Labor Relations Board (NLRB) is empowered to regulate the formation and operation of labor unions in most industries and businesses in the United States. The federal Occupational Health and Safety Administration (OSHA) is authorized to formulate and enact workplace safety and health standards for most industries and businesses in the country. And the Consumer Product Safety Commission (CPSC) is empowered to establish mandatory safety standards for products sold in this country.

Specific Government Regulation

Some administrative agencies, and the laws they enforce, are created to regulate specific industries. That is, an industry is subject to administrative laws that are specifically adopted to regulate that industry. Administrative agencies, which are industry specific, are created to administer these specific laws.

Examples The Federal Communications Commission (FCC) issues licenses and regulates the operation of television and radio stations. The Federal Aviation Administration (FAA) regulates the operation of commercial airlines. And the federal Office of the Comptroller of the Currency (OCC) regulates licensing and operation of national banks.

CONCEPT SUMMARY

GOVERNMENT REGULATION OF BUSINESS

Type of Regulation	Description
General government regulation	Government regulation that applies to many industries (e.g., antidiscrimination laws).
Specific government regulation	Government regulation that applies to a specific industry (e.g., banking laws).

► FEDERAL ADMINISTRATIVE AGENCIES

federal administrative agencies
Administrative agencies that are created by the executive or legislative branch of federal government.

Federal administrative agencies can be created by either the *legislative* or the *executive* branch of the federal government. Congress has established many federal administrative agencies. These agencies have broad regulatory powers over key areas of the national economy. Examples are the Securities and Exchange Commission (SEC), which regulates the issuance and trading in securities, and the Commodity Futures Trading Commission (CFTC), which regulates trading in commodities futures contracts.

Other federal administrative agencies are created by the president of the United States to operate the federal government. Examples are the U.S. Department of Justice, the Labor Department, and the Commerce Department.

LANDMARK LAW

Homeland Security Act of 2002

On September 11, 2001, the World Trade Center buildings in New York City were destroyed and the Pentagon in Washington, DC, was damaged by terrorist attacks. After the attacks, President George W. Bush issued an executive order to create the Office of Homeland Security. The president called for the office to be made into a cabinet-level agency. Congress responded by enacting the **Homeland Security Act (HSA)** of 2002, which created the cabinet-level **Department of Homeland Security (DHS)** [Public Law No. 107-296, 116 Stat. 2135]. The creation of the DHS was the largest government reorganization in over 50 years.

The act placed 22 existing federal agencies with more than 180,000 employees under the umbrella of the DHS. The DHS is the second largest government agency, after the Department of Defense. The DHS contains the Bureau of Customs and Border Protection, the Bureau of Citizenship and Immigration Services, the U.S. Secret Service, the Federal Emergency Management Agency, the Federal Computer Incident Response Center, the National Domestic Preparedness Office, the U.S. Coast Guard, and portions of the Federal Bureau of Investigation, Treasury Department, Commerce Department, Justice Department, and other federal government agencies.

The mission of the DHS is to prevent domestic terrorist attacks, reduce vulnerability to terrorist attacks, minimize the harm caused by such attacks, and assist in the recovery in the event of a terrorist attack. The DHS provides services in the following critical areas: (1) border and transportation security, including protecting airports, seaports, and borders and providing immigration and visa processing; (2) chemical, biological, radiological, and nuclear countermeasures, including metering the air for biological agents and developing vaccines and treatments for biological agents; (3) information analysis and infrastructure protection, including protecting communications systems, power grids, transportation networks, telecommunications, and cyber systems; and (4) emergency preparedness and response to terrorist incidents, including training first responders and coordinating government disaster relief.

▶ STATE ADMINISTRATIVE AGENCIES

All states have created administrative agencies to enforce and interpret state law. **State administrative agencies** have a profound effect on business. State administrative agencies are empowered to enforce state statutes. They have the power to adopt rules and regulations to interpret the statutes they are empowered to administer.

state administrative agencies
Administrative agencies that states create to enforce and interpret state law.

Examples Most states have corporation departments to enforce state corporation law and regulate the issuance of securities, banking departments to license and regulate the operation of banks, fish and game departments to regulate fishing and hunting within the state's boundaries, workers' compensation boards to decide workers' compensation claims for injuries that occur on the job, and environmental protection departments to regulate the land, waterways, and other environmental issues.

Local governments and municipalities create administrative agencies to administer local law.

▶ ADMINISTRATIVE LAW

Administrative law is a combination of *substantive* and *procedural law*. **Substantive law** is law that an administrative agency enforces—federal statutes enacted by Congress or state statutes enacted by state legislatures. **Procedural law** establishes the procedures that must be followed by an administrative agency while enforcing substantive laws.

administrative law
A combination of substantive and procedural law.

Examples The federal Environmental Protection Agency (EPA) was created by Congress to enforce federal environmental laws that protect the environment. This is an example of substantive law—laws to protect the environment. In enforcing these laws, the EPA must follow certain established procedural rules (e.g., notice, hearing). These are examples of procedural law.

LANDMARK LAW
Administrative Procedure Act

In 1946, Congress enacted the **Administrative Procedure Act (APA)**.[1] This act is very important because it establishes procedures that federal administrative agencies must follow in conducting their affairs. The APA establishes notice requirements of actions the federal agency plans on taking. It requires hearings to be held in most cases, and it requires certain procedural safeguards and protocols to be followed at these proceedings. The APA also establishes how rules and regulations can be adopted by federal administrative agencies. This includes providing notice of proposed rule making, granting a time period for receiving comments from the public regarding proposed rule making, and holding hearings to take evidence. The APA provides a procedure for receiving evidence and hearing requests for the granting of federal licenses (e.g., to operate a national bank). The APA also establishes notice and hearing requirements and rules for conducting agency adjudicative actions, such as actions to take away certain parties' licenses (e.g., a securities broker's licenses).

Most states have enacted administrative procedural acts that govern state administrative procedures.

Administrative Procedure Act (APA)
A federal act that establishes certain administrative procedures that federal administrative agencies must follow in conducting their affairs.

administrative law judge (ALJ)
A judge who presides over administrative proceedings and decides questions of law and fact concerning a case.

order
A decision issued by an administrative law judge.

delegation doctrine
A doctrine that says when an administrative agency is created, it is delegated certain powers; the agency can use only those legislative, judicial, and executive powers that are delegated to it.

substantive rule
A rule issued by an administrative agency that has the force of law and to which covered persons and businesses must adhere.

Administrative Law Judge

Administrative law judges (ALJs) preside over administrative proceedings. They decide questions of law and fact concerning a case. An ALJ is an employee of an administrative agency. Both the administrative agency and the respondent may be represented by counsel. Witnesses may be examined and cross-examined, evidence may be introduced, objections may be made, and such. There is no jury.

An ALJ's decision is issued in the form of an **order**. The order must state the reasons for the ALJ's decision. The order becomes final if it is not appealed. An appeal consists of a review by the agency. Further appeal can be made to the appropriate federal court (in federal agency actions) or state court (in state agency actions).

Delegation of Powers

When an administrative agency is created, it is delegated certain powers. The agency has only the legislative, judicial, and executive powers that are delegated to it. This is called the **delegation doctrine**. Thus, an agency can adopt a rule or regulation (a legislative function), prosecute a violation of the statute or rule (an executive function), and adjudicate the dispute (a judicial function). The courts have upheld this combined power of administrative agencies as being constitutional. If an administrative agency acts outside the scope of its delegated powers, it is an unconstitutional act.

Administrative agencies have been delegated legislative powers that consist of substantive rule making, interpretative rule making, issue of statements of policy, and granting of licenses. Administrative agencies have also been delegated certain executive powers and judicial powers. Legislative, executive and judicial powers are discussed in the following paragraphs.

Rule Making   Many federal statutes expressly authorize an administrative agency to issue **substantive rules**. A substantive regulation is much like a statute: It has the force of law, and covered persons and businesses must adhere to it. Violators may be held civilly or criminally liable, depending on the rule. All substantive rules are subject to judicial review.

A federal administrative agency that proposes to adopt a substantive rule must follow procedures set forth in the APA.[2] This means the agency must do the following:

1. Publish a general notice of the proposed rule making in the *Federal Register*. The notice must include:
   a. The time, place, and nature of the rule-making proceeding.
   b. The legal authority pursuant to which the rule is proposed.
   c. The terms or substance of the proposed rule or a description of the subject and issues involved.
2. Give interested persons an opportunity to participate in the rule-making process. This may involve oral hearings.

3. Review all written and oral comments. Then the agency announces its *final rule making* in the matter. This procedure is often referred to as *notice-and-comment rule making*, or *informal rule making*.
4. Require, in some instances, *formal rule making*. Here, the agency must conduct a trial-like hearing at which the parties may present evidence, engage in cross-examination, present rebuttal evidence, and such.

Administrative agencies can issue an **interpretive rule** that interprets existing statutory language. Such rules do not establish new laws. Neither public notice nor public participation is required. Administrative agencies may issue a **statement of policy**. Such a statement announces a proposed course of action that an agency intends to follow in the future. Statements of policy do not have the force of law. Again, public notice and participation are not required.

In the following case, the U.S. Supreme Court determined the lawfulness of an administrative agency's rule.

interpretive rule
A rule issued by an administrative agency that interprets existing statutory language.

statement of policy
A statement issued by an administrative agency that announces a proposed course of action that the agency intends to follow in the future.

CASE 43.1 U.S. SUPREME COURT Regulation of a Drug

Food and Drug Administration v. Brown & Williamson Tobacco Corporation

529 U.S. 120, 20 S.Ct. 1291, 146 L.Ed.2d 121, Web 2000 U.S. Lexis 2195 (2000)
Supreme Court of the United States

"The agency has amply demonstrated that tobacco use, particularly among children and adolescents, poses perhaps the single most significant threat to public health in the United States."

—Justice O'Connor

Facts

The Food and Drug Administration (FDA) is a federal administrative agency empowered to administer the Food, Drug, and Cosmetic Act (FDC Act) [21 U.S.C. Sections 301-397]. Pursuant to this act, the FDA can regulate "drugs" and medical "devices." Based on its perceived power under the FDC Act, the FDA enacted a rule regulating tobacco products. The rule:

1. Prohibits the sale of cigarettes and smokeless tobacco to persons younger than 18.
2. Requires retailers to verify through photo identification the age of all purchasers younger than 27.
3. Prohibits the sale of cigarettes in quantities smaller than 20.
4. Prohibits the distribution of free samples.
5. Prohibits sales through self-service displays and vending machines except in adult-only locations.
6. Requires that print advertising appear in black-and-white, text-only format.
7. Prohibits outdoor advertising within 1,000 feet of any public school or playground.
8. Prohibits the distribution of any promotional items, such as t-shirts or hats, bearing the manufacturer's brand.

9. Prohibits a manufacturer from sponsoring any athletic, musical, artistic, or other social or cultural event using its brand name.
10. Requires that the statement "A Nicotine-Delivery Device for Persons 18 or Older" appear on all tobacco products.

A group of tobacco manufacturers and advertisers filed a lawsuit in U.S. District Court, asserting that the FDA did not have authority to regulate tobacco as a "drug" or "device" that delivered nicotine to the body. The District Court certified the issue to the Court of Appeals, which held that the FDC Act did not grant the FDA power to regulate tobacco products. The plaintiffs appealed to the U.S. Supreme Court.

Issue

Did the Food, Drug, and Cosmetic Act grant the Food and Drug Administration authority to regulate tobacco products as a "drug" or "device"?

Language of the U.S. Supreme Court

Regardless of how serious the problem an administrative agency seeks to address, however, it may not exercise its authority in a manner that is inconsistent with the administrative structure that Congress enacted into law. Congress has foreclosed the removal of tobacco products from the market. A provision of the United States Code currently in force states that "the marketing of tobacco constitutes one of the greatest basic industries of the United States with ramifying activities which directly

(case continues)

affect interstate and foreign commerce at every point, and stable conditions therein are necessary to the general welfare." More importantly, Congress has directly addressed the problem of tobacco and health through legislation on six occasions since 1965. See Federal Cigarette Labeling and Advertising Act (FCLAA), Public Health Cigarette Smoking Act of 1969, Alcohol and Drug Abuse Amendments of 1983, Comprehensive Smoking Education Act, Comprehensive Smokeless Tobacco Health Education Act of 1986, and Alcohol, Drug Abuse, and Mental Health Administration Reorganization Act. When Congress enacted these statutes, the adverse health consequences of tobacco use were well known, as were nicotine's pharmacological effects. Nonetheless, Congress stopped well short of ordering a ban. Instead, it has generally regulated the labeling and advertisement of tobacco products.

Considering the FDC Act as a whole, it is clear that Congress intended to exclude tobacco products from the FDA's jurisdiction. A fundamental precept of the FDC Act is that any product regulated by the FDA—but not banned—must be safe for its intended use. Consequently, if tobacco products were within the FDA's jurisdiction, the FDC Act would require the FDA to remove them from the market entirely. But a ban would contradict Congress' clear intent as expressed in its more recent, tobacco-specific legislation. The inescapable conclusion is that there is no room for tobacco products within the FDC Act's regulatory scheme.

By no means do we question the seriousness of the problem that the FDA has sought to address. The agency has amply demonstrated that tobacco use, particularly among children and adolescents, poses perhaps the single most significant threat to public health in the United States. Nonetheless, no matter how important, conspicuous, and controversial the issue, an administrative agency's power to regulate in the public interest must always be grounded in a valid grant of authority from Congress. And, in our anxiety to effectuate the congressional purpose of protecting the public, we must take care not to extend the scope of the statute beyond the point where Congress indicated it would stop. Reading the FDC Act as a whole, as well as in conjunction with Congress' subsequent tobacco-specific legislation, it is plain that Congress has not given the FDA the authority that it seeks to exercise here.

Decision

The U.S. Supreme Court held that the FDA does not have authority under the Food, Drug, and Cosmetic Act to regulate tobacco products as a "drug" or "device." It affirmed the judgment of the Court of Appeals.

Case Questions

Critical Legal Thinking Did the FDA exceed its delegated authority under the FDC Act by enacting its tobacco products rules?

Business Ethics Do you think cigarette companies act unethically in the advertising and promotion of smoking? Why or why not? Do governments have a stake in cigarette sales? Explain.

Contemporary Business Did the cigarette companies benefit from the result reached in this lawsuit? Explain.

Licensing Power   Statutes often require the issuance of a government **license** before a person can enter certain types of industries (e.g., the operation of banks, television and radio stations, and commercial airlines) or professions (e.g., doctors, lawyers, dentists, certified public accountants, contractors). The administrative agency that regulates the specific area involved is granted the power to determine whether to grant a license to an applicant.

Applicants must usually submit detailed applications to the appropriate administrative agency. In addition, the agency usually accepts written comments from interested parties and holds hearings on the matter. Courts generally defer to the expertise of administrative agencies in licensing matters.

Judicial Power   Many administrative agencies have **judicial power** to adjudicate cases through an administrative proceeding. Such a proceeding is initiated when an agency serves a complaint on a party the agency believes has violated a statute or an administrative rule or order.

In adjudicating cases, an administrative agency must comply with the Due Process Clause of the U.S. Constitution (and state constitution, where applicable). **Procedural due process** requires the respondent to be given proper and timely notice of the allegations or charges against him or her and an opportunity to present evidence on the matter.

procedural due process
Due process that requires the respondent to be given proper and timely notice of the allegations or charges against him or her and an opportunity to present evidence on the matter.

Executive Power   Administrative agencies are usually granted **executive powers**, such as the power to investigate and prosecute possible violations of statutes, administrative rules, and administrative orders.

To perform these functions successfully, an agency must often obtain information from the persons and businesses under investigation as well as from other sources. If the required information is not supplied voluntarily, the agency may issue an administrative subpoena to search the business premises; this is called an **administrative search**.

An administrative agency can issue an **administrative subpoena** to a business or person subject to its jurisdiction. The subpoena directs the party to disclose the requested information to the administrative agency. The administrative agency can seek judicial enforcement of the subpoena if the party does not comply with the subpoena.

executive power
Power that administrative agencies are granted, such as the investigation and prosecution of possible violations of statutes, administrative rules, and administrative orders.

administrative subpoena
An order that directs the subject of the subpoena to disclose the requested information.

CONCEPT SUMMARY
POWERS OF ADMINISTRATIVE AGENCIES

Power	Description of Power
1. Legislative Power	
A. Substantive rule making	To adopt rules that advance the purpose of the statutes that the agency is empowered to enforce. These rules have the force of law. Public notice and participation are required.
B. Interpretive rule making	To adopt rules that interpret statutory language. These rules do not establish new laws. Neither public notice nor participation is required.
C. Statements of policy	To announce a proposed course of action the agency plans to take in the future. These statements do not have the force of law. Public participation and notice are not required.
D. Licensing	To grant licenses to applicants (e.g., television station licenses, bank charters) and to suspend or revoke licenses.
2. Judicial Power	The power to adjudicate cases through an administrative proceeding. This includes the power to issue a complaint, hold a hearing by an administrative law judge (ALJ), and issue an order deciding the case and assessing remedies.
3. Executive Power	The power to prosecute violations of statutes and administrative rules and orders. This includes the power to investigate suspected violations, issue administrative subpoenas, and conduct administrative searches.

Administrative Searches

Sometimes a physical inspection of business premises is crucial to an investigation. Most inspections by administrative agencies are considered "searches" that are subject to the **Fourth Amendment to the U.S. Constitution**. The Fourth Amendment protects persons (including businesses) from **unreasonable search and seizures**. Searches by administrative agencies are generally considered to be reasonable within the meaning of the Fourth Amendment if:

unreasonable search and seizure
Any search and seizure by the government that violates the Fourth Amendment.

- The party voluntarily agrees to the search.
- The search is conducted pursuant to a validly issued *search warrant*.
- A warrantless search is conducted in an emergency situation.
- The business is part of a special industry where warrantless searches are automatically considered valid (e.g., liquor sales, firearm sales).
- The business is part of a hazardous industry and a statute expressly provides for nonarbitrary warrantless searches (e.g., coal mines).

Evidence from an unreasonable search and seizure ("tainted evidence") is inadmissible in court. In the following case, the U.S. Supreme Court had to decide whether a warrantless search of business premises was lawful.

CASE 43.2 U.S. SUPREME COURT Search of Business Premises

New York v. Burger

482 U.S. 691, 107 S.Ct. 2636, 96 L.Ed.2d 601, Web 1987 U.S. Lexis 2725 (1987)
Supreme Court of the United States

"An expectation of privacy in commercial premises, however, is different from, and indeed less than, a similar expectation in an individual's home."

—Justice Blackmun

Facts

Joseph Burger is the owner of a junkyard in Brooklyn, New York. His business consists, in part, of dismantling automobiles and selling their parts. The state of New York enacted a statute that requires automobile junkyards to keep certain records. The statute authorizes warrantless searches of vehicle dismantlers and automobile junkyards without prior notice. One day, five plainclothes officers of the Auto Crimes Division of the New York City Police Department entered Burger's junkyard to conduct a surprise inspection. Burger did not have either a license to conduct the business or records of the automobiles and vehicle parts on his premises, as required by state law. After conducting an inspection of the premises, the officers determined that Burger was in possession of stolen vehicles and parts. He was arrested and charged with criminal possession of stolen property. Burger moved to suppress the evidence. The New York supreme court and appellate division held the search to be constitutional. The New York court of appeals reversed. New York appealed.

Issue

Does the warrantless search of an automobile junkyard pursuant to a state statute that authorizes such search constitute an unreasonable search and seizure in violation of the Fourth Amendment to the U.S. Constitution?

In the Language of the Supreme Court

The court has long recognized that the Fourth Amendment's prohibition on unreasonable searches and seizures is applicable to commercial premises, as well as to private homes. An expectation of privacy in commercial premises, however, is different from, and indeed less than, a similar expectation in an individual's home. This expectation is particularly attenuated in commercial property employed in "closely regulated" industries.

*Because the owner or operator of commercial premises in a closely regulated industry has a reduced expectation of privacy, the warrant and probable cause requirements—which fulfill the traditional Fourth Amendment standard of reasonableness for a government search—have a lessened application in this context. The nature of the regulatory statute reveals that the operation of a junkyard, part of which is devoted to vehicle dismantling, is a closely reg-*ulated business in the state of New York. A warrantless inspection of commercial premises may well be reasonable within the meaning of the Fourth Amendment.

The New York regulatory scheme satisfies the criteria necessary to make reasonable warrantless inspections. The state has substantial interest in regulating the vehicle dismantling and automobile junkyard industry because motor vehicle theft has increased in the state of New York and because the problem of theft is associated with this industry. Regulation of the vehicle dismantling industry reasonably serves the state's substantial interest in eradicating automobile theft. It is well established that the theft problem can be addressed effectively by controlling the receiver of, or market in, stolen property. Automobile junkyards and vehicle dismantlers provide the major market for stolen vehicles and vehicle parts. The New York law provides a constitutionally adequate substitute for a warrant. The statute informs the operator of a vehicle dismantling business that inspections will be made on a regular basis.

Decision

The U.S. Supreme Court held that the New York statute that authorizes warrantless searches of vehicle dismantling businesses and automobile junkyards does not constitute an unreasonable search in violation of the Fourth Amendment to the U.S. Constitution. The Supreme Court reversed the judgment of the New York court of appeals and remanded the case for further proceedings, consistent with its decision.

Case Questions

Critical Legal Thinking Should the Fourth Amendment's protection against unreasonable searches and seizures apply to businesses? Why or why not?

Business Ethics Was it ethical for the defendant to assert the Fourth Amendment's prohibition against unreasonable searches and seizures? Why did he raise this defense?

Contemporary Business Is auto theft big business? Will the New York law that regulates vehicle dismantling businesses and junkyards help to alleviate this crime?

▶ JUDICIAL REVIEW OF ADMINISTRATIVE AGENCY ACTIONS

Many federal statutes expressly provide for **judicial review of administrative agency actions**. Where an enabling statute does not provide for review, the Administrative Procedure Act (APA) authorizes judicial review of federal administrative agency actions.[3] The party appealing the decision of an administrative agency is called the **petitioner**.

Decisions of federal administrative agencies can be appealed to the appropriate federal court (see Exhibit 43.2). Decisions of state administrative agencies can be appealed to the proper state court.

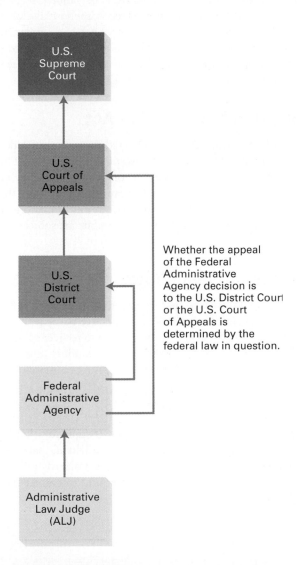

Whether the appeal of the Federal Administrative Agency decision is to the U.S. District Court or the U.S. Court of Appeals is determined by the federal law in question.

▶ Exhibit 43.2
APPEAL OF A FEDERAL ADMINISTRATIVE AGENCY DECISION

▶ DISCLOSURE OF ADMINISTRATIVE AGENCY ACTIONS

Public concern over possible secrecy of administrative agency actions led Congress to enact several statutes that promote public **disclosure of federal administrative agency actions** and protect parties from overly obtrusive agency actions. These statutes are discussed in the paragraphs that follow.

The Freedom of Information Act

Freedom of Information Act
A federal act that gives the public access to documents in the possession of federal administrative agencies. There are many exceptions to disclosure.

The **Freedom of Information Act**[4] was enacted to give the public access to most documents in the possession of federal administrative agencies. The act requires federal administrative agencies to publish agency procedures, rules, regulations, interpretations, and other such information in the *Federal Register*. The act also requires agencies to publish quarterly indexes of certain documents. In addition, the act specifies time limits for agencies to respond to requests for information, sets limits on copying charges, and provides for disciplinary action against agency employees who refuse to honor proper requests for information.

For purposes of privacy, the following documents are exempt from disclosure: (1) documents classified by the president to be in the interests of national security; (2) documents that are statutorily prohibited from disclosure; (3) records whose disclosure would interfere with law enforcement proceedings; (4) medical, personnel, and similar files; and (5) documents containing trade secrets or other confidential or privileged information. Decisions by federal administrative agencies not to publicly disclose documents requested under the act are subject to judicial review in the proper U.S. District Court.

The Government in the Sunshine Act

Government in the Sunshine Act
A federal act that opens most federal administrative agency meetings to the public.

The **Government in the Sunshine Act**[5] was enacted to open most federal administrative agency meetings to the public. There are some exceptions to this rule. These include meetings (1) where a person is accused of a crime, (2) concerning an agency's issuance of a subpoena, (3) where attendance of the public would significantly frustrate the implementation of a proposed agency action, and (4) concerning day-to-day operations. Decisions by federal administrative agencies to close meetings to the public are subject to judicial review in the proper U.S. District Court.

The Equal Access to Justice Act

Equal Access to Justice Act
A federal act that protects persons from harassment by federal administrative agencies.

Congress enacted the **Equal Access to Justice Act**[6] to protect persons from harassment by federal administrative agencies. Under this act, a private party who is the subject of an unjustified federal administrative agency action can sue to recover attorneys' fees and other costs. The courts have generally held that the agency's conduct must be extremely outrageous before an award will be made under the act. A number of states have similar statutes.

Privacy Act

Privacy Act
A federal act which states that federal administrative agencies can maintain only information about an individual that is relevant and necessary to accomplish a legitimate agency purpose.

The federal **Privacy Act**[7] concerns individual privacy. It stipulates that federal administrative agencies can maintain only information about an individual that is relevant and necessary to accomplish a legitimate agency purpose. The act affords individuals the right to have access to agency records concerning themselves and to correct these records. Many states have enacted similar privacy acts.

CONCEPT SUMMARY

ACTS THAT PROTECT INDIVIDUALS FROM FEDERAL ADMINISTRATIVE AGENCIES

Act	Provisions of the Act
Freedom of Information Act	Requires that documents of federal administrative agencies be open to the public; there are certain exemptions from this requirement. The act requires agencies to publish their procedures, rules, regulations, and other information in the *Federal Register*.
Government in the Sunshine Act	Requires that meetings of federal administrative agencies be open to the public; there are certain exemptions from this requirement.

Equal Access to Justice Act	Gives a private party who was subject to an unjustified federal administrative agency action the right to sue and recover attorneys' fees and costs.
Privacy Act	Requires that federal administrative agencies maintain only information about an individual that is relevant and necessary to accomplish a legitimate agency purpose. Also gives individuals access to these records and a right to correct the records.

TEST REVIEW TERMS AND CONCEPTS

Administrative agency
Administrative law
Administrative law judge (ALJ)
Administrative Procedure Act (APA)
Administrative search
Administrative subpoena
Delegation doctrine
Department of Homeland Security (DHS)

Disclosure of agency administrative actions
Equal Access to Justice Act
Executive branch of the federal government (President)
Executive power
Federal administrative agency
Federal Register
Fourth Amendment to the U.S. Constitution

Freedom of Information Act
Government in the Sunshine Act
Homeland Security Act
Interpretive rule
Judicial power
Judicial review of administrative agency actions
Legislative branch of the federal government (Congress)
License

Order
Petitioner
Privacy Act
Procedural due process
Procedural law
State administrative agency
Statement of policy
Substantive law
Substantive rule
Unreasonable search and seizure

CASE PROBLEMS

43.1 Administrative Procedure The Federal Deposit Insurance Corporation (FDIC) insures the deposit accounts of banks up to $100,000. Federal law [12 U.S.C. Section 1818(g)] permits the FDIC to suspend from office any officer of a federally insured bank who is criminally indicted if that person's continued service poses a threat to the interest of the bank's depositors or threatens to impair public confidence in the bank. The statute entitles suspended bank officers to a hearing before the FDIC within 30 days of a written request and to a final decision within 60 days of the hearing. At the administrative hearing, the officer may submit written material or, at the discretion of the FDIC, oral testimony.

The FDIC suspended James E. Mallen, the president and director of Farmers State Bank in Kanawha, Iowa, upon his indictment for conspiracy to commit mail fraud and for making false statements in violation of federal law. The FDIC issued an order, suspending Mallen as president and director. A hearing was scheduled to occur within 19 days after his written request. The FDIC did not permit oral testimony in this case. Mallen sued, alleging that the FDIC's refusal to allow oral testimony at the administrative hearing violated the Due Process Clause of the U.S. Constitution. Is Section 1818(g) constitutional? *Federal Deposit Insurance Corporation v. Mallen*, 486 U.S. 230, 108 S.Ct. 1780, 100 L.Ed.2d 265, **Web** 1988 U.S. Lexis 2477 (Supreme Court of the United States)

43.2 Rule Making The Food and Drug Administration (FDA), a federal administrative agency, is charged with enforcing the Food, Drug, and Cosmetic Act. This statute mandates that the FDA limit the amount of "poisonous or deleterious substances" in food. Pursuant to this authority, the FDA established certain "action levels" of unavoidable contaminants, such as aflatoxins, in food. Food producers that sell products that are contaminated above the set action level are subject to enforcement proceedings initiated by the FDA. In announcing these action levels, the FDA did not comply with the notice and comment procedure required for the adoption of a substantive or legislative rule. The FDA argued that the "action levels" are merely interpretive rules or statements of policy that do not require notice and comment. The Community Nutrition Institute, a consortium of consumer public interest groups, sued to require the FDA to follow the notice and comment procedure. Who wins? *Community Nutrition Institute v. Young*, 260 U.S. App. D.C. 294, 818 F.2d 943, **Web** 1987 U.S. App. Lexis 6385 (United States Court of Appeals for the District of Columbia Circuit)

43.3 Rule Making The Federal Communications Commission (FCC) is a federal administrative agency that is empowered to enforce the Communications Act of 1934. This act, as amended, gives the FCC power to regulate broadcasting of radio and television. The act provides that "broadcasting shall not be deemed to common carrier." In *United States v. Midwest Video Corporation*, 406 U.S. 649, 92 S.Ct. 1860, 32 L.Ed.2d 390, **Web** 1972 U.S. Lexis 166 (1972), the U.S. Supreme Court held that the FCC also has the power to regulate cable television.

The FCC promulgated rules requiring cable television operators that have 3,500 or more subscribers to (1) develop a 20-channel capacity, (2) make 4 channels available for use by public, educational, local, governmental, and leased-access users (with 1 channel assigned to each), (3) make equipment available for those utilizing these public-access channels, and (4) limit the fees cable operators charge for their services. Do these rules exceed the statutory authority of the FCC? *Federal Communications Commission v. Midwest Video Corporation*, 440 U.S. 689, 99 S.Ct. 1435, 59 L.Ed.2d 692, **Web** 1979 U.S. Lexis 82 (Supreme Court of the United States)

43.4 Administrative Regulation   George Carlin, a satiric humorist, recorded a 12-minute monologue called "Filthy Words." He began by referring to his thoughts about "the words you couldn't say on the public airwaves" and then proceeded to list those words, repeating them over and over again in a variety of colloquialisms. At about 2 o'clock in the afternoon, a New York radio station, owned by Pacifica Foundation (Pacifica), broadcast Carlin's "Filthy Words" monologue. A father who heard the broadcast while driving with his young son filed a complaint with the Federal Communications Commission (FCC), a federal administrative agency charged with regulating broadcasting. The Federal Communications Act forbids the use of "any obscene, indecent, or profane language by means of radio communications." Therefore, the FCC issued an order granting the complaint, and it informed Pacifica that the order would be considered in future licensing decisions involving Pacifica. Is the FCC regulation legal? *Federal Communications Commission v. Pacifica Foundation*, 438 U.S. 726, 98 S.Ct. 3026, 57 L.Ed.2d 1073, **Web** 1978 U.S. Lexis 135 (Supreme Court of the United States)

43.5 License   The Interstate Commerce Commission (ICC) was a federal administrative agency empowered to regulate motor carriers involved in interstate commerce. Trucking companies had to apply to the ICC to obtain a license before they could offer trucking services on a route. The Interstate Commerce Act empowered the ICC to grant an application for a license if the ICC found that (1) the applicant was fit, willing, and able to properly perform the service proposed and (2) the service proposed would be required by the present or future "public convenience or necessity."

Thirteen motor carriers applied to offer trucking services between points in the Southwest and Southeast. After reviewing the applications and hearing extensive evidence (including the testimony of more than 900 witnesses), the ICC granted licenses to three of the applicants. Arkansas-Best Freight System, Inc., a rejected applicant, brought an action, seeking to annul the ICC's order. Should the ICC's grant of the license be overturned on appeal? *Browman Transportation, Inc. v. Arkansas-Best Freight System, Inc.*, 419 U.S. 281, 95 S.Ct. 438, 42 L.Ed.2d 447, **Web** 1974 U.S. Lexis 51 (Supreme Court of the United States)

BUSINESS ETHICS CASES

43.6 Business Ethics   The Federal Mine Safety and Health Act requires the secretary of labor to develop detailed mandatory health and safety standards to govern the operation of the nation's mines. The act provides that federal mine inspectors are to inspect underground mines at least four times a year and surface mines at least twice a year to ensure compliance with these standards and to make inspections to determine whether previously discovered violations have been corrected. The act also grants mine inspectors "a right of entry to, upon or through any coal or other mine" and states that "no advance notice of an inspection shall be provided to any person."

A federal mine inspector attempted to inspect quarries owned by Waukesha Lime and Stone Company (Waukesha) to determine whether all 25 safety and health violations uncovered during a prior inspection had been corrected. Douglas Dewey, Waukesha's president, refused to allow the inspector to inspect the premises without first obtaining a search warrant. Are the warrantless searches of stone quarries authorized by the Mine Safety and Health Act constitutional? Did Dewey act ethically in refusing to allow the inspections? *Donovan, Secretary of Labor v. Dewey*, 452 U.S. 594, 101 S.Ct. 2534, 69 L.Ed.2d 262, **Web** 1980 U.S. Lexis 58 (Supreme Court of the United States)

43.7 Business Ethics   A statute of the state of Wisconsin forbids the practice of medicine without a license granted by the Examining Board (Board), a state administrative agency composed of practicing physicians. The statute specifically prohibits certain acts of professional misconduct. Board may investigate alleged violations, issue charges against a licensee, hold hearings, and rule on the matter. Board also has the authority to warn and reprimand violators, suspend or revoke their licenses, and institute criminal actions.

Dr. Larkin was a physician licensed to practice medicine in the state of Wisconsin. Board sent a notice to Larkin that it would hold a hearing to determine whether he had engaged in prohibited acts. Larkin was represented by counsel at the hearing. Evidence was introduced, and witnesses gave testimony at the hearing. Board found Larkin guilty and temporarily suspended his license to practice medicine. Larkin then filed suit, alleging that it was an unconstitutional violation of due process to permit an administrative agency to adjudicate a charge that it had investigated and brought. Is there a violation of due process? Did Larkin act ethically in challenging the authority of the administrative agency? *Withrow v. Larkin*, 421 U.S. 35, 95 S.Ct. 1456, 43 L.Ed.2d 712, **Web** 1975 U.S. Lexis 56 (Supreme Court of the United States)

ENDNOTES

1. 5 U.S.C. Section 551-706.
2. 5 U.S.C. Section 553.
3. 5 U.S.C. Section 702.
4. 5 U.S.C. Section 552.
5. 5 U.S.C. Section 552(b).
6. 5 U.S.C. Section 504.
7. 5 U.S.C. Section 552(a).

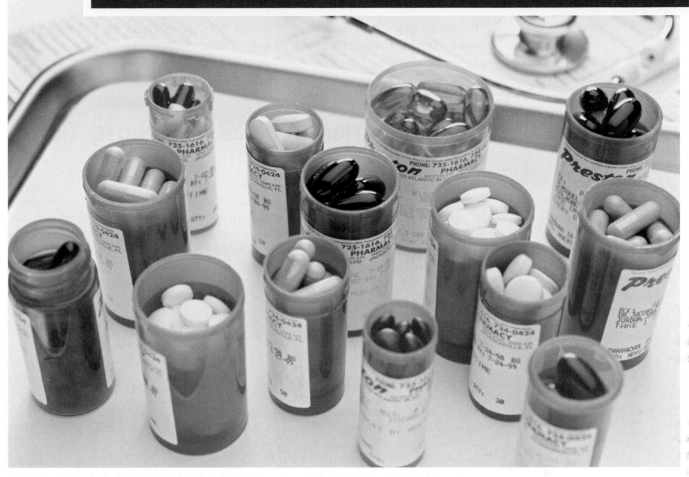

▲ **Pharmaceuticals** *The Food and Drug Administration (FDA) is a federal administration that must approve the safety of certain food additives, drugs, cosmetics, and medicinal devices before they can be sold to the public.*

CHAPTER OBJECTIVES

After studying this chapter, you should be able to:

1. Describe government regulation of food and food additives.
2. Describe government regulation of drugs, cosmetics, and medicinal devices.
3. Explain the coverage of Consumer Product Safety Acts.
4. Describe the United Nations Biosafety Protocol concerning genetically altered foods.
5. Identify and describe unfair and deceptive business practices.

CHAPTER CONTENTS

Ethics Spotlight · *Animal Testing*
▶ **PRODUCT SAFETY**
Ethics Spotlight · *State Lemon Laws*
▶ **UNFAIR AND DECEPTIVE PRACTICES**

Case 44.2 U.S. Supreme Court · Federal Trade Commission v. Colgate-Palmolive Company
Internet Law & Online Commerce · *Do-Not-Call Registry*

"I should regret to find that the law was powerless to enforce the most elementary principles of commercial morality."

—Lord Herschell
Reddaway v. Banham (1896)

▶ INTRODUCTION TO CONSUMER PROTECTION AND PRODUCT SAFETY

Originally, sales transactions in this country were guided by the principle of *caveat emptor* ("let the buyer beware"). To promote the safety of foods, cosmetics, drugs, products, and services, and to prohibit abusive, unfair, and deceptive selling practices, federal and state governments have enacted a variety of statutes that regulate the behavior of businesses that deal with consumers. These laws, collectively referred to as **consumer protection laws**, are the subject of this chapter.

consumer protection laws
Federal and state statutes and regulations that promote product safety and prohibit abusive, unfair, and deceptive business practices.

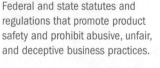 United States Department of Agriculture

▶ U.S. DEPARTMENT OF AGRICULTURE

The **United States Department of Agriculture (USDA)** is a federal administrative agency that is responsible for regulating meat, poultry, and other **food** products. The USDA conducts inspections of food processing and storage facilities, and it can initiate legal proceedings against violators. The USDA employs approximately 8,000 inspectors and spends approximately $1 billion a year on inspecting meat and poultry. Some have criticized the USDA, saying that it cares more about protecting industry interests than about public health. The USDA initiated a proceeding in the following case.

CASE 44.1 Adulterated Food

United States of America v. LaGrou Distribution Systems, Incorporated

466 F.3d 585, Web 2006 U.S. App. Lexis 25986 (2006)
United States Court of Appeals for the Seventh Circuit

"The conditions at LaGrou's cold storage warehouse at 2101 Pershing Road in Chicago were enough to turn even the most enthusiastic meat-loving carnivore into a vegetarian."

—Judge Bauer

Facts

LaGrou Distribution Systems, Incorporated, operated a cold storage warehouse and distribution center in Chicago,

Illinois. The warehouse stored raw, fresh, and frozen meat, poultry, and other food products that were owned by customers who paid LaGrou to do so. Over 2 million pounds of food went into and out of the warehouse each day.

The warehouse had a rat problem for a considerable period of time. LaGrou workers consistently found rodent droppings and rodent-gnawed products, and they caught rats in traps throughout the warehouse on a daily basis. The manager of the warehouse and the president of LaGrou were aware of this problem and discussed it weekly. The problem became so bad that workers were assigned to "rat patrols" to search for rats and to put out traps to catch rats. At one point, the rat patrols were trapping as many as 50 rats per day. LaGrou did not inform its customers of the rodent infestation. LaGrou would throw out product that had been gnawed by rats but tell the customer that the product was thrown out because of warehouse damage such as torn boxes and forklift mishaps. LaGrou employees, as a joke, would write "MM" for Mickey Mouse on product that was infested.

One day, a food inspector for the United States Department of Agriculture (USDA) went to the LaGrou warehouse and discovered the rat problem. The following morning, 14 USDA inspectors and representatives of the federal Food and Drug Administration (FDA) arrived at the warehouse to begin an extensive investigation. The inspectors found the extensive rat infestation and the contaminated meat. The contaminated meat could transmit bacterial, viral, parasitic, and fungal pathogens, including *E. coli* and *Salmonella*, which could cause severe illness in human beings.

The USDA ordered the warehouse shut down. Of the 22 million pounds of meat, poultry, and other food products stored at the warehouse, 8 million pounds were found to be adulterated and were destroyed. The remaining product had to be treated with strict decontamination procedures. The U.S. government brought charges against LaGrou for violating federal food safety laws. The U.S. District Court ordered LaGrou to pay restitution of $8.2 million to customers who lost product and to pay a $2 million fine, and it sentenced LaGrou to a five-year term of probation. LaGrou appealed.

Issue

Did LaGrou knowingly engage in the improper storage of meat, poultry, and other food products, in violation of federal food safety laws?

Language of the Court

The conditions at LaGrou's cold storage warehouse at 2101 Pershing Road in Chicago were enough to turn even the most enthusiastic meat-loving carnivore into a vegetarian. According to Dr. Bonnie Rose, the USDA microbiologist who testified, LaGrou's warehouse was the "worst case" she had seen in her 28 years with the USDA. The inspectors found and photographed the

following conditions at the Pershing Road warehouse: rat droppings and rat nesting material throughout the warehouse, including next to and on product; rodent-gnawed meat, poultry, and other food products; live rodent sightings; blood from meat product on the floor mixed with rodent droppings and rat tail marks; dirt and debris on meat product; potential rodent access points, including open sewer drains and openings under doors; holes in ceilings, walls, and floors; ice buildup on the ceilings directly above stored product and water dripping from the ceilings onto the product; mold and filth on the walls and ceilings; several inoperable bathrooms, which forced warehouse workers to use broken toilets and "flush" them with buckets of water; and raw sewage and standing water on the floors.

The instructions in this case explained that in order to convict LaGrou, the jury had to find that an authorized agent or employee of LaGrou knowingly stored products under insanitary conditions. Since 1999, LaGrou's President, managers, and several employees were aware of the unsanitary conditions in the Pershing Road warehouse. LaGrou was aware of the rodent infestation from formal reports, such as from the ASI and McCloud, LaGrou's pest control company, and from informal reports, such as LaGrou employee rat patrols and the employees' necessary sorting of rat-infested product from supposedly clean product. A crucial charge in these three offenses is that LaGrou knowingly stored these products under unsanitary conditions, which states the requisite mens rea *for the charges.*

Decision

The U.S. Court of Appeals held that LaGrou had knowingly engaged in the improper storage of meat, poultry, and other food products, in violation of federal food safety laws. The Court of Appeals affirmed the judgment of the District Court, except that it reduced the fine from $2 million to $1.5 million.

Case Questions

Critical Legal Thinking What is the USDA? What is the purpose of the USDA?

Business Ethics Did LaGrou management knowingly engage in improper storage of food products?

Contemporary Business Do you think that the penalties imposed on LaGrou were sufficient? Why or why not?

  U.S. Food and Drug Administration

LANDMARK LAW
Food, Drug, and Cosmetic Act

The federal **Food, Drug, and Cosmetic Act (FDCA or FDC Act)** was enacted in 1938. This act, as amended, regulates the testing, manufacture, distribution, and sale of foods, drugs, cosmetics, and medicinal products and devices in the United States. The **Food and Drug Administration (FDA)** is the federal administrative agency empowered to enforce the FDCA.

Before certain food additives, drugs, cosmetics, and medicinal devices can be sold to the public, they must receive FDA approval. An applicant must submit to the FDA an application that contains relevant information about the safety and uses of the product. The FDA, after considering the evidence, will either approve or deny the application.

The FDA can seek search warrants and conduct inspections; obtain orders for the seizure, recall, and condemnation of products; seek injunctions; and turn over suspected criminal violations to the U.S. Department of Justice for prosecution.

Food, Drug, and Cosmetic Act (FDCA)
A federal statute that provides the basis for the regulation of much of the testing, manufacture, distribution, and sale of foods, drugs, cosmetics, and medicinal products.

Food and Drug Administration (FDA)
The federal administrative agency that administers and enforces the federal Food, Drug, and Cosmetic Act and other federal consumer protection laws.

▶ FOOD, DRUG, AND COSMETIC SAFETY

The **Federal Food, Drug, and Cosmetic Act (FDCA)**[1] is a federal statute that regulates the safety of food, cosmetics, drugs, and medicinal devices. The specific areas regulated by the FDCA are discussed in the following paragraphs.

Regulation of Food

The FDCA prohibits the shipment, distribution, or sale of **adulterated food**. Food is deemed adulterated if it consists in whole or in part of any "filthy, putrid, or decomposed substance" or if it is otherwise "unfit for food." Note that food does not have to be entirely pure to be distributed or sold—it only has to be unadulterated.

The FDCA also prohibits **false and misleading labeling** of food products. In addition, it mandates affirmative disclosure of information on food labels, including the name of the food, the name and place of the manufacturer, a statement of ingredients, and nutrition content. A manufacturer may be held liable for deceptive labeling or packaging.

CONTEMPORARY ENVIRONMENT
Safety of Foods

You take a big bite of a peanut butter sandwich and savor the taste. It has been processed by a food manufacturer and inspected by the federal government, so you think it is pure peanut butter. Not necessarily. Under federal FDA guidelines, peanut butter may contain up to 30 insect fragments per 3 ounces and still be considered "safe" for human consumption.

The FDA has set ceilings, or "action levels," for certain contaminants—or "defects," as the FDA likes to call them—for various foods. Several of these action levels are:

- Golden raisins—35 fly eggs per 8 ounces
- Popcorn—two rodent hairs per pound
- Shelled peanuts—20 insects per 100 pounds
- Canned mushrooms—20 maggots per 3.5 ounces
- Tomato juice—10 fly eggs per 3.5 ounces

The FDA can mount inspections and raids to enforce its action levels. If it finds that the federal tolerance system has been violated, it can seize the offending food and destroy it at the owner's expense.

The courts have upheld the presence of some contamination in food as lawful under the federal FDCA. For example, in one case, the court found that 28 insect parts in 9 pounds of butter did not violate the act. The court stated, "Few foods contain no natural or unavoidable defects. Even with modern technology, all defects in foods cannot be eliminated." *United States v. Capital City Foods, Inc.*, 345 F.Supp. 277, **Web** 1972 U.S. Dist. Lexis (United States District Court for the District of North Dakota)

Food Labeling

In 1990, Congress passed a sweeping truth-in-labeling law called the **Nutrition Labeling and Education Act (NLEA)**.[2] This statute requires food manufacturers and processors to provide nutrition information on many foods and prohibits them from making scientifically unsubstantiated health claims.

The NLEA applies to packaged foods and other foods regulated by the Food and Drug Administration. The law requires food labels to disclose the number of calories derived from fat and the amount of dietary fiber, saturated fat, trans fat, cholesterol, and a variety of other substances contained in the food. The law also requires the disclosure of uniform information about serving sizes and nutrients, and establishes standard definitions for *light* (or *lite*), *low fat, fat free, cholesterol free, lean, natural, organic*, and other terms routinely bandied about by food processors.

The Department of Agriculture adopted consistent labeling requirements for the meat and poultry products that it regulates. Nutrition labeling for raw fruits and vegetables and raw seafood is voluntary. Many sellers of these products provide point-of-purchase nutrition information.

Nutrition Labeling and Education Act
A federal statute that requires food manufacturers to place on food labels that disclose nutritional information about the food.

INTERNATIONAL LAW

United Nations Biosafety Protocol for Genetically Altered Foods

In many countries, the food is not genetically altered. However, many food processors in the United States and elsewhere around the world genetically modify some foods by adding genes from other organisms to help crops grow faster or ward off pests. In the past, food processors did not notify consumers that they were purchasing genetically modified agricultural products. Although the companies insist that genetically altered foods are safe, consumers and many countries began to demand that such foods be clearly labeled so that buyers could decide for themselves.

The most concerned countries in the world regarding this issue were in Europe. Led by Germany, many European countries wanted to require genetically engineered food products to be labeled as such and be transported separately from nonaltered agricultural products. Some European countries wanted genetically altered foods to be banned completely. The United States, a major exporter of agricultural products and the leader in the development of biotech foods, argued that those countries were using this issue to erect trade barriers to keep U.S.-produced food products out of their countries, in violation of international trade treaties and conventions administered by the World Trade Organization (WTO), which had reduced or eliminated many international trade restrictions.

In January 2000, a compromise was reached when 138 countries, including the United States, agreed to the United Nations–sponsored **Biosafety Protocol**. After much negotiation, the countries agreed that all genetically engineered foods would be clearly labeled with the phrase "May contain living modified organisms." This allows consumers to decide on their own whether to purchase such altered food products. In addition, the boxes and containers in which such goods are shipped must also be clearly marked as containing genetically altered food products.

Regulation of Drugs

The FDCA gives the FDA the authority to regulate the testing, manufacture, distribution, and sale of **drugs**. The **Drug Amendment to the FDCA**,[3] enacted in 1962, gives the FDA broad powers to license new drugs in the United States. After a new drug application is filed, the FDA holds a hearing and investigates the merits of the application. This process can take many years. The FDA may withdraw approval of any previously licensed drug.

This law requires all users of prescription and nonprescription drugs to receive proper directions for use (including the method and duration of use) and adequate warnings about any related side effects. The manufacture, distribution, or sale of adulterated or misbranded drugs is prohibited.

Regulation of Cosmetics

The FDA's definition of **cosmetics** includes substances and preparations for cleansing, altering the appearance of, and promoting the attractiveness of a person. Eye shadow and other facial makeup products are examples of cosmetics subject to FDA regulation. Ordinary household soap is expressly exempted from this definition.

The FDA has issued regulations that require cosmetics to be labeled, to disclose ingredients, and to contain warnings if they are carcinogenic (cancer-causing) or otherwise dangerous to a person's health. The manufacture, distribution, or sale of adulterated or misbranded cosmetics is prohibited. The FDA may remove from commerce any cosmetics that contain unsubstantiated claims of preserving youth, increasing virility, growing hair, and such.

ETHICS SPOTLIGHT

Animal Testing

Under the law, cosmetics must be safe for human use. Potential cosmetics are often tested on animals in order to determine whether they can be safely used on humans. The cosmetics industry has been highly criticized for the use of animal testing. There is no law against animal testing for cosmetics. The federal Food and Drug Administration (FDA) issued the following statement as to its position on animal testing.

Animal Testing

The Food and Drug Administration (FDA) is responsible for assuring that cosmetics are safe and properly labeled. This mission is accomplished through enforcement of the Federal Food, Drug, and Cosmetic Act (FD&C Act), related statutes, and regulations promulgated under these laws.

The FD&C Act does not specifically require the use of animals in testing cosmetics for safety, nor does the Act subject cosmetics to FDA premarket approval. However, the agency has consistently advised cosmetic manufacturers to employ whatever testing is appropriate and effective for substantiating the safety of their products. It remains the responsibility of the manufacturer to substantiate the safety of both ingredients and finished cosmetic products prior to marketing.

Animal testing by manufacturers seeking to market new products may be used to establish product safety. In some cases, after considering available alternatives, companies may determine that animal testing is necessary to assure the safety of a product or ingredient. FDA supports and adheres to the provisions of applicable laws, regulations, and policies governing animal testing, including the Animal Welfare Act and the Public Health Service Policy of Humane Care and Use of Laboratory Animals. Moreover, in all cases where

animal testing is used, FDA advocates that research and testing derive the maximum amount of useful scientific information from the minimum number of animals and employ the most humane methods available within the limits of scientific capability. We also believe that prior to use of animals, consideration should be given to the use of scientifically valid alternative methods to whole-animal testing.

FDA supports the development and use of alternatives to whole-animal testing as well as adherence to the most humane methods available within the limits of scientific capability when animals are used for testing the safety of cosmetic products. We will continue to be a strong advocate of methodologies for the refinement, reduction, and replacement of animal tests with alternative methodologies that do not employ the use of animals.

Cruelty-Free Testing

Some cosmetic companies promote their products with claims such as "CRUELTY-FREE" or "NOT TESTED ON ANIMALS" in their labeling or advertising. The unrestricted use of these phrases by cosmetic companies is possible because there are no legal definitions for these terms.

Some companies may apply such claims solely to their finished cosmetic products. However, these companies may rely on raw material suppliers or contract laboratories to perform any animal testing necessary to substantiate product or ingredient safety. Many raw materials used in cosmetics were tested on animals years ago when they were first introduced. A cosmetic manufacturer might only use those raw materials and base their "cruelty-free" claims on the fact that the materials or products are not "currently" tested on animals.

Regulation of Medicinal Devices

In 1976, Congress enacted the **Medicinal Device Amendment to the FDCA**.[4] This amendment gives the FDA authority to regulate **medicinal devices**, such as heart pacemakers, kidney dialysis machines, defibrillators, surgical equipment, and other diagnostic, therapeutic, and health devices. The mislabeling of such devices is prohibited. The FDA is empowered to remove "quack" devices from the market.

▶ PRODUCT SAFETY

In 1972, Congress enacted the **Consumer Product Safety Act (CPSA)**[5] and created the **Consumer Product Safety Commission (CPSC)**. The CPSC is an independent federal administrative agency empowered to (1) adopt rules and regulations to interpret and enforce the CPSA, (2) conduct research on the safety of consumer products, and (3) collect data regarding injuries caused by consumer products.

Because the CPSC regulates potentially dangerous consumer products, it issues **product safety** standards for consumer products that pose unreasonable risk of injury. If a consumer product is found to be imminently hazardous—that is, if its use causes an unreasonable risk of death or serious injury or illness—the manufacturer can be required to recall, repair, or replace the product or take other corrective action. Alternatively, the CPSC can seek injunctions, bring actions to seize hazardous consumer products, seek civil penalties for knowing violations of the act or of CPSC rules, and seek criminal penalties for knowing and willful violations of the act or of CPSC rules. A private party can sue for an injunction to prevent violations of the act or of CPSC rules and regulations.

Certain consumer products, including motor vehicles, boats, aircraft, and firearms, are regulated by other government agencies.

Consumer Product Safety Act (CPSA)
A federal statute that regulates potentially dangerous consumer products and that created the Consumer Product Safety Commission.

Consumer Product Safety Commission (CPSC)
A federal administrative agency empowered to adopt rules and regulations to interpret and enforce the Consumer Product Safety Act.

ETHICS SPOTLIGHT

State Lemon Laws

In the past, consumers who purchased automobiles and other vehicles that developed nagging mechanical problems had to try to convince the dealer or manufacturer to correct the problems. If a problem was not corrected, the consumer's only recourse was to seek redress through costly and time-consuming litigation. Today, most states have enacted **lemon laws**, which give consumers a new weapon in this battle.

Lemon laws provide a procedure for consumers to follow to correct recurring problems in vehicles. These laws establish an administrative procedure that is less formal than a court proceeding. Most lemon laws require that an arbitrator decide a dispute between a consumer and a car dealer. Lemon laws stipulate that if the dealer or manufacturer does not correct a recurring defect in a vehicle and within a specified number of tries (e.g., four tries) within a specified period of time (e.g., two years), the purchaser can rescind the purchase and recover a full refund of the vehicle's purchase price.

To properly invoke a state's lemon law, a consumer should take the following steps:

1. Notify the car dealer immediately of any mechanical or other problems that appear in the vehicle.
2. Take the vehicle back to the dealer the statutory number of times to give the dealer the opportunity to correct the defect.
3. File a claim with the appropriate state agency, seeking arbitration of the claim if the defect is not corrected during the number of times and time period established by the state's lemon law.
4. Attend the arbitration hearing and present evidence to substantiate the claim that the vehicle suffered from a defect that was not corrected by the dealer or manufacturer within the statutorily prescribed period.

Federal Trade Commission (FTC)
A federal administrative agency empowered to enforce the Federal Trade Commission Act and other federal consumer protection statutes.

Section 5 of the FTC Act
A provision in the FTC Act that prohibits unfair and deceptive practices.

▶ UNFAIR AND DECEPTIVE PRACTICES

The **Federal Trade Commission Act (FTC Act)** was enacted in 1914.[6] The **Federal Trade Commission (FTC)** was created the following year. The FTC is empowered to enforce the FTC Act as well as other federal consumer protection statutes.

Section 5 of the FTC Act, as amended, prohibits **unfair and deceptive practices**. It has been used extensively to regulate business conduct. This section gives the FTC the authority to bring an administrative proceeding to attack a deceptive or unfair practice. If, after a public administrative hearing, the FTC finds a violation of Section 5, it may order a cease-and-desist order, an affirmative disclosure to consumers, corrective advertising, or the like. The FTC may sue in state or federal court to obtain compensation on behalf of consumers. A decision of the FTC may be appealed to federal court.

False and Deceptive Advertising

Advertising is **false and deceptive** under Section 5 of the FTC Act if it (1) contains misinformation or omits important information that is likely to mislead a "reasonable consumer" or (2) makes an unsubstantiated claim (e.g., "This product is 33 percent better than our competitor's"). Proof of actual deception is not required. Statements of opinion and "sales talk" (e.g., "This is a great car") do not constitute false and deceptive advertising.

Example In 2004, KFC entered into an agreement with the FTC whereby KFC withdrew television commercials in which it claimed that its "fried chicken can, in fact, be part of a healthy diet."

Bait and Switch

bait and switch
A type of deceptive advertising that occurs when a seller advertises the availability of a low-cost discounted item but then pressures the buyer into purchasing more expensive merchandise.

Bait and switch is a type of deceptive advertising under Section 5 of the FTC Act. It occurs when a seller advertises the availability of a low-cost discounted item (the "bait") to attract customers to its store. Once the customers are in the store, however, the seller pressures them to purchase more expensive merchandise (the "switch"). The FTC states that a bait and switch occurs if the seller refuses to show consumers the advertised merchandise, discourages employees from selling the advertised merchandise, or fails to have adequate quantities of the advertised merchandise available.

Door-to-Door Sales

You can fool some of the people all of the time, and all of the people some of the time, but you cannot fool all of the people all of the time.

P.T. Barnum

Some salespersons sell merchandise and services **door-to-door**. In some situations, these salespersons use aggressive sales tactics to overcome a consumer's resistance to the sale. To protect consumers from ill-advised decisions, many states have enacted laws that give the consumer a certain number of days to rescind (cancel) a door-to-door sales contract. The usual period is three days. The consumer must send a required notice of cancellation to the seller. An FTC regulation requires the salesperson to permit cancellation of the contract within the stipulated time.

The following is a classic case of false and deceptive advertising.

U.S. SUPREME COURT   CASE 44.2   Deceptive Advertising

Federal Trade Commission v. Colgate-Palmolive Company

380 U.S. 374, 85 S.Ct. 1035, 13 L.Ed.2d 904, Web 1965 U.S. Lexis 2300 (1965)
Supreme Court of the United States

"We agree with the FTC that the undisclosed use of Plexiglas in the present commercial was a material deceptive practice."

—Chief Justice Warren

Facts

The Colgate-Palmolive Co. (Colgate) manufactured and sold a shaving cream called "Rapid Shave." Colgate hired Ted Bates & Company (Bates), an advertising agency, to prepare television commercials designed to show that Rapid Shave could shave the toughest beards. With Colgate's consent, Bates prepared a television commercial that included the sandpaper test. The announcer informed the audience, "To prove Rapid Shave's super-moisturizing power, we put it right from the can onto this tough, dry sandpaper. And off in a stroke."

While the announcer was speaking, Rapid Shave was applied to a substance that appeared to be sandpaper, and immediately a razor was shown shaving the substance clean. Evidence showed that the substance resembling sandpaper was in fact a simulated prop, or "mock-up," made of Plexiglas to which sand had been glued. The Federal Trade Commission (FTC) issued a complaint against Colgate and Bates, alleging a violation of Section 5 of the FTC Act. The FTC held against the defendants. The Court of Appeals reversed. The FTC appealed to the U.S. Supreme Court.

Issue

Did the defendants engage in false and deceptive advertising in violation of Section 5 of the FTC Act?

Language of the U.S. Supreme Court

We agree with the FTC that the undisclosed use of Plexiglas in the present commercial was a material deceptive practice. Respondents claim that it will be impractical to inform the viewing public that it is not seeing an actual test, experiment or demonstration, but we think it inconceivable that the ingenious advertising world will be unable, if it so desires, to conform to the FTC's insistence that the public be not misinformed.

If it becomes impossible or impracticable to show simulated demonstrations on television in a truthful manner, this indicates that television is not a medium that lends itself to this type of commercial. Similarly unpersuasive is respondents' objection that the FTC's decision discriminates against sellers whose product claims cannot be verified on television without the use of simulation. All methods of advertising do not equally favor every seller. If the inherent limitations of a method do not permit its use in the way a seller desires, the seller cannot by material misrepresentation compensate for those limitations.

Decision

The U.S. Supreme Court held that Colgate and Bates had engaged in false and deceptive advertising. The Supreme Court reversed the decision of the Court of Appeals and remanded the case for further proceeding.

Case Questions

Critical Legal Thinking Does the government owe a duty to protect consumers from false and misleading business practices?

Business Ethics Did Colgate and Bates act ethically in this case? Do you think the viewing public believed the commercial?

Contemporary Business Do you think many companies engage in false and deceptive advertising? Can you think of any examples?

INTERNET LAW & ONLINE COMMERCE

Do-Not-Call Registry

In 2003, two federal administrative agencies—the *Federal Trade Commission (FTC)* and the **Federal Communications Commission (FCC)**—promulgated administrative rules that created the **"Do-Not-Call" Registry**, on which consumers can place their names and free themselves from most unsolicited commercial telephone calls. The FTC and FCC were given their authority to adopt their coordinated do-not-call rules in several federal statutes.

A person can place himself or herself on the Do-Not-Call Registry by calling toll-free 888-382-1222 or registering online, at **www.donotcall.gov**. Both wire-connected phones and wireless phones can be registered.

Telemarketers have three months from the date on which a consumer signs up for the registry to remove the customer's phone number from their sales call list. Customer registration remains valid for five years and can be renewed. Charitable and political organizations are exempt from the registry. Also, there is an "established business relationship" exception that allows businesses to call customers for 10 months after they sell or lease goods or services to that person or conduct a financial transaction with that person. The Do-Not-Call Registry allows consumers to designate specific companies not to call them, including those that otherwise qualify for the established business relationship exemption.

Telemarketers, who claimed they would lose substantial business and would have to fire millions of workers, sued to have the Do-Not-Call Registry declared unconstitutional as a violation of their constitutional right to free speech. A U.S. District Court in Colorado agreed with the telemarketers. On appeal, however, the U.S. Court of Appeals for the Tenth Circuit reversed, holding that the Do-Not-Call Registry did not violate telemarketers' free speech rights. The Court of Appeals held that the Do-Not-Call Registry was narrowly tailored and did not prevent marketers from reaching consumers by direct mail, advertisements, and other lawful methods. The court stated, "The Do-Not-Call Registry lets consumers avoid unwanted sales pitches that invade the home via telephone." *Mainstream Marketing Services, Inc. v. Federal Trade Commission*, 358 F.3d 1228, **Web** 2004 U.S. App. Lexis 2564 (United States Court of Appeals for the Tenth Circuit)

Business Ethics Do many telemarketers act illegally?

TEST REVIEW TERMS AND CONCEPTS

Adulterated food

Bait and switch

Biosafety Protocol

Consumer Product Safety Act (CPSA)

Consumer Product Safety Commission (CPSC)

Consumer protection laws

Cosmetics

Do-Not-Call Registry

Door-to-door sales

Drug Amendment to the FDCA

Drugs

False and deceptive advertising

False and misleading labeling

Federal Communications Commission (FCC)

Federal Trade Commission (FTC)

Federal Trade Commission Act (FTC Act)

Food

Food and Drug Administration (FDA)

Food, Drug, and Cosmetic Act (FDCA or FDC Act)

Lemon law

Medicinal device

Medicinal Device Amendment to the FDCA

Nutrition Labeling and Education Act (NLEA)

Product safety

Section 5 of the FTC Act

Unfair and deceptive practices

United States Department of Agriculture (USDA)

CASE PROBLEMS

44.1 Food Regulation Barry Engel owned and operated the Gel Spice Co., Inc. (Gel Spice), which specialized in the importation and packaging of various food spices for resale. All the spices Gel Spice imported were unloaded at a pier in New York City and taken to a warehouse on McDonald Avenue. Storage and repackaging of the spices took place in the warehouse. During three years, the McDonald Avenue warehouse was inspected four times by investigators from the Food and Drug Administration (FDA). The investigators found live rats in bags of basil leaves, rodent droppings in boxes of chili peppers, and mammalian urine in bags of sesame seeds. The investigators produced additional evidence which showed that spices packaged and sold from the warehouse contained insects, rodent excreta pellets, rodent hair, and rodent urine. The FDA brought criminal charges against Engel and Gel Spice. Are they guilty? *United States v. Gel Spice Co., Inc.*, 601 F.Supp. 1205, **Web** 1984 U.S. Dist. Lexis 21041 (United States District Court for the Eastern District of New York)

44.2 Regulation of Drugs Dey Laboratories, Inc. (Dey), was a drug manufacturer operating in the state of Texas. Dey scientists created an inhalant known as ASI. The only active ingredient in ASI was atropine sulfate. The inhalant was sold to physicians, who then prescribed the medication for patients suffering from asthma, bronchitis, and other pulmonary diseases. Dey filed a new drug application with the Food and Drug Administration (FDA). Four months later, Dey was advised that its application would not be approved. Despite the lack of FDA approval, Dey began marketing ASI. The United States filed a complaint for forfeiture of all ASI manufactured by Dey. The inhalant was seized, and Dey sued to have the FDA's seizure declared illegal. Who wins? *United States v. Atropine Sulfate 1.0 Mg. (Article of Drug)*, 843 F.2d 860, **Web** 1988 U.S. App Lexis 5817 (United States Court of Appeals for the Fifth Circuit)

44.3 Cosmetics Regulation FBNH Enterprises, Inc. (FBNH), was a distributor of a product known as "French Bronze Tablets." The purpose of the tablets was to allow a person to achieve an even tan without exposure to the sun. When ingested, the tablets imparted color to the skin through the use of various ingredients, one of which is canthaxanthin, a coloring agent. The Food and Drug Administration (FDA) had not approved the use of canthaxanthin as a coloring additive. The FDA became aware that FBNH was marketing the tablets and that each contained 30 milligrams of canthaxanthin. The FDA filed a lawsuit, seeking the forfeiture and condemnation of eight cases of the tablets in the possession of FBNH. FBNH challenged the government's right to seize the tablets. Who wins? *United States v. Eight Unlabeled Cases of an Article of Cosmetic*, 888 F.2d 945, **Web** 1989 U.S. App. Lexis 15589 (United States Court of Appeals for the Second Circuit)

44.4 Drug Regulation Joseph Wahba had a prescription filled at Zuckerman's Pharmacy (Zuckerman's) in Brooklyn, New York. The prescription was for Lomotil, a drug used to counteract stomach disorders. The pharmacy dispensed 30 tablets in a small, plastic container unequipped with a "childproof" cap. Joseph took the medicine home, where it was discovered by Wahba's two-year-old son, Mark. Mark opened the container and ingested approximately 20 pills before Mark's mother saw him and stopped him. She rushed him to a hospital but, despite the efforts of the doctors, Mark lapsed into a coma and died. The Wahbas sued H&N Prescription Center, Inc., the company that owns Zuckerman's, for damages. Who wins? *Wahba v. H&N Prescription Center, Inc.*, 539 F.Supp. 352, **Web** 1982 U.S. Dist. Lexis 12327 (United States District Court for the Eastern District of New York)

BUSINESS ETHICS CASES

44.5 Business Ethics Charles of the Ritz Distributing Corporation (Ritz) was a New York corporation engaged in the sale and distribution of a product called "Rejuvenescence Cream." The extensive advertising campaign that accompanied the sale of the cream placed emphasis upon the supposed rejuvenating powers of the product. The ads claimed that the cream would bring to the user's "skin quickly the clear radiance" and "the petal-like quality and texture of youth." Another advertisement claimed that the product would "restore natural moisture necessary for a live, healthy skin" with the result that "Your face need not know drought years." The Federal Trade Commission (FTC) learned of the ads and asked several experts to investigate the claimed benefits of Rejuvenescence Cream. The experts reported to the FTC that it is impossible for an external application of cosmetics to overcome skin conditions that result from physiological changes occurring with the passage of time. The FTC issued a cease-and-desist order with regard to the advertising. Ritz appealed the FTC's decision to a federal court. Did Ritz act ethically in making its advertising claims? Who wins? *Charles of the Ritz Distributing Corp. v. FTC*, 143 F.2d 676, **Web** 1944 U.S. App. Lexis 3172 (United States Court of Appeals for the Second Circuit)

44.6 Business Ethics Leon A. Tashof operated a store known as the New York Jewelry Company. The store was located in an area that served low-income consumers, many of whom had low-paying jobs and had no bank or charge accounts. About 85 percent of the store's sales were made on credit. The store advertised eyeglasses "from $7.50 complete," including "lenses, frames and case." Tashof advertised this sale extensively on radio and in newspapers. Evidence showed that of the 1,400 pairs of eyeglasses sold by the store, fewer than 10 were sold for $7.50; the rest were more expensive glasses. The Federal Trade Commission sued Tashof for engaging in "bait and switch" marketing. Was Tashof's conduct ethical? Who wins? *Tashof v. Federal Trade Commission*, 437 F.2d 707, **Web** 1970 U.S. App. Lexis 5809 (United States Court of Appeals for the District of Columbia Circuit)

ENDNOTES

1. 21 U.S.C. Section 301.
2. Public Law 101-535.
3. 21 U.S.C. Section 321.
4. 21 U.S.C. Section 360(c) et seq.
5. 15 U.S.C. Section 2051.
6. 15 U.S.C. Sections 41-51.

45 | ENVIRONMENTAL PROTECTION AND GLOBAL WARMING

▲ **Air Pollution** *Environmental protection is becoming a more important issue internationally as countries become aware of the pollution of their air, water and land.*

CHAPTER OBJECTIVES

After studying this chapter, you should be able to:

1. Describe an environmental impact statement and identify when one is needed.
2. Describe the Clean Air Act and national ambient air quality standards.
3. Describe the Clean Water Act and effluent water standards.

4. Explain how environmental laws regulate the use of toxic substances and the disposal of hazardous wastes.
5. Describe how the Endangered Species Act protects endangered and threatened species and their habitats.

CHAPTER CONTENTS

"All animals are equal but some animals are more equal than others."

George Orwell
Animal Farm (1945)

▶ INTRODUCTION TO ENVIRONMENTAL PROTECTION AND GLOBAL WARMING

The environment in the United States—both waterways and the air—was polluted during the Industrial Revolution of the late 1800s through a good portion of the 1900s. In addition, the automobile and other vehicles were introduced in the early 1900s, and their rapid growth and popularity since then have caused substantial air pollution. With the increased population of the United States—currently above 300 million and counting—solid wastes and toxic wastes that pollute the land and the waterways present an important current problem and an increasingly significant problem for the future. Pollution causes injury and death to various forms of wildlife, pollutes drinking water, pollutes the air we breathe, and harms human health and the environment.

Because voluntary pollution control by most businesses and industries had not been successful, and because only a small portion of the American public practiced significant pollution control, the government took on the regulation and control of pollution. The U.S. Congress has enacted federal statutes to protect the air, water, land and the environment from pollution. State governments have also enacted pollution control laws.

This chapter covers the major federal and state laws that protect the environment from pollution.

▶ ENVIRONMENTAL PROTECTION

In the 1970s, the federal government began enacting statutes to protect our nation's air and water from pollution, to regulate hazardous wastes, and to protect wildlife. In many instances, states have enacted their own environmental laws that now coexist with federal law. These laws provide both civil and criminal penalties. *Environmental protection* is one of the most important, and costly, issues facing business and society today.

Environmental Protection Agency

In 1970, Congress created the **Environmental Protection Agency (EPA)** to coordinate the enforcement of the federal **environmental protection laws**. The EPA has broad rule-making

Environmental Protection Agency (EPA)
A federal administrative agency created by Congress to coordinate the implementation and enforcement of the federal environmental protection laws.

powers to adopt regulations to advance the laws that it is empowered to administer. The agency also has adjudicative powers to hold hearings, make decisions, and order remedies for violations of federal environmental laws. In addition, the EPA can initiate judicial proceedings in court against suspected violators of federal environmental laws.

Environmental Impact Statement

National Environmental Policy Act (NEPA)
A federal statute which mandates that the federal government consider the adverse impact a federal government action would have on the environment before the action is implemented.

The **National Environmental Policy Act (NEPA)** became effective January 1, 1970.[1] The NEPA mandates that the federal government consider the "adverse impact" of proposed legislation, rule making, or other federal government action on the environment before the action is implemented.

The NEPA and rules the EPA has adopted require that an **environmental impact statement (EIS)** be prepared for any proposed legislation or major federal action that significantly affects the quality of the human environment. The purpose of an EIS is to provide enough information about the environment to enable the federal government to determine the feasibility of the project. The EIS is also used as evidence in court whenever a federal action is challenged as violating the NEPA or other federal environmental protection laws. Examples of actions that require an EIS include proposals to build new federally funded highways, to license nuclear plants, and the like.

environmental impact statement (EIS)
A document that must be prepared for any proposed legislation or major federal action that significantly affects the quality of the human environment.

An EIS must (1) describe the affected environment, (2) describe the impact of the proposed federal action on the environment, (3) identify and discuss alternatives to the proposed action, (4) list the resources that will be committed to the action, and (5) contain a cost–benefit analysis of the proposed action and alternative actions. Expert professionals, such as engineers, geologists, and accountants, may be consulted during the preparation of an EIS.

Once an EIS is prepared, it is subject to a 30-day public review, during which citizens can submit comments to the EPA. After the comments have been received and reviewed, the EPA will issue an order that states whether the proposed federal action may proceed. Decisions of the EPA are appealable to the appropriate U.S. Court of Appeals. Most states and many local governments have enacted laws that require an EIS to be prepared regarding proposed state and local government action as well as private development.

▶ AIR POLLUTION

air pollution
Pollution caused by factories, homes, vehicles, and the like that affects the air.

One of the major problems facing the United States is **air pollution**. The **Clean Air Act** was enacted in 1963 to assist states in dealing with air pollution. The act was amended in 1970 and 1977 and, most recently, by the **Clean Air Act Amendments** of 1990.[2] The Clean Air Act, as amended, provides comprehensive regulation of air quality in this country.

Clean Air Act
A federal statute that provides comprehensive regulation of air quality in the United States.

Sources of Air Pollution

Substantial amounts of air pollution are emitted by **stationary sources** (e.g., industrial plants, oil refineries, public utilities). The Clean Air Act requires states to identify major stationary sources and develop plans to reduce air pollution from these sources.

Automobile and other vehicle emissions are a major source of air pollution in this country. In an effort to control emissions from these **mobile sources of air pollution**, the Clean Air Act requires air pollution controls to be installed on motor vehicles. Emission standards have been set for automobiles, trucks, buses, motorcycles, and airplanes. In addition, the Clean Air Act authorizes the EPA to regulate air pollution caused by fuel and fuel additives.

National Ambient Air Quality Standards

national ambient air quality standards (NAAQS)
Standards for certain pollutants set by the EPA that protect (1) human beings (primary level) and (2) vegetation, matter, climate, visibility, and economic values (secondary level).

The Clean Air Act directs the EPA to establish **national ambient air quality standards (NAAQS)** for certain pollutants. These standards are set at two different levels: primary (to protect human beings) and secondary (to protect vegetation, matter, climate, visibility, and economic values). Specific standards have been established for carbon monoxide, nitrogen oxide, sulfur oxide, ozone, lead, and particulate matter.

Although the EPA establishes air quality standards, the states are responsible for their enforcement. The federal government has the right to enforce these air pollution standards if the states fail to do so. Each state is required to prepare a **state implementation plan (SIP)** that sets out how the state plans to meet the federal standards. The EPA has divided each state into **air quality control regions (AQCRs)**. Each region is monitored to ensure compliance.

Nonattainment Areas

Regions that do not meet air quality standards are designated **nonattainment areas**. A nonattainment area is classified into one of five categories—*marginal, moderate, serious, severe,* or *extreme*—based on the degree to which it exceeds the ozone standard. Deadlines are established for areas to meet the attainment level.

nonattainment area
A geographical area that does not meet established air quality standards.

States must submit compliance plans that (1) identify major sources of air pollution and require them to install pollution control equipment, (2) institute permit systems for new stationary sources, and (3) implement inspection programs to monitor mobile sources. States that fail to develop or implement approved plans are subject to the following sanctions: loss of federal highway funds and limitations on new sources of emissions (e.g., the EPA can prohibit the construction of a new pollution-causing industrial plant in a nonattainment area).

The Clean Air Act was at issue in the following case.

U.S. SUPREME COURT   CASE 45.1 Air Pollution

Whitman, Administrator of Environmental Protection Agency v. American Trucking Association

531 U.S. 457, 121 S.Ct. 903, 149 L.Ed.2d 1, Web 2001 U.S. Lexis 1952 (2001)
Supreme Court of the United States

"The EPA, based on the information about health effects contained in the technical criteria documents, is to identify the maximum airborne concentration of a pollutant that the public health can tolerate."

—Justice Scalia

Facts

Section 109 of the federal Clean Air Act requires the administrator of the EPA, a federal administrative agency, to set national ambient air quality standards (NAAQS) for air pollutants. Section 109 instructs the EPA to set NAAQS at levels "to protect the public health" with "an adequate margin of safety." Pursuant to Section 109, the EPA issued new standards for ozone and particulate matter emitted from the operation of trucks. The American Trucking Association sued the EPA, arguing that the EPA must consider the cost caused to trucking firms before issuing the NAAQS. The EPA argued that it did not have to do so under the statute. The U.S. District Court held for the American Trucking Association, but the U.S. Court of Appeals held for the EPA on this issue. The U.S. Supreme Court granted review.

Issue

Under Section 109 of the federal Clean Air Act, must the EPA consider the cost imposed on trucking firms before setting NAAQS for ozone and particulate matter emissions from trucks?

Language of the U.S. Supreme Court

Section 109 instructs the EPA to set primary ambient air quality standards "the attainment and maintenance of which are requisite to protect the public health" with "an adequate margin of safety." This text does not permit the EPA to consider costs in setting the standards. The language is absolute. The EPA, based on the information about health effects contained in the technical criteria documents, is to identify the maximum airborne concentration of a pollutant that the public health can tolerate, decrease the concentration to provide an adequate margin of safety, and set the standard at that level. Nowhere are the costs of achieving such a standard made part of that initial calculation.

Respondent argues many more factors than air pollution affect public health. In particular, the economic cost of implementing a very stringent standard might produce losses sufficient to offset the health gains achieved in cleaning the air—for example, by closing down whole industries and thereby impoverishing the workers and consumers dependent upon those industries. That is unquestionably true. Accordingly, to prevail in their present challenge, respondent must show a textual commitment of authority to the EPA to consider costs in setting NAAQS under Section 109. Congress does not alter the fundamental details of a regulatory scheme.

(case continues)

Decision

The U.S. Supreme Court held that the statutory language of Section 109 of the Clean Air Act does not require the EPA to consider the cost to trucking firms for implementing the NAAQS set by the EPA. The Supreme Court affirmed the decision of the Court of Appeals in favor of the EPA.

Case Questions

Critical Legal Thinking Do you think the statutory language of Section 109 is clear as it applies to this case?

Business Ethics Would the "public health" be compromised under the trucking firms' argument? Why did the trucking firms resist the NAAQS set by the EPA?

Contemporary Business What are the economic consequences of the Supreme Court's ruling in this case? Explain.

CONTEMPORARY ENVIRONMENT

Indoor Air Pollution

According to officials of the EPA, the air inside some buildings may be 100 times more polluted than outside air. Doctors increasingly attribute a wide range of symptoms to **indoor air pollution**, or **sick building syndrome**. Indoor air pollution has two primary causes. In an effort to reduce dependence on foreign oil, many recently constructed office buildings have been overly insulated and built with sealed windows and no outside air ducts. As a result, no fresh air enters many workplaces. This lack of fresh air can cause headaches, fatigue, and dizziness among workers.

The other chief cause of sick building syndrome, which is believed to affect up to one-third of U.S. office buildings, is hazardous chemicals and construction materials. In the office, these include everything from asbestos to noxious fumes omitted from copy machines, carbonless paper, and cleaning fluids. In the home, radon, an odorless gas that is emitted from the natural breakdown of uranium in soil, poses a particularly widespread danger. Radon gas damages and may destroy lung tissue. The costs of eliminating these conditions can be colossal.

Experts predict that sick building syndrome is likely to spawn a flood of litigation and that a wide range of parties will be sued. Manufacturers, employers, home sellers, builders, engineers, and architects will increasingly be forced to defend themselves against tort and breach of contract actions filed by homeowners, employees, and others affected by indoor air pollution. Insurance companies will undoubtedly be drawn into costly lawsuits stemming from indoor air pollution.

India *This is a photograph of a watercourse in the country of India. In the twenty-first century, governments around the world will have to take a greater interest in protecting the environment from pollution so that the peoples of the world will have safe drinking water and food supplies and so many types of fish, animals, reptiles, and other wildlife will be protected from extinction.*

▶ WATER POLLUTION

Water pollution affects human health, recreation, agriculture, and business. Pollution of waterways by industry and humans has caused severe ecological and environmental problems, including making water sources unsafe for human consumption, fish, birds, and animals. The federal government has enacted a comprehensive scheme of statutes and regulations to prevent and control water pollution.

In 1948, Congress enacted the **Federal Water Pollution Control Act (FWPCA)** to regulate water pollution. This act has been amended several times. As amended, it is simply referred to as the **Clean Water Act**.[3] This act is administered by the EPA.

Pursuant to the Clean Water Act, the EPA has established water quality standards that define which bodies of water can be used for public drinking water, recreation (e.g., swimming), propagation of fish and wildlife, and agricultural and industrial uses. States are primarily responsible for enforcing the provisions of the Clean Water Act and EPA regulations adopted thereunder. If a state fails to do so, the federal government may enforce the act.

water pollution
Pollution of lakes, rivers, oceans, and other bodies of water.

Clean Water Act
A federal statute that establishes water quality standards and regulates water pollution.

Point Sources of Water Pollution

The Clean Water Act authorizes the EPA to establish water pollution control standards for **point sources of water pollution**. Point sources are sources of pollution that are fixed and stationary. Point source dischargers of pollutants are required to maintain monitoring equipment, keep samples of discharges, and keep records.

Examples Mines, manufacturing plants, paper mills, electric utility plants, and municipal sewage plants are examples of stationary sources of water pollution.

We won't have a society if we destroy the environment.

Margaret Mead

Thermal Pollution

The Clean Water Act expressly forbids **thermal pollution** because the discharge of heated waters or materials into the nation's waterways can upset the ecological balance; decrease the oxygen content of water; and harm fish, birds, and other animals that use the waterways.[4] Sources of thermal pollution (e.g., electric utility companies, manufacturing plants) are subject to the provisions of the Clean Water Act and regulations adopted by the EPA.

Examples Electric utility plants and manufacturing plants often emit thermal pollution by discharging heated water or materials into the water. This heated water or material could harm fish in the water, as well as birds and other animals that use the water.

thermal pollution
Heated water or material discharged into waterways that upsets the ecological balance and decreases the oxygen content.

Wetlands

Wetlands are defined as areas that are inundated or saturated by surface water or ground water that support vegetation typically adapted for life in saturated soil conditions. Wetlands include swamps, marshes, bogs, and similar areas that support birds, animals, and vegetative life. The federal Clean Water Act regulates the discharge of dredged or fill material into navigable water and wetlands that have a significant nexus to navigable waters. The **Army Corps of Engineers** is authorized to enforce this statute and to issue permits for discharge of dredged or fill material into navigable waters and qualified wetlands in the United States. The Clean Water Act forbids the filling or dredging of navigable waters and qualified wetlands unless a permit has been obtained from the Army Corps of Engineers.

wetlands
Areas that are inundated or saturated by surface water or ground water that support vegetation typically adapted for life in such conditions.

Safe Drinking Water Act

The **Safe Drinking Water Act**,[5] enacted in 1974 and amended in 1986, authorizes the EPA to establish national primary drinking water standards (setting the minimum quality of water for human consumption). The act prohibits the dumping of wastes into wells used for drinking water. The states are primarily responsible for enforcing the act. If a state fails to do so, the federal government can enforce the act.

Safe Drinking Water Act
A federal statute that authorizes the EPA to establish national primary drinking water standards.

Ocean Protection

Marine Protection, Research, and Sanctuaries Act
A federal statute that extends limited environmental protection to the oceans.

The **Marine Protection, Research, and Sanctuaries Act**,[6] enacted in 1972, extends environment protection to the oceans. It (1) requires a permit for dumping wastes and other foreign materials into ocean waters and (2) establishes marine sanctuaries in ocean waters as far seaward as the edge of the Continental Shelf and in the Great Lakes and their connecting waters. The Clean Water Act authorizes the U.S. government to clean up oil spills and spills of other hazardous substances in ocean waters within 12 miles of the shore and on the Continental Shelf and to recover the cleanup costs from responsible parties.

There have been several major oil spills from oil tankers in ocean waters off the coast of the United States. These oil spills have caused significant damage to plant, animal, and human life, as well as to their habitats. In response, Congress enacted the federal **Oil Pollution Act** of 1990,[7] which is administered by the U.S. Coast Guard. This act requires the oil industry to adopt procedures and contingency plans to readily respond to and clean up oil spills. A tanker owner-operator must prove that it is fully insured to cover any liability that may occur from an oil spill. The act also requires oil tankers to have double hulls by 2015.

Oil Pollution Act
A federal statute that requires the oil industry to take measures to prevent oil spills and to readily respond to and clean up oil spills.

ETHICS SPOTLIGHT

The Exxon Valdez Oil Spill

In 1989, the *Exxon Valdez*, a 987-foot long oil tanker owned by the Exxon Corporation, was carrying 53 million gallons of crude oil when it ran aground on the treacherous Bligh Reef off the coast of Prince Edward Sound in Alaska. Eleven million gallons of crude oil was released into the sea and eventually spread over 1,200 miles of Alaskan shoreline. About 250,000 seabirds and thousands of marine mammals, covered by the crude oil, died. Thousands of fishers, cannery workers, and other Alaskan residents suffered loss of jobs and damage to property because of the oil spill.

Evidence showed that the ship's captain, prior to boarding the vessel, had gone to waterfront bars and had five double shots of 80-proof alcohol. The captain had previously been treated for alcoholism but had relapsed. When the ship ran aground, the captain was in his cabin and had left a third mate in charge. The company argued that the *Exxon Valdez*'s foul-up was merely an accident. The injured parties alleged that Exxon knew that the captain had had an alcoholic relapse and still let this person captain the monstrous ship.

A massive cleanup effort was put into place. State and federal governments brought legal actions against Exxon. More than 32,000 private plaintiffs filed a class action

lawsuit against Exxon to recover for their losses. Exxon—which is now Exxon Mobil Corporation—paid out about $3.5 billion for cleanup costs and to compensate those whose livelihoods were affected. The *Exxon Valdez*, which was only three years old when it ran aground in Alaska, was repaired and renamed by Exxon.

Legal maneuvering in the case has gone on for over 20 years. The company tries to pay less money, and the plaintiffs try to get more money. Originally the U.S. District Court awarded $4.5 billion of punitive damages against Exxon, but that amount was later reduced to $4 billion and then to $2.5 billion. Exxon would not quit; it appealed the case to the U.S. Supreme Court, arguing that maritime law did not permit the awarding of punitive damages against the owner of a vessel on the high seas.

The U.S. Supreme Court, in a decision issued in 2008, held that an award of punitive damages is permissible in maritime cases but found that a 1:1 ratio of compensatory-to-punitive damages is the appropriate limit on punitive damages in maritime tort cases. Thus, the award of punitive damages was reduced from $2.5 billion to $500 million. *Exxon Shipping Company v. Baker*, 128 S.Ct. 2605, 171 L.Ed.2d 570, **Web** 2008 U.S. Lexis 5263 (Supreme Court of the United States)

toxic substances
Chemicals used by agriculture, industry, business, mining, and households that cause injury to humans, birds, animals, fish, and vegetation.

hazardous waste
Hazardous waste that may cause or significantly contribute to an increase in mortality or serious illness or pose a hazard to human health or the environment if improperly managed.

▶ TOXIC SUBSTANCES AND HAZARDOUS WASTE

Many chemicals used by agriculture, industry, business, mining, and households contain **toxic substances** that cause cancer, birth defects, and other health-related problems in human beings, as well as injury or death to birds, fish, other animals, and vegetation. Many chemical compounds that are used in the manufacture of products are toxic (e.g., PCBs, asbestos). Each year, hundreds of chemicals and chemical compounds are found to be possibly toxic.

Agriculture, mining, industry, other businesses, and households generate wastes that often contain hazardous substances that can harm the environment or pose a danger to human health. The mishandling and disposal of **hazardous wastes** can cause air, water, and land pollution.

Examples Hazardous wastes consist of garbage, sewage, industrial discharges, old equipment, and such that are discharged or placed in the environment.

Toxic Substances Control

In 1976, Congress enacted the **Toxic Substances Control Act**[8] and gave the EPA authority to administer the act. The act requires the EPA to identify **toxic air pollutants** that presented a substantial risk of injury to human health or the environment. So far, more than 200 **chemicals** have been listed as toxic, including asbestos, mercury, vinyl chloride, benzene, beryllium, and radionuclides.

The act requires the EPA to establish standards for toxic chemicals and requires stationary sources to install equipment and technology to control emissions of toxic substances. EPA standards for toxic substances are set without regard to economic or technological feasibility. The act requires manufacturers and processors to test new chemicals to determine their effects on human health and the environment and to report the results to the EPA before the chemicals are marketed.

The EPA may limit or prohibit the manufacture and sale of toxic substances, and it can remove them from commerce if it finds that they pose an imminent hazard or an unreasonable risk of injury to human health or the environment. The EPA also requires special labeling of toxic substances.

Toxic Substances Control Act
A federal statute that authorizes the EPA to regulate toxic substances.

Insecticides, Fungicides, and Rodenticides

Farmers and ranchers use chemical pesticides, herbicides, fungicides, and rodenticides to kill insects, weeds, and pests. Evidence shows that the use of some of these chemicals on food, and their residual accumulation in soil, poses health hazards. In 1947, Congress enacted the **Insecticide, Fungicide, and Rodenticide Act**, which gave the federal government authority to regulate pesticides and related chemicals. This act, which was substantially amended in 1972,[9] is administered by the EPA. Under the act, pesticides must be registered with the EPA before they can be sold. The EPA may suspend the registration of a registered pesticide that it finds poses an imminent danger or emergency.

Insecticide, Fungicide, and Rodenticide Act
A federal statute that requires pesticides, herbicides, fungicides, and rodenticides to be registered with the EPA; the EPA may deny, suspend, or cancel registration.

Hazardous Waste

The disposal of hazardous wastes sometimes causes **land pollution**. In 1976, Congress enacted the **Resource Conservation and Recovery Act (RCRA)**,[10] which regulates the disposal of new hazardous wastes. This act, which has been amended several times, authorizes the EPA to regulate facilities that generate, treat, store, transport, and dispose of hazardous wastes. States have primary responsibility for implementing the standards established by the act and EPA regulations.

The act defines *hazardous waste* as a solid waste that may cause or significantly contribute to an increase in mortality or serious illness or pose a hazard to human health or the environment if improperly managed. The EPA has designated substances that are toxic, radioactive, or corrosive or ignitable as hazardous and can add to the list of hazardous wastes as needed.

The EPA also establishes standards and procedures for the safe treatment, storage, disposal, and transportation of hazardous wastes. Under the act, the EPA is authorized to regulate underground storage facilities, such as underground gasoline tanks.

land pollution
Pollution of the land that is generally caused by hazardous waste being disposed of in an improper manner.

Resource Conservation and Recovery Act (RCRA)
A federal statute that authorizes the EPA to regulate facilities that generate, treat, store, transport, and dispose of hazardous wastes.

LANDMARK LAW

Superfund

In 1980, Congress enacted the **Comprehensive Environmental Response, Compensation, and Liability Act (CERCLA)**, which is commonly called the **Superfund** [42 U.S.C. Sections 9601-9675]. The act, which was significantly amended in 1986, is administered by the EPA. The act gave the federal government a mandate to deal with hazardous wastes that have been spilled, stored, or abandoned. The act provides for the creation of a government fund to finance the cleanup of hazardous waste sites (hence the name *Superfund*). The fund is financed through taxes on chemicals, feedstock, motor fuels, and other products that contain hazardous substances.

The Superfund requires the EPA to (1) identify sites in the United States where hazardous wastes have been disposed, stored, abandoned, or spilled and (2) rank these sites regarding the severity of the risk. When it ranks the sites, the EPA considers factors such as the types of hazardous waste, the toxicity of the wastes, the types of pollution (i.e., air, water, land, other pollution), the number of people potentially affected by the risk, and other factors. The hazardous waste sites with the highest ranking are put on the National Priority List. The sites on this list receive first consideration for

cleanup. The EPA has the authority to clean up hazardous priority or nonpriority sites quickly to prevent fire, explosion, contamination of drinking water, and other imminent danger.

The EPA can order a responsible party to clean up a hazardous waste site. If that party fails to do so, the EPA can clean up the site and recover the cost of the cleanup. The Superfund imposes *strict liability*—that is, liability without fault. The EPA can recover the cost of the cleanup from (1) the generator who deposited the wastes, (2) the transporter of the wastes to the site, (3) the owner of the site at the time of the disposal, and (4) the current owner and operator of the site. The Superfund permits states and private parties who clean up hazardous waste sites to seek reimbursement from the fund.

Comprehensive Environmental Response, Compensation, and Liability Act (CERCLA or Superfund)
A federal statute that authorizes the federal government to deal with hazardous wastes. The act creates a monetary fund to finance the cleanup of hazardous waste sites.

radiation pollution
Emissions from radioactive wastes that can cause injury and death to humans and other life and can cause severe damage to the environment.

Nuclear Regulatory Commission (NRC)
A federal agency that licenses the construction and opening of commercial nuclear power plants.

Nuclear Waste

Nuclear-powered fuel plants create radioactive wastes that maintain a high level of *radioactivity*. Radioactivity can cause injury and death to humans and other life and can also cause severe damage to the environment. Accidents, human error, faulty construction, and such can all be causes of **radiation pollution**.

The **Nuclear Regulatory Commission (NRC)**, which was created by Congress in 1977, licenses the construction and opening of commercial nuclear power plants. It continually monitors the operation of nuclear power plants and may close a plant if safety violations are found. The EPA is empowered to set standards for radioactivity in the environment and to regulate the disposal of radioactive waste. The EPA also regulates thermal pollution from nuclear power plants and emissions from uranium mines and mills. The **Nuclear Waste Policy Act** of 1982[11] mandates that the federal government select and develop a permanent site for the disposal of **nuclear wastes**.

INTERNATIONAL LAW
Global Warming

For decades, scientists have been concerned that **greenhouse gases**—particularly from carbon dioxide created by burning coal, oil, and gas, as well as deforestation—are causing a **global warming** effect and creating a hole in the ozone layer around the earth. The effect of global warming is immediate; since the advent of weather records in the mid-1800s, the eight warmest years on record have all occurred since 1998.

Because of global warming, sea levels are rising worldwide. This is primarily due to the melting of glaciers and ice caps, including the Greenland Ice Sheet and the Antarctic Ice Sheet—resulting in more water in the oceans and a decrease of land. Increasing global temperature will increase the occurrence and intensity of extreme weather

events, changes in agricultural yields, increases in diseases, and the extinction of species.

After much debate, the countries of the world met in Kyoto, Japan, and proposed the **Kyoto Protocol**, an international treaty to reduce greenhouse gases. In 2001, 178 countries agreed to abide by the rules of the Kyoto Protocol. The Kyoto Protocol calls for the reduction of greenhouse gases worldwide to 5.2 percent below 1990 levels, with this goal to be reached by 2012. The Kyoto Protocol calls for member nations to create a fund to help developing nations adopt technology to reduce greenhouse gases. The United States has not signed the Kyoto Protocol but instead has chosen to adopt its own laws to control greenhouse gas emissions.

▶ ENDANGERED SPECIES

Many species of birds, fish, reptiles, and animals are **endangered** or threatened with extinction. The reduction of certain species of wildlife may be caused by environmental pollution, real estate development, or hunting. The **Endangered Species Act** was enacted in 1973.[12] The act, as amended, protects *endangered* and *threatened* species of wildlife. The secretary of the interior is empowered to declare a form of wildlife as endangered or threatened.

The act requires the EPA and the Department of Commerce to designate *critical habitats* for each endangered and threatened species. Real estate and other development in these areas is prohibited or severely limited. The secretary of commerce is empowered to enforce the provisions of the act as to marine species. In addition, the Endangered Species Act, which applies to both government and private persons, prohibits the taking of any endangered species. *Taking* is defined as an act intended to "harass, harm, pursue, hunt, shoot, wound, kill, trap, capture, or collect" an endangered animal.

Numerous other federal laws protect wildlife. These include (1) the Migratory Bird Treaty Act, (2) the Bald Eagle Protection Act, (3) the Wild Free-Roaming Horses and Burros Act, (4) the Marine Mammal Protection Act, (5) the Migratory Bird Conservation Act, (6) the Fishery Conservation and Management Act, (7) the Fish and Wildlife Coordination Act, and (8) the National Wildlife Refuge System. Many states have enacted statutes that protect and preserve wildlife.

Endangered Species Act
A federal statute that protects endangered and threatened species of wildlife.

LANDMARK LAW

Endangered Species: Tennessee Valley Authority v. Hill, Secretary of the Interior

"Examination of the language, history, and structure of the legislation under review here indicates beyond doubt that Congress intended endangered species to be afforded the highest of priorities."

—Chief Justice Burger

The Tennessee Valley Authority (TVA) is a wholly owned public corporation of the United States. It operates a series of dams, reservoirs, and water projects that provide electric power, irrigation, and flood control to areas in several southern states. In 1967, with appropriations from Congress, the TVA began construction of the Tellico Dam on the Little Tennessee River. When completed, the dam would impound water covering 16,500 acres, thereby converting the river's shallow, fast-flowing waters into a deep reservoir over 30 miles long. Construction of the dam continued until 1977, when it was completed.

In 1973, a University of Tennessee ichthyologist found a previously unknown species of perch called the *Percina tanasi*—or "snail darter"—in the Little Tennessee River. After further investigation, it was determined that approximately 10,000 to 15,000 of these 3-inch, tannish-colored fish existed in the river's waters that would be flooded by the operation of the Tellico Dam. The snail darter is not found anywhere else in the world. It feeds exclusively on snails and requires substantial oxygen, both supplied by the fast-moving waters of the Little Tennessee River. The impounding of the water behind the Tellico Dam would destroy the snail darter's food and oxygen supplies, thus causing its extinction. Evidence was introduced, showing that the TVA could not, at that time, successfully transplant the snail darter to any other habitat.

Also in 1973, Congress enacted the Endangered Species Act, which authorizes the secretary of the interior to declare species of animal life endangered and to identify the critical habitats of these creatures. When a species or its habitat is so listed, Section 7 of the act mandates that the secretary take such action as is necessary to ensure that actions of the federal government do not jeopardize the continued existence of such endangered species. The secretary of the interior declared the snail darter an endangered species and the area that would be affected by the Tellico Dam its critical habitat.

Congress continued to appropriate funds for the construction of the dam, which was completed at a cost of over $100 million. In 1976, a regional association of biological scientists, a Tennessee conservation group, and several individuals filed an action seeking to enjoin the TVA from closing the gates of the dam and impounding the water in the reservoir on the grounds that those actions would violate Section 7 of the act by causing the extinction of the snail darter. The District Court held in favor of the TVA. The Court of Appeals reversed and remanded with instructions to the District Court to issue a permanent injunction halting the operation of the Tellico Dam. The TVA appealed to the U.S. Supreme Court, which agreed to hear the case. The issue presented to the U.S. Supreme Court was: Would the TVA be in violation of the Endangered Species Act if it operated the Tellico Dam?

The U.S. Supreme Court held that the Endangered Species Act prohibited the impoundment of the Little Tennessee River by the Tellico Dam. The Supreme Court affirmed the injunction against the operation of the dam. The Court stated:

It may seem curious to some that the survival of a relatively small number of 3-inch fish among all the countless millions of species extant would require the permanent halting of a virtually completed dam for which Congress has expended more than $100 million.

We conclude, however, that the explicit provisions of the Endangered Species Act required precisely this result. As it was passed, the Endangered Species Act of 1973 represented the most comprehensive legislation for the preservation of endangered species ever enacted by any nation.

Eventually, after substantial research and investigation, it was determined that the snail darter could live in another habitat that was found for it. After the snail darter was removed, at government expense, to this new location, the TVA was permitted to close the gates of the Tellico Dam and begin its operation. Under the federal Endangered Species Act, a small fish was saved from extinction. *Tennessee Valley Authority v. Hill, Secretary of the Interior*, 437 U.S. 153, 98 S.Ct. 2279, 57 L.Ed.2d 117, **Web** 1978 U.S. Lexis 33 (Supreme Court of the United States)

Hoover Dam *The Hoover Dam is built on the Nevada–Arizona border. The dam, which was completed in 1936, is used for flood control, the generation of electric power, and the provision of water supplies. A reservoir named Lake Mead is created behind the dam. The dam is named after Herbert F. Hoover, the thirty-first president of the United States.*

▶ STATE ENVIRONMENTAL PROTECTION LAWS

Many state and local governments have enacted statutes and ordinances to protect the environment. Most states require that an EIS or a report be prepared for any proposed state action. In addition, under their police power to protect the "health, safety, and welfare" of their residents, many states require private industry to prepare EISs for proposed developments. Some states have enacted special environmental statutes to protect unique areas within their boundaries.

Examples Florida has enacted laws to protect the Everglades, and California has enacted laws to protect its Pacific Ocean coastline.

Harbor, St. Ignace, Michigan *This photograph is of the harbor of St. Ignace, Michigan. The city is located on the shoreline close to where Lake Michigan and Lake Huron, two of the five Great Lakes, converge. The waters of the harbor look serene and clean. But this was not always so and is not quite the case below the waterline. For over a century, the Great Lakes and its tributary streams and rivers have been subject to pollution caused by the dumping of lead and mercury from ore smelting operations, ammonia and industrial sludge from manufacturing plants, scrap from sawmills, sewage from boats, and other sources of pollution. The enactment and enforcement of federal and state antipollution laws has saved the Great Lakes.*

TEST REVIEW TERMS AND CONCEPTS

Air pollution
Air quality control regions (AQCRs)
Army Corps of Engineers
Chemicals
Clean Air Act
Clean Air Act Amendments
Clean Water Act
Comprehensive Environmental Response, Compensation, and Liability Act (CERCLA or Superfund)
Endangered species
Endangered Species Act
Environmental impact statement (EIS)

Environmental Protection Agency (EPA)
Environmental protection laws
Exxon Valdez
Federal Water Pollution Control Act (FWPCA)
Global warming
Greenhouse gases
Hazardous wastes
Indoor air pollution (sick building syndrome)
Insecticide, Fungicide, and Rodenticide Act
Kyoto Protocol
Land pollution
Marine Protection, Research, and Sanctuaries Act

Mobile source of air pollution
National ambient air quality standards (NAAQS)
National Environmental Policy Act (NEPA)
Nonattainment area
Nuclear Regulatory Commission (NRC)
Nuclear waste
Nuclear Waste Policy Act
Oil Pollution Act
Point source of water pollution
Radiation pollution
Resource Conservation and Recovery Act (RCRA)
Safe Drinking Water Act

State implementation plan (SIP)
Stationary source of air pollution
Thermal pollution
Toxic air pollutants
Toxic substances
Toxic Substances Control Act
Water pollution
Wetlands

CASE PROBLEMS

45.1 Environmental Impact Statement   The U.S. Forest Service is responsible for managing the country's national forests for recreational and other purposes. This includes issuing special-use permits to private companies to operate ski areas on federal lands. Sandy Butte is a 6,000-foot mountain located in the Okanogan National Forest in Okanogan County, Washington. Sandy Butte, like the Methow Valley it overlooks, is a pristine, unspoiled, sparsely populated area located within the North Cascades National Park. Large populations of mule deer and other animals exist in the park.

Methow Recreation, Inc. (MRI), applied to the Forest Service for a special-use permit to develop and operate its proposed Early Winters Ski Resort on Sandy Butte and a 1,165-acre parcel of private land it had acquired adjacent to the national forest. The proposed development would make use of approximately 3,900 acres of Sandy Butte to provide up to 16 ski lifts capable of accommodating 10,500 skiers at one time. Is an environmental impact statement required? *Robertson v. Methow Valley Citizens Council*, 490 U.S. 332, 109 S.Ct. 1835, 104 L.Ed.2d 351, **Web** 1989 U.S. Lexis 2160 (Supreme Court of the United States)

45.2 Clean Air Act   Pilot Petroleum Associates, Inc., and various affiliated companies distributed gasoline to retail gasoline stations in the state of New York. Pilot owned some of these stations and leased them to individual operators who were under contract to purchase gasoline from Pilot. The EPA took samples of gasoline from five different service stations to which Pilot had sold unleaded gasoline. These samples showed that Pilot had delivered "unleaded gasoline that contained amounts of lead in excess of that permitted by the Clean Air Act and EPA regulations." The United States brought criminal charges against Pilot for violating the act and EPA regulations and sought fines from Pilot. Who wins? *United States v. Pilot Petroleum Associates, Inc.*, 712 F.Supp. 1077, **Web** 1989 U.S. Dist. Lexis 6119 (United States District Court for the Eastern District of New York)

45.3 Rule Making   Placer mining is a method used to mine for gold in the streambeds of Alaska. The miner removes soil, mud, and clay from the streambed, places it in an on-site sluice box, and separates the gold from the other matter by forcing water through the pay dirt. The water in the sluice box is discharged into the stream, causing aesthetic and water-quality impacts on the water both in the immediate vicinity and downstream. Toxic metals, including arsenic, cadmium, lead, zinc, and copper, are found in higher concentrations in streams where mining occurs than in streams where there is no mining.

After public notice and comment, the EPA issued rules that require placer miners to use the best practical control technology (BPCT) to control discharges of nontoxic pollutants and the best available control technology (BACT) to control discharges of toxic pollutants. The BACT standard requires miners to construct settling ponds and recycle water through these ponds before discharging the water into the streambed. This method requires substantial expenditure. The Alaska Miners Association challenged the EPA's rule making. Who wins? *Rybachek v. U.S. Environmental Protection Agency*, 904 F.2d 1276, **Web** 1990 U.S. App. Lexis 7833 (United States Court of Appeals for the Ninth Circuit)

45.4 Wetlands   Leslie Salt Company owned a 153-acre tract of undeveloped land south of San Francisco. The property abutted the San Francisco National Wildlife Refuge and was approximately one-quarter mile from Newark Slough, a tidal arm of San Francisco Bay. Originally, the property was

pastureland. The first change occurred in the early 1900s, when Leslie's predecessors constructed facilities to manufacture salt on the property. They excavated pits and created large, shallow, watertight basins on the property. Salt production on the property was stopped in 1959. The construction of a sewer line and public roads on and around the property created ditches and culverts on the property. Newark Slough is connected to the property by these culverts, and tidewaters reach the property. Water accumulates in the ponds, ditches, and culverts, providing wetland vegetation to wildlife and migratory birds. Fish live in the ponds on the property. Over 25 years later, Leslie started to dig a ditch to drain the property and began construction to block the culvert that connected the property to the Newark Slough. The Army Corps of Engineers issued a cease-and-desist order against Leslie. Leslie challenged the order. Who wins? *Leslie Salt Co. v. United States*, 896 F.2d 354, **Web** 1990 U.S. App. Lexis 1524 (United States Court of Appeals for the Ninth Circuit)

45.5 Clean Water Act   The Reserve Mining Company (Reserve) owned and operated a mine in Minnesota that was located on the shores of Lake Superior and produced hazardous waste. In 1947, Reserve obtained a permit from the state of Minnesota to dump its wastes into Lake Superior. The permits prohibited discharges that would "result in any clouding or discoloration of the water outside the specific discharge zone" or "result in any material adverse affects on public water supplies." Reserve discharged its wastes into Lake Superior for years. Evidence showed that the discharges caused discoloration of surface waters outside the zone of discharge and contained carcinogens that adversely affected public water supplies. The United States sued Reserve for engaging in unlawful water pollution. Who wins? *United States v. Reserve Mining Company*, 543 F.2d 1210, **Web** 1976 U.S. App. Lexis 6503 (United States Court of Appeals for the Eighth Circuit)

45.6 Hazardous Waste   Douglas Hoflin was the director of the Public Works Department for Ocean Shores, Washington. During a period of seven years, the department purchased 3,500 gallons of paint for road maintenance. As painting jobs were finished, the 55-gallon drums that had contained the paint were returned to the department's yard. Paint contains hazardous substances such as lead. When 14 of the drums were discovered to still contain unused paint, Hoflin instructed employees to haul the paint drums to the city's sewage treatment plant and bury them. The employees dug a hole on the grounds of the treatment plant and dumped in the drums. Some of the drums were rusted and leaking. The hole was not deep enough, so the employees crushed the drums with a front-end loader to make them fit. The refuse was then covered with sand. Almost two years later, one of the city's employees reported the incident to state authorities, who referred the matter to the EPA. Investigation showed that the paint had contaminated the soil. The United States brought criminal charges against Hoflin for aiding and abetting the illegal dumping of hazardous waste. Who wins? *United States* *v. Hoflin*, 880 F.2d 1033, **Web** 1989 U.S. App. Lexis 10169 (United States Court of Appeals for the Ninth Circuit)

45.7 Nuclear Waste Metropolitan Edison Company owned and operated two nuclear-fueled power plants at Three Mile Island near Harrisburg, Pennsylvania. Both power plants were licensed by the NRC after extensive proceedings and investigations, including the preparation of the required environmental impact statements. When one of the power plants was shut down for refueling, the other plant suffered a serious accident that damaged the reactor. The governor of Pennsylvania recommended an evacuation of all pregnant women and small children, and many area residents did leave their homes for several days. As it turned out, no dangerous radiation was released.

People Against Nuclear Energy (PANE), an association of area residents who opposed further operation of the nuclear power plants at Three Mile Island, sued to enjoin the plants from reopening. They argued that the reopening of the plants would cause severe psychological health damage to persons living in the vicinity and serious damage to the stability and cohesiveness of the community. Are these reasons sufficient to prevent the reopening of the nuclear power plants? *Metropolitan Edison Company v. People Against Nuclear*

Energy, 460 U.S. 766, 103 S.Ct. 1556, 75 L.Ed.2d 534, **Web** 1983 U.S. Lexis 21 (Supreme Court of the United States)

45.8 Endangered Species The red-cockaded woodpecker is a small bird that lives almost exclusively in old pine forests throughout the southern United States. Its survival depends on a very specialized habitat of pine trees that are at least 30, if not 60, years old, in which they build nests and forage for insects. The population of this bird decreased substantially as pine forests were destroyed by clear-cutting. The secretary of the interior has named the red-cockaded woodpecker an endangered species.

The Forest Service, which is under the authority of the secretary of agriculture, manages federal forests and is charged with duties to provide recreation, protect wildlife, and provide timber. To accomplish the charge of providing timber, the Forest Service leases national forest lands to private companies for lumbering. When the Forest Service proposed to lease several national forests in Texas, where the red-cockaded woodpecker lives, to private companies for lumbering, the Sierra Club sued. The Sierra Club sought to enjoin the Forest Service from leasing these national forests for lumbering. Who wins? *Sierra Club v. Lyng, Secretary of Agriculture*, 694 F.Supp. 1260, **Web** 1988 U.S. Dist. Lexis 9203 (United States District Court for the Eastern District of Texas)

BUSINESS ETHICS CASES

45.9 Business Ethics The state of Michigan owns approximately 57,000 acres of land that comprise the Pigeon River County State Forest in southwestern Michigan. Shell Oil Company applied to the Michigan Department of Natural Resources (DNR) for a permit to drill 10 exploratory oil wells in the forest. Roads had to be constructed to reach the proposed drill sites. Evidence showed that the only sizable elk herd east of the Mississippi River annually used the forest as its habitat and returned to this range every year to breed. Experts testified that elk avoid roads, even when there is no traffic, and that the construction of the roads and wells would destroy the elk's habitat. Michigan law prohibits activities that adversely affect natural resources. The West Michigan Environmental Action Council sued the DNR, seeking to enjoin the DNR from granting the drilling permits to Shell. Did Shell Oil Company act socially responsibly in this case? Who wins?

West Michigan Environmental Action Council v. Natural Resources Commission, 405 Mich. 741, 275 N.W.2d 538, **Web** 1979 Mich. Lexis 347 (Supreme Court of Michigan)

45.10 Business Ethics Riverside Bayview Homes, Inc. (Riverside), owned 80 acres of low-lying marshland (wetlands) near the shores of Lake St. Clair in Macomb County, Michigan. Riverside began to place fill materials on its property as part of its preparations for construction of a housing development. Riverside did not obtain a permit from the Army Corps of Engineers. Upon discovery of Riverside's activities, the Corps sued, seeking to enjoin Riverside from discharging a pollutant (fill) onto wetlands. Is this property subject to the Corps of Engineers permit system? Did Riverside Bayview Homes act ethically in this case? *United States v. Riverside Bayview Homes, Inc.*, 474 U.S. 121, 106 S.Ct. 455, 88 L.Ed.2d 419, **Web** 1985 U.S. Lexis 145 (Supreme Court of the United States)

ENDNOTES

1. 42 U.S.C. Sections 4321–4370d.
2. 42 U.S.C. Sections 7401–7671q.
3. 33 U.S.C. Sections 1251–1367.
4. 33 U.S.C. Section 1254(t).
5. 21 U.S.C. Section 349 and 300f–300j-25.
6. 16 U.S.C. Section 1431 et seq.; 33 U.S.C. Sections 1401–1445.
7. 33 U.S.C. Sections 2701–2761.
8. 15 U.S.C. Sections 2601–2692.
9. 7 U.S.C. Sections 135 et seq.
10. 42 U.S.C. Sections 6901–6986.
11. 42 U.S.C. Sections 10101–10270.
12. 16 U.S.C. Sections 1531–1544.

▲ **Oriole Park, Baltimore, Maryland** *Most businesses and industries in the United States are subject to federal antitrust laws. In 1922, the U.S. Supreme Court was asked whether professional baseball was subject to federal antitrust laws. In that case, the established American and National Baseball Leagues enticed owners of teams in the upstart Federal League to leave the Federal League and join them. The remaining Federal League team sued, alleging that the other leagues violated antitrust laws by eliminating competition. The Supreme Court cut out a special exemption for professional baseball by holding that professional baseball was the "national pastime" and not interstate commerce and was therefore not subject to federal antitrust laws (Federal Baseball Club of Baltimore, Inc. v. National League of Professional Baseball Clubs[1]). In other cases, professional football, basketball, and hockey have not been so lucky and have been held subject to federal antitrust laws.*

CHAPTER OBJECTIVES

After studying this chapter, you should be able to:

1. Describe the enforcement of federal antitrust laws.
2. Describe the horizontal and vertical restraints of trade that violate Section 1 of the Sherman Act.
3. Identify acts of monopolization that violate Section 2 of the Sherman Act.

4. Explain how the lawfulness of mergers is examined under Section 7 of the Clayton Act.
5. Apply Section 5 of the Federal Trade Commission Act to antitrust cases.

CHAPTER CONTENTS

"While competition cannot be created by statutory enactment, it can in large measure be revived by changing the laws and forbidding the practices that killed it, and by enacting laws that will give it heart and occasion again. We can arrest and prevent monopoly."

—Woodrow Wilson
Speech, August 7, 1912

▶ INTRODUCTION TO ANTITRUST LAW AND UNFAIR TRADE PRACTICES

The U.S. economic system was built on the theory of freedom of competition. After the Civil War, however, the U.S. economy changed from a rural and agricultural economy to an industrialized and urban one. Many large industrial trusts were formed during this period. These arrangements resulted in a series of monopolies in basic industries such as oil and gas, sugar, cotton, and whiskey.

Because the common law could not deal effectively with these monopolies, Congress enacted a comprehensive system of **antitrust laws** to limit anticompetitive behavior. Almost all industries, businesses, and professions operating in the United States were affected. Although many states have also enacted antitrust laws, most actions in this area are brought under federal law.

This chapter discusses federal and state antitrust laws.

antitrust laws
A series of laws enacted to limit anticompetitive behavior in almost all industries, businesses, and professions operating in the United States.

▶ FEDERAL ANTITRUST LAW

Federal antitrust law comprises several major statutes that prohibit certain anticompetitive and monopolistic practices. The federal antitrust statutes are broadly drafted to reflect the government's enforcement policy and to allow it to respond to economic, business, and technological changes. Federal antitrust laws provide for both government and private lawsuits.

Each administration that occupies the White House adopts a policy for the enforcement of antitrust laws. These policies differ from one administration to another. From the 1940s through the 1970s, antitrust enforcement was quite stringent. From the 1980s through the first decade of the 2000s, government enforcement of antitrust laws has been more relaxed. It will be interesting to see how future administrations will enforce antitrust law.

LANDMARK LAW
Federal Antitrust Statutes

After the Civil War, the United States became a leader of the Industrial Revolution. Behemoth companies and trusts were established. The most powerful of these were John D. Rockefeller's Standard Oil Company, Andrew Carnegie's Carnegie Steel, Cornelius Vanderbilt's New York Central Railroad System, and J.P. Morgan's banking house. These corporations dominated their respective industries, many obtaining monopoly power. For example, the Rockefeller oil trust controlled 90 percent of the country's oil refining capacity. Mergers and monopolization of industries were rampant.

In response, during the late 1800s and early 1900s, Congress enacted a series of antitrust laws aimed at curbing abusive and monopoly practices by business. During this time, the following federal statutes were enacted by Congress:

- The **Sherman Act** is a federal statute, enacted in 1890, that makes certain restraints of trade and monopolistic acts illegal.
- The **Clayton Act** is a federal statute, enacted in 1914, that regulates mergers and prohibits certain exclusive dealing arrangements.
- The **Federal Trade Commission Act (FTC Act)** is a federal statute enacted in 1914, prohibits unfair methods of competition.
- The **Robinson-Patman Act** is a federal statute, enacted in 1930, that prohibits price discrimination.

Each of these important statutes is discussed in this chapter.

Government Actions

The federal government is authorized to bring actions to enforce federal antitrust laws. Government enforcement of federal antitrust laws is divided between the **Antitrust Division of the Department of Justice** and the **Bureau of Competition of the FTC**.

The Sherman Act is the only major antitrust act that includes **criminal sanctions**. Intent is the prerequisite for criminal liability under this act. Penalties for individuals include fines and prison terms; corporations may be fined.[2]

The government may seek **civil damages**, including *treble damages*, for violations of antitrust laws.[3] Broad remedial powers allow the courts to order a number of civil remedies, including orders for divestiture of assets, cancellation of contracts, liquidation of businesses, licensing of patents, and such. Private parties cannot intervene in public antitrust actions brought by the government.

The notion that a business is clothed with a public interest and has been devoted to the public use is little more than a fiction intended to beautify what is disagreeable to the sufferers.

Justice Holmes
Tyson & Bro-United Theatre Ticket Offices v. Banton (1927)

Private Actions

Section 4 of the Clayton Act permits any person who suffers antitrust injury in his or her "business or property" to bring a **private civil action** against the offenders.[4] Consumers who have to pay higher prices because of an antitrust violation have recourse under this provision.[5] To recover damages, plaintiffs must prove that they suffered **antitrust injuries** caused by the prohibited act. The courts have required that consumers must have dealt *directly* with the alleged violators to have standing to sue; indirect injury resulting from higher prices being "passed on" is insufficient.

Successful plaintiffs may recover **treble damages** (i.e., triple the amount of the damages), plus reasonable costs and attorneys' fees. Damages may be calculated as lost profits, an increase in the cost of doing business, or a decrease in the value of tangible or intangible property caused by the antitrust violation. This rule applies to all violations of the Sherman Act, the Clayton Act, and the Robinson-Patman Act. Only actual damages—not treble damages—may be recovered for violations of the FTC Act. A private plaintiff has four years from the date on which an antitrust injury occurred to bring a private civil treble-damages action. Only damages incurred during this four-year period are recoverable. This statute is *tolled* (i.e., does not run) during a suit by the government.

Effect of a Government Judgment

A government judgment against a defendant for an antitrust violation may be used as *prima facie* evidence of liability in a private civil treble-damages action. Antitrust defendants often opt to settle government-brought antitrust actions by entering a plea of *nolo contendere* in a criminal action or a **consent decree** in a government civil action. These pleas usually subject the defendant to penalty without an admission of guilt or liability.

Section 16 of the Clayton Act permits the government or a private plaintiff to obtain an injunction against anticompetitive behavior that violates antitrust laws.[6] Only the FTC can obtain an injunction under the FTC Act.

► RESTRAINTS OF TRADE: SECTION 1 OF THE SHERMAN ACT

In 1890, Congress enacted the *Sherman Act* in order to outlaw anticompetitive behavior. The Sherman Act has been called the "Magna Carta of free enterprise."[7] **Section 1 of the Sherman Act** is intended to prohibit certain concerted anticompetitive activities. It provides:

> *Every contract, combination in the form of trust or otherwise, or conspiracy, in restraint of trade or commerce among the several states, or with foreign nations, is hereby declared to be illegal. Every person who shall make any contract or engage in any combination or conspiracy hereby declared to be illegal shall be deemed guilty of a felony.*[8]

In other words, Section 1 outlaws *contracts*, *combinations*, and *conspiracies* in restraint of trade. Thus, it applies to unlawful conduct by two or more parties. The agreement may be written, oral, or inferred from the conduct of the parties. The two tests the U.S. Supreme Court has developed for determining the lawfulness of a restraint—the *rule of reason* and the *per se rule*—are discussed in the following paragraphs.

Rule of Reason

If Section 1 of the Sherman Act were read literally, it would prohibit almost all contracts. In the landmark case *Standard Oil Company of New Jersey v. United States*,[9] the Supreme Court adopted the **rule of reason** standard for analyzing Section 1 cases. This rule holds that only *unreasonable restraints of trade* violate Section 1 of the Sherman Act. Reasonable restraints are lawful. The courts examine the following factors in applying the rule of reason to a particular case:

- The pro- and anticompetitive effects of the challenged restraint
- The competitive structure of the industry
- The firm's market share and power
- The history and duration of the restraint
- Other relevant factors

People of the same trade seldom meet together, even for merriment and diversion, but that the conversation ends in a conspiracy against the public, or in some contrivance to raise prices.

Adam Smith
The Wealth of Nations (1776)

Section 1 of the Sherman Act
A section that prohibits contracts, combinations, and conspiracies in restraint of trade.

rule of reason
A rule which holds that only unreasonable restraints of trade violate Section 1 of the Sherman Act. The court must examine the pro- and anticompetitive effects of a challenged restraint.

Per Se Rule

per se rule
A rule that is applicable to restraints of trade considered inherently anticompetitive. Once this determination is made about a restraint of trade, the court will not permit any defenses or justifications to save it.

The Supreme Court adopted the *per se* **rule**, which is applicable to restraints of trade that are considered inherently anticompetitive. No balancing of pro- and anticompetitive effects is necessary in such cases: The restraint is automatically in violation of Section 1 of the Sherman Act. When a restraint is characterized as a *per se* violation, no defenses or justifications for the restraint will save it, and no further evidence need be considered. Restraints that are not characterized as *per se* violations are examined using the rule of reason.

CONCEPT SUMMARY

RESTRAINTS OF TRADE: SECTION 1 OF THE SHERMAN ACT

RULE	Description
Rule of reason	Requires a balancing of pro- and anticompetitive effects of the challenged restraint. Restraints that are found to be unreasonable are unlawful and violate Section 1 of the Sherman Act. Restraints that are found to be reasonable are lawful and do not violate Section 1 of the Sherman Act.
Per se rule	Applies to restraints that are inherently anticompetitive. No justification for the restraint is permitted. Such restraints automatically violate Section 1 of the Sherman Act.

Horizontal Restraints of Trade

horizontal restraint of trade
A restraint of trade that occurs when two or more competitors at the same *level of distribution* enter into a contract, combination, or conspiracy to restrain trade.

A **horizontal restraint of trade** occurs when two or more competitors at the *same level of distribution* enter into a contract, combination, or conspiracy to restrain trade (see Exhibit 46.1). Many horizontal restraints fall under the *per se* rule; others are examined under the rule of reason. The most common forms of horizontal restraint are discussed in the following paragraphs.

▶ **Exhibit 46.1 HORIZONTAL RESTRAINT OF TRADE**

Price-Fixing

price-fixing
A restraint of trade that occurs when competitors in the same line of business agree to set the price of the goods or services they sell, raising, depressing, fixing, pegging, or stabilizing the price of a commodity or service.

Horizontal **price-fixing** occurs when the competitors in the same line of business agree to set the price of goods or services they sell. Price-fixing is defined as raising, depressing, fixing, pegging, or stabilizing the price of a commodity or service. Illegal price-fixing includes setting minimum or maximum prices or fixing the quantity of a product or service to be produced or provided. Although most price-fixing agreements occur between sellers, an agreement among buyers to set the price they will pay for goods or services is also price-fixing. The plaintiff bears the burden of proving a price-fixing agreement.

Price-fixing is a *per se* violation of Section 1 of the Sherman Act. No defenses or justifications of any kind—such as "the price-fixing helps consumers or protects competitors from ruinous competition"—can prevent the *per se* rule from applying.

Example If the three largest automobile manufacturers agreed among themselves what prices to charge automobile dealers for this year's models, this would be sellers' illegal *per se* price-fixing.

Example If the three largest automobile manufacturers agreed among themselves what price they would pay to purchase tires from tire manufactures, this would be buyers' illegal *per se* price-fixing.

ETHICS SPOTLIGHT

The Department of Justice Flunks the Ivy League Schools

For years, the administrators of the Ivy League schools (Brown, Columbia, Cornell, Dartmouth, Harvard, Princeton, the University of Pennsylvania, and Yale) and Massachusetts Institute of Technology (MIT) met annually to trade information about student applicants seeking admission and scholarships at their universities. The universities than divided up the applicants and agreed to offer scholarships to the students they thought would attend their schools; they did not offer scholarships to those less likely to attend. The schools defended this practice as preventing "overlap"—that is, certain students getting scholarship offers from many schools and other applicants receiving no scholarship offers.

The U.S. Department of Justice sued the universities, alleging that they engaged in the horizontal restraint of trade of price-fixing, in violation of Section 1 of the Sherman Act. The Department of Justice lawyers pointed to what they learned in Economics 101 and asserted that this collegiate cartel was no different from any other cartel: It denied customers (students) the right to "comparison shop" just as they would for other services.

The eight Ivy League schools agreed to settle the case with the Department of Justice. Under the terms of the consent decree, the schools agreed not to share financial aid information or discuss future tuition levels with other schools. MIT chose to fight the case in court and lost. The court found MIT guilty of price-fixing and enjoined the challenged practices. *United States v. Brown University*, 5 F.3d 658, **Web** 1993 U.S. App. Lexis 23895 (United States Court of Appeals for the Third Circuit)

Business Ethics Do you think the schools acted ethically in this case?

Division of Markets

Competitors who agree that each will serve only a designated portion of the market are engaging in a **division of markets** (or **market sharing**), which is a *per se* violation of Section 1 of the Sherman Act. Each market segment is considered a small monopoly served only by its designated "owner." Horizontal market-sharing arrangements include division by geographical territories, customers, and products.

division of markets
A restraint of trade in which competitors agree that each will serve only a designated portion of the market.

Example Suppose that three national breweries agree among themselves that each one will be assigned one-third of the country as its geographical "territory," and each agrees not to sell beer in the other two companies' territories. This would be a *per se* illegal geographical division of markets.

Example Suppose that the three largest sellers of media software agree that each can sell media software only to one designated media software purchaser and not to any other media software purchasers. This would be a *per se* illegal product division of markets.

Group Boycotts

A **group boycott** (or **refusal to deal**) occurs when two or more competitors at one level of distribution agree not to deal with others at a different level of distribution.

group boycott
A restraint of trade in which two or more competitors at one level of distribution agree not to deal with others at another level of distribution. Also known as *refusal to deal*.

Examples If a group of sellers agreed not to sell their products to a certain buyer, this would be a group boycott by sellers. If a group of purchasers agreed not to purchase a product from a certain seller, this would be a group boycott by purchasers.

Example A group of high-fashion clothes designer and sellers agree not to sell their clothes to a certain discount retailer, such as Wal-Mart. This is a group boycott by sellers (see Exhibit 46.2).

Example A group of rental car companies agree not to purchase Chrysler automobiles for their fleets. This would be a group boycott by purchasers (see Exhibit 46.3).

In the past, the U.S. Supreme Court has held that all group boycotts were *per se* illegal. However, the Supreme Court changed this rule and held that only certain group boycotts are *per se* illegal; others are to be examined under the rule of reason. Nevertheless, most group boycotts are still found to be illegal.

▶ **Exhibit 46.2 GROUP BOYCOTT BY SELLERS**

▶ **Exhibit 46.3 GROUP BOYCOTT BY PURCHASERS**

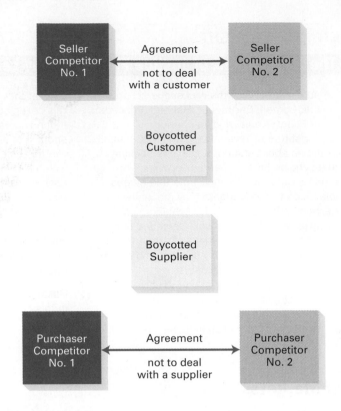

Other Horizontal Agreements

Some horizontal agreements entered into by competitors at the same level of distribution—including trade association activities and rules, exchange of non-price information, participation in joint ventures, and the like—are examined using the rule of reason. Reasonable restraints are lawful; unreasonable restraints violate Section 1 of the Sherman Act.

Vertical Restraints of Trade

vertical restraint of trade
A restraint of trade that occurs when two or more parties on *different levels of distribution* enter into a contract, combination, or conspiracy to restrain trade.

A **vertical restraint of trade** occurs when two or more parties on *different levels of distribution* enter into a contact, combination, or conspiracy to restrain trade (see Exhibit 46.4). The Supreme Court has applied both the *per se* rule and the rule of reason in determining the legality of vertical restraints of trade under Section 1 of the Sherman Act. The most common forms of vertical restraint are discussed in the following paragraphs.

▶ **Exhibit 46.4 VERTICAL RESTRAINT OF TRADE**

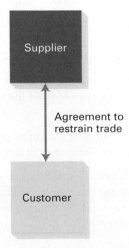

Resale Price Maintenance

Resale price maintenance (or **vertical price-fixing**) occurs when a party at one level of distribution enters into an agreement with a party at another level to adhere to a price schedule that either sets or stabilizes prices.

The U.S. Supreme Court has held that setting **minimum resale prices** is a *per se* violation of Section 1 of the Sherman Act as an unreasonable restraint of trade.[10]

Example Integral Camera Corporation manufactures digital cameras and sets a *minimum* price below which the cameras cannot be sold by retailers to consumers (e.g., the cameras cannot be sold for less than $1,000 to consumers by retailers). This constitutes *per se* illegal minimum resale price maintenance.

However, the U.S. Supreme Court has held that the setting of **maximum resale prices** will be examined under the *rule of reason* to determine whether it violates Section 1 of the Sherman Act. The Supreme Court concluded that there was insufficient economic justification for *per se* invalidation of vertical maximum price fixing.[11]

> **resale price maintenance**
> A *per se* violation of Section 1 of the Sherman Act that occurs when a party at one level of distribution enters into an agreement with a party at another level to adhere to a price schedule that either sets or stabilizes prices. Also called *vertical price-fixing*.

Non-price Vertical Restraints

The legality of **non-price vertical restraints** of trade under Section 1 of the Sherman Act is examined by using the rule of reason.[12] Non-price restraints are unlawful under this analysis if their anticompetitive effects outweigh their procompetitive effects. Non-price vertical restraints include situations in which a manufacturer assigns exclusive territories to retail dealers or limits the number of dealers that may be located in a certain territory.

> **non-price vertical restraints**
> Restraints of trade that are unlawful under Section 1 of the Sherman Act if their anticompetitive effects outweigh their procompetitive effects.

Unilateral Refusal to Deal

The U.S. Supreme Court has held that a firm can unilaterally choose not to deal with another party without being liable under Section 1 of the Sherman Act. A **unilateral refusal to deal** is not a violation of Section 1 because there is no concerted action with others. This rule was announced in *United States v. Colgate & Co.* and is therefore often referred to as the **Colgate doctrine**.[13]

Example If Louis Vuitton, a maker of expensive women's clothing, shoes, handbags, and accessories, refuses to sell its merchandise to Wal-Mart stores, this is a lawful unilateral refusal to deal.

> **unilateral refusal to deal**
> A unilateral choice by one party not to deal with another party. This does not violate Section 1 of the Sherman Act because there is not concerted action.
>
> **conscious parallelism**
> A doctrine which states that if two or more firms act the same but no concerted action is shown, there is no violation of Section 1 of the Sherman Act.

CONTEMPORARY ENVIRONMENT

Conscious Parallelism

Sometimes two or more firms act the same, but they have done so individually. If two or more firms act the same but no concerted action is shown, there is no violation of Section 1 of the Sherman Act. This doctrine is often referred to as **conscious parallelism**. Thus, if two competing manufacturers of a similar product both separately reach an independent decision not to deal with a retailer, there is no violation of Section 1 of the Sherman Act. The key is that each of the manufacturers acted on its own.

Example If Louis Vuitton, Gucci, and Chanel, makers of expensive women's clothing, shoes, handbags, and accessories, each independently make a decision not to sell their products to Wal-Mart, this is lawful conscious parallelism. There is no violation of Section 1 of the Sherman Act because the parties did not agree with one another in making their decisions.

Noerr Doctrine

The *Noerr* **doctrine** holds that two or more persons may petition the executive, legislative, or judicial branch of the government or administrative agencies to enact laws or to take other action without violating antitrust laws. The rationale behind this doctrine is that the right to petition the government has precedence because it is guaranteed by the Bill of Rights.[14]

> *Noerr* **doctrine**
> A doctrine which says that two or more persons can petition the executive, legislative, or judicial branch of the government or administrative agencies to enact laws or take other action without violating antitrust laws.

Example General Motors and Ford collectively petition Congress to pass a law that would limit the import of foreign automobiles into this country. This is lawful activity under the *Noerr* doctrine.

There is an exception to this doctrine. Under the *"sham" exception*, petitioners are not protected if their petition or lawsuit is baseless—that is, if a reasonable petitioner or litigant could not realistically expect to succeed on the merits of the petition or lawsuit. If the protection of the *Noerr* doctrine is lost, an antitrust action may be maintained against the parties who asserted its protection.

▶ MONOPOLIZATION: SECTION 2 OF THE SHERMAN ACT

By definition, monopolies have the ability to affect the price of goods and services. **Section 2 of the Sherman Act** was enacted in response to widespread concern about the power generated by this type of anticompetitive activity. Section 2 of the Sherman Act prohibits the act of monopolization. It provides:

> *Every person who shall monopolize, or attempt to monopolize, or combine or conspire with any other person or persons, to monopolize any part of the trade or commerce among the several States, or with foreign nations, shall be deemed guilty of a felony.*[15]

Proving that a defendant is in violation of Section 2 means proving that the defendant (1) possesses monopoly power in the relevant market and (2) engaged in a willful act of monopolization to acquire or maintain that power. Each of these elements is discussed in the following paragraphs.

Defining the Relevant Market

Identifying the **relevant market** for a Section 2 action requires defining the relevant product or service market and geographical market. The definition of the relevant market often determines whether the defendant has monopoly power. Consequently, this determination is often litigated.

The **relevant product or service market** generally includes substitute products or services that are reasonably interchangeable with the defendant's products or services. Defendants often try to make their market share seem smaller by arguing for a broad definition of the product or service market. Plaintiffs, on the other hand, usually argue for a narrow definition.

Example If the Anheuser-Busch Corporation InBev, which is the largest beer producer in the United States, is sued by the government for violating Section 2 of the Sherman Act, the government would argue that the relevant product market is beer sales. Anheuser-Busch, on the other hand, would argue that the relevant product market is sales of all alcoholic beverages, or even of all drinkable beverages.

The **relevant geographical market** is usually defined as the area in which the defendant and its competitors sell the product or service. This may be a national, regional, state, or local area, depending on the circumstances.

Examples If the Coca-Cola Corporation is sued by the government for violating Section 2 of the Sherman Act, the relevant geographical market would be the nation. If the largest owner of automobile dealerships in south Florida were sued for violating Section 2, the geographical market would be the counties of south Florida.

Monopoly Power

For an antitrust action to be sustained, the defendant must possess **monopoly power** in the relevant market. Monopoly power is defined by the courts as the power to control prices or exclude competition. The courts generally apply the following guidelines: Market share

---

Section 2 of the Sherman Act
A section that prohibits monopolization and attempts or conspiracies to monopolize trade.

relevant product or service market
A relevant market that includes substitute products or services that are reasonably interchangeable with the defendant's products or services.

relevant geographical market
A relevant market that is defined as the area in which the defendant and its competitors sell the product or service.

monopoly power
The power to control prices or exclude competition, measured by the market share the defendant possesses in the relevant market.

above 70 percent is monopoly power; market share under 20 percent is not monopoly power. Otherwise, the courts generally prefer to examine the facts and circumstances of each case before making a determination about monopoly power.

Willful Act of Monopolizing

Section 2 of the Sherman Act outlaws the **act of monopolizing**, not monopolies. Any act that otherwise violates any other antitrust law (e.g., illegal restraints of trade in violation of Section 1 of the Sherman Act) is an act of monopolizing that violates Section 2. When coupled with monopoly power, certain otherwise lawful acts have been held to constitute acts of monopolizing. **Predatory pricing**—that is, pricing below average or marginal cost—that is intended to drive out competition has been held to violate Section 2.[16]

> **act of monopolizing**
> An act that is required for there to be a violation of Section 2 of the Sherman Act. Possession of monopoly power without such act does not violate Section 2.

CONCEPT SUMMARY

MONOPOLIZATION: SECTION 2 OF THE SHERMAN ACT

Element	Description
Relevant product or service market	The market that includes substitute products or services that are reasonably interchangeable with the defendant's products or services.
Relevant geographic market	The geographic area in which the defendant and its competitors sell the product or service.
Monopoly power	The power to control prices or exclude competition. If the defendant does not possess monopoly power, it cannot be held liable for monopolization. If the defendant possesses monopoly power, the court will determine whether the monopolist has engaged in an act of monopolizing.
Act of monopolizing	The defendant's engagement in a willful act of monopolizing trade or commerce in the relevant market.

Attempts and Conspiracies to Monopolize

Firms that *attempt* or *conspire* to monopolize a relevant market may be found liable under Section 2 of the Sherman Act. A single firm may be found liable for monopolizing or attempting to monopolize. Two or more firms may be found liable for conspiring to monopolize.

Defenses to Monopolization

Only two narrow defenses to a charge of monopolizing have been recognized: (1) *innocent acquisition* (e.g., acquisition because of superior business acumen, skill, foresight, or industry) and (2) *natural monopoly* (e.g., a small market that can support only one competitor, such as a small-town newspaper). If a monopoly that fits into one of these categories exercises its power in a predatory or exclusionary way, the defense is lost.

> *A monopoly granted either to an individual or to a trading company has the same effect as a secret in trade or manufacture. The monopolists, by keeping the market constantly understocked, by never fully supplying the effectual demand, sell their commodities much above the natural price, and raise their emoluments greatly above their natural rate.*
>
> Adam Smith
> *Wealth of Nations (1776)*

INTERNET LAW & ONLINE COMMERCE

United States v. Microsoft Corporation

In less than 40 years, Microsoft Corporation has grown from a startup company into the world's largest software company, whose products touch the lives of virtually everyone who uses a personal computer. Microsoft dominates the software market with its Windows operating system, which is used on most of the world's personal computers.

Netscape, a competing company, developed its Navigator Internet web browser and controlled over 80 percent of that market. Microsoft began a campaign to defeat Netscape. Microsoft developed its own browser, called *Explorer*, and attached it to its Windows operating system for free. Microsoft warned Apple, a manufacturer of personal computers, that it would cancel Microsoft's all-important Office Software unless Apple used Explorer; Apple capitulated and made Explorer its web browser. Microsoft muscled AOL into offering Explorer in return for a small placement on the Windows desktop if it would not offer Netscape anywhere on its online service. AOL agreed. Microsoft gave Compaq, a maker of personal computers, a reduced price for Windows in return for placing a Microsoft icon for the Explorer web browser on Compaq's computers. Microsoft was alleged to have used "bundling" of its software products with its operating systems to eliminate competitors from the software marketplace.

After investigating, the U.S. government and 19 states sued Microsoft in a civil antitrust case. After a nine-month trial and four months of failed settlement negotiations, the U.S. District Court held that Microsoft had used predatory and anticompetitive conduct to illegally maintain its monopoly in the Windows operating system, in violation of Section 2 of the Sherman Act. The judge issued an order that prohibited Microsoft from engaging in such conduct in the future and ordered that Microsoft be split into two separate companies, one company to own the operating

systems such as Windows, and a second company to own software, Internet browsers, and other computer applications.

Microsoft appealed. On appeal, the U.S. Court of Appeals upheld the finding that Microsoft had engaged in monopolization in violation of Section 2 of the Sherman Act, but it ruled that Microsoft did not have to be broken up. The case was remanded for further proceedings. A new U.S. District Court judge reached a judgment with Microsoft Corporation wherein Microsoft agreed to refrain from engaging in coercive practices and to make some of the code for its operating systems available to other software companies under reasonable licensing arrangement so that they could design their software to be used in conjunction with Microsoft's operating system.

In exchange for agreeing to the judgment, Microsoft did not have to admit to any wrongdoing. Many commentators believe that Microsoft basically "won" this case. Do you think Microsoft acted ethically? *United States v. Microsoft Corporation*, **Web** 2002 U.S. Dist. Lexis 22864 (United States District Court for the District of Columbia)

CONCEPT SUMMARY

THE SHERMAN ACT

Section	Description
1	Prohibits contracts, combinations, and conspiracies in restraint of trade. To violate Section 1, the restraint must be found to be unreasonable under either of two tests: (1) rule of reason or (2) *per se* rule. A violation requires the concerted action of two or more parties.
2	Prohibits the act of monopolizing and attempts or conspiracies to monopolize. This act can be violated by the conduct of one firm.

▶ MERGERS: SECTION 7 OF THE CLAYTON ACT

Section 7 of the Clayton Act
A section which provides that it is unlawful for a person or business to acquire the stock or assets of another "where in any line of commerce or in any activity affecting commerce in any section of the country, the effect of such acquisition may be substantially to lessen competition, or to tend to create a monopoly."

In the late 1800s and early 1900s, *mergers* led to increased concentration of wealth in the hands of a few wealthy individuals and large corporations. In response, in 1914, Congress enacted **Section 7 of the Clayton Act**, which gave the federal government the power to prevent anticompetitive mergers. Originally, Section 7 of the Clayton Act applied only to stock mergers. The **Celler-Kefauver Act**, which was enacted in 1950, widened Section 7's scope to include asset acquisitions.

Today, Section 7 applies to all methods of external expansion, including technical mergers, consolidations, purchases of assets, subsidiary operations, joint ventures, and other combinations.

Section 7 of the Clayton Act provides that it is unlawful for a person or business to acquire stock or assets of another "where in any line of commerce or in any activity affecting commerce in any section of the country, the effect of such acquisition may be substantially to lessen competition, or to tend to create a monopoly."[17] In determining whether a merger is lawful under Section 7 of the Clayton Act, the courts must examine the elements discussed in the following paragraphs.

Line of Commerce

Determining the **line of commerce** that will be affected by a merger involves defining the relevant *product or service market*. Traditionally, the courts have done this by applying the functional interchangeability test. Under this test, the relevant line of commerce includes products or services that consumers use as substitutes. If two products are substitutes for each other, they are considered part of the same line of commerce.

Example Suppose a price increase for regular coffee causes consumers to switch to tea. The two products are part of the same line of commerce because they are considered interchangeable.

Section of the Country

Defining the relevant **section of the country** consists of determining the relevant *geographical market*. The courts traditionally identify this market as the geographical area that will feel the direct and immediate effects of the merger. It may be a local, state, or regional market; the entire country; or some other geographical area.

Example Anheuser-Busch InBev and Miller Brewing Company, two brewers, sell beer nationally. If Anheuser-Busch and Miller Brewing Company plan to merge, the relevant section of the country is the nation.

Probability of a Substantial Lessening of Competition

After the relevant product or service and geographical market have been defined, the court must determine whether a merger or an acquisition is likely to **substantially lessen competition** or to **create a monopoly**. If the court feels that a merger is likely to do either, it may prevent the merger. Section 7 tries to prevent potentially anticompetitive mergers before they occur. It deals in probabilities; an actual showing of the lessening of competition is not required.

CONCEPT SUMMARY
MERGER: SECTION 7 OF THE CLAYTON ACT

Element	Description
Line of commerce	The market that will be affected by a merger. It includes products or services that consumers use as substitutes for those produced or sold by the merging firms.
Section of the country	The geographic market that will be affected by a merger.
Probability of a substantial lessening of competition	A probability of a substantial lessening of competition after a merger, in which case the merger may be prohibited. The statute deals with probabilities; a showing of actual lessening of competition is not required.

Types of Mergers

In applying Section 7, mergers are generally classified as one of the following: *horizontal merger, vertical merger, market extension merger,* or *conglomerate merger*. These are discussed in the paragraphs that follow.

Horizontal Mergers A **horizontal merger** is a merger between two or more companies that compete in the same business and geographical market. The merger of two grocery store chains that serve the same geographical market fits this definition. Such mergers are subjected to strict review under Section 7 because they clearly result in an increase in concentration in the relevant market.

Example General Motors Corporation and Ford Motor Company are two of the largest automobile, SUV, and truck manufacturers. If General Motors Corporation and Ford Motor Company tried to merge, this would be a horizontal merger. This merger would most likely violate Section 7.

Vertical Mergers A **vertical merger** is a merger that integrates the operations of a supplier and a customer. In examining the legality of vertical mergers, the courts usually consider such factors as the past history of the firms, the trend toward concentration in the

line of commerce
The products or services that will be affected by a merger, including those that consumers use as substitutes. If an increase in the price of one product or service leads consumers to purchase another product or service, the two products are substitutes for each other.

section of the country
A division of the country that is based on the relevant geographical market; the geographical area that will feel the direct and immediate effects of a merger.

probability of a substantial lessening of competition
The probability that a merger will substantially lessen competition or create a monopoly, in which case the court may prevent the merger under Section 7 of the Clayton Act.

horizontal merger
A merger between two or more companies that compete in the same business and geographical market.

vertical merger
A merger that integrates the operations of a supplier and a customer.

industries involved, the barriers to entry, the economic efficiencies of the merger, and the elimination of potential competition caused by the merger.

Example If the book publisher Simon & Schuster acquires a paper mill, this would be a **backward vertical merger**. If the book publisher Simon & Schuster acquires a retail book-store chain such as Barnes & Noble, this would be a **forward vertical merger**.

Vertical mergers do not create an increase in market share because the merging firms serve different markets. They may, however, cause anticompetitive effects such as **foreclosing** competitors from either selling goods or services to or buying them from the merged firm.

Example A furniture manufacturer acquires a chain of retail furniture stores. The merger is unlawful if it is likely that the merged firm will not buy furniture from other manufacturers or sell furniture to other retailers.

backward vertical merger
A vertical merger in which the customer acquires the supplier.

forward vertical merger
A vertical merger in which the supplier acquires the customer.

Market Extension Mergers A **market extension merger** is a merger between two companies in similar fields whose sales do not overlap. The merger may expand the acquiring firm's geographical or product market. The legality of market extension mergers is examined under Section 7 of the Clayton Act.

Example A merger between two regional brewers that do not sell beer in the same geographical area is called a **geographical market extension merger**.

Example A merger between sellers of similar products, such as a soft drink manufacturer and an orange juice producer, is called a **product market extension merger**.

market extension merger
A merger between two companies in similar fields whose sales do not overlap.

Conglomerate Mergers **Conglomerate mergers** are mergers that do not fit into any other category. That is, they are mergers between firms in unrelated businesses.

Example If the large oil company ExxonMobil merged with Neiman-Marcus, a company that owns and operates retail clothing stores, the result would be a conglomerate merger.

The **unfair advantage theory** holds that a conglomerate merger may not give the acquiring firm an unfair advantage over its competitors in finance, marketing, or expertise. This rule is intended to prevent wealthy companies from overwhelming the competition in a given market.

Example Wal-Mart Stores, Inc., a giant discount warehouse store and one of the largest and wealthiest companies in the world, may be prevented from acquiring Almost Death Row Records, a small recording studio, under the unfair advantage theory. The court would be concerned that Wal-Mart could bring its wealth to support and grow Almost Death Row Records into an extremely large and monopolistic recording label.

conglomerate merger
A merger that does not fit into any other category; a merger between firms in totally unrelated businesses.

Defenses to Section 7 Actions

There are two primary defenses to Section 7 actions. These defenses can be raised even if the merger would otherwise violate Section 7. The defenses are:

1. **The failing company doctrine.** According to the **failing company doctrine**, a competitor may merge with a failing company if (1) there is no other reasonable alternative for the failing company, (2) no other purchaser is available, and (3) the assets of the failing company would completely disappear from the market if the anticompetitive merger were not allowed to go through.
2. **The small company doctrine.** The courts have permitted two or more small companies to merge without liability under Section 7 if the merger allows them to compete more effectively with a large company. This is called the **small company doctrine**.

Premerger Notification

In 1976, premerger notification rules were enacted pursuant to the **Hart-Scott-Rodino Antitrust Improvement Act**.[18] These rules require certain firms to notify the FTC and the Department of Justice of any proposed merger and give them time to investigate and

Hart-Scott-Rodino Antitrust Improvement Act
An act that requires certain firms to notify the FTC and the Justice Department in advance of a proposed merger. Unless the government challenges a proposed merger within 30 days, the merger may proceed.

challenge any mergers they deem anticompetitive. If a merger is reportable, the parties must file the notification form and wait 30 days. If within the waiting period the government sues, the suit is entitled to expedited treatment in the courts.

▶ TYING ARRANGEMENTS: SECTION 3 OF THE CLAYTON ACT

Section 3 of the Clayton Act prohibits tying arrangements that involve sales and leases of goods (tangible personal property).[19] **Tying arrangements** are vertical trade restraints that involve the seller's refusal to sell a product (the *tying* item) to a customer unless the customer purchases a second product (the *tied* item). Section 1 of the Sherman Act (restraints of trade) forbids tying arrangements involving goods, services, intangible property, and real property.

The defendant must be shown to have had sufficient economic power in the tying product market to restrain competition in the tied product market. A tying arrangement is lawful if there is some justifiable reason for it. For example, the protection of quality control coupled with a trade secret may make a tying arrangement lawful.

Example A manufacturer makes one patented product and one unpatented product. An illegal tying arrangement occurs if the manufacturer refuses to sell the patented product to a buyer unless the buyer also purchases the unpatented product. The patented product is the tying product, and the unpatented product is the tied product. Here, the patented product and the unpatented product can be sold separately.

> **Section 3 of the Clayton Act**
> An act that prohibits tying arrangements involving sales and leases of goods.

> **tying arrangement**
> A restraint of trade in which a seller refuses to sell one product to a customer unless the customer agrees to purchase a second product from the seller.

▶ PRICE DISCRIMINATION: SECTION 2 OF THE CLAYTON ACT

Businesses in the U.S. economy survive by selling their goods and services at prices that allow them to make a profit. Sellers often offer favorable terms to their preferred customers. **Price discrimination** occurs if a seller does this without just cause. The rules regarding this type of unlawful trade practices are found in **Section 2 of the Clayton Act**, which is commonly referred to as the **Robinson-Patman Act**. **Section 2(a) of the Robinson-Patman Act** contains the following basic prohibition against price discrimination in the sale of goods:

> *It shall be unlawful for any person engaged in commerce, either directly or indirectly, to discriminate in price between different purchases of commodities of like grade and quality, where either or any of the purchases involved in such discrimination are in commerce, where the effect of such discrimination may be substantially to lessen competition or tend to create a monopoly in any line of commerce, or to injure, destroy, or prevent competition with any person who either grants or knowingly receives the benefit of such discrimination, or with customers of either of them.[20]*

Section 2 does not apply to the sale of services, real estate, intangible property, securities, leases, consignments, or gifts. Mixed sales (i.e., sales involving both services and commodities) are controlled based on the dominant nature of the transaction.

> **Section 2(a) of the Robinson-Patman Act**
> A section that prohibits direct and indirect price discrimination by sellers of a commodity of a like grade and quality, where the effect of such discrimination may be to substantially lessen competition or to tend to create a monopoly in any line of commerce.

Direct Price Discrimination

To prove a violation of Section 2(a) of the Robinson-Patman Act, the following elements of **direct price discrimination** must be shown:

- **Commodities of like grade and quality.** A Section 2(a) violation must involve goods of "like grade and quality." To avoid this rule, sellers sometimes try to differentiate identical or similar products by using brand names. Nevertheless, as one court stated, "Four roses under any other name would still swill the same."[21]
- **Sales to two or more purchasers.** To violate Section 2(a), the price discrimination must involve sales to at least two different purchasers at approximately the same time. It

> **direct price discrimination**
> Price discrimination in which (1) the defendant sold commodities of like grade and quality, (2) to two or more purchasers at different prices at approximately the same time, and (3) the plaintiff suffered injury because of the price discrimination.

is legal to make two or more sales of the same product to the same purchaser at different prices. The Robinson-Patman Act requires that the discrimination occur "in commerce."

• **Injury.** To recover damages, the plaintiff must have suffered actual injury because of the price discrimination. The injured party may be the purchaser who did not receive the favored price (**primary line injury**), that party's customers to whom the lower price could not be passed along (**secondary line injury**), and so on down the line (**tertiary line injury**).

A plaintiff who has not suffered injury because of a price discrimination cannot recover.

Example A wholesaler sells the same-type Michelin tires to one automobile repair and tire shop at a lower price than to another similar-size repair and tire shop. If the second tire shop cannot purchase the same-type Michelin tires at this or a lower price, it has a good case of price discrimination against the wholesaler. If the second tire shop could have purchased comparable Michelin tires elsewhere at the lower price, it cannot recover for price discrimination.

Indirect Price Discrimination

indirect price discrimination
A form of price discrimination (e.g., favorable credit terms) that is less readily apparent than direct forms of price discrimination.

Because direct forms of price discrimination are readily apparent, sellers of goods have devised sophisticated ways to provide discriminatory prices to favored customers. Favorable credit terms, freight charges, and such are examples of **indirect price discrimination** that violate the Robinson-Patman Act.

Defenses to Price Discrimination

The Robinson-Patman Act establishes three statutory defenses to Section 2(a) liability: *cost justification*, *changing conditions*, and *meeting the competition*. These defenses are discussed in the following paragraphs.

cost justification defense
A defense in a Section 2(a) action which provides that a seller's price discrimination is not unlawful if the price differential is due to "differences in the cost of manufacture, sale, or delivery" of the product.

Cost Justification   Section 2(a) provides that a seller's price discrimination is not unlawful if the price differential is due to "differences in the cost of manufacture, sale, or delivery" of the product. This is called the **cost justification defense**. For example, quantity or volume discounts are lawful to the extent that they are supported by cost savings. Sellers may classify buyers into various broad groups and compute an average cost of selling to the group. The seller may then charge members of different groups different prices without being liable for price discrimination. The seller bears the burden of proving this defense.

Example If Procter & Gamble can prove that bulk shipping rates make it less costly to deliver 10,000 boxes of Tide than lesser quantities, it may charge purchasers accordingly. However, Procter & Gamble cannot simply lower its price per box because the buyer is a good customer.

changing conditions defense
A price discrimination defense that claims prices were lowered in response to changing conditions in the market for or the marketability of the goods.

Changing Conditions   Price discrimination is not unlawful, under Section 2(a), if it is in response to "changing conditions in the market for or the marketability of the goods." For example, the price of goods can be lowered to subsequent purchasers to reflect the deterioration of perishable goods (e.g., fish), obsolescence of seasonable goods (e.g., winter coats sold in the spring), a distress sale pursuant to court order, or discontinuance of a business. This is called the **changing conditions defense**.

Meeting the Competition   The **meeting the competition defense** to price discrimination is stipulated in **Section 2(b) of the Robinson-Patman Act**[22] This defense holds that a seller may lawfully engage in price discrimination to meet a competitor's price.

meeting the competition defense
A defense provided in Section 2(b) that says a seller may lawfully engage in price discrimination to meet a competitor's price.

Example Rockport sells its "Pro Walker" shoe nationally at $100 per pair, while the Great Lakes Shoe Co. (Great Lakes), which produces and sells a comparable walking shoe, sells its product only in Michigan and Wisconsin. If Great Lake sells its walking shoes at $75 per pair, Rockport can do the same in Michigan and Wisconsin. Rockport does not have to reduce the price of the shoe in the other 48 states. The seller can only meet, not beat, the competitor's price, however.

LANDMARK LAW

Federal Trade Commission Act

In 1914, Congress enacted the **Federal Trade Commission (FTC) Act** and created the **Federal Trade Commission (FTC)**. **Section 5 of the FTC Act** prohibits **"unfair methods of competition** and unfair or deceptive acts or practices" in or affecting commerce.[23]

Section 5, which is broader than the other antitrust laws, covers conduct that (1) violates any provision of the Sherman Act or the Clayton Act, (2) violates the "spirit" of those acts, (3) fills the gaps of those acts, and (4) offends public policy; is immoral, oppressive, unscrupulous, or unethical; or causes substantial injury to competitors or consumers.

The FTC is exclusively empowered to enforce the FTC Act. It can issue interpretive rules, general statements of policy, trade regulation rules, and guidelines that define unfair or deceptive practices, and it can conduct investigations of suspected antitrust violations. It can also issue cease-and-desist orders against violators. These orders are appealable to federal court. The FTC Act provides for a private civil cause of action for injured parties. Treble damages are not available.

▶ EXEMPTIONS FROM ANTITRUST LAWS

Certain industries and businesses are exempt from federal antitrust laws. The three categories of exemptions are *statutory exemptions*, *implied exemptions*, and *state action exemptions*. These are discussed in the following paragraphs.

Statutory Exemptions

Certain statutes expressly exempt some forms of business and other activities from the reach of antitrust laws. **Statutory exemptions** include labor unions,[24] agricultural cooperatives,[25] export activities of American companies,[26] and insurance business that is regulated by a state.[27] Other federal statutes exempt railroad, utility, shipping, and securities industries from most antitrust laws.

Implied Exemptions

The federal courts have implied several exemptions from antitrust laws. Examples of **implied exemptions** include professional baseball (but not other professional sports) and airlines.[28] The airline exemption was granted on the ground that railroads and other forms of transportation were expressly exempt. The Supreme Court has held that professionals such as lawyers do not qualify for an implied exemption from antitrust laws.[29] The Supreme Court strictly construes implied exemptions from antitrust laws.

State Action Exemptions

The U.S. Supreme Court has held that economic regulations mandated by state law are exempt from federal antitrust laws. The **state action exemption** extends to businesses that must comply with these regulations.

Example States may set the rates that public utilities (e.g., gas, electric, and cable television companies) may charge their customers. The states that set these rates and the companies that must abide by them are not liable for price-fixing in violation of federal antitrust law.

▶ STATE ANTITRUST LAWS

Most states have enacted antitrust statutes. These statutes are usually patterned after federal antitrust statutes. They often contain the same language as well. State antitrust laws are used to attack anticompetitive activity that occurs in intrastate commerce. When federal antitrust laws are laxly applied, plaintiffs often bring lawsuits under state antitrust laws.

Section 5 of the Federal Trade Commission Act
A section that prohibits unfair methods of competition and unfair or deceptive acts or practices in or affecting commerce.

statutory exemptions
Exemptions from antitrust laws that are expressly provided in statutes enacted by Congress.

implied exemptions
Exemptions from antitrust laws that are implied by the federal courts.

state action exemptions
Business activities that are mandated by state law and are therefore exempt from federal antitrust laws.

TEST REVIEW TERMS AND CONCEPTS

Act of monopolizing
Antitrust Division of the
　Department of Justice
Antitrust injury
Antitrust laws
Backward vertical merger
Bureau of Competition of
　the FTC
Celler-Kefauver Act
Changing conditions
　defense
Civil damages
Clayton Act
Colgate doctrine
Conglomerate merger
Conscious parallelism
Consent decree
Cost justification defense
Creation of a monopoly
Criminal sanctions
Direct price discrimination
Division of markets (market
　sharing)
Failing company doctrine
Federal Trade Commission
　(FTC)
Federal Trade Commission
　Act (FTC Act)

Foreclose
Forward vertical merger
Geographical market
　extension merger
Group boycott (refusal to
　deal)
Hart-Scott-Rodino
　Antitrust Improvement
　Act
Horizontal merger
Horizontal restraint of trade
Implied exemptions
Indirect price
　discrimination
Line of commerce
Market extension merger
Maximum resale price
Meeting the competition
　defense
Minimum resale price
Monopoly power
Noerr doctrine
Nolo contendere
Non-price vertical restraint
Per se rule
Predatory pricing
Price discrimination
Price-fixing

Primary line injury
Private civil action
Product market extension
　merger
Relevant geographical
　market
Relevant market
Relevant product or service
　market
Resale price maintenance
　(vertical price-fixing)
Robinson-Patman Act
Rule of reason
Secondary line injury
Section of the country
Section 1 of the Sherman
　Act
Section 2 of the Clayton
　Act (Robinson-Patman
　Act)
Section 2 of the Sherman
　Act
Section 2(a) of the
　Robinson-Patman Act
Section 2(b) of the
　Robinson-Patman Act
Section 3 of the Clayton
　Act

Section 4 of the Clayton
　Act
Section 5 of the FTC Act
Section 7 of the Clayton
　Act
Section 16 of the Clayton
　Act
Sherman Act
Small company doctrine
*Standard Oil Company of
　New Jersey v. United
　States*
State action exemption
Statutory exemptions
Substantial lessening of
　competition
Tertiary line injury
Treble damages
Tying arrangement
Unfair advantage theory
Unfair methods of
　competition
Unilateral refusal to deal
Vertical merger
Vertical restraint of trade

CASE PROBLEMS

46.1 Price-Fixing The Maricopa County Medical Society (Society) is a professional association that represents doctors of medicine, osteopathy, and podiatry in Maricopa County, Arizona. The society formed the Maricopa Foundation for Medical Care (Foundation), a nonprofit Arizona corporation. Approximately 1,750 doctors, who represent 70 percent of the practitioners in the country, belong to the foundation. The Foundation acts as an insurance administrator between its member doctors and insurance companies that pay patients' medical bills.

The Foundation established a maximum fee schedule for various medical services. The member doctors agreed to abide by this fee schedule when providing services to patients. The state of Arizona brought this action against the Society and the Foundation and its members, alleging price-fixing in violation of Section 1 of the Sherman Act. Who wins? *Arizona v. Maricopa County Medical Society*, 457 U.S. 332, 102 S.Ct. 2466, 73 L.Ed.2d 48, **Web** 1982 U.S. Lexis 5 (Supreme Court of the United States)

46.2 Division of Market Topco Associates, Inc. (Topco), was founded in the 1940s by a group of small, local grocery store chains to act as a buying cooperative for the member stores. In this capacity, Topco procured for and distributed to its members more than 1,000 different food and related items. Topco did not itself own any manufacturing or processing facilities, and the items it procured were shipped directly from the manufacturer or packer to Topco members. Topco members agreed to sell only Topco brand products within an exclusive territory. The United States sued Topco and its members, alleging a violation of Section 1 of the Sherman Act. Who wins? *United States v. Topco Associates, Inc.*, 405 U.S. 596, 92 S.Ct. 1126, 31 L.Ed.2d 515, **Web** 1972 U.S. Lexis 167 (Supreme Court of the United States)

46.3 Tying Arrangement Mercedes-Benz of North America (MBNA) was the exclusive franchiser of Mercedes-Benz dealerships in the United States. MBNA's franchise agreements required each dealer to establish a customer service department for the repair of Mercedes-Benz automobiles and for dealers to purchase Mercedes-Benz replacement parts from MBNA. At least eight independent wholesale distributors, including Metrix Warehouse, Inc. (Metrix), sold replacement parts for Mercedes-Benz automobiles. Because they were precluded from selling parts to Mercedes-Benz dealers, these parts distributors sold their replacement parts to independent garages that specialized in the repair of Mercedes-Benz automobiles. Evidence showed that Metrix sold replacement parts for Mercedes-Benz automobiles of equal quality and at a lower price than those sold by MBNA. Metrix sued MBNA, alleging a tying agreement violation of Section 1 of the Sherman Act. Who wins? *Metrix Warehouse, Inc. v. Mercedes-Benz of North America, Inc.*, 828 F.2d 1033, **Web** 1987 U.S. App. Lexis 12341 (United States Court of Appeals for the Fourth Circuit)

46.4 Resale Price Maintenance   The Union Oil Company (Union Oil) was a major oil company that operated a nationwide network of franchised service station dealers that sold Union Oil gasoline and other products throughout the United States. The franchise dealers leased their stations from Union Oil; they also signed a franchise agreement to purchase gasoline and other products on assignment from Union Oil. Both the lease and the franchise agreement were one-year contracts that Union Oil could cancel if a dealer did not adhere to the contract. The franchise agreement provided that all dealers must adhere to the retail price of gasoline as set by Union Oil. The retail price fixed by Union Oil for gasoline during the period in question was 29.9 cents per gallon. Simpson, a franchised dealer, violated this provision in the franchise agreement and sold gasoline at 27.9 cents per gallon to meet competitive prices. Because of this, Union Oil canceled Simpson's lease and franchise agreement. Simpson sued Union Oil, alleging a violation of Section 1 of the Sherman Act. Who wins? *Simpson v. Union Oil Company*, 377 U.S. 13, 84 S.Ct. 1051, 12 L.Ed.2d 98, **Web** 1964 U.S. Lexis 2378 (Supreme Court of the United States)

46.5 Monopolization   The International Business Machines Corporation (IBM) manufactured entire computer systems, including mainframes and peripherals, and provided software and support services to customers. IBM both sold and leased computers. Greyhound Computer Corporation, Inc. (Greyhound), was a computer leasing company that bought older computers from IBM and then leased them to businesses. Thus, Greyhound was both a customer and a competitor of IBM. Prior to 1963, IBM sold its older equipment at a 10 percent discount per year, up to a maximum of 75 percent. Thus, equipment on the market for several years could be purchased at a substantial discount from its original cost.

IBM's market share of this leasing market was 82.5 percent. The portion of the leasing market not controlled by IBM was dispersed among many companies, including Greyhound. IBM officials became concerned that the balance between sales and leases was turned too heavily toward sales and that the rapid increase in leasing companies occurred because of their ability to purchase second-generation computers from IBM at a substantial discount. In 1963, IBM reduced the annual discount to 5 percent per year, with a maximum of 35 percent. In 1964, the discount was changed to 12 percent after the first year, with no further discounts. Greyhound sued IBM, alleging that IBM engaged in monopolization in violation of Section 2 of the Sherman Act. Who wins? *Greyhound Computer Corporation v. International Business Machine*

Corporation, 559 F.2d 488, **Web** 1977 U.S. App. Lexis 11957 (United States Court of Appeals for the Ninth Circuit)

46.6 Merger   The Lipton Tea Co. (Lipton) was the second-largest U.S. producer of herbal teas, controlling 32 percent of the national market. Lipton announced that it would acquire Celestial Seasonings, the largest U.S. producer of herbal teas, which controlled 52 percent of the national market. R.C. Bigelow, Inc., the third-largest producer of herbal teas, with 13 percent of the national market, brought an action, alleging that the merger would violate Section 7 of the Clayton Act, and seeking an injunction against the merger. What type of merger was proposed? What was the relevant market? Should the merger be enjoined? *R. C. Bigelow, Inc., v. Unilever, N.V.*, 867 F.2d 102, **Web** 1989 U.S. App. Lexis 574 (United States Court of Appeals for the Second Circuit)

46.7 Antitrust Injury   The Brunswick Corporation (Brunswick) was the second-largest manufacturer of bowling equipment in the United States. In the late 1950s, the bowling industry expanded rapidly. Brunswick's sales of lanes, automatic pinsetters, and ancillary equipment to bowling alley operators rose accordingly. Because the equipment required a major capital expenditure by bowling center operators, Brunswick required a cash down payment and extended credit for the rest of the purchase price. It took a security interest in the equipment.

Brunswick's sales dropped in the early 1960s, when the bowling industry went into a sharp decline. In addition, many of the bowling center operators defaulted on their loans. By the end of 1964, Brunswick was in financial difficulty. It met with limited success when it foreclosed on its security interests and attempted to lease or sell the repossessed equipment and bowling centers. To avoid complete loss, Brunswick started running the centers that would provide a positive cash flow. This made Brunswick the largest operator of bowling centers in the country, with more than five times as many bowling centers as its next largest competitor. Because the bowling industry was so deconcentrated, however, Brunswick controlled fewer than 2 percent of the bowling centers in the country.

Pueblo Bowl-O-Mat, Inc., operated three bowling centers in markets where Brunswick had repossessed bowling centers and began operating them. Pueblo Bowl sued Brunswick, alleging that Brunswick had violated Section 7 of the Clayton Act. Pueblo Bowl alleged that it had suffered injury in the form of lost profits that it would have made had Brunswick allowed the bowling centers to go bankrupt, and it requested treble damages. Is Brunswick liable? *Brunswick Corporation v. Pueblo Bowl-O-Mat, Inc.*, 429 U.S. 477, 97 S.Ct. 690, 50 L.Ed.2d 701, **Web** 1977 U.S. Lexis 37 (Supreme Court of the United States)

46.8 Price Discrimination   Corn Products Refining Company (Corn Products) manufactured corn syrup, or glucose (a principal ingredient of low-priced candy), at two plants, one located in Chicago, Illinois, and the other in Kansas City, Missouri. Corn Products sold glucose at the same retail price to all purchasers but charged separately for freight charges. Instead of charging actual freight charges, Corn Products charged every purchaser the price it would have cost for the glucose to be shipped from Chicago, even if the glucose was shipped from its Kansas City plant. This "base point pricing" system created a favored price zone for Chicago-based purchasers and put them in a better position to compete for business. The FTC sued Corn Products, alleging that it was engaging in price discrimination in violation of Section 2(a) of the Robinson-Patman Act. Who wins? *Corn Products Refining Company v. Federal Trade Commission*, 324 U.S. 726, 65 S.Ct. 961, 89 L.Ed. 1320, **Web** 1945 U.S. Lexis 2749 (Supreme Court of the United States)

BUSINESS ETHICS CASES

46.9 Business Ethics E. I. du Pont de Nemours & Co. (Du Pont) is a manufacturer of chemicals, paints, finishes, fabrics, and other products. General Motors Corporation (General Motors) is a major manufacturer of automobiles. During the period 1917–1919, Du Pont purchased 23 percent of the stock of General Motors. Du Pont became a major supplier of finishes and fabrics to General Motors.

Du Pont's commanding position as a General Motors supplier was not achieved until shortly after its purchase of a sizable block of General Motors stock in 1917. The company's interest in buying into General Motors was stimulated by John J. Raskob, Du Pont's treasurer, and Pierre S. du Pont, Du Pont's president, who acquired personal holdings of General Motors stock in 1914. General Motors had been organized six years earlier by William C. Durant to acquire the previously independent automobile manufacturing companies Buick, Cadillac, Oakland, and Oldsmobile. Durant later brought in Chevrolet, organized by Durant when he was temporarily out of power, during 1910–1915, and a bankers' group controlled General Motors. In 1915, when Durant and the bankers deadlocked on the choice of a board of directors, they resolved the deadlock by an agreement under which Pierre S. du Pont was named chairman of the General Motors board, and Pierre S. du Pont, Raskob, and two nominees of Mr. du Pont were named neutral directors. By 1916, Durant settled his differences with the bankers and resumed the presidency and his controlling position in General Motors. He prevailed upon Pierre S. du Pont and Raskob to continue their interest in General Motors's affairs, which both did as members of the finance committee, working closely with Durant in matters of finances and operations, as well as plans for future expansion.

Raskob foresaw the success of the automobile industry and the opportunity for great profit in a substantial purchase of General Motors stock. On December 19, 1917, Raskob submitted a treasurer's report to the Du Pont finance committee, recommending a purchase of General Motors stock in the amount of $25 million. That report made it clear that more than just a profitable investment was contemplated. A major consideration was that an expanding General Motors would provide a substantial market needed by the burgeoning Du Pont organization. Raskob's summary of reasons in support of the purchase included this statement: "Our interest in the General Motors Company will undoubtedly secure for us the entire Fabrikoid, Pyralin (celluloid), paint and varnish business of those companies, which is a substantial factor."

General Motors was the colossus of the giant automobile industry. Expressed in percentages, Du Pont supplied 67 percent of General Motors's requirements for finishes in 1946 and 68 percent in 1947. In fabrics, Du Pont supplied 52.3 percent of requirements in 1946 and 38.5 percent in 1947. Because General Motors accounted for almost one-half of the automobile industry's annual sales, its requirements for automotive finishes and fabrics must have represented approximately one-half of the relevant market for these materials.

In 1949, the United States brought an antitrust action against Du Pont, alleging violation of Section 7 of the Clayton Act and seeking the divestiture of Du Pont's ownership of stock in General Motors. Does Du Pont's ownership of 23 percent of the stock of General Motors constitute a vertical merger that gave Du Pont illegal preferences over competitors in the sale of finishes and fabrics to General Motors in violation of Section 7 of the Clayton Act? Did the du Ponts act ethically in this case? *United States v. E. I. du Pont de Nemours & Co.*, 353 U.S. 586, 77 S.Ct. 872, 1 L.Ed.2d 1057, **Web** 1957 U.S. Lexis 1755 (Supreme Court of the United States)

46.10 Business Ethics Falls City Industries, Inc. (Falls City), was a regional brewer located in Nebraska. It sold its Falls City brand beer in 13 states, including Indiana and Kentucky. In Indiana, Falls City sold its beer to Vanco Beverage, Inc. (Vanco), a beer wholesaler located in Vanderburgh County. In Kentucky, Falls City sold its beer to wholesalers located in Henderson County. The two counties are directly across from each other and are separated only by the Indiana–Kentucky state line. A four-lane interstate highway connects the two counties. When other brewers raised their wholesale prices in Indiana, Falls City also raised its prices. Falls City also raised its wholesale prices in Kentucky, but less than it raised its prices in Indiana. Vanco brought a treble-damages action against Falls City, alleging that Falls City had engaged in price discrimination in violation of Section 2(a) of the Robinson-Patman Act by raising prices less in Kentucky than in Indiana. Does the meeting-the-competition defense protect Falls City from liability for price discrimination? Did Falls City act unethically in this case? *Falls City Industries, Inc. v. Vanco Beverage, Inc.*, 460 U.S. 428, 103 S.Ct. 1282, 75 L.Ed.2d 174, **Web** 1983 U.S. Lexis 148 (Supreme Court of the United States)

ENDNOTES

1. 259 U.S. 200, 42 S.Ct. 465, 66 L.Ed. 898, Web 1922 U.S. Lexis 2475 (Supreme Court of the United States).
2. Antitrust Amendments Act of 1990, P.L. 101-588.
3. Antitrust Amendments Act of 1990, P.L. 101-588.
4. 15 U.S.C. Section 15.
5. *Reiter v. Sonotone Corporation,* 442 U.S. 330, 99 S.Ct. 2326, 60 L.Ed.2d 931, Web 1979 U.S. Lexis 108 (Supreme Court of the United States).
6. 15 U.S.C. Section 26.
7. Justice Marshall, *United States v. Topco Associates,* Inc., 405 U.S. 596, 92 S.Ct. 1126, 31 L.Ed.2d 515, Web 1972 U.S. Lexis 167 (Supreme Court of the United States).
8. 15 U.S.C. Section 1.
9. 221 U.S. 1, 31 S.Ct. 502, 55 L.Ed. 619, Web 1911 U.S. Lexis 1725 (Supreme Court of the United States). The Court found that Rockefeller's oil trust violated the Sherman Act and ordered the trust broken up into 30 separate companies.
10. *Dr. Miles Medical Co. v. John D. Park & Sons, Co.,* 220 U.S. 373, 31 S.Ct. 376, 55 L.Ed. 502, Web 1911 U.S. Lexis 1685 (Supreme Court of the United States).
11. *State Oil Company v. Khan,* 522 U.S. 3, 118 S.Ct. 275, 139 L.Ed.2d 199, Web 1997 U.S. Lexis 6705 (Supreme Court of the United States).
12. *Continental T.V., Inc. v. GTE Sylvania, Inc.,* 433 U.S. 36, 97 S.Ct. 2549, 53 L.Ed.2d 568, Web 1977 U.S. Lexis 134 (Supreme Court of the United States), reversing *United States v. Arnold Schwinn & Co.,* 388 U.S. 365, 87 S.Ct. 1856, 18 L.Ed.2d 1249, Web 1967 U.S. Lexis 2965 (Supreme Court of the United States).
13. 250 U.S. 300, 39 S.Ct. 465, 63 L.Ed. 992, Web 1919 U.S. Lexis 1748 (Supreme Court of the United States).
14. This doctrine is a result of two U.S. Supreme Court decisions: *Eastern R.R. President's Conference v. Noerr Motor Freight, Inc.,* 365 U.S. 127, 81 S.Ct. 523, 5 L.Ed.2d 464, Web 1961 U.S. Lexis 2128 (Supreme Court of the United States), and *United Mine Workers v. Pennington,* 381 U.S. 657, 85 S.Ct. 1585, 14 L.Ed.2d 626, Web 1965 U.S. Lexis 2207 (Supreme Court of the United States).
15. 15 U.S.C. Section 2.
16. *William Inglis & Sons Baking Company v. ITT Continental Baking Company, Inc.,* 668 F.2d 1014, Web 1982 U.S. App. Lexis 21926 (United States Court of Appeals for the Ninth Circuit).
17. 15 U.S.C. Section 18.
18. 15 U.S.C. Section 18(a).
19. 15 U.S.C. Section 14.
20. 15 U.S.C. Section 13(a).
21. *Hartley & Parker, Inc. v. Florida Beverage Corp.,* 307, F.2d 916, 923, Web 1962 U.S. App. Lexis 4196 (United States Court of Appeals for the Fifth Circuit).
22. 15 U.S.C. Section 13(b).
23. 15 U.S.C. Section 45.
24. Section 6 of the Clayton Act, 15 U.S.C. Section 17; the Norris-LaGuardia Act of 1932, 29 U.S.C. Sections 101-155; and the National Labor Relations Act of 1935, 29 U.S.C. Section 141 et seq. Labor unions that conspire or combine with nonlabor groups to accomplish a goal prohibited by federal antitrust law lose their exemption.
25. Capper-Volstrand Act of 1922, 7 U.S.C. Section 291; and Cooperative Marketing Act of 1926, 15 U.S.C. Section 521.
26. Webb-Pomerene Act, 15 U.S.C. Sections 61-65.
27. McCarran-Ferguson Act of 1945, 15 U.S.C. Sections 1011-1015.
28. *Community Communications Co., Inc. v. City of Boulder,* 455 U.S. 40, 102 S.Ct. 835, 70 L.Ed.2d 810, Web 1982 U.S. Lexis 65 (Supreme Court of the United States).
29. *Goldfarb v. Virginia State Bar,* 421 U.S. 773, 95 S.Ct. 2004, 44 L.Ed.2d 572, Web 1975 U.S. Lexis 13 (Supreme Court of the United States).

PART X
PERSONAL AND REAL PROPERTY

47 | PERSONAL PROPERTY AND BAILMENT

▲ **Grand Hotel, Mackinac Island, Michigan** *Almost all states have enacted innkeepers' statutes that limit the liability of innkeepers for loss of guests' property if certain statutory requirements are met.*

CHAPTER OBJECTIVES

After studying this chapter, you should be able to:

1. Define *personal property*.
2. Describe the methods for acquiring and transferring ownership in personal property.
3. Describe and apply rules regarding ownership rights in mislaid, lost, and abandoned property.
4. List and describe the elements for creating a bailment.
5. Explain the liability of bailees for lost, damaged, or destroyed goods.

CHAPTER CONTENTS

"Property and law are born and must die together."

—Jeremy Bentham
Principles of the Civil Code, I Works 309

▶ INTRODUCTION TO PERSONAL PROPERTY AND BAILMENT

Private ownership of property forms the foundation of our economic system. Therefore, a comprehensive body of law has been developed to protect property rights. The law protects the rights of property owners to use, sell, dispose of, control, and prevent others from trespassing on their rights.

This chapter discusses the kinds of personal property, methods of acquiring ownership in personal property, and property rights in mislaid, lost, and abandoned property. This chapter also discusses bailment, situations in which possession of (but not title to) personal property is delivered to another party for transfer, safekeeping, or some other purpose.

▶ PERSONAL PROPERTY

There are two kinds of property: *real property* and *personal property*. Real property includes land and property that is permanently attached to it. For example, minerals, crops, timber, and buildings that are attached to land are generally considered real property. **Personal property** (sometimes referred to as *goods* or *chattels*) consists of everything that is not real property. Real property can become personal property if it is removed from the land. For example, a tree that is part of a forest is real property; a tree that is cut down is personal property.

Personal property that is permanently affixed to land or buildings is called a **fixture**. Such property, which includes things like heating systems and storm windows, is categorized as real property. Unless otherwise agreed, fixtures remain with a building when it is sold. Personal property (e.g., furniture, pictures, other easily portable household items) may be removed by the seller prior to sale.

Personal property can be either tangible or intangible. **Tangible property** includes physically defined property, such as goods, animals, and minerals. **Intangible property** represents rights that cannot be reduced to physical form, such as stock certificates, certificates of deposit, bonds, and copyrights.

Real and personal property may be owned by one person or by more than one person. If property is owned concurrently by two or more persons, there is *concurrent ownership*.

personal property
Tangible property such as automobiles, furniture, and equipment, and intangible property such as securities, patents, and copyrights.

tangible property
All real property and physically defined personal property, such as buildings, goods, animals, and minerals.

intangible property
Rights that cannot be reduced to physical form, such as stock certificates, certificates of deposit, bonds, and copyrights.

▶ ACQUIRING OWNERSHIP OF PERSONAL PROPERTY

Personal property can be acquired or transferred with a minimum of formality. Commerce would be severely curtailed if the transfer of such items were difficult. The methods for acquiring ownership in personal property are possession or capture, purchase, production, gift, will, inheritance, accession, confusion, and divorce. These methods are discussed in the following paragraphs.

Possession or Capture

A person can acquire ownership in unowned personal property by **taking possession** of it, or **capturing** it. The most notable unowned objects are things in their natural state. This type of property acquisition was important when this country was being developed. In today's urbanized society, however, there are few unowned objects, and this method of acquiring ownership in personal property has become less important.

Example Someone who obtains the proper fishing license acquires ownership of all the fish he or she catches.

Purchase

The most common method of acquiring title to personal property is by *purchasing* the property from its owner.

Example Urban Concrete owns a large piece of equipment. City Builders purchases the equipment from Urban Concrete for $100,000. Urban Concrete transfers title to the equipment to City Builders. City Builders is now the owner of the equipment.

Production

Only a ghost can exist without material property.

Ayn Rand
Atlas Shrugged (1957)

Production is a common method of acquiring ownership in personal property. A manufacturer that purchases raw materials and produces a finished product owns that product.

Gift

gift
The voluntary transfer of title to property without payment of consideration by the donee. To be a valid gift, three elements must be shown: (1) donative intent, (2) delivery, and (3) acceptance.

donor
A person who gives a gift.

donee
A person who receives a gift.

gift *inter vivos*
A gift made during a person's lifetime that is an irrevocable present transfer of ownership.

gift *causa mortis*
A gift that is made in contemplation of death.

A **gift** is a voluntary transfer of property without consideration. The lack of consideration is what distinguishes a gift from a purchase. The person making a gift is called the **donor**. The person who receives a gift is called the **donee**. There are three elements of a valid gift:

1. **Donative intent.** For a gift to be effective, the donor must have intended to make a gift. **Donative intent** can be inferred from the circumstances or language used by the donor. The courts also consider such factors as the relationship of the parties, the size of the gift, and the mental capacity of the donor.
2. **Delivery.** **Delivery** must occur for there to be a valid gift. Although **physical delivery** is the usual method of transferring personal property, it is sometimes impracticable. In such circumstances, **constructive delivery** (or *symbolic delivery*) is sufficient. For example, if the property being gifted is kept in a safe-deposit box, physically giving the key to the donee is enough to signal the gift. Most intangible property is transferred by written conveyance (e.g., conveying a stock certificate represents a transfer of ownership in a corporation).
3. **Acceptance.** **Acceptance** is usually not a problem because most donees readily accept gifts. In fact, the courts presume acceptance unless there is proof that the gift was refused. Nevertheless, a person cannot be forced to accept an unwanted gift.

CONTEMPORARY ENVIRONMENT

Gift *Inter Vivos* and Gift *Causa Mortis*

A gift can be classified as either a gift *inter vivos* or a gift *causa mortis*. A gift made during a person's lifetime that is an irrevocable present transfer of ownership is a **gift** *inter vivos*.

A **gift** *causa mortis* is a gift made in contemplation of death. A gift *causa mortis* is established when (1) the donor makes a gift in anticipation of approaching death from some existing sickness or peril and (2) the donor dies from such sickness or peril without having revoked the gift. A gift *causa mortis* can be revoked by the donor up until the time he or she dies. A gift *causa mortis* takes precedence over a prior conflicting will.

Example Sandy is a patient in a hospital. She is to have a major operation from which she may not recover. Prior to going into surgery, Sandy removes her diamond ring and gives it to her friend Pamela, stating, "In the event of my death, I want you to have this." This gift is a gift *causa mortis*. If Sandy dies from the operation, the gift is effective, and Pamela owns the ring. If Sandy lives, the requisite condition for the gift (her death) has not occurred; therefore, the gift is not effective, and Sandy can recover the ring from Pamela.

Uniform Gifts to Minors Act and Uniform Transfers to Minors Act

Many states have adopted in whole or part the **Uniform Gifts to Minors Act (UGMA)** or the **Uniform Transfers to Minors Act (UTMA)**. These acts were drafted by the National Conference of Commissioners on Uniform State Laws and do not become the law of a state until that state's legislature enacts the act as a statute. These laws establish procedures for adults to make irrevocable gifts of money and securities to minors. Gifts of money can be made by depositing the money in an account in a financial institution, with the donor or another trustee (e.g., another adult or bank) as custodian for the minor. Gifts of securities can be made by registering the securities in the name of a trustee as custodian for the minor.

Uniform Gifts to Minors Act and Uniform Transfers to Minors Act
Acts that establish procedures for adults to make gifts of money and securities to minors.

Will or Inheritance

Title to personal property is frequently acquired by **will** or **inheritance**. If the person who dies has a valid will, the property is distributed to the **beneficiaries**, pursuant to the provisions of that will. If a person dies without having executed a will, the property is distributed to the **heirs** as provided in the relevant state's inheritance statute.

Accession

Accession occurs when the value of personal property increases because it is added to or improved by natural or manufactured means. Accession that occurs naturally belongs to the owner.

accession
An increase in the value of personal property because it is added to or improved by natural or manufactured means.

Example Julie owns a mare named Echo. Echo gives birth to a colt. Pursuant to accession, Julie owns the newborn colt.

If an improvement is made wrongfully, the owner acquires title to the improved property and does not have to pay the improver for the value of the improvements.

Example Suppose a thief steals a car and puts a new engine in it. The owner is entitled to recover the car as improved and does not have to pay the thief for the improvements.

If an improvement is mistakenly made by an improver and the improvement can be easily separated from the original article, the improver must remove the improvement and pay any damages caused by such removal.

Example A builder who puts the wrong door on a house must replace that door with the correct door at his own cost.

If an improvement is mistakenly made by an improver, and the improvement cannot be removed from the original article, the owner owns title to the improved property and does not have to pay the improver for the improvement.

Example If a builder misreads blueprints and extends an addition to a building farther than the owner has contracted for, the owner of the building is entitled to keep the improvement at no extra cost.

Confusion

Confusion occurs if two or more persons commingle **fungible goods** (i.e., goods that are exactly alike, such as the same grade of oil, grain, or cattle). Title to goods can be acquired by confusion. The owners share ownership in the commingled goods in proportion to the amount of goods contributed by each owner. It does not matter whether the goods were

Personal property has no locality.

Chief Justice Lord
Loughborough
Sill v. Worswick (1971)

commingled by agreement or by accident. If goods are wrongfully or intentionally commingled without permission, the innocent party acquires title to them.

Example If three farmers voluntarily agree to store the same amount of Grade B winter wheat in a silo, each of them owns one-third. When the grain is sold, the profits are divided into three parts; if the silo burns to the ground, each farmer suffers one-third of the loss.

Divorce

When a marriage is dissolved by a **divorce**, the parties obtain certain rights in the property that comprises the marital estate. Often, a settlement of property rights is reached. If not, the court must decide the property rights of the spouses.

▶ MISLAID, LOST, AND ABANDONED PERSONAL PROPERTY

Often, people find other people's personal property. Ownership rights to found property differ, depending on whether the property was mislaid, lost, or abandoned. The following paragraphs discuss these legal rules.

Mislaid Property

mislaid property
Property that an owner voluntarily places somewhere and then inadvertently forgets.

Property is **mislaid** when its owner voluntarily places the property somewhere and then inadvertently forgets it. It is likely that the owner will return for the property upon realizing that it was misplaced.

The owner of the premises where the property is mislaid is entitled to take possession of the property against all except the rightful owner. This right is superior to the rights of the person who finds it. Such possession does not involve a change of title. Instead, the owner of the premises becomes an involuntary bailee of the property and owes a duty to take reasonable care of the property until it is reclaimed by the owner. (Bailments are discussed later in this chapter.)

Example Felicity is on a business trip and stays in a hotel during her trip. Felicity accidentally leaves her diamond engagement ring in the hotel room she has stayed in and checks out of the hotel. The engagement ring is mislaid property, and the hotel has a duty to return it to Felicity, its rightful owner.

Lost Property

lost property
Property that the owner leaves somewhere due to negligence, carelessness, or inadvertence.

Property is considered **lost property** when its owner negligently, carelessly, or inadvertently leaves it somewhere. The finder obtains title to such property against the whole world except the true owner. The lost property must be returned to its rightful owner, whether the finder discovers the loser's identity or the loser finds the finder. A finder who refuses to return the property to the loser is liable for the tort of conversion and the crime of larceny. Many states require the finder to conduct a reasonable search (e.g., place advertisements in newspapers) to find the rightful owner.

Example If a commuter finds a laptop computer on the floor of a subway station in New York City, the computer is considered lost property. The finder can claim title to the computer against the whole world except the true owner. If the true owner discovers that the finder has her computer, she may recover it from the finder. If there is identification of the owner on the computer (e.g., name, address, and telephone number), the finder owes a duty to contact the rightful owner and give back the computer.

ETHICS SPOTLIGHT

Estray Statute

Most states have enacted **estray statutes** that permit a finder of mislaid or lost property to clear title to the property if:

- The finder reports the found property to the appropriate government agency and then turns over possession of the property to this agency.
- Either the finder or the government agency posts notices and publishes advertisements describing the lost property.
- A specified time (usually a year or a number of years) has passed without the rightful owner's reclaiming the property.

Many state estray statutes provide that the government receive a portion of the value of the property. Some statutes provide that title cannot be acquired in found property that is the result of illegal activity. For example, title has been denied to finders of property and money deemed to have been used for illegal drug purchases.

Business Ethics Do estray statutes encourage ethical behavior? Explain.

The following case involves the distinction between lost and mislaid property.

estray statute
A statute that permits a finder of mislaid or lost property to clear title to the property if certain prescribed legal formalities are met.

CASE 47.1 Estray Statute

Willsmore v. Township of Oceola, Michigan

106 Mich.App. 671, 308 N.W.2d 796, Web 1981 Mich.App. Lexis 2993
Court of Appeals of Michigan

"The Lost Goods Act provides certainty of title to property by eventually vesting clear title after a set period of time. It encourages honesty in finders."

—Judge Corsiglia

Facts

While hunting on unposted and unoccupied property in Oceola Township, Michigan, Duane Willsmore noticed an area with branches arranged in a crisscross pattern. When he kicked aside the branches and sod, he found a watertight suitcase in a freshly dug hole. Willsmore informed the Michigan State Police of his find. A state trooper and Willsmore together pried open the suitcase and discovered $383,840 in cash. The state police took custody of the money, which was deposited in an interest-bearing account. Michigan's Lost Goods Act provides that the finder and the township in which the property was found must share the value of the property if the finder publishes required notices and the true owner does not claim the property within one year.

Willsmore published the required notices and brought a declaratory judgment action, seeking a determination of the ownership of the money. Thomas Powell, the owner of the land on which the suitcase was found, claimed he was the owner of the suitcase. After Powell incorrectly named the amount of money in the suitcase, he asserted his Fifth Amendment right not to testify at his deposition and at trial. The trial court awarded the money equally to Willsmore and the Township of Oceola. Powell appealed.

Issue

Who is the owner of the lost briefcase and its contents?

Language of the Court

It is a universally accepted fundamental principle of property law that the true owner, assuming he presented himself within the one-year statute of limitations of the Lost Goods Act, would be entitled to the money before any other party in this case.

Voluntarily, and perhaps wisely, claimant Powell did not present himself at trial. At Powell's deposition, virtually the only answer he would give was the bald assertion that he was the true owner of the money. When asked the sum of money in the suitcase, his answer was incorrect. When faced with questions about how he obtained the money and hid it, claimant Powell had the right to assert his constitutional privilege to remain silent. However, the court not only had the right, but also the duty, to conclude from such silence that claimant Powell did not carry his burden of proof. Claimant Powell's claim as true owner fails as a matter of law. The

(case continues)

trial court was justified in granting a directed verdict against claimant Powell, claiming as the true owner.

The Lost Goods Act provides certainty of title to property by eventually vesting clear title after a set period of time. It encourages honesty in finders. The public obtains a portion of the benefit of a find through receipt of one-half of the value by the township. The finder receives an award for his honesty by receiving one-half of the value of the property plus costs.

Decision

The court of appeals held that Willsmore and the Township of Oceola were the owners of the briefcase and its contents. The court of appeals affirmed the judgment of the trial court and ordered that Willsmore and the

township each receive one-half the proceeds of the find after Willsmore's costs were deducted.

Case Questions

Critical Legal Thinking What is an estray statute? What is the public policy underlying an estray statute?

Business Ethics If you had found the suitcase, would you have turned it in to the government? Or would you have opened it? If you had found the $383,840 in cash, would you have kept it or turned it in to the government?

Contemporary Business Should the government be entitled to half the find? Does this rule encourage finders to turn in their finds? Explain.

Abandoned Property

abandoned property
Property that an owner has discarded with the intent to relinquish his or her rights in it and mislaid or lost property that the owner has given up any further attempts to locate.

Property is classified as **abandoned property** if (1) an owner discards the property with the intent to relinquish his or her rights in it or (2) an owner of mislaid or lost property gives up any further attempts to locate it. Anyone who finds abandoned property acquires title to it. The title is good against the whole world, including the original owner.

Example Property left at a garbage dump is abandoned property. It belongs to the first person who claims it.

CONCEPT SUMMARY

MISLAID, LOST, AND ABANDONED PROPERTY

Type of Property	Ownership Rights
Mislaid property	The owner of the premises where property is mislaid is entitled to possession but does not acquire title. He or she holds the property as an involuntary bailee until the owner reclaims it.
Lost property	The finder acquires title to the property against the whole world except the true owner; the owner may reclaim his or her property from the finder.
Abandoned property	The finder acquires title to the property, even against its original owner.

▶ BAILMENT

bailment
A transaction in which an owner transfers his or her personal property to another to be held, stored, delivered, or for some other purpose. Title to the property does not transfer.

bailor
The owner of property in a bailment.

bailee
A holder of goods who is not a seller or a buyer (e.g., warehouse, common carrier).

A **bailment** occurs when the owner of personal property delivers his or her property to another person, either to be held, stored, or delivered or for some other purpose. In a bailment, the owner of the property is the **bailor**. The party to whom the property is delivered for safekeeping, storage, or delivery (e.g., warehouse, common carrier) is the **bailee** (see Exhibit 47.1). The law of bailment establishes the rights, duties, and liabilities of parties to a bailment.

A bailment is different from a sale or a gift because title to the goods does not transfer to the bailee. Instead, the bailee must follow the bailor's directions concerning the goods.

Example Hudson Corporation is relocating offices and hires American Van Lines to move its office furniture and equipment to the new location. American Van Lines (the bailee) must follow Hudson's (the bailor's) instructions regarding delivery.

► Exhibit 47.1 BAILMENT

Elements Necessary to Create a Bailment

Three elements are necessary to create a bailment:

1. **Personal property.**   Only *personal property* can be bailed. The property can be tangible (e.g., automobiles, jewelry, animals) or intangible (e.g., stocks, bonds, promissory notes).

2. **Delivery of possession.**   **Delivery of possession** involves two elements: (1) The bailee must have exclusive control over the personal property, and (2) the bailee must knowingly accept the personal property.

   Examples No bailment is created if a patron goes into a restaurant and hangs her coat on an unattended coat rack because other patrons have access to the coat. However, a bailment is created if a patron checks her coat with a coatroom attendant because the restaurant has assumed exclusive control over the coat. If valuable property was left in the pocket of the coat, there would be no bailment of that property because the checkroom attendant did not knowingly accept it.

   Most bailments are created by *physical delivery*. For example, a bailment is created if Great Lakes Shipping, Inc., delivers a vessel to Marina Repairs, Inc., for repairs. *Constructive delivery* can create a bailment, too. For example, there has been constructive delivery of an automobile if the owner gives someone the keys and registration to his car.

3. **Bailment agreement.**   The creation of a bailment does not require any formality. A bailment may be either express or implied. Most *express bailments* can be either written or oral. Under the Statute of Frauds, however, a **bailment agreement** must be in writing if it is for more than one year. An example of an *implied bailment* is the finding and safeguarding of lost property.

In the following case, the court had to decide whether a bailment had been created.

> *Laws are always useful to persons of property, and hurtful to those who have none.*
>
> Jean-Jacques Rousseau
> *Du Contrat Social (1761)*

CASE 47.2 Bailment

Ziva Jewelry, Inc. v. Car Wash Headquarters, Inc.

897 So.2d 1011, Web 2004 Ala. Lexis 238 (2004)
Supreme Court of Alabama

"Thus, Ziva Jewelry cannot claim that CWH knew or that it should have reasonably foreseen or expected that it was taking responsibility for over $850,000 worth of jewelry when it accepted Smith's vehicle for the purpose of washing it."

—Judge Stuart

Facts

Ziva Jewelry, Inc., is a jewelry wholesaler. Stewart Smith was employed by Ziva Jewelry as a traveling sales representative. In connection with the employment, Smith drove his own vehicle to meet clients and attend trade shows. Smith testified that he knew that thieves are aware of jewelry trade shows and sometimes follow jewelry sales representatives, looking for an opportunity to steal the jewelry in the possession of the sales representatives and that they are most likely to strike when the car carrying the jewelry is unattended. Smith's practice was to keep the jewelry in the trunk of his vehicle while he was traveling on business. He kept the trunk padlocked and kept the only key to the padlock on the key ring with his ignition key.

One day, when Smith was traveling from a jewelry trade show, he stopped at Rain Tunnel Car Wash, owned by Car

(case continues)

Wash Headquarters, Inc. (CWH). At Rain Tunnel, the driver leaves his or her vehicle with employees of the car wash, and the vehicle is sent through a wash "tunnel." Upon completion of the car wash cycle, an employee drives the vehicle to another area of the car-wash premises to be hand dried. Once the vehicle is dried, the driver is signaled to retrieve the vehicle.

Smith left his car and the keys with a car-wash employee. Jewelry worth $850,000 was locked in the trunk of the vehicle. Smith watched the car as it went through the car wash tunnel. He watched as an employee dried the vehicle. As Smith was standing at the counter waiting to pay the cashier, he saw the employee wave a flag, indicating that the vehicle was ready for Smith. The employee then walked away from the vehicle. While Smith was standing at the cashier counter, someone jumped into Smith's vehicle and sped off. When the police recovered Smith's vehicle about 15 minutes later, the jewelry was gone.

Ziva Jewelry sued CWH to recover the value of the jewelry, alleging that a bailment had been created between Ziva and CWH and that CWH, as the bailee, was negligent in protecting the bailed goods. CWH defended, arguing that no bailment was created and therefore it was not liable for the loss of Ziva's stolen jewelry. The trial court held that no bailment had been created and entered summary judgment for CWH. Ziva Jewelry appealed.

Issue

Was a bailment created between Ziva Jewelry and CWH?

Language of the Court

A bailment is defined as the delivery of personal property by one person to another for a specific purpose, with a contract, express or implied, that the trust shall be faithfully executed, and the property returned or duly accounted for when the special purpose is accomplished, or *kept until the bailor reclaims it. In order for a bailment to exist the bailee must have voluntarily assumed the custody and possession of the property for another.*

In this case, Ziva Jewelry cannot establish that CWH expressly or impliedly agreed to take responsibility for the jewelry hidden inside Smith's trunk. Ziva Jewelry acknowledges that the jewelry was not plainly visible; that its presence was not made known to the car-wash employees; and that there was no reason that the employees should have expected expensive jewelry to be in the trunk of Smith's vehicle. Thus, Ziva Jewelry cannot claim that CWH knew or that it should have reasonably foreseen or expected that it was taking responsibility for over $850,000 worth of jewelry when it accepted Smith's vehicle for the purpose of washing it. Thus, there is no evidence indicating that CWH expressly or impliedly accepted responsibility for the jewelry in the trunk of Smith's vehicle. Without express or implied acceptance by the purported bailee, a bailment cannot arise.

Decision

The supreme court held that no bailment had been created between Ziva Jewelry and CWH. The supreme court affirmed the trial court's ruling that granted summary judgment to CWH.

Case Questions

Critical Legal Thinking What is a bailment? What is required for a bailment to be created? Why was a bailment not created in this case? Explain.

Business Ethics Did Ziva Jewelry have a good chance of winning this case? Why or why not? Do you think Smith was negligent in this case?

Contemporary Business Do you think that jewelry sales representatives are often subject to theft?

Types of Ordinary Bailments

There are three types of ordinary bailments: *bailment for the sole benefit of the bailor*, *bailment for the sole benefit of the bailee*, and *mutual benefit bailment*. Each of these types of bailments is discussed in the following paragraphs.

bailment for the sole benefit of the bailor
A gratuitous bailment that benefits only the bailor. The bailee owes only a *duty of slight care* to protect the bailed property.

Bailment for the Sole Benefit of the Bailor A **bailment for the sole benefit of the bailor** is a **gratuitous bailment** that benefits only the bailor. This ordinary bailment arises when the bailee is requested to care for the bailor's property as a favor. The bailee owes only a **duty of slight care** to protect the bailed property—that is, he or she owes a duty not to be grossly negligent in caring for the bailed goods.

Example The Watkins family is going on vacation and asks the neighbors, the Smiths, to feed its dog, which is allowed to run free. The Smiths diligently feed the dog, but the dog runs away and does not return. The Smiths are not liable for the loss of the dog.

Bailment for the Sole Benefit of the Bailee   A **bailment for the sole benefit of the bailee** is a *gratuitous bailment* that solely benefits the bailee. This ordinary bailment arises when a bailee requests to use the bailor's property for personal reasons. In this situation, the bailee owes a **duty of great care** (or **duty of utmost care**) to protect the bailed property—that is, he or she owes a duty not to be slightly negligent in caring for the bailed goods.

Example Mitch borrows Courtney's lawn mower (free of charge) to mow his own lawn. Mitch is the bailee, and Courtney is the bailor. This bailment is for the sole benefit of the bailee. Suppose Mitch, while mowing his lawn, leaves the lawn mower in his front yard while he goes into his house to answer the telephone. While he is gone, the lawn mower is stolen. Here, Mitch will be held liable to Courtney for the loss of the lawn mower because Mitch breached his duty of great care to protect the lawn mower.

Mutual Benefit Bailment   A **mutual benefit bailment** is a bailment that *benefits both parties*. The bailee owes a **duty of reasonable care** (or **duty of ordinary care**) to protect the bailed goods. This means that the bailee is liable for any goods that are lost, damaged, or destroyed because of his or her negligence.

Example ABC Garment Co. delivers goods to Lowell, Inc., a commercial warehouser, for storage. A fee is charged for this service. ABC Garment Co. receives the benefit of having its goods stored, and Lowell, Inc., receives the benefit of being paid compensation for storing the goods. In this example, Lowell, Inc. (the bailee), owes a duty of ordinary care to protect the goods.

> **bailment for the sole benefit of the bailee**
> A gratuitous bailment that benefits only the bailee. The bailee owes a *duty of utmost care* to protect the bailed property.

> **mutual benefit bailment**
> A bailment for the mutual benefit of the bailor and bailee. The bailee owes a *duty of ordinary care* to protect the bailed property.

CONCEPT SUMMARY
ORDINARY BAILMENT

Type of Bailment	Duty of Care Owed by Bailee	Bailee Liable to Bailor for
For the sole benefit of the bailor	Slight	Gross negligence
For the sole benefit of the bailee	Great	Slight negligence
For the mutual benefit of the bailor and bailee	Ordinary	Ordinary negligence

Duration and Termination of Bailments

A bailment generally expires at a specified time or when a certain purpose is accomplished. A **bailment for a fixed term** terminates at the end of the term or sooner, by mutual consent of the parties. A party who terminates a bailment in breach of the bailment agreement is liable to the innocent party for damages resulting from the breach. A bailment without a fixed term is called a **bailment at will**. A bailment at will can be terminated at any time by either party. Gratuitous bailees can generally terminate a fixed-term bailment prior to expiration of the term.

Upon termination of a bailment, the bailee is legally obligated to do as the bailor directs with the property. Unless otherwise agreed, the bailee is obligated to return the identical goods bailed. Where commingled *fungible goods* are involved (e.g., grain), identically equivalent goods may be returned by the bailee.

> **bailment for a fixed term**
> A bailment that terminates at the end of the term or sooner, by mutual consent of the parties.

> **bailment at will**
> A bailment without a fixed term; can be terminated at any time by either party.

▶ SPECIAL BAILMENTS

Several special forms of bailment require special procedures for formation and have their own special liability rules. There bailments involve *warehouse companies*, *common carriers*, and *innkeepers*. These special types of bailments are discussed in the following paragraphs.

Warehouse Company

A **warehouser**, or **warehouse company**, is a bailee engaged in the business of storing property for compensation. Warehousers are subject to the rights, duties, and liability of an ordinary bailee. As such, they owe a *duty of reasonable care* to protect the bailed property in their possession from harm or loss.[1] Warehousers are liable only for loss or damage to the bailed property caused by their own negligence. They are not liable for loss or damage caused to bailed goods by another person's negligence or conduct. Warehousers can limit the dollar amount of their liability if they offer the bailor the opportunity to increase the liability limit for the payment of an additional charge.

Warehouse Receipt   A **warehouse receipt** is a document of title issued by a company that is engaged in the business of storing goods for hire, such as a warehouse company or a storage company.[2] A warehouse receipt that is issued to the bailor is often a preprinted form drafted by the warehouse company. A warehouse receipt includes the date of issue, a description of the goods or the packages containing the goods, the location of the warehouse where the goods are stored, and other terms related to the bailment. A warehouse company has a **lien** on the goods in its possession for necessary expenses incurred in storing and handling the goods. If the charges are not paid, the warehouse company may sell the goods at a public or private auction and apply the proceeds to pay the charges. Any excess proceeds must be held for the persons who had the right to demand delivery of the goods.

Common Carrier

Common carriers offer transportation services to the general public. For example, commercial airlines, railroads, public trucking companies, public pipeline companies, and such are common carriers. The delivery of goods to a common carrier creates a mutual benefit bailment. The person shipping the goods is the **consignor**, or **shipper** (the bailor). The transportation company is called the **common carrier** (the bailee). The person to whom the goods are to be delivered is called the **consignee**. (See Exhibit 47.2.)

Common carriers are held to a **duty of strict liability**:[3] If the goods are lost, damaged, destroyed, or stolen, the common carrier is liable even if it was not at fault for the loss. Common carriers are not liable for the loss, damage, or destruction of goods caused by (1) an act of God (e.g., a tornado), (2) an act of a public enemy (e.g., a terrorist activity), (3) an order of the government (e.g., statutes, court decisions, government regulations), (4) an act of the shipper (e.g., improper packaging), or (5) the inherent nature of the goods (e.g., perishability).

consignor
A person shipping goods. The bailor.

consignee
A person to whom bailed goods are to be delivered.

▶ **Exhibit 47.2 COMMON CARRIER CONSIGNMENT**

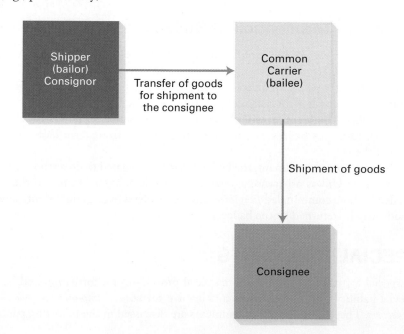

Common carriers can limit their liability to a stated dollar amount by expressly stating that in the bailment agreement. Federal law requires common carriers who take advantage of such limitation to offer shippers the opportunity to pay a premium and declare a higher value for the goods.[4]

Bill of Lading   A **bill of lading** is a document of title that is issued by a carrier-bailee to the bailor when goods are received for transportation. A carrier has a lien on the goods in its possession covered by a bill of lading for necessary charges and expenses. If the charges are not paid, the carrier can sell the goods at public or private sale and apply the proceeds to pay the charges. Any excess proceeds must be held for the person who had the right to demand delivery of the goods.[5]

Mine is better than ours.

Benjamin Franklin

innkeepers' statutes
State statutes that limit an innkeeper's common law liability. An innkeeper can avoid liability for loss caused to a guest's property if (1) a safe is provided in which the guest's valuable property may be kept and (2) the guest is notified of this fact.

CONTEMPORARY ENVIRONMENT

Innkeeper's Statute

An **innkeeper** is the owner of a facility that provides lodging to the public for compensation (e.g., hotel, motel). Under the common law, innkeepers are held to a **strict liability standard** regarding loss caused to the personal property of transient guests. Permanent lodgers are not subject to this rule.

However, almost all states have enacted **innkeepers' statutes** that change the common law and limit the liability of innkeepers. These statutes allow innkeepers to avoid liability for loss caused to guests' property if a safe is provided in which the guests' valuable property may be kept and the guests are aware of the safe's availability. Most state laws also allow innkeepers to limit the dollar amount of their liability by notifying their guests of this limit (e.g., by posting a notice on each guest room door).

Example Hospitality Hotel, Inc., operates a hotel. The hotel is located in a state that has an innkeepers' statute that (1) eliminates a hotel's liability for guests' property not placed in the safe located at the hotel's registration desk and (2) limits a hotel's liability to $500 for any guest's property stored in the hotel's safe. The hotel has proper notices posted at the registration counter and in guests' rooms, notifying guests of these limitations on liability. Gion, a guest at the hotel, leaves expensive jewelry and cameras in his room when he temporarily leaves the hotel. When Gion returns, he finds that his jewelry and cameras have been stolen. Because of the innkeepers' statute, the hotel is not liable for Gion's loss. Suppose instead that Gion had taken items to the hotel's registration desk and had the hotel place the items in the hotel safe. If the items had been stolen from the hotel's safe, the innkeepers' statute would have limited the hotel's liability to $500.

CONCEPT SUMMARY

SPECIAL BAILMENTS

Type of Bailee	Liability	Limitation on Liability
Warehouse company	Ordinary negligence	May limit the dollar amount of liability by offering the bailor the right to declare a higher value for the bailed goods for an additional charge.
Common carrier	Strictly liable except for: 1. Act of God 2. Act of a public enemy 3. Order of the government 4. Act of the shipper 5. Inherent nature of the goods	May limit the dollar amount of liability by offering the bailor the right to declare a higher value for the bailed goods for an additional charge.
Innkeeper	Strictly liable	State innkeepers' statutes limit the liability of an innkeeper for others' negligence.

TEST REVIEW TERMS AND CONCEPTS

Abandoned property	Confusion	Estray statute	Personal property
Acceptance	Consignee	Fixture	Physical delivery
Accession	Consignor (shipper)	Fungible goods	Production
Bailee	Constructive delivery	Gift	Strict liability standard
Bailment	Delivery	Gift *causa mortis*	Taking possession
Bailment agreement	Delivery of possession	Gift *inter vivos*	(capturing)
Bailment at will	Divorce	Gratuitous bailment	Tangible property
Bailment for a fixed term	Donative intent	Heir	Uniform Gifts to Minors
Bailment for the sole	Donee	Inheritance	Act
benefit of the bailee	Donor	Innkeeper	Uniform Transfer to Minors
Bailment for the sole	Duty of great care (duty	Innkeepers' statute	Act
benefit of the bailor	of utmost care)	Intangible property	Warehouser (warehouse
Bailor	Duty of reasonable care	Lien	company)
Beneficiary	(duty of ordinary care)	Lost property	Warehouse receipt
Bill of lading	Duty of slight care	Mislaid property	Will
Common carrier	Duty of strict liability	Mutual benefit bailment	

CASE PROBLEMS

47.1 Gift   For 12 years, Theodore Alexander Buder's father made substantial gifts to his minor grandchildren. Theodore Buder and his wife divorced during this period. The cash gifts, typically in the form of checks made directly payable to the children, were given to Buder with the understanding that he would safeguard the money and invest it on behalf of the children. Buder invested various amounts of the children's money in "blue chip" stocks traded over the New York and American stock exchanges. Buder also invested substantial sums of the children's money in speculative penny stocks. The stocks were purchased in Buder's name as custodian for the children, as required by the Uniform Gifts to Minors Act (UGMA). At one point, almost half of the children's money was invested in penny stocks. All the penny stocks except one suffered substantial losses. Buder's ex-wife, Sartore, sued him, alleging that he had breached his fiduciary duty owed to the children under the UGMA. She sought to recover the funds lost by Buder's investment of the children's funds in penny stocks. Who wins? *Buder v. Sartore*, 774 P.2d 1383, **Web** 1989 Colo. Lexis 227 (Supreme Court of Colorado)

47.2 Lost Property   Danny Lee Smith and his brother, Jeffrey Allen Smith, found a 16-foot fiberglass boat lying beside the roadway in Mobile County, Alabama. Seeing two sheriff's deputies, they stopped them to discuss the boat. Over the Smiths' objections, the deputies impounded the boat. The Smiths made it clear that if the true owner of the boat was not found, they wanted the boat. The true owner did not claim the boat. Mobile County claimed the boat and wanted to auction it off for sale to raise money for county recreational programs. The Smiths claimed the boat as finders. Alabama did not have an estray statute that applied to the situation. Who gets the boat? *Smith v. Sheriff Purvis*, 474 So.2d 1131, **Web** 1985 Ala. Civ. App. Lexis 1280 (Court of Civil Appeals of Alabama)

47.3 Abandoned Property   Police officers of the city of Miami, Florida, responded to reports of a shooting at the apartment of Carlos Fuentes. Fuentes had been shot in the neck and shoulder, and shortly after the police arrived, he was removed to a hospital. In an ensuing search of the apartment, the police found assorted drug paraphernalia, a gun, and cash in the amount of $58,591. The property was seized, taken to the police station, and placed in custody. About nine days later, the police learned that Fuentes had been discharged from the hospital. All efforts by police to locate Fuentes and his girlfriend, a co-occupant of Fuentes's apartment, were unsuccessful. Neither Fuentes nor his girlfriend ever came forward to claim any of the items taken by the police from his apartment. About four years later, James W. Green and Walter J. Vogel, the owners of the apartment building in which Fuentes was a tenant, sued the city of Miami to recover the cash found in Fuentes's apartment. The state of Florida intervened in the case, also claiming an interest in the money. Who wins? *State of Florida v. Green*, 456 So.2d 1309, **Web** 1984 Fla.App. Lexis 15340 (Court of Appeal of Florida)

47.4 Bailment   James D. Merritt leased a storage locker from Nationwide Warehouse Co., Ltd. (Nationwide), and agreed to pay a monthly fee to lease the locker. Merritt placed various items in the leased premises but never informed Nationwide as to the nature or quantity of articles stored therein. Merritt was free to store or remove whatever he wished without consultation with, permission from, or notice to Nationwide. Merritt locked the leased premises with his own lock and key. Nationwide was not furnished with a key. Subsequently, certain personal property belonging to Merritt disappeared from the storage space. Merritt sued Nationwide to recover damages of $5,275. Was a bailment created between Merritt and Nationwide? *Merritt v. Nationwide*

Warehouse Co., Ltd., 605 S.W.2d 250, **Web** 1980 Tenn.App. Lexis 338 (Court of Appeals of Tennessee)

47.5 Lost Goods   Clarence Williams took his wife's fur coat to Debonair Cleaners for cleaning and storage. The clerk told him that the cleaner was experienced in such matters and that the charge would be 3 percent of the stated value of the coat. Williams stated that the coat was worth $13,000, and the clerk gave Williams a claim check and informed Williams that the total fee for storage would be $390, to be paid when the coat was retrieved. That evening, Williams related the substance of his conversation with the clerk to his wife, America, and gave her the claim check. Approximately eight months later, America Williams went to Debonair Cleaners to retrieve her coat. She presented the claim check to the clerk, who, after searching the premises for the coat, told her that it could not be located. Williams was informed that the coat had probably been stolen during a break-in and burglary. Williams sued Debonair Cleaners to recover the value of the coat. Who wins? *Mahallati v. Williams*, 479 A.2d 300, **Web** 1984 D.C.App. Lexis 419 (District of Columbia Court of Appeals)

47.6 Gratuitous Bailment   Marsha Hamilton and Andrea Morris were guests at a dinner party attended by approximately 25 people. The party began about 7:00 P.M. and ended at approximately 1:00 A.M. Alcoholic beverages were served throughout the evening. At approximately 11:30, while working in the kitchen, Hamilton removed her watch and placed it on the counter. About midnight, Hamilton left the kitchen and went outside. After about 15 minutes, she became ill and fled to the bathroom. Shortly after Hamilton left the kitchen, Morris saw the watch on the counter and, fearing for its safety, picked it up and carried it in her hand as she looked for Hamilton. When Hamilton came out of the bathroom, she and her fiancé left the party. Morris was unable to find Hamilton and could not recall precisely what she did with the watch. She testified that she either gave it to Hamilton's fiancé or put it somewhere in the host's house for safekeeping. Hamilton's fiancé testified that Morris did not give him the watch. The next day, Hamilton discovered that she did not have her watch, but in a search of the host's home, the watch was not recovered. Hamilton sued Morris for damages. Who wins? *Morris v. Hamilton*, 225 Va. 372, 302 S.E.2d 51, **Web** 1983 Va. Lexis 231 (Supreme Court of Virginia)

47.7 Parking Lot's Liability   Allright, Inc., was a parking lot operator in Houston, Texas. Kirkland Strauder drove his automobile to a Houston Allright parking lot and placed it in a row of cars to be parked by the attendant. When Strauder returned two hours later to reclaim his car, it could not be found. Strauder reported the car stolen. Allright could not explain the loss of the car, which was found weeks later, wrecked and stripped. Strauder sued Allright, Inc., for damages. Who wins? *Allright, Inc. v. Strauder*, 679 S.W.2d 81, **Web** 1984 Tex.App. Lexis 6006 (Court of Appeals of Texas)

47.8 Disclaimer of Liability   Joseph Conboy, his wife, and a group of friends convened in Manhattan, New York, for a party at a club where patrons danced to recorded music. The Conboy party checked their coats, 14 in all, with the coatroom attendant. After paying a $0.75 charge per coat, they received seven check stubs. A small sign in the coatroom stated "Liability for lost property in this coat/check room is limited to $100 per loss of misplaced article." Conboy testified that he did not notice it when he checked his coat and that the coatroom attendant did not call his attention to the sign. At the end of the evening, Conboy and the other guests of the party attempted to reclaim their coats. Conboy's one-month-old $1,350 leather coat was missing. Conboy sued the club for damages. Is the disclaimer of liability enforceable? *Conboy v. Studio 54, Inc.*, 113 Misc.2d 403, 449 N.Y.S.2d 391, **Web** 1982 N.Y. Misc. Lexis 3309 (Civil Court of the City of New York)

BUSINESS ETHICS CASES

47.9 Business Ethics   When Dr. Arthur M. Edwards died, leaving a will disposing of this property, he left the villa-type condominium in which he lived, its "contents," and $10,000 to his stepson, Ronald W. Souders. Edwards left the residual of his estate to other named legatees. In administering the estate, certain stock certificates, passbook savings accounts, and other bank statements were found in Edwards's condominium. Souders claimed that these items belonged to him because they were "contents" of the condominium. The other legatees opposed Souders' claim, alleging that the disputed property was intangible property and not part of the contents of the condominium. The value of the property was as follows: condominium, $138,000; furniture in condominium, $4,000; stocks, $377,000; and passbook and other bank accounts, $124,000. Who is entitled to the stocks and bank accounts? Do you think Souders acted ethically in this case? *Souders v. Johnson*, 501 So.2d 745, **Web** 1987 Fla.App. Lexis 6579 (Court of Appeal of Florida)

47.10 Business Ethics   Darryl Kulwin was employed by Nova Stylings, Inc. (Nova), as a jewelry salesman. In that capacity, he traveled throughout the country, carrying with him jewelry owned and manufactured by Nova to show to prospective buyers. Kulwin was visiting Panoria Ruston, who was a guest registered with the Red Roof Inn in Overland Park, Kansas. Ruston and Kulwin met at the Red Roof Inn and later made plans to leave to go out for dinner. Kulwin asked Ruston to make arrangements with the desk clerk to leave his sample case in the office of the Red Roof Inn while they went out to dinner. Ruston asked the clerk if she could leave the bag in the manager's office of the Red Roof Inn, and the clerk agreed.

Ruston advised the clerk that the contents of the case were valuable but did not describe the contents of the bag.

Kansas Statute Section 36-402(b) provides:

No hotel or motel keeper in this state shall be liable for the loss of, or damage to, merchandise for sale or samples belonging to a guest, lodger, or boarder unless the guest, lodger, or boarder upon entering the hotel or motel, shall give notice of having merchandise for sale or samples in his possession, together with an itemized list of such property, to the hotel or motel keeper, or his authorized agent or clerk in the registration office of the hotel or motel office.

No hotel or motel keeper shall be liable for any loss of such property designated in this subsection (b), after notice an itemized statement having been given and delivered as aforesaid, in an amount in excess of two hundred fifty dollars ($250), unless such hotel or motel keeper, by specific agreement in writing, individually, or by an authorized agent or clerk in charge of the registration office of the hotel or motel, shall voluntarily assume liability for a larger amount with reference to such property. The hotel or motel keeper shall not be compelled to receive such guests, lodgers, or boarders with merchandise for sale or samples.

The inn posted the proper notice of the provisions of this act in all of the guests' rooms, including that of Ruston. An unidentified person obtained access to the manager's office and removed the case from the office. Nova sued Red Roof Inns for the alleged value of the jewelry, $650,000. Is Red Roof Inns liable? Did either party act unethically in this case? *Nova Stylings v. Red Roof Inns, Inc.*, 242 Kan. 318, 747 P.2d 107, **Web** 1987 Kan. Lexis 469 (Supreme Court of Kansas)

ENDNOTES

1. UCC 7-204(1), 7-403(1).
2. UCC 1-201(45).
3. UCC 7-301(1).
4. UCC 7-309(2).
5 UCC 7-308(1).

▲ **Cottages, Mackinac Island, Michigan** *A person's house is often his or her most valuable asset.*

CHAPTER OBJECTIVES

After studying this chapter, you should be able to:

1. List and describe the different types of real property.
2. Describe the different types of freehold estates and future interests in real property.
3. Identify the different types of concurrent ownership of real property.
4. Explain how ownership interests in real property can be transferred.
5. Describe the zoning laws.

CHAPTER CONTENTS

"**Without that sense of security which property gives, the land would still be uncultivated.**"

Francois Quesnay
Maximes, IV

▶ INTRODUCTION TO REAL PROPERTY

Property and ownership rights in *real property* play an important part in the society and economy of the United States. Individuals and families own houses, farmers and ranchers own farmland and ranches, and businesses own commercial and office buildings. The concept of real property is concerned with the legal rights to the property rather than the physical attributes of the tangible land. Thus, real property includes some items of personal property that are affixed to real property (e.g., fixtures) and other rights (e.g., minerals, air).

Although the United States has the most advanced private property system in the world, the ownership and possession of real estate are not free from government regulation. Pursuant to constitutional authority, federal, state, and local governments have enacted myriad laws that regulate the ownership, possession, lease, and use of real property. These laws include zoning laws, and the like.

This chapter covers the law concerning the ownership and transfer of real property.

▶ REAL PROPERTY

Property is usually classified as either real or personal property. **Real property** is immovable or attached to immovable land or buildings, whereas personal property is movable. The various types of real property are described in the following paragraphs.

Land and Buildings

Land is the most common form of real property. A landowner usually purchases the **surface rights** to the land—that is, the right to occupy the land. The owner may use, enjoy, and develop the property as he or she sees fit, subject to any applicable government regulation.

Buildings constructed on land are real property. Houses, apartment buildings, manufacturing plants, and office buildings constructed on land are real property. Such things as radio towers and bridges are usually considered real property as well.

Subsurface Rights

The owner of land possesses **subsurface rights**, or **mineral rights**, to the earth located beneath the surface of the land. These rights can be very valuable. Gold, uranium, oil, or natural gas may lie beneath the surface of the land. Theoretically, mineral rights extend to the center of the earth. In reality, mines and oil wells usually extend only several miles into the earth. Subsurface rights may be sold separately from surface rights.

Plant Life and Vegetation

Plant life and vegetation growing on the surface of land are considered real property. Such vegetation includes both natural plant life (e.g., trees) and cultivated plant life (e.g., crops). When land is sold, any plant life growing on the land is included, unless the parties agree otherwise. Plant life that is severed from the land is considered personal property.

Fixtures

Certain personal property is so closely associated with real property that it becomes part of the realty. Such items are called **fixtures**. Kitchen cabinets, carpet, and doorknobs are fixtures, but throw rugs and furniture are personal property. Unless otherwise provided, if a

real property
The land itself as well as buildings, trees, soil, minerals, timber, plants, and other things permanently affixed to the land.

Good fences make good neighbors.

Robert Frost
"Mending Wall" (1914)

subsurface rights
Rights to the earth located beneath the surface of the land.

fixtures
Goods that are affixed to real estate so as to become part thereof.

building is sold, the fixtures are included in the sale. If the sale agreement is silent as to whether an item is a fixture, the courts make their determination on the basis of whether the item can be removed without causing substantial damage to the realty.

CONTEMPORARY ENVIRONMENT

Air Rights

Common law provided that the owners of real property owned that property from the center of the earth to the heavens. This rule has been eroded by modern legal restrictions such as land use regulation laws, environmental protection laws, and air navigation requirements. Even today, however, the owners of land may sell or lease air space parcels above their land.

An **air space parcel** is the air space above the surface of the earth of an owner's real property. Air space parcels are valuable property rights, particularly in densely populated metropolitan areas, where building property is scarce.

Examples Railroads have made money by leasing or selling air rights over their railroad tracks. For example, the Grand Central Terminal in New York City sold air rights over its railroad property for the construction of the PanAm Building (now MetLife Building) next to Grand Central Terminal.

Many other developments have been built in air space parcels in New York City.

Owners of highways—including states and cities—often sell or lease **air rights** over the highways.

Example Many fast food restaurants and gasoline stations are located on air rights over freeways. In addition, air rights are often developed so that historic buildings can be preserved. This is often accomplished by the city premitting a developer to purchase air rights above the historic building in exchange for preserving the historic building.

Owners of air rights, and parties who want to build on those air rights, will continue to come up with unique solutions to meet building needs.

▶ ESTATES IN LAND

A person's ownership right in real property is called an **estate in land** (or **estate**). An estate is defined as the bundle of *legal rights* that the owner has to possess, use, and enjoy the property. The type of estate that an owner possesses is determined from the deed, will, lease, or other document that transferred the ownership rights to him or her.

estate
Ownership rights in real property; the bundle of legal rights that the owner has to possess, use, and enjoy the property.

Freehold Estate

A **freehold estate** is an estate in which the owner has a *present possessory interest* in the real property; that is, the owner may use and enjoy the property as he or she sees fit, subject to any applicable government regulation or private restraint. There are three types of freehold estates: two *estates in fee—fee simple absolute (or fee simple)* and *fee simple defeasible (or qualified fee)*—and *life estate*. These are discussed in the following paragraphs.

freehold estate
An estate in which the owner has a present possessory interest in the real property.

Fee Simple Absolute (or Fee Simple)   A **fee simple absolute** (or **fee simple**) is an estate in fee that is the highest form of ownership of real property because it grants the owner the fullest bundle of legal rights that a person can hold in real property. It is the type of ownership most people connect with "owning" real property. A fee simple owner has the right to exclusively possess and use his or her property to the extent that the owner has not transferred any interest in the property (e.g., by lease).

If a person owns real property in fee simple, his or her ownership:

- Is infinite in duration (fee)
- Has no limitation on inheritability (simple)
- Does not end upon the occurrence of any event (absolute)

fee simple absolute
A type of ownership of real property that grants the owner the fullest bundle of legal rights that a person can hold in real property. Also known as *fee simple*.

Fee Simple Defeasible (or Qualified Fee)   A **fee simple defeasible** (or **qualified fee**) grants the owner all the incidents of a fee simple absolute except that it may be taken away if a specified *condition* occurs or does not occur.

fee simple defeasible
A type of ownership of real property that grants the owner all the incidents of a fee simple absolute except that it may be taken away if a specified condition occurs or does not occur. Also known as *qualified fee*.

Example A conveyance of property to a church "as long as the land is used as a church or for church purposes" creates a qualified fee. The church has all the rights of a fee simple absolute owner except that its ownership rights are terminated if the property is no longer used for church purposes.

life estate
An interest in real property for a person's lifetime; upon that person's death, the interest is transferred to another party.

Life Estate   A **life estate** is an interest in real property that lasts for the life of a specified person, usually the grantee. For example, a conveyance of real property "to Anna for her life" creates a life estate. A life estate may also be measured by the life of a third party, which is called *estate pour autre vie* (e.g., "To Anna for the life of Benjamin"). A life estate may be defeasible (e.g., "To John for his life but only if he continues to occupy this residence").

Upon the death of the named person, the life estate terminates, and the property reverts to the grantor or the grantor's estate or another designated person.

CONCEPT SUMMARY
FREEHOLD ESTATES

Estate	Description
Fee simple absolute	Is the highest form of ownership of real property. Ownership (1) is infinite in duration, (2) has no limitation on inheritability, and (3) does not end upon the occurrence or nonoccurrence of an event.
Fee simple defeasible	Grants the owner all the incidents of a fee simple absolute except that it may be taken away if a specified condition occurs or does not occur.
Life estate	Is an interest in property that lasts for the life of a specified person. A life estate terminates upon the death of the named person and reverts back to the grantor or his or her estate or other designated person.

▶ CONCURRENT OWNERSHIP

co-ownership
A situation in which two or more persons own a piece of real property. Also called *concurrent ownership*.

Two or more persons may own a piece of real property. This is called **co-ownership**, or **concurrent ownership**. The following forms of co-ownership are recognized: *joint tenancy, tenancy in common, tenancy by the entirety, community property, condominiums,* and *cooperatives.*

Joint Tenancy

joint tenancy
A form of co-ownership that includes the right of survivorship.

To create a joint tenancy, words that clearly show a person's intent to create a joint tenancy must be used. Language such as "Marsha Leest and James Leest, as joint tenants" is usually sufficient. The most distinguished feature of a **joint tenancy** is the co-owners' **right of survivorship**. This means that upon the death of one of the **co-owners** (or **joint tenants**), the deceased person's interest in the property automatically passes to the surviving joint tenant or joint tenants. Any contrary provision in the deceased's will is ineffective. Each joint tenant has a right to sell or transfer his or her interest in the property, but such conveyance terminates the joint tenancy. The parties then become tenants in common.

Example ZiYi, Heathcliff, Manuel, and Mohammad own a large commercial building as joint tenants. They are joint tenants with the right to survivorship. Heathcliff executes a will that leaves all of his property to his alma mater university. Heathcliff dies. The surviving joint tenants—ZiYi, Manuel, and Mohammad—and not the university—acquire Heathcliff's ownership interest in the building. ZiYi, Manuel, and Mohammad are now joint tenants with a one-third interest in the building.

Example ZiYi, Heathcliff, Manuel, and Mohammad own a large commercial building as joint tenants. They are joint tenants with the right to survivorship. ZiYi sells her one-quarter interest in the building to Wolfgang. At that time, the joint tenancy is broken, and the four owners—Wolfgang, Heathcliff, Manuel, and Mohammad—become tenants in common, with no right of survivorship. Wolfgang executes a will that leaves all of his property to his alma mater university. Wolfgang dies. Because the owners are not joint tenants, but are instead tenants in common, Wolfgang's quarter interest in the building goes to the university. The university is now a tenant in common with Heathcliff, Manuel, and Mohammad.

Tenancy in Common

In a **tenancy in common**, the interests of a surviving tenant in common pass to the deceased tenant's estate and not to the co-tenants. A tenancy in common may be created by express words (e.g., "Ian Cespedes and Joy Park, as tenants in common"). Unless otherwise agreed, a tenant in common can sell, give, devise, or otherwise transfer his or her interest in the property without the consent of the other co-owners.

Example Lopez, who is one of four tenants in common who own a piece of property, has a will that leaves all his property to his granddaughter. When Lopez dies, the granddaughter receives his interest in the tenancy in common, and the granddaughter becomes a tenant in common with the other three owners.

Tenancy by the Entirety

Tenancy by the entirety is a form of co-ownership of real property that can be used only by married couples. This type of tenancy must be created by express words (e.g., "Harold Jones and Maude Jones, husband and wife, as tenants by the entirety"). A surviving spouse has the right of survivorship. Tenancy by the entirety is distinguished from joint tenancy in that neither spouse may sell or transfer his or her interest in the property without the other spouse's consent. Only about half of the states recognize tenancy by the entirety.

tenancy in common
A form of co-ownership in which the interest of a surviving tenant in common passes to the deceased tenant's estate and not to the co-tenants.

tenancy by the entirety
A form of co-ownership of real property that can be used only by married couples.

community property
A form of ownership in which each spouse owns an equal one-half share of the income of both spouses and the assets acquired during the marriage.

Property is an instrument of humanity. Humanity is not an instrument of property.

Woodrow Wilson
Speech (1912)

CONTEMPORARY ENVIRONMENT
Community Property

Nine states—Arizona, California, Idaho, Louisiana, Nevada, New Mexico, Texas, Washington, and Wisconsin—recognize a form of co-ownership known as **community property**. This method of co-ownership applies only to married couples. It is based on the notion that a husband and wife should share equally in the fruits of the marital partnership. Under these laws, each spouse owns an equal one-half share of the *income* both spouses earned during the marriage and one-half of the *assets acquired by this income during the marriage*, regardless of who earns the income. Property that is acquired through gift or inheritance either before or during marriage remains **separate property**. Interest payments, dividends, and appreciation of separate property received or accrued during marriage is also separate property.

When a spouse dies, the surviving spouse automatically receives one-half the community property. The other half passes to the heirs of the deceased spouse, as directed by will or by state intestate statute if there is no will. During the marriage, neither spouse can sell, transfer, or gift community property without the consent of the other spouse. Upon a divorce, each spouse has a right to one-half the community property.

The location of the real property determines whether community property law applies. If a married couple who lives in a non-community property state purchases real property located in a community property state, community property laws apply to that property.

Example Elma is a successful brain surgeon who makes $500,000 income per year. She meets and marries Brad, a struggling actor who makes $10,000 per year. When Elma gets married, she owns $1 million of real estate and $2 million in securities, which she retains as her separate property. Brad has no separate property when he and Elma are married. After three years, Elma and Brad get a divorce. Assume that Elma has made $500,000 and Brad has made $10,000 each of the three years of their marriage, their living expenses were $110,000 per year, and they have $1,200,000 of earned income saved in a bank account. During the marriage, Elma's real estate has increased in value to $1.5 million, and her securities have increased in value to $3 million. Upon divorce, Elma receives her $1.5 million in real estate and $3 million in securities as her separate property. If they live in a state that recognizes community property, Elma and Brad each receive $600,000 from the community property bank account.

CONCEPT SUMMARY
CONCURRENT OWNERSHIP

Form of Ownership	Right of Survivorship	Tenant may Unilaterally Transfer his or her Interest
Joint tenancy	Yes, deceased tenant's interest automatically passes to co-tenants.	Yes, tenant may transfer his or her interest without the consent of co-tenants. Transfer severs joint tenancy.
Tenancy in common	No, deceased tenant's interest passes to his or her estate.	Yes, tenant may transfer his or her interest without the consent of co-tenants. Transfer does not sever tenancy in common.
Tenancy by the entirety	Yes, deceased tenant's interest automatically passes to his or her spouse.	No, neither spouse may transfer his or her interest without the other spouse's consent.
Community property	Yes, when a spouse dies, the surviving spouse automatically receives one-half of the community property. The other half passes to the heirs of the deceased spouse, as directed by a valid will or by state intestate statute if there is no will.	No, neither spouse may transfer his or her interest without the other spouse's consent.

Condominium

condominium
A common form of ownership in a multiple-dwelling building where the purchaser has title to the individual unit and owns the common areas as a tenant in common with the other condominium owners.

Condominiums are a common form of ownership in multiple-dwelling buildings. Purchasers of a condominium (1) have title to their individual units and (2) own the common areas (e.g., hallways, elevators, parking areas, recreational facilities) as tenants in common with the other owners. Owners may sell or mortgage their units without the permission of the other owners. Owners are assessed monthly fees for the maintenance of common areas. In addition to being used for dwelling units, the condominium form of ownership is often used for office buildings, boat docks, and such.

Cooperative

cooperative
A form of co-ownership of a multiple-dwelling building in which a corporation owns the building and the residents own shares in the corporation.

A **cooperative** is a form of co-ownership of a multiple-dwelling building in which a corporation owns the building, and the residents own shares in the corporation. Each cooperative owner leases a unit in the building from the corporation under a renewable, long-term, proprietary lease. Individual residents may not secure loans for the units they occupy. The corporation can borrow money on a blanket mortgage, and each shareholder is jointly and severally liable on the loan. Usually, cooperative owners may not sell their shares or sublease their units without the approval of the other owners.

▶ FUTURE INTERESTS

future interest
The interest that a grantor retains for him- or herself or a third party.

A person may be given the right to possess property in the *future* rather than in the present. This right is called a **future interest**. The two forms of future interests are *reversion* and *remainder*.

Reversion

reversion
A right of possession that returns to the grantor after the expiration of a limited or contingent estate.

A **reversion** is a right of possession that returns to the grantor after the expiration of a limited or contingent estate. Reversions do not have to be expressly stated because they arise automatically by law.

Example Edgar, an owner of real property, conveys his property "to Harriet Lawson for life." The grantor, Edgar, has retained a reversion in the property. That is, when Harriet dies, the property reverts to Edgar or, if he is not living, to his estate.

Remainder

If the right of possession returns to a *third party* upon the expiration of a limited or contingent estate, it is called a **remainder**. The person who is entitled to the future interest is called a **remainder beneficiary**.

Example Janice, an owner of real property, conveys her property "to Joe Jackson for life, remainder to Meredith Smith." This creates a vested remainder, with Meredith being the remainder beneficiary. The only contingency to Meredith's possessory interest is Joe's death. When Joe dies, Meredith obtains ownership to the property or, if she is not living, it goes to her estate.

remainder
A right of possession that returns to a third party upon the expiration of a limited or contingent estate.

CONCEPT SUMMARY
FUTURE INTERESTS

Future interest	Description
Reversion	Right to possession of real property returns to the grantor after the expiration of a limited or contingent estate.
Remainder	Right to possession of real property goes to a third person upon the expiration of a limited or contingent estate.

▶ TRANSFER OF OWNERSHIP OF REAL PROPERTY

Ownership of real property can be transferred from one person to another. Title to real property can be transferred by sale; tax sale; gift, will, or inheritance; and adverse possession. The different methods of transfer provide different degrees of protection to the transferee.

Sale of Real Estate

A **sale**, or **conveyance**, is the most common method for transferring ownership rights in real property. An owner may offer his or her real estate for sale either by himself or herself or by using a real estate broker. When a buyer has been located and the parties have negotiated the terms of the sale, a **real estate sales contract** is executed by the parties. The Statute of Frauds in most states requires this contract to be in writing.

The seller delivers a deed to the buyer, and the buyer pays the purchase price at the **closing**, or **settlement**. Unless otherwise agreed, it is implied that the seller is conveying fee simple absolute title to the buyer. If either party fails to perform, the other party may sue for breach of contract and obtain either monetary damages or specific performance.

sale
The passing of title from a seller to a buyer for a price. Also called a *conveyance*.

Deeds

Deeds are used to convey real property by sale or gift. The seller or donor is called the **grantor**. The buyer or recipient is called the **grantee**. A deed may be used to transfer a fee simple absolute interest in real property or any lesser estate (e.g., life estate). State laws recognize different types of deeds that provide different degrees of protection to grantees. They are:

- A **warranty deed** (i.e., a deed in which the grantor warrants that he or she has clear title to the real property) contains the greatest number of warranties and provides the most protection to a grantee.
- A **quitclaim deed** (i.e., a deed in which the grantor transfers only whatever interest he or she has in the real property) provides the least amount of protection because only the grantor's interest is conveyed.

deed
A writing that describes a person's ownership interest in a piece of real property.

grantor
The party who transfers an ownership interest in real property.

grantee
The party to whom an interest in real property is transferred.

Recording Statutes

recording statute
A state statute that requires a mortgage or deed of trust to be recorded in the county recorder's office of the county in which the real property is located.

Every state has a **recording statute** which provides that copies of deeds and other documents concerning interests in real property (e.g., mortgages, liens, easements) may be filed in a government office, where they become public records, open to viewing by the public. Recording statutes are intended to prevent fraud and to establish certainty in the ownership and transfer of property. Instruments are usually filed in the **county recorder's office** of the county in which the property is located. A fee is charged to record an instrument.

Persons interested in purchasing property or lending on property should check these records to determine whether the grantor or borrower actually owns the property in question and whether any other parties (e.g., lienholders, mortgages, easement holders) have an interest in the property. The recordation of a deed is not required to pass title from the grantor to the grantee. Recording the deed gives **constructive notice** to the world of the owner's interest in the property.

Quiet Title Action

quiet title action
An action brought by a party, seeking an order of the court declaring who has title to disputed property. The court "quiets title" by its decision.

A party who is concerned about his or her ownership rights in a parcel of real property can bring a **quiet title action**, which is a lawsuit to have a court determine the extent of those rights. Public notice of the hearing must be given so that anyone claiming an interest in the property can appear and be heard. After the hearing, the judge declares who has title to the property; that is, the court "quiets title" by its decision.

Marketable Title

marketable title
Title to real property that is free from any encumbrances or other defects that are not disclosed but would affect the value of the property. Also called *good title*.

A grantor has the obligation to transfer **marketable title**, or **good title**, to the grantee. Marketable title means that the title is free from any encumbrances, defects of title, or other defects that are not disclosed but would affect the value of the property. The three most common ways of assuring marketable title are as follows:

1. **Attorney's opinion.** An attorney examines an **abstract of title** (i.e., a chronological history of the chain of title and encumbrances affecting the property) and renders an **opinion** concerning the status of the title. The attorney can be sued for any losses caused by his or her negligence in rendering the opinion.
2. **Torrens system.** The **Torrens system** is a method of determining title to real property in a judicial proceeding at which everyone claiming an interest in the property can appear and be heard. After the evidence is heard, the court issues a **certificate of title** to the person who is determined to be the rightful owner.
3. **Title insurance.** The best way for a grantee to be sure that he or she has obtained marketable title is to purchase **title insurance** from an insurance company. The title insurer must reimburse the insured for any losses caused by undiscovered defects in title. Each time a property is transferred or refinanced, a new title insurance policy must be obtained.

Tax Sale

tax sale
A method of transferring property ownership that involves a lien on property for unpaid property taxes. If the lien remains unpaid after a certain amount of time, a tax sale is held to satisfy the lien.

If an owner of real property fails to pay property taxes, the government can obtain a lien on the property for the amount of the taxes. If the taxes remain unpaid for a statutory period of time, the government can sell the property at a **tax sale** to satisfy the lien. Any excess proceeds are paid to the taxpayer. The buyer receives title to the property. Many states provide a **period of redemption** after a tax sale during which the taxpayer can redeem the property by paying the unpaid taxes and penalties. In these states, the buyer at a tax sale does not receive title to the property until the period of redemption has passed.

Gift, Will, or Inheritance

Ownership of real property can be transferred by **gift**. The gift is made when the deed to the property is delivered by the donor to the donee or to a third party to hold for the donee. No consideration is necessary.

The right of property enables an industrious man to reap where he has sown.

Anonymous

Example A grandfather wants to give his farm to his granddaughter. To do so, he only has to execute a deed and give the deed to her or to someone to hold for her, such as her parents.

Real property can also be transferred by **will**.

Example A person may leave a piece of real estate to his best friend by will when he dies. This transfer does not require the transfer of a deed during the testator's lifetime. A deed will be issued to the beneficiary when the will is probated. If a person dies without a valid will, his or her property is distributed to the heirs pursuant to the applicable state interstate statute.

Adverse Possession

In most states, a person who wrongfully possesses someone else's real property obtains title to that property if certain statutory requirements are met. This is called **adverse possession**. Property owned by federal and state governments is not subject to adverse possession.

Under the doctrine of adverse possession, the transfer of the property is involuntary and does not require the delivery of a deed. To obtain title under adverse possession, the wrongful possession must be:

- **For a statutorily prescribed period of time.** In most states, this period is between 10 and 20 years.
- **Open, visible, and notorious.** The adverse possessor must occupy the property so as to put the owner on notice of the possession.
- **Actual and exclusive.** The adverse possessor must physically occupy the premises. The planting of crops, grazing of animals, or building of a structure on the land constitutes physical occupancy.
- **Continuous and peaceful.** The occupancy must be continuous and uninterrupted for the required statutory period. Any break in normal occupancy terminates the adverse possession. This means that the adverse possessor may leave the property to go to work, to the store, on a vacation, and such. The adverse possessor cannot take the property by force from an owner.
- **Hostile and adverse.** The possessor must occupy the property without the express or implied permission of the owner. Thus, a lessee cannot claim title to property under adverse possession.

If the elements of adverse possession are met, the adverse possessor acquires clear title to the land. However, title is acquired only as to the property actually possessed and occupied during the statutory period, and not the entire tract.

Example An adverse possessor who occupies 1 acre of a 200,000-acre ranch for the statutory period of time acquires title only to the 1 acre.

In the following case, the court had to decide whether the elements for adverse possession had been met.

adverse possession
A situation in which a person who wrongfully possesses someone else's real property obtains title to that property if certain statutory requirements are met.

The disseisor must unfurl his flag on the land, and keep it flying, so that the owner may see, if he will, that an enemy has invaded his domains, and planted the standard of conquest.

Judge Ellington
Johnson v. Asfaw and Tanus
(2005)

CASE 48.1 Adverse Possession

Witt v. Miller
845 S.W.2d 665, Web 1993 Mo.App. Lexis 20 (1993)
Court of Appeals of Missouri

"Hostility does not imply animosity."
—Judge Gaertner

Facts
Edward and Mary Shaughnessey purchased a 16-acre tract in St. Louis County, Missouri. Subsequently, they subdivided 12 acres into 18 lots offered for sale and retained possession of the remaining 4-acre tract. Thirteen years later, Charles and Elaine Witt purchased lot 12, which is adjacent to the 4-acre tract. The Witts constructed and moved into a house on their lot. The next year, they cleared an area of land that ran the length of their property and extended 40 feet onto the

(case continues)

4-acre tract. The Witts constructed a pool and a deck, planted a garden, made a playground for their children, set up a dog run, and built a fence along the edge of the property line, which included the now-disputed property. Neither the Witts nor the Shaughnesseys realized that the Witts had encroached on the Shaughnesseys' property.

Twenty years later, the Shaughnesseys sold the 4-acre tract to Thomas and Rosanne Miller. When a survey showed the Witts' encroachment, the Millers demanded that the Witts remove the pool and cease using the property. When the Witts refused to do so, the Millers sued to quiet title. The Witts defended, arguing that they had obtained title to the disputed property through adverse possession. The trial court held that there was no adverse possession and ruled in favor of the Millers. The Witts appealed.

Issue

Have the elements for adverse possession been met?

Language of the Court

We address the element of "hostile possession." Hostility does not imply animosity. There is no substantial evidence to support the finding that plaintiffs' possession was not hostile. Plaintiffs testified that they intended to possess the disputed property as their own because they believed it was part of lot 12. That intent manifests itself in plaintiffs' actions which include clearing the area, maintaining the area, planting grass and a garden,

erecting a fence, installing playground equipment and a dog run, and building an above ground pool with a deck.

The evidence established plaintiffs' claim to title of the disputed property under adverse possession. The trial court's decision was not supported by substantial evidence and erroneously declared the law.

Decision

The court of appeals held that the Witts had proven the necessary elements for adverse possession under state law. The Witts' occupation of the land was open and notorious, actual and exclusive, hostile and adverse, and continuous and peaceful, and it had occurred for over the statutory period of 10 years. The court of appeals reversed the decision of the trial court and issued an order quieting title to the disputed property in the Witts' favor.

Case Questions

Critical Legal Thinking What does the doctrine of adverse possession provide? What elements need to be proven?

Business Ethics Did the Witts act ethically in claiming title to someone else's land? Should they be allowed to benefit from their own mistake?

Contemporary Business What should owners of property do to protect themselves from adverse possession claims? Explain.

▶ NONPOSSESSORY INTERESTS

nonpossessory interest
A situation in which a person holds an interest in another person's property without actually owning any part of the property.

A person can own a **nonpossessory interest** in another's real estate. Three nonpossessory interests—*easement*, *license*, and *profit*—are discussed in the following paragraphs.

Easement

easement
A given or required right to make limited use of someone else's land without owning or leasing it.

An **easement** is an interest in land that gives the holder the right to make limited use of another's property without taking anything from it. Typical easements are common driveways, party walls, and rights-of-way. Easements can be expressly created by *grant* (where an owner gives another party an easement across his or her property) or *reservation* (where an owner sells land that he or she owns but reserves an easement on the land). Easement can also be implied by (1) *implication*, where an owner subdivides a piece of property with a well, path, road, or other beneficial appurtenant that serves the entire parcel, or by (2) *necessity*—for example, where "landlocked" property has an implied easement across surrounding property to enter and exit the landlocked property. Easements can also be created by *prescription*—that is, by adverse possession.

There are two types of easements: *easements appurtenant* and *easements in gross*. These are described in the following paragraphs.

easement appurtenant
A situation created when the owner of one piece of land is given an easement over an adjacent piece of land.

Easements Appurtenant   An **easement appurtenant** is created when the owner of one piece of land is given an easement over an adjacent piece of land. The land over which the easement is granted is called the **servient estate**. The land that benefits from the easement is called the **dominant estate**. *Adjacent land* is defined as two estates that are in proximity to each other but that do not necessarily abut each other. An appurtenant easement runs with the land.

Example If an owner sells the dominant estate, the new owner acquires the benefit of the easement. If an owner sells the servient estate, the buyer purchases the property subject to the easement.

Easements in Gross An **easement in gross** authorizes a person who does not own adjacent land the right to use another person's land. An easement in gross is a personal right because it does not depend on the easement holder owning adjacent land. Thus, there is no dominant estate.

easement in gross
An easement that authorizes a person who does not own adjacent land to use another's land.

Examples Easements in gross include those granted to run power, telephone, and cable television lines across an owner's property. Commercial easements in gross run with the land.

The easement holder owes a duty to maintain and repair the easement. The owner of the estate can use the property as long as doing so does not interfere with the easement.

Example If a piece of property is subject to an easement for an underground pipeline, the owner of the property could graze cattle or plant crops on the land above the easement, subject to the easement holder's right to repair the pipeline.

In the following case, the court had to decide whether an implied easement had been created.

CASE 48.2 Implied Easement

Walker v. Ayres
Web 1993 Del. Lexis 105 (1993)
Supreme Court of Delaware

"An implied easement was created by the severance which landlocked Bluff Point."

—Judge Moore

Facts
Elizabeth Star Ayres and Clara Louise Quillen owned in fee simple absolute a tract of land in Sussex County known as "Bluff Point." The tract was surrounded on three sides by Rehoboth Bay and was landlocked on the fourth side by land owned by Irvin C. Walker. At one time, the two tracts were held by a common owner. In 1878, Bluff Point was sold in fee simple absolute apart from the other holdings, thereby landlocking the parcel. A narrow dirt road, which traversed Walker's land, connected Bluff Point to a public road and was its only means of access to Bluff Point. Ayres and Quillen sought an easement to use this road, and Walker objected. This lawsuit ensued. The trial court granted an easement to Ayres and Quillen. Walker appealed.

Issue
Should Ayres and Quillen's estate be granted an easement against Walker's estate?

Language of the Court
> Based upon our review of the record, we conclude that the factual findings of the trial court are clearly sustainable.

> There is ample evidence in the record to support the finding that the two tracts originated from the unified holdings of one owner, and that an implied easement was created by the severance which landlocked Bluff Point. The record also sufficiently supports the finding that navigable access to Bluff Point was not feasible.

Decision
The supreme court of Delaware held that an implied easement had been created. The supreme court affirmed the trial court's judgment, granting Ayres and Quillen an easement to use the road that traversed Walker's property.

Case Questions

Critical Legal Thinking What is an easement? Should easements be recognized by the law? Why or why not?

Business Ethics Did Walker act ethically in denying the easement? Did Ayres and Quillen act ethically in seeking to use Walker's property?

Contemporary Business Do easements across a person's property increase or decrease the value of their property? Does an easement increase or decrease the value of the easement holder's property?

License

license
A document that grants a person the right to enter upon another's property for a specified and usually short period of time.

A **license** grants a person the right to enter upon another's property for a specified and usually short period of time. The person granting the license is called the **licensor**; the person receiving the license is called the **licensee**.

Example A ticket to a movie theater or sporting event that grants the holder the right to enter the premises for the performance is a common license. A license does not transfer any interest in the property. A license is a personal privilege that may be revoked by the licensor at any time.

Profit

profit
A document that grants a person the right to remove something from another's real property. Also known as *profit-à-prendre*.

A *profit-à-prendre* (or **profit**) gives the holder the right to remove something from another's real property.

Examples Examples of profit are rights to remove gravel, minerals, grain, or timber from another person's property.

CONCEPT SUMMARY

NONPOSSESSORY INTERESTS

Nonpossessory Interest	Description
Easement appurtenant	Is an easement over a servient estate that benefits a dominant estate. The easement runs with the land.
Easement in gross	Is an easement that grants a person a right to use another's land. It is a personal right that does not run with the land.
License	Grants a person the right to enter upon another's real property for a specified event or time (e.g., for a concert).
Profit	Grants the holder the right to remove something from another's real property (e.g., timber, grain).

▶ ZONING

zoning ordinances
Local laws that are adopted by municipalities and local governments to regulate land use within their boundaries.

Most counties and municipalities have enacted **zoning ordinances** to regulate land use. Zoning ordinances generally (1) establish use districts within the municipality (i.e., areas are generally designated residential, commercial, or industrial); (2) restrict the height, size, and location of buildings on a building site; and (3) establish aesthetic requirements or limitations for the exterior of buildings.

A **zoning commission** usually formulates zoning ordinances, conducts public hearings, and makes recommendations to the city council, which must vote to enact an ordinance. Once a zoning ordinance is enacted, the zoning ordinance commission enforces it. If landowners believe that a zoning ordinance is illegal or that it has been unlawfully applied to them or their property, they may institute a court proceeding, seeking judicial review of the ordinance or its application.

variance
An exception that permits a type of building or use in an area that would not otherwise be allowed by a zoning ordinance.

An owner who wants to use his or her property for a use different from that permitted under a current zoning ordinance may seek relief from the ordinance by obtaining a **variance**. To obtain a variance, the landowner must prove that the ordinance causes an undue hardship by preventing him or her from making a reasonable return on the land as zoned. Variances are usually difficult to obtain.

nonconforming uses
Uses and buildings that already exist in a zoned area that are permitted to continue even though they do not fit within new zoning ordinances.

Zoning laws act prospectively; that is, uses and buildings that already exist in the zoned area are permitted to continue even though they do not fit within new zoning ordinances. Such uses are called **nonconforming uses**. For example, if a new zoning ordinance is enacted, making an area a residential zone, an existing funeral parlor is a nonconforming use.

TEST REVIEW TERMS AND CONCEPTS

Abstract of title
Adverse possession
Air rights
Air space parcel
Attorney's opinion
Buildings
Certificate of title
Closing (settlement)
Community property
Condominium
Constructive notice
Cooperative
Co-owners (joint tenants)
Co-ownership (concurrent ownership)
County recorder's office
Deed
Dominant estate

Easement
Easement appurtenant
Easement in gross
Estate in land (estate)
Estate pour autre vie
Fee simple absolute (fee simple)
Fee simple defeasible (qualified fee)
Fixtures
Freehold estate
Future interest
Gift
Grantee
Grantor
Joint tenancy
Land
License

Licensee
Licensor
Life estate
Marketable title (good title)
Nonconforming use
Nonpossessory interest
Period of redemption
Plant life and vegetation
Profit-à-prendre (profit)
Quiet title action
Quitclaim deed
Real estate sales contract
Real property
Recording statute
Remainder
Remainder beneficiary
Reversion
Right of survivorship

Sale (conveyance)
Separate property
Servient estate
Subsurface rights (mineral rights)
Surface rights
Tax sale
Tenancy by the entirety
Tenancy in common
Title insurance
Torrens system
Variance
Warranty deed
Will
Zoning commission
Zoning ordinance

CASE PROBLEMS

48.1 Subsurface Rights   In 1883, Isaac McIlwee owned 100 acres of land in Valley Township, Guernsey Country, Ohio. In that year, he sold the property to Akron & Cambridge Coal Company (Akron & Cambridge) in fee simple but reserved in fee simple "the surface of all said lands" to himself. Over the years, the interests in the land were transferred to many different parties. One hundred years after McIlwee's transfer of an interest in the property to Akron & Cambridge, the Mid-Ohio Coal Company owned the rights originally transferred to Akron & Cambridge, and Peter and Irene Minnich owned the rights reserved by Isaac McIlwee in 1883. The Minniches claimed that they possessed subsurface rights to the property except for coal rights. Who wins? *Minnich v. Guernsey Savings and Loan Company*, 36 Ohio App.3d 54, 521 N.E.2d 489, **Web** 1987 OhioApp. Lexis 10497 (Court of Appeals of Ohio)

48.2 Life Estate and Remainder   Baudilio Bowles died testate. His will devised to his sister, Julianita B. Vigil, "one-half of any income, rents, or profits from any real property located in Bull Creek or Colonias, New Mexico." The will contained another clause that left to his children "my interest in any real property owned by me at the time of my death, located in Bull Creek and/or Colonias, San Miguel County." The property referred to in both devises was the same property. Julianita died before the will was probated. Her heirs claimed a one-half ownership interest in the real property. Bowles's children asserted that they owned all his property. Who wins? *In the Matter of the Estate of Bowles*, 107 N.M.

739, 764 P.2d 510, **Web** 1988 N.M.App. Lexis 93 (Court of Appeals of New Mexico)

48.3 Reversion   W.E. and Jennie Hutton conveyed land they owned to the Trustees of Schools of District Number One of the Town of Allison, Illinois (School District), by warranty deed "to be used for school purpose only; otherwise to revert to Grantor." The School District built a school on the site, commonly known as Hutton School. The Huttons conveyed the adjoining farmland and their reversionary interest in the school site to the Jacqmains, who in turn conveyed their interest to Herbert and Betty Mahrenholz. The 1.5-acre site sits in the middle of Mahrenhoz's farmland. Over 30 years after School District built the school, School District discontinued holding regular classes at Hutton School. Instead, it used the school building to warehouse and store miscellaneous school equipment, supplies, unused desks, and the like. Mahrenholz filed suit to quiet title to the school property to them. Who wins? *Mahrenholz v. County Board of School Trustees of Lawrence County*, 188 Ill.App.3d 260, 544 N.E.2d 128, **Web** 1989 Ill.App. Lexis 1445 (Appellate Court of Illinois)

48.4 Joint Tenancy   Verna M. Chappell owned a piece of real property. On June 16, 1965, Chappell transferred the property to herself and her niece, Bertha M. Stewart, as joint tenants. When Chappell died in 1981, Chappell's gross estate was set at $28,321, which included the value of the house. Claims, debts, and charges against the estate totaled $19,451, which included a $14,040 claim by Lorna M.

Rembe for services provided as conservator. The probate assets available to pay the claims and debts came to only $1,571 if the real property went to Stewart as the joint tenant. Rembe sued, alleging that the value of the real property should be used to pay off Chappell's debts and claims. Who wins? *Rembe v. Stewart*, 387 N.W.2d 313, **Web** 1986 Iowa Sup. Lexis 1177 (Supreme Court of Iowa)

48.5 Tenancy by the Entirety Charles Jetter Eichman and his wife, Cora Paton Eichman, were married on August 12, 1965. In 1968, they purchased a house in Tallahassee, Florida, taking title in their joint names as husband and wife, thus creating a tenancy by the entirety. In 1971, they separated, and Cora moved to Vancouver, Canada. Charles continued to live in the marital home in Florida. In January 1975, Cora filed a petition for divorce. On March 31, 1975, Charles struck Cora on the head with a pipe, causing injuries that rendered her incapable of managing herself or her affairs and bringing to an end the divorce proceeding. A guardian was appointed for her. Charles was convicted of attempted murder and was sentenced to prison for 10 years. Cora's guardian filed an action, seeking to partition the marital property located in Florida. Charles answered, alleging that an estate by the entirety is not subject to partition as long as the parties remain married. Who wins? *Eichman v. Paton*, 393 So.2d 655, **Web** 1981 Fla.App. Lexis 19454 (District Court of Appeal of Florida)

48.6 Community Property Daniel T. Yu and his wife, Bernice, owned a house and two lots as community property. Yu entered into an agreement with Arch, Ltd. (Arch), whereby he agreed to exchange these properties for two office buildings owned by Arch. Yu signed the agreement, but his wife did not. At the date set for closing, Arch performed its obligations under the agreement, executed all documents, and was prepared to transfer title to its properties to Yu. Yu, however, refused to perform his obligations under the agreement. Evidence showed that the office buildings had decreased in value from $800,000 to $700,000 from the date of the agreement to the date set for closing. Arch sued Yu to recover damages for breach of contract. Who wins? *Arch, Ltd. v. Yu*, 108 N.M. 67, 766 P.2d 911, **Web** 1988 N.M. Lexis 330 (Supreme Court of New Mexico)

48.7 Easement in Gross John L. Yutterman died, leaving one piece of property, located in Fort Smith, Arkansas, to his two sons and two daughters. Each child received approximately one-fourth of the property in fee simple. A 40-foot driveway divided the property. Concerning the driveway, Yutterman's will provided as follows: "Further, a specific condition of this will and of these devises is that the forty (40) foot driveway from Free Ferry Road, three hundred (300) feet Northward, shall be kept open for the common use of the devisees in this will." Subsequently, one of the daughters wanted to sell her property to a third party. If the third party purchases the property, will that party have an easement to use the driveway? *Merriman v. Yutterman*, 291 Ark. 207, 723 S.W.2d 823, **Web** 1987 Ark. Lexis 1934 (Supreme Court of Arkansas)

48.8 Adverse Possession Joseph and Helen Naab purchased a tract of land in a subdivision of Williamstown, West Virginia. At the time of purchase, there were both a house and a small concrete garage on the property. Evidence showed that the garage had been erected sometime prior to 20 years earlier by one of the Naabs' predecessors in title. Two years after the Naabs bought their property, Roger and Cynthia Nolan purchased a lot contiguous to that owned by the Naabs. The following year, the Nolans had their property surveyed. The survey indicated that one corner of the Naabs' garage encroached 1.22 feet onto the Nolans' property and the other corner encroached 0.91 feet over the property line. The Nolans requested that the Naabs remove the garage from their property. When the Naabs refused, a lawsuit ensued. Who wins? *Naab v. Nolan*, 174 W.Va. 390, 327 S.E.2d 151, **Web** 1985 W.Va. Lexis 476 (Supreme Court of Appeals of West Virginia)

48.9 Zoning The city of Ladue is one of the wealthy suburban residential areas of metropolitan St. Louis. The homes in the city are considerably more expensive than those in surrounding areas and consist of homes of traditional design, such as colonial, French provincial, and English. The city set up an architectural board to approve plans for buildings that:

> *Conform to certain minimum architectural standards of appearance and conformity with surrounding structures, and that unsightly, grotesque, and unsuitable structures, detrimental to the stability of value and the welfare of surrounding property, structures, and residents, and to the general welfare and happiness of the community, be avoided.*

The owner of a lot in the city submitted a plan to build a house of ultramodern design. It was pyramid shaped, with a flat top and triangular-shaped windows and doors. Although the house plans met other city zoning ordinances and building codes, the architectural board rejected the owner's petition for a building permit, based on aesthetic reasons. The owner sued the city. Who wins? *State of Missouri v. Berkeley*, 458 S.W.2d 305, **Web** 1970 Mo. Lexis 902 (Supreme Court of Missouri)

BUSINESS ETHICS CASES

48.10 Business Ethics   Victor and Phyllis Garber acquired a piece of real property by warranty deed. The deed was recorded. The property consisted of 80 acres enclosed by a fence that had been in place for over 50 years. The enclosed area was used to graze cattle and produce hay. Ten years after the Garbers acquired their property, William and Herbert Doenz acquired a piece of real property adjacent to the Garbers' and employed a surveyor to locate their land's boundaries. As a result of the survey, it was discovered that the shared fence was 20 to 30 feet inside the deed line on the Doenz property. The amount of property between the old fence and the deed line was 3.01 acres. The Doenzes removed the old fence and constructed a new fence along the deed line. The Garbers brought suit to quiet title. Did the Doenzes act ethically in removing the fence? Did the Garbers act ethically in claiming title to property that originally belonged with the adjacent property? Have the Garbers acquired title to the property between the fence and the deed through adverse possession? *Doenz v. Garber*, 665 P.2d 932, **Web** 1983 Wyo. Lexis 339 (Supreme Court of Wyoming)

48.11 Business Ethics   The town of Hempstead, New Hampshire, enacted a zoning ordinance "in order to retain the beauty and countrified atmosphere of the town, and to promote health, safety, morals, order, convenience, peace, prosperity, and general welfare of its inhabitants." To preserve abutting property owners' views and light, the ordinance limits the homes in the town to one-and-one-half stories. In violation of the ordinance, John M. Alexander built a shell of a second story and a new roof on his house. After the town ordered him to halt construction and denied him permission to occupy the second floor, he applied for a variance. Should the variance be granted? Did John M. Alexander act ethically in this case? *Alexander v. Town of Hempstead*, 129 N.H. 278, 525 A.2d 276, **Web** 1987 N.H. Lexis 171 (Supreme Court of New Hampshire)

49 | LANDLORD–TENANT LAW AND LAND USE REGULATION

▲ **New York City** *Many of the businesses and professionals in New York City lease office space, retail space, warehouse space, and other space from which to conduct their businesses.*

CHAPTER OBJECTIVES

After studying this chapter, you should be able to:

1. Explain how a landlord–tenant relationship is created.
2. Identify and describe the various types of tenancy.
3. List and describe the landlord's and tenant's duties under a lease.
4. List and describe the antidiscrimination laws that apply to real estate.
5. Describe the government's power of eminent domain.

CHAPTER CONTENTS

The right of property has not made poverty, but it has powerfully contributed to make wealth.

—J. R. McCulloch
Principles of Political Economy (1825)

► INTRODUCTION TO LANDLORD–TENANT LAW AND LAND USE REGULATION

Individuals and families rent houses and apartments, professionals and businesses lease office space, small businesses rent stores, and businesses lease commercial and manufacturing facilities. In these situations, a *landlord–tenant relationship* is created. The party who owns or controls the leased space is called the *lessor*, and the party who is renting the space is called the *lessee*. The contract between them is called a *lease*. The parties to a landlord–tenant relationship have certain legal rights and duties that are governed by a mixture of real estate and contract law.

The ownership and possession of real estate in the United States is commonly a private affair. However, the ownership and leasing of real property is not free from government regulation. Pursuant to constitutional authority, federal, state, and local governments have enacted a myriad of laws that regulate the ownership, possession, lease, and use of real property. These laws include antidiscrimination laws in leasing and selling real property. The government may also take private property for public use under its power of eminent domain, assuming that certain requirements are met and just compensation is paid to the owner.

This chapter covers the law concerning landlord–tenant relationships and the government regulation of real estate.

► LANDLORD–TENANT RELATIONSHIP

A **landlord–tenant relationship** is created when the owner of a freehold estate (i.e., an estate in fee or a life estate) transfers a right to exclusively and temporarily possess the owner's property. The tenant receives a *nonfreehold estate* in the property; that is, the tenant has a right to possession of the property but not title to the property.

The tenant's interest in the property is called a **leasehold estate**, or **leasehold**. The owner who transfers the leasehold estate is called the **landlord**, or **lessor**. The party to whom the leasehold estate is transferred is called the **tenant**, or **lessee**. A landlord–tenant relationship is illustrated in Exhibit 49.1.

leasehold
A tenant's interest in property.

landlord
An owner who transfers a leasehold.

tenant
The party to whom a leasehold is transferred.

Lease

A rental agreement between a landlord and a tenant is called a **lease**. Leases can generally be either oral or written, but most Statutes of Frauds require that leases for periods of time longer than one year be in writing. A lease must contain the essential terms of the parties' agreement. A lease is often a form contract that is prepared by the landlord and presented to the tenant. This practice is particularly true of residential leases. Other leases are negotiated between the parties. For example, Bank of America's lease of a branch office would be negotiated with the owner of the building.

There are four types of *tenancies*: *tenancy for years*, *periodic tenancy*, *tenancy at will*, and *tenancy at sufferance*. They are described in the following paragraphs.

lease
A transfer of the right to the possession and use of real property for a set term in return for certain consideration; the rental agreement between a landlord and a tenant.

Tenancy for Years

A **tenancy for years** is created when a landlord and a tenant agree on a specific duration for a lease. Any lease for a stated period—no matter how long or short—is called a tenancy for

tenancy for years
A tenancy created when a landlord and a tenant agree on a specific duration for a lease.

▶ **Exhibit 49.1**
LANDLORD–TENANT
RELATIONSHIP

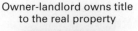

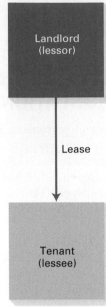

Owner-landlord owns title
to the real property

Landlord
(lessor)

Lease

Tenant
(lessee)

Tenant acquires a
nonfreehold estate in the
real property that gives
the tenant a right to
possession of the property

years. A tenancy for years terminates automatically, without notice, upon the expiration of the stated term.

Examples A business leases an office in a high-rise office building on a 10-year lease. This lease terminates after 10 years. A family leases a cabin for the month of July in the summer. This lease expires on July 31.

Periodic Tenancy

periodic tenancy
A tenancy created when a lease specifies intervals at which payments are due but does not specify how long the lease is for.

A **periodic tenancy** is created when a lease specifies intervals at which payments are due but does not specify the duration of the lease. A lease that states, "Rent is due on the first day of the month" establishes a periodic tenancy. Many such leases are created by implication. A periodic tenancy may be terminated by either party at the end of any payment interval, but adequate notice of the termination must be given. Under common law, the notice period equaled the length of the payment period. That is, a month-to-month tenancy required a one-month notice of termination.

Tenancy at Will

tenancy at will
A tenancy created by a lease that may be terminated at any time by either party.

A lease that may be terminated at any time by either party creates a **tenancy at will**. A tenancy at will may be created expressly (e.g., "to tenant as long as landlord wishes") but is more likely to be created by implication. Most states have enacted statutes requiring minimum advance notice for the termination of a tenancy at will. The death of either party terminates a tenancy at will.

Tenancy at Sufferance

tenancy at sufferance
A tenancy created when a tenant retains possession of property after the expiration of another tenancy or a life estate without the owner's consent.

A **tenancy at sufferance** is created when a tenant retains possession of property after the expiration of another tenancy or a life estate without the owner's consent. That is, the owner suffers the **wrongful possession** of his or her property by the holdover tenant. This is not a true tenancy but merely the possession of property without right. Technically, a tenant at sufferance is a trespasser. A tenant at sufferance is liable for the payment of rent during the period of sufferance. Most states require an owner to go through certain legal proceedings, called *eviction proceedings* or *unlawful detainer actions*, to evict a holdover tenant. A few states allow owners to use self-help to evict a holdover tenant, as long as force is not used.

CONCEPT SUMMARY
TYPES OF TENANCIES

Types of Tenancy	Description
Tenancy for years	Continues for the duration of the lease and terminates automatically upon expiration of the stated term without requiring notice. It does not terminate upon the death of either party.
Periodic tenancy	Continues from payment interval to payment interval. It may be terminated by either party with adequate notice. It does not terminate upon the death of either party.
Tenancy at will	Continues at the will of the parties and may be terminated by either party at any time with adequate notice. It terminates upon the death of either party.
Tenancy at sufferance	Arises when a tenant wrongfully occupies real property after the expiration of another tenancy or life estate. It continues until the owner either evicts the tenant or holds him or her over for another term. It terminates upon the death of the tenant.

▶ LANDLORD'S DUTIES TO A TENANT

In a landlord–tenant relationship, the law imposes certain legal duties on the landlord. That is, the tenant has lawful rights that can be enforced against the landlord. The duties that a landlord owes to a tenant are discussed in the following paragraphs.

Landlord's Duty to Deliver Possession

A lease grants the tenant **exclusive possession** of the leased premises until (1) the term of the lease expires or (2) the tenant defaults on the obligations under the lease. The landlord is obligated to deliver possession of the leased premises to the tenant on the date the lease term begins. A landlord may not enter leased premises unless the right is specifically reserved in the lease.

Property has its duties as well as its rights.

Benjamin Disraeli
Sybil, Book II, Chapter XI (1845)

Landlord's Duty Not to Interfere with a Tenant's Right to Quiet Enjoyment

The law implies a **covenant of quiet enjoyment** in all leases. Under this covenant, the landlord may not interfere with the tenant's quiet and peaceful possession, use, and enjoyment of the leased premises. The covenant is breached if the landlord, or anyone acting with the landlord's consent, interferes with the tenant's use and enjoyment of the property. This interference is called **wrongful eviction**, or **unlawful eviction**.

covenant of quiet enjoyment
A covenant that says a landlord may not interfere with the tenant's quiet and peaceful possession, use, and enjoyment of the leased premises.

Examples If a landlord evicts a tenant by physically preventing him or her from possessing or using the leased premises, this is wrongful eviction. If a landlord constructively evicts a tenant by causing the leased premises to become unfit for their intended use (e.g., by failing to provide electricity), this is also wrongful eviction.

If the landlord refuses to cure a defect after a reasonable time, a tenant who has been *constructively evicted* may (1) sue for damages and possession of the premises or (2) treat the lease as terminated, vacate the premises, and cease paying rent. The landlord is not responsible for wrongful acts of third persons that were done without his or her authorization.

Landlord's Duty to Maintain the Leased Premises

At common law, the doctrine of *caveat lessee*—"lessee beware"—applied to leases. The landlord made no warranties about the quality of leased property and had no duty to repair it. The tenant took the property "as is." Modern real estate law, however, imposes certain statutory and judicially implied duties on landlords to repair and maintain leased premises.

building codes
State and local statutes that impose specific standards on property owners to maintain and repair leased premises. Also called *housing codes*.

States and local municipalities have enacted statutes called **building codes**, or **housing codes**. These statutes impose specific standards on property owners to maintain and repair leased premises. They often provide certain minimum standards regarding heat, water, light, and other services. Depending on the statute, violators may be subject to fines by the government, loss of their claim for rent, and imprisonment for serious violations.

In the following case, the court held that a landlord was liable for negligence to a tenant.

CASE 49.1 Negligence

New Haverford Partnership v. Stroot

772 A.2d 792, Web 2001 Del. Lexis 2278 (2001)
Supreme Court of Delaware

"The presumption in Delaware is that a jury verdict is 'correct and just.'"

—Justice Berger

Facts

Elizabeth Stroot was a tenant at Haverford Place apartments, which was owned by New Haverford Partnership. Stroot was 33-year-old graduate student. After moving into her apartment, Stroot noticed mold around the windows and in the bathroom. Although she attempted to remove the mold with bleach, the mold kept returning. There were also water leaks in the bathroom ceiling and in the kitchen and bathroom.

Stroot moved to another apartment at Haverford Place. Here, the bathroom ceiling leaked. Within a few months, the leaks caused holes in the drywall, and the edges of the holes were covered with a black substance. When Stroot showered, black water ran out of the holes. Stroot complained to the management, but nothing was done. One evening, Stroot's bathroom ceiling collapsed, and water flooded her floor. The exposed ceiling was covered with black, green, orange, and white mold. The room had a strong, nauseating odor. Stroot slept in the apartment that night. The next morning she could not breathe. Stroot called an ambulance and was taken to the hospital. When she was released from the hospital, Stroot decided she could no longer live at Haverford Place.

Subsequently, the symptoms of Stroot's allergies and asthma, which she had suffered from since childhood, increased significantly. She was forced to go to the emergency room of the hospital seven times. She spent time as an inpatient at the hospital. Stroot incurred over $28,000 in medical expenses. Stroot sued New Haverford Partnership to recover damages for negligence for causing her medical problems because it permitted the water leaks and mold problem to persist in her apartments.

Stroot offered testimony from several expert witnesses. Michael Lynn, an architect, examined the property and discovered excessive mold. Dr. Yang, a mycologist and microbiologist, testified that mold levels at Haverford Place posed a serious health risk to Stroot. Dr. Johanning, an environmental and occupational medical expert, testified that the toxic mold significantly and permanently increased the severity of Stroot's asthma. Dr. Rose, an expert in pulmonary medicine, testified that Stroot developed osteopenia. And Dr. Gordon, a neuropsychologist, testified that Stroot suffered from permanent cognitive defects caused by exposure to the mold.

The jury found the landlord liable for negligence and awarded Stroot $1 million, reduced by 22 percent based on Stroot's own negligence. The landlord appealed the finding of negligence and also made a motion for remittitur, asking the court that if it was held liable for negligence to reduce the amount of the award from $1 million to $250,000.

Issue

Was New Haverford Partnership liable for negligence, and if so, was the amount of the award of damages to Stroot appropriate?

Language of the Court

To state a claim for negligence one must allege that defendant owed plaintiff a duty of care; defendant breached that duty; and defendant's breach was the proximate cause of plaintiff's injury. In sum, we find no error in the trial court's decision allowing plaintiffs to pursue an ordinary, or common law, negligence claim.

Landlord argues that the amount awarded to Stroot was so excessive that it shocks the conscience. At best, according to Landlord, these injuries could support an award of $250,000, not the $1,000,000 set by the jury. The presumption in Delaware is that a jury verdict is *"correct and just." A Motion for Remittitur may be granted only with great reluctance. The jury obviously accepted Dr. Johanning's and Dr. Rose's medical testimony in this case that despite other triggers which could cause her to have an asthma attack, Stroot's asthma was nevertheless significantly exacerbated or worsened by her exposure to microbial contamination at the apartment complex, and that her need for medication increased significantly after she moved to Haverford Place. The Court is satisfied that Stroot showed to a reasonable degree of medical probability that her asthma symptoms decreased, but did not return to her pre-exposure baseline, after she left the apartment complex. Further, the jury may have also chosen to accept Dr. Wayne Gordon's testimony that Stroot's cognitive deficits in three areas—attention, concentration, and executive functioning—were proximately caused by her long-term exposure to microbial contamination at Haverford Place.*

Given the permanent nature of Plaintiff's injuries as well as the physical and emotional pain and suffering Stroot will have to endure for the remainder of her life, the Court does not find the $1,000,000 verdict to Stroot unreasonable, nor is its conscience shocked.

Decision

The supreme court of Delaware held that New Haverford Partnership was negligent and the award of damages to Stroot was supported by the evidence. The supreme court affirmed the trial court's judgment in favor of Stroot.

Case Questions

Critical Legal Thinking What is negligence? Do you think the landlord was negligent in this case?

Business Ethics Did New Haverford Partnership act ethically in this case? Do you think Stroot was partially at fault in this case?

Contemporary Business Do you think the award of damages in this case was appropriate? Why or why not?

Implied Warranty of Habitability

The courts of many jurisdictions hold that an **implied warranty of habitability** applies to residential leases for their duration. This warranty provides that the leased premises must be fit, safe, and suitable for ordinary residential use.

Examples Unchecked rodent infestation, leaking roofs, unworkable bathroom facilities, and the like have been held to breach the implied warranty of habitability. On the other hand, a small crack in a wall or some paint peeling from a door does not breach this warranty.

State statutes and judicial decisions provide various remedies that can be used if a landlord's failure to maintain or repair leased premises affects the tenant's use or enjoyment of the premises. Generally, the tenant may (1) withhold from his or her rent the amount by which the defect reduced the value of the premises to him or her, (2) repair the defect and deduct the cost of repairs from the rent due for the leased premises, (3) cancel the lease if the failure to repair constitutes constructive eviction, or (4) sue for damages in the amount by which the landlord's failure to repair the defect reduced the value of the leasehold.

In the following case, the court had to address the issue of implied warranty of habitability.

implied warranty of habitability
A warranty that provides that leased premises must be fit, safe, and suitable for ordinary residential use.

CASE 49.2 Implied Warranty of Habitability

Poyck v. Bryant

13 Misc.3d 699, 820 N.Y.S.2d 774, Web 2006 N.Y. Misc. Lexis 2278 (2006)
Civil Court of the City of New York

"Secondhand smoke is just as insidious and invasive as the more common conditions such as noxious odors, smoke odors, chemical fumes, excessive noise, and water leaks and extreme dust penetration."

—Judge Hagler

Facts

Peter Poyck was the owner and landlord of condominium unit No. 5-D, located in a building at 22 West 15th Street, New York City. Poyck leased his condominium to Stan and Michelle Bryant (Tenants). After living in the premises for three years, Tenants signed a new two-year lease. Two months into the new term, neighbors moved in next door, in unit No. 5-C. The new neighbors constantly smoked in the common fifth-floor hallway and in apartment 5-C. The tobacco smoke—secondhand smoke—penetrated into Tenants' unit. Tenants immediately complained to the building's superintendent, who

(case continues)

talked to the smokers, to no avail. The incessant smoke continued unabated.

Tenants then complained to landlord Poyck, but the landlord took no action. Tenants vacated the premises 16 months before their lease was up. Poyck sued Tenants for the unpaid rent. Tenants countered that the second-hand smoke breached the implied warranty of habitability and thus caused constructive eviction. The landlord made a motion to strike Tenants' defense of breach of the implied warranty of habitability and constructive eviction.

Issue

Does secondhand smoke emanating from a neighbor's unit constitute a breach of the implied warranty of habitability and cause constructive eviction?

Language of the Court

Most urban dwelling in New York City comprises "vertical living" in high-rise apartment buildings with possibly multiple neighbors in all directions. With multiple neighbors living beside each other comes basic duties and responsibilities. There is a duty to protect each other's right to privacy and a responsibility not to invade a neighbor's privacy. The unwanted invasion of privacy comes in many guises such as noise, smells, odors, fumes, dust, water and even secondhand smoke.

The key to avoiding such unneighborly behavior is for the neighbor to follow the often forgotten "Golden Rule"—You shall love your fellow or neighbor as yourself. The Golden Rule is a general principle of ethics which essentially admonishes neighbors as follows: What is hateful to you, do not do to your neighbor. The landlord also has an obligation to ensure that the conditions do not render the apartment "unsafe and uninhabitable" or prevent the premises from serving their intended function of residential occupation. When

neighbors fail to respect each other and the landlord does not act, the law imposes its will on landlords and tenants through the statutorily enacted implied warranty of habitability pursuant to Real Property Law § 235-b.

Secondhand smoke is just as insidious and invasive as the more common conditions such as noxious odors, smoke odors, chemical fumes, excessive noise, and water leaks and extreme dust penetration. Indeed, the United States Surgeon General, the New York State Legislature and the City of New York City Council declared that there is a substantial body of scientific research that breathing secondhand smoke poses a significant health hazard. Therefore, this court holds as a matter of law that secondhand smoke qualifies as a condition that invokes the protections of Real Property Law § 235-b under the proper circumstances. As such, it is axiomatic that secondhand smoke can be grounds for a constructive eviction.

Decision

The court held as a matter of law that secondhand smoke can cause a breach of the implied warranty of habitability and constructive eviction of a tenant. The court denied the landlord's motion to strike these issues.

Case Questions

Critical Legal Thinking What is the implied warranty of habitability? What is constructive eviction?

Business Ethics Did the neighbors in unit No. 5-C breach a duty owed to a neighbor? Was there justification for the tenants in unit No. 5-D to vacate the premises before their lease was up?

Contemporary Business Did the landlord have any power over the situation? Explain.

▶ TENANT'S DUTIES TO A LANDLORD

In a landlord–tenant relationship, the law imposes certain legal duties on the tenant. That is, the landlord has lawful rights that can be enforced against the tenant. The duties that a tenant owes to a landlord are discussed in the following paragraphs.

Tenant's Duty to Pay Rent

A commercial or residential tenant owes a duty to pay the agreed-upon amount of **rent** for the leased premises to the landlord at the agreed-upon time and terms. Generally, rent is payable in advance (e.g., on the first day of the month for use that month), although the lease may provide for other times and methods for payment. Reasonable late charges may be assessed on rent that is overdue. In a **gross lease**, the tenant pays a gross sum to the landlord. The landlord is responsible for paying the property taxes and assessments on the property.

Several of the most common commercial rental arrangements are:

- **Net lease.** In a **net lease** arrangement, the tenant is responsible for paying rent and property taxes.
- **Double net lease.** In a **double net lease** arrangement, the tenant is responsible for paying rent, property taxes, and utilities.
- **Net, net, net lease (or triple net lease).** In a **net, net, net lease(triple net lease)** arrangement, the tenant is responsible for paying rent, property taxes, utilities, and insurance.

Upon nonpayment of rent, the landlord is entitled to recover possession of the leased premises from the tenant. This may require the landlord to *evict* the tenant. Most states provide a summary procedure called **unlawful detainer action** that a landlord can bring to evict a tenant. The landlord may also sue to recover the unpaid rent from the tenant. The more modern rule requires the landlord to make reasonable efforts to *mitigate damages* (i.e., to make reasonable efforts to re-lease the premises).

unlawful detainer action
A legal process that a landlord must complete to evict a holdover tenant.

CONCEPT SUMMARY
TENANT'S DUTY TO PAY RENT

Rental Agreement	Description
Gross lease	The tenant is responsible for paying rent.
Net lease	The tenant is responsible for paying rent and property taxes.
Double net lease	The tenant is responsible for paying rent, property taxes, and utilities.
Triple net lease	The tenant is responsible for paying rent, property taxes, utilities, and insurance.

Tenant's Duty Not to Use Leased Premises for Illegal or Nonstipulated Purposes

A tenant may use leased property for any lawful purposes permitted by the lease. Leases often stipulate that the leased premises can be used only for specific purposes. If the tenant uses the leased premises for unlawful purposes (e.g., operating an illegal gambling casino) or nonstipulated purposes (e.g., operating a restaurant in a residence), the landlord may terminate the lease, evict the tenant, and sue for damages.

Tenant's Duty Not to Commit Waste

A tenant is under a **duty not to commit waste** to the leasehold. Waste occurs when the tenant causes substantial and permanent damage to the leased premises that decreases the value of the property and the landlord's reversionary interest in it. Waste does not include ordinary wear and tear. The landlord can recover damages from the tenant for waste.

Example It would be waste if the floor of the premises buckled because a tenant permitted heavy equipment to be placed on the premises. It would not be waste if the paint chipped from the walls because of the passage of time.

Tenant's Duty Not to Disturb Other Tenants

A tenant owes a **duty not to disturb other tenants** in the same building. A landlord may evict a tenant who interferes with the use and quiet enjoyment of other tenants.

Example A tenant in an apartment building breaches the duty not to disturb other tenants if he or she disturbs the sleep of other tenants by playing loud music throughout the night.

CONTEMPORARY ENVIRONMENT

Premises Liability

"We hold that in all areas of the leasehold, particularly in the areas under his control, the landlord is under a duty to provide adequate security to protect his tenants from the foreseeable criminal actions of third persons."

—Judge Cirillo

Landlords owe a *duty of reasonable care* to tenants and third parties not to negligently cause them injury. This duty is based on the foreseeability standard of ordinary negligence actions. A landlord who breaches this duty is liable to the injured tenant or third party for tort damages. The liability of landlords to tenants injured on their premises is called **premises liability**.

Consider this case. Cedarbrook was a complex of approximately 1,000 apartment units located on a 36-acre tract of land in Cheltenham, Pennsylvania, owned by John W. Merriam. Vehicles could enter the grounds through two entrances. Automobiles parked in garages located beneath each apartment building. The parking facility under Building No. 1 had spaces for 160 cars. Access to the garages could be gained through two open entrances. The garages were not well lit. Over a five-year period, the crime rate in Cedarbrook had risen. During the three-month period preceding the criminal incident at issue in this case, 21 separate incidents of criminal activity, including robberies, burglaries at apartments, car thefts, and an assault on a tenant, were reported.

One night, at approximately 9:00 P.M., Samuel and Peggy Feld, tenants in Building No. 1, drove into the Cedarbrook complex and parked their car in the garage. After getting out of their car, they walked toward the pedestrian exit. Three armed men emerged from behind a parked car, accosted them, and robbed them at gunpoint. They then raped Mrs. Feld. Following the incident, Mrs. Feld began

psychotherapy to help alleviate her severe emotional distress. Her psychiatrist testified that she would never recover from the emotional trauma of the event. Following the incident, Mr. Feld was constantly in a fearful, nervous, and agitated state.

Mr. and Mrs. Feld sued Cedarbrook for damages. The issue was whether the landlord was liable to Mr. and Mrs. Feld for the injuries caused to them by third parties. The jury said "yes" and returned a verdict that awarded $2 million compensatory damages to Mrs. Feld, $1 million compensatory damages to Mr. Feld, and $1.5 million punitive damages to each of them. Cedarbrook appealed, but the superior court of Pennsylvania upheld the verdict, except that it reduced the punitive damages awarded to Mr. Feld from $1.5 million to $750,000. The court stated:

We hold that in all areas of the leasehold, particularly in the areas under his control, the landlord is under a duty to provide adequate security to protect his tenants from the foreseeable criminal actions of third persons. In order to establish a prima facie case of negligence against a landlord for his failure to provide adequate security, a plaintiff must present evidence showing that the landlord had notice of criminal activity that posed risk of harm to his tenants, that he had the means to take precautions to protect the tenant against this risk of harm, and that his failure to do so was the proximate cause of the tenant's injuries.

Thus, the court held the landlord liable to the tenants under the doctrine of premises liability. *Feld v. Merriam*, 314 Pa.Super. 414, 461 A.2d 225, **Web** 1983 Pa. Super. Lexis 3092 (Superior Court of Pennsylvania)

---

premises liability
The liability of landlords and tenants to persons injured on their premises.

assignment
A transfer by a tenant of his or her rights under a lease to another.

assignor
A party who transfers rights under a lease.

assignee
A party to whom rights are transferred under a lease.

▶ TRANSFER OF RIGHTS TO LEASED PROPERTY

Landlords may sell, gift, devise, or otherwise transfer their interests in leased property. For example, a landlord can sell either the right to receive rents, his or her reversionary interest, or both. If complete title is transferred, the property is subject to the existing lease. The new landlord cannot alter the terms of the lease (e.g., raise the rent) during the term of the lease unless the lease so provides.

The tenant's right to transfer possession of the leased premises to another depends on the terms of the lease. Many leases permit the tenants to *assign* or *sublease* their rights in the property. Assignment and subleases are discussed in the following paragraphs.

Assignment of a Lease

If a tenant transfers all of his or her interests under a lease, it is an **assignment**. The original tenant is the **assignor**, and the new tenant is the **assignee** (see Exhibit 49.2). Under an assignment, the assignee acquires all the rights that the assignor had under the lease. The

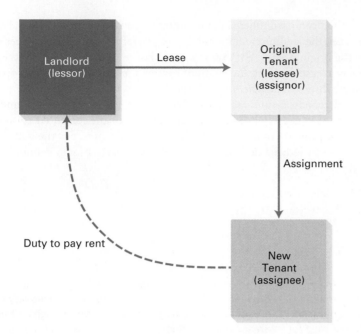

assignee is obligated to perform the duties that the assignor had under the lease. That is, the assignee must pay the rent and perform other covenants contained in the original lease.

The assignor remains responsible for his or her obligations under the lease unless specifically released from doing so by the landlord. If the landlord recovers from the assignor, the assignor has a course of action to recover from the assignee. Many leases contain a provision that prohibits a lessee from assigning a lease without the lessor's consent.

Sublease

If a tenant transfers only some of his or her rights under a lease, it is a **sublease**. The original tenant is the **sublessor**, and the new tenant is the **sublessee** (see Exhibit 49.3). The sublessor is not released from his or her obligations under the lease unless specifically released by the landlord.

sublease
A situation in which a tenant transfers only some of his or her rights under the lease.

sublessor
The original tenant in a sublease situation.

sublessee
The new tenant in a sublease situation.

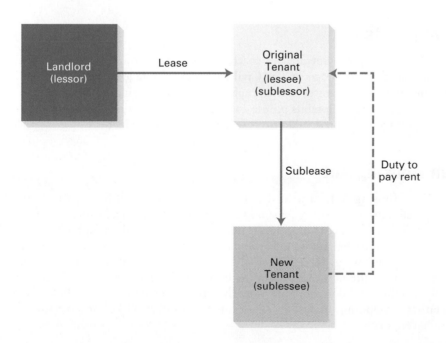

Subleases differ from assignments in important ways. In a sublease, no legal relationship is formed between the landlord and the sublessee. Therefore, the sublessee does not acquire rights under the original lease. For example, a sublessee would not acquire the sublessor's option to renew a lease. Further, the landlord cannot sue the sublessee to recover rent payments or enforce duties under the original lease.

In most cases, tenants cannot assign or sublease their leases without the landlord's consent. This right protects the landlord from the transfer of the leasehold to someone who might damage the property or not have the financial resources to pay the rent. Most states, either by statute or by judicial decision, hold that the owner's consent cannot be unreasonably withheld.

CONTEMPORARY ENVIRONMENT

Rent Control

Many local communities across the country have enacted **rent control ordinances** that stipulate an amount of rent a landlord can charge for residential housing. Most of these ordinances fix the rent at a specific amount and provide for minor annual increases. Although many communities have adopted rent control ordinances, New York City is the most famous one.

Landlords, of course, oppose rent control, arguing that rent control ordinances are merely a "regulatory tax" that transfers wealth from landowners to tenants. Tenants and proponents of rent control say that it is necessary to create affordable housing, particularly in high-rent urban areas. The U.S. Supreme Court has upheld the use of rent control [*Yee v. City of Escondido, California*, 503 U.S. 519, 112 S.Ct. 1522, 118 L.Ed.2d 153, **Web** 1992 U.S. Lexis 2115 (Supreme Court of the United States)].

▶ CIVIL RIGHTS ACTS AND REAL ESTATE

Federal and state laws guarantee civil rights in the purchase, sale, and lease of real estate, as well as in the use of public property. Several major federal statutes that regulate real estate are the *Civil Rights Act*, the *Fair Housing Act*, and *Title III of the Americans with Disabilities Act*. These federal statutes are discussed in the following paragraphs.

Civil Rights Act

Civil Rights Act
A federal statute that prohibits racial discrimination in the transfer of real property.

Federal and state governments have enacted statutes that prohibit discrimination in the sale and rental of real property. The **Civil Rights Act**,[1] a federal statute, prohibits racial discrimination in the transfer of real property, including housing, commercial, and industrial property. The act prohibits private and public discrimination and permits lawsuits to recover damages and obtain injunctions against offending conduct.

Fair Housing Act

Fair Housing Act
A federal statute that makes it unlawful for a party to refuse to rent or sell a dwelling to any person because of his or her race, color, national origin, sex, or religion.

The **Fair Housing Act**,[2] a federal statute, makes it unlawful for a party to refuse to rent or sell a dwelling to any person because of his or her race, color, national origin, sex, or religion. The act also prohibits discrimination by real estate brokers, mortgage lenders, and advertisers concerning the sale or rental of real property. The law does not apply to the following: (1) a person who owns a building of four or fewer units and occupies one of the units and leases the others and (2) a person who leases a single-family dwelling and does not own more than three single-family dwellings. To qualify for either exemption, the lessor cannot use a real estate broker or advertise in a discriminating manner.

Title III of the Americans with Disabilities Act

The **Americans with Disabilities Act (ADA)**,[3] a federal statute, became effective January 26, 1992. The ADA is a broad civil rights statute that prohibits discrimination against disabled individuals in employment, public services, public accommodations and services, and telecommunications. **Title III of the ADA** prohibits discrimination on the basis of disability in places of public accommodation operated by private entities. The U.S. Department of Justice is empowered to issue regulations that interpret and enforce the ADA.

Title III of the ADA applies to public accommodations and commercial facilities such as motels, hotels, restaurants, theaters, recreation facilities, colleges and universities, department stores, retail stores, and office buildings. It does not generally apply to residential facilities (single- and multifamily housing).

Title III requires covered facilities to be designed, constructed, and altered in compliance with specific accessibility requirements established by regulations issued pursuant to the ADA. This includes constructing ramps to accommodate wheelchairs, installing railings next to steps, placing signs written in Braille in elevators and at elevator call buttons, and so on.

New construction must be built in such a manner as to be readily accessible to and usable by disabled individuals. Any alterations made to existing buildings must be made so that the altered portions of the building are readily accessible to disabled individuals to the maximum extent feasible. With respect to existing buildings, architectural barriers must be removed if such removal is readily achievable. In determining when an action is readily achievable, the factors to be considered include the nature and cost of the action, the financial resources of the facility, and the type of operations of the facility.

The ADA provides for both private right of action and enforcement by the attorney general. Individuals may seek injunctive relief and monetary damages, while the attorney general may seek equitable relief and civil fines for any violation.

Title III of the Americans with Disabilities Act
A federal statute that prohibits discrimination on the basis of disability in places of public accommodation by private entities.

State and Local Antidiscrimination Laws

Many states and local communities have enacted statutes and ordinances that prohibit discrimination in the sale or lease of real property. These laws usually prohibit discrimination based on race, color, national origin, sex, or religion and also often prohibit discrimination based on other protected classes, such as age, sexual orientation, and receipt of government assistance.

Property is the most ambiguous of categories. It covers a multitude of rights which have nothing in common except that they are exercised by persons and enforced by the state.

R. H. Tawney
*The Acquisitive Society, Chapter V
(1921)*

▶ EMINENT DOMAIN AND THE "TAKING" OF REAL PROPERTY

The government may use its power of **eminent domain** to acquire private property for public purposes. However, the **Due Process Clause** of the Fifth Amendment to the U.S. Constitution (and state constitutions, where applicable) requires that the government only take property for "public use." The government must allow the owner of the property to make a case for keeping the property.

The **Just Compensation Clause** of the Fifth Amendment to the U.S. Constitution requires the government to compensate the property owner (and possibly others, such as lessees) when it exercises the power of eminent domain. Anyone who is not satisfied with the compensation offered by the government can bring an action to have the court determine the compensation to be paid.

Example IT-Corporation owns a large piece of property, with the intention of erecting a 10-story commercial building at some future time. Suppose that the government enacts a zoning law that restricts buildings in the area to 5 stories. Although IT-Corporation would suffer a substantial economic loss, the zoning law, nevertheless, would not constitute a "taking" that required the payment of compensation.

eminent domain
The government's power to take private property for public use, provided that just compensation is paid to the private property holder.

Just Compensation Clause
A clause of the U.S. Constitution that requires the government to compensate the property owner, and possibly others, when the government takes property under its power of eminent domain.

CONTEMPORARY ENVIRONMENT

The *Kelo* "Takings" Case

"The concept of the public welfare is broad and exclusive. The values it represents are spiritual as well as physical, aesthetic as well as monetary."

—Justice Stevens

Obviously the government can "take" an owner's real property to use the property for a public use such as building a highway, school, fire station, and such. However, the extent of what qualifies as "public use" was tested in a recent major U.S. Supreme Court ruling. A discussion of the facts of the case and the Supreme Court's ruling follows.

The City of New London is located in southeastern Connecticut, at the junction of the Thames River and Long Island Sound. The city has suffered decades of economic decline, including the closing of the federal military base in the Fort Trumbull area of the city. The city's unemployment rate was nearly double the state's unemployment rate, and the city's population of 24,000 was the lowest since 1920.

To try to remedy the situation, state and local officials targeted the City of New London for economic revitalization. The government created the New London Development Corporation (NLDC) to assist the city in planning economic redevelopment. The NLDC finalized an integrated redevelopment plan for 90 acres in the Fort Trumbull area of the city. The redevelopment plan included a waterfront conference hotel, restaurants, stores, a marina, 80 new residences, and office buildings. Importantly, these projects were to be constructed and owned by private developers and parties selected by the city. The stated purposes were to make the city more attractive, create jobs, and increase tax revenue.

The only problem was that some of the property needed for the redevelopment was owned by individual homeowners. The city purchased most of the land needed for the redevelopment from private owners. However, Susette Kelo and several other homeowners in the redevelopment district (collectively Kelo) refused to sell their properties. Their properties were well kept and were not blighted.

A Connecticut state statute authorized the use of eminent domain to take property to promote economic development. Thus, the NLDC initiated eminent domain actions to take the properties. Kelo defended, arguing that the taking violated the "public use" requirement of the Fifth Amendment to the U.S. Constitution because the properties were being taken from one private party—Kelo and the other holdout homeowners—and were being transferred to other private owners—the developers. The state trial court held for Kelo. However, the Connecticut supreme court held that the taking of private property by the NLDC was valid. Kelo appealed to the U.S. Supreme Court. The issue directed at the U.S. Supreme Court was: Does the City of New London's decision to take Kelo's property by eminent domain for the purpose of economic development satisfy the "public use" requirement of the Fifth Amendment?

The U.S. Supreme Court, in a 5–4 decision, held that the general benefit a community enjoys from economic growth qualifies as a permissible "public use" to support the taking of private property for such redevelopment plans under the Takings Clause of the Fifth Amendment. In the majority opinion, Justice Stevens wrote:

The disposition of this case therefore turns on the question whether the City's development plan serves a "public purpose." Without exception, our cases have defined this concept broadly. The concept of the public welfare is broad and exclusive. The values it represents are spiritual as well as physical, aesthetic as well as monetary. It is within the power of the legislature to determine that the community should be beautiful as well as healthy, spacious as well as clean, well-balanced as well as carefully patrolled.

The U.S. Supreme Court upheld the state of Connecticut's statute that permitted the taking of private property for the purposes of economic development. Thus, Kelo's property could be taken by the redevelopment agency and transferred to another private party—the developers—who in turn would build and own commercial property where Kelo's house once stood. The Supreme Court opinion stated, "In affirming the City's authority to take petitioners' properties, we do not minimize the hardship that condemnations may entail, notwithstanding the payment of just compensation."

The response to the *Kelo* case was swift: The Supreme Court's decision was widely criticized by members of the public who believed the decision violated private property rights. State politicians were quick to respond, with over half of the states enacting state laws that make it more difficult for state and local governments to acquire private property by eminent domain than the standard permitted in the *Kelo* ruling. *Kelo v. City of New London, Connecticut*, 545 U.S. 469, 125 S.Ct. 2655, 162 L.Ed.2d 439, **Web** 2005 U.S. Lexis 5011 (Supreme Court of the United States).

TEST REVIEW TERMS AND CONCEPTS

Americans with Disabilities Act (ADA)	Assignee Assignment of a lease	Assignor Building codes (housing codes)	Civil Rights Act Covenant of quiet enjoyment

Double net lease	Implied warranty of	Net lease	Sublessor
Due Process Clause	habitability	Net, net, net lease (triple	Tenancy at sufferance
Duty not to commit	Just Compensation Clause	net lease)	Tenancy at will
waste	Landlord–tenant	Periodic tenancy	Tenancy for years
Duty not to disturb other	relationship	Premises liability	Title III of the ADA
tenants	Lease	Rent	Unlawful detainer action
Eminent domain	Leasehold estate (leasehold)	Rent control ordinance	Wrongful eviction
Exclusive possession	Lessee (tenant)	Sublease	(unlawful eviction)
Fair Housing Act	Lessor (landlord)	Sublessee	Wrongful possession

CASE PROBLEMS

49.1 Constructive Eviction   T&W Building Company (Landlord) entered into a five-year lease agreement with Merrillville Sport & Fitness, Inc. (Tenant), to lease space in a building to be used as a sports and fitness center. The lease provided that Landlord was to keep the heating and cooling plant "in good order, repair, and condition" and was to commence required repairs as soon as reasonably practicable after receiving written notice of problems. Tenant complained of several problems throughout the first year of its tenancy. First, the heating system did not work properly, causing the premises to be extremely cold, particularly in the winter months. Second, there was no water on many occasions. Third, there was only one electrical outlet installed on the premises. Landlord failed to rectify the problems. As a result, Tenant lost members. It gave notice and vacated the premises within one year of signing the lease. Tenant and Landlord ended up in a lawsuit regarding the lease. Who wins? *T&W Building Co. v. Merrillville Sport & Fitness, Inc.*, 529 N.E.2d 865, **Web** 1988 Ind.App. Lexis 805 (Court of Appeals of Indiana)

49.2 Implied Warranty of Habitability   Sharon Love entered into a written lease agreement with Monarch Apartments (Monarch) for apartment 4 at 441 Winfield in Topeka, Kansas. Shortly after moving in, she experienced serious problems with termites. Her walls swelled, clouds of dirt came out of the walls, and when she checked on her children one night, she saw termites flying around the room. She complained to Monarch, which arranged for the apartment to be fumigated. When the termite problem persisted, Monarch moved Love and her children to apartment 2. Upon moving in, Love noticed that roaches crawled over the walls, ceilings, and floors of the apartment. She complained, and Monarch called an exterminator, who sprayed the apartment. When the roach problem persisted, Love vacated the premises. Did Love lawfully terminate the lease? Who wins? *Love v. Monarch Apartments*, 13 Kan.App.2d 341, 771 P.2d 79, **Web** 1989 Kan.App. Lexis 219 (Court of Appeals of Kansas)

49.3 Lease   Susan Nylen, Elizabeth Lewis, and Julie Reed, students at Indiana University, signed a rental agreement as cosigners to lease an apartment from Park Doral Apartments. The rental term was from August 26 until August 19 of the following year. The lessees agreed to pay a monthly rent for the apartment. The tenants paid a security deposit, constituting prepayment of rent for the last month of the lease term. At the end of the fall semester, Reed moved out of the apartment and refused to pay any further rent. Nylen and Lewis remained in possession of the apartment, paying only two-thirds of the total rent due for the month for several months. Nylen and Lewis made a full payment of the rent for March and then vacated the apartment. The landlord, who was unable to re-lease the apartment during the lease term, sued Reed, Nylen, and Lewis for the unpaid rent. Who wins? *Nylen v. Park Doral Apartments*, 535 N.E.2d 178, **Web** 1989 Ind.App. Lexis 185 (Court of Appeals of Indiana)

49.4 Tort Liability   William Long, d/b/a Hoosier Homes, owned an apartment building in Indianapolis, Indiana. He rented a second-story apartment to Marvin Tardy. Almedia McLayea visited Tardy with her one-month-old nephew, Garfield Dawson. As McLayea was leaving the apartment, she walked down the stairway, carrying Dawson in an infant seat. As she came down 4 steps to a landing, which led to a flight of 10 stairs, she caught her heel on a stair, slipped, and fell forward. There was no handrail along the stairway (as required by law) by which she could break her fall. Instead, her shoulder struck a window at the landing, the window broke, the rotted screen behind it collapsed, and Dawson fell through the opening to the ground below. He sustained permanent injuries, including brain damage. Dawson (through his mother) sued the landlord to recover damages for negligence. Who wins? *Dawson v. Long*, 546 N.E.2d 1265, **Web** 1989 Ind.App. Lexis 1225 (Court of Appeals of Indiana)

49.5 Tort Liability   Luis and Barbara Chavez leased a house they owned in Arizona to Michael and Terry Diaz. The lease provided that no pets were to be kept on the premises without prior written approval of the landlords. The Diazes, without the landlords' consent or knowledge, kept a Pit Bull and another dog, which was half Pit Bull and half Rottweiler, at the leased premises. Two weeks later, the Diazes' two dogs escaped from the backyard and attacked and injured Josephine Gibbons. Gibbons sued the landlords for damages. Are the landlords liable? Are the tenants liable? *Gibbons v. Chavez*, 160 Ariz. 73, 770 P.2d 377, **Web** 1988 Ariz.App. Lexis 373 (Court of Appeals of Arizona)

BUSINESS ETHICS CASES

49.6 Business Ethics   Moe and Joe Rappaport (Tenants) leased space in a shopping mall owned by Bermuda Avenue Shopping Center Associates, L.P. (Landlord), to use as an indoor golf arcade. The lease was signed, and Tenants were given possession of the leased premises. Landlord did not tell Tenants about the extensive renovations planned for the mall. For one month, the golf arcade was busy and earned a net profit. However, at the end of the month, renovation of the mall began in front of the arcade. According to Tenants, their store sign was taken down, there was debris and dust in front of the store, the sidewalks and parking spaces in front of the store were taken away, and their business "died." Tenants closed their arcade approximately one month later and sued Landlord for damages. Landlord counterclaimed, seeking to recover lost rental income. Did Landlord act ethically in not explaining the planned renovations to Tenants? Did Tenants act ethically in terminating the lease? Were Tenants constructively evicted from the leased premise? Who wins? *Bermuda Avenue Shopping Center Associates v. Rappaport*, 565 So.2d 805, **Web** 1990 Fla.App. Lexis 5354 (Court of Appeal of Florida)

49.7 Business Ethics   The Middleton Tract consisted of approximately 560 acres of land located in the Santa Cruz Mountains in San Mateo County, California. The land, which had once been owned by William H. Middleton, had been subdivided into 80 parcels of various shapes and sizes that were owned by various parties. The original deeds of conveyance from Middleton to purchasers contained certain restrictive covenants. One covenant limited use of the land exclusively for "residential purposes." Most of the land consisted of thickly wooded forest with redwood and Douglas fir trees. The Holmeses, who owned parcels totaling 144 acres, proposed to engage in commercial logging activities on their land. The plaintiffs, who owned other parcels in the tract, sued the Holmeses, seeking an injunction against such commercial activities. Did the Holmeses act ethically in this case? Who wins? *Greater Middleton Assn. v. Holmes Lumber Co.*, 222 Cal.App.3d 980, 271 Cal.Rptr. 917, **Web** 1990 Cal.App. Lexis 816 (Court of Appeal of California)

ENDNOTES

1. 42 U.S.C. Section 1971 et seq.
2. 42 U.S.C. Section 360 et seq.
3. 42 U.C.C. Section 1201 et seq.

Part XI

SPECIAL TOPICS

▲ **Los Angeles, California** *Automobile accidents are a primary cause of injury and death in the United States. Most states require automobile owners to carry automobile insurance. The required amount is often low, however.*

CHAPTER OBJECTIVES

After studying this chapter, you should be able to:

1. Describe an insurance contract and define *insurable interest*.
2. List and describe the various types of life, health, and disability insurance.
3. Identify the risks covered by a standard fire insurance policy and a homeowners' policy.
4. Describe automobile insurance and explain no-fault insurance.
5. List and describe special forms of business insurance.

CHAPTER CONTENTS

"The underwriter knows nothing and the man who comes to him to ask him to insure knows everything."

—Lord Justice Scrutton
Rozanes v. Bowen (1928)

▶ INTRODUCTION TO INSURANCE

Insurance is a means for persons and businesses to protect themselves against the risk of loss. For example, a business can purchase fire insurance to cover its buildings. If there is a fire and the property is damaged, the insurance company will pay for all or part of the loss, depending on the policy. Similarly, an individual who purchases automobile insurance may be reimbursed by the insurer if his or her car is stolen. Insurance is crucial to personal, business, and estate planning.

This chapter covers the formation of an insurance contract, types of insurance, defenses of insurance companies to liability, and other topics of insurance law.

▶ INSURANCE

Insurance is defined as a contract whereby one party undertakes to indemnify another against loss, damage, or liability arising from a contingent or unknown event. It is a means of transferring and distributing risk of loss. The risk of loss is *pooled* (i.e., spread) among all the parties (or **insureds**) who pay premiums to a particular insurance company. The insurance company—also called the **insurer**, or **underwriter**—is then obligated to pay insurance proceeds to members of the pool who experience losses.

An insurance contract is called a **policy**. The money paid to the insurance company is called a **premium**. Premiums are based on an estimate of the number of parties within the pool who will suffer the risks insured against. The estimate is based on past experience.

Insurance policies are often sold by insurance agents or brokers. An **insurance agent** usually works exclusively for one insurance company and is an agent of that company. An **insurance broker** is an independent contractor who represents a number of insurance companies. The broker is the agent of the insured. Some insurance is sold directly by the insurer to the insured (e.g., by direct mail).

The **McCarran-Ferguson Act**[1] which was enacted by the federal government, gave the regulation of insurance to the states.

Insurable Interest

Anyone who would suffer a pecuniary (monetary) loss from the destruction of real or personal property has an **insurable interest** in that property. If the insured does not have an insurable interest in the property being insured, the contract is treated as a wager and cannot be enforced. Ownership creates an insurable interest. In addition, mortgagees, lienholders, and tenants have an insurable interest in property. The insurable interest in property must exist at the time of loss.

In the case of life insurance, a person must have a close family relationship or an economic benefit from the continued life of another to have an insurable interest in that person's life. Thus, spouses, parents, children, and sisters and brothers can insure each others' lives. Other more remote relationships (e.g., aunts, uncles, cousins) require additional proof of an economic interest (e.g., proof of support). The insurable interest must exist when the life insurance policy is issued but need not exist at the time of death.

A person can insure his or her own life and name anyone as the **beneficiary**. The named beneficiary or beneficiaries receive the proceeds from the life insurance policy when the insured dies. The beneficiary does not have to have an insurable interest in the insured's life.

insurance
A means for persons and businesses to protect themselves against the risk of loss.

insured
A party who pays a premium to a particular insurance company for insurance coverage.

insurer
An insurance company that underwrites insurance coverage.

policy
An insurance contract.

premium
Money paid to an insurance company.

insurable interest
A requirement that a person who purchases insurance have a personal interest in the insured item or person.

beneficiary
A person who is to receive life insurance proceeds when the insured dies.

Insurance Policy

insurance policy
An insurance contract.

An insurance contract, called an **insurance policy**, is governed by the law of contracts. Most policies are prepared on standardized forms. Some states even make that a requirement. Often, state statutes mandate that specific language be included in different types of insurance contracts. These statutes concern coverage for certain losses, how limitations on coverage must be stated in the contract, and the like. The insurance coverage is in place as soon as the insurance policy is issued. If both the insurer and the insured agree, an insurance policy may be modified. Modification is usually done either by adding an **endorsement** to the policy or through the execution of a document called a **rider**.

In most instances, an insured can cancel an insurance policy at any time. An insurer can cancel an insurance policy for nonpayment of premiums. Many insurance policies provide a *grace period* during which an insured can pay an overdue premium. The insurance usually remains in effect during the grace period.

Duties of Insured and Insurer

The parties to an insurance contract are obligated to perform the duties imposed by the contract. The insured owes the following duties: (1) to pay the premiums stipulated by the policy, (2) to notify the insurer after the occurrence of an insured event within the time period stated in the policy or within a reasonable time, and (3) to cooperate with the insurer in investigating claims made against the insurer.

The insurer owes two primary duties. First, the insurer owes a **duty to defend** against any suit brought against the insured that involves a claim within the coverage of the policy. Thus, the insurer must provide and pay for the lawyers and court costs necessary to defend the lawsuit. Second, the insurer owes the **duty to pay** legitimate claims up to the policy limit. Insurers who wrongfully refuse to perform these duties are liable for damages.

Deductible Clause

deductible clause
A clause in an insurance policy which provides that insurance proceeds are payable only after the insured has paid a specified amount toward the damage or loss.

Many insurance policies, such as automobile insurance and health insurance policies, contain **deductible clauses**. A deductible clause provides that insurance proceeds are payable only after the insured has paid a certain amount toward the damage or loss. For example, typical deductibles for automotive collision insurance are $500 and $1,000.

Example Suppose that an insured has a $50,000 automobile collision policy with a $1,000 deductible, and her car suffers $10,000 damages in an accident. The insured must pay the first $1,000; the insurer will pay the remaining $9,000.

An insurance policy is like old underwear. The gaps in its cover are only shown by accident.

David Yates

Exclusions from Coverage

Most insurance policies include certain **exclusions from coverage**. For example, standard fire insurance policies often exclude coverage for damage caused by the storage of explosives or flammable liquids unless a special premium is paid for this coverage. Many health insurance policies exclude coverage for preexisting undisclosed medical conditions.

Coinsurance Clause

coinsurance clause
A clause in an insurance policy that requires the insured to pay a percentage of an insured loss. One type of coinsurance clause is a *copay clause*.

A **coinsurance clause** requires an insured to pay a percentage of the cost of an insured loss. These clauses are sometimes structured as **copay clauses**, in which case the insured must pay a flat amount rather than a percentage.

Example If a health insurance policy has a 10% coinsurance clause and an insured's medical bills are $50,000, the insurance company will pay $45,000, and the insured will have to pay $5,000.

ETHICS SPOTLIGHT

Incontestability Clause

Insurance companies can require applicants to disclose certain information to help determine whether they will insure the risk and to calculate the premium. The insurer can avoid liability on a policy (1) if its decision is based on a material misrepresentation on the part of the applicant or (2) if the applicant concealed material information from the insurer. This rule applies whether the misrepresentation was intentional or not intentional.

Many states have enacted laws that require **incontestability clauses** be placed in insurance agreements. An incontestability clause prevents insurers from contesting statements made by insureds in applications for insurance after the passage of a stipulated number of years (the typical length of time is two to five years).

Business Ethics Why are incontestability clauses required by law to be included in insurance policies? Do they prevent unethical conduct by insurance companies? Do they promote unethical behavior by insureds?

An incontestability clause was at issue in the following case.

incontestability clause
A clause that prevents insurers from contesting statements made by insureds in applications for insurance after the passage of a stipulated number of years.

CASE 50.1 Incontestability Clause

Amex Life Assurance Company v. Slome Capital Corp.

14 Cal.4th 1231, 60 Cal.Rptr.2d 898, 930 P.2d 1264, Web 1997 Cal. Lexis 404 (1997)
Supreme Court of California

"The beneficiaries should be assured they will receive the expected benefits, and not a lawsuit, upon the insured's death."

—Judge Chin

Facts

Jose Morales applied for a life insurance policy from Amex Life Assurance Company (Amex). Morales knew he was HIV (human immunodeficiency virus) positive, but he lied on the application form and denied having AIDS (acquired immune deficiency syndrome). As part of the application process, Amex required Morales to have a medical examination. A paramedic working for Amex met a man claiming to be Morales and took blood and urine samples from him. On his application, Morales had listed his height as 5 feet 6 inches and his weight as 147 pounds. The examiner registered the man taking the examination as 5 feet 10 inches tall, weighing 172 pounds, and appearing to be "older than the stated age." The blood samples tested HIV negative. Amex issued Morales a life insurance policy; the policy included a two-year incontestability clause, as required by state law. All premiums were paid.

Two years and one month after the life insurance policy was issued, Morales died of AIDS-related causes. When Morales's life insurance policy was presented to Amex for payment, Amex refused to pay, alleging that Morales had engaged in fraud and had had an imposter take his physical examination for him. The trial court denied Amex's summary judgment motion. The court of appeals held that the incontestability clause prevented Amex from denying coverage. Amex appealed.

Issue

Does the two-year incontestability clause prevent Amex from raising the insured's fraud as a reason not to pay the life insurance proceeds?

Language of the Court

Amex argues it insured, if anyone, the person who appeared for the medical examination, not Morales, and that to the extent the policy purported to insure Morales, it was void from the beginning. But imposter fraud is similar to other frauds the incontestability clause covers. When the named insured applies for the policy, and the premiums are faithfully paid for over two years, the beneficiaries should be assured they will receive the expected benefits, and not a lawsuit, upon the insured's death. The incontestability clause requires the insurer to investigate fraud before it issues the policy or within two years afterwards. The insurer may not accept the premiums for two years

(case continues)

and investigate a possible defense only after the beneficiaries file a claim. Here, with minimal effort, Amex could have discovered the fraud at the outset, as it did finally from information available before it issued the policy.

Decision

The supreme court held that the incontestability clause prevented Amex from denying coverage. The supreme court affirmed the judgment of the court of appeals, ordering Amex to pay the proceeds of Morales's life insurance policy.

Case Questions

Critical Legal Thinking Should the law contain incontestability clauses? What public policy is served by these clauses?

Business Ethics Did Morales act ethically in this case? Should unethical conduct be rewarded?

Contemporary Business Who pays the cost of insurance fraud? Explain.

▶ LIFE INSURANCE

life insurance
A form of insurance in which the insurer is obligated to pay a specific sum of money upon the death of the insured.

Life insurance is really "death insurance" because the insurer is normally obligated to pay a specified sum of money upon the death of the insured. Some life insurance policies provide for the payment of all or a portion of the proceeds to the insured before death if he or she is suffering from a terminal illness. This allows the insured to pay for medical and other costs associated with the illness. The most common forms of life insurance are described in Exhibit 50.1.

▶ **Exhibit 50.1 TYPES OF LIFE INSURANCE**

Type	Description
Whole life insurance	Whole life insurance (also called ordinary life or straight life) provides coverage during the entire life of the insured. Premiums are paid during the life of the insured or until the insured reaches a certain age. Whole life insurance involves an element of savings. That is, premiums are set to cover both the death benefit and an additional amount for investment by the insurance company. This builds up a cash surrender value that may be borrowed against by the insured. Premiums for such insurance tend to be high.
Limited-payment life insurance	Limited-payment life insurance premiums are paid for a fixed number of years (e.g., 10 years) even though coverage is provided during the entire life of the insured. This form of insurance has cash surrender value. Premiums are higher than those for whole life insurance. Insurance companies have introduced single-premium life insurance where the insured pays the entire premium in a lump-sum payment.
Term life insurance	Term life insurance is issued for a limited period of time (e.g., five years), with premiums payable and coverage effective only during this term. Because term life insurance involves no savings feature, there is no cash surrender value. Because term life is "pure" insurance, premiums are less than for whole life or limited-payment life insurance. Term life policies usually provide for renewal or conversion to other forms of life insurance.
Universal life insurance	Universal life insurance combines features of both term and whole life insurance. The premium payment—called a contribution—is divided between the purchase of term insurance and an amount invested by the insurance company. The cash value grows at a variable interest rate rather than at a fixed rate.
Endorsement and annuity contracts	Endorsement and annuity contracts are forms of retirement and life insurance contracts. An endorsement contract is an agreement by an insurance company to pay an agreed-upon lump sum of money either to the insured when he or she reaches a certain age or to his or her beneficiary if he or she dies before that age. An annuity contract is an agreement by an insurance company to pay periodic payments (e.g., monthly) to the insured once he or she reaches a certain age.
Double indemnity	Double indemnity life insurance stipulates that the insurer will pay double the amount of the policy if death is caused by accident. Double indemnity insurance does not apply if the insured dies of a natural cause.

Parties to a Life Insurance Contract

There are four parties to a life insurance contract:

1. The **insurance company** issues the policy.
2. The **owner** of the policy is the person who contracts with the insurance company and pays the premiums.
3. The **insured** is the person whose life is insured.

4. The **beneficiary** is the person who is to receive the insurance proceeds when the insured dies.

The owner of the policy has the power to name the beneficiary of the insurance proceeds. Most life insurance contracts permit the owner to change beneficiaries. If no beneficiary is named, the proceeds go to the insured's estate. Often, the owner and the insured are the same person. For example, an owner can take out an insurance policy on his or her own life. The owner and beneficiary can also be the same person.

A life insurance policy where the insured takes out life insurance on her own life and names a beneficiary is illustrated in Exhibit 50.2.

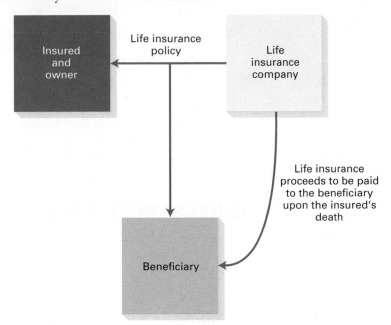

▶ **Exhibit 50.2 LIFE INSURANCE**

suicide clause
A clause in a life insurance contract which provides that if an insured commits suicide before a stipulated date, the insurance company does not have to pay the life insurance proceeds.

CONTEMPORARY ENVIRONMENT

Suicide Clause

A common feature of a life insurance policy is a **suicide clause**, which states that if the insured commits suicide within a certain period after taking out a life insurance policy on him or her, the insurance company does not have to pay the life insurance proceeds to the named beneficiary. The usual time period for which a suicide clause is valid is two years.

If the insured commits suicide before the specified date, the insurance company does not have to pay the policy proceeds but must refund the premiums paid to the deceased insured's estate. If the insured commits suicide after the specified date, the insurance company must pay the life insurance proceeds to the insured's designated beneficiary or, if there is none, to the deceased insured's estate.

▶ HEALTH AND DISABILITY INSURANCE

An individual may require certain expenses to be covered if he or she becomes ill or disabled. The insurance industry provides two types of insurance—*health insurance* and *disability insurance*—that pay benefits for health-related costs during a person's lifetime.

Health Insurance

A person who is injured or sick may have to have medical treatment, surgery, or hospital care. **Health insurance** can be purchased to help cover the costs of such medical care. Health insurance usually covers only a portion of the costs of medical care. Many insurance companies also offer **dental insurance**. Many employers pay for health insurance coverage for their employees, but most require an employee to pay a portion of the health insurance premium.

health insurance
Insurance that is purchased to help cover the costs of medical treatment, surgery, or hospital care.

Disability Insurance

disability insurance
Insurance that provides a monthly income to an insured who is disabled and cannot work.

A person who is injured or becomes sick may not be able to continue gainful employment. **Disability insurance**, which provides a monthly income to an insured who is disabled and cannot work, can be purchased to protect the insured against such an eventuality. The monthly benefits are usually based on the degree of disability. Many employers pay for disability insurance for their employees, but most require an employee to pay a portion of the disability insurance premium.

CONCEPT SUMMARY
HEALTH AND DISABILITY INSURANCE

Type	Description
Health	Insurance that covers the cost of medical treatment, surgery, and hospital care.
Dental	Insurance that covers the costs of dental care.
Disability	Insurance that provides monthly income to an insured who is disabled and cannot work. Benefits are based on the degree of disability.

▶ FIRE AND HOMEOWNERS' INSURANCE

Two major forms of insurance are available for residences: a *standard fire insurance policy* and a *homeowners' policy*. Such insurance is often required on real property that is mortgaged. Renters can also purchase insurance policies. These types of policies are discussed in the paragraphs that follow.

Standard Fire Insurance Policy

A standard **fire insurance** policy protects real and personal property against loss resulting from fire and certain related perils. It does not, however, provide **liability insurance** for personal injury.

standard fire insurance form
A standard fire insurance policy that protects the homeowner from loss caused by fire, lightning, smoke, and water damage.

Most states require insurance companies to use a **standard fire insurance form** as the standard fire insurance policy. This standard policy protects the homeowner from loss caused by fire, lightning, smoke, and water damage. The coverage of a standard policy can be enlarged by adding *riders* or *endorsements* to the policy. Riders are often added to cover damage caused by windstorms, rainstorms, hail, explosions, theft, and personal injury liability. Additional coverage requires the payment of increased premiums.

Most standard fire insurance policies exclude coverage for loss caused by enemy attack, civil war, revolution, landslides, and floods. In the case of property located in a designated flood area, a separate flood insurance policy is required.

Most policies limit recovery to damage caused by *hostile fires* (e.g., fire caused by faulty electrical wiring) and not *friendly fires* (e.g., damage caused by a fire contained in a fireplace). No personal liability coverage is provided. Most modern fire insurance policies provide **replacement cost insurance**. That is, the insurance will pay the cost to replace the damaged or destroyed property up to the policy limits (and subject to coinsurance). The insurer has the right to either pay the insured for the loss or pay to have the property restored or replaced.

replacement cost insurance
Insurance that pays the cost to replace the damaged or destroyed property up to the policy limits.

Homeowners' Policy

A **homeowners' policy** is a comprehensive insurance policy that includes coverage for the real and personal risks covered by a fire insurance policy and also includes **personal liability insurance**.

homeowners' policy
A comprehensive insurance policy that includes coverage for the risks covered by a fire insurance policy as well as personal liability insurance.

A homeowners' policy covers (1) the dwelling, (2) any appurtenant structures (e.g., garage, storage building), and (3) personal property (e.g., furniture, clothing). A homeowners' policy also provides protection for losses caused by theft, whether the items are taken from the home or workplace or taken while traveling.

Personal liability coverage homeowners' policy provides comprehensive *personal liability insurance* for the insured and members of his or her family. The insurer must pay property damage, personal injuries, and medical expenses to persons injured on the insured's property (e.g., a guest slipping on the sidewalk) and to persons injured by the insured or members of the insured's immediate family away from the insured's property (e.g., while golfing).

Personal Articles Floater

An insured might want to obtain insurance for specific valuable items (e.g., jewelry, works of art, furs). This is accomplished by adding a **personal articles floater**, or **personal effects floater**, to a homeowners' policy. The insured must submit a list of the items he or she wants covered, along with a statement of the value of each item, to the insurance company. The insurance company will charge an increased premium based on the articles insured. A personal articles floater provides coverage for loss or damage to the articles while traveling.

personal articles floater
An addition to a homeowners' policy that covers specific valuable items.

Renters' Insurance

Renters can purchase insurance to cover loss or damage to their possessions. A **renters' insurance** policy covers a renter's possessions against the same perils as a homeowners' broad-form policy and provides personal liability coverage.

renters' insurance
Insurance that renters purchase to cover loss or damage to their possessions.

CONCEPT SUMMARY
FIRE AND HOMEOWNERS' INSURANCE

Type	Description
Standard fire insurance policy	Insurance that protects real and personal property against loss resulting from fire, lightning, smoke, water damage, and related perils. Most policies limit recovery to damage caused by *hostile fires* (e.g., fire caused by faulty electrical wiring) and not *friendly fires* (e.g., damage caused by a fire contained in a fireplace). No personal liability coverage is provided.
Homeowners' policy	A comprehensive insurance policy that includes coverage for the risks covered by a standard fire insurance policy as well as personal liability insurance. It includes coverage for property damage, personal injury, and medical expenses of persons injured on the insured's property.
Personal liability coverage	Insurance for the insured and members of his or her family. The insurer must pay property damage, personal injuries, and medical expenses to persons injured on the insured's property (e.g., a guest slipping on the sidewalk) and to persons injured by the insured or members of the insured's immediate family away from the insured's property (e.g., while golfing).
Personal articles floater	Insurance that covers specific valuable items (e.g., jewelry, works of art, furs) that are usually excluded from standard fire and homeowners' policies.
Renters' insurance	Insurance that covers loss and damage to renters' possessions and provides personal liability coverage. Insures against the same perils as a homeowners' policy.

Title Insurance

Owners of real property can purchase **title insurance** to ensure that they have clear title to the property. Mortgagees and other lienholders can purchase title insurance on property on which they have a lien.

Title insurance protects against defects in titles and liens or encumbrances that are not disclosed on the title insurance policy. An owner of real property or a mortgagee pays only

title insurance
Insurance that owners of real property purchase to ensure that they have clear title to the property.

one premium for title insurance, usually at closing. Each new owner or mortgagee who wants this coverage must purchase a new title insurance policy. Mortgagees sometimes require a debtor to purchase such a policy as a prerequisite for making a loan.

CONTEMPORARY ENVIRONMENT

Mold Damage

When the residents of a home become seriously ill and doctors cannot find the cause of their illness, what may have caused the illness? Possibly mold. Thousands of sick homeowners and residents are having their homes tested for mold, and thousands of cases have been found. Mold usually develops when there have been leaks of water in a house or an apartment. Mold grows on water-soaked wood, stucco, and other building materials.

Whose headache is mold? Definitely that of the homeowner or resident. But it is also a problem for the insurance company that wrote the homeowners' insurance policy covering the home or residence. Thousands of claims have been filed against insurance companies concerning

mold-related damages. The claims not only include the cost of removing the mold and making the home livable again but also include claims for the personal suffering caused by the mold-related illnesses, pain and suffering, and other damages. The illnesses related to mold include sore throats, asthma, respiratory problems, and memory loss.

Mold is quickly becoming one of the most costly problems for the insurance industry as the number of lawsuits grows all over the country. Juries have awarded many multimillion-dollar judgments in toxic-mold verdicts. Some experts estimate that toxic-mold liability is in the billions of dollars and may exceed the asbestos liability paid for by the insurance industry.

▶ AUTOMOBILE INSURANCE

Several types of *automobile insurance* policies include both property and liability insurance. Many states require proof of automobile insurance before license plates are issued. The basic types of automobile insurance policies are discussed in the paragraphs that follow.

Collision Insurance

collision insurance
Insurance that a car owner purchases to insure his or her car against risk of loss or damage.

An owner of an automobile can purchase **collision insurance** that insures his or her car against risk of loss or damage. This form of property insurance pays for damages caused if the car is struck by another car. The coverage is in effect whether the insured's car is moving or standing still. Usually the premium is less if the policy has a high deductible.

Example A motorist hits an insured's automobile while it is parked on the street. Collision insurance would pay for the damages.

Comprehensive Insurance

comprehensive insurance
A form of property insurance that insures an automobile from loss or damage due to causes other than collision.

Comprehensive insurance is a form of property insurance that insures an automobile from loss or damage due to causes other than collision, such as fire, theft, explosion, windstorm, hail, falling objects, earthquakes, floods, hurricanes, vandalism, and riot. Many insureds purchase both collision and comprehensive insurance when they insure their automobiles against damage.

Liability Insurance

automobile liability insurance
Automobile insurance that covers damages that the insured causes to third parties.

Automobile liability insurance covers damages that the insured causes to third parties, including both bodily injury and property damage. The limits of liability insurance are usually stated in three numbers, such as "200/500/50." This level of liability limits the insurer's obligation to pay insurance proceeds arising from one accident to $200,000 for bodily injury or death to one person, $500,000 total for bodily injury or death to all persons, and $50,000 for property damage. States often require insureds to carry minimum liability insurance specified by statute. The minimum legal required liability insurance for injury or death is usually quite low (e.g., 25/50/5).

A basic automobile liability policy protects the insured when he is driving his own automobile. The owner, however, might want to expand coverage by adding (1) an **omnibus clause**, or **other-driver clause**, which protects the owner when someone else drives the car with his or her permission, and (2) a **D.O.C. (drive-other coverage)**, which protects the insured while driving other automobiles (e.g., rental cars). Some omnibus clauses extend coverage to third parties who drive automobiles with permission from a person to whom the owner gave permission to drive the car. Additional premiums are charged for this coverage.

Medical Payment Coverage

An automobile owner can obtain a **medical payment coverage** policy that covers medical expenses incurred by him- or herself, other authorized drivers of the car, and passengers in the car who are injured in an automobile accident. Coverage includes payments for reasonable medical, surgical, and hospital services.

Uninsured Motorist Coverage

Usually, people injured in an automobile accident look to the insurer of the party at fault to recover for their personal injury. But what if the person who is at fault has no insurance? An owner of an automobile can purchase **uninsured motorist coverage** that provides coverage to the driver and passengers who are injured by an uninsured motorist or a hit-and-run driver. Certain states require uninsured motorist coverage to be included in automobile insurance policies.

uninsured motorist coverage
Automobile insurance that provides coverage to a driver and passengers who are injured by an uninsured motorist or a hit-and-run driver.

no-fault automobile insurance
An automobile insurance system used by some states in which the driver's insurance company pays for any injuries or death the driver suffers in an accident, no matter who caused the accident.

CONTEMPORARY ENVIRONMENT
No-Fault Automobile Insurance

Until fairly recently, most automobile insurance coverage in this country was based on the principle of "fault," whereby a party injured in an accident relied on the insurance of the at-fault party to pay for his or her injuries. This system led to substantial litigation, and many accident victims were unable to recover because the at-fault party had either inadequate insurance or no insurance at all.

To remedy this problem, more than half of the states have enacted legislation that mandates **no-fault insurance** for automobile accidents. Under this system, a driver's insurance company pays for any injuries or death he or she suffers in an accident, no matter who caused the accident. No-fault insurance assures insureds that coverage is available if they are injured in an automobile accident.

No-fault insurance policies provide coverage for medical expenses and lost wages. Pain and suffering are sometimes covered. No-fault insurance usually covers the insured, members of the insured's immediate family, authorized drivers of the automobile, and passengers.

CONCEPT SUMMARY
AUTOMOBILE INSURANCE

Type	Description
Collision	Property insurance that covers the insured's vehicle against risk of loss or damage when it is struck by another vehicle.
Comprehensive	Property insurance that covers the insured's vehicle against risk of loss or damage from causes other than collision, such as fire, theft, explosion, hail, windstorm, falling objects, earthquakes, floods, hurricanes, vandalism, and riots.
Liability	Insurance that covers damage and loss that the insured causes to third parties. This includes both bodily injury and property damage. States often require individuals to carry minimum liability insurance, specified by statute. Additional coverage may be purchased: Other-driver coverage is liability coverage that protects the owner of a vehicle when someone else drives his or her vehicle with his or her permission, and drive-other coverage is liability coverage that protects the insured while driving other vehicles.

Medical payment	Insurance that covers medical expenses incurred by the owner, passengers, and other authorized drivers of his or her car who are injured in an automobile accident.
Uninsured motorist	Insurance that provides coverage to the driver and passengers of a vehicle who are injured by an uninsured motorist or a hit-and-run driver.
No-fault	Insurance required in some states whereby the driver's insurance company pays for any injuries or death the driver suffers in an accident, no matter who caused the accident.

Marine Insurance

marine insurance
Insurance that owners of a vessel can purchase to insure against loss or damage to the vessel and its cargo caused by perils on the water.

Owners of a vessel can purchase **marine insurance** to insure against loss or damage to the vessel and its cargo caused by perils on the water. Marine insurance is often comprehensive, covering property damage to the vessel or its cargo and liability insurance. Shippers can purchase marine insurance to cover the risk of loss to their goods during shipment. Marine insurance policies sometimes distinguish between *inland marine insurance* (for inland waters) and *ocean marine insurance* (for perils on the ocean).

Umbrella Insurance Policy

Liability coverage under most insurance policies, such as automobile and homeowners' insurance, is usually limited to a certain dollar amount. Insureds who want to increase their liability coverage beyond the original coverage can purchase an **umbrella insurance policy**. Coverage under an umbrella policy is usually at least $1 million and often reaches $5 million. An umbrella policy pays only if the basic policy limits on other insurance policies have been exceeded. An insurer will issue an umbrella policy only if a stipulated minimum amount of basic coverage on other insurance policies has been purchased by the insured.

Example An insured purchases automobile liability insurance that pays up to $500,000 per accident and an umbrella policy with an additional $3 million of coverage. If the insured's negligence causes an automobile accident in which injuries to other persons total $2 million, the basic automobile policy will pay the first $500,000, and the umbrella policy will pay the remaining $1.5 million.

▶ BUSINESS INSURANCE

Businesses usually purchase automobile insurance, property and casualty insurance, liability insurance, and other types of insurance previously discussed in this chapter. In addition, businesses often purchase insurance to cover risks uniquely applicable to conducting business. These types of business insurance are discussed in the following paragraphs.

Business Interruption Insurance

business interruption insurance
Insurance that reimburses a business for loss of revenue incurred when the business has been damaged or destroyed by fire or some other peril.

When a business is severely damaged or destroyed by fire or some other peril, it usually takes time to repair or reconstruct the damaged property. During this time, the business loses money. A business can purchase a **business interruption insurance** policy that will reimburse it for any revenues lost during such a period.

Example A retail store that is covered by business interruption insurance is destroyed by fire, and it takes nine months to rebuild the store. During this nine-month period, the owner of the store will be paid the insurance proceeds provided in the business interruption insurance policy to cover the lost revenues the store would have made had it been open for business.

Workers' Compensation Insurance

Employees are sometimes injured while working within the scope of their employment. All states have enacted legislation that compensates employees for such injuries.

Employers can purchase **workers' compensation insurance** to cover this risk. Many states require companies to purchase this form of insurance.

Under a workers' compensation system, an injured worker submits a claim to the appropriate workers' compensation court or administrative agency for a determination of payment for loss. In most instances, the injured employee cannot sue his or her employer for liability because the workers' compensation award is the exclusive remedy.

Example Mary is injured while working on an assembly line of an automobile manufacturer and loses the use of one of her arms. Assume that the manufacturer has purchased appropriate workers' compensation insurance. In this case, Mary can pursue her claim and be awarded money for her injury from workers' compensation insurance. Mary cannot, however, sue her employer in court to recover tort damages in a normal court action.

> **workers' compensation insurance**
> Insurance that compensates employees for work-related injuries.

Key-Person Life Insurance

In many small businesses, such as partnerships, limited liability companies, and close corporations, the death of one of the owners may cause a loss to the business. To compensate for such loss, the business often purchases **key-person life insurance** on owners and other important persons who work for the business. The business pays the premiums for the key-person life insurance policies. Upon the death of the insured person, the proceeds of the key-person life insurance are paid to the business.

Sometimes key-person life insurance is used to fund buy–sell agreements among the owners of the business. Thus, if an insured owner dies, the insurance proceeds are paid to the deceased's beneficiaries, and the deceased's interest in the business then reverts to either the other owners or the business, according to the terms of the buy–sell agreement.

> **key-person life insurance**
> Life insurance purchased and paid for by a business that insures against the death of owners and other key executives and employees of the business.

Directors' and Officers' Liability Insurance

Most large and medium corporations carry **directors' and officers' liability insurance (D&O insurance)** to protect directors and officers from liability for the actions they take on behalf of the corporation. Smaller companies tend to forgo this type of insurance because of the expense involved.

Example The iDot Computer Corporation has purchased D&O insurance. Assume that the shareholders of the corporation sue the board of directors, alleging that the directors were negligent in not catching a fraud perpetrated by management that caused a loss to the shareholders. If the court finds that the directors were negligent, the D&O insurance will pay the award and court costs.

> **directors' and officers' liability insurance**
> Insurance that protects directors and officers of a corporation from liability for actions taken on behalf of the corporation.

Professional Malpractice Insurance

Professionals—such as attorneys, accountants, physicians, dentists, architects, and engineers—are liable for injuries resulting from their negligence in practicing their professions. These professionals can purchase **professional malpractice insurance** (or simply **malpractice insurance**) to insure against liability. Premiums for malpractice insurance are often quite high.

Example Ms. Jones, Ms. Chen, and Ms. Smith form the law firm Jones, Chen, and Smith. The law firm purchases professional malpractice insurance. Assume that Ms. Smith is negligent and fails to file legal documents with the court, and this negligence causes the client's case to be dismissed. The client successfully sues the law firm for malpractice. In this case, the professional malpractice insurance will cover the client's award, up to its policy limits.

> **professional malpractice insurance**
> Insurance that insures professionals against liability for injuries caused by their negligence. Also known as *malpractice insurance*.

Product Liability Insurance

Manufacturers and sellers of products can be held liable for injuries caused by defective products. These businesses can purchase **product liability insurance** specifically to insure against this risk.

> **product liability insurance**
> Insurance that protects sellers and manufacturers against injuries caused by defective products.

Example The Children's Toy Company purchases product liability insurance. The company produces a toy that is defectively designed and causes injury to a child using the toy. The child sues the company for product liability. The court finds the company liable and issues a judgment for monetary damages against the company. In this case, the company's product liability insurance would pay the judgment up to the policy limit of the insurance.

TEST REVIEW TERMS AND CONCEPTS

Automobile liability
  insurance
Beneficiary
Business interruption
  insurance
Coinsurance clause
Collision insurance
Comprehensive insurance
Copay clause
Deductible clause
Dental insurance
Directors' and officers'
  liability insurance (D&O
  insurance)
Disability insurance
D.O.C. (drive-other
  coverage)

Duty to defend
Duty to pay
Endorsement
Exclusions from coverage
Fire insurance
Health insurance
Homeowners' policy
Incontestability clause
Insurable interest
Insurance
Insurance agent
Insurance broker
Insurance company
Insurance policy
Insured
Insurer (underwriter)
Key-person life insurance

Liability insurance
Life insurance
Marine insurance
McCarran-Ferguson Act
Medical payment coverage
No-fault insurance
Omnibus clause (other-
  driver clause)
Owner
Personal articles floater
  (personal effects floater)
Personal liability coverage
  homeowners' policy
Personal liability insurance
Policy
Premium
Product liability insurance

Professional malpractice
  insurance (malpractice
  insurance)
Renters' insurance
Replacement cost insurance
Rider
Standard fire insurance
  form
Suicide clause
Title insurance
Umbrella insurance policy
Uninsured motorist
  coverage
Workers' compensation
  insurance

CASE PROBLEMS

50.1 Exclusion Richard Usher's home was protected by a homeowners' policy issued by National American Insurance Company of California. The policy included personal liability insurance. A provision in the policy read: "Personal liability and coverage do not apply to bodily injury or property damage arising out of the ownership, maintenance, use, loading, or unloading of a motor vehicle owned or operated by, or rented or loaned to any insured." Usher parked a Chevrolet van he owned in his driveway. He left the van's side door open while he loaded the van in preparation for a camping trip. While Usher was inside his house, several children, including two-year-old Graham Coburn, began playing near the van. One of the children climbed into the driver's seat and moved the shift lever from *park* to *reverse*. The van rolled backward, crushing Coburn and killing him. Coburn's parents sued Usher for negligence. Is the accident covered by Usher's homeowners' policy? *National American Insurance Company of California v. Coburn*, 209 Cal.App.3d 914, 257 Cal.Rptr. 591, **Web** 1989 Cal.App. Lexis 356 (Court of Appeal of California)

50.2 Insurance Premiums Mutual Life Insurance Company of New York (Mutual Life) issued a $100,000 life insurance policy on the life of 65-year-old Alex Brecher. In consideration for the policy, Brecher agreed to pay an annual insurance premium of $7,830 in 12 monthly installments. Brecher provided a written request and authorization to have

the insurance company withdraw the premiums directly from his checking account at Citibank. The insurance company's first attempt to do so was returned unpaid. Mutual Life and Brecher were informed that one of Brecher's creditors had placed a restraining order on the bank account. Mutual Life sent Brecher a returned check notice, advising him that the withdrawal had been dishonored by his bank and that to keep the policy in force, the unpaid premiums would have to be paid before August 28. Mutual Life received Brecher's check for the outstanding amounts on August 26. When Mutual Life tried to cash the check, which was drawn on the Citibank account, the bank returned it unpaid, marked "refer to maker." Brecher made no further attempts to pay the insurance premiums. He died on September 18. His widow, the beneficiary of the life insurance policy, filed a claim to recover $100,000 from Mutual Life. When Mutual Life refused to pay, the widow sued. Who wins? *Brecher v. Mutual Life Insurance Company of New York*, 120 A.D.2d 423, 501 N.Y.S.2d 879, **Web** 1986 N.Y.App. Div. Lexis 56512 (Supreme Court of New York)

50.3 Duty to Defend Judith Isenhart purchased a Dodge station wagon. She then contacted Ed Carpenter, an agent of the National Automobile and Casualty Insurance Company (National) and told him she was interested in obtaining "full coverage" for the car. The policy that Carpenter provided to Judith provided coverage for bodily injury, property damage, medical costs, and collision damage. The policy specifically exempted coverage for accidents involving "non-owned automobiles." One and one-half years later, Judith's 16-year-old son Matt purchased a Volkswagen automobile. Insurance for this car was obtained from Allstate Insurance Company (Allstate). Two months after buying the car, Matt had an accident in which a passenger in the Volkswagen, Thea Stewart, was severely injured. Stewart sued Matt and Judith. Allstate agreed to defend the suit up to the limits of its policy. When National was contacted regarding the accident, the company refused to defend Judith in the suit and denied coverage, based on the policy's exclusion. Must National defend Judith? *National Automobile and Casualty Insurance Company v. Stewart*, 223 Cal.App.3d 452, 272 Cal.Rptr. 625, **Web** 1990 Cal.App. Lexis 941 (Court of Appeal of California)

50.4 Automobile Insurance Jowenna Surber owned a Mercedes-Benz automobile that she insured through an insurance broker, Mid-Century Insurance Company (Mid-Century). Mid-Century secured a policy for Surber with the Farmers Insurance Company (Farmers). Surber gave permission to her friend, Bruce Martin, to use the car. Martin held a valid California driver's license. Surber did not receive any compensation for allowing Martin to use the car. While driving the car, Martin was involved in a collision with another vehicle, driven by Loretta Haynes, who suffered severe injuries. Martin admitted that his negligence was the cause of the accident. Surber's policy stipulates that the policy covers "you or any family member or any person using your insured car." Is Farmers liable to Haynes? *Mid-Century Insurance Company v. Haynes*, 218 Cal.App.3d 737, 267 Cal.Rptr. 248, **Web** 1990 Cal.App. Lexis 219 (Court of Appeal of California)

50.5 Automobile Insurance Antonio Munoz and Jacinto Segura won some money from two unidentified men in a craps game in a Los Angeles park. When Munoz and Segura left the park in Segura's car, the two men followed them in another car. They chased Segura's car for several miles and then pulled beside it on a freeway. The men in the other car fired several gunshots at Segura's car, killing Munoz. At the time he was killed, Munoz had an automobile insurance policy issued by Nationwide Mutual Insurance Company (Nationwide). A provision in the policy covered damages from "an accident arising out of the use of an uninsured vehicle." Munoz's widow and child filed a claim with Nationwide to recover for Munoz's death. Nationwide rejected the claim. Who wins? *Nationwide Mutual Insurance Company v. Munoz*, 199 Cal.App.3d 1076, 245 Cal.Rptr. 324, **Web** 1988 Cal. App. Lexis 259 (Court of Appeal of California)

50.6 Malpractice Insurance Donald Barker, a wealthy Oregon resident, went to the law firm Winokur, Schoenberg, Maier, Hamerman & Knudson to have his estate planned. An attorney at the firm repeatedly told Barker that he could convey half of his $20-million estate to his wife tax free under Oregon's marital deduction. Barker had his will drawn based upon the law firm's advice. It was not until after Barker died three years later that Barker's family learned that Oregon does not recognize the marital deduction. As a result, the will's beneficiaries were subject to significant estate taxes. The beneficiaries sued the law firm for negligence, and the case was settled for $2 million. At the time Barker was being advised by the law firm, it had a professional malpractice insurance policy with the Travelers Insurance Company (Travelers) that covered "all sums which the insured shall become legally obligated to pay as damages because of any act or omission of the insured arising out of the performance of professional services for others in the insured's capacity as a lawyer." The policy expired one year prior to Barker's death. Is Travelers liable for the $2 million settlement? *Travelers Insurance Company v. National Union Fire Insurance Company of Pittsburgh*, 207 Cal.App.3d 1390, 255 Cal.Rptr. 727, **Web** 1989 Cal.App. Lexis 130 (Court of Appeal of California)

50.7 Duty to Defend When Michael A. Jaffe, a child psychiatrist practicing in California, was accused of Medi–Cal fraud and theft, he requested that his malpractice insurer, Cranford Insurance Company (Cranford), provide his criminal defense. Cranford refused to defend Jaffe, citing the terms of Jaffe's malpractice insurance policy. The policy describes the insured risk as "psychiatrist's professional liability in respect of insured's practice of psychiatry." Another clause of the policy states that Cranford "agrees to pay such damages as may be awarded in respect of professional services rendered by Jaffe, or which should have been rendered by him, resulting from any claims or suits based solely upon malpractice, error, or mistake." After Cranford refused to defend him, Jaffe hired his own criminal defense lawyer. The case went to trial, and Jaffe was found innocent of all charges. After his acquittal, Jaffe demanded that Cranford reimburse him for the expenses incurred during trial. When Cranford refused this request, Jaffe sued. Who wins? *Jaffe v. Cranford Insurance Company*, 168 Cal.App.3d 930, 214 Cal.Rptr. 567, **Web** 1985 Cal.App. Lexis 2153 (Court of Appeal of California)

BUSINESS ETHICS CASES

50.8 Business Ethics Lewis Coe bought a $500,000 life insurance policy from Farmers New World Life Insurance Company (Farmers) from its authorized agent, Hannify. The policy, which was payable in monthly installments, contained a clause allowing for the insurance to remain in effect for a 31-day grace period if the insured failed to pay a premium by the due date. In February of the following year, Lewis informed Hannify that he wanted to cancel the policy. Farmers sent Lewis a cancellation form, which he signed and returned on or about March 1. At the time Farmers received the written cancellation notice, Lewis had paid the monthly premium for February, covering the period ending March 10. Lewis died April 8. His widow sued Farmers for the policy proceeds, claiming that Lewis died during the 31-day grace period provided by the policy. Farmers claimed that the policy had been canceled and the grace period did not apply. Who wins? Did either party act unethically in this case? *Coe v. Farmers New World Life Insurance Company*, 209 Cal.App.3d 600, 257 Cal.Rptr. 411, **Web** 1989 Cal.App. Lexis 328 (Court of Appeal of California)

50.9 Business Ethics A federal regulation adopted pursuant to the Resource Conservation and Discovery Act required certain manufacturers to insure against pollution hazards. Advanced Micro Devices, Inc. (AMD), a company covered by the regulation, purchased the required insurance from Great American Surplus Lines Insurance Company (Great American). Before issuing the policy, Great American asked AMD to disclose any preexisting conditions that could give rise to a claim. AMD warranted that there were none. AMD made this statement despite the existence of a prior company memorandum written by AMD's environmental supervisor. The memo warned that toxic waste was escaping from an underground steel tank in AMD's acid neutralization system "C" and that AMD was "far from being in compliance" with environmental laws. Great American issued the insurance policy. One year later, the government ordered AMD to undertake a $1.5 million cleanup of the toxic contaminants surrounding the steel tank in system "C." AMD filed a claim for this amount with Great American, which refused to pay. AMD sued. Who wins? Did AMD's management act ethically in this case? *Advanced Micro Devices, Inc. v. Great American Surplus Lines Insurance Company*, 199 Cal.App.3d 791, 245 Cal.Rptr. 44, **Web** 1988 Cal.App. Lexis 226 (Court of Appeal of California)

ENDNOTE

1. 5 U.S.C. Sections 1011–1015.

▲ **Wall Street** *This is Wall Street, which is located in Manhattan, New York City. The street received its name because it was the location of a wall built in the 1600s by the Dutch for protection. The wall was later taken down, but the name "Wall Street" was attached to the street located where the wall once stood. Today, the name "Wall Street" is synonymous with securities trading. The New York Stock Exchange, NASDAQ, and other stock markets and exchanges are located on Wall Street and in the financial district surrounding Wall Street. Public accountants audit the firms listed on these exchanges.*

CHAPTER OBJECTIVES

After studying this chapter, you should be able to:

1. Describe an accountant's liability to his or her client for breach of contract and fraud.
2. Describe an accountant's liability to third parties under the *Ultramares* doctrine.
3. Describe an accountant's liability to third parties under the *Restatement (Second) of Torts* and the foreseeability standard.
4. Describe an accountant's civil liability and criminal liability under federal securities laws.
5. Describe the duties of accountants under the Sarbanes-Oxley Act.

CHAPTER CONTENTS

▶ **INTRODUCTION TO ACCOUNTANTS' LIABILITY**
▶ **PUBLIC ACCOUNTING**

Contemporary Environment · *Auditor's Opinions*
▶ **LIMITED LIABILITY PARTNERSHIP (LLP)**

> **"In our complex society the accountant's certificate and the lawyer's opinion can be instruments for inflicting pecuniary loss more potent than the chisel or the crowbar."**
>
> —Justice Blackman
> *Dissenting Opinion, Ernst & Ernst v. Hochfelder, (1976)*

▶ INTRODUCTION TO ACCOUNTANTS' LIABILITY

Although accountants provide a wide variety of services to corporations and other businesses, their primary functions are (1) auditing financial statements and (2) rendering opinions about those audits. Accountants also prepare unaudited financial statements for clients, render tax advice, prepare tax forms, and provide consulting and other services to clients.

Audits generate the majority of litigation against accountants. Lawsuits against accountants are based on the common law (e.g., breach of contract, misrepresentation, negligence) or on violation of certain statutes (particularly federal securities laws). Accountants can be held liable both to clients and to third parties. This chapter examines the legal liability of accountants.

▶ PUBLIC ACCOUNTING

The term **accountant** applies to persons who perform a variety of services, including bookkeepers, tax preparers, and so on. The term **certified public accountant (CPA)** applies to accountants who meet certain educational requirements, pass the CPA examination, and have a certain number of years of auditing experience. A person who is not certified is generally referred to as a **public accountant**.

Accounting Standards and Principles

certified public accountant (CPA)
An accountant who has met certain educational requirements, has passed the CPA examination, and has had a certain number of years of auditing experience.

generally accepted accounting principles (GAAPs)
Standards for the preparation and presentation of financial statements.

Certified public accountants must comply with two uniform standards of professional conduct. They are (1) **generally accepted accounting principles (GAAPs)**, which are standards for the preparation and presentation of financial statements,[1] and (2) **generally accepted auditing standards (GAASs)**, which specify the methods and procedures that must be used to conduct audits.[2]

Audits

generally accepted auditing standards (GAASs)
Standards for the methods and procedures that must be used to conduct audits.

audit
A verification of a company's books and records pursuant to federal securities laws, state laws, and stock exchange rules that must be performed by an independent CPA.

Audit can be defined as a verification of a company's books and records. Pursuant to federal securities laws, state laws, and stock exchange rules, an audit must be performed by an independent CPA. The CPA must review the company's financial records, check their accuracy, and otherwise investigate the financial position of the company.

The auditor must also (1) conduct a sampling of inventory to verify the figures contained in the client's financial statements and (2) verify information from third parties (e.g., contracts, bank accounts, real estate, accounts receivable). An accountant's failure to follow GAASs when conducting audits constitutes negligence.

CONTEMPORARY ENVIRONMENT

Auditor's Opinions

After an audit is complete, the auditor must render an *opinion* about how fairly the financial statements of the client company represent the company's financial position, results of operations, and change in cash flows. The **auditor's opinion** may be unqualified, qualified, or adverse. Alternatively, the auditor may offer a disclaimer of opinion. Most auditors give unqualified opinions. The various types of opinions are described in the following paragraphs.

Unqualified Opinion

An **unqualified opinion** represents an auditor's finding that the company's financial statements fairly represent the company's financial position, the results of its operations, and the change in cash flows for the period under audit, in conformity with generally accepted accounting principles (GAAPs). This is the most favorable opinion an auditor can give.

Qualified Opinion

A **qualified opinion** states that the financial statements are fairly represented except for, or subject to, a departure from GAAPs, a change in accounting principles, or a material uncertainty. The exception, departure, or uncertainty is noted in the auditor's opinion.

Adverse Opinion

An **adverse opinion** determines that the financial statements do not fairly represent the company's financial position, results of operations, or change in cash flows in conformity with GAAPs. This type of opinion is usually issued when an auditor determines that a company has materially misstated certain items on its financial statements.

Disclaimer of Opinion

A **disclaimer of opinion** expresses the auditor's inability to draw a conclusion about the accuracy of the company's financial records. This opinion is generally issued when the auditor lacks sufficient information about the financial records to issue an overall opinion.

The issuance of other than an *unqualified opinion* can have substantial adverse effects on the company audited.

Examples A company that receives an opinion other than an unqualified opinion may not be able to sell its securities to the public, merge with another company, or obtain loans from banks. The Securities and Exchange Commission (SEC) has warned publicly held companies against "shopping" for a favorable opinion.

► LIMITED LIABILITY PARTNERSHIP (LLP)

Most public accounting firms are organized and operated as **limited liability partnerships (LLPs)**. In this form of partnership, all the partners are limited partners who lose only their capital contribution in the LLP if the LLP fails. The limited partners are not personally liable for the debts and obligations of the LLP (see Exhibit 51.1). A limited partner whose negligent or intentional conduct causes injury is personally liable for his or her own conduct.

auditor's opinion
An opinion of an auditor about how fairly the financial statements of the client company represent the company's financial position, results of operations, and change in cash flows.

► **Exhibit 51.1**
ACCOUNTING FIRM LLP

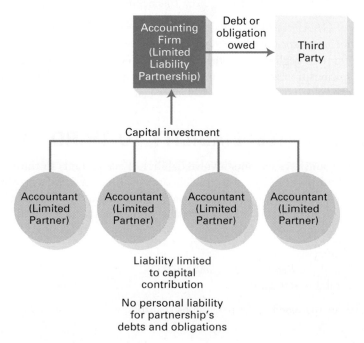

limited liability partnership (LLP)
A special form of partnership in which all partners are limited partners.

▶ ACCOUNTANTS' LIABILITY TO THEIR CLIENTS

Accountants are employed by their clients to perform certain accounting services. Under the *common law*, accountants may be found liable to the clients who hire them under several legal theories, including breach of contract, fraud, and negligence.

Breach of Contract

engagement
A formal entrance into a contract between a client and an accountant.

The terms of an **engagement** are specified when an accountant and a client enter into a contract. An accountant who fails to perform may be sued for damages caused by the **breach of contract**. Generally, the courts consider damages to be the expenses the client incurs in securing another accountant to perform the needed services as well as any fines or penalties incurred by the client for missed deadlines, lost opportunities, and such.

Fraud

Where an accountant has been found liable for actual or constructive **fraud**, the client may bring a civil lawsuit and recover any damages proximately caused by that fraud. Punitive damages may be awarded in cases of actual fraud. **Actual fraud** is defined as intentional misrepresentation or omission of a material fact that is relied on by the client and causes the client damage. Such cases are rare. **Constructive fraud** occurs when an accountant acts with "reckless disregard" for the truth or the consequences of his or her actions. This type of fraud is sometimes categorized as *gross negligence*.

Negligence

negligence
Negligence in which the accountant breaches the duty of reasonable care, knowledge, skill, and judgment that he or she owes to a client when providing auditing and other accounting services to the client. Also known as *accountant malpractice*.

Accountants owe a duty to use *reasonable care*, *knowledge*, *skill*, and *judgment* when providing auditing and other accounting services to a client. In other words, an accountant's actions are measured against those of a "reasonable accountant" in similar circumstances. The development of GAAPs, GAASs, and other uniform accounting standards has generally made this a national standard.

An accountant who fails to meet this standard may be sued for **negligence** (also called **accountant malpractice**).

Example An accountant who does not comply with GAASs when conducting an audit and thereby fails to uncover a fraud or embezzlement by an employee of the company being audited can be sued for damages arising from this negligence.

Violations of GAAPs or GAASs are *prima facie* evidence of negligence, although compliance does not automatically relieve the accountant of such liability. Accountants can also be held liable for their negligence in preparing **unaudited financial statements**. If an audit turns up a suspicious transaction or entry, the accountant is under a duty to investigate it and to inform the client of the results of the investigation.

▶ ACCOUNTANTS' LIABILITY TO THIRD PARTIES

Many lawsuits against accountants involve liability of accountants to third parties. The plaintiffs are third parties (e.g., shareholders and bondholders, trade creditors, banks) who relied on information supplied by the auditor. There are three major rules of liability that a state can adopt in determining whether an accountant is liable in negligence to third parties:

1. The *Ultramares* doctrine
2. Section 552 of the *Restatement (Second) of Torts*
3. The foreseeability standard

These rules are discussed in the paragraphs that follow.

The *Ultramares* Doctrine

The landmark case that initially defined the liability of accountants to third parties was *Ultramares Corporation v. Touche*[3] In that case, Touche Niven & Co. (Touche), a national firm of certified public accountants, was employed by Fred Stern & Co. (Stern), to conduct an audit of the company's financial statements. Touche was negligent in conducting the audit and did not uncover over $700,000 of accounts receivable that were based on fictitious sales and other suspicious activities. Touche rendered an unqualified opinion and provided 32 copies of the audited financial statements to Stern. Stern gave one copy to Ultramares Corporation (Ultramares). Ultramares made a loan to Stern on the basis of the information contained in the audited statements. When Stern failed to repay the loan, Ultramares brought a negligence action against Touche.

In his now-famous opinion, Judge Cardozo held that an accountant could not be held liable for negligence unless the plaintiff was in either *privity of contract* or a *privity-like relationship* with the accountant. Judge Cardozo wrote:

> *If liability for negligence exists, a thoughtless slip or blunder, the failure to detect a theft or forgery beneath the cover of deceptive entries may expose accountants to a liability in an indeterminate amount for an indeterminate time to an indeterminate class. The hazards of a business conducted on these terms are so extreme as to enkindle doubt whether a flaw may not exist in the implication of a duty that exposes to these consequences.*

For this purpose, a privity of contract relationship would occur in which a client employed an accountant to prepare financial statements to be used by a third party for a specific purpose. For example, if (1) a client employs an accountant to prepare audited financial statements to be used by the client to secure a bank loan and (2) the accountant is made aware of this special purpose, the accountant is liable for any damages incurred by the bank because of a negligently prepared report. The *Ultramares* **doctrine** remains the majority rule for accountants' liability for negligence in this country.

In the following case, the court reaffirmed the *Ultramares* doctrine and held accountants not liable to the third-party plaintiffs.

Ultramares doctrine
A rule which says that an accountant is liable only for negligence to third parties who are in *privity of contract* or in a *privity-like relationship* with the accountant. It provides a narrow standard for holding accountants liable to third parties for negligence.

CASE 51.1 *Ultramares* Doctrine

Credit Alliance Corporation v. Arthur Andersen & Co.

65 N.Y.2d 536, 493 N.Y.S.2d 435, Web 1985 N.Y. Lexis 15157 (1985)
Court of Appeals of New York

"The facts as alleged by plaintiffs fail to demonstrate the existence of a relationship between the parties sufficiently approaching privity."

—Judge Jasen

Facts

L.B. Smith, Inc., of Virginia (Smith) was a Virginia corporation engaged in the business of selling, leasing, and servicing heavy construction equipment. It was a capital-intensive business that regularly required debt financing. Arthur Andersen & Co. (Andersen), a large national firm of certified public accountants, was employed to audit Smith's financial statements. Andersen audited Smith's financial statements for two years. During that period of time, Andersen issued unqualified opinions concerning Smith's financial statements. Without Andersen's knowledge, Smith gave copies of its audited financial statements to Credit Alliance Corporation (Credit Alliance). Credit Alliance, in reliance on these financial statements, extended over $15 million of credit to Smith to finance the purchase of capital equipment through installment sales and leasing arrangements.

The audited financial statements overstated Smith's assets, net worth, and general financial position. In performing the audits, Andersen was negligent and failed to conduct investigations in accordance with generally accepted auditing standards. Because of this negligence, Andersen failed to discover Smith's precarious financial condition. The next year, Smith filed a petition for bankruptcy. Smith defaulted on obligations owed Credit

(case continues)

Alliance in an amount exceeding $8.8 million. Credit Alliance brought this action against Andersen for negligence. The trial court denied Andersen's motion to dismiss. The appellate division affirmed. Andersen appealed.

Issue

Is Andersen liable under the *Ultramares* doctrine?

Language of the Court

Upon examination of Ultramares, *certain criteria may be gleaned. Before accountants may be held liable in negligence to noncontractual parties who rely to their detriment on inaccurate financial reports, certain prerequisites must be satisfied, (1) the accountants must have been aware that the financial reports were to be used for a particular purpose or purposes, (2) in the furtherance of which a known party or parties was intended to rely, and (3) there must have been some conduct on the part of the accountants linking them to that party or parties, which evinces the accountants' understanding of that party or parties' reliance.*

In the appeal we decide today, application of the foregoing principles presents little difficulty. The facts as alleged by plaintiffs fail to demonstrate the existence of a relationship between the parties sufficiently approaching privity. While the allegations in the complaint state that Smith sought to induce plaintiffs to extend credit, no claim is made that Andersen was being employed to prepare the

reports with that particular purpose in mind. Moreover, there is no allegation that Andersen had any direct dealings with plaintiffs, had specifically agreed with Smith to prepare the report for plaintiffs' use or according to plaintiffs' requirements, or had specifically agreed with Smith to provide plaintiffs with a copy or actually did so. Indeed there is simply no allegation of any word or action on the part of Andersen directed to plaintiffs or anything contained in Andersen's retainer agreement with Smith that provided the necessary link between them.

Decision

The court of appeals held that the state should follow the *Ultramares* doctrine in examining the liability of accountants to third parties for negligence. The court reversed the lower court's decision and dismissed Credit Alliance's cause of action for negligence against defendant Andersen.

Case Questions

Critical Legal Thinking What does the *Ultramares* doctrine provide? Do you think this standard should be used for assessing accountants' liability?

Business Ethics Should an accountant's ethical duty parallel the *Ultramares* doctrine?

Contemporary Business Do you think accountants favor the *Ultramares* doctrine? Why or why not?

Section 552 of the *Restatement (Second) of* Torts

Section 552 of the *Restatement*
***(Second) of* Torts**
A rule which says that an accountant is liable only for negligence to third parties who are *members of a limited class of intended users* of the client's financial statements. It provides a broader standard for holding accountants liable to third parties for negligence than does the *Ultramares* doctrine.

Section 552 of the *Restatement (Second) of Torts* provides a broader standard for holding accountants liable to third parties for negligence than the *Ultramares* doctrine. Under the *Restatement* standard, an accountant is liable for his or her negligence to any member of *a limited class of intended users* for whose benefit the accountant has been employed to prepare the client's financial statements or to whom the accountant knows the client will supply copies of the financial statements. In other words, the accountant does not have to know the specific name of the third party. Many states have adopted this standard.

Example A client employs an accountant to prepare financial statements to be used to obtain investors for the company. The accountant is negligent in preparing these statements and overstates the company's earnings. If the company provides copies of the financial statements to potential investors, the accountant may be held liable to any investor who relies on the information in the financial statements, purchases securities in the company, and is injured thereby. This is so even though the accountant does not know the identity of these investors when the financial statements are prepared.

The Foreseeability Standard

foreseeability standard
A rule which says that an accountant is liable for negligence to third parties who are *foreseeable users* of the client's financial statements. It provides the broadest standard for holding accountants liable to third parties for negligence.

A few states have adopted a broad rule known as the **foreseeability standard** for holding accountants liable to third parties for negligence. Under this standard, an accountant is liable to any foreseeable user of the client's financial statements. The accountant's liability does not depend on his or her knowledge of the identity of either the user or the intended class of users.

Example A corporation makes a tender offer for the shares of a target corporation whose financial statements have been audited by a CPA. If the CPA negligently prepared the financial statements and the tender offeror relied on them to purchase the target corporation, the accountant is liable for injuries suffered by the tender offeror.

In the following case, the court had to decided whether accountants were liable to a third party.

CASE 51.2   Accountant's Liability

Johnson Bank v. George Korbakes & Company, LLP

472 F.3d 439, Web 2006 U.S. App. Lexis 31058 (2006)
United States Court of Appeals for the Seventh Circuit

"The audit report might flunk Accounting 101, but if the report didn't mislead anyone toward whom the auditor had a duty of care, the auditor would not have committed a tort."

—Judge Posner

Facts

Brandon Apparel Group, Inc. (Brandon), made and sold clothing and licensed the making and selling of clothing in exchange for a percentage of the licensees' sales revenues. Brandon began borrowing money from Johnson Bank and in two years owed the bank $10 million. George Korbakes & Company, LLP (GKCO) was the auditor of Brandon during the period at issue in this case. When Brandon was seeking an additional loan from the bank, Brandon instructed GKCO to give the bank the audit report that GKCO had just completed, which GKCO gave to Johnson Bank.

The audit report summarized Brandon's financial results for the year and revealed that Brandon had serious problems. But the audit report contained several errors. First, the audit report classified a $1 million lawsuit Brandon had brought against a third party as an asset, but it was in fact only a contingency that should not have been listed as an asset. Second, Brandon's sales were inflated by 50 percent because sales of a licensee were treated as if they were Brandon's sales. However, footnotes in the audit report indicated that Brandon might not prevail in the lawsuit and that Brandon's sales included those of a licensee.

After receiving the audit report, Johnson Bank made further loans to Brandon. Brandon did not repay Johnson Bank the new money it borrowed. Johnson Bank sued GKCO, alleging that GKCO committed the tort of negligent misrepresentation and was therefore liable for the money lost by the bank as a result of the errors in the audit report prepared by GKCO. The U.S. District Court entered judgment in GKCO's favor. Johnson Bank appealed.

Issue

Is GKCO, the auditor of Brandon, liable to Johnson Bank for negligent misrepresentation?

Language of the Court

The tort of negligent misrepresentation does not create liability for violating accounting conventions, as such; the elements of the tort must be present. In addition, under Illinois law an auditor is liable to a third party, that is, to someone different from the firm that hired it to audit its books, only if the auditor knew that the firm wanted to use the audit report to influence a third party. The audit report might flunk Accounting 101, but if the report didn't mislead anyone toward whom the auditor had a duty of care, the auditor would not have committed a tort.

At root the bank's argument for liability is that it was entitled to look no farther than the bottom-line numbers in the audit report. That is incorrect; it had no right to ignore the footnotes in the report, which together with the numbers in it gave the reader an accurate picture of Brandon's financial situation. The bank cannot base a claim for damages on a refusal to read. The audit report even says that "the notes on the accompanying pages are an integral part of these financial statements."

The bank imputes to GKCO a duty to advise it whether lending more money to this faltering firm (throwing good money after bad, as the saying goes) would make commercial sense. But an auditor's duty is not to give business advice; it is merely to paint an accurate picture of the audited firm's financial condition, insofar as that condition is revealed by the company's books and inventory and other sources of an auditor's opinion. An auditor who fulfills that duty, or fails but manages not to mislead the intended readers of the audit report, has no tort liability. Erroneous characterizations can mislead, but not when the facts mischaracterized are fully and accurately disclosed in the audit report, as they were here.

(case continues)

The district judge was right, moreover, to find that the bank did not rely on the mischaracterizations. It kept lending money to Brandon in the hope of keeping the firm from going broke and thus keeping alive the hope of eventual repayment. That decision—the cause of the bank's undoing—had nothing to do with the audit.

The losses the bank incurred as a result of the additional loans that it made could not be recovered as damages even if GKCO had been guilty of negligent misrepresentation. GKCO could not have predicted how much money the bank would lend to Brandon in reliance on the audit and with what consequences. Damages so speculative are not recoverable in a lawsuit.

Decision

The U.S. Court of Appeals held that GKCO, the auditor of Brandon, was not liable to Johnson Bank for negligent misrepresentation. The Court of Appeals upheld the District Court's judgment in favor of GKCO.

Case Questions

Critical Legal Thinking Which of the following three legal theories did the Court apply in making its decision in this case?

a. *Ultramares* doctrine
b. Section 552 of the *Restatement (Second) of Tort*
c. Foreseeability standard

Business Ethics Should GKCO have listed the lawsuit as a contingency rather than an asset? Was the footnote sufficient disclosure of this information? Should GKCO have included the licensee's sales in Brandon's sales? Was the footnote sufficient disclosure of this information?

Contemporary Business How could Johnson Bank have better protected itself rather than rely on the audited reports of Brandon Apparel that were prepared by GKCO?

CONCEPT SUMMARY

ACCOUNTANTS' NEGLIGENCE LIABILITY TO THIRD PARTIES

Legal Theory	To Whom Liable
Ultramares doctrine	Any person in *privity of contract* or a privity-like relationship with the accountant.
Section 552 of the *Restatement (Second) of* Torts	Any member of a *limited class* of intended users for whose benefit the accountant has been employed to prepare the client's financial statements or whom the accountant knows will be supplied copies of the client's financial statements.
Foreseeability standard	Any *foreseeable user* of the client's financial statements.

Fraud

Like a gun that fires at the muzzle and kicks over at the breach, a cheating transaction hurts the cheater as much as the man cheated.

Henry Ward Beecher
Proverbs from Plymouth Pulpit
(1887)

If an accountant engages in *actual* or *constructive fraud*, a third party who relies on the accountant's fraud and is injured thereby may bring a tort action against the accountant to recover damages.

Example Salvo Retailers, Inc. (Salvo), applies for a bank loan, but the bank requires audited financial statements of the company before making the loan. Salvo hires a CPA to do the audit, and the CPA falsifies the financial position of the company. The bank extends the loan to Salvo, and the loan is not repaid. The bank can recover its losses from the CPA who committed fraud.

Breach of Contract

privity of contract
The state of two specified parties being in a contract.

Third parties usually cannot sue accountants for breach of contract because the third parties are merely incidental beneficiaries who do not acquire any rights under the accountant–client contract. That is, they are not in **privity of contract** with the accountants.

Example An accountant contracts to perform an audit for Kim Manufacturing Company (Kim) but then fails to do so. A supplier to Kim cannot sue the accountant. This is because the supplier is not in privity of contract with the accountant.

ETHICS SPOTLIGHT

Accountant's Duty to Report Client's Illegal Activity

In the course of conducting an audit of a client company's financial statements, an accountant could uncover information about the client's illegal activities. In 1995, Congress added **Section 10A to the Securities Exchange Act of 1934** [15 U.S.C. Section 78j-1]. Section 10A imposes duties on auditors to detect and report illegal acts committed by their clients. Under Section 10A, an *illegal act* is defined as an "act or omission that violates any law, or any rule or regulation having the force of law." Section 10A imposes the following reporting requirements on accountants:

- Unless an illegal act is "clearly inconsequential," the auditor must inform the client's management and audit committee of the illegal act.
- If management fails to take timely and appropriate remedial action, the auditor must report the illegal act

to the client's full board of directors if (a) the illegal act will have a material effect on the client's financial statements and (b) the auditor expects to issue a nonstandard audit report or intends to resign from the audit engagement.
- Once the auditor reports the illegal act to the board of directors, the board of directors must inform the Securities and Exchange Commission (SEC) of the auditor's conclusion within one business day; if the client fails to do so, the auditor must notify the SEC the next business day.

Business Ethics Should accountants report illegal activities of their clients without the law requiring them to do so? Should accountants report unethical conduct of clients that is not considered illegal conduct? Why or why not?

▶ SECURITIES LAW VIOLATIONS

Accountants can be held liable for violating various federal and state securities laws. This section examines the civil and criminal liability of accountants under these statutes.

Section 11(a) of the Securities Act of 1933

The Securities Act of 1933 requires that before a corporation or another business sells securities to the public, the issuer must file a registration statement with the Securities and Exchange Commission (SEC). Accountants are often employed to prepare and certify financial statements that are included in the registration statements filed with the SEC. Accountants are considered experts, and the financial statements they prepare are considered an **expertised portion** of the registration statement.

Section 11(a) of the Securities Act of 1933 imposes civil liability on accountants and others for (1) making misstatements or omissions of material facts in a registration statement or (2) failing to find such misstatements or omissions.[4] Accountants can be held liable for fraud or negligence under Section 11(a) if the financial statements they prepare for a registration statement contain such errors.

Accountants can, however, assert a **due diligence defense** to liability. An accountant avoids liability if he or she had, after reasonable investigation, reasonable grounds to believe and did believe, at the time the registration statement became effective, that the statements made therein were true and there was no omission of a material fact that would make the statements misleading.

Example While conducting an audit, accountants fail to detect a fraud in the financial statements. The accountants' unqualified opinion is included in the registration statement and prospectus for the offering. An investor purchases the securities and suffers a loss when the fraud is uncovered. The investor can sue the makers of the misrepresentations for fraud and the accountants for negligence.

The plaintiff may recover the difference between the price he or she paid for the security and the value of the security at the time of the lawsuit (or at the time the security was sold, if it was sold prior to the lawsuit). The plaintiff does not have to prove that he or she relied on the misstatement or omission. Privity of contract is irrelevant.

Section 11(a)
A section of the Securities Act of 1933 that imposes civil liability on accountants and others for (1) making misstatements or omissions of material facts in a registration statement or (2) failing to find such misstatements or omissions.

Section 10(b) of the Securities Exchange Act of 1934

Section 10(b)
A section of the Securities Exchange Act of 1934 that prohibits any manipulative or deceptive practice in connection with the purchase or sale of a security.

Section 10(b) of the Securities Exchange Act of 1934 prohibits any manipulative or deceptive practice in connection with the purchase or sale of any security.[5] **Rule 10b-5** makes it unlawful for any person, by the use or means or instrumentality of interstate commerce, to employ any device or artifice to defraud; to make misstatements or omissions of material fact; or to engage in any act, practice, or course of conduct that would operate as a fraud or deceit upon any person in connection with the purchase or sale of any security.[6]

The scope of these antifraud provisions is quite broad, and the courts have implied a civil private cause of action. Thus, plaintiffs injured by a violation of these provisions can sue the offending party for monetary damages. Only purchasers and sellers of securities can sue under Section 10(b) and Rule 10b-5. Privity of contract is irrelevant.

Accountants are often defendants in Section 10(b) and Rule 10b-5 actions. The U.S. Supreme Court has decided that only intentional conduct and recklessness of accountants and others, but not ordinary negligence, violates Section 10(b) and Rule 10b-5.[7]

Section 18(a) of the Securities Exchange Act of 1934

Section 18(a)
A section of the Securities Exchange Act of 1934 that imposes civil liability on any person who makes false or misleading statements in any application, report, or document filed with the SEC.

Section 18(a) of the Securities Exchange Act of 1934 imposes civil liability on any person who makes false or misleading statements of material fact in any application, report, or document filed with the SEC.[8] Because accountants often file reports and other documents with the SEC on behalf of clients, they can be found liable for violating this section.

Like Section 10(b), Section 18(a) requires a showing of fraud or reckless conduct on the part of the defendant. Thus, the plaintiffs in a Section 18(a) action must prove that they relied on the misleading statement and that it affected the price of the security. Negligence is not actionable.

There are two ways an accountant or another defendant can defeat the imposition of liability under Section 18(a). First, the defendant can show that he or she acted in *good faith*. Second, he or she can show that the plaintiff had knowledge of the false or misleading statement when the securities were purchased or sold.

Private Securities Litigation Reform Act of 1995

Private Securities Litigation Reform Act of 1995
A federal statute that limits a defendant's liability to its proportionate degree of fault.

The **Private Securities Litigation Reform Act of 1995**, a federal statute, changed the liability of accountants and other securities professionals in the following ways:

- The act imposes pleading and procedural requirements that make it more difficult for plaintiffs to bring class action securities lawsuits.
- The act replaces **joint and several liability** of defendants (where one party of several at-fault parties could be made to pay all of a judgment) with **proportionate liability**. This new rule limits a defendant's liability to its *proportionate* degree of fault. Thus, the act relieves accountants from being the "deep pocket" defendant except up to their degree of fault. The only exception to this rule—where joint and several liability is still imposed—is if the defendant acted knowingly.[9]

Example Consider a case involving plaintiffs who are victims of a securities fraud perpetrated by a firm, and they suffer $1 million in damages. If the accountants for the firm are found to be 25 percent liable, the accountants are required to pay only their proportionate share in damages—$250,000. If the accountants knowingly participated in the fraud, they would be jointly and severally liable for the entire $1 million in damages, however.

 **ETHICS SPOTLIGHT**

U.S. Supreme Court Finds Aiders and Abettors Not Liable

"There is no private right of action for aiding and abetting a Section 10(b) violation."
—Justice Kennedy

Are parties that **aid and abet** a securities fraud liable under Section 10(b) of the Securities Exchange Act of 1934? That question had been answered with mixed results by U.S. Courts of Appeal, so the U.S. Supreme Court chose to decide the issue. It did so in the case ***Stoneridge Investment Partners, LLC v. Scientific-Atlanta, Inc.*** The facts of that case and the decision of the U.S. Supreme Court follow.

Charter Communications, Inc. (Charter), fraudulently issued financial statements that affected the value of its securities. Charter was a cable operator that provided cable service to subscribers. Charter wanted to show increased subscriber growth and cash flow. To do so, Charter obtained the knowing assistance of two companies, Scientific-Atlanta, Inc. (Scientific), and Motorola, Inc. Scientific and Motorola supplied Charter with digital cable converters—set-top boxes—that Charter's cable subscribers needed to receive cable service.

Charter entered into a fraudulent arrangement with Scientific and Motorola whereby Charter would overpay $20 for each box it purchased from Scientific and Motorola. Charter would then capitalize these payments over years rather than expense them during the current year. In addition, the parties agreed that Scientific and Motorola would repay the overpayments by purchasing advertising from Charter at higher prices than fair value. This two-part fraudulent scheme would increase Charter's revenues and profits for the year. Charter was the primary fraudulent party, and Scientific and Motorola were aiders and abettors to Charter's fraud.

Charter gave its fraudulent financial statements to its outside auditor, Arthur Andersen LLP (Andersen), to audit. During its audit of the financial statements, Andersen was fooled and did not discover Charter's fraud. Andersen certified Charter's financial statements, which Charter filed with the Securities and Exchange Commission (SEC) and made public. The fraud was discovered, and the price of Charter's stock plummeted.

Stoneridge Investment Partners, LLC, which owned stock in Charter, brought a class action civil lawsuit against Scientific and Motorola on behalf of itself and other Charter shareholders (collectively Stoneridge). Stoneridge relied on the ability to bring its civil action on the implied private cause of action under Section 10(b) that previous U.S. Supreme Court decisions had created. The lawsuit alleged that Scientific and Motorola—the aiders and abettors to Charter's fraud—violated Section 10(b) and Rule 10b-5 and were liable to the plaintiffs for monetary damages. The U.S. Supreme Court said no and held that there was no implied civil cause of action against aiders and abettors under Section 10(b). In its decision, the U.S. Supreme Court stated:

We conclude the implied right of action does not reach the customer/supplier companies because the investors did not rely upon their statements or

representations. At most, respondents had aided and abetted Charter's misstatement of its financial results; but, there is no private right of action for aiding and abetting a Section 10(b) violation. The Section 10(b) implied private right of action does not extend to aiders and abettors. Concerns with the judicial creation of a private cause of action caution against its expansion. The decision to extend the cause of action is for Congress, not for us. Though it remains the law, the Section 10(b) private right should not be extended beyond its present boundaries.

The U.S. Supreme Court held that there was no implied civil private right of action under Section 10(b) against aiders and abettors of securities fraud. *Stoneridge Investment Partners, LLC v. Scientific-Atlanta, Inc.*, 128 S.Ct. 761, 169 L.Ed.2d 627, **Web** 2008 U.S. Lexis 1091 (Supreme Court of the United States)

Application to Auditors

Although the *Stoneridge* case did not involve public accountants, the case has important implications for auditors. If an auditor (here, Andersen) aids and abets a primary party's securities fraud (here, Charter), the auditor would stand in the same shoes as other aiders and abettors (here, Scientific and Motorola) and not be civilly liable because the U.S. Supreme Court's decision in this case eliminated an implied civil right of action against aiders and abettors under Section 10(b). However, an injured party (here, Stoneridge) could bring a civil common law action in state court against an auditor (here, Andersen) for negligence for not discovering the fraud.

Although the U.S. Supreme Court held that there was no implied private cause of action under Section 10(b) against aiders and abettors (here, Scientific and Motorola), it did not disturb the implied right of plaintiffs to bring private civil actions against the primary party who commits the securities fraud (here, Charter). Therefore, Stoneridge would have an implied civil cause of action against Charter to recover monetary damages for securities fraud in violation of Section 10(b).

Under the *express* right of action provided in Section 10(b), the Securities Exchange Commission (SEC) can bring civil cases against aiders and abettors, and the U.S. government can bring criminal charges against aiders and abettors. An injured party (here, Stoneridge) can bring a civil common law fraud action in state court against aiders and abettors (here, Scientific and Motorola) to recover monetary damages.

Business Ethics Did Charter act ethically in this case? Why do think Scientific and Motorola participated in Charter's fraud?

▶ CRIMINAL LIABILITY OF ACCOUNTANTS

Many statutes impose criminal penalties on accountants who violate their provisions. These criminal statutes are discussed in the following paragraphs.

Section 24 of the Securities Act of 1933

Section 24
A section of the Securities Act of 1933 that makes it a criminal offense for any person to (1) willfully make any untrue statement of material fact in a registration statement filed with the SEC, (2) omit any material fact necessary to ensure that the statements made in the registration statement are not misleading, or (3) willfully violate any other provision of the Securities Act of 1933 or rule or regulation adopted thereunder.

Section 24 of the Securities Act of 1933 makes it a criminal offense for any person to (1) willfully make any untrue statement of material fact in a registration statement filed with the SEC, (2) omit any material fact necessary to ensure that the statements made in the registration statement are not misleading, or (3) willfully violate any other provision of the Securities Act of 1933 or rule or regulation adopted thereunder. Because accountants prepare the financial reports included in the registration statements, they are subject to criminal liability for violating this section. Penalties for a violation of this statute include fines, imprisonment, or both.[10]

Section 32(a) of the Securities Exchange Act of 1934

Section 32(a)
A section of the Securities Exchange Act of 1934 that makes it a criminal offense for any person willfully and knowingly to make or cause to be made any false or misleading statement in any application, report, or other document required to be filed with the SEC pursuant to the Securities Exchange Act of 1934 or any rule or regulation adopted thereunder.

Section 32(a) of the Securities Exchange Act of 1934 makes it a criminal offense for any person willfully and knowingly to make or cause to be made any false or misleading statement in any application, report, or other document required to be filed with the SEC pursuant to the Securities Exchange Act of 1934 or any rule or regulation adopted thereunder. Because accountants often file reports and documents with the SEC on behalf of clients, they are subject to this rule. Insider trading also falls within the parameters of this section.

Upon conviction under Section 32(a), an individual may be fined, imprisoned, or both. A corporation or another entity may be fined. A person cannot be imprisoned under Section 32(a) unless he or she had knowledge of the rule or regulation violated.[11]

If the SEC finds evidence of fraud or other willful violation of federal securities laws, or other federal law (e.g., mail and wire fraud statutes), the matter may be referred to the U.S. Department of Justice, with a recommendation that the suspected offending party be criminally prosecuted. The Department of Justice determines whether criminal charges will be brought.

Tax Reform Act of 1976

Tax Reform Act of 1976
An act that imposes criminal liability on accountants and others who prepare federal tax returns if they (1) willfully understate a client's tax liability, (2) negligently understate the tax liability, or (3) aid or assist in the preparation of a false tax return.

The **Tax Reform Act of 1976** imposes criminal liability on accountants and others who prepare federal tax returns and commit wrongdoings.[12] The act specifically imposes the following penalties: (1) fines for the willful understatement of a client's tax liability, (2) fines for the negligent understatement of a client's tax liability, and (3) fines and imprisonment for an individual and imprisonment and fines for a corporation for aiding and assisting in the preparation of a false tax return. Accountants who have violated these provisions can be enjoined from further federal income tax practice.

Racketeer Influenced and Corrupt Organizations Act (RICO)

Racketeer Influenced and Corrupt Organizations Act (RICO)
A federal act that provides for both criminal and civil penalties for securities fraud.

Accountants and other professionals can be named as defendants in lawsuits that assert violations of the **Racketeer Influenced and Corrupt Organizations Act (RICO)**.[13] Because securities fraud falls under the definition of racketeering activity, the government often brings a RICO allegation in conjunction with a securities fraud allegation.

Persons injured by a RICO violation can bring a private *civil* action against the violator and recover treble (triple) damages. But to bring a private civil RICO action based on securities fraud, the defendant has to have first been criminally convicted in connection with the securities fraud.[14] A third-party independent contractor (e.g., an outside accountant) must have participated in the operation or management of the enterprise to be liable for civil RICO.[15]

State Securities Laws

Most states have enacted securities laws, many of which are patterned after federal securities laws. State securities laws provide for a variety of civil and criminal penalties for violations of these laws. Many states have enacted all or part of the **Uniform Securities Act**, a model act promulgated by the National Conference of Commissioners on Uniform State Laws. *Section 101* of this act makes it a criminal offense for accountants and others to willfully falsify financial statements and other reports.

PCAOB®

▶ SARBANES-OXLEY ACT

During the late 1990s and early 2000s, many corporations in the United States engaged in fraudulent accounting in order to report inflated earnings or to conceal losses. Many public accounting firms that were hired to audit the financial statements of these companies failed to detect fradulent accounting practices.

In response, Congress enacted the federal **Sarbanes-Oxley Act of 2002**.[16] Sometimes called **SOX** or **SarBox**, this act imposes new rules that affect public accountants. The goals of these rules are to improve financial reporting, eliminate conflicts of interest, and provide government oversight of accounting and audit services. Several major features of the act are:

- **Established the Public Company Accounting Oversight Board.** The act creates the Public Company Accounting Oversight Board, which consists of five financially literate members who are appointed by the SEC for five-year terms. Two of the members must be CPAs, and three must not be CPAs. The SEC has oversight and enforcement authority over the board. The board has the authority to adopt rules concerning auditing, accounting quality control, independence, and ethics of public companies and public accountants.
- **Requires public accounting firms to register with the Public Company Accounting Oversight Board.** In order to audit a public company, a public accounting firm must register with the board. Registered accounting firms that audit more than 100 public companies annually are subject to inspection and review by the board once a year; all other public accounting firms must be audited by the board every three years. The board may discipline public accountants and accounting firms and order sanctions for intentional or reckless conduct, including suspending or revoking registration with the board, placing temporary limitations on activities, and assessing civil money penalties.
- **Separates audit and nonaudit services.** The act makes it unlawful for a registered public accounting firm to simultaneously provide audit and certain nonaudit services to a public company. If a public accounting firm audits a public company, the accounting firm may not provide the following nonaudit services to the client: (1) bookkeeping services; (2) financial information systems; (3) appraisal or valuation services; (4) internal audit services; (5) management functions; (6) human resources services; (7) broker, dealer, or investment services; (8) investment banking services; (9) legal services; or (10) any other services the board determines. A certified public accounting firm may provide tax services to audit clients if such tax services are preapproved by the audit committee of the client.
- **Requires audit report sign-offs.** Each audit by a certified public accounting firm is assigned an audit partner of the firm to supervise the audit and approve the audit report. The act requires that a second partner of the accounting firm review and approve audit reports prepared by the firm. All audit papers must be retained for at least seven years. The lead audit partner and reviewing partner must rotate off an audit every five years.
- **Prohibits certain employment.** Any person who is employed by a public accounting firm that audits a client cannot be employed by that client as the chief executive officer (CEO), chief financial officer (CFO), controller, chief accounting officer, or equivalent position for a period of one year following the audit.

Sarbanes-Oxley Act
A federal act that imposes new rules that affect public accountants. The act:
· Created the Public Company Accounting Oversight Board (PCAOB)
· Requires public accounting firms to register with the PCAOB
· Separates audit services and certain nonaudit services provided by accountants to clients
· Requires an audit partner of the accounting firm to supervise an audit and approve an audit report prepared by the firm and requires a second partner of the accounting firm to review and approve the audit report
· Prohibits employment of an accountant by a previous audit client for certain positions for a period of one year following the audit.

By certifying the public reports that collectively depict a corporation's financial status, the independent auditor assumes a public responsibility transcending any employment relationship with the client.

Justice Burger
United States v. Arthur Young & Co. (1984)

accountant–client privilege
A state statute which provides that an accountant cannot be called as a witness against a client in a court action.

► ACCOUNTANT'S PRIVILEGE AND WORK PAPERS

In the course of conducting audits and providing other services to clients, accountants obtain information about their clients and prepare work papers. Sometimes clients are sued in court, and the court seeks information about the client from the accountant. The following paragraphs discuss the law that applies to these matters.

Accountant–Client Privilege

Sometimes clients of accountants are sued in court. About 20 states have enacted statues that create an **accountant–client privilege**. In these states, an accountant cannot be called as a witness against a client in a court action. The majority of the states follow the common law, which provides that an accountant may be called at court to testify against his or her client.

The U.S. Supreme Court has held that there is no accountant–client privilege under federal law.[17] Thus, an accountant could be called as a witness in cases involving federal securities laws, federal mail or wire fraud, federal RICO, or other federal criminal statutes.

Accountants' Work Papers

Accountants often generate substantial internal *work papers* as they perform their services. These papers often include plans for conducting audits, work assignments, notes regarding the collection of data, evidence about the testing of accounts, notes concerning the client's internal controls, notes reconciling the accountant's report and the client's records, research, comments, memorandums, explanations, opinions, information regarding the affairs of the client, and so on.

work product immunity
A state statute which provides that an accountant's work papers cannot be used against a client in a court action.

Some state statutes provide **work product immunity**, which means an **accountant's work papers** cannot be discovered in a court case against the accountant's client. Most states do not provide this protection, and an accountant's work papers can be discovered. Federal law allows for discovery of an accountant's work papers in a federal case against the accountant's client.

TEST REVIEW TERMS AND CONCEPTS

Accountant
Accountant–client
  privilege
Accountant's work papers
Actual fraud
Adverse opinion
Aid and abet
Audit
Auditor's opinion
Breach of contract
Certified public accountant
  (CPA)
Constructive fraud
Disclaimer of opinion
Due diligence defense
Engagement
Expertised portion
Foreseeability standard
Fraud

Generally accepted
  accounting principles
  (GAAPs)
Generally accepted auditing
  standards (GAASs)
Joint and several liability
Limited liability partnership
  (LLP)
Negligence (accountant
  malpractice)
Private Securities Litigation
  Reform Act of 1995
Privity of contract
Proportionate liability
Public accountant
Qualified opinion
Racketeer Influenced and
  Corrupt Organizations
  Act (RICO)

Rule 10b-5
Sarbanes-Oxley Act of
  2002 (SOX or SarBox)
Section 10A of the
  Securities Exchange Act
  of 1934
Section 10(b) of the
  Securities Exchange Act
  of 1934
Section 11(a) of the
  Securities Act of 1933
Section 18(a) of the
  Securities Exchange Act
  of 1934
Section 24 of the Securities
  Act of 1933
Section 32(a) of the
  Securities Exchange Act
  of 1934

Section 552 of the
  *Restatement (Second) of
  Torts*
*Stoneridge Investment
  Partners, LLC v.
  Scientific-Atlanta, Inc.*
Tax Reform Act of 1976
Uniform Securities Act
*Ultramares Corporation v.
  Touche*
Ultramares doctrine
Unaudited financial
  statements
Unqualified opinion
Work product immunity

CASE PROBLEMS

51.1 Audit Opinion Stephens Industries, Inc. (Stephens), agreed to purchase the stock of Colorado Rent-A-Car, Inc. (Rent-A-Car), subject to an audit of the car rental company by Haskins and Sells (Haskins & Sells), a national accounting and CPA firm. When Haskins & Sells conducted the audit, it found that the accounts receivable records were so poorly maintained that the figures could not be reconciled. Haskins & Sells issued a qualified opinion which clearly stated that the account receivable had not been audited. The purchase agreement between Stephens and Rent-A-Car stated that the accounts receivable had not been adjusted to reflect the fact that they could not be collected. Stephens later sued Haskins & Sells regarding the audit of accounts receivable. Does the qualified opinion protect the accountants from liability? *Stephens Industries, Inc. v. Haskins and Sells*, 438 F.2d 357, **Web** 1971 U.S. App. Lexis 11628 (United States Court of Appeals for the Tenth Circuit)

51.2 Auditor's Liability to Third Party Michael H. Clott was chairman and chief executive officer of First American Mortgage Company, Inc. (FAMCO), which originated loans and sold them to investors, including E. F. Hutton Mortgage Corp. (Hutton). FAMCO employed Ernst & Whinney, a national CPA firm, to conduct audits of its financial statements. Hutton received a copy of the financial statements with an unqualified certification by Ernst & Whinney. Hutton bought more than $100 million of loans from FAMCO. As a result of massive fraudulent activity by Clott, which was undetected by Ernst & Whinney during its audit, many of the loans purchased by Hutton proved to be worthless. Ernst & Whinney had no knowledge of Clott's activities. Hutton's own negligence contributed to most of the losses it suffered. Hutton sued Ernst & Whinney for fraud and negligence. Is Ernst & Whinney liable? *E. F. Hutton Mortgage Corporation v. Pappas*, 690 F.Supp. 1465, **Web** 1988 U.S. Dist. Lexis 6444 (United States District Court for the District of Maryland)

51.3 Auditor's Liability Guarente-Harrington Associates was a limited partnership formed for the purpose of investing in securities. There were 2 general partners and 40 limited partners. The partnership agreement provided that no partner could withdraw any part of his or her interest in the partnership except at the end of the fiscal year and with not less than 30 days' prior notice. Arthur Andersen & Co. (Arthur Andersen), a national CPA firm, was hired to audit the books of the limited partnership. In certifying the financial statements of the partnership and preparing its tax returns, Arthur Andersen failed to report that the general partners had withdrawn $2 million of their $2.6 million capital investment at times other than at the end of the fiscal year and without proper notice. The partnership suffered losses because of this lack of capital. Shelby White, a limited partner, sued Arthur Andersen for accounting malpractice. Is Arthur Andersen liable under the *Ultramares* doctrine? *White v. Guarente*, 43 N.Y.2d 356, 372 N.E.2d 315, 401 N.Y.S.2d 474, **Web** 1977 N.Y. Lexis 2470 (Court of Appeals of New York)

51.4 Accountant's Liability to Third Party Giant Stores Corporation (Giant) hired Touche Ross & Co. (Touche), a national CPA firm, to conduct audits of the company's financial statements for two years. Touche gave an unqualified opinion for both years. Touche was unaware of any specific use of the audited statements by Giant. After receiving copies of these audited financial statements from Giant, Harry and Barry Rosenblum (Rosenblums) sold their retail catalog showroom business to Giant in exchange for 80,000 shares of Giant stock.

One year later, a major fraud was uncovered at Giant that caused its bankruptcy. Because of the bankruptcy, the stock that the Rosenblums received became worthless. In conducting Giant's audits, Touche had failed to uncover that Giant did not own certain assets that appeared on its financial statements and that Giant had omitted substantial amounts of accounts payable from its records. The Rosenblums sued Touche for accounting malpractice. Is Touche liable for accounting malpractice under any of the three negligence theories discussed in this chapter? *H. Rosenblum, Inc. v. Adler*, 93 N.J. 324, 461 A.2d 138, **Web** 1983 N.J. Lexis 2717 (Supreme Court of New Jersey)

51.5 *Ultramares* Doctrine Texscan Corporation (Texscan) was a corporation located in Phoenix, Arizona. The company was audited by Coopers & Lybrand (Coopers), a national CPA firm that prepared audited financial statements for the company. The Lindner Fund, Inc., and the Lindner Dividend Fund, Inc. (Lindner Funds), were mutual funds that invested in securities of companies. After receiving and reviewing the audited financial statements of Texscan, Lindner Funds purchased securities in the company. Thereafter, Texscan suffered financial difficulties, and Lindner Funds suffered substantial losses on its investment. Lindner Funds sued Coopers, alleging that Coopers was negligent in conducting the audit and preparing Texscan's financial statements. Can Coopers be held liable to Lindner Funds for accounting malpractice under the *Ultramares* doctrine, Section 552 of the *Restatement (Second) of Torts*, or the foreseeability standard? *Lindner Fund v. Abney*, 770 S.W.2d 437, **Web** 1989 Mo.App. Lexis 490 (Court of Appeals of Missouri)

51.6 Section 10(b) The Firestone Group, Ltd. (Firestone), a company engaged in real estate development, entered into a contract to sell nursing homes it owned to a buyer. The buyer paid a $30,000 deposit to Firestone and promised to pay the remainder of the $28 million purchase price in the future. The profit on the sale, if consummated, would have been $2 million.

To raise capital, Firestone planned on issuing $7.5 million of securities to investors. Firestone hired Laventhol, Krekstein, Horwath & Horwath (Laventhol), a national CPA firm, to audit the company for the fiscal year. When Laventhol proposed to record the profit from the sale of the nursing homes as unrealized gross profit, Firestone threatened to withdraw its account from Laventhol. Thereafter, Laventhol decided to recognize $235,000 as profit and to record the balance of $1,795,000 as "deferred gross profit." This was done even though, during the course of the audit, Laventhol learned that there was no corporate resolution approving the sale, the sale transaction was not recorded in the minutes of the corporation, and the buyer had a net worth of only $10,000. Laventhol also failed to verify the enforceability of the contracts.

Gerald M. Herzfeld and other investors received copies of the audited financial statements and invested in the securities issued by Firestone. Later, when the buyer did not purchase the nursing homes, Firestone declared bankruptcy. Herzfeld and the other investors lost most of their investment. Herzfeld sued Laventhol for securities fraud, in violation of Section 10(b) of the Securities Exchange Act of 1934. Is Laventhol liable? *Herzfeld v. Laventhol, Krekstein, Horwath & Horwath*, 540 F.2d 27, **Web** 1976 U.S. App. Lexis 8008 (United States Court of Appeals for the Second Circuit)

51.7 Accountant–Client Privilege For five years, Chaple, an accountant licensed by the state of Georgia, provided accounting services to Roberts and several corporations in which Roberts was an officer and shareholder (collectively called Roberts). During this period, Roberts provided Chaple with confidential information, with the expectation that this information would not be disclosed to third parties. Georgia statutes provide for an accountant–client privilege. When the IRS began investigating Roberts, Chaple, voluntarily and without being subject to a subpoena, released some of this confidential information about Roberts to the IRS. Roberts sued Chaple, seeking an injunction to prevent further disclosure, requesting return of all information in Chaple's possession, and seeking monetary damages. Who wins? *Roberts v. Chaple*, 187 Ga.App. 123, 369 S.E.2d 482, **Web** 1988 Ga.App. Lexis 554 (Court of Appeals of Georgia)

BUSINESS ETHICS CASES

51.8 Business Ethics The archdiocese of Miami established a health and welfare plan to provide medical coverage for its employees. The archdiocese purchased a stop-loss insurance policy from Lloyd's of London (Lloyd's), which provided insurance against losses that exceeded the basic coverage of the plan. The archdiocese employed Coopers & Lybrand (Coopers), a national firm of CPAs, to audit the health plan every year for 12 years.

The audit program required Coopers to obtain a copy of the current stop-loss policy and record any changes. After 2 years, Coopers neither obtained a copy of the policy nor verified the existence of the Lloyd's insurance. Nevertheless, Coopers repeatedly represented to the trustees of the archdiocese that the Lloyd's insurance policy was in effect, but in fact it had been canceled. During this period of time, Dennis McGee, an employee of the archdiocese, had embezzled funds that were to be used to pay premiums on the Lloyd's policy. The archdiocese sued Coopers for accounting malpractice and sought to recover the funds stolen by McGee. Did Coopers act ethically in this case? Is Coopers liable? *Coopers*

& Lybrand v. Trustees of the Archdiocese of Miami, 536 So.2d 278, **Web** 1988 Fla.App. Lexis 5348 (Court of Appeal of Florida)

51.9 Business Ethics Milton Mende purchased the Star Midas Mining Co., Inc., for $6,500. This Nevada corporation was a shell corporation with no assets. Mende changed the name of the corporation to American Equities Corporation (American Equities) and hired Bernard Howard to prepare certain accounting reports so that the company could issue securities to the public. In preparing the financial accounts, Howard (1) made no examination of American Equities's books, (2) falsely included an asset of over $700,000 on the books, which was a dormant mining company that had been through insolvency proceedings, (3) included in the profit and loss statement companies that Howard knew American Equities did not own, and (4) recklessly stated as facts things of which he was ignorant. The United States sued Howard for criminal conspiracy in violation of federal securities laws. Is Howard criminally liable? *United States v. Howard*, 328 F.2d 854, **Web** 1964 U.S. App. Lexis 6343 (United States Court of Appeals for the Second Circuit)

ENDNOTES

1. GAAPs are official standards promulgated by the Financial Accounting Standards Board (FASB) and predecessor accounting ruling bodies. GAAPs also include unofficial pronouncements, interpretations, research studies, textbooks, and the like.
2. GAASs are issued by the Auditing Standards Committee of the American Institute of Certified Public Accountants (AICPA).
3. 255 N.Y. 170, 174 N.E. 441, **Web** 1931 N.Y. Lexis 660 (Court of Appeals of New York).
4. 15 U.S.C. Section 77k(a).
5. 15 U.S.C. Section 78j(b).
6. 17 C.F.R. Section 240.10b–5.
7. *Ernst & Ernst v. Hochfelder*, 425 U.S. 185, 96 S.Ct. 1375, 47 L.Ed.2d 668, **Web** 1976 U.S. Lexis 2 (Supreme Court of the United States).
8. 15 U.S.C. Section 78r(a).
9. 15 U.S.C. Section 78u-4(g).
10. 15 U.S.C. Section 77x.
11. 15 U.S.C. Section 78ff.
12. 26 U.S.C. Sections 7206(1), 7206(2).
13. 18 U.S.C. Sections 1961–1968.
14. Private Securities Litigation Reform Act of 1995.
15. *Reves v. Ernst & Young*, 507 U.S. 170, 113 S.Ct. 1163, 122 L.Ed.2d 525, **Web** 1993 U.S. Lexis 1940 (Supreme Court of the United States).
16. Public Law No. 107-204, 16 Statute 745, also known as the Public Company Accounting Reform and Investor Protection Act of 2002.
17. *Couch v. U.S.*, 409 U.S. 322, 93 S.Ct. 611, 34 L.Ed.2d 548, **Web**, 1973 U.S. Lexis 23 (Supreme Court of the United States).

▲ **Wills** *Wills let the deceased dictate exactly where property should go when they die. However, laws differ regarding wills state by state with every state maintaining its one Statue of Wills.*

CHAPTER OBJECTIVES

After studying this chapter, you should be able to:

1. List and describe the requirements for making a valid will.
2. Describe the different types of testamentary gifts.
3. Identify how property is distributed under intestacy statutes if a person dies without a will.

4. Define *trust* and *living trust* and identify the parties to a trust.
5. Describe living wills and health care directives.

CHAPTER CONTENTS

► TRUST
► LIVING TRUST

► LIVING WILL AND HEALTH CARE DIRECTIVE
U.S. Supreme Court Case 52.2 · Gonzales, Attorney General
v. Oregon

"When you have told someone you have left him a legacy, the only decent thing to do is to die at once."

—Samuel Butler

► INTRODUCTION TO WILLS, TRUSTS, AND ELDER LAW

Wills and trusts are means of transferring property. *Wills* transfer property upon a person's death. They permit people to state exactly where they want their property to go when they die. If a person dies *intestate*—that is, without a will—the deceased's property is distributed to relatives according to state statute. The property escheats (goes) to the state if there are no relatives.

Trusts are used to transfer property that is to be held and managed for the benefit of another person or persons. A trust can be created to come into effect during one's lifetime. Trusts may also be created during one's lifetime and be worded to become effective only upon the trustor's (or grantor's) death. A *living trust* is a special type of trust used for estate planning.

A living will and health care directive can be created by an individual. A *living will* states a person's wishes regarding emergency medical treatment and decisions regarding being kept alive on life support systems. A *health care directive* names an individual or individuals who can make health care decisions if the maker of the directive is unable to do so.

This chapter discusses the use of wills, trusts, living trusts, living wills, health care directives, and elder law.

► WILL

A **will** is a declaration of how a person wants his or her property to be distributed upon his or her death. It is a testamentary deposition of property. The person who makes a will is called a **testator** (male) or **testatrix** (female). The persons designated in the will to receive the testator's property are called **beneficiaries** (see Exhibit 52.1).

will
A declaration of how a person wants his or her property to be distributed upon death.

testator or testatrix
A person who makes a will.

beneficiary
A person or an organization designated in a will to receive all or a portion of the testator's property at the time of the testator's death.

► **Exhibit 52.1 PARTIES TO A WILL**

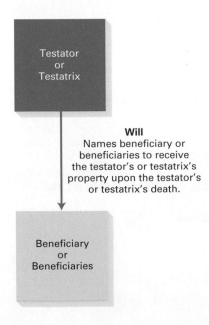

Testator or Testatrix

Will
Names beneficiary or beneficiaries to receive the testator's or testatrix's property upon the testator's or testatrix's death.

Beneficiary or Beneficiaries

Requirements for Making a Will

Every state has a **Statute of Wills** that establishes the requirements for making a valid will in that state. These requirements are:

- **Testamentary capacity.** The testator must have been of legal age and "sound mind" when the will was made. The courts determine **testamentary capacity** on a case-by-case basis. The legal age for executing a will is set by state statute.
- **Writing.** Wills must be in **writing** to be valid (except for dying declarations, discussed later in this chapter). The writing may be formal or informal. Although most wills are typewritten, they can be handwritten (see the later discussion of holographic wills). The writing may be on legal paper, other paper, scratch paper, envelopes, napkins, or the like. A will may incorporate other documents by reference.
- **Testator's signature.** Wills must be signed. Most jurisdictions require the **testator's signature** to appear at the end of the will. This step is to prevent fraud that could occur if someone added provisions to the will below the testator's signature.

Example Courts have held that initials (*R.K.H.*), a nickname (*Buffy*), title (*mother*), and even an *X* is a valid signature on a will if it can be proven that the testator intended it to be his or her signature.

Attestation by Witnesses

Wills must be **attested** to by mentally competent witnesses. Although state law varies, most states require two or three witnesses. The witnesses do not have to reside in the jurisdiction in which the testator is domiciled. Most jurisdictions stipulate that interested parties (e.g., a beneficiary under the will, the testator's attorney) cannot be witnesses. If an interested party has attested to a will, state law either voids any clauses that benefit such person or voids the entire will. Witnesses usually sign a will following the signature of the testator. These signatures are called the **attestation clause**. Most jurisdictions require that each witness attest to the will in the presence of the other witnesses.

A will that meets the requirements of the Statute of Wills is called a **formal will**. A sample will is shown in Exhibit 52.2.

Codicil

A will cannot be amended by merely striking out existing provisions and adding new ones. Adding **codicils** is the legal way to change an existing will. A codicil is a separate document that must be executed with the same formalities as a will. In addition, it must incorporate by reference the will it is amending. The codicil and the will are then read as one instrument.

Revoking a Will

A will may be **revoked** by acts of the testator. A will is revoked if the testator intentionally burns, tears, obliterates, or otherwise destroys it.

A properly executed **subsequent will** revokes a prior will if it specifically states that it is the testator's intention to do so. If the second will does not expressly revoke the prior will, the wills are read together. If any will provisions are inconsistent, the provisions in the second will control.

Wills can also be revoked by operation of law. For example, divorce or annulment revokes disposition of property to the former spouse under a will. The remainder of the will is valid. The birth of a child after a will has been executed does not revoke the will but does entitle the child to receive his or her share of a parents' estate, as determined by state statute.

Joint and Mutual Wills

If two or more testators execute the same instrument as their will, the document is called a **joint will**. A joint will may be held invalid as to one testator but not the other(s). **Mutual**

Statute of Wills
A state statute that establishes the requirements for making a valid will.

attestation
The action of a will being witnessed by two or three objective and competent people.

codicil
A separate document that must be executed to amend a will. It must be executed with the same formalities as a will.

revocation
Termination of a will.

joint will
A will that is executed by two or more testators.

mutual wills
A situation in which two or more testators execute separate wills that leave their property to each other on the condition that the survivor leave the remaining property on his or her death as agreed by the testators. Also known as *reciprocal wills*.

Last Will and Testament of Florence Winthorpe Blueblood

I, FLORENCE WINTHORPE BLUEBLOOD, presently residing at Boston, County of Suffolk, Massachusetts, being of sound and disposing mind and memory, hereby make, publish, and declare this to be my Last Will and Testament.

FIRST. I hereby revoke any and all Wills and Codicils previously made by me.

SECOND. I direct that my just debts and funeral expenses be paid out of my Estate as soon as practicable after my death.

THIRD. I am presently married to Theodore Hannah Blueblood III.

FOURTH. I hereby nominate and appoint my husband as the Personal Representative of this my Last Will and Testament. If he is unable to serve as Personal Representative, then I nominate and appoint Mildred Yardly Winthorpe as Personal Representative of this my Last Will and Testament. I direct that no bond or other security be required to be posted by my Personal Representative.

FIFTH. I hereby nominate and appoint my husband as Guardian of the person and property of my minor children. In the event that he is unable to serve as Guardian, then I nominate and appoint Mildred Yardly Winthorpe Guardian of the person and property of my minor children. I direct that no bond or other security be required to be posted by any Guardian herein.

SIXTH. I give my Personal Representative authority to exercise all the powers, rights, duties, and immunities conferred upon fiduciaries under law with full power to sell, mortgage, lease, invest, or reinvest all or any part of my Estate on such terms as he or she deems best.

SEVENTH. I hereby give, devise, and bequeath my entire estate to my husband, except for the following specific bequests:

I give my wedding ring to my daughter, Hillary Smythe Blueblood.
I give my baseball card collection to my son, Theodore Hannah Blueblood IV.
In the event that either my above-named daughter or son predeceases me, then and in that event, I give, devise, and bequeath my deceased daughter's or son's bequest to my husband.

EIGHTH. In the event that my husband shall predecease me, then and in that event, I give, devise and bequeath my entire estate, with the exception of the bequests in paragraph SEVENTH, to my beloved children or grandchildren surviving me, per stirpes.

NINTH. In the event I am not survived by my husband or any children or grandchildren, then and in that event, I give, devise, and bequeath my entire estate to Harvard University.

IN WITNESS WHEREOF, I, Florence Winthorpe Blueblood, the Testatrix, sign my name to this Last Will and Testament this 3rd day of January, 2010.

Florence Winthorpe Blueblood
(Signature)

Signed, sealed, published and declared by the above-named Testatrix, as and for her Last Will and Testament, in the presence of us, who at her request, in her presence, and in the presence of one another, have hereunto subscribed our names as attesting witnesses, the day and year last written above.

Witness	Address
Norm Peterson	100 Beacon Hill Rd Boston, Massachusett
Clifford Claven	200 Minute Man Drive Boston, Massachusetts
Rebecca Howe	300 Charles River Place Boston, Massachusett

▶ **Exhibit 52.2 WILL**

wills, or **reciprocal wills,** arise where two or more testators execute separate wills that make testamentary dispositions of their property to each other on the condition that the survivor leave the remaining property on his or her death as agreed by the testators. The wills are usually separate instruments with reciprocal terms. Because of their contractual nature, mutual wills cannot be unilaterally revoked after one of the parties has died. Valid mutual wills are enforceable.

Special Types of Wills

The law recognizes several types of wills that do not meet all the requirements discussed previously. The special types of wills admitted by the courts include:

- **Holographic wills. Holographic wills** are entirely handwritten and signed by the testator. The writing may be in ink, pencil, crayon, or some other medium. Many states recognize the validity of such wills even though they are not witnessed.
- **Nuncupative wills. Nuncupative wills** are oral wills that are made before witnesses. Such wills are usually valid only if they are made during the testator's last illness and before he or she is about to die. They are sometimes called **dying declarations**, or **deathbed wills**.

Simultaneous Deaths

Sometimes people who would inherit property from each other **die simultaneously**. If it is impossible to determine who died first, the question becomes one of inheritance. The **Uniform Simultaneous Death Act**, a model act adopted by many states, provides that each deceased person's property is distributed as though he or she had survived.

Example A husband and wife make wills that leave their entire estate to each other. The husband and wife are killed simultaneously in an airplane crash. Here, the husband's property would go to his relatives, and the wife's property would go to her relatives.

Undue Influence

A will may be found to be invalid if it was made as a result of **undue influence** on the testator. Undue influence can be inferred from the facts and circumstances surrounding the making of a will.

Example If an 85-year-old woman leaves all her property to the lawyer who drafted her will and ignores her blood relatives, the court is likely to presume undue influence.

Undue influence is difficult to prove by direct evidence, but it may be proved by circumstantial evidence. The court considers elements such as the following to determine the presence of undue influence:

- The benefactor and beneficiary are involved in a relationship of confidence and trust.
- The will contains substantial benefit to the beneficiary.
- The beneficiary caused or assisted in effecting execution of the will.
- There was an opportunity to exert influence.
- The will contains an unnatural disposition of the testator's property.
- The bequests constitute a change from a former will.
- The testator was highly susceptible to undue influence.

In the following case, the court had to decide if there had been undue influence in a will contest.

---

holographic will
A will that is entirely handwritten and signed by the testator.

noncupative will
An oral will that is made before a witness during the testator's last illness. Also known as a *dying declaration* or *deathbed will.*

Uniform Simultaneous Death Act
An act which provides that if people who would inherit property from each other die simultaneously, each person's property is distributed as though he or she had survived.

undue influence
A situation in which one person takes advantage of another person's mental, emotional, or physical weakness and unduly persuades that person to make a will; the persuasion by the wrongdoer must overcome the free will of the testator.

Disinherit: The prankish action of the ghosts in cutting the pockets out of trousers.

Frank McKinney Hubbard
The Roycroft Dictionary (1923)

CASE 52.1 Undue Influence

Medlock v. Mitchell

Web 2006 Ark.App. Lexis 320 (2006)
Court of Appeals of Arkansas

"**There must be a malign influence resulting from fear, coercion, or any other cause which deprives the testator of his free agency in disposing of his property.**"

—Judge Hart

Facts

Richard Mitchell executed a will leaving his estate equally to two of his children, Mark and Michelle. Four months later, Richard married Glenda Kay. On the same day, Richard created a revocable living trust. The trust was to

(case continues)

terminate 10 years after Richard's death. Upon termination of the trust, the trust corpus was to be distributed to Mark and Michelle. Five years later, Richard was diagnosed with terminal lung cancer. Three months later, he executed another will, leaving his entire $3.5 million estate to Kay. Richard died two months later.

Michelle filed her father's earlier will for probate. Kay filed Richard's most recent will for probate, arguing that Richard's earlier will had been revoked by the most recent will. Michelle responded that her father's most recent will was invalid because of Richard's incompetence at the time it was executed and was a product of undue influence by Kay. Kay died pending trial, and her son Jerald pursued the lawsuit. The trial court found that there was a confidential relationship between Richard and Kay, and therefore the burden shifted to Jerald to prove that there was no undue influence in the making of Richard's last will.

After hearing numerous witnesses, the trial court held that Jerald had not rebutted the presumption of undue influence, and judgment was ordered to probate the earlier will, leaving all of Richard's property to his children, Mark and Michelle. Jerald appealed.

Issue

Has Jerald rebutted the presumption of undue influence?

Language of the Court

Whether two individuals have a confidential relationship is a question of fact. We cannot say that the trial court clearly erred in finding under the facts of the case that a confidential relationship existed between Kay and Richard, either because of their confidential relationship as husband and wife and Richard's terminal illness or because Kay had Richard's durable power of attorney. It is the combination of both confidential relationships that gives rise to a presumption of undue influence in the present case. We affirm on this point.

It is not enough that a confidential relationship exist in order to void a testamentary instrument; there must be a malign influence resulting from fear, coercion, or any other cause which deprives the testator of his free agency

in disposing of his property. Undue influence on a testator may be inferred from the facts and circumstances. First, we consider the fact that Richard was in the hospital in a weakened state at the time the instruments were prepared. This could indicate undue influence. According to Michelle, during Richard's hospitalization, Kay indicated that she wanted Richard's will changed, suggesting that Kay was the driving force behind the changes. By her own testimony, Kay admitted to being present when Richard discussed the will and amendments to the trust with the Attorney Pierces, another possible sign of undue influence. She was also present at the execution of the will and the trust amendments, another factor indicating undue influence if other factors are present.

A will may also be invalidated for undue influence under certain circumstances where a person makes false statements and accusations to a testator concerning the natural objects of his bounty. Here, the trial court specifically found that Kay's statements to Richard that Mark broke into the office and wanted Richard taken off of life support precipitated the changes to the will and trust.

Decision

The court of appeals held that, given the facts of the case, Jerald was required to rebut the presumption of Kay's undue influence, which he failed to do. The court of appeals affirmed the judgment of the trial court that enforced Richard's prior will, which left his estate to his two children, Mark and Michelle.

Case Questions

Critical Legal Thinking What does the doctrine of undue influence provide? Explain.

Business Ethics Do you think Kay acted ethically in this case? Do you think there was undue influence in this case?

Contemporary Business Do you think that there are many cases of undue influence in the making of wills? Explain.

CONTEMPORARY ENVIRONMENT

Videotaped Will

Many acrimonious will contests involve written wills. The contesters allege such things as mental incapacity of the testator at the time the will was made, undue influence, fraud, or duress. Although a written will speaks for itself,

the mental capacity of the testator or testatrix and the voluntariness of his or her actions cannot be determined from the writing alone. To prevent unwarranted will contests, a testator or testatrix can use a **videotaped will** to supplement a written will. Videotaping a will that can withstand challenges by disgruntled relatives and alleged heirs involves a certain amount of planning.

The following procedures should be followed. A written will should be prepared to comply with the state's Statute of Wills. The video session should not begin until after the testator has become familiar with the document. The video should begin with the testator reciting the will verbatim. Next, the lawyer should ask the testator questions to demonstrate the testator's sound mind and understanding of the implications of his or her actions. The execution ceremony—the signing of the will by the testator and the attestation by the witnesses—should also be

videotaped. The videotape should then be stored in a safe place.

In video wills, the testator or testatrix often explains to relatives and others the reasons he or she has or has not left them any of his or her estate. These types of statements are often referred to as the deceased "reaching out from the grave" to commend or condemn relatives or others.

With the testator's actions crystallized in video, a judge or jury will be able to determine the state of the testator's mental capacity at the time the will was made and the voluntariness of his or her testamentary gifts. In addition, fraudulent competing wills will fall in the face of such proof.

Probate

When a person dies, his or her property must be collected, debts and taxes paid, and the remainder of the estate distributed to the beneficiaries of the will or the heirs under the state intestacy statute. This process is called **probate**, or **settlement of the estate**. The process and procedures for settling an estate are governed by state statute. A specialized state court, called the **probate court**, usually supervises the administration and settlement of estates.

A **personal representative** must be appointed to administer an estate during its settlement phase. If a testator's will designates a personal representative, that person is called an **executor** (male) or **executrix** (female). If no one is named or if the decedent dies intestate, the court appoints an **administrator** (male) or **administratrix** (female). Usually, this party is a relative of the deceased or a bank. An attorney is usually appointed to help administer the estate and to complete the probate.

probate
The process of a deceased's property being collected, debts and taxes being paid, and the remainder of the estate being distributed. Also called *settlement of the estate*.

probate court
A specialized state court that supervises the administration and settlement of estates.

▶ TESTAMENTARY GIFT

A gift of real estate by will is called a **devise**. A gift of personal property by will is called a **bequest**, or **legacy**. Gifts in wills can be specific, general, or residuary:

- **Specific gift. Specific gifts** in a will are gifts of specifically named pieces of property.

Examples A gift of a ring, a boat, or a piece of real estate in a will is a specific gift.

- **General gift. General gifts** are gifts that do not identify the specific property from which the gift is to be made.

Example A gift of $100,000 to a named beneficiary is an example of a general gift. The cash can come from any source in the decedent's estate.

- **Residuary gift. Residuary gifts** are gifts that are established by a **residuary clause** in a will.

Example A clause in a will that states "I give my daughter the rest, remainder, and residual of my estate" is an example of a residuary gift. This clause means that any portion of the estate left after the debts, taxes, and specific and general gifts have been paid belongs to the decedent's daughter.

A person who inherits property under a will or an intestacy statute takes the property subject to all the outstanding claims against it (e.g., liens, mortgages). A person can **renounce** an inheritance and often does where the liens or mortgages against the property exceed the value of the property.

devise
A gift of real estate by will.

bequest
A gift of personal property by will. Also known as a *legacy*.

specific gift
A gift of a specifically named piece of property.

general gift
A gift that does not identify the specific property from which the gift is to be made.

residuary gift
A gift of an estate left after the debts, taxes, and specific and general gifts have been given.

Lineal Descendants

lineal descendants
Children, grandchildren, great-grandchildren, and so on of a testator.

per stirpes **distribution**
A distribution of an estate in which grandchildren and great-grandchildren of the deceased inherit by representation of their parent.

The power of making a will is an instrument placed in the hands of individuals for the prevention of private calamity.

Jeremy Bentham
Principles of the Civil Code (1748)

per capita **distribution**
A distribution of an estate in which each grandchild and great-grandchild of the deceased inherits equally with the children of the deceased.

A testator's will often states that property is to be left to his or her **lineal descendants** (e.g., children, grandchildren, great-grandchildren) either *per stirpes* or *per capita*. The differences between these two methods are discussed in the following paragraphs.

Per Stirpes Distribution   Pursuant to *per stirpes* **distribution**, the lineal descendants *inherit by representation of their parent;* that is, they split what their deceased parent would have received. If their parent is not deceased, they receive nothing.

Example   Anne dies without a surviving spouse, and she had three children, Bart, Beth, and Bruce. Bart, who survives his mother, has no children. Beth has one child, Carla, and they both survive Anne. Bruce, who predeceased his mother, had two children, Clayton and Cathy; and Cathy, who predeceased Anne, had two children, Deborah and Dominic, both of whom survive Anne. If Anne leaves her estate to her lineal descendants *per stirpes*, Bart and Beth each get one-third, Carla receives nothing because Beth is alive, Clayton gets one-sixth, and Deborah and Dominic each get one-twelfth. See Exhibit 52.3.

Per Capita Distribution   Pursuant to *per capita* **distribution**, the lineal descendants *equally share the property of the estate.* That is, children of the testator share equally with grandchildren, great-grandchildren, and so forth.

Example   Suppose the facts are the same as in the previous example, except that Anne leaves her estate to her lineal descendants *per capita*. In this case, all the surviving lineal descendants—Bart, Beth, Carla, Clayton, Deborah, and Dominic—share equally in the estate. That is, they each get one-sixth of Anne's estate. See Exhibit 52.4.

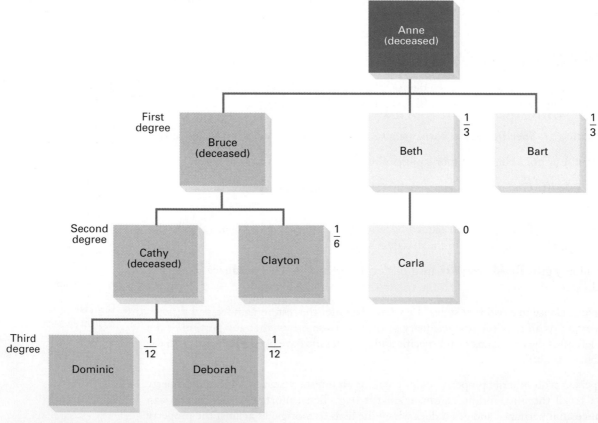

▶ **Exhibit 52.3 *PER STIRPES* DISTRIBUTION**

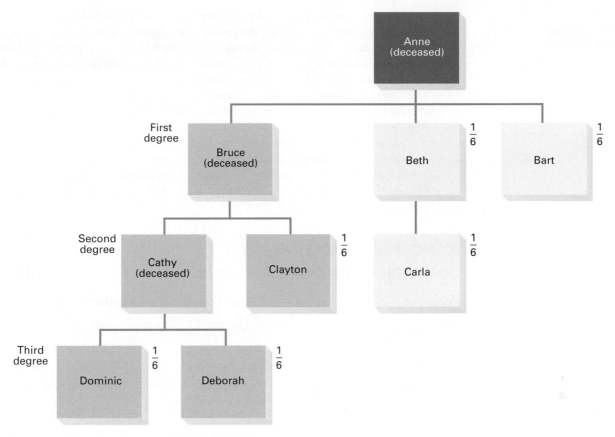

▶ **Exhibit 52.4 *PER CAPITA* DISTRIBUTION**

Ademption

If a testator leaves a specific gift of property to a beneficiary, but the property is no longer in the estate of the testator when he or she dies, the beneficiary receives nothing. This doctrine is called the doctrine of **ademption**.

Abatement

If a testator's estate is not large enough to pay all the devises and bequests, the doctrine of **abatement** applies. The doctrine works as follows:

• If a will provides for both general and residuary gifts, the residuary gifts are abated first.

Examples A testator executes a will when he owns $500,000 of property that leaves (1) $100,000 to the Red Cross, (2) $100,000 to a university, and (3) the residual to his niece. If the testator died with this $500,000 estate, the Red Cross and the university would each receive $100,000, and the niece would receive $300,000. However, if when the testator died, his estate was worth only $225,000, the Red Cross and the university would each receive $100,000, and the niece would receive $25,000.

• If a will provides only for general gifts, the reductions are proportionate.

Example A testator's will leaves $200,000 to each of two beneficiaries. However, when the testator died, his estate was worth only $100,000. Here, each beneficiary would receive $50,000.

▶ INTESTATE SUCCESSION

If a person dies without a will—that is, **intestate**—or if his or her will fails for some legal reason, the property is distributed to his or her relatives pursuant to the state's **intestacy statute**.

ademption
A principle that says if a testator leaves a specific devise of property to a beneficiary, but the property is no longer in the estate when the testator dies, the beneficiary receives nothing.

abatement
A doctrine that says if the property a testator leaves is not sufficient to satisfy all the beneficiaries named in a will and there are both general and residuary bequests, the residuary bequest is abated first (i.e., paid last).

intestate
The state of having died without leaving a will.

intestacy statute
A state statute that specifies how a deceased's property will be distributed if he or she dies without a will or if the last will is declared void and there is no prior valid will.

heir
The receiver of property under intestacy statutes.

Relatives who receive property under intestacy statutes are called **heirs**. Although intestacy statutes differ from state to state, the general rule is that the deceased's real property is distributed according to the intestacy statute of the state where the real property is located, and the deceased's personal property is distributed according to the intestacy statute of the state where the deceased had his or her permanent residence.

Intestacy statutes usually leave the deceased's property to his or her heirs in this order: spouse, children, lineal heirs (e.g., grandchildren, parents, brothers and sisters), collateral heirs (e.g., aunts, uncles, nieces, nephews), and other next of kin (e.g., cousins). If the deceased has no surviving relatives, then the deceased's property **escheats** (goes) to the state. In-laws do not inherit under most intestacy statutes.

To avoid the distribution of an estate as provided in an intestacy statute, a person should have a properly written, signed, and witnessed will that distributes the estate property as the testator wishes.

CONCEPT SUMMARY
COMPARISON OF DYING WITH AND WITHOUT A VALID WILL

Situation	Parties Who Receive Deceased's Property
Deceased dies with a valid will	Beneficiaries named in the will.
Deceased dies without a valid will	Heirs set forth in the applicable state intestacy statute. If there are no heirs, the deceased's property escheats to the state.

▶ TRUST

trust
A legal arrangement established when one person transfers title to property to another person to be held and used for the benefit of a third person.

A **trust** is a legal arrangement under which one person (the **settlor**, **trustor**, or **transferor**) delivers and transfers legal title to property to another person, bank, or other entity (the **trustee**), to be held and used for the benefit of a third person or entity (the **beneficiary**). The property and assets held in trust are called the **trust corpus**, or **trust res**. The trustee has legal title to the trust corpus, and the beneficiary has equitable title. Unlike wills, trusts are not public documents, so property can be transferred in privacy. An **express trust** is voluntarily created by the settlor. It is usually written. The written agreement is called a **trust instrument**, or **trust agreement**. Exhibit 52.5 shows the parties to a trust.

settlor
A person who creates a trust. Also known as a *trustor* or *transferor*.

A trust can be created and becomes effective during a trustor's lifetime, or it can be created during a trustor's lifetime to become effective upon the trustor's death. During the existence of a trust, the trustee collects money owed to the trust, pays taxes and necessary expenses of the trust, makes investment decisions, pays the income to the income beneficiary, and keeps necessary records of transactions.

trustee
A person or an entity that holds legal title to a trust corpus and manages the trust for the benefit of the beneficiary or beneficiaries.

Beneficiaries

trust corpus
Property and assets held in trust. Also known as *trust res*.

Trusts often provide that any trust income is to be paid to a person or an entity called the **income beneficiary**. The person or entity to receive the trust corpus upon the termination of the trust is called the **remainder beneficiary**. The income beneficiary and the remainder beneficiary can be the same person or different persons. The designated beneficiary can be any identifiable person, animal (e.g., a pet), charitable organization, or other institution or cause that the settlor chooses. There can be multiple income and remainder beneficiaries. An entire class of persons—for example, "my grandchildren"—can be named.

express trust
A trust created voluntarily by a settlor.

income beneficiary of a trust
A person or an entity to be paid income from a trust.

A trust can allow the trustee to invade (use) the trust corpus for certain purposes. These purposes can be named (e.g., "for the beneficiary's college education"). The trust agreement usually specifies how the receipts and expenses of the trust are to be divided between the income beneficiary and the remainder beneficiary.

remainder beneficiary of a trust
A person or an entity to receive the trust corpus upon the termination of a trust.

Generally, the trustee has broad management powers over the trust property. Thus, the trustee can invest the trust property to preserve its capital and make it productive. The trustee must follow any restrictions on investments contained in the trust agreement or state statute.

Inter Vivos Trust

An ***inter vivos* trust** is created and its assets are distributed to the trust while the settlor is alive. The settlor transfers legal title of property to a named trustee to hold, administer, and manage for the benefit of named beneficiaries. The trust can be for a stated period of time (e.g., 10 years) or until some event happens (e.g., the settlor dies). The trust sometimes provides that an income beneficiary will receive income from the trust until the trust ends. The trust provides what will happen to the trust assets when the trust ends, such as being distributed to named beneficiaries.

Testamentary Trust

A **testamentary trust** is created by will. In other words, the trust comes into existence when the settlor dies. If the will that establishes a trust is found to be invalid, the trust is also invalid.

Constructive Trust

A **constructive trust** is an equitable trust that is implied by law to avoid fraud, unjust enrichment, and injustice. In constructive trust arrangements, the holder of the title to property (i.e., the trustee) holds the property in trust for its rightful owner. When a constructive trust is imposed, the party who is the implied trustee cannot sell or otherwise transfer ownership to the property or give a mortgage on the property.

Example Thad and Kaye are partners. Kaye embezzles partnership funds and uses the stolen funds to purchase a piece of real estate. In this case, the court can impose a constructive trust whereby Kaye (who holds actual title to the land) is considered a trustee who is holding the property in trust for Thad, its rightful owner.

inter vivos **trust**
A trust that is created while the settlor is alive.

testamentary trust
A trust created by will; the trust comes into existence when the settlor dies.

constructive trust
An equitable trust that is implied by law to avoid fraud, unjust enrichment, and injustice.

A constructive trust is the formula through which the conscience of equity finds expression.

Justice Cardozo
*Beatty v. Guggenheim
Exploration Co. (1919)*

Resulting Trust

resulting trust
A trust that is implied from the conduct of the parties.

A **resulting trust** is implied from the conduct of the parties.

Example Henry is purchasing a piece of real estate but cannot attend the closing. He asks his brother, Gregory, to attend the closing and take title to the property until he can return. In this case, Gregory holds the title to the property as trustee for Henry until he returns.

Special Types of Trusts

Trusts may be created for special purposes. Three types of special trusts are fairly common:

1. **Charitable trusts.** A **charitable trust** is created for the benefit of a segment of society or society in general.

   Example A trust that is created for the construction and maintenance of a public park is an example of a charitable trust.

2. **Spendthrift trusts.** A **spendthrift trust** is designed to prevent a beneficiary's personal creditors from reaching his or her trust interest. All control over the trust is removed from the beneficiary. Personal creditors still can go after trust income that is paid to the beneficiary, however.

3. **Totten trusts.** A **Totten trust** is created when a person deposits money in a bank account in his or her own name and holds it as a trustee for the benefit of another person. A totten trust is a tentative trust because (a) the trustee can add or withdraw funds from the account, and (b) the trust can be revoked at any time prior to the trustee's death or prior to completing delivery of the funds to the beneficiary.

Termination of a Trust

A trust is **irrevocable** unless the settlor reserves the right to revoke it. Many trusts fall into the first category. Usually, a trust either contains a specific termination date or provides that it will terminate upon the occurrence of an event (e.g., when the remainder beneficiary reaches a certain age). Upon termination, the trust corpus is distributed as provided in the trust agreement.

▶ LIVING TRUST

living trust
A method for holding property during a person's lifetime and distributing the property upon that person's death. Also called a *grantor's trust* or a *revocable trust*.

grantor
A person who creates a living trust. Also called a *trustor*.

Living trusts have become a popular means of holding property during a person's lifetime and distributing the property upon that person's death. A living trust works as follows. During his or her life, a person establishes a living trust, which is a legal entity used for estate planning. A living trust is also referred to as a **grantor's trust**, or a **revocable trust**. The person who creates the trust is called the **grantor** (or the **trustor**).

Benefits of a Living Trust

The primary purpose of using a living trust is to avoid *probate* associated with using a will. If a person dies with a will, the will must be probated so the deceased's assets can be properly distributed according to the will. A probate judge is named to oversee the probate process, and all documents, including the will, are public record. A living trust, on the other hand, is private. When the grantor dies, the assets are owned by the living trust and are therefore not subject to probate proceedings. In addition, if real property is owned in more than one state and a will is used, ancillary probate must be conducted in the other state. If a living trust is used, ancillary probate is avoided.

   Living trusts are often promoted for claimed benefits that do not exist. The true facts are that a living trust:

- Does not reduce estate taxes any more than a will.
- Does not reduce the grantor's income taxes. All the income earned by the trust is attributed to the grantor, who must pay income taxes on the earnings just as if the trust did not exist.

Another good thing about being poor is that when you are seventy your children will not have declared you legally insane in order to gain control of your estate.

Woody Allen

- Does not avoid creditors. Thus, creditors can obtain liens against property in the trust.
- Is subject to property division upon divorce.
- Is usually not less expensive to create than a will. Both require payments to lawyers and usually to accountants and other professionals to draft and probate a will or draft and manage a living trust.
- Does not avoid controversies upon the grantor's death. Like wills, living trusts can be challenged for lack of capacity, undue influence, duress, and other legal grounds.

Funding and Operation of a Living Trust

To fund a living trust, the grantor transfers title to his or her property to the trust. This property is called the **trust corpus**. Bank accounts, stock certificates, real estate, personal property, intangible property, and other property owned by the grantor must be retitled to the trust's name. For example, the grantor must execute deeds transferring title to real estate to the trust. Once property is transferred to the trust, the trust is considered funded. A living trust is revocable during the grantor's lifetime. Thus, a grantor can later change his or her mind and undo the trust and retake title of the property in his or her own name.

A living trust names a **trustee** who is responsible for maintaining, investing, buying, or selling trust assets. The trustee is usually the grantor. Thus, the grantor who establishes the trust does not lose control of the property placed in the trust and may manage and invest trust assets during his or her lifetime. The trust should name a **successor trustee** to replace the grantor-trustee if the grantor becomes incapacitated or too ill to manage the trust.

trustee
A person named in a living will to administer the trust assets. This is usually the grantor.

Beneficiaries

A living trust names a **beneficiary** or **beneficiaries** who are entitled to receive income from the living trust while it is in existence and to receive the property of the trust when the grantor dies. Usually the grantor is the **income beneficiary**, who receives the income from the trust during his or her lifetime. Upon the death of the grantor, assets of the trust are distributed to the **remainder beneficiary** or beneficiaries named in the trust. The designated trustee has the fiduciary duties of identifying assets, paying creditors, paying income and estate taxes, transferring assets to named beneficiaries, and rendering an accounting.

income beneficiary of a living trust
A person who receives the income from a living trust during his or her life. This is usually the grantor.

remainder beneficiary of a living trust
A person who receives the assets of a living trust upon the death of the grantor.

▶ LIVING WILL AND HEALTH CARE DIRECTIVE

Technological breakthroughs have greatly increased the life span of human beings. This same technology, however, permits life to be sustained long after a person is "brain dead." Some people say they have a right to refuse life-extending treatment. Others argue that human life must be preserved at all costs. In 1990, the U.S. Supreme Court was called upon to decide the *right to die* issue. In the ***Cruzan v. Director, Missouri Department of Health***[1] case, the U.S. Supreme Court acknowledged that the right to refuse medical treatment is a personal liberty protected by the Due Process Clause of the U.S. Constitution. The Court stated that this interest must be expressed through clear and convincing proof that the patient did not want to be sustained by artificial means.

Living Will

The clear message of the Supreme Court's opinion in the *Cruzan* case is that people who do not want their life prolonged indefinitely by artificial means should sign a **living will** that stipulates their wishes before catastrophe strikes and they become unable to express it themselves because of an illness or an accident. The living will should state which life-saving measures the signor does and does not want. In addition, the signor can specify that he or she wants any such treatments withdrawn if doctors determine that there is no hope of a meaningful recovery. A living will provides clear and convincing proof of a patient's wishes with respect to medical treatment.

living will
A document that states which life-saving measures the signor does and does not want, and can specify that he or she wants such treatments withdrawn if doctors determine that there is no hope of a meaningful recovery.

Health Care Directive

health care directive (health care proxy)
A document in which the maker names someone to be his or her health care agent to make all health care decisions in accordance with his or her wishes, as outlined in the living will.

In a living will or in a separate document, usually called a **health care directive**, or **health care proxy**, the maker should name someone, such as a spouse or another relative or trusted party, to be his or her **health care agent** to make all health care decisions in accordance with the wishes outlined in the maker's living will. An alternative person should also be named in case the originally designated health care agent is unable or chooses not to serve in that capacity.

Example A well-known example of a case in which a person did not have a living will and health care proxy was the Terri Schiavo case. In February 1990, Terri collapsed and was placed on life support systems. For 15 years, Terri remained in a vegetative state. Her husband wanted Terri to be taken off life support systems, but her parents did not. After years of legal battles that included more than 50 trial and appellate court hearings, in April 2005, the Florida supreme court ordered Terri to be taken off life support systems. Days later, she died. Much of the legal battle concerned what Terri's intention would have been about staying on or being removed from life support systems. If Terri had had a living will and health care proxy, her intentions would have been clear.

The Right to Die

One legal issue that has been prominent in the news is whether an individual has the right to choose to die when he or she is terminally ill and has less than a certain time to live. This issue has been debated many times in the past. Today, many persons in the United States support this **right to die**, while others are against having such a law.

In the following case, the U.S. Supreme Court was called upon to decide the legality of **Oregon Death with Dignity Act**[2] when the federal government asserted that an existing federal law prohibited the Oregon law.

U.S. SUPREME COURT CASE 52.2 Oregon's Death with Dignity Law

Gonzales, Attorney General v. Oregon

546 U.S. 243, 126 S.Ct. 904, 163 L.Ed.2d 748, Web 2006 U.S. Lexis 767 (2006)
Supreme Court of the United States

"Americans are engaged in an earnest and profound debate about the morality, legality, and practicality of physician-assisted suicide."

—Justice Kennedy

Facts

The state of Oregon became the first state to legalize assisted suicide when voters approved a ballot measure enacting the Oregon Death with Dignity Act (ODWDA). The Oregon law exempts from civil or criminal liability state-licensed physicians who, in compliance with the safeguards in ODWDA, dispense or prescribe a lethal dose of drugs upon the request of a terminally ill patient.

For Oregon residents to be eligible to request a prescription under ODWDA, they must receive a diagnosis from their attending physician that they have an incurable and irreversible disease that, within reasonable medical judgment, will cause death within six months. Attending physicians must also determine whether a patient has made a voluntary request, ensure that a patient's choice is informed, and refer patients to counseling if they might be suffering from a psychological disorder or depression causing impaired judgment. A second consulting physician must examine the patient and the medical record and confirm the attending physician's conclusions. Oregon physicians may dispense or issue a prescription for the requested drug but may not administer it. Physicians who dispense medication pursuant to ODWDA must also be registered with both the state's Board of Medical Examiners and the federal Drug Enforcement Administration (DEA).

The drugs Oregon physicians prescribe pursuant to ODWDA are regulated under a federal statute, the **Controlled Substances Act (CSA)** [21 U.S.C. Section 801 et seq.]. The CSA allows covered drugs to be available only by written prescription from a registered physician. To prevent the diversion of controlled substances, the physician must obtain a registration from the U.S. attorney general. The attorney general may deny, suspend, or revoke this registration if the physician's registration would be "inconsistent with the public interest."

The U.S. attorney general issued an interpretive rule announcing his intent to restrict the use of controlled substances for physician-assisted suicide. The U.S. attorney general ruled that assisting suicide is not a legitimate medical purpose and that prescribing or dispensing federally controlled substances to assist suicide violates the federal CSA. The interpretive rule also stated that a physician who prescribes controlled substances for assisted suicides violates the public interest and would be subject to suspension or revocation of his or her medical license.

In response, the state of Oregon, joined by a physician, a pharmacist, and some terminally ill patients, all from Oregon, challenged the interpretive rule in federal court. The U.S. District Court entered a permanent injunction against the federal government's enforcement of the interpretive rule. The U.S. Court of Appeals agreed and held the interpretive rule invalid. The U.S. attorney general appealed to the U.S. Supreme Court.

Issue

Does the U.S. attorney general have the statutory power pursuant to the federal Controlled Substances Act to issue the interpretive rule criminalizing medical practices authorized by the state of Oregon law?

Language of the U.S. Supreme Court

Americans are engaged in an earnest and profound debate about the morality, legality, and practicality of physician-assisted suicide. The dispute before us is in part a product of this political and moral debate, but its resolution requires an inquiry familiar to the courts: interpreting a federal statute to determine whether Executive action is authorized by, or otherwise consistent with, the enactment.

In deciding whether the CSA can be read as prohibiting physician-assisted suicide, we look to the statute's text and design. The statute and our case law amply support the conclusion that Congress regulates medical practice insofar as it bars doctors from using their prescription-writing powers as a means to engage in illicit drug dealing and trafficking as conventionally understood. Beyond this, however, the statute manifests no intent to

regulate the practice of medicine generally. The silence is understandable given the structure and limitations of federalism, which allow States great latitude under their police powers to legislate as to the protection of the lives, limbs, health, comfort, and quiet of all persons. Oregon's regime is an example of the state regulation of medical practice that the CSA presupposes. Rather than simply decriminalize assisted suicide, ODWDA limits its exercise to the attending physicians of terminally ill patients, physicians who must be licensed by Oregon's Board of Medical Examiners.

The Government, in the end, maintains that the prescription requirement delegates to a single Executive officer the power to effect a radical shift of authority from the States to the Federal Government to define general standards of medical practice in every locality. The text and structure of the CSA show that Congress did not have this far-reaching intent to alter the federal-state balance and the congressional role in maintaining it.

Decision

The U.S. Supreme Court held that the federal Controlled Substances Act did not authorize the U.S. attorney general to issue the interpretive rule in this case. The Supreme Court affirmed the judgment of the Court of Appeals, which held that the interpretive rule was invalid and permanently enjoined from enforcement. Thus, the Oregon Death with Dignity Act can be administered as written.

Case Questions

Critical Legal Thinking What does the Oregon Death with Dignity Act provide? Explain.

Business Ethics Do you think it is morally right for a terminally ill patient to request physician-assisted suicide? Explain.

Contemporary Business Would you want the ability to be provided physician-assisted suicide if you were diagnosed with a terminal illness?

TEST REVIEW TERMS AND CONCEPTS

Abatement	Controlled Substances Act (CSA)	Health care agent	Intestate
Ademption		Health care directive (health care proxy)	Irrevocable trust
Administrator or administratrix	*Cruzan v. Director, Missouri Department of Health*	Heir	Joint will
Attestation	Devise	Holographic will	Lineal descendants
Attestation clause	Escheat	Income beneficiary of a living trust	Living trust (grantor's trust or revocable trust)
Beneficiary	Executor or executrix	Income beneficiary of a trust	Living will
Bequest (legacy)	Express trust	*Inter vivos* trust	Mutual (reciprocal) wills
Charitable trust	Formal will	Intestacy statute	Nuncupative will (dying declaration or deathbed will)
Codicil	General gift		
Constructive trust	Grantor (trustor)		

Oregon Death with
    Dignity Act
Per capita distribution
Per stirpes distribution
Personal representative
Probate (settlement of the
    estate)
Probate court
Remainder beneficiary of a
    living trust
Remainder beneficiary of a
    trust

Renounce
Residuary clause
Residuary gift
Resulting trust
Revocation
Right to die
Settlor (trustor,
    transferor)
Simultaneous deaths
Specific gift
Spendthrift trust
Statute of Wills

Subsequent will
Successor trustee
Testamentary capacity
Testamentary trust
Testator or testatrix
Testator's (or testatrix's)
    signature
Totten trust
Trust
Trust corpus of a living
    trust
Trust corpus (trust res)

Trustee
Trustee of a living trust
Trust instrument (trust
    agreement)
Undue influence
Uniform Simultaneous
    Death Act
Videotaped will
Will
Writing

CASE PROBLEMS

52.1 Will Martha Jansa executed a will, naming her two sons as executors and leaving all her property to them. The will was properly signed and attested to by witnesses. Thereafter, Martha died. When Martha's safe-deposit box at a bank was opened, the original of this will was discovered, along with two other instruments that were dated after the will. One was a handwritten document that left her home to her grandson, with the remainder of her estate to her two sons; this document was not signed. The second document was a typed version of the handwritten one; this document was signed by Martha but was not attested to by witnesses. Which of the three documents should be admitted to probate? *In re Estate of Jansa*, 670 S.W.2d 767, **Web** 1984 Tex. App. Lexis 5503 (Court of Appeals of Texas)

52.2 Mental Capacity Everett Clark met with William Wham, an attorney, to discuss the preparation of a will. Clark, who had never married and who lived with his sister, was to return the following day to execute his will. Clark was hospitalized that evening with a perforated ulcer. He underwent surgery on March 19. From the surgery until the time of his death, he was in intensive care and unable to communicate verbally. On March 23, Clark's cousin John Bailey retrieved the will prepared by Wham and took it to attorney Frank Walker to have him finalize it. Walker testified that he took the will to the hospital on March 25. Immediately prior to the execution of the will, Walker asked Clark a few questions. Walker testified that Clark knew what he was doing. Dorothy Smith, an attesting witness, testified that Clark could not talk but answered her questions by nodding yes or no. She asked Clark "if he knew me and if he knew we were all there and he shook his head yes." She testified that he also shook his head yes to the question "Is this your will and testament?" "Is John Bailey your cousin?" and "Do you want to leave everything to John Bailey?" Clark signed the will with an *X*. On March 26, Clark passed into a coma and died. Bailey introduced the will into probate, but another relative of Clark's challenged it. Is the will valid? *Bailey v. Bailey*, 203 Ill.App.3d 1017, 561 N.E.2d 367, **Web** 1990 Ill.App. Lexis 1541 (Appellate Court of Illinois)

52.3 Lineal Descendants In October 1973, Mr. and Mrs. Pate executed separate wills that followed a common plan in

disposing of their respective estates. Each will provided for the establishment of trusts with a life estate to their son Billy, and upon his death, the estate was to be distributed "in equal shares *per stirpes* to my natural born grandchildren." Mr. and Mrs. Pate had two sons, Billy and Wallace. Billy's first marriage ended in divorce without children. Billy's second marriage also ended in divorce without children, although his second wife had a daughter by her previous marriage. Billy married again, and to the time of this action, no children had been born to his 32-year-old wife. Wallace first married in 1952. Of that marriage, five children were born, each before the time that the Pates made their wills. After that marriage ended in divorce, Wallace married his present wife. There were no children of the second marriage, but there were stepchildren by Wallace's second wife. One of Wallace's daughters had two children by her marriage. Mr. Pate died on November 9, 1979, leaving an estate of $1.6 million. Mrs. Pate died on October 21, 1983, leaving an estate of $6.7 million. Who inherits the estate? *Pate v. Ford*, 293 S.C. 268, 360 S.E.2d 145, **Web** 1987 S.C.App. Lexis 363 (Court of Appeals of South Carolina)

52.4 Ademption Mrs. Mildred D. Potter executed a will which provided that her residence in Pompano Beach, Florida, was to go to her daughter and an equivalent amount of cash to her son upon her death. Evidence showed that Mrs. Potter's intent was to treat the daughter and son equally in the distribution of her estate. When she died, her will was admitted into probate. At the time, she still possessed her home in Pompano Beach. Unfortunately, there were insufficient assets to pay Mrs. Potter's son the equivalent amount of cash. Can the son share in the value of the house so that his inheritance is equal to his sister's? *In re Estate of Potter*, 469 So.2d 957, **Web** 1985 Fla.App. Lexis. 14338 (Court of Appeal of Florida)

52.5 Will During his first marriage to Miriam Talbot, Robert Mirkil Talbot executed a will in multiple originals that bequeathed his entire estate to Miriam, or if she should predecease him, to his friend J. Barker Killgore. After his first wife's death, Robert married Lois McClen Mills. After consulting a Louisiana intestacy chart, the Talbots determined that if Robert died, Lois would receive Robert's entire estate because he had no descendants, surviving parents, or siblings.

However, Lois did have descendants. Lois wanted to leave Robert a portion of her estate. Robert and his new wife went to an attorney to execute the new wife's will. While there, the attorney took Robert aside and showed him his prior will that made Killgore the contingent beneficiary. The attorney asked Robert if he wanted to leave his estate to his new wife, and Robert answered "yes." Robert then tore the old will in half in the attorney's presence. After leaving the attorney's office, Robert and Lois went shopping for furnishings for their new house. That night, Robert became short of breath and was taken to a hospital, where he died. Killgore retrieved a multiple original of Robert's 1981 will and petitioned to have it probated. Lois opposed the petition. Who wins? *Succession of Talbot*, 530 So.2d 1132, **Web** 1988 La. Lexis 1597 (Supreme Court of Louisiana)

52.6 Intestacy Mr. and Mrs. Campbell were out in a small boat on Hyatt Lake near Ashland, Oregon. The boat capsized near the middle of the lake sometime in the afternoon. No one saw the capsizing or either of the Campbells in the water. The deputy sheriff was called to the lake about 5 o'clock, after the Campbells' boat was found. Numerous people searched the shoreline and lake, but the Campbells were not located by nightfall. The body of Mrs. Campbell was found the next morning. The body of Mr. Campbell was found four days later. The pathologists who conducted the autopsies testified that both Mr. and Mrs. Campbell died of drowning but could not determine the exact time of death. Both parties died intestate. Mr. Campbell was survived by three sisters and a brother, and Mrs. Campbell was survived by a daughter and son from a prior marriage. Who inherits the Campbells' property? *In re Estate of Campbell*, 56 Ore.App. 222, 641 P.2d 610, **Web** 1982 Ore.App. Lexis 2448 (Court of Appeals of Oregon)

52.7 Murder Dr. Duncan R. Danforth, a 75-year-old man of substantial means, married 21-year-old Loretta Ollison. Immediately following the ceremony, the newlyweds went to a lawyer's office, where Danforth executed a newly prepared will, naming Ollison a principal beneficiary of his estate. Four days later, Danforth was murdered by Michael Stith, Ollison's lover. In a criminal trial, Ollison was convicted of conspiracy to commit murder and was sentenced to 10 years in prison. Can Ollison recover under the will or take her elective share of the estate under the state's intestacy statute? *In re the Estate of Danforth*, 705 S.W.2d 609, **Web** 1986 Mo.App. Lexis 3757 (Court of Appeals of Missouri)

BUSINESS ETHICS CASES

52.8 Business Ethics Homer and Edna Jones, husband and wife, executed a joint will that provided "We will and give to our survivor, whether it be Homer Jones or Edna Jones, all property and estate of which the first of us that dies may be seized and possessed. If we should both die in a common catastrophe, or upon the death of our survivor, we will and give all property and estate then remaining to our children, Leonida Jones Eschman, daughter, Sylvia Marie Jones, daughter, and Grady V. Jones, son, share and share alike."

When Homer died 18 years later, Edna Jones received his entire estate under the will. Two years later, Edna executed a new will that left a substantially larger portion of the estate to her daughter, Sylvia Marie Jones, than to the other two children. Edna Jones died in 1982. Edna's daughter introduced her mother's will for probate. The other two children introduced the earlier joint will for probate. Did Edna act ethically in this case? Who wins? *Jones v. Jones*, 718 S.W.2d 416, **Web** 1986 Tex.App. Lexis 8929 (Court of Appeals of Texas)

52.9 Business Ethics Wilmer Breeden, an active socialist, was a very wealthy individual. When he died, his will designated the bulk of his estate to be placed in the Breeden-Schmidt Foundation. This testamentary trust was to be administered by the trustees named in Breeden's will, and the funds of the foundation were to be distributed:

> *TO persons, entities and causes advancing the principles of socialism and those causes related to socialism. This shall include, but not be limited to, subsidizing publications, establishing and conducting reading rooms, supporting radio, television and the newspaper media and candidates for public office.*

Breeden's nephew and niece petitioned the court to have the trust provision declared invalid and the estate residue given to them as intestate heirs. Des the language in Breeden's will create a valid testamentary charitable trust? Did the nephew and niece act ethically in this case? *In re Estate of Breeden*, 208 Cal.App.3d 981, 256 Cal.Rptr. 813, **Web** 1989 Cal.App. Lexis 215 (Court of Appeal of California)

ENDNOTES

1. 497 U.S. 261, 110 S.Ct. 2841, 11 L.Ed.2d 224, Web 1990 U.S. Lexis 3301 (Supreme Court of the United States).
2. Oregon Revised Statute Section 127.800 et seq.

▲ **Florence Lorraine and Henry Benjamin Cheeseman** *The author's parents, who celebrated 50 years of marriage.*

CHAPTER OBJECTIVES

After studying this chapter, you should be able to:

1. Define *marriage* and enumerate the legal requirements of marriage.
2. Explain adoption and describe how adoption proceedings work.
3. Define *divorce* and *no-fault divorce* and describe divorce proceedings.

4. Describe how assets are distributed upon the termination of marriage and explain the requirements for awarding spousal support.
5. Explain child custody, visitation rights, joint custody of children, and child support.

CHAPTER CONTENTS

"The happiest moments of my life have been the few which I have passed at home in the bosom of my family."

—Thomas Jefferson
Letter to Francis Willis, Jr. (April 18, 1790)

▶ INTRODUCTION TO FAMILY LAW

Family law and domestic relations is a broad area of the law, involving marriage, prenuptial agreements, dissolution of marriage, division of property upon dissolution of marriage, spousal and child support, child custody, and other family law issues. This chapter covers family law and domestic relations issues.

▶ PREMARRIAGE ISSUES

Prior to marriage, several legal issues may arise. These include *promises to marry*, *engagement*, and *prenuptial agreements*.

Promise to Marry

In the nineteenth century, many courts recognized an action for breach of a **promise to marry**. This usually would occur if a man proposed marriage, the woman accepted, and then the man backed out before the marriage took place. The lawsuit was based on a breach-of-contract theory. Today, most courts do not recognize a breach of a promise-to-marry lawsuit. The denial of such lawsuits is based on current social norms.

Example Heather and Harold promise to marry each other, and to prove their commitment, they sign a written contract to marry each other one year from the signing of the contract. They get engaged and move in together. After six months, Heather calls off the engagement. Harold cannot enforce Heather's promise to marry him. Heather is free to leave Harold even though she breaks the contract.

If the potential groom backs out close to the wedding date, after many of the items for the pending marriage have been purchased or contracted for (e.g., flowers, rental of a reception hall), he may be responsible for paying these costs.

Engagement

As a prelude to getting married, many couples go through a period of time known as **engagement**. The engagement usually begins when the male proposes marriage to the female, and if the female accepts, he gives her an engagement ring (usually a diamond ring). The engagement period runs until the wedding is held or the engagement is broken off. If the couple gets married, they often exchange wedding rings at the marriage ceremony.

Sometimes the engagement is broken off prior to the wedding. Then the issue becomes: Who gets the engagement ring if the engagement is broken off?

Fault Rule   Some states follow a **fault rule**, which works as follows:

• If the prospective groom breaks off the engagement, the prospective bride gets to keep the engagement ring.
• If the prospective bride breaks off the engagement, she must return the engagement ring to the prospective groom.

The fault rule is sometimes difficult to apply. Questions often arise as to who broke off the engagement, which then requires a trial to decide the issue.

Objective Rule   The modern rule and trend is to abandon the fault rule and adopt an **objective rule**: If the engagement is broken off, the prospective bride must return the

A successful marriage requires falling in love many times, always with the same person.

Mignon McLaughlin

objective rule
A rule which states that if an engagement is broken off, the prospective bride must return the engagement ring, regardless of which party broke off the engagement.

engagement ring, regardless of who broke off the engagement. This objective rule is clear and usually avoids litigation unless the female refuses to return the ring.

CONTEMPORARY ENVIRONMENT

Prenuptial Agreement

In today's society, many spouses sign prenuptial agreements in advance of their marriage. **Prenuptial agreements**—also called **premarital agreements**—are contracts that specify how property will be distributed upon termination of the marriage or death of a spouse. To be enforced, a prenuptial agreement must be in writing.

Prenuptial agreements are often used where each party to a marriage has his or her own career and has accumulated assets prior to the marriage, or where one of the spouses has significant assets prior to the marriage. Prenuptial agreements are also often used where there are children from a prior marriage and the agreement guarantees that those children will receive a certain share of the assets of the remarrying spouse if he or she dies or the marriage is terminated.

Prenuptial agreements often include the following:

- **Separate property.** An agreement usually lists each party's separate property that he or she is bringing into the marriage and a statement that the listed property shall remain separate property unless changed by writing during the course of the marriage.
- **Income.** A common part of a prenuptial agreement is an agreement as to how income will be treated during the marriage. For example, a high income earner may be awarded a certain percentage or dollar amount of his or income as separate property.

- **Alimony.** A prenuptial agreement can set forth the alimony that will be paid if the parties are divorced.
- **Child custody.** A prenuptial agreement can provide for child custody and visitation rights.
- **Marital property.** A prenuptial agreement can address the division of marital property upon divorce.
- **Other issues.** A prenuptial agreement can describe the treatment of other issues that can arise in a marriage.

For a prenuptial agreement to be enforceable, each party must make full disclosure of his or her assets and liabilities, and each party should be represented by his or her own attorney. Prenuptial agreements must be voluntarily entered into, without threats or undue pressure. They must provide for fair distribution of assets and must not be unconscionable. Generally, courts will enforce a properly negotiated prenuptial agreement even if the agreement provides for an unequal distribution of assets and eliminates financial support of a spouse in case the marriage is terminated.

Sometimes the parties enter into an agreement during the marriage, setting forth the distribution of property upon death or termination of the marriage. This is called an **antenuptial agreement**. With these agreements, the courts apply the same standards for enforceability as to prenuptial agreements.

---

prenuptial agreement
A contract entered into prior to marriage that specifies how property will be distributed upon the termination of the marriage or death of a spouse. Also called a *premarital agreement*.

marriage
A legal union between spouses that confers certain legal rights and duties upon the spouses and upon the children born of the marriage.

▶ MARRIAGE

Each state has marriage laws that recognize a legal union between a man and a woman. **Marriage** confers certain legal rights and duties upon the spouses, as well as upon the children born of the marriage. A couple wishing to marry must meet the legal requirements established by the state in which they are to be married. The following paragraphs discuss marriage requirements the legal rights and duties of spouses.

Marriage Requirements

State law establishes certain requirements that must be met before two people can be married. Most states require that the parties be a man and a woman. The parties must be of a certain age (usually 18 years of age). States will permit younger persons to be married if they have the consent of their parents or if they are emancipated from their parents. *Emancipation* means that the person is not supported by his or her parents and provides for himself or herself.

All states provide that persons under a certain age, such as 14 or 15 years of age, cannot be married. States also prohibit marriages between persons who are closely related, usually by blood.

Example A brother could not marry his sister or half-sister. Cousins may marry in some states.

Another requirement of marriage is that neither party can currently be married to someone else.

Marriage License

In order for two people to be legally married, certain legal procedures must be followed. State law requires that the parties obtain a **marriage license** issued by the state. Marriage licenses are usually obtained at the county clerk's office. Some states require that the parties take a blood test prior to obtaining a license. This is to determine whether the parties have certain diseases, particularly sexually transmitted diseases.

Some states require that, in addition to a marriage license, there must be some sort of **marriage ceremony**. This ceremony usually is held in front of a justice of the peace or similar government officer, or at a church, temple, synagogue, or mosque, in front of a minister, priest, rabbi, or imam. At the ceremony, the parties exchange wedding vows, in which they make a public statement that they will take each other as wife and husband.

After the wedding ceremony, the marriage license is recorded. Some states require a waiting period between the time the marriage license is obtained and when the wedding ceremony takes place.

marriage license
A legal document issued by a state which certifies that two people are married.

Financial Support

Most states require a spouse to financially support the other spouse and their children during their marriage. This includes providing for the necessities such as food, shelter, clothing, and medical care. A spouse is obligated only up to the level he or she is able to provide. In some states, this duty exists even if the spouses are living apart. The spouses are free to agree on additional duties in separate contracts. Contracts to provide sex violate public policy and are therefore illegal.

Common Law Marriage

Several states recognize a form of marriage called a **common law marriage**. A common law marriage is one in which the parties have not obtained a valid marriage license, nor have they participated in a legal marriage ceremony. Instead, a common law marriage is recognized if the following requirements are met: (1) The parties are eligible to marry, (2) the parties voluntarily intend to be husband and wife, (3) the parties must live together, and (4) the parties hold themselves out as husband and wife.

There are several misconceptions about common law marriages. First, cohabitation is not sufficient in and of itself to establish a common law marriage. Second, the length of time the parties live together is not sufficient alone to establish a common law marriage. For example, couples who immediately live together and intend a common law marriage have one, whereas couples who live together a long time but do not intend a common law marriage do not have one.

When a state recognizes a common law marriage and the necessary requirements are met to establish one, the couple has a legal and formal marriage. All the rights and duties of a normal licensed marriage apply. A court decree of divorce must therefore be obtained to end a common law marriage.

common law marriage
A type of marriage some states recognize, in which a marriage license has not been issued but certain requirements are met.

CONTEMPORARY ENVIRONMENT
Same-Sex Marriage

Many couples of the same sex cohabit as if they are married couples. These same-sex couples have fought legal battles in many states to have the law changed to recognize **same-sex marriage**. These couples argue that the Equal Protection Clause of the U.S. Constitution and state constitutions require that their unions be accorded the same legal recognition as marriage unions between a man and a woman.

In 2004, the state of Massachusetts granted equal rights for gay couples to get married. In 2008, although the California supreme court ruled that gay couples could marry, a subsequent state constitutional amendment overruled this decision. Several other states provide that gay partners can enter into "civil unions" that grant gay partners rights similar to those of heterosexual marriage partners.

Many states have adopted statutes stating that same-sex marriages obtained in other states will be not recognized as legal in their state. Over half of the states have enacted constitutional amendments to their state constitutions that ban gay marriages.

In 1996, the federal Congress enacted the **Defense of Marriage Act (DOMA)** [28 U.S.C. Section 1738C], which bars same–sex couples from enjoying federal benefits (e.g., Social Security benefits due the spouse of a married couple). This federal act also provides that states cannot be forced to recognize same-sex marriages performed in other states.

The battle between the sides that want and do not want same-sex marriages to be recognized as legal will continue for years to come. Most of these battles will be fought in state courts, in state legislatures, and by state referendums. There is also lobbying by both sides to have federal laws enacted that would weigh in on this issue.

▶ PARENTS AND CHILDREN

In many instances, a major purpose of marriage is to have children. Couples who have children have certain legal rights and duties that develop from their parental status.

Parents' Rights and Duties

emancipation
A minor's act of legally separating from his or her parents and providing for himself or herself.

Parents have an obligation to provide food, shelter, clothing, medical care, and other necessities to their children until a child reaches age 18 or until **emancipation**. A child becomes emancipated if he or she leaves his or her parents and voluntarily lives on his or her own. The law imposes certain other duties on parents as well.

Examples A parent must see to it that his or her child attends school up until 16 or 18 years of age, depending on the state, unless the child is home-schooled. Parents may be legally responsible for a child beyond the age of majority if the child has a disability.

Parents also have the right to control the behavior of their children. Parents have the right to select schools for their children and the religion they will practice. Parents have the right to use corporal punishment (physical punishment) as long as it does not rise to the level of child abuse. For example, mild slapping or spanking is legally permitted.

child neglect
A parent's failure to provide a child with the necessities of life or other basic needs.

Child neglect occurs when a parent fails to provide a child with the necessities of life or other basic needs. The state may remove a child, either temporarily or permanently, from situations of child neglect. A parent's refusal to obtain medical care for a child can be punished as a crime.

Parent's Liability for a Child's Wrongful Act

Law cannot stand aside from the social changes around it.

William J. Brennan, Jr.

Generally, parents are not liable for their children's negligent acts. However, parents are liable if their negligence caused their child's act.

Example If a child negligently injures another child while they are playing, the parents of the child who caused the injury are not liable.

Example If a parent lets a child who does not have a driver's license drive an automobile and the child-driver injures someone, the parents are liable.

About half of the states have enacted child liability statutes that make the parents financially liable for the intentional torts of their children. This liability is usually limited to a specified dollar amount, such as $5,000.

adoption
A situation in which a person becomes the legal parent of a child who is not his or her biological child.

Adoption

Adoption occurs when a person becomes the legal parent of a child who is not his or her biological child. A married couple can adopt a child together, a single parent can adopt a child, and a spouse can adopt the child of his or her new spouse.

The process for adoption is complicated and is regulated by state law. Basically, the procedure for adoption consists of the following requirements:

- All procedures of the state law for adoption are met.
- The biological parents' legal rights as parents are terminated by legal decree or death.
- A court formally approves the adoption.

The two main ways by which persons can become adoptive parents are *agency adoptions* and *independent adoptions*

Agency Adoption   An **agency adoption** occurs when a person adopts a child from a social service organization of a state. The state often obtains jurisdiction over children who are born out of wedlock and whose biological parents give them up for adoption by terminating their parental rights. The state also may obtain jurisdiction over a child if the child has been permanently removed from parents who are judged unsuitable to be parents or where parents are deceased and no relative wants or qualifies to become the child's parents.

In the past, the identity of the biological parents of adopted children was kept confidential in an agency adoption. Currently, many states allow for disclosure of the identity of the biological parents in certain circumstances. Usually, the court will notify the other side—either the child or the biological parent—that the other wishes to meet with them. If both sides consent, a meeting will be arranged.

In many cases today, **open adoption** procedures are being used. In these cases, the biological and adoptive parents are introduced prior to the adoption. The biological parents may screen the prospective adoptive parents to ensure that the adoptive parents are suitable for the child. In many instances, the adoptive and biological parents remain in contact with each other, and the biological parents are given visitation rights to see the child.

Independent Adoption   An **independent adoption** occurs when there is a private arrangement between biological and adoptive parents of a child. Often, an intermediary, such as a lawyer, doctor, or private adoption agency, introduces the two parties. The biological parents and the adoptive parents enter into a private arrangement for adoption of the child. Adoptive parents usually pay intermediaries a fee for their services, as well as pay the costs of the adoption.

Many divorced people who have children remarry. Often, a new stepparent formally adopts the child or children of his or her new spouse. To do so, the other biological parent of the child must relinquish his or her legal rights concerning the child. This can be done voluntarily or by order of the court if it is in the best interests of the child.

Foster Care

A child may become the responsibility of the state under several circumstances. The first is if a child's parents or parent dies and there are no relatives to take the child or no other arrangements have been made for the care of the child. Another situation occurs if the state institutes a proceeding to remove a child from the parents' or parent's custody, based on the parent being unfit to care for the child or because the child is in danger (e.g., from child abuse).

Today, the primary means of caring for children under the state's jurisdiction is to place children in **foster care**. This is usually a temporary arrangement. The state pays the foster family for the care given to a foster child. This temporary arrangement will be terminated if the child is returned to his or her biological parents or if the child is legally adopted. Sometimes the foster parents will legally adopt a child who has been placed in their care.

▶ MARRIAGE TERMINATION

Once a state has recognized the marital status of a couple, only the state can terminate this marital status. This is so even if the couple separate and live apart from one another. As long as they are married, they continue to have certain legal rights and duties to one another. The law recognizes two methods for legally terminating a marriage: *annulment* and *divorce.*

agency adoption
An adoption that occurs when a person adopts a child from a social service organization of a state.

independent adoption
An adoption that occurs when there is a private arrangement between biological and adoptive parents of a child.

Annulment

annulment
An order of the court which declares that a marriage did not exist.

An **annulment** is an order of the court, declaring that a marriage did not exist. The order invalidates the marriage. Annulments are rarely granted now that most states recognize no-fault divorces.

Certain grounds must be asserted to obtain a legal annulment. One ground is that the parties lacked capacity to consent. Examples are: (1) One of the parties was a minor and had not obtained his or her parents' consent to marry, (2) one of the parties was mentally incapacitated at the time of marriage, (3) one of the parties was intoxicated at the time of the marriage, or (4) the marriage was never consummated. Marriage can also be annulled if the parties are too closely related to one another or there was bigamy (one of the parties was already married). A marriage can also be annulled if there was duress or fraud leading to the marriage (e.g., one of the parties declared that he or she could conceive children when the person knew in fact that he or she could not).

The law considers children born of a marriage that is annulled to be legitimate. When a marriage is annulled, issues of child support, child custody, spousal support, and property settlement must be agreed upon by the couple or decided by the court.

Divorce

divorce
An order of the court that terminates a marriage.

The most common option used by married partners to terminate their marriage is divorce. **Divorce** is a legal proceeding whereby the court issues a decree that legally orders a marriage terminated.

Traditionally, a married person who sought a divorce had to prove that the other person was **at fault** for causing a major problem with continuing the marriage. Grounds for granting a divorce consisted of adultery, physical or emotional abuse, abandonment, substance or alcohol abuse, or insanity.

no-fault divorce
A divorce recognized by the law of a state whereby neither party is blamed for the divorce.

Beginning in the 1960s, states began to recognize **no-fault divorce**. A spouse wishing to obtain a divorce merely had to assert *irreconcilable differences* with his or her spouse. In a no-fault divorce, neither party is blamed for the divorce. Today, every state recognizes no-fault divorce. A spouse may still decide to assert that the other party was at fault for causing the divorce in those states that consider fault when deciding how to divide marital assets and award spousal support.

petition for divorce
A document filed with the proper state court that commences a divorce proceeding.

Divorce Proceedings   A divorce proceeding is commenced by a spouse filing a **petition for divorce** with the proper state court. The petition must contain required information, such as the names of the spouses, date and place of marriage, names of minor children, and reason for the divorce. The petition must be served on the other spouse. That spouse then has a certain period of time (usually 20 to 30 days) to file an answer to the petition.

If the spouses do not reach a settlement of the issues involved in the divorce—such as property division, custody of the children, and spousal and child support—the case will go to trial. The parties are permitted to conduct discovery, which includes taking depositions and producing documents. If the case goes to trial, each side is permitted to call witnesses, including expert witnesses (e.g., financial experts), to testify on his or her behalf. Both parties are also allowed to introduce evidence to support their claims.

decree of divorce
A court order that terminates a marriage.

Many states require a certain waiting period from the date a divorce petition is filed to the date the court grants a divorce. A typical waiting period is six months. The public policy for this waiting period is to give the parties time for reconciliation. After the waiting period has passed, a court will enter a **decree of divorce**, which is a court order that terminates the marriage. The parties are then free to marry again. The decree of divorce may be granted even if the other issues concerning the divorce, such as the division of property or support payments, have not yet been settled or tried.

If there is a showing that one partner is likely to injure the other spouse, a court may issue a **restraining order**. This places limitations on the ability of the dangerous partner to go near the innocent partner.

***Pro se* Divorce**   In a *pro se* **divorce**, the parties do not have to hire lawyers to represent them but may represent themselves in the divorce proceeding. Most states permit *pro se*—commonly called "do-it-yourself"—divorces. If there are substantial assets at stake in the divorce, or if there are other complicated issues involving child custody, child support, or spousal support, the parties usually hire lawyers to represent them in the divorce proceeding.

Settlement Agreement   Approximately 90 percent of divorce cases are settled between the parties prior to trial. The parties often engage in negotiations to try to settle a divorce lawsuit in order to save the time and expense of a trial and to reach an agreement that is acceptable to each side. These negotiations are usually conducted between the parties with the assistance of their attorneys.

Some divorcing parties use mediation to try to reach a settlement of the issues involved in terminating their marriage. Some states require mediation before divorcing couples can use the court to try the case. In *mediation*, a neutral third party—often an attorney, a retired judge, or another party—acts as a *mediator* between the parties. A mediator is not empowered to make a decision but, instead, acts as a go-between and facilitator to try to help the parties reach an acceptable settlement of the issues. Mediation is often successful because it forces the parties to consider all facets of the case, even the position of the opposing side.

If a settlement is reached, a **settlement agreement** is drafted, usually by the attorneys. After being signed by the parties, the settlement agreement is presented to the court. The court accepts the terms of the settlement agreement if the judge believes that the settlement is fair and that the rights of the parties and minor children are properly taken care of. If a case is not settled, the case goes to trial.

settlement agreement
A written document signed by divorcing parties that evidences their agreement settling property rights and other issues of their divorce.

CONTEMPORARY ENVIRONMENT

Paul McCartney's Divorce

Paul McCartney is one of the four original Beatles, a group from England that took the music scene by storm in the 1960s and into the 1970s. Of the four Beatles—John Lennon, Paul McCartney, George Harrison, and Ringo Starr—Lennon and McCartney are credited with writing most of the songs that the Beatles sung. Eventually the Beatles broke up as a group, and Paul McCartney continued a career as a solo artist. Lennon was fatally shot, and Harrison has passed away. Paul McCartney was knighted by the Queen of England and is sometimes referred to as Sir Paul McCartney.

Paul McCartney's first wife passed away. He waited four years and then, in 2004, he married Heather Mills. McCartney and Mills did not sign a prenuptial agreement. McCartney and Mills had a daughter named Beatrice.

After four years of marriage, the marriage fell apart, and the parties separated. In a protracted and nasty divorce proceeding, the parties argued about how much Heather Mills should get of Paul McCartney's money and assets. At the time of divorce, McCartney's net worth was estimated to be over $800 million. McCartney had made almost all of his fortune prior to marrying Heather Mills. In the divorce proceedings, Heather Mills claimed that McCartney's fortune totaled $1.6 billion and that she was entitled to $250 million of it.

After firing her attorneys, Mills took over her own case and represented herself in court during the divorce proceedings. After a lengthy trial in which both sides presented evidence, the judge awarded Mills $48.6 million. Over Mills's objection, the judge allowed the judgment to be made public. The lengthy judgment goes through the details of the couple's marriage, claims, divorce, and other details. Sir Paul should not have believed the words of a Beatles's song that "All you need is love."

Business Ethics   Do you think Paul McCartney should have required a prenuptial agreement as a prerequisite to marrying Heather Mills? Do you think that the amount that Heather Mills received was appropriate? Or was it too little or too much?

▶ DIVISION OF ASSETS

Upon termination of a marriage, the parties may own certain assets, including property owned prior to marriage, gifts and inheritances received during marriage, and assets purchased with income earned during the marriage. In most cases, the parties reach a settlement as to how these assets are to be divided. If no settlement agreement is reached, the court orders the division of assets.

Separate Property

separate property
Property owned by a spouse prior to marriage, as well as inheritances and gifts received by a spouse during the marriage.

In most states, each spouse's separate property is awarded to the spouse who owns the separate property. **Separate property** includes property owned by a spouse prior to the marriage, as well as inheritances and gifts received during the marriage. In most states, upon the termination of a marriage, each spouse is awarded his or her separate property.

However, if separate property is commingled with marital property during the course of the marriage, or if the owner of the separate property changes title to the separate property by placing the other spouse's name on title to the property (e.g., real estate), the separate property is then considered a marital asset.

Marital Property

marital property
Property acquired during the course of marriage using income earned during the marriage, and separate property that has been converted to marital property.

Marital property consists of property acquired during the course of the marriage using income earned by the spouses during the marriage, and separate property that has been converted to marital property. There are two major legal theories that different states adhere to when dividing marital assets upon the termination of a marriage. These are the theories of *equitable distribution* and *community property*.

equitable distribution
A law used by many states where the court orders a fair distribution of marital property to the divorcing spouses.

Equitable Distribution   In states that follow the rule of **equitable distribution**, the court may order the *fair distribution* of property. The fair distribution of property does not necessarily mean the equal distribution of property. In determining the fair distribution of property, the court may consider factors such as:

- Length of the marriage
- Occupation of each spouse
- Standard of living during the marriage
- Wealth and income-earning ability of each spouse
- Which party is awarded custody of the children
- Health of the individuals
- Other factors relevant to the case

In most states, the house is usually awarded to the parent who is granted custody of the children. A court may order the house to be sold and the proceeds divided fairly between the individuals.

community property
A law used by some states where the court orders an equal division of marital property to the divorcing spouses.

Community Property   Under the doctrine of **community property**, all property acquired during the marriage using income earned during the marriage is considered marital property. It does not matter which spouse earned the income or which spouse earned higher income. Money placed in pension funds, stock options, the value of businesses, the value of professional licenses, and such, are considered community property.

In community property states, marital property is divided *equally* between the individuals. This does not necessarily mean that each piece of property is sold and the proceeds are divided equally between the individuals. Usually each of the marital assets is valued using appraisers and expert witnesses. The court then awards the property to the spouses. If one spouse is awarded the house, the other spouse is awarded other property of equal value.

CONCEPT SUMMARY

DIVISION OF MARITAL ASSETS

Law	Description
Equitable distribution	Marital property is fairly distributed. This does not necessarily mean equal distribution of the property.
Community property	Marital property is divided *equally* between the parties.

Division of Debts

Individuals often have debts that must be divided upon termination of the marriage. How these debts are divided depends on the type of debt and on state law. In most states, each spouse is personally liable for his or her own premarital debts, and the other spouse is not liable for those debts. This is because the debt was incurred prior to the marriage. Student loans are a good example of these types of debts.

Debts that are incurred during the marriage for necessities and other joint needs, including but not limited to shelter, clothing, automobiles, medical expenses, and such, are **joint marital debts** and are the joint responsibility of the spouses. The court may equally distribute these debts upon termination of the marriage. Spouses are jointly liable for taxes incurred during their marriage. If a debt is not paid by the spouse to whom the court has distributed the debt, the third-party creditor may recover payment of the debt from the other spouse, however. This individual's only recourse is to recover the amount paid from his or her prior spouse.

Upon the termination of a marriage, it is wise for the individuals to notify prior creditors that they will no longer be responsible for the other's debts. This is particularly true if the individuals have joint credit cards.

In the following case, the court had to decide whether certain property was marital property or separate property.

Our legal system faces no theoretical dilemma but a single continuous problem: how to apply to ever changing conditions the never changing principles of freedom.

Earl Warren

joint marital debts
Debts incurred during the marriage for joint needs.

CASE 53.1 Separate Property

In the Matter of the Marriage of Joyner
196 S.W.3d 883, Web 2006 Tex.App. Lexis 5691 (2006)
Court of Appeals of Texas

"Belinda Joyner filed for divorce from Thomas Joyner. The day after the final hearing, Thomas purchased a winning lottery ticket worth $2,080,000."

—Judge Carter

Facts

Belinda Ann Joyner filed for divorce from Thomas Stephen Joyner. The parties engaged in three mediation sessions to negotiate the settlement of property disputes. After the end of their third mediation session, the parties signed a mediated settlement agreement that delineated and partitioned their property. Each of the parties' lawyers also signed the agreement. Subsequently, the parties appeared in court for the final hearing, to argue a few personal property issues that remained, including ownership of a ring and a broach that had been given to Thomas by his mother. The court clearly and explicitly decided which party should have ownership of these items. Although Belinda argued that she should have them because Thomas had made them gifts to their daughter earlier, the court awarded Thomas's mother's rings and broach to Thomas. The judge then stated: "You've elected not to make yourself a gift of these items to your daughter. And that's your prerogative. You have every legal right to do so. And it may be that—your divorce is granted—so I'll now say—your former wife has made all this up."

The day after the final hearing, Thomas purchased a lottery ticket. He won the lottery, worth $2,080,000. The judge subsequently signed the final decree of divorce. Belinda filed a motion, claiming that the divorce had not yet been finalized and that she was still married to Thomas because the judge had not yet signed the final decree of divorce. Belinda argued that the $2,080,000 lottery winnings should be divided equally with her. Thomas alleged that the divorce was final and that the $2,080,000 was his separate property and was his and his only. The trial court agreed with Thomas and awarded him the money. Belinda appealed.

Issue

Was the $2,080,000 lottery winning separate property that Thomas could keep, or was it community property that needed to be divided equally between Thomas and Belinda?

Language of the Court

Belinda Joyner filed for divorce from Thomas Joyner. The day after the final hearing, Thomas purchased a winning lottery ticket worth $2,080,000. The issue in this case is whether the trial court's actions constituted an oral rendition of judgment on the Joyners' divorce. A judgment is

(case continues)

rendered when the court makes an announcement, either in writing or orally in open court, of its decision on the matter submitted for adjudication. Once a judgment is rendered by oral pronouncement, the entry of a written judgment is purely a ministerial act. In order to be an official judgment, the trial court's oral pronouncement must indicate intent to render a full, final, and complete judgment at that point in time.

In this case, the words granting a divorce are undeniably there. The statement by the trial court was made in open court while officiating as the presiding judge after all evidence had been presented and in the presence of all parties and attorneys. During the process of ruling on some personal property items, the court then stated, "You've elected not to make yourself a gift of these items to your daughter. And that is your prerogative. You have every legal right to do so. And it may be that—your divorce is granted—so I'll now say—your former wife has made all this up." We interpret that as a clear statement granting the divorce. The trial court then referred to Belinda as "your former wife." Once a

couple is divorced, they can no longer accumulate community property, for there is no longer a community.

Decision

The court of appeals held that the Joyners' divorce was final when the trial court made its oral pronouncement of such. The court of appeals affirmed the judgment of the trial court that awarded the $2,080,000 lottery winnings to Thomas Joyner as his separate property.

Case Questions

Critical Legal Thinking What is the difference between separate and community property? Explain.

Business Ethics Did Belinda act ethically in this case? Did Thomas act ethically in this case?

Contemporary Business If a person brings separate property into a marriage and wants it to remain separate property, what should he or she do—or not do?

▶ SPOUSAL SUPPORT, CHILD SUPPORT, AND CHILD CUSTODY

When a marriage is terminated, spousal support and child support may be awarded. In addition, custody of the children must be decided. These issues are discussed in the following paragraphs.

Spousal Support

spousal support
Payments made by one divorced spouse to the other divorced spouse. Also called *alimony*.

In some cases where a marriage is terminated, a court may award **spousal support**—also called **alimony**—to one of the divorced spouses. The other divorced spouse is usually ordered to pay the alimony in monthly payments. The parties may agree to the amount of alimony to be paid. If an agreement is not reached, the court determines whether the payment of alimony is warranted and, if so, the amount of alimony to be paid. In the past, alimony has usually been awarded to the female. Today, with the female often earning more than the male, the male has been awarded alimony in some cases.

Alimony is usually awarded for a specific period of time. This is called **temporary alimony**, or **rehabilitation alimony**. This alimony is designed to provide the receiving individual with payment for a limited time during which the individual can obtain the education or job skills necessary to enter the job force. Alimony is also awarded in cases where a parent, usually the female, needs to care for a disabled child and must remain home to care for the child. The amount of alimony is based on the needs of the individual who will receive the alimony and the income and ability of the other individual to pay.

Spousal support payments usually terminate if the former spouse dies, remarries, or otherwise becomes self-sufficient. Spousal support awards can be modified by the court if circumstances change. This usually occurs if the paying individual loses his or her job or his or her income decreases, or if the receiving individual's income increases. A party wishing to have a spousal support award changed must petition the court to *modify* the award of spousal support.

Permanent alimony—sometimes called **lifetime alimony**—is usually awarded only if the individual to receive the alimony is of an older age and if that individual has been a homemaker who has little opportunity to obtain job skills to enter the workplace. Permanent alimony must be paid until the individual receiving it dies or remarries.

Child Support

The non-custodial parent is obligated to contribute to the financial support of his or her biological and adopted children. This includes a child's costs for food, shelter, clothing, medical expenses, and other necessities of life. This payment is called **child support**. The custodial and non-custodial parents may agree to the amount of child support. If they do not, the court determines the amount of child support to be paid.

In awarding child support, the court may consider several factors, including the number of children, the needs of the children, the net income of the parents, the standard of living of the children prior to termination of the marriage, any special medical or other needs of the children, and other factors the court deems relevant. The duty to pay child support usually continues until a child reaches the age of majority, graduates from high school, or emancipates himself or herself by voluntary choosing to live on his or her own.

To help in the determination of child support, about half of the states have adopted a formula for computing the amount of child support. These formulas are usually based on a percentage of the non-custodial parent's income. A court is permitted to deviate from the formula if a child has special needs, such as if the child has a disability or requires special educational assistance.

An award of child support may be modified if conditions change. For example, an award of child support may be decreased if the non-custodial parent loses his or her job. The amount of child support may be modified if the child's needs change, such as if the child needs special care because of a disability. The parent wishing to obtain modification of child support must petition the court to change the award of child support.

child support
Payments made by a non-custodial parent to help financially support his or her children.

ETHICS SPOTLIGHT

Federal Family Support Act

In the past, many non-custodial parents failed to pay child support when it was due. In many cases, the custodial parent had to initiate long and expensive legal procedures to obtain child support payments. To remedy this situation, the federal government enacted the **Family Support Act** [Public Law 100-485]. This federal law, effective in 1994, provides that all original or modified child support orders require automatic wage withholding from a non-custodial parent's income. The Family Support Act was designed primarily to prevent non-custodial parents from failing to pay required support payments.

Assume that a court order requires a non-custodial parent to pay 25 percent of his or her gross monthly income for child support. In this case, the court will order the non-custodial parent's employer to deduct this amount from that parent's income and send a check in that amount to the custodial parent. The non-custodial parent receives a check for the remainder of his or her income.

Business Ethics What is the stated goal of the federal Family Support Act? Do you think that there are many deadbeat parents who do not pay child support as ordered by the court?

Child Custody

When a couple terminates their marriage and they have children, the issue of who is legally and physically responsible for raising the children must be decided, either by settlement or by the court. The legal term *custody* is used to describe who has legal responsibility for raising a child. **Child custody** is one of the most litigated issues of divorcing couples.

Traditionally, the court almost always granted custody of a child to the mother. Today, with fathers taking a more active role in childrearing, and with many mothers working, this is not always the case. In child custody disputes where both parents want custody of a child, the courts determine what is in the *best interests of the child* in awarding custody. Some of the factors that a court considers are:

- The ability of each parent to provide for the emotional needs of the child
- The ability of each parent to provide for other needs of the child, such as education
- The ability of each parent to provide a stable environment for the child
- The ability of each parent to provide for the special needs of a child if the child has a disability or requires special care

child custody
The award of legal custody of a child to a parent, based on the best interests of the child. The parent awarded custody is called the *custodial parent.*

- The desire of each parent to provide for the needs of the child
- The wishes of the child (This factor is given more weight as the child gets older.)
- The religion of each parent
- Other factors the court deems relevant

The awarding of custody to a **custodial parent** is not permanent. Custody may be altered by the court if circumstances change. The parent who is awarded custody has **legal custody** of the child. This usually includes physical custody of the child. The custodial parent has the right to make day-to-day decisions and major decisions concerning the child's education, religion, and other such matters.

The court does not award custody to a parent, and sometimes not to either parent, if it is in the child's best interest not to be awarded to a parent, or if there has been child abuse, or if there are other extenuating circumstances. In such cases, the court may award custody to other relatives, such as grandparents, or place the child in a foster home.

joint custody
A custody arrangement that gives both parents responsibility for making major decisions concerning the child.

Joint Custody   Most states now permit joint custody of a child. **Joint custody** means that both parents are responsible for making major decisions concerning the child, such as his or her education, religion, and other major matters.

Parents are sometimes awarded **joint physical custody** of a child as well. This means that the child spends a certain portion of time being raised by each parent. For example, the child may spend every other week with each parent, or the child might spend the weekdays with one parent and the weekends with the other parent. These arrangements are awarded only if the child's best interests are served, such as the child being able to remain in the same school while in the physical custody of each parent.

visitation rights
Rights of a non-custodial parent to visit with the child for limited periods of time.

Visitation Rights   If the parents do not have joint custody of a child, the non-custodial parent is usually awarded **visitation rights**. This means that the non-custodial parent is given the right to visit the child for limited periods of time, as determined by a settlement agreement or by the court.

If the court is concerned about the safety of a child, the court may grant only supervised visitation rights to a non-custodial parent. This means that a court-appointed person must be present during the non-custodial parent's visitation with the child. This is usually done if there has been a history of child abuse or there is a strong possibility that the non-custodial parent might kidnap the child.

TEST REVIEW TERMS AND CONCEPTS

Adoption	Defense of Marriage Act	Joint physical custody	Prenuptial agreement
Agency adoption	(DOMA)	Legal custody	(premarital agreement)
Annulment	Divorce	Marital property	Promise to marry
Antenuptial agreement	Emancipation	Marriage	*Pro se* divorce
At fault	Engagement	Marriage ceremony	Restraining order
Child custody	Equitable distribution	Marriage license	Same-sex marriage
Child neglect	Family Support Act	No-fault divorce	Separate property
Child support	Fault rule	Objective rule	Settlement agreement
Common law marriage	Foster care	Open adoption	Spousal support (alimony)
Community property	Independent adoption	Permanent alimony	Temporary alimony
Custodial parent	Joint custody	(lifetime alimony)	(rehabilitation alimony)
Decree of divorce	Joint marital debts	Petition for divorce	Visitation rights

CASE PROBLEMS

53.1 Marital Assets   George Neville and Tina Neville were married. At the time, George was 31 years old and a practicing attorney; Tina was a 23-year-old medical student. After 7 years, Tina became a licensed physician. Soon after, George filed for divorce from Tina because she was having an adulterous affair with another doctor. At the time of the divorce, George was earning $55,000 per year practicing law; Tina was earning $165,000 per year as a physician.

The divorce was filed in Mississippi, where the couple lived. Mississippi follows the doctrine of equitable distribution. George sought to have Tina's medical license and medical practice valued as an ongoing business, and he claimed a portion of the value. The court refused George's request and instead applied the doctrine of equitable distribution and awarded him rehabilitative alimony of $1,400 per month for 120 months. The aggregate amount of the alimony was $168,000. George appealed this award, alleging on appeal that Tina's medical license and practice should be valued, and he should receive a portion of this value. Under the doctrine of equitable distribution, was the trial court's award fair, or should George win on appeal? *Neville v. Neville*, 734 So.2d 352, **Web** 1999 Miss.App. Lexis 68 (Court of Appeals of Mississippi)

53.2 Marital Assets   Ronald R. and Edith Johnston were married and had three sons ranging in age from 12 to 16 when the parties separated. Edith filed for divorce the same year. The Johnstons owned a primary residence worth $186,000, with no mortgage on it. Ronald was a successful entrepreneur. He owned Depot Distributors, Inc., a business involved in selling and installing bathroom cabinets. He also owned several other businesses. In the four years leading up to the divorce, Ronald's income was $543,382; $820,439; $1,919,713; and $1,462,712. Ronald invested much of his income in commercial and residential real estate that was held in his name only. At the time of the divorce trial, the real estate was valued at $11,760,000 and was subject to mortgages of $4,966,343.

After their separation, Ronald engaged in certain transfers of property and distributions of property, in violation of the court's order, that obfuscated his income and net worth. The trial court judge therefore accepted Edith's appraisals of the value of the real estate. The trial court judge applied the equitable distribution doctrine of Massachusetts and awarded Edith real estate totaling $2,446,000, the family residence, and alimony of $1,200 per month. The trial court judge

awarded Ronald real estate valued at $9,314,000 subject to mortgages of $4,966,343, for a net value of $4,347,657. The judge characterized this as a roughly 60–40 split of the real estate (i.e., 60 percent for Ronald and 40 percent for Edith). Ronald appealed the split of real estate and the award of alimony as violating the equitable distribution doctrine. Under the doctrine of equitable distribution, was the trial court's award fair, or should Ronald win on appeal? *Johnston v. Johnston*, 38 Mass.App.Ct. 531, 649 N.E.2d 799, **Web** 1995 Mass.App. Lexis 429 (Appeals Court of Massachusetts)

53.3 Child Custody   Randolph J. Schweinberg and Sandra Faye Click were married. Thirteen years later, Sandra Click moved out of the couple's home, and the couple was divorced the same year. At the time of the divorce, the couple had two minor children, Randolph II and Russell. Randolph II had cerebral palsy and walked with difficulty. The children lived with Randolph after Sandra moved out. Randolph was a sergeant in the U.S. Air Force, stationed in South Carolina; he considered Florida as his permanent home, however.

In the divorce proceeding, the court awarded custody of the two minor children to Randolph. The two children were doing well in school, and the court found that Randolph II needed the emotional support provided by his brother Russell. Sandra was permitted visitation rights to see the children. Sandra later married a new husband, who had previously been convicted of lewd and lascivious behavior on a female child and was under court supervision for 15 years.

Sandra petitioned the court to modify the custody order to grant her custody of the two minor children. The trial court granted the petition and awarded custody to Sandra. Randolph appealed the trial court's decision. Under the best interests test, should Randolph or Sandra be awarded custody of the two minor children? *Schweinberg v. Click* 627 So.2d 548, **Web** 1993 Fla.App. Lexis 11660 (Court of Appeal of Florida)

BUSINESS ETHICS CASES

53.4 Business Ethics   Mrs. Barbara Chadwick filed for divorce in Pennsylvania from Mr. H. Beatty Chadwick. During an equitable distribution conference, Mr. Chadwick informed the divorce court that he had transferred more than $2.5 million of the marital estate to pay an alleged debt he owed to Maison Blanche, Ltd., a Gibraltar partnership. It was later discovered that the principals of Maison Blanche had transferred approximately $1 million to a bank account in Switzerland in Mr. Chadwick's name and had purchased approximately $950,000 of insurance annuity contracts in Mr. Chadwick's name. Mr. Chadwick redeemed these annuity contracts and received the money. In addition, Mr. Chadwick claimed that $550,000 of stock certificates in his name had been "lost."

The divorce court ordered Mr. Chadwick to return the $2,500,000 to an account under the jurisdiction of the court.

When Mr. Chadwick refused, the court held Mr. Chadwick in civil contempt of court and ordered him jailed. During a seven-year period of incarceration, Mr. Chadwick applied 14 times to be released from prison, and each request was denied. Mr. Chadwick filed another request to be released from prison, alleging that he should be released because it was unlikely that he would comply with the divorce court's order to turn over the money and that, therefore, the civil contempt order had lost its coercive effect. The District Court agreed and granted Mr. Chadwick's petition to be released from prison. The government appealed the case to the U.S. Court of Appeals. Did Mr. Chadwick act ethically in this case? Should Mr. Chadwick be released from prison? *Chadwick V. Janecka Warden*, 312 F.3d 597, **Web** 2002 U.S. App. Lexis 25263 (United States Court of Appeals for the Third Circuit)

Part XII
GLOBAL ENVIRONMENT

▲ **Pyongyang, North Korea** *This is a presentation at the mass games of the Arirang Festival in Pyongyang, North Korea. The mass games involve up to 100,000 participants. The North Korean flag shown here is made of cards held by fans in Pyongyang's 150,000-seat stadium. Countries around the world have various political systems—democracy, communist, dictatorship, socialist, and variations of these. North Korea—officially the Democratic People's Republic of Korea (DPRK)—is a socialist dictatorship. In the past 50 years, the country has been ruled by the late Kim Il-sung and then by his son Kim Jong-il. Because of its isolationist policy, North Korea is often referred to as the "Hermit Kingdom."*

CHAPTER OBJECTIVES

After studying this chapter, you should be able to:

1. Describe the U.S. government's power under the Foreign Commerce Clause and Treaty Clause of the U.S. Constitution.
2. Describe nations' courts jurisdiction over international disputes.
3. Describe the functions and governance of the United Nations.

4. Describe the North American Free Trade Agreement (NAFTA) and other regional economic organizations.
5. Describe the World Trade Organization (WTO) and explain how its dispute resolution procedure works.

CHAPTER CONTENTS

"International law, or the law that governs between nations, has at times, been like the common law within states, a twilight existence during which it is hardly distinguishable from morality or justice, till at length the imprimatur of a court attests its jural quality."

—Justice Cardozo
New Jersey v. Delaware (1934)

▶ INTRODUCTION TO INTERNATIONAL AND WORLD TRADE LAW

International law, important to both nations and businesses, has many unique features. First, there is no single legislative source of international law. All countries of the world and numerous international organizations are responsible for enacting international law. Second, there is no single world court that is responsible for interpreting international law. There are, however, several courts and tribunals that hear and decide international legal disputes of parties that agree to appear before them. Third, there is no world executive branch that can enforce international law. Thus, nations do not have to obey international law enacted by other countries or international organizations. Because of these uncertainties, some commentators question whether international law is really law.

As technology and transportation bring nations closer together and as American and foreign firms increase their global activities, international law will become even more important to governments and businesses. This chapter introduces the main concepts of international law and discusses the sources of international law and the organizations responsible for its administration.

international law
Law that governs affairs between nations and that regulates transactions between individuals and businesses of different countries.

▶ THE UNITED STATES AND FOREIGN AFFAIRS

The U.S. Constitution divides the power to regulate the internal affairs of this country between the federal and state governments. On the international level, however, the Constitution gives most of the power to the federal government. Two constitutional provisions establish this authority: the Foreign Commerce Clause and the Treaty Clause.

Foreign Commerce Clause

Article I, Section 8, Clause 3 of the U.S. Constitution—the **Foreign Commerce Clause**—vests Congress with the power "to regulate commerce with foreign nations." The Constitution does not vest exclusive power over foreign affairs in the federal government, but any state or local law that unduly burdens foreign commerce is unconstitutional, as a violation of the Foreign Commerce Clause.

Foreign Commerce Clause
A clause of the U.S. Constitution that vests Congress with the power "to regulate commerce with foreign nations."

Treaty Clause

Treaty Clause
A clause of the U.S. Constitution which states that the president "shall have the power . . . to make treaties, provided two-thirds of the senators present concur."

Article II, Section 2, Clause 2 of the U.S. Constitution—the **Treaty Clause**—states that the president "shall have power, by and with the advice and consent of the Senate, to make treaties, provided two-thirds of the senators present concur."

Under the Treaty Clause, only the federal government can enter into treaties with foreign nations. Under the Supremacy Clause of the Constitution, treaties become part of the "law of the land," and conflicting state or local law is void. The president is the agent of the United States in dealing with foreign countries.

Treaties and conventions are the equivalents of legislation at the international level. A **treaty** is an agreement or a contract between two or more nations that is formally signed by an authorized representative and ratified by the supreme power of each nation. **Bilateral treaties** are between two nations; **multilateral treaties** involve more than two nations. **Conventions** are treaties that are sponsored by international organizations, such as the United Nations. Conventions normally have many signatories. Treaties and conventions address such matters as human rights, foreign aid, navigation, commerce, and the settlement of disputes. Most treaties are registered with and published by the United Nations.

treaty
The first source of international law, consisting of an agreement or a contract between two or more nations that is formally signed by an authorized representative and ratified by the supreme power of each nation.

convention
A treaty that is sponsored by an international organization.

▶ UNITED NATIONS

United Nations (UN)
An international organization created by a multilateral treaty in 1945 to promote social and economic cooperation among nations and to protect human rights.

One of the most important international organizations is the **United Nations (UN)**, which was created by a multilateral treaty on October 24, 1945.[1] Most countries of the world are members of the UN. The goals of the UN, which is headquartered in New York City, are to maintain peace and security in the world, promote economic and social cooperation, and protect human rights (see Exhibit 54.1).

Our respective Governments, through representatives assembled in the city of San Francisco, who have exhibited their full powers found to be in good and due form, have agreed to the present Charter of the United Nations and do hereby establish an international organization to be known as the United Nations.

Chapter 1. Purposes and Principles

Article 1 The Purposes of the United Nations are:
(1) To maintain international peace and security, and to that end: to take effective collective measures for the prevention and removal of threats to the peace, and for the suppression of acts of aggression or other breaches of the peace, and to bring about by peaceful means, and in conformity with the principles of justice and international law, adjustment or settlement of international disputes or situations which might lead to a breach of the peace;
(2) To develop friendly relations among nations based on respect for the principle of equal rights and self-determination of peoples, and to take other appropriate measures to strengthen universal peace;
(3) To achieve international co-operation in solving international problems of an economic, social, cultural, or humanitarian character, and in promoting and encouraging respect for human rights and for fundamental freedoms for all without distinction as to race, sex, language, or religion; and
(4) To be a centre for harmonizing the actions of nations in the attainment of these common ends.

▶ **Exhibit 54.1 CHARTER OF THE UNITED NATIONS (SELECTED PROVISIONS)**

The UN is governed by the General Assembly, the Security Council, and the Secretariat, which are discussed in the following paragraphs.

General Assembly

The **General Assembly** is composed of all UN member nations. As the legislative body of the UN, it adopts resolutions concerning human rights, trade, finance and economics, as well as other matters within the scope of the UN Charter. Although resolutions have limited force, they are usually enforced through persuasion and the use of economic and other sanctions.

Security Council

The UN **Security Council** is composed of 15 member nations, 5 of which are permanent members (China, France, Russia, the United Kingdom, and the United States), and 10 other countries selected by the members of the General Assembly to serve two-year terms. The council is primarily responsible for maintaining international peace and security and has authority to use armed forces.

Secretariat

The **Secretariat** administers the day-to-day operations of the UN. It is headed by the **secretary-general**, who is elected by the General Assembly. The secretary-general may refer matters that threaten international peace and security to the Security Council and use his office to help solve international disputes.

When Kansas and Colorado have a quarrel over the water in the Arkansas River they don't call out the National Guard in each state and go to war over it. They bring a suit in the Supreme Court of the United States and abide by the decision. There isn't a reason in the world why we cannot do that internationally.

Harry S. Truman
Speech (1945)

United Nations, New York City *Almost all of the countries of the world are members of the United Nations.*

United Nations Agencies

The UN is composed of various autonomous agencies that deal with a wide range of economic and social problems. These include the **United Nations Educational, Scientific, and Cultural Organization (UNESCO)**, the **United Nations International Children's Emergency Fund (UNICEF)**, the International Monetary Fund (IMF), the World Bank, and the **International Fund for Agricultural Development (IFAD)**.

INTERNATIONAL LAW

International Monetary Fund (IMF)

The **International Monetary Fund (IMF)**, an agency of the United Nations, was established by treaty in 1945 to help promote the world economy following the Great Depression of the 1930s and following the end of World War II in 1945. The IMF comprises more than 180 countries that are each represented on the board of directors, which makes the policy decisions of the IMF. The IMF is funded by monetary contributions of member nations, assessed based on the size of each nation's economy. The IMF's headquarters is located in Washington, DC.

The primary function of the IMF is to promote sound monetary, fiscal, and macroeconomic policies worldwide by providing assistance to needy countries. The IMF responds to financial crises around the globe. It does so by providing short-term loans to member countries to help

them weather problems caused by unstable currencies, to balance payment problems, and to recover from the economic policies of past governments. The IMF examines a country's economy as a whole and its currency accounts, inflation, balance of payments with other countries, employment, consumer and business spending, and other factors to determine whether the country needs assistance. In return for the financial assistance, a country must agree to meet certain monetary, fiscal, employment, inflation, and other goals established by the IMF.

International Monetary Fund

INTERNATIONAL LAW

World Bank

The **World Bank** is a United Nations agency that comprises more than 180 member nations. The World Bank is financed by contributions from developed countries, with the United States, the United Kingdom, Japan, Germany, and France being its main contributors. The World Bank has employees located in its headquarters in Washington, DC, and regional offices elsewhere throughout the world.

The World Bank provides money to developing countries to fund projects for humanitarian purposes and to relieve poverty. The World Bank provides funds to build roads, construct dams and build other water projects, establish

hospitals and provide medical assistance, develop agriculture, and provide humanitarian aid. The World Bank provides outright grants of funds to developing countries for such projects, and it makes long-term low-interest-rate loans to those countries. The bank routinely grants debt relief for these loans.

The World Bank
IBRD & IDA: Working for a World Free of Poverty

The International Court of Justice

International Court of Justice (ICJ)

The judicial branch of the United Nations that is located in The Hague, the Netherlands. Also called the *World Court*.

The **International Court of Justice (ICJ)**, also called the **World Court**, is located in The Hague, the Netherlands. It is the judicial branch of the UN. Only nations, not individuals or businesses, can have cases decided by this court. The ICJ hears cases that nations refer to it as well as cases involving treaties and the UN Charter. A nation may seek redress on behalf of an individual or a business that has a claim against another country. The ICJ is composed of 15 judges who serve nine-year terms.

▶ REGIONAL INTERNATIONAL ORGANIZATIONS

There are several significant regional organizations whose members have agreed to work together to promote peace and security as well as economic, social, and cultural development. The most important of these organizations are discussed in the following paragraphs.

European Union

One of the most important international regional organizations is the **European Union (EU)**, formerly called the *European Community*, or *Common Market*. The EU, which was created in 1957, is composed of many countries of western and eastern Europe. Member nations are Austria, Belgium, Bulgaria, Cyprus (the Greek part), Czech Republic, Denmark, Estonia, Finland, France, Germany, Greece, Hungary, Ireland, Italy, Latvia, Lithuania, Luxembourg, Malta, the Netherlands, Poland, Portugal, Romania, Slovakia, Slovenia, Spain, Sweden, and the United Kingdom of Great Britain and Northern Ireland. The EU represents more than 500 million people and a gross community product that exceeds that of the United States, Canada, and Mexico combined.

The EU's **Council of Ministers** is composed of representatives from each member country, who meet periodically to coordinate efforts to fulfill the objectives of the treaty. The council votes on significant issues and changes to the treaty. Some matters require unanimity, whereas others require only a majority vote. The member nations have surrendered substantial sovereignty to the EU. The **EU Commission**, which is independent of its member nations, is charged to act in the best interests of the union. The member nations have delegated substantial powers to the commission, including authority to enact legislation and to take enforcement actions to ensure member compliance with the treaty.

The EU treaty creates open borders for trade by providing for the free flow of capital, labor, goods, and services among member nations. Under the EU, customs duties have been eliminated among member nations. Common customs tariffs have been established for EU trade with the rest of the world.

A single monetary unit, the **euro**, has been introduced. Not all EU countries have voted to use the euro. However, the euro can be used in all countries that comprise the **Eurozone**. An EU central bank, equivalent to the U.S. Federal Reserve Board, has been established to set common monetary policy.

A unanimous vote of existing EU members is needed to admit a new member. Other nonmember European countries are expected to apply for and be admitted as members of the EU. A map of the EU is shown in Exhibit 54.2.

European Union
A regional international organization that comprises many countries of western and eastern Europe and was created to promote peace and security as well as economic, social, and cultural development.

▶ **Exhibit 54.2 MAP OF EUROPEAN UNION (EU) COUNTRIES**

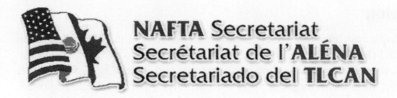

North American Free Trade Agreement (NAFTA)

North American Free Trade Agreement (NAFTA)
A treaty that has removed or reduced tariffs, duties, quotas, and other trade barriers between the United States, Canada, and Mexico.

In 1990, Mexico asked the United States to set up a two-country trade pact. Negotiations between the two countries began. Canada joined the negotiations, and on August 12, 1992, the **North American Free Trade Agreement (NAFTA)** was signed by the leaders of the three countries. The treaty creates a free-trade zone stretching from the Yukon to the Yucatan, bringing together more than 400 million people in the three countries.

NAFTA has eliminated or reduced most of the duties, tariffs, quotas, and other trade barriers between Mexico, the United States, and Canada. Agriculture, automobiles, computers, electronics, energy and petrochemicals, financial services, insurance, telecommunications, and many other industries are affected. The treaty contains a safety valve: A country can reimpose tariffs if an import surge from one of the other nations hurts its economy or workers. Like other regional trading agreements, NAFTA allows the bloc to discriminate against outsiders and to cut deals among its members. NAFTA also includes special protection for favored industries that have a lot of lobby muscle. Thus, many economists assert that NAFTA is not a "free trade" pact but a *managed trade* agreement.

NAFTA forms a supranational trading region that more effectively competes with Japan and the EU. Consumers in all three countries began to pay lower prices on a wide variety of goods and services as trade barriers fell and competition increased. Critics contend that NAFTA shifted U.S. jobs—particularly blue-collar jobs—south of the border, where Mexican wage rates are about one-tenth those in the United States. Environmentalists criticize the pact for not doing enough to prevent and clean up pollution in Mexico.

A map of NAFTA countries is shown in Exhibit 54.3.

Association of Southeast Asian Nations (ASEAN)

Only when the world is civilized enough to keep promises will we get any kind of international law.

Julius Henry Cohen

In 1967, the **Association of Southeast Asian Nations (ASEAN)** was created. The countries that belong to ASEAN are Brunei Darussalam, Cambodia, Indonesia, Laos, Malaysia, Myanmar, Philippines, Singapore, Thailand, and Vietnam. This is a cooperative association of diverse nations.

Two of the world's largest countries, Japan and China, do not belong to any significant economic community. Although not a member of ASEAN, Japan has been instrumental in providing financing for the countries that make up that organization. China also works closely with the countries of ASEAN and is a potential member of ASEAN.

Organization of the Petroleum Exporting Countries (OPEC)

One of the most well-known economic organizations is the **Organization of the Petroleum Exporting Countries (OPEC)**. OPEC consists of oil-producing and exporting countries from Africa, Asia, the Middle East, and South America. The member nations are Algeria, Angola, Ecuador, Indonesia, Iran, Iraq, Kuwait, Libya, Nigeria, Qatar, Saudi Arabia, United Arab Emirates (UAE), and Venezuela. OPEC sets quotas on the output of oil production by member nations.

Other Regional Economic Organizations

Countries of Latin America and the Caribbean have established several regional organizations to promote economic development and cooperation. Mexico, the largest industrialized country in Latin America and the Caribbean, has entered into a free trade agreement with all the countries of Central America as well as Chile, Colombia, and Venezuela. Other regional economic organizations include countries of Central America and South America. Several regional economic communities have been formed in Africa as well.

INTERNATIONAL LAW

Dominican Republic–Central America Free Trade Agreement (DR-CAFTA)

After years of negotiations, the United States and several Central American countries formed the **Central America Free Trade Agreement (CAFTA)**. The agreement originally encompassed the United States and the Central American countries of Costa Rica, El Salvador, Guatemala, Honduras, and Nicaragua. The Dominican Republic subsequently joined CAFTA, which is now commonly called **Dominican Republic–Central America Free Trade Agreement (DR-CAFTA)**. This agreement lowered tariffs and reduced trade restrictions among the member nations. The

United States has bilateral trade agreements with several other Central American countries that are not members of DR-CAFTA.

The formation of DR-CAFTA is seen as a stepping stone toward the creation of the **Free Trade Area of the Americas (FTAA)**, which would be an ambitious free trade agreement that would encompass most of the countries of Central America, North America, and South America. The negotiation of the FTAA is difficult because of the different interests of the countries that would be members.

▶ WORLD TRADE ORGANIZATION (WTO)

World Trade Organization (WTO)

An international organization of more than 130 member nations created to promote and enforce trade agreements among member nations.

In 1995, the **World Trade Organization (WTO)** was created as part of the Uruguay Round of trade negotiations on the **General Agreement on Tariffs and Trade (GATT)**. GATT is a multilateral treaty that establishes trade agreements and limits tariffs and trade restrictions among its 150 member nations.

The WTO is an international organization whose headquarters is located in Geneva, Switzerland. WTO members have entered into many trade agreements among themselves, including international agreements on investments, sale of goods, provision of services, intellectual property, licensing, tariffs, subsidies, and the removal of trade barriers.

The WTO, which has been referred to as the "Supreme Court of Trade," has become the world's most important trade organization. The WTO has jurisdiction to enforce the most important and comprehensive trade agreements in the world among its more than 130 member nations. Many herald the WTO as a much-needed world court that can peaceably solve trade disputes among nations.

WTO Dispute Resolution

One of the primary functions of the WTO is to hear and decide trade disputes between member nations. Before the creation of the WTO, GATT governed trade disputes between signatory nations. That system was inadequate because any member nation that was found to have violated any GATT trade agreement could itself veto any sanctions imposed by GATT's governing body. The WTO solved this problem by adopting a "judicial" mode of dispute resolution to replace GATT's more politically based one.

WTO panel

A body of three WTO judges that hears trade disputes between member nations and issues a "panel report."

A member nation that believes that another member nation has breached one of the trade agreements can initiate a proceeding to have the WTO hear and decide the dispute. The dispute is first heard by a three-member **WTO panel**, which issues a "panel report." The members of the panel are professional judges from member nations. The report, which is the decision of the panel, contains the panel's findings of fact and law, and it orders a remedy if a violation has been found. The report is then referred to the **WTO dispute-settlement body**. This body is required to adopt the panel report unless the body, by consensus, agrees not to adopt it.

There is a **WTO appellate body** to which a party can appeal a decision of the dispute-settlement body. This appeals court is composed of seven professional justices selected from member nations. Appeals are limited to issues of law, not fact.

If a violation of a trade agreement is found, the panel report and appellate decision can order the offending nation to cease engaging in the violating practice and to pay damages to the other party. If the offending nation refuses to abide by the order, the WTO can order retaliatory trade sanctions (e.g., tariffs) by other member nations against the noncomplying nation.

WTO dispute settlement body
A board composed of one representative from each WTO member nation that reviews panel reports.

WTO appellate body
A panel of seven judges selected from WTO member nations that hears and decides appeals from decisions of the dispute-settlement body.

NATIONAL COURTS AND INTERNATIONAL DISPUTE RESOLUTION

The majority of cases involving international law disputes are heard by **national courts** of individual nations. This is primarily the case for commercial disputes between private litigants that do not qualify to be heard by international courts. Some countries have specialized courts that hear international commercial disputes. Other countries permit such disputes to proceed through their regular court systems. In the United States, commercial disputes between U.S. companies and foreign governments or parties may be brought in U.S. District Court.

national courts
The courts of individual nations.

Judicial Procedure

A party seeking judicial resolution of an international dispute faces several problems, including which nation's courts will hear the case and what law should be applied to the case. Jurisdiction is often a highly contested issue. Absent an agreement providing otherwise, a case involving an international dispute will be brought in the national court of the plaintiff's home country.

Many international contracts contain a **choice of forum clause** (or **forum-selection clause**) that designates which nation's court has jurisdiction to hear a case arising out of a contract. In addition, many contracts also include a **choice of law clause** that designates which nation's laws will be applied in deciding such a case. Absent these two clauses, and without the parties agreeing to these matters, an international dispute may never be resolved.

choice of forum clause
A clause in an international contract that designates which nation's court has jurisdiction to hear a case arising out of the contract. Also known as a *forum-selection clause*.

choice of law clause
A clause in an international contract that designates which nation's laws will be applied in deciding a dispute.

CONCEPT SUMMARY
INTERNATIONAL CONTRACT CLAUSES

Clause	Description
Forum-selection	A clause that designates the judicial or arbitral forum that will hear and decide a case.
Choice of law	A clause that designates the law to be applied by the court or arbitrator in deciding a case.

Act of State Doctrine

A general principle of international law is that a country has absolute authority over what transpires *within* its own territory. In furtherance of this principle, the **act of state doctrine** states that judges of one country cannot question the validity of an act committed by another country within that other country's own borders. In *United States v. Belmont*,[2] the U.S. Supreme Court declared, "Every sovereign state must recognize the independence of every other sovereign state; and the courts of one will not sit in judgment upon the acts of the government of another, done within its own territory." This restraint on the judiciary is justified under the doctrine of separation of powers and permits the executive branch of the federal government to arrange affairs with foreign governments.

act of state doctrine
A doctrine which states that judges of one country cannot question the validity of an act committed by another country within that other country's borders. It is based on the principle that a country has absolute authority over what transpires within its own territory.

Example Suppose the country of North Korea outlaws the practice of all religions in that country. Paul, a Christian who is a citizen of, and living in, the United States, disagrees with North Korea's law. Paul brings a lawsuit against North Korea in a U.S. District Court located in the state of Idaho, arguing to the court that the North Korean law should be declared illegal. The U.S. District Court will apply the act of state doctrine and dismiss Paul's lawsuit again North Korea. The U.S. District Court will rule that North Korea's law is an act of that state (country) and that a U.S. court does not have authority to hear and decide Paul's case.

In the following case, the court was called upon to apply the act of state doctrine.

CASE 54.1 Act of State Doctrine

Glen v. Club Mediterranee, S.A.
450 F.3d 1251, Web 2006 U.S. App. Lexis 13400 (2006)
United States Court of Appeals for the Eleventh Circuit

"The act of state doctrine is a judicially-created rule of decision that precludes the courts of this country from inquiring into the validity of the public acts a recognized foreign sovereign power committed within its own territory."

—Judge Cox

Facts

Prior to the Communist revolution in Cuba, Elvira de la Vega Glen and her sister, Ana Maria de la Vega Glen, were Cuban citizens and residents who jointly owned beachfront property on the Peninsula de Hicacos in Varadero, Cuba. On or about January 1, 1959, in conjunction with Fidel Castro's Communist revolution, the Cuban government expropriated the property without paying the Glens. Also in 1959, the sisters fled Cuba. Ana Maria de la Vega Glen died and passed any interest she had in the Varadero beach property to her nephew Robert M. Glen.

In 1997, Club Mediterranee, S.A., and Club Mediterranee Group (Club Med) entered into a joint venture with the Cuban government to develop the property. Club Med constructed and operated a five-star luxury hotel on the property that the Glens had owned. The Glens sued Club Med in a U.S. District Court located in the state of Florida. The Glens alleged that the original expropriation of their property by the Cuban government was illegal and that Club Med had trespassed on their property and had been unduly enriched by its joint venture with the Cuban government to operate a hotel on their expropriated property. The Glens sought to recover the millions of dollars in profits earned by Club Med from its alleged wrongful occupation and use of the Glens' expropriated property. The U.S. District Court held that the act of state doctrine barred recovery by the Glens and dismissed the Glens' claims against Club Med. The Glens appealed.

Issue

Does the act of state doctrine bar recovery by the Glens?

Language of the Court

The act of state doctrine is a judicially-created rule of decision that precludes the courts of this country from inquiring into the validity of the public acts a recognized foreign sovereign power committed within its own territory. The doctrine prevents any court in the United States from declaring that an official act of a foreign sovereign performed within its own territory is invalid. It requires that the acts of foreign sovereigns taken within their own jurisdictions shall be deemed valid. The act of state doctrine is a product of judicial concern for separation of powers, a result of the judiciary's recognition that it is the province of the executive and legislative branches to establish and pursue foreign policy and that judicial determinations regarding the validity of the acts of foreign sovereigns might negatively affect those policies.

The validity of the Cuban government's act of expropriation is directly at issue in this litigation. The act of state doctrine is properly applied to claims, like the Glens', that necessarily require U.S. courts to pass on the legality of the Cuban government's expropriation of property within Cuba from then–Cuban citizens. Because the act of state doctrine requires the courts deem valid the Cuban government's expropriation of the real property at issue in this case, the Glens cannot maintain their claims for trespass and unjust enrichment against Club Med.

Decision

The U.S. Court of Appeals applied the act of state doctrine and affirmed the judgment of the U.S. District Court that dismissed the Glens' claim against Club Med.

Case Questions

Critical Legal Thinking What does the act of state doctrine provide? Explain.

Business Ethics Did the Cuban government act ethically when it expropriated the Glens' property? Did Club Med

act ethically when it entered into a joint venture with the Cuban government to develop the property that had been expropriated from the Glens?

Contemporary Business What is the expropriation of property by a government?

Doctrine of Sovereign Immunity

One of the oldest principles of international law is the **doctrine of sovereign immunity**. Under this doctrine, *countries* are granted immunity from suits in courts in other countries. For example, if a U.S. citizen wanted to sue the government of China in a U.S. court, he or she could not (subject to certain exceptions).

Originally, the United States granted absolute immunity to foreign governments from suits in U.S. courts. In 1952, the United States switched to the principle of **qualified immunity**, or **restricted immunity**, which was eventually codified in the **Foreign Sovereign Immunities Act (FSIA)** of 1976.[3] This act now exclusively governs suits against foreign nations in the United States, whether in federal or state court. Most Western nations have adopted the principle of restricted immunity. Other countries still follow the doctrine of absolute immunity.

Exceptions to the Sovereign Immunities Act

The FSIA provides that a foreign country is not immune from lawsuits in U.S. courts in the following situations:

- If the foreign country has waived its immunity, either explicitly or by implication
- If the action is based on a commercial activity carried on in the United States by the foreign country or carried on outside the United States but causing a direct effect in the United States

What constitutes "commercial activity" is the most litigated aspect of the FSIA. With commercial activity, the foreign sovereign is subject to suit in the United States; without it, the foreign sovereign is immune from suit in this country.

Example The country of Cuba has state-owned enterprises. The government of Cuba wants to raise capital for these state-owned enterprises. To do so, the Cuban government sells 20-year bonds in these companies to investors in the United States. The bondholders are to be paid 10 percent interest annually. By selling bonds to investors in the United States, the government of Cuba is involved in commercial activity in the United States. If Cuba defaults and does not pay the U.S. investors the 10 percent interest on the bonds, the bondholders can sue Cuba in U.S. court under the commercial activity exception to the doctrine of sovereign immunity to recover the unpaid interest.

doctrine of sovereign immunity
A doctrine which states that countries are granted immunity from suits in courts of other countries.

Foreign Sovereign Immunities Act (FSIA)
An act that exclusively governs suits against foreign nations that are brought in federal or state courts in the United States. It codifies the principle of *qualified, or restricted, immunity.*

My nationalism is intense internationalism. I am sick of the strife between nations or religions.

Gandhi

CONCEPT SUMMARY

ACT OF STATE AND SOVEREIGN IMMUNITY DOCTRINES COMPARED

Doctrine	Description
Act of state	A doctrine that states that an act of a government in its *own country* is not subject to suit in a foreign country's courts.
Sovereign immunity	A doctrine that states that an act of a government in a *foreign country* is not subject to suit in the foreign country. Some countries provide absolute immunity, and other countries (such as the United States) provide limited immunity.

INTERNATIONAL LAW

Jewish Law and the Torah

Jewish law, which has existed for centuries, is a complex legal system based on the ideology and theology of the **Torah**. The Torah prescribes comprehensive and integrated rules of religious, political, and legal life that together form Jewish thought. Jewish law is decided by rabbis who are scholars of the Torah and other Jewish scriptures. Rabbinic jurisprudence, known as **Halakhah**, is administered by rabbi-judges sitting as the **Beis Din**, Hebrew for the "house of judgment." As a court, the *Beis Din* has roots that go back 3,000 years.

Today, Jews are citizens of countries worldwide. As such, they are subject to the criminal and civil laws of their host countries. But Jews, no matter where they live, abide by the principles of the Torah in many legal matters, such as marriage, divorce, inheritance, and other family matters.

Thus, the legal principles embedded in the Torah coexist with the secular laws of Jews' home countries.

Rabbinical judges tend to be actively involved in cases. True to its roots, the *Beis Din* is more a search for the truth than it is an adversarial process.

Israel

INTERNATIONAL LAW

Islamic Law and the Qur'an

Approximately 20 percent of the world's population is Muslim. Islam is the principal religion of Afghanistan, Algeria, Bangladesh, Egypt, Indonesia, Iran, Iraq, Jordan, Kuwait, Libya, Malaysia, Mali, Mauritania, Morocco, Niger, North Yemen, Oman, Pakistan, Qatar, Saudi Arabia, Somalia, South Yemen, Sudan, Syria, Tunisia, Turkey, and the United Arab Emirates. **Islamic law** (or **Shari'a**) is the only law in Saudi Arabia. In other Islamic countries, the *Shari'a* forms the basis of family law but coexists with other laws.

The Islamic law system is derived from the **Qur'an**, the **Sunnah** (decisions and sayings of the prophet Muhammad), and reasonings by Islamic scholars. By the tenth century A.D., Islamic scholars had decided that no further improvement of the divine law could be made, closed the door of *ijtihad* (independent reasoning), and froze the evolution of Islamic law at that point. Islamic law prohibits *riba*, or the making of unearned or unjustified profit. Making a profit from the sale of goods or the provision of services is permitted. The most notable consequence of *riba* is that the payment of interest on loans is forbidden. To circumvent this result, the party with the money is permitted to purchase the item and resell it

to the other party at a profit or to advance the money and become a trading partner who shares in the profits of the enterprise.

Today, Islamic law is primarily used in the areas of marriage, divorce, and inheritance and, to a limited degree, in criminal law. To resolve the tension between *Shari'a* and the practice of modern commercial law, the *Shari'a* is often not applied to commercial transactions.

Uzbekistan

INTERNATIONAL LAW

Hindu Law—*Dharmasastra*

Over 20 percent of the world's population is Hindu. Most Hindus live in India, where they make up 80 percent of the population. Others live in Burma, Kenya, Malaysia, Pakistan, Singapore, Tanzania, and Uganda. **Hindu law** is a religious

law. As such, individual Hindus apply this law to themselves, regardless of their nationality or place of domicile.

Classical Hindu law rests neither on civil codes nor on court decisions but on the works of private scholars that were passed along for centuries by oral tradition and eventually were recorded in the **smitris** (law books). Hindu law—called **dharmasastra** in Sanskrit ("the doctrine of proper behavior")—is linked to the divine revelation of Veda (the holy collection of Indian religious songs, prayers, hymns, and sayings written between 2000 and 1000 B.C.). Most Hindu law is concerned with family matters and the law of succession.

After India became a British colony, British judges applied a combination of Hindu law and common law in solving cases. This Anglo-Hindu law, as it was called, was ousted when India gained its independence. In the mid-1950s, India codified Hindu law by enacting the Hindu Marriage Act, the Hindu Minority and Guardianship Act, the Hindu Succession Act, and the Hindu Adoptions and Maintenance Act. Outside India, Anglo-Hindu law applies in most other countries populated by Hindus.

Nepal

TEST REVIEW TERMS AND CONCEPTS

Act of state doctrine
Association of Southeast
  Asian Nations (ASEAN)
Beis Din
Bilateral treaty
Central America Free Trade
  Agreement (CAFTA)
Choice of forum clause
  (forum-selection clause)
Choice of law clause
Convention
Council of Ministers
Dharmasastra
Doctrine of sovereign
  immunity
Dominican
  Republic–Central
  America Free Trade
  Agreement
  (DR-CAFTA)

EU Commission
Euro
European Union (EU)
Eurozone
Foreign Commerce
  Clause
Foreign Sovereign
  Immunities Act
  (FSIA)
Free Trade Area of the
  Americas (FTAA)
General Agreement on
  Tariffs and Trade
  (GATT)
General Assembly
Halakhah
Hindu law
International Court of
  Justice (ICJ) (World
  Court)

International Fund for
  Agricultural
  Development (IFAD)
International law
International Monetary
  Fund (IMF)
Islamic law (*Shari'a*)
Koran
Multilateral treaty
National courts
North American Free Trade
  Agreement (NAFTA)
Organization of the
  Petroleum Exporting
  Countries (OPEC)
Qualified immunity
  (restricted immunity)
Secretariat
Secretary-general
Security Council

Smitris
Sunnah
Torah
Treaty
Treaty Clause
United Nations (UN)
United Nations Educational,
  Scientific, and Cultural
  Organization (UNESCO)
United Nations
  International Children's
  Emergency Fund
  (UNICEF)
World Bank
World Trade Organization
  (WTO)
WTO appellate body
WTO dispute-settlement
  body
WTO panel

CASE PROBLEMS

54.1 Act of State Doctrine Prior to 1918, the Petrograd Metal Works, a Russian corporation, deposited a large sum of money with August Belmont, a private banker doing business in New York City under the name August Belmont & Co. (Belmont). In 1918, the Soviet government nationalized the corporation and appropriated all its property and assets wherever situated, including the deposit account with Belmont. As a result, the deposit became the property of the Soviet government. In 1933, the Soviet government and the United States entered into an agreement to settle claims and

counterclaims between them. As part of the settlement, it was agreed that the Soviet government would take no steps to enforce claims against American nationals (including Belmont) and assigned all such claims to the United States. The United States brought an action against the executors of Belmont's estate to recover the money originally deposited with Belmont by Petrograd Metal Works. Who owns the money? *United States v. Belmont*, 301 U.S. 324, 57 S.Ct. 758, 81 L.Ed. 1134, **Web** 1937 U.S. Lexis 293 (Supreme Court of the United States)

54.2 Act of State Doctrine   Banco Nacional de Costa Rica is a bank wholly owned by the government of Costa Rica. It is subject to the rules and regulations adopted by the minister of finance and the central bank of Costa Rica. The bank borrowed $40 million from a consortium of private banks located in the United Kingdom and the United States. The bank signed promissory notes, agreeing to repay the principal plus interest on the loan in four equal installments due on July 30, August 30, September 30, and October 30 of the following year. The money was to be used to provide export financing of sugar and sugar products from Costa Rica. The loan agreements and promissory notes were signed in New York City, and the loan proceeds were tendered to the bank there.

The bank paid the first installment on the loan. The bank did not, however, make the other three installment payments and defaulted on the loan. The lending banks sued the bank in U.S. District Court in New York to recover the unpaid principal and interest. The bank alleged in defense that the minister of finance and the central bank of Costa Rica had issued a decree forbidding the repayment of loans by the bank to private lenders, including the lending banks in this case. The action was taken because Costa Rica was having trouble servicing debts to foreign creditors. The bank alleged that the act of state doctrine prevented the plaintiffs from recovering on their loans to the bank. Who wins? *Libra Bank Limited v. Banco Nacional de Costa Rica*, 570 F.Supp. 870, **Web** 1983 U.S. Dist. Lexis 14677 (United States District Court for the Southern District of New York)

54.3 Forum-Selection Clause   Zapata Off-Shore Company (Zapata) is a Houston, Texas–based American corporation that engages in drilling oil wells throughout the world. Unterweser Reederei, GMBH (Unterweser), is a German corporation that provides ocean shipping and towing services. Zapata requested bids from companies to tow its self-elevating drilling rig *Chaparral* from Louisiana to a point off Ravenna, Italy, in the Adriatic Sea, where Zapata had agreed to drill certain wells. Unterweser submitted the lowest bid and was requested to submit a proposed contract to Zapata, which it did. The contract submitted by Unterweser contained the following provision: "Any dispute arising must be treated before the London Court of Justice." Zapata executed the contract without deleting or modifying this provision.

Unterweser's deep sea tug *Bremen* departed Venice, Louisiana, with the *Chaparral* in tow, bound for Italy. While

the flotilla was in international waters in the middle of the Gulf of Mexico, a severe storm arose. The sharp roll of the *Chaparral* in Gulf waters caused portions of it to break off and fall into the sea, seriously damaging the *Chaparral*. Zapata instructed the *Bremen* to tow the *Chaparral* to Tampa, Florida, the nearest port of refuge, which it did. Zapata filed suit against Unterweser and the *Bremen* in U.S. District Court in Florida, alleging negligent towing and breach of contract. The defendants asserted that suit could be brought only in the London Court of Justice. Who is correct? *M/S Bremen and Unterweser Reederei, GMBH v. Zapata Off-Shore Company*, 407 U.S. 1, 92 S.Ct. 1907, 32 L.Ed.2d 513, **Web** 1972 U.S. Lexis 114 (Supreme Court of the United States)

54.4 International Arbitration   Alberto-Culver Company is an American company that is incorporated in Delaware and has its principal office in Illinois. It manufactures and distributes toiletries and hair care products in the United States and other countries. Fritz Scherk owned three interrelated businesses organized under the laws of Germany and Liechtenstein that were engaged in the manufacture of toiletries. After substantial negotiations, in February 1969, Alberto-Culver entered into a contract with Scherk to purchase his three companies, along with all rights held by these companies to trademarks in cosmetic goods. The contract contained a number of express warranties whereby Scherk guaranteed the sole and unencumbered ownership of these trademarks. The contract also contained a clause which provided that "any controversy or claim that shall arise out of this agreement or breach thereof" was to be referred to arbitration before the International Chamber of Commerce in Paris, France. The transaction closed in Geneva, Switzerland.

Nearly one year later, Alberto-Culver allegedly discovered that the trademark rights purchased under the contract were subject to substantial encumbrances that threatened to give other parties superior rights to the trademarks and to restrict or preclude Alberto-Culver's use of them. Alberto-Culver sued Scherk in U.S. District Court in Illinois, alleging fraudulent misrepresentation in violation of Section 10(b) of the federal Securities Exchange Act of 1934. Scherk asserted in defense that the case was subject to mandatory arbitration in Paris. Who is correct? *Scherk v. Alberto-Culver Co.*, 417 U.S. 506, 94 S.Ct. 2449, 41 L.Ed.2d 270, **Web** 1974 U.S. Lexis 73 (Supreme Court of the United States)

BUSINESS ETHICS CASES

54.5 Business Ethics   Bank of Jamaica is wholly owned by the government of Jamaica. Chisholm & Co. was a Florida corporation owned by James Henry Chisholm, a Florida resident. The U.S. Export–Import Bank (Ex-Im Bank) provides financial services and credit insurance to export and import companies. The Bank of Jamaica and

Chisholm & Co. agreed that Chisholm & Co. would arrange lines of credit from various banks and procure $50 million of credit insurance from Ex-Im Bank to be available to aid Jamaican importers. Chisholm & Co. was to be paid commissions for its services.

Chisholm & Co. negotiated and arranged for $50 million of credit insurance from Ex-Im Bank and lines of credit from

Florida National Bank, Bankers Trust Company, and Irving Trust Company. Chisholm also arranged meetings between the Bank of Jamaica and the U.S. banks. Unbeknownst to Chisholm & Co., the Bank of Jamaica went directly to Ex-Im Bank to exclude Chisholm & Co. from the Jamaica program and requested that the credit insurance be issued solely in the name of the Bank of Jamaica. As a result, Chisholm & Co.'s Ex-Im Bank insurance application was not considered. The Bank of Jamaica also obtained lines of credit from other companies and paid them commissions. Chisholm & Co. sued the Bank of Jamaica in U.S. District Court in Miami, Florida, alleging breach of contract and seeking damages. The Bank of Jamaica filed a motion to dismiss the complaint, alleging that its actions were protected by sovereign immunity. Who wins? Did the Bank of Jamaica act ethically in trying to avoid its contract obligations? *Chisholm & Co. v. Bank of Jamaica*, 643 F.Supp. 1393, **Web** 1986 U.S. Dist. Lexis 20789 (United States District Court for the Southern District of Florida)

54.6 Business Ethics Nigeria, an African nation, while in the midst of a boom period due to oil exports, entered into $1 billion of contracts with various countries to purchase huge quantities of Portland cement. Nigeria was going to use the cement to build and improve the country's infrastructure. Several of the contracts were with American companies, including Texas Trading & Milling Corporation (Texas Trading). Nigeria substantially overbought cement, and the country's docks and harbors became clogged with ships waiting to unload. Unable to accept delivery of the cement it had bought, Nigeria repudiated many of its contracts, including the one with Texas Trading. When Texas Trading sued Nigeria in a U.S. District Court to recover damages for breach of contract, Nigeria asserted in defense that the doctrine of sovereign immunity protected it from liability. Who wins? *Texas Trading & Milling Corp. v. Federal Republic of Nigeria*, 647 F.2d 300, **Web** 1981 U.S. App. Lexis 14231 (United States Court of Appeals for the Second Circuit)

ENDNOTES

1. The Charter of the United Nations was entered into force October 24, 1945, and it was adopted by the United States October 24, 1945 (59 Stat. 1031, T.S. 993, 3 Bevans 1153, 1976 Y.B.U.N. 1043).

2. 301 U.S. 324, 57 S.Ct. 758, 81 L.Ed. 1134, Web 1937 U.S. Lexis 293 (Supreme Court of the United States).

3. 28 U.S.C. Sections 1602–1611.

We the People of the United States, in Order to form a more perfect Union, establish Justice, insure domestic Tranquility, provide for the common defense, promote the general Welfare, and secure the Blessings of Liberty to ourselves and our Posterity, do ordain and establish this Constitution for the United States of America.

Article I

Section 1. All legislative Powers herein granted shall be vested in a Congress of the United States, which shall consist of a Senate and House of Representatives.

Section 2. The House of Representatives shall be composed of Members chosen every second Year by the People of the several states, and the Electors in each State shall have the Qualifications requisite for Electors of the most numerous Branch of the State Legislature.

No Person shall be a Representative who shall not have attained to the Age of twenty five Years, and been seven Years a Citizen of the United States, and who shall not, when elected, be an Inhabitant of that State in which he shall be chosen.

Representatives and direct Taxes shall be apportioned among the several states which may be included within this Union, according to their respective Numbers, which shall be determined by adding to the whole Number of free Persons, including those bound to Service for a Term of Years, and excluding Indians not taxed, three fifths of all other Persons. The actual Enumeration shall be made within three Years after the first Meeting of the Congress of the United States, and within every subsequent Term of ten Years, in such Manner as they shall by Law direct. The number of Representatives shall not exceed one for every thirty Thousand, but each State shall have at Least one Representative; and until such enumeration shall be made, the State of New Hamp-shire shall be entitled to chuse three, Massachusetts eight, Rhode Island and Providence Plantations one, Connecticut five, New York six, New Jersey four, Pennsylvania eight, Delaware one, Maryland six, Virginia ten, North Carolina five, South Carolina five, and Georgia three.

When vacancies happen in the Representation from any State, the Executive Authority thereof shall issue Writs of Election to fill such vacancies.

The House of Representatives shall chuse their Speaker and other Officers; and shall have the sole Power of Impeachment.

Section 3. The Senate of the United States shall be composed of two Senators from each State, chosen by the Legislature thereof, for six Years; and each Senator shall have one Vote.

Immediately after they shall be assembled in Consequence of the first Election, they shall be divided as equally as may be into three Classes. The Seats of the Senators of the first Class shall be vacated at the Expiration of the second Year, of the second Class at the Expiration of the fourth Year, and the third Class at the Expiration of the sixth Year, so that one third may be chosen every second Year; and if Vacancies happen by Resignation, or otherwise, during the Recess of the Legislature of any State, the Executive thereof may make temporary Appointments until the next meeting of the Legislature, which shall then fill such Vacancies.

No person shall be a Senator who shall not have attained to the Age of thirty Years, and been nine Years a Citizen of the United States, and who shall not, when elected, be an Inhabitant of that State for which he shall be chosen.

The Vice President of the United States shall be President of the Senate, but shall have no Vote, unless they be equally divided.

The Senate shall chuse their other Officers, and also a President pro tempore, in the Absence of the Vice President, or when he shall exercise the Office of President of the United States.

The Senate shall have the sole power to try all Impeachments. When sitting for that Purpose, they shall be an Oath or Affirmation. When the President of the United States is tried, the Chief Justice shall preside: And no Person shall be convicted without the Concurrence of two thirds of the Members present.

Judgment in Cases of Impeachment shall not extend further than to removal from Office, and disqualification to hold and enjoy any Office of honor, Trust or Profit under the United States: but the Party convicted shall nevertheless be liable and subject to Indictment, Trial, Judgment and Punishment, according to Law.

Section 4. The Times, Places and Manner of holding Elections for Senators and Representatives, shall be prescribed in each State by the Legislature thereof: but the Congress may at any time by Law make or alter such Regulations, except as to the Places of choosing Senators.

The Congress shall assemble at least once in every Year, and such Meeting shall be on the first Monday in December, unless they shall by Law appoint a different day.

Section 5. Each House shall be the Judge of the Elections, Returns and Qualifications of its own Members, and a Majority of each shall constitute a Quorum to do Business; but a smaller Number may adjourn from day to day, and may be authorized to compel the Attendance of absent Members, in such Manner, and under such Penalties as each House may provide.

Each House may determine the Rules of its Proceedings, punish its Members for disorderly Behaviour, and, with the Concurrence of two thirds, expel a Member.

Each House shall keep a Journal of its Proceedings, and from time to time publish the same, excepting such Parts as may in their Judgment require Secrecy; and the Yeas and Nays of the Members of either House on any question shall, at the Desire of one fifth of those Present, be entered on the Journal.

Neither House, during the Session of Congress, shall, without the Consent of the other, adjourn for more than three days, nor to any other Place than that in which the two Houses shall be sitting.

Section 6. The Senators and Representatives shall receive a Compensation for their Services, to be ascertained by Law, and paid out of the Treasury of the United States. They shall in all Cases, except Treason, Felony and Breach of the Peace, be privileged from Arrest during their Attendance at the Session of their respective Houses, and in going to and returning from the same; and for any Speech or Debate in either House, they shall not be questioned in any other Place.

No Senator or Representative shall, during the Time for which he was elected, be appointed to any civil Office under the Authority of the United States, which shall have been created, or the Emoluments whereof shall have been encreased during such time; and no Person holding any Office under the United States, shall be a Member of either House during his Continuance in Office.

Section 7. All Bills for raising Revenue shall originate in the House of Representatives; but the Senate may propose or concur with Amendments as on other Bills.

Every Bill which shall have passed the House of Representatives and the Senate, shall, before it become a Law, be presented to the President of the United States; If he approve he shall sign it, but if not he shall return it, with his Objections to that House in which it shall have originated, who shall enter the Objections at large on their Journal, and proceed to reconsider it. If after such Reconsideration two thirds of that House shall agree to pass the Bill, it shall be sent, together with the Objections, to the other House, by which it shall likewise be reconsidered, and if approved by two thirds of that House, it shall become a Law. But in all such Cases the Votes of both Houses shall be determined by Yeas and Nays, and the Names of the Persons voting for and against the Bill shall be entered on the Journal of each House respectively. If any Bill shall not be returned by the President within ten Days (Sundays excepted) after it shall have been presented to him, the Same shall be a Law, in like Manner as if he had signed it, unless the Congress by their Adjournment prevent its Return, in which Case it shall not be a Law.

Every Order, Resolution, or Vote to which the Concurrence of the Senate and House of Representatives may be necessary (except on a question of Adjournment) shall be presented to the President of the United States; and before the Same shall take Effect, shall be approved by him, or being disapproved by him, shall be repassed by two thirds of the Senate and House of Representatives, according to the Rules and Limitations prescribed in the Case of a Bill.

Section 8. The Congress shall have Power to lay and collect Taxes, Duties, Imposts and Excises, to pay the Debts and provide for the common Defence and general Welfare of the United States; but all Duties, Imposts and Excises shall be uniform throughout the United States;

To borrow Money on the credit of the United States;

To regulate Commerce with foreign Nations, and among the several States, and with the Indian Tribes;

To establish an uniform Rule of Naturalization, and uniform Laws on the subject of Bankruptcies throughout the United States;

To coin Money, regulate the Value thereof, and of foreign Coin, and fix the Standard of Weights and Measures;

To provide for the Punishment of counterfeiting the Securities and current Coin of the United States;

To establish Post Offices and post Roads;

To promote the Progress of Science and useful Arts, by securing for limited Times to Authors and Inventors the exclusive Right to their respective Writings and Discoveries;

To constitute Tribunals inferior to the supreme Court;

To define and punish Piracies and Felonies committed on the high Seas, and Offenses against the Law of Nations;

To declare War, grant Letters of Marque and Reprisal, and make Rules concerning Captures on Land and Water;

To raise and support Armies, but no Appropriation of Money to that Use shall be for a longer Term than two Years;

To provide and maintain a Navy;

To make Rules for the Government and Regulation of the land and naval Forces;

To provide for calling forth the Militia to execute the Laws of the Union, suppress Insurrections and repel Invasions;

To provide for organizing, arming, and disciplining, the Militia, and for governing such Part of them as may be employed in the Service of the United States, reserving to the States respectively, the Appointment of the Officers, and the Authority of training the Militia according to the discipline prescribed by Congress;

To exercise exclusive Legislation in all Cases whatsoever, over such District (not exceeding ten Miles square) as may, by Cession of particular States, and the Acceptance of Congress, become the Seat of the Government of the United States, and to exercise like Authority over all Places purchased by the Consent of the Legislature of the State in which the Same shall be, for the Erection of Forts, Magazines, Arsenals, dock-Yards, and other needful Buildings;—And

To make all Laws which shall be necessary and proper for carrying into Execution the foregoing Powers, and all other Powers vested by this Constitution in the Government of the United States, or in any Department or Officer thereof.

Section 9. The Migration or Importation of such Persons as any of the States now existing shall think proper to admit, shall not be prohibited by the Congress prior to the Year one thousand eight hundred and eight, but a Tax or Duty may be imposed on such Importation, not exceeding ten dollars for each Person.

The Privilege of the Writ of Habeas Corpus shall not be suspended, unless when in Cases of Rebellion or Invasion the public Safety may require it.

No Bill of Attainder or ex post facto Law shall be passed.

No Capitation, or other direct, Tax shall be laid, unless in Proportion to the Census or Enumeration herein before directed to be taken.

No Tax or Duty shall be laid on Articles exported from any State.

No Preference shall be given by any Regulation of Commerce or Revenue to the Ports of one State over those of another; nor shall Vessels bound to, or from, one State, be obliged to enter, clear, or pay Duties in another.

No Money shall be drawn from the Treasury, but in Consequence of Appropriations made by Laws; and a regular Statement and Account of the Receipts and Expenditures of all public Money shall be published from time to time.

No Title of Nobility shall be granted by the United States: And no Person holding any Office of Profit or Trust under them, shall, without the Consent of the Congress, accept of any present, Emolument, Office, or Title, of any kind whatever, from any King, Prince, or foreign State.

Section 10. No State shall enter into any Treaty, Alliance, or Confederation; grant Letters of Marque and Reprisal; coin Money; emit Bills of Credit; make any Thing but gold and silver Coin a Tender in Payment of Debts; pass any Bill of Attainder, ex post facto Law, or Law impairing the Obligation of Contracts, or grant any Title of Nobility.

No State shall, without the Consent of the Congress, lay any Imposts or Duties on Imports or Exports, except what may be absolutely necessary for executing its inspection Laws: and the net Produce of all Duties and Imposts, laid by any State on Imports or Exports, shall be for the Use of the Treasury of the United States; and all such Laws shall be subject to the Revision and Control of the Congress.

No State shall, without the Consent of Congress, lay any Duty of Tonnage, keep Troops, or Ships of War in time of Peace, enter into any Agreement or Compact with another State, or with a foreign Power, or engage in War, unless actually invaded, or in such imminent Danger as will not admit of delay.

Article II

Section 1. The executive Power shall be vested in a President of the United States of America. He shall hold his Office during the Term of four Years, and, together with the Vice President, chosen for the same Term, be elected, as follows:

Each State shall appoint, in such Manner as the Legislature thereof may direct, a Number of Electors, equal to the whole Number of Senators and Representatives to which the State may be entitled in the Congress: but no Senator or Representative, or Person holding an Office of Trust or Profit under the United States, shall be appointed an Elector.

The Electors shall meet in their respective States, and vote by Ballot for two Persons, of whom one at least shall not be an Inhabitant of the same State with themselves. And they shall make a list of all the Persons voted for, and of the Number of Votes for each; which List they shall sign and certify, and transmit sealed to the Seat of the Government of the United States, directed to the President of the Senate. The President of the Senate shall, in the presence of the Senate and House of Representatives, open all the Certificates, and the Votes shall be counted. The Person having the greatest Number of Votes shall be the President, if such Number be a Majority of the whole Number of Electors appointed; and if there be more than one who have such Majority, and have an equal Number of Votes, then the House of Representatives shall immediately choose by Ballot one of them for President; and if no Person have a Majority, then from the five highest on the List the said House shall in like Manner choose the President. But in chusing the President, the Votes shall be taken by States, the Representation from each State having one Vote; A quorum for this Purpose shall consist of a Member or Members from two thirds of the States, and a Majority of all the States shall be necessary to a Choice. In every Case, after the Choice of the President, the Person having the greatest Number of Votes of the Electors shall be the Vice President. But if there should remain two or more who have equal Votes, the Senate shall chuse from them by Ballot the Vice President.

The Congress may determine the Time of Chusing the Electors, and the Day on which they shall give their Votes; which Day shall be the same throughout the United States.

No Person except a natural born Citizen, or a Citizen of the United States, at the time of the Adoption of this Constitution, shall be eligible to the Office of President; neither shall any Person be eligible to that Office who shall not have attained to the Age of thirty five Years, and been fourteen Years a Resident within the United States.

In Case of the Removal of the President from Office, or of his Death, Resignation, or Inability to discharge the Powers and Duties of the said Office, the Same shall devolve on the Vice President, and the Congress may by Law provide for the Case of Removal, Death, Resignation or Inability, both of the President and Vice President, declaring what Officer shall then act as President, and such Officer shall act accordingly, until the Disability be removed, or a President shall be elected.

The President shall, at stated Times, receive for his Services, a Compensation, which shall neither be encreased nor diminished during the Period for which he shall have been elected, and he shall not receive within that Period any other Emolument from the United States, or any of them.

Before he enter on the Execution of his Office, he shall take the following Oath or Affirmation:—"I do solemnly swear (or affirm) that I will faithfully execute the Office of President of the United States, and will to the best of my Ability, preserve, protect and defend the Constitution of the United States."

Section 2. The President shall be Commander in Chief of the Army and Navy of the United States, and of the Militia of the several States, when called into the actual Service of the United States; he may require the Opinion, in writing, of the principal Officer in each of the executive Departments, upon any Subject relating to the Duties of their respective Offices, and he shall have Power to grant Reprieves and Pardons for Offences against the United States, except in Cases of Impeachment.

He shall have Power, by and with the Advice and Consent of the Senate, to make Treaties, provided two thirds of the Senators present concur; and he shall nominate, and by and with the Advice and Consent of the Senate, shall appoint Ambassadors, other public Ministers and Consuls, Judges of the supreme Court, and all other Officers of the United States, whose Appointments are not herein otherwise provided for, and which shall be established by Law: but the Congress may by Law vest the Appointment of such inferior Officers, as they think proper, in the President alone, in the Courts of Law, or in the Heads of Departments.

The President shall have Power to fill up all Vacancies that may happen during the Recess of the Senate, by granting Commissions which shall expire at the End of their next Session.

Section 3. He shall from time to time give to the Congress Information of the State of the Union, and recommend to their Consideration such Measures as he shall judge necessary and expedient; he may, on extraordinary Occasions, convene both Houses, or either of them, and in Case of Disagreement between them, with Respect to the Time of Adjournment, he may adjourn them to such Time as he shall think proper; he shall receive Ambassadors and other public Ministers; he shall take Care that the Laws be faithfully executed, and shall Commission all the Officers of the United States.

Section 4. The President, Vice President and all civil Officers of the United States, shall be removed from Office on Impeachment for, and Conviction of, Treason, Bribery, or other high Crimes and Misdemeanors.

Article III

Section 1. The judicial Power of the United States, shall be vested in one supreme Court, and in such inferior Courts as the Congress may from time to time ordain and establish. The Judges, both of the supreme and inferior Courts, shall hold their Offices during good Behaviour, and shall, at Times, receive for their Services, a Compensation, which shall not be diminished during their Continuance in Office.

Section 2. The judicial Power shall extend to all Cases, in Law and Equity, arising under this Constitution, the Laws of the United States, and Treaties made, or which shall be made, under their Authority;—to all Cases affecting Ambassadors, other public Ministers and Consuls;—to all Cases of admiralty and maritime Jurisdiction;—to Controversies to which the United States shall be a Party;—to controversies between two or more States;—between a State and Citizens of another State;—between Citizens of different States;—between Citizens of the same State claiming Lands under Grants of different States, and between a State, or the Citizens thereof, and foreign States, Citizens or Subjects.

In all Cases affecting Ambassadors, other public Ministers and Consuls, and those in which a State shall be Party, the supreme Court shall have original Jurisdiction. In all the other Cases before mentioned, the supreme Court shall have appellate Jurisdiction, both as to Law and Fact, with such Exceptions, and under such Regulations as the Congress shall make.

The Trial of all Crimes, except in Cases of Impeachment, shall be by Jury; and such Trial shall be held in the State where the said Crimes shall have been committed; but when not committed within any State, the Trial shall be at such Place or Places as the Congress may by Law have directed.

Section 3. Treason against the United States, shall consist only in levying War against them, or in adhering to their Enemies, giving them Aid and Comfort. No Person shall be convicted of Treason unless on the Testimony of two Witnesses to the same overt Act, or on Confession in open Court.

The Congress shall have Power to declare the Punishment of Treason, but no Attainder of Treason shall work Corruption of Blood, or Forfeiture except during the Life of the Person attainted.

Article IV

Section 1. Full Faith and Credit shall be given in each State to the public Acts, Records, and judicial Proceedings of every other State. And the Congress may by general Laws prescribe the Manner in which such Arts, Records, and Proceedings shall be proved, and the Effect thereof.

Section 2. The Citizens of each State shall be entitled to all Privileges and Immunities of Citizens in the several States.

A person charged in any State with Treason, Felony, or other Crime, who shall flee from Justice, and be found in another State, shall on Demand of the executive Authority of the State from which he fled, be delivered up, to be removed to the State having Jurisdiction of the Crime.

No Person held to Service or Labour in one State, under the Laws thereof, escaping into another, shall, in Consequence of any Law or Regulation therein, be discharged from such Service or Labour, but shall be delivered up on Claim of the Party to whom such Service or Labour may be due.

Section 3. New States may be admitted by the Congress into this Union; but no new state shall be formed or erected within the Jurisdiction of any other State; nor any State be formed by the Junction of two or more States, or Parts of States, without the Consent of the Legislatures of the States concerned as well as of the Congress.

The Congress shall have Power to dispose of and make all needful Rules and Regulations respecting the Territory or other Property belonging to the United States; and nothing in this Constitution shall be so construed as to Prejudice any Claims of the United States, or of any particular State.

Section 4. The United States shall guarantee to every State in this Union a Republican Form of Government, and shall protect each of them against Invasion; and on Application of the Legislature, or of the Executive (when the Legislature cannot be convened) against domestic Violence.

Article V

The Congress, whenever two thirds of both Houses shall deem it necessary, shall propose Amendments to this Constitution, or, on the Application of the Legislatures of two thirds of the several States, shall call a Convention for proposing Amendments, which, in either Case, shall be valid to all Intents and Purposes, as Part of this Constitution, when ratified by the Legislatures of three fourths of the several States, or by Conventions in three fourths thereof, as the one or the other Mode of Ratification may be proposed by the Congress; Provided that no Amendment which may be made prior to the Year One thousand eight hundred and eight shall in any Manner affect the first and fourth Clauses in the Ninth Section of the first Article; and that no State, without its Consent, shall be deprived of its equal Suffrage in the Senate.

Article VI

All Debts contracted and Engagements entered into, before the Adoption of this Constitution, shall be as valid against the United States under this Constitution, as under the Confederation.

This Constitution, and the Laws of the United States which shall be made in Pursuance thereof; and all Treaties made, or which shall be made, under the Authority of the United States, shall be the supreme Law of the Land; and

the Judges in every State shall be bound thereby, any Thing in the Constitution or Laws of any State to the Contrary notwithstanding.

The Senators and Representatives before mentioned, and the Members of the several State Legislatures, and all executive and judicial Officers, both of the United States and of the Several States, shall be bound by Oath or Affirmation, to support this Constitution; but no religious Test shall ever be required as a Qualification to any Office or public Trust under the United States.

Article VII

The Ratification of the Conventions of nine States, shall be sufficient for the Establishment of this Constitution between the States so ratifying the Same.

Amendment I [1791]

Congress shall make no law respecting an establishment of religion, or prohibiting the free exercise thereof; or abridging the freedom of speech, or the press; or the right of the people peaceably to assemble, and to petition the Government for a redress of grievances.

Amendment II [1791]

A well regulated Militia, being necessary to the security for a free State, the right of the people to keep and bear Arms, shall not be infringed.

Amendment III [1791]

No Soldier shall, in time of peace be quartered in any house, without the consent of the Owner, nor in time of war, but in a manner to be prescribed by law.

Amendment IV [1791]

The right of the people to be secure in their persons, houses, papers, and effects, against unreasonable searches and seizures, shall not be violated, and no Warrants shall issue, but upon probable cause, supported by Oath or Affirmation, and particularly describing the place to be searched, and the persons or things to be seized.

Amendment V [1791]

No person shall be held to answer for a capital, or otherwise infamous crime, unless on a presentment or indictment of a Grand Jury, except in cases arising in the land or naval forces, or in the Militia, when in actual service in time of War or public danger; nor shall any person be subject for the same offense to be twice put in jeopardy of life or limb; nor shall be compelled in any criminal case to be a witness against himself, nor be deprived of life, liberty, or property, without due process of law; nor shall private property be taken for public use, without just compensation.

Amendment VI [1791]

In all criminal prosecutions, the accused shall enjoy the right to a speedy and public trial, by an impartial jury of the State and district wherein the crime shall have been committed, which district shall have been previously ascertained by law, and to be informed of the nature and cause of the accusation; to be confronted with the Witnesses against him; to have compulsory process for obtaining witnesses in his favor, and to have the Assistance of counsel for his defence.

Amendment VII [1791]

In suits at common law, where the value in controversy shall exceed twenty dollars, the right of trial by jury shall be preserved, and no fact tried by a jury, shall be otherwise reexamined in any Court of the United States, than according to the rules of the common law.

Amendment VIII [1791]

Excessive bail shall not be required, nor excessive fines imposed, nor cruel and unusual punishments inflicted.

Amendment IX [1791]

The enumeration in the Constitution, of certain rights, shall not be construed to deny or disparage others retained by the people.

Amendment X [1791]

The powers not delegated to the United States by the Constitution, nor prohibited by it to the States, are reserved to the States respectively, or to the people.

Amendment XI [1798]

The judicial power of the United States shall not be construed to extend to any suit in law or equity, commenced or prosecuted against one of the United States by Citizens of another State, or by Citizens or Subjects of any Foreign State.

Amendment XII [1804]

The Electors shall meet in their respective states and vote by ballot for President and Vice-President, one of whom, at least, shall not be an inhabitant of the same state with themselves; they shall name in their ballots the person voted for as President, and in distinct ballots the person voted for as Vice-President, and they shall make distinct lists of all persons voted for as President, and of all persons voted for as Vice-President, and of the number of votes for each, which lists they shall sign and certify, and transmit sealed to the seat of the government of the United States, directed to the President of the Senate;—The President of the Senate shall, in the presence of the Senate and House of Representatives,

open all the certificates and the votes shall then be counted;—The person having the greatest number of votes for President, shall be the President, if such number be a majority of the whole number of Electors appointed; and if no person have such majority, then from the persons having the highest numbers not exceeding three on the list of those voted for as President, the House of Representatives shall choose immediately, by ballot, the President. But in choosing the President, the votes shall be taken by states, the representation from each state having one vote; a quorum for this purpose shall consist of a member or members from two-thirds of the states, and a majority of all the states shall be necessary to a choice. And if the House of Representatives shall not choose a President whenever the right of choice shall devolve upon them, before the fourth day of March next following, then the Vice-President shall act as President, as in the case of the death or other constitutional disability of the President. The person having the greatest number of votes as Vice-President, shall be the Vice-President, if such number be a majority of the whole number of Electors appointed, and if no person have a majority, then from the two highest numbers on the list, the Senate shall choose the Vice-President; a quorum for the purpose shall consist of two-thirds of the whole number of Senators, and a majority of the whole number shall be necessary to a choice. But no person constitutionally ineligible to the office of President shall be eligible to that of the Vice-President of the United States.

Amendment XIII [1865]

Section 1. Neither slavery nor involuntary servitude, except as a punishment for crime whereof the party shall have been duly convicted, shall exist within the United States, or any place subject to their jurisdiction.

Section 2. Congress shall have power to enforce this article by appropriate legislation.

Amendment XIV [1868]

Section 1. All persons born or naturalized in the United States, and subject to the jurisdiction thereof, are citizens of the United States and of the State wherein they reside. No State shall make or enforce any law which shall abridge the privileges or immunities of citizens of the United States; nor shall any State deprive any person of life, liberty, or property, without due process of law; nor deny to any person within its jurisdiction the equal protection of the laws.

Section 2. Representatives shall be appointed among the several States according to their respective numbers, counting the whole number of persons in each State, excluding Indians not taxed. But when the right to vote at any election for the choice of electors for President and Vice President of the United States, Representatives in Congress, the Executive and Judicial officers of a State, or the members of the Legislature thereof, is denied to any of the male inhabitants of such State, being twenty-one years of age, and citizens of the United States, or in any way abridged, except for participation in rebellion, or other crime, the basis of representation therein shall be reduced in the proportion which the number of such male citizens shall bear to the whole number of male citizens twenty-one years of age in such State.

Section 3. No person shall be a Senator or Representative in Congress, or elector of President and Vice President, or hold any office, civil or military, under the United States, or under any State, who, having previously taken an oath, as a member of Congress, or as an officer of the United States, or as a member of any State legislature, or as an executive or judicial officer of any State, to support the Constitution of the United States, shall have engaged in insurrection or rebellion against the same, or given aid or comfort to the enemies thereof. But Congress may by a vote of two-thirds of each House, remove such disability.

Section 4. The validity of the public debt of the United States, authorized by law, including debts incurred for payment of pensions and bounties for services in suppressing insurrection or rebellion, shall not be questioned. But neither the United States nor any State shall assume or pay any debt or obligation incurred in aid of insurrection of rebellion against the United States, or any claim for the loss or emancipation of any slave; but all such debts, obligations and claims shall be held illegal and void.

Section 5. The Congress shall have power to enforce, by appropriate legislation, the provisions of this article.

Amendment XV [1870]

Section 1. The right of citizens of the United States to vote shall not be denied or abridged by the United States or by any State on account of race, color, or previous condition of servitude.

Section 2. The Congress shall have power to enforce this article by appropriate legislation.

Amendment XVI [1913]

The Congress shall have power to lay and collect taxes on incomes, from whatever source derived, without apportionment among the several States, and without regard to any census or enumeration.

Amendment XVII [1913]

The Senate of the United States shall be composed of two Senators from each State, elected by the people thereof, for six years; and each Senator shall have one vote. The electors in each State shall have the qualifications requisite for electors of the most numerous branch of the State legislatures.

When vacancies happen in the representation of any State in the Senate, the executive authority of each State

shall issue writs of election to fill such vacancies; *Provided,* That the legislature of any State may empower the executive thereof to make temporary appointments until the people fill the vacancies by election as the legislature may direct. This amendment shall not be so construed as to affect the election or term of any Senator chosen before it becomes valid as part of the Constitution.

Amendment XVIII [1919]

Section 1. After one year from the ratification of this article the manufacture, sale, or transportation of intoxicating liquors within, the importation thereof into, or the exportation thereof from the United States and all territory subject to the jurisdiction thereof for beverage purposes is hereby prohibited.

Section 2. The Congress and the several States shall have concurrent power to enforce this article by appropriate legislation.

Section 3. This article shall be inoperative unless it shall have been ratified as an amendment to the Constitution by the legislatures of the several States, as provided in the Constitution, within seven years from the date of the submission hereof to the States by the Congress.

Amendment XIX [1920]

The right of citizens of the United States to vote shall not be denied or abridged by the United States or by any State on account of sex.

Congress shall have power to enforce this article by appropriate legislation.

Amendment XX [1933]

Section 1. The terms of the President and Vice President shall end at noon on the 20th day of January, and the terms of Senators and Representatives at noon on the 3rd day of January, of the years in which such terms would have ended if this article had not been ratified; and the terms of their successors shall then begin.

Section 2. The Congress shall assemble at least once in every year, and such meeting shall begin at noon on the 3rd day of January, unless they shall by law appoint a different day.

Section 3. If, at the time fixed for the beginning of the term of the President, the President elect shall have died, the Vice President elect shall become President. If a President shall not have been chosen before the time fixed for the beginning of his term, or if the President elect shall have failed to qualify, then the Vice President elect shall act as President until a President shall have qualified; and the Congress may by law provide for the case wherein neither a President elect nor a Vice President elect shall have qualified, declaring who shall then act as President, or the manner in which one who is to act shall be selected, and such person shall act accordingly until a President or Vice President shall have qualified.

Section 4. The Congress may by law provide for the case of the death of any of the persons from whom the House of Representatives may choose a President whenever the right of choice shall have devolved upon them, and for the case of the death of any of the persons from whom the Senate may choose a Vice President whenever the right of choice shall have devolved upon them.

Section 5. Sections 1 and 2 shall take effect on the 15th day of October following the ratification of this article.

Section 6. This article shall be inoperative unless it shall have been ratified as an amendment to the Constitution by the legislatures of three-fourths of the several States within seven years from the date of its submission.

Amendment XXI [1933]

Section 1. The eighteenth article of amendment to the Constitution of the United States is hereby repealed.

Section 2. The transportation or importation into any State, Territory, or possession of the United States for delivery or use therein of intoxicating liquors, in violation of the laws thereof, is hereby prohibited.

Section 3. This article shall be inoperative unless it shall have been ratified as an amendment to the Constitution by conventions in the several States, as provided in the Constitution, within seven years from the date of the submission hereof to the States by the Congress.

Amendment XXII [1951]

Section 1. No person shall be elected to the office of the President more than twice, and no person who has held the office of President, or acted as President, for more than two years of a term to which some other person was elected President shall be elected to the office of the President more than once. But this Article shall not apply to any person holding the office of President when this article was proposed by the Congress, and shall not prevent any person who may be holding the office of President, or acting as President, during the term within which this Article becomes operative from holding the office of President, or acting as President during the remainder of such term.

Section 2. This article shall be inoperative unless it shall have been ratified as an amendment to the Constitution by the legislatures of three-fourths of the several States within seven years from the date of its submission to the States by the Congress.

Amendment XXIII [1961]

Section 1. The District constituting the seat of government of the United States shall appoint in such manner as the Congress may direct:

A number of electors of President and Vice President equal to the whole number of Senators and Representatives in Congress to which the District would be entitled if it were a State, but in no event more than the least populous State; they shall be in addition to those appointed by the States, but they shall be considered, for the purposes of the election of President and Vice President, to be electors appointed by a State; and they shall meet in the District and perform such duties as provided by the twelfth article of amendment.

Section 2. The Congress shall have power to enforce this article by appropriate legislation.

Amendment XXIV [1964]

Section 1. The right of citizens of the United States to vote in any primary or other election for President or Vice President, for electors for President or Vice President, or for Senator or Representative in Congress, shall not be denied or abridged by the United States or any State by reason of failure to pay any poll tax or other tax.

Section 2. The Congress shall have power to enforce this article by appropriate legislation.

Amendment XXV [1967]

Section 1. In case of the removal of the President from office or of his death or resignation, the Vice President shall become President.

Section 2. Whenever there is a vacancy in the office of the Vice President, the President shall nominate a Vice President who shall take office upon confirmation by a majority vote of both Houses of Congress.

Section 3. Whenever the President transmits to the President pro tempore of the Senate and the Speaker of the House of Representatives his written declaration that he is unable to discharge the powers and duties of his office, and until he transmits to them a written declaration to the contrary, such powers and duties shall be discharged by the Vice President as Acting President.

Section 4. Whenever the Vice President and a majority of either the principal officers of the executive departments or of such other body as Congress may by law provide, transmit to the President pro tempore of the Senate and the Speaker of the House of Representatives their written declaration that the President is unable to discharge the powers and duties of his office, the Vice President shall immediately assume the powers and duties of the office as Acting President.

Thereafter, when the President transmits to the President pro tempore of the Senate and the Speaker of the House of Representatives his written declaration that no inability exists, he shall resume the powers and duties of his office unless the Vice President and a majority of either the principal officers of the executive department or of such other body as Congress may by law provide, transmit within four days to the President pro tempore of the Senate and the Speaker of the House of Representatives their written declaration that the President is unable to discharge the powers and duties of his office. Thereupon Congress shall decide the issue, assembling within forty-eight hours for that purpose if not in session. If the Congress, within twenty-one days after receipt of the latter written declaration, or, if Congress is not in session, within twenty-one days after Congress is required to assemble, determines by two-thirds vote of both Houses that the President shall continue to discharge the same as Acting President; otherwise, the President shall resume the powers and duties of his office.

Amendment XXVI [1971]

Section 1. The right of citizens of the United States, who are 18 years of age or older, to vote, shall not be denied or abridged by the United States or any State on account of age.

Section 2. The Congress shall have the power to enforce this article by appropriate legislation.

Amendment XXVII [1992]

No law, varying the compensation for the services of the Senators and Representatives, shall take effect, until an election of Representatives shall have intervened.

Article 2. Sales

Part 1. Short Title, General Construction and Subject Matter

§ 2–101. Short Title.

This Article shall be known and may be cited as Uniform Commercial Code—Sales.

§ 2–102. Scope; Certain Security and Other Transactions Excluded From This Article.

Unless the context otherwise requires, this Article applies to transactions in goods; it does not apply to any transaction which although in the form of an unconditional contract to sell or present sale is intended to operate only as a security transaction nor does this Article impair or repeal any statute regulating sales to consumers, farmers or other specified classes of buyers.

§ 2–103. Definitions and Index of Definitions.

(1) In this Article unless the context otherwise requires
    (a) "Buyer" means a person who buys or contracts to buy goods.
    (b) "Good faith" in the case of a merchant means honesty in fact and the observance of reasonable commercial standards of fair dealing in the trade.
    (c) "Receipt" of goods means taking physical possession of them.
    (d) "Seller" means a person who sells or contracts to sell goods.
(2) Other definitions applying to this Article or to specified Parts thereof, and the sections in which they appear are:

"Acceptance"	Section 2–606.
"Banker's credit"	Section 2–325.
"Between merchants"	Section 2–104.
"Cancellation"	Section 2–106(4).
"Commercial unit"	Section 2–105.
"Confirmed credit"	Section 2–325.
"Conforming to contract"	Section 2–106.
"Contract for sale"	Section 2–106.
"Cover"	Section 2–712.
"Entrusting"	Section 2–403.
"Financing agency"	Section 2–104.

(3) The following definitions in other Articles apply to this Article:

(4) In addition Article 1 contains general definitions and principles of construction and interpretation applicable throughout this Article.

§ 2–104. Definitions: "Merchant"; "Between Merchants"; "Financing Agency".

(1) "Merchant" means a person who deals in goods of the kind or otherwise by his occupation holds himself out as having knowledge or skill peculiar to the practices or goods involved in the transaction or to whom such knowledge or skill may be attributed by his employment of an agent or broker or other intermediary who by his occupation holds himself out as having such knowledge or skill.

(2) "Financing agency" means a bank, finance company or other person who in the ordinary course of business makes advances against goods or documents of title or who by arrangement with either the seller or the buyer intervenes in ordinary course to make or collect payment due or claimed under the contract for sale, as by purchasing or paying the seller's draft or making advances against it or by merely taking it for collection whether or not the documents of title accompany the draft. "Financing agency" includes also a bank or other person who similarly intervenes between persons who are in the position of seller and buyer in respect to the goods (Section 2–707).

(3) "Between merchants" means in any transaction with respect to which both parties are chargeable with the knowledge or skill of merchants.

§ 2–105. Definitions: Transferability; "Goods"; "Future" Goods; "Lot"; "Commercial Unit".

(1) "Goods" means all things (including specially manufactured goods) which are movable at the time of identification to the contract for sale other than the money in which the price is to be paid, investment securities (Article 8) and things in action. "Goods" also includes the unborn young of animals and growing crops and other identified things attached to realty as described in the section on goods to be severed from realty (Section 2–107).

(2) Goods must be both existing and identified before any interest in them can pass. Goods which are not both existing and identified are "future" goods. A purported present sale of future goods or of any interest therein operates as a contract to sell.

(3) There may be a sale of a part interest in existing identified goods.

(4) An undivided share in an identified bulk of fungible goods is sufficiently identified to be sold although the quantity of the bulk is not determined. Any agreed proportion of such a bulk or any quantity thereof agreed upon by number, weight or other measure may to the extent of the seller's interest in the bulk be sold to the buyer who then becomes an owner in common.

(5) "Lot" means a parcel or a single article which is the subject matter of a separate sale or delivery, whether or not it is sufficient to perform the contract.

(6) "Commercial unit" means such a unit of goods as by commercial usage is a single whole for purposes of sale and division of which materially impairs its character or value on the market or in use. A commercial unit may be a single article (as a machine) or a set of articles (as a suite of furniture or an assortment of sizes) or a quantity (as a bale, gross, or car load) or any other unit treated in use or in the relevant market as a single whole.

§ 2–106. Definitions: "Contract"; "Agreement"; "Contract for Sale"; "Sale"; "Present Sale"; "Conforming" to Contract; "Termination"; "Cancellation".

(1) In this Article unless the context otherwise requires "contract" and "agreement" are limited to those relating to the present or future sale of goods. "Contract for sale" includes both a present sale of goods and a contract to sell goods at a future time. A "sale" consists in the passing of title from the seller to the buyer for a price (Section 2–401). A "present sale" means a sale which is accomplished by the making of the contract.

(2) Goods or conduct including any part of a performance are "conforming" or conform to the contract when they are in accordance with the obligations under the contract.

(3) "Termination" occurs when either party pursuant to a power created by agreement or law puts an end to the contract otherwise than for its breach. On "termination" all obligations which are still executory on both sides are discharged but any right based on prior breach or performance survives.

(4) "Cancellation" occurs when either party puts an end to the contract for breach by the other and its effect is the same as that of "termination" except that the cancelling party also retains any remedy for breach of the whole contract or any unperformed balance.

§ 2–107. Goods to Be Severed From Realty: Recording.

(1) A contract for the sale of minerals or the like (including oil and gas) or a structure or its materials to be removed from realty is a contract for the sale of goods within this Article if they are to be severed by the seller but until severance a purported present sale thereof which is not effective as a transfer of an interest in land is effective only as a contract to sell.

(2) A contract for the sale apart from the land of growing crops or other things attached to realty and capable of severance without material harm thereto but not described in subsection (1) or of timber to be cut is a contract for the sale of goods within this Article whether the subject matter is to be severed by the buyer or by the seller even though it forms part of the realty at the time of contracting, and the parties can by identification effect a present sale before severance.

(3) The provisions of this section are subject to any third party rights provided by the law relating to realty records, and the contract for sale may be executed and recorded as a document transferring an interest in land and shall then constitute notice to third parties of the buyer's right under the contract for sale.

Part 2. Form, Formation and Readjustment of Contra

§ 2–201. Formal Requirements; Statute of Frauds.

(1) Except as otherwise provided in this section a contract for the sale of goods for the price of $500 or more is not enforceable by way of action or defense unless there is some writing sufficient to indicate that a contract for sale has been made between the parties and signed by the party against whom enforcement is sought or by his authorized agent or broker. A writing is not insufficient because it omits or incorrectly states a term agreed upon but the contract is not enforceable under this paragraph beyond the quantity of goods shown in such writing.

(2) Between merchants if within a reasonable time a writing in confirmation of the contract and sufficient against the sender is received and the party receiving it has reason to know its contents, it satisfies the requirements of subsection (1) against such party unless written notice of objection to its contents is given within 10 days after it is received.

(3) A contract which does not satisfy the requirements of subsection (1) but which is valid in other respects is enforceable

   (a) if the goods are to be specially manufactured for the buyer and are not suitable for sale to others in the ordinary course of the seller's business and the seller, before notice of repudiation is received and under circumstances which reasonably indicate that the goods are for the buyer, has made either a substantial beginning of their manufacture or commitments for their procurement; or

   (b) if the party against whom enforcement is sought admits in his pleading, testimony or otherwise in court that a contract for sale was made, but the contract is not enforceable under this provision beyond the quantity of goods admitted; or

   (c) with respect to goods for which payment has been made and accepted or which have been received and accepted (Section 2–606).

§ 2–202. Final Written Expression: Parol or Extrinsic Evidence.

Terms with respect to which the confirmatory memoranda of the parties agree or which are otherwise set forth in a writing intended by the parties as a final expression of their agreement with respect to such terms as are included therein may not be contradicted by evidence of any prior agreement or of a contemporaneous oral agreement but may be explained or supplemented

(a) by course and dealing or usage of trade (Section 1–205) or by course of performance (Section 2–208); and

(b) by evidence of consistent additional terms unless the court finds the writing to have been intended also as a complete and exclusive statement of the terms of the agreement.

§ 2–203. Seals Inoperative.

The affixing of a seal to a writing evidencing a contract for sale or an offer to buy or sell goods does not constitute the writing a sealed instrument and the law with respect to sealed instruments does not apply to such a contract or offer.

§ 2–204. Formation in General.

(1) A contract for sale of goods may be made in any manner sufficient to show agreement, including conduct by both parties which recognizes the existence of such a contract.

(2) An agreement sufficient to constitute a contract for sale may be found even though the moment of its making is undetermined.

(3) Even though one or more terms are left open a contract for sale does not fail for indefiniteness if the parties have intended to make a contract and there is a reasonably certain basis for giving an appropriate remedy.

§ 2–205. Firm Offers.

An offer by a merchant to buy or sell goods in a signed writing which by its terms gives assurance that it will be held open is not revocable, for lack of consideration, during the time stated or if no time is stated for a reasonable time, but in no event may such period of irrevocability exceed three months; but any such term of assurance on a form supplied by the offeree must be separately signed by the offeror.

§ 2–206. Offer and Acceptance in Formation of Contract.

(1) Unless otherwise unambiguously indicated by the language or circumstances

(a) an offer to make a contract shall be construed as inviting acceptance in any manner and by any medium reasonable in the circumstances;

(b) an order or other offer to buy goods for prompt or current shipment shall be construed as inviting acceptance either by a prompt promise to ship or by the prompt or current shipment of conforming or non-conforming goods, but such a shipment of non-conforming goods does not constitute an acceptance if the seller seasonably notifies the buyer that the shipment is offered only as an accommodation to the buyer.

(2) Where the beginning of a requested performance is a reasonable mode of acceptance an offeror who is not notified of acceptance within a reasonable time may treat the offer as having lapsed before acceptance.

§ 2–207. Additional Terms in Acceptance or Confirmation.

(1) A definite and seasonable expression of acceptance or a written confirmation which is sent within a reasonable time operates as an acceptance even though it states terms additional to or different from those offered or agreed upon, unless acceptance is expressly made conditional on assent to the additional or different terms.

(2) The additional terms are to be construed as proposals for addition to the contract. Between merchants such terms become part of the contract unless:

(a) the offer expressly limits acceptance to the terms of the offer;

(b) they materially alter it; or

(c) notification of objection to them has already been given or is given within a reasonable time after notice of them is received.

(3) Conduct by both parties which recognizes the existence of a contract is sufficient to establish a contract for sale although the writings of the parties do not otherwise establish a contract. In such case the terms of the particular contract consist of those terms on which the writings of the parties agree, together with any supplementary terms incorporated under any other provisions of this Act.

§ 2–208. Course of Performance or Practical Construction.

(1) Where the contract for sale involves repeated occasions for performance by either party with knowledge of the nature of the performance and opportunity for objection to it by the other, any course of performance accepted or acquiesced in without objection shall be relevant to determine the meaning of the agreement.

(2) The express terms of the agreement and any such course of performance, as well as any course of dealing and usage of trade, shall be construed whenever reasonable as consistent with each other; but when such construction is unreasonable, express terms shall control course of performance and course of performance shall control both course of dealing and usage of trade (Section 1–205).

(3) Subject to the provisions of the next section on modification and waiver, such course of performance shall be relevant to show a waiver or modification of any term inconsistent with such course of performance.

§ 2–209. Modification, Rescission and Waiver.

(1) An agreement modifying a contract within this Article needs no consideration to be binding.

(2) A signed agreement which excludes modification or rescission except by a signed writing cannot be otherwise modified or rescinded, but except as between merchants such a requirement on a form supplied by the merchant must be separately signed by the other party.

(3) The requirements of the statute of frauds section of this Article (Section 2–201) must be satisfied if the contract as modified is within its provisions.

(4) Although an attempt at modification or rescission does not satisfy the requirements of subsection (2) or (3) it can operate as a waiver.

(5) A party who has made a waiver affecting an executory portion of the contract may retract the waiver by reasonable notification received by the other party that strict performance will be required of any term waived, unless the retraction would be unjust in view of a material change of position in reliance on the waiver.

§ 2–210. Delegation of Performance; Assignment of Rights.

(1) A party may perform his duty through a delegate unless otherwise agreed or unless the other party has a substantial interest in having his original promisor perform or control the acts required by the contract. No delegation of performance relieves the party delegating of any duty to perform or any liability for breach.

(2) Except as otherwise provided in Section 9–406, unless otherwise agreed all rights of either seller or buyer can be assigned except where the assignment would materially change the duty of the other party, or increase materially the burden or risk imposed on him by his contract, or impair materially his chance of obtaining return performance. A right to damages for breach of the whole contract or a right arising out of the assignor's due performance of his entire obligation can be assigned despite agreement otherwise.

(3) The creation, attachment, perfection, or enforcement of a security interest in the seller's interest under a contract is not a transfer that materially changes the duty of or increases materially the burden or risk imposed on the buyer or impairs materially the buyer's chance of obtaining return performance within the purview of subsection (2) unless, and then only to the extent that, enforcement actually results in a delegation of material performance of the seller. Even in that event, the creation, attachment, perfection, and enforcement of the security interest remain effective, but (i) the seller is liable to the buyer for damages caused by the delegation to the extent that the damages could not reasonably be prevented by the buyer, and (ii) a court having jurisdiction may grant other appropriate relief, including cancellation of the

contract for sale or an injunction against enforcement of the security interest or consummation of the enforcement.

(4) Unless the circumstances indicate the contrary a prohibition of assignment of "the contract" is to be construed as barring only the delegation to the assignee of the assignor's performance.

(5) An assignment of "the contract" or of "all my rights under the contract" or an assignment in similar general terms is an assignment of rights and unless the language or the circumstances (as in an assignment for security) indicate the contrary, it is a delegation of performance of the duties of the assignor and its acceptance by the assignee constitutes a promise by him to perform those duties. This promise is enforceable by either the assignor or the other party to the original contract.

(6) The other party may treat any assignment which delegates performance as creating reasonable grounds for insecurity and may without prejudice to his rights against the assignor demand assurances from the assignee (Section 2–609).

Part 3. General Obligation and Construction of Contract

§ 2–301. General Obligations of Parties.

The obligation of the seller is to transfer and deliver and that of the buyer is to accept and pay in accordance with the contract.

§ 2–302. Unconscionable Contract or Clause.

(1) If the court as a matter of law finds the contract or any clause of the contract to have been unconscionable at the time it was made the court may refuse to enforce the contract, or it may enforce the remainder of the contract without the unconscionable clause, or it may so limit the application of any unconscionable clause as to avoid any unconscionable result.

(2) When it is claimed or appears to the court that the contract or any clause thereof may be unconscionable the parties shall be afforded a reasonable opportunity to present evidence as to its commercial setting, purpose and effect to aid the court in making the determination.

§ 2–303. Allocation or Division of Risks.

Where this Article allocates a risk or a burden as between the parties "unless otherwise agreed", the agreement may not only shift the allocation but may also divide the risk or burden.

§ 2–304. Price Payable in Money, Goods, Realty, or Otherwise.

(1) The price can be made payable in money or otherwise. If it is payable in whole or in part in goods each party is a seller of the goods which he is to transfer.

(2) Even though all or part of the price is payable in an interest in realty the transfer of the goods and the seller's obligations with reference to them are subject to this Article, but not the transfer of the interest in realty or the transferor's obligations in connection therewith.

§ 2–305. Open Price Term.

(1) The parties if they so intend can conclude a contract for sale even though the price is not settled. In such a case the price is a reasonable price at the time for delivery if
(a) nothing is said as to price; or
(b) the price is left to be agreed by the parties and they fail to agree; or
(c) the price is to be fixed in terms of some agreed market or other standard as set or recorded by a third person or agency and it is not so set or recorded.

(2) A price to be fixed by the seller or by the buyer means a price for him to fix in good faith.

(3) When a price left to be fixed otherwise than by agreement of the parties fails to be fixed through fault of one party the other may at his option treat the contract as cancelled or himself fix a reasonable price.

(4) Where, however, the parties intend not to be bound unless the price be fixed or agreed and it is not fixed or agreed there is no contract. In such a case the buyer must return any goods already received or if unable so to do must pay their reasonable value at the time of delivery and the seller must return any portion of the price paid on account.

§ 2–306. Output, Requirements and Exclusive Dealings.

(1) A term which measures the quantity by the output of the seller or the requirements of the buyer means such actual output or requirements as may occur in good faith, except that no quantity unreasonably disproportionate to any stated estimate or in the absence of a stated estimate to any normal or otherwise comparable prior output or requirements may be tendered or demanded.

(2) A lawful agreement by either the seller or the buyer for exclusive dealing in the kind of goods concerned imposes unless otherwise agreed an obligation by the seller to use best efforts to supply the goods and by the buyer to use best efforts to promote their sale.

§ 2–307. Delivery in Single Lot or Several Lots.

Unless otherwise agreed all goods called for by a contract for sale must be tendered in a single delivery and payment is due only on such tender but where the circumstances give either party the right to make or demand delivery in lots the price if it can be apportioned may be demanded for each lot.

§ 2–308. Absence of Specified Place for Delivery.

Unless otherwise agreed
(a) the place for delivery of goods is the seller's place of business or if he has none his residence; but
(b) in a contract for sale of identified goods which to the knowledge of the parties at the time of contracting are in some other place, that place is the place for their delivery; and
(c) documents of title may be delivered through customary banking channels.

§ 2–309. Absence of Specific Time Provisions; Notice of Termination.

(1) The time for shipment or delivery or any other action under a contract if not provided in this Article or agreed upon shall be a reasonable time.

(2) Where the contract provides for successive performance but is indefinite in duration it is valid for a reasonable time but unless otherwise agreed may be terminated at any time by either party.

(3) Termination of a contract by one party except on the happening of an agreed event requires that reasonable notification be received by the other party and an agreement dispensing with notification is invalid if its operation would be unconscionable.

§ 2–310. Open Time for Payment or Running of Credit; Authority to Ship Under Reservation.

Unless otherwise agreed

(a) payment is due at the time and place at which the buyer is to receive the goods even though the place of shipment is the place of delivery; and

(b) if the seller is authorized to send the goods he may ship them under reservation, and may tender the documents of title, but the buyer may inspect the goods after their arrival before payment is due unless such inspection is inconsistent with the terms of the contract (Section 2–513); and

(c) if delivery is authorized and made by way of documents of title otherwise than by subsection (b) then payment is due at the time and place at which the buyer is to receive the documents regardless of where the goods are to be received; and

(d) where the seller is required or authorized to ship the goods on credit the credit period runs from the time of shipment but post-dating the invoice or delaying its dispatch will correspondingly delay the starting of the credit period.

§ 2–311. Options and Cooperation Respecting Performance.

(1) An agreement for sale which is otherwise sufficiently definite (subsection (3) of Section 2–204) to be a contract is not made invalid by the fact that it leaves particulars of performance to be specified by one of the parties. Any such specification must be made in good faith and within limits set by commercial reasonableness.

(2) Unless otherwise agreed specifications relating to assortment of the goods are at the buyer's option and except as otherwise provided in subsections (1) (c) and (3) of Section 2–319 specifications or arrangements relating to shipment are at the seller's option.

(3) Where such specification would materially affect the other party's performance but is not seasonably made or where one party's cooperation is necessary to the agreed performance of the other but is not seasonably forthcoming, the other party in addition to all other remedies

(a) is excused for any resulting delay in his own performance; and

(b) may also either proceed to perform in any reasonable manner or after the time for a material part of his own performance treat the failure to specify or to cooperate as a breach by failure to deliver or accept the goods.

§ 2–312. Warranty of Title and Against Infringement; Buyer's Obligation Against Infringement.

(1) Subject to subsection (2) there is in a contract for sale a warranty by the seller that

(a) the title conveyed shall be good, and its transfer rightful; and

(b) the goods shall be delivered free from any security interest or other lien or encumbrance of which the buyer at the time of contracting has no knowledge.

(2) A warranty under subsection (1) will be excluded or modified only by specific language or by circumstances which give the buyer reason to know that the person selling does not claim title in himself or that he is purporting to sell only such right or title as he or a third person may have.

(3) Unless otherwise agreed a seller who is a merchant regularly dealing in goods of the kind warrants that the goods shall be delivered free of the rightful claim of any third person by way of infringement or the like but a buyer who furnishes specifications to the seller must hold the seller harmless against any such claim which arises out of compliance with the specifications.

§ 2–313. Express Warranties by Affirmation, Promise, Description, Sample.

(1) Express warranties by the seller are created as follows:

(a) Any affirmation of fact or promise made by the seller to the buyer which relates to the goods and becomes part of the basis of the bargain creates an express warranty that the goods shall conform to the affirmation or promise.

(b) Any description of the goods which is made part of the basis of the bargain creates an express warranty that the goods shall conform to the description.

(c) Any sample or model which is made part of the basis of the bargain creates an express warranty that the whole of the goods shall conform to the sample or model.

(2) It is not necessary to the creation of an express warranty that the seller use formal words such as "warrant" or "guarantee" or that he have a specific intention to make a warranty, but an affirmation merely of the value of the goods or a statement purporting to be merely the seller's opinion or commendation of the goods does not create a warranty.

§ 2–314. Implied Warranty: Merchantability; Usage of Trade.

(1) Unless excluded or modified (Section 2–316), a warranty that the goods shall be merchantable is implied in a contract for their sale if the seller is a merchant with

respect to goods of that kind. Under this section the serving for value of food or drink to be consumed either on the premises or elsewhere is a sale.

(2) Goods to be merchantable must be at least such as

   (a) pass without objection in the trade under the contract description; and

   (b) in the case of fungible goods, are of fair average quality within the description; and

   (c) are fit for the ordinary purposes for which such goods are used; and

   (d) run, within the variations permitted by the agreement, of even kind, quality and quantity within each unit and among all units involved; and

   (e) are adequately contained, packaged, and labeled as the agreement may require; and

   (f) conform to the promises or affirmations of fact made on the container or label if any.

(3) Unless excluded or modified (Section 2–316) other implied warranties may arise from course of dealing or usage of trade.

§ 2–315. Implied Warranty: Fitness for Particular Purpose.

Where the seller at the time of contracting has reason to know any particular purpose for which the goods are required and that the buyer is relying on the seller's skill or judgment to select or furnish suitable goods, there is unless excluded or modified under the next section an implied warranty that the goods shall be fit for such purpose.

§ 2–316. Exclusion or Modification of Warranties.

(1) Words or conduct relevant to the creation of an express warranty and words or conduct tending to negate or limit warranty shall be construed wherever reasonable as consistent with each other, but subject to the provisions of this Article on parol or extrinsic evidence (Section 2–202) negation or limitation is inoperative to the extent that such construction is unreasonable.

(2) Subject to subsection (3), to exclude or modify the implied warranty of merchantability or any part of it the language must mention merchantability and in case of a writing must be conspicuous, and to exclude or modify any implied warranty of fitness the exclusion must be by a writing and conspicuous. Language to exclude all implied warranties of fitness is sufficient if it states, for example, that "There are no warranties which extend beyond the description on the face hereof."

(3) Notwithstanding subsection (2)

   (a) unless the circumstances indicate otherwise, all implied warranties are excluded by expression like "as is", "with all faults" or other language which in common understanding calls the buyer's attention to the exclusion of warranties and makes plain that there is no implied warranty; and

   (b) when the buyer before entering into the contract has examined the goods or the sample or model as fully as he desired or has refused to examine the goods there is no implied warranty with regard to

defects which an examination ought in the circumstances to have revealed to him; and

   (c) an implied warranty can also be excluded or modified by course of dealing or course of performance or usage of trade.

(4) Remedies for breach of warranty can be limited in accordance with the provisions of this Article on liquidation or limitation of damages and on contractual modification of remedy (Sections 2–718 and 2–719).

§ 2–317. Cumulation and Conflict of Warranties Express or Implied.

Warranties whether express or implied shall be construed as consistent with each other and as cumulative, but if such construction is unreasonable the intention of the parties shall determine which warranty is dominant. In ascertaining that intention the following rules apply:

   (a) Exact or technical specifications displace an inconsistent sample or model or general language of description.

   (b) A sample from an existing bulk displaces inconsistent general language of description.

   (c) Express warranties displace inconsistent implied warranties other than an implied warranty of fitness for a particular purpose.

§ 2–318. Third Party Beneficiaries of Warranties Express or Implied.

> Note: *If this Act is introduced in the Congress of the United States this section should be omitted. (States to select one alternative.)*

Alternative A. A seller's warranty whether express or implied extends to any natural person who is in the family or household of his buyer or who is a guest in his home if it is reasonable to expect that such person may use, consume or be affected by the goods and who is injured in person by breach of the warranty. A seller may not exclude or limit the operation of this section.

Alterntive B. A seller's warranty whether express or implied extends to any natural person who may reasonably be expected to use, consume or be affected by the goods and who is injured in person by breach of the warranty. A seller may not exclude or limit the operation of this section.

Alternative C. A seller's warranty whether express or implied extends to any person who may reasonably be expected to use, consume or be affected by the goods and who is injured by breach of the warranty. A seller may not exclude or limit the operation of this section with respect to injury to the person of an individual to whom the warranty extends.

§ 2–319. F.O.B. and F.A.S. Terms.

(1) Unless otherwise agreed the term F.O.B. (which means "free on board") at a named place, even though used only in connection with the stated price, is a delivery term under which

(a) when the term is F.O.B. the place of shipment, the seller must at that place ship the goods in the manner provided in this Article (Section 2–504) and bear the expense and risk of putting them into the possession of the carrier; or

(b) when the term is F.O.B. the place of destination, the seller must at his own expense and risk transport the goods to that place and there tender delivery of them in the manner provided in this Article (Section 2–503);

(c) when under either (a) or (b) the term is also F.O.B. vessel, car or other vehicle, the seller must in addition at his own expense and risk load the goods on board. If the term is F.O.B. vessel the buyer must name the vessel and in an appropriate case the seller must comply with the provisions of this Article on the form of bill of lading (Section 2–323).

(2) Unless otherwise agreed the term F.A.S. vessel (which means "free alongside") at a named port, even though used only in connection with the stated price, is a delivery term under which the seller must

(a) at his own expense and risk deliver the goods alongside the vessel in the manner usual in that port or on a dock designated and provided by the buyer; and

(b) obtain and tender a receipt for the goods in exchange for which the carrier is under a duty to issue a bill of lading.

(3) Unless otherwise agreed in any case falling within subsection (1)(a) or (c) or subsection (2) the buyer must seasonably give any needed instructions for making delivery, including when the term is F.A.S. or F.O.B. the loading berth of the vessel and in an appropriate case its name and sailing date. The seller may treat the failure of needed instructions as a failure of cooperation under this Article (Section 2–311). He may also at his option move the goods in any reasonable manner preparatory to delivery or shipment.

(4) Under the term F.O.B. vessel or F.A.S. unless otherwise agreed the buyer must make payment against tender of the required documents and the seller may not tender nor the buyer demand delivery of the goods in substitution for the documents.

§ 2–320. C.I.F. and C. & F. Terms.

(1) The term C.I.F. means that the price includes in a lump sum the cost of the goods and the insurance and freight to the named destination. The term C. & F. or C.F. means that the price so includes cost and freight to the named destination.

(2) Unless otherwise agreed and even though used only in connection with the stated price and destination, the term C.I.F. destination or its equivalent requires the seller at his own expense and risk to

(a) put the goods into the possession of a carrier at the port for shipment and obtain a negotiable bill or bills of lading covering the entire transportation to the named destination; and

(b) load the goods and obtain a receipt from the carrier (which may be contained in the bill of lading) showing that the freight has been paid or provided for; and

(c) obtain a policy or certificate of insurance, including any war risk insurance, of a kind and on terms then current at the port of shipment in the usual amount, in the currency of the contract, shown to cover the same goods covered by the bill of lading and providing for payment of loss to the order of the buyer or for the account of whom it may concern; but the seller may add to the price the amount of the premium for any such war risk insurance; and

(d) prepare an invoice of the goods and procure any other documents required to effect shipment or to comply with the contract; and

(e) forward and tender with commercial promptness all the documents in due form and with any indorsement necessary to perfect the buyer's rights.

(3) Unless otherwise agreed the term C. & F. or its equivalent has the same effect and imposes upon the seller the same obligations and risks as a C.I.F. term except the obligation as to insurance.

(4) Under the term C.I.F. or C. & F. unless otherwise agreed the buyer must make payment against tender of the required documents and the seller may not tender nor the buyer demand delivery of the goods in substitution for the documents.

§ 2–321. C.I.F. or C. & F.: "Net Landed Weights"; "Payment on Arrival"; Warranty of Condition on Arrival.

Under a contract containing a term C.I.F. or C. & F.

(1) Where the price is based on or is to be adjusted according to "net landed weights", "delivered weights", "out turn" quantity or quality or the like, unless otherwise agreed the seller must reasonably estimate the price. The payment due on tender of the documents called for by the contract is the amount so estimated, but after final adjustment of the price a settlement must be made with commercial promptness.

(2) An agreement described in subsection (1) or any warranty of quality or condition of the goods on arrival places upon the seller the risk of ordinary deterioration, shrinkage and the like in transportation but has no effect on the place or time of identification to the contract for sale or delivery or on the passing of the risk of loss.

(3) Unless otherwise agreed where the contract provides for payment on or after arrival of the goods the seller must before payment allow such preliminary inspection as is feasible; but if the goods are lost delivery of the documents and payment are due when the goods should have arrived.

§ 2–322. Delivery "Ex-Ship".

(1) Unless otherwise agreed a term for delivery of goods "ex-ship" (which means from the carrying vessel) or in equivalent language is not restricted to a particular ship

and requires delivery from a ship which has reached a place at the named port of destination where goods of the kind are usually discharged.

(2) Under such a term unless otherwise agreed
   (a) the seller must discharge all liens arising out of the carriage and furnish the buyer with a direction which puts the carrier under a duty to deliver the goods; and
   (b) the risk of loss does not pass to the buyer until the goods leave the ship's tackle or are otherwise properly unloaded.

§ 2–323. Form of Bill of Lading Required in Overseas Shipment; "Overseas".

(1) Where the contract contemplates overseas shipment and contains a term C.I.F. or C. & F. or F.O.B. vessel, the seller unless otherwise agreed must obtain a negotiable bill of lading stating that the goods have been loaded on board or, in the case of a term C.I.F. or C. & F., received for shipment.

(2) Where in a case within subsection (1) a bill of lading has been issued in a set of parts, unless otherwise agreed if the documents are not to be sent from abroad the buyer may demand tender of the full set; otherwise only one part of the bill of lading need be tendered. Even if the agreement expressly requires a full set
   (a) due tender of a single part is acceptable within the provisions of this Article on cure of improper delivery (subsection (1) of Section 2–508); and
   (b) even though the full set is demanded, if the documents are sent from abroad the person tendering an incomplete set may nevertheless require payment upon furnishing an indemnity which the buyer in good faith deems adequate.

(3) A shipment by water or by air or a contract contemplating such shipment is "overseas" insofar as by usage of trade or agreement it is subject to the commercial, financing or shipping practices characteristic of international deep water commerce.

§ 2–324. "No Arrival, No Sale" Term.

Under a term "no arrival, no sale" or terms of like meaning, unless otherwise agreed.
   (a) the seller must properly ship conforming goods and if they arrive by any means he must tender them on arrival but he assumes no obligation that the goods will arrive unless he has caused the non-arrival; and
   (b) where without fault of the seller the goods are in part lost or have so deteriorated as no longer to conform to the contract or arrive after the contract time, the buyer may proceed as if there had been casualty to identified goods (Section 2–613).

§ 2–325. "Letter of Credit" Term; "Confirmed Credit".

(1) Failure of the buyer seasonably to furnish an agreed letter of credit is a breach of the contract for sale.

(2) The delivery to seller of a proper letter of credit suspends the buyer's obligation to pay. If the letter of credit is dishonored, the seller may on seasonable notification to the buyer require payment directly from him.

(3) Unless otherwise agreed the term "letter of credit" or "banker's credit" in a contract for sale means an irrevocable credit issued by a financing agency of good repute and, where the shipment is overseas, of good international repute. The term "confirmed credit" means that the credit must also carry the direct obligation of such an agency which does business in the seller's financial market.

§ 2–326. Sale on Approval and Sale or Return; Rights of Creditors.

(1) Unless otherwise agreed, if delivered goods may be returned by the buyer even though they conform to the contract, the transaction is
   (a) a "sale on approval" if the goods are delivered primarily for use, and
   (b) a "sale or return" if the goods are delivered primarily for resale.

(2) Goods held on approval are not subject to the claims of the buyer's creditors until acceptance; goods held on sale or return are subject to such claims while in the buyer's possession.

(3) Any "or return" term of a contract for sale is to be treated as a separate contract for sale within the statute of frauds section of this Article (Section 2–201) and as contradicting the sale aspect of the contract within the provisions of this Article on parol or extrinsic evidence (Section 2–202).

§ 2–327. Special Incidents of Sale on Approval and Sale or Return.

(1) Under a sale on approval unless otherwise agreed
   (a) although the goods are identified to the contract the risk of loss and the title do not pass to the buyer until acceptance; and
   (b) use of the goods consistent with the purpose of trial is not acceptance but failure seasonably to notify the seller of election to return the goods is acceptance, and if the goods conform to the contract acceptance of any part is acceptance of the whole; and
   (c) after due notification of election to return, the return is at the seller's risk and expense but a merchant buyer must follow any reasonable instructions.

(2) Under a sale or return unless otherwise agreed
   (a) the option to return extends to the whole or any commercial unit of the goods while in substantially their original condition, but must be exercised seasonably; and
   (b) the return is at the buyer's risk and expense.

§ 2–328. Sale by Auction.

(1) In a sale by auction if goods are put up in lots each lot is the subject of a separate sale.

(2) A sale by auction is complete when the auctioneer so announces by the fall of the hammer or in other customary manner. Where a bid is made while the hammer is

falling in acceptance of a prior bid the auctioneer may in his discretion reopen the bidding or declare the goods sold under the bid on which the hammer was falling.

(3) Such a sale is with reserve unless the goods are in explicit terms put up without reserve. In an auction with reserve the auctioneer may withdraw the goods at any time until he announces completion of the sale. In an auction without reserve, after the auctioneer calls for bids on an article or lot, that article or lot cannot be withdrawn unless no bid is made within a reasonable time. In either case a bidder may retract his bid until the auctioneer's announcement of completion of the sale, but a bidder's retraction does not revive any previous bid.

(4) If the auctioneer knowingly receives a bid on the seller's behalf or the seller makes or procures such a bid, and notice has not been given that liberty for such bidding is reserved, the buyer may at his option avoid the sale or take the goods at the price of the last good faith bid prior to the completion of the sale. This subsection shall not apply to any bid at a forced sale.

Part 4. Title, Creditors and Good Faith Purchasers

§ 2–401. Passing of Title; Reservation for Security; Limited Application of This Section.

Each provision of this Article with regard to the rights, obligations and remedies of the seller, the buyer, purchasers or other third parties applies irrespective of title to the goods except where the provision refers to such title. Insofar as situations are not covered by the other provisions of this Article and matters concerning title become material the following rules apply:

(1) Title to goods cannot pass under a contract for sale prior to their identification to the contract (Section 2–501), and unless otherwise explicitly agreed the buyer acquires by their identification a special property as limited by this Act. Any retention or reservation by the seller of the title (property) in goods shipped or delivered to the buyer is limited in effect to a reservation of a security interest. Subject to these provisions and to the provisions of the Article on Secured Transactions (Article 9), title to goods passes from the seller to the buyer in any manner and on any conditions explicitly agreed on by the parties.

(2) Unless otherwise explicitly agreed title passes to the buyer at the time and place at which the seller completes his performance with reference to the physical delivery of the goods, despite any reservation of a security interest and even though a document of title is to be delivered at a different time or place; and in particular and despite any reservation of a security interest by the bill of lading

(a) if the contract requires or authorizes the seller to send the goods to the buyer but does not require him to deliver them at destination, title passes to the buyer at the time and place of shipment; but

(b) if the contract requires delivery at destination, title passes on tender there.

(3) Unless otherwise explicitly agreed where delivery is to be made without moving the goods.

(a) if the seller is to deliver a document of title, title passes at the time when and the place where he delivers such documents; or

(b) if the goods are at the time of contracting already identified and no documents are to be delivered, title passes at the time and place of contracting.

(4) A rejection or other refusal by the buyer to receive or retain the goods, whether or not justified, or a justified revocation of acceptance revests title to the goods in the seller. Such revesting occurs by operation of law and is not a "sale".

§ 2–402. Rights of Seller's Creditors Against Sold Goods.

(1) Except as provided in subsections (2) and (3), rights of unsecured creditors of the seller with respect to goods which have been identified to a contract for sale are subject to the buyer's rights to recover the goods under this Article (Sections 2–502 and 2–716).

(2) A creditor of the seller may treat a sale or an identification of goods to a contract for sale as void if as against him a retention of possession by the seller is fraudulent under any rule of law of the state where the goods are situated, except that retention of possession in good faith and current course of trade by a merchant-seller for a commercially reasonable time after a sale or identification is not fraudulent.

(3) Nothing in this Article shall be deemed to impair the rights of creditors of the seller

(a) under the provisions of the Article on Secured Transactions (Article 9); or

(b) where identification to the contract or delivery is made not in current course of trade but in satisfaction of or as security for a pre-existing claim for money, security or the like and is made under circumstances which under any rule of law of the state where the goods are situated would apart from this Article constitute the transaction a fraudulent transfer or voidable preference.

§ 2–403. Power to Transfer; Good Faith Purchase of Goods; "Entrusting".

(1) A purchaser of goods acquires all title which his transferor had or had power to transfer except that a purchaser of a limited interest acquires rights only to the extent of the interest purchased. A person with voidable title has power to transfer a good title to a good faith purchaser for value. When goods have been delivered under a transaction of purchase the purchaser has such power even though

(a) the transferor was deceived as to the identity of the purchaser, or

(b) the delivery was in exchange for a check which is later dishonored, or

(c) it was agreed that the transaction was to be a "cash sale", or

(d) the delivery was procured through fraud punishable as larcenous under the criminal law.

(2) Any entrusting of possession of goods to a merchant who deals in goods of that kind gives him power to transfer all rights of the entruster to a buyer in ordinary course of business.

(3) "Entrusting" includes any delivery and any acquiescence in retention of possession regardless of any condition expressed between the parties to the delivery or acquiescence and regardless of whether the procurement of the entrusting or the possessor's disposition of the goods have been such as to be larcenous under the criminal law.

(4) The rights of other purchasers of goods and of lien creditors are governed by the Articles on Secured Transactions (Article 9). [Bulk Transfers/Sales (Article 6)* and Documents of Title (Article 7)].

Part 5. Performance

§ 2–501. Insurable Interest in Goods; Manner of Identification of Goods.

(1) The buyer obtains a special property and an insurable interest in goods by identification of existing goods as goods to which the contract refers even though the goods so identified are non-conforming and he has an option to return or reject them. Such identification can be made at any time and in any manner explicitly agreed to by the parties. In the absence of explicit agreement identification occurs.

(a) when the contract is made if it is for the sale of goods already existing and identified;

(b) if the contract is for the sale of future goods other than those described in paragraph (c), when goods are shipped, marked or otherwise designated by the seller as goods to which the contract refers;

(c) when the crops are planted or otherwise become growing crops or the young are conceived if the contract is for the sale of unborn young to be born within twelve months after contracting or for the sale of crops to be harvested within twelve months or the next normal harvest season after contracting, whichever is longer.

(2) The seller retains an insurable interest in goods so long as title to or any security interest in the goods remains in him and where the identification is by the seller alone he may until default or insolvency or notification to the buyer that the identification is final substitute other goods for those identified.

(3) Nothing in this section impairs any insurable interest recognized under any other statute or rule of law.

§ 2–502. Buyer's Right to Goods on Seller's Insolvency.

(1) Subject to subsections (2) and (3) and even though the goods have not been shipped a buyer who has paid a part or all of the price of goods in which he has a special property under the provisions of the immediately preceding section may on making and keeping good a tender of any unpaid portion of their price recover them from the seller if:

(a) in the case of goods bought for personal, family, or household purposes, the seller repudiates or fails to deliver as required by the contract; or

(b) in all cases, the seller becomes insolvent within ten days after receipt of the first installment on their price.

(2) The buyer's right to recover the goods under subsection (1)(a) vests upon acquisition of a special property, even if the seller had not then repudiated or failed to deliver.

(3) If the identification creating his special property has been made by the buyer he acquires the right to recover the goods only if they conform to the contract for sale.

§ 2–503. Manner of Seller's Tender of Delivery.

(1) Tender of delivery requires that the seller put and hold conforming goods at the buyer's disposition and give the buyer any notification reason ably necessary to enable him to take delivery. The manner, time and place for tender are determined by the agreement and this Article, and in particular

(a) tender must be at a reasonable hour, and if it is of goods they must be kept available for the period reasonably necessary to enable the buyer to take possession; but

(b) unless otherwise agreed the buyer must furnish facilities reasonably suited to the receipt of the goods.

(2) Where the case is within the next section respecting shipment tender requires that the seller comply with its provisions.

(3) Where the seller is required to deliver at a particular destination tender requires that he comply with subsection (1) and also in any appropriate case tender documents as described in subsections (4) and (5) of this section.

(4) Where goods are in the possession of a bailee and are to be delivered without being moved

(a) tender requires that the seller either tender a negotiable document of title covering such goods or procure acknowledgment by the bailee of the buyer's right to possession of the goods; but

(b) tender to the buyer of a non-negotiable document of title or of a written direction to the bailee to deliver is sufficient tender unless the buyer seasonably objects, and receipt by the bailee of notification of the buyer's rights fixes those rights as against the bailee and all third persons; but risk of loss of the goods and of any failure by the bailee to honor the non-negotiable document of title or to obey the direction remains on the seller until the buyer has had a reasonable time to present the document or direction, and a refusal by the bailee to honor the document or to obey the direction defeats the tender.

(5) Where the contract requires the seller to deliver documents
   (a) he must tender all such documents in correct form, except as provided in this Article with respect to bills of lading in a set (subsection (2) of Section 2–323); and
   (b) tender through customary banking channels is sufficient and dishonor of a draft accompanying the documents constitutes non-acceptance or rejection.

§ 2–504. Shipment by Seller.

Where the seller is required or authorized to send the goods to the buyer and the contract does not require him to deliver them at a particular destination, then unless otherwise agreed he must
(a) put the goods in the possession of such a carrier and make such a contract for their transportation as may be reasonable having regard to the nature of the goods and other circumstances of the case; and
(b) obtain and promptly deliver or tender in due form any document necessary to enable the buyer to obtain possession of the goods or otherwise required by the agreement or by usage of trade; and
(c) promptly notify the buyer of the shipment.

Failure to notify the buyer under paragraph (c) or to make a proper contract under paragraph (a) is a ground for rejection only if material delay or loss ensues.

§ 2–505. Seller's Shipment Under Reservation.

(1) Where the seller has identified goods to the contract by or before shipment:
   (a) his procurement of a negotiable bill of lading to his own order or otherwise reserves in him a security interest in the goods. His procurement of the bill to the order of a financing agency or of the buyer indicates in addition only the seller's expectation of transferring that interest to the person named.
   (b) a non-negotiable bill of lading to himself or his nominee reserves possession of the goods as security but except in a case of conditional delivery (subsection (2) of Section 2–507) a non-negotiable bill of lading naming the buyer as consignee reserves no security interest even though the seller retains possession of the bill of lading.
(2) When shipment by the seller with reservation of a security interest is in violation of the contract for sale it constitutes an improper contract for transportation within the preceding section but impairs neither the rights given to the buyer by shipment and identification of the goods to the contract nor the seller's powers as a holder of a negotiable document.

§ 2–506. Rights of Financing Agency.

(1) A financing agency by paying or purchasing for value a draft which relates to a shipment of goods acquires to the extent of the payment or purchase and in addition to its own rights under the draft and any document of title securing it any rights of the shipper in the goods including the right to stop delivery and the shipper's right to have the draft honored by the buyer.
(2) The right to reimbursement of a financing agency which has in good faith honored or purchased the draft under commitment to or authority from the buyer is not impaired by subsequent discovery of defects with reference to any relevant document which was apparently regular on its face.

§ 2–507. Effect of Seller's Tender; Delivery on Condition.

(1) Tender of delivery is a condition to the buyer's duty to accept the goods and, unless otherwise agreed, to his duty to pay for them. Tender entitles the seller to acceptance of the goods and to payment according to the contract.
(2) Where payment is due and demanded on the delivery to the buyer of goods or documents of title, his right as against the seller to retain or dispose of them is conditional upon his making the payment due.

§ 2–508. Cure by Seller of Improper Tender or Delivery; Replacement.

(1) Where any tender or delivery by the seller is rejected because non-conforming and the time for performance has not yet expired, the seller may seasonably notify the buyer of his intention to cure and may then within the contract time make a conforming delivery.
(2) Where the buyer rejects a non-conforming tender which the seller had reasonable grounds to believe would be acceptable with or without money allowance the seller may if he seasonably notifies the buyer have a further reasonable time to substitute a conforming tender.

§ 2–509. Risk of Loss in the Absence of Breach.

(1) Where the contract requires or authorizes the seller to ship the goods by carrier
   (a) if it does not require him to deliver them at a particular destination, the risk of loss passes to the buyer when the goods are duly delivered to the carrier even though the shipment is under reservation (Section 2–505); but
   (b) if it does require him to deliver them at a particular destination and the goods are there duly tendered while in the possession of the carrier, the risk of loss passes to the buyer when the goods are there duly so tendered as to enable the buyer to take delivery.
(2) Where the goods are held by a bailee to be delivered without being moved, the risk of loss passes to the buyer
   (a) on his receipt of a negotiable document of title covering the goods; or
   (b) on acknowledgment by the bailee of the buyer's right to possession of the goods; or
   (c) after his receipt of a non-negotiable document of title or other written direction to deliver, as provided in subsection (4)(b) of Section 2–503.
(3) In any case not within subsection (1) or (2), the risk of loss passes to the buyer on his receipt of the goods if the seller is a merchant; other wise the risk passes to the buyer on tender of delivery.

(4) The provisions of this section are subject to contrary agreement of the parties and to the provisions of this Article on sale on approval (Section 2–327) and on effect of breach on risk of loss (Section 2–510).

§ 2–510. Effect of Breach on Risk of Loss.

(1) Where a tender or delivery of goods so fails to conform to the contract as to give a right of rejection the risk of their loss remains on the seller until cure or acceptance.

(2) Where the buyer rightfully revokes acceptance he may to the extent of any deficiency in his effective insurance coverage treat the risk of loss as having rested on the seller from the beginning.

(3) Where the buyer as to conforming goods already identified to the contract for sale repudiates or is otherwise in breach before risk of their loss has passed to him, the seller may to the extent of any deficiency in his effective insurance coverage treat the risk of loss as resting on the buyer for a commercially reasonable time.

§ 2–511. Tender of Payment by Buyer; Payment by Check.

(1) Unless otherwise agreed tender of payment is a condition to the seller's duty to tender and complete any delivery.

(2) Tender of payment is sufficient when made by any means or in any manner current in the ordinary course of business unless the seller demands payment in legal tender and gives any extension of time reason ably necessary to procure it.

(3) Subject to the provisions of this Act on the effect of an instrument on an obligation (Section 3–310), payment by check is conditional and is defeated as between the parties by dishonor of the check on due presentment.

§ 2–512. Payment by Buyer Before Inspection.

(1) Where the contract requires payment before inspection nonconformity of the goods does not excuse the buyer from so making payment unless
   (a) the non-conformity appears without inspection; or
   (b) despite tender of the required documents the circumstances would justify injunction against honor under this Act (Section 5–109(b)).

(2) Payment pursuant to subsection (1) does not constitute an acceptance of goods or impair the buyer's right to inspect or any of his remedies.

§ 2–513. Buyer's Right to Inspection of Goods.

(1) Unless otherwise agreed and subject to subsection (3), where goods are tendered or delivered or identified to the contract for sale, the buyer has a right before payment or acceptance to inspect them at any reasonable place and time and in any reasonable manner. When the seller is required or authorized to send the goods to the buyer, the inspection may be after their arrival.

(2) Expenses of inspection must be borne by the buyer but may be recovered from the seller if the goods do not conform and are rejected.

(3) Unless otherwise agreed and subject to the provisions of this Article on C.I.F. contracts (subsection (3) of Section 2–321), the buyer is not entitled to inspect the goods before payment of the price when the contract provides
   (a) for delivery "C.O.D." or on other like terms; or
   (b) for payment against documents of title, except where such payment is due only after the goods are to become available for inspection.

(4) A place or method of inspection fixed by the parties is presumed to be exclusive but unless otherwise expressly agreed it does not postpone identification or shift the place for delivery or for passing the risk of loss. If compliance becomes impossible, inspection shall be as provided in this section unless the place or method fixed was clearly intended as an indispensable condition failure of which avoids the contract.

§ 2–514. When Documents Deliverable on Acceptance; When on Payment.

Unless otherwise agreed documents against which a draft is drawn are to be delivered to the drawee on acceptance of the draft if it is payable more than three days after presentment; otherwise, only on payment.

§ 2–515. Preserving Evidence of Goods in Dispute.

In furtherance of the adjustment of any claim or dispute
   (a) either party on reasonable notification to the other and for the purpose of ascertaining the facts and preserving evidence has the right to inspect, test and sample the goods including such of them as may be in the possession or control of the other; and
   (b) the parties may agree to a third party inspection or survey to determine the conformity or condition of the goods and may agree that the findings shall be binding upon them in any subsequent litigation or adjustment.

Part 6. Breach, Repudiation and Excuse

§ 2–601. Buyer's Rights on Improper Delivery.

Subject to the provisions of this Article on breach in installment contracts (Section 2–612) and unless otherwise agreed under the sections on contractual limitations of remedy (Sections 2–718 and 2–719), if the goods or the tender of delivery fail in any respect to conform to the contract, the buyer may
   (a) reject the whole; or
   (b) accept the whole; or
   (c) accept any commercial unit or units and reject the rest.

§ 2–602. Manner and Effect of Rightful Rejection.

(1) Rejection of goods must be within a reasonable time after their delivery or tender. It is ineffective unless the buyer seasonably notifies the seller.

(2) Subject to the provisions of the two following sections on rejected goods (Sections 2–603 and 2–604),
   (a) after rejection any exercise of ownership by the buyer with respect to any commercial unit is wrongful as against the seller; and

(b) if the buyer has before rejection taken physical possession of goods in which he does not have a security interest under the provisions of this Article (subsection (3) of Section 2–711), he is under a duty after rejection to hold them with reasonable care at the seller's disposition for a time sufficient to permit the seller to remove them; but

(c) the buyer has no further obligations with regard to goods rightfully rejected.

(3) The seller's rights with respect to goods wrongfully rejected are governed by the provisions of this Article on Seller's remedies in general (Section 2–703).

§ 2–603. Merchant Buyer's Duties as to Rightfully Rejected Goods.

(1) Subject to any security interest in the buyer (subsection (3) of Section 2–711), when the seller has no agent or place of business at the market of rejection a merchant buyer is under a duty after rejection of goods in his possession or control to follow any reasonable instructions received from the seller with respect to the goods and in the absence of such instructions to make reasonable efforts to sell them for the seller's account if they are perishable or threaten to decline in value speedily. Instructions are not reasonable if on demand indemnity for expenses is not forthcoming.

(2) When the buyer sells goods under subsection (1), he is entitled to reimbursement from the seller or out of the proceeds for reasonable expenses of caring for and selling them, and if the expenses include no selling commission then to such commission as is usual in the trade or if there is none to a reasonable sum not exceeding ten percent on the gross proceeds.

(3) In complying with this section the buyer is held only to good faith and good faith conduct hereunder is neither acceptance nor conversion nor the basis of an action for damages.

§ 2–604. Buyer's Options as to Salvage of Rightfully Rejected Goods.

Subject to the provisions of the immediately preceding section on perishables if the seller gives no instructions within a reasonable time after notification of rejection the buyer may store the rejected goods for the seller's account or reship them to him or resell them for the seller's account with reimbursement as provided in the preceding section. Such action is not acceptance or conversion.

§ 2–605. Waiver of Buyer's Objections by Failure to Particularize.

(1) The buyer's failure to state in connection with rejection a particular defect which is ascertainable by reasonable inspection precludes him from relying on the unstated defect to justify rejection or to establish breach

(a) where the seller could have cured it if stated seasonably; or

(b) between merchants when the seller has after rejection made a request in writing for a full and final written statement of all defects on which the buyer proposes to rely.

(2) Payment against documents made without reservation of rights precludes recovery of the payment for defects apparent on the face of the documents.

§ 2–606. What Constitutes Acceptance of Goods.

(1) Acceptance of goods occurs when the buyer

(a) after a reasonable opportunity to inspect the goods signifies to the seller that the goods are conforming or that he will take or retain them in spite of their non-conformity; or

(b) fails to make an effective rejection (subsection (1) of Section 2–602), but such acceptance does not occur until the buyer has had a reasonable opportunity to inspect them; or

(c) does any act inconsistent with the seller's ownership; but if such act is wrongful as against the seller it is an acceptance only if ratified by him.

(2) Acceptance of a part of any commercial unit is acceptance of that entire unit.

§ 2–607. Effect of Acceptance; Notice of Breach; Burden of Establishing Breach After Acceptance; Notice of Claim or Litigation to Person Answerable Over.

(1) The buyer must pay at the contract rate for any goods accepted.

(2) Acceptance of goods by the buyer precludes rejection of the goods accepted and if made with knowledge of a non-conformity cannot be revoked because of it unless the acceptance was on the reasonable assumption that the non-conformity would be seasonably cured but acceptance does not of itself impair any other remedy provided by this Article for non-conformity.

(3) Where a tender has been accepted

(a) the buyer must within a reasonable time after he discovers or should have discovered any breach notify the seller of breach or be barred from any remedy; and

(b) if the claim is one for infringement or the like (subsection (3) of Section 2–312) and the buyer is sued as a result of such a breach he must so notify the seller within a reasonable time after he receives notice of the litigation or be barred from any remedy over for liability established by the litigation.

(4) The burden is on the buyer to establish any breach with respect to the goods accepted.

(5) Where the buyer is sued for breach of a warranty or other obligation for which his seller is answerable over

(a) he may give his seller written notice of the litigation. If the notice states that the seller may come in and defend and that if the seller does not do so he will be bound in any action against him by his buyer by any determination of fact common to the two litigations, then unless the seller after seasonable receipt of the notice does come in and defend he is so bound.

(b) if the claim is one for infringement or the like (subsection (3) of Section 2–312) the original seller may demand in writing that his buyer turn over to him control of the litigation including settlement or else be barred from any remedy over and if he also agrees to bear all expense and to satisfy any adverse judgment, then unless the buyer after seasonable receipt of the demand does turn over control the buyer is so barred.

(6) The provisions of subsection (3), (4) and (5) apply to any obligation of a buyer to hold the seller harmless against infringement or the like (subsection (3) of Section 2–312).

§ 2–608. Revocation of Acceptance in Whole or in Part.

(1) The buyer may revoke his acceptance of a lot or commercial unit whose non-conformity substantially impairs its value to him if he has accepted it
   (a) on the reasonable assumption that its non-conformity would be cured and it has not been seasonably cured; or
   (b) without discovery of such non-conformity if his acceptance was reasonably induced either by the difficulty of discovery before acceptance or by the seller's assurances.
(2) Revocation of acceptance must occur within a reasonable time after the buyer discovers or should have discovered the ground for it and before any substantial change in condition of the goods which is not caused by their own defects. It is not effective until the buyer notifies the seller of it.
(3) A buyer who so revokes has the same rights and duties with regard to the goods involved as if he had rejected them.

§ 2–609. Right to Adequate Assurance of Performance.

(1) A contract for sale imposes an obligation on each party that the other's expectation of receiving due performance will not be impaired. When reasonable grounds for insecurity arise with respect to the performance of either party the other may in writing demand adequate assurance of due performance and until he receives such assurance may if commercially reasonable suspend any performance for which he has not already received the agreed return.
(2) Between merchants the reasonableness of grounds for insecurity and the adequacy of any assurance offered shall be determined according to commercial standards.
(3) Acceptance of any improper delivery or payment does not prejudice the aggrieved party's right to demand adequate assurance of future performance.
(4) After receipt of a justified demand failure to provide within a reasonable time not exceeding thirty days such assurance of due performance as is adequate under the circumstances of the particular case is a repudiation of the contract.

§ 2–610. Anticipatory Repudiation.

When either party repudiates the contract with respect to a performance not yet due the loss of which will substantially impair the value of the contract to the other, the aggrieved party may
(a) for a commercially reasonable time await performance by the repudiating party; or

(b) resort to any remedy for breach (Section 2–703 or Section 2–711), even though he has notified the repudiating party that he would await the latter's performance and has urged retraction; and
(c) in either case suspend his own performance or proceed in accordance with the provisions of this Article on the seller's right to identify goods to the contract notwithstanding breach or to salvage unfinished goods (Section 2–704).

§ 2–611. Retraction of Anticipatory Repudiation.

(1) Until the repudiating party's next performance is due he can retract his repudiation unless the aggrieved party has since the repudiation cancelled or materially changed his position or otherwise indicated that he considers the repudiation final.
(2) Retraction may be by any method which clearly indicates to the aggrieved party that the repudiating party intends to perform, but must include any assurance justifiably demanded under the provisions of this Article (Section 2–609).
(3) Retraction reinstates the repudiating party's rights under the contract with due excuse and allowance to the aggrieved party for any delay occasioned by the repudiation.

§ 2–612. "Installment Contract"; Breach.

(1) An "installment contract" is one which requires or authorizes the delivery of goods in separate lots to be separately accepted, even though the contract contains a clause "each delivery is a separate contract" or its equivalent.
(2) The buyer may reject any installment which is non-conforming if the non-conformity substantially impairs the value of that installment and cannot be cured or if the non-conformity is a defect in the required documents; but if the non-conformity does not fall within subsection (3) and the seller gives adequate assurance of its cure the buyer must accept that installment.
(3) Whenever non-conformity or default with respect to one or more installments substantially impairs the value of the whole contract there is a breach of the whole. But the aggrieved party reinstates the contract if he accepts a non-conforming installment without seasonably notifying of cancellation or if he brings an action with respect only to past installments or demands performance as to future installments.

§ 2–613. Casualty to Identified Goods.

Where the contract requires for its performance goods identified when the contract is made, and the goods suffer casualty without fault of either party before the risk of loss passes to the buyer, or in a proper case under a "no arrival, no sale" term (Section 2–324) then
(a) if the loss is total the contract is avoided; and
(b) if the loss is partial or the goods have so deteriorated as no longer to conform to the contract the buyer may nevertheless demand inspection and at his option either

treat the contract as avoided or accept the goods with due allowance from the contract price for the deterioration or the deficiency in quantity but without further right against the seller.

§ 2–614. Substituted Performance.
(1) Where without fault of either party the agreed berthing, loading, or unloading facilities fail or an agreed type of carrier becomes unavailable or the agreed manner of delivery otherwise becomes commercially impracticable but a commercially reasonable substitute is available, such substitute performance must be tendered and accepted.
(2) If the agreed means or manner of payment fails because of domestic or foreign governmental regulation, the seller may withhold or stop delivery unless the buyer provides a means or manner of payment which is commercially a substantial equivalent. If delivery has already been taken, payment by the means or in the manner provided by the regulation discharges the buyers obligation unless the regulation is discriminatory, oppressive or predatory.

§ 2–615. Excuse by Failure of Presupposed Conditions.
Except so far as a seller may have assumed a greater obligation and subject to the preceding section on substituted performance:
(a) Delay in delivery or non-delivery in whole or in part by a seller who complies with paragraphs (b) and (c) is not a breach of his duty under a contract for sale if performance as agreed has been made impracticable by the occurrence of a contingency the non-occurrence of which was a basic assumption on which the contract was made or by compliance in good faith with any applicable foreign or domestic governmental regulation or order whether or not it later proves to be invalid.
(b) Where the causes mentioned in paragraph (a) affect only a part of the seller's capacity to perform, he must allocate production and deliveries among his customers but may at his option include regular customers not then under contract as well as his own requirements for further manufacture. He may so allocate in any manner which is fair and reasonable.
(c) The seller must notify the buyer seasonably that there will be delay or non-delivery and, when allocation is required under paragraph (b), of the estimated quota thus made available for the buyer.

§ 2–616. Procedure on Notice Claiming Excuse.
(1) Where the buyer receives notification of a material or indefinite delay or an allocation justified under the preceding section he may by written notification to the seller as to any delivery concerned, and where the prospective deficiency substantially impairs the value of the whole contract under the provisions of this Article relating to breach of installment contracts (Section 2–612), then also as to the whole,
  (a) terminate and thereby discharge any unexecuted portion of the contract; or

  (b) modify the contract by agreeing to take his available quota in substitution.
(2) If after receipt of such notification from the seller the buyer fails so to modify the contract within a reasonable time not exceeding thirty days the contract lapses with respect to any deliveries affected.
(3) The provisions of this section may not be negated by agreement except in so far as the seller has assumed a greater obligation under the preceding section.

Part 7. Remedies

§ 2–701. Remedies for Breach of Collateral Contracts Not Impaired.
Remedies for breach of any obligation or promise collateral or ancillary to a contract for sale or not impaired by the provisions of this Article.

§ 2–702. Seller's Remedies on Discovery of Buyer's Insolvency.
(1) Where the seller discovers the buyer to be insolvent he may refuse delivery except for cash including payment for all goods therefore delivered under the contract, and stop delivery under this Article (Section 2–705).
(2) Where the seller discovers that the buyer has received goods on credit while insolvent he may reclaim the goods upon demand made within ten days after the receipt, but if misrepresentation of solvency has been made to the particular seller in writing within three months before delivery the ten day limitation does not apply. Except as provided in this subsection the seller may not base a right to reclaim goods on the buyer's fraudulent or innocent misrepresentation of solvency or of intent to pay.
(3) The seller's right to reclaim under subsection (2) is subject to the rights of a buyer in ordinary course or other good faith purchaser under this Article (Section 2–403). Successful reclamation of goods excludes all other remedies with respect to them.

§ 2–703. Seller's Remedies in General.
Where the buyer wrongfully rejects or revokes acceptance of goods or fails to make a payment due on or before delivery or repudiates with respect to a part or the whole, then with respect to any goods directly affected and, if the breach is of the whole contract (Section 2–612), then also with respect to the whole undelivered balance, the aggrieved seller may
(a) withhold delivery of such goods;
(b) stop delivery by any bailee as hereafter provided (Section 2–705);
(c) proceed under the next section respecting goods still unidentified to the contract;
(d) resell and recover damages as hereafter provided (Section 2–706);
(e) recover damages for non-acceptance (Section 2–708) or in a proper case the price (Section 2–709);
(f) cancel.

§ 2–704. Seller's Right to Identify Goods to the Contract Notwithstanding Breach or to Salvage Unfinished Goods.

(1) An aggrieved seller under the preceding section may

    (a) identify to the contract conforming goods not already identified if at the time he learned of the breach they are in his possession or control;

    (b) treat as the subject of resale goods which have demonstrably been intended for the particular contract even though those goods are unfinished.

(2) Where the goods are unfinished an aggrieved seller may in the exercise of reasonable commercial judgment for the purposes of avoiding loss and of effective realization either complete the manufacture and wholly identify the goods to the contract or cease manufacture and resell for scrap or salvage value or proceed in any other reasonable manner.

§ 2–705. Seller's Stoppage of Delivery in Transit or Otherwise.

(1) The seller may stop delivery of goods in the possession of a carrier or other bailee when he discovers the buyer to be insolvent (Section 2–702) and may stop delivery of carload, truckload, planeload or larger shipments of express or freight when the buyer repudiates or fails to make a payment due before delivery or if for any other reason the seller has a right to withhold or reclaim the goods.

(2) As against such buyer the seller may stop delivery until

    (a) receipt of the goods by the buyer; or

    (b) acknowledgment to the buyer by any bailee of the goods except a carrier that the bailee holds the goods for the buyer; or

    (c) such acknowledgment to the buyer by a carrier by reshipment or as warehouseman; or

    (d) negotiation to the buyer of any negotiable document of title covering the goods.

(3)(a) To stop delivery the seller must so notify as to enable the bailee by reasonable diligence to prevent delivery of the goods.

    (b) After such notification the bailee must hold and deliver the goods according to the directions of the seller but the seller is liable to the bailee for any ensuing charges or damages.

    (c) If a negotiable document of title has been issued for goods the bailee is not obliged to obey a notification to stop until surrender of the document.

    (d) A carrier who has issued a non-negotiable bill of lading is not obliged to obey a notification to stop received from a person other than the consignor.

§ 2–706. Seller's Resale Including Contract for Resale.

(1) Under the conditions stated in Section 2–703 on seller's remedies, the seller may resell the goods concerned or the undelivered balance thereof. Where the resale is made in good faith and in a commercially reasonable manner the seller may recover the difference between the resale price and the contract price together with any incidental damages allowed under the provisions of this Article (Section 2–710), but less expenses saved in consequence of the buyer's breach.

(2) Except as otherwise provided in subsection (3) or unless otherwise agreed resale may be at public or private sale including sale by way of one or more contracts to sell or of identification to an existing contract of the seller. Sale may be as a unit or in parcels and at any time and place and on any terms but every aspect of the sale including the method, manner, time, place and terms must be commercially reasonable. The resale must be reasonably identified as referring to the broken contract, but it is not necessary that the goods be in existence or that any or all of them have been identified to the contract before the breach.

(3) Where the resale is at private sale the seller must give the buyer reasonable notification of his intention to resell.

(4) Where the resale is at public sale

    (a) only identified goods can be sold except where there is a recognized market for a public sale of futures in goods of the kind; and

    (b) it must be made at a usual place or market for public sale if one is reasonably available and except in the case of goods which are perishable or threaten to decline in value speedily the seller must give the buyer reasonable notice of the time and place of the resale; and

    (c) if the goods are not to be within the view of those attending the sale the notification of sale must state the place where the goods are located and provide for their reasonable inspection by prospective bidders; and

    (d) the seller may buy.

(5) A purchaser who buys in good faith at a resale takes the goods free of any rights of the original buyer even though the seller fails to comply with one or more of the requirements of this section.

(6) The seller is not accountable to the buyer for any profit made on any resale. A person in the position of a seller (Section 2–707) or a buyer who has rightfully rejected or justifiably revoked acceptance must account for any excess over the amount of his security interest, as hereinafter defined (subsection (3) of Section 2–711).

§ 2–707. "Person in the Position of a Seller".

(1) A "person in the position of a seller" includes as against a principal an agent who has paid or become responsible for the price of goods on behalf of his principal or anyone who otherwise holds a security interest or other right in goods similar to that of a seller.

(2) A person in the position of a seller may as provided in this Article withhold or stop delivery (Section 2–705) and resell (Section 2–706) and recover incidental damages (Section 2–710).

§ 2–708. Seller's Damages for Non-Acceptance or Repudiation.

(1) Subject to subsection (2) and to the provisions of this Article with respect to proof of market price (Section 2–723), the measure of damages for non-acceptance or

repudiation by the buyer is the difference between the market price at the time and place for tender and the unpaid contract price together with any incidental damages provided in this Article (Section 2–710), but less expenses saved in consequence of the buyer's breach.

(2) If the measure of damages provided in subsection (1) is inadequate to put the seller in as good a position as performance would have done then the measure of damages is the profit (including reasonable overhead) which the seller would have made from full performance by the buyer, together with any incidental damages provided in this Article (Section 2–710), due allowance for costs reasonably incurred and due credit for payments or proceeds of resale.

§ 2–709. Action for the Price.

(1) When the buyer fails to pay the price as it becomes due the seller may recover, together with any incidental damages under the next section, the price
   (a) of goods accepted or of conforming goods lost or damaged within a commercially reasonable time after risk of their loss has passed to the buyer; and
   (b) of goods identified to the contract if the seller is unable after reasonable effort to resell them at a reasonable price or the circumstances reasonably indicate that such effort will be unavailing.

(2) Where the seller sues for the price he must hold for the buyer any goods which have been identified to the contract and are still in his control except that if resale becomes possible he may resell them at any time prior to the collection of the judgment. The net proceeds of any such resale must be credited to the buyer and payment of the judgment entitles him to any goods not resold.

(3) After the buyer has wrongfully rejected or revoked acceptance of the goods or has failed to make a payment due or has repudiated (Section 2–610), a seller who is held not entitled to the price under this section shall nevertheless be awarded damages for non-acceptance under the preceding section.

§ 2–710. Seller's Incidental Damages.

Incidental damages to an aggrieved seller include any commercially reasonable charges, expenses or commissions incurred in stopping delivery, in the transportation, care and custody of goods after the buyer's breach, in connection with return or resale of the goods or otherwise resulting from the breach.

§ 2–711. Buyer's Remedies in General; Buyer's Security Interest in Rejected Goods.

(1) Where the seller fails to make delivery or repudiates or the buyer rightfully rejects or justifiably revokes acceptance then with respect to any goods involved, and with respect to the whole if the breach goes to the whole contract (Section 2–612), the buyer may cancel and whether or not he has done so may in addition to recovering so much of the price as has been paid

(a) "cover" and have damages under the next section as to all the goods affected whether or not they have been identified to the contract; or
(b) recover damages for non-delivery as provided in this Article (Section 2–713).

(2) Where the seller fails to deliver or repudiates the buyer may also
   (a) if the goods have been identified recover them as provided in this Article (Section 2–502); or
   (b) in a proper case obtain specific performance or replevy the goods as provided in this Article (Section 2–716).

(3) On rightful rejection of justifiable revocation of acceptance a buyer has a security interest in goods in his possession or control for any payments made on their price and any expenses reasonably incurred in their inspection, receipt, transportation, care and custody and may hold such goods and resell them in like manner as an aggrieved seller (Section 2–706).

§ 2–712. "Cover"; Buyer's Procurement of Substitute Goods.

(1) After a breach within the preceding section the buyer may "cover" by making in good faith and without unreasonable delay any reasonable purchase of or contract to purchase goods in substitution for those due from the seller.

(2) The buyer may recover from the seller as damages the difference between the cost of cover and the contract price together with any incidental or consequential damages as hereinafter defined (Section 2–715), but less expenses saved in consequence of the seller's breach.

(3) Failure of the buyer to effect cover within this section does not bar him from any other remedy.

§ 2–713. Buyer's Damages for Non-Delivery or Repudiation.

(1) Subject to the provisions of this Article with respect to proof of market price (Section 2–723), the measure of damages for nondelivery or repudiation by the seller is the difference between the market price at the time when the buyer learned of the breach and the contract price together with any incidental and consequential damages provided in this Article (Section 2–715), but less expenses saved in consequence of the seller's breach.

(2) Market price is to be determined as of the place for tender or, in cases of rejection after arrival or revocation of acceptance, as of the place of arrival.

§ 2–714. Buyer's Damages for Breach in Regard to Accepted Goods.

(1) Where the buyer has accepted goods and given notification (subsection (3) of Section 2–607) he may recover as damages for any non-conformity of tender the loss resulting in the ordinary course of events from the seller's breach as determined in any manner which is reasonable.

(2) The measure of damages for breach of warranty is the difference at the time and place of acceptance between the value of the goods accepted and the value they

would have had if they had been as warranted, unless special circumstances show proximate damages of a different amount.

(3) In a proper case any incidental and consequential damages under the next section may also be recovered.

§ 2–715. Buyer's Incidental and Consequential Damages.

(1) Incidental damages resulting from the seller's breach include expenses reasonably incurred in inspection, receipt, transportation and care and custody of goods rightfully rejected, any commercially reasonable charges, expenses or commissions in connection with effecting cover and any other reasonable expense incident to the delay or other breach.

(2) Consequential damages resulting from the seller's breach include

(a) any loss resulting from general or particular requirements and needs of which the seller at the time of contracting had reason to know and which could not reasonably be prevented by cover or otherwise; and

(b) injury to person or property proximately resulting from any breach of warranty.

§ 2–716. Buyer's Right to Specific Performance or Replevin.

(1) Specific performance may be decreed where the goods are unique or in other proper circumstances.

(2) The decree for specific performance may include such terms and conditions as to payment of the price, damages, or other relief as the court may deem just.

(3) The buyer has a right of replevin for goods identified to the contract if after reasonable effort he is unable to effect cover for such goods or the circumstances reasonably indicate that such effort will be unvailing or if the goods have been shipped under reservation and satisfaction of the security interest in them has been made or tendered. In the case of goods bought for personal, family, or household purposes, the buyer's right of replevin vests upon acquisition of a special property, even if the seller had not then repudiated or failed to deliver..

§ 2–717. Deduction of Damages From the Price.

The buyer on notifying the seller of his intention to do so may deduct all or any part of the damages resulting from any breach of the contract from any part of the price still due under the same contract.

§ 2–718. Liquidation or Limitation of Damages; Deposits.

(1) Damages for breach by either party may be liquidated in the agreement but only at an amount which is reasonable in the light of the anticipated or actual harm caused by the breach, the difficulties of proof of loss, and the inconvenience of nonfeasibility of otherwise obtaining an adequate remedy. A team fixing unreasonably large liquidated damages is void as a penalty.

(2) Where the seller justifiably withholds delivery of goods because of the buyer's breach, the buyer is entitled to restitution of any amount by which the sum of his payments exceeds.

(a) the amount to which the seller is entitled by virtue of terms liquidating the seller's damages in accordance with subsection (1), or

(b) in the absence of such terms, twenty percent of the value of the total performance for which the buyer is obligated under the contract or $500, whichever is smaller.

(3) The buyer's right to restitution under subsection (2) is subject to offset to the extent that the seller establishes

(a) a right to recover damages under the provisions of this Article other than subsection (1), and

(b) the amount or value of any benefits received by the buyer directly or indirectly by reason of the contract.

(4) Where a seller has received payment in goods their reasonable value or the proceeds of their resale shall be treated as payments for the purposes of subsection (2); but if the seller has notice of the buyer's breach before reselling goods received in part performance, his resale is subject to the conditions laid down in this Article on resale by an aggrieved seller (Section 2–706).

§ 2–719. Contractual Modification or Limitation of Remedy.

(1) Subject to the provisions of subsections (2) and (3) of this section and of the preceding section on liquidation and limitation of damages,

(a) the agreement may provide for remedies in addition to or in substitution for those provided in this Article and may limit or alter the measure of damages recoverable under this Article, as by limiting the buyer's remedies to return of the goods and repayment of the price or to repair and replacement of non-conforming goods or parts; and

(b) resort to a remedy as provided is optional unless the remedy is expressly agreed to be exclusive, in which case it is the sole remedy.

(2) Where circumstances cause an exclusive or limited remedy to fail of its essential purpose, remedy may be had as provided in this Act.

(3) Consequential damages may be limited or excluded unless the limitation or exclusion is unconscionable. Limitation of consequential damages for injury to the person in the case of consumer goods is prima facie unconscionable but limitation of damages where the loss is commercial is not.

§ 2–720. Effect of "Cancellation" or "Rescission" on Claims for Antecedent Breach.

Unless the contrary intention clearly appears, expressions of "cancellation" or "rescission" of the contract or the like shall not be construed as a renunciation or discharge of any claim in damages for an antecedent breach.

§ 2–721. Remedies for Fraud.

Remedies for material misrepresentation or fraud include all remedies available under this Article for non-fraudulent breach. Neither rescission or a claim for rescission of the contract for sale nor rejection or return of the goods shall bar or be deemed inconsistent with a claim for damages or other remedy.

§ 2–722. Who Can Sue Third Parties for Injury to Goods.

Where a third party so deals with goods which have been identified to a contract for sale as to cause actionable injury to a party to that contract

(a) a right of action against the third party is in either party to the contract for sale who has title to or a security interest or a special property or an insurable interest in the goods; and if the goods have been destroyed or converted a right of action is also in the party who either bore the risk of loss under the contract for sale or has since the injury assumed that risk as against the other,

(b) if at the time of the injury the party plaintiff did not bear the risk of loss as against the other party to the contract for sale and there is no arrangement between them for disposition of the recovery, his suit or settlement is, subject to his own interest, as a fiduciary for the other party to the contract;

(c) either party may with the consent of the other sue for the benefit of whom it may concern.

§ 2–723. Proof of Market Price: Time and Place.

(1) If an action based on anticipatory repudiation comes to trial before the time for performance with respect to some or all of the goods, any damages based on market price (Section 2–708 or Section 2–713) shall be determined according to the price of such goods prevailing at the time when the aggrieved party learned of the repudiation.

(2) If evidence of a price prevailing at the times or places described in this Article is not readily available the price prevailing within any reasonable time before or after the time described or at any other place which in commercial judgment or under usage of trade would serve as a reasonable substitute for the one described may be used, making any proper allowance for the cost of transporting the goods to or from such other place.

(3) Evidence of a relevant price prevailing at a time or place other than the one described in this Article offered by one party is not admissible unless and until he has given the other party such notice as the court finds sufficient to prevent unfair surprise.

§ 2–724. Admissibility of Market Quotations.

Whenever the prevailing price or value of any goods regularly bought and sold in any established commodity market is in issue, reports in official publications or trade journals or in newspapers or periodicals of general circulation published as the reports of such market shall be admissible in evidence. The circumstances of the preparation of such a report may be shown to affect its weight but not its admissibility.

§ 2–725. Statute of Limitations in Contracts for Sale.

(1) An action for breach of any contract for sale must be commenced within four years after the cause of action has accrued. By the original agreement the parties may reduce the period of limitation to not less than one year but may not extend it.

(2) A cause of action accrues when the breach occurs, regardless of the aggrieved party's lack of knowledge of the breach. A breach of warranty occurs when tender of delivery is made, except that where a warranty explicitly extends to future performance of the goods and discovery of the breach must await the time of such performance the cause of action accrues when the breach is or should have been discovered.

(3) Where an action commenced within the time limited by subsection (1) is so terminated as to leave available a remedy by another action for the same breach such other action may be commenced after the expiration of the time limited and within six months after the termination of the first action unless the termination resulted from voluntary discontinuance or from dismissal for failure or neglect to prosecute.

(4) This section does not alter the law on tolling of the statute of limitations nor does it apply to causes of action which have accrued before this Act becomes effective.

Sarbanes-Oxley Act of 2002 (Excerpts)

Title I—Public Company Accounting Oversight Board

Sec. 101 Establishment; Administrative Provisions.

(a) Establishment of Board.—There is established the Public Company Accounting Oversight Board, to oversee the audit of public companies that are subject to the securities laws, and related matters, in order to protect the interests of investors and further the public interest in the preparation of informative, accurate, and independent audit reports for companies the securities of which are sold to, and held by and for, public investors. The Board shall be a body corporate, operate as a nonprofit corporation, and have succession until dissolved by an Act of Congress.

Sec. 102 Registration with the Board.

(a) Mandatory Registration.—It shall be unlawful for any person that is not a registered public accounting firm to prepare or issue, or to participate in the preparation or issuance of, any audit report with respect to any issuer.

(b) Application for Registration.—

   (1) Form of application.—A public accounting firm shall use such form as the Board may prescribe, by rule, to apply for registration under this section.

Sec. 104 Inspections of Registered Public Accounting Firms.

(a) In General.—The Board shall conduct a continuing program of inspections to assess the degree of compliance of each registered public accounting firm and associated persons of that firm with this Act, the rules of the Board, the rules of the Commission, or professional standards, in connection with its performance of audits, issuance of audit reports, and related matters involving issuers.

(b) Inspection Frequency.—

   (1) In general.—Subject to paragraph (2), inspections required by this section shall be conducted—

      (A) annually with respect to each registered public accounting firm that regularly provides audit reports for more than 100 issuers; and

      (B) not less frequently than once every 3 years with respect to each registered public accounting firm that regularly provides audit reports for 100 or fewer issuers.

Sec. 105 Investigations and Disciplinary Proceedings.

(a) In General.—The Board shall establish, by rule, subject to the requirements of this section, fair procedures for the investigation and disciplining of registered public accounting firms and associated persons of such firms.

(c) Disciplinary Procedures.—

   (4) Sanctions.—If the Board finds, based on all of the facts and circumstances, that a registered public accounting firm or associated person thereof has engaged in any act or practice, or omitted to act, in violation of this Act, the rules of the Board, the provisions of the securities laws relating to the preparation and issuance of audit reports and the obligations and liabilities of accountants with respect thereto, including the rules of the Commission issued under this Act, or professional standards, the Board may impose such disciplinary or remedial sanctions as it determines appropriate, subject to applicable limitations under paragraph (5), including—

      (A) temporary suspension or permanent revocation of registration under this title;

      (B) temporary or permanent suspension or bar of a person from further association with any registered public accounting firm;

      (C) temporary or permanent limitation on the activities, functions, or operations of such firm or person (other than in connection with required additional professional education or training);

      (D) a civil money penalty for each such violation, in an amount equal to—

         (i) not more than $100,000 for a natural person or $2,000,000 for any other person; and

         (ii) in any case to which paragraph (5) applies, not more than $750,000 for a natural person or $15,000,000 for any other person;

      (E) censure;

      (F) required additional professional education or training; or

      (G) any other appropriate sanction provided for in the rules of the Board.

(5) Intentional or other knowing conduct.—The sanctions and penalties described in subparagraphs (A) through (C) and (D)(ii) of paragraph (4) shall only apply to—

(A) intentional or knowing conduct, including reckless conduct, that results in violation of the applicable statutory, regulatory, or professional standard; or

(B) repeated instances of negligent conduct, each resulting in a violation of the applicable statutory, regulatory, or professional standard.

Title II—Auditor Independence

Sec. 201 Services Outside the Scope of Practice of Auditors.

(a) Prohibited Activities.—Section 10A of the Securities Exchange Act of 1934 (15 U.S.C. 78j–1) is amended by adding at the end of the following:

"(g) Prohibited Activities.—Except as provided in subsection (h), it shall be unlawful for a registered public accounting firm (and any associated person of that firm, to the extent determined appropriate by the Commission) that performs for any issuer any audit required by this title or the rules of the Commission under this title or, beginning 180 days after the date of commencement of the operations of the Public Company Accounting Oversight Board established under section 101 of the Sarbanes-Oxley Act of 2002 (in this section referred to as the 'Board'), the rules of the Board, to provide to that issuer, contemporaneously with the audit, any non-audit service, including—

"(1) bookkeeping or other services related to the accounting records or financial statements of the audit client;

"(2) financial information systems design and implementation;

"(3) appraisal or valuation services, fairness opinions, or contribution-in-kind reports;

"(4) actuarial services;

"(5) internal audit outsourcing services;

"(6) management functions or human resources;

"(7) broker or dealer, investment adviser, or investment banking services;

"(8) legal services and expert services unrelated to the audit; and

"(9) any other service that the Board determines, by regulation, is impermissible.

"(h) Preapproval Required for Non-Audit Services.—A registered public accounting firm may engage in any non-audit service, including tax services, that is not described in any of paragraphs (1) through (9) of

subsection (g) for an audit client, only if the activity is approved in advance by the audit committee of the issuer, in accordance with subsection (i)."

Sec. 206 Conflicts of Interest.

Section 10A of the Securities Exchange Act of 1934 (15 U.S.C. 78j–1), as amended by this Act, is amended by adding at the end the following:

"(l) Conflicts of Interest.—It shall be unlawful for a registered public accounting firm to perform for an issuer any audit service required by this title, if a chief executive officer, controller, chief financial officer, chief accounting officer, or any person serving in an equivalent position for the issuer, was employed by that registered independent public accounting firm and participated in any capacity in the audit of that issuer during the 1-year period preceding the date of the initiation of the audit."

Title III-Corporate Responsibility

Sec. 301 Public Company Audit Committees.

Section 10A of the Securities Exchange Act of 1934 (15 U.S.C. 78f) is amended by adding at the end the following:

"(m) Standards Relating to Audit Committees.—

"(2) Responsibilities relating to registered public accounting firms.—The audit committee of each issuer, in its capacity as a committee of the board of directors, shall be directly responsible for the appointment, compensation, and oversight of the work of any registered public accounting firm employed by that issuer (including resolution of disagreements between management and the auditor regarding financial reporting) for the purpose of preparing or issuing an audit report or related work, and each such registered public accounting firm shall report directly to the audit committee.

"(3) Independence.—

"(A) In general.—Each member of the audit committee of the issuer shall be a member of the board of directors of the issuer, and shall otherwise be independent.

"(B) Criteria.—In order to be considered to be independent for purposes of this paragraph, a member of an audit committee of an issuer may not, other than in his or her capacity as a member of the audit committee, the board of directors, or any other board committee—

"(i) accept any consulting, advisory, or other compensatory fee from the issuer; or

"(ii) be an affiliated person of the issuer or any subsidiary thereof.

Sec. 302 Corporate Responsibility for Financial Reports.

(a) Regulations Required.—The Commission shall, by rule, require, for each company filing periodic reports under section 13(a) or 15(d) of the Securities Exchange Act of 1934 (15 U.S.C. 78m, 78o(d)), that the principal executive officer or officers and the principal financial officer or officers, or persons performing similar functions, certify in each annual or quarterly report filed or submitted under either such section of such Act that—

(1) the signing officer has reviewed the report;

(2) based on the officer's knowledge, the report does not contain any untrue statement of a material fact or omit to state a material fact necessary in order to make the statements made, in light of the circumstances under which such statements were made, not misleading;

(3) based on such officer's knowledge, the financial statements, and other financial information included in the report fairly present in all material respects the financial condition and results of operations of the issuer as of, and for, the periods presented in the report;

(4) the signing officers—

(A) are responsible for establishing and maintaining internal controls;

(B) have designed such internal controls to ensure that material information relating to the issuer and its consolidated subsidiaries is made known to such officers by others within those entities, particularly during the period in which the periodic reports are being prepared;

(C) have evaluated the effectiveness of the issuer's internal controls as of a date within 90 days prior to the report; and

(D) have presented in the report their conclusions about the effectiveness of their internal controls based on their evaluation as of that date;

(5) the signing officers have disclosed to the issuer's auditors and the audit committee of the board of directors (or persons fulfilling the equivalent function)—

(A) all significant deficiencies in the design or operation of internal controls which could adversely affect the issuer's ability to record, process, summarize, and report financial data and have identified for the issuer's auditors any material weaknesses in internal controls; and

(B) any fraud, whether or not material, that involves management or other employees

who have a significant role in the issuer's internal controls; and

(6) the signing officers have indicated in the report whether or not there were significant changes in internal controls or in other factors that could significantly affect internal controls subsequent to the date of their evaluation, including any corrective actions with regard to significant deficiencies and material weaknesses.

Sec. 303 Improper Influence on Conduct of Audits.

(a) Rules to Prohibit.—It shall be unlawful, in contravention of such rules or regulations as the Commission shall prescribe as necessary and appropriate in the public interest or for the protection of investors, for any officer or director of an issuer, or any other person acting under the direction thereof, to take any action to fraudulently influence, coerce, manipulate, or mislead any independent public or certified accountant engaged in the performance of an audit of the financial statements of that issuer for the purpose of rendering such financial statements materially misleading.

Title IV-Enhanced Financial Disclosures

Sec. 401 Disclosures in Periodic Reports.

(a) Disclosures Required.—Section 13 of the Securities Exchange Act of 1934 (15 U.S.C. 78m) is amended by adding at the end the following:

"(i) Accuracy of Financial Reports.—Each financial report that contains financial statements, and that is required to be prepared in accordance with (or reconciled to) generally accepted accounting principles under this title and filed with the Commission shall reflect all material correcting adjustments that have been identified by a registered public accounting firm in accordance with generally accepted accounting principles and the rules and regulations of the Commission.

"(j) Off–Balance Sheet Transactions.—Not later than 180 days after the date of enactment of the Sarbanes-Oxley Act of 2002, the Commission shall issue final rules providing that each annual and quarterly financial report required to be filed with the Commission shall disclose all material off-balance sheet transactions, arrangements, obligations (including contingent obligations), and other relationships of the issuer with unconsolidated entities or other persons, that may have a material current or future effect on financial condition, changes in financial condition, results of operations, liquidity, capital expenditures, capital resources, or significant components of revenues or expenses."

(b) Commission Rules on Pro Forma Figures.—Not later than 180 days after the date of enactment of the Sarbanes-Oxley Act of 2002, the Commission shall issue final rules providing that pro forma financial information included in any periodic or other report filed with the Commission pursuant to the securities laws, or in any public disclosure or press or other release, shall be presented in a manner that—

(1) does not contain an untrue statement of a material fact or omit to state a material fact necessary in order to make the pro forma financial information, in light of the circumstances under which it is presented, not misleading; and

(2) reconciles it with the financial condition and results of operations of the issuer under generally accepted accounting principles.

Sec. 402 Enhanced Conflict of Interest Provisions.

(a) Prohibition on Personal Loans to Executives.—Section 13 of the Securities Exchange Act of 1934 (15 U.S.C. 78m), as amended by this Act, is amended by adding at the end the following:

"(k) Prohibition on Personal Loans to Executives.—

"(1) In general.—It shall be unlawful for any issuer (as defined in section 2 of the Sarbanes-Oxley Act of 2002), directly or indirectly, including through any subsidiary, to extend or maintain credit, to arrange for the extension of credit, or to renew an extension of credit, in the form of a personal loan to or for any director or executive officer (or equivalent thereof) of that issuer. An extension of credit maintained by the issuer on the date of enactment of this subsection shall not be subject to the provisions of this subsection, provided that there is no material modification to any term of any such extension of credit or any renewal of any such extension of credit on or after that date of enactment.

Sec. 406 Code of Ethics for Senior Financial Officers.

(a) Code of Ethics Disclosure.—The Commission shall issue rules to require each issuer, together with periodic reports required pursuant to section 13(a) or 15(d) of the Securities Exchange Act of 1934, to disclose whether or not, and if not, the reason therefor, such issuer has adopted a code of ethics for senior financial officers, applicable to its principal financial officer and comptroller or principal accounting officer, or persons performing similar functions.

(b) Changes in Codes of Ethics.—The Commission shall revise its regulations concerning matters requiring prompt disclosure on Form 8-K (or any successor thereto) to require the immediate disclosure by means of the filing of such form, dissemination by the Internet or by other electronic means, by any issuer of any change in or waiver of the code of ethics for senior financial officers.

(c) Definition.—In this section, the term "code of ethics" means such standards as are reasonably necessary to promote—

(1) honest and ethical conduct, including the ethical handling of actual or apparent conflicts of interest between personal and professional relationships;

(2) full, fair, accurate, timely, and understandable disclosure in the periodic reports required to be filed by the issuer; and

(3) compliance with applicable governmental rules and regulations.

Title V—Analyst Conflicts of Interest

Sec. 501 Treatment of Securities Analysts by Registered Securities Associations and National Securities Exchanges.

(a) Rules Regarding Securities Analysts.—The Securities Exchange Act of 1934 (15 U.S.C. 78a et seq.) is amended by inserting after section 15C the following new section:

"Sec. 15D. Securities Analysts and Research Reports

"(a) Analyst Protections.—The Commission, or upon the authorization and direction of the Commission, a registered securities association or national securities exchange, shall have adopted, not later than 1 year after the date of enactment of this section, rules reasonably designed to address conflicts of interest that can arise when securities analysts recommend equity securities in research reports and public appearances, in order to improve the objectivity of research and provide investors with more useful and reliable information, including rules designed—

"(1) to foster greater public confidence in securities research, and to protect the objectivity and independence of securities analysts, by—

"(A) restricting the prepublication clearance or approval of research reports by persons employed by the broker or dealer who are engaged in investment banking activities, or persons not directly responsible for investment research, other than legal or compliance staff;

"(B) limiting the supervision and compensatory evaluation of securities analysts to officials employed by the broker or dealer who are not engaged in investment banking activities; and

"(C) requiring that a broker or dealer and persons employed by a broker or dealer who are involved with investment banking activities may not, directly or indirectly, retaliate against or threaten to retaliate against any securities analyst employed by that broker or dealer or its affiliates as a result of an adverse, negative, or otherwise unfavorable research report that may adversely affect the present or prospective investment banking relationship of the broker or dealer with the issuer that is the subject of the research report, except that such rules may not limit the authority of a broker or dealer to discipline a securities analyst for causes other than such research report in accordance with the policies and procedures of the firm;

"(2) to define periods during which brokers or dealers who have participated, or are to participate, in a public offering of securities as underwriters or dealers should not publish or otherwise distribute research reports relating to such securities or to the issuer of such securities;

"(3) to establish structural and institutional safeguards within registered brokers or dealers to assure that securities analysts are separated by appropriate informational partitions within the firm from the review, pressure, or oversight of those whose involvement in investment banking activities might potentially bias their judgment or supervision; and

"(4) to address such other issues as the Commission, or such association or exchange, determines appropriate.

"(b) Disclosure.—The Commission, or upon the authorization and direction of the Commission, a registered securities association or national securities exchange, shall have adopted, not later than 1 year after the date of enactment of this section, rules reasonably designed to require each securities analyst to disclose in public appearances, and each registered broker or dealer to disclose in each research report, as applicable, conflicts of interest that are known or should have been known by the securities analyst or the broker or dealer, to exist at the time of the appearance or the date of distribution of the report, including—

"(1) the extent to which the securities analyst has debt or equity investments in the issuer that is the subject of the appearance or research report;

"(2) whether any compensation has been received by the registered broker or dealer, or any affiliate thereof, including the securities analyst, from the issuer that is the subject of the appearance or research report, subject to such exemptions as the Commission may determine appropriate and necessary to prevent disclosure by virtue of this paragraph of material non-public information regarding specific potential future investment banking transactions of such issuer, as is appropriate in the public interest and consistent with the protection of investors;

"(3) whether an issuer, the securities of which are recommended in the appearance or research report, currently is, or during the 1-year period preceding the date of the appearance or date of distribution of the report has been, a client of the registered broker or dealer, and if so, stating the types of services provided to the issuer;

"(4) whether the securities analyst received compensation with respect to a research report, based upon (among any other factors) the investment banking revenues (either generally or specifically earned from the issuer being analyzed) of the registered broker or dealer; and

"(5) such other disclosures of conflicts of interest that are material to investors, research analysts, or the broker or dealer as the Commission, or such association or exchange, determines appropriate.

"(c) Definitions.—In this section—

"(1) the term 'securities analyst' means any associated person of a registered broker or dealer that is principally responsible for, and any associated person who reports directly or indirectly to a securities analyst in connection with, the preparation of the substance of a research report, whether or not any such person has the job title of 'securities analyst'; and

"(2) the term 'research report' means a written or electronic communication that includes an analysis of equity securities of individual companies or industries, and that provides information reasonably sufficient upon which to base an investment decision."

(b) Enforcement.—Section 21B(a) of the Securities Exchange Act of 1934 (15 U.S.C. 78u–2(a)) is amended by inserting "15D," before "15B".

(c) Commission Authority.—The Commission may promulgate and amend its regulations, or direct a registered securities association or national securities exchange to promulgate and amend its rules, to carry out section 15D of the Securities Exchange Act of

1934, as added by this section, as is necessary for the protection of investors and in the public interest.

Title VI—Commission Resources and Authority

Sec. 602 Appearance and Practice Before the Commission.

The Securities Exchange Act of 1934 (15 U.S.C. 78a et seq.) is amended by inserting after section 4B the following:

"Sec 4C. Appearance and Practice Before the Commission

"(a) Authority to Censure.—The Commission may censure any person, or deny, temporarily or permanently, to any person the privilege of appearing or practicing before the Commission in any way, if that person is found by the Commission, after notice and opportunity for hearing in the matter—

"(1) not to possess the requisite qualifications to represent others;

"(2) to be lacking in character or integrity, or to have engaged in unethical or improper professional conduct; or

"(3) to have willfully violated or willfully aided and abetted the violation of, any provision of the securities laws or the rules and regulations issued thereunder.

Title VII—Studies and Reports

Sec. 705 Study of Investment Banks.

(a) GAO Study.—The Comptroller General of the United States shall conduct a study on whether investment banks and financial advisers assisted public companies in manipulating their earnings and obfuscating their true financial condition. The study should address the rule of investment banks and financial advisers—

(1) in the collapse of the Enron Corporation, including with respect to the design and implementation of derivatives transactions, transactions involving special purpose vehicles, and other financial arrangements that may have had the effect of altering the company's reported financial statements in ways that obscured the true financial picture of the company;

(2) in the failure of Global Crossing, including with respect to transactions involving swaps of fiberoptic cable capacity, in the designing transactions that may have had the effect of altering the company's reported financial statements in ways that obscured the true financial picture of the company; and

(3) generally, in creating and marketing transactions which may have been designed solely to enable companies to manipulate revenue streams, obtain loans, or move liabilities off balance sheets without altering the economic and business risks faced by the companies or any other mechanism to obscure a company's financial picture.

Title VIII—Corporate and Criminal Fraud Accountability

Sec. 801 Short Title.

This title may be cited as the "Corporate and Criminal Fraud Accountability Act of 2002".

Sec. 802 Criminal Penalties for Altering Documents.

(a) In General.—Chapter 73 of title 18, United States Code, is amended by adding at the end the following:

§1519. Destruction, alteration, or falsification of records in Federal investigations and bankruptcy

"Whoever knowingly alters, destroys, mutilates, conceals, covers up, falsifies, or makes a false entry in any record, document, or tangible object with the intent to impede, obstruct, or influence the investigation or proper administration of any matter within the jurisdiction of any department or agency of the United States or any case filed under Title 11, or in relation to or contemplation of any such matter or case, shall be fined under this title, imprisoned not more than 20 years, or both.

§1520. Destruction of corporate audit records

"(a)(1) Any accountant who conducts an audit of an issuer of securities to which section 10A(a) of the Securities Exchange Act of 1934 (15 U.S.C. 78j–1(a)) applies, shall maintain all audit or review workpapers for a period of 5 years from the end of the fiscal period in which the audit or review was concluded.

Sec. 807 Criminal Penalties for Defrauding Shareholders of Publicly Traded Companies.

(a) In General.—Chapter 63 of title 18, United States Code, is amended by adding at the end the following:

§1348. Securities fraud

"Whoever knowingly executes, or attempts to execute, a scheme or artifice—

"(1) to defraud any person in connection with any security of an issuer with a class of securities registered under section 12 of the Securities Exchange Act of 1934 (15 U.S.C. 78l) or that is required to file reports under section 15(d) of the Securities Exchange Act of 1934 (15 U.S.C. 78o(d)); or

"(2) to obtain, by means of false or fraudulent pretenses, representations, or promises, any money or property in connection with the purchase or sale of any security of an issuer with a class of securities registered under section 12 of the Securities Exchange Act of 1934 (15 U.S.C. 78l) or that is required to file reports under section 15(d) of the Securities Exchange Act of 1934 (15 U.S.C. 78o(d));

shall be fined under this title, or imprisoned not more than 25 years, or both."

Title IX—White-Collar Crime Penalty Enhancements

Sec. 901 Short Title.

This title may be cited as the "White-Collar Crime Penalty Enhancement Act of 2002".

Sec. 906 Corporate Responsibility for Financial Reports.

(a) In General.—Chapter 63 of title 18, United States Code, is amended by inserting after section 1349, as created by this Act, the following:

$1350. Failure of corporate officers to certify financial reports

(a) Certification of Periodic Financial Reports.—Each periodic report containing financial statements filed by an issuer with the Securities Exchange Commission pursuant to section 13(a) or 15(d) of the Securities Exchange Act of 1934 (15 U.S.C. 78m(a) or 78o(d)) shall be accompanied by a written statement by the chief executive officer and chief financial officer (or equivalent thereof) of the issuer.

"(b) Content.—The statement required under subsection (a) shall certify that the periodic report containing the financial statements fully complies with the requirements of section 13(a) or 15(d) of the Securities Exchange Act of 1934 (15 U.S.C. 78m or 78o(d)) and that information contained in the periodic report fairly presents, in all material respects, the financial condition and results of operations of the issuer.

"(c) Criminal Penalties.—Whoever—

"(1) certifies any statement as set forth in subsections (a) and (b) of this section knowing that the periodic report accompanying the statement does not comport with all the requirements set forth in this section shall be fined not more than $1,000,000 or imprisoned not more than 10 years, or both; or

"(2) willfully certifies any statement as set forth in subsections (a) and (b) of this section knowing that the periodic report accompanying the statement does not comport with all the requirements set forth in this section shall be

fined not more than $5,000,000, or imprisoned not more than 20 years, or both."

(b) Clerical Amendment.—The table of sections at the beginning of chapter 63 of title 18, United States Code, is amended by adding at the end the following:
"1350". Failure of corporate officers to certify financial reports."

Title X—Corporate Tax Returns

Sec. 1001 Sense of the Senate Regarding the Signing of Corporate Tax Returns by Chief Executive Officers.

It is the sense of the Senate that the Federal income tax return of a corporation should be signed by the chief executive officer of such corporation.

Title XI—Corporate Fraud Accountability

Sec. 1101 Short Title.

This title may be cited as the "Corporate Fraud Accountability Act of 2002".

Sec. 1102 Tampering with a Record or Otherwise Impeding an Official Proceeding.

Section 1512 of title 18, United States Code, is amended—

(1) by redesignating subsections (c) through (i) as subsections (d) through (j), respectively; and

(2) by inserting after subsection (b) the following new subsection:

"(c) Whoever corruptly—

"(1) alters, destroys, mutilates, or conceals a record, document, or other object, or attempts to do so, with the intent to impair the object's integrity or availability for use in an official proceeding; or

"(2) otherwise obstructs, influences, or impedes any official proceeding, or attempts to do so, shall be fined under this title or imprisoned not more than 20 years, or both."

Sec. 1105 Authority of the Commission to Prohibit Persons from Serving as Officers or Directors.

(a) Securities Exchange Act of 1934.—Section 21C of the Securities Exchange Act of 1934 (15 U.S.C. 78u–3) is amended by adding at the end the following:

"(f) Authority of the Commission to Prohibit Persons from Serving as Officers or Directors.—In any cease-and-desist proceeding under subsection (a), the Commission may issue an order to prohibit, conditionally or unconditionally, and permanently or for such period of time as it shall determine, any person who has violated section 10(b) or the rules or regulations thereunder, from acting as an officer or director of any issuer that has a class of securities registered pursuant to section 12, or that is required to file reports pursuant to section 15(d), if the conduct of that person demonstrates unfitness to serve as an officer or director of any such issuer."

(b) Securities Act of 1933.—Section 8A of the Securities Act of 1933 (15 U.S.C. 77h–1) is amended by adding at the end of the following:

"(f) Authority of the Commission to Prohibit Persons from Serving as Officers or Directors.—In any cease-and-desist proceeding under subsection (a), the Commission may issue an order to prohibit, conditionally or unconditionally, and permanently or for such period of time as it shall determine, any person who has violated section 17(a)(1) or the rules or regulations thereunder, from acting as an officer or director of any issuer that has a class of securities registered pursuant to section 12 of the Securities Exchange Act of 1934, or that is required to file reports pursuant to section 15(d) of that Act, if the conduct of that person demonstrates unfitness to serve as an officer or director of any such issuer."

GLOSSARY

abandoned property Property that an owner has discarded with the intent to relinquish his or her rights in it and mislaid or lost property that the owner has given up any further attempts to locate.

abatement A doctrine that says if the property a testator leaves is not sufficient to satisfy all the beneficiaries named in a will and there are both general and residuary bequests, the residuary bequest is abated first (i.e., paid last).

abusive filing A Chapter 7 filing that is found to be an abuse of Chapter 7 liquidation bankruptcy. In such a case, the court can dismiss the case or convert the case to a Chapter 13 or Chapter 11 proceeding, with the debtor's consent.

acceptance "A manifestation of assent by the offeree to the terms of the offer in a manner invited or required by the offer as measured by the objective theory of contracts." (Section 50 of the Restatement (Second) of Contracts. An act that occurs when a buyer or lessee takes any of the following actions after a reasonable opportunity to inspect the goods: (1) signifies to the seller or lessor in or by conduct that the goods are conforming or that the buyer or lessee will take or retain the goods despite their nonconformity or (2) fails to effectively reject the goods within a reasonable time after their delivery or tender by the seller or lessor. Acceptance also occurs if a buyer acts inconsistently with the seller's ownership rights in the goods.

acceptance method A method whereby the court confirms a plan of reorganization if the creditors accept the plan and if other requirements are met.

accession An increase in the value of personal property because it is added to or improved by natural or manufactured means.

accommodation A shipment that is offered to a buyer as a replacement for the original shipment when the original shipment cannot be filled.

accord An agreement whereby the parties agree to accept something different in satisfaction of the original contract.

accord and satisfaction The settlement of a contract dispute.

accountant–client privilege A state statute which provides that an accountant cannot be called as a witness against a client in a court action.

act of monopolizing An act that is required for there to be a violation of Section 2 of the Sherman Act. Possession of monopoly power without such act does not violate Section 2.

act of state doctrine A doctrine which states that judges of one country cannot question the validity of an act committed by another country within that other country's borders. It is based on the principle that a country has absolute authority over what transpires within its own territory.

action for an accounting A formal judicial proceeding in which the court is authorized to (1) review the partnership and the partners' transactions and (2) award each partner his or her share of the partnership assets.

actual cause The actual cause of negligence. A person who commits a negligent act is not liable unless actual cause can be proven. Also called causation in fact.

actus reus "Guilty act"—the actual performance of a criminal act.

ademption A principle that says if a testator leaves a specific devise of property to a beneficiary, but the property is no longer in the estate when the testator dies, the beneficiary receives nothing.

adequate assurance of performance Adequate assurance of performance from the other party if there is an indication that the contract will be breached by that party.

adjudged insane Declared legally insane by a proper court or administrative agency. A contract entered into by a person adjudged insane is void.

administrative agencies Agencies (such as the Securities and Exchange Commission and the Federal Trade Commission) that the legislative and executive branches of federal and state governments are empowered to establish.

administrative dissolution Involuntary dissolution of a corporation that is ordered by the secretary of state if a corporation has failed to comply with certain procedures required by law.

administrative law judge (ALJ) A judge who presides over administrative proceedings and decides questions of law and fact concerning a case. A federal act that establishes certain administrative procedures that federal administrative

administrative law Substantive and procedural law that governs the operation of administrative agencies.

Administrative Procedure Act (APA) Agencies must follow in conducting their affairs.

administrative subpoena An order that directs the subject of the subpoena to disclose the requested information.

adoption A situation in which a person becomes the legal parent of a child who is not his or her biological child.

adverse possession A situation in which a person who wrongfully possesses someone else's real property obtains title to that property if certain statutory requirements are met.

advertisement An invitation to make an offer, or an actual offer.

affirmative action A policy which provides that certain job preferences will be given to minority or other protected-class applicants when an employer makes an employment decision.

AFL-CIO The 1955 combination of the AFL and the CIO.

Age Discrimination in Employment Act (ADEA) of 1967 A federal statute that prohibits age discrimination practices against employees who are 40 and older.

agency The principal–agent relationship; the fiduciary relationship "which results from the manifestation of consent by one person to another that the other shall act in his behalf and subject to his control, and consent by the other so to act" [Restatement (Second) of Agency].

agency adoption An adoption that occurs when a person adopts a child from a social service organization of a state.

agency by ratification An agency that occurs when (1) a person misrepresents him- or herself as another's agent when in fact he or she is not and (2) the purported principal ratifies the unauthorized act.

agency coupled with an interest A special type of agency that is created for the agent's benefit and that the principal cannot revoke.

agency law The large body of common law that governs agency; a mixture of contract law and tort law.

agency shop A workplace where an employee does not have to join the union but must pay a fee equal to the union dues.

agent A party who agrees to act on behalf of another. A person who has been authorized to sign a negotiable instrument on behalf of another person.

905

agent's duty of loyalty A fiduciary duty owed by an agent not to act adversely to the interests of the principal.

agreement of conversion A document that states the terms for converting an existing business to an LLC.

agreement The manifestation by two or more persons of the substance of a contract.

air pollution Pollution caused by factories, homes, vehicles, and the like that affects the air.

alien corporation A corporation that is incorporated in another country.

allonge A separate piece of paper attached to an instrument on which an indorsement is written.

altered check A check that has been altered without authorization and thus modifies the legal obligation of a party.

alternative dispute resolution (ADR) Methods of resolving disputes other than litigation.

American Inventors Protection Act A federal statute that permits an inventor to file a provisional application with the U.S. Patent and Trademark Office three months before the filing of a final patent application, among other provisions.

Americans with Disabilities Act (ADA) A federal statute that imposes obligations on employers and providers of public transportation, telecommunications, and public accommodations to accommodate individuals with disabilities.

annual financial statement A statement provided to shareholders that contains a balance sheet, an income statement, and a statement of changes in shareholder equity.

annual shareholders' meeting A meeting of the shareholders of a corporation that must be held by the corporation to elect directors and to vote on other matters.

annulment An order of the court which declares that a marriage did not exist.

answer The defendant's written response to a plaintiff's complaint that is filed with the court and served on the plaintiff.

anti-assignment clause A clause that prohibits the assignment of rights under the contract.

antideficiency statute A statute that prohibits deficiency judgments regarding certain types of mortgages, such as those on residential property.

anti-delegation clause A clause that prohibits the delegation of duties under the contract.

antitakeover statutes Statutes enacted by a state legislature that protect against the hostile takeover of corporations incorporated in or doing business in the state.

anticipatory breach A breach that occurs when one contracting party informs the other that he or she will not perform his or her contractual duties when due.

anticipatory repudiation The repudiation of a sales or lease contract by one of the parties prior to the date set for performance.

antifraud provision Section 14(a) of the Securities Exchange Act of 1934, which prohibits misrepresentations or omissions of a material fact in the proxy materials.

antitrust laws A series of laws enacted to limit anticompetitive behavior in almost all industries, businesses, and professions operating in the United States.

apparent agency Agency that arises when a franchisor creates the appearance that a franchisee is its agent when in fact an actual agency does not exist. Agency that arises when a principal creates the appearance of an agency that in actuality does not exist.

appeal The act of asking an appellate court to overturn a decision after the trial court's final judgment has been entered.

appellant The appealing party in an appeal. Also known as the petitioner.

appellee The responding party in an appeal. Also known as the respondent.

arbitration A form of ADR in which the parties choose an impartial third party to hear and decide the dispute.

arbitration clause A clause in a contract that requires disputes arising out of the contract to be submitted to arbitration.

arraignment A hearing during which the accused is brought before a court and is (1) informed of the charges against him or her and (2) asked to enter a plea.

arrest warrant A document for a person's detainment, based upon a showing of probable cause that the person committed a crime.

arson The willful or malicious burning of a building.

Article 2 (Sales) An article of the UCC that governs sale of goods.

Article 2A (Leases) An article of the UCC that governs leases of goods.

Article 3 of the UCC A model code that establishes rules for the creation of, transfer of, enforcement of, and liability on negotiable instruments.

Article 3 of the UCC An article of the UCC that sets forth the requirements for negotiable instruments, including checks.

Article 4 of the UCC An article of the UCC that establishes the rules and principles that regulate bank deposit and collection procedures.

Article 4A of the UCC An article of the UCC that establishes rules regulating the

creation and collection of and liability for wire transfers.

articles of incorporation The basic governing documents of a corporation. It must be filed with the secretary of state of the state of incorporation. Also known as a corporate charter.

articles of organization The formal documents that must be filed at the secretary of state's office of the state of organization of an LLC to form the LLC.

assault (1) The threat of immediate harm or offensive contact or (2) any action that arouses reasonable apprehension of imminent harm. Actual physical contact is unnecessary.

assignee A party to whom a right has been transferred. A party to whom rights are transferred under a lease. A transferee in an assignment situation.

assignment A transfer by a tenant of his or her rights under a lease to another. The transfer of contractual rights by an obligee to another party. The transfer of rights under a contract.

assignor A party who transfers rights under a lease. A transferor in an assignment situation. An obligee who transfers a right.

assumption of duties A situation in which a delegation of duties contains the term assumption, I assume the duties, or other similar language. In such a case, the delegatee is legally liable to the obligee for nonperformance.

assumption of the risk A defense a defendant can use against a plaintiff who knowingly and voluntarily enters into or participates in a risky activity that results in injury.

attestation The action of a will being witnessed by two or three objective and competent people.

attorney–client privilege A rule that says a client can tell his or her lawyer anything about the case without fear that the attorney will be called as a witness against the client.

at-will LLC An LLC that has no specified term of duration.

auction with reserve An auction in which the seller retains the right to refuse the highest bid and withdraw the goods from sale. Unless expressly stated otherwise, an auction is an auction with reserve.

auction without reserve An auction in which the seller expressly gives up his or her right to withdraw the goods from sale and must accept the highest bid.

audit A verification of a company's books and records pursuant to federal securities laws, state laws, and stock exchange rules that must be performed by an independent CPA.

auditor's opinion   An opinion of an auditor about how fairly the financial statements of the client company represent the company's financial position, results of operations, and change in financial position.

authorized shares   The number of shares provided for in the articles of incorporation.

automatic stay   The suspension of certain legal actions by creditors against a debtor or the debtor's property.

automobile liability insurance Automobile insurance that covers damages that the insured causes to third parties.

backward vertical merger   A vertical merger in which the customer acquires the supplier.

bailee   A holder of goods who is not a seller or a buyer (e.g., warehouse, common carrier).

bailment   A transaction in which an owner transfers his or her personal property to another to be held, stored, delivered, or for some other purpose. Title to the property does not transfer.

bailment at will   A bailment without a fixed term; can be terminated at any time by either party.

bailment for a fixed term   A bailment that terminates at the end of the term or sooner, by mutual consent of the parties.

bailment for the sole benefit of the bailee A gratuitous bailment that benefits only the bailee. The bailee owes a duty of utmost care to protect the bailed property.

bailment for the sole benefit of the bailor A gratuitous bailment that benefits only the bailor. The bailee owes only a duty of slight care to protect the bailed property.

bailor   The owner of property in a bailment.

bait and switch   A type of deceptive advertising that occurs when a seller advertises the availability of a low-cost discounted item but then pressures the buyer into purchasing more expensive merchandise.

bank check   A certified check or a cashier's check, the payment for which a bank is solely or primarily liable.

Bankruptcy Abuse Prevention and Consumer Protection Act of 2005   A federal act that substantially amended federal bankruptcy law. This act makes it more difficult for debtors to file for bankruptcy and have their unpaid debts discharged.

Bankruptcy Code   The name given to federal bankruptcy law, as amended.

bankruptcy courts   Special federal courts that hear and decide bankruptcy cases.

bankruptcy estate   The debtor's property and earnings that comprise the estate of a bankruptcy proceeding.

Bankruptcy Reform Act of 1978   A federal act that substantially changed federal bankruptcy law. The act made it easier for debtors to file for bankruptcy and have their unpaid debts discharged. This act was considered debtor friendly.

bargained-for exchange   Exchange that parties engage in that leads to an enforceable contract.

battery   Unauthorized and harmful or offensive direct or indirect physical contact with another person that causes injury.

bearer paper   An instrument that is negotiated by delivery; indorsement is not necessary.

beneficiary   A person or an organization designated in a will to receive all or a portion of the testator's property at the time of the testator's death. A person who is to receive life insurance proceeds when the insured dies.

bequest   A gift of personal property by will. Also known as a legacy.

bilateral contract   A contract entered into by way of exchange of promises of the parties; "a promise for a promise."

Bill of Rights   The first 10 amendments to the Constitution, which were added to the U.S. Constitution in 1791.

blank indorsement   An indorsement that does not specify a particular indorsee. It creates bearer paper.

board of directors   A panel of decision makers who are elected by the shareholders.

bona fide occupational qualification (BFOQ)   A true job qualification. Employment discrimination based on a protected class (other than race or color) is lawful if it is job related and a business necessity. This exception is narrowly interpreted by the courts.

bond   A long-term debt security that is secured by some form of collateral.

breach   Failure of a party to perform an obligation in a sales or lease contract.

breach of contract   A contracting party's failure to perform an absolute duty owed under a contract.

breach of the duty of care   A failure to exercise care or to act as a reasonable person would act.

bribery   A crime in which one person gives another person money, property, favors, or anything else of value for a favor in return. A bribe is often referred to as a *payoff* or *kickback*.

building codes   State and local statutes that impose specific standards on property owners to maintain and repair leased premises. Also called housing codes.

burglary   The taking of personal property from another's home, office, or commercial or other type of building.

business interruption insurance   Insurance that reimburses a business for loss of revenue incurred when the business has been damaged or destroyed by fire or some other peril.

business judgment rule   A rule that protects the decisions of a board of directors that acts on an informed basis, in good faith, and in the honest belief that the action taken was in the best interests of the corporation and its shareholders. A rule that says directors and officers are not liable to the corporation or its shareholders for honest mistakes of judgment.

buy-and-sell agreement   An agreement that requires selling shareholders to sell their shares to the other shareholders or to the corporation at the price specified in the agreement.

buyer in the ordinary course of business A person who in good faith and without knowledge that the sale violates the ownership or security interests of a third party buys goods in the ordinary course of business from a person in the business of selling goods of that kind. A buyer in the ordinary course of business takes the goods free of any third-party security interest in the goods.

buyer's or lessee's cancellation   A buyer or lessee has the right to cancel a sales or lease contract if the seller or lessor fails to deliver conforming goods or repudiates the contract or if the buyer or lessee rightfully rejects the goods or justifiably revokes acceptance of the goods.

bylaws   A detailed set of rules adopted by the board of directors after a corporation is incorporated that contains provisions for managing the business and the affairs of the corporation.

cancellation   The termination of a contract by a contracting party upon the material breach of the contract by the other party.

cashier's check   A check issued by a bank for which the customer has paid the bank the amount of the check and a fee. The bank guarantees payment of the check.

certificate of deposit (CD)   A two-party negotiable instrument that is a special form of note created when a depositor deposits money at a financial institution in exchange for the institution's promise to pay back the amount of the deposit plus an agreed-upon rate of interest upon the expiration of a set time period agreed upon by the parties.

certification   A process in which the accepting bank writes or stamps the word certified on an ordinary check of an account holder and sets aside funds from that account to pay the check.

certified check   A type of check for which a bank agrees in advance (certifies) to accept the check when it is presented for payment.

chain of distribution   All manufacturers, distributors, wholesalers, retailers, lessors, and subcomponent manufacturers involved in a transaction.

check   A distinct form of draft drawn on a financial institution and payable on demand. An order by a drawer to a drawee bank to pay a specified sum of money from the drawer's checking account to the named payee (or holder).

checks and balances   A system built into the U.S. Constitution to prevent any one of the three branches of the government from becoming too powerful.

choice-of-law clause   A contract provision that designates a certain state's law or country's law that will be applied in any dispute concerning nonperformance of the contract.

C.O.D. shipment   A type of shipment contract in which the buyer agrees to pay the shipper cash upon the delivery of the goods.

collateral   Security against repayment of a note that lenders sometimes require; can be a car, a house, or other property.

collecting bank   The depository bank and other banks in the collection process (other than the payer bank).

Commerce Clause   A clause of the U.S. Constitution that grants Congress the power "to regulate commerce with foreign nations, and among the several states, and with Indian tribes."

commercial impracticability   Nonperformance that is excused if an extreme or unexpected development or expense makes it impractical for the promisor to perform.

commercial speech   Speech used by businesses, such as advertising. It is subject to time, place, and manner restrictions.

commercial wire transfer   An electronic transfer of funds from one party to another party. Also known as a wholesale wire transfer.

common law   Law developed by judges who issued their opinions when deciding a case. The principles announced in these cases became precedent for later judges deciding similar cases.

common law of contracts   Contract law developed primarily by state courts.

comparative fault   A doctrine that applies to strict liability actions that says a plaintiff who is contributorily negligent for his or her injuries is responsible for a proportional share of the damages.

comparative negligence   A doctrine under which damages are apportioned according to fault.

compensatory damages   An award of money intended to compensate a non-breaching party for the loss of the bargain. Compensatory damages place the non-breaching party in the same position as if the contract had been fully performed by restoring the "benefit of the bargain." Damages that are generally equal to the difference between the value of the goods as warranted and the actual value of the goods accepted at the time and place of acceptance.

competent party's duty of restitution   A rule which states that if a minor has transferred money, property, or other valuables to the competent party before disaffirming the contract, that party must place the minor in status quo.

complaint   The document a plaintiff files with the court and serves on the defendant to initiate a lawsuit.

complete performance   A situation in which a party to a contract renders performance exactly as required by the contract. Complete performance discharges that party's obligations under the contract.

conciliation   A form of ADR in which the parties use a third party to help them resolve their dispute.

concurrent condition   A condition that exists when the parties to a contract must render performance simultaneously; each party's absolute duty to perform is conditioned on the other party's absolute duty to perform.

concurrent jurisdiction   Jurisdiction shared by two or more courts.

condition   A qualification of a promise that becomes a covenant if it is met. There are three types of conditions: conditions precedent, conditions subsequent, and concurrent conditions.

condition precedent   A condition that requires the occurrence of an event before a party is obligated to perform a duty under a contract.

condition subsequent   A condition whose occurrence or nonoccurrence of a specific event automatically excuses the performance of an existing contractual duty to perform.

consequential damages   Foreseeable damages that arise from circumstances outside a contract. To be liable for these damages, the breaching party must know or have reason to know that the breach will cause special damages to the other party.

consideration   Something of legal value given in exchange for a promise.

consignment   An arrangement in which a seller (the consignor) delivers goods to a buyer (the consignee) to sell.

conspicuous   A requirement that warranty disclaimers be noticeable to the reasonable person.

consolidation   The act of a court to combine two or more separate lawsuits into one lawsuit.

Constitution of the United States of America   The supreme law of the United States.

consumer expectation test   A test to determine merchantability based on what the average consumer would expect to find in food products.

Consumer Leasing Act (CLA)   An amendment to the TILA that extends the TILA's coverage to lease terms in consumer leases.

contract contrary to public policy   A contract that has a negative impact on society or that interferes with the public's safety and welfare.

contract in restraint of trade   A contract that unreasonably restrains trade.

contributory negligence   A defense that says a person who is injured by a defective product but has been negligent and has contributed to his or her own injuries cannot recover from the defendant. A doctrine that says a plaintiff who is partially at fault for his or her own injury cannot recover against the negligent defendant.

copyright infringement   An infringement that occurs when a party copies a substantial and material part of a plaintiff's copyrighted work without permission. A copyright holder may recover damages and other remedies against the infringer.

Copyright Revision Act   A federal statute that (1) establishes the requirements for obtaining a copyright and (2) protects copyrighted works from infringement.

corporate criminal liability   Criminal liability of corporations for actions of their officers, employees, or agents.

counteroffer   A response by an offeree that contains terms and conditions different from or in addition to those of the offer. A counteroffer terminates the previous offer.

Court of Appeals for the Federal Circuit   A U.S. Court of Appeals in Washington, DC, that has special appellate jurisdiction to review the decisions of the Court of Federal Claims, the Patent and Trademark Office, and the Court of International Trade.

covenant   An unconditional promise to perform.

covenant not to compete   A contract which provides that a seller of a business or an employee will not engage in a similar business or occupation within a specified geographical area for a specified time following the sale of the business or termination of employment. Also called a noncompete clause.

covenant of good faith and fair dealing An implied covenant under which the parties to a contract not only are held to the express terms of the contract but are also required to act in "good faith" and deal fairly in all respects in obtaining the objective of the contract.

cover A licensee's right to engage in a commercially reasonable substitute transaction after the licensor has breached the contract.

crashworthiness doctrine A doctrine that says automobile manufacturers are under a duty to design automobiles so they take into account the possibility of harm from a person's body striking something inside the automobile in the case of a car accident.

credit report Information about a person's credit history that can be secured from a credit bureau reporting company.

creditor The lender in a credit transaction.

creditor beneficiary An original creditor who becomes a beneficiary under the debtor's new contract with another party.

creditor beneficiary contract A contract that arises in the following situation: (1) a debtor borrows money, (2) the debtor signs an agreement to pay back the money plus interest, (3) the debtor sells the item to a third party before the loan is paid off, and (4) the third party promises the debtor that he or she will pay the remainder of the loan to the creditor.

creditor–debtor relationship A relationship that is created when a customer deposits money into the bank; the customer is the creditor, and the bank is the debtor.

crime A violation of a statute for which the government imposes a punishment.

criminal conspiracy A crime in which two or more persons enter into an agreement to commit a crime and an overt act is taken to further the crime.

criminal fraud A crime that involves obtaining title to property through deception or trickery. Also known as *false pretenses* or *deceit*.

cure An opportunity to repair or replace defective or nonconforming goods.

damages Damages a buyer or lessee recovers from a seller or lessor who fails to deliver the goods or repudiates the contract. Damages are measured as the difference between the contract price (or original rent) and the market price (or rent) at the time the buyer or lessee learned of the breach.

debenture A long-term unsecured debt instrument that is based on a corporation's general credit standing.

debt securities Securities that establish a debtor–creditor relationship in which the corporation borrows money from the investor to whom a debt security is issued.

debtor The borrower in a credit transaction.

debtor-in-possession A debtor who is left in place to operate the business during the reorganization proceeding.

decree of divorce A court order that terminates a marriage.

deductible clause A clause in an insurance policy which provides that insurance proceeds are payable only after the insured has paid a specified amount toward the damage or loss.

deed A writing that describes a person's ownership interest in a piece of real property.

deed of trust An instrument that gives a creditor a security interest in the debtor's property that is pledged as collateral.

defamation of character False statement(s) made by one person about another. In court, the plaintiff must prove that (1) the defendant made an untrue statement of fact about the plaintiff and (2) the statement was intentionally or accidentally published to a third party.

defect in design A defect that occurs when a product is improperly designed.

defect in manufacture A defect that occurs when a manufacturer fails to (1) properly assemble a product, (2) properly test a product, or (3) adequately check the quality of the product.

defect in packaging A defect that occurs when a product has been placed in packaging that is insufficiently tamperproof.

deferred posting rule A rule that allows banks to fix an afternoon hour of 2:00 p.m. or later as a cutoff hour for the purpose of processing items.

deficiency judgment A judgment of a court that permits a secured lender to recover other property or income from a defaulting debtor if the collateral is insufficient to repay the unpaid loan.

delegatee A party to whom a duty has been transferred.

delegation doctrine A doctrine that says when an administrative agency is created, it is delegated certain powers; the agency can use only those legislative, judicial, and executive powers that are delegated to it.

delegation of duties A transfer of contractual duties by an obligor to another party for performance.

delegator An obligor who has transferred his or her duty.

demand instrument An instrument payable on demand.

demand note A note payable on demand.

deponent A party who gives his or her deposition.

deposition Oral testimony given by a party or witness prior to trial. The testimony is given under oath and is transcribed.

depository bank The bank where the payee or holder has an account.

derivative lawsuit A lawsuit a shareholder brings against an offending party on behalf of a corporation when the corporation fails to bring the lawsuit.

destination contract A contract that requires the seller to deliver the goods either to the buyer's place of business or to another destination specified in the sales contract. A sales contract that requires the seller to deliver the goods to the buyer's place of business or another specified destination. The seller bears the risk of loss during transportation.

devise A gift of real estate by will.

Digital Millennium Copyright Act (DMCA) A federal statute that prohibits unauthorized access to copyrighted digital works by circumventing encryption technology or the manufacture and distribution of technologies designed for the purpose of circumventing encryption protection of digital works.

direct price discrimination Price discrimination in which (1) the defendant sold commodities of like grade and quality, (2) to two or more purchasers at different prices at approximately the same time, and (3) the plaintiff suffered injury because of the price discrimination.

directors' and officers' liability insurance Insurance that protects directors and officers of a corporation from liability for actions taken on behalf of the corporation.

disability insurance Insurance that provides a monthly income to an insured who is disabled and cannot work.

disaffirmance The act of a minor to rescind a contract under the infancy doctrine. Disaffirmance may be done orally, in writing, or by the minor's conduct.

discharge A court order that relieves a debtor of the legal liability to pay his or her debts that were not paid in the bankruptcy proceeding.

discovery A legal process during which each party engages in various activities to discover facts of the case from the other party and witnesses prior to trial.

dishonored instrument An instrument that is presented for payment and payment is refused.

disparate-impact discrimination   A form of discrimination that occurs when an employer discriminates against an entire protected class. An example would be discrimination in which a racially neutral employment practice or rule causes an adverse impact on a protected class.

disparate-treatment discrimination   A form of discrimination that occurs when an employer discriminates against a specific individual because of his or her race, color, national origin, sex, or religion.

dissenting shareholder appraisal rights   The rights of shareholders who object to a proposed merger, share exchange, or sale or lease of all or substantially all of the property of a corporation to have their shares valued by the court and receive cash payment of this value from the corporation.

dissolution   The change in the relation of the partners caused by any partner ceasing to be associated in the carrying on of the business [UPA Section 29].

distinctive   Being unique and fabricated.

distributional interest   A member's ownership interest in an LLC that entitles the member to receive distributions of money and property from the LLC.

diversity of citizenship   A means for bringing a lawsuit in federal court that involves a nonfederal question if the parties are (1) citizens of different states or (2) a citizen of a state and a citizen or subject of a foreign country.

dividend   A distribution of profits of the corporation to shareholders.

dividend preference   The right to receive a fixed dividend at stipulated periods during the year (e.g., quarterly).

division of markets   A restraint of trade in which competitors agree that each will serve only a designated portion of the market.

divorce   An order of the court that terminates a marriage.

doctrine of sovereign immunity   A doctrine which states that countries are granted immunity from suits in courts of other countries.

document of title   An actual piece of paper, such as a warehouse receipt or bill of lading, that is required in some transactions of pickup and delivery.

domain name   A unique name that identifies an individual's or company's website.

domestic corporation   A corporation in the state in which it was formed.

domestic limited partnership   A limited partnership in the state in which it was formed.

donee   A person who receives a gift.

donee beneficiary   A third party on whom a benefit is to be conferred.

donee beneficiary contract   A contract entered into with the intent to confer a benefit or gift on an intended third party.

donor   A person who gives a gift.

double Jeopardy Clause   A clause of the Fifth Amendment that protects persons from being tried twice for the same crime.

draft   A three-party instrument that is an unconditional written order by one party that orders a second party to pay money to a third party.

drawee of a check   The bank where a check drawer has his or her account. The party who must pay the money stated in a draft. Also called the acceptor of a draft.

drawer of a check   The checking account holder and writer of a check.

drawer of a draft   The party who writes an order for a draft.

dual-purpose mission   An errand or another act that a principal requests of an agent while the agent is on his or her own personal business.

due diligence defense   A defense to a Section 11 action that, if proven, makes the defendant not liable.

Due Process Clause   A clause which provides that no person shall be deprived of "life, liberty, or property" without due process of the law.

duress   A situation in which one party threatens to do a wrongful act unless the other party enters into a contract.

duty of care   A duty of corporate directors and officers to use care and diligence when acting on behalf of the corporation. A duty owed by a member of a member-managed LLC and a manager of a manager-managed LLC not to engage in (1) a known violation of law, (2) intentional conduct, (3) reckless conduct, or (4) grossly negligent conduct that injures the LLC. The obligation partners owe to use the same level of care and skill that a reasonable person in the same position would use in the same circumstances. A breach of the duty of care is negligence. The obligation people owe each other not to cause any unreasonable harm or risk of harm.

duty of loyalty   A duty owed by a member of a member-managed LLC and a manager of a manager-managed LLC to be honest in his or her dealings with the LLC and to not act adversely to the interests of the LLC. A duty that a partner owes not to act adversely to the interests of the partnership. A duty that directors and officers have not to act adversely to the interests of the corporation

and to subordinate their personal interests to those of the corporation and its shareholders.

duty of obedience   A duty that directors and officers of a corporation have to act within the authority conferred upon them by state corporation statutes, the articles of incorporation, the corporate bylaws, and the resolutions adopted by the board of directors. A duty that requires partners to adhere to the provisions of the partnership agreement and the decisions of the partnership.

duty to account   A duty that an agent owes to maintain an accurate accounting of all transactions undertaken on the principal's behalf. Also known as the duty of accountability.

duty to compensate   A duty that a principal owes to pay an agreed-upon amount to the agent either upon the completion of the agency or at some other mutually agreeable time.

duty to inform   A duty a partner owes to inform his or her co-partners of all information he or she possesses that is relevant to the affairs of the partnership.

duty to perform   An agent's duty to a principal that includes (1) performing the lawful duties expressed in the contract and (2) meeting the standards of reasonable care, skill, and diligence implicit in all contracts.

easement   A given or required right to make limited use of someone else's land without owning or leasing it.

easement appurtenant   A situation created when the owner of one piece of land is given an easement over an adjacent piece of land.

easement in gross   An easement that authorizes a person who does not own adjacent land to use another's land.

e-commerce   The sale of goods and services by computer over the Internet.

effect of illegality   A doctrine which states that the courts will refuse to enforce or rescind an illegal contract and will leave the parties where it finds them.

electronic funds transfer system (EFTS)   Computer and electronic technology that makes it possible for banks to offer electronic payment and collection systems to bank customers. E-banking and e-money consists of: (1) Automated teller machines (ATMs); (2) Point-of-sale terminals; (3) Direct deposit and withdrawal; (4) Online banking; and (5) Debit cards.

electronic mail (e-mail)   Electronic written communication between individuals using computers connected to the Internet.

e-mail and web contracts   Contracts that are entered into by e-mail and over the World Wide Web.

emancipation   A minor's act of legally separating from his or her parents and providing for himself or herself.

embezzlement   The fraudulent conversion of property by a person to whom that property was entrusted.

eminent domain   The government's power to take private property for public use, provided that just compensation is paid to the private property holder.

Employee Retirement Income Security Act (ERISA)   A federal act designed to prevent fraud and other abuses associated with private pension funds.

employer lockout   An act of an employer to prevent employees from entering the work premises when the employer reasonably anticipates a strike.

employer–employee relationship   A relationship that results when an employer hires an employee to perform some task or service but the employee has not been authorized to enter into contracts on behalf of his employer.

Endangered Species Act   A federal statute that protects endangered and threatened species of wildlife.

engagement   A formal entrance into a contract between a client and an accountant.

entrepreneur   A person who forms and operates a new business either by him- or herself or with others.

enumerated powers   Certain powers delegated to the federal government by the states.

environmental impact statement (EIS)   A document that must be prepared for any proposed legislation or major federal action that significantly affects the quality of the human environment.

Environmental Protection Agency (EPA)   A federal administrative agency created by Congress to coordinate the implementation and enforcement of the federal environmental protection laws.

Equal Access to Justice Act   A federal act that protects persons from harassment by federal administrative agencies.

Equal Credit Opportunity Act (ECOA)   A federal statute that prohibits discrimination in the extension of credit based on sex, marital status, race, color, national origin, religion, age, or receipt of income from public assistance programs.

equal dignity rule   A rule which says that agents' contracts to sell property covered by the Statute of Frauds must be in writing to be enforceable.

Equal Employment Opportunity Commission (EEOC)   The federal administrative agency that is responsible for enforcing most federal antidiscrimination laws.

equal opportunity in employment   The right of all employees and job applicants (1) to be treated without discrimination and (2) to be able to sue employers if they are discriminated against.

Equal Pay Act   A federal statute that protects both sexes from pay discrimination based on sex. It extends to jobs that require equal skill, equal effort, equal responsibility, and similar working conditions.

Equal Protection Clause   A clause which provides that a state cannot "deny to any person within its jurisdiction the equal protection of the laws."

equitable distribution   A law used by many states where the court orders a fair distribution of marital property to the divorcing spouses.

equity   A doctrine that permits judges to make decisions based on fairness, equality, moral rights, and natural law.

equity securities   Representation of ownership rights to a corporation. Also called stocks.

Establishment Clause   A clause to the First Amendment that prohibits the government from either establishing a state religion or promoting one religion over another.

estate   Ownership rights in real property; the bundle of legal rights that the owner has to possess, use, and enjoy the property.

estray statute   A statute that permits a finder of mislaid or lost property to clear title to the property if certain prescribed legal formalities are met.

ethical fundamentalism   A theory of ethics that says a person looks to an outside source for ethical rules or commands.

ethical relativism   A moral theory which holds that individuals must decide what is ethical based on their own feelings about what is right and wrong.

ethics   A set of moral principles or values that governs the conduct of an individual or a group.

European Union   A regional international organization that comprises many countries of western and eastern Europe and was created to promote peace and security as well as economic, social, and cultural development.

exclusionary rule   A rule that says evidence obtained from an unreasonable search and seizure can generally be prohibited from introduction at a trial or an administrative proceeding against the person searched.

exclusive agency contract   A contract a principal and agent enter into that says the principal cannot employ any agent other than the exclusive agent.

exclusive jurisdiction   Jurisdiction held by only one court.

exclusive license   A license that grants the licensee exclusive rights to use informational rights for a specified duration.

exculpatory clause   A contractual provision that relieves one (or both) of the parties to a contract from tort liability for ordinary negligence. Also known as a release of liability clause.

executed contract   A contract that has been fully performed on both sides; a completed contract.

executive branch   The part of the U.S. government that enforces the federal law; it consists of the president and vice president.

executive order   An order issued by a member of the executive branch of the government.

executive power   Power that administrative agencies are granted, such as the investigation and prosecution of possible violations of statutes, administrative rules, and administrative orders.

executory contract   A contract that has not been fully performed by either or both sides.

executory contract or unexpired lease   A contract or lease that has not been fully performed. With the bankruptcy court's approval, a debtor may reject executory contracts and unexpired leases in bankruptcy.

exempt property   Property that may be retained by the debtor pursuant to federal or state law that does not become part of the bankruptcy estate.

express agency   An agency that occurs when a principal and an agent expressly agree to enter into an agency agreement with each other.

express authorization   A stipulation in an offer that says the acceptance must be by a specified means of communication.

express contract   An agreement that is expressed in written or oral words.

express powers   Powers given to a corporation by (1) the U.S. Constitution, (2) state constitutions, (3) federal statutes, (4) state statues, (5) articles of incorporation, (6) bylaws, and (7) resolutions of the board of directors.

express trust   A trust created voluntarily by a settlor.

express warranty   A warranty that is created when a seller or lessor makes an affirmation that the goods he or she is selling or leasing meet certain standards of quality, description, performance, or condition.

extortion   A threat to expose something about another person unless that other person gives money or property. Often referred to as blackmail.

failure to provide adequate instructions   A defect that occurs when a manufacturer does not provide detailed directions for safe assembly and use of a product.

failure to warn   A defect that occurs when a manufacturer does not place a warning on the packaging of products that could cause injury if the danger is unknown.

Fair Credit and Charge Card Disclosure Act   An amendment to the TILA that requires disclosure of certain credit terms on credit card and charge card solicitations and applications.

Fair Credit Reporting Act (FCRA)   An amendment to the TILA that protects a consumer who is the subject of a credit report by setting out guidelines for credit bureaus.

Fair Debt Collection Practices Act (FDCPA)   A federal act that protects consumer-debtors from abusive, deceptive, and unfair practices used by debt collectors.

Fair Housing Act   A federal statute that makes it unlawful for a party to refuse to rent or sell a dwelling to any person because of his or her race, color, national origin, sex, or religion.

Fair Labor Standards Act (FLSA)   A federal act enacted in 1938 to protect workers. It prohibits child labor and spells out minimum wage and overtime pay requirements.

fair price rule   A rule that says any increase in price paid for shares tendered must be offered to all shareholders, even those who have previously tendered their shares.

fair use doctrine   A doctrine that permits certain limited use of a copyright by someone other than the copyright holder without the permission of the copyright holder.

false imprisonment   The intentional confinement or restraint of another person without authority or justification and without that person's consent.

Family and Medical Leave Act (FMLA)   A federal act that guarantees workers up to 12 weeks of unpaid leave in a 12-month period to attend to family and medical emergencies and other specified situations.

family farmer   An individual, a corporation, or a partnership that engages in farming operations and meets the requirements for filing for a Chapter 12 proceeding.

family fisherman   An individual, a corporation, or a partnership that engages in commercial fishing operations and meets the requirements for filing for a Chapter 12 proceeding.

federal administrative agencies   Administrative agencies that are created by the executive or legislative branch of federal government.

Federal Arbitration Act (FAA)   A federal statute that provides for the enforcement of most arbitration agreements.

Federal Dilution Act   A federal statute that protects famous marks from dilution, erosion, blurring, or tarnishing.

Federal Patent Statute   A federal statute that establishes the requirements for obtaining a patent and protects patented inventions from infringement.

federal question case   A case arising under the U.S. Constitution, treaties, or federal statutes and regulations.

Federal Reserve System   A system of 12 regional Federal Reserve banks that assist other banks in the collection of checks.

Federal Trade Commission (FTC)   A federal administrative agency empowered to enforce the Federal Trade Commission Act and other federal consumer protection statutes.

Federal Unemployment Tax Act (FUTA)   A federal act that requires employers to pay unemployment taxes; unemployment compensation is paid to workers who are temporarily unemployed.

federalism   The U.S. form of government, in which the federal government and the 50 state governments share powers.

fee simple absolute   A type of ownership of real property that grants the owner the fullest bundle of legal rights that a person can hold in real property. Also known as fee simple.

fee simple defeasible   A type of ownership of real property that grants the owner all the incidents of a fee simple absolute except that it may be taken away if a specified condition occurs or does not occur. Also known as qualified fee.

felony   The most serious type of crime; inherently evil crime. Most crimes against persons and some business-related crimes are felonies.

fiduciary duties   The duties of obedience, care, and loyalty owed by directors and officers to their corporation and its shareholders.

final settlement   A situation in which a payer bank (1) pays a check in cash, (2) settles for a check without having a right to revoke the settlement, or (3) fails to dishonor a check within certain statutory time periods.

finance lease   A three-party transaction consisting of a lessor, a lessee, and a supplier.

fixed amount of money   A requirement that a negotiable instrument contain a promise or an order to pay a fixed amount of money.

fixed amount requirement   A requirement of a negotiable instrument that ensures that the value of the instrument can be determined with certainty.

fixtures   Goods that are affixed to real estate so as to become part thereof.

Food and Drug Administration (FDA)   The federal administrative agency that administers and enforces the federal Food, Drug, and Cosmetic Act and other federal consumer protection laws.

Food, Drug, and Cosmetic Act (FDCA)   A federal statute that provides the basis for the regulation of much of the testing, manufacture, distribution, and sale of foods, drugs, cosmetics, and medicinal products.

force majeure **clause**   A clause in a contract in which the parties specify certain events that will excuse nonperformance.

foreclosure sale   A legal procedure by which a secured creditor causes the judicial sale of the secured real estate to pay a defaulted loan.

Foreign Commerce Clause   A clause of the U.S. Constitution that vests Congress with the power "to regulate commerce with foreign nations."

foreign corporation   A corporation in any state or jurisdiction other than the one in which it was formed.

foreign limited partnership   A limited partnership in all other states besides the one in which it was formed.

Foreign Sovereign Immunities Act (FSIA)   An act that exclusively governs suits against foreign nations that are brought in federal or state courts in the United States. It codifies the principle of qualified, or restricted, immunity.

foreign substance test   A test to determine merchantability based on foreign objects found in food.

foreseeability standard   A rule which says that an accountant is liable for negligence to third parties who are foreseeable users of the client's financial statements. It provides the broadest standard for holding accountants liable to third parties for negligence.

forged indorsement   The forged signature of a payee or holder on a negotiable instrument.

forged instrument   A check with a forged drawer's signature on it.

forgery   The fraudulent making or alteration of a written document that affects the legal liability of another person.

formal contract   A contract that requires a special form or method of creation.

forum-selection clause A contract provision that designates a certain court to hear any dispute concerning nonperformance of the contract.

forward vertical merger A vertical merger in which the supplier acquires the customer.

Fourteenth Amendment An amendment added to the U.S. Constitution in 1868 that contains the Due Process, Equal Protection, and Privileges and Immunities clauses.

franchise An arrangement that is established when one party (the franchisor) licenses another party (the franchisee) to use the franchisor's trade name, trademarks, commercial symbols, patents, copyrights, and other property in the distribution and selling of goods and services.

franchise agreement An agreement that a franchisor and franchisee enter into that sets forth the terms and conditions of a franchise.

fraud by concealment Fraud that occurs when one party takes specific action to conceal a material fact from another party.

fraud in the inception Fraud that occurs if a person is deceived as to the nature of his or her act and does not know what he or she is signing. Also known as fraud in the factum.

fraud in the inducement Fraud that occurs when the party knows what he or she is signing but has been fraudulently induced to enter into the contract.

fraudulent misrepresentation An event that occurs when one person consciously decides to induce another person to rely and act on a misrepresentation. Also called fraud.

fraudulent transfer A transfer of a debtor's property or an obligation incurred by a debtor within two years of the filing of a petition, where (1) the debtor had actual intent to hinder, delay, or defraud a creditor or (2) the debtor received less than a reasonable equivalent in value, and the debtor was insolvent or unable to pay at the time the transfer was made or the obligation was incurred.

Free Exercise Clause A clause to the First Amendment that prohibits the government from interfering with the free exercise of religion in the United States.

Freedom of Information Act A federal act that gives the public access to documents in the possession of federal administrative agencies. There are many exceptions to disclosure.

freedom of speech The right to engage in oral, written, and symbolic speech protected by the First Amendment.

freehold estate An estate in which the owner has a present possessory interest in the real property.

fresh start The goal of federal bankruptcy law, to grant a debtor relief from some of his or her burdensome debts, while protecting creditors by requiring the debtor to pay more of his or her debts than would otherwise have been required prior to the 2005 act.

frolic and detour A situation in which an agent does something during the course of his or her employment to further his or her own interests rather than the principal's.

FTC franchise rule A rule set out by the FTC that requires franchisors to make full presale disclosures to prospective franchisees.

FTC notice A statement required by the FTC to appear in at least 12-point boldface type on the cover of a franchisor's required disclosure statement to prospective franchisees.

fully disclosed agency An agency in which a contracting third party knows (1) that the agent is acting for a principal and (2) the identity of the principal.

future goods Goods not yet in existence (e.g., ungrown crops, unborn stock animals).

future interest The interest that a grantor retains for him- or herself or a third party.

gambling statutes Statutes that make certain forms of gambling illegal.

gap-filling rule A rule that says an open term can be "read into" a contract.

general duty A duty that an employer has to provide a work environment free from recognized hazards that are causing or are likely to cause death or serious physical harm to employees.

general gift A gift that does not identify the specific property from which the gift is to be made.

general partners Partners in a limited partnership who invest capital, manage the business, and are personally liable for partnership debts. Persons liable for the debts and obligations of a general partnership. Also known simply as partners.

general partnership An association of two or more persons to carry on as co-owners of a business for profit [UPA Section 6(1)]. Also known as an ordinary partnership.

general-jurisdiction trial court A court that hears cases of a general nature that are not within the jurisdiction of limited-jurisdiction trial courts. Testimony and evidence at trial are recorded and stored for future reference.

generally accepted accounting principles (GAAPs) Standards for the preparation and presentation of financial statements.

generally accepted auditing standards (GAASs) Standards for the methods and procedures that must be used to conduct audits.

generally known dangers A defense that acknowledges that certain products are inherently dangerous and are known to the general population to be so.

generic name A term for a mark that has become a common term for a product line or type of service and therefore has lost its trademark protection.

genuineness of assent The requirement that a party's assent to a contract be genuine.

gift The voluntary transfer of title to property without payment of consideration by the donee. To be a valid gift, three elements must be shown: (1) donative intent, (2) delivery, and (3) acceptance.

gift causa mortis A gift that is made in contemplation of death.

gift inter vivos A gift made during a person's lifetime that is an irrevocable present transfer of ownership.

gift promise A promise that is unenforceable because it lacks consideration. Also known as a gratuitous promise.

good faith Honesty in fact in the conduct or transaction concerned. The good faith test is subjective.

good faith purchaser for value A person to whom good title can be transferred from a person with voidable title. The real owner cannot reclaim goods from a good faith purchaser for value.

good faith subsequent lessee A person to whom a lease interest can be transferred from a person with voidable title. The real owner cannot reclaim the goods from the subsequent lessee until the lease expires.

Good Samaritan law A statute that relieves medical professionals from liability for ordinary negligence when they stop and render aid to victims in emergency situations.

goods Tangible things that are movable at the time of their identification to a contract.

government contractor defense A defense that says a contractor who was provided specifications by the government is not liable for any defect in the product that occurs as a result of those specifications.

Government in the Sunshine Act A federal act that opens most federal administrative agency meetings to the public.

grantee The party to whom an interest in real property is transferred.

grantor The party who transfers an ownership interest in real property. A person who creates a living trust. Also called a *trustor*.

greenmail The purchase by a target corporation of its stock from an actual or perceived tender offeror at a premium.

group boycott   A restraint of trade in which two or more competitors at one level of distribution agree not to deal with others at another level of distribution. Also known as refusal to deal.

guarantee of collection   A form of accommodation in which the accommodation party guarantees collection of a negotiable instrument; the accommodation party is secondarily liable on the instrument.

guarantee of payment   A form of accommodation in which the accommodation party guarantees payment of a negotiable instrument; the accommodation party is primarily liable accommodation party. A party who signs an instrument and lends his or her name (and credit) to another party to the instrument.

guarantor   A person who agrees to pay a debt if the primary debtor does not.

guaranty arrangement   An arrangement in which a third party promises to be secondarily liable for the payment of another's debt.

guaranty contract   A promise in which one person agrees to answer for the debts or duties of another person. It is a contract between the guarantor and the original creditor.

Hart-Scott-Rodino Antitrust Improvement Act   An act that requires certain firms to notify the FTC and the Justice Department in advance of a proposed merger. Unless the government challenges a proposed merger within 30 days, the merger may proceed.

hazardous waste   Hazardous waste that may cause or significantly contribute to an increase in mortality or serious illness or pose a hazard to human health or the environment if improperly managed.

health care directive (health care proxy)   A document in which the maker names someone to be his or her health care agent to make all health care decisions in accordance with his or her wishes, as outlined in the living will.

health insurance   Insurance that is purchased to help cover the costs of medical treatment, surgery, or hospital care.

heir   The receiver of property under intestacy statutes.

holder   A person who is in possession of a negotiable instrument that is drawn, issued, or indorsed to him or his order, or to bearer, or in blank.

holder in due course (HDC)   A holder who takes a negotiable instrument for value, in good faith, and without notice that it is defective or overdue.

holographic will   A will that is entirely handwritten and signed by the testator.

homeowners' policy   A comprehensive insurance policy that includes coverage for the risks covered by a fire insurance policy as well as personal liability insurance.

homestead exemption   Equity in a debtor's home that the debtor is permitted to retain.

honor   To pay a drawer's properly drawn check.

horizontal merger   A merger between two or more companies that compete in the same business and geographical market.

horizontal restraint of trade   A restraint of trade that occurs when two or more competitors at the same level of distribution enter into a contract, combination, or conspiracy to restrain trade.

hung jury   A jury that cannot come to a unanimous decision about the defendant's guilt. In the case of a hung jury, the government may choose to retry the case.

identification of goods   Distinguishing the goods named in a contract from the seller's or lessor's other goods.

illegal consideration   A promise to refrain from doing an illegal act. Such a promise will not support a contract.

illegal contract   A contract that has an illegal object. Such contracts are void.

illusory promise   A contract into which both parties enter but one or both of the parties can choose not to perform their contractual obligations. Thus, the contract lacks consideration. Also known as an illusory contract.

immoral contract   A contract whose objective is the commission of an act that is society considers immoral.

immunity from prosecution   The government's agreement not to use against a person granted immunity any evidence given by that person.

impairment of right of recourse   A situation in which certain parties (holders, indorsers, accommodation parties) are discharged from liability on an instrument if the holder (1) releases an obligor from liability or (2) surrenders collateral without the consent of the parties who would benefit by it.

implied authorization   A mode of acceptance that is implied from what is customary in similar transactions, usage of trade, or prior dealings between the parties.

implied exemptions   Exemptions from antitrust laws that are implied by the federal courts.

implied term   A term in a contract that can reasonably be supplied by the courts.

implied warranties   Certain warranties that the law implies on transferors of negotiable instruments. There are two types of implied warranties: transfer and presentment warranties.

implied warranty of authority   A warranty of an agent who enters into a contract on behalf of another party that he or she has the authority to do so.

implied warranty of fitness for a particular purpose   A warranty that arises where a seller or lessor warrants that the goods will meet the buyer's or lessee's expressed needs.

implied warranty of fitness for human consumption   A warranty that applies to food or drink consumed on or off the premises of restaurants, grocery stores, fast-food outlets, and vending machines.

implied warranty of habitability   A warranty that provides that leased premises must be fit, safe, and suitable for ordinary residential use.

implied warranty of merchantability   Unless properly disclosed, a warranty that is implied that sold or leased goods are fit for the ordinary purpose for which they are sold or leased, as well as other assurances.

implied-in-fact condition   A condition that can be implied from the circumstances surrounding a contract and the parties' conduct.

implied-in-fact contract   A contract in which agreement between parties has been inferred from their conduct.

impossibility of performance   Nonperformance that is excused if a contract becomes impossible to perform. It must be objective impossibility, not subjective.

imputed knowledge   Information that is learned by an agent that is attributed to the principal.

in pari delicto   A situation in which both parties are equally at fault in an illegal contract.

in personam jurisdiction   Jurisdiction over the parties to a lawsuit.

in rem jurisdiction   Jurisdiction to hear a case because of jurisdiction over the property of the lawsuit.

inaccessibility exception   A rule that permits employees and union officials to engage in union solicitation on company property if the employees are beyond reach of reasonable union efforts to communicate with them.

incidental damages   Reasonable expenses incurred in stopping delivery, transportation charges, storage charges, sales commissions, and so on.

income beneficiary of a living trust   A person who receives the income from a living trust during his or her life. This is usually the grantor.

income beneficiary of a trust   A person or an entity to be paid income from a trust.

incontestability clause A clause that prevents insurers from contesting statements made by insureds in applications for insurance after the passage of a stipulated number of years.

incorporator The person or persons, partnerships, or corporations that are responsible for incorporation of a corporation.

indemnification The right of a partner to be reimbursed for expenditures incurred on behalf of the partnership.

indenture agreement A contract between a corporation and a holder that contains the terms of a debt security.

independent adoption An adoption that occurs when there is a private arrangement between biological and adoptive parents of a child.

independent contractor "A person who contracts with another to do something for him who is not controlled by the other nor subject to the other's right to control with respect to his physical conduct in the performance of the undertaking" [Restatement (Second) of Agency]. A person or business that is not an employee but is employed by a principal to perform a certain task on behalf of the principal.

indictment The charge of having committed a crime (usually a felony), based on the judgment of a grand jury.

indirect price discrimination A form of price discrimination (e.g., favorable credit terms) that is less readily apparent than direct forms of price discrimination.

indorsee A person to whom a negotiable instrument is indorsed.

indorsee of a check A party to whom a check is indorsed.

indorsement The signature (and other directions) written by or on behalf of the holder somewhere on an instrument.

indorsement for deposit or collection An indorsement that makes the indorsee the indorser's collecting agent (e.g., "for deposit only").

indorsement of a check A payee's signing of the back of a check in order to turn it over to another party.

indorser A person who indorses a negotiable instrument.

indorser of a check A payee who indorses a check to another party.

infancy doctrine A doctrine that allows minors to disaffirm (cancel) most contracts they have entered into with adults.

informal contract A contract that is not formal. Valid informal contracts are fully enforceable and may be sued upon if breached.

information The charge of having committed a crime (usually a misdemeanor), based on the judgment of a judge (magistrate).

injunction A court order that prohibits a person from doing a certain act.

injury A plaintiff's personal injury or damage to his or her property that enables him or her to recover monetary damages for the defendant's negligence.

innkeepers' statutes State statutes that limit an innkeeper's common law liability. An innkeeper can avoid liability for loss caused to a guest's property if (1) a safe is provided in which the guest's valuable property may be kept and (2) the guest is notified of this fact.

innocent misrepresentation Fraud that occurs when a person makes a statement of fact that he or she honestly and reasonably believes to be true even though it is not.

insane but not adjudged insane Being insane but not having been adjudged insane by a court or an administrative agency. A contract entered into by such person is generally voidable. Some states hold that such a contract is void.

Insecticide, Fungicide, and Rodenticide Act A federal statute that requires pesticides, herbicides, fungicides, and rodenticides to be registered with the EPA; the EPA may deny, suspend, or cancel registration.

inside director A member of the board of directors who is also an officer of the corporation.

insider trading A situation in which an insider makes a profit by personally purchasing shares of the corporation prior to public release of favorable information or by selling shares of the corporation prior to the public disclosure of unfavorable information.

Insider Trading Sanctions Act A federal statute that permits the SEC to obtain a civil penalty of up to three times the illegal benefits received from insider trading.

installment contract A contract that requires or authorizes goods to be delivered and accepted in separate lots.

insurable interest A requirement that a person who purchases insurance have a personal interest in the insured item or person.

insurance A means for persons and businesses to protect themselves against the risk of loss.

insurance policy An insurance contract.

insured A party who pays a premium to a particular insurance company for insurance coverage.

insurer An insurance company that underwrites insurance coverage.

intangible property Rights that cannot be reduced to physical form, such as stock certificates, certificates of deposit, bonds, and copyrights.

integration of several writings The combination of several writings to form a single contract.

intellectual property rights Patents, copyrights, trademarks, and trade secrets. Federal and state laws protect intellectual property rights from misappropriation and infringement.

intended third-party beneficiary A third party who is not in privity of contract but who has rights under the contract and can enforce the contract against the promisor.

intentional infliction of emotional distress A tort that says a person whose extreme and outrageous conduct intentionally or recklessly causes severe emotional distress to another person is liable for that emotional distress. Also known as the tort of outrage.

intentional interference with contractual relations A tort that arises when a third party induces a contracting party to breach the contract with another party.

intentional misrepresentation A deceit in which an agent makes an untrue statement that he or she knows is not true. A tort in which a seller or lessor fraudulently misrepresents the quality of a product and a buyer is injured thereby. The intentional defrauding of a person out of money, property, or something else of value. Also known as fraud or deceit. Also known as *fraud* or *deceit*.

intentional tort A category of torts that requires that the defendant possessed the intent to do the act that caused the plaintiff's injuries.

inter vivos **trust** A trust that is created while the settlor is alive.

intermediary bank A bank in the collection process that is not the depository bank or the payer bank.

intermediate appellate court An intermediate court that hears appeals from trial courts.

intermediate scrutiny test A test that is applied to classifications based on protected classes other than race (e.g., sex, age).

International Court of Justice (ICJ) The judicial branch of the United Nations that is located in The Hague, the Netherlands. Also called the World Court.

international law Law that governs affairs between nations and that regulates transactions between individuals and businesses of different countries.

internet A collection of millions of computers that provide a network of electronic connections between the computers.

interpretive rule   A rule issued by an administrative agency that interprets existing statutory language.

interrogatories   Written questions submitted by one party to another party. The questions must be answered in writing within a stipulated time.

interstate commerce   Commerce that moves between states or that affects commerce between states.

intervention   The act of others to join as parties to an existing lawsuit.

intestacy statute   A state statute that specifies how a deceased's property will be distributed if he or she dies without a will or if the last will is declared void and there is no prior valid will.

intestate   The state of having died without leaving a will.

intoxicated person   A person who is under contractual incapacity because of ingestion of alcohol or drugs to the point of incompetence.

intrastate offering exemption   An exemption from registration that permits local businesses to raise capital from local investors to be used in the local economy without the need to register with the SEC.

involuntary petition   A petition filed by creditors of a debtor that alleges that the debtor is not paying his or her debts as they become due.

issued shares   Shares that have been sold by a corporation.

joint and several liability   Tort liability of partners together and individually. A plaintiff can sue one or more partners separately. If successful, the plaintiff can recover the entire amount of the judgment from any or all of the defendant-partners.

joint custody   A custody arrangement that gives both parents responsibility for making major decisions concerning the child.

joint liability   Liability of partners for contracts and debts of the partnership. A plaintiff must name the partnership and all of the partners as defendants in a lawsuit.

joint marital debts   Debts incurred during the marriage for joint needs.

joint tenancy   A form of co-ownership that includes the right of survivorship.

joint venture   An arrangement in which two or more business entities combine their resources to pursue a single project or transaction.

joint venture corporation   A corporation owned by two or more joint venturers that is created to operate a joint venture.

joint venture partnership   A partnership owned by two or more joint venturers that is formed to operate a joint venture.

joint will   A will that is executed by two or more testators.

judicial branch   The part of the U.S. government that interprets the law. It consists of the Supreme Court and other federal courts.

judicial decision   A decision about an individual lawsuit issued by a federal or state court.

judicial dissolution   Dissolution of a corporation through a court proceeding instituted by the state.

jurisprudence   The philosophy or science of law.

jury instructions   Instructions given by the judge to the jury that inform them of the law to be applied in the case.

Just Compensation Clause   A clause of the U.S. Constitution that requires the government to compensate the property owner, and possibly others, when the government takes property under its power of eminent domain.

Kantian ethics   A moral theory which says that people owe moral duties that are based on universal rules, such as the categorical imperative "Do unto others as you would have them do unto you." Also known as *duty ethics*.

key-person life insurance   Life insurance purchased and paid for by a business that insures against the death of owners and other key executives and employees of the business.

land pollution   Pollution of the land that is generally caused by hazardous waste being disposed of in an improper manner.

land sales contract   An arrangement in which the owner of real property sells property to a purchaser and extends credit to the purchaser.

landlord   An owner who transfers a leasehold.

Lanham Act   An amended federal statute that (1) establishes the requirements for obtaining a federal mark and (2) protects marks from infringement.

larceny   The taking of another's personal property other than from his or her person or building.

law   That which must be obeyed and followed by citizens, subject to sanctions or legal consequences; a body of rules of action or conduct prescribed by controlling authority and having binding legal force.

lease   A transfer of the right to the possession and use of named goods for a set term in return for certain consideration. A transfer of the right to the possession and use of real property for a set term in return for certain consideration; the rental agreement

between a landlord and a tenant. The transfer of the right to use real property for a specified period of time.

leasehold   A tenant's interest in property.

legal insanity   A state of contractual incapacity, as determined by law.

legal value   Support for a contract when either (1) the promisee suffers a legal detriment or (2) the promisor receives a legal benefit.

legally enforceable contract   A contract in which if one party fails to perform as promised, the other party can use the court system to enforce the contract and recover damages or other remedy.

legislative branch   The part of the U.S. government that makes federal laws. It is known as Congress (the Senate and the House of Representatives).

lessee   A person who acquires the right to possession and use of goods under a lease.

lessor   A person who transfers the right of possession and use of goods under a lease.

libel   A false statement that appears in a letter, newspaper, magazine, book, photograph, movie, video, and so on.

license   A contract that transfers limited rights in intellectual property and informational rights. A document that grants a person the right to enter upon another's property for a specified and usually short period of time.

licensee   A party who is granted limited rights in or access to intellectual property or informational rights owned by a licensor.

licensee's damages   Monetary damages that a licensee may recover from a licensor who breaches a contract.

licensing   A business arrangement that occurs when the owner of intellectual property (the *licensor*) contracts to permit another party (the *licensee*) to use the intellectual property.

licensing agreement   A detailed and comprehensive written agreement between a licensor and a licensee that sets forth the express terms of their agreement.

licensing statute   A statute that requires a person or business to obtain a license from the government prior to engaging in a specified occupation or activity.

licensor   An owner of intellectual property or informational rights who transfers rights in the property or information to the licensee.

licensor's damages   Monetary damages that a licensor may recover from a licensee who breaches a contract.

life estate   An interest in real property for a person's lifetime; upon that person's death, the interest will be transferred to another party.

life insurance A form of insurance in which the insurer is obligated to pay a specific sum of money upon the death of the insured.

limited liability The liability of LLC members for the LLC's debts, obligations, and liabilities only to the extent of their capital contributions.

limited liability company (LLC) An unincorporated business entity that combines the most favorable attributes of general partnerships, limited partnerships, and corporations.

limited liability limited partnership (LLLP) A special type of limited partnership that has both general partners and limited partners where both the general and limited partners have limited liability and are not personally liable for the debts of the LLLP.

limited liability of limited partners The limited liability of limited partners of a limited partnership only up to their capital contributions to the limited partnership; limited partners are not personally liable for the debts and obligations of the limited partnership.

limited liability of shareholders A general rule of corporate law which provides that generally shareholders are liable only to the extent of their capital contributions for the contracts and debts of their corporation and are not personally liable for the contracts and debts of the corporation.

limited liability partnership (LLP) A special form of partnership in which all partners are limited partners, and there are no general partners.

limited partners Partners in a limited partnership who invest capital but do not participate in management and are not personally liable for partnership debts beyond their capital contributions.

limited partnership A type of partnership that has two types of partners: (1) general partners and (2) limited partners.

limited partnership agreement A document that sets forth the rights and duties of general and limited partners; the terms and conditions regarding the operation, termination, and dissolution of a partnership; and so on.

limited-jurisdiction trial court A court that hears matters of a specialized or limited nature.

line of commerce The products or services that will be affected by a merger, including those that consumers use as substitutes. If an increase in the price of one product or service leads consumers to purchase another product or service, the two products are substitutes for each other.

lineal descendants Children, grandchildren, great-grandchildren, and so on of a testator.

liquidated damages Damages that parties to a contract agree in advance should be paid if the contract is breached. Damages that will be paid upon a breach of contract that are established in advance.

liquidation preference The right to be paid a stated dollar amount if a corporation is dissolved and liquidated.

litigation The process of bringing, maintaining, and defending a lawsuit.

living trust A method for holding property during a person's lifetime and distributing the property upon that person's death. Also called a grantor's trust or a revocable trust.

living will A document that states which life-saving measures the signor does and does not want, and can specify that he or she wants such treatments withdrawn if doctors determine that there is no hope of a meaningful recovery.

long-arm statute A statute that extends a state's jurisdiction to nonresidents who were not served a summons within the state.

lost property Property that the owner leaves somewhere due to negligence, carelessness, or inadvertence.

Magnuson-Moss Warranty Act A federal statute that regulates written warranties on consumer products.

mailbox rule A rule that states that an acceptance is effective when it is dispatched, even if it is lost in transmission. Also known as the acceptance-upon-dispatch rule.

main purpose exception An exception to the Statute of Frauds which states that if the main purpose of a transaction and an oral collateral contract is to provide pecuniary benefit to the guarantor, the collateral contract does not have to be in writing to be enforced.

maker of a CD The financial institution that issues a CD (borrower).

maker of a note The party who makes a promise to pay (borrower).

malicious prosecution A lawsuit in which the original defendant sues the original plaintiff. In the second lawsuit, the defendant becomes the plaintiff and vice versa.

manager-managed LLC An LLC that has designated in its articles of organization it is a manager-managed LLC and whose non-manager members give their management rights over to designated managers.

marine insurance Insurance that owners of a vessel can purchase to insure against loss or damage to the vessel and its cargo caused by perils on the water.

Marine Protection, Research, and Sanctuaries Act A federal statute that extends limited environmental protection to the oceans.

marital property Property acquired during the course of marriage using income earned during the marriage, and separate property that has been converted to marital property.

mark The collective name for trademarks, service marks, certification marks, and collective marks that can be trademarked.

market extension merger A merger between two companies in similar fields whose sales do not overlap.

marketable title Title to real property that is free from any encumbrances or other defects that are not disclosed but would affect the value of the property. Also called good title.

marriage A legal union between spouses that confers certain legal rights and duties upon the spouses and upon the children born of the marriage.

marriage license A legal document issued by a state which certifies that two people are married.

master limited partnership A form of limited partnership that is listed on stock exchanges and is publicly traded to provide liquidity.

material breach A breach that occurs when a party renders inferior performance of his or her contractual duties.

maximizing profits A theory of social responsibility that says a corporation owes a duty to take actions that maximize profits for shareholders.

means test A new test added by the 2005 act that applies to debtors who have family incomes that exceed the state's median income for families of the same size.

mechanic's lien A contractor's, laborer's, and material person's statutory lien that makes the real property to which services or materials have been provided security for the payment of the services and materials.

mediation A form of ADR in which the parties use a mediator to propose a settlement of their dispute.

meeting of the creditors A meeting of the creditors in a bankruptcy case that must occur within a reasonable time after an order for relief. The debtor must appear at this meeting.

meeting the competition defense A defense provided in Section 2(b) that says a seller may lawfully engage in price discrimination to meet a competitor's price.

member An owner of an LLC.

member-managed LLC An LLC that has not designated it is a manager-managed

LLC in its articles of organization and is managed by its members.

mens rea "Evil intent"—the possession of the requisite state of mind to commit a prohibited act.

merchant A person who (1) deals in the goods of the kind involved in a transaction or (2) by his or her occupation holds himself or herself out as having knowledge or skill peculiar to the goods involved in the transaction.

merchant protection statutes Statutes that allow merchants to stop, detain, and investigate suspected shoplifters without being held liable for false imprisonment if (1) there are reasonable grounds for the suspicion, (2) suspects are detained for only a reasonable time, and (3) investigations are conducted in a reasonable manner.

merger A situation in which one corporation is absorbed into another corporation and ceases to exist.

merger clause A clause in a contract that stipulates that it is a complete integration and the exclusive expression of the parties' agreement. Also known as an integration clause.

midnight deadline The midnight of the next banking day following the banking day on which the bank received an "on them" check for collection.

minor A person who has not reached the age of majority.

minor breach A breach that occurs when a party renders substantial performance of his or her contractual duties.

minor's duty of restoration A rule which states that a minor is obligated only to return the goods or property he or she has received from the adult in the condition it is in at the time of disaffirmance.

mirror image rule A rule which states that for an acceptance to exist, the offeree must accept the terms as stated in the offer.

misdemeanor A less serious crime; not inherently evil but prohibited by society. Many crimes against property are misdemeanors.

mislaid property Property that an owner voluntarily places somewhere and then inadvertently forgets.

misuse A defense that relieves a seller of product liability if the user abnormally misused the product. Products must be designed to protect against foreseeable misuse.

mitigation A nonbreaching party's legal duty to avoid or reduce damages caused by a breach of contract.

mixed sale A sale that involves the provision of a service and a good in the same transaction.

monetary damages An award of money.

Money Laundering Control Act A federal statute that makes it a crime to (1) knowingly engage in a money transaction through a financial institution involving property from an unlawful activity worth more than $10,000 and (2) knowingly engage in a *financial transaction* involving the proceeds of an unlawful activity.

search warrant A warrant issued by a court that authorizes the police to search a designated place for specified contraband, articles, items, or documents. A search warrant must be based on probable cause.

monopoly power The power to control prices or exclude competition, measured by the market share the defendant possesses in the relevant market.

moral minimum A theory of social responsibility that says a corporation's duty is to make a profit while avoiding causing harm to others.

moral obligation A sense of honor that prompts a person to make a promise. Promises made out of a sense of moral obligation lack consideration.

mortgage An interest in real property given to a lender as security for the repayment of a loan. A collateral arrangement in which a property owner borrows money from a creditor, who uses real estate as collateral for repayment of the loan.

mortgagee The creditor in a mortgage transaction.

mortgagor The owner-debtor in a mortgage transaction.

motion for summary judgment A motion which asserts that there are no factual disputes to be decided by the jury and that the judge can apply the proper law to the undisputed facts and decide the case without a jury. These motions are supported by affidavits, documents, and deposition testimony.

motion for judgment on the pleadings A motion which alleges that if all the facts presented in the pleadings are taken as true, the party making the motion would win the lawsuit when the proper law is applied to these asserted facts.

motivation test A test that determines whether an agent's motivation in committing an intentional tort is to promote the principal's business; if so, the principal is liable for any injury caused by the tort.

mutual benefit bailment A bailment for the mutual benefit of the bailor and bailee. The bailee owes a duty of ordinary care to protect the bailed property.

mutual mistake of fact A mistake made by both parties concerning a material fact that is important to the subject matter of a contract.

mutual mistake of value A mistake that occurs if both parties know the object of the contract but are mistaken as to its value.

mutual wills A situation in which two or more testators execute separate wills that leave their property to each other on the condition that the survivor leave the remaining property on his or her death as agreed by the testators. Also known as reciprocal wills.

national ambient air quality standards (NAAQS) Standards for certain pollutants set by the EPA that protect (1) human beings (primary level) and (2) vegetation, matter, climate, visibility, and economic values (secondary level).

national courts The courts of individual nations.

National Environmental Policy Act (NEPA) A federal statute which mandates that the federal government consider the adverse impact a federal government action would have on the environment before the action is implemented.

National Labor Relations Board (NLRB) A federal administrative agency that oversees union elections, prevents employers and unions from engaging in illegal and unfair labor practices, and enforces and interprets certain federal labor laws.

necessaries of life Food, clothing, shelter, medical care, and other items considered necessary to the maintenance of life. Minors must pay the reasonable value of necessaries of life for which they contract.

negligence A tort related to defective products in which the defendant has breached a duty of due care and caused harm to the plaintiff. Failure of a corporate director or officer to exercise the duty of care while conducting the corporation's business. Negligence in which the accountant breaches the duty of reasonable care, knowledge, skill, and judgment that he or she owes to a client when providing auditing and other accounting services to the client. Also known as *accountant malpractice*.

negligence per se A tort in which the violation of a statute or an ordinance constitutes the breach of the duty of care.

negligent infliction of emotional distress A tort that permits a person to recover for emotional distress caused by the defendant's negligent conduct.

negotiable instrument A special form of contract that satisfies the requirements established by Article 3 of the UCC. Also called commercial paper or instrument.

negotiation The transfer of a negotiable instrument by a person other than the issuer to a person who thereby becomes a holder.

No Electronic Theft Act (NET Act) A federal statute that makes it a crime for a person to willfully infringe on a copyright work that exceeds $1,000 in retail value.

no evidence of forgery, alteration, or irregularity requirement A requirement that says a holder cannot become an HDC to an instrument that is apparently forged or altered or is so otherwise irregular or incomplete as to call into question its authenticity.

Noerr **doctrine** A doctrine which says that two or more persons can petition the executive, legislative, or judicial branch of the government or administrative agencies to enact laws or take other action without violating antitrust laws.

no-fault automobile insurance An automobile insurance system used by some states in which the driver's insurance company pays for any injuries or death the driver suffers in an accident, no matter who caused the accident.

no-fault divorce A divorce recognized by the law of a state whereby neither party is blamed for the divorce.

nominal damages Damages awarded when the nonbreaching party sues the breaching party even though no financial loss has resulted from the breach. Nominal damages are usually $1 or some other small amount.

nonattainment area A geographical area that does not meet established air quality standards.

nonconforming uses Uses and buildings that already exist in a zoned area that are permitted to continue even though they do not fit within new zoning ordinances.

noncupative will An oral will that is made before a witness during the testator's last illness. Also known as a dying declaration or deathbed will.

non-intent crime A crime that imposes criminal liability without a finding of mens rea (intent).

nonnegotiable contract A contract that fails to meet the requirements of a negotiable instrument and, therefore, is not subject to the provisions of UCC Article 3.

nonpossessory interest A situation in which a person holds an interest in another person's property without actually owning any part of the property.

non-price vertical restraints Restraints of trade that are unlawful under Section 1 of the Sherman Act if their anticompetitive effects outweigh their procompetitive effects.

nonrestrictive indorsement An indorsement that has no instructions or conditions attached to the payment of the funds.

North American Free Trade Agreement (NAFTA) A treaty that has removed or reduced tariffs, duties, quotas, and other trade barriers between the United States, Canada, and Mexico.

note A debt security with a maturity of five years or less. An instrument that evidences a borrower's debt to the lender.

notice of dishonor The formal act of letting the party with secondary liability to pay a negotiable instrument know that the instrument has been dishonored.

novation agreement An agreement that substitutes a new party for one of the original contracting parties and relieves the exiting party of liability on the contract. Also known as simply a novation.

Nuclear Regulatory Commission (NRC) A federal agency that licenses the construction and opening of commercial nuclear power plants.

Nutrition Labeling and Education Act A federal statute that requires food manufacturers to place on food labels that disclose nutritional information about the food.

objective rule A rule which states that if an engagement is broken off, the prospective bride must return the engagement ring, regardless of which party broke off the engagement.

objective theory of contracts A theory that says the intent to contract is judged by the reasonable person standard and not by the subjective intent of the parties.

obligation An action a party to a sales or lease contract is required by law to carry out.

obscene speech Speech that (1) appeals to the prurient interest, (2) depicts sexual conduct in a patently offensive way, and (3) lacks serious literary, artistic, political, or scientific value.

Occupational Safety and Health Act A federal act enacted in 1970 that promotes safety in the workplace.

offensive speech Speech that is offensive to many members of society. It is subject to time, place, and manner restrictions.

offer "The manifestation of willingness to enter into a bargain, so made as to justify another person in understanding that his assent to that bargain is invited and will conclude it." (Section 24 of the Restatement (Second) of Contracts).

offeree The party to whom an offer to enter into a contract is made.

offeror The party who makes an offer to enter into a contract.

officers Employees of a corporation who are appointed by the board of directors to manage the day-to-day operations of the corporation.

Oil Pollution Act A federal statute that requires the oil industry to take measures to prevent oil spills and to readily respond to and clean up oil spills.

Older Workers Benefit Protection Act (OWBPA) A federal statute that prohibits age discrimination in employee benefits.

one-year "on sale" doctrine A doctrine that says a patent may not be granted if the invention was used by the public for more than one year prior to the filing of the patent application.

one-year rule A rule which states that an executory contract that cannot be performed by its own terms within one year of its formation must be in writing.

operating agreement An agreement entered into among members that governs the affairs and business of the LLC and the relations among members, managers, and the LLC.

order A decision issued by an administrative law judge.

order for relief An order that occurs upon the filing of either a voluntary petition or an unchallenged involuntary petition, or an order that is granted after a trial of a challenged involuntary petition.

order paper An instrument that is negotiated by (1) delivery and (2) indorsement.

order to pay A drawer's unconditional order to a drawee to pay a payee.

ordinance Law enacted by local government bodies, such as cities and municipalities, counties, school districts, and water districts.

organizational meeting A meeting that must be held by the initial directors of a corporation after the articles of incorporation are filed.

original tenor The original amount for which the drawer wrote a check.

outside director A member of a board of directors who is not an officer of the corporation.

overdraft The amount of money a drawer owes a bank after it has paid a check despite the drawer's account having insufficient funds.

parol evidence Any oral or written words outside the four corners of a written contract.

parol evidence rule A rule that says if a written contract is a complete and final statement of the parties' agreement, any prior or contemporaneous oral or written statements that alter, contradict, or are in addition to the terms of the written contract are inadmissible in court regarding a dispute over the contract. There are several exceptions to this rule.

part performance   An equitable doctrine that allows the court to order an oral contract for the sale of land or transfer of another interest in real property to be specifically performed if it has been partially performed and performance is necessary to avoid injustice.

partially disclosed agency   An agency in which a contracting third party knows that the agent is acting for a principal but does not know the identity of the principal.

participating preferred stock   Stock that allows the stockholder to participate in the profits of the corporation along with the common stockholders.

partnership agreement   A written agreement that partners sign. Also called articles of partnership.

partnership at will   A partnership created with no fixed duration.

partnership for a term   A partnership created for a fixed duration.

past consideration   A prior act or performance. Past consideration (e.g., prior acts) will not support a new contract. New consideration must be given.

patent infringement   Unauthorized use of another's patent. A patent holder may recover damages and other remedies against a patent infringer.

payable on demand or at a definite time requirement   A requirement that a negotiable instrument be payable either on demand or at a definite time.

payee of a CD   The party to whom a CD is made payable; usually the depositor (lender).

payee of a check   The party to whom a check is written.

payee of a draft   The party who receives the money from a draft.

payee of a note   The party to whom a promise to pay is made (lender).

payer bank   The bank where the drawer has a checking account and on which a check is drawn.

penal code   A collection of criminal statutes.

per capita distribution   A distribution of an estate in which each grandchild and great-grandchild of the deceased inherits equally with the children of the deceased.

per se **rule**   A rule that is applicable to restraints of trade considered inherently anticompetitive. Once this determination is made about a restraint of trade, the court will not permit any defenses or justifications to save it.

per stirpes **distribution**   A distribution of an estate in which grandchildren and great-grandchildren of the deceased inherit by representation of their parent.

perfect tender rule   A rule that says if the goods or tender of a delivery fail in any respect to conform to the contract, the buyer may opt either (1) to reject the whole shipment, (2) to accept the whole shipment, or (3) to reject part and accept part of the shipment.

periodic tenancy   A tenancy created when a lease specifies intervals at which payments are due but does not specify how long the lease is for.

permanency requirement   A requirement of negotiable instruments that says they must be in a permanent state, such as written on ordinary paper.

personal articles floater   An addition to a homeowners' policy that covers specific valuable items.

personal defense   A defense that can be raised against enforcement of a negotiable instrument by an ordinary holder but not against an HDC.

personal liability of general partners   The unlimited personal liability of general partners of a limited partnership for the debts and obligations of the general partnership.

personal property   Tangible property such as automobiles, furniture, and equipment, and intangible property such as securities, patents, and copyrights.

personal satisfaction test   A subjective test that applies to contracts involving personal taste and comfort.

petition for certiorari   A petition asking the Supreme Court to hear a case.

petition for divorce   A document filed with the proper state court that commences a divorce proceeding.

petition   A document filed with a bankruptcy court that starts a bankruptcy proceeding.

physical or mental examination   A court-ordered examination of a party to a lawsuit before trial to determine the extent of the alleged injuries.

picketing   The action of strikers walking in front of an employer's premises, carrying signs announcing their strike.

piercing the corporate veil   A doctrine that says if a shareholder dominates a corporation and uses it for improper purposes, a court of equity can disregard the corporate entity and hold the shareholder personally liable for the corporation's debts and obligations. Also called the *alter ego doctrine.*

plaintiff   The party who files a complaint.

plan of reorganization   A plan that sets forth a proposed new capital structure for a debtor to assume when it emerges from Chapter 11 reorganization bankruptcy.

plea bargain   An agreement in which the accused admits to a lesser crime than charged.

In return, the government agrees to impose a lesser sentence than might have been obtained had the case gone to trial.

pleadings   The paperwork that is filed with the court to initiate and respond to a lawsuit.

police power   Power that permits states and local governments to enact laws to protect or promote the public health, safety, morals, and general welfare.

policy   An insurance contract.

portability requirement   A requirement of negotiable instruments that says they must be able to be easily transported between areas.

postdated check   A check that a drawer does not want cashed until sometime in the future.

power of attorney   An express agency agreement that is often used to give an agent the power to sign legal documents on behalf of the principal.

power of sale   A power stated in a mortgage or deed that permits foreclosure without court proceedings and sale of the property through an auction.

precedent   A rule of law established in a court decision. Lower courts must follow the precedent established by higher courts.

preemption doctrine   The concept that federal law takes precedence over state or local law.

preemptive rights   Rights that give existing shareholders the option of subscribing to new shares being issued in proportion to their current ownership interests.

preexisting duty   Something a person is already under an obligation to do. A promise lacks consideration if a person promises to perform a preexisting duty.

preferred stock   A type of equity security that is given certain preferences and rights over common stock.

preferred stockholder   A person who owns preferred stock.

prefiling period   A period of time that begins when the issuer first contemplates issuing securities and ends when the registration statement is filed. The issuer may not condition the market during this period.

premises liability   The liability of landlords and tenants to persons injured on their premises.

premium   Money paid to an insurance company.

prenuptial agreement   A contract entered into prior to marriage that specifies how property will be distributed upon the termination of the marriage or death of a spouse. Also called a premarital agreement.

presentment   A demand for acceptance or payment of an instrument made upon the maker, acceptor, drawee, or other payer by or on behalf of the holder.

presentment across the counter   A situation in which a depositor physically presents a check for payment at the payer bank instead of depositing an "on them" check for collection.

presentment warranties   Three warranties that a person who presents a draft or check for payment or acceptance makes to a drawee or an acceptor who pays or accepts the instrument in good faith: (1) The presenter has good title to the instrument or is authorized to obtain payment or acceptance of the person who has good title; (2) the instrument has not been materially altered; and (3) the presenter has no knowledge that the signature of the maker or drawer is unauthorized.

presentment warranty   A guarantee in which each prior transferor warrants that a check has not been altered.

pretrial motion   A motion a party can make to try to dispose of all or part of a lawsuit prior to trial.

price-fixing   A restraint of trade that occurs when competitors in the same line of business agree to set the price of the goods or services they sell, raising, depressing, fixing, pegging, or stabilizing the price of a commodity or service.

primary liability   Absolute liability to pay a negotiable instrument, subject to certain universal (real) defenses.

principal   A person who authorizes an agent to sign a negotiable instrument on his or her behalf.

principal–agent relationship   A relationship formed when an employer hires an employee and gives that employee authority to act and enter into contracts on his or her behalf.

Privacy Act   A federal act which states that federal administrative agencies can maintain only information about an individual that is relevant and necessary to accomplish a legitimate agency purpose.

private corporation   A corporation formed to conduct privately owned business.

private placement exemption   An exemption from registration that permits issuers to raise capital from an unlimited number of accredited investors and no more than 35 nonaccredited investors without having to register the offering with the SEC.

Private Securities Litigation Reform Act of 1995   A federal statute that limits a defendant's liability to its proportionate degree of fault.

Privileges and Immunities Clause   A clause that prohibits states from enacting laws that unduly discriminate in favor of their residents.

privity of contract   The state of two specified parties being in a contract.

pro rata rule   A rule that says shares must be purchased on a pro rata basis if too many shares are tendered.

probability of a substantial lessening of competition   The probability that a merger will substantially lessen competition or create a monopoly, in which case the court may prevent the merger under Section 7 of the Clayton Act.

probate   The process of a deceased's property being collected, debts and taxes being paid, and the remainder of the estate being distributed. Also called settlement of the estate.

probate court   A specialized state court that supervises the administration and settlement of estates.

procedural due process   A category of due process which requires that the government give a person proper notice and hearing of the legal action before that person is deprived of his or her life, liberty, or property. Due process that requires the respondent to be given proper and timely notice of the allegations or charges against him or her and an opportunity to present evidence on the matter.

product defect   Something wrong, inadequate, or improper in the manufacture, design, packaging, warning, or instructions about a product.

product disparagement   False statements about a competitor's products, services, property, or business reputation. Also known as trade libel, product disparagement and slander of title.

product liability   The liability of manufacturers, sellers, and others for the injuries caused by defective products.

product liability insurance   Insurance that protects sellers and manufacturers against injuries caused by defective products.

production of documents   A request by one party to another party to produce all documents relevant to the case prior to the trial.

professional corporation   A corporation formed by lawyers, doctors, or other professionals.

professional malpractice   The liability of a professional who breaches his or her duty of ordinary care.

professional malpractice insurance   Insurance that insures professionals against liability for injuries caused by their negligence. Also known as malpractice insurance.

profit   A document that grants a person the right to remove something from another's real property. Also known as profit-à-prendre.

profit corporation   A corporation created to conduct a business for profit that can distribute profits to shareholders in the form of dividends.

promise to pay   A maker's (borrower's) unconditional and affirmative undertaking to repay a debt to a payee (lender).

promissory estoppel   An equitable doctrine that prevents the withdrawal of a promise by a promisor if it will adversely affect a promisee who has adjusted his or her position in justifiable reliance on the promise. An equitable doctrine that permits enforcement of oral contracts that should have been in writing. It is applied to avoid injustice. Also known as *equitable estoppel*.

promissory note   A two-party negotiable instrument that is an unconditional written promise by one party to pay money to another party.

promoter   A person or persons who organize and start a corporation, negotiate and enter into contracts in advance of its formation, find the initial investors to finance the corporation, and so forth.

promoters' contracts   A collective term for such things as leases, sales contracts, contracts to purchase property, and employment contracts entered into by promoters on behalf of the proposed corporation prior to its actual incorporation.

proof of claim   A document required to be filed by a creditor that states the amount of his or her claim against the debtor.

proof of interest   A document required to be filed by an equity security holder that states the amount of his or her interest against the debtor.

proper dispatch   The proper addressing, packaging, and posting of an acceptance.

prospectus   A written disclosure document that must be submitted to the SEC along with the registration statement and given to prospective purchasers of the securities.

provisional credit   A situation in which a collecting bank gives credit to a check in the collection process prior to its final settlement. Provisional credits may be reversed if the check does not clear.

proximate cause   A point along a chain of events caused by a negligent party after which this party is no longer legally responsible for the consequences of his or her actions. Also called legal cause.

proxy   A written document that a shareholder signs, authorizing another person to vote his or her shares at the shareholders' meetings in the event of the shareholder's absence. Also called a *proxy card*.

proxy contest A contest in which opposing factions of shareholders and managers solicit proxies from other shareholders; the side that receives the greatest number of votes wins the proxy contest.

proxy statement A document that fully describes (1) the matter for which a proxy is being solicited, (2) who is soliciting the proxy, and (3) any other pertinent information.

publicly held corporation A corporation that has many shareholders and whose securities are often traded on national stock exchanges.

punitive damages Monetary damages that are awarded to punish a defendant who either intentionally or recklessly injured the plaintiff.

qualified individual with a disability A person who (1) has a physical or mental impairment that substantially limits one or more of his or her major life activities, (2) has a record of such impairment, or (3) is regarded as having such impairment.

qualified indorsement An indorsement that includes the notation "without recourse" or similar language that disclaims liability of the indorser.

qualified indorser An indorser who signs a qualified indorsement to an instrument.

qualified indorsers Those who disclaim liability and are not secondarily liable on instruments they endorse.

quasi in rem jurisdiction Jurisdiction that allows a plaintiff who obtains a judgment in one state to try to collect the judgment by attaching property of the defendant located in another state.

quasi-contract (implied-in-law contract) An equitable doctrine whereby a court may award monetary damages to a plaintiff for providing work or services to a defendant even though no actual contract existed. The doctrine is intended to prevent unjust enrichment and unjust detriment.

quiet title action An action brought by a party, seeking an order of the court declaring who has title to disputed property. The court "quiets title" by its decision.

quorum The required number of shares that must be represented in person or by proxy to hold a shareholders' meeting. The RMBCA establishes a majority of outstanding shares as a quorum.

Racketeer Influenced and Corrupt Organizations Act (RICO) A federal act that provides for both criminal and civil penalties for racketeering.

radiation pollution Emissions from radioactive wastes that can cause injury and death to humans and other life and can cause severe damage to the environment.

ratification A situation in which a principal accepts an agent's unauthorized contract. The act of a minor after the minor has reached the age of majority by which he or she accepts a contract entered into when he or she was a minor.

rational basis test A test that is applied to classifications not involving a suspect or protected class.

reaffirmation agreement An agreement entered into by a debtor with a creditor prior to discharge, whereby the debtor agrees to pay the creditor a debt that would otherwise be discharged in bankruptcy. Certain requirements must be met for a reaffirmation agreement to be enforced.

real property The land itself, as well as buildings, trees, soil, minerals, timber, plants, crops, fixtures and other things permanently affixed to the land or buildings.

reasonable person test An objective test that applies to commercial contracts and contracts involving mechanical fitness.

receiving stolen property To (1) knowingly receive stolen property and (2) intend to deprive the rightful owner of that property.

record date A date specified in corporate bylaws that determines whether a shareholder may vote at a shareholders' meeting.

recording statute A state statute that requires a mortgage or deed of trust to be recorded in the county recorder's office of the county in which the real property is located.

red light doctrine A doctrine that says a holder cannot qualify as an HDC if he or she has notice of an unauthorized signature or an alteration of the instrument or any adverse claim against or defense to its payment.

redeemable preferred stock Stock that permits a corporation to buy back the preferred stock at some future date.

reformation An equitable doctrine that permits the court to rewrite a contract to express the parties' true intentions.

registered agent A person or corporation that is empowered to accept service of process on behalf of a corporation.

registration statement A document that an issuer of securities files with the SEC that contains required information about the issuer, the securities to be issued, and other relevant information.

Regulation A A regulation that permits the issuer to sell securities pursuant to a simplified registration process.

Regulation Z A regulation that sets forth detailed rules for compliance with the TILA.

regulatory statute A licensing statute enacted to protect the public.

regulatory statutes Statutes such as environmental laws, securities laws, and antitrust laws that provide for criminal violations and penalties.

rejection Express words or conduct by the offeree that rejects an offer. Rejection terminates the offer.

release of lien A written document signed by a contractor, subcontractor, laborer, or material person, waiving his or her statutory lien against real property. Also known as a *lien release*.

relevant geographical market A relevant market that is defined as the area in which the defendant and its competitors sell the product or service.

relevant product or service market A relevant market that includes substitute products or services that are reasonably interchangeable with the defendant's products or services.

religious discrimination Discrimination against a person solely because of his or her religion or religious practices.

remainder A right of possession that returns to a third party upon the expiration of a limited or contingent estate.

remainder beneficiary of a living trust A person who receives the assets of a living trust upon the death of the grantor.

remainder beneficiary of a trust A person or an entity to receive the trust corpus upon the termination of a trust.

renters' insurance Insurance that renters purchase to cover loss or damage to their possessions.

replacement cost insurance Insurance that pays the cost to replace the damaged or destroyed property up to the policy limits.

replevin An action by a buyer or lessor to recover scarce goods wrongfully withheld by a seller or lessor.

reply A document filed by the original plaintiff to answer the defendant's cross-complaint.

res ipsa loquitur A tort in which the presumption of negligence arises because (1) the defendant was in exclusive control of the situation and (2) the plaintiff would not have suffered injury but for someone's negligence. The burden switches to the defendant to prove that he or she was not negligent.

resale price maintenance A *per se* violation of Section 1 of the Sherman Act that occurs when a party at one level of distribution enters into an agreement with a party at another level to adhere to a price schedule that either sets or stabilizes prices.

rescission   An action to rescind (undo) a contract. Rescission is available if there has been a material breach of contract, fraud, duress, undue influence, or mistake.

residuary gift   A gift of an estate left after the debts, taxes, and specific and general gifts have been given.

Resource Conservation and Recovery Act (RCRA)   A federal statute that authorizes the EPA to regulate facilities that generate, treat, store, transport, and dispose of hazardous wastes.

respondeat superior   A rule that says an employer is liable for the tortious conduct of its employees or agents while they are acting within the scope of its authority.

Restatement of the Law of Contracts   A compilation of model contract law principles drafted by legal scholars. The Restatement is not law.

restitution   The return of goods or property received from the other party to rescind a contract. If the actual goods or property are not available, a cash equivalent must be made.

restrictive indorsement   An indorsement that contains some sort of instruction from the indorser.

resulting trust   A trust that is implied from the conduct of the parties.

revenue-raising statute   A licensing statute with the primary purpose of raising revenue for the government.

reverse discrimination   Discrimination against a group that is usually thought of as a majority.

reversion   A right of possession that returns to the grantor after the expiration of a limited or contingent estate.

Revised Article 3   A comprehensive revision of the UCC law of negotiable instruments that reflects modern commercial practices.

Revised Model Business Corporation Act (RMBCA)   A 1984 revision of the MBCA that arranges the provisions of the act more logically, revises the language to be more consistent, and makes substantial changes in the provisions.

Revised Uniform Limited Partnership Act (RULPA)   A 1976 revision of the ULPA that provides a more modern, comprehensive law for the formation, operation, and dissolution of limited partnerships.

revocation   Termination of a will. Withdrawal of an offer by the offeror which terminates the offer.

revocation of acceptance   Reversal of acceptance.

reward   An award given for performance of some service or attainment. To collect a reward, the offeree must (1) have knowledge of the reward offer prior to completing the requested act and (2) perform the requested act.

right of first refusal   An agreement that requires a selling shareholder to offer his or her shares for sale to the other parties to the agreement before selling them to anyone else.

right of redemption   A right that allows the mortgagor to redeem real property after default and before foreclosure. It requires the mortgagor to pay the full amount of the debt incurred by the mortgagee because of the mortgagor's default.

right to cover   The right of a buyer or lessee to purchase or lease substitute goods if a seller or lessor fails to make delivery of the goods or repudiates the contract or if the buyer or lessee rightfully rejects the goods or justifiably revokes their acceptance.

right to dispose of goods   The right to dispose of goods in a good faith and commercially reasonable manner. A seller or lessor who is in possession of goods at the time the buyer or lessee breaches or repudiates a contract may in good faith resell, release, or otherwise dispose of the goods in a commercially reasonable manner and recover damages, including incidental damages, from the buyer or lessee.

right to participate in management   A situation in which, unless otherwise agreed, each partner has a right to participate in the management of a partnership and has an equal vote on partnership matters.

right to reclaim goods   The right of a seller or lessor to demand the return of goods from the buyer or lessee under specified situations.

right to recover damages for breach of contract   A seller's or lessor's right to recover damages measured as the difference between the contract price (or rent) and the market price (or rent) at the time and place the goods were to be delivered, plus incidental damages, from a buyer or lessee who repudiates the contract or wrongfully rejects tendered goods.

right to recover goods from an insolvent seller or lessor   The right of a buyer or lessee who has wholly or partially paid for goods before they are received to recover the goods from a seller or lessor who becomes insolvent within 10 days after receiving the first payment; the buyer or lessee must tender the remaining purchase price or rent due under the contract.

right to recover the purchase price or rent   A seller's or lessor's right to recover the contracted-for purchase price or rent

from the buyer or lessee (1) if the buyer or lessee fails to pay for accepted goods, (2) if the buyer or lessee breaches the contract and the seller or lessor cannot dispose of the goods, or (3) if the goods are damaged or lost after the risk of loss passes to the buyer or lessee.

right to reject nonconforming goods or improperly tendered goods   A situation in which a buyer or lessee rejects goods that do not conform to the contract. If the goods or the seller's or lessor's tender of delivery fails to conform to the contract, the buyer or lessee may (1) reject the whole, (2) accept the whole, or (3) accept any commercial unit and reject the rest.

right to stop delivery of goods in transit   The right of a seller or lessor to stop delivery of goods in transit if he or she learns of the buyer's or lessee's insolvency or if the buyer or lessee repudiates the contract, fails to make payment when due, or gives the seller or lessor some other right to withhold the goods.

right to withhold delivery   A seller's or lessor's right to refuse to deliver goods to a buyer or lessee upon breach of a sales or lease contract by the buyer or lessee or the insolvency of the buyer or lessee.

robbery   The taking of personal property from another person by the use of fear or force.

Rule 10b-5   A rule adopted by the SEC to clarify the reach of Section 10(b) against deceptive and fraudulent activities in the purchase and sale of securities.

rule of reason   A rule which holds that only unreasonable restraints of trade violate Section 1 of the Sherman Act. The court must examine the pro- and anticompetitive effects of a challenged restraint.

Racketeer Influenced and Corrupt Organizations Act (RICO)   A federal act that provides for both criminal and civil penalties for securities fraud.

Safe Drinking Water Act   A federal statute that authorizes the EPA to establish national primary drinking water standards.

sale on approval   A type of sale in which there is no actual sale unless and until the buyer accepts the goods.

sale or return contract   A contract in which the seller delivers goods to a buyer with the understanding that the buyer may return them if they are not used or resold within a stated or reasonable period of time.

sale   The passing of title from a seller to a buyer for a price. Also called a *conveyance*.

Sarbanes-Oxley Act   A federal act that imposes new rules that affect public accountants. The act: created the Public Company

Accounting Oversight Board (PCAOB); requires public accounting firms to register with the PCAOB; separates audit services and certain nonaudit services provided by accountants to clients; requires an audit partner of the accounting firm to supervise an audit and approve an audit report prepared by the firm and requires a second partner of the accounting firm to review and approve the audit report; and prohibits employment of an accountant by a previous audit client for certain positions for a period of one year following the audit.

satisfaction   The performance of an accord.

scienter   Intentional conduct. Scienter is required for there to be a violation of Section 10(b) and Rule 10b-5. Knowledge that a representation is false or that it was made without sufficient knowledge of the truth.

secondary boycott picketing   A type of picketing in which a union tries to bring pressure against an employer by picketing the employer's suppliers or customers.

secondary liability   Liability on a negotiable instrument that is imposed on a party only when the party primarily liable on the instrument defaults and fails to pay the instrument when due.

"secondary meaning"   A brand name that has evolved from an ordinary term.

Section 1 of the Sherman Act   A section that prohibits contracts, combinations, and conspiracies in restraint of trade.

Section 2 of the Sherman Act   A section that prohibits monopolization and attempts or conspiracies to monopolize trade.

Section 2(a) of the Robinson-Patman Act   A section that prohibits direct and indirect price discrimination by sellers of a commodity of a like grade and quality, where the effect of such discrimination may be to substantially lessen competition or to tend to create a monopoly in any line of commerce.

Section 3 of the Clayton Act   An act that prohibits tying arrangements involving sales and leases of goods.

Section 5 of the Federal Trade Commission Act   A section that prohibits unfair methods of competition and unfair or deceptive acts or practices in or affecting commerce.

Section 5 of the FTC Act   A provision in the FTC Act that prohibits unfair and deceptive practices.

Section 7 of the Clayton Act   A section which provides that it is unlawful for a person or business to acquire the stock or assets of another "where in any line of commerce or in any activity affecting commerce in any section of the country, the effect of such acquisition may be substantially to lessen competition, or to tend to create a monopoly."

Section 7 of the NLRA   A law that gives employees the right to join together to form a union.

Section 8(a) of the NLRA   A law that makes it an unfair labor practice for an employer to interfere with, coerce, or restrain employees from exercising their statutory right to form and join

Section 10(b)   A provision of the Securities Exchange Act of 1934 that prohibits the use of manipulative and deceptive devices in the purchase or sale of securities in contravention of the rules and regulations prescribed by the SEC.

Section 10(b)   A section of the Securities Exchange Act of 1934 that prohibits any manipulative or deceptive practice in connection with the purchase or sale of a security.

Section 11   A provision of the Securities Act of 1933 that imposes civil liability on persons who intentionally defraud investors by making misrepresentations or omissions of material facts in the registration statement or who are negligent for not discovering the fraud.

Section 11(a)   A section of the Securities Act of 1933 that imposes civil liability on accountants and others for (1) making misstatements or omissions of material facts in a registration statement or (2) failing to find such misstatements or omissions.

Section 12   A provision of the Securities Act of 1933 that imposes civil liability on any person who violates the provisions of Section 5 of the act.

Section 14(a)   A provision of the Securities Exchange Act of 1934 that gives the SEC the authority to regulate the solicitation of proxies.

Section 14(e)   A provision of the Williams Act that prohibits fraudulent, deceptive, and manipulative practices in connection with a tender offer.

Section 16(b)   A section of the Securities Exchange Act of 1934 that requires that any profits made by a statutory insider on transactions involving short-swing profits belong to the corporation.

Section 18(a)   A section of the Securities Exchange Act of 1934 that imposes civil liability on any person who makes false or misleading statements in any application, report, or document filed with the SEC.

Section 24   A provision of the Securities Act of 1933 that imposes criminal liability on any person who willfully violates the 1933 act or the rules or regulations adopted thereunder.

Section 24   A section of the Securities Act of 1933 that makes it a criminal offense for any person to (1) willfully make any untrue statement of material fact in a registration statement filed with the SEC, (2) omit any material fact necessary to ensure that the statements made in the registration statement are not misleading, or (3) willfully violate any other provision of the Securities Act of 1933 or rule or regulation adopted thereunder.

Section 32   A provision of the Securities Exchange Act of 1934 that imposes criminal liability on any person who willfully violates the 1934 act or the rules or regulations adopted thereunder.

Section 32(a)   A section of the Securities Exchange Act of 1934 that makes it a criminal offense for any person willfully and knowingly to make or cause to be made any false or misleading statement in any application, report, or other document required to be filed with the SEC pursuant to the Securities Exchange Act of 1934 or any rule or regulation adopted thereunder.

Section 552 of the Restatement (Second) of Torts   A rule which says that an accountant is liable only for negligence to third parties who are members of a limited class of intended users of the client's financial statements. It provides a broader standard for holding accountants liable to third parties for negligence than does the Ultramares doctrine.

section of the country   A division of the country that is based on the relevant geographical market; the geographical area that will feel the direct and immediate effects of a merger.

secured credit   Credit that requires security (collateral) that secures payment of the loan.

Securities Act of 1933   A federal statute that primarily regulates the issuance of securities by corporations, partnerships, associations, and individuals.

Securities and Exchange Commission (SEC)   The federal administrative agency that is empowered to administer federal securities laws. The SEC can adopt rules and regulations to interpret and implement federal securities laws.

Securities Exchange Act of 1934   A federal statute that primarily regulates the trading in securities.

security   (1) An interest or instrument that is common stock, preferred stock, a bond, a debenture, or a warrant; (2) an interest or instrument that is expressly mentioned in securities acts; and (3) an investment contract.

self-incrimination   A person being a witness against himself or herself. The Fifth Amendment prevents self-incrimination in any criminal case.

seller's or lessor's cancellation   A seller or lessor has the right to cancel a sales or lease contract if the buyer or lessee rejects or revokes acceptance of the goods, fails to pay for the goods, or repudiates the contract in part or in whole.

separate property   Property owned by a spouse prior to marriage, as well as inheritances and gifts received by a spouse during the marriage.

service mark   A mark that distinguishes the services of the holder from those of its competitors.

service of process   A summons being served on the defendant to obtain personal jurisdiction over him or her.

settlement agreement   A written document signed by divorcing parties that evidences their agreement settling property rights and other issues of their divorce.

settlement conference   A hearing before a trial in order to facilitate the settlement of a case. Also called a pretrial hearing.

settlor   A person who creates a trust. Also known as a trustor or transferor.

sex discrimination   Discrimination against a person solely because of his or her gender.

sexual harassment   Lewd remarks, touching, intimidation, posting of indecent materials, and other verbal or physical conduct of a sexual nature that occurs on the job.

share exchange   A situation in which one corporation acquires all the shares of another corporation, and both corporations retain their separate legal existence.

shareholder resolution   A resolution that a shareholder who meets certain ownership requirements may submit to other shareholders for a vote. Many shareholder resolutions concern social issues.

shareholder voting agreement   An agreement between two or more shareholders that stipulates how they will vote their shares.

shipment contract   A contract that requires the seller to ship the goods to the buyer via a common carrier. A sales contract that requires the seller to send the goods to the buyer but not to a specifically named destination. The buyer bears the risk of loss during transportation.

short-form merger   A merger between a parent corporation and a subsidiary corporation that does not require the vote of the shareholders of either corporation or the board of directors of the subsidiary corporation.

sight draft   A draft payable on sight. Also called a demand draft.

signature   Any name, word, or mark used in lieu of a written signature; any symbol that is (1) handwritten, typed, printed, stamped, or made in almost any other manner and (2) executed or adopted by a party to authenticate a writing.

signature liability   Liability in which a person cannot be held contractually liable on a negotiable instrument unless his or her signature appears on the instrument. Also called contract liability.

signature requirement   A requirement which states that a negotiable instrument must be signed by the drawer or maker. Any symbol executed or adopted by a party with a present intent to authenticate a writing qualifies as his or her signature.

signer   A person signing an instrument who acts in the capacity of (1) a maker of notes or certificates of deposit, (2) a drawer of drafts or checks, (3) a drawee who certifies or accepts checks or drafts, (4) an indorser who indorses an instrument, (5) an agent who signs on behalf of others, or (6) an accommodation party.

slander   Oral defamation of character.

small claims court   A court that hears civil cases involving small dollar amounts.

small offering exemption   An exemption from registration that permits the sale of securities not exceeding $1 million during a 12-month period.

social contract   A moral theory that says each person is presumed to have entered into a social contract with all others in society to obey moral rules that are necessary for people to live in peace and harmony.

Social Security   A federal system that provides limited retirement and death benefits to covered employees and their dependents.

sole proprietorship   A form of business in which the owner is actually the business; the business is not a separate legal entity.

special federal courts   Federal courts that hear matters of specialized or limited jurisdiction.

special indorsement   An indorsement that contains the signature of the indorser and specifies the person (indorsee) to whom the indorser intends the instrument to be payable. It creates order paper.

special shareholders' meetings   Meetings of shareholders that may be called to consider and vote on important or emergency issues, such as a proposed merger or amending the articles of incorporation.

specific duty standard   An OSHA standard that addresses a safety problem of a specific duty nature (e.g., requirement for a safety guard on a particular type of equipment).

specific gift   A gift of a specifically named piece of property.

specific performance   A decree of the court that orders a seller or lessor to perform his or her obligations under the contract; usually occurs when the goods in question are unique, such as art or antiques. A remedy that orders the breaching party to perform the acts promised in the contract. Specific performance is usually awarded in cases in which the subject matter is unique, such as in contracts involving land, heirlooms, and paintings.

spousal support   Payments made by one divorced spouse to the other divorced spouse. Also called *alimony*.

stakeholder interest   A theory of social responsibility that says a corporation must consider the effects its actions have on persons other than its shareholders.

stale check   A check that has been outstanding for more than six months.

standard fire insurance form   A standard fire insurance policy that protects the homeowner from loss caused by fire, lightning, smoke, and water damage.

standing to sue   Some stake in the outcome of a lawsuit.

stare decisis   Latin: "to stand by the decision." Adherence to precedent.

state action exemptions   Business activities that are mandated by state law and are therefore exempt from federal antitrust laws.

state administrative agencies   Administrative agencies that states create to enforce and interpret state law.

state median income   For any size family, income for which half of the state's families of this size have incomes above this figure and half of the state's families of this size have incomes less than this figure.

State Supreme Court   The highest court in a state court system; it hears appeals from intermediate appellate state courts and certain trial courts.

statement of disassociation   A document filed with the secretary of state that gives constructive notice that a member has disassociated from an LLC.

statement of opinion   A commendation of goods, made by a seller or lessor, that does not create an express warranty. Also known as puffing.

statement of policy   A statement issued by an administrative agency that announces a proposed course of action that the agency intends to follow in the future.

statute   Written law enacted by the legislative branch of the federal and state governments that establishes certain courses of conduct that must be adhered to by covered parties.

statute of frauds A state statute that requires certain types of contracts to be in writing.

statute of limitations A statute that establishes the period during which a plaintiff must bring a lawsuit against a defendant. A statute that establishes the time period during which a lawsuit must be brought; if the lawsuit is not brought within this period, the injured party loses the right to sue. A statute that requires an injured person to bring an action within a certain number of years from the time that he or she was injured by a defective product.

statute of repose A statute that limits the seller's liability to a certain number of years from the date when the product was first sold.

statute of wills A state statute that establishes the requirements for making a valid will.

statutory exemptions Exemptions from antitrust laws that are expressly provided in statutes enacted by Congress.

stock dividend Additional shares of stock distributed as a dividend.

stop-payment order An order by a drawer of a check to the payer bank not to pay or certify a check.

straight voting A system in which each shareholder votes the number of shares he or she owns on candidates for each of the positions open. Also called noncumulative voting.

strict liability A tort doctrine that makes manufacturers, distributors, wholesalers, retailers, and others in the chain of distribution of a defective product liable for the damages caused by the defect, *irrespective of fault*. Liability without fault.

strict scrutiny test A test that is applied to classifications based on race.

strike A cessation of work by union members in order to obtain economic benefits or correct an unfair labor practice.

sublease A situation in which a tenant transfers only some of his or her rights under the lease.

sublessee The new tenant in a sublease situation.

sublessor The original tenant in a sublease situation.

substantial performance Performance by a contracting party that deviates only slightly from complete performance.

substantive due process A category of due process which requires that government statutes, ordinances, regulations, or other

laws be clear on their face and not overly broad in scope.

substantive rule A rule issued by an administrative agency that has the force of law and to which covered persons and businesses must adhere.

subsurface rights Rights to the earth located beneath the surface of the land.

suicide clause A clause in a life insurance contract which provides that if an insured commits suicide before a stipulated date, the insurance company does not have to pay the life insurance proceeds.

summons A court order directing the defendant to appear in court and answer the complaint.

superseding or intervening event An event for which a defendant is not responsible. The defendant is not liable for injuries caused by the superseding or intervening event.

supervening event or intervening event An alteration or a modification of a product by a party in the chain of distribution that absolves all prior sellers from strict liability.

supervening illegality The enactment of a statute, regulation, or court decision that makes the object of an offer illegal. This action terminates the offer.

supramajority voting requirement A requirement that a greater than majority of shares constitutes a quorum of the vote of the shareholders.

Supremacy Clause A clause of the U.S. Constitution which establishes that the U.S. Constitution and federal treaties, laws, and regulations are the supreme law of the land.

surety arrangement An arrangement in which a third party promises to be primarily liable with the borrower for the payment of the borrower's debt.

taking for value requirement A requirement that says a holder must give value for a negotiable instrument in order to qualify as an HDC.

taking in good faith requirement A requirement that says a holder must take the instrument in good faith in order to qualify as an HDC.

taking without notice of defect requirement A requirement that says a person cannot qualify as an HDC if he or she has notice that the instrument is defective in certain ways.

tangible property All real property and physically defined personal property, such as buildings, goods, animals, and minerals.

target corporation The corporation that is proposed to be acquired in a tender offer situation.

Tax Reform Act of 1976 An act that imposes criminal liability on accountants and others who prepare federal tax returns if they (1) willfully understate a client's tax liability, (2) negligently understate the tax liability, or (3) aid or assist in the preparation of a false tax return.

tax sale A method of transferring property ownership that involves a lien on property for unpaid property taxes. If the lien remains unpaid after a certain amount of time, a tax sale is held to satisfy the lien.

tenancy at sufferance A tenancy created when a tenant retains possession of property after the expiration of another tenancy or a life estate without the owner's consent.

tenancy at will A tenancy created by a lease that may be terminated at any time by either party.

tenancy by the entirety A form of co-ownership of real property that can be used only by married couples.

tenancy for years A tenancy created when a landlord and a tenant agree on a specific duration for a lease.

tenancy in common A form of co-ownership in which the interest of a surviving tenant in common passes to the deceased tenant's estate and not to the co-tenants.

tenant The party to whom a leasehold is transferred.

tender of delivery The obligation of a seller to transfer and deliver goods to the buyer or lessee in accordance with a sales or lease contract.

tender of performance An unconditional and absolute offer by a contracting party to perform his or her obligations under a contract. Also known as tender.

tender offer An offer that an acquirer makes directly to a target corporation's shareholders in an effort to acquire the target corporation.

tender offeror The party that makes a tender offer.

Term LLC An LLC that has a specified term of duration.

testamentary trust A trust created by a will; the trust comes into existence when the settlor dies.

testator or testatrix A person who makes a will.

thermal pollution Heated water or material discharged into waterways that upsets the ecological balance and decreases the oxygen content.

time draft A draft payable at a designated future date.

time instrument An instrument payable (1) at a fixed date, (2) on or before a stated date, (3) at a fixed period after sight, or (4) at a time readily ascertainable when the promise or order is issued. An instrument that specifies a definite date for payment of the instrument.

time note A note payable at a specific time.

tippee A person who receives material nonpublic information from a tipper.

tipper A person who discloses material nonpublic information to another person.

title Legal, tangible evidence of ownership of goods.

Title I of the ADA A title of a federal statute that prohibits employment discrimination against qualified individuals with disabilities in regard to job application procedures, hiring, compensation, training, promotion, and termination.

Title I of the Landrum-Griffin Act Labor's "bill of rights," which gives each union member equal rights and privileges to nominate candidates for union office, vote in elections, and participate in membership meetings.

Title III of the Americans with Disabilities Act A federal statute that prohibits discrimination on the basis of disability in places of public accommodation by private entities.

Title VII of the Civil Rights Act of 1964 A title of a federal statute enacted to eliminate job discrimination based on five protected classes: race, color, religion, sex, and national origin.

title insurance Insurance that owners of real property purchase to ensure that they have clear title to the property.

tort of misappropriation of the right to publicity An attempt by another person to appropriate a living person's name or identity for commercial purposes.

tortfeasor A person who intentionally or unintentionally (negligently) causes injury or death to another person. A person liable to persons he or she injures and to the heirs of persons who die because of his or her conduct.

toxic substances Chemicals used by agriculture, industry, business, mining, and households that cause injury to humans, birds, animals, fish, and vegetation.

Toxic Substances Control Act A federal statute that authorizes the EPA to regulate toxic substances.

trade acceptance A sight draft that arises when credit is extended (by a seller to a buyer) with the sale of goods. The seller is both the drawer and the payee, and the buyer is the drawee.

trade secret A product formula, pattern, design, compilation of data, customer list, or other business secret.

trade secrets Ideas that make a franchise successful but that do not qualify for trademark, patent, or copyright protection.

trademark A distinctive mark, symbol, name, word, motto, or device that identifies the goods of a particular business.

trademark infringement Unauthorized use of another's mark. The holder may recover damages and other remedies from the infringer.

trademark or service mark A distinctive mark, symbol, name, word, motto, or device that identifies the goods or services of a particular franchisor.

transfer Any passage of an instrument other than its issuance and presentment for payment.

transfer warranties Any of the following five implied warranties: (1) The transferor has good title to the instrument or is authorized to obtain payment or acceptance on behalf of one who does have good title; (2) all signatures are genuine or authorized; (3) the instrument has not been materially altered; (4) no defenses of any party are good against the transferor; and (5) the transferor has no knowledge of any insolvency proceeding against the maker, the acceptor, or the drawer of an unaccepted instrument.

Treaty Clause A clause of the U.S. Constitution which states that the president "shall have the power . . . to make treaties, provided two-thirds of the senators present concur."

treaty A compact made between two or more nations. The first source of international law, consisting of an agreement or a contract between two or more nations that is formally signed by an authorized representative and ratified by the supreme power of each nation.

trier of fact The jury in a jury trial; the judge where there is not a jury trial.

trust A legal arrangement established when one person transfers title to property to another person to be held and used for the benefit of a third person.

trust corpus Property and assets held in trust. Also known as trust res.

trustee A legal representative of the debtor's estate. A person named in a living will to administer the trust assets. This is usually the grantor. A person or an entity that holds legal title to a trust corpus and manages the trust for the benefit of the beneficiary or beneficiaries.

Truth-in-Lending Act (TILA) A federal statute that requires creditors to make certain disclosures to debtors in consumer transactions and real estate loans on the debtor's principal dwelling.

tying arrangement A restraint of trade in which a seller refuses to sell one product to a customer unless the customer agrees to purchase a second product from the seller.

U.S. Constitution The fundamental law of the United States of America. It was ratified by the states in 1788.

U.S. courts of appeals The federal court system's intermediate appellate courts.

U.S. district courts The federal court system's trial courts of general jurisdiction.

U.S. Supreme Court The highest court in the United States, located in Washington, DC. The Supreme Court was created by Article III of the U.S. Constitution.

U.S. trustee A federal government official who is responsible for handling and supervising many of the administrative tasks of a bankruptcy case.

UCC Statute of Frauds Section 2-201(1) A section of the Uniform Commercial Code which states that sales contracts for the sale of goods costing $500 or more must be in writing.

UCC Statute of Frauds Section 2A-201(1) A section of the Uniform Commercial Code which states that lease contracts involving payments of $1,000 or more must be in writing.

UCC Statute of Frauds A rule that requires all contracts for the sale of goods costing $500 or more and lease contracts involving payments of $1,000 or more to be in writing.

UCC statute of limitations A rule which provides that an action for breach of any written or oral sales or lease contract must commence within four years after the cause of action accrues. The parties may agree to reduce the limitations period to one year.

ultra vires **act** An act by a corporation that is beyond its express or implied powers.

ultramares doctrine A rule which says that an accountant is liable only for negligence to third parties who are in privity of contract or in a privity-like relationship.

unauthorized signature A signature made by a purported agent without authority from the purported principal.

unconditional Not conditional or limited. Promises to pay and orders to pay must be unconditional in order for them to be negotiable.

unconditional promise or order to pay requirement A requirement that says a negotiable instrument must contain either an unconditional promise to pay (note or CD) or an unconditional order to pay money. A "medium of exchange authorized or adopted by a domestic or foreign government" [UCC 1-201(24)].

unconscionable contract   A contract that courts refuse to enforce in part or at all because it is so oppressive or manifestly unfair as to be unjust.

undisclosed agency   An agency in which a contracting third party does not know of either the existence of the agency or the principal's identity.

undue influence   A situation in which one person takes advantage of another person's mental, emotional, or physical weakness and unduly persuades that person to enter into a contract; the persuasion by the wrongdoer must overcome the free will of the innocent party.

unduly burden interstate commerce   A concept which says that states may enact laws that protect or promote the public health, safety, morals, and general welfare, as long as the laws do not unduly burden interstate commerce.

unenforceable contract   A contract in which the essential elements to create a valid contract are met but there is some legal defense to the enforcement of the contract.

Uniform Commercial Code (UCC)   A comprehensive statutory scheme which includes laws that cover aspects of commercial transactions. A model act that includes comprehensive laws that cover most aspects of commercial transactions. All the states have enacted all or part of the UCC as statutes.

Uniform Computer Information Transactions Act (UCITA)   A model state law that creates contract law for the licensing of information technology rights.

Uniform Computer Information Transactions Act (UCITA)   A model act that establishes uniform legal rules for the formation and enforcement of electronic contracts and licenses.

Uniform Franchise Offering Circular (UFOC)   A uniform disclosure document that requires a franchisor to make specific presale disclosures to prospective franchisees.

Uniform Gifts to Minors Act and Uniform Transfers to Minors Act   Acts that establish procedures for adults to make gifts of money and securities to minors

Uniform Limited Liability Company Act (ULLCA)   A model act that provides comprehensive and uniform laws for the formation, operation, and dissolution of LLCs.

Uniform Partnership Act (UPA)   A model act that codifies partnership law. Most

states have adopted the UPA in whole or in part.

Uniform Simultaneous Death Act   An act which provides that if people who would inherit property from each other die simultaneously, each person's property is distributed as though he or she had survived.

unilateral contract   A contract in which the offeror's offer can be accepted only by the performance of an act by the offeree; a "promise for an act."

unilateral mistake   A mistake in which only one party is mistaken about a material fact regarding the subject matter of a contract.

unilateral refusal to deal   A unilateral choice by one party not to deal with another party. This does not violate Section 1 of the Sherman Act because there is not concerted action.

uninsured motorist coverage   Automobile insurance that provides coverage to a driver and passengers who are injured by an uninsured motorist or a hit-and-run driver.

unintentional tort   A doctrine that says a person is liable for harm that is the foreseeable consequence of his or her actions. Also known as negligence.

union shop   A workplace where an employee must join the union within a certain number of days after being hired.

United Nations (UN)   An international organization created by a multilateral treaty in 1945 to promote social and economic cooperation among nations and to protect human rights.

universal defense   A defense that can be raised against both holders and HDCs. Also called a real defense.

unlawful detainer action   A legal process that a landlord must complete to evict a holdover tenant.

unprotected speech   Speech that is not protected by the First Amendment and may be forbidden by the government.

unqualified indorsement   An indorsement whereby the indorser promises to pay the holder or any subsequent indorser the amount of the instrument if the maker, drawer, or acceptor defaults on it.

unqualified indorser   An indorser who signs an unqualified indorsement to an instrument.

unqualified indorsers   Those who are secondarily liable on negotiable instruments they endorse.

unreasonable search and seizure   Any search and seizure by the government that violates the Fourth Amendment.

unsecured credit   Credit that does not require any security (collateral) to protect the payment of the debt.

usury law   A law that sets an upper limit on the interest rate that can be charged on certain types of loans.

utilitarianism   A moral theory that dictates that people must choose the action or follow the rule that provides the greatest good to society.

valid contract   A contract that meets all the essential elements to establish a contract; a contract that is enforceable by at least one of the parties.

variance   An exception that permits a type of building or use in an area that would not otherwise be allowed by a zoning ordinance.

venue   A concept that requires lawsuits to be heard by the court with jurisdiction that is nearest the location in which the incident occurred or where the parties reside.

vertical merger   A merger that integrates the operations of a supplier and a customer.

vertical restraint of trade   A restraint of trade that occurs when two or more parties on different levels of distribution enter into a contract, combination, or conspiracy to restrain trade.

violation   A crime that is neither a felony nor a misdemeanor that is usually punishable by a fine.

visitation rights   Rights of a non-custodial parent to visit with the child for limited periods of time.

void contract   A contract that has no legal effect; a nullity.

void title   A situation in which a thief acquires no title to goods he or she steals. Also known as a void leasehold interest.

voidable contract   A contract in which one or both parties have the option to avoid their contractual obligations. If a contract is avoided, both parties are released from their contractual obligations.

voidable title   A title that a purchaser has if the goods were obtained by (1) fraud, (2) a check that is later dishonored, or (3) impersonation of another person. Also known as *voidable leasehold interest*.

voir dire   The process whereby prospective jurors are asked questions by the judge and attorneys to determine whether they would be biased in their decisions.

voluntary dissolution   Dissolution of a corporation that has begun business or issued shares upon recommendation of the board of directors and a majority vote of the shares entitled to vote.

voluntary petition   A petition filed by a debtor that states that the debtor has debts.

voting trust   An arrangement in which the shareholders transfer their stock certificates to a trustee who is empowered to vote the shares.

warranty A seller's or lessor's express or implied assurance to a buyer or lessee that the goods sold or leased meet certain quality standards.

warranty disclaimer A statement that negates express and implied warranties.

warranty against interference A warranty in which the lessor warrants that no person holds a claim or an interest in the goods that arose from an act or omission of the lessor that will interfere with the lessee's enjoyment of his or her leasehold interest. An automatic warranty of a seller or lessor who is a merchant who regularly deals in goods of the kind sold or leased which warrants that the goods are delivered free of any third-party patent, trademark, or copyright claim. Also known as the *warranty against infringements*.

warranty of no security interests A warranty in which sellers of goods warrant that the goods they sell are delivered free from any third-party security interests, liens, or encumbrances that are unknown to the buyer.

warranty of good title A warranty in which the seller warrants that he or she has valid title to the goods being sold and that the transfer of title is rightful.

water pollution Pollution of lakes, rivers, oceans, and other bodies of water.

wetlands Areas that are inundated or saturated by surface water or ground water that support vegetation typically adapted for life in such conditions.

will A declaration of how a person wants his or her property to be distributed upon death.

winding up The process of liquidating a partnership's assets and distributing the proceeds to satisfy claims against the partnership.

winding up and liquidation The process by which a dissolved corporation's assets are collected, liquidated, and distributed to creditors, shareholders, and other claimants.

Williams Act An amendment to the Securities Exchange Act of 1934 made in 1968 that specifically regulates tender offers.

World Wide Web An electronic connection of millions of computers that support a standard set of rules for the exchange of information.

work-related test A test that determines whether an agent committed an intentional tort within a work-related time or space; if so, the principal is liable for any injury caused by the agent's intentional tort.

workers' compensation Compensation paid to workers and their families when workers are injured in connection with their jobs.

Worker Adjustment and Retraining Notification (WARN) Act A federal act that requires employers with 100 or more employees to give their employees 60 days' notice before engaging in certain plant closings or layoffs.

workers' compensation insurance Insurance that compensates employees for work-related injuries.

work product immunity A state statute which provides that an accountant's work papers cannot be used against a client in a court action.

World Trade Organization (WTO) An international organization of more than 130 member nations created to promote and enforce trade agreements among member nations.

writ of certiorari An official notice that the Supreme Court will review a case.

writ of garnishment An order of the court that orders that wages, bank accounts, or

other property of the breaching party held by third persons be paid to the nonbreaching party to satisfy a judgment.

writ of attachment An order of the court that enables a government officer to seize property of the breaching party and sell it at auction to satisfy a judgment.

wrongful dishonor A situation in which there are sufficient funds in a drawer's account to pay a properly payable check, but the bank does not do so.

wrongful termination The termination of an agency contract in violation of the terms of the agency contract. The nonbreaching party may recover damages from the breaching party.

wrongful dissolution A situation in which a partner withdraws from a partnership without having the right to do so at that time.

wrongful disassociation When a member withdraws from (1) a term LLC prior to the expiration of the term or (2) an at-will LLC when the operating agreement eliminates a member's power to withdraw.

wrongful termination Termination of a franchise without just cause.

writ of certiorari An official notice that the Supreme Court will review a case.

WTO panel A body of three WTO judges that hears trade disputes between member nations and issues a "panel report."

WTO appellate body A panel of seven judges selected from WTO member nations that hears and decides appeals from decisions of the dispute-settlement body.

WTO dispute settlement body A board composed of one representative from each WTO member nation that reviews panel reports.

zoning ordinances Local laws that are adopted by municipalities and local governments to regulate land use within their boundaries.

CASE INDEX

Cases cited or discussed are in roman type.
Principle cases are in **bold type.**

SUBJECT INDEX